THE OXFORD HA

NAMES
AND NAMING

OXFORD HANDBOOKS IN LINGUISTICS

Recently Published

THE OXFORD HANDBOOK OF THE HISTORY OF LINGUISTICS
Edited by Keith Allan

THE OXFORD HANDBOOK OF LINGUISTIC TYPOLOGY
Edited by Jae Jung Song

THE OXFORD HANDBOOK OF CONSTRUCTION GRAMMAR
Edited by Thomas Hoffman and Graeme Trousdale

THE OXFORD HANDBOOK OF LANGUAGE EVOLUTION
Edited by Maggie Tallerman and Kathleen Gibson

THE OXFORD HANDBOOK OF ARABIC LINGUISTICS
Edited by Jonathan Owens

THE OXFORD HANDBOOK OF CORPUS PHONOLOGY
Edited by Jacques Durand, Ulrike Gut, and Gjert Kristoffersen

THE OXFORD HANDBOOK OF LINGUISTIC FIELDWORK
Edited by Nicholas Thieberger

THE OXFORD HANDBOOK OF DERIVATIONAL MORPHOLOGY
Edited by Rochelle Lieber and Pavol Štekauer

THE OXFORD HANDBOOK OF HISTORICAL PHONOLOGY
Edited by Patrick Honeybone and Joseph Salmons

THE OXFORD HANDBOOK OF LINGUISTIC ANALYSIS
Second Edition
Edited by Bernd Heine and Heiko Narrog

THE OXFORD HANDBOOK OF THE WORD
Edited by John R. Taylor

THE OXFORD HANDBOOK OF INFLECTION
Edited by Matthew Baerman

THE OXFORD HANDBOOK OF LANGUAGE AND LAW
Edited by Peter M. Tiersma and Lawrence M. Solan

THE OXFORD HANDBOOK OF DEVELOPMENTAL LINGUISTICS
Edited by Jeffrey Lidz, William Snyder, and Joe Pater

THE OXFORD HANDBOOK OF LEXICOGRAPHY
Edited by Philip Durkin

THE OXFORD HANDBOOK OF NAMES AND NAMING
Edited by Carole Hough

For a complete list of Oxford Handbooks in Linguistics, please see pp. 773–4

THE OXFORD HANDBOOK OF

NAMES
AND NAMING

Edited by
CAROLE HOUGH

With assistance from
DARIA IZDEBSKA

OXFORD
UNIVERSITY PRESS

OXFORD
UNIVERSITY PRESS

Great Clarendon Street, Oxford, OX2 6DP,
United Kingdom

Oxford University Press is a department of the University of Oxford.
It furthers the University's objective of excellence in research, scholarship,
and education by publishing worldwide. Oxford is a registered trade mark of
Oxford University Press in the UK and in certain other countries

Published in the United States of America by Oxford University Press
198 Madison Avenue, New York, NY 10016, United States of America

British Library Cataloguing in Publication Data
Data available

Library of Congress Cataloging in Publication Data
Data available

ISBN 978–0–19–965643–1 (Hbk.)
ISBN 978–0–19–881553–2 (Pbk.)

This volume is dedicated to the memory of Eva Brylla,
an outstanding name scholar, colleague, and friend
1944–2015

PREFACE

....

NAMES are a linguistic universal. All known languages make use of names—most commonly, but not exclusively, to identify individual people and places. The study of names, known as onomastics, is central to the work of scholars in various disciplines. It is also of enduring interest to the wider public, many of whom participate enthusiastically in societies formed to investigate names of different kinds. Indeed, name studies is an area where it is often essential for academics and non-academics to work closely together, with local knowledge making an important contribution to scholarly research. This volume aims to provide an up-to-date account of the state of the art in different areas of name studies, in a format that is both useful to specialists in related fields and accessible to the general reader.

The main focus is on general principles and methodologies, with case studies from a range of languages and cultures. The editors are grateful to the many leading scholars from different parts of the world who have agreed to contribute, and who have made this Handbook what it is. We are also grateful to our colleagues in the subject area of English Language at the University of Glasgow for their support, and to the editorial team at Oxford University Press for their unfailing helpfulness, wise guidance, and good humour. They have been a pleasure to work with.

Contents

PART III ANTHROPONOMASTICS

PART IV LITERARY ONOMASTICS

PART V SOCIO-ONOMASTICS

PART VI ONOMASTICS AND OTHER DISCIPLINES

PART VII OTHER TYPES OF NAMES

List of Figures

LIST OF ABBREVIATIONS

A	Austria
AUS	Australia
CH	Switzerland
CHL	Chile
COK	Cook Islands
D	Germany
DNK	Denmark
Engl.	English
F	France
FJI	Fiji
Fr.	French
GBR	Great Britain
Germ.	German
Gr.	Greek
GUF	French Guiana
I	Italy
It.	Italian
KIR	Kiribati
Lat.	Latin
NCL	New Caledonia
NEZ	New Zealand
NOR	Norway
OE	Old English
ON	Old Norse
Rtr.	Raeto-Romance
SHN	Saint Helena, Ascension and Tristan da Cunha

Slav.   Slavonic
SLB   Solomon Islands
Sp.   Spanish
SWE   Sweden
TKL   Tokelau
VUT   Vanuatu

LIST OF CONTRIBUTORS

Terhi Ainiala is University Lecturer in Finnish Language at the University of Helsinki. After her doctoral dissertation on Finnish place-names in change (1997), her research has been focused on socio-onomastics and place-naming. She is one of the three authors of *Names in Focus: An Introduction to Finnish Onomastics* (2012).

Emilia Aldrin is Senior Lecturer at Halmstad University, Sweden. She received a PhD in Scandinavian Languages from the University of Uppsala in 2011. She has published a monograph on the choice of first names as an act of identity, *Namnval som social handling* [*Naming as a social act*] (Uppsala University Press, 2011), as well as a number of articles on the subject. Her research interests also include socio-onomastics and anthroponyms.

Katarzyna Aleksiejuk has a PhD in Russian Studies from the University of Edinburgh for her thesis 'Names on the Internet: Towards Electronic Socio-onomastics'. She is interested in anthroponomastics from both historical and contemporary perspectives as well as in internet linguistics and the concept of identity.

Marc Alexander is Senior Lecturer in Semantics and Lexicology at the University of Glasgow. His work primarily focuses on digital humanities and the study of meaning in English, with a focus on lexicology, semantics, and stylistics through cognitive and corpus linguistics. He is Director of the *Historical Thesaurus of English*, and works mainly on applications of the *Thesaurus* in digital humanities, most recently through the AHRC/ESRC-funded SAMUELS and Mapping Metaphor projects. He also directs the STELLA Digital Humanities lab at Glasgow.

Ellen S. Bramwell is Research Associate at the University of Glasgow. Her PhD, awarded in 2012, examined personal naming practices in five communities within Scotland with differing social profiles, including both immigrant and indigenous communities. In addition to research into anthroponymy, she works on semantics and lexicography with a particular interest in conceptual metaphor.

Serge Brédart is Professor in the Cognitive Psychology Unit at the University of Liège (Belgium). His research bears upon the processes involved during the identification of familiar persons, including person naming. In his more recent work, he has investigated different aspects of self-related cognition such as self-recognition and self-reference effects in memory.

Stefan Brink is Sixth Century Professor of Scandinavian Studies, Adjunct Professor of Archaeology, and Director of the Centre for Scandinavian Studies at the University of Aberdeen. He is also *Docent* (Associate Professor) of Scandinavian Languages, especially Onomastics, at Uppsala University, Fellow of The Royal Swedish Academy of Letters, History and Antiquities, Stockholm, and Fellow of The Royal Gustavus Adolphus Academy for Swedish Folk Culture, Uppsala.

Eva Brylla† was Docent (Senior Lecturer) in Scandinavian Languages at Uppsala University, specializing in name research. Her doctoral thesis was on the inflection of place-names in Old Swedish, and she published extensively on both place-names and personal names. She was formerly the Head of the Department of Names at the Institute of Language and Folklore Research in Uppsala. Her death in March 2015 was a great loss to scholarship as well as to her family, colleagues, and friends.

Paul Cavill teaches Old English at the University of Nottingham. He is Editor of the *Journal of the English Place-Name Society*. He is author of many essays and several monographs on Old English literature including *Maxims in Old English Poetry* (1999), and, most recently, articles on the *Battle of Brunanburh*. He has edited *The Christian Tradition in Anglo-Saxon England* (2004) and co-edited *Language Contact in the Place-Names of Britain and Ireland* (2007).

Richard Coates is Professor of Linguistics/Onomastics at the University of the West of England, Bristol, Honorary Director of the Survey of English Place-Names, and principal investigator of the Family Names of the United Kingdom project (2010–16). He has special interests in the philological origins of place-names and surnames, especially in England, and also in the linguistic theory of names and naming, being responsible for The Pragmatic Theory of Properhood.

Elwys De Stefani is Professor of Italian Linguistics and Director of the research unit Multimodality, Interaction & Discourse (MIDI) at KU Leuven, Belgium. His research interests range from historical onomastics to the analysis of naturally occurring interactions. His previous academic appointments include the Universities of Basel, Neuchâtel, Berne (Switzerland), the University of Freiburg im Breisgau (Germany), and the University of Lyon 2 (France).

Peter Drummond has an MSc by Research from Edinburgh University on the hill-names of southern Scotland, and a PhD on place-names in the upper Kelvin basin from Glasgow University. He is the author of *Place-Names of the Monklands* (1982) and *Scottish Hill Names* (2007), and co-author of *Pentland Place-Names* (2011). He is also a leading member of the Scottish Place-Name Society.

Birgit Falck-Kjällquist is Senior Lecturer and was previously employed at the Institute for Languages and Folklore, Department of Onomastics in Uppsala, later Archive Manager of the Department of Dialectology, Onomastics and Folklore Research in Gothenburg. She has also been Editor at the Board of the Swedish Academy Dictionary.

She is now working on linguistic interpretations of place-names designating lakes, rivers, mountains, and so on, including minor names. Her research interests also include coastal names and literary onomastics.

Gillian Fellows-Jensen is Reader Emerita in Name Studies at the Department of Scandinavian Research of the University of Copenhagen, where she taught from 1961 to 2003. She has published widely in the field of place-names and is still actively interested in settlement history in the British Isles and Normandy, as well as in the care and conservation of manuscripts.

Peder Gammeltoft has researched place-names since 1996, focussing on place-names of Scandinavian origin outside of Scandinavia. His major contributions include a survey of the Old Norse place-name element *bólstaðr*, regional studies of place-names containing Old Norse *tóft* in the former Viking-Age colonies, island names, and managing the digitization of the Danish place-name collections. He also takes an active part in the standardization of place-names through the Danish Place-Name Commission and UNGEGN.

Alison Grant has a PhD in place-names and language contact from the University of Glasgow. She is Senior Editor with *Scottish Language Dictionaries* in Edinburgh, and is currently working on the revision of the *Concise Scots Dictionary*. She is also the Convener of the Scottish Place-Name Society, and is the author of *The Pocket Guide to Scottish Place-Names*.

Patrick Hanks is Lead Researcher on the Family Names Project at the University of the West of England. He is Editor-in-chief of the *Dictionary of American Family Names* and the forthcoming *Dictionary of Family Names in Britain and Ireland* (both Oxford University Press). He is co-author of the *Oxford Dictionary of First Names*. In addition, he holds a part-time position as Professor in Lexicography at the University of Wolverhampton. From 1990 to 2000 he was Chief Editor of Current English Dictionaries at Oxford University Press.

Carole Hough is Professor of Onomastics at the University of Glasgow. Her research interests include Scottish and English place-names and personal names, names in literature, and onomastic theory. She has around 300 publications on these and other topics. A former President of the International Council of Onomastic Sciences and Convener of the Scottish Place-Name Society, she is currently President of the International Society of Anglo-Saxonists, Vice-President of the Society for Name Studies in Britain and Ireland, and a Council Member of the English Place-Name Society.

Malcolm Jones retired from the School of English at Sheffield University in 2010. Before joining the university he had worked as a lexicographer and museum curator. To date he has published two books concerned with art history: *The Secret Middle Ages* (2002), and *The Print in Early Modern England* (2010), and he is currently working on a book on Gaelic place-names and their associated folklore.

Richard Jones is Senior Lecturer in Landscape History based in the Centre for English Local History, University of Leicester. His research focuses on the rural communities and environments of medieval England. His books include *Medieval Villages in an English Landscape: Beginnings and Ends* (2006), *Thorps in a Changing Landscape* (2011), *Manure Matters: Historical, Archaeological and Ethnographic Perspectives* (2012), *Sense of Place in Anglo-Saxon England* (2012), and *The Medieval Natural World* (2013).

Andreas H. Jucker is Dean of the Faculty of Arts and Social Sciences and Professor of English Linguistics at the University of Zurich. His current research interests include historical pragmatics, politeness theory, speech act theory, and the grammar and history of English. His recent publications include *English Historical Pragmatics* (Edinburgh University Press, 2013) co-authored with Irma Taavitsainen and *Diachronic Corpus Pragmatics* (Benjamins, 2014) co-edited with Irma Taavitsainen and Jukka Tuominen.

Adrian Koopman is Professor Emeritus of the University of KwaZulu-Natal in Pietermaritzburg, South Africa. He has taught Zulu linguistics and literature for over thirty-five years but his major research interest has always been in onomastics. He is currently the President of the Names Society of Southern Africa, and the Editor of its journal *Nomina Africana*, and has served on the Executive of the International Council of Onomastic Sciences, including being Vice-President from 2008 to 2010.

Laura Kostanski is the CEO and Director of Geonaming Solutions Pty Ltd. She holds a PhD in Geography and History, a Graduate Certificate in Tertiary Education and a Bachelor of Arts (Honours) in Linguistics and History. Her professional and research interests centre on developing robust geospatial, addressing, and geographic naming policies and systems for government and private clients at national and international levels.

Julia Kuhn is full Professor of Romance Linguistics at the Friedrich Schiller Universität Jena, Germany. Her main research interests are Onomastics, Discourse Analysis, Construction Grammar and Systemic Linguistics. From 2005 to 2011 she was a member of the Board of Directors of the International Council of Onomastic Sciences, and a member of the editorial boards of the journals *Namenkundliche Informationen* and *Onoma*. She worked on the project *St. Galler Namenbuch* initiated by Gerold Hilty and Hans Stricker, University of Zürich, Switzerland, and for the *Lexikon der schweizerischen Gemeindenamen* edited by Andres Kristol, University of Neuchatel, Switzerland. She has published numerous articles and books on onomastic subjects.

Edwin D. Lawson is Professor Emeritus of Psychology at the State University of New York, Fredonia. His doctorate is from the University of Illinois, Urbana-Champaign. Before coming to Fredonia, he taught at the State University of New York, Albany, and Acadia University, Nova Scotia. He has published many articles in social psychology and also in onomastics. Work in onomastics has included annotated bibliographies and several names websites.

Katharina Leibring received her PhD in Scandinavian Studies at the University of Uppsala in 2000, and became Reader at the same university in 2006. She is currently employed as Senior Research Archivist at the Department of Onomastics, Institute for language and folklore in Uppsala. Her main research interests include animal names, personal names, and contemporary name-giving. She is an editor of *Studia anthroponymica Scandinavica* and is a former member of the Board of Directors of the International Council of Onomastic Sciences.

Kay Muhr read Celtic Studies at Edinburgh 1966–70 and gained a PhD on Gaelic literature from the same university. After postgraduate fellowships in Cambridge, Dublin, and Queen's University Belfast, she became Senior Researcher of the Northern Ireland Place-Name Project in Irish & Celtic Studies, from its foundation in 1987 until 2010. A former president of the Society for Name Studies in Britain and Ireland, and chairman of the Ulster Place-Name Society, she is now a private scholar.

Bertie Neethling is currently Senior Emeritus Professor at the University of the Western Cape in South Africa. His research interests vary, but he has lately focused entirely on onomastics. Contributions have been on anthroponymy (first names, family names, bynames), toponymy (street names, school names), names in the economy, names in songs, and animal names. His most significant publication is the monograph *Naming among the Xhosa of South Africa* (Edwin Mellen Press, 2005).

Staffan Nyström is Professor (chair) in Scandinavian Onomastics at Uppsala University, Sweden. He is active in the Place Names Advisory Board of Sweden (member), the Name Drafting Committee of Stockholm (chair), the Place Name Society of Uppsala (chair), the International Council of Onomastic Sciences (treasurer), and United Nations Group of Experts on Geographical Names (convenor of its working group on toponymic terminology). His research interests include field names, microtoponymy, urban names, national and international name standardization, and name theory.

Harry Parkin is Research Associate on the Family Names Project at the University of the West of England, Bristol. He is a linguist with particular interests in the history of English surnames, the methodology of surname research, and the use of historical onomastic data in philology, demography, and Middle English dialectology.

Guy Puzey is a postdoctoral researcher at the University of Edinburgh, Scotland, where he also teaches Norwegian and works as a course organizer for lifelong learning courses in Germanic and Slavonic languages. In the field of language policy, he has carried out extensive research on the relative visibility of languages in public spaces and language activism, while in critical toponomastic studies, he has incorporated the linguistic landscape approach into studies of power and place-naming.

George Redmonds works as a freelance historian in Yorkshire, specializing in Name Studies, Language and Local History. He has lectured widely in Europe, North America, Australia, and New Zealand, and in 2001 presented the BBC Radio 4 series *Surnames. Genes and Genealogy*. His numerous books include *Surnames and Genealogy* (1997) and

Christian Names in Local and Family History (2004). In 2011 he co-authored *Surnames, DNA, and Family History* with Turi King and David Hey.

Berit Sandnes wrote her doctoral thesis on Old Norse place-names in Orkney with special focus on contact linguistic aspects. She has worked with Onomastics in Norway and Denmark. Since 2006, she has been Research Archivist at the Institute for Language and Folklore, Department of Dialectology in Lund, Sweden. One area of interest is how speakers interpret and adapt names.

Margaret Scott is Lecturer in English Literature and English Language at the University of Salford. She formerly worked as a lexicographer for the Historical Thesaurus of English at the University of Glasgow, the *Oxford English Dictionary*, and Scottish Language Dictionaries in Edinburgh. She edited *Nomina*, the journal of the Society for Name Studies in Britain and Ireland, from 2008 to 2013. Her research interests include Onomastics and the History and Lexicography of English and Scots.

Paula Sjöblom is Senior Lecturer and Docent in Finnish language at the University of Turku, Finland. Her main interests are in commercial naming, theoretical and methodological questions of onomastics, cognitive linguistics, text linguistics, and business language. Her doctoral thesis (2006) on Finnish company names presents new methods for name studies. She is one of the three authors of *Names in Focus* (2012), and she has published a number of scholarly articles about commercial naming and name theory.

Grant W. Smith is Professor of English and Coordinator of Humanities at Eastern Washington University. He has served as President of the American Name Society, Vice President of the International Council of Onomastic Sciences, Regional Secretary for the American Dialect Society, and is a long-time member of the Washington Board on Geographic Names. His current scholarship emphasizes literary onomastics, especially Shakespeare, but previous publications include American Indian languages and the emotive effects of language sounds.

Svante Strandberg presented his doctoral thesis at Uppsala University in 1991: *Studier över sörmländska sjönamn: Etymologi, namnbildning och formutveckling* ('Studies of Södermanland lake names: Etymology, name formation and morphological development'). From 1994 to 2007 he held the chair of Scandinavian Languages, especially Onomastics, at Uppsala University. Since 2006 he has been the Editor of the journal *Namn och bygd*. He has published a large number of articles, many of them dealing with hydronyms.

Irma Taavitsainen is Professor Emerita of English Philology at the University of Helsinki. Her interests cover historical pragmatics and corpus linguistics, genre studies and historical discourse analysis. She has published widely in these fields. Her most recent co-edited volume is *Developments in English: Expanding Electronic Evidence* (Cambridge University Press, 2015) with Merja Kytö, Claudia Claridge, and Jeremy Smith. Her research team has produced two electronic corpora, and a third, *Late Modern English Medical Texts 1700–1800*, is under way.

Simon Taylor is Lecturer at the University of Glasgow specializing in Scottish topo-nymics. He has published extensively on the subject including five volumes of the place-names of Fife (2006–12) and individual volumes on the place-names of Kinross-shire and Clackmannanshire (forthcoming). He co-founded the Scottish Place-Name Society in 1996. He has been Editor of the annual *Journal of Scottish Name Studies* since its inception in 2007, the first academic, peer-reviewed publication devoted to Scottish onomastics.

Andreas Teutsch worked as a translator for a French company in the automotive sec-tor, after graduating in Applied Linguistics and Cultural Studies. In 2001 he joined the trademark department of the Swiss Federal Institute of Intellectual Property in Berne as a linguistic consultant and trademark examiner. In 2007 he received his PhD in General Linguistics. His main fields of research are language and law as well as onomastics with special focus on product names.

Karina van Dalen-Oskam's research interests focus on the digital and computational humanities, especially on stylometry and (comparative) literary onomastics. She is head of the department of Literary Studies at Huygens Institute for the History of the Netherlands (Royal Netherlands Academy of Arts and Sciences) and Professor of Computational Literary Studies at the University of Amsterdam. She is currently president of EADH, the European Association for Digital Humanities.

Mark Van de Velde is a researcher at Llacan, a research lab of CNRS dedicated to the study of African languages, where he is currently Deputy Director. He is interested in linguistic typology, linguistic documentation, and especially the grammatical analy-sis of previously undescribed sub-Saharan languages. Traditionally a specialist in the Bantu languages, he has recently started working on the Adamawa languages of Nigeria.

Willy Van Langendonck was Professor of Linguistics at the University of Leuven until 2003. He started as a structuralist, became a generativist, turned to Generative Semantics, and became interested in cognitive linguistic theories. His research interests include markedness and iconicity, reference and semantics (especially proper names), grammatical categories such as definiteness, genericness, number, grammatical rela-tions, prepositions, dependency syntax, and word-order. He has published widely on proper names.

CHAPTER 1

INTRODUCTION

CAROLE HOUGH

1.1 INTRODUCTION

THE study of names, known as 'onomastics', is both an old and a young discipline. Since Ancient Greece, names have been regarded as central to the study of language, throwing light on how humans communicate with each other and organize their world. Socrates, Plato, Aristotle, and others were keenly interested in the relationship between names and referents, and this has continued to be a major theme of both philosophical and linguistic enquiry throughout the history of Western thought. The investigation of name origins, on the other hand, is more recent, not developing until the twentieth century in some areas, and being still today at a formative stage in others. Here the emphasis is on etymology, systematically tracing the derivation of individual names back through time, and the resulting data have provided a rich evidence base for the investigation of historical and linguistic topics. Relatively new is the study of names in society, which draws on techniques from sociolinguistics and has gradually been gathering momentum over the last few decades.

Whereas these approaches encompass names of all kinds, others prioritize particular types of names, such as place-names or personal names. A wide range of inter-disciplinary research bearing on archaeology, geography, and landscape studies focuses largely on the names of places, while research bearing on anthropology and genealogy focuses largely on the names of people. Fictional as well as real names repay attention, most obviously in the study of names in literature, but also in relation to areas such as commerce, law, psychology, and religion. Named entities are not limited to people and places, but extend to other living creatures, man-made objects, and celestial bodies, all reflecting different aspects of the interaction between humans and their surroundings.

Much research in the field begins at the level of the individual name, but only reaches full significance when the results are grouped together, allowing patterns to emerge. Comparative analysis of large datasets has been facilitated enormously by advances in technology, as some of the contributions to this volume explain. Also important is the sharing of knowledge through national and international collaboration. Many name scholars are closely involved in subject societies, whether focusing on names of a particular type or within a particular geographical area, and the over-arching organization, the International Congress of Onomastic Sciences, brings together research into names of all types throughout the world at its triennial conferences.

The structure of this volume reflects the emergence of the main branches of name studies, in roughly chronological order. First, a section on name theory outlines key issues about the role of names in language. Some of these will be revisited in later chapters, often from different viewpoints. Many aspects of the subject are controversial, and the volume does not aim to present a party line, but rather to reflect the rich diversity of scholarship. Part II deals with toponomastics, the study of place-names, with an opening chapter on methodology followed by chapters on different types of referents. Part III turns to anthroponomastics, the study of personal names, beginning with an overview of naming systems in different parts of the world, followed by chapters on the individual components of those systems. Part IV outlines contrasting approaches to the study of names in literature, otherwise known as literary onomastics, with case studies from different languages and time periods. Part V introduces a range of recent scholarship within the field of socio-onomastics, with chapters relating to the names of people, places, and commercial products. Part VI focuses on the inter-disciplinarity of name studies, outlining some of the ways in which other disciplines both draw on, and contribute to, this field of research. Finally, Part VII presents a selection of animate and inanimate referents, and explores the naming strategies adopted for them. Strikingly, each has distinctive naming patterns, some esoteric, some idiosyncratic, and some developed with great ingenuity according to a complex system.

1.2 ONOMASTIC THEORY

What are names, and how do they function in language? As Coates (2006e: 7) explains, name theory is 'arguably the most ancient topic area in the whole of linguistics since it was first problematized by Plato in his *Cratylus*, and it is, notwithstanding its antiquity, one with foundational problems still to be resolved'. In the English-speaking world, names are traditionally regarded as a type of noun or noun phrase, sometimes referred to as 'proper nouns'. Whether they are atypical or prototypical nouns has been hotly debated, and attempts have also been made to reclassify them as determinatives (Anderson 2003, 2004, 2007). This volume therefore begins with the crucial issue of the definition of names—a definition which, like other key questions addressed in subsequent chapters, must be universally applicable rather than language-specific. To this end, Willy Van Langendonck and Mark Van de Velde advocate a cognitive approach, focusing on the pragmatic-semantic properties of names as distinct from language-specific grammatical categories. Drawing on data from a range of European and African languages, they argue that names are definite nouns with unique denotation, an inherent basic level sense, no defining sense, and optional connotative meanings.

In the following chapter, Staffan Nyström picks up on the issue of meaning, elaborating on the different types of meaning attributed to names by different scholars, and outlining the main arguments relating to this highly controversial area of name theory. Despite the influential view that absence of semantic meaning is a defining characteristic of a name, some theorists argue that names have certain types of semantic meaning, while many—perhaps all—accept that names have non-semantic meaning. This chapter too takes a cognitive approach, focusing particularly on the interface between lexical and proprial meaning, such that lexically transparent components of names may bring to mind their non-proprial meanings. Nyström also provides a cogent exposition of the range of potential presuppositional meanings, including categorical (basic level) meaning, associative (connotative) meaning, and emotive (affective) meaning. Like Van Langendonck and Van de Velde, who identify a 'cline of nameworthiness' from more to less typical types of names, he argues that 'names and words should not be seen as completely isolated from each other but instead as two communicating and integrated parts of the total network, the mental lexicon'. Both chapters thus situate names within a language continuum, rather than proposing a cut-off point separating them from other linguistic items.

The third and final chapter in this section shifts the perspective from the internal properties of names to their uses in spoken language. Elwys De Stefani introduces the concept of interactional onomastics, applying techniques from conversation analysis to the study of names in discourse. Again pragmatic analysis is key to the investigation, but whereas traditional approaches to onomastic theory have been dominated by issues relating to the denotative function of names, this chapter raises broader questions about their social and cultural significance. In so doing, de Stefani introduces a number of themes that will be revisited in later sections of the volume, particularly in connection with anthropology and socio-onomastics.

1.3 TOPONOMASTICS

The study of place-names is known as 'toponomastics', the term recommended in the list of key onomastic terms produced by the International Congress of Onomastic Sciences (ICOS 2011). An alternative term 'toponymy' is preferred by some scholars but is ambiguous, as it also refers to a corpus of place-names, otherwise known as 'toponyms'. Much research in toponomastics is organized geographically, surveying the place-names of an area by compiling and analysing sequences of historical spellings in order to establish etymological origins. The opening chapter of Part II offers an introduction to sources and methodologies, focusing on the recently-inaugurated Survey of Scottish Place-Names. Simon Taylor draws on his extensive experience of place-name research to discuss key issues relating to the collection, organization, storage, analysis, and presentation of data, including evidence from both written and oral sources. Although Scotland is a small country, its toponymy draws on an unusually wide range of languages including both Celtic and Germanic strata, and hence the examples presented here have a much broader relevance.

The following chapters deal with the names of different types of geographical entities, including both the natural and the built environment. The prototypical place-name is that of a human settlement such as a town, city, or village, and there are many parallels between those found in different parts of the world. Some parallels result from similar naming strategies being applied independently by unrelated groups of speakers; others result from names being transferred directly from one area to another. Carole Hough outlines the main structures of settlement names, grouped broadly into descriptive and non-descriptive names. The former tend to predominate in Indo-European languages, whereas the latter, which include commemorative, transferred, and incident names, are characteristic not only of some non-Indo-European languages but of the names created by European settlers in the African, American, and Australian continents during the Age of Exploration. The second part of Hough's chapter discusses some of the evidence preserved in both groups, particularly for settlement patterns, settlement chronologies and historical linguistics. Examples are mostly from the mainland of Britain, but again the underlying principles have a broader relevance.

The most ancient toponyms are those of large geographical features. The names of major rivers are among the earliest evidence for language and population movement, with some dating back two millennia or more. Svante Strandberg analyses the linguistic and chronological strata reflected in different types of formations, as well as the implications of identical or related river names in areas of Britain and continental Europe. His chapter includes a discussion of some of the most common roots in European river names, alongside semantic and morphological factors. A controversial area is the stratigraphy of 'Old European' hydronymy, a system of river naming dating back to a period before the emergence of individual branches of Indo-European. This has been a major focus of scholarship throughout the twentieth and early twenty-first centuries, and the chapter traces the development of the debate.

Other large geographical features include hills and mountains, whose names are the subject of Peter Drummond's chapter. These tend to be recorded later than the names of settlements and of rivers, a factor attributed to their economic marginality. It is also more common for more than one name to be attached to a single feature, partly due to lack of communication between rural societies on different sides of a single mountain. Something similar accounts for the fact that the names of ranges tend to be later than those of individual hills, since the concept of a local hill being part of a larger group depends on a degree of mobility. Changes over time are also relatively common in hill names, as are uncertainties regarding the precise referent, which may comprise the whole massif, its main or subsidiary summit, a shoulder, or another prominent part. Alongside such issues, Drummond gives an account of research into the defining elements or 'generics' of mountain names in Scotland, Ireland, Switzerland, and France, followed by a discussion of selected types of qualifying elements or 'specifics', focusing in particular on the application of personal names to summits in the former European colonies, the USA, and Europe.

The naming strategies of the European colonizers are also reflected in many island names, since islands are often among the first places to be settled and named by new groups of incomers. For the same reason, they provide unique evidence for language history and migration patterns. Peder Gammeltoft explores these and other issues, with particular attention to the mindsets of the namers. Case studies include island names of Scandinavian origin in the British Isles, and island names from Polynesian *motu* 'island' in the Pacific Ocean. Both illustrate the central role of island names in tracing the spread of people and their languages throughout the world.

Julia Kuhn deals with a more disparate set of entities, linked by being 'uninhabited, delimited objects in rural settings and surroundings'. Her chapter on rural names covers the names of fields, meadows, forests, single trees, and so on, many of which are associated with the agricultural exploitation of land. Changes in farming practices are leading to the loss of such names, so there is a real urgency to the task of documenting and studying them. Their main purpose is orientation and the identification of areas within small and limited units, and they provide fine-grained evidence for local conditions and dialects. Kuhn offers a detailed analysis of semantic and morphological patterns, followed by an outline of methods of collection and interpretation. Many examples are from Romance and Germanic languages, and the chapter demonstrates the value and importance of this often neglected group of toponyms.

Whereas rural names serve to organize uninhabited space, street names fulfil the corresponding purpose in towns and cities. There are, however, marked contrasts, not least in that whereas rural names are gradually diminishing in use, street names represent the most productive area of the present-day toponymicon. Bertie Neethling begins by outlining the characteristic structures of street names, and moves on to examine their functions, both referential and symbolic. His chapter focuses particularly on the renaming of streets, with case studies from South Africa. The high emotive value of commemorative names is strikingly illustrated, reinforcing the key role of such formations in the naming environments treated in previous chapters.

The final chapter in this section deals not with a type of referent but with a type of naming strategy, touched on in previous chapters but here brought centre-stage. Stefan Brink presents an in-depth treatment of place-name transfers, including different ways of adapting existing names, and the importance of analogy and patterning in name formation. Many examples are from Scandinavia; others from Polynesia and the European colonies.

1.4 ANTHROPONOMASTICS

Also referred to as 'anthroponymy', anthroponomastics encompasses the study of names given to individuals or to groups of people. As in toponomastics, etymological investigation is a major thrust of investigation, but there is in addition a greater emphasis on the historical development of naming patterns and on synchronic research into name choices. This section outlines the development and uses of different kinds of personal names, and concludes by discussing links with related areas of research.

Unlike place-names, where there are different naming strategies for different referents, personal names all refer to the same type of referent—people—but the system itself comprises different types of names, including given names, family names, nicknames, and so on. The various components of the personal naming system are selected and combined in different ways in different cultures, and the opening chapter in this section presents a comparative analysis of fifteen languages across the world. Edwin D. Lawson assembles a range of specialists to outline the naming practices in their language of expertise, and then correlates the data in order to identify shared features. The results show that naming practices in the UK have the most overlap with others, followed respectively by those found in Greek, German, Dutch, the USA, French, Portuguese, Hungarian, Polish, Chinese, Maltese, Jewish, Zulu, Māori, and the Bible.

The following chapter by Katharina Leibring focuses on given names, otherwise known as first names. After defining and categorizing given names both morphologically and semantically, she presents a diachronic survey of their evolution and selection in a wide range of European naming systems from pre-Christian times to the present day. Despite differences between countries and regions, a number of common features are identified, including a bias towards male, upper class names in the extant records. Changes in naming practices are linked to historical developments, and the survey concludes with a discussion of the current trend in many European countries for individualization in given names, through such strategies as unorthodox spellings and the creation of new, innovatory names.

In many naming systems, one or more given names are followed by a surname, otherwise known as a family name since its function is to identify an individual as a member of a family. Patrick Hanks and Harry Parkin address the origins and typology of hereditary surnames in different parts of the UK, drawing both on previous scholarship and on examples from the ongoing *Family Names of Britain and Ireland* research project at the University of the West of England. They also discuss the influence of migration on the world's family-name stocks, such that, for instance, present-day surnames in the UK reflect origins in languages as diverse as Arabic, Chinese, English, French, Gaelic, Hebrew, Indian, Latin, Persian, Turkish, and Yiddish. The chapter goes on to present an account of scholarship in continental Europe, Asia, and the Indian subcontinent, and concludes by drawing attention to the potential of large surname databases to underpin further research in the field.

As Hanks and Parkin explain, an intermediate stage before the development of hereditary family names was the use of non-hereditary bynames. These, alongside nicknames, are the focus of the next chapter by Eva Brylla. She begins by defining the terms, before turning to issues relating to function, syntax, semantics, and morphology. Coverage extends to the names both of individuals and of groups such as football clubs, and there is also a brief analysis of internet names, to which the next section will return. Similarly, the concluding discussion of bynames as a mirror of society raises issues that will be addressed in further detail within Part V.

The names of ethnic groups are known as 'ethnonyms', and Adrian Koopman discusses the relationship between the names themselves and a range of factors often linked to ethnicity, including race, nationality, geographical area, language, and religion. Case studies focus on Scottish and Zulu clan names, and the chapter addresses theoretical issues concerning the linguistic status of ethnonyms.

The remaining two chapters in this section deal with areas of research which both draw on and contribute to anthroponomastics. Ellen S. Bramwell outlines the role of names within anthropological frameworks, with examples from different parts of the world. Examining the close connection between names and the cultural contexts in which they appear, she argues that despite some existing cross-over between the two disciplines through, for instance, the use of ethnographic fieldwork methods, there is potential for much closer theoretical engagement. Finally, George Redmonds explores the key role of personal naming patterns in tracing ancestry. While the significance of surnames for genealogy has long been recognized, he argues that the importance of given names in this connection has been undervalued. His chapter presents a compelling analysis of patterns of distribution, showing how they can be used not only to reveal the origins of individual names, but also to trace migration, whether between countries or between counties. The complexities associated with the development of surname variants, abbreviations, and contractions are illustrated by a wealth of examples, and the chapter emphasizes the role of the genealogist as contributor to, as well as beneficiary from, name research.

1.5 LITERARY ONOMASTICS

Despite an exponential growth of publications on literary onomastics in recent decades, the development of methodologies for the study of names in literature is at a much earlier stage than for the study of either toponomastics or anthroponomastics. This section discusses the theoretical basis of literary onomastics and offers a survey of different kinds of approaches.

The opening chapter by Grant W. Smith takes as its starting point the philosophical debate concerning the meaning of names, and provides a magisterial survey of competing theories. Supporting the semiotic approach advocated by C. S. Peirce, he analyses literary uses of names in terms of iconic associations, indexical associations, and symbolic associations. The chapter concludes by emphasizing the importance of systematic analysis.

In contrast to this broad theoretical approach, Bertie Neethling presents a comparative analysis of uses of names in two songs from the late twentieth century: Billy Joel's *We Didn't Start The Fire* and Christopher Torr's *Hot Gates*. Both are remarkable for the sheer number of names included in the lyrics. Torr uses place-names exclusively, while Joel brings in a variety of place-names, personal names, brand names, and others. Particular significance is attached to connotative meanings, bringing out the ways in which they enrich the artistic experience.

Some uses of names are genre-specific, so a number of literary onomastic studies approach names through groups of texts related by genre. Birgit Falck-Kjällquist outlines previous research in connection with a variety of genres, including nineteenth-century novels, twentieth-century detective fiction, sequels, comics, fantasy literature, drama, films, heroic poetry, medieval romance, and parodies. The main focus is on English and German literature.

Advances in technology are transforming many branches of name studies, not least in this field. Karina van Dalen-Oskam outlines the development of literary onomastic scholarship from the qualitative analysis of selected names to the quantitative analysis of the entire 'onymic landscape', an approach facilitated by the availability of electronic databases. As yet, only relatively small text corpora are available for this kind of study, but the chapter demonstrates the immense potential of a computational approach.

Paul Cavill's chapter on language-based approaches to names in literature traces the history of literary onomastics from the earliest written traditions to the present day. It relates literary names to contemporary naming practices, showing how and why they sometimes differ. There is a particular focus on Old and Middle English literature, Shakespeare, and later modern novelists.

1.6 SOCIO-ONOMASTICS

The emerging subdiscipline of socio-onomastics offers new approaches to names of all kinds, including both personal names and place-names. As Terhi Ainiala explains, this branch of onomastics examines names in society, focusing particularly on name variation. Names vary according to the social, cultural, and situational fields in which they are used, and socio-onomastics draws on techniques from sociolinguistics in order to trace and to analyse this phenomenon. Ainiala's chapter offers a state-of-the-art account of the field, and concludes by presenting folk onomastics as a sub-category of socio-onomastics.

The role of names is key to the construction of identity and to notions of selfhood, but has only recently begun to be critically examined. Emilia Aldrin gives an overview of theoretical and methodological tools, and outlines current trends and gaps within the field. Her chapter focuses mainly on contemporary names, primarily those of individuals.

Turning from personal names to place-names, Guy Puzey introduces linguistic land-scape research, an approach that has emerged in recent years to reflect issues relating to the language(s) used on public signs (e.g. roads, railway stations, shops) in areas occu-pied by different speech communities. These issues are crucial to the field of language planning. Puzey details major theoretical and methodological developments here and in the related fields of geosemiotics and semiotic landscapes. He then turns to the ono-mastic potential, including opportunities to apply linguistic landscape fieldwork tech-niques to study observable onomastic practice, to facilitate the collection of names, and to study names in relation to language policy.

Recent work on place attachment (comprising place identity and place dependence) has led to a new theory of 'Toponymic attachment', with particular relevance to areas of the world with both indigenous and immigrant populations. Toponymic attachment is defined as a positive or negative association made by individuals and groups with real or imagined place-names. It was developed by Laura Kostanski, whose chapter makes comparisons between existing geographical-domain-based theories and potential new avenues for exploration, while also investigating and explaining the sub-domains of 'Toponymic identity' and 'Toponymyic dependence'. Most examples are from the Grampians National Park in Australia.

The names used to address a person may not be the names used to refer to him or her, and may indeed vary substantially in different situations and social environ-ments. As much if not more than names themselves, forms of address reflect chang-ing cultural values and attitudes both synchronically and diachronically. As Irma Taavitsainen and Andreas H. Jucker explain, address terms are used by speakers to appeal to their hearer(s) and to convey both interpersonal and expressive meanings, with a scale extending from endearment to deference and to terms of abuse. Their chapter outlines alternative semantic classifications, and presents a diachronic over-view of changes in both the frequency and the semantic types of address terms. The focus is on English, but there is also some consideration of developments in other languages.

Unlike personal names and nicknames, which are generally bestowed by other peo-ple, and also unlike surnames, which are inherited, pseudonyms are chosen by the indi-vidual, and hence offer specific insights into naming and self-presentation. Katarzyna Aleksiejuk introduces pseudonyms as a category of names, and describes practices of use from various angles. She goes on to outline the historical development of schol-arly approaches to anonymity and pseudonymity, and the functions of pseudonyms in different contexts, including literature, entertainment, politics, religion, and selected non-European traditions. Her chapter also discusses the recent phenomenon of internet usernames, and puts forward a proposed typology.

Another area of naming that has come to prominence in recent years is commer-cial nomenclature, often but not always referring to businesses and products. Paula Sjöblom explores the increasing commercialization of the Western way of life and its impact on names. Her chapter casts light on the history of commercial naming and introduces different approaches to linguistic analysis. There is a particular focus on the semantics and functions of names, and Sjöblom explains how English, as the global language of business, is pervasive in commercial names throughout the world.

1.7 ONOMASTICS AND OTHER DISCIPLINES

Onomastics is essentially inter-disciplinary, and it might be difficult to identify any major subject area to which it is completely unrelated. The chapters in this section explore some of the most prominent connections between name studies and other fields of research, but are by no means exhaustive. Their number could easily have been multiplied, and readers will no doubt be able to think of other topics that could have been included.

First, Richard Jones discusses names and archaeology, explaining how place-names and field names can be used to locate sites of archaeological interest, while examination of material culture can contribute to the understanding of when and why places were named. The emergence of cognitive approaches has also led to place-names being used as evidence for the mental world of past communities.

Cognitive approaches are also central to Serge Brédart's chapter on names and cognitive psychology. He begins by summarizing empirical evidence demonstrating that personal names are both more difficult to retrieve than other biographical information about people, and more difficult to retrieve than other words. Then he outlines competing hypotheses that attempt to explain these difficulties, respectively on the grounds that personal names lack descriptiveness, that person naming requires the retrieval of one specific label, that the set size of plausible phonology is larger for personal names, and that the frequency of personal name usage is relatively low. The conclusion is that a combination of factors makes personal names hard to recall.

Maggie Scott's chapter on names and dialectology explores the relationship between the study of language varieties and the study of names, taking account of historical developments in theory and methodology. The oral corpus of local names is usually more detailed than that represented on maps, and such 'unofficial' names can provide a range of insights into the sociolinguistic and pragmatic functions of non-standard, slang, and dialectal terminology. Place-names also preserve important evidence for dialect geography, and Scott draws on Nicolaisen's concept of the *onomastic dialect* to provide an explanatory framework for instances where onomastic isoglosses do not parallel their lexical counterparts.

Peder Gammeltoft also focuses largely on place-names for his chapter on names and geography. A challenge in using place-names in this connection is to establish when a name was established and the significance of the naming focus. In addition, later onomastic developments may create a mismatch between the current denotation and the original place-name meaning. These and other issues are explored here, alongside a discussion of the role of Geographical Information Systems and geospatial databases in both onomastic research and geography.

Turning to names and history, Gillian Fellows-Jensen outlines the various linguistic layers of place-names in England in reverse chronological order. She moves from names of French origin to those from Norse, Anglo-Saxon, and Celtic languages, tracing the principal areas where each group is found, and also touching on river names of Old European origin.

Richard Coates's chapter on historical linguistics looks at names as evidence for the nature and progress of linguistic change, and for prehistoric languages which have since disappeared. The relationship between names and other vocabulary items is also addressed, and the chapter concludes with a description and evaluation of the practice of the etymological study of names.

As Berit Sandnes explains, place-names are easily borrowed in language contact situations, probably because sharing a place-name is the easiest way to point out a specific location. Loan names are regularly adapted to the sound system of the recipient language, and adaptations occur sporadically on other linguistic levels, including grammar and syntax. Elements may be translated or substituted by similar-sounding words in the new language. Sandnes also draws attention to the key role of the speaker in contact onomastics, as processes such as translations, replacement of elements, and syntactic adaptations can only be explained as the result of a speaker's interpretation and adaptation.

Personal names feature prominently in Andreas Teutsch's chapter on names and law, since they are closely connected with personal rights. Teutsch presents an overview of legal regulations concerning personal names in different countries, but also attempts to define universal tendencies and to discuss the challenge of legal harmonization on an international level. Since law regulates social interaction, it can also be a decisive institution for conflicts relating to other types of names, including those of places, streets, undertakings, and commercial products.

Alison Grant charts the increasing use of onomastic source material in English lexicography, from its marginal consideration in the first edition of the *Oxford English Dictionary* to the much more inclusive policy of the ongoing third edition. In Scotland, the situation is less well advanced, and name evidence is used unsystematically in the major dictionaries of Scots, a language for which reliable onomastic source material is also less readily available. However, toponymic and anthroponymic evidence can provide valuable ante-datings and reinterpretations for existing dictionary entries, as well as providing new additions to the lexicon.

Kay Muhr discusses the interface between names and religion, focusing particularly on place-names in Ireland. Her chapter presents some place-name elements from Ireland illustrating the sacredness of water, hills, and burial and assembly sites. She analyses problematic terms such as *findabair, temair*, the Otherworld dwelling *síd*, the pagan grave *fert*, and the human house *tech*, as well as ecclesiastical terminology borrowed from Latin: *domnach, cell, dísert, aireagal, martar*, and *reilic*.

1.8 OTHER NAMES

Names are given to many animate and inanimate referents, with distinctive patterns even for apparently similar referents such as boats and ships, locomotives and trains, or pets and farm animals. The shorter chapters in this section explore some of these patterns. Again, their number could have been expanded exponentially, but the aim is to provide a representative cross-section, illustrating a variety of naming strategies.

Guy Puzey covers aircraft names, presenting an outline history of approaches to naming British military aircraft types. Civil aircraft naming practices are illustrated with the example of the Boeing Company's 700-series of airliners, and the chapter also discusses aircraft naming in international development projects. Finally, examples are given of names and nicknames for individual machines.

Two of the chapters in Part I drew attention to similarities between personal names and pet names, and Katharina Leibring now treats the names of domestic animals in fuller detail both diachronically and synchronically. She focuses on the names of production animals and companion animals in European countries from the eighteenth century onwards, but also includes some coverage of African and Arctic animal names. Changes in the name stock for different species are related to changes in agriculture, and differences between the names of male and female animals are also addressed.

Marc Alexander introduces the study of astronomical naming practices, showing how they relate to scientific and general culture. His chapter focuses on constellation names, star names, and planet names, and addresses both the historical background and the complex modern conventions.

Adrian Koopman discusses the names of private dwellings, outlining the various semantic categories and levels of meaning. He focuses particularly on the functions and meanings of Zulu homestead names, with an emphasis on their use to communicate messages aimed at relieving tension and conflict.

The two remaining chapters deal with land and sea transport. Richard Coates describes the history of the names of steam locomotives, showing a progression from attributive to arbitrary names. He also more briefly considers the names of trains. Finally, Malcolm Jones discusses the names given to ships from the earliest records to the present day. Political and religious motivations for the giving and changing of names are illustrated from the English, French, and Russian Revolutions. Categories of name are illustrated from medieval and early modern English and Spanish fleets, and modern navies, merchantmen, and cruise-lines.

1.9 CONCLUSION

As well as outlining the current state of name studies in its various branches, the chapters in this volume show the discipline continuing to expand and to develop into new areas.

To mention a few examples from different sections, de Stefani introduces the concept of interactional onomastics, Neethling argues for song lyrics as a legitimate area of investigation for literary onomastics, Sandnes introduces contact onomastics as a branch of contact linguistics, and some of the legal cases cited by Teutsch show changes still in progress through ongoing rulings with a binding effect. Research within name studies is vigorous, vibrant, and innovative, and if this volume had been produced twenty or even ten years ago, many of the chapters would have been radically different or even absent. We can be confident that a similar undertaking in another ten or twenty years would be as different again.

PART I

ONOMASTIC THEORY

CHAPTER 2

··

NAMES AND GRAMMAR

··

WILLY VAN LANGENDONCK
AND MARK VAN DE VELDE

2.1 INTRODUCTION

THE study of names and grammar involves establishing the grammar of proper names (henceforth: names) in one or more languages. First, we should have a workable idea of what is to be understood by *names* and by *grammar*, because '... finally onomastics is a branch of linguistics' (Algeo 2010: 93). Thus, we first have to deal with a long-standing distinction. In recent decades, many scholars have adopted Ronald Langacker's (1987) distinction between the 'established linguistic convention' (formerly *langue* or competence) and 'language use' (formerly *parole* or performance), which appear to form a reasonable continuum. As a rule, grammar deals with the morphosyntactic peculiarities of a specific language. In this, we follow Haspelmath (2010: 663), who contends: 'Descriptive formal categories cannot be equated across languages because the criteria for category-assignment are different from language to language'. Thus, grammar is language-specific (compare Algeo 1985, 2010). The Chomskyan universal grammar seems to be a remote ideal in approaching language research. By contrast, Haspelmath (2010) introduces the notion of 'comparative concept', thus avoiding speaking of 'universal categories'. In this chapter, we advocate a cognitive view, and more specifically, an approach with a constructionist flavour.

In construction grammar (Croft 2001), it is argued that the semantics of a linguistic expression determines its (morpho)syntax to a considerable extent. Thus, the semantic status of names is mirrored by certain syntactic (called 'symbolic') constructions (see also Van Langendonck 2007b: ch. 2). Unfortunately, as Croft (1990: 268, fn. 24) notes, only few data about names are available in the linguistic typological literature because 'most grammatical descriptions do not include information on proper names'. So far as Bantuist studies go, Van de Velde (2003) speaks of 'a lack of the study of proper names, at least from a grammatical point of view'. Anderson (2004: 438) complains that 'little theoretical attention in general linguistics has been paid to the morphosyntax of names'. To make things worse, contemporary 'pragmatic' or 'discourse' approaches to names show little interest in looking for grammatical criteria to characterize names, if only because their attention is focused on language use, not on established linguistic convention, whose rules are described by grammar. Often, established linguistic convention and grammar are hardly taken into consideration, see, among others Coates (2006a, 2006b, 2009b, 2012c), De Stefani and Pepin (2006: 132, 142, 2010), Brendler (2008), and even Algeo (2010: 95), who writes '...the individual use of names may form an important part of the theory of onomastics'. Nevertheless, all these scholars refer to (proper) names, common nouns, though seldom pronouns, without defining these nominal categories. It is apparently left to the speaker to determine what a name is in discourse since grammarians are sometimes said to just make a mess of it. We cannot of course share this defeatism, although the limited data available on names are undoubtedly insufficient to constitute a representative sample of the world's languages (but see Anderson 2007; Van Langendonck 2007b, 2010). A bias towards Indo-European (Western European, and especially English) will be unavoidable here. This will not prevent us from taking into account old and new morphosyntactic criteria for name status in some 'exotic' as well as more familiar languages.

We will start from a semantic-pragmatic 'comparative concept' applying to the essence of 'properhood', as Coates (2006a, 2006b) calls it. Thus, we regard a name as a nominal expression that denotes a unique entity at the level of established linguistic convention to make it psychosocially salient within a given basic level category. The meaning of the name, if any, does not (or not any longer) determine its denotation (Van Langendonck 2007b: 125).

Our task here is to find out to what extent the comparative concept of name corresponds to language-specific descriptive (sub-)categories in the languages for which we have data, and to what extent these categories formally mirror the denotative and semantic properties of names. As far as possible, morphosyntactic criteria will be connected with each of the semantic-pragmatic characteristics, that is, nominal status, unique denotation, categorical (or: basic level) presupposition, and the lack of defining sense. We will use a well-established convention in the typological literature to distinguish the universally applicable semantic-pragmatic comparative concept of name from the language-specific grammatical categories of Name, by using initial capitalization for the latter. Two important distinctions are to be made first: established linguistic onomastic convention vs. the use of language and names, and name vs. name lemma. Section 2.2 will then provide a characterization of proper names. The chapter will conclude with a partial typology of names, organized according to a scale of typicality.

2.1.1 Established Linguistic and Onomastic Convention vs. the Use of Language and Names

The view that names have a unique denotation and can refer in discourse is in accordance with Langacker's (1987) notion of established linguistic convention (formerly *langue* or competence), forming a continuum with language use (formerly *parole* or performance). Just as denotation is an abstraction from reference, established linguistic convention is an abstraction from language use. Only in established linguistic convention does it make sense to speak of grammar or morphosyntax, which most linguists call the heart of the linguistic system. In this way, names can be given a genuine place in grammar as a structural category, like all other word classes.

The grammar of names describes their peculiarities in established linguistic and onomastic convention. Langacker's (1987) concept of established linguistic convention is flexible and useful, also for names. As a part of it, we discern established onomastic convention. Names enter established onomastic convention via bestowal or via gradual onymization. This allows us to make three observations.

First, although it is admitted that acts of reference fix the denotation of proper nouns (Coates 2006b: 39, 2012c: 121), it is not clear where this denotation finds its place if names are defined in terms of reference in language use. Clearly, unique denotation pertains to established linguistic convention. The rejection of this uniqueness in Coates (2012c) prohibits a distinction between names and pronouns since in this framework, both essentially refer in language use, even if they appear to denote as well, but not uniquely according to Coates (2012c). The lack of the notion of established linguistic convention led philosophers like Bertrand Russell (1919: 179; 1964 [1918]: 201) to claim that genuine names were 'logically proper names', that is, referring words like *this* or *that* (compare Kripke 1972: 345, fn. 16). Russell called ordinary names 'shorthand descriptions'. Surely, referring words like *this* or *that* refer uniquely in a certain context, but the reference will differ in another context. However, taking Kripke's term 'rigid designator' seriously, names denote uniquely in any context.

Second, there is a continuum from established onomastic convention to the use of names in speech and writing. We may use a name just once, and then forget it, so it does not enter established onomastic convention. For instance, referring to an unpopular guest, we could say: *Hitler is coming tonight*. In this example, *Hitler* is a new referent in discourse only, not yet a denotatum in established onomastic convention. That is one extreme. The other extreme for names is that many have been functioning in society for centuries, for instance family names, city, country, or river names, and the like.

Third, the notion of established onomastic convention allows us to recognize that there are well established names known and used only in small communities, such as nicknames in a family, for example, Dutch *Ons Pop* 'Our Doll', called that by her father. This is an established name in this minimal community (Van Langendonck 2007b: 286). The other extreme is that there exist names known worldwide, such as *Africa* or *Mandela*.

2.1.2 Name vs. Name Lemma (Proprial, Appellative, other Lemmas)

Another important distinction is between lexical items and the way they are used in different contexts. Thus, names need to be distinguished from name lemmas. The term *name lemma* indicates a dictionary entry with an onomastic valency. For instance, the lemma *Mary* has the potential to be used as a name with one or more sublemmas that each underlie a name. Thus, the lemma *Mary* underlies a large number of names, such as Mary the mother of Jesus, Mary Stuart, and so on. Since the lemma *Mary* is typically used as a name, it can be called a *proprial lemma*. Proprial lemmas always allow common noun uses, albeit marginally, as in *I was thinking of a different Mary*. Proprial lemmas could be further subdivided into personal name lemmas, place-name lemmas, and so on, according to the type of name they are most typically used to denote. Again, this does not exclude a personal name lemma such as *Mary* from being used to denote the name of a boat, for instance. We have seen that a proprial lemma can be used as a common noun (*a different Mary*). Conversely, names can be based on all kinds of lemmas. Thus, for instance, an appellative lemma is assigned to a name like the film name *Gladiator*, and a phrasal lemma to a novel name such as *The Old Man and the Sea*. In many languages the etymology of most personal names is transparent, and it is sometimes stated that 'names have a meaning' in such languages. A more accurate way to characterize these languages is to say that they have no or few proprial lemmas and that personal names tend to be based on appellative lemmas. Finally, common nouns can be derived from names metaphorically or metonymically, as are *Napoleon* and *Jane* in (1)–(2). Such common nouns are called *deproprial* in Van de Velde (2009).

(1)   That soldier is a second Napoleon.
(2)   She purports to be another Jane.

2.2 CHARACTERIZATION OF NAMES

In this section we will characterize names as nouns (2.2.1) with unique denotation (2.2.2) that have an inherent basic level sense (2.2.3), no defining sense (2.2.5), but optionally connotative meanings. We will argue that names can be considered to be the most prototypical nominal category (2.2.4), and we will compare names with pronouns (2.2.6).

2.2.1 Names and Nouns

From Antiquity onwards, it has been held that names are nouns (or possibly noun phrases). Classical terminology speaks of *onoma kyrion* (*nomen proprium*), and *onoma proseigorikon* (*nomen appellativum*). Therefore both names and appellatives are considered to be nouns (Gary-Prieur 1994: 243). Following Hudson (1990: 170), personal (and other) pronouns can also be regarded as nouns. According to this, we have three kinds of nouns. Few scholars seem to dispute the thesis that names are nouns or at least nominal expressions. For Coates (2006a: 373), names are noun phrases though not typically nouns. Anderson (2004: 436; 2007) contends that names 'are no more nouns than are pronouns or determiners'. If a pronoun is a kind of noun there is no problem. However, it seems difficult to view a name as a kind of determiner, at least syntactically, even if the determiner is considered to be the head of the 'noun phrase' (Anderson 2004: 456; but see Van Langendonck 1994).

From a cross-linguistic perspective, trying to determine whether names are nouns may not be the most meaningful goal, since the answer depends on how one chooses to define the comparative concept of *noun*, especially in languages such as Straits Salish where parts of speech distinctions are not very clear cut. The question can better be answered on the language specific level, where the semantic-pragmatic comparative concept of name provided in the introduction can correspond to zero, one or more than one grammatical category of Name. The grammatical characteristics of Names in a given language should be compared to those of Common Nouns in that language. In English, for instance, Names can take (non-restrictive) determiners, just like Nouns but unlike Pronouns, for example *that* modifying *George Bush* in (3), and *Britain's* modifying *Jeremy Irons* in (4). See Section 2.2.6 for more discussion of the difference between names and pronouns.

(3) That George Bush is a nice guy. (Vandelanotte and Willemse 2002: 22)
(4) Britain's Jeremy Irons was present at the premiere in New York. (Vandelanotte and Willemse 2002: 25)

Still in English, Names can be grammatically differentiated from Common Nouns due to their ability to appear as the identifying element in close appositional patterns of the form [(definite article +) noun + (definite article +) noun], for example *Fido the dog*. (Van Langendonck 2007b: 4, 131; Idiatov 2007).[1] The unit that does not characterize but identifies is a name (noun), that is, *Fido*. The appellative *dog* indicates the categorical presupposition.[2] This grammatical criterion for distinguishing Names from Common Nouns seems to be valid for most Indo-European languages (e.g. French *la ville de Paris*, Dutch *de stad Amsterdam*, or Polish *miasto Kraków* '(the) city (of) Cracow'). In other languages, such as the Gabonese Bantu language Orungu, this criterion cannot be used to distinguish Names from Common Nouns, but agreement provides a grammatical criterion (see Van de Velde and Ambouroue 2011 for Orungu and Van de Velde 2009 for Kirundi).

---

[1] Moltmann (2013) deals with 'sortals' and close appositions with names from a different perspective.
[2] Of course, not all close appositions give us the basic level meaning, e.g. *President Obama* does not indicate that Obama is necessarily a president. Mostly, the basic level meaning is not overtly expressed, especially not in prototypical names such as personal names, where it is taken for granted.

2.2.2 The Unique Denotation of Names

The unique denotation of names entails their definiteness, as well as their incompatibility with restrictive relative clauses and their inability to refer back anaphorically.

2.2.2.1 *Names as Definite Noun Phrases*

Definiteness is well-established both as an inherent feature of names (cf. among others Sørensen 1958; Dalberg 1985: 129; Löbner 1985: 299; Pamp 1985: 113; Wotjak 1985: 7, 13; Abbott 2002; but see Allerton 1987; Lyons 1999; Anderson 2003: 351, 394, 2004), and as of personal pronouns (Löbner 1985: 300). The feature 'definite' is often understood as displaying a presupposition of existence in the universe of discourse, at least in its prototypical occurrences (Van Langendonck 1979; cf. 1981; Kleiber 1992). It does not come as a surprise that names, which have a fixed denotation, suggesting uniqueness and existence, are bound to have this grammatical meaning. The syntactic evidence we will adduce for the definiteness of names will pertain only to their denotative use as arguments (see Van Langendonck 1981). Sometimes, languages show an overt distinction between this use and other uses. Greek, for instance, puts a definite article before personal names in argument position, that is, in the denotative use of names, though not in vocatives or name-giving utterances (e.g. *I name this child X*, Anderson 2004: 441–2, 456).

A diagnostic for the definiteness of names in (colloquial) English can be found in the following observation: NPs that occur in right dislocation and are announced by a cataphoric personal pronoun, have to be definite. It turns out then that, like other definite NPs, names can occur in right dislocation in this way, at least in colloquial speech (Quirk, et al. 1985: 632):

(5)   a. He's a complete idiot, *that brother of yours.*
       b. It went on far too long, *your game.*
(6)   *He's a complete idiot, *a neighbour.*
(7)   He's a complete idiot, *John.*

Announced by a personal pronoun (*he, it*), the definite NPs of a proprial, pronominal, or appellative nature *that brother of yours, your game, John* are able to appear in right dislocation. For the indefinite appellative NP *a neighbour*, this possibility is excluded. Apparently, it is only definite NPs, with their presupposition of existence and uniqueness, that can occur as 'afterthoughts', in this case; well-known referents that the speaker wants to recall, just to ensure the hearer will think of the right person or thing.

Since names are inherently definite, the addition of an overt definiteness marker is superfluous, and definite articles with names are often used to express notions other than definiteness. Certain types of names have a fixed determiner in English (e.g. *the Nile*), which can be argued to have a classifying function. We shall return to this in Section 2.3.2. We also find an expressive use of the article, such as the augmentative use of the article with Flemish forenames in certain dialectal areas, for example *de Jan* 'the John'. In German, the article has almost lost its expressivity with first names because of its frequency in discourse (e.g. *der Johann*). In other contexts, the addition of a definite article is honorific: *La Callas*.

When a name appears with an indefinite article in English, the latter expresses merely countable singularity (its original function), while the propriality and therefore the definiteness of the name are preserved, as in:

(8)   a. *A* devastated Claes entered the court room.
         (= Claes entered the court room as a devastated man)
(9)   b. This idiot of *a* Jack!
         (= Jack is such an idiot!)

It is useful at this point to remind ourselves of the distinction between names and the name lemma on which they are based. In the Gabonese Bantu language Orungu, nouns are marked for definiteness by means of their tone pattern. Many personal names are based on an appellative lemma with an indefinite tone pattern, for example *ŋguwa* 'a shield'. Used as names, these nouns are definite, as is the phrasal name of the French movie *Un prophète* (A prophet).

2.2.2.2 *No Restrictive Relative Clauses with Names*

Restrictive modifiers limit the extension of a given NP. Therefore, names are incompatible with such modifiers (see Sørensen 1958; Seppänen 1971, 1982; Vandelanotte and Willemse 2002). The most conspicuous of restrictive modifiers is the relative clause. As a rule, the English relative pronoun *that* refers to inanimate appellative antecedents and introduces a restrictive clause. A zero form can be used for any restrictive clause if it is not intended to 'replace' the clause's subject, for example

(10)   The city **that** I visited was nice.

By contrast, proprial antecedents do not allow such restrictive devices because of their unique denotation, for example

(11)   *Ghent **that** is the most beautiful city in Flanders, was one of the biggest in medieval Europe.
(12)   *Mary I saw smiled.

2.2.2.3 *Anaphoric Relations*

Since names display a fixed denotation, it is predictable that they cannot refer back in the discourse to any other kind of NP, at least in the standard anaphoric way. Lakoff

(1968: 17–19) and Cole (1974: 671) pointed this out, setting up a cline going from the strongest anaphoric elements (clitic pronouns) to the weakest (names) (Van Langendonck 2007b: 153). Examples could be:

(13)   a. Napoleon was the emperor of France. He lost at Waterloo.
        b. *He was the emperor of France. Napoleon lost at Waterloo.
(14)   a. Quisling was at power during the war. The prime minister betrayed his country.
        b. ?*The prime minister was at power during the war. Quisling betrayed his country.

With this criterion, the most marked difference between personal pronouns and names is brought to the fore. Personal pronouns display the least specific denotation whereas names show the most rigid reference because of their fixed extension. At the same time, we can see that in this respect, names differ least from multidenotative NPs like *the prime minister* in (14).

2.2.3 Names (not Lemmas) Have an Inherent Basic Level Sense

A crucial characteristic of names is that they have an inherent categorical presupposed sense (compare Coates 2012c: 125). Philosophers such as Geach (1957: section 16) and Searle (1958) argue that this categorical sense is necessary for every use of a name to preserve the identity of the referent. Likewise, certain psychologists see a categorical, and more precisely a basic level sense in names. La Palme Reyes et al. (1993: 445) establish

(15)   [Freddy: *dog*] = [*this*: *dog*]

which is to be read as 'Freddy in the category DOG' is 'this in the category DOG'.

Thus, there is a deictic component in names (*this*), as in pronouns, but there is also a categorical appellative sense (*dog*). Names can therefore be situated between pronouns and common nouns from a semantic viewpoint (see Molino 1982: 19; Valentine et al. 1996; Hollis and Valentine 2001; James 2004; Van Langendonck 2007b: 169–171).

The inherent categorical sense of names is presupposed and therefore cannot be negated. *A fortiori*, in a sentence like *London is on the Thames*, the existence of London is presupposed, as is its basic level category *city*. Obviously, we can say *London is not a city*. But in this special case, the asserted sense contradicts the presupposition. The basic level categories for which the individual members typically receive a name, are to a certain extent culture specific. Thus cows typically have a name in Kirundi (Bantu, Burundi), but not, or much less often, in present-day English. Note that *person* is usually not the basic level category for personal names, nor is *place* the one for place-names. In such highly salient categories the basic level tends to be lower on the hierarchy, *man* and *woman* for human beings, *city, country, village*, etc. for places.

The rest of this section will adduce neurolinguistic and morphosyntactic evidence for the presupposed inherent categorical meaning of names. Neurolinguistic evidence is reported in Bayer (1991) (see Van Langendonck 2007b: 110–13 for discussion), who worked with a patient (H.J.) suffering from so-called deep dyslexia, which means that she can observe written texts exclusively via a semantic route and not by means of a transmission from grapheme to phoneme. Such patients cannot read nonsense words, they have difficulties reading abstract words or grammatical morphemes, and reading concrete common nouns often gives rise to paralexia, for example reading *hammer* when *axe* is written. H.J. is unable to read names. However, she always recognizes them as names and for personal names she could usually specify whether the name bearer is a man or a woman. She could also identify place-names as names for cities, countries, or rivers. Bayer concludes that there must exist a minimal lexical categorical sense belonging to the semantic memory, specifying the categorical presupposition. Bayer also reports on a different type of response that H.J. gave when asked to read names, *viz.* connotations. Thus, the name *Australia* triggered the basic level sense 'country', but also connotations such as 'far away' and 'kangaroos'. We will come back to these non-lexical connotative meanings in Section 2.2.7.

Strong morphosyntactic evidence for the categorical sense of names can be found in the Burundese Bantu language Kirundi (Van de Velde 2009). As in the great majority of Bantu languages, nouns trigger noun class agreement in Kirundi. Noun classes are overtly marked by means of a nominal prefix, so that the agreement pattern triggered by a noun is largely predictable from its prefix. This is not the case for Kirundi Names, however, which trigger the same agreement pattern as the common noun that is used to refer to their basic level category. Thus, names for dogs agree according to the noun class of the common noun *imbwa* 'dog' (class 9), and personal names agree according to the class of the common noun *umuuntu* 'person' (class 1). This is illustrated in (16) by means of the name *Rukara*, based on the lemma that underlies the common noun *urukara* 'blackness' (class 11). Agreement prefixes are marked by means of roman numbers in the glosses.[3]

(16) a. Rukara   a-rikó   a-rafuungura
          Rukara   I-is   I-eating
          'Rukara (a person) is eating.'
      b. Rukara   i-rikó   i-iraryá
          Rukara   IX-is   IX-eating
          'Rukara (a dog) is eating.'

[3] Arabic numerals are used to gloss overt noun class markers in examples of Bantu languages, whereas Roman numerals mark noun class agreement prefixes. Wherever possible, we follow the Leipzig Glossing Rules, with the following additions: NTP non-definite tone pattern, PROP proper name.

More grammatical evidence for the basic level sense of names can be found in the choice of an interrogative pro-word in name questions such as *What is x's name* (Idiatov 2007: 61–94, 2010). In languages that differentiate between 'who' and 'what', the choice between both is determined by two independent parameters, *viz.* entity type and type of reference. Entity type distinguishes between PERSONS and THINGS (i.e. non-persons). Type of reference distinguishes between IDENTIFICATION and CLASSIFICATION or categorization. 'Who' is prototypically used in questions for the identification of a person, whereas 'what' is used to ask for a categorization of a thing. The name question *What is x's name* is non-canonical in that it asks for the identification of a thing (i.e. a name). In order to deal with this non-canonical situation, many languages avoid the choice between 'who' and 'what', using other interrogatives such as 'how', 'which', or 'where'. In languages that do not use this avoidance strategy, the choice between 'who' and 'what' very often depends on the categorical sense of the name that is expected as an answer. If the name of a human being is expected, 'who' will be selected. If the basic level category of the name is non-human or inanimate (depending on the language), 'what' is selected. This is illustrated in (17) with an example from the Sepik-Ramu language Namia from Papua New Guinea (cited from Idiatov 2007, who obtained the example from Becky Feldpausch, p.c.). Note that English selects 'what' in such questions, irrespective of the categorical sense of the expected answer.

(17) [A:]   ne-k(a)   ilei   tal(a)?   [B:]   John
            2SG-POSS   name   who   PROP
      [A:]   'What is your name?'   [B:]   'John'

Finally, the presence or absence of a categorical sense distinguishes names from other words with unique reference, such as *the internet, the universe*, or *the sun.* These words for singleton categories lack a basic level categorical presupposition: [the x (the) internet] and [the x (the) universe].

2.2.4 Names as the Most Prototypical Nominal Category

If we look at the grammatical features that are relevant for names, it is striking that names tend to have the unmarked feature value. Therefore, it could be argued that names are the most prototypical nominal category. This conclusion runs counter to Langacker (1991: ch. 1).

We saw in Section 2.2.1 that names are definite. As regards DEFINITENESS, it has been argued in Van Langendonck (1979) that it is the unmarked counterpart of the feature [+/– definite]. Karmiloff-Smith (1979), Mayerthaler (1988), and Croft (1990) have come to the same conclusion on various grounds: early acquisition, experiential and typological evidence. In fact, definiteness is the most natural state of a referring expression, that is, definite and referential go together (Van Langendonck 1994). As regards the feature

NUMBER, names are mostly singular (and countable): *Kevin, Mary, London, the Rhine,* and so on. Sometimes they show a collective plural: *the Andes, the Philippines.*

As regards the features DEFINITENESS and NUMBER, there is an essential difference from common nouns: where we have a dichotomy of plus and minus in the features of one and the same common noun, e.g. *the city* vs. *a city; city* vs. *cities*, there is no such opposition in one and the same name. *Pluralia tantum* such as *the Andes* and *the Philippines* are rare, and are not even ordinary plurals since they are not quantifiable: **(the) many Andes.* Even in such plural names we find an element of singularity: the plurality is construed as a unity, a singularity, a fact we have accounted for by calling *pluralia tantum* collective plurals.

2.2.5 Names have no Defining Sense

To get to grips with the notion of 'sense', we can put specific questions asked by Stephen Ullmann and other scholars, such as: *What does the word 'table' mean?* Or *What do you understand by 'table'?* If these are questions that make sense, then the word has 'sense', that is, definitional lexical meaning. Indeed, we can give a definition of the word *table*, as found in dictionaries. Usually, such words, in this case the common noun *table*, show polysemy, that is, a coherent set of semantic features, of which one is often prototypical. For instance, Webster's dictionary defines *a table as* a piece of furniture consisting of a smooth flat slab fixed on legs; this sense is akin to the sense of a tablet or a contents list, and so on. On the basis of these senses, we can find the referents. By contrast, in the case of names, the designation prevails over the meanings. As Ullmann (1969: 33) contends: 'One cannot possibly say that one understands a name; one can only say that one knows whom it refers to, whose name it is'.[4] It does not make sense to ask: *What does the word 'London' mean?* or: *What do you understand by 'London'?* This applies to pronouns as well. It does not make sense to ask: *What do you understand by 'he/she',* or *'this'?* Therefore neither names nor pronouns appear to have sense, that is, definitional lexical meaning, let alone a polysemous structure. The rest of this section will discuss three morphosyntactic patters that reflect the absence of a defining sense of names.

2.2.5.1 *The Non-restrictive Relative Construction with* which

Predicate nominals, nouns or NPs that function as a predicate, contain only an intension, not an extension. In English, they can be modified by non-restrictive relative clauses introduced by *which.*

(18)   Obama is (the) president, *which* McCain will probably never be.

---

[4] Similar observations were made by Nicolaisen (1995b: 391); for German: Boesch (1957: 32) and Debus (1980: 194). However, Brendler (2005: 108–9) rejects the relevance of such statements since he adheres to a kind of maximum meaningfulness theory for names, although he (2008) refers to *nomeme* (equivalent to 'name'), *archinomeme* (equivalent to 'proprial lemma'), and a number of other terms.

Since for names, as well as for personal pronouns, it is essential to have denotation and not descriptive meaning, neither names nor personal pronouns can appear in these structures (Van Langendonck 2007b: 146–8):

(19)   *The president is Obama / him, *which* McCain will probably never be.

2.2.5.2 *The [for + NP] Construction*

For similar reasons, names and pronouns are excluded from the constructions exemplified in (20):

(20)   For *a* schoolboy he is not performing badly.

The *for*-phrase can be paraphrased as: 'although he is a schoolboy'. This makes clear that the object NP of the preposition *for* behaves as a kind of a predicate nominal. Normally, predicate nominals can be definite, as in: *Obama is the president.* That seems, however, not to be the case in this structure:

(21)   *For *the* schoolboy he is not performing badly.

To patch up the pattern with a definite NP, a few stratagems are necessary. First, a relative *be*-clause has to be added; second, a qualitative, evaluative element has to be inserted, either an evaluative noun or qualitative adjective accompanying the noun. Compare:

(22)   For the idiot that he is, he is not performing badly.
(23)   For the modest schoolboy that he is, he is not performing badly.

However, if the noun in question is not a common noun but a name, the sentence cannot be patched up:

(24)   ?*For the modest Leroy that he is, he is not performing badly.

For non-personal names, the test works even better. An example involving place-names is the following:

(25)   a.   For the hectic river that it is, the Rhine is not that polluted yet.
      b.   *For the hectic Rhine that it is, this river is not that polluted yet.

2.2.5.3 *Names and Homophonous Coordination*

It has been observed by McCawley (1968: 144) that homophonous NPs cannot be coordinated.[5]

(26)   *The employees and the employees are male and female respectively.

Instead, a single NP must be used:

(27)   The employees are male and female respectively.

However, this rule is not always valid. For instance, with names homophonous conjunction is permitted to a certain extent (Van Langendonck 1981). At least two different cases are possible:

(28)   a. Johnson and Johnson have set up a new subsidiary.
       b. London and London are two different cities.

In (28a) we have to do with the name of a company formed by the coordination of two occurrences of the same family name; (28b) is about the capital of the UK, the name of which emigrated to the USA to become the name of another place.

Different again is an example from German (Dobnig-Jülch 1977):

(29)   Toni, also die Tochter von nebenan, und Toni, der Sohn der anderen Nachbarn,
           kommen heute nicht.
       'Toni, next door's daughter, and Toni, the other neighbors' son, are not coming
           today.'

In (29), first names with identical lemmas are coordinated. After each name, a loose apposition is inserted so as to clarify the identity of the referent without affecting the proprial character of the lemmas. Cases such as (29) in particular are similar to those of personal pronouns and demonstratives employed deictically, that is, with a pointing gesture:

(30)   a. Yóu and yóu should leave.
       b. Thís and thís will have to be removed.

---

[5] McCawley's (1968: 144) generative semantic rule runs as follows: 'There is a transformation which obligatorily collapses the conjoined subject *the employees and the employees* into a single occurrence of *the employees*'.

The rationale behind these examples may be that no two homophonous NPs containing a lexical sense could be conjoined. In Hansack's (2004) framework, we would have to say that no two homophonous NPs with *denotata* belonging to the same set could be conjoined. However, two such NPs containing a combination of a deictic word and a common noun are possible, for example

(31)   This man and thís man will be fired.

In (31), *man* has the same meaning each time and belongs to the same set of *denotata*. The rule would then have to be qualified as follows: two (or more) homophonous NPs cannot be coordinated unless they emphasize some deictic element (extension) in them, whether an intensional element is present or not. Apparently, names come closest to such ambivalent expressions as *thís man*. It should be recalled that this ambivalent structure combining a deictic (extensional) element and a categorical (intensional but presupposed) element is inherent in names. The difference from the type [deictic + appellative], for example *this man* lies in the fact that this NP shows the ambivalent status on the level of the construction, while names unite the two aspects in common on word level. This resemblance explains the grammaticality of (28a), (28b), and (31).

2.2.6 Names between Pronouns and Appellatives

Language philosophers have tended to view names as a kind of indexical, closer to personal pronouns or demonstratives than to common nouns. Although this view is also supported by some linguists (e.g. Anderson 2004, 2007), most linguists seem to find it more difficult to distinguish names grammatically from common nouns. Section 2.2.1 has already pointed out that English Names can take determiners, just as Common Nouns, but unlike pronouns. Moreover, we have seen that names and pronouns are at opposite ends of a cline in anaphoricity (Section 2.2.2.3), bringing to the fore the most marked difference between pronouns and names. This section compares names and pronouns in more detail, pointing out differences and commonalities. Overall, names share more commonalities with common nouns than with pronouns. We will limit ourselves here to giving three differences between names and pronouns.

First, in Dutch both proprial and appellative NPs can be construed in left dislocation such that the coreferential demonstrative *die/dat* features in the sentence proper, for example

(32)   Karel / De baas, *die* lacht altijd.
       lit. 'Charles / The boss, that laughs all the time.'

However, we cannot do the same with personal pronouns (Van Langendonck 2007b: 170):

(33)   *Hij, *die* lacht altijd.
       lit. 'He, that laughs all the time.'

Second, English and Dutch personal pronouns still display case distinctions (*I—me/ ik—mij*, etc.) while common nouns and names do not. Third, as Anderson recognizes (2007: 118, 197–8, 201–3), derivation and compounding are typical of names and appellatives, but not of pronouns. Often, names and appellatives share the same classifiers or affixes, for example

(34)   a.   Compounding: Sherwood Forest / rainforest
       b.   Derivation: Spain > Span-ish / fever > fever-ish
                                      (Anderson 2007: 197)
            Elizabeth-an / republic-an   (Anderson 2007: 198)

Anderson (2007: 201) argues that 'the inflectional and derivational morphology of names ... cannot be identified with noun morphology', but it is not clear why.

Coates (2006a, 2006b) argues in favour of the thesis that is the opposite of Anderson's, that is, that names are nouns and noun phrases. He does not even mention pronouns in this context. In fact, names are said to be distinguishable from common nouns only at the (pragmatic) level of language use. Perhaps the truth lies in the middle: names can be considered a nominal category to be situated between pronouns and appellatives (Van Langendonck 2007b: 169–71). Names are a kind of noun and form an open class, *pace* the opposite claim of Anderson (2004, 2007). A number of arguments have been provided for this thesis in Van Langendonck (2007b).

2.2.7 Names Can Have Connotations

An aspect of the meaning of names that we have not mentioned so far is the different types of optional connotative meanings that they can have. These are not essential for the characterization of names and have no or far fewer morphosyntactic correlates. At least four types of connotative meanings can be distinguished.

First, names with a transparent etymology can give rise to associative meanings related to the name form. Thus, the family name *Baker* may remind us of a baker. This type of connotative meaning is exploited in personal name-giving in many cultures. Old English dithematic names such as *Ælf-weald* 'elf-king' (Insley 2007), for instance, had an aspirational character. In literature too, this type of connotation is often exploited, as in the name *Snowwhite*. Second, there are connotations that arise via the *denotatum* and can be exploited in discourse to identify or to characterize the name-bearer. No polysemy is involved here (see also Semenza 2009), for example Obama is president of the United States, Obama has a wife and children, Obama does not eat hamburgers, and so on. The third type of connotative meanings that can be distinguished are emotive meanings such as augmentative, diminutive, or honorific. These can be inherent in certain names, for instance if the name contains a diminutive or augmentative suffix, as in the Dutch first names *Jan-tje, Marie-ke,* and *Bert-ie,* where *-tje, -ke, and -ie* are diminutive suffixes. Needless to state, bynames and nicknames tend to have strong emotive connotations. Although connotative meanings are not part of the lexical meaning of names, contrary to their categorical presupposition, morphosyntactic correlates can be found. In Kirundi, for instance, personal names can trigger diminutive or augmentative agreement patterns in order to add an endearing or deprecating connotation. Example (35) shows three possible agreement patterns with the personal name controller *Taama*. The first is agreement of class 1, according to the noun class of the basic level term 'person' (see ex (16) above). The second (32b) and third (32c) are augmentative agreement of class 7 and diminutive agreement of class 12, respectively (Meeussen 1959: 191, cited via Van de Velde 2009: 234).

(35)   a.   Taama a-raaje
            Taama I-arrives
            'Taama arrives'
       b.   Taama ki-raaje
            Taama VII-arrives
            'Taama arrives' (augmentative)
       c.   Taama ka-raaje
            Taama XII-arrives
            'Taama arrives' (diminutive)

Fourth, there are what Cislaru (2006, 2012) calls 'facets' of meaning. Although the basic level meaning of city names is 'city', and that of country names is 'country', these geographical names often adopt additional meanings (animate), induced by metonymy. English examples are:

(36)   Paris elected a new mayor < The citizens of Paris elected a new mayor
(37)   America decided to declare war on terror < The Government of The United States of America decided to declare war on terror

Personal names, especially of artists, can stand for the work the artists produced:

(38)   Rodin se trouve dans la troisième salle du musée. (Lemghari 2014: 354)
       '(The work of) Rodin is to be found in the third room of the museum.'

2.3 A Partial Typology of Names

This section provides a partial typological classification of names, in which we will show that there is a grammatically relevant cline from more to less typical types of names. A fuller account dealing with more types of names can be found in Van Langendonck (2007b: 183–255). Individuals in the psychosocially highly relevant categories of people and settlements normally have a name. The names for settlements and especially persons are also the most typical names from a grammatical point of view. Towards the bottom of the cline we often find mismatches between what counts as a name from a semantic-pragmatic point of view (cf. our comparative concept in Section 2.1) and what is construed as a Name from a grammatical point of view in individual languages. We find categories for which only some members have a name that behaves as a Name, whereas names of other members are construed as Common Nouns, for example the category of diseases. Non-prototypical names can have unusual properties such as being non-count, or recursive. For the analysis of certain types of names, such as brand names, the distinction between name and proprial lemma turns out to be crucial.

2.3.1 Personal Names

Personal names are arguably the most prototypical names. The number and types of names that are bestowed on people are highly culture specific, as are the principles that guide the choice of a name. A discussion of personal names in European societies can be found in Van Langendonck (2007b: 187–96). Before moving on to other types of names, it is useful to point out that personal names do not always originate in a name giving act. The process of onymization, the gradual evolution of a name, can be observed with personal names as with other types of names. Van Langendonck (2007b: 194) gives the example of the Flemish first name—byname combination *Suske de Verver* 'Francis the Painter', in which the byname has a transparent origin in the appellative *painter*. In the process of onymization, the primary accent moved from the first syllable of the first name to that of the byname (*Súske de Verver* → *Suske de Vérver*). At the same time, *de verver* was semantically bleached, losing its asserted lexical meaning, so that the byname could continue to be used when its name bearer was no longer a painter. When animals such as pets receive a name, this name tends to have the properties of personal names.

2.3.2 Place-names

Often, interesting insights and generalizations can be gained through recognizing the validity of a synchronic view. A case in point is the synchronic semantic and formal place-name hierarchy, as defended in Van Langendonck (1998, 2007b: 204–12). Here, we can observe a synchronic formal cline, based on basic level categories:

ZERO MARKING, as in city and town names: *London, Berlin*;
SUFFIXING, as in country names: *Fin-land, German-y*;
ARTICLE PREPOSING, as in names of, e.g. fields, regions, and rivers: *the Highlands, the Rhine*;
The use of CLASSIFIERS plus possibly an article, as in names of seas, oceans, or deserts: *the North Sea, the Gobi Desert*.

This formal markedness hierarchy apparently corresponds to a cline in human organizational involvement: maximal in cities and countries, but minimal in regions, rivers, seas, or desert. Anderson calls it an 'anthropocentric' cline. If only English examples are cited (as in Anderson 2007: 115, 187), we see no distinctions in gender since in English all place-names exhibit neuter gender. Hence we cannot observe the interesting interaction between gender and basic level sense that occurs in languages like German, where the prototypical articleless names of cities and countries have neuter gender, whilst the more marked categories systematically construed with articles (*der Rhein* 'the Rhine', *die Nordsee* 'the North Sea') continue the historical appellative gender. Last but not least, English shows the humanized place-names (e.g. settlement names) omitting the article, whilst the non-human place-names (e.g. river names) tend to adopt the article. This can be observed where the names of former colonies or regions lose their article when they become independent countries: the Ukraine > Ukraine, The Congo > Congo, the Lebanon > Lebanon.

2.3.3 Names of Months

Names of months are ambiguous between a non-recursive (39a) and a recursive/generic (39b) reading, which is admittedly an untypical feature for names.

(39) a. *June was hot*
       b. *June is always hot*

This semantic characteristic of month names has been adduced to argue against their name status. However, non-recursivity is not a defining semantic characteristic of names in our view. Grammatical evidence in a typologically and genealogically diverse set of languages shows that the category of months is rather similar to those of people and places in that its individual members typically receive a name. From that perspective, names of months are typical names.

According to the close appositional test, names of months are Names in English, since we can speak of *the month of June*. In the Bantu Language Kirundi too, names of months display the grammatical properties of Names, including agreement according to the basic level categorical term *ukwêzi* 'month' (Van de Velde 2009: 229). Likewise in Rapa Nui, spoken on Easter Island, names of months are marked by the morpheme *a*, indicating onymic status, for example *i a hori iti* 'in August' (Idiatov 2007; Van Langendonck and Van de Velde 2007: 459–61).

2.3.4 Trade and Brand Names

When dealing with trade and brand names, the distinction between name and name lemma is of crucial importance, since the same lemma is typically used as a name and as a common noun. Lemmas such as *Ford* can therefore be called proprio-appellative lemmas. In example (40a) *Ford* is the name of a brand, whereas in (40b) it is a common noun used to refer to a product of this brand. In the latter use, *Ford* has a defining sense.

(40)   a.   Ford is a familiar brand.
       b.   Jane bought a Ford yesterday.

Note that several names are based on the multidenotative lemma *ford*, for individuals of different categories. In (41a) *Ford* is the name of a person, in (41b) that of a company. Thus, in the examples (40)–(41) we are dealing with three different names and one common noun, all of which are semantically linked by metonymy.

(41)   a.   Ford founded a car industry.
       b.   Ford is an American car company.

2.3.5 Numbers

Numerals have a versatility comparable to that of the proprio-appellative lemmas underlying trade and brand names. They can certainly be construed as names (42a), (42b), as appellatives (42c) and, probably most frequently, in an attributive function (42d) (likewise Langacker 1991: 86):

(42)   a.   Three is a sacred number.
       b.   the number seven
       c.   He has millions of books.
       d.   People normally have ten fingers.

Grammatical evidence for analysing numerals as names in some uses can be seen in (42b), where *seven* occurs in a close appositional construction. The Bantu languages also provide grammatical evidence. In the Gabonese language Orungu, numbers trigger an agreement pattern typical for Names in subject position of clauses similar to that in (42a) (Van de Velde and Ambouroue 2011: 135). Kirundi is interesting, in that the same number can be alternatively construed as a Name (43b) or as something in between a Name and a Common Noun (43a), with a preference for the latter.

(43) a.   Ga-taanu   ga-kwirikira   ka-ne
           12-five   XII-follows   12-four
           'Five comes after four.'
      b.   Ga-taanu   gi-kwirikira   ka-ne
           12-five   VII-follows   12-four
           'Five comes after four.'

In (43b), the number five has the two typical grammatical characteristics of Names in Kirundi, *viz.* the absence of the so-called augment—a word-initial grammatical morpheme—and an agreement pattern determined by the class 7 categorical term *igitigiri* 'number' (see Section 2.2.3). In (40a) the augment is lacking, but the agreement pattern is the one predicted by the overt class prefix *ga-*, *viz.* agreement pattern 12. The Name construction in (43b) is stylistically marked as learned, or even pedant. This seems to be typical in situations where the same item can be construed as a Name or as Common Noun.

2.3.6 Names of Diseases and Biological Species

As we move further away from the most prototypical types of names, we encounter categories for which only some members receive a name, whereas other members are designated by means of an appellative. The distinction is not random. Phenomena that are familiar tend to be treated as one of a kind, that is, categories of their own, and they are not designated by means of a name. On the other hand, unfamiliar phenomena tend to be treated as belonging to a category of which the individual members receive a name. We will look at names for diseases and biological species here.

Names of diseases are apparently never Names in English, but in Dutch it depends on the disease (compare Van Osta 1995). Apart from the fact that names of diseases behave as mass nouns in common noun use, they seem to differ regarding the capacity of taking on a proprial function, and to appear in close apposition. As the close appositional constructions in (44) show, names of diseases that are new, exotic, and/or are to be taken seriously appear to be treated as genuine names. They are also capitalized in spelling.

(44) a.   *De ziekte Aids* breidt uit in Afrika.
           'The Aids disease expands in Africa.'
      b.   *De ziekte Ebola* heeft vreselijke gevolgen.
           'The Ebola disease has terrible effects.'

By contrast, ordinary diseases are not capitalized and cannot appear in apposition except in coordinate structures, compare:

(45) a. *De ziekte (de) griep komt elk jaar terug.
          'The influenza disease returns every year.'
      b. De ziektes griep, mazelen en rodehond vind je overal.
          'The diseases influenza, measles and rubella are found everywhere.'
      c. Griep kan nog gevaarlijk zijn.
          'Influenza can still be dangerous.'

It therefore seems that words for ordinary or older diseases are rarely construed as names, but that new and exotic terms for illnesses can be given name status more easily.

From a grammatical point of view, names of subspecies low on the biological taxonomy are sometimes Names in Bantu languages. Evidence can be found in the Cameroonian language Eton (Van de Velde 2006: 232, 2008: 111) and in Kirundi, where all names for species of beans agree according to the noun *i-gi-haragé* 'bean' (Van de Velde 2009).

2.3.7 Autonyms

In Section 2.1.2, we saw that proprial lemmas such as *Mary* are construed as common nouns in certain contexts. Likewise, any other lemma can be construed as a name with the presupposed categorical sense of 'word'. In this usage, called *autonymy*, linguistic expressions refer to themselves. Autonyms have the grammatical characteristics of names in English, as they can occur in close appositional constructions (46).

(46) The words *stand for* and *about* (Meyer 1992: 84)

Moreover, autonyms need not be preceded by an article in English.

(47) *Bank* is a homonymous word.

Languages differ as to whether autonyms have the grammatical properties of Names. One language that is like English, in that autonyms belong to the grammatical category of Names, is Orungu (Bantu, Gabon). In this language, Names trigger agreement of class 1 on verbal targets. This can be seen in the metalinguistic statement on the word ònέmέ 'tongue, language' in (48). If ònέmέ were construed as a common noun, it would trigger a prefix of agreement pattern 5 on the copula (Van de Velde and Ambouroue 2011).

(48)   ònémé   èrê   n   ìmpìβínyí   mbání
       ònémé.NTP I.is with 10.meaning x.two
       '*Oneme* has two meanings.'

2.4 CONCLUSIONS

Starting from the comparative concept of (proper) name, we distinguish between established linguistic convention and the use of language, and subsequently between name and name lemma. Names are nouns with unique denotation, they are definite, have no restrictive relative modifiers, and occupy a special place in anaphoric relations. They display an inherent basic level and can be argued to be the most prototypical nominal category. Names have no defining sense. They can have connotative meanings, but this has little grammatical relevance. We have stressed the need to rely on grammatical criteria, which are too often ignored in approaches to names.

The approach developed in this chapter aims at being universally valid in two ways. First, the pragmatic-semantic concept of names defined in the introduction is cross-linguistically applicable. It is distinct from language-specific grammatical categories of Proper Names for which language-specific grammatical criteria should be adduced. Second, our approach takes into account all types of proper names. The question of what counts as a name, very often debated in the literature, should be answered on two levels, keeping in mind the distinction between proprial lemmas and proper names. The language specific question as to what belongs to the grammatical category of Names does not necessarily yield the same answer as the question of what can be considered to be a name from a semantic-pragmatic point of view. Mismatches are most likely to be found at the bottom of the cline of nameworthiness introduced in Section 2.3.

CHAPTER 3

....

NAMES AND MEANING

....

STAFFAN NYSTRÖM

Do names have meaning? To most people such a question might seem strange. Of course names have meaning, they would probably say, even if the meaning is sometimes difficult to grasp. *Long Island* means 'long island', which is obvious if you know English. *Costa Blanca* means 'the white coast' to anyone who speaks Spanish. *Lago Maggiore* and *East River* mean 'the greater lake' and 'the river to the east' to people speaking Italian and English respectively. Surnames such as Eng. *White*, Germ. *Müller* 'miller' and Sw. *Svärd* 'sword' do not have to be explained. The meaning of all these names is obvious—you do not need to be a trained onomastician to realize that—and if the meaning is obscured by time or otherwise, there are name scholars to help us interpret and explain such opaque names as well. So yes, names do have meaning.

3.1 ARE NAMES 'MEANINGLESS' OR 'MEANINGFUL'?

....

In fact it is not as simple as suggested above. Many scholars from different disciplines have claimed for a long time that names do not have meaning, names only have reference. In the examples mentioned in the opening paragraph it is the corresponding words (*long, island, costa, maggiore, east, river, white*, etc.) that have meaning, not the names as such. A name has an illusory lexical and etymological meaning, while the real 'meaning' of the name is actually the place carrying the name, the named object. Thus the meaning of *Stockholm* is 'the city that is the capital of Sweden situated on a group of islands where Lake Mälaren meets the Baltic Sea and where . . .' or something like that. The fact that the words *stock* 'log' and *holm* 'islet' were once used to form the name is not at all important to the people using the name today. A meaning 'the islet with the logs; log island' is completely irrelevant. The name *Stockholm* has a clearly identifying function, but no meaning. The name is just a label.

The same arguments apply to personal names. Given names in Sweden like *Karl* and *Sten*, as well as the surnames *Gren* and *Modig*, still have equivalents in the Swedish lexicon (*karl* 'man', *sten* 'stone', *gren* 'branch, twig', *modig* 'brave'), which in some sense enables us to 'understand' the names, but despite that fact the words and their meanings are normally not relevant to us at all. Roger *Black* was a **white**, very successful British athlete in the 1990s. Almost 40 people in Sweden today bear the surname *Löpare* 'runner' (how many of them run on a regular basis?) and also a very short person can answer to the surname *Lång* 'long; tall'. It is only the identifying function of the names—their reference—that is important, not the lexical meaning of the words they are based on.

Names do not need to contain recognizable words at all and they function equally well when they are completely unintelligible to the name users. All proper names (i.e. place-names and personal names, as in the examples above, animal names, names of vehicles, products, etc.) are a type of word that people use to identify and refer to objects individually without having to describe them. When a linguistic expression turns into a proper name, the deictic, referring function of the name becomes more or less the only function. The former lexical meaning (if there ever was one) ceases to exist. The 'meaning' of a proper name, therefore, is only the place, person, animal, or whatever the name identifies and refers to; in all other respects, names are 'meaningless'. This scientific position, represented for instance by Saul Kripke (1972) and Keith Donnellan (1972, 1974), has been referred to as 'the meaninglessness thesis'.

Other scholars disagree. According to them names do have meaning, at least some kind of meaning. A crucial point is what we mean by *meaning*. In my opinion we cannot ignore the importance of lexical meaning when discussing the meaning of names. Names and words (with lexical meaning) interact and influence each other to a varying degree in different situations. And even if names do not have an asserted lexical or etymological meaning, they normally have other kinds of meanings, presuppositional meanings. Names are not only practical labels, instead they are packed with meaning in many senses. Based on such an assumption, 'the maximum meaningfulness thesis', represented for instance by Otto Jespersen (1924) and Jerzy Kuryłowicz (1980), has attracted many followers.

So who is right? Do names have meaning or not, that is do they have both meaning and reference or do they only have reference? This question is closely connected to the dichotomy *proper name—common noun* (or to use another pair of terms *name—appellative*) and also to the idea of names being more or less 'namelike', showing a lower or higher degree of propriality or 'nameness'. Can a certain name be a more 'namelike' name than another? I believe it can. To support such an assertion one might argue that a name is not a physical, material object. It is an abstract conception. A name is the result of a complex mental process: sometimes (when we hear or see a name) the result of an individual analysis of a string of sounds or letters, sometimes (when we produce a name) the result of a verbalization of a thought. We shall not ask ourselves what a name *is* but what a name *does*. To use a name means to start a process in the brain, a process which in turn activates our memories, fantasy, linguistic abilities, emotions, and many other things. With an approach like that, it would be counterproductive to state that names do not have meaning, that names are meaningless. So let us look a little closer at what the meaningful element in a name can be.

3.2 Denotation—Connotation

We can all agree that the identifying function of a name is important, and perhaps the most important. Using a name is an efficient way to individualize an object (the referent) and to point at it with a concentrated linguistic expression (the name) instead of describing or 'explaining' it. The relationship between a name and its referent is sometimes called *denotation*; at least that is how the term is used in British and Scandinavian onomastics. The named object is called the *denotatum* (plur. *denotata*). *Oxford* is the linguistic sign (the name) while the city itself with the old university is the object (the referent) that the name *Oxford* nowadays *denotes*. Depending on, for instance, my personal knowledge and experiences of the city of Oxford, the name *Oxford* evokes certain *connotations* when I hear it: greyish buildings, a cosy book-shop, hot tea, heavy rain, etc.

Connotations like these (scattered images, associations, information) might be individual or commonly shared by a smaller or larger group of people. Comparatively few people in Sweden have visited Gottröra, a rural parish north of Stockholm. But the name *Gottröra* evokes similar connotations in many Swedes since 27 December 1991 when Scandinavian Airlines Flight 751 managed to make an emergency landing there shortly after the engines of the aircraft had ceased to function. The plane was broken into three parts when forced to land in a field but the crew and all the passengers survived. The lexical, etymological meaning of *Gottröra* is probably 'Gutte's barrow', true or not, referring to an old tradition with a Viking named *Gutte* being buried there, while the connotative, associative meaning of the name *Gottröra* since 1991 to many people is something like 'plane crash ending miraculously well'.

3.3 Lexical and Proprial Meaning

As I have shown with the examples *Long Island, Lago Maggiore*, etc. above, it has been argued that only the corresponding words (*long, island, costa, maggiore*) have meaning, not the names as such. In my opinion this is a much too simplified way to view the problem. In fact a constant interplay takes place between the proprial part of our mental lexicon (the onomasticon) and the non-proprial part (the common words), which makes even the idea of lexical meaning more complicated and more important than it appears. The lexical meaning and the proprial meaning (i.e. the meaning of a certain word used as a name or a name element) depend, or at least can depend, on each other. The proprial meaning of for example the name element (name part) *island* in the name *Long Island* does not necessarily have to be exactly the same as the lexical meaning of the word used in a phrase like 'let us row to that little island over there'. I will elaborate on this with some examples.

Stockholm is the well-known name of the capital of Sweden. *Storsjön* is a frequent lake name. The names *Stockholm* and *Storsjön* are compounds including the still very common words *stock* 'log' + *holm(e)* 'small island' and *stor* 'big' + *sjö* 'lake' respectively. *Bromma* is the name of a district in Stockholm (an old village and parish name), *Kalmar* is a town in the south-east of Sweden, and *Vättern* is the second largest lake in the country. The last three names are completely unintelligable to people without onomastic skills. So let us compare the transparent names *Stockholm* and *Storsjön* with the strange *Bromma*, *Kalmar*, and *Vättern*, names in which modern name users can hardly find a meaning besides the identifying, deictic place-name meaning (the reference). As already mentioned, such opaque names do function equally well when we use them in daily life, even though we cannot identify or understand their linguistic content. So is there—concerning the meaning of the names—no difference in principle between transparent names like *Stockholm* and *Storsjön* on the one hand and completely opaque names such as *Bromma*, *Kalmar*, and *Vättern* on the other? No, some scholars say, there is no difference. Names are names and as such meaningless. Yes, other scholars say, there is a difference. The fact that the name *Storsjön* has something to do with the words *stor* and *sjö* can hardly be questioned, and in that respect the name includes a dimension— a lexical intelligibility—that the names *Bromma*, *Kalmar*, and *Vättern* do not include (what is a *brom* or *bromma*, a *kalm* or a *vätt(er)*?). But if, despite this quality, *Storsjön* does not have meaning, what does it have that the other names do not? Well, the name *Storsjön* has open, working connections to the living vocabulary, the mental lexicon.

In the same way, certain personal names have open connections to the living lexicon. We take *Björn* as an example. A meaningless sequence of sounds (if that is what a name is?) cannot be translated from one language into another, but still a man *Björn* can sometimes be called *Bear*. His name has obviously—besides its identifying function—a living connection to the appellative *björn* 'bear' in the lexicon, and with that an associative meaning 'björn' is available and also possible to be expressed in other languages. The name *Björn* might thus activate several functions in the brain apart from guiding us to the right person. Also many surnames and earlier bynames, alongside their dominating, identifying function, still retain something of the meaning we see in the corresponding words. For instance, nouns for professions and ordinary adjectives are the basis of many Swedish surnames like *Målare*, *Snickare*, *Karsk*, *Svensk*, and *Säker* (*målare* 'painter', *snickare* 'carpenter', *karsk* 'plucky', *svensk* 'Swedish', *säker* 'secure, safe'). The correspondence between these names and their equivalent words may cause facetious comments if reality does not match the names. And when people in today's Sweden apply for new given names such as *Mango* 'mango', *Prins* 'prince', *Solstråle* 'sunbeam', and *Summercloud*, or for surnames as *Cyklist* 'cyclist', *Måndroppe* 'moondrop', *Nightlove*, *Rymdport* 'spacegate', *Stenriker* 'made of money', and *Tvärnit* 'sudden braking', it is hardly because the names are without meaning, but, on the contrary, because the meanings of the names are clear and important to them, associatively and emotionally.

The human brain can be described as a dictionary, a mental lexicon, where words and names are organized and stored in a gigantic network. Within this network the names as such—the mental name stock—form an onomasticon. Names occupy a place in the brain just as much as other linguistic units. What we learn through life and through our experiences is collected in this lexicon. Figuratively speaking, we can 'look up' words and names in the lexicon when we need to interpret and understand them as well as choose the relevant word or name when we need to use it ourselves. Exactly how this works in the brain is uncertain: the brain is immensely complex, but nevertheless we can have some ideas.

One such idea that I have presented previously is that names and words should not be seen as completely isolated from each other but instead as two communicating and integrated parts of the total network, the mental lexicon (Nyström 1998). When we hear or see a name in use, the network is activated and the place, person, animal, company, vehicle, etc. is identified. But at the same time personal memories can be awakened, different associations take place (see Section 3.5.2), and in addition the common words forming the name (if they still exist in our lexicon) are crying out for attention with their lexical meaning, adding to the overall meaning of the name in our brain. As long as the words *stor* 'big' and *sjö* 'lake' are alive in the brain, we simply cannot cut off the connection between these and the name *Storsjön* 'the big lake'. *Storsjön* is quite obviously a place-name, in most cases we know that instinctively from the situational context when we use it, but the name does not exist in splendid isolation. Should Storsjön turn out to be a very small lake we will no doubt be surprised. The linguistic expression *Storsjön* has not only identified the lake and told us that its name is *Storsjön*, it has also led us to certain assumptions about the lake, certain presuppositions. And as long as *snickare* 'carpenter', *svensk* 'Swedish', *prins* 'prince', and *cyklist* 'cyclist' are common words in the Swedish language there is always the potential to activate everything these words mean to us even if the expression we hear or see (*Snickare, Svensk, Prins*, or *Cyklist*) is only meant to be a name. The risk of misunderstanding, of making the wrong choice between name and word, should be greatest when the name is new to the person hearing it. Concurrently with him or her hearing or using *Storsjön, Snickare, Svensk*, etc. in their function as names in real situations, the deictic, onomastic meaning—the reference—will become more and more evident and dominant while the descriptive lexical meaning will be correspondingly repressed.

Thus, the exclusive name character in a name can be weakened or 'blurred' through influence from a living homonymous appellative or from other words. The common words do have meanings which can make themselves felt in certain situations. This makes it hard to claim that, for instance, *Storsjön, Snickare*, and *Björn* are completely without meaning. If meanings, qualities and characteristics in the appellatives 'leak' to the names, these may assume an associative or characterizing meaning as well. If that happens we easily presume for instance that Storsjön 'the big lake' is a big lake. Personal names such as *Annika, Roland*, and *Bodin*, and place-names such as *Bromma, Kalmar*, and *Vättern*, on the other hand, have no living connections whatsoever to recognizable appellatives or other words, and this makes it easier for us to accept them as being without meaning.

3.4 THE WORD AND PLACE-NAME ELEMENT *ÅRD*

Another way of describing the mutual influence and interrelations between lexical and proprial meaning will be illustrated through a single word and place-name element, the terrain denoting *ård*, known only from the island of Gotland in the Baltic Sea. The example is partly fictional, partly real.[1] Names in -*ård* have previously been thoroughly examined by Ingemar Olsson (1959). An *ård* can be described as 'a promontory sticking out into the sea, mainly consisting of rocks, stones and gravel'. In the following, and mostly for pedagogical reasons, I will discuss one type of possible influence at a time, following a chronological framework (see Fig. 3.1). Reality is of course less simple. Much happens simultaneously, and the individual language user and name user lives in a buzz of linguistic and emotional forces.

Fig. 3.1 is divided into two: on the right is the onomasticon, that is, the proprial part of the mental lexicon, on the left is the non-proprial lexicon. On the far left there is a time axis. We imagine a diacronic development from the top downwards and we watch what is happening at some specific points (1–6) in time.

1. At the starting point a word *ård* (an appellative) exists in the non-proprial part of the lexicon.
2. Based on the word *ård* in the lexicon, some place-names ending in -*ård(en)* are formed (*Grasården, Grundården, Klasården*, etc.). Most Swedish place-names are compounds with the generic as the second element and the specific as the first. The final -*en* in -*ården* is the definite article in non-neuter words. The names are stored in the onomasticon of an individual person or of a smaller or larger group of people depending on how well known the names are. Every filled circle in the figure represents such a place-name. There are connections between the two systems, i.e. between the onomasticon and the non-proprial lexicon, in that the linguistic element *ård* is used both as a common noun and as a name element. The influences go from lexicon to onomasticon, shown as arrow A in Fig. 3.1.
3. Time passes and the appellative *ård* becomes more and more frequent, perhaps at the expense of other words. The word frequency is illustrated in Fig. 3.1 by the increasingly wider arrow (the 'striped tie') from the top downwards. At the same time, new names ending in -*ård(en)* are formed continuously, partly influenced by

---

[1] This example is largely a translation from Swedish of my article 'Lexikon och onomastikon—två samverkande system' (Nyström 1995).

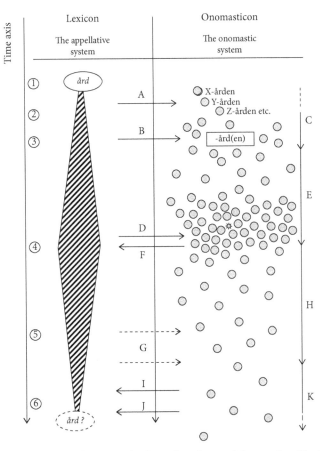

FIGURE 3.1 The interrelations between the lexical and proprial meaning illustrated with the Swedish (Gotland) word and place-name element *ård* 'promontory in the sea'.

Adapted from Nyström (1995).

the living and frequently used appellative *ård* in the lexicon (arrow B), partly due to analogical patterns (ready-made structures) in the growing number of names ending in -*ård*(*en*), i.e. internal influences within the onomasticon, the proprial system (arrow C). In time these names become so numerous that a productive, type forming place-name element -*ård*(*en*) can be said to exist.

4. We move further on in time. To the individual name user, the meaning of the place-name element -*ård*(*en*) is the synthesis of all the individual names in -*ård*(*en*) that exist in his onomasticon, a sort of lowest common denominator for a lot of places. If the creation of new names in -*ård*(*en*) increases or decreases over time, the centre of gravity of the semantic content of the name element -*ård*(*en*) will be affected as well (the centre of gravity is shown as ✳). Periods with many new names in -*ård*(*en*) will put a greater mark on the collective meaning of the name element (the lowest common denominator) than periods with few new *ård*-names.

Exactly where in time we find the point of gravity in a place-name element is unimportant providing the meaning does not change over time. It does not matter if the inspiration for creating new *ård*-names comes from older or younger names in -*ård(en)*, and it matters little whether the basis is an older or younger lexical meaning providing the meaning has not changed over time. However, if the meaning of the appellative, the lexical meaning, shifts over time (through widening, narrowing, or polysemy), so also will the semantic point of gravity change in the place-name element, since the appellative to some extent also affects the creation of new names (arrow D).

But, as I have claimed above, new names are just as much formed from internal forces within the onomasticon. This means that older names with an older meaning represented will also play a role when new names are formed (arrow E). The onomasticon is constantly present to the name users as well as the non-proprial lexicon; the connections between them are available and open, which means that the many names which include older meanings of *ård* will affect new *ård*-names and more or less counteract the changing lexical meaning of the appellative *ård*. In other words: a change in lexical meaning (in the appellative) could probably have been more dramatic if the preservative powers of the onomasticon had not dampened it. We see here a possible influence from the onomasticon to the non-proprial lexicon according to arrow F.

5. Later on, the appellative *ård* starts to be used less frequently, perhaps being considered as increasingly old fashioned or dialectal. Perhaps it is outcompeted by other words. Meanwhile, but not to the same extent, new place-names in -*ård(en)* are created. The influences behind these new names are now only to a limited and decreasing degree coming from the lexicon (arrow G). But due to analogical and other internal powers within the onomasticon, new names in -*ård(en)* may still be produced long after the appellative has become obsolete.

6. Places (localities) carrying names in -*ård(en)* change in appearance, something that also might affect the lexical meaning of the appellative *ård*. And this is what has actually happened in the island of Gotland. The land is slowly rising from the sea, a gradual shoaling is taking place, slowly covering the 'årds', the original stone formations, with soil, sand, and vegetation. The places with names in -*ård(en)* no longer look the same as they did when the majority of them were given their names, and this fact also affects people's sense of what the meaning of the place-name element -*ård(en)* is.

If, at the same time, the appellative is going out of use, and the uncertainty regarding its actual meaning is increasing, the place-name element through its *denotata* will be more and more influential in relation to the lexical meaning of the appellative. We see an obvious influence from the onomasticon on the non-proprial lexicon (arrow I). Sometimes this helps to keep a vanishing appellative alive. Still, in the final stage of its life cycle the word *ård* can be 'filled' with a semantic content, which is basically retrieved by the individual language user from his onomasticon. The fact that informants extract the meaning of words (the lexical meaning) from (certain) place-names is well-known to many name scholars and name collectors, and the explanation for that is simply that the connections between the two systems, the two parts of the mental lexicon, are still open and available for use, while the internal connections within the lexicon are obsolete. There is nothing better on which to base one's understanding of the word than how it has been used in place-names (arrow J).

A possible concluding phase in this scenario could be that *ård* completely dies out as an appellative. It will then be impossible to talk about, for instance, 'a great ård in the sea' without confusing people. The communication will not work. But if someone in the future gives a name to a promontory in the sea, a name in -*ård*(*en*) will still be an option, an internal onomastic pattern available to be copied. But gradually too the name element -*ård*(*en*) will appear more and more obscure and difficult to use in a new name. Not only are the connections between *ård* and other elements in the lexicon cut off, but also the connections between the proprial and the non-proprial lexicon will cease to exist, and like the Swedish examples *Bromma* (possibly from an Old Swedish agricultural word **brumma* meaning 'place to harvest leaves') and *Kalmar* (from the dialectal word *kalm* 'pile of stones' and an old *arin* 'island of gravel'), they can only be restored by onomasticians and other scholars with knowledge of Old Swedish.

3.5 PRESUPPOSITIONAL MEANINGS

Apart from the lexical meaning and the proprial meaning (as used above), every proper name in a given situation gives rise to one or more presuppositional meanings, varying from person to person, from group to group: categorical meaning, associative meaning, and emotive meaning, to mention the most important ones.

3.5.1 Categorical Meaning

The notion of names having a categorical meaning is very much debated. It is based on the presumption that human beings mentally divide objects and other phenomena in our world into categories of some kind (such as animals, horses, people, fruit, cities, cars, etc.), that we use words to gather and group referents that belong to such common categories, and that such a categorization also forms an underlying structure when names and name giving are concerned. Certainly, it is not evident that we know for sure which category should be brought to the fore when we hear a certain name, but that does not prevent the idea of categorical meaning from being correct. We make an assumption about a certain category—a categorical presupposition—when we hear a name, an assumption that later can prove to be right or wrong. Willy van Langendonck (2007b) argues that the supposed proprial categories are closely linked to what Eleanor Rosch

(1977) called 'basic level concept'. To show what this concept is, an often used example of a hierarchy with three levels can be presented: *animal—dog—basset*. Here *dog* is the basic level concept, that is, the conceptually and perceptually most available word (or term), while the other words are either of too vague and abstract a level, or of too specific or technical a kind. It has been said that children normally acquire the basic level concepts before words from the other levels.

Transposed into names, a categorical presupposition should mean for instance that when we hear a certain name, we draw the conclusion that the name must belong to a dog, not to an animal of any kind and not to a bassett, beagle, or labrador retriever. Other possible name categories could include human beings, male human beings, female human beings, cats, rivers, cities, countries, companies, aircraft, or something else. Certainly, movements within the onomasticon do take place (Andersson 1997) so that, for instance, given names and surnames are used as place-names (the names of the church parishes *Fredrika* and *Vilhelmina* in the north of Sweden, and the city and state *Washington* in the USA), place-names are used as personal names (for instance, the Norwegian surnames *Haugen, Lund, Moen, Strand*, and *Bakken*) and today personal names are frequently used also to name our pets (the animals are made human, almost personified: a dog *Erik*, a cat *Lisa*, etc.). However, in principle there are still onomastic patterns and models sufficiently impressed on us to make our brains categorize the name bearer as soon as we hear a name. In many cases, the category is explicitly shown in the name phrase itself: *the river Nile, the city of New York, Fritz the cat*, etc.

The fact that names have or may have a categorical meaning leads to the result that people in a real situation easily ascribe a name a categorical presupposition.

3.5.2 Associative Meaning

Associative meaning (connotative meaning) implies that a name user—or a group of name users—when hearing a certain name comes to think of something else or something more, apart from reacting to the primary function of the name, namely the function of individualizing and localizing the referent. Something comes to his or her mind, an association with a person, a point in time, a milieu, a certain mood or an event, as in the case described above with the Swedish place-name *Gottröra* and the airplane crash. Associations can differ from one name user to another according to the attitude or point of view they have as regards the place, person, company, etc. in question; a variety of thoughts, hopes, feelings, and memories emerge when the brain is confronted with a name. Associations like this are often personal, others are commonly shared by many people.

The boy's name *Adolf* has not been bestowed upon many people in Sweden since the Second World War. Not until recently, almost seventy years after the end of the war, do we see children occasionally being given that name. Of course this is not the result of some emerging linguistic problem with the name *Adolf* (spelling, inflection, pronunciation), nor of the fact that the lexical (etymological) meaning of the name has become inappropriate in some way. Instead it is all about the negative associations we may have towards the most famous name bearer from the twentieth century. The associative meaning (the connotations) of *Adolf* is still strong and unpleasant to many people. Other given names, borne by stars from cinema, TV, sports, or the music business, conversely give rise to positive associations—often during a shorter period of time—and thus are reflected in many children's names around the world.

For similar reasons many politicians, city planners, and marketing people today try to avoid urban place-names that could cause negative associations. Instead they prefer names that are supposed to have a positive meaning, names sending signals of well-being and of a good life, that is, names including elements like *beach, garden, park,* or *village*. Older, supposedly strained names of streets, squares, districts, and parks, they try to get rid of, despite the fact that it is the places as such that are the real problem, not the names. Branding and re-branding of places is a huge business today (Alderman 2008; Ashworth and Kavaratzis 2010).

In cases like the ones above it is quite obvious that names are not 'meaningless'. On the contrary, names show themselves as linguistic expressions of great symbolic value and bearers of important associative meanings.

In connection with this aspect of names and meaning it is appropriate to mention also the so-called folk etymologies (especially concerning place-names). In many cases people wish to find a meaning, a common sense, in a name. They look for an understandable reason why a certain place is called the way it is. They want the name of the place to be explained. And if there is no explanation available or acceptable (the scientific interpretation might be too complicated, too difficult to grasp), it quite often happens that an explanation is created by the name users themselves. Several places in Sweden are called *Bälinge* (two parishes and an old jurisdictional district). These names are probably formed from an Old Swedish word *bal* or *bale* meaning 'height; hill', but they may alternatively contain another word corresponding to the present day Swedish word *bål* 'fire'. They have not been definitively interpreted. An old, local explanation of the parish name in the province Uppland refers to a particular event a long time ago. The story tells us that all the men in Bälinge were gathered at the *thing* (the old district court) to decide upon a suitable name for their parish. They agreed that a good name would be something ending in *-inge* or maybe *-linge*, both of which are common endings used in many names in the neighbourhood. Such a name should fit in well. At that point in the process, one of the sheep close by bleated—*bäääää* (sheep in Sweden sound like that)—and that solved the problem. The name must be *Bälinge*. Of course no one takes this explanation seriously today, but still it has emerged: it is known, and it shows that names make people associate, in this case with bleating sheep.

In the *Bälinge* case, it is a question of phonological resemblance, which is a well-known reason for associations. A very thorough investigation of how parents in Sweden choose or reject names for their children (Aldrin 2011) shows, among many other things, that they sometimes avoid names that rhyme with 'unfavourable' words of different kinds. They want to protect their child from being teased at school and also later in life. *Johan* (pronounced /jo:an/) is an old traditional name form in Sweden, but still we can hear comments like 'we don't want to call him Johan because it rhymes with toan' (and *boan; toan* means 'toilet' and *boan* means 'boa constrictor'). Johan might be called *Johan Toan* or *Johan Boan*! So phonological resemblance can give rise to unwanted associations in cases like this.

3.5.3 Emotive Meaning

The associative meaning of names as described in the previous subsection is closely related to the emotive (or affective) meaning that names may have. Positive or negative associations (connotations) caused by or connected to a certain name might be of an emotional character. Certainly most place-names are emotionally neutral and objectively descriptive, like Sw. *Mörtsjön* 'roach lake', *Järnvägsgatan* 'railway street', *Råggärdet* 'rye field', *Smedstorp* 'smith's hamlet', and *Aspholmen* 'aspen island', but many others are instead loaded with emotions, values, hope, or anger. Fishing spots on the Swedish coast named *Jämmerdalen* 'vale of tears' and *Eländet* 'misery' or *Guldtunnan* 'gold barrel' and *Riksdalergrundet* 'riksdaler sunken rock' bear witness to that (*riksdaler* is an old Swedish currency used before the present-day *krona* 'crown'). Also, many replicated names of fields or small hamlets in Sweden, such as *Amerika* (Eng. America) and *Sibirien* (Eng. Siberia), show traces of hope, dreams, and longing, or of toil and hard work respectively. In cases like these, the names are not only coined as unbiased references, but equally as a means of communicating emotions and sharing them with others.

Modern examples of emotionally based place-names can easily be found in developing urban environments from the late twentieth century. From my personal experience, growing up in a small town in central Sweden, I take the name of a new residential area that was planned and built in the 1960s on land that had earlier been the main fields of the old farm Salsta with its roots in the Iron Age. The location close to a lake was excellent and the houses as well as the apartments in them were innovative and different. A fresh, new thinking characterized the—in some peoples' eyes—posh area, causing jealousy as well as sarcastic remarks about those who chose to move there. The area was called *Salsta gärde* 'Salsta field' in the official, municipal administration, but *Guldkusten* 'gold coast' in popular parlance (not a unique name in situations like this). As the years passed, however, Guldkusten deteriorated, the former freshness disappeared, the town saw many industrial closures, the housing company had serious problems, rents were raised, buildings and yards were not as carefully managed as before. People started to leave the area, to move away. Others moved in, but the newcomers were mostly immigrants from other parts of the world, who had had apartments assigned to them after having lived temporarily in the town's local refugee camp. To the surrounding and name giving population, *Guldkusten* 'gold coast' was no longer an apposite name. Instead, the well-known *Ångermanland* turned up with a new reference, as a somewhat sarcastic name, based on the resemblance between the ancient and now obsolete topographical word *ånger* (*anger*) '(narrow) bay in the sea' and the word *ånger* meaning 'repentance'. *Ångermanland*, with the topographical reference, is the name of a province in Northern Sweden.

In personal names, the emotive presuppositions might be inherent in the stem or in the suffix used in the name itself. Hypocoristic name forms or certain name endings like German -*chen* or Spanish -*ito*/-*ita* can be found in many languages, perhaps characterizing the name bearer at some point in life, and still more clearly showing the special relation between the name bearer and the name user. Emotive meaning may also be caused by associative (connotative) emotions, as in the case of *Adolf* mentioned above.

CHAPTER 4

....

NAMES AND DISCOURSE

....

ELWYS DE STEFANI

4.1 INTRODUCTION

....

THIS chapter presents an overview of several methods of investigation that analyse names in the context of their discursive and interactional appearance. Various disciplines within the humanities and social sciences are concerned with exploring names as resources that may serve a plethora of socially relevant purposes, and with describing their discursive functions and related interactional practices. The focus of this chapter will thus be on those approaches that examine how speakers, that is, social actors, use names in their everyday lives.

4.2 ANTHROPOLOGY

....

For some authors, an anthropological approach to names is the reverse of that developed in historical onomastics, which is believed to be mainly preoccupied with organizing names in complex onomastic taxonomies. With regard to the study of personal names, Bromberger (1982: 104) states that 'rather than analysing how societies classify the individuals through the names that they bestow on them, they (i.e. the onomasticians) remain attached to classifying the names by adopting (formal and semantic) criteria that are external to the culture investigated'.[1] In the light of studies such as Walther and Schultheis (1989 [1974]) and Kohlheim (1977), which address the issue of the social significance of personal names from a

---

[1] '[Or, paradoxalement, la plupart des études anthroponymiques se sont situées aux antipodes d'un tel programme:] plutôt qu'à analyser comment les sociétés *classent les individus* à travers les noms qu'elles leur assignent, on s'est attaché à *classer les noms*, selon des critères (formels ou sémantiques) extérieurs aux cultures considérées. . . .'

historical perspective, Bromberger's criticism is only partially acceptable. However, the anthropologist's vision foregrounds the necessity of studying names—just like any other cultural phenomenon—from an emic perspective, or, as Malinowski (1922: 25) puts it, 'to grasp the native's point of view, his relation to life, to realize his vision of his world'. Two consequences follow from this standpoint: first, names cannot be studied as isolated entities but need to be described in a contextualized way, encompassing the linguistic as well as the broader social environment in which they occur; second, anthropology makes researchers aware of the fact that the analytical categories conventionally used in onomastics are themselves rooted in a historical and epistemological tradition, and cannot simply be transferred to societies in which these categories have no cultural significance. This holds true not only for the highly particularized onomastic nomenclature, but also for broader concepts such as 'place-name' and 'personal name' (see section 4.6).

In fact, anthropology developed an early interest in the contextualized analysis of both place- and personal names. Franz Boas' (1934) pioneering examination of the place-names of the Kwakiutl (today named Kwakwaka'wakw), an indigenous people living in northern Vancouver Island, is a milestone for the anthropological approach to name studies. The excellence of Boas' fieldwork practices allowed him to deliver not only a precise formal description of some 2,500 toponyms and their respective geographical locations, but also to investigate the practical and mythological uses that the members of the community make of these names. In his book, Boas effectively illustrates his claim that the study of place-names provides understanding of how a community conceptualizes environmental phenomena. Boas' interest in place-names already emanates from earlier work (Boas 1901–07), and has been influential for American anthropology (see Thornton 1997). Many of his disciples carry out analyses of Native American place-names, among them Harrington (1916), who publishes a fine-grained and monumental analysis of Tewa place-names, and Sapir (1912), who maintains that 'the physical environment is reflected in language only in so far as it has been influenced by social factors' (1912: 227). In other words, place-names do not emerge from descriptions of visible features of the landscape, their use rather reveals the community's perception and experience of the environment.

Later work includes Lounsbury's (1960) work on Iroquois place-names and de Laguna's (1972) monograph on the Tlingit, which contains a significant focus on place-names. In his article on Apache narratives, Basso (1984: 23) neatly describes the anthropological relevance of places and their names: 'A native model of how stories work to shape Apaches' conceptions of the landscape, it is also a model of how stories work to shape Apaches' conceptions of themselves.' The anthropological perspective thus stresses the fact that place-names are culturally constructed and that the analysis of place-names has to take into account the community's beliefs and practices. In this sense, Iteanu (2006) shows that among the Orokaiva (New Guinea), places are defined with regard to kinship or exchange relations, rather than to territorial extensions.

Consequently, a place-name may be used to refer to a variety of localities and rarely solidifies as a fixed name.

Clearly, from the point of view of anthropology, the study of place-names goes beyond the mere etymological explanation of isolated units of language. Instead, it begins with a contextualized examination of names as they appear in narratives, witnessed through (participant) observation. However, recent developments in the anthropological analysis of names are surprisingly close to the historical onomastic tradition, see for example Senft (2008) on the place-names of the Trobriand Islands.

As far as personal names are concerned, they are examined with regard to their social significance, that is, social identification and the embedding of an individual within a community. Personal names have been described as a means to index aspects of identity (such as gender, descent, religion, etc.) and mark biographical changes (transition to adulthood, marriage, maternity, etc.). Therefore, they are of great importance for the social organization of communities. In Britain, for instance, parents are required by law to register the name of a baby within six weeks of the birth (Bodenhorn and Vom Bruck 2006: 2). Thus, with regard to naming practices, anthropologists are typically interested not only in the source of names (or onomastic basis), but also in when a name is assigned and by whom, whether or not it is gender-specific.

Anchored in an evolutionary approach to the study of communities, Morgan (1860) provides a first description of *The Indian Method of Bestowing and Changing Names*. But it is Lévi-Strauss (1962) who makes a major contribution to how naming practices and name usage are related to social and religious life, maintaining that naming is a practice of social classification. In a similar vein, Geertz and Geertz (1964) publish an analysis of teknonymy in Bali—whereby adults are designated with respect to the names of their children—and find it to be 'a coherent system of ideas, a consistent set of beliefs, a theory even, about the way in which social life is, and ought to be, organized' (1964: 103). Subsequently, a comprehensive overview of naming practices is provided by Alford (1988), who offers a cross-cultural investigation of naming practices and related phenomena, such as how communities classify and individualize their members through names, and how names may change in the course of one's life, and who also describes the social and religious relevance of name usage vs. name avoidance in social interaction.

While anthropology has not developed a consistent methodology for the analysis of personal names, there is a general view that understanding how a community bestows and uses personal names is of paramount importance in anthropological fieldwork, precisely because it provides a grasp of the community's understanding of identity, kinship, genealogy, and social life. This is also true for urban settings, as Rymes (1996) shows in her analysis of names used by gang members of a Los Angeles barrio. In this study, the author analyses excerpts from narratives by a gang member and thus provides a contextualized understanding of the practical meaning of gang names. Her strong focus on speech situates her work in the proximity of linguistic pragmatics, which I outline in the subsequent section.

4.3 PRAGMATICS OF NAMES

The pragmatic analysis of names is largely indebted to the philosophy of language, more specifically to the theories of reference that have emerged from logic. John Stuart Mill's (1973 [1843]: 43) observation, according to which 'proper names . . . have, strictly speaking, no signification', is often reported as a starting point for the different accounts that subsequent philosophers developed with respect to proper names. While in Mill's view proper names merely refer to an object, authors such as Frege (1892) and Russell (1973 [1905]) maintain that they can have a meaning (*Sinn* in Frege's terms), or at least a connotation. These authors see names as 'descriptions of single objects' (Frege 1892) or as 'abbreviated definite "descriptions"' (Russell 1973 [1905]). Such descriptivist theories of names are challenged by authors adopting a causal approach to names and reference, such as Kripke (1972), who describes names as 'rigid designators'. A much lesser influence on the study of naming and reference was exerted by Charles S. Peirce's reflections on names, which have been keenly discussed only since the 1980s (see Pietarinen 2010 for an overview).

The influence that philosophy of language exerted on linguistics in the 1960s and 1970s is also visible in the work on proper names stemming from that time. Continuing the language philosophical tradition, authors such as Searle (1958) and Zabeeh (1968) reflect on the 'classical' logical problems of name reference and meaning. In line with the pragmatic conception, authors aim at describing the different functions that names can have in the speakers' utterances (see Coates 2006a and Van Langendonck 2007b for an overview). However, these analyses are generally based on invented examples emanating from the researchers' introspection, thereby manifesting their solid philosophical roots. Yet an empirically more grounded account has also emerged within the field, mainly in the German research tradition. Dobnig-Jülch's (1977) book bears the revealing title *Pragmatik und Eigennamen* [Pragmatics and Proper Names] and proposes an analysis of how farmers use the names of their breeding animals. The author's innovative approach is echoed in later work by German scholars, such as Werner (1986, 1995) and Hoffmann (1999), who analyse names beyond the traditional, language philosophical approaches concerned with understanding the referential and semantic properties of names.

Within pragmatics, the topic most frequently investigated in relation to names is probably their use as forms of address (see chapter 29 in this book). However, the topics currently analysed from a pragmatic perspective are varied. Pang (2009) studies the eponymic use of names, as in *Lounge Lover. The Naomi Campbell of Bars* (2009: 333), and provides the narrative and cognitive backgrounds that make such uses possible. A further line of research examines the use of personal names in social interaction with regard to Brown and Levinson's (1987) politeness theory. Anchimbe (2011) shows, for instance, that while in Western communities it appears to be polite to use a person's name when engaging in interaction, this is not the case in postcolonial African countries, such as

Cameroon, where using someone's name can be perceived as disrespectful and impolite. In these communities, kinship terms and other social titles are typically used to address someone. Gehweiler (2008) provides instead a historical take on pragmatics, and analyses the transition that led in the English language from the name *Jesus* to the interjection *gee!*

While the first linguistic studies on the pragmatics of names (e.g. Dobnig-Jülch 1977) are largely indebted to Austinian and Searlian speech act theory, recent investigations offer a wide spectrum of approaches and methodologies. At present, the pragmatics of names does not denote a sharply defined method of investigation, and its analytical interests regularly overlap with those of other approaches.

4.4 Discourse Analysis

While in the field of pragmatics the study of names is mainly concerned with the oral use of proper names (actual, imagined, or enacted, e.g. in literature), discourse oriented approaches mostly deal with the 'public' use of names as observed throughout various kinds of media. For example, Clifton (2013) analyses the construction of national identity through naming practices. He focuses on the political debate triggered by the French nationalist party *Front National*, whose leader Marine Le Pen maintains that children of immigrants should be given traditional French names in order to better assimilate into the French culture. In this article, the author shows how personal names are used to create membership categories leading to social inclusion or exclusion, and thus to fostering what has been termed 'new racism'. Similarly, Bertrand (2010) analyses the use of place-names as a device of 'discursive deracialization', that is, the veiled indexing of race. She bases her analysis on focus group discussions about the quality of education in California. In the discussions among two groups of parents with different ethnic backgrounds, the participants' use of place-names and school names can frequently be seen to index racialized communities, that is, members of a community that are ultimately categorized on the basis of race. This line of research is anchored in critical discourse analysis (Fairclough 1995), with its focus on langue practices and the exertion of power and domination. In particular, the studies of Bertrand (2010) and Clifton (2013) are soundly inspired by Van Dijk's (1992) work on racist discourse. In a similar vein, Galasiński and Skowronek (2001) discuss issues of social categorization and show how proper names are used in political addresses to the nation to represent an 'ideologically preferred reality' (2001: 63). Names are thus paramount resources for the implementation of institutional power and ideology, precisely because power 'comes to appear as something other than itself, indeed, it comes to appear as a name' (Butler 1997: 36).

A further study that should be mentioned here is Kalverkämper's (1977) analysis of (personal and place) names that the author situates in the field of text linguistics. On the basis of a corpus of literary data, Kalverkämper analyses not only the traditional pragmatic dimensions of naming, but also what he calls their communicative and rhetorical functions. His interest thus goes beyond the single speech act and encompasses the relevance of names for the organization of larger passages of text.

4.5 SOCIO-ONOMASTICS AND THE SOCIOLOGY OF NAMES

The application of sociolinguistic and sociological methods to the investigation of names has led to two main fields of investigation, socio-onomastics and the sociology of names respectively. Because these approaches address names within the context of society, they receive a short but indispensable treatment in this chapter. For an extensive presentation of the research methods and topics see part V of this volume. I draw a distinction between socio-onomastics and the sociology of names by observing divergent methodological procedures and research topics in the two fields. Socio-onomasticians apply methods inherited from sociolinguistics to the analysis of names. They use interviews, focus group discussions or questionnaires as the basis of their analyses, and describe name usage with respect to previously defined social categories (e.g. 'male', 'female', 'young', 'native', 'migrants', etc.). In this line of research, name variants as used by different populations in urban settings constitute a privileged topic of investigation (Ainiala and Vuolteenaho 2006; Pablé 2009). By contrast, the sociology of names mainly addresses larger societal questions, arising for instance from language contact, in particular in the presence of so-called minority languages or dialects. The use of names in the construction of an individual's or a community's identity is a central topic of investigation, as exemplified for example by numerous studies on linguistic landscapes (Puzey 2012; see chapter 27).

4.6 INTERACTIONAL ONOMASTICS

This section subsumes studies of names carried out with methods of investigation developed in conversation analysis and interactional linguistics. Interactional onomastics differs from the approaches previously discussed at various levels, for example with respect to the data on which the analysis is based, which generally emanate from recordings of non-elicited, naturally occurring interactions. Hence interactional onomastics contrasts with approaches that use experimental set-ups for data collection as a basis of investigation, such as interviews or questionnaires (e.g. socio-onomastics), observation, and photography (sociology of names), etc. The latter kinds of data are perceived as a construction of the researcher (who decides on the basis of his assumptions, preconceptions, interests, what he or she considers relevant phenomena), rather than as a product of the participants actually engaged in social interaction. The empiricist background of interactional onomastics provides the researcher with the possibility of documenting name usage in everyday settings of interaction. Moreover, the naturalistic take on the data furnishes recordings that are rich in empirical detail, which could not be imagined by the researcher's introspection. A further difference concerns the analytical procedure adopted by interactional onomasticians, who analyse how participants use specific linguistic forms (i.e. names) to achieve their interactional goals. Hence, this approach is concerned both with formal aspects of language and with their praxeological embedding, thus mirroring the research agenda developed in interactional linguistics (Ochs et al. 1996; Selting and Couper-Kuhlen 2001). This latter approach emanated in the 1990s from conversation analysis, which manifests an early (though not declared) interest in names as used, for example, in referring to persons or places. Conversation analysis is rooted in ethnomethodology (Garfinkel 1967). One of Harold Garfinkel's students, Harvey Sacks, began using conversational telephone data to study the 'methods' that social actors employ to construct social order. The analysis of data collected in the 1960s at the Los Angeles Suicide Prevention Center, an institution offering anonymous consultation to persons with suicidal tendencies, led Sacks to describe the sequential organization and the orderliness of talk-in-interaction. Interestingly, in the first of his *lectures on conversation* held in autumn 1964, Sacks discusses an excerpt that reveals the social dimension of name usage, and, more specifically, of name avoidance (Sacks 1992: 3–11). The excerpt reproduces the opening of a phone call between a consultant (A) and an anonymous caller (B) and reads as follows:

(1)   A: This is Mr Smith may I help you
       B: I can't hear you.
       A: This is Mr <u>Smith</u>.
       B: Sm<u>i</u>th. (Sacks 1992: 3)

Sacks uses this excerpt to illustrate a recurrent phenomenon that he encounters in his data: various callers display a problem in the second turn of the phone call (represented here by the words 'I can't hear you.'), that is, in the caller's reply to the call-taker's self-identification. While a hasty explanation could relate this problem to a trouble of hearing or to a potentially bad quality of the connection, Sacks offers a sequential explanation accounting for this recurrent phenomenon. Indeed, in phone-calls to service providers, the second turn habitually houses the caller's self-identification, which the caller typically achieves by introducing his or her name. Hence, by saying 'I can't hear you.' when facing their first opportunity to talk, callers delay their self-identification to a later part of the phone call (or possibly get out of the obligation of self-identifying). In addition, the excerpt above shows that the call-taker understands 'I can't hear you.' as addressing a communicative problem. The call-taker thus tries to solve this problem by repeating his name with more emphasis (indicated by the underline: 'This is Mr <u>Smith</u>.'). Next, the caller ratifies the call-taker's name ('Sm<u>i</u>th.') without further developing that turn. At this point, the call-taker has the right and obligation to take the subsequent turn (not reproduced here). As a result, the caller manages to get through the opening sequence of the telephone call without ever having to mention his or her own name. For this reason, Sacks describes 'I can't hear you.' as a resource that many callers to the Suicide Prevention Center adopt to resolve a practical problem, which consists of avoiding self-identification.

This short example provides a sketch of the way in which names, and the absence of names, have been studied in early conversation analytic studies. Conversation analysts do not perceive names as language units with particular properties, rather, they examine them with respect to specific, routinely occurring interactional practices—such as initiating a phone call, self-identification, avoiding self-identification, etc. Hence, conversation analysts are not interested in names per se, but in the actions that participants accomplish through the use of names (and other resources). The contrast with (theoretical) onomasticians is striking. While the latter understand reference as an intrinsic property of names (see Van Langendonck 2007b), which are said to point directly to their referents (Mill (1973 [1843])), conversation analysts describe reference as a practical achievement by which participants create the interactional relevance of a referent. Consequently, names are analysed alongside other (linguistic) resources that participants use to establish reference, such as pronouns, formulations, etc.

The investigation of names as resources for establishing reference is just one overlapping concern of onomastics and conversation analysis. In addition, both approaches share a common interest in two specific kinds of referents, namely persons and places. These referential categories are of course the main pillars of onomastic research, which has extensively studied personal names (anthroponyms) and place-names (toponyms) from a diachronic perspective. It appears thus—perhaps surprisingly—that interactionally oriented research on names and onomastics have common interests. The emergence of interactional onomastics can therefore be seen as an attempt to respond to central research questions of onomastics by using the tools developed within conversation analysis and interactional linguistics.

With regard to personal names, it is worthwhile to look at the research that conversation analysts have devoted to person reference. In Sacks and Schegloff's (1979) paper on practices of reference to absent persons, the authors delineate two principles that emerge from their data. On the one hand, they observe that speakers tend to use single linguistic forms when referring to absent persons. While speakers could use an infinite number of referential forms when talking about an individual (e.g. 'Susan', 'Tom's mother', 'the lady I met yesterday', 'my teacher' may be used to refer to the 'same' person), Sacks and Schegloff (1979) observe that speakers overwhelmingly use one single referential device. Hence, they speak of a 'preference for minimization' of reference forms. On the other hand, the authors show that referential devices tend to be recipient designed. According to the 'preference for recipient design' (1979: 17), speakers choose specific referential forms 'for' their interlocutor, that is, forms that allow the interlocutor to easily identify the person that the speaker is referring to. The authors number (first) names among the most frequently used reference forms, which they call 'recognitionals'. According to the authors

> names are prototypical and ideal recognitionals in part because they are minimized reference forms as well; and the stock of minimized forms includes a set (of which names are only one sort) that is for use as recognitionals. (It should be noted that names do not have their uniqueness of reference serve to account for their recognitional usage—for they are, of course, not characteristically unique). (Sacks and Schegloff 1979: 25)

Sacks and Schegloff's (1979) paper set in motion research on two interconnected objects among interactionally oriented scholars. Several authors continued to investigate the practices of person reference (Enfield and Stivers 2007; Lerner and Kitzinger 2007; Schegloff 2007), while others focused specifically on the use of personal names in conversation as resources that serve referential purposes but also a plethora of other interactional achievements (see Downing 1996; De Stefani 2009a). Names may be used to address co-present participants in a conversation (Schwitalla 1995, 2010), speakers may use them to display disalignment or disaffiliation with what has been said (De Stefani 2004; Clayman 2010), and they are also used to organize a collaborative activity, as Mondada (2004) shows in her analysis of a work meeting during which psychiatrists discuss their 'cases', each of which is introduced by a patient's name.

The interest of conversation analysts both in the practical accomplishment of reference and in the formal (linguistic) resources that speakers employ to establish reference is also visible in Schegloff's (1972: 87) paper on what the author calls 'place formulations'. In this contribution, Schegloff shows that speakers have at their disposition various linguistic resources for establishing place reference (e.g. 'there', 'in London', 'at Peggy's house', etc.) and that they choose the appropriate formulation in a situated way, that is, in connection with the specific interactional constellation. The author identifies five kinds of place formulations that he calls 'geographical formulations' (addresses, latitude–longitude indications), 'relation to members formulations' (i.e. place formulations related to a person, such as 'Chuck's house'), 'relation to landmarks formulations' (such as 'nearby the bridge'), 'course of action places' (e.g. 'where they put the dustbins'), and finally 'place names'.[2] Among these, relation to members formulations are used preferentially. In other words, if a speaker formulates a place by relationship to a person that the hearer knows, then it is more likely that the hearer will recognize that place. Names instead 'are to be used only when expectably recognizable' (Schegloff 1972: 92), that is, when the speaker can reasonably assume that the hearer knows the place bearing that name. Schegloff's concern is to understand on

---

[2] Rather surprisingly, Schegloff (1972) mentions only briefly deictic formulations (such as 'here' and 'there'), which he calls 'locational pro-terms' (1972: 87) and which do not constitute, according to the author, a separate category of formulations.

what grounds speakers choose the appropriate formulation, and his analyses lead him to identify three analytic procedures that speakers carry out when selecting a place formulation: (a) on the basis of a 'location analysis' (Schegloff 1972: 83) speakers select the appropriate place formulation with regard to the location in which each participant is positioned and thus with respect to the shared spatial knowledge (for instance, the author explains that an American planning to travel to France would very likely speak of a journey to Europe with a fellow citizen, whereas announcing a trip 'just to France' would have to be accounted for (Schegloff 1972: 86)); (b) participants also perform a 'membership analysis', which allows them to see their interlocutors as members of a specific social category (e.g. 'neighbours', 'tourists', 'foreigners', etc.) and to choose the appropriate place formulation with regard to that categorization. For instance, a tourist visiting Birmingham and wishing to ask for directions will most likely choose an interlocutor whom he identifies as a 'local', and the person eventually giving directions will probably use 'official' place-names rather than popular names only used by locals. Hence, when talking to each other, inhabitants of Birmingham may refer to the area around 'Saint Philips Place' by using the popular name 'Pigeon Park' (see Pires 2007), but when interacting with a tourist they would more likely use the official name; (c) finally, the selection of the adequate place formulation also relies on a 'topic or activity analysis'. Schegloff maintains that speakers may prefer certain place formulations over others, depending on the topic that is being discussed or the activity in which the interactants are engaged (e.g. asking the way).

With its interest in practices of reference both to persons and to places, conversation analysis offers a thought-provoking stimulus for the analysis of the linguistic resources that speakers use for this purpose. Because of their strong praxeologic concern, many conversation analysts would probably consider that an analysis of names alone (i.e. of one single category of possible reference formulations) would be too restrictive and incapable of informing us about how the selection of a reference formulation is intertwined with interactional contingencies. However, onomasticians may fruitfully put into practice the methods developed by interactionally oriented scholars in order to investigate how interactants use names in their everyday encounters. The following subsection sketches a procedure for the investigation of names from the vantage point of interactional onomastics.

4.6.1 Method

Interactional onomastics takes over from conversation analysis its empiricist and naturalistic standpoint. Therefore, any investigation should be carried out on the basis of (audio or video) recordings that document language usage (and thus 'name usage') in the natural habitat of its occurrence. This means that researchers refrain from using experimental set-ups (such as interviews, focus group discussions, etc.) for eliciting and collecting data, because such data are considered to be 'produced' by the researcher (and thus reflect his or her opinions, assumptions, attitudes, etc.) and hence do not reveal the 'natural use' of names.[3] In order to obtain natural data, a preparatory phase of ethnographic fieldwork is necessary, which allows the researcher to have a first perception of the social event that he or she is going to record and possibly to discover recurring name related phenomena, to identify (more active) participants, to decide where to place the recording devices, etc.[4] But the empiricist backbone of interactional onomastics is visible also in the way in which researchers approach their data. While the recordings allow for a repeated observation of the phenomenon that caught the researcher's interest, the detailed transcription of the data (encompassing pauses, overlaps, laughter, etc.) enables the analyst to observe the environment in which a participant uses a name and to take into account phenomena that the researcher would not have access to if he or she had just taken notes on the spot. These phenomena are 'seen but unnoticed' (Garfinkel 1967) and may be relevant for the accurate analysis of names in usage—see for instance De Stefani and Ticca's (2011) investigation of the concepts of 'endonymy' and 'exonymy' from an interactional perspective, in which the authors show the importance of documenting the precise pronunciation of (foreign) names. This example also reveals a paradox that researchers in interactional onomastics have to come to terms with. Indeed, interactional onomastics seeks to combine a research procedure aiming at an emic description of social action (such as conversation analysis) with analytical, etic categories that are crucial for onomasticians (such as 'endonyms', 'exonyms', etc.), but that generally do not have any relevance for ordinary interactants. This holds true also for categories whose validity is taken for granted, such as 'toponyms' and 'anthroponyms', as De Stefani and Pepin (2006) show in their analysis of family bynames used in an Alpine community of Northern Italy. Indeed, the members of that community use the 'same' family bynames when referring to a place (i.e. a house or a neighbourhood), but also when referring to persons. Moreover, the authors document usages in which the nature of the referent (place or person) cannot be specified and show that the members of the community do not systematically make a conceptual distinction between place-names and personal names. In other words, the distinction between toponyms and anthroponyms is not always relevant for the members of that community.

The basic methodological principles of interactional onomastics evolve around the following three ideas:

1. Social interaction is the natural habitat of language, both from an ontogenetic and a phylogenetic perspective. It is through language that interactants construct their relevant social identities and create social order. In this respect, names are of course of central importance.

2. Interaction is organized in an orderly manner, for instance as regards the way in which speakers take turns in ordinary conversation, but also with respect to how

---

[3] Of course, interviews can also occur naturally in a given community (e.g. news interviews), and may hence constitute an object of investigation (see Clayman and Heritage 2002; Clayman 2010).

[4] For a hands-on introduction to the methodological and analytic procedures in conversation analysis, see Ten Have (1999).

actions are sequentially organized (Sacks et al. 1974). In this perspective, a contextualized analysis of names needs to take into account not only their syntactic
positioning within an utterance, but also their sequential placement within the
ongoing conversation. For instance, in telephone calls, the names of the interactants typically occur during the opening of the conversation (where they serve the
mutual identification of the participants), whereas in the subsequent parts of the
conversations referential pro-forms are generally used (but see Schegloff 1996).

3. Interaction is always situated. It is anchored in a spatial environment and in a tem-
porality that is constantly evolving and re-negotiated by the participants, who may
alter the focus of their attention, move in space, etc. In this respect, interactional
onomastics can contribute to understanding the relationship that speakers establish between a name and its referent.

With regard to place-names, Mondada (2000) and De Stefani (2009b) show that interactants may modify, negotiate, redefine the territorial extension of the area indicated by
a specific geographical name. Referring to a place thus becomes visible as a practice by
which participants actively constitute the object that is interactionally relevant.

From an epistemological point of view, 'name' or 'proper name' are categories that
pertain to the domains of linguistics and philosophy. As mentioned above, interactional
onomasticians face a twofold problem when using these categories for the analysis
of their data. To begin with, the analyst does not know in advance whether these (or
other) categories are actually relevant for the specific interaction in which the participants are engaged. In many cases participants do not seem to orient towards 'name'
as a specific category; in other cases they may use the word 'name' for language units
that would not be treated as names by linguists (see ex. (2)). Moreover, even among linguists and language philosophers there is a vigorous debate about how a 'name' should
be defined—and it is not likely that a unanimously accepted description will arise soon.
While in language philosophy the discussion is vibrant, the absence of theoretical studies on names from a strictly linguistic point of view is notable (see Van Langendonck
2007b).[5] Given these premises, the analysis of names as they occur in interaction may
appear problematic. However, there are at least two ways forward. One possibility consists of looking at how speakers use the word 'name' (or even 'proper name') in their
interactions. Such an analysis might result in an endogenous reconsideration of that
concept and possibly lead to an empirically grounded understanding of what a 'name'
is from the perspective of the speakers. A further, and probably more viable procedure,
consists of taking as a starting point the analyst's concept of 'name', although it is advis-
able to dismiss any strict definition of that concept. Preferably, the analyst should be a

---

[5] Note in this respect that proper names are excluded very early from the realm of linguistic
investigation. In Ferdinand de Saussure's *Cours de Linguistique Générale* they are mentioned just
once. We know, however, that the father of structural linguistics had studied the etymology of specific
toponyms present in communities neighbouring Geneva (Testenoire 2008) and that he was particularly
interested in the Germanic personal naming system (Caprini 2001).

member of the wider community in which the interaction was recorded. This allows him or her to share a common understanding of what ordinary members of that community may consider a 'name'. Rather than adopting a static definition of the concept, the analyst should bear in mind that interactants display varying understandings of what a name is. The analysis of interactional data shows that names are actually malleable language units: 'Proper names . . . seem in fact to be categorially quite labile and to be referential only, or at least chiefly, in a social and interactive context' (Hopper 1990: 162). This is visible in the following short excerpt, taken from an interaction between two ladies (Maria and Teresa) who browse through a supermarket in Southern Switzerland. They are looking at and manipulating duvets, and comment on their actions as follows:

(2)   (cons45111/43:38–44:01)[6]
1   MAR   ((chuckles))
2   (1.7)
3   MAR   piumino di seta sel<u>va</u>tica ti piace- ti piace il nome?
              wild silk duvet do you like- do you like the name?
4   TER   eh?
              huh?
5   (0.4)
6   MAR   di seta selvatica
              (of) wild silk
7   TER   oh pora me
              oh poor me
8   MAR   ((laughs)) fai vedere comè la seta sel[vatica
              ((laughs)) *let me see how wild silk is*
9   TER   [non lo so
                                                   I don't know

On the one hand, this excerpt shows what kind of linguistic units speakers label as a 'name'; on the other hand, it allows us to see how the very same linguistic material serves other purposes in the subsequent conversation. At l. 3 Maria is first reading a text fragment printed on the box of the duvet she is manipulating ('piumino di seta sel<u>va</u>tica', 'wild silk duvet'), and she then categorizes it as a 'name', asking Teresa whether she 'likes that name' (l. 3). Subsequently, Teresa utters a request for reformulation (or repair initiation, l. 4) and after a short pause (l. 5) Maria says 'di seta selvatica' ('(of) wild silk'). From a linguistic point of view, what Maria produces here is a prepositional phrase, thus a syntactic category that linguists and onomasticians would in all likelihood not consider a 'name'. However, from an interactional perspective the mere repetition of the prepositional phrase is accountable, since it allows Maria to pinpoint what she treats as being an exceptional, surprising wording. At l. 7 Teresa assesses the 'name' with the words 'oh

---

[6] I use the Jeffersonian notation system for the transcription of speech (see Jefferson 2004).

pora me' ('oh poor me'), after which the participants start inspecting the 'wild silk' by manipulating the duvet (l. 8–9). Note that at line 8 'seta selvatica' ('wild silk') no longer appears as a name, but rather as a term that Teresa uses to identify an extralinguistic referent.

This brief analysis can only provide a glimpse of the analytical procedures and questionings that disclose themselves when working with interactional data. The findings emerging from interactional onomastics should ultimately contribute to a better understanding of what we 'do' when we use names in conversation.

4.7 Concluding Remarks

In this chapter I tried to set apart the different disciplines that analyse names as discursive and interactional resources of social organization, by identifying research traditions anchored in anthropology, language philosophy and pragmatics, (critical) discourse analysis, sociology and sociolinguistics, and finally interactional linguistics. In doing so, I disentangled areas of research that were much more inter-connected at the beginning. For instance, in the first sentence of his book on Kwaiakutl place-names, the anthropologist Boas (1934) refers to Egli (1876), a Swiss geographer who published two volumes on place-names: 'F. J. [sic!] Egli in his "Nomina geographica" has demonstrated that geographical names, being an expression of the mental character of each people and each period, reflect their cultural life and the line of development belonging to each cultural area' (1934: 9). Adopting an evolutionary viewpoint, Egli indeed claims that descriptive, semantically transparent place-names are typically found in less developed communities, whereas in developed (European) communities place-names are generally semantically opaque. Although this conclusion is incompatible with current studies and beliefs, it shows anthropology's and geography's early interest in the relationship between the formal aspects of a name and its conceptual counterpart. Similarly, in recent anthropological work on names, authors often refer to other disciplines, such as philosophy and linguistics, when describing their research agenda (see Rymes 1996; Bodenhorn and Vom Bruck 2006). Names appear as an ideal object of investigation for cross-disciplinary research, because they are cultural artefacts and because their bestowal, change, and everyday usage are so manifestly related to the social organization of a community. According to Alford (1988), names are found in every society and can be considered cultural universals, and historical linguistics describes the word 'name' as one of the most ancient words, with cognates in all the languages of the Indo-European family. The approaches presented in this chapter address precisely the point of convergence between language and society. Although they emanate from different, and sometimes conflicting epistemological backgrounds, they all aim to contribute to a better understanding of the roles that names play in society. Some fields of study offer a macro-level analysis of name usage, resulting in a description of models, practices that have community-wide validity (e.g. anthropology, sociology of names), while others operate on the micro-level of specific social encounters (e.g. interactional onomastics). Both perspectives are necessary and they can be fruitfully combined, as for instance the studies carried out in (critical) discourse analysis show.

The synopsis outlined above shows a fertile research activity on names in discursive and interactional environments. The topics most investigated are linked, in different ways, to the use of names as referential devices, and thus continue a long-established language philosophical line of research. A further object of attention is the role that names play in the construction of individual and community identity. It is striking—but given the epistemological antecedents perhaps not surprising—that research has so far focused mostly on place- and personal names, while other kinds of names (of objects, etc.) have been ignored, with few exceptions (e.g. De Stefani 2007; Janner 2013). Discursive and interactional research would certainly benefit from investigations into such less prototypical name categories, which may open up new research questions and contribute to a better understanding of the nature of 'properhood' (Coates 2006a). The approaches outlined above certainly contribute to documenting name usage in everyday settings, but hope remains that they will also be able to advance a long-awaited linguistic theory of names.

PART II

TOPONOMASTICS

CHAPTER 5

··

METHODOLOGIES IN PLACE-NAME RESEARCH

··

SIMON TAYLOR

5.1 FOREWORD

··

ALL of what I have to say about methodology of place-name surveys is born of several years spent at the toponymic coalface, the main output of which are detailed
surveys of the county of Fife in Scotland, containing approximately 3,000 head
names (now published in five volumes as Taylor with Márkus 2006–12, and including in volume 5 a 300-page elements glossary), as well as of the Scottish counties of
Kinross-shire (one volume forthcoming, as Taylor with McNiven and Williamson)
and Clackmannanshire (one volume forthcoming, as Taylor with McNiven and
Williamson).[1] I am very much what may be termed a historical toponymist, viewing
place-nomenclature as an important historical and historico-linguistic tool. While
fully recognizing, and appreciating, the socio-onomastic, and more general sociolinguistic, aspects of place-names as part of contemporary discourse, there is no doubt
that the historical toponymist in me determines much of the shape and content of
this chapter.

---

[1] These two forthcoming volumes are part of the output of the *Scottish Toponymy in Transition:
Progressing County Surveys of the Place-Names of Scotland* (STIT) Project, funded by the Arts and
Humanities Research Council (AHRC) and based at the University of Glasgow from 2011 to 2014. For
more details, see <www.gla.ac.uk/stit>. My colleague and collaborator on the Fife volumes, Gilbert
Márkus, went on to produce a substantial volume on the place-names of Bute (2012) using the same
format and methodologies. This constitutes volume one of an eventual two-volume work on the
place-names of Buteshire. The Survey consistently uses as its geographical and administrative framework
the counties of Scotland as they were before complete reconfiguration in 1975.

5.2 INTRODUCTION

Place-names are generated by humans as language-users in response to their environment. This environment is first and foremost a place in which to dwell and to sustain life, in which to pursue various kinds of recreation and ritual, and in and through which to travel. This response perforce changes over time as our relationship with our environment changes. For example, in Europe over the past 1,000 years there has been a distinct move away from an almost complete dependence on the immediate environment for sustenance and other basic needs to one where international trade, manufacture, services, and state support have come to dominate. This shift is reflected in the way, and what, humans choose to name. The recent controversial naming of a beach Giro Bay on an official navigational chart of Loch Lomond north of Glasgow is a good example of this. The name was later withdrawn and the charts pulped, but I suspect the name lingers on, at least amongst the Loch Lomond and The Trossachs National Park rangers, the most recent stewards of the loch, who commissioned the chart and were behind this and several other new names.[2]

Place-names can thus be seen as cultural artefacts which arise from the interaction between language and environment. This means that to understand a place-name, when it was coined, by whom and with what motivation(s) in mind, it is important to collect as much information as possible from both sides of this interaction. While the environment is studied by site-visits, conversations with local people, and through detailed maps and plans, the language is approached above all through the collection of early forms and their context, although of course conversations with local people can play an important role here too. I have written elsewhere that early forms could be said to be the basic currency of the toponymist, and generally speaking the earlier the form, the more valuable the coin (*PNF* 5: 134). It is not hard to understand why this should be so. While many place-names start life as part of the lexicon or lexis, that is, as part of ordinary speech, they soon become part of the onomasticon, the technical term for that part of language which consists of all names or proper nouns.[3] These are items of language which are generally untranslatable, or rather, what they mean as words is not necessarily important for their everyday usage, although, as the above-mentioned Giro Bay shows, this does not mean that they are always semantically inert or empty of meaning. It remains true, however, that you do not need to know the meaning of Paris to know where it is, how to get there, and what it has to offer.

---

[2] See Anonymous (2011). I am grateful to Coinneach Maclean for drawing this controversy to my attention.

[3] This is greatly simplifying a complex situation, well summarized in Hough (2009). See also Coates (2013).

5.3 EARLY FORMS

Nevertheless, the most commonly asked question of any place-name, or rather of anyone who admits to some expertise in the subject, is: 'what does it mean?' And in a country such as Scotland, where five languages have made major contributions to its toponymy (British, Pictish, Gaelic, Old English, Scots and Norse; see Taylor 2001), the other most commonly asked question is: 'what language is it from?'. These are valid questions, and in their answering much can be revealed about the history of the place and the wider area, often going back to pre-documentary times.

It is therefore at least part of the toponymist's role, one might even say social duty, to provide a coherent, intelligible, and at the same time honest answer to both these questions. And this is where the early forms come in. They become especially important when they span a change in language, such as the one which occurred in Fife in east central Scotland in the twelfth and thirteenth centuries, in the course of which Scots spread rapidly at the expense of Gaelic (for details see *PNF* 5:169–72). Thus names of Gaelic origin which were recorded from the mouths of Gaelic-speakers, before about 1200, will reflect the underlying Gaelic name many times more faithfully than the same names recorded from Scots-speakers a hundred years later.

To illustrate the importance of early forms, I will take one example amongst many from Fife. Baldinnie (Ceres parish, *PNF* 2) is clearly a name of Gaelic origin, containing as its generic the common Gaelic element *baile* 'farm'. Early forms going back to 1448 are variously *Baldun(n)y, Baldony*, and *Baldinny*. If these were the earliest forms we had (and in many parts of Scotland fifteenth-century forms, even of old-established settlements, are often by far the earliest), we would be forgiven for thinking the second element might be Gaelic *dùn* 'a fort' or Old Gaelic *dind* 'a height, a fortress', the latter in fact suggested by Scotland's two foremost place-name scholars, W. J. Watson (1926: 143) and W. F. H. Nicolaisen (2001: 139). However, before 1448 there is a gap in the record of over 200 years, until the first half of the thirteenth century, when we come upon forms such as *Balemacdunechin* 1140 and *Balemacduneg'* 1228, showing that the specific or qualifying element is a personal name '(of the) sons of Donnchad (Duncan)'. Without these forms of the name, recorded possibly within a few years or decades of its coining, there would be absolutely no chance of analysing it correctly.

5.4 EARLY FORMS NOT THE BE ALL AND END ALL

We must not fetishize early forms, however. Place-names are more than simply inert linguistic items, the end-product of decades, centuries, even millennia of development. They are constantly evolving, reflecting our changing relationship with and perceptions of an ever-changing world. Modern forms, usages, additions to place-names which were originally coined in, say, the tenth century, are as important as a form recorded in the eleventh century: not in terms of linguistic analysis of the original name, but in terms of referent, usage, and associations.[4] Also, we must bear in mind that even in our earliest stratum of recorded names the processes by which an etymology or derivation is obscured may have been at work. The toponymist knows such processes well: they include analogical re-formation and the re-interpretation of names through place-name stories (for more detail, see Coates 1987 and Nicolaisen 1987). We see examples of both in our earliest text in Scottish Gaelic, known as *The Gaelic Notes in the Book of Deer* (see Jackson 1972 and Forsyth 2008). These are property records relating to the church of Deer in Buchan, Aberdeenshire, written into a tenth-century gospel book in the early twelfth century, and detailing grants made at least as far back as the early eleventh century.[5] It might be expected that the forms of the place-names in this text bring us closer to the forms used by the coiners of these names than almost any other text in Scotland. In many instances, this is indeed the case. However, re-interpretation has already been at work. The name of the church, Deer, which came also to be applied to a large medieval parish, later divided into the parishes of New Deer and Old Deer, probably derives from a Pictish word *derw-* meaning 'oak'. However, already in the Gaelic Notes, the name has been re-interpreted as Old Gaelic *déar* 'tear', the reason being that St Drostan, to whom the church of Deer was dedicated, shed tears (*déara*) as he was parting from St Columba, and so Columba said 'Let *déar* be its name from now on' (Taylor 2008: 275–6). The name Turriff, now an important Buchan town, has probably already been subjected to similar processes as Deer before it is first recorded in the Gaelic Notes, appearing as *Turbrud* and *Turbruaid* (genitive), remarkably like Old Gaelic *turbród* or *turbrúd* 'penalty, violation, infringement', as such an unlikely place-name. It was probably coined (either in Gaelic or Pictish) as a topographical name, which was then re-interpreted in the light of a now lost explanatory narrative, the re-interpretation then affecting how it was written (re-formation) (for more detail, see Taylor 2008: 280).

Behind these earliest forms of Deer and Turriff, already transmuted by story and tradition, with one at least (Deer) having probably made the transition from Pictish to Gaelic, we are able to glimpse what was nearer to the intention of the original name-givers. It is, however, just as important to record and engage with the re-interpretations, which in the case of the Gaelic Notes reflect either an increasing christianization of the landscape, or the ecclesiastical milieu through which the names were mediated, or both.

As I see it, the fundamental challenge to the toponymist is to capture as much information as can satisfy the basic needs of onomasticians, as well as satisfying those of other disciplines and scholarly enterprises, both academic and lay, which will be enhanced and enriched by a better understanding of place-names: disciplines such as archaeology,

---

[4] Scott and Clark (2011) challenge the strongly historical basis of traditional toponymics in their useful and constructively provocative article.

[5] For the dating of these records, see Broun (2008: 313–14 and fn 4). For a detailed study of their place-names, see Taylor (2008) and Cox (2008).

linguistics, lexicography, historical geography, and various branches of local and national history, social, judicial, agricultural, industrial, and genealogical.

5.5 SOURCES

While every place-name, wherever it is in the world, will have spatial details that can be expressed in terms of latitude, longitude, and altitude, when it comes to the sources for the forms of any particular name, these can range from an oral item, captured either by sound-recording equipment or by written notes from an interview (or by a mixture of both), to an ancient piece of parchment. In European terms Scotland is a land of contrasts when it comes to sources, with some areas document-rich as far back as the twelfth century, while others remain document-poor until the later eighteenth or even the nineteenth century. This means that the 'historical' toponymist has to engage seriously with many different kinds of sources, medieval and modern, published and unpublished, written and oral.

5.5.1 Written Sources

It is an unfortunate fact that in any transcription of a text, be it within a medieval context of one scribe copying the work of another, or for editorial and publication purposes, the items most subject to errors are names, in particular place-names. This means that each source needs to be evaluated separately, and in those cases where one single early form might have an important bearing on its interpretation, original documents need to be checked whenever possible. If the source document supplies an important early stratum of name-forms in the survey-area, and has clearly been poorly edited, then a new edition is a desideratum. Several such editions were produced for the *PNF* volumes (see e.g. *PNF* 3, 564–622; *PNF* 5, 625–56), an unplanned additional tranche of work, but one that justified itself from the point of view both of linguistic and toponymic analysis and of political, ecclesiastical, economic, and local history. The medieval recording of place-names is closely bound up with ownership, management, and exploitation of individual units of land and their inhabitants by aristocratic and gentry families, as well as by institutions, both lay and religious. These tenurial and exploitative relationships have both direct and indirect bearing on the formation and survival of place-names. Their direct toponymic influence is discussed in section 5.7, 'Context'. Here I am more concerned with source evaluation. It is important to be able to identify a place-name as coming from a particular source or archive, and this is usually quite clear from the source details themselves. However, this is not always the case. If using printed sources of medieval texts, it is always desirable to use the most up-to-date edition. This can, however, obscure the provenance of the text in question. The excellent series of Scottish royal charters, ordered by reign, starting with G. W. S. Barrow's edition of the charters of David I (1124–53) (*David*

I Chrs.), and continuing with those of Malcolm IV (*RRS* i) and William I (the Lion) (*RRS* ii)[6] is a case in point. The ordering principle of each volume is that of chronology. Citing any of these as the source of a particular form gives the best available printed reading, but at the same time obscures the more general source-context. It is therefore important to keep references to certain older printed sources alongside more recent ones, whether or not the readings are the same. For example the earliest reference to Tullibody, a parish and territory in Clackmannanshire near Stirling in central Scotland, is 'terram de *Dunbodeuin*', the date being 1147, the source *David I Chrs.* no. 159. From this information alone it is not obvious that the provenance of this form is a charter from a sixteenth-century register belonging to the abbey of Cambuskenneth by Stirling, first printed in 1872 as *Registrum Monasterii S. Marie de Cambuskenneth* (*Camb. Reg.*), this charter being *Camb. Reg.* no. 51.[7] There is therefore good reason to record the forms from both printed sources, with some kind of cross-reference between the two. A further good reason to include references to older printed sources is because these will be the ones cited by earlier scholarship.

5.5.2 Oral Sources

The importance of recording how a place-name is pronounced is discussed in section 5.8 under Fifth Section, which also briefly considers some methodological aspects of oral collection. Beyond the value of pronunciations to the analysis of well-established place-names, oral sources can also supply names which rarely if ever find expression in the written record. Examples of such are certain field names and fishing places, both on the shore and at sea. From 1965 till the late 1990s Ian Fraser of the Scottish Place-Name Survey, School of Scottish Studies, University of Edinburgh, visited many parts of the Highlands and Islands of Scotland armed with OS 6 inch maps and recording equipment.[8] His main aim was to collect minor names (microtoponyms) such as field names, pool names, and rock names, known only very locally, and chiefly in oral tradition only, and to particular user-groups, such as fishermen, farmers, and crofters. Fraser describes the methodology as follows: 'A six-inch Ordnance Survey plan is used. The informant and the fieldworker discuss the names on the map, the conversation being recorded on tape. Care is taken to record pronunciations for each name already in use on the map, and in addition, the informant supplies the names of all the places which do not appear, thus providing a complete place-name coverage for the village [or township], as far as

---

[6] Beyond this the series contains *RRS* iv (Alexander III), *RRS* v (Robert I) and *RRS* vi (David II).

[7] The forthcoming Acts of Henry I of England organize the royal documents by beneficiary archive, then chronologically within that archive. This automatically supplies important aspects of the context lost in an entirely chronological ordering. For more details, see *The Charters of William II and Henry I* (n.d.).

[8] Initially the School of Scottish Studies concentrated on Gaelic-speaking areas, especially where Gaelic was seen to be on the decline, although later collection work (of field names in particular) was also undertaken in Scots-speaking areas. See Fraser (1980).

the informant's knowledge goes and his memory serves' (Fraser 1970: 192–3). These plans were also annotated, indicating the exact position of each name.[9]

5.6 FIELDWORK

There is much in the life and work of the toponymist which involves sitting at a desk, whether at home, in a library, or in an archive. Equally, there are aspects essential to the work which involve 'getting out and about': for the purposes not just of interrogating those who live in a landscape, as in the collection of oral material, but of interrogating the landscape itself. There are many cases in which the landscape offers the key to the interpretation of a name. Ambiguity and doubt abound especially in the interpretation of names which have been mediated by a language or languages different from the one in which they were originally coined, and it is often only a careful consideration of the physical configuration of the landscape, past and present, which can offer any chance of certainty. While some of this can be done through maps, and with the recently available online resources such as Google Earth and the 3D modelling of maps in such programs as Fugawi UK, there is, for the foreseeable future at least, no substitute for being in and moving through the actual landscape.

Even in cases in which there is little or no doubt concerning a given element, a detailed engagement with the landscape can shed much light on the precise definition and application of the element involved, bringing us closer to the mindset and motivations of the original name-givers. The work of Margaret Gelling and Ann Cole in England with topographical terms convincingly develops the thesis that Old English topographical vocabulary was far richer and more nuanced than its modern English equivalent, as well as being relatively consistently applied over wide swathes of the country (see Gelling and Cole 2000; Cullen 2013). Such a thesis is relevant to other toponymies. For the application of some of these ideas to a Highland, Gaelic toponymy, see Murray 2014: 43–67.

5.7 CONTEXT

The context in which a place-name occurs can be almost as important as the place-name itself. For example, it can provide crucial evidence in the identification and disambiguation of places with the same or very similar names. Particularly important in this process is tenurial data, that is information about who held the named entity, or who granted it and who received it. In medieval Fife there were three

---

[9] Although the School of Scottish Studies has not undertaken any systematic oral collection since Ian Fraser retired in 2000, the valuable collection of these annotated OS maps is still housed there, and a programme of digitization has begun.

settlements called Kinnaird,[10] and the only way to create a satisfactory toponymic profile for each one is through context, above all tenurial. Tenurial data can also have even more direct bearing on the place-name itself, with the names of land-holders or tenants incorporated into the place-name in different ways, either as specifics[11] or as affixes.[12] These tenurial affixes can come and go depending on the vagaries of tenure, or can become an integral part of a place-name without which it cannot function. Examples of the latter are to be found in some of the many parts of the territory of Beath in west Fife which was divided up into twenty or more units, many of which contain or contained a personal name affix, for example Keirsbeath (*PNF* 1: 325–6) and Leuchatsbeath (*PNF* 1: 177–8). Careful documentation of the context of each land-holder also allows us to judge the time-lag involved between tenurial fact and evolution of the tenurial specific or affix, and what other factors might be at play to explain why some such affixes are overwritten every time there was a change of tenant, while others survived several such changes.

5.8 A Sample Name

In what follows I will attempt to explain the thinking that has gone into a typical entry which could be taken from any of the new Survey of Scottish Place-Names volumes. I will take a more recently created one, since there has been a certain amount of refinement to the model over the years. The protocols which underlie this have now been adopted as those of the recently established Survey of Scottish Place-Names, whose aim is to produce a series of volumes covering the whole of Scotland using the pre-1975 counties and *quoad omnia* parishes as the framework.

[First Section] BALQUHARN   AVA, LOI CLA S NS866972 1 E366 29m SOF

[Second Section]   totam terram de *Balecharne* 1315 × 1321 *RMS* i no. 85 [Robert I to Henry of Annan (*Anand*) all the land of Sauchie (*Salacheth*) ALL and 'all the land of Balquharn, with pertinents within the land of Menstrie' (cum pertinenciis infra terram de *Mestry*); assigned in index to sheriffdom of Stirling]

---

[10] Gaelic *ceann* 'head, end' + *àird* (f.) *or àrd* (m.) 'height', so '(settlement located at the) end of a height or substantial hill'.

[11] Most commonly in the form of personal names, but also sometimes in the form of occupational names. An example of the latter would be Friarton in north-east Fife, an estate belonging to the canons (friars) of St Andrews Augustinian priory. In the thirteenth century this name ousted the older name Melcrether following its acquisition by the priory in the mid-twelfth (see *PNF* 4: 413–15, 424–5).

[12] An affix is an adjective or noun attached to an older, existing place-name to describe later divisions. Typical affixes are Scots *west(er)*, *east(er)*, *hill*, *nether*, *laigh*, *heich or high*, *new*, *over*, *meikle*. Such affixes usually describe the position or size of different divisions of a settlement area relative to each other. They can also consist of personal names denoting land-holding.

Ballequharne 1536 *RMS* iii, no. 1646

Balquharne 1608 *Stirling Tests.*, 161 [William Thomson, cottar in, LOI]

Bowharn 1635 CC6/5/22/149 [Walter Rob in, LOI; *Bowquharn* in margin]

terris de *Balquhairne* 1684 *Retours* CLA no. 52 ['the lands of Balquharn']

Boquharn 1734 *Dunb. Tests.*, 71 [John Guild in, LOI]

Bewharn c.1750 Roy

Balquharn 1783 Stobie

Nether Balquharn 1783 Stobie

the farm of *Boquharn* 1862 OS1/32/2/5

Balquharn 1866 OS 6 inch 1st edn PER & CLA CXXXIII

[**Third Section**] G *baile* +? G *an* + G *càrn*

[**Fourth Section**] This is either *baile chàirn* 'cairn-farm' or *baile a' chàirn*, earlier *baile an chàirn* 'farm of the cairn' . . . The presence of the definite article preceding *càrn* is uncertain. G *càrn* 'cairn' in place-names in eastern lowland Scotland usually refers to a prehistoric burial mound. However, there is no surviving record of such a feature in the vicinity in NMRS.

[**Fifth Section**] /balˈhwɔrn/ or /bəlˈhwɔrn/, also /bəˈhwɔrn/.

Let us lo ok more closely at each segment of this entry, taking the top line first.

First Section

BALQUHARN AVA, LOI CLA S NS866972 1 E366 29m SOF

The name in bold upper case is the modern or latest form of the name. 'Latest' is of course a moving target, and has to be defined. In the case of the Clackmannanshire volume, from which this example is taken, the default form of the head name is that of the Ordnance Survey (OS) 1:25,000 Explorer series, published 2001, the relevant sheet being 366. If the name does not occur on that map, then an X appears where the OS Explorer number would be expected.

This raises the important question as to what defines the corpus of names to be fully analysed. For the latest volumes of the Survey of Scottish Place-Names, those for Clackmannanshire and Kinross-shire, the corpus was determined by (a) all names appearing on the OS 6 inch to the mile first edition maps, surveyed and published in the 1850s and 1860s; and (b) all names on the OS Explorer map. This results in a remarkably fine-grained coverage of the study areas. For names not on either of these map series, a certain amount of discretion is used: for example, names of settlements are included which the record tells us were important in the medieval or early modern period, but which never made it onto any Ordnance Survey map. Such names may have entirely dropped out of use or have survived only as field names or other such microtoponyms. Nevertheless, their former importance justifies them a place amongst the head names.

BALQUHARN AVA, LOI CLA

After the head name come one or more three-letter abbreviations. These capture in a minimalist way the administrative history of the place, siting it in its parish and county. The importance of this cannot be overemphasized. These administrative units are the building-blocks of the medieval kingdom, and their boundaries were extant in one form or another when the bulk of our place-names were coined. They thus form an integral part of the toponymic matrix.

Three-letter abbreviations for all pre-1975 *quoad omnia* parishes in Scotland have existed since the 1980s, and these have been augmented by abbreviations for those parishes which had ceased to exist by the early twentieth century. At the moment the list stands at 1,256 parishes.[13] Three-letter abbreviations also exist for all thirty-three pre-1975 Scottish counties.[14] AVA is the parish of Alva, which formed a detached part of Stirlingshire STL until 1891, when it was made part of Clackmannanshire. At the same time (1891) the town of Menstrie and its territory, which had until then lain in the Clackmannanshire part of the parish of Logie (LOI), was made part of Alva parish. Also until 1891 the parish of Logie was divided between three counties, namely Clackmannanshire, Perthshire, and Stirlingshire. In 1891 what remained of it after the Menstrie part had been hived off was placed entirely in Stirlingshire. Three-letter abbreviations separated by commas indicate change through time: so at a glance (and with the key beside us) we can tell that Balquharn not only lies in the parish of Alva, Clackmannanshire, but also that at some time in the past it lay in that part of the parish of Logie which lay in Clackmannanshire. For features such as hill ranges and rivers which extend beyond a single parish, the various parishes and counties through which the feature passes, or which it touches, are separated by a forward slash. The Balquharn Burn, which is now entirely in the parish of Alva (AVA), formed a county and parish boundary up until 1891. This would be expressed as:

BALQUHARN BURN ~ [15]   AVA, AVA STL/LOI CLA

[13] This list, which is still very much a 'work in progress', can be accessed online (Taylor n.d.). It includes very brief notes on individual parishes, with some information on the dedication of the parish kirk, as well as the names of scholars who have worked or are working on parish evolution in different parts of Scotland. Similar, but more extensive, notes on individual parishes, but without dedicatory information, can be found on Scotlandsplaces (n.d.), which also brings together a very useful set of sources relating to individual parishes in their most recent incarnation (i.e. 1891–1975), and makes available the relevant sections of Shennan (1892).

[14] See Nicolaisen (2001: xxvii–xxviii); they were first introduced (for England, Scotland, and Wales) in Nicolaisen et al. (1970), but only Scotland has continued using them. See also Taylor and Cox (2013: 90).

[15] The tilde following the head name indicates that the named feature extends over more than one kilometre (the dimension of a grid square).

The parish and county also help to distinguish place-names containing the same elements, of which there are many in Scotland.[16] The year of 1975 is not an arbitrary cut-off point. In that year in Scotland the *quoad omnia* parishes (civil and ecclesiastical) were abolished as legally valid administrative units, and thereafter their boundaries were no longer shown on OS maps. Furthermore the counties were also abolished, and a two-tier system of Regions and Districts was created. These in turn were phased out in 1996, to be replaced by Unitary Council Areas (UCAs). These UCAs bear a strong resemblance to the pre-1975 councils, but do not map exactly onto them, with important smaller counties such as Kincardineshire and Kinross-shire, which disappeared in 1975, remaining disappeared.

BALQUHARN   AVA, LOI CLA S NS866972 1 E366 29m SOF

The rest of the top line contains physical and spatial information which further ties the name to its environment. These will be dealt with briefly, later in this section.[17] The letter following the three-letter parish and county abbreviations indicates the kind of feature to which the head name refers, defining the named feature as it appears on the OS Explorer map or, failing that, on the OS 6 inch first edition. If the name is no longer extant, then it is defined as it was when it was last recorded. This follows a simple classification system, devised by the Ordnance Survey and used in R. A. Hooker's (1990) *Pathfinder Gazetteer*, such as S for settlement (anything from a house to a city), R for relief feature, W for a water feature.

Next comes the Ordnance Survey National Grid Reference (NGR). This is of course something peculiar to Britain, with a similar grid system applied in Ireland. A 6-digit NGR is usually used, which ties a place to a 100-metre square patch of the Earth's surface,[18] and programs exist to convert this to the international latitude and longitude system.

Linear features present a particular challenge to this system. There are various ways to meet this challenge, none of which is of itself right or wrong. However, once a methodology has been decided upon, it is important to state it clearly and apply it consistently. For example, for a watercourse the NGR can be given of its mid-point, its lowest point, or its highest point, or a combination of the latter two. The Survey of Scottish Place-Names gives the NGR of the lowest point, that is where it joins the sea, a loch, or another watercourse, or of the furthest point downstream at which the name changes. This last is sometimes approximate. The mid-nineteenth-century Ordnance Survey Object Name Books[19] are very useful here, as they typically define where such a name-change takes

---

[16] We have seen that there were three places called Kinnaird in medieval Fife; in Scotland as a whole there are at least nine.

[17] Full details of their usage can be found in any of the Introductions to *PNF* 1–4; also in Márkus (2012: 7–11).

[18] Instructions on how to calculate an NGR are given on every published Ordnance Survey map.

[19] These are the note-books of the surveyors of the first edition Ordnance Survey maps in the mid-nineteenth century. They contain valuable details about every single name on those maps, such as

place: for example, the OS Name Book describes the Benbuck Burn, a small water-course in the Ochils, as follows: 'A small burn, has its source in the moorland district east from Craighorn, from its junction with Benever Burn it afterwards takes the name of Glenwinnel Burn' (OS1/32/2/14). As is so often the case with burn names, the map itself is ambiguous as to where the name Benbuck Burn gives way to the Glenwinnel Burn, but with this extra information we can confidently give NN889005 as the NGR for this feature.[20]

Each NGR is followed by a single digit between 1 and 5 indicating its accuracy, with 1 signalling 'Accurate Position: clearly identifiable from reliable sources' and 5 'Vague Location'. There are several problems in tying a place-name to a place, and not only in respect of names that are no longer in use. For example, many land units have been divided over the centuries into separate farms distinguished by affixes such as *easter* and *wester*, or *nether (lower)* and *over (upper)*. It is therefore not always possible to say with complete certainty where the older, unaffixed name was originally applied. One such example might be Balgedie, Portmoak parish, Kinross-shire, which appears on maps from the seventeenth century onwards only with affixes. There is thus no indica-tion of the exact whereabouts of the original settlement to which the name Balgedie was applied. In a case like this the accuracy code 2 is used, 'Assumed Location'.

Next comes the OS 1:25,000 map sheet number, but only if the head name is found on that map series (see discussion at the start of this section). This is followed by the approximate height in metres: unless the place is marked with a spot height on the map, it is given to the nearest multiple of five.

And finally there is orientation or aspect, which of course is only given if the feature is on a slope. This has obvious implications as regards both drainage and exposure to sun-light. Eight airts or compass points are used, from NOF 'north facing' moving sunwise to NWF 'north-west facing'.

The information contained in this top line also creates a profile not just of the place-name itself but also of the elements which make up the name in question. For example, we might find that the element *muir* commonly occurs above a certain alti-tude, or that Gaelic *pett* and *baile* names are more likely to occur on slopes with certain aspects. Such correspondence between toponymy and topography can help us define place-name elements more precisely and understand them more fully.

---

alternative forms, names of informants, and descriptions of the named feature ranging from translations of names from Gaelic to English (chiefly in the then Gàidhealtachd), local place-name lore to short archaeological reports, the names of contemporary owners and tenants, vegetation cover, land-use etc. They constitute an extremely important resource for many disciplines, and may be termed a toponymic goldmine. Digital images of them, with an excellent name-searching facility, have recently been made available on *Scotland's Places* (n.d.). For a full description of the OS Name Books as they relate to Fife and Kinross, see *PNF* 5: 142–6.

[20] King (2008) also locates burns and rivers in this way. It could be argued that a more accurate system of locating water-courses would be to give the NGR of where the name begins as well as where the name ends. However, as with other aspects of toponymic methodology, it is sometimes necessary to apply workable compromises.

Second Section

The second section of each entry consists of the early forms of the place-name in question.

[1.] totam terram de [2.] *Balecharne* [3.] 1315 x 1321 [4.] *RMS* i no. 85 [5.] [Robert I to Henry of Annan (*Anand*) all the land of Sauchie (*Salacheth*) ALL[21] and 'all the land of Balquharn, with pertinents within the land of Menstrie' (cum pertinenciis infra terram de *Mestry*); assigned in index to sheriffdom of Stirling]

These are set out as follows, with reconstructed letters in angled brackets < >:

1. (optional) the referent, e.g. land of, ecclesia de, Thomas de. If the referent has been translated into English from another language, it appears in round brackets;
2. the early form itself, which is always italicized;
3. the date or date-range of the document from which the early form is taken, always using the modern year-beginning of 1 January rather than 25 March (Lady Day) year-beginning, which obtained in Scotland until 1600;
4. the abbreviated source reference, including page, document number, or folio number;
5. (optional) in square brackets other information about the source, especially whether it is an original document or a late copy, as well as the relevant wider context in which the form occurs, such as the person, family, or institution granting or receiving the land. Within these source notes early forms are always given in italics. For further discussion of this 'square bracket' unit, see under *Sources* and *Context*, sections 5.5 and 5.7 above.

Third Section

The elements analysis summary gives the elements (both words and names) which can be identified with varying degrees of certainty as making up the head name. The most frequently occurring languages in central eastern Scotland are Gaelic (G) and Scots (Sc). Personal names (pn) and existing place-names (en) are not assigned to any particular language-group. The nominative singular forms of all words (including the definite article) are used in this section. Reconstructed or hypothetical forms (indicated by an asterisk) are given for all Pictish and British words, since none has survived in sources independently of place-names. Modern Scottish Gaelic forms are given as the standard form of Gaelic elements, using the most recent Gaelic orthographic conventions. For Scots elements, modern Scots forms are also given, usually using the main *CSD* form.

The decision to present the elements in this way was not easily reached. It can be argued that in Fife, for example, modern Gaelic was not used to coin the bulk

---

[21] ALL = Alloa parish, Clackmannanshire.

of the place-names of Gaelic origin since this coining took place in the Old Gaelic period, in a form of the language much closer to Middle Irish (defined as the form of the Gaelic language of Ireland c.900 to c.1200 AD). It might therefore make more sense to use these older forms, which are often spelled differently, with, for example, only acute accents to indicate vowel length.[22] However, from the point of view of a Scotland-wide survey, in areas where Gaelic has been toponymically productive into the modern period, the elements would have to be adjusted accordingly, since the use of an Old Gaelic form would be inappropriate for a Gaelic name coined in, say, the eighteenth century. And what about those names in the present or recent Gàidhealtachd which are first recorded in the nineteenth century, but may—or may not—be much older. Is an older form of the element to be chosen to reflect this possibility? And if so, then implicit in the choice of the form of the element is a decision about the age of the name in question, when in so many cases no such decision can be made with any confidence. By using the modern form of the elements wherever possible, in every part of Scotland which has place-names of Gaelic origin (which is most of the country), all such agonizing over dating and language stages is obviated. It should be said that the Survey of English Place-Names has gone down the opposite route, taking the oldest attested forms of elements (usually Old English and Old Norse), even when a name was coined many centuries after that form of the language had become obsolete.[23] There is no ideal solution here, and open acknowledgement and awareness of the problems and limitations of each approach, consistently applied, are probably best.

Fourth Section

The fourth section consists of a set of discursive notes, which can vary greatly in length and content. It always starts with a suggested meaning, or meanings, of the head name, if this can be established, followed by some discussion of the elements involved, and, where relevant, their syntax and morphology.

Fifth Section: Pronunciation

It is very important to record how a place-name is pronounced, since this can yield vital clues for its correct analysis. For example it is a general, though by no means universal, rule that place-names which are stressed on the first element are in languages of Germanic origin, such as Scots or Norse, while place-names which are stressed on the second or third element are of Celtic origin, such as Pictish or Gaelic. It would be more accurate to say that in both language groups it is the specific element which

---

[22]   According to the most recent recommendations, modern Scottish Gaelic uses only grave accents as length-indicators.

[23]   See Taylor (2009) for some of the anomalies this approach can create. For example, the common Durham place-name element *myr, myre, myer*, etc. is clearly the (northern) Middle English word *myre* or *mire*, modern English *mire* 'mire, marsh'. However, in Watts' (2007) Elements Index, its basic form appears as ON **mýrr**.

bears the stress, but that in Scots and Norse names the specific usually comes first, the generic second, while in names of Celtic origin it is usually the other way round. It is a remarkable fact that the original stress pattern of a name tends to survive, even when the original language of coining has not been spoken locally for many hundreds of years.

I would contend that pronunciations are always best given using the International Phonetic Alphabet (IPA). While this script might seem a little daunting to the uninitiated at first, it brings with it advantages which far outweigh any initial strangeness. There might be an argument for using a home-made system if it did not need its own key, but in using a system based on English orthography a key is still needed: if one is not provided, such a system will always be open to confusion and ambiguity.

There is not always one correct way to pronounce a place-name, and it can be said that spoken forms are considerably more contested than written ones. Where more than one pronunciation is given for a place-name, it is always important to indicate the user group of each. It should also be borne in mind that throughout those parts of Scotland where Scots is still spoken (i.e. most of the country) there exist two pronunciations, especially of names containing recognizable Scottish Standard English elements (see, for example, *PNF* 4: 8, for details).

In the Introductions to *PNF* 1–4 (e.g. *PNF* 4: 8) I wrote that pronunciation is not given '(a) where it is unambiguous or (b) it was not collected, because, for example, it was no longer known locally'. I realize that there is a problem with (a), as it might be argued that no word or name in such a non-phonetic orthography as that of (Scottish Standard) English is unambiguous. And even in names consisting of elements whose pronunciation would be familiar to any speaker of English, such as Barnhill, it is not clear where the stress might fall, whether on the first element, or equally on both. Ideally, therefore, the pronunciation(s) should be given for every current name.

This begs the question as to how pronunciations are collected. There is a premium on the recording of names embedded in conversation or ordinary discourse rather than as an item isolated for special attention. Just as context matters in the written milieu, so it does in the spoken. Sometimes the current, everyday (and thus more unselfconsciously traditional) pronunciation of a place-name can only be discerned in ordinary discourse. When the informant isolates the name for the fieldworker, it is often much more influenced by the written form, or by expectations of what the informant thinks the fieldworker might want to hear.

5.9 Minimal and Maximal

The above model for the Survey of Scottish Place-Names (SSPN) has been very much informed by other, earlier surveys in Britain and Ireland, above all the Survey of English Place-Names (SEPN), which has been producing volumes in its county series since 1923, and the Northern Ireland Place-Name Project (NIPNP), which ran from 1987–97. The main way in which they differ from each other is in the amount of information collected for each name. On a scale of minimal to maximal, the survey methodologies move from SEPN towards the minimal end of the scale, with the SSPN towards the maximal, and the NIPNP between the two. SEPN, for example, gives no absolute spatial data such as NGR or altitude, no referents, no context, no source-specific details and no pronunciations. Typical of the former is the most recent volume, volume 90, part six of *The Place-Names of Leicestershire: Sparkenhoe Hundred* by Barrie Cox (2014).[24] As is the case with all three survey methodologies, the overall structure of this volume is provided by the parish, which is especially appropriate given that the old administrative unit of the hundred defines the scope of the volume itself.

During its active life-span, the Northern Ireland Place-Name Project produced eight volumes covering parts of each of the six counties of Northern Ireland. The methodology is clearly set out in the General Introduction to each volume. Typical is Volume 7 (Mac Gabhann 1997), which covers the six civil parishes which make up the barony of Carey in the north-east corner of Co. Armagh. The corpus is defined by these parish names, each of which forms a separate chapter section, in alphabetical order, with all the townland names[25] arranged alphabetically within the parish (the biggest parish in the volume containing 72 and the smallest 14). Within each parish the townland names come first, followed by another section called 'Other Names' which, to quote the General Introduction (p. xv) 'deals with names of towns, villages, hills and water-features which appear on the OS 1:50,000 map, but which are not classified as townlands. This section may also include a few names of historical importance which do not appear on the map but which may be of interest to the reader'. For each name a four-figure NGR is given, and for names of Irish origin a recommended modern Irish form is also included. In the early forms, each of which is numbered, there are few referents and no context. Under early forms are usefully included interpretations by earlier writers, as is the pronunciation (sometimes more than one).

5.10 ELECTRONIC STORAGE

Electronic storage of systematically collected place-name data opens up analytic and comparative possibilities which would otherwise be practically unfeasible in terms of the vast datasets involved. A fully populated database can be interrogated within

---

[24] The methodology and lay-out is described in the introductory section 'Notes on Arrangement': xix–xx. For more detailed exposition on the methodology underpinning the English Survey, see Sedgefield (1924).

[25] The townland is the basic land unit throughout Ireland, and the building-block of the parish. In Northern Ireland there are 269 parishes consisting of 9,600 townlands, with over 60,000 townlands in the whole of Ireland.

seconds, producing, for example, lists and/or distribution maps of individual elements or place-name types both regionally and nationally, of names recorded before a certain date, and of names from one particular source. The methodology and layout of both the Scottish and the Northern Irish survey volumes have been developed very much with such electronic storage and interrogation in mind,[26] while in England, despite the fact that the bulk of the survey volumes were produced before concepts such as digital databases and online resources were even dreamt of, great strides are being made towards putting all the data online in various user-friendly interactive ways.[27] In 2000–01 the Scottish Place-Name Database was developed in Access 97.[28] The concepts and structures underlying this Database have been developed by the Database of Scottish Hagiotoponyms as part of the Leverhulme-funded project 'Commemoration of Saints in Scottish Place-Names', to create a searchable, online relational database.[29] The lay-out of individual head names, as described above, was designed to be fed into the Scottish Place-Name Database through a parsing program. A pilot project has successfully implemented this, creating the core of an online database.[30] Both Wales and the Republic of Ireland have databases based on otherwise unpublished paper archives: Wales with the Melville Richards Archive/Archif Melville Richards (n.d.), Ireland with the index cards and notes from the archives of the Placenames Branch, a government body (FIONTAR 2008–14a) The Irish database, while not having searchable historical forms, has several other very useful functions, such as a detailed mapping facility, sound files, and distribution maps and lists of all the more commonly used place-names elements.

5.11 CONCLUDING REMARKS

The methodology of place-name analysis set out in this chapter is in the first instance descriptive of one that has evolved through my own and others' close dialogue with a wide range of place-name data over the last 25 years. It seems to satisfy the basic criteria of place-name surveying as set out, above, and is as internally consistent as any system can be when trying to capture the complexities and contradictions of a non-systematic

---

[26] The NIPP's database is now partly available online at <Placenamsni.org> (2013).

[27] See *Key to English Place-Names* (2015); see also Jisc (2011–13), with its Digital Exposure of English Place-Names. This latter, still under development, aims to make all the information in the published EPNS volumes available online.

[28] This built on an earlier Scottish place-name database in FoxPro developed by the late Terry James of CADW (the Welsh equivalent of Historic Scotland and English Heritage) using a structure he had created in the early 1990s for *Enwau*, a relational database to store and analyse the place-names of Carmarthenshire.

[29] For details, see: *Commemorations of Saints in Scottish Place-Names* (2010–13).

[30] Thanks are due to the John Robertson Bequest and Brian Aitken of the University of Glasgow for making this possible. The results of this project can be viewed on <scottish-placenames.glasgow.ac.uk/Fife>.

corpus, the result of millennia of evolution, both linguistic and paralinguistic. It is prescriptive only in terms of the Survey of Scottish Place-Names, and even in these terms it is not sacrosanct: indeed for it to remain robust and usable for the long road ahead, in terms of collection and analysis, it must be capable of adaptation and evolution. It is hoped, however, that it can form the basis of a system which will last the course, both for the needs of hard-copy and digital user-groups.

CHAPTER 6

··

SETTLEMENT NAMES

··

CAROLE HOUGH

6.1 INTRODUCTION

SETTLEMENT names are the prototypical type of place-name, designating areas where people live together in communities. These communities range from tiny hamlets to large cities, but size may have little relevance to the names themselves, which often pre-date the historical developments that led to the growth of some settlements but not of others. Many settlement names in Western Europe were created during the Early Middle Ages; many of those in other parts of the Western Hemisphere during the European Age of Exploration in the fifteenth to seventeenth centuries. However, others are much older, while some continue to be created at the present day. Since names can be used without understanding of semantic content, incoming groups of speakers characteristically take over some of the existing names while creating others of their own. This means that in almost all areas where successive phases of migration have occurred, the names represent a palimpsest of formations from different languages and time-periods. This chapter will outline the main structures represented in settlement names, and discuss some of the types of evidence that they preserve.[1]

6.2 STRUCTURES

6.2.1 Descriptive Names

Many settlement names from Indo-European languages are descriptive, and originate as noun phrases containing one or more terms known as 'elements'. Some comprise

---

[1] Further information on the English place-names used as examples within this chapter can be found in the Survey of English Place-Names. For those from other parts of the world, see especially Room (1997), Mills (2003), and Everett-Heath (2005).

a headword only, known as the 'generic' or 'defining element', as with Aachen in Germany (Old High German *aha* 'water'), Bruges in Belgium (Flemish *brugge* 'bridges'), and Cahors in France (Latin *Cadurci*, the name of a Celtic tribe). These are known as 'simplex' names, and the examples illustrate the three main types of referents: the natural environment, the built environment, and the inhabitants. However, the majority of settlement names are compound, combining the generic with a modifier known as the 'specific' or 'qualifying element'. Examples include Casablanca in Morocco (Portuguese *casa* 'house' + *branca* 'white'), Copenhagen in Denmark (Danish *køpmann* 'merchant' + *havn* 'harbour'), and Glasgow in Scotland (Brittonic *glas* 'green' + *cau* 'hollow'). Element order is determined by the characteristic structures of noun phrases in the different languages, so the Portuguese formation has the generic first followed by the qualifier, while the Danish and Brittonic formations have the qualifier first followed by the generic.

A minority of both simplex and compound names also contain a third type of element, known as the 'affix', which is generally a later addition to differentiate between two places with the same name. Hence the common settlement name Newton in England (Old English *nīwe* 'new' + *tūn* 'village') appears in a variety of forms including Long Newton, Maiden Newton, Newton Abbot, Newton Blossomville, Newton Ferrers, Newton-le-Willows, Newton St Cyres, and North Newton. Affixes are more flexible in position, although again standard syntactic patterns tend to be influential. Newton Blossomville and Newton Ferrers exemplify 'manorial' affixes, referring to possession by the *de Blosseville* and *de Ferers* families respectively in the thirteenth century. Cameron (1996: 112–13) compiles a 'representative collection' of 177 English settlement names with affixes comprising French family names, of which 172 are post-fixed—the standard position for a family name in the European personal naming system.[2] Whereas many affixes refer to possession,[3] the other main type is descriptive, referring for instance to size (Long Newton) or geographical position (Newton-le-Willows, North Newton).[4] Here it is striking that whereas post-fixed adjectival affixes are not precluded, occurring for instance in formations such as Gilling East, Gilling West, Lydbury North, and Stuckeridge South, they are vanishingly rare in comparison to names where the descriptive affix is prefixed, occupying the same position as a modifier in an English noun phrase. Table 6.1 shows the proportion of pre- and post-fixed compass points used as affixes in names represented on the Ordnance Survey 1:50,000 Gazetteer of Britain.

Many elements only function as qualifiers, others only as generics or affixes, but some are entirely flexible. Fig. 6.1 shows place-names in Britain from Old English (OE)

---

[2] The five exceptions are Marks Tey, Mersey Hampton, Furneux Pelham, Mavis Enderby, and Goose Bradon.

[3] Newton Abbot refers to possession by Torre Abbey; Maiden Newton may refer to possession by nuns. Newton St Cyres is a reference to the church dedication, another common type of affix generally grouped with possession.

[4] A more detailed classification is offered by Bölcskei (2010).

Table 6.1 Pre- and post-fixed compass points used as affixes in place-names

	pre-fixed	%	post-fixed	%	total	%
East	663	98.81%	8	1.19%	671	25.10%
West	787	97.89%	17	2.11%	804	30.08%
North	655	99.39%	4	0.61%	659	24.65%
South	536	99.44%	3	0.56%	539	20.16%
TOTAL	2641	98.80%	32	1.20%	2673	100.00%

FIGURE 6.1 Place-names in Britain from OE *mynster* 'large church, minster' and its reflexes.

Map was created using GenMap UK software and contains Ordnance Survey data © Crown copyright and database right 2013.

mynster 'large church, minster' and its later reflexes.[5] Where this is used as a qualifying element, it tends to denote monastic property, as with Minsterworth in Gloucestershire, which belonged to St Peter's Gloucester. More often, however, it appears as a generic, as with Axminster in Devon 'church by the River Axe' and Southminster in Essex 'southern church'. In such instances the name of the building has come to denote the settlement around it, a form of metonymy common in place-names. In other instances, as with Iwerne Minster in Dorset, the term is used as an affix to differentiate between two settlements with the same name. Here the corresponding settlement is Iwerne Courtney, with the two names referring to possession respectively by the Courtenay family and by Shaftesbury Abbey. Minster in Kent is a simplex name, as originally were Little Minster and Minster Lovell in Oxfordshire. In all three instances, the element functions as a generic, but since the thirteenth century the two Oxfordshire names have been differentiated by affixes relating, on the one hand, to size and, on the other, to possession by the Lovell family.

Some descriptive names are not literal but metaphorical, conceptualizing the environment as something other than it is. Cann in England is a simplex name from OE *canne* 'can, cup', used with reference to a deep valley. The same metaphorical pathway is reflected in other English names such as Beedon (OE *byden* 'tub; valley'), Chettle (OE **ceotol* 'kettle; valley'), Combe (OE *cumb* 'vessel; valley'), and Trow (OE *trog* 'trough; valley'), as also in names from other languages, such as Cwm in Wales (Welsh *cwm* 'bowl; valley'). Possibly universal across all languages is the transfer of anatomical terms to landscape features, as with Chale on the Isle of Wight (Old English *ceole* 'throat; ravine'), Delphi in Greece (Greek *delphys* 'womb; cavity'), Drumcliff in Ireland (Gaelic *drum* 'back; ridge' + *cliabh* 'baskets'), Halifax in England (Old English *halh* 'nook' + *feax* 'hair; grass'), and Stromness in Orkney (Old Norse *straumr* 'current' + *nes* 'nose; headland'). An extension of the metaphor from body parts to clothing may be represented in names such as Taupo in New Zealand (Māori *taupo* 'cloak'—a contracted form of *Taupo nui a Tia* 'great cloak of Tia', from the name of a Māori chief).

Descriptive names are highly repetitive, both within and across languages. In areas of Scandinavian settlement in the north of England, the place-name Newton mentioned above exists alongside occurrences of the synonymous Newby, where the generic is Old Norse (ON) *bý* 'village'. Further parallels are found not only in the doublet Newbie in Scotland and the cognate name Nyby in Denmark and Sweden, but in unrelated formations such as Novgorod in Russia (Russian *novyj* 'new' + *gorod* 'town') and Dzankoy in Ukraine (Turkic *dzhan* 'new' + *koy* 'village').

Even more common is the repetition of generics, or of synonymous generics in different languages. The most common generic in English settlement names, OE *tūn*

---

[5] All maps in this chapter are based on the Ordnance Survey 1:50,000 Gazetteer.

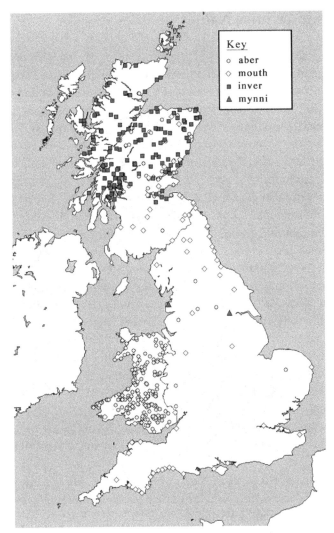

FIGURE 6.2 Place-names in Britain from P-Celtic *aber*, Gaelic *inbhir*, OE *muþa*, and ON *mynni*, all meaning 'river-mouth'.

Map was created using GenMap UK software and contains
Ordnance Survey data © Crown copyright and database right 2013.

'farmstead, village', occurs in hundreds of formations, and the same is true of other generics both in Britain and elsewhere. Fig. 6.2 shows place-names in Britain referring to a river-mouth, from P-Celtic *aber* (e.g. Aberdeen in Scotland, Abergavenny in Wales), Gaelic *inbhir* (e.g. Inverness in Scotland), OE *muþa* (e.g. Yarmouth in England), and ON *mynni* (e.g. Stalmine in England). Excluded are later, metaphorical names such as Devil's Mouth and Lion's Mouth in England, which tend to designate landscape features rather than settlements.

6.2.2 Non-descriptive Names

Non-descriptive names identify a settlement by means of an association, often with a historical or legendary event, or with a person. The latter are known as 'commemorative' names, and are particularly common among the settlements founded or renamed by European settlers in the African, American, and Australian continents during the Age of Exploration that began in the early fifteenth century. Hence Aukland in New Zealand was named after the Viceroy of India, George Eden, Earl of Aukland (1784–1849), Durban in South Africa after the governor of Cape Colony, Sir Benjamin D'Urban (1777–1849), New Orleans in the USA after the French Regent, Philippe, Duc d'Orléans (1674–1723), and Sydney in Australia after the British Home Secretary, Thomas Townshend, 1st Viscount Sydney (1733–1800). Both Adelaide in Australia and Adelaide in South Africa were named after Queen Adelaide (1792–1849), the wife of William IV, while Victoria in Canada was named after his niece, Queen Victoria (1819–1901). A more ancient example is Alexandria in Egypt, founded by and named after Alexander the Great c.331 BC.

Another type of commemorative name transfers the name of an existing settlement to another locality. Waterloo in Belgium is a descriptive name (Flemish *water* 'water' + *loo* 'sacred wood'), but other occurrences of the name in England and the USA commemorate the battle that took place there in 1815 during the Napoleonic wars. Many European explorers and immigrants to other parts of the world have re-used place-names from their native countries. Sometimes these are differentiated from the parent place-name by the affix *New*, as with New Glasgow, New Liskeard, and New Waterford in Canada, named after places in Scotland, England, and Ireland respectively. More commonly, the name is simply replicated as it stands, as with occurrences of Glasgow in Jamaica and the USA, and the transfer of the English place-name London to Canada and the USA.

Names referring to an event are known as 'incident' names. Again, many are associated with the Age of Exploration. Santa Barbara in the USA was named by Spanish explorers who landed on the feast day of St Barbara (4 December 1602), while São Paulo in Brazil was named by Portuguese monks on the feast day of the Conversion of St Paul (25 January 1554). Although less prevalent as a name-type in the UK, Battle in south-east England was named from the abbey founded to commemorate the 1066 Battle of Hastings; and there is a strong possibility that Burntisland in east Scotland 'arose because fishers' huts had been burnt on an islet east of the present harbour of Burntisland, and since incorporated into Burntisland docks' (*PNF* 1: 191).

Incident names are particularly common in some non-Indo-European naming traditions. They may indeed be among the earliest name-types, as Stewart (1975: 106) suggests, drawing attention to their high incidence in names created by the Inuit, Māori, Tonganese, and ancient Israelites. Nice in France was named after *Nike*, the Greek goddess of victory, by Massillian Greeks following a victory over the Ligurians c.350 BC, and Nicopolis in Greece (Greek *nikē* 'victory' + *polis* 'city') was founded by Augustus to celebrate a victory over Marc Antony in 31 BC. More recently, Vitoria in Brazil commemorates a victory over native Americans in 1551, while Weenen in South Africa (Afrikaans *geween* 'weeping') refers to the massacre of Boers by the Zulus in

1838. Abeokuta in Nigeria (Yoruba *abe* 'on the' + *okuta* 'rock') was founded in 1830 by refugees fleeing from inter-tribal wars. As Odebode (2010: 214) explains: 'The name of the town was derived from the protection which the fleeing settlers sought under the rock'.

6.2.3 Connections between Descriptive and Non-descriptive Names

Although the distinction between descriptive and non-descriptive names appears at first sight to be clear-cut, there are fuzzy boundaries between them. In some instances, the selection of transferred names may be motivated by similarities between the old and new locations, so that the original description remains salient. As Nicolaisen (1982b: 97) points out in connection with the Scandinavian settlements in Scotland, transferred names 'are most easily detected when their overt word meaning apparently does not fit the place to which they apply, as for instance, a typical shore name found in the middle of an island, or when they are one of a kind on both sides of the North Sea'. A corollary to this is that where the meaning *does* fit the place, transferred names may not only be less easy to detect, but may to some extent represent descriptive names in their own right. Nicolaisen (1982b) goes on to argue:

> Once a certain association has been made with regard to a certain place requiring a name, then only one specific name and none other could be given. If, for example, the major association for a particular island was that it was linked with the mainland or another island at low tide but separated from it at high tide, then it had, of necessity and not from choice, to be called **Ørfiris-ey*, 'tidal island', because this was the name given to such islands in the homeland. The same principle appears to have applied also to human settlements—farms, villages, and the like—that were built near such natural features . . . (Nicolaisen 1982b: 98)

Here, then, transferred names and descriptive names begin to merge into each other.

Incident names too may be difficult to differentiate from descriptive names. Many place-name qualifiers comprise terms for wild animals, and these are usually taken to be descriptive, referring to animals commonly found at the location. However, an alternative view is that such names result from an incident involving a particular animal. This is demonstrably the case in at least a few documented instances, and although Stewart's (1975: 107) claim that 'the majority of animal-names originated thus' is surely an over-statement, the actual proportion of names that may be accounted for in this way is unknown. Even when an incident is on record, it may be difficult to determine the type of name. Although Abeokuta 'on the rock' is treated above as an incident name (Section 6.2.2), it could alternatively be regarded as descriptive of the rock that provided shelter to the fleeing refugees. Conversely, whereas Taupo 'cloak' is treated above as a descriptive name (Section 6.2.1), the connection between a nearby landscape feature

and a cloak is reputed to have been made on a particular occasion by the Māori chief
Tia, motivated by a garment that he was wearing at the time, and so it could arguably be
classed as an incident name.

6.3 TYPES OF EVIDENCE

Settlement names preserve various types of evidence, particularly for settlement patterns, settlement chronologies, and historical linguistics (see also Chapters 36, 37, 40).
As regards the first two in particular, attention tends to focus on place-name generics.
As regards the third, qualifiers are also useful, since they are more varied and hence preserve a wider range of linguistic data. Again, however, generics provide a larger corpus
of comparative material. Examples within this section will focus mainly on England and
Scotland; however, the underlying principles are also applicable to settlement names in
other parts of the world.

6.3.1 Settlement Patterns

The value of place-names for tracing settlement patterns stems from two of the points
mentioned above. First, the repetitive nature of place-name formations; second, the tendency of immigrants and explorers to re-use familiar place-name types from their own
countries. Both result in large datasets for comparative analysis.

Because place-name generics are so repetitive, they can be used to plot areas of
settlement by speakers of different languages. The Picts, a group of P-Celtic speakers who inhabited north-east Scotland from the early part of the first millennium
to the ninth century, are poorly recorded in documentary sources, but their geographical location has been established from the distribution of place-names from
the Pictish term *pett 'piece of land', shown in Fig. 6.3. The modern reflex is Pit-,
as in Pitliver, Pitlochry, and Pitlurg. In all three examples, as well as in most other
*pett compounds, the qualifying element is from Gaelic (leabhar 'book'; cloichreach
'stones'; lurg 'shank; strip of land'—another anatomical term used topographically),
reflecting close communication with the Gaelic speakers who conquered the Picts
in the ninth century. Whether this communication took place largely before or after
the fall of the Pictish kingdom is uncertain, and it is also controversial whether the
hybrids represent Gaelic names incorporating Pictish loan-words or if they are
part-translations of earlier Pictish names. On the one hand, some words are known
to have been borrowed from Pictish into Gaelic either as place-name-forming elements or as vocabulary words (e.g. Cox 1997); on the other, the distribution pattern
suggests Pictish origin, as names containing *pett do not occur in other areas settled
by Gaelic speakers.

FIGURE 6.3 Place-names in Scotland from Pictish **pett* 'piece of land'.

Map was created using GenMap UK software and contains
Ordnance Survey data © Crown copyright and database right 2013.

Similarly, areas of Danish settlement in Britain are defined by the distribution of place-names from the recurrent generic ON *bý* 'village', as in Newby mentioned above, and others such as Ashby (ON *askr* 'ash tree'), Derby (ON *djúr* 'deer'), and Westby (ON *vestr* 'west'). Their distribution is shown in Fig. 6.4, with a high concentration in north-east England.[6] This includes the area known as the Danelaw, the part of England

---

[6] A version of Figure 6.4 also appears in Hough (2015: 638).

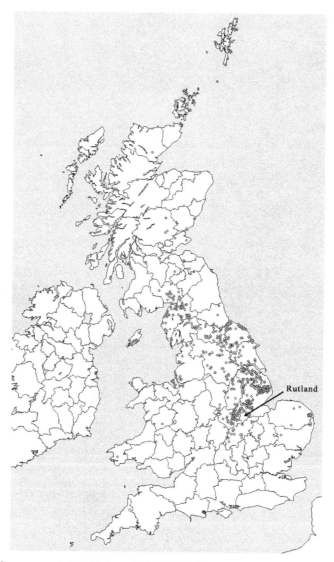

FIGURE 6.4 Place-names in Britain from ON *bý* 'village'.

Map was created using GenMap UK software and contains
Ordnance Survey data © Crown copyright and database right 2013.

allocated to the Danish invaders under the terms of a treaty with the Anglo-Saxon king Alfred the Great in 877. An apparent anomaly is the striking dearth of settlement names containing *bý* or other Scandinavian elements in the small historical county of Rutland, surrounded on all sides by heavy Norse settlement. As Cox (1989) has argued, this appears to represent key evidence that Rutland was excluded from the area ceded to the Danes.[7]

---

[7] This conclusion is also supported by evidence from field names (Cox 1989–90).

Because immigrants and explorers tend to re-use place-name types from their native countries, comparison between the place-names of different areas can also throw light on settlement patterns. Room (1997: 8–9) notes that:

> While English names are found throughout North America, French names are mainly concentrated in eastern Canada, especially around Ottawa and in the St. Lawrence basin. Spanish names are chiefly in the southwest of the United States. . . . A further pocket of French names is found in Louisiana, as attested by such familiar names as New Orleans, Lafayette, and Baton Rouge. . . . The extensive territory of Central and South America, from Mexico to Tierra del Fuego, is dominated by Spanish and Portuguese placenames of colonial origin.

Similarly, immigration from Scotland to New Zealand is attested by transferred names such as Balmoral, Hamilton, and Kilbirnie on North Island, and Abbotsford, Dumbarton, and Roxburgh on South Island. The motivations for such names range from nostalgic to territorial, even where comparatively short distances are involved. Owen (2013: 353) discusses the 'deliberate implantation' of some English settlement names in Wales, while noting that 'others are the by-products of military occupation, religion, industry, tourism, commerce, transport, travel and agriculture'. Estonian settlement names have been influenced by periods of German, Russian, and Swedish rule, and loan names from all three languages are analysed by Laansalu and Alas (2013).

The transfer to the USA of Dutch settlement names such as Amsterdam, Breukelen (Brooklyn), Haarlem (Harlem), Hoboken, and Utrecht has been used to work out migration routes, and Udolph (2012) applies the same methodology to trace the continental origins of the Anglo-Saxon settlers in Britain. By comparing the distribution of cognate elements on either side of the North Sea and the English Channel, he argues against the traditional model of migration from Denmark and Schleswig across the North Sea, proposing instead that the Anglo-Saxons reached Britain from Flanders, northern Germany and the Netherlands via the English Channel.

6.3.2 Settlement Chronologies

As mentioned in Section 6.1, the place-names of many areas reflect successive phases of settlement by different groups of incomers. In England, an early core of Celtic settlement names is overlaid by formations in Old English created by the Anglo-Saxon settlers of the fifth century onwards, and then further overlaid by formations in Old Norse in areas of subsequent Danish and Norwegian settlement. Even within individual languages, however, some name-types are earlier or later than others, and these can help to trace different stages of settlement by a single group of speakers. Among the earliest Old English place-name elements are *hām* 'homestead' (e.g. Grantham, Nottingham), *-ingahām* 'homestead of the followers of . . .' (e.g. Walsingham, Whittingham), and *-ingas* 'followers of . . .' or 'people associated with . . .' (e.g. Hastings, Reading). Of these, the most ancient is *hām*, which has a high incidence in early records and is found in proximity to Roman sites and material finds, and which was followed chronologically by names in -*ingahām* and -*ingas* (Cox 1972–73, 1975–76). Place-names containing these elements are therefore believed to represent an early stage of Anglo-Saxon settlement both in England, where the Anglo-Saxons settled first, and in southern Scotland, where they later expanded their territory.

Also indicative of early settlement are place-names referring to religious or other customs that were later superseded. Place-names referring to Anglo-Saxon paganism represent an early stratum which must pre-date the conversion to Christianity around 627. In England they fall into two main groups: those containing the names of pagan gods, and those containing a word for a heathen shrine or temple. Examples of the former are Tysoe (Tiw + OE *hōh* 'heel; hill-spur'),[8] Wensley (Woden + OE *lēah* 'wood, clearing'), Thursley (Thunor + OE *lēah* 'wood, clearing'), and Friden (Frig + *denu* 'valley'); examples of the latter are Harrow (OE *hearg* 'temple') and Weeford (OE *wēoh* 'shrine' + *ford* 'ford'). The absence of either type from the corpus of Old English place-names in Scotland is usually taken to indicate that the Anglo-Saxons did not move north until after the conversion to Christianity, although this has been challenged on the grounds that pagan names are also absent from large areas of England (Hough 1997b).

Also early are place-name elements drawn from the language(s) of previous groups of settlers. Latin words borrowed into Old English reflect contact between the Anglo-Saxon settlers and Latin speakers among the existing population of Britain. An example is OE **wīc-hām*, from Latin *vicus* 'village'. This appears to refer to Roman settlements that survived into early Anglo-Saxon times, and is represented in the recurrent place-name Wickham and its variants Wykeham, Wykham, and Wycomb. OE *camp*, from Latin *campus* 'field', occurs in place-names such as Camps, Campsey, and Campsfield, all from areas of early Anglo-Saxon settlement in south-east England. Most place-names from OE *camp* are associated with known Romano-British sites, as also are place-names from OE *port* 'harbour', a borrowing from Latin *portus* found in coastal names such as Porlock, Portishead, Portland, Portslade, and Portsmouth. OE **wīc-hām* is attested in place-names only, as also is OE **funta* 'spring', a loan-word from Latin *fons, fontis* referring to a spring characterized by Roman building work (e.g. Boarhunt, Cheshunt). Like other types of names, settlement names are a major source of vocabulary unattested in documentary sources, although it cannot always be assumed that terms used in name formation were in general use as vocabulary items (see Hough 2010).

Conversely, some elements may be dated to a later phase of settlement on semantic or other grounds. Place-names from OE *wīc* 'specialized farm' are indicative of established farming communities, and are considered unlikely to have been coined before the eighth century AD. Examples from England include Butterwick (butter), Cheswick (cheese), Gatwick (goats), and Shapwick (sheep); examples from Scotland include Berwick (barley), Hedderwick (heather), and Sunwick (pigs).

---

[8] Another metaphorical use of an anatomical term.

Syntactic structures may also repay investigation. As noted above (Section 6.2.1), element order varies according to the syntax of individual languages. The geographical scatter of Brittonic *tref* 'farm' in Scotland is related to its position either as a first or as a second element. In the area of historical Pictland in east and north-east Scotland, *tref* occurs only as a second element, as in Cantray (Brittonic *canto 'white' + *tref*). In south and south-west Scotland, on the other hand, it occurs only as a first element, as in Tranent (*tref* + Brittonic *neint* 'streams') and Traprain (*tref* + Brittonic *pren* 'tree'). This may have chronological implications. Whether in first or second position, *tref* consistently functions as a generic. In north-eastern names, it is preceded by the qualifier, whereas in south-western names, the qualifier follows it. The key point here is that a reversal of element order in Celtic place-names took place around the sixth century AD, when the characteristic structure changed from qualifier + generic to generic + qualifier. The different groups of *tref*-names may therefore represent different stages of settlement, with the earliest in north-east Scotland, and later settlements in the south-west (Hough 2001a).

Also relevant is land quality, since it is reasonable to suppose that the earliest settlements will be on the most attractive sites. The three most common types of Scandinavian place-names in the English Danelaw are those combining an Old Norse personal name with OE *tūn* 'farmstead' (e.g. Gamston, Thoroton), those from ON *bý* 'village' (e.g. Grimsby, Skegby), and those from ON *þorp* 'secondary settlement' (e.g. Gunthorpe, Ullesthorpe). The first group are found on the best ground, and are believed to represent existing Anglo-Saxon settlements that were partially renamed by the Danes. Names from ON *bý* occur on slightly less attractive sites, and are thought to represent new settlements, established as a result of a later immigration from Denmark following the Danish conquest. Names from ON *þorp* tend to refer to outlying settlements of less importance than the *bý*-names, representing a still later stage of settlement. Moreover, the *þorp*-names include English as well as Danish qualifiers, again pointing to a later stratum of name-giving, when a degree of integration had taken place between Scandinavians and Anglo-Saxons. The chronology was established in a seminal series of studies by Cameron (1965, 1970, 1971); understanding of these and other formations has been further advanced by subsequent scholarship (e.g. Abrams and Parsons 2004; Cullen et al. 2011).

A problematic issue is the extent to which differences in geographical scatter reflect differences in time, such that elements confined to a limited geographical area reflect an early chronological phase, while elements with a more widespread distribution reflect a later chronological phase. This principle underlies a series of distribution maps produced by Nicolaisen (2001) to chart the progress and extent of the Norwegian settlements in northern Scotland from *c*.800 AD onwards, and of the Gaelic settlements in western Scotland from the fifth century onwards. The methodology has not gone unchallenged, and indeed Nicolaisen (1994) acknowledges that regional naming factors may account for a particular type of place-name remaining productive in one area without spreading elsewhere. Moreover, distribution patterns are not always clear-cut. A concentration of names from Gaelic *sliabh* 'hill' in western Scotland, with a few occurrences in the central belt but none in the north or north-east, appeared to indicate that the element was most productive when the Gaels arrived in the west during the fifth century, still in use during the period of expansion in the sixth and seventh centuries, but obsolete by the time the Gaels reached the area of historical Pictland in the ninth. However, the more recent identification of additional *sliabh*-names in other parts of Scotland has cast doubt on this chronology by suggesting that the element may have continued in use later than was previously thought, and the implications continue to be debated (Nicolaisen 2007; Taylor 2007a).

6.3.3 Historical Linguistics

Settlement names provide rich data for historical linguistics. Many of those referring to the natural environment can be compared directly with the referent in order to establish a more precise meaning for individual place-name elements. Pioneering fieldwork by Gelling and Cole (2000) has revealed a system of finely-differentiated topographical vocabulary in Old English, such that terms previously regarded as synonyms are now known to have had distinctive meanings. As regards words for marsh, for instance, OE *ēg* refers to an area of raised ground in wet country (e.g. Bardney, Selsey), OE *strōd* to marshy land overgrown with brushwood (e.g. Strood, Stroud), and OE *wæsse* to land by a river which floods and drains quickly (e.g. Buildwas, Broadwas). River-crossings could be designated not only by the general term *ford* 'ford' (e.g. Bedford, Bradford), but by more specialized terms for difficult crossings, including *fær* 'difficult passage' (e.g. Denver, Laver) and *gelād* 'difficult river-crossing' (e.g. Cricklade, Linslade). Whereas the general term for a road was OE *weg* 'road' (e.g. Garmondsway, Thoresway), OE *strǣt* referred to a Roman road (e.g. Stratford, Stretton), and OE *stīg* to an upland path (e.g. Bransty, Gresty). Except for a pilot study of Scots by Pratt (2005), this methodology has not yet been applied to settlement names from other historical languages in Britain or elsewhere, so it is not yet known whether the subtlety of the Anglo-Saxon topographical naming system is exceptional, or if it is paralleled by those of other Indo-European or non-Indo-European cultures.

As well as semantic distinctions, settlement names can reveal regional differences in terminology. Fig. 6.5 shows the distribution of the habitative generic OE *worð* 'enclosure' and its variant *worðig*.[9] According to the place-name evidence, the latter appears to be a distinctively south-west form, whereas the literary evidence points to a more widespread use. The implications of this are not straightforward. One explanation relates to the difference between toponymic and lexical terminology, such that *worðig* was only productive as a place-name element in the south-west, despite being used as a

---

[9] The important factor is not the present-day spelling of the name but its derivation, so the map includes names such as Cessford and Jedburgh in Scotland, recorded respectively as *Cesseworth* in 1296 and *Gedwearde* in c.1060, and Cotchford in England, recorded as *Cocheworth* in 1265.

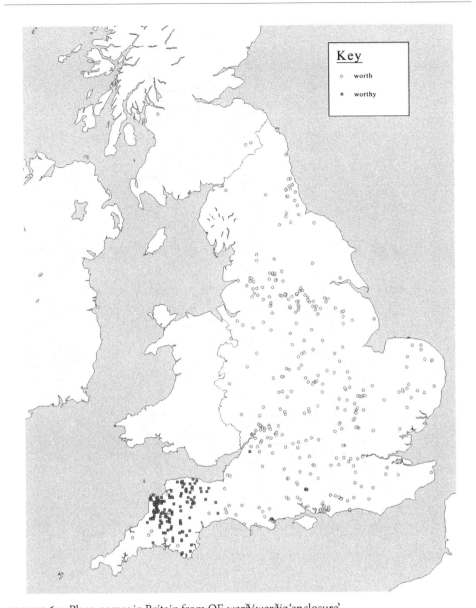

FIGURE 6.5 Place-names in Britain from OE *worð/worðig* 'enclosure'.

Map was created using GenMap UK software and contains
Ordnance Survey data © Crown copyright and database right 2013.

vocabulary word elsewhere. An alternative possibility is that since most extant manu-scripts of Old English are written in a standardized literary language based on the Late West Saxon dialect, the place-name distribution of *worð* and *worðig* may be a more reli-able indicator of word geography.

The repetitive nature of place-name generics also means that they can be used to map different regional developments over time. Most names from OE *ford* survive as

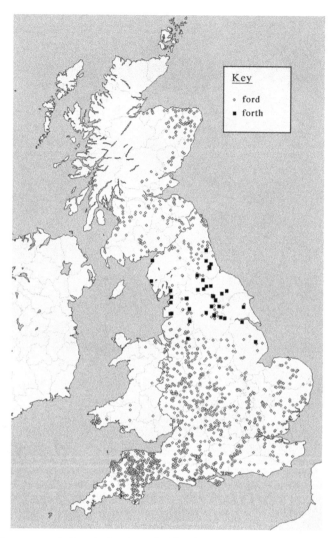

FIGURE 6.6 Place-names in Britain from OE *ford* 'ford'.

Map was created using GenMap UK software and contains
Ordnance Survey data © Crown copyright and database right 2013.

<ford>, as in Chelmsford, Dartford, Guildford, Hereford, Milford, and Oxford, but some become <forth>, particularly in northern England, where examples include Ampleforth, Gateforth, Gosforth, and Hartforth. The distribution of the two variants is shown on Fig. 6.6.[10]

---

[10] Occurrences as a qualifying element are excluded, as are names where *ford* has replaced a different generic, as with Cessford and Cotchford mentioned in note 9, or has itself been replaced by another element, as with the English names Brafferton, Claverton, Harvington, Milverton, Nettlebridge, Redbridge, and Tiverton.

6.4 CONCLUSIONS

Many of the examples in this chapter are from Britain, partly because that is the area with which the author is most familiar, but also because research into settlement names is at a more advanced stage in Britain than in some other parts of the world. The Survey of English Place-Names (SEPN) was inaugurated in the 1920s, and the ninety volumes so far published make available a wealth of primary material as well as serving as a model for other national place-name surveys. Initially focusing on settlement names, SEPN subsequently extended its remit to include other toponyms such as field names, but this has had the result of slowing progress. Comprehensive coverage of the settlement names of the whole country will be needed in order to undertake fully robust analyses of the distribution and significance of individual elements and name-types. But the ultimate objective is systematic survey work on a global scale. Only then will it be possible to fit all the pieces of the jigsaw together, and to address questions relating to fundamental issues such as the potential existence of universal name-types, and the primacy of descriptive or non-descriptive formations.

CHAPTER 7

RIVER NAMES

SVANTE STRANDBERG

7.1 THE CHARACTER AND IMPORTANCE OF RIVER NAMES

RIVER names constitute an important body of linguistic and historical material, owing to their considerable age, wide linguistic range, and role in society. 'Jedes Volk, jeder Stamm hinterläßt so seine sprachlichen Spuren in der Hydronymie der Landschaft' (Nicolaisen 1957). Names of rivers provide the most important evidence of an early linguistic European community. They can bear witness to human thought, activities, and conditions in very remote ages, and naturally to early stages of language development (lexicon, phonology, morphology, and semantics). Names like Scottish *Dee* 'goddess', English *Gaunless* 'useless river', Norwegian *Helvitesfossen* 'hellish rapids', *Illåi* 'evil river', *Ogna* 'fright river', and Swedish *Matfors* 'food-giving rapids' reflect human attitudes towards, and feelings for, watercourses. Greule (2009b: 145) quotes the theologian Matthias Blum: 'Gibt es überhaupt irgendetwas, das nicht materiell oder symbolisch, direkt oder indirekt mit Wasser zu tun hat?' Studies of river names which seek to demonstrate the earlier distribution of different peoples or tribes and their languages, for example, are of great interest. The title of an article by Greule (2009a) is illustrative: 'Danube, Rhine, Moldau and the Indo-Germanisation of Europe'. A much-discussed question concerning some parts of Europe is whether a Germanic or Celtic origin for river names is to be assumed. A case in point is *Hull* in Yorkshire, which has been considered Celtic, but also Scandinavian.

Hydronymic research in a country like Sweden has concerned itself to a very great extent with lake names; these can be as old as river names and contain the same words or roots. River names formed from names of lakes are common in Sweden. In Denmark and Norway, too, much research has been done on lake names. For topographical reasons, in areas of Europe such as England and Germany more attention has been paid to river names than to lake names.

7.2 TERMINOLOGY

The term *river name* refers to names of bodies of running water: rivers large and small, streams, brooks, rapids, and so on: *Thames, Duddon, Merry Brook, Falls of Clyde*, etc. A river name is a *hydronym*, a name of a body of water. The whole stock of hydronyms in a district, territory, country, or the like is called its *hydronymy*.

A river name is either uncompounded (coined by directly name-forming derivation or as a secondary name formation) or compound (with a specific, e.g. *Black-*, and a generic, e.g. *-water*). *Primary name formation* (by derivation or composition) involves the generation of a new word. *Secondary name formation* is the use of an existing word (common noun or adjective, e.g. PrGmc **aitra-* 'swelling') as a toponym (a German term for such names, by contrast, is *primäre Bildung*). A *formally secondary* river name emanates from another, older toponym, whereas a *formally primary* river name has not been coined on the basis of another place-name.

The river name *Mosel* (*Moselle*), for instance, is a derivative of *Maas* (*Meuse*, Lat. *Mosa*) and thus a formally secondary name. Another derivative of *Maas* is *Maasje* in the Netherlands. An old and famous formally secondary hydronym is *Bodensee* (Lake Constance) in Austria, Germany, and Switzerland; it contains the settlement name *Bodman*. The Ukrainian river name *Donets* is a diminutive derivative of the Russian *Don*, the latter a secondary name formation meaning 'river'. Another secondary name formation is the English river name *Avon*, which contains a Celtic word for 'water(course)'. Some formally secondary river names are the results of *back-formation* (see section 7.6). The river name *Amstel* in the Netherlands has been explained as secondary in a semantic sense (earlier attached to another denotatum), but its etymology is considered uncertain.

A specific kind of naming is *eponymization* (transfer of an existing toponym to denote another place as well).

Over time, river names have changed in many ways. One phenomenon is *epexegesis*, the addition of an explanatory or defining element to an older river name. In *Devils Water* (Northumberland, England), the element *water* defines a Celtic river name, corresponding to the Irish and Scottish *Douglas* 'black stream'. Ger. *Aiterbach* (from an older *Aitra, Eitra*) contains the epexegetically added *Bach* 'brook'. The Danish river name *Guden* was expanded into *Gudenå*, containing Scand. *å* 'river'. In many cases Eng. *brook* was added to an earlier name (e.g. *Glaze Brook, Humber Brook*); it is even possible to find *Bourne Brook* (*Bourne* means 'brook').

Ellipsis is the intentional reduction of an entire element (often the generic) in a toponym. *Eamont* (Cumberland and Westmorland, England) may be elliptical and originate from an **Eamōt-ēa* or the like 'the river of Eamot' ('junction of streams'). A typical Swedish example is *Hedesjön > Heden*. One type of ellipsis is reduction of the middle element of a hydronym (German *Klammerform*): Dan. *Fokkebæk < Fokkebrobæk*, Ger. *Sindelbach* instead of **Sindelfingerbach*, etc.

The term *polynymy* refers to the simultaneous existence of more than one name for a body of water.

7.3 CHRONOLOGY AND STRATIFICATION

Hydronyms are considered the oldest and most enduring of all preserved place-names in Europe: 'Sie übertreffen in ihren frühesten Schichten alle anderen Namen an Alter und Altertümlichkeit' (Krahe 1964). Many European river names are recorded before, or not long after, the birth of Christ; Caesar, for example, has the forms *Arar* (the Saône), *Liger, Ligeris* (Loire), *Mosa* (Maas/Meuse), *Scaldim* (Schelde/l'Escaut), and *Tamesis* (Thames); Tacitus has *Albis* (Elbe), *Moenum* (Main), and *Sabrina* (Severn); and Ptolemy *Iska* (Exe) and *Varar* (Farrar). Scandinavian river names occur much later in written sources, although that does not mean that names of great antiquity are lacking; the oldest stratum of preserved Germanic hydronyms in Scandinavia dates back to Proto-Indo-European times.

It has been assumed—for obvious reasons—that large rivers, as a rule, have older names than smaller ones. This is a vexed question, however. There are in any case exceptions; the geographical location of the denotatum and special societal circumstances connected with it may have prompted early naming. Schmid (1981, 1995) stresses that less impressive rivers, too, may bear very old names. The Oare Water in Somerset, England, for instance, is not very large, but its name is considered pre-Celtic (*alteuropäisch*).

7.3.1 Linguistic and Chronological Strata

When trying to establish the age of a river name, scholars have to consider word formation (derivation or composition, primary or secondary name formation, which suffix?), lexicon (words lost early?), extralinguistic circumstances, and the occurrence of identical or related river names in other countries.

The linguistic and chronological stratification of river names in Britain and on the continent may be complicated. *Ambra/Amber/Ammer* names in England and other European countries have been considered Celtic, but names in northern Germany and Sweden seem to make it necessary also to ponder another origin for European river names in *Amb-/Amm-*.

The hydronymic evidence for the distribution of different languages and peoples in the distant past is of great historical importance. Much attention has been paid to the chronological stratigraphy of river names in different parts of Europe. Among English river names, Ekwall (1928) discerned pre-English names ('mainly British or possibly pre-British'), Anglo-Saxon and later English names, Scandinavian names, and names containing French elements. Later, Nicolaisen defined a great many river names in Britain as pre-Celtic (pre-British).

Pre-English river names are numerous. They are predominant among the names of more important rivers: the Avon, Thames, Tyne, etc. Early Celtic river names are for the most part uncompounded. Scandinavian river names are not uncommon in England; they chiefly denote watercourses of small or medium size, are mostly compounded, and occur in districts where Scandinavians settled.

Krahe (1963, 1964, 1965) identifies the following strata: the *alteuropäische Hydronymie* (see below, section 7.3.2), with uncompounded river names, for example *Drava* (a river flowing, *inter alia*, through Croatia, Hungary, and Slovenia), *Farrar* in Scotland, *Nidd* in England, and *Saale* in Germany; Celtic river names, for example *Dover* in England and *Kamp* in Austria; and German(ic) river names, which include very old uncompounded river names, for example **Aitra, Nette, Streu*, younger uncompounded river names, for example *Glatt, Krumm, Lauter*, and compound river names (with generics like -*aha* 'river' and -*bach* 'brook'). Among old Germanic river names, Krahe highlights the groups containing PrGmc **aitra-* 'swelling, flooding' (Ger. *Aitrach* < *Aitra* and *Eitra*, Swed. *Ätran*, and other names) or **nat-* 'wet; water', which seems to be contained, for example, in Ger. *Nathe* and *Notter* (< *Natra*) and in the Swedish settlement name *Nätra* (< **Natriōn-*), originally a river name. (The *e*-grade of IE **nod-* and PrGmc **nat-* is assumed to be the basis of the Celtic or pre-Celtic river name *Ness* in *Inverness* and *Loch Ness*, Scotland.)

Greule (1973, 1996a, 2007) has stratified river names in several parts of German-speaking Europe. In a territory surrounding the Oberrhein (in Alsace, northern Switzerland, and Südbaden), he distinguished Germanic and pre-Germanic river names. The oldest river names of all in that study belong under the *alteuropäische Hydronymie*, while Celtic river names make up the youngest stratum among the pre-Germanic names. Characteristic of the pre-Germanic and the oldest Germanic river names is that they are uncompounded. Greule later stratified river names in Germany thus: *alteuropäisch*, Celtic, old Germanic, Slavic and German river names. For an area of Germany between the Baltic and the Erzgebirge and between the Elbe–Saale and the Oder–Neisse, Eichler (1981) distinguished pre-Slavic river names (including *Elbe, Oder, Saale*), old Slavic river names (none of the major rivers bears a Slavic name), older German river names, and younger German river names. In linguistically homogeneous countries such as Denmark, Norway, and Sweden, stratification is chiefly a question of chronology.

7.3.2 Old European Hydronymy (*alteuropäische Hydronymie*)

A most important and influential contribution to hydronymic research was Hans Krahe's (1963, 1964, 1965) structural description of many groups of very old European river names, closely related to each other and dating back to a period before the existence of fully developed Indo-European subfamilies (Baltic, Celtic, Germanic, etc.). Such river names are not *einzelsprachlich*, that is they are pre-dialectal and cannot be ascribed to any Indo-European subfamily (*Einzelsprache*). Fundamental to this reconstructed 'network' (the *alteuropäische Hydronymie*), according to Krahe (1963, 1964, 1965), are words and suffixes of Indo-European (not *einzelsprachlich*) origin, a time of establishment before 1,500 BC, and a range from western Europe with Britain to the Baltic states and from Scandinavia to the Mediterranean. The most characteristic semantic feature of this hydronymy is its many 'water roots', IE *adu-/*adro-* 'watercourse', *el-/*ol-* 'flow, stream', *sal-* 'brook, flowing water, current', *ser-/*sor-* 'flow, stream', and the like.

Krahe's hydronymic 'network' has given rise to much discussion (Nicolaisen 1957, 1971, 2001, 2004; Andersson 1972, 1980, 1988, 2004; Kousgård Sørensen 1972; Greule 1973, 1996a, 1996b, 2007, 2009b; Schmid 1981, 1995; Udolph 1995b, 1996, 2004; and other scholars), and also to criticism. Controversial issues include the chronology of *alteuropäisch* river names and the necessity or otherwise of studying topographical features as possible reasons for the naming of rivers. The likelihood of there being very old secondary name formations among these river names makes the chronological assessment of names and suffixes more difficult. Patterns (including eponymization) may have played a very important role in the creation and distribution of 'old European' river names.

Schmid (1981, 1995) modified Krahe's chronology, explaining *alteuropäisch* as *Proto-Indo-European* (*pre-Germanic, pre-Celtic, pre-Slavonic*, etc.) and arguing that river names belonging to that stratum may be much younger in some parts of Europe than in others. The territory with Baltic languages and the Mosel region are assumed to be continuity centres of the *alteuropäische Hydronymie*.

Nicolaisen (1957, 1971, 2001, 2004) made important contributions to the discussion as regards Britain. Unlike Ekwall (1928), he is convinced that there are pre-Celtic (Proto-Indo-European) river names in England. His discussion of *Farrar* in Scotland is stratigraphically illuminating; according to Nicolaisen, this river name goes back to a pre-Celtic *Varar*, belonging to the IE root *μor-* 'water, rain, river'.

The extralinguistic aspects of the toponymic interpretation process have been much stressed in Scandinavia, and this can be seen in the semantic discussion of Krahe's 'system'. The German scholar assigned the Norwegian river name *Orma* to IE *μer-/*μor-/*μr* 'water, rain, river', whereas Hovda (1971) called attention to the very winding form of the watercourse and associated its name with Scand. *orm* 'snake'. According to Krahe, the Norwegian lake name *Vermunden* can also be traced to IE *μer-/*μor-/*μr-* 'water etc.'; Nyman (2000), however, prefers the interpretation 'warm lake'; a trait of the denotatum is that it has places with rapid-flowing (and probably often ice-free) water. (Conversely, Særheim (2007), considering a derivation from *μer-/*μor-* 'water etc.', is persuaded by topographical reasons to reject the interpretation 'warm river' for a Norwegian river name *Vorma* (< *Varma*).)

A case in which the *alteuropäisch* interpretation has been criticized in Scandinavia is that of river names in *Al-/El-* (> *Il-*). Continental scholars—following Krahe—explain such names, among them Ger. *Aller, Alster, Elster*, and *Elz*, as containing an IE *el-/*ol-* 'flow, stream'. Særheim (2007) does not rule out the possibility of such an origin for some Norwegian hydronyms (*Aln-, *Alra, *Jalsi, *Qlund*). Andersson, however, reckons with a Gmc *al- 'grow; nourish' (referring to swelling water) in river names like Ger. *Alster* and Swed. *Alster* and *Alma*. Greule derives (*Weiße*) *Elster* from Gmc *ala- 'grow; nourish'. A number of European river names are assumed to contain IE *ueis-/*uis- 'flow', a typical 'water root'; they include *Wyre* in Lancashire, England, *Vesdre* in Belgium, *Wisła* (*Vistula*) in Poland, and Ger. *Werra* and *Weser*.

At all events, it is evident that there are groups of very old European river names that are related to each other and contain the same stem and a very old suffix. A semantically reasonable interpretation can be found for several river names associated with IE *eis-, *ois-, or *is- 'move fast or violently': river names outside Scandinavia derived from this Indo-European root include *Aire* and *Ure* in Yorkshire and, on the continent, *Ijssel* in the Netherlands, *Isar* in Germany, *Isonzo* in Italy, and *Isère* in France. Scandinavian river names in this context are, among others, Norw. *Eisand* and the reconstructed Danish names *Esa* and *Isen*. According to Schmid (1981, 1995), it is impossible to confirm etymological interpretations of *alteuropäisch* river names extralinguistically, because their semantic content is so vague and the topographical background so hard to judge. The topographical conditions for a hydronym containing *eis- 'move fast' are, however, excellent—the existence of rapids—in cases like Swed. *Esla* (*Eslo*), *Esman*, *Gesunden* (< *Esund-*), and *Gesunda* (< *Esunda*).

IE *er-/*or-, (originally) 'set in motion' or the like, is another Indo-European root regarded as the basis for numerous European river names, among them *Ayr* in Scotland, *Oare* (*Water*) in Somerset, England, *Ara* in Spain, *Aar* in the Netherlands, *Aare* in Switzerland, *Arl* in Austria, and *Arno* in Italy. Several river names are associated with IE *neid-/*nid- 'flow', including *Nidd* (Yorkshire, England), *Neth* (Cornwall, England), *Nedd/Neath* (Wales), *Neer* (Netherlands), *Niedà* (Lithuania), and *Nida* (Poland).

7.4 MORPHOLOGY

A priori, there are good reasons to expect feminine gender for an old derived and formally primary Germanic hydronym denoting a major river. The character of the denotatum is important in this regard; in Scandinavia, masculine gender is natural for names of streams and rapids. In Britain and on the continent (with, among others, Celtic languages and Old Latin), the gender structure is more complicated. Masculine river names like *Inn* and *Rhein* are not of Germanic origin. *Le Rhône* and *la Seine* in France have retained the gender of their Old Latin forms (Caesar: *Rhodanus, Sequana*).

In early prehistoric times, derivation or secondary name formation based on a common noun (appellative) or adjective were the predominant ways of coining names. Composition gained ground as time went on and finally became the normal mode of Germanic name formation.

Derived river names are important for the study of suffixes and their functions. Of great interest are suffixes that are better documented in toponyms than in common nouns or adjectives, and suffixes with semantic functions characteristic only of toponyms. Scholars have spoken of 'place-name suffixes': 'typischen Namensuffixen, die per definitionem inhaltsleer sind' (Schmid 1981: 8).

The suffixes -na-/-nō-, -ra-/-rō-, and -nt(i)a-, for instance, play an important part in the discussion about the *alteuropäische Hydronymie*. Much research, however, remains to be done on the chronological stratigraphy, distribution, and earlier functions of suffixes. A very comprehensive and thorough study has been made of the old Germanic suffix -*und*, which occurs in many Scandinavian hydronyms and island names.

When trying to establish an approximate *terminus ante quem* for the use of a suffix and to ascertain the name-forming function of that suffix, scholars have to take into account the distinction between primary and secondary name formation. A common noun or adjective may contain a suffix that had fallen into disuse long before the word in question became a proper name. The Norwegian fjord name *Sogn* refers to streaming water, containing an -*n*-derivative of the stem of the verb *suga* 'to suck'. This hydronym is probably very old; however, a corresponding common noun *sugn* is still preserved in Scandinavia: Norw. *Sogn* may be a secondary name formation, and its *n*-suffix cannot tell us much about its age as a fjord name. The name of a rapid in the river Dnieper, Ukraine, is recorded in a tenth-century source as *Strukun*; its origin is a Scand. *Strukn*, closely related to the Old Swedish lake name *Strukni* (and the Swedish verb *stryka* 'stroke'). How likely is it that a Scandinavian river name was coined by means of the *n*-suffix as late as the Viking Age? Is it more plausible to explain *Strukun* as a secondary name formation? Eponymization with a Norwegian river name *Skirna* as the pattern has been considered for *Skerne Beck* in Yorkshire (a river name in *Skirn*-), but an -*n*-derivative (of *skīr/scīr* 'clear') coined by Scandinavians is another possibility. Here, too, a crucial question is whether derivation with the -*na*/-*nō*-suffix was possible as late as Viking times. Place-names provide evidence of a function of the -*n*-suffix that may seem striking, set against classical teachings on word formation.

A particular kind of secondary name formation in the hydronymy is nominalization. (Because of the change from adjective to noun, it is even theoretically possible to classify nominalized adjectives (Greule 1996a: *Konversionsprodukte*) as primary name formations.) The river names in question form an important and well-known category, instances of which include the European **aitra* names (see section 7.3.1 above); *Stour* ('strong'?), *Wensum* (OE **wendsum* 'winding'), and, it has been suggested, *Writtle* (OE **writol* 'babbling') in England; *Glatt* ('shining') and *Lauter* ('clean') in Germany; *Vorma* ('warm') in Norway; and *Blakka* ('pale') in Sweden. However, there are also hydronyms that look like nominalized adjectives, but are in fact the result of sound reduction or intended ellipsis. The French river name *Brune* 'the dark or brown river', for instance, has been explained as an elliptical name, as has Fr. *Morte* 'the dead river'. A Swedish lake name *Svarten* may be a reduced form of *Svartsjö(n)*. Sometimes it can be difficult to decide whether a hydronymic form is the result of ellipsis (of a compound) or sound change or represents a genuine nominalization (perhaps enlarged for some time by epexegesis). Does the Ger. *Schwarza* 'black river' go back to a compound in -*aha* or a simplex form?

Dehydronymic derivatives are indisputable examples of primary name formation and may thus provide information on suffixal functions in ancient times. Diminutive forms are a well-documented type, including river names like French *Aubette* from *Aube* and *Garonelle* from *Garonne*, and the above-mentioned Ukrainian *Donets* from *Don*. *Styric* (the upper Cam) and the lost river name *Sturkel* in Dorset, England are assumed to be diminutive forms of *Stour*. The river name *Riccal* 'the calf of the [river] Rye' in Yorkshire, England is a dehydronymic compound, functioning in semantic terms like a derivative.

Compound river names, too, may be very old. Some river names containing the much-discussed generic -*apa* 'water' have even been regarded as belonging in the *alteuropäische Hydronymie*.

The shape of old hydronyms has often been dramatically transformed, by sound change, ellipsis, misunderstanding, 'popular etymology', and/or analogy (on analogy, see below, section 7.6).

7.5 Name Change and Polynymy

Name change is a common phenomenon in the history of hydronyms. In England, *Blyth* was replaced by *Ryton*, *Granta* by *Cam*, *Hail* by *Kym*, *Writtle* by *Wid*, etc. During a transitional stage of polynymy, there must often have existed both an older name and a new one. *Trent* (< *Terente*) is an alternative name for the river Piddle in Dorset. In Denmark, an older *Guden* and a younger *Storå(en)* were for a long time used in parallel for the same river.

Polynymy may also involve the simultaneous existence of different names for different parts of a (long) river. There are, for example, cases where the upper and lower reaches of a river have different names. The upper part of the Wylye in Wiltshire, England is called the *Deverill*, and the source of the French river Marne has the name *Marnotte*. A present-day name for a long river may have replaced several old ones denoting different stretches of it. The Nyköpingsån is a long and large river in Sweden; its name is formally secondary, containing the town name *Nyköping*. Two lost partial names of the Nyköpingsån (*Blakka*, *Sølnoa*) are recorded in medieval sources, while others, like *Sledh* and *Vrena, may be or probably are preserved in names denoting settlements on the river; the current partial name *Morjanån* most likely goes back to an OSwed. *Morgha.

7.6 Semantics

The semantic range of river names is very wide. They may tell us about distinctive features of the rivers or their beds, the nearby topography, human activities in or near the watercourses, or settlements and people connected with them. Stems or words in hydronyms may express meanings such as 'large', 'long', 'broad', 'narrow', 'deep', 'shallow', 'fast', 'violent', 'slow', 'winding' 'abounding in water', 'clear', 'light', 'shining', 'dark', 'black, white, brown, red or the like', 'misty', 'sandy', 'gravelly', 'stony', 'muddy', 'full of vegetation', 'silent', 'loud', 'chattering', 'warm', 'cold', 'profitable', 'dangerous', 'injurious', and 'sacred'.

Greule (1996a) identifies twelve different reasons for naming in the hydronymy: *primary reasons* are connected with the water (the sense 'water, river' or the like) and its qualities (e.g. colour, motion, abundance or shortage of water, character of the river bed); *secondary reasons* are connected with the form of the watercourse, its location and its environment (e.g. striking curves, animals, vegetation, features of the ground); and *tertiary reasons* are connected with human use of the water (e.g. artefacts, individuals, historical circumstances, settlements).

Hydronyms with the sense 'water', 'river', 'lake', or the like form an important semantic group. They figure prominently in the *alteuropäische Hydronymie*, but examples are easily found in other contexts as well. *Avon* in England and *Rhein* (*Rhine*) stand for 'stream, river'. The river names *Don* in Durham and Yorkshire, England, *Don* in Russia, and *Donau* (*Danube*) are assumed to contain an old word for 'water, river'. *Bourne* (*Burn*) 'the stream, the brook' is the name of several English rivers. In Scandinavia, PrGmc and PrScand. *laghu- 'water' (OE *lagu* 'sea', OWScand. *lǫgr* 'lake', corresponding to *Loch* in *Loch Ness* and other Scottish lake names) occurs in names of important bodies of water, including the river names *Lågen* in Norway and *Lagan* in Sweden.

Many formally secondary river names refer to a settlement. Among them are back-formations, a type well-known from Britain and Germany; Eng. *Cam* (from *Cambridge*) and Ger. *Wilde* (from the settlement name *Wildungen*) are two examples. 'Most often back-formations arose because the first element of a compound name or the first syllable of a derivative was mistaken for a river-name' (Ekwall 1928). River names with a settlement name as specific are frequent in Scandinavia: *Odense Å* (Denmark), *Motala ström* (Sweden), etc. Often, an older name for such a river is known. A name change of this kind (e.g. OSwed. *Næria* > Swed. *Eskilstunaån*) is due to the development of society: in later periods, more attention has been paid to the settlements than to the watercourses.

Rivers have been described as the most living and individual element in nature. Their names may express human or animal activities or qualities of the denotata. River names reported from Norway include *Dansarhora* 'dancing whore', *Hyggjande* 'sober river', and *Pissaren* 'piddling stream'. Norw. *Ork* (now *Orkla*) means 'working [probably eroding] river'. Among English river names, *Blyth* has been interpreted as 'gentle or pleasant river' and *Webburn* as 'raging stream'. A stream name *Morðingi* 'murderer' is mentioned from Iceland. Examples in Germany include *Hungerbach* 'hunger brook' (periodically dry), *Neckar* 'impetuous, furious, rapid river', and the contrasting *Wilde Gera* and *Zahme Gera* 'the wild Gera' and 'the tame Gera'. A French *Folru* is interpreted as 'silly brook' (often dry).

Metaphorical river names are a kind of secondary name formation. *Sence* in Leicestershire, England, is explained as 'cup'. Lebel (1956) interpreted a French *Loup* as a metaphor ('wolf'), denoting a small stream 'qui devient furieux après les orages'.

Norw. *Systrene* 'the sisters' is also metaphorical, referring to two streams running close together.

Analogy may result in eponymization (where the new river name and its model are morphologically identical), but it may also work in other ways. An *alteuropäisch* pattern may have generated river names in later periods. Sometimes it is difficult to know whether a name is due to eponymization or not. There are German river names (*Rhein, Rhin*) that are assumed to have been transferred from the large and well-known Rhine. However, there is a common noun *Rin*; it is considered possible that this noun is a dehydronymic one, originating from the river name *Rhein* (*Rhine*). A French stream name *Jourdan* is said to have been modelled on the *Jordan* in the Holy Land. Hydronymic research has devoted a good deal of attention to analogy in recent years.

7.7 LEXICON AND RECONSTRUCTION

Two widely occurring Germanic elements (generics) are **ahwō* f. (OE *ēa*, OHG *aha*, OScand. *ā*) 'river' (Lat. *aqua* 'water') and **baki-/*bakja-* (Eng. *beck*, Ger. *Bach*, Dan. *bæk*, Norw. *bekk*) 'stream'. Krahe described *-bach* as the typical German 'Flußnamengrundwort' and *-aha* as 'das germanische'; while *ēa* (the specific in *Eton* and the generic in *Romney*) has been called 'the standard word' for a river in Old English. *Beck* was brought to England by the Scandinavians, with stream names containing it found in parts of the country where they settled. Very important generics in England are *brook* (OE *brōc*) and *burn* (OE *burna*). They are not used for major rivers, but may denote watercourses of considerable size. The functional relationship between *brook* and *burn* is complex and much discussed. Eng. *brook* corresponds to OHG *bruoh* 'marsh'. 'There is no "bright" brook... and no "foul" bourn' (Gelling and Cole 2000).

Reconstruction is very important in the field of hydronymic research. Many river names are long since lost and forgotten. The purpose of reconstruction may be to ascertain an older, unrecorded form of a still-surviving name, such as **Frankina* for *Frenke* in Switzerland, **Isura* for *Ure* in Yorkshire, **Oghn* for *Ljungan* in Sweden, and **Wultahwa* for *Vltava* in the Czech Republic. The process may also, however, involve extracting lost, unrecorded hydronyms from other, recorded toponyms. Such reconstructions may be very convincing, but naturally there are also uncertain and complicated cases. An illustrative example is *Leicester*; it seems difficult to ascertain, but possible, that the farthest origin of the specific in this English town name (*Ligera ceastre* 917) is a river name corresponding to the French *Loire* (< *Liger*). Greater certainty attaches to the well-known reconstruction of the river name PrGmc **Wermōn-*, OSwed. **Værma*, the derivation basis of the lake name *Värmeln* (PrScand. **Wermilaʀ*) and the earliest origin of the specific of the Swedish province name *Värmland*.

Numerous European river names have survived only in settlement names, which may thus contribute significantly to our knowledge of ancient hydronymy. A river name **Amber* can for example be extracted from the district name *Ambergau*, and an **Erphesa* from the town name *Erfurt* (Germany). The above-mentioned Norwegian hydronyms *Aln-*, *Alra*, *Jalsi*, and *Qlund* are all reconstructed from settlement names. Innumerable reconstructions are inevitable in a study of older hydronymic strata in Denmark, where the original river names are generally lost: *Brusn* 'swelling(?) river', *Farandi* 'moving river', *Røthn* 'red river', *Thrima* 'noisy river', *Wærn* (IE *uer-* 'water'), etc.

The great age of so many river names often makes comparisons with other languages rewarding. The occurrence of a word or stem in the hydronymy of one European country may be of importance for the interpretation or reconstruction and the structural assessment of a river name in another. In a reconstruction of the Danish river name *Isen* (IE *eis-/*ois-/*is-* 'move fast'), Kousgård Sørensen (1972) refers to continental river names like *Eisen*, *Isen*, and *Isina* (now *Eisbach*) in Germany and *Iwoine* (< *Isna*) in Belgium. The interpretation of the Swedish lake name *Ekoln* as referring to rough sea is strengthened by the existence of OE *ācol* 'frightened'. The Swedish morpheme *strö(-)* is not unambiguous; however, the hydronymic alternative *strø* 'stream' (secondary name formation) is quite acceptable for some Scandinavian toponyms: *Strö* (Sweden), *Strøy* (Norway) and *Strø* (Denmark), not least in the light of the German river name *Streu*. MHG *gelster* 'loud' and the German river name *Gelster* support the reconstruction of a corresponding river name from the Swedish hundred name *Göstring* (OSwed. *Gilstring-*). The Swedish settlement name *Skuttunge* probably contains a lost river name in *Skut-* referring to rapid water; this reconstruction is supported not only by a reconstructed Old Scandinavian (Danish and Swedish) river name element *Skut-*, but also by the existence of the German river names *Schussen* (PrGmc *Skut-*) and *Schutter* (PrGmc *skutr-*), both traceable to IE *skeud-/*skud-*, Gmc *skeut-/*skut-* 'rush ahead, dash, speed', and by the extraction of a river name *Schöttel* (< PrGmc *Skutil-*) from the presumably epexegetic German river name *Schöttelbach*.

Fortunately, the lexicological basis for an interpretation is very often solid. This is the case regarding the river names *Meden* (Nottinghamshire, England), *Medina* (Isle of Wight), *Mettma* (Germany), and the convincingly reconstructed OScand. *Meðumō, OSwed. *Miædhm* 'middle part or river'. Here, scholars can refer to words for 'middle' like OE *medume* (adj.), OLG *medamo* (adj.), and Goth. *miduma* (noun). In many other cases, however, they have to reconstruct lost words contained in old river names and other toponyms. The Czech river name *Ohře* (Ger. *Eger*) is assumed to contain an adjective, Celt. *agro-*, derived from IE *ag-* 'drive'. Two Swedish parishes called *Ving* (OSwed. *Vighn*) seem to preserve lost hydronyms, being nominalized forms of an adjective PrIE *uiknó-*, PrGmc *wigná-* 'bent', corresponding to Latvian *wīkns* 'flexible'. The Swedish hundred name *Lagunda* illustrates one of the problems connected with reconstruction: *Lag-* contains PrGmc *laghu-* 'water', but it is difficult to decide in this case between the common noun and a hydronym.

CHAPTER 8

···

HILL AND MOUNTAIN NAMES

···

PETER DRUMMOND

THIS chapter will deal with the names of high ground, above the habitable and cultivable land, and particularly its peaks and summits. It will outline some of the research that has been done, illustrating it with examples, and will discuss some salient features of mountain names. Historically, high ground was economically marginal, although it may be have been used for pasture (especially of a transhumant nature), hunting, or mining. However, over the last century and a half, the human activity of climbing mountains simply for pleasure has led to a greater focus on their names, with in some cases new names being coined, either to replace an older extant name, or to fill a gap where no name existed.

The historic marginality resulted in a relative lateness in the recording of oronyms (hill and mountain names). In the British Isles, for instance, whilst most major rivers and many settlements were on record by the eleventh century, only Snowdon (*Snawdune* 1095) and The Cheviot (*Chiuiet* 1181) appear to have been recorded by the twelfth century. Scotland and England's highest peaks, Ben Nevis and Scafell respectively, were first recorded in the sixteenth century (1590s and 1578); Mont Blanc was not apparently recorded as such until the seventeenth century, superseding the older name of Mont Maudit (still used for its subsidiary summit); and even the striking Alpine peaks Eiger and Jungfrau only emerge in the seventeenth century (Blaeu 1654; map of Aargau: *Mons Junckfrau, Eiger mons*), with the third member of the now-famous trio, the Mönch, a late arrival.[1] Relatively lower peaks were recorded earlier: Switzerland's Mount Pilatus, barely half the height of the country's highest, and standing only 585m above Lake Lucerne, was recorded in 1307; Scotland's Tinto and Cairn Table hills were recorded in the fourteenth century (in 1315),[2] long before any of the many higher Scottish summits; and in the English Lakes, minor hills like Rest Dodd, Latrigg, and Caw were on record before the well-known high top of Skiddaw (*Skydehow*, 1247), whilst many other

---

[1] From 1790 it was *Grossmonch*, from 1860 *Monch*.
[2] Both hills marked the boundaries of James Douglas' lands (Thomson et al. 1882–1914: I, 77).

low hills were recorded before the sixteenth century when Scafell (*Skallfeild*, 1578), Blencathra (*Blenkarthure*, 1589) and Helvellyn (*Helvillon*, 1577) appeared. This pattern is logical from the point of view of those who worked the land, or owned the productive areas, in that the lower hills or mountains closer to them, and more easily accessible for transhumance, would be significant enough to name and record. Conversely, the names of the highest and less accessible summits were of little interest until relatively modern times. It is no surprise that in Cassini's magisterial survey map of France in the seventeenth century, the very highest peaks in the Dauphiné (such as Mont Pelvoux) are displayed graphically but their names not recorded.

It is also logical that names of ranges, expressed as plural formations (e.g. the Cairngorms, the Andes) are late developments, because in a settled rural society where people rarely moved any distance, the concept of the local hill being part of a much larger group would have been problematic. The ancient Greeks and Romans typically but not always used 'mountain' in the singular to mean one or a range, for example *Appeninus Mons*: the earliest references to the Pyrenees appear to be singular (*Pyrene*); and the (correct) singular form of Himalaya is from Sanskrit, meaning 'abode of the snow'. In the USA, the Appalachians only became established as the plural formation for this long eastern range after the 1861 publication of an important geological study by geographer Guyot (he had hesitated between that name and Alleghenies), a book which subsequently impacted school geography lessons and thus popular usage (Stewart 1945: 334). In the British Isles, late formations like the Cairngorms, the Pentlands, and the Brecon Beacons[3] were derived from one peak bearing the name (e.g. Cairn Gorm) spreading to include its neighbours as a range: the Pennines were a 1747 invention in a forged treatise by Bertram, inspired perhaps by Camden's 1586 comparison of elements like the *pen* of Pen-y-Ghent, with the Apennines of Italy (Watts 2004).

One noteworthy feature of many oronyms, compared to names of watercourses or of settlements, is that they often bear more than one appellation, either contemporaneously, or over time. In Asia, Mount Everest is also Quomolungma, in North America Mount McKinley is also Denali, and in Europe the Matterhorn is also Cervin: in the British Isles Snowdon is also Yr Wyddfa, Blencathra is also Saddleback, and Ben Arthur is more commonly The Cobbler. None of these alternative names represents a translation of meaning to another language, nor a reflex of an original form. The Matterhorn, a name coined by German speakers from *Matte*, 'meadow', was earlier Mons Silvius (from the Latin *silva*), 'wood, forest', whilst the French and Italian forms are from *cervin/cervino*, 'deer': local people meanwhile used the names *Horu* (from *Horn*, 'sharp peak') and *Gran Becca* (from *bec*, 'peak') for the mountain (<Swissworld. org> n.d.). In Drummond (2009), I compared Scottish borders hill names recorded on seventeenth- and eighteenth-century maps with today's, noting that *c.*40 per cent of them had changed, either in the specific (e.g. *Great Law* to Drummelzier Law), or the generic (e.g. *Cairn Edge* to West Cairn Hill), or both (e.g. *Cala Cairn* to Wether

---

[3] First recorded in 1804, 1642, and 1536, respectively.

Law); this in addition to some significant summits becoming lost names (e.g. *Three Lairds Cairn*). Clearly, a factor in generic change will be the local toponymicon, and any changes in it: for instance, the term *edge* seemed to go 'out of fashion' in the nineteenth century in Scotland. Similarly, in the Irish Mourne Mountains, the name *Benn mBoirchi* was replaced by *Sliabh Dónairt*, probably on account of the generic *sliabh* being common in that area (Tempan 2004).

There are several reasons for this plurality and changeability of names. The simple fact of having people living on the several sides of a mountain, in valleys very poorly connected to each other, means it may have a different name on either side, in different languages or dialects, or from a different perception of its qualities from another angle. These alternatives may co-exist for centuries, until the advent of systematic cartographic surveys, whose surveyors select which name to put 'on the map'. Thus in the Scottish border hills, a significant hill on the watershed between the rivers Esk (to the south) and Ettrick (to the north), was known as the *Penn of Es[k]dale Moore* on the south (Blaeu 1654: Eskdale map), and the *Penn of Ettrick* on the north (Blaeu 1654: Tweeddale map): the 1860s Ordnance Survey cartographers chose Ettrick Pen, the name that still applies. In other areas the arrival of new political masters with a new language meant many toponyms were freshly-coined, especially in North America where many indigenous names were lost. Thus Mount Washington, highest peak of north-east USA, known to the various indigenous peoples living in the environs as *Kodaak Wadjo*, 'summit of the highest mountain', but also as *Waumbik*, 'white rocks' and as *Agiochook*, possibly 'place of the great spirit'. In 1628 English mariner Leavett named it *Christall Hill*, and later English governor Winthrop designated it both *White Hill* and *Sugarloaf* (the then-ubiquitous term for a peak of a certain shape). However, in 1792, the report of a 1784 scientific expedition to the mountain named it Mount Washington, in honour of the then US President. The name took some time to establish itself—two decades later on an expedition led by Joseph Bigelow called it *Mount Sugarloaf*, but also recognized *Mount Agiochook*—but subsequently it led to neighbouring peaks, in what is now called the Presidential Range, being named after Presidents Adams, Jefferson, Madison, Monroe, and Eisenhower (Julyan and Julyan 1993: 125, 159–60). Further, the economic marginality of montane terrain to settled society meant that it was not important enough to record in the early documents of land transfers or rents, unlike productive farmland and habitations, thus making it comparatively easy for an old name to be lost, especially as the area would be thinly inhabited. Finally, the very topography of a mountain or a massif can make precision in locating a name difficult: does a local oronym refer to the main or subsidiary summit, or to a shoulder that may dominate the valley? Ben Arthur in the Scottish Highlands (recorded as *Suy [suidhe] Arthire*, 'Arthur's seat', in Pont's 1590s map) is now widely known as The Cobbler, from the name (translated from Gaelic *An Greasaiche Crom*, 'the crooked shoe-maker') applying to the central of its three main peaks. In France, Mont Maudit was probably used as the name for the massif although it now only refers to a northern shoulder of Mont Blanc, dominating the view from Chamonix below.

8.1 ORONYMIC GENERICS

Oronyms may be studied from the perspective of their generics (i.e. the element indicating that it is a hill, mountain, etc.), or their specifics (i.e. the descriptive element distinguishing it from other instances). In an early example of a study of the former, the eighteenth-century Scottish map-maker Mostyn Armstrong commented on the oronymic generics (not that he used that term) on his Peeblesshire map in the Scottish borders, thus:

> These piles of stones are often termed Cairn, Pike, Currough, Cross etc, and Hills are as variously named, according to their magnitude; as Law, Pen, Kipp, Coom, Dod, Craig, Fell, Top, Drum, Tor, Watch, Rig, Edge, Know, Knock, Mount, Kaim, Bank, Hope-head, Cleugh-head, Gare, Scarr, Height, Shank, Brae, Kneis, Muir, Green etc. (Armstrong 1775)

Many of these elements are found throughout the Scottish border hills, and also in northern England. Armstrong did not attempt to analyse his collection of terms, and indeed was imprecise in attributing the variety 'according to magnitude', because a generic may refer to aspects such as shape; for instance, *kip(p)* in a hill name signifies a pointed top (or a jutting-out feature on a slope), whilst *dod(d)* represents a lumpy hill. The 'choice' of generic used will also reflect the locally-available toponymicon, itself representing past linguistic layers: for instance, whilst *fell* and *law* usually tend to describe substantial hills in southern Scotland,[4] the former is found south-west of the main Borders watershed, the former to the north-east, with almost complete mutual exclusivity. Such a geographically-circumscribed toponymicon reflects the prevalence of the two terms in their neighbouring southern 'source regions', *fell* from Cumbria—of Scandinavian origin in *fell or fjall*—and *law* from north-east England—of Old English origin in *hlāw*.

Six of the Scots elements noted by Armstrong in 1775, i.e. *craig, dod, fell, knowe, law, rig*, were first systematically investigated by Matley (1990), with distribution maps plotted for northern England and southern Scotland, and a discussion of their etymologies. Earlier, for Scotland as a whole, a selection of Gaelic oronymic generics was investigated by Nicolaisen (1969), i.e. *beinn, cnoc, druim, maol, meall, sliabh*, and *tòrr*. He noted: 'Of the seven [elements] chosen not one has the same distribution as any other...' (although three occur throughout the area where Gaelic was once spoken). He says further research is necessary to determine 'whether these differences in distribution... were of a purely dialectal nature, [or] were determined by non-linguistic factors such as the differing shapes of hills in different parts of Scotland, or might be attributable to different historical stages in the expansion of Gaelic [in Scotland]'. His conclusions might apply

---

[4] In Drummond (2007b) I analysed a sample of large hills bearing the generics *fell* and *law*, and concluded that there was 'no apparent topographical distinctions between the two'.

to the distribution pattern of oronymic elements in many languages and countries, not just Scotland.

Matley (1990) as noted, examined the distribution of some six oronymic elements occurring in northern England as well as Scotland, only three of which (*dod*, *hlāw*, and *hrycg*—the latter two respectively modern *law* and *rig/ridge*) receive any discussion in *English Place-name Elements* (Smith 1956b), although it does have substantial material on *dūn*, 'hill', the root of the English oronym *down* 'hill, or expanse of open country', as in the South Downs. Gelling and Cole (2000) have a chapter on elements for 'hills, slopes and ridges', but since the book's central theme is explanation of settlement names containing such elements, they tend to refer to lower hills, on which settlements stand.

Whaley's *Dictionary of Lake District Place-Names* (2006) includes a 'List of Common Elements' of its toponyms, and there is considerable analysis not only of *crag*, *dod(d)*, and *fell*, but also of other oronymic generics characteristic of the area, including *barrow*, *bell*, *edge*, *how*, and *knott*. Owen and Morgan's *Dictionary of the Place-Names of Wales* (2007) contains some entries listing Welsh hills, with their dated early records, and an interpretation of the individual name, but has a limited glossary, briefly treating elements such as *bryn* 'hill' and *mynydd* 'mountain; hill; common, unenclosed land, mountain land, moorland' (and giving instances of the element in hill names, e.g. Bryn-gwyn), but without discussion of the element. Flanagan and Flanagan's *Irish Place Names* (1994) is laid out principally as a glossary of toponymic elements, each discussed in some detail: it includes Irish (Gaelic) oronyms such as *beann*, *cruach*, *meall*, and *sliabh*, and gives instances of each. Tempan (2004) explores in more detail five Gaelic oronyms in Ireland, that is: *binn*, *cnoc*, *cruach*, *mullach*, and *sliabh*. He concludes: 'The patterns which do bear closer scrutiny [unlike any link between height and generic] are related more to location and to characteristics such as shape and ruggedness.' *Sliabh*—the oldest attested generic—is, he finds, in the north a substantial mountain, often isolated, while in the south it is often a range, whilst all across the country it refers to an area of mountain moor or pasture. *Binn* is a rugged mountain, often with significant peaks, while *cruach* is a triangular or sometimes pointed shape seen from some directions. Although many Scottish Gaelic oronyms are formally identical to Irish Gaelic (e.g. *beinn*, *meall*), in some cases they differ in meaning: *carn* in Ireland is a cairn of stones, usually marking a burial, while in Scotland *càrn* usually refers to a high mountain—of conical appearance in the west, but of rounded skyline in the eastern Highlands. Some important Scottish Gaelic words do not come from Irish Gaelic at all: *sgùrr*, always indicating a rocky peak, appears to be a loan-word from Old Norse (Drummond 2007a: 54), whereas *monadh* is a loan-word from Brittonic *mynydd*. *Monadh* is discussed in detail in Watson (1926: 391–407), using the term a 'survival' from 'British'. Apart from *monadh*, Watson discusses very few other oronyms (or indeed any topographical elements) in any detail,[5] his *magnum opus* being laid out in a way that analyses individual place-names as it

[5] The distribution of elements *bàrr* and *tulach* are discussed on page 184, and elsewhere there is a passing reference to the etymology of *aonach*, *beinn*, *carn*, *sliabh*, and *suidhe*.

comes to them. Scottish oronyms, both Gaelic and Scots, are pulled together in glossary fashion in Drummond (2007a: 16–63), where over seventy Gaelic and nearly forty Scots oronyms are listed and discussed as regards their etymology, distribution, and meaning.

Julyan (1984) is a selective dictionary of mountain names from all round the world, but naturally (given its provenance) has entries for many[6] individual North American peaks (e.g. Mount Rainier) and ranges (e.g. Tetons). However, being a 'global picture', there is no attempt at a glossary of North American oronymic elements, a task that was perhaps hinted at in Stewart (1945), whose work traces the historical development of place-naming in the USA, tracing the onomastic operation of its many languages (both indigenous and European). He does deal with some individual names, like the appellation Blue Ridge, linked to the eighteenth-century explorer Colonel William Byrd, who saw them as blue from a considerable distance—as indeed distant hills are anywhere. But he also touched on how, since the English had no word 'for a mountain that stands up sharply by itself' (Stewart 1945: 132), they began to use the term *knob*; whilst the terms *mesa*, 'flat-topped hill', and *butte* 'a sharp hill rising from a plain', were borrowed into English from, respectively, the Spaniards and French who occupied much of the continent before the English. Stewart also observed that in consequence of the ubiquitous American cultural referencing of the Christian Bible, there are a plethora of peaks named after those in the good book, such as Mounts Pisgah, Carmel, Hermon, and Gilead, all occurring in many States. Stewart (1945: 133) also noted: 'From Biblical usage also sprang perhaps another strange custom, that Mount should precede and Mountain should follow. Thus they said Mount Tom, and Black Mountain.' This might seem to account for the number of substantial US peaks in whose name the generic *mount* precedes the specific (e.g. Mount Adams, Mount Washington, and Mount Whitney), contrary to normal English word order in which the specific precedes the generic. However, the form *Mount X* is also widespread in Canada, Australia, and New Zealand, areas heavily colonized and named by migrants from the UK: *mount*, and indeed *mountain*, are rarely used in hill names in the UK (there are Black Mount and Black Mountain), although it does occur more often in Ireland (e.g. Brandon Mountain). Conceivably, the name-coining practice in these UK colonies was influenced by the oronymic forms of the Romance languages, especially France and Spain (both with huge territories in North America), in which *mont* or *monte* is the first element, in names like Mont Blanc or Monte Perdido.

Studies of continental European oronymic elements include the work of Zinsli (1945), who researched oronyms in the German-speaking areas of Switzerland. His *Grund und Grat* (1945, essentially 'Valley and Ridge'), is sub-titled *Die Bergwelt im Spiegel der Schweizerdeutscher Alpenmundarten*, which translates as 'the mountain world in the alpine dialects of Swiss German'. He examines generic elements that are found throughout the area, such as *Horn* (also *Hoore(n)*), literally 'horn', that was so widely used to indicate a peak that it was sometimes dropped from toponyms because it was

---

[6] *c*.95 in USA, *c*.10 in Canada.

understood: the Jungfrau, for instance, was earlier known as *Jungfrau-horn*. Originally, noted Zinsli, *Horn* referred precisely to a 'sharp towering pyramid in the mountain landscape, curving up like the horn of an animal'.[7] It came not simply to refer to a 'rocky tower' or a 'single towering summit' but also to an 'imposing mountain massif'. He also recorded terms that were limited in their area of use, such as *Graffel*, found only in the Bernese Oberland for a rocky summit, from its root meaning of a sharp tool. In Wallis canton, a rock resembling a human is a *Stein-hirte*, literally 'stone herd', whereas in other cantons it tends to be known as *Stein-mannli*, literally 'little stone man'. Huge rock pillars in Unterwalden canton are *Stolle(n)*, whereas in the Berner Oberland they are *Guetsch(en)*. In inner Switzerland a smaller peak is often a *Nosse*, whereas a bigger peak, or one on a projecting ridge, is a *Schnarz*: however, in the Riggisberg area, this latter can mean a more rounded hill. Zinsli's book contains a glossary (1945: 310–41) listing the elements covered in his discussion.

A methodology similar to Zinsli's underlies much work on oronyms in the French-speaking area of the Alps. Bessat and Germi (2001) focus on six elements of '*relief sommital*' [summit topography], viz. *bric, forclaz, frette, pelvoux, serre*, and *truc*. They examine the use of these elements both in the local lexicon (including the variant spellings—for example for *serre*, the variants *sarre, sarret*, and *chèr/char* are found) and in the toponymicon (i.e. in oronyms). *Serre* 'elongated summit, crest, hill' (related to Spanish *sierra*) is found as an oronym throughout the French alpine area, whilst by contrast other elements are in concentrated clusters, as *forclaz* is in the Alpes du Nord, and *bric* is in the Alpes du Sud. For *pelvoux*, the authors note that they chose this form rather than one of its other variants (e.g. *pelve, peuve*) because of the renown of Mont Pelvoux, one of the highest summits of the Écrins massif in the Dauphiné; they record sixteen attestations of the oronym in the French Alps, half in the Hautes-Alpes department.

8.2 ORONYMIC SPECIFICS

The specifics of oronyms often relate to their colour, size, shape, or other aspect of appearance. Among colour references, one of the commonest is white, usually relating to ice or snow—as in Mont Blanc, Weisshorn, or Dhaulagiri—although it can also relate to local rock (as in Sgùrr Bàn and Stob Bàn in the Scottish Highlands, which are composed of quartzite), or to comparatively pale vegetation (as in Scottish Gaelic's many instances of Geal Chàrn, or the ubiquitous White Hills): black and red are also common as hues. Julyan (1984: 6–8) has a discussion of global 'white' oronyms; Drummond (2007a: 144–5) has a discussion of the several Scottish Gaelic words for 'white' in oronyms, and several sections devoted to an analysis of other Gaelic and Scots/English colours in hill names.

---

[7] The Gaelic *beinn* 'mountain', derives from an earlier Gaelic *benn*, which had the same meaning of 'animal horn'.

Some significant peaks, and their specifics, have understandably been explored in depth in mountaineering literature. Several of the world's best-known high peaks carry associative European personal names, reflecting the history of European colonialism. The world's highest and best-known mountain is in the Himalaya, and is widely known as Mount Everest, a name given by British surveyors. The peak was 'discovered' by Europeans (in the sense that America was 'discovered' by Columbus) in the mid-nineteenth century, specifically by British India's Great Trigonometric Survey. The highest peak recognized, it was classed initially as Peak XV.[8] In 1856 the Surveyor-General Andrew Waugh proposed naming it Mont Everest, after his 'illustrious predecessor' Sir George Everest;[9] 'Mount' replaced 'Mont' in 1857. Waugh claimed that the Survey had tried but failed to find a reliable local name for the peak. Imposing a European's personal name on an Asian mountain might not have troubled many eminent Victorians (although Everest himself objected on the grounds that one should always use a local name if possible), but there was an immediate challenge from Hodgson, a British resident of Darjeeling, who claimed the Nepalese name was Devadhunga ('God's Seat') or Bhairathan. A committee was set up to investigate this, but concluded that the former was applied to many places, not just to this one peak, and that the latter had little factual basis. Chomolungma (various spellings, 'Goddess Mother of the Earth') is the long-standing local Tibetan name, although Tibet was not readily accessible to the British in the 1850s. Its onomastic claim is supported by French cartographer Jean Baptiste D'Anville, who based his 1733 map 'Tibet ou Bou-tan' [Tibet or Bhutan] on reports from French missionaries in China: he records *Tchoumour lancma M[ont]*, an apparent phonetic representation of Chomolungma. The name was used in the inter-titles of the official film of the British 1924 expedition to the mountain, a *de facto* acceptance of its claim: but since the first ascent in 1953, the sheer volume of news stories concerning the peak have forefronted the Everest form of the name, imperialistic in origin though it may be.

The Asian continent is not alone in having a name of its highest peak given by Westerners: Antarctica (where there never were indigenous peoples) is dominated by Vinson Massif, named after an American senator; Australasia's highest peak is Mount Wilhelm in the Bismarck Range of Papua New Guinea, formerly a German colony (although it does have a local name Enduwa Kombuglu), while Australia's highest is Mount Kosciuszko, named by a Polish-born explorer in honour of a Polish expatriate hero of the American Civil War. North America's highest mountain in Alaska certainly had a native Koyukon Athabaskan name, *Dinale* or *Denali*, meaning 'high one' or 'great one': however, the name Mount McKinley, given by an Alaskan prospector in the 1890s in honour of a US senator, became common currency when he became US President (and particularly after his assassination in 1901). Late twentieth-century attempts to

---

[8] In fact, first identifications classed it as 'b' (1849), then 'h' (1849), until Waugh decided to re-label all high peaks counting from east to west.

[9] Everest is a contracted form of the English surname *Deveraux*, itself from Norman French *de Ebrois* (1086). See Reaney (1997).

revert the name to Denali were approved by Alaska's state government, but blocked nationally by Congressmen from McKinley's home state of Ohio (Julyan 1984: 136–7).

New Zealand's highest peak, reckoned by some mountaineers to be harder than Everest, has a Māori name *Aorangi* ('white cloud'), but is widely known as Mount Cook, after the British explorer. In Australia, that stunning desert monolith known to Aborigines as Uluru, was named Ayers Rock by the 1873 explorer William Gosse, after the then Chief Secretary of South Australia. In both New Zealand and Australia, dual-naming policies now put the indigenous name first, for example Uluru/Ayers Rock. In Australia's state of Victoria lies Mount Niggerhead, whose name unsurprisingly became the subject of controversy in the late twentieth century: more surprisingly, however, opposition to changing it to an 'indigenous' name came not only from white people who felt the name to be 'of historical significance', but also from indigenous groups who could not reach a consensus on an appropriate Aboriginal name (Kostanski and Clark 2009: 199–200).

The application of personal names to summits was not confined to the remits of colonial powers, as the widespread American practice of naming peaks after Presidents, or other members of the great and the good, shows. And not just the great and good, but also little people: in the USA's White Mountains, for instance, Butters Mountain is from a family who cleared the land here, while Carlo Mountain was after the local inn's dog, companion to a well-known hiker (Julyan and Julyan 1993). The growth of mountaineering led to the application of mountaineers' names, partly because the peaks they climbed were often at that point nameless, being beyond the toponymic world of the nearest farmers: not for nothing was French climber Lionel Terray's autobiography called *Conquistadors of the Useless*. In the Swiss Alps, the names of guides—contained for instance, in Ulrichspitze and Punta Carrel—and of their climbers—for instance in Gertrudspitze and Pic Tyndall—were coined in the nineteenth century, the Golden Age of Alpinism. Perhaps surprisingly, the highest peak in Switzerland was also given a personal name, not from a mountaineer but a nineteenth-century military man and cartographer: this peak, on the Monte Rosa massif, was known as the *Hochste Spitze* ('highest peak'), but was named Dufourspitze in 1863 in honour of Guillaume-Henri Dufour, who led the first Swiss national geographic survey—in that respect, he was a forerunner of Everest. In Scotland's Cuillin range on Skye, several of the rocky spires had apparently no earlier Gaelic name when they were first scaled in the late nineteenth century: thus Sgùrr Alasdair, highest in the range, was named after Sheriff Alexander Nicolson,[10] its first recorded climber (1873), and Sgùrr Mhic Choinnich after the Cuillin guide, John MacKenzie.

Although the use of personal names in oronyms is essentially a late development, pre-industrial peoples did not eschew the practice completely. Scotland's second-highest summit, Ben MacDhui, is named after its historic landowner MacDuff (Drummond 2007a: 117–18), while Wales' Cadair Idris, 'fort of Idris', is said in legend to be after a lost

---

[10] Local guide John MacKenzie said it was earlier locally *Sgùrr Bhiorach*, 'pointed peak'.

(and unidentified) prince or giant (Owen and Morgan 2007: 61). Some mountains are even given nicknames: Provence's Mont Ventoux is 'le petit-fils' (the grandson), while the Pyrenees' Pic du Midi d'Ossau is locally 'Jean-Pierre'.

Lastly, some studies focus not on the generics or the specifics in mountain names, but on area studies, often in dictionary layout, where the focus is on explaining the meaning of individual oronyms in conjunction with individual settlement names or river names. In this category are the Julyans' 1993 *Place Names of the White Mountains* (the range in Vermont, USA), Whaley's 2006 *A Dictionary of Lake District Place-Names* (the English region), and Baldwin and Drummond's 2011 *Pentland Place-Names* (the Pentland hills near Edinburgh).

CHAPTER 9

··

ISLAND NAMES

··

PEDER GAMMELTOFT

No man is an island, as John Donne put it in 1624, but he is most definitely living on one. All landmasses on Earth are, when all comes to all, surrounded by water. However, we do not consider all land to be islands—the biggest are normally referred to as *continents*. In this chapter, all landmasses are considered to be islands by definition. Thus, island names are here defined as names used of archipelagos, island states, islands, islets, atolls, skerries, and rocky outcrops—basically anything with (permanent or tidal) water around them, etc. Even the names of the continents will be used to highlight various aspects of island names and naming of islands.

Mankind has always been fascinated by islands. They appeal to our inquisitive nature, offering us something to explore, albeit just outside of reach—at least not without us transcending the water in between. We have probably all felt the lure of that narrow stretch of land just visible in the distance, wishing to go and take a look and see what may be found there. At the same time, islands offer solitude and an escape from the helter-skelter of our everyday worlds. Sometimes, however, this solitude may be transformed into a prison—not allowing us to return to our daily lives. This is also a strong theme in mankind's encounter with islands, detracting from islands as livable places.

When the lake of Filsø, DNK,[1] was drained in order to make room for farming land in the late nineteenth century, new islands appeared in the ever-diminishing lake. Two of these were named *Sankt Helene* and *Djævleøen*, Danish name forms of the penal colonies *Saint Helena*, SHN, and *île du Diable*, GUF.[2] The exact reason for these names are now lost but it is imaginable it was the barren and uninhabitable appearance of these newly emerged places that stimulated the connection with these feared island prisons that had become so infamous in the preceding decades.

---

[1] The country codes used in this chapter are the so-called *ISO 3166-1 alpha-3* codes, a system of three-letter country codes as defined in the ISO 3166-1 standard published by the International Organization for Standardization (ISO). See List of Abbreviations.

[2] The location of *Sankt Helena* and *Djævleøen* are known from maps and place-name registries but nowadays they are no longer remembered, owing to the fact that they are no longer islands. Djævleøen is today a barely recognizable elevation in a field, whereas Sankt Helena has recently become a recognized Stone Age archaeological site known locally as *Gammeltoft Pold*, or *Gammeltoft Odde* on official maps.

9.1 Why Are Island Names Worth Studying?

Islands have a tendency to be the first to be named by the first people to settle, or just set eyes on, them. This means that islands are usually among the first localities to be named, in both monolingual, multilingual, and language change areas. Thus, island names provide valuable evidence not only of language historical developments, they also allow us to get a glimpse of earlier migration patterns, the mental history of our naming ancestors, and later in history how far-flung islands became entangled in the geopolitical power struggles of colonial nations hungry for new territories to rule and administer. We shall see examples of these research areas in this chapter.[3]

9.2 Island Names and their Importance to Language History

Since island names tend to belong to the earliest language strata, old linguistic traits can be observed with a fair number of island names. By combining language history with historically known migrations, it is possible to indicate at which times certain linguistic traits were in force and when certain linguistic changes must have taken place.

A couple of examples of this can be explored in relation to the island names of Scandinavian origin in the British Isles. These names are the result of a large-scale migration from Scandinavia to the British Isles, probably mainly during the ninth–tenth centuries. The island names in the Northern Isles—Orkney and Shetland, GBR, are usually either compound formations such as: *Foula* 'Bird Island' from Old Norse *fugl* 'bird' and Old Norse *ey* 'island' and *Vementrie*, 'Island belonging to Vémundr', from the Old Norse male personal name *Vémundr* + Old Norse *ey*; or they are uncompounded comparative names such as: *Wyre*, from Old Norse *vígr* 'spear', owing to its tapering, spearhead like shape (Gammeltoft 2005: 258–9). A couple of instances of reversed generic–specific word order are also known, always in the form *Eyin Helga* 'The holy isle', now *Eynhallow* but also known as a Viking Age and Medieval Scandinavian name for *Iona*.[4]

---

[3] Many of the examples given in this chapter are also applicable to all other types of place-names, as island names do not differ principally in type, origin, history, or usage from other place-name types.

[4] This trait seems to have been in lively use in the Northern Isles, and several examples exist today, e.g. in the Shetland sea stack name *Stackingroo*, GBR, from the definite form of Old Norse *stakkr* 'a sea rock, stack' + *grá* 'grey'.

By surveying the island name types of the Viking Age colonies, we can establish a typology for Scandinavian island name formations in the ninth–tenth centuries. When turning back to Scandinavia, we of course encounter the same name types, as seen in the examples *Håøya* 'High island', NOR (Gammeltoft 2005: 257), and *Saltholm* 'Salty islet', DNK (Jørgensen 2008: 244). And there are also historical examples of reversed word order in the current *Helgøya* of Lake Mjøsa, NOR, which is also attested as *Eyin Helga*. [5]

It is, however, striking that a substantial number of Scandinavian island names are of a different type altogether from those in the Viking Age colonies, namely suffixed place-names with a varied and diverse stock of derivations, ranging from *k*-derivation in **Stork* (now *Sturkö*), SWE, possibly 'The large [one]' (SOL: 300),[6] over *ia*-derivations, as in **Eria* (now *Ærø*), DNK, possibly 'The curvy [one]' (Jørgensen 2008: 344), to *s*-derivations, as in **Samps* (now Samsø), DNK, conceivably 'The joined [one]' (Jørgensen 2008: 244), and the commonly occurring *und*-derived *Borgund* (now *Borgann* and *Borgundøya*), NOR, 'The large [one]', **Jalund* (now *Jeløya*), NOR, perhaps 'The howling [one]' (NSL: 101, 243). These names belong to an earlier stratum of island names (NSL: 46–9), and owing to the complete lack of this name-type, it is possible to say that derived island names comfortably predate the ninth century. On the other hand, the instances of reversed word order can be seen in, for example, *Eyin Helga*, now where the generic + specific word order seen in historical sources is a typical trait of early Scandinavian. However, its existence in the Viking Age colonies testifies to it being a longer-lived trait than derivation formations.

At the same time, there are also differing traits between island names in the Viking Age colonies and the Scandinavian homeland. There is a greater tendency to 'update' the island names to newly emerged naming structures in Scandinavia, not least the reversion of the post-positioned adjective in Eyin Helga to present Helgøya, NOR, whose exact parallel is to be found in the Orcadian *Eynhallow*, GBR (NSL: 206). This seemingly did not occur in the Viking Age colonies, thus probably retaining a more conservative form of Norse—as is visible in Iceland today.

9.3 ISLAND NAMES
AND MIGRATION PATTERNS

By testing the language origin of island name formations, a picture may be gained of the spread of peoples and their languages throughout the world. By adding language

---

[5] Post-positioned adjective (noun + adjective) was the standard in Common Scandinavian and is observable until the twelfth century. From the Viking Age and onwards, today's word order in Scandinavian, adjective + noun, becomes increasingly common.

[6] The *Sturkö* article is somewhat unclear and is not explicitly stating that this is an original *k*-derivation. However, this must be the case, as there is no other way in which the current -*k*- should occur in the name.

historical evidence to the equation, however, it is possible to say when certain languages spread to where. If we return briefly to the islands discussed above, the presence of island names of Scandinavian origin in the Scottish Isles proves that there was a Scandinavian presence in those archipelagos at some time. The time of Scandinavian presence there can be judged by examining the structure of the name formations and their content. So, if we look at two Hebridean examples: *Miughalaigh/Mingulay*, GBR, and *Eirisgeigh/Eriskay*, GBR, and look beneath their present Gaelic and Anglicised 'varnish', we see that they are compound formations of which the second element is Old Norse *ey* 'island'. The first element of the former name is Old Norse *mikill* 'large, great'; whereas the specific of the latter contains the genitive singular form of an Old Norse personal name *Eirikr*. From this, it is clear that the word order is *specific + generic*. This proves that these names are definitely of non-Gaelic origin, since Gaelic word order normally dictates native Gaelic place-names to have a *generic + specific* word order. The fact that *Miughalaigh* and *Eirisgeigh* are compound formations puts them firmly within the later layer of Scandinavian island names. However, the occurrence of the pre-Christian Old Norse personal name, *Eirikr*, is evidence of a formation most probably not later than the conversion of Scandinavians to Christianity. In Scandinavia, the conversion occurred from *c.*1000 AD and later, although it is thought that the conversion took place rather earlier in the Viking Age colonies. Thus, by looking at a couple of island names, we can state (with a fair degree of certainty) that Scandinavians had migrated to the Scottish Isles in the last centuries of the first millennium.

Migration patterns can naturally be followed throughout the world and over much greater distances. If we make a long, long leap to the other side of our planet to the Pacific Ocean, we reach the home of countless far-flung islands. Owing to the great distance of the islands in the Pacific, the languages there are very numerous but are usually divided into Melanesian, Micronesian, and Polynesian languages, all belonging to the so-called Austronesian language family. The common Polynesian word *motu* 'island' is a good example of how migrations can be traced. Being mostly confined to the Polynesian languages today, a mapping of all names containing this element (grey dots on Fig. 9.1) shows that the name element is also found particularly in the Melanesian language area and to some extent in the Micronesian one as well. High concentrations are found in New Zealand (especially the northern parts), French Polynesia, and in Fiji. Being part of the Melanesian language area, Fiji may have its concentration of names in *Motu-* as a result of Tongan influence from the tenth century onwards, but since the element is virtually unknown (Geraghty 2005b)—certainly as an independent noun—it is altogether more likely that *motu* was indigenous to Fiji, which saw its first Melanesian settlement *c.*2,500–2,000 BC.

If this is the case, then the distribution of names containing *motu* can be seen to visualize the spread of the Austronesian languages in the Pacific over three to five millennia from, probably, the Maritime South East Asia via Melanesia into the Pacific with its furthest outlyers, Easter Island and New Zealand colonized after the tenth–thirteenth centuries. This articulates well with archaeological and genetic evidence suggesting that the spread of the Austronesian culture and peoples took place in a semi-circular

FIGURE 9.1 Map showing the distribution of island names containing Polynesian *motu* 'island'

eastward move from Maritime South East Asia into the Pacific (Pawley 2002: 251–73; see also Anonymous 2008). The most compelling piece of onomastic evidence we have for an eastward migration into the Pacific, however, lies in the name of *Fiji*, FJI,[7] and one of its isles. One of the most westerly islands in the archipelago is called *Naviti*, FJI, which literally means 'the east' or 'the sunrise' (Geraghty 2005a). Such a name would not make sense if it had not been named from further west of the isles, such as the Solomon Islands, SLB, or Vanuatu, VUT (Geraghty 2005a: 7). The current name *Fiji*, or *Viti*, locally thus ultimately derives from the same name, being possibly an abbreviation of **Navitilevu* 'Large Naviti'.

The important thing to note here is that only place-names can say something about what language a migrating people spoke. Therefore, with careful attention to place-names, their origins, and language historical developments, it is possible to

[7] The name Fiji is actually not an original local name for this archipelago but rather of Tongan origin. The establishment of a Tongan name form for these islands is owing to Captain James Cook, who learnt of the existence of Fiji through his extended stay in Tonga in the 1770s. The current form of the name, Fiji [feːjeː], reflects the Tongan pronunciation of the time. Today, Tongans call Fiji for *Fisi*. The local Fijian name, on the other hand, is *Viti*, from which the Tongan name form also originates (see Geraghty 2005a: 6).

quantify evidence from other scientific disciplines and create a more rounded picture of (pre)historical events.

9.4 Island Names and Geopolitics

A more sinister side to migration is also visible in many island names throughout the world—and in particular in the Indian and Pacific Ocean areas—namely Western European expansionism and colonialism. With the rise of the great competing seafaring nations, Portugal, the Netherlands, Great Britain, and France, and to a lesser extent nations such as Imperial Russia and Denmark, a quest for new lands which could bring new fortunes and exotic commodities back to Europe spurred a series of explorations into unknown parts of the world which usually ended up with territorial claims to far-flung lands. One very effective way for an explorer to claim a territory for his own country or ruler was achieved by naming a place in his own language—and usually commemorating an aspect of the explorer's cultural and social background.

In this battle for new lands, islands were often given names with potent cultural and national associations, owing to their strategic importance not only as potential sources of income and goods but also as bridgeheads for further explorations and land claiming. Thus, very large or strategically important islands often have several names. For instance, *Australia*, AUS, has been known under a great number of names, such as: *Terra Australis (Incognita)* (Unknown South Land), *Nova Hollandia* (New Holland), *New South Wales, Notasia,* and *Ulimaroa.* The first of these names are instances of what may be called an 'exploration name' and whether it is to be considered to be a place-name or merely a descriptive label is arguable. In the seventeenth century, however, with the increase of Dutch activities in the Indian Ocean, the name *Nova Hollandia* was bestowed on the sparsely chartered continent by the famous Dutch seafarer Abel Tasman (Forsyth 1967). His choice of name can hardly have been coincidental, as it is an effective and simple way of stating the Netherlands' alleged right to this new, vast continent by naming it after one of the provinces of the Netherlands. As the British grew hungry for new colonies, Captain Cook undertook a journey into what had hitherto been a Dutch sea domain and claimed the eastern parts of Australia in 1770 in the name of *New South Wales* (Anonymous 1966), again making use of the same naming principles as Abel Tasman—naming after a region in the country under which it is claimed. Western Australia, however, retained the name Nova Hollandia/New Holland (until 1833). Noting the potential problems in having two names for the Australian continent, Matthew Flinders, the first person to circumnavigate Australia, proposed the name Australia as an umbrella term for the territories of New Holland and New South Wales, and this eventually became the name under which we know Australia today. The two remaining names, Notasia and Ulimaroa, are best termed cartographic curiosities. *Notasia* appeared on a number of maps and in some literary works in the first quarter of the nineteenth century (Tent 2010). The origin of *Notasia* is not entirely certain but is thought to derive from Greek *notos* + *asia*, that is, 'South Asia' (Tent 2010). The name of Ulimaroa for Australia, on the other hand, has its unlikely origin in Sweden, having been used by Daniel Djurberg in his geography from 1776 (Djurberg 1776), and subsequently on a map from 1780 (Djurberg and Åkerman 1780). The name gained a certain amount of currency in other Swedish, German, Czech, and Austrian maps over the next forty years (Geraghty and Tent 2010; Du Rietz 1961: 84), but derives from some of the conversations between Captain James Cook and the Polynesian priest, chief, and navigator of Ra'iatea in 1769–70, where it is described as 'a country of great extent, called *Ulimaroa*, to which some people had sailed in a very large canoe' (Hawkesworth 1773). The name appears to go back to Māori **Rimaroa* and is seems to mean something like 'Long arm' (Tent and Geraghty 2012: 15), presumably describing the shape of the island.[8]

Not only did a continent like Australia have many names bestowed to it, as a result of the rival aspirations of seafaring nations and cartographers' misconceptions, but also smaller entities like the above-mentioned *Fiji*, FJI, had before James Cook's usage of the Tongan name form for the isles, been called as varied names as *Prins Wyllem's Eylanden* (Abel Tasman) and *Bligh's Islands, Sandalwood Islands*, and *Cannibal Islands* (Geraghty 2005a: 7). None of these names was in use very long. However, more often than not, island peoples saw their traditional names vanish into oblivion when their islands were 'discovered' and subsequently named by Western European explorers and colonizers. Thus, an island group like *Tokelau*, TKL, was renamed *Union Islands* by European explorers during the nineteenth century and retained this name until 1946 when the islands were called *Tokelau Island*, and subsequently shortened to *Tokelau* in 1976. Tokelau consists of three coral atolls, *Atafu, Nukunonu*, and *Fakaofo*, TKL. When Atafu was discovered in 1765, it was given the name *Duke of York's Island*, and when Nukunonu was first visited by Europeans it was given the name *Duke of Clarence's Island*. Fakaofo long stayed off the radar of Western explorers, but when it was finally discovered, it was given the name *D'Wolf's Island*, thus effectively alienating its inhabitants from their own islands by exchanging their traditional names for colonial ones. The same was the case with *New Zealand*, NEZ, which is called *Aotearoa* by its indigenous Māori populations. In the twentieth century, however, most of the island names reflecting exploratory and colonial efforts of the seventeenth–nineteenth centuries have now been renamed, such as the abovementioned *Tokelau*, TKL or given double name forms, as in the case of New Zealand, NEZ, which is also officially known under both its Māori and English names: *Aotearoa* and *New Zealand*. In other cases, a great variety of names have been retained, both European and indigenous, as in the case of *Penrhyn*, COK, the largest and most remote atoll in Kūki 'Āirani/Cook Islands, which is also known as: *Tongareva, Mangarongaro, Hararanga*, and *Te Pitaka*.[9]

---

[8] The place *Ulimaroa* is thought to refer to is no longer believed to be Australia but rather *New Caledonia*, NCL, or *Kadavu* and *Vitilevu*, FJI (Tent and Geraghty 2012: 10).

[9] The name *Penrhyn* derives from the ship *Lady Penrhyn* who landed on the island in 1788, a ship noted for being one of the ships that founded the earliest convict colony in Australia. *Tongareva* seemingly means 'Tonga floating in space', 'Tonga-in-the-skies', or possibly 'A way from the South' (see Kloosterman 1976).

In a number of instances, however, the current indigenous or official name of Pacific islands and island nations are merely adaptations of Western European names, for example *Kūki ʻĀirani*, COK, for *Cook Islands*; *Kiribati*, KIR, for *Gilbert Islands*; *Kiritimati*, KIR, for *Christmas Island*. Some of these islands were uninhabited at the time of discovery, such as *Kiritimati*, which is the reason why the island name has not reverted back to its original name—there simply was not one. With *Kiribati* and *Kūki ʻĀirani*, where most of the islands within these nations had been settled at the time of European 'discoveries', the reasons for retaining an adapted form of a European name must be sought elsewhere. The most obvious reason is that no traditional collective name for these present-day island states ever existed.

9.5 ISLAND NAMES AND MENTALITY HISTORY

It is also possible to use island names to create a mentality history of naming. Early island names appear mainly descriptive, the earliest stratum, derived formations, seemingly only describe characteristics and not what the denotation is, as in the above *Borgund* and *Jalund*, NOR, meaning 'The hilly (one)' and 'The noisy (one)', respectively, without saying what is hilly or noisy. Later, stating the locality type becomes dominant and compounded and uncompounded names abound, for example as in the above *Eynhallow* and *Miughalaig*, GBR, clearly stating that they denote islands + what is special about them: religious significance and size. During this period comparative names are found, for example *Giltarump* and *Noss*, from Shetland, GBR, deriving from ON *gyltarumpa* 'hogs rump' and ON *noss* 'nose, nostril'. These naming possibilities live on until today.

With the Renaissance and the Enlightenment, a notable change is observable in many island names coined from then on. Where the focus of naming was previously on the feature itself, naming with the namer in focus becomes normal. This applies particularly to the so-called commemorative names, where naming focuses on people, places, or items special to the namer. Examples are *Cook Islands*, COK, or *Nepean Island* off Norfolk Island, AUS, named from Evan Nepean, the Undersecretary for the Home Office, shortly after the beginning of the First Settlement period on Norfolk (1788–1814). There is a difference between the two names in as much as the former, Cook Islands, is a truly commemorative name naming after a person of the past. The name first appeared on a Russian Naval chart, commemorating explorer James Cook, who discovered the islands. Incidentally, Cook himself called the islands *Hervey Islands*, after Augustus John Hervey (1724–79), later Third Earl of Bristol, a naval officer who became a Lord of the Admiralty. Hervey was a strong supporter and friend of James Cook (Erskine 1953: xxi). In bestowing a name like *Nepean Island* and, for that matter, *Hervey Islands*, the naming motive is commemorative in a different way—naming after a benefactor or a sponsor. This will also be the reason for a significant proportion of the numerous names of regents and their nearest families in colonial settings.

Another naming principle which evolves with the Enlightenment is naming according to events of significance to the namer, or naming circumstances such as celebrating discovery on a certain day or after having been saved from a storm. Well-known examples of the former are the instances of Christmas Island, KIR and AUS, and the well-known Easter Island, CHL. The Pacific *Christmas Island* was discovered by James Cook on 24 December 1777, whereas the Australian *Christmas Island*, situated in the Indian Ocean, was named by captain William Mynors, who encountered the island on Christmas Day 1643. This island was, however, also known by other names such as *Moni* and *Selam*, and the name form *Christmas Island* did not gain currency until well into the nineteenth century (Tent 2013). *Easter Island* was named by the island's first recorded European visitor, Jacob Roggeveen from the Netherlands, who encountered the island on Easter Sunday 1722. Roggeveen named it *Paasch-Eyland*, which has subsequently been translated as Easter Island and Isla de Pascua, the official Spanish name of the island (owing to it being part of Chile). The current Polynesian name of the island is *Rapa Nui*.

Names bestowed according to Renaissance and Enlightenment principles exist to a large extent even today, but with the steady decline of colonialism since World War II, more and more of these names have been replaced by indigenous name forms. In a large number of cases, the old island name exists concurrently with the new, indigenous name for the island, for example the abovementioned *Union Island*, TKL, which was renamed *Tokelau Island* in 1946 (and shortened to *Tokelau* in 1976)—either as officially sanctioned dual name forms, or as unsanctioned entities living on, owing to the fact that the old, colonial form is better known internationally. It can be argued that this latest trend in island naming is a way of giving the islands back to the original inhabitants. However, there can be very little doubt that renaming island names in the languages of the inhabitants reflects the growing awareness and need for taking the local population into consideration in naming questions.

9.6 ROUNDING OFF

The name category island names are in many ways similar to all other place-names. This is only natural, as islands as physical entities are found among all other nameable entities, such as settlements, hills, mountains, fields, rivers and lakes, etc., and thus form part of the same cognitive framework of the naming community. Thus, they are bestowed in the same way as all other relevant physical entities and according to the naming principles of the day.

Island names do, however, offer us a gateway into the minds of the namers through time in a better way than most other name types. This is probably owing to the locality type of islands—being isolated in water—so that the reference is virtually always to the island itself and not, for example, a metonymically transferred name form from another, original, locality. The study of island names is ripe for providing insights not only into the *what* (etymology) and *why* (motivation) of naming but even more so into the *who* (namer) and *when* (time of naming) questions and particularly into the principles, trends, and ideologies behind naming. The door is open ...

CHAPTER 10

....

RURAL NAMES

....

JULIA KUHN

10.1 DEFINITION

....

RURAL names are the names of uninhabited, delimited objects in rural settings and surroundings. Examples of rural names are the names of acres, fields, vineyards, hatches, meadows, forests, isolated trees, and borders, such as Engl. *Little Round Meadow* (Broderick 2000: 118); Fr. *Sault* (Vaucluse, F) < Lat. SALTUS here meaning 'forest' (Astor 2002: 718), Fr. *Fouillouse* (Hautes Alpes, F) (Astor 2002: 331).

Following Dittmaier (1963) and Šrámek (1996: 1462), one can even consider buildings (like chapels, wayside crosses, Christian wayside shrines, mills) as naming motives for rural names, for example Fr. *Moulinet* (Astor 2002: 528), Engl. *Chapel field* (Kirk Broddan) 'Now only applies to the field in which the chapel was situated' (Broderick 2000, 78), Fr. *La Croisette* (Barret-le-bas, Hautes Alpes, F) (Astor 2002: 278), Sp. *Crucellas* (Valle de Tena, Spain) (Guillén Calvo 1981: 159–60), Germ. *Kreuzacker* (Salurn, Südtirol, I) (Finsterwalder 1990–5: III, 1164); It. *La Crus, I Crus d'öcch* (Castel S. Pietro, I) (Lurati 1983: 65).

The definition of 'rural names' can be seen in two ways: a more restricted and a wider definition. The more restricted way (cf. e.g. Hornung 1994: 43) focuses only on the names of small entities, so-called microtoponyms. The broader way includes the names of larger areas or entities, commonly called macrotoponyms. This larger definition includes names like hydronyms as the names of rivulets, rivers, ponds, and shore areas as well as oronyms, such as the names of hills, mountains, rocks, or street names (Schnetz 1952, 1997; Hornung 1994: 44; Tyroller 1996a, 1996b; Šrámek 1996), which are excluded in the case of the narrower definition. The broader definition, including macrotoponyms, focuses on the distinction between inhabited and uninhabited areas. Sonderegger (1985a, 1985b) amplifies this distinction and considers the names of uninhabited land and water and keeps apart 'Verkehrsverbindungen und Abgrenzungen'— 'streets and boundaries' (Sonderegger 1985a: 2070; 1985b: 450).

Even if some definitions treat hydronyms as rural names and others do not, it has to be taken into account that it is not always easy to draw a clear dividing line between land and water. After the melting of snow in winter, water or watery ground might remain for a certain period in spring; after heavy rainfall, the ground might be muddy; swamps are neither land nor water, rivers might change their positions, etc.; therefore it is not always clear whether names of these areas should be included or excluded in the domain of rural names.

Besides the smallness of the named object, another characteristic of rural names (Ramge 1998: 82–3, 2002: 28; Windberger-Heidenkummer 2001, 2011: 290) is their limited communicative value, since the knowledge of rural names can be restricted to a few people, for instance the inhabitants of a village.

In general, rural names designate uninhabited areas. Nevertheless, a connection to settlement names might exist. This is the case if an originally uninhabited area becomes inhabited and the settlement takes the name of the originally uninhabited area. Swiss onomasticians (Sonderegger 1960: 197, 1966–7: 286–7, 1997–8: 9–10; Waser 2004: 351) call these names *sekundäre Siedlungsnamen* 'secondary settlement names'. Examples for such names are *Gäll* (St Gallen, CH) < Lat. RUNCALIA (Kuhn 2002: 197) 'wood clearance', *Laui* (Kuhn 2002: 229–30) < Lat. LABINA 'avalanche', the name of the village *Buchrain* < 1257 *Bůchrein* originally meaning 'hillside with beeches' (Waser 2004: 352), or Fr. *Capendut* < camp pendut (Aude, F) (Astor 2002: 589) originally meaning 'field on a hillside'.

Names directly designating a settlement, so-called *primäre Siedlungsnamen* 'primary settlement names', are covered separately in this handbook in chapter 6: 'Settlement Names'. The phenomenon whereby one entity is named after another can be observed in the case of rural names that can also be based on street names, for instance Germ. *An der Weinstraße* (Ramge 1987: 80).

Šrámek (2002: 889) brings a specialized notion for economically usable and especially agrotecnically used surfaces that he calls *agronyms* (< Gr. Agrós 'field, acre').

To sum up, this chapter presents *rural names* as *microtoponyms* designating uninhabited entities in rural surroundings and excludes (to a large extent) hydronyms, oronyms, and street names, which are covered in separate chapters of this handbook (7: 'River Names', 8: 'Hill and Mountain Names', 11: 'Street Names').

10.2 SEMANTIC ASPECTS

The primary motivation for rural names is orientation and identification of areas within small and limited units that can be further subdivided.

The basis of rural names are (frequently) appellatives designating areas within a landscape, which are cultivated, needed or used in mostly agricultural contexts. Therefore, many name-giving appellatives stand in agricultural contexts and form the so-called *cultural names* that can be distinguished from the so-called *natural names*. Cultural names reflect human influence on the named area, whereas natural names are based on natural facts and can describe the characteristics of the named object. So, for instance, an elevation can be called *Buel* in Switzerland, which can be found in names like *Rofenbüel* Eschen (Stricker et al. 1999: 266ff.) or *Stornenbüel* a secondary settlement name in the canton St Gallen CH (Kuhn 2002: 282); in France we find *saut* with a similar meaning, for example *Saut du Loup* (Ferrières-les-Verreries, F) (Astor 2002: 718).

Further examples for natural names reflect climatic conditions. In Slavonic contexts, sunny areas in wind protected positions can contain the Slavonic element **toplъ/*teplъ*, for instance sloven. *Topli Vrh, Topla Reber, Topla Jama* (Bezlaj 1956–61: II, 265–6) or Czech *Teplá, Teplice* (Profous 1947–60: IV, 326ff.; Bergermayer 2005: 268), the German rural name *Sonnenhöchfelln* 'fields in a sunny position in the mountains' (Kaisergebirge, Tirol, A) (Finsterwalder 1990–5: II, 465) reflect a similar naming motivation. Also the position of the named area can motivate the name. The Slovenian rural names *Stranik, Stranica, Stranice* (Bezlaj 1956–61: II, 223–4, cfr. Slovenian *stran, strana* 'side') designate the position on a slope or a hillside.

Other examples indicate the existence of water, like *Zammes* < rom. *Mediamnes* 'land between rivers' (Finsterwalder 1990–5: I, 366), or the Swiss name *Zwüschewassere* (Waser 2004: 352).

A frequent naming motive is the existence of animals in the area. As for example in France: *La Loubière* (Bozouls, Aveyron, F); *Loubières* (Ariège, Foix, F), *Loubère* (Beychac, Gironde, F) (Astor 2002: 447) 'place where wolves dwell'; or *Servières* (Lozère, F) (Astor 2002: 792), a collective derivation of *cerv, cerf* 'stag', meaning 'forests where stags and similar animals live'.

Another frequent naming motive is plants, often trees: the Czech rural name *Javorovec* (Czech Republic) < slav. **(j)avorъ* 'maple' (Šrámek 2007: 337) reflects the former existence of maple trees. This is similar for Bohemia: *Javor, Javorecko, Javůrkovský, Javůří*; and Moravia: *Javor, Javorek, Javorka, Javornik*, etc. (Šrámek 2007: 340). The same naming motive 'maple' is the basis of Rtr. *Naserina* (St Gallen, CH) < Lat. ACER (Kuhn 2002: 254ff.). Rtr. *Säls* (St Gallen, CH) < SALIX reflects the former existence of willows (Kuhn 2002: 275); linden trees are the basis of the Polish rural name *Trzylipy* 'three linden trees' (Bezlaj 1957–61: II, 273–4); Fern was the basis of names such as Slovenian *Prapače, Prapence, Praponca, Prapoše, Paraprotišče, Praprtnik* (Bezlaj 1956–61: II, 115–16) < Slav.**Popracъ* 'fern' (Skok 1972: 602; Bergermayer 2005: 190–1). The French name *Longe-Faye* (St-Prix, Ardèche, F) 'longue hêtraie' (Astor 2002: 446) < Lat. FAGUS reflects the existence of beech trees. The It. name *Miurína* (Nuree, I) 'zona piantata a miglio' (Lurati 1983: 80) reflects the cultivation of millet. It. *Cas'gnöla* (Balerna, I) (Lurati 1983: 60) was named after a small chestnut tree. It. *Albaréda* (Campora, I) (Lurati 1983: 49) is the name of a forest that is based on Lat. ALBARUS 'poplar' (Lurati 1983: 49). Span. *Olivar* (Rioja, Spain) (Ortiz Trifol 1982: 74) designates an area where olive trees grow. *Fagüeñas* (Valle de Tena, Sp.) (Guillén Calvo 1981: 117) reflects the existence of beech trees, *Pinillos* (Rioja, Spain) (Ortiz Trifol 1982, 74) < Lat. PINUS + -ELLU, *Pinaralto, Pino* (Valle de Tena, Sp.) (Guillén Calvo 1981: 122) the existence of pine trees.

Soil properties are reflected in rural names like *Arschitz* (St Gallen, CH) (Kuhn 2002: 56) < Lat. AGER 'acre' + Lat. EXSUCTUS 'dry'.

Apart from plants growing in an area, wood clearances can also motivate names. As forest clearings reflect human influence, names of forest clearings belong to cultural names. Thus, for example *Ragore* (St Gallen, CH) (Kuhn 2002: 107), *Hinggalina* (St Gallen, CH) (Kuhn 2002: 224–5) < Lat. *RUNCU 'clearance' < Lat. RUNCARE, and *Gafedur* (St Gallen, CH) < Lat. CAPRITURA here 'clearance' (Vincenz 1992: 86–7); or in France *Sauveplane* (Aveyron, Lozère), *Salveplane* (Aujac) (Astor 2002: 726) < SILVAM PLANAM 'cleared wood'.

Forest areas that have been cleared can provide space for meadows. Rural names reflecting meadows are, for instance, Engl. *Little Round Meadow* (Broderick 2000: 118), Slovenian *Loka* (Bezlaj 1956–61: I, 355) < *lǫka* 'meadow'; perhaps also Slovak *Turá Lúka*, Polish *Łęka*, Sorbian *Łuka* (Germ. *Wiesa*) (Šmilauer 1970: 115).

Some names show that animals (sheep and goats) were shepherded in an area like Slovenian *Koznik* (Bezlaj 1956–61: I, 295) < *Kozъnikъ ,goat-,... derivation with suffix *-ik—< *kozъnъ (Bergermayer 2005: 121–2) or Slovenian *Kozljak* (Bezlaj 1956–61: I, 295–6) < *Kozъl'a 'male goat' (Bergermayer 2005: 122). The Czech name *Ovčin, Ovčinec* (Profous 1947–60: III, 314; Hosák and Šramek 1970–80: II, 212) reflects the existence of flocks of sheep in the area. In France, the name *Pas de la Fède* (Astor 2002: 576) < FETA indicates a place where flocks of sheep used to pass from one area to another.

A clear differentiation as to whether a name is cultural or natural is not always possible. Some names consist of compound nouns and can combine elements of the two groups (natural and cultural names), for example Germ. *Galgenbühl* 'gallows hill' (Dittmaier 1963; Schnetz 1997) or Germ. *Luigacker* (Innsbruck Land, A) < Old High German *Luog*—'whole, burrow, hallow' + Germ. *Acker* 'field, acre' (Hausner and Schuster 1999: 690).

A yet more detailed differentiation than the one of cultural and natural names is given by Dittmaier (1963), who distinguishes further within the natural names: names indicating extension and delimitation, general designations for parts of the area, general form and appearance, natural limitation, natural position, form of the territory, flatness, vertical variation (ground depression, elevation and rising terrain), geology, hydrology, hydronyms as microtoponyms, fountains, running water and stagnant water, names of parts of rivers and lakes, swamps, land in water or by the side of water, flora and fauna, forests, woods and trees, grass, uncultivated land, cultural names, forest clearance, arable land, lawn, meadow and grassland, animal husbandry, farming, special cultures, measures and numbers, forestry, trade, objects named after people, buildings, soil resources, equipment, embankments, transitions and borders, locations of prehistoric finds, and tax systems, legal conditions, religion and church, popular belief, legends and events.

Besides natural and cultural names, another way to distinguish types of rural names is the differentiation of *direct* and *indirect* names (Schwarz 1950: 259), whereby direct names designate the object directly, like *Hanfland* (St Gallen, CH) (Stricker 1981: 349), indirect names identify an object via other entities; they often use prepositions like *Hinterburg* 'behind the castle' (Going Tirol, A) (Finsterwalder 1990–5: I, 286) or *Vorreith (1618 Vorreit)* 'in front of the wood clearance' (Finsterwalder 1990–5: II, 577).

10.3 MORPHOLOGY OF RURAL NAMES

Rural names are, in general, based on appellatives that largely follow the morphology of the language spoken in the area at the time of naming. Frequent morphological patterns for rural names are simplex forms, derivations with affixes or compound nouns. Some rural names consist of syntagmatic structures, nominal phrases containing articles, prepositions, or adjectives besides the nucleus.

Derivations as one of the frequent morphological patterns often contain suffixes that can designate collectives. In German, for instance, the suffix *-ahi* (Old High German), Germ. *-ach* like *Forchach* (Bozen, Südtirol, I) < Old High German *For(a)ha* 'pine tree' + collective suffix *-ahi* (Hausner and Schuster 1999: 373).

Collective suffixes in France can be *-eda* or *-era* as in *Espéchèdes* (Pyrénées Atlantiques, F) < Occitan *espès, espèssa* 'thick', an adjective transformed into a substantive + suffix *-eda* meaning 'thicket' (Astor 2002: 304). The suffix *-era* appears in *Cerbère* (Pyrénées Orientales, F) < Lat. CERVUS 'stag' (Astor 2002: 732), meaning 'area with many stags'. Similarly Span. *Cervera (del Rio Alhama)* < Lat. CERVUS + -ARIA (Rioja, Spain) (Ortiz Trifol 1982: 65).

Derivations indicating diminutives or augmentatives are also frequent. A diminutive is, for instance, *La Croisette* 'little cross' < Lat. CRUCEM (Barret-le-bas, Hautes Alpes, F) (Astor 2002); Fr. *Moulinet* (Alpes Maritimes) 'little Mill' (Astor 2002: 528); It. *Selvítt* 'small woods at Corteglia' (Lurati 1983: 97) < SILVA+-ITTU; It. *Pradèla* (Monte Generoso, I) (Lurati 1983: 90) < Lat. PRATUM + -ELLU; It. *Ciarèll* (Corteglia, I) (Lurati 1983: 62) < Lat. CERRUM + -ELLU; Rtr. Runggeldin (Sax, CH) < *RUNCARE + -ITTU + -INU (Vincenz 1992: 115) 'little wood clearance'; Rtr. *Refina* < *Rova (Oberschan, CH) + -INA (Stricker 1981: 376); *Molinet* (Valle de Tena, Spain) (Guillén Calvo 1981: 159) containing Lat. -ITTU, *Crucellas* (Guillén Calvo 1981: 159–60) containing *-ella* < Lat. -ELLU.

In Romance languages the so-called *suffixes prédiaux* frequently occur. These indicate property in combination with personal names, for example the suffix *-asco* in combination with Celtic and Roman names, for instance in Italy and the Italian-speaking part of Switzerland such as in *Vernasca, Godiasco* (Vassere 1996: 1447). Other suffixes of that kind are Celtic *-acum, -anu, -anicum*, but also *-ate, -ing, -ossu, ate*; as in Span. *Campos Suliáns* (Valle de Tena, Spain) (Guillén Calvo 1981: 163) reflecting *-anum*.

Prefixes can indicate the localization of a place, like *anter-, enter-, vor-, auf-* as in *Vorreith* 'in front of the wood clearance' (Finsterwalder 1990–5: II, 577), or can form collectives like Germ. *ge-*, such as *Geplätt* < *Ge-* + *Platte* (Bichlbacher Alpe, D) (Finsterwalder 1990–5: II, 773); *Gestaige* (Ötztal, A) (Finsterwalder 1990–5: II, 790).

A second morphological pattern (besides derivation) is composition. Compound nouns as rural names can further differentiate already existing names. They are often similar to the corresponding appellative, like *Alp* > *Vorder-alp*.

Compounds can consist of two nouns, as in Germ. *Luigacker* (Innsbruck Land, Österreich) < Old High German *Luog* 'Höhle, Schlupfwinkel, Lagerstätte des Wildes' + Germ. *Acker* 'acre'.

Compounds can consist of a noun and an adjective: Germ. *Vorderalp, Hinderalp* (St Gallen, CH) (Vincenz 1992: 66); Fr. *Viellespesse* 'the old forest' (St-Cernin, Cantal, F) (Astor 2002: 304); Fr. Le Bois de *Longuefeuille* 'long leaf' (Concoules, Lozère, F) (Astor 2002: 446); Fr. *Bonpas* 'good step' (Avignon Vaucluse, F) (Astor 2002: 577), Fr. *Maupas* 'bad step' (Gers, F) (Astor 2002: 577), a place difficult to pass; Fr. *Salvanère* 'black forest' (Montfort-sur-Boulzanne, Aude, F) (Astor 2002: 726) < Lat. SILVAM NIGRAM; Fr. *Camplong, Chanlon, Longchamp* 'long field' (Mareugheol, Puy-de-Dôme, F) (Astor 2002: 446) < Lat. CAMPU- + LONG-.

Compounds can consist of a numeral and a noun: Germ. *Fünfeich* 'Five oaks' (Engerstheim, Passau, D) < Old High German *funf, fünf* (Förstemann 1967: 970).

Compound nouns can also be more complex and consist of several elements, such as Germ. *Ochsgrubenlehn* (Tirol, A) (Finsterwalder 1990–5: II, 639), *Kapphahnsberge* (Magdeburg D) (Zschieschang 2005: 190), *Schüsselbergstücke* (Magdeburg D) (Zschieschang 2005: 194).

Rural names containing a noun and an adjective do not necessarily have to be written as one word—for instance: Fr. *Silve Longue* < SILVAM + LONGAM 'long forest' (Alpes Maritimes) (Astor 2002: 726); Fr. *Longe-Faye* (St-Prix, Ardèche, F) (Astor 2002: 446) < LONG- + FAGUS; Engl. *Hilly Flatt* (Kirk Santan) (Broderick 2000: 244); Engl. *Lag evel* (Kirk Patrick) 'hollow of poor ground' (Broderick 1994: 136); It. *Sélva scüra* (Corteglia, I) (Lurati 1983: 97) < Lat. SILVAM + OSCURAM; It. *Praa Grand* (Zocche di Gorla, I) (Lurati 1983: 89); It. *Tre Pini* 'three pinetrees' (Corteglia, I) (Lurati 1983: 1029); Czech *Tři Stolice* (Bezlaj 1956–61: II, 273–4), Slav. * *Tri Pol'ica* 'three small fields' < *tri* 'three' + * *pol'ica, *poljica* (Skok 1972: 698).

Syntagmatic constructions containing prepositions and articles occur frequently in Romance languages. So NP + preposition + NP, such as Fr. *La Croix de la penderie* (Plagnol, Ardèche, F) (Astor 2002: 278); Fr. *Saut du Loup* (Ferrières-les-Verreries, F) (Astor 2002: 718); or Germ. *Lehmkeutenstücken hintern Weinbergen, Lehmkeutenstücken beim Dorfe* (Magdeburg, D) (Zschieschang 2005: 190).

Rural names contain verbal stems as compounds like *Bleichstatt* or *Schleifweg* (Tyroller 1996a: 1433) or derived forms like *Penchot* (Livinhac-le-Haut, F) < Occitan *penchar* 'pendre pour évoquer la déclivité du terrain' (Astor 2002: 589); or Slav. *Stanoviska, Staniska* < *stát* 'to stand, stay or linger somewere' (Šrámek 2007: 333).

Rural names can also consist of adjectives used as substantives: Lat. ROTUNDUS 'round' > + *Radunn* (Grabs, CH) (Stricker 1981: 125); It. *Nuaa* < novale 'new' name of a recently cleared area (Gorteglia, I) (Lurati 1983: 84); It. *Grass* (Génur, I) (Lurati 1983: 74) < Lat. GRASSUS 'fat' name of a productive meadow; or Occitan adj. *espès, espèssa* > *Espès* (Cornillon, Gard, F) (Astor 2002: 304) a name of a forest that regularly has to be cut down; stock-farming introduced expressions for places where herds, especially sheep, can stay in protected areas or close to water.

Rural names are close to their appellatival counterparts and may even be used with articles, which is, in general, rarely the case if they are officialized. Examples of rural names containing the article: Engl. *The little Field, The Flatt* (Kirk Santan) (Broderick 2000: 244); Fr. *La Feuillade* (Dordogne) (Astor 2002: 331), Fr. *La Salvage* (La Roque-Sainte-Marguerite, Aveyron, France) (Astor 2002: 725), *Les Sauvades* (Dore L'Eglise, Puy-de-Dôme, F) (Astor 2002: 726) both < Lat. SILVAM 'forest', Fr. *La Loubière* (Bozouls, Aveyron, F) (Astor 2002: 447), Sp. *La Pinaza, La Salz, La Salzosa* (Valle de Tena, Sp.) (Guillén Calvo 1981: 122–3).

The frequent use of articles in microtoponymy leads to another phenomenon: the agglutination or deglutination of articles and prepositions, for instance in *Delebio* (Sondrio) (Vassere 1996: 1446); or *Fergoda* (St Gallen, CH) (Kuhn 2002: 38) < Germ. prep. *uf*, '*auf* + Lat. RADICATA, Rtr. *ragau* 'fir tree uprooted by the wind'.

10.4 HOW TO COLLECT RURAL NAMES?

The collection of rural names essentially consists of the following factors: the collection of names *in situ* (in place), the collection of historical name-forms in historical documents, and the linguistic and historical interpretation of the names.

For collection in place, names can be looked up in a list of properties (Germ. *Ortskataster* and *Riedübersichten*). This helps to localize the names in the landscape. Furthermore, the possibility of extracting information guarantees a certain completeness of the collection of (at least the larger) rural names. Parallel interviews with people who know the area very well allow the name form to be registered and transcribed phonetically, and eventually, articles and prepositions used can be added. These interviews often lead to the additional mention of rural names not contained in the written sources. Another important factor is knowledge of the place, its position, soil properties, and agricultural use that prevents errors in interpretation. Bach (1953–4: 248–50), Waser (1998: 19), Ramge (1998: 85) call this aspect the *Realprobe*.

The second essential step is the collection of previous references to the rural name in historical documents. As these older forms go back in time, they can be closer to the etymon, which can be of particular importance in areas where language change took place.

The historical forms are evaluated and then the names are interpreted, explained, and traced back to the etymon. So the naming motivation and the origin of the name are revealed. In an ideal case, all the elements of the rural name at the time when the name was given can be explained, which can be difficult since rural names are often shortened, for example, *Gäll* < Lat. RUNCALIA (Kuhn 2002: 197). If it is not possible to explain all the elements of a name, either because historical documentation is missing or because a name found in the historical documents is no longer in use and cannot be localized, the linguist can give hints and suggest his ideas concerning the etymology of the rural name, but he has to leave the definitive etymological interpretation open.

10.5 Added Values and Conclusion

Not all rural names reflect real conditions. Some are used metaphorically, like Germ. *Teufelsgsäß*, *Teufelsgrat* (Wettersteingebirge) (Finsterwalder 1990–5: II, 769) or French *Pas du Loup* 'wolves step' (Astor 2002: 576) for a difficult path. The element *devil* is also contained in Slavonic contexts like Slavon. *Běsьnica* (Kronsteiner 1967–8: 84) > Slovenian *Besenik, Besnica, Besnik* (Bezlaj 1956–61: I, 57). The It. name *Pian dal Giöch* (Obino, I) < *giöch* 'barlotto delle streghe' (Lurati 1983: 86) designates a flat area in the mountains where reunions of witches were thought to take place.

Even if rural names do not necessarily refer to real conditions, like the examples given above, most of them do. Thus rural names can reflect earlier conditions of the natural and cultural landscape, they can provide information about former inhabitants, their languages and dialects, their way of life or former agricultural techniques (Kleiber 1985; Ramge 1998: 88–93).

Even though rural names are often close to the language spoken in the area, they can nevertheless provide information about the linguistic development of the area. This is especially the case in areas where language change has taken place: for instance in St Gallen (Switzerland), Vorarlberg and Tirol (Austria) where, until some centuries ago, the language was Raeto-Romance and then changed to German. In these areas, rural names of Latin origin (either relics or loan names) persist in German-speaking areas nowadays (cf. Stricker 1981; Vincenz 1983, 1992; Finsterwalder 1990–5; Kuhn 2002; and other scholars).

Even if the language remained the same in an area, dialects there could have changed or disappeared. Rural names can help to reveal such developments and can show how people speaking certain dialects moved within a certain area and at which times. A good example is the *Walser* in Switzerland and in Vorarlberg, whose settlement activities are shown by the persistence of names formed with characteristic words of the *Walser* dialect, such as *Holiecht, Jatz, Chinn* (Zinsli 1963, 1975, 1984, 1991).

Rural names can indicate ancient possessors of areas, like Germ. *Chlosterwald* 'forest of the cloister', Fr. *Silvereal* < SELVE < SILVAM (Gard, petit Rhône, Vauvert, F) 'forest under the authority of the king' (Astor 2002: 726), Germ. *Kaiserau* (Admont, Österreich) < Old High German *ouwa* 'land by the side of the water' + Old High German *Keisur* 'emperor', 'Property based on imperial rights' (Hausner and Schuster 1999: 573).

Even if rural names are intensively analysed (Nübling 2012: 239), they do not always receive the same attention as other name types. One reason might be the enormous number of rural names and their sometimes poor historical documentation. Printed historical documents contain mostly settlement names and anthroponyms. The historical sources containing rural names, on the other hand, are often neither printed nor published, and thus rural names have to be extracted from handwritten sources. Systematic collections of rural names are often lacking or unavailable.

Rural names are actually among the most threatened name types. Changes in the exploitation of soils, the structure of farms, new buildings, streets and houses, and new agricultural techniques lead to the loss of rural names. However, the danger that rural names may disappear correspondingly increases the interest in them, since it is recognized that rural names in particular contain interesting data for research into language, history, and culture.

CHAPTER 11

....

STREET NAMES

A Changing Urban Landscape

....

BERTIE NEETHLING

11.1 INTRODUCTION

WITHIN the onomastics discipline, toponymy forms an important sub-section, referring to various types of place-names. One of these is street names or odonyms, a phenomenon common all across the world. Odonymy therefore concerns itself with the
names and naming of public streets, roads, and highways; how and why such names
are selected; the approval, cataloguing, and standardizing of these names; and making
information about these names available (Toussaint 2007: 1–5). They are commonly
found in towns and cities, and a street name usually forms an important part of an
address. An exception is Japan, where not all streets have names, and those street names
that do exist often do not feature in addresses.

A common form of street names in English speaking countries is the so-called
two-part form. The first is the individual name, a specific one, followed by the generic
form, that is, the type of street, for example Street, Road, Avenue, etc. Well-known
examples could be Main Road, Fleet Street, and Park Avenue. In some other languages, for example French, the order is changed around with the generic part coming
first followed by the specific individual name: Rue de Saussure (de Saussure Street), or
Boulevard Saint Michele (Saint Michele Boulevard).

The purpose of this contribution is to exemplify the general nature and functions
of street names or odonyms. The basic concept of a street has probably developed in
various ways from medieval to present times, but the focus will be on the present-day
context. There will also be a closer look at the renaming of streets in cities of South
Africa.

11.2 STREET NAMES AND SPACE

All the various place-name categories which also include street names basically function in a geospatial domain. Regardless of where these places are situated, they are essentially concerned with and strongly linked to space. At first view, however, street names appear to be extremely commonplace. Place and space are a precondition of human existence which is always situated 'in place' as people move 'in culture'. As a result of modern scientific approaches and the resulting technological advances in communication and transport, people's sense of place and space is, however, constantly changing (Entrikin 1991).

The basic function of street names remains, however, a common one—the organization of space in towns and cities. As cities and towns grow, the need for new names constantly arises, and local authorities are usually responsible for assigning these new names. This sometimes happens in conjunction with the developers who may have suggestions. In this everyday context streets have become indispensable indicators regarding geographical orientation. They basically then have a referential function, designating entities. Light (2004: 154) describes this function as to 'serve the purpose of orientation within the built environment'.

In essence street names, once allocated, merely become an organization of space. In any city map anywhere in the world street names are the guiding principles; one is lost and it will not be possible for a stranger to the area to find his way without them. It is a common sight in cities all across the world to see tourists on street corners trying to make sense of where they are by scrutinizing the maps in their hands. Azaryahu (1996: 312) describes this function as follows:

> the primarily practical function of street names, . . . is to distinguish between different streets, to provide the users of the city with spatial orientation, and to regulate administrative control over the city.

Street names are therefore also extremely important in finding the physical addresses of all the businesses within an economic context. The global positioning systems (GPS) nowadays common in vehicles, use street name references as primary indicators towards a particular destination within a town or city. The actual meaning of the street name that has been in existence for a long time has become of less importance; it is subordinate to the practical function and few people still think about that. Space orientation is primarily all that counts. As time goes by, little of the traditional society that initially assigned meaning to the naming of spaces like street names remains. A journalist, referring to the street names in Durban, a city in South Africa, noted that the names, particularly those connected with an individual, come from a colonial past, and remarked that 'most people have forgotten who the hell they are anyway' (Davis 1999: 17). The names have become indicators of address or direction and therefore serve as nothing more than an orientation point (Entrikin 1991: x).

11.3 STREET NAMES, SEMIOTICS, AND COMMEMORATION

Street names form part of signs and symbols. Koopman (2012a) states the following:

> Street names are always visible. They are there when one travels around the urban environment, on each corner and intersection. They are needed when an envelope or parcel is addressed. Newspaper and television advertisements exhort us to buy at such-and-such an establishment on such-and-such a street. (Koopman 2012a: 100)

It is quite obvious then that there is a strong link between street names and semiotics, and from this viewpoint they become the means through which urban space becomes authoritative which elevates common life to the sublime. At this level street names appear to have a transcendental dimension elevating them above the mere mundane or the referential function.

There seem to be various types of street names in terms of their importance as signs or symbols that lead to their association with semiotics. Some are exceptionally neutral and do not arouse any emotion or strong feelings. This is sometimes referred to as the objective viewpoint in which a decentralized approached is followed (Moll 2011: 4). In many towns and cities all across the world, the indigenous fauna and flora often serve as the inspiration for the names in a particular area. Local authorities and developers are continuously looking for suitable street names. Fauna occurring in the area like birds, small mammals, and antelopes are often used, as well as the common flora prevalent in an area, such as trees and flowers. One may refer to these types of names as thematic. Proximity to other geographical features like mountains, rivers, and parks may also inspire names. Other 'neutral' names are sometimes linked with a structure such as a church (Church Street), a station (Station Road), or reflect its role as a popular and centrally located throughway (Main Road). These types are often referred to as descriptive names. There are many other similar possibilities.

The street names of the commemorative type are more symbolic in nature, going beyond the referential function. Light (2004) describes it thus:

> Those names which commemorate key events or personalities from a country's history are a manifestation of political order, and can be significant expressions of national identity with a powerful symbolic importance. They represent a particular view of the national past which is directly mapped onto urban geography. (Light 2004: 154)

Although the symbolic function of a street name as a vehicle for commemoration is considered as subordinate to the practical function—that of signifying spatial orientation—Azaryahu (1996) emphasizes how politicians manage through commemoration to cleverly impact on the everyday consciousness of the city dwellers:

> The utilization of street names for commemorative purposes enables an official version of history to be incorporated into spheres of social life which seem to be totally detached from political contexts or communal obligations, and to be integrated into intimate realms of human interactions and activities. (Azaryahu 1996: 321)

Pfukwa (2012: 119), dealing with street names in Zimbabwe, regards them as statements of identity, being a socio-historical peg that anchors the community and users of that name in a specific social, political, or cultural context. The symbolic value of naming streets is also echoed by Yeoh (1992) when she says the following about street naming in Singapore:

> naming a place, whether as a deliberate act or informally, is also a social activity; it embodies some of the struggle for control over the means of symbolic production in the urban landscape . . . (Yeoh 1992: 313)

The symbolic value of street names through commemoration is strongly inspired through collective memory, involving history and cultural heritage. Azaryahu and Kook (2002: 199) emphasize the fact that collective memory is always construed and experienced through shared symbols and representations, and to be socially effective, such a collective identity must be culturally shared. Current political interests and power relations often determine the symbolic construction of identity. Political manipulation may occur: 'In particular it reflects certain needs of political elites and their ability to manipulate symbols and notions of common heritage' (Azaryahu and Kook 2002: 199).

The occurrence of street names reflecting commemoration, whether of individuals who played a significant role in historical events or the events themselves, is fairly common all across the world. This commemoration is a general feature of the modern political culture and such streets perpetuate the memory of historical figures or events that those in control deem important enough to be commemorated within the urban landscape (Moll 2011: 5). In such a way such commemorative street names through their use convert an urban environment into a nearly full political environment, and the ability to change the meanings of such environments and to control it, is an important demonstration of power (Entrikin 1991: 52).

The commemorative street names define history in terms of locality and form part of the historical memory of the city dwellers. Although seemingly mundane, street name-giving becomes a representation of complex events reflecting the collective identity of a cultural group of inhabitants. Those with the power to determine the symbolic infrastructure of the community, use commemorative street names as a sanctioned representation of history within everyday life. They decide who is worthy of commemoration and in that way the naming of streets becomes part of the public political veneration and commemoration of individuals or events (Azaryahu and Kook 2002: 199; Moll 2011: 6).

11.4 RENAMING OF STREETS

All kinds of names, whether of people or places, seldom change once allocated, unless there are compelling reasons to do so. Perhaps street name changes are the most common, and are often linked to a change in government. It is indeed difficult to think of a more likely scenario where an existing system would be subjugated to a new one than the case of South Africa. With the dramatic change from a minority government in power since 1948 to a full democratic society in 1994 when the African National Congress (ANC) came into power, it was likely that name changes would follow, particularly because the former government was associated with the concept of segregation policies that became known worldwide as *apartheid*. This was linked to many discriminatory practices of different kinds, and many of the leaders of the former dispensation were commemorated through their names (see Hilterman and Koopman 2003; Lubbe 2003; Moll 2011; Koopman 2012a).

The all important function assigned to street names, that of spatial orientation, simply takes a back seat when a street name change is proposed. The issue that now moves to the fore, is the actual interpretation or meaning of the old one compared with the proposed new one (Neethling 2013: 20). Should one regard the change in South Africa as a kind of a bloodless revolution, the following view by Lefebvre (1991) on the coming into being of a new space, is noteworthy:

> A revolution that does not produce a new space has not realized its full potential: indeed, it has failed in that it has not changed life itself, but has merely changed ideological superstructures, institutions and political apparatuses. A social transformation, to be truly revolutionary in character, must manifest a creative capacity in its effects on daily life, on language and on space—though its impact need not occur at the same time, or with equal force, in each of these areas. (Lefebvre 1991: 54)

The quotation above advocates strongly that 'new space' has to be created in order for a new government to realize its full potential when coming into power. In the case of street names it may simply mean that 'new space' has been created when a street name is replaced by another (Lefebvre 1991: 27).

The ANC realized the importance of 'decolonizing' South Africa, and the great value contained in names and symbols. The title of a newspaper column '*Apartheid came to taunt us in the naming of streets*' clearly expresses the strong feelings the ANC had. The columnist continued:

> We would restore our pride and dignity and then would forever remove all vestiges
> and reminders of apartheid, and with the full participation of our people, change
> these names and symbols to ones that would instill national pride and acceptance.
> (Mowzer 1998: 12)

The so-called 'full participation of our people' has, up to now, seldom materialized and
nearly all the changes were effectively spearheaded by the local politicians and some
supporters. Surrounded by decolonized countries like Angola, Mozambique, and
Namibia, South Africa was preceded in this respect. South Africa was the last country
to move to a full democracy with a general election held on 27 April 1994, and 27 April
has become Freedom Day. South Africa became a republic in 1961, no longer officially
linked to any colonial entity in the years after that prior to 1994, but there were many
traces of the former British colonialism, which also embittered the ANC.

The rest of this contribution will deal with street renaming in some South African
cities. These are Pretoria, Johannesburg, Bloemfontein, Durban, Pietermaritzburg, and
Cape Town. Not all effected or proposed changes can be discussed, and only some significant ones will be singled out for brief discussion.

11.4.1 Pretoria (Gauteng Province)

Pretoria is the administrative capital of South Africa, with the imposing Union
Buildings as the centre of the current and previous governments. A raging battle concerns the name of the city: the present government wants to change that to Tshwane
whereas opponents are happy to accept Tshwane for the municipality or metro but want
to retain Pretoria, named after the Voortrekker leader Sarel Pretorius, for the city. The
fight started in 2003 and is ongoing.

Regarding the streets, a ruling by the North Gauteng High Court in Pretoria
demanded that the old names that were removed should be put back (June 2013), pending the conclusion of an adjudication process. The Tshwane executive mayor agreed
that fresh public participation meetings would be held because 'proper records of the
proceedings were not kept' and that it was an 'embarrassment' (Hlahla 2013). It is not
surprising that a blogger, Tia Mysoa (2008–) posted the following heading in April
2012: 'The Pretoria street name-changing fiasco has begun!'

Some proposals were to be expected. Hendrik Verwoerd (Drive), often referred to as
the architect of apartheid, is to be replaced by Johan Heyns (Drive). This is a sensible
proposal: both were Afrikaans speaking but Heyns was an influential Afrikaner Calvinist
theologian and moderator of the Dutch Reformed Church. He was widely known for his
criticism of apartheid, and was tragically assassinated one night in his own home playing
with his grandchildren. His murderer was never found (Wikipedia 2015a).

D.F. Malan (Drive) was the Prime Minister of South Africa when the National
Party came into power in 1948. He is seen as a champion of Afrikaner nationalism and
began the comprehensive implementation of apartheid. He is seemingly to be replaced

by Es'kia Mphahlele (Drive) who was a writer, academic, artist, and activist. He lived mainly as an exile outside of South Africa but returned in 1977 when he joined the University of the Witwatersrand. He was born as Ezekiel but changed his own name to Es'kia in 1977 (Wikipedia 2014a).

Gen. Louis Botha (Drive) was the leader of the South African Party and also became the Prime Minister of the Union of South Africa in 1910. A close inspection of his history in South Africa reveals that he played no significant role in the coming into being of discriminatory practices in South Africa. He actually, after the Anglo-Boer war of 1899–1902, tried hard to reconcile the Afrikaners with the British, and managed to establish the Union of South Africa by involving Lord Alfred Milner. As a historical figure he was important, and it makes little sense to have him replaced with January Masilela (Drive). Masilela was the Secretary of Defence of the ANC government when he died in 2008 at the age of 53 in a horrific car accident when he burned to death. Although he was considered to be an activist, few people will remember him.

Azaryahu (1996: 317) stresses the point that a politically motivated renaming is a two-fold process that often causes conflict and strife. Verwoerd, Malan, and Botha, formerly commemorated through street naming, will be 'de-commemorated' should these proposals be implemented. Heyns, Mphahlele, and Masilela in turn will then be the newly commemorated ones.

11.4.2 Johannesburg (Gauteng Province)

Johannesburg is the biggest city in South Africa and is considered as the economic heartbeat. The first street name change was in 2001 when D.F. Malan (also mentioned as an example in Pretoria) was replaced by Beyers Naudé, a prominent anti-apartheid and controversial clergyman. He was of the same calibre as Johan Heyns. It was again commendable that an Afrikaans-speaking politician was replaced by an Afrikaans-speaking clergyman, suggesting that Afrikaans leaders, from the same cultural background, may have very different convictions on sensitive issues.

The name changing of streets carrying the names from the apartheid era only picked up momentum again in 2007. In the Randburg suburb, Verwoerd was changed to Bram Fischer Road and Strijdom to Malibongwe Road. Both of them were considered as heroes in the fight against the oppression of blacks. J. G. Strijdom was the premier of the 'apartheid' South Africa (1954–58) and known as *The Lion of the North* because he was seen as an uncompromising Afrikaner Nationalist. The view of Sepotokele (2004: 9) that people 'form an association with street names and want names to which they can relate' started to surface.

An interesting development took place in the Newtown suburb in 2004. Various artists who suffered from censorship and banning, as well as the demolishing of Sophiatown, managed to survive and flourish (see Moll 2011: 11). The focus here was then obviously on history and cultural heritage, and the argument was that the renaming should also honour the prominent artists in the black culture. The names that were 'de-commemorated' were mainly from non-important individuals that hardly anybody knew or places not playing a significant role in South African history. Such renaming is indeed to be welcomed. A few examples of these are:

- Becker was changed to Gerard Sekoto, a well-known painter and pioneer of modern African art;
- Bezuidenhout to Miriam Makeba, a cultural icon through her singing;
- Wolhuter to Margaret Mcingana, known worldwide for 'Mama Tembu's Wedding';
- Goch to Henry Nxumalo, respected for his exposé over working conditions on potato farms;
- Sydenham to Noria Mabasa, known for her clay and wooden statues in galleries worldwide (Cox 2004)
- In 2006 Harrow Street, named after an English town and private school, was renamed after Joe Slovo, an advocate who defended the ANC leaders in the so-called Treason trial of 1956 and the Rivonia trial of 1963 (Cox 2006).

Towards the end of 2008, the Johannesburg City Council decided to honour one of the ANC icons and stalwarts, 'Ma' Albertina Sisulu by renaming no fewer than eighteen streets in various suburbs after her. Some of these streets were well-known such as Mark Street, Kitchener Avenue, Broadway Extension, Maraisburg Street, Delville Street, Hamberg Street, and Hoofd Street (A. Cox 2008). In this manner, important historical figures like Lord Herbert Kitchener, who was the Commander-in-chief of the British forces in the Anglo-Boer war (1899–1902) in South Africa, simply disappear off the radar although he admittedly did not play a heroic role in the eyes of South Africans. The same happens to Delville: the Battle of Delville Wood during World War I in 1916 took place in Northern France. The casualties sustained by the 1st Infantry Brigade of South Africa were of catastrophic proportions. Honouring these soldiers through the place name where they fell in battle is praiseworthy, but clearly not recognized by many who probably do not know that chapter of the South African history.

Renaming streets is a sensitive issue. Aside from the grave effect that it has on the once firmly established space orientation, it may interfere with the symbolic role of an existing name and hence wide consultation should take place before any changes are recommended. This seldom happens.

11.4.3 Bloemfontein (Free State Province)

Bloemfontein is known as the judicial capital of South Africa. Various proposed changes as part of the cultural heritage led to extremely ardent debates between the ANC and opposition parties, but it was only in 2000 that reports emerged regarding the possible changes of street names, and involving Nelson Mandela, the first president of the 'new' South Africa. The important street in question was Voortrekker Street which received its name in 1938 a hundred years after the Groot Trek took place. Initially, with Bloemfontein under British control in the first half of the nineteenth century, the street was named after a lieutenant of the Royal Artillery, St John. When the city council in 1946 changed to Afrikaner control, it was renamed Voortrekker Street (Lubbe 2003: 12–13).

The commemorative nature of Voortrekker Street, linked to the pioneering Voortrekkers, was extremely important to the white members in the Legislative Assembly, and they recommended that Eeufeesweg (= Centenary Road) should become Mandela Road (Lubbe 2003: 16). The black majority, however, felt that there was less sentiment connected to Eeufeesweg than to Voortrekker Street and it would not send a strong signal of dramatic new change. The fairly well-known objection of the high cost of such a name change, involving the addresses of many important concerns, requiring new signboards and city maps, was voiced by many, but to no avail: Voortrekker Street became Mandela Road.

The pace at which streets were renamed picked up in 2012. A number of former ANC stalwarts were commemorated after the Mangaung Metro approved the proposals. Andries Pretorius Street, a Voortrekker leader, was renamed Raymond Mhlaba Street. Haldon Road became Walter Sisulu Road, the husband of the commemorated Albertina Sisulu, particularly in Pretoria. Curie Avenue became Govan Mbeki Avenue, father of the second president of the new South Africa, Thabo Mbeki. The former president of Zambia, Kenneth Kaunda (1964–91), replaced Eeufees Road.

The ANC Women's League (ANCWL) kicked off the women's month of August 2012 by renaming Maitland Street to Charlotte Maxeke. Maxeke was considered the founder of the women's rights movement in South Africa. At the same time she was considered as a prominent religious leader, a social worker, and a political activist. Many of the cities recognize her through street name commemoration.

The commemorative street names form part of the symbolic infrastructure of power, hence when political changes occur, they become targets. A politically inspired renaming includes a twofold process starting with 'decommemoration' and then moving to commemoration which inevitably leads to conflict, or at least some form of reaction (Azaryahu 1996: 317).

11.4.4 Pietermaritzburg and Durban (KwaZulu-Natal Province)

These are the two big cities in KwaZulu-Natal and because they are in the same province (and incidentally only around 80 kilometres apart) will be treated together. Some experienced name scholars in South Africa live in the two cities, and it comes as no surprise that street renaming has featured in their work (Hilterman and Koopman 2003; Turner 2009; Koopman 2012a). What follows is largely derived from their work.

It is also sensible to compare the renaming processes in both cities because it appears as if they differ from one another. The changes started and were effected in the first decade of the twenty-first century. Turner (2009) suggests that around 181 name changes took place in Durban, whereas Koopman (2012a) indicates that only twenty names were changed in Pietermaritzburg. In both cities there were extensive letter-writing campaigns to local newspapers complaining about and challenging the changes, but in Pietermaritzburg this died down after the changes had been effected, whereas in Durban the protests continue and the defacing of signs has been common. Not surprisingly, Turner referred to the Durban context as 'odonymic warfare' in the title of her article (2009).

Perhaps one should also comment on the names of the two cities. Both are populated by diverse communities, with Zulu and English the two strongest language communities. There are two interpretations regarding the name of Pietermaritzburg. The first is that it was named after two Voortrekker leaders, Piet(er) Retief and Gerrit Maritz. The second is that it was named after Retief only, because his full names were Pieter Maurits Retief. The first one is more popular, and the city is often shortened to Maritzburg when people refer to it. As the capital of KwaZulu-Natal, it is noteworthy that the Voortrekker history is commemorated by the name. In other cities (e.g. Bloemfontein), getting rid of Voortrekker Street was a big priority.

Durban, by stark contrast, was initially named after Sir Benjamin D'Urban, then the Governor of the Cape Colony. The Borough of Durban was proclaimed in 1854 and the apostrophe was dropped from the name. Its population is similar to that of Pietermaritzburg, except that a large Indian population has settled in Durban having been brought to the city as indentured labourers in the sugarcane fields.

The similarities in both cities regarding name changes were that (a) major thoroughfares that were symbolically or economically important were targeted for renaming, and (b) all the changes were commemorative with no descriptive or thematic names (Koopman 2012a: 97). Aside from the difference in the total of street name changes mentioned above, it is interesting to note the type of person commemorated in Pietermaritzburg compared to the ones in Durban. In Pietermaritzburg the commemorated people came from a wide range of backgrounds but all contributed in significant ways to the history and the social fabric of the city. As a matter of policy the Pietermaritzburg officials avoided changing the names of streets that already carried names, that is, those that were commemorative in nature. That suggested that the politicians in Pietermaritzburg acknowledged the role that individuals played in the past and were prepared not to tamper with them. By contrast the authorities in Durban were not shy in 'decommemorating' a great number of individuals and replacing them with an exceptionally high proportion of ANC stalwarts and so-called 'giants of the struggle' that were not linked to the history of Durban.

Although citizens in both cities reacted to the proposed name changes, once renaming in Pietermaritzburg had taken place, it seemed to be accepted. In Durban it was different: after many complaints from the citizens, it was followed by court challenges and interdictions, violent street marches, and protests. New names that went up were defaced. An important aspect that contributed to this was the role of the Inkatha Freedom Party (IFP), led by Mangosuthu Buthelezi. The IFP opposed the ANC in KwaZulu-Natal and this led to many clashes.

Some of the name changes effected in Pietermaritzburg, are the following:

- Durban Road became Alan Paton Road. Paton was an author and a political activist. He is well-known for his book *Cry, the Beloved Country* published in 1948.
- Newpost Drive became Archie Gumede Drive. Gumede was also an anti-apartheid activist and lawyer.
- Bishopstowe Road became Harriette Colenso. She was the daughter of Bishop John Colenso of Natal, and devoted herself to the interests of the Zulu people. It is praiseworthy that the name-givers retained the 'Bishop' connotation through her naming.
- Berg Street became Hoosen Haffejee. Haffejee was a political activist, a dentist and a political detainee. At the young age of 26 he suffered his death through hanging which was symptomatic of the brutality of the secret police.

Aside from Harriette Colenso, the others all grew up in Pietermaritzburg. All the commemorative individuals represent different cultures although they shared political views.

The name changes in Durban were often of the 'de-commemorated' category, removing an old name from history, and replacing it with one of the ANC stalwarts. A few examples:

- Mansfield Road (an early resident family), became Stephen Bantu Biko Road (a major ANC martyr).
- Beatrice Street (Queen Victoria's fifth daughter), became Charlotte Maxeke Street (a longtime president of the ANC Women's league).
- Russell Street (Lord John Russell, Prime Minister of Great Britain in 1846) became Gen. Joseph Nduli Street (a political activist, ANC organizer and MK commander).
- West Street (Martin West, 1st Lieut-Governor of Natal 1845–49) became Pixley Ka Seme Street (a political activist, lawyer, and founder of the ANC).

As said earlier, nearly all the changes in Durban were of the commemorative kind and even well-known streets suffered this fate. Whether the Durbanites have all now accepted these changes, remains to be seen.

11.4.5 Cape Town (Western Cape Province)

Cape Town is the legislative capital of South Africa, because the Parliament is situated there. In spite of that, the changing of street names after 1994 was slow in taking off. There are many possible reasons for this. This southern tip of Africa was identified as a refreshment post for passing ships, and the Dutch under the leadership of Jan van Riebeeck landed there with three ships in 1652 to establish that post. The settlement grew steadily and developed into a city with a number of influences playing a role. There was some interaction between the Dutch and the roaming Khoi and San people, many of them being hunter-gatherers. From a colonial perspective it was mainly the Dutch and the British that played a prominent role. The development of Afrikaans out of seventeenth-century Dutch alongside Malaysian influences was also an important development as the language of communication between different cultures in one household. The cosmopolitan nature of the early Cape Town still persists today (Neethling 2013: 21)

Another reason linked to the above situation, was that Cape Town is the most southern city and has never been the stronghold of the black communities of South Africa, hence the pressure, and also political force, has never been as great as in other parts of the country. The so-called 'Coloured' community, a fusion between the early white settlers and the Khoi and Malay slaves, is strongly represented in and around Cape Town. They are politically less active and, because of language considerations, often side with the white population. Cape Town (and the Western Cape province) is currently also ruled by the Democratic Alliance. Couple all of these factors with the traditional cosmopolitan character of Cape Town, and it becomes clear that street name changes may have been a low priority (Neethling 2013: 22).

A lack of policy contributed to the slow progress. Developing a policy started in 2001, but it was repeatedly amended. The first attempt at changing street names in Cape Town was launched in 2001 by the then Unicity Mayor Peter Marais. He wanted to change the names of Wale and Adderley Streets to honour the Nobel Peace Prize Laureates, former presidents F. W. de Klerk and Nelson Mandela respectively (see Younge 2006: 76). His so-called 'public participation' exercise was exposed as being seriously manipulated, and the renaming never took place.

Then followed a number of years with occasional requests for name changes. The lack of a proper policy delayed progress. Councillor Owen Kinahan was a prominent author of the eventual policy. In one of his statements he concluded: 'This city belongs to its citizens, not its politicians' (City of Cape Town 2007). A team of experts was appointed and more than 200 suggestions were received during a public participation period in 2007. An independent panel of fifteen members examined these submissions and put forward thirty-one streets to be renamed. This report, however, was withdrawn with no clear reason. An official policy only seemed to have been arrived at in December 2010.

Since 2011 a few changes have been effected, all names which appeared on the list of thirty-one. Eastern Boulevard became Nelson Mandela Boulevard, Cape Town following the other cities in commemorating Nelson Mandela. Then followed Western Boulevard, named after Helen Suzman, the former veteran politician and anti-apartheid campaigner who sat on the opposition benches of parliament for thirty-six years. The Mayor, Patricia de Lille, stressed the fact that the city had begun to build a more cohesive and inclusive community (Neethling 2013: 27). Another two changes, involving Albert Luthuli and a Khoi woman Krotoa, still have to be implemented.

That left twenty-seven recommendations of the original thirty-one still not finally dealt with, and, from March to June 2012, an extensive public participation process took place in which the public was asked to comment on the proposed renaming of twenty-four streets, two civic centres, and a footbridge. Nearly 19,000 comments were received.

Some of the recommended changes and repercussions are:

- Hendrik Verwoerd Drive (apartheid architect) to Beyers Naude Drive (a cleric and activist strongly opposed to apartheid). Ironically this was inexplicably not effected and Beyers Naude gave way to the poet and playwright, Uys Krige.
- Jip de Jager (mayor and community leader) to Dulcie September (activist murdered while in exile in Paris). Respondents claimed that De Jager did a lot for the area and all its inhabitants, and his name should not change. It was left unchanged. The Athlone Civic Centre was replaced with the Dulcie September Centre.
- Coen Steytler (vital individual in Roggebaai development) to Walter Sisulu (prominent ANC stalwart). Many objected to the proposed change. Of 1,466 respondents, 835 (57%) were in favour, a very close majority. Steytler's family and friends felt 'deeply offended' that his name should be changed, but the City Council stuck to its majority decision.

Another interesting development was that suggestions to rename all streets named after Lord Alfred Milner, Governor of the Cape Colony and the High Commissioner of Southern Africa, should be subjected to a new process of public participation. There were six altogether, and the proposals were that they be renamed after prominent individuals in the literary context: P. J. Philander, Uys Krige (now already named), Jan Rabie, S. V. Petersen, Ingrid Jonker, and Adam Small. The Milner Road in Woodstock, identified for Adam Small, has fallen away, perhaps because Small is still alive or because Krige has already been named. Nobody knows how this matter will unfold.

The last two name changes that were effected, were Modderdam Road to Robert Sobukwe (founder of PAC) Road, a descriptive name giving way to a commemorative one. The NY 1 in Gugulethu gave way to Steve Biko (an ANC martyr) Drive, and this was historic because it was the first NY (= Native Yard) street to be renamed and it coincided with Heritage Day on 24 September 2012 (see Nicholson 2012). The NY names had been considered an offensive remnant of the apartheid era and considered a 'derogatory' type of name. Another ninety-one street names have been identified for future renaming in Gugulethu.

Although Cape Town had a stumbling start, it looks as if it has generally found its way given the existing policy document. It seems to carefully analyse the responses from the public regarding a possible change, and is sensitive in taking into consideration all the responses of various communities which are representative of diverse cultural groupings in the city. This is an encouraging development which is superior to the processes followed in other South African cities.

11.5 CONCLUSION

Soon after their names allocation, streets, through their names and wherever they are found, become intimate and indispensable indicators regarding geographical orientation. They are the guiding principles regarding the organization of space.

It is true that at the time of name bestowal, there exists a strong link between a street name and its reflected meaning, and at this level street names appear to have a transcendental and authoritative dimension elevating them above the mere referential function. These signs or symbols may reflect various types of names, some like the commemorative ones, carrying strong sentimental and historical-ideological values.

Not long after these name bestowals, there is a gradual return to its basic function, that is, the organization of space. This function, however, has to retreat in favour of the transcendental dimension when a street name change is called for. When it is suggested that an existing commemorative street name be replaced with another commemorative name, it is seen as a centralized view of reality, representing a subjective viewpoint at a specific time. It is this process that is still taking place in South Africa since 1994. The tensions evoked by it range from extreme to modest, and are likely to continue for some time. Once the changes have been effected, there is a slow return to the primary function of street names—space organization—albeit a new one.

CHAPTER 12

TRANSFERRED NAMES AND ANALOGY IN NAME-FORMATION

STEFAN BRINK

OUR place-name corpus consists of two main types: *primary names* and *transferred names*. The former represents (we believe) the normal way of naming in early societies, the latter are predominantly to be found in the 'New World'. This is, however, a qualified truth. That place-names were brought over from Europe to Australia, Canada, USA, etc., and reused there, is undeniable. But what about a transfer of place-names in early societies in Europe? We can see that this cannot have been a major principle in name-giving, but was this way of naming non-existing? Probably not.

In this chapter I will discuss the transfer of place-names, the different backgrounds to the transfers, and also the important role of analogy and patterns in name-formation. The cases to illustrate this are mainly taken from Scandinavia, but the motifs and forces lying behind these phenomena are general in all onymic cultures.

To fully understand why we have name transfers, we must introduce the concept of an *onomasticon*. Everyone who speaks a language has a *lexicon*, a set of words from which we choose when communicating (see e.g. Aitchison 2012). Each individual's lexicon is, of course, unique for that person. In the same way, every individual has a unique *onomasticon*, the set of names to be used for geographical orientation and social integration. The former represents place-names, which we need to function spatially as a collective, the latter are the names of human beings and other (named) living creatures that we need for addressing and referring to other people and animals. An onomasticon is to be understood as a subdivision of a lexicon.

The term *onomasticon*, with this specific meaning, was introduced into onomastic research by the Scottish/German onomastician W. F. H. Nicolaisen. When analysing Scandinavian place-names in Scotland, he found that 'the early Scandinavian settlers in the Scottish north and west brought with them, and used, in addition to a *lexicon* reflecting the vocabulary of the homeland, an *onomasticon* which was the product of the *onomastic dialect* of that same homeland' (Nicolaisen 1978: 46), and on another occasion he stated that 'all speakers of any language have and use a discrete onomasticon or repertoire of names' (Nicolaisen 1982b: 211).

The term *onomasticon* has, of course, been used before, but then in a wider meaning as 'an inventory of names', as in *Onomasticon Anglo-Saxonicum* by W. G. Searle (1897), or 'the stock of names', as used by Hans Walther (1978: 6): 'Der Namenschatz, das Onomasticon'.

Hence, in the way Nicolaisen has defined *onomasticon*, the concept becomes a useful tool when discussing the frequent use of patterns and analogy in name-giving situations. When a name-giver forms a new name, her mind is, of course, not a total blank. In her onomasticon she has patterns which indicate how names for that particular feature should normally be formed. This framework may be called the individual's onomastic competence. And this is the reason why we find a palpable uniformity amongst place-names within a certain area. In these cases, when new names are formed, we can see that the name-givers are seldom adventurous and inventive. They accommodate to the toponymic standard used in that collective. However, when existing names are reused, hence transferred, we cannot talk about name-giving, but instead a choice of names.

There are two different ways of (re)using an onomasticon and one's onomastic competence when moving to an alien environment: to create names from the individual's repertoire of name elements, which are hence brought from the abandoned homeland, these names are by definition primary constructions, but result in new, alien types of names for the 'new' environment; to transfer already existing names.

The former we find in, for example, the Danelaw in England and northern Scotland, where Scandinavian settlers have created new names, congruent with and mirroring the actual landscape and settlement, but using their homeland's place-name elements, creating names such as *Sandwic < sand—vík* 'bay', *Lerwick < leira* 'clay'—*vík* 'bay', *Fladdabister < flati* 'flat'—*bólstaðr* 'farm', *Laimeseadar < Lambasetr < lamb—setr* 'farm', *Swansea* 'Sveinn's sær/ey', *Ashby < askr* 'ash tree'—*by* 'settlement' etc.[1] These are primary names.

An even earlier case concerns the question of whether the place-name (elements) may shed light on where the Anglo-Saxons came from when migrating to Britain in the Merovingian Period. A traditional view is that these settlers came from the Jutland peninsula, the area of modern Schleswig-Holstein and Denmark, but this has been questioned in recent years by several scholars, who claim that the Germanic tribes who invaded Britain during the fifth century did not come directly from Schleswig and Denmark across the North Sea, but rather from parts of Northern Germany, the Netherlands and Flanders across the Channel, and that this might be substantiated by toponymic evidence (Piroth 1979; Udolph 1994, 1995a, 1995b, 2006, 2012; Fellows-Jensen 1995).

---

[1] See for example Fellows-Jensen (2008) and the bibliography in Brink (2012: 47–51).

The latter case, the transfer of already existing names, we find in abundance when we go to the New World where we find names such as *Cambridge, Avon, Christchurch, Boston, York, Plymouth, Balmoral, Stockholm, Karlstad,* and so on, which are place-names that have clearly been transferred. These names could be described as *commemorative names,* names which have been reused to bring out some sentiment or nostalgia, to commemorate the settlers' old home environment.

An interesting case of name transfer is when the Scottish Free Church and the Church of England planned a new settlement on the south island of New Zealand (Matthews 1972: 270–2). The Free Church of Scotland drew up the plans for the southern region of the island, with a landscape very similar to the Scottish countryside. For the major settlement they wanted the name *Edinburgh* but chose to use the old Gaelic form *Dunedin,* and in the same spirit they named the river in the vicinity *Clutha,* the old name of the river *Clyde.* Oddly enough, they used a Māori name for the actual district, *Otago,* but it became scattered with names such as *Ben Nevis, Roslyn, Bannockburn.* A curiosity is the name *Mossgiel,* which was the name of Robert Burns' farm in Ayrshire. This name was actually given by the poet's great-nephew, who was one of the leaders of this resettling enterprise.

A special type of transferred commemorative name can be called the *vogue names.* There might be an original name bearer in these cases, but not always. The coining of these names relied on a kind of fashion that spread. In Sweden we have a couple of very frequent names of this kind in *Fridhem* and *Rosenhill.* Internationally we find names such as *Bellevue, Belmont, Athens, Frescati, Clairvaux,* etc. As we can see, many of these vogue names have a background in the Classical World, some in famous medieval castles or monasteries.

A big question in research has been whether this kind of name transfer is a 'modern' phenomenon or if we may expect the same or similar actions to have taken place in the past. It seems obvious that we cannot assume the same magnitude of transferred names in the past as in the nineteenth century, but there is the odd example which forces us not to exclude this possibility totally. One such example seems to be the name *Uppsala,* obviously given after the famous place in central Sweden, today *Gamla Uppsala* 'Old Uppsala'.[2] This enigmatic, and historically very contested, place was a regal seat for the early Swedish kings and saw the first Swedish archbishop's cathedral. There are hundreds of *Uppsala* names in Scandinavia and also two to be found in England. Many of them might be rather young, but there is a substantial group of names which seems to be old. The most probable explanation for this spread of the *Uppsala* name is the reputation the place acquired from its occurrence in Old Norse mythology, mentioned in many Old Icelandic sagas and also by the German clerical historian Adam of Bremen, where he describes a famous pagan temple in Uppsala and some sacrificial gatherings every ninth year.

---

[2] For a discussion of the *Uppsala* names as transferred names, see Brink (1996: 63), Vikstrand (2013), *pace* Sandnes (1998).

The scholarly term for the kind of name that constitutes the base for all these new *Cambridges*, *Uppsalas*, etc. is *eponym* 'person (or place) that has given its name to someone or something', and the new 'namesakes' may be termed *transferred* or *eponymized* names, and the act of renaming thus *eponymization*.[3]

It is to be noted that this eponymization has not always emanated from the Old World, going to the New World. There has been another direction as well, which can be illustrated by place-names in Europe such as *Lombok, Amerika, Jeruzalem* in the Netherlands, *Kaanaa (Caanan), Bethlehem*, and *Egypti* in Finland and so on. A special case here are the commemorative battle names, such as *Waterloo, Portobello, Krim, Transvaal, Lombok*, and *Korea*.

The transfer of names by a Church when resettling with an emigrating congregation, as described above for New Zealand, is rather unique. However, even more unique is when a whole set of names is transferred from one location to another. One such case we find in the province of Västergötland in western Sweden. In the ancient district of Falbygden we find names such as *Friggeråker, Lovene, Slöta, Holma, Synneröl*, and *Saleby*, which all seem to have a prehistoric origin (prehistoric in the Scandinavian sense of the concept, hence pre *c*.1100). We find this set of names *c*.50 km to the north-west of Falbygden, in the same province, just south of the city of Lidköping (Brink 1996: 66). It seems fairly obvious that these latter names are younger than the former, and they cannot be understood as primary formations, but must be looked upon as transferred names. But why transfer a whole set of names *c*.50 km? We have no idea!

A similar move of a set of names happened fairly recently when the United States unfortunately decided to use the Bikini atoll for nuclear tests. At that time, 1945–46, about 170 people lived on the Bikini atoll. The United States relocated these people, which took place in several steps, first to the nearby island of Rongerik, then finally to the previously uninhabited Kili Island. One notable thing with this forced and tragic relocation was that the inhabitants also brought with them their place-names from the Bikini Island to Kili Island, so that nearly all the Kili tract names were former names of Bikini tracts (Bender 1970: 183).

Sometimes we can see that names have 'travelled' over rather great distances, names that are odd birds in their new environment, hence cannot be understood or etymologized within their local language context. Such a case occurs in some place-names found in the north Atlantic: *Stóra* and *Lítla Dímun* in the Faroes, *de Dimons*, two standing rocks in the sea west of the island of Yell, Shetland, a place-name *Dímun* on Greenland, and in Iceland we have several occurrences of the same name, found in, for example *Dímundarklakkar* for two craggy islands at Breiðafjörður (Brink 1996: 67–8). This name, *Dímun*, comes from a Celtic/Irish compound containing *di* 'two' (in the feminine) and *muinn* 'top, neck' (Craigie 1897: 450; Bugge 1905: 355; Jakobsen 1957: 77). In this case we have an eponymized toponym, which has been used for similar topographical features, where the common denominator is that the natural feature should have two peaks, tops,

---

[3] For the role of eponymization, see a case study from the Netherlands (Rentenaar 1984).

islands, or whatever. We cannot assume that the Celtic language was spoken over the whole of the north Atlantic, wherefore we must suppose that there has been a 'progenitor', which has been the prototype for this transferred name, a topographical feature with two peaks or two close-neighbouring islands. It is namely typical that all these names, containing a *Dímun*, have this characteristic feature, of two peaks, two small islands, etc.

I became aware of an illuminating case when visiting Australia, where Prof. Hank Nelson, Canberra, an authority on Papua New Guinea, told me of the following: In the highlands along the Sepik river, Nelson had noticed that the Biami people, when moving in unfamiliar territory, used their familiar place-names from back home for similar topographical features in the new territory. Nelson's explanation for this odd behaviour was that by rattling these familiar names for 'new' natural features in (hostile) territory, they felt secure and safe in the new surroundings (Brink 1996: 68).

A really special case of a name transfer is the case of *Hawaiki/Hawai'i* in the eastern South Pacific (Brink 1996: 73–4). This is named for the ancestral homeland, *Hawaiki*, for the Polynesians in their mythology. The name is found on the biggest island of Samoa, *Savai'i*, as the name of one of the Hawai'ian islands, *Hawai'i*, as the name of an island in the Marquesas, *Havai'i*. The name is also known as some supernatural land in the Tuamotus (*Havaiki*), in the Cook Islands (*Avaiki*) and in Māori New Zealand (*Hawaiki*) (Orbell 1991). The common idea is that there must be one place of origin for all these names, and it is believed to be the island *Savai'i* in Samoa (Geraghty 1993). A similar idea is to be found in the western South Pacific, where the ancestral homeland is thought to be *Pulotu*, which is found in several cases in western Polynesia (Geraghty 1993). In these cases of *Hawaiki* and *Pulotu* we must reckon with some kind of transfer of name, which was a vital part of the mythology for the Polynesians.

When analysing these kind of aspects of the *onomasticon*, we must distinguish between a *name transfer* or *eponymization* or *renaming* (i.e. taking a place-name with one as one moves, calling a place after another place, or giving a place a name that has become fashionable) from the coining of new names according to a toponymic pattern or by analogy. The latter, *analogy*, has been understood to be perhaps the main driving force behind all naming (Nicolaisen 1991: 147) and has been a subject of some really interesting discussions and analyses by two Finnish onomasticians, Kurt Zilliacus (1966: 9) and Eero Kiviniemi (1973, 1974, 1991).[4] The concept of *analogy* has, for onomastics, been defined as 'Partial resemblance created through the imitation of models or patterns' (Nicolaisen 1991: 148) or 'a choice of name from the name-giver's name repertoire or according to the name pattern they make up' (Kiviniemi 1973: 4; my trans.). What Kiviniemi (1973) correctly describes is a situation within a more mature society where new names are coined within an existing name system, so that these new names were more or less a choice of names from among those known or modelled upon them, rather than primary formations from the appellative lexicon. We can substantiate this observation by looking at regional or local name corpora, which are remarkably similar,

---

[4] See now also Leino (2007) for discussions regarding analogy found in the formation of Finnish lake names.

where certain name elements are predominant, while the appellative vocabulary could offer much more variety in the stock of names. And the answer to this is of course that analogy plays a vital role in a name-giving situation. Analogical name-giving is hence the choice of a name from amongst those which the name-giver knows of, that is, the corpus of her onomasticon. She can reuse an already existing name or form a new name according to a given toponymic pattern.

Kiviniemi (1973) makes a distinction between *analogically* transferred names, resulting from an association with or resemblance to the place; *metaphorically* transferred names, resulting from an association with or resemblance to the concept, for example the name *Siberia* for a distant farm; *metonymically* transferred names, resulting from an association by connection, such as a farm *Big Lake* beside a lake *Big Lake*; and finally *language associations*, which simply is a play with words, where a low-lying (wet?) meadow can be called *the Netherlands*. Closely associated to these cases are the *contrast names*, where we find a *Little Lake* beside a *Big Lake*, or a ridge name, *Neck*, beside a hill name, *Head*, etc.[5]

We find all these possibilities in name formation and I would like to add the case where a name has been reused for reasons of sentiment, instances which we saw were very common in North America, Australia, and New Zealand. This case could perhaps be called a *psychological* transfer of names.

I have (Brink 1996: 78–80) tried to systemize and structure different kinds of name formation reflecting the use of the onomasticon:

12.1 NAME FORMATION REFLECTING THE USE OF AN ONOMASTICON

(1) 'New' name by analogy or association (i.e. renewal of a name):
    (a) analogical transfer of a name;
    (b) metaphorical transfer of a name;
    (c) metonymical transfer of a name;
    (d) psychological transfer of a name;
    (e) socially conditioned transfer of a name.
(2) New name by association or from a pattern:
    (a) different kinds of association;
    (b) homogeneous dialectical pattern;
    (c) grammatical connection;
    (d) patterns in word or name formation;
    (e) partial eponymization;
    (f) analogical affix formation.

---

[5] For a discussion of analogy and patterns in name-giving, see for example Strandberg (1987); Albøge *et al.* (1991); Kiviniemi (1991); Pamp (1991); Nyström (1996); and Dalberg (2008).

The first case lists mostly 'new' names given by analogy or association, which, hence, is the transfer of a name or the reuse of an old name. Here we can distinguish the following types:

(a) An *analogical* transfer of a name, due to association with or resemblance to a place, for example, the coining of a name *Dímun* for a two-peaked island, due to its resemblance to or association with some known 'prototype', some two-peaked island or natural feature.

(b) A *metaphorical* transfer of a name, due to association with or resemblance to the concept, for example, the aforementioned case of calling a distant farm *Siberia*, or a low-lying meadow *the Netherlands* (cf. Nilsson 1987).

(c) A *metonymical* transfer of a name, due to association by connection, which is a frequent and very normal case. For example by giving a railway station the name *Big Hill*, when it is located nearby a hill called *Big Hill*, or by using the name *Bear Lake* for a settlement by the lake *Bear Lake*. (This in its turn of course leads to the situation that a new name must be found for the actual lake, which in the Swedish onymic system results in a lake name *Björnsjösjön* 'Bear Lake's Lake', where the last *-sjön* is an epexegetic addition. This example also reveals another interesting theoretical aspect in onomastics, namely the importance of a *name hierarchy*, where a settlement name is 'higher' up in the onymic system than a nature name, so that the former has a kind of precedence over the latter in the toponymic usage.)

(d) A *psychological* transfer of a name, for example, out of sentiment, like the above-mentioned *Canterbury, Christchurch*, or *Avon*; or following the vital force of eponymization, commonly from a stock of vogue or fashion names, such as *Bellevue, Balmoral, Rosenthal*, or *Uppsala*; or for a feeling of security, as in the Papua New Guinea case, where the Biami people used familiar names in unfamiliar territory to feel more secure and safe.

(e) A *socially conditioned* transfer of a name (or a name element), for example, where highly prestigious names are used for new settlements normally owned by a social elite, as was the case in, for example, Sweden with settlements and castles owned by the nobility, where these settlements or castles were often given a name in *-hus*, which was a loan from German *hus* 'fortified house, castle' (Mattisson 1982), or in *-holm*, where the word *holm* 'island, peninsula' was used with a new meaning 'fortified house, castle' (Mattisson 1986), or by using existing, well-known German castle or monastery names such as *Rosendal* (< *Rosenthal*), *Fågelsång* (< *Vogelsang*), *Landskrona* (< *Lantzcrona*), or *Raseborg* (< *Ratzeburg*) (Ejder 1950).

In the second case, in which we have new names made up on the basis of some kind of association or a well-known and well-used pattern for a region, we can distinguish the formation of names with the following origins.

(a) Different kinds of *associations*, such as with a name, word, concept, or sound. For example, when a settlement is established by a lake called *The Box*, the name *The Lid* may be chosen; a small lake beside a larger lake may be given a name meaning 'The Calf' (which is very common in Sweden, Sw. *Kalven*); a play on words may result in a ridge being called *The Cat's Tail*, etc.

(b) The force of using a *homogeneous dialectical pattern* for a region, hence with similar names occurring within a local or regional toponymical context.

(c) The possibility of *grammatical connection*, for example, in a region names may occur with stereotyped case suffixes (nominative, genitive, dative, accusative, etc.). A most illustrative case are some Swedish simplex names, such as *Berg* 'hill', *Lund* 'grove', etc. which may occur in fossilized grammatical forms. In central Sweden the plural accusative seems to have been favoured, resulting in names such as *Berga(r)*, *Lunda(r)*, whereas in the province of Hälsingland very often we find fossilized singular dative forms, *Berge*, *Lunde*, while in the province of Ångermanland the plural dative is often found, *Bergom*, *Lundom*. In the same way it has been noted for Norway that regionally some place-names of feminine gender in the definite singular form have taken on the stereotyped ending *-(e)n*, which has become a kind of norm for those areas (Helleland 1991).

(d) The use of *patterns in word and name formation*, for example, in the province of Skåne, Sweden, we have a river *Alma*. A short tributary to this river is called *Silma*, containing the stem *sil* 'to flow slowly', and this latter river has taken the ending *-ma* from the river name *Alma*, not as a regular and ancient *m*-suffix, but in association with *Alma* (Moberg 1987).

(e) *Partial eponymization*, for example, the older name for *Bathford* (in Avon, England) was *Ford*, but some time before 1575 *Bath* was added from the town situated nearby (Room 1985: 7). A Scandinavian example is the town name *Borgholm* on the island of Öland. The name contains the word *borg* 'castle' (or a name *Borg*) and the 'suffix' *holm*, modelled on *Stockholm* (Mattisson 1986: 148–50; Pamp 1991: 159). A special case of partial eponymization is the adding of the prefix *New* to a place-name, such as *New York, New Jersey, New England*.[6]

(f) An *analogical affix-formation*. It is a well-known fact that some place-name elements have decayed down to a suffixoid element, in which the etymological meaning has become obscured, as is the case with the Scandinavian *-vin* '(probably) meadow', *-hult* 'grove', *-röd/-rød* 'clearing' and *-boda* 'booths, sheds', all of which have a secondary usage with a general meaning of 'farm'.[7]

---

[6] For a discussion of the concept and term *partial eponymization*, see Hallberg (1976: 5–6) and Rentenaar (1991: 173).

[7] For a discussion of a secondary usage of toponymic generics, where the older meaning has been watered down to 'farm, settlement' etc., see Benson (1972); Ståhl (1976: 90); Kousgård Sørensen (1984); Brink (1988: 72–5); and Pamp (1991).

Name transfer has been a frequent phenomenon, especially in recent centuries, but it is also notable in earlier periods of history. Such name transfers may be the result of a migration of people, or in the case of eponymization, the desire of the name-giver to be fashionable or go-with-the-flow. The underlying motive may be a feeling of nostalgia for one's old home, resemblances to a well-known geographical feature, or simply a geographical misidentification. Also the role of analogy and patterns in name formation is very important. It is a rather romantic belief to assume that the name-giver in a society is totally unaffected by already existing onymic patterns. As in all human intellectual behaviour, we tend to associate and create from learned and acquired knowledge, patterns, and frameworks.

PART III

ANTHROPONOMASTICS

CHAPTER 13

··

PERSONAL NAMING SYSTEMS

··

EDWIN D. LAWSON

13.1 INTRODUCTION

WHEN we look at our own country's naming system and then see the naming systems of other countries, we see some similarities and some differences. There have been cross-cultural studies that have focused on various aspects of naming in different societies. Alford (1988) searched the literature from 1871 to 1980 to report on forty-seven naming practices in sixty societies. Among those included were Ashanti, Kurds, Lapps, Truk, and Blackfoot. These societies were non-industrialized. The reports show the tremendous range of practices with regard to forms of address, titles, nicknames, change of name, patronymy, and many other aspects of naming. Another study by Caffarelli and Gerritzen (2002) focused on first name popularity in forty nations and autonomous communities to examine the theory of fashionable name-giving.

One series of reports on names and naming practices in thirty-five languages was done by the CIA. These reports are described by Lawson (1996a); they have a similar form and were produced mainly in the 1960s during the period of the Cold War. Among the languages included were Arabic, Chinese, Estonian, and Russian. Many of the CIA reports are now online at Lawson and Sheil (2013).

Another work on cross-cultural naming is that of Teresa Norman (2003 [1996]). She listed names and their meanings in thirty-one language categories including African-America, Chinese, Irish, American Indian, and Scottish. Presentations there have information that is not found elsewhere. The coverage of first names is excellent but the inclusion of family names is variable.

There are many studies that are cross-cultural but only involve one or two groups. Among them are the work on Ashanti (Jahoda 1954), Truk (Goodenough 1965), and Ojibway (Rogers and Rogers 1978).

All of these studies contributed to our knowledge of the naming practices in different parts of the world. They have contributed to the first two methods of the scientific approach to a subject: Description and Classification. Caffarelli and Gerritzen (2002) went a bit further in their work, examining the relationship of current popular names in forty countries with the names in an earlier period.

This investigation focuses on going one step further: relationships. What I propose is to examine the relationships of naming systems to one another. This investigation is directed to exploring the similarities and differences of naming systems. Are there some common threads? And, with respect to the differences, what are they?

To answer these questions, I selected the following experts in representative languages and asked them to describe their naming systems: Ellen S. Bramwell, United Kingdom; Mario Cassar, Maltese; Aaron Demsky, Bible, Jewish; Cleveland K. Evans, United States; Tamás Farkas, Hungarian; Rosa and Volker Kohlheim, German; Adrian Koopman, Zulu; Li Zhonghua, Chinese; Philip W. Matthews, Māori; Anastasia Parianou, Greek; Mariusz Rutkowski, Polish; Maria Trigoso, Portuguese; Willy Van Langendonck, Dutch; and Julie Sullivan Winn, French.

13.2 METHOD

To learn about different systems without biasing results with leading questions, I simply asked each author to describe in a limited number of words the system he/she was responsible for.

Here are the reports in alphabetical order by language:

13.2.1 Biblical Names by Aaron Demsky

The Hebrew Bible provides a reservoir of personal names found in Judaism, Christianity and Islam. Hebrew names are one branch of the ancient Semitic onomasticon documented in Akkadian, South Arabic, Ugaritic, Canaanite, and Aramaic.

Hebrew names can be divided into propositional names and epithetic (descriptive, short) names. Propositional names are either full or shortened (hypocoristic) verbal or nominal sentences, that is, either subject + predicate or predicate + subject, where the subject is a divinity, for example, YHWH (Yeho/Yahu/Ya/Yo), El, Baal, Shaddai or by titles of authority (melekh, sar, 'adon, i.e. king, prince, lord, etc.) or by kinship terms ('ab, 'am, 'aḥ, i.e. father, uncle/patron, brother). The verbal form is either in the qatal perfect-tense (Netanel or Elnatan—'God (El) has given') or in the yiqtol imperfect-tense (Yekhonyahu or Yehoyakhin—'May YHWH establish').

This typology helps in appreciating the fashions and veracity of the biblical narrative as well as the theological developments over a period of a thousand years. For instance in the so-called patriarchal period, that is, the mid- and late second millennium BCE, we find the popular yiqtal + El form: Yishma + El (Ishmael), Yisra + El (Israel), and frequently without the divine element Yaqov (Jacob), Yosef (Joseph), Yitzhaq (Isaac), identical to contemporary Amorite names, adding credence to the early dating of these biblical traditions.

An important theological development noting the advent of Israelite monotheism was the appearance of the ineffable divine name YHWH, that is, the self-proclaimed personal name of the Israelite deity: 'I am the Lord. I appeared to Abraham, Isaac and Jacob as El Shaddai, but I did not make myself known to them by My name YHWH' (Exodus 6:2–3). The pronunciation of the tetragrammaton is misconstrued in modern scholarly literature making it the causative Yahweh as well as misreading it as Jehovah in Christian circles. Significantly, it was Moses who created the first Israelite name by introducing this theophoric element when renaming his protégé Yehoshua (Joshua) (Numbers 13:16). This divine name of the national deity became more popular in biblical Israel during the Monarchy (Iron Age) as reflected in the Minor Prophets. Note the abridged forms: Yeho/Yo at the beginning (Yehonatan/Jonathan) or Yahu/Yah at the end (Yeshayahu/Isaiah) of the name.

Some female names have a divine element, for example Elisheba, Bitiah, or a kinship substitute Ahinoam. Notable are animal names: Rebecca (fatted calf), Leah (cow), and Rachel (sheep), reflecting the high regard for these bovines held by the ancient Hebrews. Moses' wife was Zipporah (bird), while two other prominent ladies from the period of the Judges were Jael (gazelle) and Deborah (bee).

Foreign names were introduced in various exiles only to be accepted as Hebrew names in a later period: the Egyptian sojourn has given Moses, Aaron, and Phineas. The Babylonian-Persian exile provided Mordecai, Esther, and Cyrus.

Because of the positive associations, religious authority, and literary beauty of the biblical stories, many Hebrew names have become in their local vernacular form the most popular in Western culture.

13.2.2   Chinese Names by Li Zhonghua

In China, people set a high value on names. About 2,500 years ago, Confucius said: 'If a name is not proper, then what is said cannot be followed. If what is said cannot be followed, then nothing can be accomplished'. That idea still plays a role in the ideas and wishes of parents for a good and proper name.

In Chinese naming, the family name is placed before the given name. The leading position of the family name reveals the importance of the idea of the family in the individual's identity as well as the early appearance of the family name in history. The format of a typical Chinese name is: family name + given name (consisting of one or two characters, or even more).

China was the first country to use family names. Family names were recorded about the tenth century BC. From the early thirty family names discovered on the ancient Bronze Inscription, the number today is about 6,000 family names.

Chinese names are comprised of meaningful characters. Both family and given names have specific meaning and function. The main sources of family names include: clan totems; names of a feudal holding, or a state; occupation of ancestors; ancestral habitations; names of clans adopted as family names; posthumous titles of rulers; names conferred by a ruler; and from minority nationalities.

While the family name is inherited, the choice of a given name is up to the parents. There are four main types:

1. five-element oriented names (names to keep the balance of Metal, Wood, Water, Fire, and Earth);
2. generation names (the part of a personal name indicating the position of the bearer in the family hierarchy and to siblings);
3. birth order names (usually a Chinese character that has a numerical function);
4. patronymic linkage names (the last or the middle character of a father's name is the beginning of the son's given name; the son will use the same practice to name his son(s).

There are many other ways to name babies. For the female, parents like to select delicate characters; for the male, characters representing masculinity, strength, and good luck. Some parents name their children by the birth hour, the day, the month, the year, or by the Chinese zodiac.

In Chinese culture, it is taboo to name children after relatives. In contemporary society, women, single or married, have the right to keep their birth family name and given name while in the past they identified themselves by the traditional marriage name.

Traditionally, there are two Chinese characters in a given name. Usually, one is the generation name. At times, one-character given names were popular. However, this popularity led to duplicate names. With the increase of two-character given names, name repetitions (duplication) began to show a decline. Generation names have been retained more in rural areas than urban.

Overseas Chinese, when settling in a foreign land, usually take up a name from the local culture for easy and better communications.

13.2.3 Dutch Personal Name System
by Willy Van Langendonck

The Dutch personal name system in the Low Countries, that is, the Netherlands and Flanders (Belgium), has a history similar to that of other Germanic, and most Indo-European anthroponymic systems. The one-name system was the beginning, with some monothematic (unary) names like Otto, Hugo, but especially a number of productively construed dithematic (binary) names like Bern-hard 'bear-strong'. Remarkably, the feminine names display the same structure, for example Hilde-gonde 'fight-fight'. By the year 1000, the names were no longer understood, and the pre-medieval system was gradually replaced by a two-name paradigm consisting of Christian names like Johannes or Elisabeth, which were rather scarce at first. This situation led to the addition of surnames, which gave rise to the order [first name + surname]. Besides Christianization, the growth of the population was a factor. These surnames were nicknames, or other types of bynames. Concerning their motivational structure, I distinguish between relational and characterizing names.

The motivation of relational naming can be captured by the meaning of the genitive case, or the basic sense of the prepositions of/from. Here, the name-bearer has a fixed relationship with a different entity, a person or family, or a place. In this binary relation, the name-bearer belongs to some other entity, for example a son 'belonging' to his father. Thus, these relations are not features of the name-bearers as such. I distinguish two further subclasses: a familial relationship, and a relation to a place or space.

Patronymics with genitive -s occur, or derivations in -sen, -se, which are reduced forms of *sone, soen* 'son': Peeter-s, Geert-s, Jan-sen, David-se. Later on, we sometimes find the preposition *van* 'of/from', as in Van Geert. Much less frequent are matronymics, displaying the feminine ending -en, as in Mariën 'Mary's child'. The term 'origin' is inadequate in instances where a wife is called after her husband. Sometimes, this relation is reversed: Anneman(s) 'Ann's man'.

Local bynames appear as inhabitant names or ethnonyms: De Vlaeminck 'the Fleming', D'Hollander 'the Dutchman', or toponymic names, referring to a city, town, or village. The preposition *van* 'from' is often retained, as in Van Mechelen. One could also add -man: Brusselman(s) 'man from Brussels'; other names go back to appellatives denoting dwelling-places, for example with *van*, but also other prepositions, such as *uit* 'out of', *in* 'in', or *op* 'on', for example Vandevelde 'from the field', Opdenbosch 'on the bush', Indestege 'in the lane', Uyttebroeck 'out of the swamp'. Here too, the suffix -*man* could be added: Bosman(s) 'man from the wood'. Finally, all function words disappeared in names like Bos 'wood'.

In characterizing names, the name-bearers are presented as the persons to whom something pertains or applies, that is, they display salient characteristics of themselves. We observe a continuum from activities to physical properties, that is, from professions, occupations, or other activities, social behaviour, social status, personality features, psychological peculiarities, to physical appearance, e.g., Desmet/Smit 'the blacksmith'; Meyer and De Schout 'the sheriff'. Less official occupations are: De Jager 'the hunter', De Rover 'the robber'. Metonymy is used: Tanghe 'fire-tongs', for a blacksmith. Habits were often designated by the construction [verb + noun], as in Storte-wagen 'cants the wagon', Breck-pot 'breaks pots'. Another habit refers to delocutives, that is, nicknames referring to habitual sayings of the name-bearer, for example Deogracias 'thank God'. A particular behaviour or psychological characteristic is found in: De Stuyver 'dust-maker', Ruysschaert 'noise-maker', Dewilde 'the wild'. Physical features are also well-known: Dewit 'the white'. Animal names like Devos/Vos 'Fox' underlie a metonymy that is not always clear.

In Holland's Golden Age, a three-name system was fashionable, for example Pieter Corneliszoon Hooft, with a patronymic and a byname (see Gerritzen 2007a).

Napoleon's Civil Code imposed the adoption of official family names (the father's name) in Flanders in 1796, and in the Netherlands, around 1811. From 1998, Dutch parents have been allowed to decide themselves whether their children would bear the father's or the mother's surname. In Belgium, this change in the law is still under discussion. In the Low Countries, there is considerable freedom concerning the choice of first names. In the dialects, modern nicknames have come into use since family names became fixed and lost their initial sense.

13.2.4   French Names by Julie Sullivan Winn

France has an unusual diversity of family names. (Oddly, the vast majority of them, and the names of most French people, are from the first half of the alphabet.) It seems that hereditary names became fixed in France for nobles by the end of the 1100s, for ordinary people by the end of the 1400s. French family names can be classified into four main groups:

1. Nicknames with characteristics of the original bearer: LeGros, LeGrand, LeBoeuf, LeJeune, Roux.
2. Place or terrain names: Dupont [from the bridge], Fontaine, Picard, Langlois [the Englishman], and de names (contrary to popular belief, de names are not a marker of nobility). Basque family names are usually land names.
3. Nicknames from given names: Martin, Jacquot, Matte, Bertin. This includes names from a father, like the Flemish Colson [son of Nicolas]. Corsican names are often a given name plus -ini, -etti, -oni, or -ucci.
4. Names from occupations: Lefebvre [blacksmith], Marchand, Saulnier [salt-raker]. This type of name is much less common in France than in England or Germany, except in Alsace. Breton family names often began with Ab- [son of; cognate to Welsh Ap] or Ker- [house of; hamlet; from Latin castrum or fortified camp] or ended in -ic [son of].

After the French revolution, everyone, including Jews and Protestants, had to register children's names with the government, no longer with the Church. This was the beginning of the French état civil, or civil status. From 1803, children were required to have a name from the saints' calendar or attested from history. Old Testament, other people's family names, and city names were expressly prohibited. By the end of the nineteenth century, most French people had two or even three or more personal names, a custom begun by the nobility.

In the twentieth century, the tendency towards unique and regional names became stronger. After World War I and until the 1970s, there was a flood of prénoms composés: Jean-Pierre, Jean-Claude, Jean-Luc; Anne-Marie, Marie-Thérèse, Anne-Sophie. This type of name seems to be fading today.

In 1966 a new law made naming more flexible; parents could now give their child any name that was not invented (for example, a grandparent's name or a foreign name)

Table 13.1 Most common French names

Family names—most common

Martin	Richard
Bernard	Petit
Dubois	Durand
Thomas	Leroy
Robert	Moreau

Female names—most common

Newborns	Total population
Emma	Marie
Jade	Natalie
Zoé	Isabelle
Chloé	Catherine
Léa	Monique
Manon	Sylvie
Inès	Françoise
Maëlys	Jacqueline
Louise	Martine
Lilou	Anne

Male names—most common

Newborns	Total population
Nathan	Jean
Lucas	Michel
Jules	Pierre
Enzo	Philippe
Gabriel	Alain
Louis	Nicolas
Arthur	Patrick
Raphaël	Bernard
Mathis	Christophe
Ethan	Daniel

but in case of doubt, the local authorities could still simply refuse to register a name. Since 1993, after growing pressure, it is the authorities who must go to court. This has led to an explosion in the number of names invented or taken from television series and movies, especially American or Celtic-sounding: Ryan, Tiffany, Cindy; Sullivan, Dylan, Brandon.

Between 1970 and 2000, the number of Muslims and other immigrants skyrocketed in France. In 2010, Jean-Baptiste came second as *prénom composé* to Mohamed-Amine (Fatima-Zahra was fourth for girls). In 2011, Mohamed was the most common name given to newborns in Marseilles. Muslim parents in France often try to give their child a name that is familiar to non-Muslims: Nadia, Nora, Sara for girls; Adam, Sami for boys (Table 13.1).

13.2.5 German Names by Rosa and Volker Kohlheim

The original personal name system of the German-speaking countries (Germany, Austria, and part of Switzerland) is similar to that of other Germanic and most Indo-European name systems. Until the twelfth century people bore a single name. Most names consisted of two word-stems which were often related to the semantic fields of war, victory, glory: *Lud-wig* 'famous-war[rior]', *Sieg-mund* 'victory-protector'. Strong, fearful animals were also frequent: *Bern-hard, Wolf-hard* 'strong like a bear/wolf'. In addition, a few monothematic names (*Ernst, Karl*) were in use. Women's names were semantically similar: *Adel-gund* 'noble-fight[ress]', *Maht-hilt* 'strong-fight[ress]'. Originally the inventory of names was very extensive because the word-stems were continually used for new combinations. Later on they were no longer understood and the formation of new names ceased. Name-choice concentrated on a few names, mainly dynastic names like *Heinrich, Konrad.* In the twelfth century a twofold revolution took place. Inspired by Romance customs and favoured by the development of administration, surnames came to be used. Simultaneously names with Christian connotations were introduced, mainly New Testament names (Johannes/Hans, Peter, Paul, Andreas, Anna) and saints' names (Georg, Martin, Nikolaus, Margarete, Katharina, Elisabeth). By the end of the fifteenth century this innovation had been generally accepted, although Maria did not become a popular name until the sixteenth century. The Reformation did not fundamentally change the inventory of first names: Old Testament names were not frequent among Protestants, saints' names continued to be bestowed. Later on new saints' names like Xaver and Theresia became typical Catholic names.

By the end of the fifteenth century most people had fixed surnames. They can be classified according to the main motives for bestowing bynames: 1. The name-bearer's relationship to a person, mostly the father. There are unmarked patronyms (*Peter*), in the genitive (*Peters*), or derivations in *-sen/-son* (*Petersen/Peterson*). 2. The place of origin accounts for ethnonyms like *Bayer* (Bavarian), *Böhm* (Bohemian) and toponymic surnames like *Hildesheim, Wiener.* 3. The place of residence has led to surnames like *Bach* (stream) and derivations like *Bacher/Bachmann* (who lives near a stream). 4. Occupation is the origin of today's most frequent German surnames: *Müller* 'miller', *Schmidt* 'blacksmith', *Schneider* 'tailor'. 5. Personal characteristics have led to surnames like *Kraus* (curly), *Grimm* (furious/grim), *Stolz* (proud). Metonymical names like *Hammer* may contain an allusion to a blacksmith; *Fuchs* (fox) can be a metaphor for a smart person. The Jews in the different German states had to adopt fixed surnames from the late eighteenth century onwards; apart from some restrictions, they were allowed to choose their surnames freely. Patronymics (*Mendelssohn*), names derived from toponyms (*Feuchtwanger*), and names derived from house signs (*Strauss* 'ostrich') were frequent.

There are some legal restrictions concerning first names. They must designate gender unambiguously; surnames, toponyms, and offensive expressions are forbidden. Today women may keep their maiden names after marriage, parents may determine whether the father's or the mother's surname shall become the child's family name. Surname change is allowed in special circumstances (e.g. offensive surnames, divorce).

13.2.6 Greek Personal Names by Anastasia Parianou

From Antiquity, Greek proper names used for identifying a person have been formed by combining nouns, adjectives, and verbs; this results in names that reflect a rich linguistic, cultural, and religious background. Many of these names are still in existence today and many young Greek parents choose them for their children: for example Ἀλέξανδρος [Alexandros], Ἀλκιβιάδης [Alkibiadis], Ἀχιλλέας [Achilleas], for boys and Ἀλεξάνδρα [Alexandra], Ἀθηνά [Athina], Ἑλένη [Eleni], Ἰφιγένεια [Ifigenia] for girls.

In Greece today, there still is a tradition of naming the first-born boy/girl after the paternal grandfather/-mother, and the second after the maternal grandfather/-mother. During the last few decades, this old tradition of giving names has changed: for example Δανάη Παρασκευή [Danai Paraskevi] is a name for a girl (the first being the parents' choice, the second the grandmother's name) or Φοίβος Ἀθανάσιος [Foivos Athanasios] for a boy (the first being the parents' choice, the second the grandfather's name); because of the low birth rate there are cases where a child gets both its grandparents' names: for example Κωνσταντίνος Ἰωάννης [Konstantinos Ioannis] for a boy or Καλλιόπη Ἀσπασία [Kalliopi Aspasia] for a girl.

13.2.6.1 *Origin and Form of Greek Names*

1. From Christian times (with some names originating from the Old Testament), for example: Ἀπόστολος [Apostolos], Χρῆστος [Christos], Θεόδωρος [Theodoros], Ἰωάννης [Ioannis], Πέτρος [Petros], Νικόλαος [Nikolaos], Δημήτριος [Dimitrios], Κωνσταντίνος [Konstantinos] for boys and Μαρία [Maria], Ἄννα [Anna], Χριστίνα [Christina], Ἀγγελική [Angeliki], Σοφία [Sofia], Δέσποινα [Despoina], Κωνσταντίνα [Konstantina] for girls.

2. Saints' names: Σπυρίδων [Spyridon] or Σπυριδούλα [Spyridoula] (Corfu), Μάρκελλος [Markellos] or Μαρκέλλα [Markella] (Chios).

3. Common Greek first names: Ἀλέξανδρος [Alexandros], Κωνσταντίνος [Konstantinos], Ἰωάννης [Ioannis], Δημήτριος [Dimitrios], Γεώργιος [Georgios], Νικόλαος [Nikolaos] for boys, and Μαρία [Maria], Ἄννα [Anna], Ἑλένη [Eleni], Ἀλεξάνδρα [Alexandra], Δήμητρα [Dimitra], Ἰωάννα [Ioanna], and Αἰκατερίνη [Aikaterini] or Κατερίνα [Katerina] (as it is used today in oral speech) for girls.

4. Modern Greek names used today are for example Ἀλέξανδρος [Alexandros], Κωνσταντίνος [Konstantinos], Ἰάσων [Iason], Ὀρφέας [Orfeas] for boys and Ἀριάδνη [Ariadni], Φαίδρα [Phaidra], Νεφέλη [Nefeli], Ἰσμήνη [Ismini] for girls.

5. Hypocoristic (diminutive) termination for boys' names: Ἀλέξανδρος [Alexandros] becomes Ἀλέξης [Alexis], Ἄλεξ [Alex], Ἀλέκος [Alekos], Ἀλεκάκος [Alekakos];

Κωνσταντίνος [Konstantinos] becomes Κώστας [Kostas], Κωστής [Kostis], Κωστάκης [Kostakis], Ντίνος [Ntinos] and Ντινάκος [Ntinakos].

6. Hypocoristic (diminutive) termination for girls' names: Ελένη [Eleni] becomes Ελενίτσα [Elenitsa], Νίτσα [Nitsa], Ελενάκι [Elenaki], Λένα [Lena], Λενάκι [Lenaki], Λένιω [Lenio], and Έλενα [Elena].

13.2.6.2 *Greek Surnames*

Greek surnames are usually created from given names with the addition of suffixes, for example in many cases the suffix -πουλος ['-poulos', meaning 'son of'] is added to the given name. By way of example, let us consider the Greek surname Δημητρόπουλος [Dimitropoulos]. It is derived from the name Δημήτριος [Dimitrios] together with the suffix -poulos. The daughter's family name is the same as the father's, but is always declined in the genitive form, so in our example, it will be Δημητροπούλου [Dimitropoulou].

Most common surnames in Greece: Παπαδόπουλος [Papadopoulos], Παππάς [Pappas]; common surnames also derive from first names, for example Ιωάννης [Ioannis] forms the surnames Ιωαννίδης [Ioannidis], Γιαννόπουλος [Giannopoulos], and Ιωάννου [Ioannou]. But we also often encounter combinations from παππάς [pappas] and a first name, such as Παπαγεωργίου [Papageorgiou], Παπαιωάννου [Papaioannou] etc.

13.2.6.3 *Married Women's Surnames*

Traditionally, a married woman would adopt her husband's family name. This changed in 1983 and a married woman could now legally keep her paternal surname. In 2008, a new law allowed the married woman to choose her last name. She now has the option to keep her surname or add her husband's surname to it. Examples are Μαρία Παπαδοπούλου [Maria Papadopoulou] or Μαρία Παπαδοπούλου-Ιωαννίδου [Maria Papadopoulou-Ioannidou]. The same goes for married men.

13.2.7 Hungarian Names by Tamás Farkas

The family name followed by the given name ranks unique in Europe. This feature is attributed to the syntax of Hungarian (a Uralian agglutinative language): more precisely to the sequence of the attribute + noun structure, which has not been overwritten as a result of foreign cultural and linguistic influence (unlike in other Uralian languages like Finnish or Estonian). In Hungarian, there is no grammatical gender nor corresponding name endings. However, in other countries with Hungarian minorities, the use of Hungarian names is influenced by the official language.

Hungarians settled in Central Europe at the end of the ninth century and joined Western Christianity a century later. Therefore, old Hungarian names were replaced by Christian given names during the Middle Ages. In the eighteenth and nineteenth centuries, the stock of given names was enriched by new (revived and newly coined) Hungarian names and newer loan names. The most common elements of the current stock of given names are traditional names of an ecclesiastical origin; nonetheless, other names are also quite popular. A person can hold at most two given names suited to his/her sex. At present, approximately 3,500 given names can be registered in Hungary and, following linguistic assessment, their number is on the increase. Nowadays female names constitute a larger proportion. The use of hypocoristics is common, and some have acquired official status as given names. The onomastic corpora of minorities in Hungary are contained in a separate book of given names. The most common male, female, and family names are shown in Table 13.2.

Following the use of thirteenth-century bynames, hereditary family names became common in the fourteenth–sixteenth centuries, with their official registration at the beginning of the nineteenth century. The most characteristic of such names are ones originating from place-names, which bear the ending -*i* (an attributive affix, in archaic spelling -*y*). Through the Hungarianization of family names of foreign origin during the nineteenth–twentieth centuries, the stock of family names was enriched by numerous neologisms. Reflecting former nationalities, there are quite a few family names of foreign origin (especially Slavic and German), and Hungarian names of ethnonymic origin are also frequent.

The range of married names is incomparably unique thanks to traditional names ending in the affix -*né* (from the word *nő* 'woman) and to the newly introduced name forms. If a woman called Anna Kiss marries Nagy Pál, she has the option of choosing from seven types of married names. (The examples are written according to the Hungarian surname + given name order.) Besides the traditional Nagy Pálné, she may opt for Nagy Pálné Kiss Anna, Nagyné Kiss Anna, Nagy Anna, Kiss Anna, and recent name forms including Nagy-Kiss Anna or Kiss-Nagy Anna. The husband may opt for Nagy Pál, Kiss Pál, Nagy-Kiss Pál, or Kiss-Nagy Pál.

Table 13.2 The ten most common Hungarian male, female, and family names

Male	Female	Family
László	Mária	Nagy
István	Erzsébet	Kovács
József	Ilona	Tóth
János	Katalin	Szabó
Zoltán	Éva	Horváth
Sándor	Anna	Varga
Ferenc	Margit	Kiss
Gábor	Zsuzsanna	Molnár
Attila	Julianna	Németh
Péter	Judit	Farkas

13.2.8 Jewish Names by Aaron Demsky

The reservoir of Jewish personal names reflects a 3,500 year heritage, beginning with names in the Bible until modern ones in Israel.

Two characteristics that influenced Jewish naming practices are the widespread use of papponymy, that is, the naming after a grandparent, and the acceptance of a foreign name equivalent (Persian: Mordecai; Greek: Alexander; Latin: Julius; and Aramaic: Yose). These developments reduced the number of traditional Hebrew names in the post-biblical periods when Jews participated in multi-lingual communities and cultures.

Some biblical names thrived. Children were named for the heroes of the Maccabean revolt (165–156 BCE): Judah, Johanan, Eleazar, Jonathan, and Simeon the sons of Matthias. Less common biblical names were resurrected: Hillel, Gamliel, others were transformed: Jacob becoming Yehoaqab > Aqabiah > Akiva, or created: Meir and Beruriah. New Testament names reflect the first-century onomastic fashions featuring the names Joseph and Joshua (Yeshua, Jesus) and particularly the very common female names of Miriam (Mary, Maria), Hannah/Anna, and Salome (Shelom-Zion).

Rabbi Judah He-Hassid (1150–1217) influenced naming customs among Ashkenazic Jewry by ruling that: children should be named only after the deceased; one should not marry a person with the same name as one's parents. These restrictions may have led to the greater frequency among Ashkenazic Jewry of giving a child two Hebrew names. Other customs related to aiding a sick person by adding a second name like Chaim/ Chaya 'life' or Rephael 'God heals' or an apotropaic device to save an infant from death by calling it Alter/Zeida (masc.) or Alta/Bubbe (fem.) meaning 'elder/grandparent'.

There is early evidence of double names—a traditional Hebrew and a vernacular one, characteristic of social contact with gentile surroundings. In general, there was a higher percentage of women bearing non-Hebrew names in the Diaspora up until the modern age (Spanish: Gracia; Greek: Zoe; Arabic: Hamama 'pigeon'; Yiddish: Shprinze from Esperanza).

Double names found especially among Yiddish speaking Eastern European Jewry were generally a sacred Hebrew anthroponym and a secular Yiddish translation or complementary name. Some were simple transliterations (Yitzkaq/Isaac); others were diminutives (Yaacov/Koppel); while others were more sophisticated, formed by two consecutive words in the Hebrew Bible: Yehudah Aryeh > Layb (Genesis 49:9), Benjamin Zeev > Wolf (Genesis 49:27) or combinations like Jacob Joseph (Genesis 37:2) and Chaya Sarah (Genesis 23:1).

Jewish hereditary surnames were found in Medieval Spain, for example patronymics like Ibn Ezra or Abravenel (derived from Abraham). After the expulsion from Spain and Portugal (1492–96), many Sephardic Jews took family names that recalled their origin (Cordevero, Toledano). In the late eighteenth and early nineteenth centuries, in Austria-Hungary, Poland, Russia, and Germany it was decreed that Jews take family names. In addition to patronymics, for example Jacob (Jacobson, Yakobowsky), there were occupational names (Shuster, Schneider), geographic/habitational appellations

(Hamburger, Turkel), names reflecting personal characteristics (Ehrlich 'honest', Gottesmann 'man of God'), or physical traits (Langer 'tall', Kurtzer 'short'). Other typically Jewish family name types were: metronymics (Rifkin 'Rebecca's child', Chaikin—'Chaya's child'), artificial names (Goldstein, Steinfeld), titular names from the Jewish religious establishment (Rabinowitch, Chasen) or lineage (Cohen, Levi), and, particularly, names created from acrostics based on several Hebrew words (Katz, Charlap).

With the twentieth-century Hebrew language renaissance and the return to the Land of Israel, the Hebrew onomasticon has flourished. Non-traditional biblical names (Nimrod, Yoram, and Hagar) came into fashion followed by names linked to nature (Erez 'cedar', Ilan, Ilana 'tree'). Names with the element -*am*, formally a theophoric meaning 'patron', were now given the meaning of 'people', personalizing a national identity (Yehiam, Amihai). A current trend in Israel is to give children monosyllabic Hebrew names that are not gendered, nor particularly religious in meaning, and are homophonous with unrelated foreign counterparts (Gai, Ron, Tom). This trend reflects developments in Western society, namely the blurring of gender roles and cultural boundaries. It is a Hebrew expression of a more universalistic egalitarian identity of the modern Israeli.

13.2.9 Maltese Names by Mario Cassar

Maltese onomastics is polystratal and polyglot, because names have reached the island over many centuries in complicated historical and linguistic conditions, and because Malta has always been a place for the coexistence of various ethnic groups and their respective languages.

Some of the oldest Maltese surnames are of Arabic origin. The local vernacular itself developed from a medieval variety of dialectal Arabic during the Saracen occupation (870–1091). Some of the obvious Semitic surnames are Abdilla, Buhagiar, Farrugia, Saliba, and Zammit.

Since the end of the Arab-Muslim period and the complete re-Christianization of the island, the two major strata on the Maltese anthroponymic map have been overwhelmingly Romance and British. For four whole centuries (1130–1530), Malta was merely a geographical entity within the Kingdom of Sicily and enjoyed the same political status as any Sicilian commune. These close cultural connections continued during the rule of the Knights Hospitallers of St John (1530–1798), which guaranteed a constant influx of Neo-Latin speakers into Malta. Family names which reached the island via these channels include: Baldacchino, Debono, Pace, Falzon, and Vella.

Up until the early twentieth century, social interaction between the British and the Maltese was minimal, but the two world wars brought the two peoples into closer contact, and this resulted in a considerable number of mixed marriages. This then explains the present abundance of English, Scottish, Welsh, and Irish surnames: Jones, Mackay/Mckay, Smith, Martin, and Turner.

For whole centuries, and up until very recently, two main strands in the origin of Maltese given names could be singled out: kinship naming traditions and religious traditions. Many new-borns were given names recalling those of deceased grandparents or close relatives. Since the Middle Ages, the calendar of the saints was a popular repertoire from which names were chosen. Needless to say, patron saints were always honoured by bestowing their names on new-borns.

Since the Late Middle Ages, Maltese given names were overwhelmingly drawn from the Italian/Sicilian onomastic pool due to the long-standing political, economic, and cultural affinities between these peoples. Baptismal names in parish records were always entered in their full Italian form; however, in everyday practice, such names were usually rendered in their vernacular and hypocoristic forms, often echoing Sicilian sound patterns (e.g. Fraġisku/Ċikku < Francesco, Ġużeppi/Żeppi < Giuseppe).

The British period (1800–1964), as expected, ushered in a new predilection for typical English names: George, Albert, Edward, Victoria, Therese, and Margaret. This trend, however, only became overtly evident after the 1920s. More recent additions include: Jason, Keith, Brian, Janice, Diane, and Simone. Nowadays, one also encounters names from other linguistic sources, mainly Germanic (e.g. Kurt, Ingrid), Spanish (e.g. Ramon, Romina), and French (e.g. Gabrielle, Etienne).

Kinship and religious naming traditions in modern Malta have lost much of their appeal. Vernacular names have literally vanished, except for the sporadic *Xandru* and *David*. At the same time, Christian votive names are now conferred with less and less frequency, even though biblical names (mostly in their English version) have lately made a formidable comeback: Samuel, Gabriel, Aaron, Rebecca, Deborah.

Nowadays, many names are simply bestowed for their supposed phonetic beauty or for their perceived exotic quality. Most modern names are derived from the realm of pop culture. The names of renowned actors and rock stars lead the way, but fictional character names derived from novels, films, ad television serials have also furnished their quotas.

13.2.10   Māori Names by Philip W. Matthews

Māori are the indigenous inhabitants of New Zealand. From the mid-eighteenth century they came into contact with non-Māori explorers, sealers, whalers, and others, and from the 1840s, with foreign colonizers, mostly from Great Britain.

Precolonization Māori usually had a single name, for example Hokotahi, which could include a definitive prefix, for example Te Apurangi. Sexual distinction between names was minimal but a few female names contained *hine* ('woman') and a few male names *tane* ('man') or *tama* ('man'). Names could be commemorative (Williams 1912), describe the person (Taylor 1974 [1855]: 157), or refer to a person's occupation. Persons of high rank could have at least two names: a baby name and a later name. Names could be changed, for example by taking the name of a dead person, by celebrating success in a battle or some other activity, or by adding to the existing name.

Missionaries arrived in 1814. The first baptisms took place in 1825 and subsequently many Māori took biblical names, for example Enoka (Enoch). However, over several decades there were widespread counter movements, rejecting Christian names. For example, Erueti (Edward) Te Whiti (a religious leader) reverted to his birth name Te Whiti-o-Rongomai.

Three processes got underway resulting in Māori using both given names and surnames. First, missionaries insisted that Māori have both. Second, the hundreds of Pākeha Māori (i.e. Europeans who lived with and often as Māori) Westernized their wives and children (Bentley 1999: 203) and by the 1830s had given them at least one non-Māori name. Third, the schools often gave children English given names and surnames. By the time of World War I, almost all Māori had given names and surnames (see soldier lists in Pugsley 2006: *passim*). O'Regan points out the main Māori reason for this change: 'The motivation behind assimilation into the Pākeha world was . . . one of survival' (2001: 137).

The situation today is that Māori use Māori names (M), non-Māori names (N) and Māorified non-Māori names (X). When used in surnames (s) and given names (g), several patterns are evident. For example:

1. Ms and Mg: Parekura Tureia Horomia, Te Puea Herangi, Apirana Turupa Ngata, and Moana-nui-a-Kiwa Ngarimu.
2. Ms and M/X/Ng: Hohepine (shortened to Whina) (Josephine) Te Wake, Hone (John) Heke Ngapua, Hamuera (Samuel) Tamahau Mahupuku, and William James Te Wehi Taitoko.
3. Xs and Xg: Kingi Ihaka (King Isaac), Tiaki Omana (Jack Ormond), Tamati Matiu (Thomas Matthew(s)) and Wiremu Paora (William Paul).
4. Xs and M/X/Ng: Taurekareka Henare (Henry), Darrin Haimona (Simon), Ruia Āperahama (Abraham), and Henry Edward Perenara (Bernard).
5. Ns and M/X/Ng: Moana Jackson, Wynton Alan Whai Rufer, Doris Te Parekohe Vercoe, Thomas Rangiwahia Ellison, and Hokimai Chong.
6. Ns and Ng: Peter Russell Sharples, Kees Junior Meeuws, Zinzan Valentine Brooke, Leilani Joyce, and Leonida Christos Bertos.

Finally, it should be noted that many Māori have two sets of names, the Māori or Māorified set for use in Māori contexts and the non-Māori set in non-Māori contexts. For example: Te Rangi Hiroa/Peter Buck and Hemi Wiremu Kereama/James William Graham. Occasionally there is a mixed language double-barrelled surname, for example Te Rauhi Horomona-Solomon.

13.2.11 Polish Names by Mariusz Rutkowski

Currently, the Polish language has a two-class pattern of a personal name: the first name + the last name (surname). This system began in the fifteenth century, when on a wider scale the additional elements of identity, nicknames, or sobriquets, toponymic, and other expressions were added to the first names. The two-class system finally took shape in the nineteenth century. This type of naming has a formal character, in official relations a personal name can be represented by the last name solely, but in unofficial relations only the first name is generally used. In common usage, the official full form of the first name is replaced with an unofficial form, a diminutive, or a hypocorism (Magda from Magdalena, Aga/Agnisia from Agnieszka, Grześ from Grzegorz, etc.).

The spectrum of first names currently given in Poland has been formed within a few centuries. One can distinguish several layers of naming: pre-Christian first names, many of which derive from pre-Slavic times, as indicated by many similarities to the first names of other Slavic languages. The second group consists of Christian names, which, as propagated by the Church began to dominate from the fifteenth century. The third group is composed of names borrowed from other languages and cultures: French (Arleta, Żaneta, Luiza), Lithuanian (Aldona), or Russian (Olga, Igor, Natasza). In recent years one can notice a new trend of giving names characterized by a high originality, which stand out from the majority and are often derived from popular culture (films, TV). Not without significance is the dominance of American culture, which contributes to naming types such as Dżesika (Jessica). One can also see a tendency towards globalization, which manifests itself through names that are universal, culturally neutral, or suitable in different languages: Julia, Weronika (Veronica), Dawid (David), Patryk (Patrick), or Damian.

A second name (surname) is the second element of the full personal name. In Poland surnames are compulsory, unchangeable, and hereditary. It is assumed stereotypically that a typical Polish surname has a suffix -ski (feminine version: -ska) or -owicz/-ewicz. With regard to their origin, Polish names can be divided into three large groups: cognominal (from common words), patronymic, and toponymic. On the basis of a complicated history, a lot of surnames used today in Poland have foreign origins, particularly German, East Slavonic, Lithuanian, Czech, and Slovak, with, more rarely, Italian or French. Some foreign surnames have kept their authentic spellings, others have undergone graphical and phonetic adaptation to Polish.

13.2.12 Portuguese Names by Maria Trigoso

The present Portuguese practices of personal naming seem to want to recover, although necessarily through other paths, part of the old national tradition of freely choosing and establishing the order of surnames, as well as the flexibility in choosing and/or adapting given names.

In fact, in terms of surnames, the present law allows parents the freedom to choose from amongst their surnames, one (it does not need to be the last—the most important one) or four family names and place them in the order they desire.

The progressive discarding of the husband's surname by married women is a return to the tradition in Portugal where women only started to adopt their husbands' surnames in the nineteenth century, influenced by French bourgeoisie. The adoption, being optional and not implying the loss of one's own surname, has been seen as the fusion of the old Portuguese matriarchal custom of daughters taking their mothers', aunts', and grandmothers' family names (both amongst the nobility and the lower classes), and sons taking their surnames from fathers, uncles, and grandfathers. Similarly, there is a crossed custom of the firstborn son taking the full name (given name and surname) of the grandfather on the father's side, and the second son taking the full name of the grandfather on the mother's side or, for daughters, with the first daughter adopting the full name of the grandmother on the mother's side, and the second adopting the full name of the grandmother on the father's side.

Portuguese onomastic freedom in the use and transmission of family names explains why in ancient times it was very common for people to use different surnames from their parents and siblings, taking them indiscriminately from father, mother, grandparents, uncles, etc.

Although the use of surnames started to spread in the sixteenth century, it was only with the establishment of the mandatory Civil Registry, in the early twentieth century, that their use was extended to the whole population.

As in other European countries, Portuguese surnames originated in patronymics (e.g. the surname Viegas (in Castilian Benegas or Venegas) originated from a patronymic made from the Godo name Egas and the Arab *iben* son); in first names, in toponyms identifying the locality where the family originated (Castelo-Branco), or domain; in sacred names (e.g. São-Paio, the common form now being Sampaio); and in nicknames that replace the surname of an individual (e.g. Cara d'Anjo).

From the eighteenth century, some changes in the naming practices are worth noticing: the nobility has followed the fashion of using very long names, some with more than thirty names; amongst the working classes many women abandoned their surnames using only their first names or devotion names (e.g. hieronyms as Francisca Teresa de Santa Rosa, Ana Joaquina do Espírito Santo, Teresa Leocádia de São José still exist today). From the beginning of the nineteenth century, it became common practice to use the mother's surname first and the father's last, the latter becoming the most important, contrary to Portuguese tradition in which the first family name was the most important and was used with the abbreviated signature (as still happens in Spain).

With first names, the broadening process has been slower and supported more by social changes than legal ones. Names of things, hypocorisms and foreign names continue to be forbidden. Variants of the same English name such as Rosemary, Rosemeire, Rosemere, Rosemery, Rosimeire, Rosimere, Rosimeri, Rozemeire, acceptable in Brazil, are reduced in Portugal, to Rosa Maria, as not even Rosamaria would be accepted as a Portuguese name—but the use of religious names has recently been authorized for religious minorities.

In the present-day naming process, still governed by a positive list that enumerates possible alternatives (names from Catholic saints and from historical figures) and by a negative list that registers all officially refused first names, the progressive increase of heterodox names is evident: invented names (Kia given to a girl when the letter 'k' was not officially part of the Portuguese alphabet); names of foreign origin (Igor, Larissa); names formed by words from the lexicon (Violeta, Lua, or with the 'wrong' gender considering the sex of the bearer of that name (Jasmim and Jade, masculine nouns accepted as girls' names).

Underlying the changes in Portuguese onomastics is the integration, in Portuguese society, of thousands of people, with 'different' names, originating from old Portuguese African and Asian colonies, and more recently, from Eastern European countries and from Brazil; as well as, at a more general level, the cultural globalization process itself, where imagination plays, as is known, a relevant role.

13.2.13 Names in the United Kingdom by Ellen Bramwell

The state of the United Kingdom of Great Britain and Northern Ireland (UK) is composed of four countries (England, Northern Ireland, Scotland, and Wales). English is spoken throughout the UK with variation between dialects alongside Standard British English. The Celtic languages Welsh, Scottish Gaelic, and Irish are also important in parts of the UK on a historical and cultural level. Christianity is still the dominant religion, with 72 per cent of the population self-identifying as Christian (Office for National Statistics 2004), most of whom are Protestant.

Hereditary surnames were adopted amongst the nobility in southern parts of England after the Norman Conquest of 1066. They slowly spread to the upper classes throughout the rest of the British Isles and over the course of several centuries were adopted throughout society, in some remote parts as late as the early nineteenth century. Recent immigration has re-introduced non-hereditary surnames to the UK on a small scale. Women usually assume their husband's surname on marriage.

Many surnames descend from bynames identifying an individual through a relationship, usually to the father. The patronymics which arose in the English language often contain the suffix -son (e.g. Johnson), or its equivalent -s (e.g. Roberts), although others simply contain a name with no suffix. In the Celtic languages, surnames which contain prefixes showing relationship are most common. Scottish Gaelic surnames typically contain the prefix Mac 'son of'. Irish surnames can begin Mac/Mc, but instead often contain the prefix O' 'grandson/descendant of'. In Wales, the prefix Ap- means 'son of' and has been Anglicized in many surnames to P-, for example in Pugh and Price.

Locative surnames arose from the ownership of estates by the upper classes and places of origin or abode amongst the lower classes. Occupational terms are more common in English and have produced surnames such as Cooper and, the most common surname of all, Smith. Nickname-derived surnames are more varied but have still produced common surnames such as White.

Forenames are chosen by the parents in the UK, and that choice became freer during the course of the twentieth century with the abandonment of systems which encouraged naming after relatives. The turn-over of most popular forenames for babies has increased over the past hundred years but, most markedly, the number of separate names bestowed has multiplied. There is a much lesser likelihood of a child being given a name that is in the top ten that year. Hypocoristic forms have now become popular

Table 13.3 Top male, female, and family names in the United Kingdom

	England and Wales[a]	Scotland[b]	Northern Ireland[c]
Top 10 male names 2010	Oliver	Jack	Jack
	Jack	Lewis	Daniel
	Harry	James	James
	Alfie	Logan	Matthew
	Charlie	Daniel	Ryan
	Thomas	Ryan	Harry
	William	Aaron	Ethan
	Joshua	Oliver	Charlie
	George	Liam	Adam
	James	Jamie	Conor
Top 10 female names 2010	Olivia	Sophie	Sophie
	Sophie	Olivia	Katie
	Emily	Ava	Grace
	Lily	Emily	Emily
	Amelia	Isla	Olivia
	Jessica	Lucy	Lucy
	Ruby	Chloe	Ellie
	Chloe	Lily	Jessica
	Grace	Ellie	Emma
	Evie	Emma	Anna

Top 10 Surnames[d] (England, Northern Ireland, Scotland, and Wales combined)

Smith	Davies
Jones	Wilson
Williams	Evans
Brown	Thomas
Taylor	Roberts

[a] Office of National Statistics (ONS) official figures (data are collected together for England and Wales by the ONS, but separately by the agencies of the other home nations).

[b] General Register Office for Scotland (2013) official figures.

[c] NISRA—Northern Ireland Statistics and Research Agency (2015) official figures.

[d] Tucker (2004).

as official forms (see Jack and Ellie in Table 13.3). The country-level statistics also mask variations between regions and social classes.

Given names in the UK come from a variety of sources including biblical names, Classical names, a small number of Germanic names, Continental names (many of which were adopted after the Norman Conquest), surnames, place-names (often through surnames), and Celtic names (particularly in parts of the UK with recent Celtic heritage). Some names have the same original source but have been modified through different languages, for example John (English), Sean (Irish), Iain (Scottish Gaelic), Evan (Welsh).

13.2.14 Names in the United States by Cleveland K. Evans

American names are similar to those in all English-speaking countries, but show variations related to the unique history of the United States.

Colonial era differences from English naming amplified British trends. English Puritans used words for spiritual virtues as names in the 1600s. The custom was brought to New England, where many girls had names like Thankful, Submit, and Mindwell. A few, such as Patience and Prudence, are still used.

More important were names drawn from the Hebrew Scriptures. Names like Isaiah, Jeremiah, Caleb, Leah, and Naomi are still typically American.

The most important source of new given names has been surnames. During colonial times, most boys receiving such names were given the surnames of relatives or godfathers.

After the Revolution this became a way to honour famous men. Presidents like Washington and Madison; statesmen like Franklin; religious leaders like Calvin, Luther, and Wesley; and authors like Byron and Irving provided popular male names.

The Classical Revival of the early 1800s also affected naming. Admiration for Greece and Rome inspired names like Homer, Myron, Virgil, Cynthia, and Minerva.

When continental Europeans immigrated to America, many adopted English forms of their names. For example, Italian Antonios became Anthonys. If an English equivalent was not well-known, names shifted to something with a similar sound. Many Polish Stanisławs became Stanleys.

Immigrants who want children to fit in tend to give them American names. However, since they are not fully assimilated, they use the names of adult native-born acquaintances. In 2013 most newborn American girls named Jennifer or Ashley, generally popular a few decades ago, have Hispanic or Asian immigrant parents.

After immigrants become assimilated, later generations proudly re-adopt names from their ancestral culture. These often then become generally popular. For example, in the 1950s Irish names like Kevin, Sean, and Kathleen became widely used.

American parents have the legal right to give any name. This allows formerly male names like Ashley, Beverly, and Madison to shift into names for girls. Because of sexism, shifts from female to male are rare.

Since the 1960s African-Americans have developed distinctive naming patterns. Newly created names like Lakeisha and Dayquan are common. African or Islamic names like Kwame, Ashanti, Jamal, and Latifah are also popular with Black Americans.

Since 1950 American parents as a whole have become more likely to prefer uncommon names. The percentage of infants given the most popular names has fallen. In 1960 28.6 per cent of boys and 16.5 per cent of girls received one of the top ten names. In 2010 only 8.4 per cent of boys and 8.0 per cent of girls did so.

In a nation as vast as the United States, groups and regions differ. Hispanics, Jews, Mormons, Muslims, Native Americans, Hawaiians, South Asians, and different social classes have distinctive naming patterns. Regional variations such as the continued popularity of William in the south-east and the use of Nizhoni (beautiful, in Navajo) in the south-west are discernible. These factors, combined with the individualism of modern culture, mean American given names will become even more varied in the future.

13.2.15 Zulu Names by Adrian Koopman

There are basically six categories of personal names within the Zulu anthroponymic system, to which we must add the teknonymous mode of address.

The *igama lasekhaya* (literally 'home name') is the name given to a child at birth. The lexical meaning is always transparent, and may link the child to the circumstance of the birth, to other siblings, to the parent's religious beliefs, be a description of the child, or simply express the parents' joy at the birth of a healthy baby. Common names are Jabulani (be happy), Sipho (gift), Sibusiso (blessing), Bhekuyise (look up to your father), Mandlenkosi (strength of the Lord), and Bongani (give thanks) for boys; and Thokozile (being happy), Nomusa (Miss Grace), Sibongile (we are grateful), Ntombifuthi (another girl), and Ntombizinhle (the girls are beautiful) for girls.

The *igama lesilungu* (European name) is regarded as a colonial imposition on the Zulu people, and is fast losing popularity. Such names are commonly drawn from the English onomasticon (James, David, Edward, Mary, Gertrude, Helen), from biblical names and the names of saints (Rebecca, Ruth, Aaron, Cleopas, Boniface, Innocent), and from English words never used as personal names (Pretty, Insurance, Happygirl, Lucky, President).

All Zulu people belong to clans sharing the same chief and same progenitor. The clan name (*isibongo*) functions in modern society as a surname. These names are usually semantically opaque. Common clan names are Dlamini, Buthelezi, Cele, Hadebe, Khumalo, Maphumulo, Mkhize, Ngubane, and Zungu. All clan names have attached clan praises (*izithakazelo*, singular *isithakazelo*), and the best known praise name of each clan is often used as a substitute for the clan name. Thus Dlamini may be referred to as Sibalukhulu, Buthelezi as Shenge, Cele as Ndosi, Hadebe as Mthimkhulu, Khumalo as Mthungwa, Maphumulo as Mashimane, Mkhize as Khabazela, Ngubane as Bomvu, and Zungu as Manzini. Clan praises may be extensive and run into twenty, thirty, or more words. These must be recited in full at important ceremonial occasions.

Before the arrival of colonial administrators with their insistence on the use of a surname, most Zulu people would have identified themselves with their given name and the name of their father. The use of such a patronymic is once again becoming popular, particularly among writers and journalists, with a number of people insisting, for instance, that their public persona is Jabulani kaBhekuyise (Jabulani, son of Bhekuyise) rather than Jabulani Dlamini.

The nickname, for which there is no generally accepted Zulu term, is commonly used for men, less so for women, and nicknames may be given at any time of a person's life. Nicknames frequently consist of more than one word and, like *izithakazelo*, may often run into several words and phrases, in which case they are more like personal praise poems than names. The following are examples: Nsimbikayigobi ('the iron does not bend'—a strong fighter), Ngangozipho ('as big as a finger-nail'—a short and thin person), Mthunzi wokuphumula amatshitshi ('shade giving rest to young maidens'—a tall and handsome youth), Nncwincwi ephuza kwezokude iziziba ('honeysucker bird drinking at many and distant pools'—young man with many girlfriends).

The teknonymous mode of address is used of married people with children. Such persons may be addressed as 'Father of so-and-so' and 'Mother of so-and-so'. Thus a man may be called Baba kaSipho (father of Sipho) and a woman Mama kaNomusa (mother of Nomusa) where Sipho is usually the eldest son and Nomusa the eldest daughter. This is a very common form of address in Zulu society, even between husband and wife. For further reading and more extensive information, see Koopman (2002b, 2008).

13.3 RESULTS

Each of the fifteen naming system descriptions was examined for its description and analysis of onomastic terms. Far more terms (73) appeared than had been originally predicted. There were some terms that were shared by several cultures.

To get an overall picture of the types of names used in the different language groups, all the reports were examined to identify common trends and categories. The main categories were identified: FAM for names related to family, FIRST for names related to first names, and PERS for Personal Names. These are shown in Table 13.4.

Preliminary thoughts were that there would be several name terms or types that would be common to many languages, some that would be common to several languages, and some showing up in just a few. After examining the descriptions that were submitted, it became apparent that, even allowing for differences in the original language of the scholars who had all submitted their descriptions in English, onomastic terms had to be clarified. Here are some examples:

Terms used to indicate the name of the family unit: family name, surname, last name, and marital name. Family name should be understood to include all these terms. indicated in Table 13.4 as FAM (Family).

Terms used to indicate the unique name of an individual in a family unit: first name, Christian name, and forename. First name should be understood to include all of these terms, indicated in Table 13.4 as FIRST.

Table 13.4 Comparisons of naming practices

Name terms	Bible	Chinese	Dutch	French	German	Greek	Hungarian	Jewish	Maltese	Māori	Polish	Portuguese	United Kingdom	United States	Zulu	Totals
FAM Family name, has		1	1	1	1	1	1		1		1	1	1	1	1	12
FAM Inherited family name		1	1	1	1	1	1		1		1	1	1	1	1	12
FAM Patronym		1	1	1	1	1	1		1		1	1	1	1		11
FAM Hereditary/inherited overlap w patronyms		1	1	1	1	1	1	1	1		1		1	1		11
FAM Clan name		1														1
FAM Clan name functioning as surname															1	1
FAM Residential/location/toponymic/habitational		1	1	1	1		1	1				1	1			8
FAM Metonymic/occupational			1	1	1	1	1	1								6
FAM Personal/physical characteristics		1	1		1			1								4
FAM Nickname derived from personal characteristics			1					1				1	1			4
FAM Delocutives nickname (habitual sayings)			1													1
FAM Transparent (has meaning)		1														1
FAM Given names, derived from, ex. Martin				1		1										2
FAM Schools gave family names									1							1
FAM Choice of allowed for 18th cent Jews					1											1
FAM Cognominal (from common words)											1					1
FAM Acrostic								1								1
FAM Birth name kept after marriage allowed		1				1	1					1				4
FAM Dithematic early period			1		1											2
FAM Ethnonyms			1		1		1						1			4

(continued)

Table 13.4 (Continued)

Name terms	Bible	Chinese	Dutch	French	German	Greek	Hungarian	Jewish	Maltese	Maori	Polish	Portuguese	United Kingdom	United States	Zulu	Totals
FAM Family first in entry/index	1	1														2
FAM Minority nationalities, derived from		1					1		1							3
FAM House-sign					1											1
FAM Matronym			1					1								2
FAM Posthumous titles of rulers		1														1
FAM Sacred including saints				1								1				2
FIRST Apotropaic								1								1
FIRST Bible						1		1	1	1			1	1	1	7
FIRST Christian						1				1						2
FIRST Devotion names, hieronyms												1				1
FIRST Ecclesiastical							1									1
FIRST New Testament influence					1	1										2
FIRST Saints' influence					1	1			1			1			1	5
FIRST transparent (has meaning and/or function)	1	1														2
FIRST Patronymic link to father's name		1														1
FIRST Favourable, date, time, zodiac		1														1
FIRST Relational (name bearer has relation to family, etc.)			1						1							2

FIRST Personality, physical characteristics	2
FIRST Schools gave names	1
FIRST Globalization names suitable in diff. langs.	3
FIRST Hypocoristic	5
FIRST Imported	3
FIRST Chosen by parents	6
FIRST Connection to land and nature	1
FIRST Cultural group's distinctive patterns, Muslim, etc.	1
FIRST *igama lasekhaya* ('home name')	1
FIRST *igama lesilungu* ('European name')	1
FIRST Media influence	3
FIRST Names after political, religious, classical figures	2
FIRST Names, prénoms composé/double names	2
FIRST Papponymy	2
FIRST pre-Christian	3
FIRST Relatives naming after living permitted	1
FIRST Relatives, taboo to name a child after	1
FIRST Relatives only after deceased	2
FIRST Restrictions/gender appropriate	2
FIRST Unisex	3
PERS Commemorative	1
PERS Propositional (divinity, relationship)	3
PERS Epithetic (descriptive, short; divinity or authority)	2
PERS One-name system original	2
PERS Birth order names	2

(continued)

Table 13.4 (Continued)

Name terms	Bible	Chinese	Dutch	French	German	Greek	Hungarian	Jewish	Maltese	Māori	Polish	Portuguese	United Kingdom	United States	Zulu	Totals
PERS Divine element in many names	1	1														2
PERS Five-element oriented names		1														1
PERS Foreign names introduced	1	1									1			1		4
PERS Generation names		1														1
PERS Languages blend		1									1					2
PERS Indigenous lang. & English system										1					1	2
PERS Nicknames used											1				1	2
PERS Teknonymous form of address															1	1
Totals	5	22	15	18	16	13	11	16	13	6	14	11	12	11	11	194

FAM = Family name

FIRST = First name

PERS = Personal name or miscellaneous

Terms that do not fit neatly into either the FAM or FIRST are categorized as PERS (Personal). For example, the names of Bible figures, the teknonymous form of address, and so on.

Summarizing and tabulating the 196 entries with 73 practices was a challenging task. All the sections were read carefully. Each type of naming was marked and listed. Then, the process was repeated. Classification of many of the practices listed was subjective. Perhaps other observers would classify the practices differently. Nevertheless, there is reasonable confidence that other experienced observers would make the bulk of the classifications in a similar way.

Studying Table 13.4, and the fifteen reports, one can make several observations:

1. There is a large and varied number of naming practices.
2. Patronyms are closely associated with the family name and the influence of the father in the majority of the reports.
3. There is a greater variety of first names today than in previous historical periods.
4. The role of religion in naming children has declined in recent history
5. The role of the media (TV, film, and press) has emerged as an important factor in naming children.
6. The British and Americans appear to have similar in naming patterns, as do the Dutch and German.
7. Hyphenated names for married couples are increasing in frequency.

For family names (FAM), the most reported practices are: family names (12), hereditary (12), patronyms (11), occupations (6), and residential/toponymic (8). For first names (FIRST), the most shared practices are: Bible (7), chosen by parents (6), influence of saints (5), and hypocoristic (5). In the personal name (PERS) category, the most frequent practice is introduction of foreign names.

While there are many naming practices that are followed in several language groups, it is also true that there are many practices that were unique to a single language: generation names (Chinese), apotropaic first names [warding off evil spirits] (Jewish), and first names after political, religious, or classical figures (USA).

So, now we come to the major question of how the relationship between systems be answered? For this question, we have to go to Table 13.5, The Index of Similarity. Here we have compared the similarities among the fifteen systems. We tallied all the practices in Table 13.4. For example, when we compare the Dutch practices to the Chinese, we find they share twenty-nine naming practices. When we compare the Dutch to the French, we find thirty-five shared practices. All the practices shared by the languages were tabulated and evaluated for patterns of similarity. The British pattern, Table 13.5, demonstrates more shared practices with other languages than any other, forty-seven with German; forty-four with Portuguese; forty-one with Greek, etc. The total number of shared practices reported for the UK was 432. The languages that have the least amount in common with other languages are Bible (17) and Māori (66). The second part of Table 13.5 lists the languages in order of the amount of shared practices.

Table 13.5 Index of Similarity

	Bible	Chinese	Dutch	French	German	Greek	Hungarian	Jewish	Maltese	Māori	Polish	Portuguese	United Kingdom	United States	Zulu	Totals
Bible		14	0	0	0	0	0	0	0	6	5	6	0	0	0	31
Chinese	0		29	26	21	20	26	18	14	5	19	19	26	25	12	260
Dutch	0	29		35	53	21	25	23	16	0	25	25	40	17	14	323
French	0	26	35		30	31	17	21	23	0	30	26	33	20	0	292
German	0	21	53	30		33	35	23	15	0	17	24	47	19	17	334
Greek	0	20	21	31	33		26	15	33	12	25	28	41	35	25	345
Hungarian	0	26	25	17	35	26		8	28	11	22	31	39	15	11	294
Jewish	0	18	23	21	23	15	8		13	5	21	17	29	19	11	223
Maltese	0	14	16	23	15	33	28	13		6	30	19	33	38	19	287
Māori	6	5	5	0	0	12	11	5	5		0	0	7	7	7	70
Polish	5	19	25	30	17	25	22	21	21	0		20	32	30	18	285
Port	6	19	25	26	24	28	31	17	17	0	20		44	18	21	296
UK	0	26	40	33	47	41	39	29	29	7	32	44		35	26	428
USA	0	25	17	30	19	35	15	19	19	7	30	18	35		29	298
Zulu	0	12	14	0	17	25	11	11	11	7	18	21	26	29		202
	17	274	328	302	334	345	294	223	244	66	294	298	432	307	210	3968

The following languages are listed in the order of similarity to other languages or as shared cultural naming practices. Thus, Britain has more in common with other languages than Zulu.

United Kingdom	432
Greek	345
German	334
Dutch	328
United States	307
French	302
Portuguese	298
Hungarian	294
Polish	294
Chinese	273
Maltese	244
Jewish	223
Zulu	210
Māori	66
Bible	17

13.4 DISCUSSION AND CONCLUSIONS

Looking at the final table showing each language and the amount of naming practices, the UK heads the list followed by Greek and German. One view is that British naming practices represent the strongest shared culture with other languages, followed by Greek and German. Another interpretation is that the British naming practices have more power and influence on other systems than occurs in the opposite direction. Other observers may offer different interpretations.

Other languages show shared cultural relationships in a descending order. We can also see affinities between other languages. For example, Dutch and German are very close, as are the UK and Portuguese practices. In this way, this investigation has shown the relationships between fifteen naming systems.

CHAPTER 14

GIVEN NAMES IN EUROPEAN NAMING SYSTEMS

KATHARINA LEIBRING

14.1 INTRODUCTION

In this chapter, my aim is to outline the historical development of given names in European naming systems. I write systems in the plural form, although it could be argued that European given names traditionally are parts of the same naming system. Even so, we find many regional subsystems in Europe: the different phases in them have taken place at very different times, and the subsystems have undergone more or less deep-rooted changes. However, seen from a distance, the major traits are the same in all countries in Europe as opposed to many naming systems in, for example Africa or Asia (see Saarelma 2012b).

The chapter begins with the discussion of the meaning of the term *given name*, and a section on what written sources can and cannot tell us about given names in a historical context. After that follows a diachronic overview, beginning before the Christian era, over 2,000 years ago, where the most important characteristics of the given names for each period are presented. Name examples of different features are given from different countries and languages, with some bias towards northern Europe, as that is the region with which I am most familiar. The chapter also contains a discussion of the recent trend in many European countries for individualization in given names, through, for example, unorthodox spellings and the creation of new names, and a few words on the different ways in which personal or given names have been chosen during history.

14.2 WHAT IS A GIVEN NAME?

How should one define the term *given name* in European naming systems? My definition is: a *given name* is the name (or those names) bestowed on an individual person, in most instances a very young child, with the purpose of individualizing this child; to separate him or her as a person from other people in the vicinity. This purpose is combined with the aim of including the child in the family and in the (local) society. In many European languages, an equivalent to *given name* would be *first name*, as that name is commonly placed in front of the surname in the name phrase referring to a certain person. In Europe, the opposite position is found in Hungary, where the family name is put in front of the given name. In some older onomastic literature, the terms *Christian name* or *baptismal name* are used. I will avoid them here, as they connect the names with rites in the Christian religion.

The given name is not to be confused with the byname (which can sometimes be used instead of, or more often together with, the given name) or the family name or surname. These are in many societies hereditary names signifying that people belong to the same family, clan or 'house'. Depending on name regulations in specific countries, more than one 'given name' can be bestowed on one person, and, depending on social and cultural habits, one or two of them (rarely three) can be used in daily speech. This name (or these names) can be termed the *call name(s)*.

Given names can be categorized according to morphological aspects, that is, if they are simple names, compound names, derivations of other names with suffixes, etc., but also according to semantic or etymological aspects. As has been shown by many scholars, given names often contained meaningful elements in earlier times. The word meaning 'wolf' has been used as a male name in many languages (*Ulf, Wolf, Vlk, Vuk*), probably denoting strength. Words for weapons and fame have also been used, for example Germanic *helm* 'helmet', *gerr* 'spear', and Slavonic *slava*, 'rumour, fame'. In contrast to these war-alluding name elements, many names have also contained elements meaning 'peace' (Germ. *fried*, Slav. *mir*) and 'love' (Slav. *mil*). In most languages and cultures, there has been a division between semantic content concerning positive or wished-for qualities in male as opposed to female names. Words for the qualities of strength, power, and bellicosity are more often found in male names, while female names often contain words representing beauty and peacefulness. It should be remembered, though, that in Old Germanic names, female names could contain warlike elements. One example is the Nordic name *Gunnhildr*, where the elements *gunnr* and *hildr* both mean 'fight'. Most European naming systems share a division between male and female names. Because the male has been regarded as prototypical in all European societies, it follows that many female names have been derived from male names, for example Latin *Julia* from *Julius*, and German *Wilhelmina* from *Wilhelm*.

Many or most of the meaningful given names were created from words having positive qualities or praising elements. Over time, in several cultures, the phenomenon of names denoting negative components has, however, also been used. These so-called apotropeic names are thought to have been given as protection against evil spirits.

14.3 THE DEVELOPMENT OF GIVEN NAMES IN EUROPEAN NAMING SYSTEMS

14.3.1 The Transmission of Personal Names from Earlier Times

Most countries in Europe share at least some common historical developments regarding their given names. Before the massive dissemination of Christianity and suppression of local religions, we have, from many areas, sources that reveal that many different indigenous (vernacular) names were used. These names and name-forms were naturally dependent on the language(s) used in the area. There are large differences between countries and regions concerning the amount of sources preserved for names from these early times, due to social, cultural, linguistic, or demographic factors. From all areas, however, there are fewer women's names than men's names preserved, and most of the name stock emanates from people belonging to the upper strata of society.

One should bear in mind that the written-down form in, for example, a baptismal register, or on a rune stone or an epitaph, on many occasions does not represent the name-form in daily use. The scribe may have deemed it more proper to record a name in its 'full' form, as *Margaret*, although the bearer may have been called *Meg* or *Maggie* by most people in her vicinity. From later times we can often find examples of varying name-forms for most individuals in different types of name registers. Likewise, the notion of set orthographic rules is a rather recent innovation, as many students of archival records can testify, meaning that up until the nineteenth century, it would sometimes be natural for people to spell even their own names differently at different times.

14.3.2 Before Christianization

If we return to the earliest period from which we have records of names in Europe, most people in many areas were given only one name—if there were too many namesakes in the area, bynames would be coined, often characterizing the bearer, sometimes alluding to his ancestry or homeland, at times alluding to an event in his life. The Roman naming system differs as it was more elaborate, and I will come back to that presently. Some language groups from which we have pre-Christian names preserved are the Balto-Slavonic, Celtic, Finno-Ugric, Germanic (including Nordic), Greek, Illyrian, Latin, and Slavonic groups.

As stated above, many of these pre-Christian names were originally semantically meaningful and created from words from the ordinary language. In many cultures, a large proportion of the given names were compound names, where each part would originally have had an independent meaning. This is especially characteristic of Germanic, Celtic, Greek, and Slavonic names. Name elements in those languages could be combined fairly freely, thus in time making the original meaning of the name elements obsolete, and making the combinations illogical or absurd. One Scandinavian example could be *Arnbjǫrn*, where the two parts mean 'eagle' (< *arin*) and 'bear' (*bjǫrn*). It should be noted, however, that, even though the name elements were mixed, the second element in most instances denoted the child's gender. A Scandinavian name ending in *-rún* was given to girls, while names ending on *-sten* were given to boys. In addition to the compounds, the name stock consisted of simplex names (e.g. *Bjǫrn*) as well as short forms of the compound names (e.g. *Arni* < *Arnsten*).

A large number of different Germanic pre-Christian names are preserved in Scandinavia, mostly from runic inscriptions. The quantity is partly due to the fact that Scandinavia was Christianized very late, and because the art of writing with runic letters was fairly widespread, thus producing many artefacts containing personal names. An overall reason for the large number of Germanic names is the widespread custom of creating new compound names by combining name elements from the parents' respective names. Parallels to this, active creation of new names are found among the Slavonic-speaking people, where several name elements (see section 14.2 above) were recycled and combined in compound names.

Another impetus for creating new names among Germanic-speaking people was the tradition of alliteration, where names in a certain family for several generations would begin with the same letter. This custom can be regarded in connection with names found in Germanic heroic literature. It was mostly used in the higher social strata, as in the names of the kings of the Sviones *Dómaldi, Dómar, Dyggvi*, or the heroes of three generations in the German Hildebrandslied *Heribrand, Hiltibrand*, and *Hadubrand*. The latter names combine alliteration with the transmission of the later name element *-brand*.

A corresponding system of compound names is found among the oldest preserved names of Baltic-Finnic people, where name elements such as *toivo* 'hope', *valta* 'power', and *mieli* 'pleasant' were used. Scholars are divided as to whether this compound name system was indigenous or modelled on the Germanic fashion. In favour of the latter view is the fact that names of this type are not known among the eastern Finno-Ugric speaking people, but only in the western part of the area (Saarelma 2012b).

14.3.2.1 *Given Names in the Roman Empire*

The one-name system described above was also used originally in the Italic areas that would become the Roman Empire, although it became increasingly more sophisticated over time (Solin 1998). Towards the end of the seventh century BC a complex naming system had already been established. The name of a free male citizen would, during the classical era, always consist of three parts, the *prænomen* (forename), the *nomen gentilicum* (family name), and the *cognomen* (surname or byname). An example is M. (for *Marcus*) *Tullius Cicero*. To these three names, the father's name and a tribal designation could be added, although those elements were often omitted in the name phrase. In this context, only the *prænomen* and later, the *cognomen*, are of interest. The forenames have their roots in the old individual names, of which there were originally plenty. However, as their role in the new naming system became mostly to distinguish individuals in the same family from each other, the name corpus dwindled. During the late Republican period, only eighteen forenames were in use, and they were often represented only by their initial (*M* for *Marcus*) in the name phrase. To differentiate persons, the bynames (which were first used among patrician families, and later in all social classes) became individual names that, already in the early stages of the Caesarian era, took over the forename's role as identifier. The *cognomina* stem from many areas, both linguistically and semantically. Among the languages used Latin and Greek were the most common, but Semitic, Thracian, Illyrian, and Celtic names are also known.

Women in ancient Rome had of old a *praenomen*, mostly consisting of a feminine form of a male forename (*Livia* from *Livius*), or a name describing the bearer's place among siblings (e.g. *Tertia* for the third child), but during the Republic these names were not much used. Women instead had their father's family name (*nomen gentilicum*) in a feminine form, coupled with a patronymic. During the later Roman Empire, most free-born women used *cognomina* similar to those used by men (Solin 1998).

14.3.3 Christianization and Given Names during the Middle Ages

The process of Christianization took place at different times in different areas of Europe, starting in Rome and Greece, spreading outwards from the third century, and continuing well into the twelfth century, in the more remote parts of Europe, for example Finland and the Baltic countries.

Long before the fall of the Western Roman Empire in 476, indeed already as early as during the fourth century AD, several Germanic tribes had immigrated into (or invaded) the Roman Empire (in Gaul, Italy, and farther east) and created autonomous regions inside the Empire. Many men of Germanic origin became powerful officers in the Roman army, and these Germans brought their names with them. Many of the Latin names, especially in the northern parts of the Empire, fell into disuse, as the Germanic dithematic names became fashionable. Of those Roman names that survived the Middle Ages, many were names that had been borne by saints or martyrs in the early Christian Church. Christianity became the state religion in 380 in the Roman Empire. Names borne by Christians could also be of Greek or Hebrew origin, as the early Church did not deem it necessary that adult people should change their name to a more Christian-sounding name. Indeed, even names originally of pagan gods were borne by early Church dignitaries, as the name of the third-century Bishop Dionysius shows, according to Wilson (1998: 59).

From the sixth or seventh century, on occasions when adults converted to Christianity, the converts regularly adopted new names, often from the Bible or from the names of apostles, saints, and martyrs. Baptized children had, however, much earlier been given names that were approved by the Church, again, names from the Bible, or the names of saints and martyrs, of Hebrew, Greek, or Latin origin.

The stock of religious names approved by the Church grew bigger and more popular. During the Middle Ages these names diffused and gradually began to dominate the name pools in (mostly) all European countries. As stated above, most regions of Europe had become Christianized before or in the twelfth century. As several pagan religions were suppressed by the new creed, many vernacular names fell into disuse.

One consequence of the West–East divide of the Roman Empire (formally finalized in 395), was that different names (or name-forms) began to appear in the areas dominated by either the Roman-Catholic or the Greek-Orthodox creed. The onomastic outcome can be categorized as a rough division between Western and Eastern Europe, based on either the Latin or the Greek formation of the religious names. As a further consequence of these two creeds each dominating one part of Europe, some saints had become more popular in Eastern than in Western Europe and vice versa, which of course influenced the name stock. However, it is easy to identify a large pool of religious names that were popular all over Christianized Europe. Many of these very popular names soon began to evolve into new forms according to the different indigenous languages in the regions, and they have kept their popularity over time in many European countries. Some examples of these well-known names and name-forms are: *Iohannes*, from which (among others) the forms *Euan, Hans, Ivan, Jan, Jean, Johan, John, Juan*, etc. are found. *Katharina—Catalina, Catherine, Catriona, Kajsa, Karin, Katalin, Katarzyna, Katrin*, etc. *Michael—Michel, Mihály, Mikael, Mikhail, Miguel, Miklos. Margareta—Margaret, Margarita, Margit, Marguerite, Marit. Stefanos—Esteban, István, Staffan, Stefan, Stéphane, Stephen*, etc. Later on, many pet forms and short forms for daily use were created for these names, forms that later have evolved into given names in their own right, for example *Greta* from *Margareta, Lisa* from *Elisabet*, or *Jack* from *John*.

Many of the Germanic names that had become popular during the early Middle Ages continued to be used both in southern, western, and northern Europe. In England, some of these names were transmitted through the Norman Conquest with aristocratic bearers. In Scandinavia, High and Low Germanic names arrived with the Hanseatic merchants who exploited the new towns among the coasts and in many instances became high ranking members of society. Several of the Germanic names that had reached southern Europe during the era of the Great Migration were continuously in use in Spain and Italy during the Middle Ages. In Ireland, many indigenous Celtic names were still frequent, although they were mixed with the newer names of Christianity of which many soon received forms more adapted to the Irish language, for example the female names *Caitriona* and *Siobhán* from *Catherine* and *Joan*, and *Seán* or *Euan* from *John*.

14.3.4 Given Names during the Renaissance

During the Renaissance period, many classical given names from Rome and Greece were revived, especially among the learned professions and in the upper classes. In Italy, these names had never really gone out of fashion, and as Italian culture and style became popular in England and France in connection with the humanist movement, influences from antiquity are perceptible in these countries. The French forms of the names of well-known classical figures, for example *Achille, Alexandre, Hélène,* and *Hercule,* were used, while in England we find *Ambrose* and *Virgil,* in English forms, paired with *Diana, Caesar, Cassandra,* and *Hannibal.* However, the dominance of the religious names continued in both western and eastern countries even though many of the Germanic names lived on in both north and south. In Scandinavia, a name stock similar to that during the medieval period was used, consisting of a mixture for both sexes of primarily Christian names and German names. Male Nordic names continued to be in use, while the reduction of the stock of female Nordic names increased. The indigenous Nordic names were best preserved in Iceland, although religious names, especially female, gained a certain popularity even in that country.

14.3.5 Given Names during the Early Modern Age (*c.*1550–1750)

One of the most striking features concerning given names during the Early Modern Age (*c.*1550–1750) is the great name conformity and the surprisingly great diminishing of the name stock, especially regarding women's names. Many vernacular names seem to have virtually disappeared. It is important, however, to bear in mind that sources of given names for this period are not as rich for women as for men, especially for the lower classes. Even with this reservation, there is no doubt that the size of the name stock in use was substantially reduced compared to earlier periods all over Europe.

In the Catholic parts of Europe, one reason for this was the decisions taken at the council of Trent (1545–63), where certain rules for the Roman Catholic church were consolidated. Among the more direct religious declarations, it was decided that only names found in the saints' calendar, and names of national importance, were to be used as given names in Roman Catholic countries. This obviously led to an increased use of a limited number of very popular names. To distinguish people from each other, more different short forms and hypocoristic forms of popular names came into use, as well as bynames and hereditary family names. For the historical development of these name-types, see chapter 16 in this handbook.

However, we find the same reduction of the name stock in the Protestant countries where the council of Trent had no authority. In those countries, one reason why so few names were in use was the purification of 'heathen' names. Lutheran or Calvinist ministers could refuse to baptize children with names they considered unsuitable in a Christian (Protestant) society. In northern Europe, this meant that a number of Old Nordic or Germanic names were relegated to the collective junk room, some to be revived later. In the more remote areas of Scandinavia, several Nordic names, mostly male, were, however continuously used.

The time of the great religious wars, mainly during the late sixteenth and most of the seventeenth centuries, and the polarization of different types of Christianity (especially Protestantism and Catholicism) also led to a preference for somewhat different names for people of the respective creed. After the Reformation, we find less use of non-prestigious saints' names in Protestant countries than in Catholic countries. The usage of such names was also discouraged by the Church in several Protestant countries.

During the Middle Ages, names from the Old Testament were rather rare as given names, but after the rise of Protestantism, they became quite common in Lutheran countries. Some examples are the male names *Abraham, Benjamin, Joseph, Samuel*, and *Zacharias*. Among the rarer female names are *Rachel* and *Rebecca*. There are indications that show that these names continued to be less popular in Catholic or Orthodox countries. In Jewish societies in Europe, names from the Old Testament were dominant. The Orthodox Church had early stipulated that only names from the Orthodox saints' roll should be used, which resulted in many names of Greek origin, or in the Greek form, becoming common in Russia and other countries in the east. Another new name category at that time, mostly found in English-speaking Protestant countries, consists of names that allude to moral qualities: *Faith, Hope, Prudence*, etc. To this category can be coupled the Pietistic names that ask for God's help or allude to God's love, for example the German *Gottlieb* ('God's love') and *Traugott* ('true to God').

An important change in the giving of female names in northern Europe was the rise of the name *Maria* as a very popular name for girls. In earlier days, as the name of God's mother and the object of intensive worship, it had been regarded as too holy to give to mortals, and it was not until after the Reformation that it came into use in Scandinavia and Germany. In southern Europe, for example in Spain and Portugal, *Maria* was already a very frequent female name during the Middle Ages. It has also inspired new female names in the Iberian Peninsula through the use of commemorative names of festive days for God's mother as given names: *Maria del Dolores, Maria del Pilar, Maria del Carmen*, etc., from which the names *Dolores, Pilar*, and *Carmen* later came to be used independently. In Catholic countries, *Maria* can also be combined with a male name and be given to boys, for example *Carlos Maria, Juan Maria*.

Parts of (Eastern) Europe belonged to the Ottoman Empire for several centuries, and there, for example in Bulgaria, some names of Turkish or Arabic origin found roots. The main stock of names in the Greek-Orthodox countries continued to be based on the names of saints and Biblical people found in the Orthodox calendar, although in divers forms according to the local languages spoken. Traditional Slavonic names were not much favoured during this period, however some popular saints' names of Slavonic origin, for example *Vladislav* and *Borislav*, stayed in use. The widespread use of suffixes in the Slavonic languages meant that many new forms of Christian names, hypocorisms or short forms, were developed over time in different countries. Some examples are Bulgarian *Petko* (< *Peter*), Croatian *Katina* (< *Katarina*), Macedonian *Betka* (< *Elisabet*) and *Miha* (< *Mihail* < *Michael*), Serbian *Perica* (< *Peter*), and Slovakian *Kuba* (< *Jacob*).

To conclude, all over Europe during the seventeenth century, the name stock still mainly consisted of such names, based on the Christian tradition, that had become popular during the Middle Ages. Most of these names had been adapted to different languages, so we find many various forms that can be regarded as fully integrated in the particular language in question. Some vernacular names lived on in most areas, not least among rural people. In Sweden, several old Nordic names, for example *Erik, Olof, Ingeborg*, and *Ingrid*, continued to be used, although their popularity can in part be said to be related to sanctified name-bearers. The situation was similar in Norway, Iceland, and the northern parts of Scotland.

14.3.5.1 *Name Transmission*

An important reason for the diminishing name stock is of course the different systems of 'Nachbenennung' or transmission of names along regular patterns. This transmission was often made either from one generation to the next, or by alternating between generations (from grandfather to grandson). Furthermore, dead older siblings could be commemorated as namesakes. The system of family transmission of names was more elaborate and was apparently used more for boys than girls in most countries. However, as it is more difficult to trace female ancestors, the question of the extent of transmission of female names has not yet been sufficiently investigated. Over time, this system led to a certain set of names being used very often, thus reducing the name stock. There are examples from several countries where as few as ten names were used for over 80 per cent of the population of one sex in a certain parish. This custom enhanced the creation and use of regional name forms that were utilized as official names as well, a feature that is discernible in for example the Netherlands, where many local forms of names in the saints' calendar flourished.

Another kind of transmission of names is the tradition of naming children after godparents. This became common in England in the late Middle Ages, and was a frequent naming pattern in several northern countries in the seventeenth and eighteenth centuries.

In England, and in North America, where it became very common, original surnames were taken into use as first names. It was not uncommon for the mother's surname to be bestowed on a son as a given name. This custom began in the seventeenth century among the upper classes and continued well into the nineteenth century, then often in the middle classes. Some of these names were the now well-known independent first names *Douglas, Stanley*, and *Sidney*, which all started out as surnames. The custom of adapting surnames to given names has never been very frequent either in continental Europe or in Scandinavia.

14.3.5.2 *The Origin of Multiple Given Names*

The shrinkage of the name pool described above can be regarded as one reason for the development of systems with multiple (two or more) given names, although this phenomenon had already started in southern Europe during the early Middle Ages. Regarding this feature from a distance, we find that there are large chronological differences between countries, as well as differences between social groups in each country. It is thus hard to give a succinct overview of the diffusion history. However, as early as during the ninth century in Italy, people belonging to the higher classes had two given names, although the custom did not become frequent in that country before the high Middle Ages. The custom trickled down the social strata and spread in time to other countries, first to Spain and France, where examples of two given names are found from the twelfth century onwards. We find them regularly among the German upper classes during the sixteenth century, as well as in the Netherlands, and somewhat later in Britain. In Sweden and Denmark, the first examples date from the late sixteenth century. All early examples in those countries come from people belonging to the very high nobility, mostly in families with German connections. The custom did not, however, become really common in Scandinavia before the late eighteenth century. In England, it was established in all social classes around 1800. In several countries of Eastern Europe, for example Serbia, the custom of bestowing two or more given names has never been much in use. In many countries, after (and even during) the introductory phase of multiple name systems, it has been more frequent for two or more given names to be bestowed on girls.

One distinction to bear in mind while discussing the giving of multiple first names is the formal difference between multiple names and composite names. The first term indicates that the bearer gets more than one given name (but in many cases only uses one of them as his/her spoken name), while the second denotes that the bearer uses a combination of two names regularly as the spoken name-form. Due to its orthographic form, where a hyphen can be inserted to illustrate that both names are meant to be used, this fashion has sometimes been called hyphenated names.

14.3.6   New Influences during the Eighteenth and Nineteenth Centuries

At the time of the Enlightenment in the eighteenth century, new name trends came to light. French culture and the French language were fashionable, so many French names and names in French forms became popular in many countries. Some examples are *André, Émile, Charlotte, Henriette, Julie*, and *Marie*.

A revived interest in antiquity resulted in names from Greek and Roman mythology and history becoming popular again, for example *Diana* and *Flora*, *Julius* and *Augustus*. Even classical authors were used as name sources, for example *Horace* or *Horatius*. These names could be adapted to the languages into which they were borrowed, for example *Jules* and *Auguste* in French, and *Julius* and *August* in German. Female names used in England were *Flavia* and *Octavia*, feminine forms of the well-known Latin male names *Flavius* and *Octavius*. The custom of using classical names began, as many onomastic trends, among the upper social classes and the learned clergy, and gradually trickled down to the middle and lower classes. It became common in Italy, France, Germany, and England, and to a lesser extent in Scandinavia.

The Romantic era, during the late 1700s and early 1800s, saw the birth of nationalistic feelings in many European countries. This, in combination with the new interest in traditional folk culture and the breaking-up of some of the old empires in Europe, led to the rediscovery and revival of old vernacular names. In Eastern Europe, many old Slavonic names were taken into use again; in Scandinavia, translations of the Norse Sagas from Old Icelandic into Swedish and Danish led to the names of their heroes becoming popular, etc. Later during the nineteenth century, old Finnish and Baltic names became popular in Finland and the Baltic countries. As Finnish nationalism grew stronger under the Russian government, people would change their Swedish-sounding names to the Finnish equivalents. Both in Finland and in several other countries, new names were created on the patterns of old name types, and abstract appellatives and adjectives were used as names. Some Finnish examples of the latter are *Toivo* 'hope' and *Armas* 'beloved'. Nordic names created during the nineteenth century using well-known old elements are, for example, *Gulbret* and *Solfrid*. This custom was most common in Norway, as part of the constitution of a new national feeling after centuries of having been under domination by Denmark and Sweden. New names created from Hungarian language elements, or revivals of old indigenous names, became common in Hungary as part of the nationalistic movement. The same situation can be seen in Latvia, albeit starting not before the late nineteenth century. In contrast to this awakening awareness of national feelings, many Gaelic names and name-forms in Ireland were anglicized during the eighteenth and nineteenth centuries.

In some countries, the use of vernacular traditional names was prohibited for political or religious reasons. In catholic countries in southern and mid-Europe, names from the Catholic Church Saints' calendar still held the name-givers in a firm grip, as did the Orthodox calendar in eastern Europe. In the Netherlands, it was not until 1815 that the name laws permitted the usage of old names from outside the Calendar.

Another onomastic outcome of the romantic Sturm und Drang period was an increased usage of literary names, not least those from the Ossian Cycle (by James Macpherson). Several of his pseudo-Celtic names, for example *Oscar, Malvina*, and *Selma*, became popular in many countries. Other names made famous through literature, mostly female, that won approval by name-givers are *Julie* and *Heloise* by Rousseau, and *Lotte* and *Felix* by Goethe, as well as some names from the Arthurian cycle: *Tristan, Arthur*, and *Isolde*. Earlier examples of literary names becoming popular as given names are *Pamela* and *Clarissa* by Richardson, and several names in plays by Shakespeare (*Jessica, Miranda, Ophelia*).

Naming after royals was another new trend in the eighteenth and nineteenth centuries. In Sweden, the names *Oskar, Josefina*, and *Karl Johan* in the new royal family became popular during the first half of the nineteenth century, and in England *Augusta, Charlotte*, and *Albert*.

Later on in the nineteenth century, name creativity blossomed in many countries. The tradition of name transmission began to become unfashionable, as new political and ideological ideas became known, ideas putting more emphasis on the freedom of the individual. As ordinary people got the opportunity to travel with the new means of transportation (steamships and trains), and as literacy increased in many countries, a broader view of society was possible for many. Generally speaking, there were now more potential sources when choosing given names. One could argue that the revolutions in the mid-nineteenth century, where several countries were liberated and empires dissolved, and nationalistic feelings rekindled, paved the ground not only for name revivals but also for the coinage of new names from indigenous language elements, and the borrowing of foreign names.

A larger name stock has been in use for girls than for boys since the nineteenth century in many countries, and the lifespan of popular girls' names is often shorter than for boys' names. Probably, this mirrors a traditionalistic view where boys have been regarded as more important for upholding the family name and hereditary first names in the family.

14.3.7 Naming during the Twentieth Century

If the history of European naming systems were to be regarded as an entity, without stressing any regional differences, one striking impression would be that the stock of given names has become more and more international, and more transferable during the secularized twentieth century. Many of the popular names from the onomastically more restricted Christian era, which over time had developed vernacular forms, have kept these different forms inside the different countries, but many of these forms have also wandered over national borders. The devastating wars and political upheavals that have taken place have also been influential on name-givers. One example of this is the inflow of popular North American names after World War II. This includes both male names borrowed from the soldiers and names of popular film stars and music artists of both sexes. Other examples could be the Russian names that were tributes to the revolution and the communist leadership, or similar names in Albania.

By giving a child the name of a revolutionary hero, or the name of a dictator, different signals are transmitted. The choice of a certain name could also stress a regional identity, so much so that under different rulers certain names or name forms are forbidden, as were Catalan name forms under the Franco regime in Spain. Certain name categories could also be discouraged, as was the use of religious names in Albania during the communist era, and Turkish names in Bulgaria.

14.3.8 The Present-day Situation

During recent decades we have seen a great influx of names from cultures outside Europe. This is partly due to immigration, but it is also an obvious indicator of the undisputed internationalization and globalization of the world. One cannot, however, speak of any total globalization of the stock of given names in Europe. Not many names of, for example, Chinese or Arabian origin have gained popularity in Europe outside the circles of immigrants or their descendants. Many names and name types popular in North America are, however, used in European countries, displaying both the onomastic affinity between these continents and the impact of North American popular culture. In connection with this, one can also detect some inclinations towards the usage of more gender-neutral names. This is of course only found in countries where there are no regulations stipulating that names should reveal the bearer's sex. This custom is perhaps inspired by the United States, where many given names are regularly bestowed on children of either sex.

Over the most recent decades, one can identify a yearning or ambition by parents in many European countries to give their children unique names, or at least unique spellings of their names. This is, in my opinion, part of the present quest for individuality and uniqueness in social and cultural circumstances. The custom has seen the creation of many hitherto unknown names, some made by new combinations of already existing name elements, some by extending the sources of given names to words not used before as names, and some by combining sounds and letters in new ways. We can also see a tendency whereby even more pet forms, nicknames, and hypocorisms are used as official names. In earlier times, these forms would be spoken in daily communication, while the full form would be reserved for written documents and official transactions.

A contemporary but contrasting trend shows an increased usage of more international names, as well as names from idols in popular culture, something that has made the stock of popular names more similar in different countries. In a way, this could be regarded as an up-dated return to the earlier days when most names in European countries had their common roots in the names of saints and Biblical persons. Among the most popular names for children born in 2010–12 in many European countries were *Emma* and *Sofia*, *Lucas* and *Oliver*. Of these names, *Lucas* is a Greek name from the Bible, and *Emma* is a short form of Old Germanic names beginning in *Ermin-*. *Sophia* is a Greek name used first in the Orthodox countries, but since the eighteenth century widely used all over Europe, while *Oliver*, from the chronicles of Charlemagne, is sometimes said to be Latin (from the Latin family name *Olivarius*), sometimes thought to be an interpretation of the Germanic name elements *Alf-heri* or *Wolf-heri*. In this eclectic mixture of popular names, more than one facet of the roots of modern European name-giving is thus demonstrated.

During the last few years, there has also been a trend in many countries to use names of a more nationalistic colour, and the custom of name transmission from older relatives has had a renaissance. The three-generation-cycle of name popularity seems to be valid in many cases, that is, young parents avoid names popular in their own and in their parents' generations, choosing instead names known from the age of their grandparents.

14.4 How to Choose a Given Name?

Several ways of choosing, selecting, or creating given names can be identified throughout history. These ways are, as the rest of our language usage, dependent on time, social and political situation, as well as on individual preferences. Some ways in Europe have been:

- total or partial naming after older relatives or godparents (name transfer);
- variation by combining name elements;
- naming after the Calendar name of the birthday (very common, and indeed at some times almost obligatory in the Catholic church to give the child the name of the day in the Saints' Calendar);
- naming after famous persons, real or fictional;
- naming after an event at or time of birth;
- giving a negatively connoted name to protect the child from evil spirits, etc.;
- giving a positive name, a 'Wunschname';
- choosing a certain name because of its euphony.

The choice of a given name could also be a way of commemorating deceased ancestors, in combination with a wish that this person's positive characteristics would follow the name. The system of multiple given names could make it easier to combine some of these different choices, thus perhaps settling more demands, spoken or unspoken, that are often made on new parents when they are in the name-giving process.

14.5 SUMMING UP

I consider it worth repeating, that the historical names here studied and discussed are mostly those conveyed to us through written forms. How these forms are related to such name forms that were used in everyday life is for older periods very hard, maybe impossible, to define. Having that reservation in mind, one could sum up the devolution of the European systems of given names in a few paragraphs: According to the earliest sources, they often consisted of originally meaningful names created from the stuff of many languages. After the Christianization of Europe, from the Middle Ages until the Age of Enlightenment, the stock of given names was broadly speaking limited to such names that were related to the Christian faith and church, and the name stock dwindled in size. From the eighteenth century onwards, an overwhelming quantity of newly created names evolved, in combination with names revived from earlier cultures and periods and the basic stock of Christian names. This evolution, combined with the fact that many names of similar origin are still used in several countries over Europe, makes the many national European naming subsystems parts of one larger common system.

14.5.1 Literature

Possibly the only modern comprehensive book on European personal names is the anthology *Europäische Personennamensysteme*, edited by Brendler and Brendler (2007). For each language, an onomastic specialist has written a chapter on the historical development of the personal names as well as on the contemporary name situation. References to further reading are also given. Combined with different chapters in *Namenforschung/Name studies/Les noms propres*, edited by Ernst Eichler et al. (1995–6), the most important areas in the field of given names are covered. I have consulted these works continuously when writing this chapter. In addition, a paper by Heikki Solin (1998) was used on the Roman naming system, as was Minna Saarelma's (2012b) chapter on the Finnish names and Thorsten Andersson's (1998) on Germanic names. For various details on the historical development of naming systems in Western Europe, Stephen Wilson's (1998) monograph *The Means of Naming* proved very valuable. There are many name dictionaries and handbooks published for separate languages and countries, and I have used them when necessary. Some of the more important for this chapter are listed here: Seibicke (1996–2007); Hanks and Hodges (2001); Brylla (2004); Peterson (2007); and Kohlheim and Kohlheim (2013); Kruken (2013).

CHAPTER 15

··

FAMILY NAMES

··

PATRICK HANKS AND HARRY PARKIN

15.1 ORIGINS OF HEREDITARY SURNAMES

15.1.1 Personal Naming Systems of the World

Every human society has a naming system for identifying individuals within it (see chapter 13). This normally consists of one or more given names (see chapter 14) and an additional name whose function is to identify the individual as a member of a family within society. With very few exceptions, there are just three such systems of personal naming throughout the world: the patronymic system, the binomial system, and the Arabic system. The focus of this chapter will be on family names within the binomial system, but first we give a brief account of the other two systems, both of which have contributed to the development of family names within the binomial system in the English-speaking world and in other European languages.

In the Arabic personal naming system a person's name comprises up to five elements. These are: *kunya* (a kind of aspirational nickname, for example *Abu-Fazl* 'father of bounty' and *Umm-Abdullah* 'mother of Abdullah', which could be adopted regardless of whether any child called Abdullah actually exists), *ism* (given name), *nasab* (patronymic), *nisba* (locative name), and *laqab* (distinguishing nickname such as *al-Aswad* 'the Black'). Kunya, nasab, nisba, and laqab have all been adopted as 'surnames' among people from the Islamic world who have migrated to English-speaking countries and to other countries where the binomial system of personal naming is prevalent.

While this is the standard system of Arabic personal naming, used throughout the Islamic world, there is much variation in different countries, with the different elements being used in different ways (for more information see Schimmel 1989; Ahmed 1999; Roochnik and Ahmed 2003). One of these differences concerns the use of fixed family names. Ahmed (1999) comments:

> In some Muslim countries, e.g. Egypt, Iran and Turkey, family names are well established, but in the Indian subcontinent a complete liberty in selecting names means

that there is no necessary continuation of the surname from father to son. Also, there is little distinction between a surname and first name and they are freely interchanged. (Ahmed 1999: xiii)

The patronymic system was once the norm throughout most of Europe. People were named according to their parentage, so that along with a given name, they would be identified by the given name of their father and very often by reference to previous generations too (see, for example, section 15.1.2.4, on Welsh surnames). The patronymic system survived in Sweden well into the nineteenth century and still exists today in Iceland, where people are typically known by a given name and a patronym. Thus, the son or daughter of a man with the given name *Sven* would be *Svensson* or *Svensdóttir* respectively. This system is also found in English medieval records such as the fourteenth-century poll tax returns, where, for example, Alicia *Robertdoghter* is recorded in Rigton, West Riding of Yorkshire, in 1379. However, no names of this *-daughter* type have survived in England today. This example shows how the patronymic system, which is not hereditary, is distinct from the binomial system, in which an individual inherits a hereditary surname[1] as well as being given a forename at or soon after birth. The binomial system is used today throughout the English-speaking world, in Europe, and in certain other countries.

The binomial system has been established in most European countries since the fourteenth century. Between the twelfth and the fourteenth centuries (and in some places earlier) descriptive, non-hereditary bynames—typically derived from locations, relationships, nicknames, or occupations—gradually became fixed within family groups and passed down to subsequent generations. Throughout Europe there is remarkable uniformity in the types of names used, with comparatively few local differences. An example of a local difference is that family names of locative origin are very rare in Ireland but very common in England. This is predominantly due to differences in the historical development of bynames and hereditary family names, which we will now summarize by giving a brief account of surname history in Britain and Ireland.

15.1.2 The Origin and Typology of Surnames in Britain and Ireland

15.1.2.1 *English Surnames*

There is no simple answer to the question when and why hereditary family names first came into use in England. The history of their development is complex, with much variation in different parts of the country and different social classes, over several centuries. However, some broad generalizations can be made. It was very rare for a person to be

---

[1] The term *surname*, which used to mean no more than 'additional name', is now used interchangeably with *family name*.

recorded with more than one name before the Norman Conquest. Hey (2000: 51) comments that 'the Englishmen who were recorded in Domesday Book as the holders of land before the Conquest did not possess hereditary surnames but were known simply by a personal name, such as Alric, Thorald or Wulfstan'. However, in some pre-Conquest records, 'it was often found convenient to identify a man by describing him as son of his father'. Therefore, it could be said that some people bore second names at this time, but 'such names were not family names; they died with the man' (Reaney 1967: 75).

The next step toward the adoption of hereditary family names in England was the use of non-hereditary bynames. These names had a rather different semantic value from that of surnames today. They were used to describe some aspect or feature of their bearer, distinguishing him (or her) from other people by reference to occupation, geographical location or origin, relationship to another person, or some physical or behavioural characteristic.

Bynames and surnames are classified under one of the following four broad categories: locative names, nicknames, occupational names, and relationship names. Each category can be further subdivided. Thus, locative bynames can be either topographical (derived from a feature of the landscape, e.g. *Hill, Ford, Marsh*) or toponymic (taken from the pre-existing name of a town, farm, or other habitation, e.g. *Burford, Blakeway, Copplestone*). Many occupational names are straightforward and self-explanatory even today (e.g. *Baker, Smith*) but others are fossils, from a term that is no longer used (e.g. *Wright, Chandler*). Some occupational names originated as metonymic nicknames, for example the surname *Cheese* denoted a maker or seller of cheese. The surname *Wastell*, denoting someone who made or sold fine cakes, is a metonymic nickname from a Norman French word that is the equivalent of modern French *gâteau*. Status names such as *Knight* and *Squire* are usually classified as a subdivision of occupational names.

Bynames were coined mainly in Middle English—the vernacular language of the time—although names of Norman French origin were also adopted. The adoption of bynames following the Norman Conquest may have been accelerated by an increase in medieval bureaucracy. Hey (2000: 54) attributes the development of hereditary surnames at least in part to the fact that 'whereas the Anglo-Saxons and Vikings had used a wide range of personal names, the Normans favoured very few', some of which are still strikingly frequent today, such as the traditional male names *John, Robert*, and *William* and the female names *Juliana, Isobel*, and *Elizabeth*. The smaller stock of given names in use among the Normans and the gradual abandonment of most Anglo-Saxon given names meant that a larger number of people were known by the same name, so there was a need to distinguish between individuals in some other way than the use of a sole given name. Bynames were used for this purpose. As each byname was particular to the individual, it would not have been passed on to any offspring. This non-hereditary characteristic meant that any one individual might be known by two or more bynames. An example is 'Ricardus filius Walteri, de Cliue' (Reaney 1997: xii), recorded in a Worcestershire assize roll from 1221. This court record identifies the individual both by his parentage and by the location (Cleeve) from which he came.

Throughout this period (eleventh–fourteenth centuries) hereditary surnames were gradually coming into use, but they were by no means stable. There is 'evidence that...nicknames and "bynames" continued to replace or modify established surnames into the nineteenth century at least' (Redmonds 1997: 96). On the other hand, it is clear that certain names began to be passed from father to son from soon after the Norman Conquest and that this practice established itself as the norm by the end of the fourteenth century. Thus some people were known by what we today would call surnames, while others during the same period were known by non-hereditary bynames. Some of these bynames came to be transmitted along family lines and so established themselves as hereditary surnames, while others died out during the medieval period. Sturges and Haggett (1987) have shown, by purely statistical modelling, given reasonable assumptions about the number of marrying sons in each family, that there is a general tendency for common surnames to become more common, while rare names become rarer and many of them die out.

The use of hereditary names in England was highly socially stratified from the beginning, soon after the Conquest, and was influenced by their use in Normandy, where 'some of the more important and wealthier noble families...already possessed hereditary surnames' (McKinley 1990: 25). Indeed, it was the wealthy landholders who were the first to adopt hereditary surnames in England, 'in the two centuries or so after the Conquest' (McKinley 1990: 28), while other social classes continued to use non-hereditary bynames. These landholders typically used toponymic names—that is, they were typically identified by the names of estates from which they came.

While the development of surnames was by no means uniform throughout the country, most authorities agree that hereditary surnames were in the majority in the south of England by about 1350 and by 1450 in the north (Reaney 1967: 315; McKinley 1990: 32; Hey 2000: 53). Some hereditary surnames 'had genuinely late origins, evolving in parts of northern England well into the 1700s' (Redmonds 1997: 57). The development of hereditary surnames in England was a complex, long-drawn-out process.

15.1.2.2 *Irish, Manx, and Scottish Gaelic surnames*

The Scottish Gaelic language and the Irish language are closely related and this was even more true in the Middle Ages, at the time of surname formation. Scottish Gaelic is spoken in the Highlands and Islands and was, until the sixteenth century, in Galloway in the south-west. A traditional view is that Scottish Gaelic was brought to Scotland from Ireland in the fourth–fifth centuries AD, but it seems more likely that there was continuous interchange from earliest times around the Irish Sea, for example in the ancient maritime kingdom called Dál Riata, which extended from northern Ireland up into the Hebrides.

Many similarities can be perceived between the Irish Gaelic names of Ireland and the Scottish Gaelic names of Scotland. Attempting to distinguish between the two risks making a false distinction. Nevertheless, many surnames can be identified as distinctively Irish, while a smaller number are distinctively Scottish. In particular, the latter include names in the clan system, a distinctively Scottish social institution according to which people were associated by birth, servitude, or locality with the hegemony of a clan chief, either taking the clan name as a surname or taking a surname of a 'sept' (a subordinate group) of one of the major clans.

Initially, Gaelic patronymics were formed by use of the prefix *Mac* and (in Ireland) by *Ó* 'grandson of', giving patronymics such as *Mac Cárthaigh* 'son of *Cárthach*' and *Ó Conall* 'grandson of *Conall*'. Non-hereditary names of this form 'will be found in the records relating to centuries before the tenth', with their use as hereditary surnames having come 'into being fairly generally in the eleventh century' (MacLysaght 1985: ix). Names that became hereditary yielded anglicized forms such as *McCarthy* and *O'Connell*. Woulfe (1923: 15) observes that 'Irish surnames came into use gradually from about the middle of the tenth to the end of the thirteenth century'.

After the convention for prefixing names with *Mac* and *Ó* had become common, further changes in Irish surnames took place. Some included the words *giolla* and *maol*, meaning 'follower' or 'servant', 'in the sense of devotee of some saint e.g. *Mac Giolla Mhártain* (modern Gilmartin or Martin) or *Ó Maoilbhreanainn* (modern Mulrennan) from St. Martin and St. Brendan' (MacLysaght 1985: ix). Surnames deriving from occupations and nicknames were also formed, such as *Mac Giolla Easpaig* 'son of the servant of the bishop' and *Mac Dubhghaill* 'son of Dubhghall', a personal name meaning 'dark stranger'. Most Irish surnames acquired one or more anglicized form in the sixteenth century. For example, the two names just mentioned yielded the anglicized forms *Gillespie* and *McDowell*. Many Irish surnames yielded two distinct sets of anglicized forms, due to the phonetic phenomenon of lenition. For example, in the Irish surname *Mac Daibhéid* 'son of David', the D- came to be pronounced as a gutteral voiced fricative, yielding the anglicized surname *McKevitt* alongside the more etymological form *McDevitt*. The same phenomenon in Scottish Gaelic yielded both *McWhan* (lenited) and *McSwan* (unlenited) as anglicizations of *Mac Suain* 'son of Sveinn'. Similarly, *Mac Domhnuill* 'son of Donal or Donald' is the source of both *McDonnell* (*McDonald*) and *McConnell*. In a further development, the patronymic *Mac-* was often dropped or reduced to a residual C-, yielding anglicized surnames such as *Connell* and *Donald*. Patronymic prefixes in Ireland 'were very widely dropped during the period of submergence of Catholic and Gaelic Ireland which began in the early seventeenth century' (MacLysaght 1985: x). Some Irish names were translated to give English equivalents, with the Irish *Mac a'ghobhainn* 'son of the smith' sometimes being anglicized as *Smith* and *Mac an tSionnaigh* 'son of the fox' as *Fox*. Sometimes, Irish names were mistranslated due to folk etymology, as in the case of *Bird*, which, as an Irish name, represents quite a large number of Irish names that happen to contain the letters *éan*, for the Irish word *éan* does indeed mean 'bird', although this has nothing to do with the surnames *Ó hÉanna* (Heaney), *Ó hÉanacháin* (Heneghan), or *Mac an Déaghanaigh* (McEneaney), which are among those for which *Bird* has been adopted.

The development of Irish surnames into their modern forms was sometimes even more complex, as MacLysaght (1985) shows in a discussion of *Abraham* as an Irish surname:

Of course that is Jewish elsewhere, but in Ireland it is the modern corrupt or distorted form of an ancient Gaelic surname, Mac an Bhreitheamhan (son of the judge).
It was first anglicized MacEbrehowne, etc., which was shortened to MacEbrehan and
MacAbrehan, later MacAbreham and so to Abraham. Other anglicized forms of this
name are Breheny and Judge. (MacLysaght 1985: xii)

The prefixes *Mac* and *Ó* in Irish surnames re-emerged in an anglicized form in the late
nineteenth century. MacLysaght (1985: x) suggests this began as a result of a 'revival of
national consciousness', and comments that there was a steady increase in the number of people adopting *O* in the name *O'Sullivan* from 1866 to 1944. Similarly, Yurdan
(1990: 3) notes that 'during the renaissance of interest in things Irish during the period
1930–60, the "O"s and "Mac"s were reinstated to their former positions'. Since the 1960s
there has been an equally noticeable resurgence in the use of Irish-language (Gaelic)
forms of family names in Ireland.

As noted by Hanks and Muhr (2012), there has been considerable exchange of surnames between Britain and Ireland for almost a millennium. In the twelfth and thirteenth centuries, English kings and Norman barons brought family names such as
Butler, Clare, FitzGerald, and *Bermingham* to Ireland, and in the sixteenth and seventeenth centuries many other family names of English, Welsh, and Scots origin became
established there. In the early seventeenth century, King James I of England (and VI
of Scotland) encouraged the settlement of 'plantations' in Ireland, particularly northern Ireland, as a result of which the family names of Scottish Border reivers and others (*Nixon, Armstrong, Paisley*, etc.) became established in Ireland, mainly northern
Ireland. In the nineteenth and twentieth centuries, the flow was reversed and most Irish
surnames, in their anglicized forms, became established in Britain: notably in south
Lancashire, Lanarkshire (Glasgow), the coal-mining region of south Wales, and the
industrial west Midlands.

While many Irish and Scottish Gaelic hereditary surnames were in existence as early
as the eleventh century, non-hereditary names persisted, as can be seen in this late
example noted by Black (1946: xxv): 'Gideon Manson . . . died in Foula in March, 1930.
His father's name was James Manson (Magnus's son) and his grandfather was called
Magnus Robertson.'

Before leaving the topic of Gaelic family names, we should note that there are approximately 200 distinctively Manx family names in Britain today. Many of these begin with
an initial *C-* (*Clague, Cretney*) or *Q-* (*Quirk, Quinney*), residues of Gaelic *Mac-*.

15.1.2.3 *Surnames in Scots-speaking Scotland*

Scotland is a country with a rich variety of linguistic and cultural heritages. In addition
to Gaelic, Scottish family names are also of Cumbric origin,[2] Scandinavian (also known

---

[2] Notably among the so-called 'Strathclyde Britons', who, up to at least the fourteenth century, spoke a
language closely related to Welsh and lived in an area around the lower Clyde valley.

as Old Norse), and Anglian (the northern dialect of Old and Middle English). The latter in Scotland developed into distinctively Scottish varieties of English, sometimes called Lallans (the language of the Lowlands), the Scots *leid* (the Scottish language), or simply Scots, which is the term we shall use here.

Hereditary surnames first occurred in Scots-speaking regions at around the same time as in England, and many were 'introduced into Scotland through the Normans' (Black 1946: xiii), usually with names of toponymic origin. Following this, the 'spread of surnames in Scotland seems to have been slow' (McKinley 1990: 45). While most landholders seem to have 'acquired surnames...by about 1300' (McKinley 1990: 45), it seems that 'the general spread of hereditary surnames was not complete in the Scots-speaking regions until at least the sixteenth century' (McKinley 1990: 46). The establishment of hereditary surnames in the country occurred later than in England.

An important influence on the development of Scots family names was the importation of a Norman bureaucracy in the twelfth century, for which the person most responsible was King David I (reigned 1124–53). David had been brought up at the English court of King Henry I and had married Maud, Countess of Huntingdon. When, at the age of 39 or 40, he unexpectedly succeeded to the throne of Scotland, he took with him a cohort of Norman retainers from eastern England with surnames like *Lindsay, Ramsay, Sinclair,* and *Hamilton.*

Scots surnames can be classified using the same typology as for England (see section 15.1.2.1). Black (1946: xxix) notes that 'contrary to the common view, I have found few of our [Scottish] surnames to be derived from nicknames'.

15.1.2.4 *Welsh Surnames*

The development of hereditary surnames in Wales was very different from the English, Irish, and Scottish patterns. Even though Norman lords acquired land in Wales soon after the Conquest, 'neither this, nor the increasing use of hereditary surnames by English settlers in Wales, seems to have had much influence among the Welsh population' (McKinley 1990: 41). Even by 1500, hereditary surnames were still rare in Wales. The Welsh patronymic naming system involved using Welsh *mab* 'son' to create names in the form of 'X *mab* Y'. The word *mab* would have become *fab* due to grammatically triggered lenition, which subsequently became *ab* because 'the Welsh *f* sound was probably bilabial and therefore more easily lost' (Morgan and Morgan 1985: 10). Generally, *ab* occurred before names with initial vowels, and *ap* before those with initial consonants, resulting in names such as 'Madog *ab* Owain' and 'Madog *ap* Rhydderch' (Rowlands and Rowlands 1996: 8), although not all recorded names conform to this rule.

In Wales, not until the mid-sixteenth century did 'the change to settled surnames begin to filter through different levels of society' (Rowlands and Rowlands 1996: 25), resulting in the loss of *ab* or *ap* in a number of names. This explains why such a large proportion of surnames in Wales today are derived from given names. *Jones* and *Williams* are typically Welsh names: the English genitive *-s* apparently replaced Welsh *ab/ap* in many cases, with such genitive *-s* names having 'been common in Wales since at least the sixteenth century' (McKinley 1990: 226), coinciding with increased adoption of hereditary surnames in the country.

The Welsh patronymic form is still retained, to some extent, in certain hereditary surnames, where *ab/ap* has become incorporated with the following name through metanalysis, 'thus Thomas *ap* Howell would become Thomas Powell' (Rowlands 1999: 166–7). This was, and is, most common in areas of 'greatest and earliest English influence' (Rowlands 1999: 167), close to the English border. In other parts of Wales, the Welsh patronymic system appears to have been retained much longer, with names in *ap* occurring as late as the eighteenth century 'in upland Glamorgan parishes and in western Monmouthshire' (Rowlands and Rowlands 1996: 25–6). There are some personal names found today in Wales with the form X *ap* Y. These can be attributed to 'renewed national awareness and growing interest in the past', leading to a revival of patronymic names 'in the second half of the twentieth century' (Rowlands and Rowlands 1996: 34).

15.1.3 The Effects of Migration on the World's Family Name Stocks

While each country and indeed each region has its own histories and patterns of family name development, worldwide migration has meant that present-day name stocks tend to be much more ethnically and culturally diverse than they were a few decades ago. Therefore, any attempt to survey current family name stocks in any one country generally requires a wide variety of linguistic expertise. In the UK in particular, a reasonably comprehensive account of present-day surnames requires not only traditional expertise in Old and Middle English, Latin, Anglo-Norman French, and the Celtic languages but also expertise in Yiddish and Hebrew, other modern and medieval European languages, Arabic, Persian, Turkish, Indian languages, and Chinese, among others. Only in this way can a reasonably comprehensive account of modern family names in countries such as Britain, Australia, and America be developed. Family name dictionaries and surveys have been compiled in several but by no means all countries of the world.

15.2 STUDIES OF FAMILY NAMES IN BRITAIN AND IRELAND

The most reliable traditional introductions to the study of surnames in Britain are those by Reaney (1967) and McKinley (1990), which offer a philologist's and a historian's perspective respectively. Because they are essentially national surveys, they have little to say about surnames outside Great Britain, while at the other end of the spectrum they can do little more than exemplify fine-grained local details and regionally specific patterns of surname development and distribution that are now recognized as an essential component of the study of surnames. McKinley (1990) himself identifies the problem thus:

> It is impossible to examine the surnames present in several counties, from different parts of England, without being struck by the very sizable differences which existed in the Middle Ages, and which in large measure persisted into later periods, between the different English regions. (McKinley 1990: 20)

An ideal introduction to the study of surnames would be interdisciplinary, bringing together the expertise of historians, historical linguists, demographers, statisticians, genealogists, and (more recently) geneticists. Increasingly, this interdisciplinary approach is beginning to be adopted, but at present no such survey exists. An international perspective beyond English can be gleaned from the 108 pages of introductory essays in the *Dictionary of American Family Names* (DAFN 2003).

15.2.1 England

Compared with other onomastic fields such as place-names, family name research has received relatively little scholarly attention in Britain until recently. The earliest work offering information about surnames is a chapter in Camden's (1605) *Remains Concerning Britain*, which includes an alphabetical list of 253 locative surnames, mostly the surnames of gentry of Norman French origin. Over two centuries were to elapse before the next relevant work, namely Lower (1849), which outlines the chronology of hereditary surname adoption. It organizes the discussion of surnames by categories, though these are different from those that are generally used today.

The next important work is Bardsley (1875), which categorizes surnames using a typology of five types: 'Baptismal or personal names', 'local surnames', 'official surnames', 'occupative surnames', and 'sobriquet surnames or nicknames'. Building on this, Bardsley (1901) produced the first reasonably comprehensive inventory of English surnames. Among other innovations, it makes a systematic attempt to support etymologies with examples of early bearers. In the early twentieth century, studies of English surnames were published by Weekley (1916) and Ewen (1931, 1938) among others.

'The standard work on the etymology or meaning of surnames' (Redmonds et al. 2011: 4) is P. H. Reaney's (1958) *Dictionary of British Surnames*, published in a revised third edition as *A Dictionary of English Surnames* (Reaney 1997). Explanations are terse and sometimes cryptic, but they are grounded in traditional scholarship. Most importantly, they are supported by a wide selection of early bearers from medieval records. Recent research has shown, however, that the Reaney (1997) dictionary must be used with caution. Reaney was a great scholar, but we now know that some of his magisterial pronouncements are simply wrong. For example, Redmonds (2014) has shown that *Gaukroger* is a locative surname meaning, roughly, 'cuckoo crag' and not, as Reaney asserts, a nickname meaning 'foolish Roger'. Others of Reaney's explanations are 'fudges', which blur the issue to the point of being misleading. Typical is *Ramshaw*, which Reaney has merely as a cross-reference to *Ravenshaw*. Etymologically these two surnames are indeed related, but in fact *Ramshaw* is a toponym from a place near Bishop Auckland in county Durham (a place not mentioned by Reaney), while *Ravenshaw* (the main entry in Reaney), which is now rare or extinct as a surname, is from a place in Warwickshire. They explain a cluster of eight different toponymic surnames (*Ravenshaw, Ravenshear, Ramshaw, Ramshire, Ranshaw, Renshaw, Renshall, Renshell*) as 'dweller by the raven-wood', appearing to imply that they are variant spellings of a single topographic name—but the fact is, there is no such thing as a 'raven-wood' and no one was ever named as a dweller by one. The family names concerned are from different place-names, and these places were named hundreds of years before surnames came into existence.

Such problems were compounded by the fact that, for many names, Reaney's terse explanations regularly give only an Old English, Old Norse, or Continental Germanic etymology, bypassing intermediate steps such as Middle English and Old French. Reaney adopted this policy mainly because of space constraints imposed by his publisher due to post-war paper shortages, but it is particularly misleading because surnames were formed in the Middle English and early modern English periods; there is no such thing as an Old English surname.

Perhaps Reaney's greatest weakness was his almost complete failure to take account of the statistical relationships between surnames and locations. It must also be mentioned that literally thousands of well-established English surnames do not appear at all in Reaney's dictionary, which has been described as a dictionary of medieval surnames arranged under their modern derivative forms. If Reaney had nothing to say about a name, he simply omitted it. We mention these points, not to carp at Reaney's achievement, which is remarkable by any standard, but in order to illustrate the enormous amount of fine-grained detailed research that is needed before studies of surnames and family names can take their place as adequately informative and reliable works alongside place-name studies and works of historical lexicography.

One recent work that is better focused and stands up to scrutiny is Redmonds' *Dictionary of Yorkshire Surnames* (2015). This is based on detailed evidence of many kinds: medieval local records, local dialects (past and present), genealogical and genetic tracking, and contrastive geographical distribution. It will serve as a model for future county and areal studies. Hopefully, in years to come, a range of comparable county-by-county studies will be created, emulating Redmonds' achievement for Yorkshire.

Two other works of surname lexicography that must be mentioned here are Cottle (1967) and Titford (2009). Cottle's is an admirably succinct and reliable work, which proved popular for over forty years. It contains a few entries that were not explained by Reaney and an occasional dry witticism. For example *Butlin*, the surname of the founder of a chain of holiday camps, is explained as being derived from Old French *boute-vilain* 'hustle the churl'; Cottle adds, 'suggesting an ability to herd the common people'. Titford (2009) is an expanded edition of Cottle's work. It made extensive use of previous publications: not only Cottle and Reaney but also Hanks and Hodges (1988) and DAFN (see section 15.6 below).

Rigorous scholarship is a feature of the *Lund Studies in English*, inspired by Professor Eilert Ekwall, himself a great surname and place-name scholar. These works are far from comprehensive, but their focus on surname typology makes them useful sources of particular early name bearers and etymological information. For example, Fransson's (1935) *Middle English Surnames of Occupation 1100–1350* provides a list of occupational names with early bearers and suggested etymologies; Löfvenberg (1942) explains a selection of medieval locative surnames; and Jönsjö (1979) does the same for nicknames. Other relevant works in this series are Thuresson (1950) and Kristensson (1967–2002). However, these works are not without problems. Fransson (1935) studied names from only ten English counties. Jönsjö's (1979) etymological explanations are sometimes ambiguous and his treatment of names that share an element is not always consistent. McClure (1981b) comments:

> If one dimension of information is chiefly lacking in the comparative methods used in Lund Studies of ME bynames it is that of local and biographical history. The name is treated as 'word' rather than 'person', as a manifestation of linguistic form rather than social life. (McClure 1981b: 101)

Clark (2002: 116) makes a similar point, that 'to study in purely lexical and etymological terms a form recorded as a name, and sometimes solely so, may be to study something that never, and certainly not in the given context, existed at all'. Nevertheless, the Lund studies made an important contribution to the identification and understanding of English surnames.

The *English Surnames Series* (ESS), funded by the Marc Fitch Foundation at the University of Leicester, set out to investigate surnames historically county by county. Only seven volumes were published (Redmonds 1973; McKinley 1975, 1977, 1981, 1988; Postles 1995, 1998), but these have provided a wealth of detailed information on surnames in the particular counties and regions studied. Clark (1995) recognized the importance of this approach, noting that the works of the ESS

> never lose sight of the special nature of naming, as distinct from common vocabulary, and so proceed consistently in terms of social status, of domicile and landholding, of migration-patterns, of economic activity, of gender and familial relationships, of types of milieu, and of ramification of individual clans. (Clark 1995: 384)

However, it is not necessarily the case that county-based research is suitable for investigating regional surname patterns. Postles (1995: 4), in his ESS volume for Devon, concedes that 'counties can never be' regional societies, while Redmonds (2004b: xiv) has also commented that 'many of the counties are made up of several distinct regions, and these can be linked to marked differences in their topography, history and language'. Future surname research could benefit from focusing on socially, topographically, culturally, and linguistically distinct regions, perhaps investigating particularly localized patterns of development, as Hey (2000: xi) has suggested:

> The research that will forward our understanding of how surnames arose and spread will need to be focused on particular parts of the country, looking at how groups of names were formed at different times in particular local communities. (Hey 2000: xi)

In 2009–10 Oxford University Press and the Arts and Humanities Research Council of Great Britain were persuaded to initiate an ambitious research project called *Family Names of the United Kingdom* (FaNUK)). Eventually, this found a home at the University of the West of England under the direction of Richard Coates, with Patrick Hanks as lead researcher. It is due to be published in 2016 as the *Dictionary of Family Names in Britain and Ireland* (FaNBI). The entry list is based on a comparison of 1881 Census data with a more recent inventory based on 1997 electoral rolls, so that in principle almost every surname in the UK, no matter how rare, can be considered. People often ask, how many surnames are there in the UK? Unfortunately, a simple answer cannot be given, because among the hundreds of thousands of very low-frequency items, genuine surnames (most of which are recent immigrant names—i.e. names that came to the UK after 1945) merge imperceptibly into misprints and transcription errors. FaNBI contains entries for all family names with 100 or more bearers in the UK in 1997, regardless of ethnic or cultural origins. To these were added entries for names that are in other British surname dictionaries and 'established names' that are of particular historical or philological interest. 'Established names' in this context is a term that contrasts with 'recent immigrant names'. In practical terms, established names are those found in both the 1881 census and the 1997 data.

The result is a headword list of over 45,000 family names. There are almost 20,000 main entries and over 25,000 current spelling variants, together with innumerable examples of historical spelling variants. The spelling of family names in the UK is much more volatile than the spelling of place-names or English vocabulary words. Particular spellings of a widespread name sometimes come to be accepted as conventional in different families or in different local areas. There are at least three ways in which FaNBI differs from previous works: (1) early bearers, (2) information about geographical location, and (3) recent immigrant names.

Following the lead set by Bardsley and Reaney, examples of medieval and post-medieval early bearers are systematically included in FaNBI under each main entry, extracted from sources such as medieval tax records, court records, wills, and parish registers, many of which are now available for analysis in digitized form. These lists show the linguistic development and geographical spread of each surname since the time of its first use, while in many cases early forms provide evidence for etymological origins.

The main location of early bearers in Archer's (2011) *British 19th Century Surname Atlas* (see section 15.3.1) is summarized briefly but systematically for almost every FaNBI entry. An attempt is made to record the earliest known bearer in the main geographical location with which the name is associated. In many cases, especially among locative surnames, the geographical distribution of a surname correlates with the locality in which it originated, and this can provide useful evidence for the identification of lost place-names. The information about the main 1881 location also makes FaNBI a useful genealogical resource, pointing family historians toward the county or counties in which their research is most likely to be productive.

In addition, FaNBI provides a picture of immigration to Britain through the centuries. The Celtic, Anglo-Saxon, Scandinavian, and Norman population stocks were augmented in substantial numbers from time to time over the centuries. Flemish weavers migrated to England, having been first invited in the fourteenth century by Edward III with the aim of maintaining and improving the English wool and cloth industry. Huguenots entered Britain during the seventeenth century, fleeing to avoid religious persecution. Sephardic Jewish surnames from Spain, Portugal, and other Mediterranean countries arrived from the seventeenth century onwards, and waves of Ashkenazic surnames from central and eastern Europe arrived in the nineteenth and twentieth centuries.

Following the collapse of the British Empire in the second half of the twentieth century, ethnic diversity in Britain greatly increased as many people holding (or acquiring) British passports chose to migrate to England for economic and other reasons. As a result, many names borne by recent immigrants have been pressed into service as family names in Britain. Approximately 3,800 recent immigrant names with more than 100 bearers are recorded in FaNBI and more than 1,600 of these are from the Indian subcontinent, with Muslim, Hindu, Sikh, and other religious affiliations, each of which provides a rich set of etymological and cultural traditions. Muslim names in the subcontinent are mostly of Arabic etymology, with some Persian; Sikh names are derived from Panjabi, while Hindu names come from many different Indian languages. The Indian family name *Patel* is the 32nd most frequent surname in FaNBI's 1997 data with 95,177 bearers, followed by *Khan* with 63,795. Muhammad has only 15,016 bearers, but that is because there are seventeen variant spellings in the dictionary (plus a lot more that are too rare to be included).

Over 400 family names in Britain are of Chinese origin, many of them being Hong Kong romanizations of Chinese names in the Cantonese dialect, as opposed to the Mandarin forms, which are regarded as standard in China itself. Other family names of Chinese origin arrived via Malaysia and Singapore. English surnames of Chinese origin are particularly complex: a single 'English' orthographic form may represent up to twenty-two different Chinese surnames ('different' in that they are represented by different Chinese ideographs, each of which may have more than one explanation as to its origins). Ambiguity is avoided because Chinese is a tonal language: most apparently homophonous surnames in Chinese are distinguished by different tones, which are lost in English transcriptions.

In many entries, FaNBI gives additional information about family names, over and above the etymology, for example information about Scottish clans or historical information on great and powerful families such as *Cecil* and *Cavendish*. In other cases, brief summaries of obsolete occupations are given, as for the surname *Reeve*:

In medieval England a reeve was an administrative official responsible for the administration of a manor, including organizing work done by the peasants on the land for their lord, collecting rents, selling produce, and so on.

Elsewhere, explanations of relevant terms in the feudal system of land tenure are given, for example at *Ackerman*. Reaney's (1997: 2) explanation of this surname says tersely:

> OE [i.e. Old English] *æcermann* 'farmer', a husbandman or ploughman.

The FaNBI entry, having the luxury of greater space, is able to explain:

> An ackerman was a bond tenant of a manor holding half a virgate of arable land, for which he paid by serving as a ploughman.

For further information about FaNBI methodology, see Hanks et al. (2012).

15.2.2 Multidisciplinary Surname Research

Redmonds et al. (2011) have clearly shown the benefits of a multidisciplinary approach to surname research, coordinating philology, history, and genealogy with geographical and biographical evidence, where (for example) they consider a wide range of historical sources to determine the origin of the name *Tordoff*. The 1881 distribution shows that this surname was concentrated in the West Riding of Yorkshire, encouraging the researcher to search local records from this area. However, Redmonds et al. (2011) established that

> the surname survived in Dumfriesshire into the late fifteenth century. The next references place it in York between 1499 and 1524, where the family were pewterers, and then in and around Leeds and Bradford by 1572, where it ramified successfully in the village of Wibsey. More than 95 per cent of the 707 Tordoffs in 1881 lived in the West Riding, with Bradford (386) and Leeds (145) the major centres; the surname is still numerous in both places at the present day. (Redmonds et al. 2011: 99)

The Dumfriesshire origin of the name led to the conclusion that the surname *Tordoff* 'derives from a locality known as Tordoff Point on the Scottish side of the Solway Firth'. Without the prosopographical evidence, this origin may not have been so easily found or so confidently asserted.

Redmonds (1997) has also shown the advantages of considering a wide range of historical sources in determining a surname's etymology, particularly in his analysis of *alias* names. With a purely philological approach, a surname's origin can often be identified through the comparison of similar name forms. However, where a name has been altered by scribal influence to such an extent that its form is no longer etymologically representative, linguistic comparison is of little help, and a different approach is required. Redmonds' investigation of a large number of sources has allowed him to discover certain *alias* names, where a person is recorded with two or more names, which suggest an etymological connection between two surnames which might not appear to be related on form alone. One such example is the case of 'Simon Woodhouse alias Wydis' from Thornton le Moor in 1611 (Redmonds 1997: 125).

DNA evidence is also relevant (see Sykes and Irven 2000; Jobling 2001; Bowden, et al. 2008; King and Jobling 2009). Redmonds et al. (2011: 156) argue that 'just as a father passes on his surname to all his children, so he passes on his Y chromosome type to all his male children,' and they then pass the same Y chromosome type to their children, and so on. By comparing the Y chromosomal DNA of different people with the same surname, it is possible to demonstrate that the bearers share a common ancestor. In this way, Sykes and Irven (2000) showed that the English surname *Sykes* is most probably monogenetic, despite previous work that predicted it to be polygenetic.

The multidisciplinary approach has not only involved the application of wider historical knowledge and DNA evidence to surname study, but also the use of surname data in other historical studies. McClure (1979) used toponymic surname data to investigate rural and urban patterns of medieval migration, and the value of this methodology led to its use in further migration studies (see Penn 1983; Rosser 1989; Kowaleski 1995). Researchers in demography and geographical information science have made use of surname evidence (Schürer 2002, 2004; Longley et al. 2005), while lexicographical research using surname evidence has also been carried out (see, for example, Mawer 1930; McClure 2010a, 2010b, and the Swedish works, predominantly by students at Lund University, which provided antedatings for a large number of words, such as Fransson 1935; Löfvenberg 1942; Thuresson 1950; Jönsjö 1979).

15.2.3 Ireland

As a result of the complex development and anglicization of Irish Gaelic names, the construction of an Irish surname dictionary is no simple task. The standard work was Woulfe (1923), which took full account of this difficulty, being a dictionary in two parts, the first of which lists Irish Gaelic surnames with their anglicized and English equivalents, while the second contains etymological and historical discussion. This important work was followed by MacLysaght's (1957, 1985) *The Surnames of Ireland*.

Both Woulfe and MacLysaght were redoubtable scholars with a deep knowledge of Irish family histories and an understanding of the linguistic vicissitudes that have affected family names in Ireland over the centuries. As a result, Ireland is better served by its surname dictionaries than other European countries including England. However, neither of them includes evidence for early bearers, which makes it difficult for subsequent scholars to evaluate their more controversial etymologies. By contrast, FaNBI includes early bearers from several Irish sources, notably the Annals of Ulster, the Tudor Fiants, and a list of nearly 60,000 individuals (*Flaxgrowers*) published by the Irish Linen Board in 1796. A more recent work, providing etymological, historical, and distributional information and based on the 1980s Irish telephone directory, is by de Bhulbh (1997).

15.2.4 Scotland

The standard work on Scottish surnames is Black (1946). This is a remarkable work of scholarship, all the more remarkable because it was compiled in the New York Public Library. It contains over 8,000 surnames recorded in Scottish historical documents since the medieval period. Wherever possible, entries in this dictionary include etymology, information about early bearers, and variant spellings. Entries for surnames derived from Scottish place-names are particularly thorough and informative.

A more concise, though readable, work on Scottish surnames is Dorward (1978), which contains entries for over 1,000 common Scottish surnames, explaining their etymological origins and geographical distribution.

15.2.5 Wales

Dictionaries of Welsh surnames tend to be short in comparison to those from England, Scotland, and Ireland. The dominant patronymic naming system of Wales (see section 15.1.2.4) means that there are a relatively small number of different family names in the country. For this reason, Welsh surname dictionaries have sufficient space to give thorough accounts of surname origins and development. The two main works are Morgan and Morgan (1985) and Rowlands and Rowlands (1996, 2014), which between them give a comprehensive account of surnames in Wales. Entries in the Morgan and Morgan volume represent the medieval Welsh personal names that are the etymons of most surnames of Welsh-language origin. Rowlands and Rowlands is a more user-friendly work, of particular usefulness for genealogists.

15.3 STUDIES OF FAMILY NAMES
IN CONTINENTAL EUROPE

Not every country in Europe has a reliable dictionary or other study of family names, while even those that do exist are rarely comprehensive. Some local historical and regional studies are available, but much work remains to be done by way of investigation of the family names in Europe.

Where national surname dictionaries are not available, DAFN provides at least a starting point. American family names come from all over the world, so DAFN may be regarded as roughly equivalent to an international comparative dictionary of world surnames. In some cases, DAFN is all there is; in other cases, not even DAFN includes information about family names in certain regions of the world.

15.3.1 The German-speaking Lands

The main dictionaries of German family names are by Gottschald (1932), Brechenmacher (1936, 1957), and Bahlow (1967, 1993). Gottschald's work has extensive lists of name variants and etymological explanations for some of the names, but no examples of early bearers. Bahlow includes an occasional mention of some early bearers under certain entries, while Brechenmacher includes more extensive explanations, often supported by early bearers.

A major research project currently in progress in Germany is *Der Deutsche Familiennamenatlas* (DFA), a collaborative project based at the universities of Mainz and Freiburg, under the direction of Damaris Nübling (Mainz), Konrad Kunze (Freiburg), and Peter Auer (Freiburg). The research involves the systematic analysis of surnames, using telephone directories, with geographical distribution maps of selected surnames and surname features. This kind of distributional analysis represents a key development in family name study, with a focus on the systematic computational analysis of large datasets. Eventually, a new etymological dictionary of family names in Germany will be based on the Atlas, superseding existing works. There are several local studies of surnames of particular German regions, while Zamora (1992) provides an account of Huguenot names in the German states of the seventeenth and eighteenth centuries.

The standard work on Austrian family names is Hornung (1989), while Finsterwalder (1978) provides a more closely focused account of family names in Tyrol. The standard reference work for Swiss names is Meier (1989), which includes all family names borne by Swiss citizens in 1962. Each entry contains a list of the Cantons in which bearers of the family name are found, the year or period when the family name first appeared in the country, and the cantons in which the name has occurred previously but has since died out. For names that are not of Swiss origin, the bearer's previous country of residence is given.

15.3.2 Belgium and the Netherlands

A major scholarly and comprehensive dictionary of surnames in Belgium (including entries for the majority of Dutch surnames that have any substantial frequency) is Debrabandere (1993), in which the entries contain etymologies, variant forms, and early bearers. Not only surnames from Dutch- and French-speaking Belgium but also surnames from northern France, where there was once Flemish influence, are included.

A database showing the geographical distribution of surnames is the *Nederlandse Familienamenbank*, hosted at The Hague's Centraal Bureau voor Genealogie (2000–). However, there is still no prospect of a comprehensive dictionary of Dutch family names.

15.3.3 Scandinavia (Denmark, Norway, Sweden) and Finland

While the languages of Denmark, Norway, and Sweden are very closely related, patterns of surname development in Scandinavia show distinctive national and regional differences. There are generalizable differences in the types of surnames used in the different countries, with, for example, the majority of Danish and Swedish family names being patronymic, while most Norwegian family names are of locative origin.

Scholarly works on Scandinavian family names and their origins include Modéer's (1989) survey of the history of Swedish personal naming and family naming, Veka's (2000) dictionary of Norwegian family names, and Knudsen et al.'s (1936–64) study of Old Danish forenames and nicknames.

Finland has its own history of family naming, with perhaps the most characteristic feature of its names being the common ending -*nen*, originally a diminutive and possessive suffix, which was later simply added to patronyms as a way of creating surnames. Studies of Finnish family names include Mikkonen and Sirkka (1992) and Pöyhönen (1998).

15.3.4 France

The standard reference works for the surnames of France are Dauzat (1945, 1951) and Morlet (1991). These dictionaries are extensive collections of names, giving etymologies and variant forms under each entry. However, neither dictionary provides information about early bearers.

15.3.5 Italy

A comprehensive dictionary of Italian surnames is DeFelice (1978), in which most entries include a list of variant forms, etymologies, and the geographical distribution of the name, although early bearers are not provided. DeFelice (1980) is a more discursive work, providing information on the history, typology, and geography of Italian family names.

15.3.6 Spain and Portugal

The nearest to a comprehensive dictionary of Spanish family names is Tibón (1995 [1988]), a heroic one-man effort to provide etymological and other information on surnames throughout the Spanish-speaking world, without access to the necessary apparatus in support, such as databases of medieval records, distributional surveys, census data, and so on.

There are several surveys of family names in certain areas. Notably, Catalan is well served by Moll (1982) and Coromines (1989–97), while Basque names are described by Michelena (1973).

Machado (1984) includes information about Portuguese family names as well as vocabulary words.

15.3.7 Hungary

Kálmán's (1978) work provides an account of the origins and history of Hungarian family names, along with discussion on given names and place-names.

15.3.8 The Slavic and Baltic Countries

A selection of the numerous works on family names from Slavic countries are: Rymut (1990–4, 1999–2002) on Polish names; Beneš (1998) and Moldanová (1983) on Czech surnames; Unbegaun (1972) on Russian surnames; Red'ko (1966) on Ukrainian surnames; and Merku (1982) on Slovenian surnames in north-east Italy. Mention may also be made here of Maciejauskienė (1991) on Lithuanian surname history and Siliņš (1990) on the vocabulary of Latvian surnames.

15.4 STUDIES OF JEWISH FAMILY NAMES

As Jewish family names belong to members of a large religious community, rather than the people from a particular country, Jewish family name study requires the analysis of records from many parts of Europe and the Near East. Jewish family name studies tend to focus on particular countries or particular Jewish ethnic divisions (notably Ashkenazic vs. Sephardic), which helps to keep them down to a manageable size. Major works on Jewish surnames are Beider (1993, 1995, 1996) and Menk (2005). Jewish names are also well represented in Hanks and Hodges (1988) and DAFN.

15.5 FAMILY NAMES IN ASIA

15.5.1 China

Chinese surnames are much older than those from other countries, in some cases reputedly dating back to the third millennium BC, to the time of the legendary 'Yellow

Emperor' Huang Di, and before. The earliest known account of Chinese surname origins is written in *Shi Ben*, from the Warring States period (475–221 BC), but it is not clear whether the names in this, and other such early writings, were borne by people who lived at the time or have simply been drawn from characters of Chinese myths and legends. Even so, it seems clear that surnames emerged in China during the Western Zhou dynasty (1046–771 BC) and the Spring and Autumn period (770–476 BC). Most of today's Chinese surnames have their origin in the Han people, an ethnic group originally from North China, who migrated across much of the country and whose culture was adopted by many other ethnic groups.

The most comprehensive reference work for Chinese surnames available today is by Yida and Jiaru (2010). It includes a collection of 23,813 surnames from historic sources, also containing names that do not have their origin among the Han Chinese people. Corresponding English spellings are also provided alongside the ideographic Chinese surnames. It is worth noting, however, that the central core of conventional Chinese surnames consists of only a few hundred items. An extensive work on the genealogical origins of Chinese surnames is by Chao (2000), which also provides information on etymology and the geographical distribution of surnames in China today.

15.5.2 Japan

Two scholarly and comprehensive works on the names of Japan are Niwa's (1981) etymological study and his (1985) dictionary of Japanese surnames.

15.5.3 Korea

While studies of the etymologies and histories of Korean family names are few, genealogical information has been published by clan organizations for the majority of the 260 or so Korean surnames, and is available in collections such as *Han'gukin ŭi Sŏngbo: Ch'oidae Sŏngssi wa pon'gwan* (Korean Genealogies: updated surnames and clan seats).

15.5.4 The Indian Subcontinent

The contributions of Professor R. V. Miranda to DAFN and FaNBI have given a tantalizing glimpse of the rich variety of historical, cultural, religious, and linguistic facts that can be gleaned from the study of family names in the countries of the Indian subcontinent. Regrettably, however, there does not seem to be any immediate prospect of either a scholarly or even a popular study of family names in India, Bangladesh, or Sri Lanka. Names in Pakistan are accounted for by Ahmed (1999) insofar as they are of Muslim religious affiliation and therefore Arabic or Persian etymology. Schimmel (1989) offers a richly informative discursive study of Muslim names and culture.

15.6 International and Comparative Surveys

A Dictionary of Surnames by Hanks and Hodges (1988) is a dictionary with different aims and different scope from any of the works mentioned so far. Rather than taking medieval records as the starting point for compiling a list of surnames, Hanks and Hodges used modern data collected from selected 1980s telephone directories. They also attempted systematic coverage of European surnames. Their target audience was the whole English-speaking world and beyond, not just the UK. People migrate; they move around; so a modern study of family names must not be insular or parochial. It must contrast local stability with national and international patterns of migration. Therefore, this dictionary was the first to contain entries for surnames from all over the European continent, including extensive comparative lists of cognates and derivative forms in different languages. This work was well received in North America, where the majority of surnames are of non-English origin. This led ultimately to a larger and better-focused project, the *Dictionary of American Family Names* (DAFN), which is the standard reference work for family names in the USA. Because the USA has a great mix of names from many different countries, this dictionary included contributions by onomastic and linguistic scholars from all around the world. As a result, it is not just a source of information for those interested in the names of the USA, but also a reference work with worldwide relevance. It is published in three volumes, and contains over 70,000 entries drawn from the computational analysis of over 88 million names of US telephone subscribers.

15.7 Data Analysis—Documents and Distribution

15.7.1 Geographical Distribution of Surnames

An important new approach to the study of surnames was developed by Guppy (1890), whose work showed that there was often an enduring connection between a surname's present-day distribution and its place of origin. Guppy's approach was an important precursor to the present-day analysis of surname distribution, as in Archer's (2011) *19th Century Surname Atlas*, which has necessitated revision of what is considered the most likely origin of many UK surnames, as well as enhancing understanding of how migration within Britain has affected surname distribution patterns.

Archer's atlas is available as a CD. It shows the distribution and frequency of each surname recorded in the 1881 British census. Distributions can be viewed both by county and by poor law union (PLU), both in actual numbers and proportionally (per 100,000 of population). An advanced search option allows the distribution of a selected group of names to be shown, so that patterns of a certain surname feature, rather than just an individual name, can be plotted. This approach can be used to further our understanding of the distribution and origins of regionally specific naming features and patterns in the UK.

A comparable CD resource for the names of Ireland is Grenham (2003), which gives the distribution of surnames drawn from a variety of nineteenth-century sources. Most of the data are organized by household, and so distribution maps are not quite as detailed as those in Archer's (2011) British atlas, although Grenham's Irish atlas is still a valuable onomastic and genealogical resource.

The distribution of a family name is information that is not just of use to genealogists, who can sometimes uncover the probable geographical origin of a surname through such information, but can also inform linguistic study. Medieval dialect lexis and phonology is preserved in many present-day surnames, so an analysis of their national distribution can aid investigation of historical dialects. By comparing family name data from different periods, the continuity or change of dialect distribution can be studied. Barker et al. (2007) show the value of this approach in their analysis and comparison of surname distribution using records from the sixteenth century to the present day.

15.7.2 Computational Analysis of Large Databases

There is an ever-increasing availability of large digitized surname databases from different periods, which are only just beginning to be systematically analysed. Resources such as the International Genealogical Index (IGI) (FamilySearch 2012), which contains hundreds of millions of UK parish register entries, could in principle be used for the statistical analysis of surname frequency, geographical distribution, and the frequency and distribution of particular surname features. Such analysis could, for example, lead to a more accurate account of distributional contrasts, of which an already known example is that between patronymic surnames ending in -son, which tend to be characteristic of Northern England and Scotland, and patronymic surnames ending in -s, which are more typical of the South Midlands and Wales. Another known example concerns the distribution of locative surnames ending in -er, such as *Chalker* and *Streeter*, which are characteristic of Kent, Sussex, and Hampshire. Many similar linguistic features of surnames are no doubt waiting to be discovered as more and more data become available for computational analysis.

Certain historical records with representative national coverage have only recently become available, such as the English fourteenth-century poll tax returns (see Fenwick 1998–2005) and the Irish Fiants (see Nicholls 1994). The large amount of data these records provide can be analysed computationally, so that national family name distribution patterns and changes over a number of centuries can be discovered, which will fill a large hole in our knowledge of surname development. Rogers (1995: 224) recognized the importance of the fourteenth-century poll tax returns specifically for this purpose, stating 'it is . . . clear that, the rarer the name, the less likely it is that the distribution of its early examples will be visible in the fourteenth-century sources until the Poll Tax becomes widely available'.

Now that these records, and other large collections of family name data, are accessible, and historical records are being continually digitized, computerized systematic analysis of family name characteristics can be carried out on a much larger scale than has been previously possible, to give a more complete picture of surname development than is currently available. To this end, medieval and early modern spellings of surnames will need to be linked, drawing on the expertise of philologists, historians, and demographers.

Demographic studies of, for example, the rates of surname death over time and the effects of migration from region to region, as well as from country to country, on surname development and change, will also become possible, but only when even larger quantities of machine-readable data from many different periods are available for comparison.

Such approaches will require careful consideration of many different sources of varying onomastic value, but this kind of research will greatly improve our understanding of family name distribution and history, for example through tests for statistical significance in the relationship between a surname's geographical origin and its distribution at different periods, in order to determine the extent to which its distribution can be taken as a reliable indicator of its geographical, historical, and linguistic origins. It is therefore hoped that future work in the field of family name studies will systematically analyse very large digitized datasets, using techniques that have been developed in corpus linguistics among other subject areas, potentially leading to important new discoveries on many different aspects of family names and naming.

CHAPTER 16

BYNAMES AND NICKNAMES

EVA BRYLLA†

THIS chapter deals with byname systems in the North and West Germanic areas, particularly in the Nordic, German, and English speaking countries.[1] A byname (or a nickname, see below) is a name a person bears added to his or her official or 'real' name. It is commonly believed that in pre-medieval times a one-name system was applied among Germanic tribes, and that the use of bynames gradually arose and became especially frequent in the early Middle Ages in connection with Christianization, urbanization, and population increase. There was an increasing need to characterize people by indicating either their origin or some striking personal feature (Kohlheim 1996: 1247; Van Langendonck 1996: 1228, 2007b: 193; Nübling et al. 2012: 146).

16.1 THE TERMS *BYNAME* AND *NICKNAME* (AND OTHER COMPARABLE TERMS)

The terms *byname* and *nickname* need some clarification. A byname (or a nickname, see below) is an unofficial name. Bynames can be positive, derogatory, or neutral. The term *nickname* is often limited to characterization, and is one of the sources for bynames.

It is true that *byname* and *nickname* are etymologically synonymous terms with the meaning 'an added name', but here I employ *byname* as an inclusive term and consider *nickname* as a term for a subcategory (synonymous with e.g. German *Übername*, physical or mental characteristics). There is a reason to use the inclusive term *byname* instead of *nickname*, because it corresponds well to German *Beiname*, Dutch *bijnaam*, and Swedish *binamn*. In German onomastic literature *Beiname* is often—but not

---

[1] Bynames are found within all categories of proper names. This chapter discusses personal bynames only.

always—used as a superordinate term (see e.g. Debus 1980: 188, 2010: 36, 2012: 29, 104ff.; Andersson 2012: 133ff.; Nübling et al. 2012: 46–7). On using the term *byname* as superordinate, see also Van Langendonck (1996: 1228).

Although terminological issues have been discussed a great deal in onomastic literature, there is still much uncertainty and fluctuation. When names are meant to express some characteristic of the name bearer, one often speaks of *nicknames* (Dalberg 2000: 39; Van Langendonck 2007b: 192; Neethling 2012: 24). In German anthroponymic research, the term *Beiname* is sometimes used as a subordinated term, and it has no fixed definition (see further Andersson 2012 with cross references, 135–6). Furthermore, in recent German research (Nübling et al. 2012: 106, 172, 295), another term, *Spitzname*, is employed as a hyperonym, at the same time as the term is also the counterpart of *Übername*. The latter term plays a conspicuous role in German anthroponymic literature. According to the name scholar Teodolius Witkowski (1964: 84), there is a tendency to use *Übername* in a derogatory sense. The term *Spitzname* is also employed with this meaning, as well as *Spottname*, *Schimpfname*. According to Witkowski (1964), *Übername* seems to be a superordinate term for negatively-charged names. On the other hand, Konrad Kunze (2004: 11) has noticed that *Übername* is used as a hyperonym for all unofficial names (see recently Andersson 2012: 133ff.).

Also, in current publications in English, confusion between the terms *byname* and *nickname* continues (for instance see a recently published introduction to Finnish onomastics, Ainiala et al. 2012: 190ff.).

The terminology of bynaming is a Germanic problem. Agreement on terminology is necessary. If no agreement can be reached on a terminology common to Germany, England, and Scandinavia, it will not be possible to draw comparisons within the Germanic speech area.

16.2 FUNCTIONS OF BYNAMES

A byname (or a nickname, see section 16.1) is a name a person bears added to his or her 'real' name. In pre-medieval times we imagine that a one-name system was applied, that is, a person bore an individual name/a given name. But the need to separate persons with identical names gradually arises, and in medieval documents people are often distinguished by additional names. The function of a byname is to individualize, to identify, and to differentiate people with the same given name. Bynames are unofficial names in contradistinction to official ones, that is, given names and surnames/family names. The bynames are personal and not hereditary.

The basic condition for a byname or a byname element is that the name in an unchangeable form is used by a larger or lesser group of people in various social circles, for members of certain societies, among family members, among ordinary people in a community, a school, a club, etc. A byname can have the function either of creating affinity or of raising social barriers within a circle or a society.

Bynames can carry positive connotations, they are pet names, for example *Honey, Darling*, or pet forms of official names (hypocorisms, from Greek *hypokorisma, hypokorismos* 'affective words'), for example *Bill(y)* for *William, Lizzie* for *Elizabeth*. They can be derogatory, often labelled nicknames, for example *Piggy, Fatty* (fat people), *Stinky* (a nasty-smelling person). They can also be neutral, for example *Smith* designating a smith, or *Fleming* 'a person from Flanders' or *Brooks, Wood* formed from a place-name or a location.

Bynames, like other names, are subject to some syntactical rules. One such rule is that a byname should be able to occur independently, for example to be used together with or instead of an official name. Two syntactical types of bynames meet this criterion:

1. Bynames used instead of an official name, e.g. *Twiggy* (an English model, actress and singer), *The Boss* (Bruce Springsteen), *Der Bomber der Nation* (Gerd Müller, a German football player), *The Iron Lady* (Margaret Thatcher).
2. Bynames used together with or instead of an official name, e.g. *Fredrik Barbarossa* (Italian for *Red Beard*), *Tricky Dick Nixon* (Richard Nixon).

There is, however, a third type of byname that does not meet the requirement of independence, for example *Long* in *Long John, Robinson* in Swedish *Robinson-Emma* (referring to the person's connection with a reality television series). Such elements are not proper names, but can be classed as byname elements. It is notable—at least for Scandinavia—that prefixed additional words as in Swedish *Blonda Anna* 'blonde Anna', are usually not transferred to a surname (a hereditary byname), while for instance *Lange* in Swedish *Erik lange/Lange* from being an attributive has, via a byname element, acquired proprial status and eventually developed into a surname. In many European countries, we can see present-day surname stocks originating from earlier attributes/bynames, for example hereditary patronymics, other kinship designations, occupational and local designations, etc.

In historical sources such as Scandinavian Viking Age runic inscriptions, there are instances of individually characterizing bynames used absolutely, that is, without the person's given name. Examples are *Ōnīðingʀ* (from Runic Swedish *ōnīðingʀ* 'not a vandal, an honourable person'), *Oflāti* (from Old West Scandinavian *oflāti* 'a person with high-and-mightiness'), *Grīma* (from Old West Scandinavian *grīma* 'face mask') (Peterson 2007). The reason why the carver has chosen to exclude a given name is uncertain, but the most probable explanation is linguistic economy: the carver needed space for as much information as possible, and therefore chose to use an identifying byname instead of a given name (or a given name + a byname) (Otterbjörk 1983: 43). On the use of bynames in Viking Age runic inscriptions see Jacobsson (2012: 49ff.) and Källström (2012: 65ff.).

16.3 Demarcation of Bynames

A recurring issue in onomastics is the demarcation of the category bynames. The function of bynames is to identify and distinguish between people with identical given names, for example to separate John Black from John the carpenter. A fundamental criterion underlying the claim that a byname/byname element is a proper name is that it is used regularly and in an unchanged form by a large or limited circle of persons.

There are different types of name phrases that are defined either as bynames or alternatively as appellatives. A large group of such phrases consist of a given name + an additional designation, often characterizing the bearer. From Scandinavian sources we know for example Old Swedish *Sven svarte/Svarte* 'Sven the Black/black'. In such examples the byname is usually written with a lower-case letter showing that it is not a proper name. But what is the difference between *Sven svarte* and *Sven Tveskägg* (Danish *Svend Tveskæg* 'Forkbeard')? In the last example, the attribute is clearly a byname. Functionally the phrases are not different (Brylla 2012: 9ff.).

However, there are some types of phrases which are variously classified as bynames or as appellative attributes, that is, patro-/metronymics. On the one hand patro-/metronymics in (-)*son* and (-)*dotter/datter/dóttir* are not generally included among bynames (even if they have gradually been regarded as such). Primary patronymics in Iceland today occupy an intermediate position between proper names and appellatives. People are not really called *Sigmundsson* or *Sigurðardóttir*, they are a son or a daughter, respectively, of Sigmund.[2] On the other hand, bynames are often exemplified by names denoting kinship, that is, Old Swedish -*brodher* 'brother', -*modher* 'mother' -*bonde* 'husband', -*magher* 'male relative' and also wives' names as *Gydhukulle* (*kulle* 'husband'). Thus, the demarcation is not clear (Brylla 2012: 11).

Both in historical documents and in unofficial practice, people are named by their given name, a preposition, and a place-name used as an attribute, for example Old Swedish *magnus...j Walsta* (1429), Middle High German *Agnes von Auzpurkch* (Augsburg; 1370). Middle English *Adam de Cokefeld* (Cockfield; c.1130). In Scandinavia these name phrases with a preserved preposition are usually not seen as a proper name. When the preposition is omitted we can refer to a proper name, for example *Sven Tumba* (*Tumba* is a place-name in Sweden). The very common surnames in Norway today, for example *Helleland, Sandnes*, originate from this type of byname (Helleland 1997: 56ff.; 1999: 163; Andersson 2011: 7). When the preposition is missing, the attribute has changed into a byname. The phrase has been lexicalized. The development from an appellation into a name can also happen even if the preposition survives. There are examples of prepositional phrases which have developed into hereditary bynames, that is surnames, for example *Nash* (< Middle English *atten ashe*), *Ingendal* (> Middle Low

---

[2] The Old West Scandinavian word *sonr* (Icelandic *sonur*) occurs as a second element in the form -*son* without a nominative ending (Andersson 2011: 2).

German *in dem Tal*) (Reaney 1967: 36, 49; Brylla 1999: 17; Insley 2007: 167; Kohlheim and Kohlheim 2008: 26).

Occupational designations are often seen as non-proper nouns. Scholars have often maintained that if *John the carpenter* is a carpenter the phrase might be an description, but if he is not it may be a byname (for instance his father can be a carpenter). But in a social context where John is identified as *the carpenter* the description can function as a byname.

Moreover, there are no clearly defined limits between bynames and given names. In former times the demarcation between a byname and a given name was unclear. Many original bynames have developed into given names, for example German *Wolf*, Swedish *Ulf* 'wolf', *Björn* 'bear', *Sten* 'stone'. From being a description, the phrase has developed into a byname, been inherited, and spread as a forename. The semantic meaning has most likely been bleached. In that way we can understand derogative names on Viking Age rune stones as *Óspakr* 'unwise', *Óþveginn* 'unwashed'. Likewise, many original hypocorisms such as *Timmy, Jenny* have been transformed into official forenames.

Drawing a line between bynames and hereditary surnames is not easy, especially concerning historical data. A byname is connected with a specific person and is as a rule not hereditary. Bynames have an individual characterizing function, whereas by contrast, hereditary surnames are designating. They do not characterize the bearer. Surnames are also hereditary. But bynames can develop into hereditary surnames.

Thus, the boundaries between names and appellatives are not easy to draw. For practical reasons I have chosen to use a broad definition of the byname category in this chapter. Byname elements are included as well as occupational bynames, locative bynames, bynames of relationship and other additions to the given name (Brylla 2013: 114–15).

16.4 Semantics

The ancient byname stock is characterized by great imagination and creativity. The semantics of names, that is, their meaning and for what reason they were given, is a constant challenge for name scholars. The semantic categories principally represented are: home district, birthplace and residence, family and social function, physical and mental characteristics, and characteristic incidents, habits, and expressions.[3]

Bynames can be grouped into five categories, which will be discussed in the following subsections.

---

[3] Many bynames in Britain and the European continent have developed into hereditary surnames, which are an excellent source of medieval bynames. By contrast, the hereditary surnames of Scandinavia started to spread at a relatively late stage and do not usually contain old bynames.

16.4.1 Locative and Topographical Bynames

In the Middle Ages it was usual to add a description to the given name denoting the place from which the person came, a locative, or a topographical byname. It might concern place of birth, place of residence, or an attribute denoting a place where the person in question used to be found.

In Britain there was a widespread tendency after 1066 for Normans holding land in England to adopt bynames derived from the names of places in their newly-acquired English estates. On the whole, the tendency for landholders to adopt bynames (and later hereditary surnames) from the names of places where they held property can be observed. It was important for the landowners to adopt these bynames and let them develop into hereditary surnames to consolidate their position as hereditary property owners (McKinley 1990: 26ff.).

The origin of bynames (and also hereditary surnames) in Germany coincides with the time of urbanization. The urban population originated from places in the neighbourhood and it became natural to name the new citizens from the places where they originated. For example, a list (1370) of residents of Regensburg in Germany includes many people with bynames originating from towns and villages in a circumference of c.80 km from the city, for example *Ott von Oetershausen* (1370; today's Etterzhausen), *Steffan der Tündorffer* (today's Thundorf in der Oberpfalz) (Kohlheim and Kohlheim 2008: 25).

Likewise terms of nationality are used, such as *Danish, Welch* (a person from Wales), *Bayer* (a person from Bayer), *Fleming* (a person from Flanders), *Bremer* (a person from Bremen), and so on.

By contrast with bynames of origin which were given to people from foreign districts, names from place of residence have arisen from one's own native district. In order to identify people in the neighbourhood, the site of the farm or the nature of the ground is a common motive for naming. Locative bynames like English *York, Norton* derive from the names of particular places.

Topographical bynames are those derived from terms for features of the landscape, for example English *Brooks, Hill, Bridge*, German *Acker, Bach, Horst, Busch*. It is sometimes impossible to say whether the name originates from one of the places so called, or from the use of a topographical term.

Originally locative bynames were formed from places (place-names) by means of different prepositions (*de, von/van, aus/ut*) and the definite article, for example German *von der Au*(e) 'from the land by the sea', *In dem Tal* 'in the valley'. Also English surnames can originate from the place whence the first name bearer came, for example *Richard de Clara* (1086) from Clare in Suffolk, which was the name of the family estate (Reaney 1997: 98). After the Norman Conquest, the prefix *de* became the most common preposition before both English and French place-names. Other prepositions which were used are English *at, under, over, beneath, above*, Germ. *an, in, von*. Such name phrases, preposition (+ definite article) + byname, can be seen in recent hereditary surnames, for example *Nash* (< Middle English *atten ash* 'at the ash', *Oak* < Middle English *atte oke* 'at the oak', *Amthor* (< *an dem Tor* 'at the port'), *Vonderlind* (< *von der Linde* < 'of the lime') (Reaney 1967: 36ff.; McKinley 1990: 51ff., 72ff.; Van Langendonck 1996: 1228ff.; Kohlheim and Kohlheim 2008: 27ff.; Debus 2012: 110–11).

In medieval Sweden there are many examples of adding a description to the given name denoting the origin of the person, usually the name of a farm or village, for example *magnus...j walsta* (1429). Examples like *Andres j kiællaren* (1484), *hustru Kadrin j mwr*en (1492) denote that the person is frequently found in the basement or lives near the wall, respectively. Origin may also be described by inhabitant designations: *-bo(e)* 'inhabitant' as in *Biærghbo* 'inhabitant of the place Berg', *-fari* 'he who travels' as in *Hallandsfari* 'he who lives in the county of Halland' (see Fridell 1998: 19–20), and *-ing(e)*, for example in *Bleking(e)* 'he who lives in the county of Blekinge' (Brylla 1999: 16–17).

16.4.2 Bynames Denoting Relationship

A convenient way to identify a person was by a patronymic or a metronymic, that is, to describe him or her as a son or a daughter of the father or mother. On the Continent and in Britain some of these designations became real family names, but in Scandinavia it was a long time before such descriptions were fixed and became hereditary and used as family names.

The most common way to designate kinship is to add *-son* to the first name of the father. In England before 1066 there are instances of men being identified as the son of someone by the use of Latin *filius* 'son', for example *Johannes filius Edwardi* for 'Johannes son of Edward'. This phrase is very probably inserted to help to identify individuals. Later bynames (often as hereditary surnames), for example *Robertson, Harrison*, became numerous in all parts of England (McKinley 1990: 110ff.).

In medieval Germany as well, bynames formed from given names were a popular way to identify individuals. There are many examples of genitive formations, for example *Henrici, Hinrichs Sohn, Hinrichson, Hinrichsen, Hinrichs*. The word *son* could be transparent and also be shortened to *-s*, or *-o*. In Germany today, suffixes in hereditary surnames without an ending are in the majority, for example *Friedrich, Konrad, Walther* (Debus 2012: 109–10).

In medieval Scandinavia, patronymics and metronymics were the most common way to describe kinship, that is the father's and mother's given name, respectively, + *son* or *dotter/dóttir* 'daughter', for example *Sven Hakonarson, Sven Estridson, Kristin Karlsdotter, Margit Katerinadotter*. There are also other ways to express relationships, for example relating to brothers, brothers-in law, husbands, and so on. In Old Swedish sources there are many examples such as bynames containing Old Swedish *magher* 'male relative', for example *jap person sutor bakaramagh* (1450), or *-bonde*, *-kulle* 'husband', for example *Pæthers Ammokulla* (1393), *Eric sømquinne bonde* (1516–17) (Brylla 1999: 17).

16.4.3 Bynames Denoting Social Function

Bynames of occupation were very frequent in former times, as is reflected in the large number of such surnames today. In medieval societies we can find many bynames formed from terms for crafts or trade such as English *Baker, Brewer, Webber*, German *Fischer* 'fisherman', *Bauer* 'peasant', *Schneider* 'tailor'. In a list of the most common surnames in today's Germany, the top fourteen positions are held by occupational names, with *Müller* 'miller' and *Schmidt* 'smith' as the most common (McKinley 1990: 131ff.; Debus 2012: 111–12). The modern surnames give an excellent description of the medieval societies.

There is also a group of bynames derived from words for high rank or positions in Church or state, for example *King, Prince, Bishop, Abbot*. Such names are not necessarily occupational names. They could be individual characteristic bynames, nicknames, given in order to speak ironically of a person, for example a pretentious person. The very large number of people so named points to the fact that many of them were in reality nicknames. Opinions about the conduct of, for example, Church functionaries may have led to bynames such as *Archdeacon* and *Abbot* being given to persons who were thought to be grasping or greedy. Such bynames might have arisen when individuals played the parts of kings, bishops, and so on in a play (McKinley 1990: 135–6).

Names in medieval Scandinavia contain many examples of occupational terms in *-are*: Old Swedish *Akare* 'haulier', *Bakare* 'baker'. The corresponding feminine suffix is *-erska*: *Bakerska* 'bakeress', *Krøgherska* 'inn-keeperess'. There are also names ending in *-drængher* 'hind', for example *Bryggiaradrænger* 'brewer hind', *Fædrænger* 'cattle hind', and *-karl* 'man', Very frequent is the element *-man*, for example *Alderman* 'alderman', *Boleman* 'parish constable' (Brylla 1999: 17).

16.4.4 Bynames Denoting Physical or Mental Characteristics (Nicknames)

16.4.4.1 *Bynames Denoting Physical Characteristics*

Bynames, that is nicknames, alluding to physical characteristics are frequent: *Long, Tall*, for example *Long Tall Sally, Short* (denoting bodily structure), *Brown, Black* (alluding to hair colour), *Lisping and lame* (a Swedish king Erik *Läspe och halte* living in the thirteenth century). A common type in medieval Scandinavia is compounds alluding to a specific part of the body, for example Old Swedish *Bunkafoter* 'club foot', *Klenefoter* 'small foot'. If a person had a striking neck, he might be called *Skamhals* 'short neck'. Bynames with a prefixed *mædh* 'with' usually denote a characteristic part of the body (or lack of such a one): *Mædh axlana* 'a person with striking shoulders' or *Mædh ena øghat* 'a person with one eye' (Brylla 1999: 13, 16).

16.4.4.2 *Bynames Denoting Mental Characteristics*

Inner characteristics also serve as a reason for naming. Maybe Old Swedish *Karl Dængenæf* (*dengenæf* 1298) was a fighter and hit someone on the nose. Drunkards might be called *Ølvit* 'beer + sense', *Øhovudh* 'beer + head' or *Ølskalle* 'beer + head'.

Derogatory bynames (nicknames) occur for women to a great extent in Swedish medieval documents, for example *Ingridh Thiuvafinger* 'thievish', *katerin papeguya* 'parrot', probably referring to a garrulous woman (Brylla 1999: 16).

This type of byname can also be flattering, as can be seen in the modern nicknames of the German football players *Der Kaiser* 'the emperor' (Franz Beckenbauer) and *Der Terrier* (Berti Vogts).

16.4.5 Bynames Denoting Special Situations, Occurrences, Habits and Expressions

Bynames arose spontaneously from accidental occurrences in ancient times as well as in modern times. It is not always possible to trace the origin of the form of the byname, and the origin of many bynames is often obscure. In many cases we have to rely on guesswork. In medieval Swedish juridical registers, bynames such as *skytit smør* 'filthy butter' (1502), *Jønis Klokaraadh* 'wise advice' (1403) occur, which can be attributed to special occurrences or habits (Brylla 1999: 17–18).

Bynames can also be derived from expressions such as oaths or greetings, for example *Pardew, Pardy, Pardoe* < French *par Dieu*, English *Goodenday* 'good day' (McKinley 1990: 161).

16.5 MORPHOLOGY

Byname formation is interesting from a morphological point of view. In what way are bynames formed, and are there formations that are special for bynames?

Above all, already existing words or phrases are used in byname formation, so called *secondary name formation*. The term *primary name formation*, on the other hand, indicates that the name is an independent creation.

Thus, most bynames are nominal derivations, that is they are formed from nouns and adjectives. Properly speaking, the base words are not personal designations, but metaphorical descriptions. Particularly common are designations for animals: English *Fox*, German *Fuchs*, Swedish *Räv*, probably designating a red-haired or a sly person, English *Pig*, German *Schwein*, Swedish *Gris*, names for a filthy or fat person. In Old Swedish there are even examples of men who are designated by feminine words as *Anka* 'duck', *Birna* 'she-bear', *Flugha* 'fly'. Words for articles of clothing are also used, for example

Old West Scandinavian (Haraldr) *Grafeldr* 'the one with a grey furmantle' (Ragnarr) *Loðbrók* 'the one wearing trousers covered with hair'. Other underlying nouns are words for trees and plants, for example *Ek* 'oak', *Hafre* 'oats', natural phenomena, for example *Eld* 'fire', *Frost* 'frost', parts of the body, for example *Blafot* 'black leg', *Kroknæf* 'hooked nose' (Hellquist 1912: 84ff.). In names like Old Swedish *Spiut* 'spear', *Alboghi* 'elbow' the words are used metonymically: 'the one having a spear', 'the one with a peculiar elbow'.

As can be expected, adjectives have also often been used as bynames. Physical characteristic bynames are often formed describing the size of the body, or hair (colour, length, structure), for example *Long, Big, Grey, Curly*, etc. In Old Swedish there are postpositive bynames such as (Ketil) *Gamal* 'old', or prepositive bynames such as *Langhe* (Jøns). It goes without saying that adjectival participles are also well represented: Old Swedish *Drukken* 'drunken', *Friborin* 'freeborn', *Skitin* 'filthy', etc.

Compounds are represented by names like English *Gentleman* 'a man of gentle birth', German *Hinkefuss, Dollfuss* 'club foot', Old Swedish *Pækkilhuva* 'spiked helmet'. Those are ordinary compounds, but quite a few have a personal characteristic as their last element, such as Old Swedish *-bo(e)* 'inhabitant', *-bonde* 'husband', *magher* 'male relative', *-smedher* 'smith'. Among these bynames both primary and secondary formations are to be found. The latter type is represented by Old Swedish *Klokkaradrænger* 'organist tool', *Badhstughukarl* 'public baths man'.

Furthermore, group-compounds made up of two or more elements might occur as bynames, for example Old Swedish *Dyrt køp* 'expensive bargain', *Nat ok dagh* 'night and day'. Even phrases like *Mædh inga hænder* 'a person with no hands', Latin *Cum vacca* 'a person with a cow' are to be found in medieval Swedish sources.

Phrases (German *Satznamen*) also occur, mostly consisting of a verb + object, English *Shakespeare* 'shake the spear', German *Schützeichel* 'shake the sickle' (Reaney 1967: 285; Brylla 1990: 224ff.; McKinley 1990: 156ff.; Nübling et al. 2012: 174–5).

There are bynames in abundance formed by derivation and compounding. Bynames can be formed with suffixes, for example the agential suffix *-are*, which was borrowed from Latin in pre-literary times and is found in all Germanic languages. The suffix *-are* is considerably older than the corresponding Low German *-er*. In Middle Low German, feminine equivalents to the masculine personal nouns in *-er* were formed by adding the ending *-sche*, for example *borgersche* 'burgher's wife'. In Old Swedish the corresponding ending is *-erska*, for example *Bagerska* 'bakeress', *Krøghirska* 'landlady', etc., which seem to be patterned on Middle German feminine bynames ending in *-se, -sche, -ske* (Brylla 1990: 224–5; Kohlheim and Kohlheim 2008: 15).

Likewise there are primary byname derivations, that is those that cannot be classified as existing words. Such ones can in Scandinavia, for instance, be formed with the masculine suffix *-i/-e*, and the corresponding feminine *-a*. Examples like Old Swedish *Diure* from *diur* 'animal', *Korpe* from *korper* 'raven', and *Bokke* from *bokker* 'he-goat' are usually cited. In this type of formation, the derivative has the purpose of designating or individualizing a person. This function is assumed to be closely related to the semantic role attained by an adjective used as a noun, that is, as a noun the adjective denotes something more than it expresses in itself.

The derivative ending in this case is originally a possessive suffix. Examples are Old Swedish *Skapte* 'he with the spear', *Skægge* 'he with the beard', and such bynames are formed by means of a specializing and individualizing *e-(a)*-derivation from all kinds of basic words.

Compound bynames can also be regarded as primary formations, for example Old Swedish *Svartkulle* 'black' + 'head', 'he who is blackhaired', *Bredhemunder* 'broad' + 'mouth', 'he with a broad mouth' (Brylla 1990: 226ff. with cross-references; Andersson 2003: 603–4).

So called hypocoristic (affectionate) forms can be created in the Germanic languages. Such names are substitutes for a given name, for example English *Bill* < *William*, *Pat* < *Patricia*, or for a surname, for example Swedish *Linkan* < *Lindkvist*. Especially pet forms (sometimes called short forms), were created from dithematic first names, for example German *Otto* < (names in) *Ot-*, *Siggi* < *Sig-*, *Wolfi* < *Wolf-*, Old West Scandinavian *Fasti* and *Stein* from *Stein-*, *Fast-*, *-fastr*, *-steinn*. Feminine pet/short forms are Old West Scandinavian *Arna* from *Arn-*, *Hilda* from *Hild/-hild*. Such forms often have an affectionate and emotive character but they can be quite neutral, too, and they serve as identification in special circles. Such derivations, originally, are also primary formations.

In German, pet forms are formed with the suffix *-i/-ie/-y*, and diminutive suffixes such as *-el*, *-chen*, *-lein* are frequent, for example *Lutzi*, *Klausi*, *Steffi*, *Charlie*, *Kläuschen*, *Christalein*. Family names can also be the basis for pet forms, for example in sport, *Schumi* (< *Schuhmacher*), *Poldi* (< *Podolski*) (Nübling et al. 2012: 171ff.). Similar English suffixes like *-y/-ie* are also productive, for example *Poldy* (Leopold Bloom in *Ulysses*), *Maggie* (Margaret Thatcher).

Pet forms related to the official names are to be separated from pet names, for example *Mouse*, *Sweetie*, *Honey*, *Mausi*, *Bärchen*, etc.

16.6 COLLECTIVE BYNAMES

There are names referring to groups of people. Hereditary surnames (family names) belong to this type. But what attitude is one to take to collective bynames? Are they to be classified as proper names?

At first we have to decide whether some personal groups are names at all. There are names of, for instance, artist groups, for example *Abba*; sports teams, for example *Fußball-Club Bayern München*, *Manchester United Football Club*. Such designations are collectives who keep together by some kind of solidarity. They are names of groups consisting of people but the individuals vary and it is the collective or the organization that is in focus. However, it is not easy to draw a dividing line between the concept of personal names and the group.[4]

---

[4] The designation of inhabitants as *Bremer* (a person from Bremen), *Fleming* (a person from Flanders), etc., as well as ethnonyms like *Sioux*, *German*, *Swede*, are according to Scandinavian terminology to be classified as appellatives. Such examples have been regarded as names in the German

Nevertheless, there are also bynames of such groups, for example *Spurs*, another designation for Tottenham Hotspur F.C., *Änglarna* 'the Angles' for IFK Göteborg, a Swedish football club, *die Königsblauen* for Fußball-Club Gelsenkirchen-Schalke 04, *The Three Musketeers*, *The Gang of Four*, a derogative designation of a group of leaders in the Chinese Communist party, and so on (see Andersson 1983: 12ff.; Kunze 2004: 181; Nübling et al. 2012: 295). Such designations are to be classified as phenomena somewhere between *nomina propria* and appellatives.

16.7 INTERNET NAMES

On the internet a special name practice exists where names are created all the time. You have to choose a user name, sometimes your e-mail address. In participating in discussions on the internet you also have to choose a user name, sometimes called a nick(name). Such a name serves as a means of identification on the web. Usually you do not use your official name but a new self-created name. The names should not be offensive or discriminating. They have to be of a certain length, contain letters, numbers, and symbols. These names serve both for identification and anonymization. Internet names are a communicative phenomenon within a well-defined social, written context.

The Swedish scholar Jonas Carlquist (2005: 89ff.) stresses three important functions of internet names: they are emotive and ideological tools for communication as well as creating a social kinship.

Identification is especially important in the process of name formation. But the user also has the option of remaining anonymous. The most important difference between internet names and other personal names is that the former is chosen by oneself.

The practical function should not be forgotten: The internet name must be easy to remember both for the bearer and for other visitors on the net. The name must also be conspicuous.

Types of internet names:

1. *Letter combinations*. This function is purely practical. This is a way to hide your identity. By this you do not reveal, for example, age, e.g. *girlorwoman*, interests, e.g. *FitnessLiza*, gender, e.g. *FruKarlssson, lady dracula*.
2. *Real proper names*. These names can be the bearer's official name but can also be a new name used in the virtual world.
3. *Naming after someone* (German *Benennungsnamen*). This subgroup is predominant. Illustrative examples from comic strip characters and fantasy

research tradition (see Ainiala, *et al.* 2012: 135; Andersson 2012: 132–3; and cf. Kunze 2004: 10; Van Langendonck 2007b: 64, 196).

characters occur: *Donald Duck, Gandalf*, etc. Names of rock stars and movie stars are also involved. Such names often allude to special interests or ideologies. Often a description follows the name, prefixed, e.g. *Gollumnisse, Kejsar Danne*, or suffixed, e.g. *Robnyc23, Ralph the Wonder Llama*.

4. *Nominal phrases.* The purpose of such user names is to create a unique identification, which characterizes the bearer, *oldslowguy, Raw_Swede*. Internet names consisting of whole clauses, e.g. *Burn the Witch, Iloveuhan*, are unusual according to Carlquist (2005), partly due to the fact that the number of signs is strictly limited.

According to Carlquist, name choices can be compared to a play on words (Carlquist 2005: 89ff., 2012: 168ff.). For further reading, see Martin (2006). See also Chapter 30, this volume.

16.8 BYNAMES—A MIRROR OF SOCIETY

Bynames provide information about descent and kinship, how people act in society, and what their vices and shortcomings are. They also give us a glimpse of how people regard each other and which values are prevalent in society.

It is also interesting to look at bynames from a gender perspective. From the types of bynames that have been given to women in Scandinavia at least, a patriarchal society can be discerned. Views of the position of women in society have fluctuated down the centuries, and these variations are reflected in their names. In medieval judgement books, wives' names (andronymics) are a conspicuous feature, *Birgeta Gøtstafs* (the widow of Gøtstaf Karlsson). The byname of a wife could also be formed from the byname of her husband, for example *Ingegærdh Bangx* (married to Larins Bang). Bynames of women in medieval Sweden were mirrored in a masculine dominated world.

During the Middle Ages and in the modern period, until very recently, the dependence of women on men has been the dominant factor, as the use of patronymics and wives' name makes clear. But during certain periods and in certain circles, metronymics—names derived from the name of a mother—have also occurred, for example *Håkan Ingeborgsson*. In Sweden today they feature to some extent in efforts to achieve greater equality between the sexes (Brylla 2001b: 13ff.).

Studies of modern bynames give glimpses into naming within different groups. Personal groups of different kinds often develop a name usage of their own keeping the group together. It may concern associations, unions, young people, staff colleagues, practitioners, etc. In sport, bynames have an obvious place, for example *Ibra* (Zlatan Ibrahimowić). Bynames or byname elements are also still very much alive in different media, for example *Robinson-Emma* (a participant in a TV soap), *Beautiboxen* 'the vanity case'/*Gucci-Helle* (the present prime minister of Denmark) (Farø 2005: 61).

Bynames on the internet can also be seen from a social point of view. In this case, the question is how one wishes to present oneself, to which group one wishes to belong, etc.

Many name scholars have focused on bynames in historical times. But this involves the risk of speculation and misinterpretation of early data since it is not always easy to find naming motives. However, studying modern bynames can support the interpretation of early bynames. The way people regard each other is in many respects probably the same now as in former times.

CHAPTER 17

··

ETHNONYMS

··

ADRIAN KOOPMAN

17.1 INTRODUCTION

··

ETHNONYMS fall under the wider onomastic category of anthroponyms, a category which can be divided into two broad sub-categories: the names of individuals, and the names of groups. Under the former are personal names ('Christian' names, first names, given names), nicknames, and baptismal names; under the latter are family names (surnames), and the names of a number of different types of groups (sports teams, performing groups, religious denominations, and so on). Ethnonyms refer to the type of group known by a wide variety of different terms: race, nation, population, polity, tribe, clan, kingdom, chiefdom, and 'ethnic group'.

Two caveats must be noted here, one arising from the definition of *ethnonym* given in the onomastic terminology list on the website of the International Council of Onomastic Sciences (ICOS); the other arising from the elusive nature of ethnicity.

The ICOS terminology list says the following:

> Ethnonym—proper name of an ethnic group (a tribe, a folk, a clan etc.), or a member of this group, e.g. *Italians, Bavarians, Croat, Frenchman, Zulu.* (NOTE: Ethnonyms are not treated as proper names in some languages and by some scholars, e.g. *ingleses* in Spanish. According to some theories, ethnonyms are proper names both in plural and singular, in other theories, ethnonyms in the plural are proper names, in the singular appellatives.

While noting the point that ethnonyms are not treated as proper names in some languages and by some scholars, clearly that cannot be a guiding principle in the writing of this chapter in a book about proper names. But it does show that there is a lack of standardization and general agreement about ethnonymy among onomastic scholars. The same could be said about the last sentence, reflecting different treatments of singularity and plurality in ethnonyms. In this chapter I assume all ethnonyms to be proper names, in both singular and plural forms.

The second caveat concerns the nature of the entity to which an ethnonym refers. An example of the difficulty in pinning down just what a 'tribe', a 'folk' or a 'clan' is, can be seen in comparing the definitions of 'ethnic' and 'race' below:

> ethnic: 1. Of or pertaining to a social group within a cultural and social system that claims or is accorded a special status on the basis of complex, often variable traits including religions, linguistic, ancestral or physical characteristics. 2. Broadly, characteristic of a religious, *racial*, national, or cultural group. (Nuessel 2008: 29, quoting Morris 1979)
>
> Race is a classification system used to categorise humans into large and distinct populations or groups by anatomical, cultural, *ethnic*, genetic, geographical, historical, linguistic, religious or social affiliations. (Wikipedia 2013a)
>
> [my emphasis in both quotations]

As can be seen, according to one source, one of the defining elements of ethnicity is 'race'; according to the other, one of the defining elements of 'race' is ethnicity. This kind of circularity in definition occurs frequently in anthropological and ethnographic literature.

In the sections that follow, consideration will be given to the relationship between ethnonyms and race, nationality, geography, language, and religion. The chapter will then continue to investigate various onomastic dynamics where ethnonyms play a role, under the headings 'Ethnonyms, clans and surnames', 'Variations of ethnonyms', 'Alternative ethnonyms', 'Derogatory ethnonyms' and ' "Non-ethnonyms" and "ethnonymic gaps"'.

17.2   ETHNONYMS AND RACE

In the latter part of the nineteenth century and the first decades of the twentieth century, dividing humans into racial groups was a popular pastime for anthropologists, and such racial classification was based on physical categories. For example, for Seligman the 'chief criteria of race ... include skin colour, hair form, stature, head shape, and certain characters of the face, e.g. prognathism, and of the nose' (1966: 2), and for him the term 'race' connotes 'a group of peoples who have certain well-marked physical features in common'. These physical characteristics allow him to classify the peoples of Africa into the racial categories *Hamites, Semites, Negroes, Khoisan* (*Bushmen* and *Hottentots*), and *Negrillos*—names which would be regarded by most onomasticians as ethnonyms.

By the twenty-first century, however, the notion of 'race' and/or of classifying people according to their race had become decidedly dated and politically incorrect, with

Oppenheimer, for example, stating ' "Race" . . . is now a politically incorrect term, and in some circles, so is "ethnicity". (2003: 2). He suggests a reason for this:

> A by-product of the fight against racism has been to render discussion of race taboo. Even the word 'race' itself, tainted forever by the Nazi era, is outlawed by many anthropologists as unscientific, derogatory, meaningless, and giving the misleading impression that races are discrete entities when in fact variation, gradation, and admixture occur everywhere. (Oppenheimer 2003: 196)

His comment that '. . . most alternative terms for race such as "population" or "ethnic group" are so vague as to be misleading. . .' (2003: 197) echoes the point made above about the difficulties in establishing the nature of entities referred to by ethnonyms.

Despite Oppenheimer's misgivings about 'racial' classification, he uses terms like 'Caucasoid', 'Mongoloid', and 'Negrito' to describe physical types, 'not because they are accurate, but because they have common usage' (2003: 197). The names he uses for the major groups of the world, based on 'the geographical area of indigenous populations who appear broadly related on a wide range of biological attributes' (2003: 197) are *Sub-Saharan Africans, Negritos, Caucasoids, Australoids, Melanesians, Southern Mongoloids*, and *Northern Mongoloids*, again, names which would be accepted by most onomasticians as ethnonyms, or possibly 'ethnonymic phrases' ('Sub-Saharan African', 'Southern Mongoloid').

17.3 Ethnonyms, Nationality, and Geographical Area

Few onomasticians would dispute the ethnonymic status of the following names: *Australian, Canadian, Briton, Italian, German, Ukrainian, Russian*, and *Swiss/Switzer*), and would understand these names to refer, respectively, to inhabitants or citizens of Australia, Canada, Great Britain, Italy, Germany, the Ukraine, Russia, and Switzerland. There are, however, problems in regarding nationality as a factor defining an ethnonym. Meredith points out that when various European nations staked claims in Africa at the end of the nineteenth century, they simply drew straight lines on the map 'taking little or no account of the myriad of traditional monarchies, chiefdoms, and other African societies that existed on the ground' (2011: 1). He goes on to say:

> [many of] Europe's new colonial territories enclosed hundreds of diverse and independent groups, with no common history, culture, languages or religion. Nigeria, for example, contained as many as 250 ethno-linguistic groups. Officials sent to the Belgian Congo eventually identified six thousand chiefdoms there. (Meredith 2011: 1)

It is this that led the Yoruba leader Obafemi Awolowo, who dominated Western Nigerian politics for more than thirty years, to write in 1947:

> Nigeria is not a nation. It is a mere geographical expression. There are not 'Nigerians' in the same sense as there are 'English', 'Welsh' or 'French'. The word 'Nigerian' is merely a distinctive appellation to distinguish those who live within the boundaries of Nigeria and those who do not. (Cited in Meredith 2011: 8)

At first glance, the name *Nigerian* would appear to be as much an ethnonym as *Canadian*, *Belgian*, and *Croatian*. But if one takes the points made by both Meredith and Awolowo, *Nigerian* could perhaps be better termed a 'false ethnonym'. Given these doubts about the link between ethnonymy and nationality, it may be useful to look at ethnonyms as they relate to the inhabitants of a specific geographical area, which may not necessarily be and often are NOT a nation. Such geographical areas may be continents, producing ethnonyms like *Asian*, *American*, and *European*. Certainly, countries are highly productive sources of ethnonyms: *Kenyan*, *Bolivian*, *German*, *Dane*, *Peruvian*, *Japanese*, and hundreds of others. Most onomasticians would accept that such names at regional or provincial level are also ethnonyms for example *Queenslander*, *Cornishman*, *Bohemian*, *Fleming* (c.f. *Walloon*), *Tuscan*, *Texan*, and *Natalian*.[1] Once we move to the urban level, there is some debate. Not all onomasticians consulted in the writing of this chapter[2] accept the following as ethnonyms: *Londoner*, *New Yorker*, *Glaswegian*, *Berliner*, *Neapolitan*, *Parisian*, *Durbanite*, and *Capetonian*.

17.4 ETHNONYMS AND LANGUAGE

Seligman makes the following connection between language and ethnonyms:

> ...names [i.e. ethnonyms] based on linguistic criteria are constantly applied to large groups of mankind, and, indeed, if intelligently used, often fit quite well. Hence, in describing the great racial groups of Africa, terms such as 'Bantu', which strictly speaking have no more than a linguistic significance, are habitually employed... (Seligman 1966: 1)[3]

McConvell (2006) makes the same link between ethnic group and language when he says that the approximately 300 language names in Australia are effectively also the

---

[1] In post-1994 South Africa, the erstwhile Natal was renamed KwaZulu-Natal. This toponym is yet to produce a related ethnonym.

[2] During the last week of September 2012, when the Names Society of Southern Africa was holding its biennial congress, I had many fruitful discussions with Elwyn Jenkins (South Africa), Willy Van Langendonck (Belgium), Michael Walsh (Australia), and Michel Rateau (France).

[3] The term 'Bantu' is indeed more commonly used by linguists to refer to a group of closely-related languages spoken mostly south of the equator in Africa, but for many years in apartheid South Africa the word was used as an ethnonym in reference to black South Africans. See Neethling (2010b).

names of ethnic groups, while the many more thousand dialects share a name with the associated clan. He points out that 'Quite a number of these [language] names are opaque: they have no meaning other than that they are ethnonyms today' (McConvell 2006: 185). He expands on this point a few pages later:

> The great majority of these names function as both the name of the language (*glossonym*), and the name of the group which speaks the language, or, as is common these days, which inherits affiliation with the language, whether or not they speak it (*ethnonym*). (McConvell 2006: 189)

Language—or, at least, the manipulation of language—can even create ethnonyms or ethnic identities where none existed before. Meredith (2011) discusses how colonial officials in West Africa attempted to simplify the multitude of small chiefdoms into bigger, more manageable administrative units, and says:

> Missionary endeavour added to the trend. In the process of transcribing hitherto unwritten languages into written forms, missionaries reduced Africa's innumerable dialects to fewer written languages, each helping to define a tribe. The effect was to establish new frontiers of linguistic groups and to strengthen the sense of solidarity between them. Yoruba, Igbo, Ewe, Shona and many others were formed this way. (Meredith 2011: 155)

An interesting feature of the relation between ethnonym and language can be seen in what McConvell (2006: 196) describes as a 'shibbolethnonym', which he explains as '[t]he use of a distinctive feature of the speech of the group to form the ethnonym'. Such ethnonyms take the form of 'the people who say X', where 'X' is an unusual linguistic feature. For example, among a related group of Australian aboriginal tribes, the common word for 'get' is *marra*, but one particular tribe uses the word *manjil* instead. They are consequently known as *Manjiljarra* (<*manjil* 'get' + *jarra* 'having'; lit. '[those] having *manjil* [in their speech]'.

A similar example may be that of *Barbarian*, explained by *The Wordsworth Dictionary of Phrase and Fable* (Evans 1993: 77) as 'The Greeks and Romans called all foreigners barbarians ("babblers"); men who spoke a language not understood by them'. A further example can be found in South Africa today, when immigrants from other African countries (e.g. Nigeria, Ghana, Congo) who speak languages not recognizably one of the South African Bantu languages, are collectively dismissed by the derogative term *amaKwerekwere* ('those who, when they speak, go *kwerekwerekwere*'). Yet another example is the ethnonym *amaLala*, a reference to one of the ethnic groups in what is now KwaZulu-Natal, before the rise of the Zulu kingdom under Shaka. The Lala people were noted for their distinct dialect, and their name is explained by one of James Stuart's informants as follows:

> The amaLala were so-called by the Zulus and Qwabes because they speak in the *tekela* dialect and thereby speak with their tongues lying down *(lala).* (Webb and Wright 1976–2001: I, 117)

While still in South Africa, the ethnonym *Hottentot* can be noted. Now a derogatory term for the early pastoralist people the Khoikhoi, the term was supposedly coined by early white explorers in imitation of the clicking sound of the Khoikhoi language.

And as a final example, the term 'gringo', used in the United States for a non-Spanish speaking white person, is originally a Spanish word meaning 'foreigner' (i.e. non-Spaniard). Such a person 'hablar en griego, en guirigay, en *gringo*' (Wikipedia 2013b) (effectively, 'such a person is speaking Greek to me').

17.5 ETHNONYMS AND RELIGION

Onomasticians who have been consulted are quite definite that religion on its own is not a defining element of an ethnic identity, and the following names cannot be regarded as ethnonyms: *Buddhist, Shintoist, Muslim*, and *Christian*. Clearly this also applies to sub-groups of these major world religions, such as *Sunni* and *Shi'ite* Muslims, and *Protestants, Congregationalists, Baptists, Catholics, Methodists, Calvinists*, and so on.

Various authors, while not specifically discussing ethnonyms and ethnonymic status on onomastic grounds, make it clear that they agree with the above. For example, Dawkins (2006), writing about the sectarian civil war between Sunni and Shia Muslims in Iraq as a consequence of the Anglo-American invasion of 2003, says that this was

> … clearly a religious conflict—yet in *The Independent* of 20 May 2006 the front-page headline and first leading article described it as 'ethnic cleansing'. 'Ethnic' in this context is another euphemism. What we are seeing in Iraq is religious cleansing. (Dawkins 2006: 21)

He goes on to say:

> The original usage of 'ethnic cleansing' in the former Yugoslavia is also arguably a euphemism for religious cleansing, involving Orthodox Serbs, Catholic Croats and Muslim Bosnians. (Dawkins 2006: 43)

And yet the very fact that such 'religious cleansing' is so widely known as 'ethnic cleansing' suggests that in many situations there is confusion between ethnicity and religion.

17.6 ETHNONYMS, CLANS, AND SURNAMES

Note that the ICOS definition of ethnonym, given in the introductions to this chapter, gave *Zulu* as an example of an ethnonym. But the Zulu ethnic group itself can be sub-divided into smaller ethnic groups, as explained in the following:

The ethnonym *Zulu* is used in two ways in KwaZulu-Natal, the home of 'the Zulu peo-ple': *first*, in the same way as the rest of the world uses it, to refer to the 11 million or more people who speak the language Zulu; and *secondly*, to refer to the people who are mem-bers of the Zulu clan, and use the clan name Zulu as their surname. The Zulu language itself makes this distinction quite clear: *amaZulu* (the Zulu people, in the wider sense) and *abakwaZulu* (literally 'those of the house of Zulu'—the Zulu clan itself). Wright (2008) sees the first usage—the wider sense—as a much later development in the history of 'the Zulu people':

> For most of the history of the Zulu kingdom . . . few of its members would have regarded themselves as Zulu. Until perhaps the time of Cetshwayo, people inside the kingdom applied the term solely to members of the ruling Zulu descent group. Outside the kingdom, though, the term came to be used quite differently, particu-larly by white people. (Wright 2008: 37)

Prior to this mid-nineteenth-century 'expansion' of the ethnic sense of Zulu, the area which is now the province KwaZulu-Natal was inhabited by a number of independent clans (often referred to in the literature as 'tribes'), each occupying its own geographical area, and each with its own chief, and its own name. Wright and Hamilton, commenting on Zulu clans, quote A. T. Bryant's (1929) definition of a clan:

> the magnified family, in which all alike were descended from the same original ancestor, all were now ruled by that ancestor's living representative, and all dwelt and moved together in one great block . . . (Bryant 1929: 53)

Wright and Hamilton (1989) continue:

> The clan was thus at once a political unit, a descent group, and a residential group, with a high degree of internal cohesion. (Wright and Hamilton 1989: 53)

Despite the fact that today these clans are known collectively by the single ethnonym [*the*] *Zulus*, they have not lost their sense of independent identity and have certainly not lost their clan names. Clan names such as *Bhengu, Buthelezi, Cele, Dlamini*, and *Dlomo*, to give just five out of the several hundred still used today, are used adminis-tratively in South Africa as surnames: it is this name which is invariably filled in, by Zulu-speaking people, in the box marked 'surname' on official forms. Some might argue that if these are surnames, then they cannot be ethnonyms, as these are two discreet onomastic categories. I argue here, as I have argued previously (Koopman 2002b: 76–85), that there is a distinct difference between a surname in the onomastic sense, and a clan name—and the Zulu clan simply *functions* as a surname in official administrative contexts, as there is no equivalent of the surname in the Zulu anthro-ponymic system.

Many of the features of Zulu clans also apply to the notion of clan in Scotland:[4]

- a strong sense of clan identity, with a perception that all others with the same clan names are 'brothers' and 'sisters';
- the acknowledgement of a certain individual as 'clan chief';
- the acknowledgement of a certain geographical area as being the 'clan homeland';
- the sharing of distinct clan praises (*izithakazelo* in Zulu);
- the frequent sharing of certain visual 'clan markers' (scarification, particular head-dress styles, distinctive bead-work styles, amputation of finger joints, and so on).

I argue then, that Zulu names like *Bhengu, Buthelezi, Cele, Dlamini*, and *Dlomo*, as well as Scottish names like *Buchanan, Bruce, Campbell, Douglas, Gordon, MacDonald*, and *MacGregor*, while appearing in identity books, in passports, and on drivers' licences as 'surnames', are really ethnonyms. A synonym of 'surname' is 'family name', and the names mentioned above refer to groups which are much wider than a family. They refer to descent groups with a recognized chief, and like other chiefdoms all over the world, they are referred to by ethnonyms.

17.7 VARIATIONS OF ETHNONYMS

There are two basic types of variations among ethnonyms: morphological variations and exonymic variations.

17.7.1 Morphological Variations

Morphological variations include variation between singular and plural forms, such as *Englishman/The English, Briton/The British*, and *umZulu/amaZulu*, and informal abbreviated forms, often with the diminutive suffix -*ie*, as in *Australian/Aussie, Tasmanian/Tassie*, and *Transvaaler/Vaalie*.

17.7.2 Endonymic and Exonymic Forms of Ethnonyms

The terms 'exonym' and 'endonym' are more commonly used of place-names as in the endonymic forms *London, Firenze*, and *München*, and their exonymic equivalents *Londres, Florence*, and *Munich*. There is, of course, no reason why these terms should

---

[4] To support this claim I have relied on *Bartholomew's CLAN MAP: Scotland of Old* (n.d.) and Maclean (1990).

not also be used of ethnonyms. The terms *autethnonym* (= endonym) and *allethnonym* (= exonym) have also been used. The exonymic variants of ethnonyms may be radically different (based on different roots), as in *Deutschers, The Germans, Les Allemands*, and *Saksalainen*, or they may be based on the same root as in the exonymic forms of *The English* given below, where the historical root *Angle* is to a greater or lesser extent still recognizable.

Les Anglais (French)
Englantilainen[5] (Finnish)
Het Engelse (Dutch)
ingleses (Spanish)
iNgisi(mani) (sing) *amaNgisi* (plur) (Zulu)
mwIngereza (sing) *waIngereza* (plur) (Swahili)
awuInjilisi (sing) *awaInjilisi* (plur) (Lamba)
omuEngelisa (sing) *ovaEngelisa* (plur) (Kwanyama)
iNgesi (sing) *amaNgesi* (plur) (Xhosa)

17.8 Alternative Ethnonyms

Names like *Limey, John Bull, Pommy*, and *Rooinek*[6] for an Englishman, *Digger* for an Australian, and *Kiwi* for a New Zealander can be considered to be in the same relationship to ethnonyms as nicknames are to personal names. Indeed, there is no reason why they should not be called 'ethnonymic nicknames', or possibly even 'ethnonicks'. Examples abound from all over the world: *Apple-Islander* and *Mountain-devil* for a Tasmanian; *Canecutter* and *Bananalander* for a Queenslander, *Cabbage-Patcher* and *Yarra-yabbie*[7] for an inhabitant of the Australian state Victoria, *Canuck* for a Canadian (earlier especially a French Canadian, c.f. *Jean Baptiste*), *Celestials* for the Chinese, and the curious *Blue Hen's Chickens* for the inhabitants of the State of Delaware in the USA (Evans 1993: 126).

The website Lexicus (n.d.), in giving a list of 'specialized synonyms' for the term *ethnos*, includes the following: 'Abo, Aboriginal, Australian Aborigine, Native Australian...'. This group of four variants for the same reference is similar to the group [Native American, American Indian, Red Indian, redskin, Lo[8]], with each group

---

[5] *-lainen* is a Finnish ethnonymic suffix indicating 'inhabitant of' or 'of X nationality'.

[6] The Afrikaans word for the British during the South African Wars, because their necks characteristically burnt red in the South African sun. The English translation of this—*redneck*—does not have the same reference. *Redneck* is a disparaging term in the south-western USA for a poor, uneducated white farm worker. Is it an ethnonym?

[7] The Yarra-Yarra river runs through Melbourne.

[8] Michener (1974) quotes from a Denver newspaper in 1864:

constituting a sliding scale between formal and informal, and neutral and derogatory. *Australian Aborigine/Native Australian* and *American Indian/Native American* could be considered to be on the formal and neutral end of the scale, while *abo, redskin*, and the curious *Lo* are clearly both informal and derogatory.

17.9 DEROGATORY ETHNONYMS

Bryson (1994: 176) explains the reference and the etymology of *chink, kike, dago, polack, spic, hebe, bohunk, wop, sheeny, guinea, greaser, greaseball, skibby*, and *gu-gu*, all derogatory 'ethnonicknames' used in America to refer to minority groups who were not White Anglo-Saxon Protestants (WASPs). Many of these, he says, 'have mercifully fallen by the wayside' (1994: 177).

Nuessel (2008: 29) re-introduces the term 'ethnophaulism' for an insulting ethnonym ('ethnic slur'). Based on combining the Greek words *ethnos* and *phaulisma* ('disparage'), the term was originally coined by Abraham Roback (1979 [1944]). Nuessel explains:

> Ethnophaulisms are pejorative names or designations for people who belong to an ethnic group and they are usually based on several observable phenomena including skin color, clothing customs, culturally-determined eating and drinking practices, and other aspects commonly associated with a particular group. (Nuessel 2008: 29)

Nuessel goes on to say:

> One type of an ethnophaulism is the use of given names commonly associated with a particular ethnic group such as the Irish, the Jews, the Italians, the French, and so forth. Because these given names are so frequent in particular cultures, their use serves to identify a person as a member of a particular ethnic group. Creative writers often employ such names as a way of identifying a person's ethnicity. Another

> . . . Forty-three dead Indians for one missing horse might seem excessive to our weak sisters in Vermont and Pennsylvania . . . who are always telling us how to handle our Indians, but to those of us who have to live with Lo at close quarters, it is clear that only the most stern reprisals will keep him from slaughtering all white men along the Platte. (Michener 1974: 394)

> Michener explains 'Lo' as follows:

> The use of Lo . . . for the Indian was universal in the west and came about because the English poet, Alexander Pope, in his rhymed *Essay on Man*, introduced these thoughtful lines:

> Hope springs eternal in the human breast;
> Man never is, but always is to be blest . . .
> Lo, the poor Indian! Whose untutored mind,
> Sees God in clouds, or hears him in the wind . . .

> Many newspapers, such as *Zendt's Farm Clarion* . . . used the whole phrase, Lo, the poor Indian, but more sophisticated papers preferred the simple Lo. (Michener 1974)

example is the use of a national or ethnic designation before a noun to denote inferiority or a negative quality of the associated noun. (Nuessel 2008: 30)

Nuessel makes two points here, but exemplifies neither. His first is the (often derogatory) use of personal names to refer to ethnic groups; the second is the use of ethnonyms as adjectives to pejoratively qualify a noun.

Examples of the first could be considered to be the interface between personal names and ethnonyms, and would include the well-known examples *Hymie* (< *Hyman* < Hebrew name *Chayyim*) and *Abe/Abie* (< *Abraham*) for Jewish men, *Taffy* (< *Dafydd* 'David') for a Welshman, and *Paddy* (< *Padraig*) for an Irishman.

As regards Nuessel's second point, examples are given by both Bryson (1994: 176) and Branford (1980: 126) using respectively the ethnonyms *Irish* and *Kaffir*.

Bryson's examples are *Irish buggy* (wheelbarrow), *Irish clubhouse* (police station), *Irish confetti* (bricks), and *Irish beauty* (woman with two black eyes). Branford (1980) gives many examples of how the word *kaffir* has been used as a derogatory epithet in South Africa, including *kaffir dog* (nondescript mongrel), *kaffir sheeting* (inferior quality cloth), and *kaffir eating house*. The ethnonym-based adjective *Dutch* produces *Dutch courage, Dutch bargain, Dutch comfort*, and *Dutch nightingales.*[9]

17.10 'NON-ETHNONYMS' AND 'ETHNONYMIC GAPS'

Branford (1980), on the use of 'European' in South Africa, states:

> A white-skinned person i.e. descended from the Caucasian races, is so-called in S.A. without any regard or any actual ties with Europe; now largely replaced by *White* . . . (Branford 1980: 79)

Given that for 'non-South Africans' the ethnonym European still means 'someone from Europe', there is a potential for confusion, amusingly captured by Branford in a quotation taken from the Durban newspaper *The Natal Mercury* of 8 April 1973:

> . . . my wife . . . walked through the door marked 'non-European' at Jan Smuts Airport.[10] 'But you're White!' I hissed. 'I'm not European!' She hissed back. 'I'm American'. (Branford 1980: 79)

---

[9] Respectively 'the courage exerted by alcohol', 'a bargain settled over drinks', 'cold comfort (no comfort at all)', and 'a frog'. Evans (1993: 353) notes 'the derogatory implications of some of the phrases derive from the Anglo-Dutch war of the seventeenth century'.

[10] After 1994, Jan Smuts Airport became, briefly, Johannesburg International Airport, and is now Oliver Tambo International Airport.

In apartheid South Africa (and indeed in South Africa in the twenty-first century), the four main racial/ethnic groups were and are Black Africans,[11] Indians,[12] Coloureds,[13] and Europeans or Whites. Apartheid policy gave privileges to the Europeans or Whites, which meant that the other three groups needed to be known collectively by a single name. There being no such suitable ethnonym, the 'reverse ethnonyms' *Non-European* and *Non-White* were adopted (in Afrikaans *Nie-Blankes*). As Walsh has pointed out,[14] such terms 'fill a lexical gap in ethnonymy'. He adds that in Australia, the term 'non-Aborigines' is used informally to refer to all the ethnic groups in Australia who are not aboriginal Australians.

17.11 SUMMARY AND CONCLUSION

In this chapter I have tried to show that while 'ethnonym' is a commonly used term among onomastic scholars, not all regard ethnonyms as proper names. This anomalous status is linked to uncertainties about defining the entity which is named with an ethnonym, with (for example) terms like 'race' and 'ethnic group' being at times synonymous, and at other times part of each other's set of defining elements. Together with 'race' and 'ethnicity', other defining elements have included language, nationality, religion, geographical area, and culture. The links between ethnonyms and some of these elements, such as religion, are both complex and debatable; while other links, such as between ethnonyms and language, and ethnonyms and nationality, produce intriguing onomastic dynamics. Ethnonyms display the same kind of variations and alternatives as can be found for personal names and place-names: morpho-syntactic variations, endonymic and exonymic forms, and alternative names for the same ethnic entity, generally regarded as falling into the general spectrum of nicknames. Examples have been given of the interface between ethnonyms, personal names, toponyms, and glossonyms.

In conclusion, although ethnonyms have an anomalous status among onomastic scholars, they display the same kinds of linguistic, social, and cultural characteristics as proper names generally.

---

[11] Known at various times as *Natives* and *Bantu(s)*.

[12] Also known as Asians, these are the descendants of indented agricultural labourers brought out to Natal in the 1860s, from India, to work in the sugarcane fields.

[13] People of mixed blood, especially the descendants of Europeans and Malay slaves in the Cape in the seventeenth century.

[14] Michael Walsh, personal communication, September 2012.

CHAPTER 18

....

PERSONAL NAMES
AND ANTHROPOLOGY

....

ELLEN S. BRAMWELL

WITHIN onomastics, or name-studies, names have often been viewed in a way which privileges etymological meaning above all else. Names, whether of places or of people, are investigated as a single element or in a cluster and subjected to detailed philological and historical research. This is a valuable process and can tell us much about people and society in the past. However, there are other approaches to names which, until the recent rise of socio-onomastics, have had seemingly little intersection with the people who view names as their primary object of study. One important method is that taken in anthropology, particularly with regard to the names of people.

Despite being a wide, varied and long-established discipline, anthropological studies which look particularly at names have been fairly few and far between. This is surprising, as it seems evident that personal names have an important function in society, and so it might be expected that they would be of great interest to social and cultural anthropologists. There have been a small number of specialized conferences in the past: one 'Processes of Naming and the Significance of Names: Towards a Unified Analysis?' at Cambridge in 1999 and an earlier meeting in 1980, run by the American Ethnological Society and on the topic of 'Naming Systems' (Iteanu 2000). Both resulted in collected volumes of papers on names from an anthropological perspective (Tooker 1984; Vom Bruck and Bodenhorn 2006a). In the first, Tooker (1984: vii) wrote that 'relatively little attention has been paid to [names] in the literature'. By the latter publication there had clearly been an increase of interest within the field into names and naming but in his report on the 1999 conference Iteanu (2000: 24) echoes Tooker in pointing out that 'Naming processes remain under-theorised'. Joseph (2004) has also recently called for the study of personal names to be integrated more closely into anthropological linguistics.

This chapter will provide a brief summary of some major theories in anthropology and discuss how anthropologists have dealt with names, and particularly personal names, in their research outputs. In addition to this there will be consideration of how names might be seen in relation to wider anthropological movements at a more theoretical level. This will provide an outline of the role of names, and their potential role, within specific anthropological frameworks. The chapter is not intended to provide a complete inventory, nor even a regional survey, of anthropological studies which relate to naming. For a large-scale, comparative study, see Alford (1988); for an overview of social science contributions to naming up to the 1980s, see Lawson (1984); and for extensive annotated bibliographies on naming including anthropological studies, see Lawson (1987, 1995) and Lawson and Dance (2008). Instead, the scope is of an overview and discussion of the potential implications of anthropological methods for the way names are studied more generally.

More precisely, the first section of this chapter deals with our objects of study: names, societies, and cultural contexts of people. The second discusses anthropology itself and how names might fit in with various strands of research within the discipline. The third section concentrates on specific anthropologically-based studies of naming from a variety of contexts and perspectives.

18.1 Objects of Study

18.1.1 Names

There is not a single society yet studied where members do not use names (Alford 1988). Labelling people and their surrounding landscape seems to be something which is ingrained into human cultural practice. Names are considered by anthropologists to be a human universal: something which is part of the global human condition, rather than a phenomenon developed only within particular cultural frameworks (Murdock 1945; Brown 1991). Within anthropological studies, it is easier to find evidence of personal names, particularly alongside kinship terminology, but there have been a small number of studies which also consider place-names. Despite the universal characteristic of having personal names, the systems underlying these names are not uniform across cultures (Alford 1988; Hickerson 2000). Names are given to people at different stages of life; they change or remain constant; they contain different elements; they connect with relatives or tribes or they do not; they are used freely or they are kept secret. There are as many ways of enacting naming practices as there are communities to enact them and an understanding of these culturally-specific patterns of personal names within their context is the goal within anthropological studies of naming. Duranti (1997: 334) suggests that it does not matter if we start from a standpoint of universalism or diversity, as long as we are aware of both. Theories as to exactly what defines a name are discussed elsewhere in the volume, and Bean (1980) advocates that anthropologists use philosophical understanding of the nature of proper names to guide their own enquiry. Antoun (1968: 158) declares his object of study to be 'the full range of terms of address and reference' and this broad approach to names is a useful one. It allows a more tailored picture of the usage, bestowal, and meaning of names within communities and societies to emerge from research into individual cultures.

18.1.2 Society and Community

On the one hand, the object of study within this volume is clearly names and naming practices. On the other hand, it is impossible to discuss names in anthropological terms without also considering the people who use these names. In describing the practices of a particular group of people, it is important to understand what it is that makes those people a cohesive group (if indeed they are at all) and therefore whether it makes sense to think about them as sharing a cultural framework. So the society or community in which names are being studied is as much an object of study as the names themselves. These terms, society and community, are not necessarily synonymous, although they are often used as if they were. The ideas of Tönnies (2002 [1887]), although more closely associated with sociology, are useful in separating the two. He made a distinction between *Gemeinschaft* (community) and *Gesellschaft* (society), with the crucial difference being in the nature of the two concepts. Within the description of human existence, the former embodies 'real and organic life', while the latter denotes 'imaginary and mechanical structure' (Tönnies 2002 [1887]: 33). If we accept this model, the arrangement of shared ties within *society* are deliberately constructed with specific intentions and are, necessarily, fairly abstract (Heberle 1973: 52). They might describe arrangements such as the official organization of people within a region or country. Conversely, the ties within *communities* are created and maintained around more concrete or physical concerns such as kinship, a shared locality or the collaboration of people in a common pursuit (Tönnies 2002 [1887]: 42).

It is tempting to simply equate community with place. However, that relationship needs to be investigated as a part of a study rather than assumed and the reality can often be far more complex, which becomes clear when we consider the nature of many modern urban settlements. Brunt (2001: 81) has argued that there is in essence no real difference between rural and urban societies, as the most basic social ties between people are based on 'proximity and social contact', whether they live in a remote village or the centre of a city. These basic social ties correspond most closely with Tönnies's concept of community regardless of location.

The term 'society' is commonly employed within the social sciences, but rarely with a precise explanation of how it is being used. Eriksen (2004: 23) emphasizes that Tönnies's two concepts should not be seen as being in opposition to each other; small-scale societies should be considered as existing within the framework of larger social systems. In this manner, communities can be viewed as existing within the wider context of regional, national, and global societies (Fillitz 2002: 217). There is undoubtedly a lack of distinction between these multi-layered and entwined ideas of community and society, and it is clear that what we are dealing with is not an easily delineated whole, but an amorphous and complex entity. Hymes (1996) provides a useful viewpoint when discussing speech communities specifically:

> Clearly the boundary (and the internal organization) of a speech community is not a question solely of degree of interaction among persons … but a question equally of attributed and achieved membership, of identity and identification. (Hymes 1996: 32)

This perspective at once problematizes the direct relationship between community and ties/interactions, and introduces the issue of identification with the group as another important factor to consider. This is a significant observation for our purposes, as naming practices often play an important role in the construction of identity both in individuals and in groups of people.

18.1.3 Culture

Culture is another area which is both hugely complex and essential to the discussion of naming practices. Although the term has altered in meaning over time, Tylor defined it as early as 1871 in a sense that is recognizable today as an anthropological conception of culture:

> Culture or Civilization, taken in its wide ethnographic sense, is that complex whole which includes knowledge, belief, arts, morals, law, custom, and any other capabilities and habits acquired by man as a member of society. (Tylor 1871: 1).

Tylor's view on culture more generally would be challenged and reworked by later anthropologists but this quotation at least touches on the vast scope of the term. Riley (2007: 21) reflects on the influential work of Kroeber and Kluckhohn in 1952, which discussed 160 approaches to culture, and the myriad definitions which have appeared since then. He writes that:

> more recent examinations of the topic … have simply strengthened their conclusions: the term is highly polysemic, not to say frustratingly ambiguous, and yet it is at the same time the defining epistemological structure of social anthropology and is essential to any understanding of the modern social sciences. (Riley 2007: 21)

Eriksen's (2010) definition is straightforward but its simplicity perhaps encapsulates more than an exhaustive list of terms. He defines culture as 'that which makes it possible for two or several actors to understand each other' (2010: 82).

Research in anthropology seeks to understand culture from an insider's perspective, yet culture itself has many aspects and can vary from individual to individual. Given that a major aim of ethnographic research is to build a picture of cultural practices within a community or society, with naming practices as one facet of this, the untangling of whose practices are being recorded and how representative these are can be extremely problematic. This can be partially resolved through the use of frameworks such as 'communities of practice', as set out by Eckert and McConnell-Ginet (1992), where identities are seen as being constructed through practices and norms created amongst social groups. This is a nuanced view, as it allows for an individual to be part of many groups, reflecting multi-layered identities. However, it can make it even more difficult to say something general about the culture of a community as a whole. Eriksen (2010: 83) advocates anthropologists first discovering what networks of relationships are important to the inhabitants of a society and only then choosing which to research in depth.

18.1.4 Summary

In sum, our objects of study within the scope of this chapter are names and the practices which affect their bestowal, use, maintenance, and social meaning. Naming practices must be viewed as part of a wider set of cultural practices which may encompass any aspect of the human condition and which are enacted by groups of individuals. These groups are difficult to delineate, as concepts such as individual social ties, identity, community, and society are all elements of complexity in the task of understanding whose names we are researching.

18.2 ANTHROPOLOGICAL THEORIES

18.2.1 Anthropological Methods and Onomastics

While onomasticians and anthropologists have traditionally seemed part of different academic worlds, and certainly different faculties and departments, their methods are not always so dissimilar. In the very first volume of the onomastic journal *Nomina*, Fraser (1977) described the process of studying minor place-names in a small rural community and the camaraderie with community members that this task required. These attempts to gain an insider's perspective on an aspect of culture through local informants are common within onomastics (e.g. Taylor with Márkus 2006–2012: ix) and would also seem familiar to the anthropologist. This shared requirement for detailed fieldwork in both disciplines is something that links the two subjects and suggests that researchers may be well-served in learning from one other. Indeed, Bernard (2011: 1–2), when discussing ways of accessing information about society, noted that 'there are no anthropological or sociological or psychological methods. The questions we ask about the human condition may differ across the social sciences, but methods belong to all of us.'

The fieldwork method most recognizable to the onomastician in the anthropological context is the interview. In place-name studies, this will often consist of discussing names while jointly poring over maps of the landscape or walking around the land itself while asking about the toponymy. It is also used to some extent as a tool in the study of personal names, and has been used to discuss, for example, nicknames used within coalmines in a way that is ethnographically-orientated (Skipper 1986). A more typically anthropological method of gaining information on cultural practices is participant-observation, or ethnography, where the researcher integrates themselves within the community over a period of time and records their findings by writing extensive field-notes. The ultimate goal of this fieldwork is to gain an understanding of what is done, how it is done and why, from a local perspective. This is subject to theoretical scrutiny and cross-cultural comparison, either once removed from the field or in dialogue with members of the community. In fact, it is difficult to separate the act of recording from the act of theorizing: Hymes (1963: 3) describes this mode of research as a task which was both descriptive and theoretical. Most studies into names which use a participant-observation approach have been within the discipline of anthropology. The naming practices used within societies are sometimes collected in the course of ethnographic research, often alongside kinship terms, although the latter have assumed more importance in anthropological theory. A selection of anthropological studies into naming will be discussed further in section 18.3. These observations are sometimes published in anthropological journals but in many cases this information is not published at all, particularly if the researcher is more interested in another aspect of that community. In his comparative study of the naming practices of sixty societies, Alford (1988) found that much of the anthropological data on names was incomplete, even if it had been published. There have been only a small number of studies within the onomastic tradition which have used participant-observation (e.g. Mashiri 2004; Bramwell 2012).

18.2.2 Theoretical Frameworks

A fundamental tenet of anthropological enquiry is that social reality is constructed through interaction and association between people, and between and within social groups. Personal names seem particularly well placed for analysis along these lines of investigation. However, anthropological theory has differed over time so beyond the use of anthropological fieldwork methods it can be difficult for a disciplinary outsider to unpick these different theoretical paradigms. This is complicated by the fact that there are distinct strands of anthropological tradition within different countries. See Barth et al. (2005) for a detailed exposition of the disciplinary histories of anthropology in Britain, France, Germany, and North America. This section will concentrate on the development of early anthropology, functionalism and structuralism with reference to their relationship to the study of names.

The British anthropological tradition was influenced by the experiences of the wider world afforded by participation in the British Empire. Victorian interest in the customs of other, 'exotic' people around the world led to the formation of the Ethnological Society of London in the mid-nineteenth century, which resulted in publication of the *Journal of the Ethnological Society of London*. The articles varied considerably in their approach, and descriptions of naming practices could be patchy and incidental, ranging from the simple listing of the names of some Native Americans (Bollaert 1850) to a much more sophisticated account of naming practices in the African Gold Coast, based on detailed observation (Daniell 1856). A holistic approach was taken by J. G. Frazer (2004 [1890]) in the popular volume *The Golden Bough*, which looked at religious, magical, and folkloric practices in different societies. This included some discussion of naming in 'primitive' cultures, taking a comparative viewpoint. This evolutionist understanding of culture as being on a continuum from primitive to advanced was more explicitly theorized by E. B. Tylor (1871). His understanding of ethnography was entirely from the perspective of a theorist, rather than as a researcher in the field, and he looked at social groups in a comparative way. His understanding of culture was, as discussed in section 18.1.3, broad and influential. It was also rather different from later interpretations, as he saw culture not as something which explained people's traits, but as the phenomenon itself (Risjord 2007: 402). Although he rejected Tylor's evolutionary assumptions, the idea of culture as a collection of behaviours influenced the German-American scholar Franz Boas, who produced vast amounts of field-notes in his ethnographic research collecting data on the traits of Native American communities. He slowly began to view behavioural traits as having a strong relationship with context (Risjord 2007: 404). Names, within this changing perspective, might be seen as determined by their cultural environment. As Boas established anthropology as an academic discipline in the USA in the late nineteenth century, the development of his ideas were important and set the tone for American anthropology.

In the United Kingdom in the early twentieth century, Bronisław Malinowski and A. R. Radcliffe-Brown were establishing the foundations of a British form of social anthropology. This was distinguished from American anthropology, which encompassed cultural anthropology, anthropological linguistics, archaeology, and biological anthropology, by a narrower focus on synchronic research (Barnard 2000: 4; Erickson and Murphy 2013: 91). Malinowski in particular is associated with functionalism, while Radcliffe-Brown emphasized social structures. The former was focused on ethnographic fieldwork as being essential to anthropology, with the researcher involved in extensive participant-observation, writing that:

> we are demanding a new line of anthropological field-work: the study by direct observation of the rules of custom as they function in actual life. Such study reveals that the commandments of law and custom are always organically connected and not isolated; that their very nature consists in the many tentacles which they throw out into the context of social life; that they only exist in the chain of social transactions in which they are but a link. (Malinowski 2002 [1926]: 125)

This asserts that aspects of culture are interconnected within societies and exist through what people actually do when they are interacting. An alteration of one aspect, or 'link in the chain', has the potential to alter the culture as a whole entity through the actions of individuals. Malinowski's emphasis on fieldwork is still seen as central to anthropological enquiry. As Barnard (2000: 5) notes, 'theory without ethnography is pretty meaningless, since the understanding of cultural difference is at least one of the most important goals of anthropological enquiry'. The linked, organic view of culture created within this framework places names as part of a larger system, which will be affected by changes elsewhere in the cultural order. However, the framework need not be a universal one, but one which fits naming practices in each case with reference to how that specific culture functions.

In the mid-twentieth century, Claude Lévi-Strauss, a French anthropologist who had spent time with Boas in New York, came to critical attention (McGee and Warms 2013). Lévi-Strauss drew inspiration from structural linguistics and focused on linking the cognitive structures of people with structures of human culture. He was a universalist, interested in the general principles which might underlie all human behaviour. Earlier, Radcliffe-Brown had been interested in applying structural principles to social behaviour; Lévi-Strauss was interested in these principles as applied to human thought, with social behaviour as the expression of these mental structures (Layton 1997: 63). He used kinship systems as one means of discussing social structures, and was also interested in investigating personal naming practices for the same purpose. The task of investigating names was separated by him into the part of the linguist, who would be interested in finding the place of names within the language system, and that of the anthropologist, who should investigate names as a way of assigning positions in a social group (Lévi-Strauss 1966: 187). Lévi-Strauss reflects on the nature of names themselves in *The Savage Mind*:

> At one extreme, the name is an identifying mark which, by the application of a rule, establishes that the individual who *is named* is a member of a preordained class (a social group in a system of groups, a status by birth in a system of statuses). At the other extreme, the name is a free creation on the part of the individual who *gives the name* and expresses a transitory and subjective state of his own by means of the person he names. (Lévi-Strauss 1966: 181)

Lévi-Strauss sees all acts of naming as allotting classes either to the name-bearer or the name-giver, rather than as a way of individualizing people. If we accept this then:

> One therefore never names: one classes someone else if the name is given to him in virtue of his characteristics and one classes oneself if, in the belief that one need not follow a rule, one names someone else 'freely', that is, in virtue of characteristics of one's own. And most commonly one does both at once. (Lévi-Strauss 1966: 181)

While many anthropologists and onomasticians might criticize this as over-emphasizing the classificatory role of names while underplaying the individualizing role, it is a compelling argument and a welcome theoretical standpoint to support or assault. Glasse (1987) explicitly tests these processes in his study of Huli names in Papau New Guinea and finds that the personal naming practices he has researched do broadly support the theory. Ellen (1983) interrogates notions of social structure, and warns against trying to simplify complexity in naming to create neat structural patterns. Goodenough (1965) provides a comparative study of two Oceanic cultures, the results of which might suggest a more nuanced approach. He found that the name-giving practices of one, the Lakalai, strongly emphasized the child's place in the social group whereas the other, the Trukese, was much more based on individualizing the child. More recently, Bodenhorn and Vom Buck (2006: 3) unconsciously express a similar view to Lévi-Strauss from a social perspective as they state that: 'the act of naming has the potential to implicate infants in relations through which they become inserted into and, ultimately will act upon, a social matrix'.

Erickson and Murphy (2013: 178) state that most within social and cultural anthropology still accept the ideas of Boas, Malinowski, Lévi-Strauss, and others as 'more or less valid', despite the further development of anthropological theory during the later twentieth century and beyond. More recent preoccupations within critical approaches, such as feminism and postcolonialism, advance the discipline but do not have to invalidate what has come before.

> While advocates of critical anthropology tell us not to take received authority at face value, they do not advocate a descent into epistemological anarchy or solipsism. To the contrary, they encourage us to be more exacting in our search for real social and cultural processes, in the hope that true knowledge will bring us to a more just and humane global society. (Erickson and Murphy 2013: 179)

The central pillars of anthropology were established during the twentieth century, but it seems clear that approaches which problematize culture, authority, authenticity, and ethnography are also important for naming studies. It is possible to engage, for example, with Marxism to investigate personal names as linguistic markers of people's socio-economic class; with feminism to show how the use of names can be restricted in order either to label or to exclude; and with postcolonialism to provide a more complex discussion as to the relationship between the researchers investigating naming practices and their objects of research. Bourdieu (1991: 105) advocates studying the 'social operations' of names, their associated institutions, and their relationship to the power which is assumed by classifying people.

18.2.3 Summary

In sum, while occasionally using similar research methods, onomastics has had little interaction with the more theoretical aspects of anthropology. The theoretical paradigms discussed in this section can provide new ways of looking at names beyond etymologies and systematic collection; they have the potential to allow us to better understand the relationships between names and society.

18.3 ANTHROPOLOGICAL STUDIES
INTO NAMING

As discussed in the introductory section, anthropological literature on naming is relatively sparse. Bean (1980) feels that anthropologists have largely engaged with personal names only as an incidental part of their research in the past. Alford (1988) sees this as a matter of focus, with anthropologists not uninterested in names while they are undertaking ethnographic research, but simply lacking the well-established methodological and theoretical frameworks that have been developed for other aspects of culture.

> But while ethnographers usually entered fieldwork with a systematic set of questions to be answered about the society's kinship system, for example, ethnographers rarely asked a systematic set of questions about or applied a systematic set of terms to the naming practices they encountered. To this day, there is no uniform vocabulary for describing naming systems. (Alford 1988: 6)

Nevertheless, the published studies on naming practices display an abundance of culturally-rich ethnographic description. The emphasis of each individual study differs according to the perspective of the researcher but when viewed together these varied examinations provide a fascinating and wide-ranging picture of naming within human culture. D'Anglure (2010) suggests that ethnographers routinely record names and naming processes as 'it enables one to perceive a group's social and symbolic relationships with others in time and space'. The examples below, although by no means exhaustive, serve to explore some of the common threads running through the published literature, including discussion of naming practices perceived in terms of systems, as social actions, and as entities.

18.3.1 Naming Systems

Alford's (1988) large-scale analysis of naming systems, using the Human Relations Area Files (HRAF),[1] is designed to reflect cultural variability across the world and provides a valuable overview of naming systems as a whole. While every known culture uses names in some form, he finds that, of the sixty he chose as his sample, 40 per cent used a single personal name for each individual, and no other name (Alford 1988: 54); 33 per cent employed surnames or patronyms, 15 per cent had a clan name, while 12 per cent bore sacred names (Alford 1988: 53). Nicknames were also

---

[1] The Human Research Area Files, Inc. was formerly known as the Cross-Cultural Survey and is a collection of cultural materials developed at Yale University. For more information, see HRAF (2015).

used, either habitually or occasionally, by two-thirds of the sample societies (Alford 1988: 83). Other comparative studies have been attempted within an anthropological context, but these have generally been either narrower in focus or less systematic than Alford's. Charles (1951) uses the HRAF files to gain a comparative perspective on drama in first-naming ceremonies. She finds that these ceremonies generally emphasized the relationship of the child both to the spirit world and to the world of man. Bregenzer (1968) is interested in the complexity and communality of societies and the effect of this on naming patterns in South America, although his distinction between naming practices is criticized as unclear by Alford (1988: 9). Bean (1980) surveys the literature to identify universal features of naming systems, using name theories from the philosophy of language to tie these features to a wider theoretical context. Akinnaso (1981) provides a detailed comparison of two diverse cultures to gain a cross-cultural perspective, while also drawing on wider scholarship.

Personal names have many forms and, fitting with a systematic approach, are generally classified in relation to their function rather than their specific manifestations in societies and communities. To ethnographically study the names of a society from a functional perspective involves discerning which types of name are in use, how they are used and by whom, and the meaning attributed to their use by members of the community. This relates strongly to the classificatory and individualizing functions of names for people, as discussed in section 18.2.2. Beyond a first name, the names given often provide a classificatory function. This includes explicitly referencing kin relationships, as in patronyms, metronyms, and teknonyms, hereditary or shared surnames, or wider clan names. Alford (1988: 55) identifies surnames and patronyms as by far the most common ways of demonstrating family ties within naming systems. Besides relationship names, secondary names which give information such as occupation or place of origin or ancestry could be considered as having a classificatory function. These secondary names can be used together with names for individuals. For the latter, the classificatory and individualizing functions can vary depending on the cultural and anthroponymic context. Examples could include name-bearers being given entirely unique names, or common nouns which have preconceived associations, or anthroponyms with particular connotations of gender, social class, or religion. These more standard forms of name might also be used in parallel with practices such as nicknames, ritual names, and spirit names (for a variety of approaches to the analysis of names as a system, see Goodenough 1965; Yassin 1978; Maxwell 1984; Agyekum 2006; Iteanu 2006).

The systems of names used within a community can include both official and unofficial elements. Official names are those which are recorded and endorsed by the state or other authorities, while unofficial names are usually maintained within oral tradition. Dickinson (2007) discusses practices within the context of a Ukrainian village. The official personal naming practices are closely associated with former Soviet influence and power. They operate within official domains and comprise a standard Ukranian first name, a patronymic name, and an official last name (Dickinson 2007: 125). These exist in a diglossic relationship with unofficial names, which are used only within the community.[2] Local people use dialect versions of the standard Ukrainian names and family nicknames, alongside alternative first names, locative names, occupational terms, and even terms relating to possessions such as specific cars or horses. This fuzzy classification of naming is in the tradition of categories of names emerging from ethnographic analysis. Dickinson (2007: 121) suggests that one potential function of this diglossic system is to signify insiders and outsiders through use of the local or official names. Ethnographic studies within other small and rural communities in Europe have found patterns of official and unofficial names (e.g. Breen 1982; Bramwell 2007; Lele 2009). As well as indexing group membership, the unofficial naming practices have been found to provide various functions, including allotting places within the community (Mewett 1982), and particularly within the immediate kinship group (Fox 1963), providing a sense of in-group solidarity (Brandes 1975), as a strategy for dominance (Gilmore 1982), enforcing social control (Pitt-Rivers 1954), and to identify individuals when the official naming system proves too indistinct (Dorian 1970). The official practices work in some cases as a rough 'translation' of the authentic name for practical reasons, for example in Fox's (1963) study of Irish Gaelic speakers on Tory island.

Outside the European context, there have been many studies into personal naming systems, including in the Middle East (e.g. Antoun 1968; Yassin 1978; Salih and Bader 1999; Borg and Kressel 2001), the Americas (e.g. Collier and Bricker 1970; Bamberger 1974; Mertz 1983; Maybury-Lewis 1984; Mithun 1984; Aceto 2002; Hugh-Jones 2006; Lombard 2011), Africa (e.g. Beidelman 1974; Akinnaso 1980; Suzman 1994; Mashiri 2004; Agyekum 2006; Bloch 2006; Lambek 2006), and Asia and Oceania (e.g. Geertz 1973; Stokhof 1983; Maxwell 1984; Rosaldo 1984; Humphrey 2006; Iteanu 2006; De Grave 2011). The results of these studies have implications for name theories which are based largely on European names which have a predominantly referential function. Akinnaso (1980) describes the prototypical African name as being very different to that of the European, as there is a clear semantic link between the form of the name and real-world meaning. He analyses Yoruba naming practices, where children are given names which correspond to common nouns or full sentences in the language. These reflect concerns such as specific events in the parents' lives around the time of the baby's birth, for example *omó kó olá dé* meaning 'child brings wealth' (Akinnaso 1980: 281). In this way, they 'serve as an open diary' within the community (Akinnaso 1980: 279). Suzman (1994) also demonstrates that names in African societies are meaningful, but points towards rapid changes in the Zulu anthroponymic system. Alford (1988: 59–65) found that most of the cultural groups within his sample had meaningful names, some of which were thought to have a real, experiential effect on the individual's life. This is not to imply that all non-European names exist in a cultural framework where they are expected to

---

[2] Diglossia refers to the situation when two language varieties exist within the same society but are spoken or written in different contexts; usually these will correspond to more official and less official domains. Bramwell (2012: 373) has suggested the term 'dionomia' for this relationship when applied to names.

have semantic meaning. Geertz (1973: 369) describes the seemingly haphazard nature of Balinese names which are 'arbitrarily coined nonsense syllables'. This practice has an individualizing function, however, as no two people are given the same name. The individualizing nature of the personal names is offset by other methods of categorization used within the referential system, such as birth order names and teknonyms.

18.3.2 Naming as Social Practice

There is some dispute as to the function of names, with some scholars arguing that their role is purely pragmatic. Bloch (2006) strongly disagrees with the notion that names classify. He sees them as 'tools used in social interaction', but stresses that they 'do not form a bounded system', and cannot see how they, as words, can be said to reflect social reality (Bloch 2006: 98–9). The rejection of names as a bounded system causes him to include a much wider set of terms in his research than might be expected if limiting to prototypical proper names. However, this approach to names as a broad fuzzy set, the salient parts of which are to be discovered as part of an ethnographic study, is long-established (e.g. Antoun 1968). Mertz (1983: 55–6) argues that we must view names as more than simply pragmatic or indexical items; if we do not then we miss their key connection to culture.

Blum (1997) provides a thorough picture of the pragmatic role of personal names in China. She includes a wide range of reference and address terms within the wider category of names and stresses that naming 'is an active set of practices rather than a static system' (Blum 1997: 358). In her analysis, the relationship between, and status of, interlocutors dynamically affected which names were selected, and the use of names formed part of the wider system of face, or public self-image, within Chinese culture. Her characterization is of naming practices as a dynamic system with fuzzy boundaries, which plays an important role in power relations. This echoes Rymes (1996), who uses an in-depth ethnographic example, of a young gang member in Los Angeles, to discuss the nature of naming as part of wider social context. She sees meaning as bound to group membership and to the experience within a community, and traces the nickname of 'Little Creeper' from the 'Diamond Street' gang through several domains of use (Rymes 1996: 257–8).

Studying the usage of names can be valuable in understanding identity and naming practices as well as in investigating pragmatic functions. In the Mongolian naming system, it is only necessary to have one name, which is lexically meaningful and which cannot be the same as anyone else known to the name-giver (Humphrey 2006: 159). However, names are rarely used after childhood as it is seen as harmful to point people out by naming them, so respect terms are employed instead for address and, often, reference. These generic constructions such as 'old woman' are seen as polite and so not using names in interaction, but using categorical markers, is the norm (Humphrey 2006: 170). The Balinese names discussed in section 18.3.1, though semantically meaningless, fulfil the same super-individualizing function while also using generic markers for actual social interaction (Geertz 1973). It is possible to use names to subvert cultural norms, rather than be bound by them. The Meithei people of north-east India use different styles of personal name both to assert their Meithei identity and to reject or accept a wider Indian identity (Chelliah 2005).

The Ilongots of the Philippines acquire different names as they pass through life. In discussing these practices, Rosaldo (1984: 12) shifts his analytical paradigm from one based on systems which individualize and differentiate, to one which suggests that analysing verbal play is the real key to understanding names within the society: it allows new names to be invented, and naming children and in-laws means that adults can tease them as is expected within the culture. In some contexts, naming can only really be understood with reference to social actions within other aspects of the wider culture such as ritual events (e.g. Hugh-Jones 2006; De Grave 2011).

18.3.3 Names as Entities

Names do not only identify, categorize, tell stories, and provide social tools for interaction; within some cultures names are a physical or spiritual entity in themselves. Maybury-Lewis (1984) studied the naming practices of seven tribes in central Brazil. For these tribes, names are not seen as being given to people; instead people enter the name: 'Names do not therefore function primarily to identify individuals. Their purpose is rather to transform individuals into persons' (Maybury-Lewis 1984: 7). A personality is acquired with a name, and many of the tribes do not name young children as the burden might be physically too great. The transmission of a name can emphasize biological descent or it can even replace it in terms of social relationships. Lambek (2006), in his work on Mayotte and north-west Madagascar, found that names were being used as 'a vehicle for identity' for spirits that were being called forth: 'The names not only help to realize the identities of spirits, they render the matter of identity live and salient' (Lambek 2006: 135). Names in this case are being used as a tool to give an earthly form to something which was indistinct. This could be seen as similar to ideas that the soul is an entity in itself, as the Ainu people of northern Japan believe (Charles 1951: 34–5).

This belief in the soul as an actor is shared by the Inuit people. Giving a baby a name within this culture is considered equivalent to giving it a soul. Every child is given the name of another person, usually after their death, and possessing their 'name-soul' means that you are a physical embodiment, or reincarnation, of the other person (Searles 2007). People can have multiple names, and therefore multiple name-souls. Searles (2008: 242–3) describes the consequences of this conception of a name for social identity: 'The name-soul gives a child an Inuit ethnic identity, a family or community identity, and a personal identity. A name can transmit all those substances attached to the soul, like memories and distinctive personality traits'. Alia (2007) asserts that the naming system is the central aspect of Inuit society and explains the, sometimes complex, implications of becoming a physical embodiment of another person. As kinship depends on the name-soul, if a person is given the name of your grandmother then it is perceived that they have actually become your grandmother. Similarly, gender follows the name-soul rather than biological sex and a person can have multiple name-souls of different genders. An Inuit informant was named after a recently deceased man, so was known as 'younger brother' to that man's family. However, as her middle name had been passed on from her father's younger sister, she was known as 'sister' to her aunts and father: 'Her biological family treats her as female, but the family whose brother is her namesake treats her as male' (Alia 2007: 27).

There is a gulf between concepts of the name in European culture, where it is seen as an essentially arbitrary label, through many African and other cultures, where a proto-typical name is seen as fundamentally meaningful and motivated by circumstance, to names in Inuit, Central Brazilian, and further cultures in which names are actual mani-festations of the essential elements of people.

18.3.4 Place-names

Anthropologists have concentrated on personal names rather than names of places and this chapter continues this focus. This may seem reasonable: anthropological research relates most closely to how people function within communities and how they inter-act with each other. However, it is clear that the relationship between people and the landscape is an important element of culture and is also worthy of study. Basso (1984), in presenting an ethnographic account of Apache place-names, describes the interest in the early twentieth century into place-names within Native American anthropology, including studies by influential figures such as Boas and Sapir. On the other side of the Atlantic, place-names were also being recorded and collected within ethnographic stud-ies (e.g. Evans-Pritchard 1946).

More recently, place-names have been studied in a variety of ways using an anthro-pological approach, including alongside personal names within the same community (e.g. Marlett 2008), as regions delineating both territories and social groups (Takaki 1984), and in relation to the power of the state (e.g. Roberts 1993; Faraco and Murphy 1997). These studies show that focusing on people's relationship to place as well as to other people when studying names is a productive ethnographic endeavour. As Basso (1984: 79) states, 'place-name terminologies provide access to cultural principles with which members of human communities organize and interpret their physical surround-ings'. Therefore they should form part of any holistic view of cultural and community practices.

18.4 CONCLUSION

In conclusion, there is great deal within anthropology with which onomasticians might engage. Currently, there is some cross-over between the two disciplines through the use of ethnographic fieldwork methods, but there is the potential for much closer theoretical engagement. An understanding of a concept as seemingly basic as that of a name can be interrogated through the comparison of different cultural practices. The detailed and often complex results allow us to access a truer representation of what it is we are studying and how it functions. As we have seen in this chapter, names individualize, classify, and tie people's identity into the practices of their communities: to employ names is to create social action through language and culture. Having the opportunity to see a broad, anthropological view of human society means that we can appreciate that names in a certain cultural context can signify everything from arbitrary labels, to meaningful announcements, to the human soul.

CHAPTER 19

PERSONAL NAMES AND GENEALOGY

GEORGE REDMONDS

IN Great Britain the name we bear identifies us within our family and community.[1] We all have at least one first name, which is chosen for us by others and subject to naming practices that can vary chronologically and from region to region, but we inherit our surname and that is a vital link in a chain that in most cases will stretch back several hundred years to the first name-bearer. In combination the two are the family historian's most useful research tool, vital to the successful identification of generations of ancestors. Separately and together they must therefore be a priority for genealogists who have a vested interest in establishing the facts which relate to their origins and development.

19.1 FIRST NAMES

The importance of first names in genealogy has been undervalued. Although researchers have recognized their significance within the family, they have placed little emphasis on the influence that the godparents had in the naming process. In earlier centuries, especially when the church was Roman Catholic, our ancestors had their natural family and also a spiritual family which included the godparents, referred to as their 'affinity'. It was customary for children to be named after a godparent and the practice continued to be important into the late seventeenth century, influencing local naming habits.[2]

Many of those names were unusual, favoured initially by a particular gentry family or socially important individual, and used by them to demonstrate the links they had with their tenantry, fellow parishioners, and kin. The result is that from the Tudor period we

---

[1] Surnames quoted in support of ideas put forward in this chapter mostly have no footnote reference. The evidence is developed more fully in Redmonds (forthcoming).

[2] Smith-Bannister (1997) has valuable frequency lists for the first names of both boys and girls.

can find clusters of distinctive first names in particular localities. For example, the Kay or Kaye family of Bury in Lancashire used the first name *Giles* from at least the 1400s and it passed from them to their kinsmen in the parish of Almondbury, across the county boundary. It was an uncommon name generally in the mid-sixteenth century but Giles Kaye of Almondbury was the godfather of numerous children from *c.*1560 and at least fifteen families in the parish used the name *Giles* in that period (Redmonds 2004a: 54).

The same practice influenced the use of women's names, although the information in such cases may be less valuable to genealogists. In 1565, for example, a Staffordshire lady named Cassandra Swynnerton made bequests to four goddaughters, all called Cassandra, whose surnames were Gyfforde, Congreve, Westonne, and Berdmore.[3] Such practices were responsible for the regional and relatively short-term popularity of many distinctive first names and the evidence can be found in the parish registers. *Dorothy*, for instance, was a saint's name which had been revived in the 1400s but it was not among the top ten listed in 1560–70. Nevertheless, in Swillington near Leeds, thirteen of the fourteen girls who were baptised in the years 1569 and 1570 were named Dorothy: it had first been used in 1549 when William Mallett, gentleman, gave the name to his daughter.

Consequently, some first names had patterns of distribution which can tell the genealogist where they originated. In 1636–39 two brothers in Massachusetts became freemen of the fledgling colony: their names were Joseph and Godfrey Armitage and later they feature regularly in the records of Lynn and Boston. There is no direct evidence to say exactly where they came from in England but their surname was distinctive enough to link it with the West Riding of Yorkshire where it has been traced to the township of South Crosland. A manorial survey of 1340 lists *Adam del Hermitage* who owed his surname to a house erected close to the hermitage near the bridge, the locality now known as Armitage Bridge (Redmonds 1992: 3). Armitage families were recorded there subsequently in a wide variety of records and it was still essentially a West Riding surname in 1881: more than 80 per cent of the name-bearers lived in Yorkshire and neighbouring parts of Lancashire, and in Huddersfield alone the total was 1,561.

The first name *Joseph* was generally quite popular by the 1630s and would not, on its own, be particularly helpful to a genealogist. On the other hand *Godfrey* was missing from national frequency lists at that time but enjoyed considerable popularity in parts of south Yorkshire. One close-knit kinship group or affinity can be traced to the Holme valley, south of Huddersfield. Godfrey Armitage's age is known to us from depositions made in New England and that information almost certainly identifies him as the Godfrey Armitage of Hagg near Honley who was baptised 2 February 1612. That evidence incidentally pinpoints the origin of Joseph Armitage and other family members who settled later in America: such examples should alert genealogists to the value of identifying distinctive regional practices and widening the scope of their enquiries.

Some preferences of that kind could actually survive for long periods: the Godfrey Hirst who was a prominent mill-owner in Geelong in Australia in the 1880s is known to

---

[3] Ex info Pauline Litton.

have moved there from Meltham, just a mile or two from Hagg in Honley. His surname *Hirst* was also characteristic of that region.

The records in New England contain numerous examples of combinations which were equally distinctive, sometimes for other reasons. *Jonas* was a favourite choice among Puritans in the Halifax and Haworth area from 1562, and this seems certain to be where Jonas Pickles of Scituate in Massachusetts originated. Just when he crossed over to New England is uncertain but his inventory is dated 1665 (Bangs 1997: 1, 18). *Pickles* is a prolific surname with a very local distribution and even in 1881 almost 94 per cent of the name-bearers were living in neighbouring parts of Yorkshire and Lancashire.[4] It accounted for sixteen taxpayers in the hearth tax for Haworth in 1672, two of them named Jonas, and there were many more name-bearers in adjoining parts of Bradford and Halifax.

In the records for Scituate were surnames such as *Barstow, Fairbanks, Ferniside, Holsworth, Ingham, Sutliffe*, and *Wormall*, all of which had long histories in the same part of the Pennines, and the inference is that these families had origins similar to that of Pickles. The same may have been true of less-distinctive names such as *Briggs, Hudson*, and *Mitchell* for these were all current in the same region. Family historians can be alerted to such groups by a single distinctive first name, and overseas genealogists can clearly benefit from the study of surname distribution and first name practices in Britain.

First names can similarly help to trace migration from one county to another. In Cheshire the Masseys were an important family whose use of the first name *Hamo* is first evidenced in Domesday Book. It remained a popular choice for generations, some-times in its diminutive form *Hamlet*, and came to enjoy a wider measure of popularity in the county, probably among the Masseys' kith and kin. Quite often it identifies indi-viduals in other counties who had Cheshire origins, for example 1543 *Hamlet Masse* of Giggleswick, in Yorkshire; 1594 *Hamlet Ashton* of Glazebrook, in Lancashire. The link can be explicit: in the Leeds parish register the wife of *Haunlett* [sic] *Hyd* of Cheshire had her child buried in 1585. The surname *Hyde* here reinforces the Cheshire origin.

The same name served a dual purpose in the 1590s when a man named Hamlet Kennerley was living in the Elland area, between the West Riding towns of Huddersfield and Halifax. *Hamlet* seldom occurred at that time in Yorkshire records and it imme-diately suggests a Cheshire connection: his surname provides additional confirmation, since *Kennerley* was an unexpected variant of the Cheshire place-name Kenworthy. The alias is explicit in the unpublished parish register of Slaithwaite: 1718 *William Kenworthy vulgo Kennerlay* and also in examples of the place-name (Dodgson 1970: 236).

Frequency lists have been established for first names in England in the period 1377–1700 and any name not included there may be of value to a genealogist (Redmonds 2004a: 173). *Bertram* or *Bartram*, for example, is a distinctive omission and yet there are

---

[4] This information is derived from Archer (2011), which provides maps showing the distribution of all the surnames and first names in the 1881 census for England, Scotland, and Wales. The distribution maps and statistics are the key to the history and origin of British surnames.

numerous references to it in the north, almost always associated with Northumberland and Durham. One prominent name-bearer was Bertram Anderson of Newcastle upon Tyne, a merchant and alderman whose will was registered in 1571. His son and at least one nephew were also called Bertram, and Bertram Carr was a kinsman. *Barty* was the diminutive, for example 1572 *Bartye Andersonne son of Mr Bartyrem Anderson* (Raine 1967 [1835]: 388).

Previously, another merchant named Bertram Dawson had been resident in York where he was obliged to prove his origins. In 1506 he was 'senysterly defamed that he shulde be a Scottysshman borne' but it was said in his defence that he 'was borne in the towne of Warmeden in the parishe of Bamburght', which may mean that his Northumberland accent had aroused suspicion. He owed his name to his godfather Bertram Fenkyll of Newham, one of many families to use Bertram in that region. These included the Lumleys, Bewicks, and Sharpes and such evidence again points to the influence of an affinity (Skaife 1872: 105).

Lancelot was in occasional use in different parts of Britain but it was associated early in its history with the counties that form modern Cumbria: it was current there from the 1400s in families named Threlkeld, Hutton, and Lowther, hinting at a common affinity. It was absent from the national frequency lists for 1640–49 but Angus Winchester (2011: 42) noted its popularity in the north-west in 1642: he counted 123 examples in Cumberland and a further 73 in north Westmorland. There are practical implications for genealogists. In 1647 Lancelot Langhorne was living in Kirkgate in Leeds: this was the first reference in the parish register to any person with that surname, and the combination of first name and surname provides evidence of his ancestral ties with Westmorland (Simons 1997: 3–20).

In New England at roughly the same time was Gowen Wilson who in 1654 gave his age as 36 under oath in court. Early descendants claimed an origin in Scotland and that information, in conjunction with his rare first name, suggest that he may have been the *Gawen Wilsone* who was christened in the parish church of Prestonpans in 1618 (Stevens 2008: 174–80). *Gawen* and *Gowen* are different spellings of the name inspired by Sir Gawain who was, like Sir Lancelot, one of the knights of the Round Table. The Arthurian epic was responsible also for the choice of names such as *Tristram* and *Perceval*, not to mention *Arthur* itself, and these can all be valuable clues to family historians (Redmonds 2004a: 107–10, 114–19).

The variety of the first names in different parts of Britain can also help to locate the national origins of some early migrants and their influence on the surname's spelling. Black (1946) described the scarce surname *Gledstone* as a form of Gladstone and these both derive from a locality in Lanarkshire which is now a farm in the Upper Ward of Clydesdale. *Gladstone* was not uncommon in 1881, still well-established in Scotland, whereas only fifty-six people had the name *Gledstone*, none of them in Scotland: there were two main clusters in England, one in Tynemouth and the other in the neighbourhood of Skipton in the West Riding (Archer 2011). *Gledstone*'s history there goes back to Fergus or Fargus Gledstone who purchased land from the Marton family in East and West Marton in 1589, a parish known as Martons Both. The two places lie close to

Skipton, and Gledstone Hall is on the site of the family's former residence. *Fergus* on its own is enough to associate the name with Scotland and in combination with *Gledstone* it solves the origin of this distinctive surname. The connection between the family and Gledstone Hall had not been made by place-name specialists (Smith 1961c: 40).

19.2 SURNAMES

As useful as first names can be, it is essentially the surname which provides genealogists with the evidence that links one generation to another and, in ideal circumstances, to the progenitor or first name-bearer. The question of what the name might mean can be taken into account when such facts have been established but even then it will not always be possible to be certain of the origin and meaning. This approach gives precedence to matters such as distribution, expansion, and linguistic development, and it emphasizes the important contribution that historians, genealogists, and geneticists can make to surname studies.

In major works on the surnames of Ireland, Scotland, and Wales the significance of family history is clearly in evidence whereas that is not the case in some recent English studies. In 1958 P. H. Reaney stated in the introduction to his new dictionary of British surnames that it was not his intention 'to treat of genealogy and family history', even though he was aware that 'each surname has its pedigree which must be traced before the meaning can be discovered'. In what he considered to be a logical approach he searched the records for early references, and assumed a connection with modern surnames which had the same or very similar spellings: he apparently failed to recognize that many of those early examples were actually bynames, that is to say they were second names which never became hereditary.

The spelling of a byname may be identical with that of a modern surname but there need be no connection between the two. His dictionary took little account of where a surname occurred at different times in its history or how numerous it was, and there was no real attempt to establish a chain of evidence that linked surnames to particular families and places (Reaney 1958).[5] Such matters directly concern the genealogist for they place the name in a historical context and indicate how it may have originated.

The evidence for *Dyson* illustrates some of those points, especially the transition from byname to surname. It has spellings which pose no real problems of identification and its history and distribution place it in the Colne valley, to the south-west of Huddersfield: it is on record there continuously from the early fourteenth century in court rolls, deeds, the parish registers, and other major sources. It was a prolific surname in 1881 with a total of 9,712 but most of its expansion had taken place within a short

---

[5] The revised editions of this work by R. M. Wilson were entitled *A Dictionary of English Surnames*, but the methodology remained unchanged and many of the more than 4,000 surnames added were not represented in Britain in 1881.

distance of the locality where it originated and almost 80 per cent of the name-bearers still lived in adjoining parts of Yorkshire and Lancashire. Recent DNA tests have established that nearly 90 per cent of the men named Dyson who were tested had the same or closely related Y chromosomes and there seems no doubt that it has a single origin, even though similar bynames have been noted (Sykes 2003).[6]

The progenitor was John Dison, first mentioned in 1316 and also called the son of *Dionisia de Linthwaite*: his mother was occasionally named as *Dionisia de Mollesheved* and both her bynames derived from local place-names. In that period her son might easily have been called 'de Linthwaite' or 'de Mollesheved' but instead he was identified by the pet form of his mother's first name. The abandoned bynames are of interest to local and family historians, relevant to the origin of Dyson but not to its meaning.

Certain matters which have to do with the interpretation of such names are seldom commented on. *Dyson* in the early 1300s was clearly in a transitional stage and it became a surname only when it was inherited by John's son and retained by later generations. Its meaning may seem absolutely clear but the first bearer of the surname was actually the son of John, not the son of Dionisia. Furthermore the name *Dionisia* has a history and etymology which may be of interest to family historians but they are not essential to an understanding of how the surname originated. It is intriguing that John was identified as Dionisia's son, especially as it was more usual in that area of scattered settlement to inherit a name such as 'de Linthwaite' which identified an individual's place of residence.

Other topics which touch on the name's interpretation fall directly within the scope of the genealogist: they include the use of 'Di' as a short form of *Dionisia* and the question of whether the male equivalent *Dionisius* had a similar short form. Also important are the popularity of this unfamiliar first name *c.*1300 and the fact that John was identified by his relationship to a woman and not a man: that was not at all unusual but such matters influence the question of how many origins the surname might have had.

19.2.1 Expansion and Decline

Once we have accepted that each surname has a progenitor, we understand that no name should be taken for granted, not even the very prolific *Smith*. One 'smith' may have shod horses; another may have worked in an iron forge: the byname may have been given to a man employed by a smith but not related to him, or it may have developed at a later stage in its history as a convenient abbreviation of a compound name such as *Combsmith* or *Goldsmith*. At almost any time it may simply have translated the name of an immigrant. These are clearly matters which concern the family historian: *Smith* certainly has multiple origins but each origin is unique.

Frequency in itself is not a clue to multiple origins. The topic is one that must be looked at in a national context since high totals in different regions can result from

---

[6] Genealogists should read Sykes and Irven (2000).

different naming practices. Wales, for example, is the source of many of Britain's most popular surnames, simply because they developed at a relatively late date in a patronymic system where a few first names predominated. Consequently *Jones, Williams, Davies, Evans, Thomas*, and *Roberts* were among the twelve most common surnames in Britain in 1881, each of them certain to have had multiple origins. Prolific English surnames with numerous origins include many derived from occupations, for example *Taylor, Walker*, and *Wright* but others were patronymics of different kinds, for example *Phillips* and *Robinson*. A few nicknames such as *King* and *White* also had huge numbers, as did surnames derived from common minor place-names, notably *Hill* and *Wood*.

On the other hand *Dyson* is very common but has a single origin and in that respect it is typical of family names in the central part of the Pennines. The extensive parishes of Rochdale and Halifax in particular gave rise to numerous surnames which ramified in an extraordinary way and had national totals well above the average. Typical Lancashire examples in 1881 were *Butterworth* (10,757) and *Clegg* (10,206). Surnames in the Lowlands of Scotland may have developed in a similar way, for example *Crawford, Pringle*, and *Moffat* whereas almost all the distinctive surnames of Cornwall were quite uncommon in 1881, certainly in Britain (Redmonds et al. 2011: 77–9).

If the evidence in Britain suggests that the expansion in numbers of a surname probably had something to do with where it was located, it is worth noting that some surnames in America which are of English origin are very popular there but have declined dramatically or become extinct in Britain, for example *Dearborn, Frothingham*, and *Sanborn*. The Kent surname *Blechenden* has apparently ramified in Australia but it was not recorded in England in 1881: *Colpitts* is more numerous in Canada than in Northumberland where it originated. Surname studies and genealogy have a role to play in demographic studies.

19.2.2 Origins

Surnames are not less significant just because they fail to multiply, and those which are now extinct remain part of our ancestry. Indeed, uncommon names can provide specialists in other fields of research with vital information. *Nendick* had only eighty-nine name-bearers in 1881, almost all of them in east Yorkshire, and a series of spellings places the name in the East Riding village of Cottingham: 1533 *John Nendyke*; 1465 *John Nandik*; 1454 *William Naundike*; 1381 *William Nauendyk*. A survey of Cottingham in 1282 referred to sheepcotes for thirty tenants 'upon Nauendike' so the source was evidently a place-name (Brown 1892: 240). It is not mentioned though in the East Riding volume of the English Place-Name Society (Smith 1937). It cannot surely be a coincidence that 'Nauenby' in Kesteven in Lincolnshire was among the knights' fees that belonged to Cottingham in 1282: this probably originated as a Danish settlement in the ninth century, and *Nafni* is the Old Danish personal name that survives in both place-names and the Cottingham surname.

The nature of *Nendick*'s origin is of interest to genealogists, not least because in 1381 five married couples in Cottingham were so called, possibly unrelated tenants with rights to sheepcotes 'upon Nauendike'. The name also posed problems for clerks and transcribers: for example *Katherine Nendyke* was the prioress of Wykeham but she was called *Katherine Endyk* in 1530, probably a case of metanalysis. Other spellings of the surname include: 1381 *William Naudyk*, Cottingham; 1630 *John Mendicke*, Great Habton; 1673 *William Newdike*, Habton. The indexes of published documents can sometimes conceal vital information.

In fact many reference works have to be treated with care, especially dictionaries which take no account of the historic distribution of surnames. *Rushton* is a name with several potential place-name sources and it has been usual to say that it derives from one or other of the places named Rushton in Cheshire, Dorset, Northamptonshire, Shropshire, and Staffordshire. These cannot be ignored but they can have had little to do with *Rushton*'s remarkable expansion in Lancashire where the source is Rishton near Blackburn. The spelling *Rishton* was frequent in early records and the change to the modern form was quite late, for example 1555–58 *Ralph Ryshton or Russheton of Trawden*. The surname *Rushworth* has a similar spelling change for it derives from Rishworth near Halifax. Dictionaries which ignore historic distribution wrongly give *Cowburn* a place-name source whereas it actually derives from the personal name *Colbrand*: conversely they derive *Thirkell* and its variants from a personal name whereas evidence in the north links it with *Threlkeld*, from the place of that name near Keswick. Errors are less likely when the modern and early spellings are connected by examples over the generations.

Few writers have been able to resist suggesting an etymology for the Kent name *Hogben* or *Hogbin*. For Lower (1996 [1860]) it meant a pig-sty and was possibly occupational for a swineherd. This suggestion was derided by Bardsley (1901) who had 'no solution to offer' but could not help thinking that it referred to 'an immigrant from the Low Countries'. Reaney was of the opinion that it derived from *huck-bone*, the hip bone that is, and he compared it to the Scottish surname *Cruickshanks*. He based his opinion on an example which he had located in a Canterbury document, that is, 1479 *Thomas Huckebone* and if that had been the original spelling we could hardly quarrel with his theory. However, 1479 is quite late in terms of surname heredity and earlier examples in the poll tax returns for Canterbury throw new light on the origin: 1377 *Nicholas Hulkebon*; 1381 Nicholas *Holkebone* (Fenwick 1998–2005: I). In Middle English the prefix seems to be the word *holke* or *hulke* which means 'hollow', but that still leaves us wondering how the name should be interpreted.

In those cases where a surname derives from a place-name it can be difficult to identify the source. *Collingwood* was quite numerous in 1881, with a national total of 1,648, and it had a wide distribution. Recently more than one writer has said that it derives from 'Collingwood' in Staffordshire, although I find no evidence that Collingwood is a Staffordshire place-name. I take it to be a reference to Callingwood near Burton upon Trent which I suppose may sometimes have interchanged with Collingwood. On the other hand, earlier writers who studied its distribution said that *Collingwood* 'belonged' to the north-east: Lower and Bardsley both thought that it originated in

Northumberland but could not 'discover' the locality: it was Guppy (1890) who claimed that Durham was the county where it was most numerous and that is evident also in the 1881 census. The Durham link is made clear in the county's Quarter Sessions records of 1471 which detail an offence against Peter Colynwod 'apud Colynwod in comitatu Dunelmensi' (Fraser 1991: 45). This single spelling suggests that it meant 'the wood belonging to Colin'—a diminutive of *Nicholas* based on the pet form 'Col'. I have found no mention of this place-name in the usual sources.

19.2.3 Migration

Early migration can obscure the origins of a name even when no significant linguistic changes are involved. For instance *Wikeley* was a rare Yorkshire surname in 1881 with clusters in the Thirsk area. It has no obvious source there but is on record in lower Wharfedale continuously from the thirteenth century. The key to its origin is an inquisition of 1277 in which it was said that *Mauger le Vavasour* had estates in Wharfedale and also held 'Wykele Manor' in Northamptonshire (Brown 1892: 174). The present spelling of that place-name is *Weekley*, located near Kettering. The family must therefore have taken their name from the Northamptonshire estate and moved north to Wharfedale. The preservation of the early spelling invites comparison with *Gledstone*.

The origin of the Derbyshire surname *Levick* is more complicated. It has been said that it derives from *l'évêque*, the French word for the bishop, or from a personal name, and bynames have been quoted in support of both theories. The present spelling has a history in Derbyshire back to the late sixteenth century when Richard Levick was recorded in Norton parish register but an explicit alias in Eckington links *Levick* with *Leathwick* which looks like a place-name. Dr Anne Giller understood the importance of this example and she used it to follow a sequence of forms back to *Lethewayk* and *Lathewek* in 1350, a source which has not yet been identified.[7]

Even minor spelling differences can make identification difficult. Black (1946) found no Scottish origin for *Sherlaw* and *Shirlaw*, which have a long history in Lanarkshire and Berwickshire, and speculated that they might derive from places in England named Shirley. In fact the early spellings correspond with those for Skirlaugh in Holderness and that is likely to be the source: movement of families up and down Britain's coastline was not unusual.

19.2.4 Linguistic Development

More frequently migration could be responsible for the development of numerous variants, especially if the surname's meaning was not transparent. *Tattersall* is such a case: it

---

[7] Ex info David Hey.

probably derives from Tattershall in Lincolnshire but name-bearers were taxed in different parts of Yorkshire and Lancashire from the thirteenth century, possibly through the links the three counties had with the Duchy of Lancaster. In 1881 over 75 per cent of the name-bearers lived in Lancashire and the totals for adjoining parts of Yorkshire and Cheshire would increase that percentage to nintey-three. Just four people had the name in Lincolnshire. Among its numerous variants were *Tattershaw*, *Tattersdale*, *Tattersfield*, *Tattersley*, *Tatterson*, and *Tatterton*, many of them found in the Dewsbury area, whilst popular etymology transformed *Tattershall* into *Tortoiseshell* in Derbyshire and Staffordshire.[8]

Tortoiseshell shows how the linguistic rules are broken when it comes to popular etymology, for all that is required in such cases is an association in the mind of the clerk. Bardsley linked the surname *Regester* or *Register* with 'registrar' and was followed by Weekley (1917: 111), who described it as belonging 'to the official class'. It is actually a variant of *Rochester*, for example 1678 *Ralph Register alias Rochester* of New Malton and is likely to derive from Rochester in Northumberland rather than Rochester in Kent. It totalled only 162 in 1881 and most name-bearers lived in Norfolk and Yorkshire.

Many new names were produced in this way at quite a late date. The Scottish *Carruthers* gave rise to *Cardus* in Lancashire, *Carrodus* in Yorkshire, and *Cruddass* in the north-east; *Wheen* was an alternative spelling of *Queen* and possibly therefore of *McQueen*. Morgan and Morgan's (1985) work on registers from the border counties of England and Wales reveals how *Cadwalleder* was abbreviated there to *Wallet* and also produced the apparently derogatory nickname *Cutwallet*. The surname *Kerfoot* may have arrived in Lancashire via Cheshire, as a variant of *Griffith* or *Griffiths*: *Burtbee* is an American variant of *Birkby*.

Clerks were in the habit of converting what they heard into what their experience told them was a plausible alternative. Thus it was that *Passbusk* and *Plasterer* became *Pashby* and *Plaxton*, made to resemble place-names for which no source exists. They have similarities with *Parnaby* which has been ignored by most writers but has important lessons for genealogists. It totalled 344 in 1881 and occurred mostly in Durham and east Yorkshire. However, its spelling and distribution are misleading for it has been noted in that region only from the seventeenth century and the origin remains uncertain. I can find no evidence of *Parnaby* as a place-name and the earliest examples in the IGI are from Cambridgeshire, from c.1550 (FamilySearch 2012). It may derive from the French 'parlebien', that is 'speak well' which was a byname in several counties, including Cambridgeshire (McKinley 1990: 166). That connection has not yet been proved but possible links include: 1533 *John Parlebeyn*, Kirton, Lincolnshire; 1593 *John Parlabye*, Hickling, Nottinghamshire.

The suffix -*by* was such a common element in place-names in certain regions that it proved irresistible to clerks and that may lie behind the development of the surnames

---

[8] For an in-depth discussion of this topic, see Redmonds (1997: 205–7).

Glaisby, Glasbey, Glasby, and *Glassby*. No English source has been found so these may be English variants of the Scottish surname *Gillespie* which Black (1946) claimed had 'invaded' Northumberland: *Gilaspy* in 1477 and *Gillaspy* in 1528 were typical spellings. In Quarter Sessions documents for the West Riding the connection is more specific for 'James Gelasby, a Scotchman' was arrested as a dangerous person in 1745: under examination he was referred to as James Glasbey from Stirling.

The uncommon Sussex names *Cherriman* and *Cherryman* were dealt with by Reaney under Cherry and said to be occupational in origin, whereas Richard McKinley (1988: 177) found *Chyriam* in Horsham to be the earliest spelling. His sixteenth-century examples link it with Cherryholme in east Yorkshire which derives from a place-name. Migration in the reverse direction saw *Verrill* established in the Whitby area from the mid-seventeenth century and by 1881 it was almost exclusively a North Riding surname with most of the 205 name-bearers living in Whitby or close by. The family's earlier history is in Sussex and Kent where McKinley traced its development from 'atte Fayrhale' in the subsidy roll for Lindfield in 1332: he quoted transitional spellings such as *Fyrrall* and *Verrall* which show the voicing of 'f' to 'v', a characteristic of regional speech in south-east England.

Migration brought together surnames which had similar spellings but quite different origins and meanings and that almost inevitably led to confusion. *Maxfield*, for example, derives from Macclesfield in Cheshire and this spelling of the place-name goes back to the twelfth century (Dodgson 1970: 114). In Nottinghamshire, though, it was confused with the Scottish surname *Maxwell*: in 1616, for example, *William Maxfelde* of Harworth was buried in Wadworth but he was listed as *William Maxewell* of Harworth in the registry of wills. Similar examples are commonplace, linking *Tittensor* and *Tidswell; Hayward* and *Heywood; Laycock* and *Lowcock*. David Hey (1992) noted how the Derbyshire *Levick* was assimilated to *Levitt* in south Yorkshire, and confusion in many cases is expressed in explicit aliases, for example 1748 *John Corbutt otherwise Calvert*; 1754 *William Tinsley otherwise Tildsley*.

Many surnames have a spelling which is identical with that of a well-known place-name but in such cases the genealogist should not assume that the two must be linked. *Harrogate*, for example, is a rare north-country surname and it is tempting to see the Yorkshire spa town of Harrogate as the source. However, it occurs only occasionally in Yorkshire records and I have found no reference in the county earlier than 1775. Earlier name-bearers were living in Northumberland: in 1570 Richard *Harrigaite* was a master mariner with premises on the Quayside in Newcastle upon Tyne and in 1646 John *Harrigate* was the master of the *May Flower* sailing out of Newcastle. In 1881 only thirteen people in Britain had the name and twelve of them lived in Durham and Northumberland. The source remains uncertain. Nor should it be assumed that surnames with very similar spellings share the same origin. *Muscroft* is chiefly a West Riding name, likely to derive from *Molescroft* near Beverley, whereas *Moscroft* is found chiefly in Lancashire and Cumberland where the spellings suggest that it may be a variant of the Scottish *Moscrop*, a nickname from 'mosscrop' or cotton-grass noted by Black (1946).

19.2.5 Abbreviation and Contraction

An unexpected problem faced by genealogists is that it was formerly not uncommon for surnames to be abbreviated or contracted and only rarely are such developments confirmed by an explicit alias, for example 1592 *Bennet Smyth alias Combsmyth* of Batley. I have no such evidence for the Lancashire surname *Hayhirst* but careful research shows that it had abbreviations or contractions such as *Hairst*, *Haste*, and *Hirst*, all of which survived. Similarly there is proof in the parish registers that *Tweed* and *Jerrison* can be short forms of *Tweeddale* and *Margerison*; developments which obscure the line of descent and mask the full extent of a name's ramification or decline.

The history of the distinctive Westmorland surname *Lickbarrow* makes that point. Little has been written about it but it derives from Lickbarrow in Bowness on Windermere and may have had a single family origin. It was numerous in the Kendal area by the seventeenth century, especially in Long Sleddale, and *Peter Lickbarrowe* of Sleddale was among the first entries in the Kendal register: in the hearth tax return of 1670 seven male taxpayers were resident there not to mention a dozen others in different parts of the county. By the standards of the time it was a common and well-established surname. Things changed dramatically in the centuries that followed and in 1881 only two individuals in Westmorland were so called. There were a few others away from the north-west but on the face of it the decline was spectacular. The truth is that it had the short form *Barrow*: when the *Signe of the Bull* in Doncaster changed hands in May 1640 part of the property was described as 'late the inheritance of William Barrowe alias Lick Barrow' formerly an alderman in the town (Hall 1914: 74). The high total for *Barrow* in 1881 no doubt includes families who were originally named *Lickbarrow*.

Less obviously *Walsh* can pose a similar problem. Usually it derives from the Middle English *walsche* which can be interpreted as 'foreigner' or even 'welshman', and that is no doubt an acceptable explanation of bynames such as *John le Walsche*, taxed in Suffolk in 1327. That is certainly the correct origin for many families now named Walsh although in Lancashire and Yorkshire it was often an abbreviation for *Walshaw*. There are occasional aliases, for example 1746 *John Walsh otherwise Walshaw* but usually the abbreviation can be confirmed only by rigorous genealogical research. In the Birstall register, for example, *Nicholas Walsh* of Wyke was buried in August 1624 and he was almost certainly the *Nicholas Walshey* of Wyke mentioned in 1606. There is similar evidence in Slaidburn, more than thirty miles to the north-west, but in such cases it is difficult to be absolutely sure: *Barrow* and *Walsh* pose problems that DNA might help to solve.[9]

---

[9] Abbreviation is just one of numerous linguistic and social developments that create difficulties for the genealogist. For a much fuller treatment of the subject, see Redmonds (1997).

19.3 CONCLUSION

Numerous books have been written about surnames in the last 150 years or so but only recently have scholars in other fields begun to recognize the potential significance of surname studies throughout Great Britain. This coincides with a change in methodology which emphasizes the important role of the genealogist, who stands to benefit from the new approach but also has a vital contribution to make. The shift in emphasis, away from etymology, means that historians, linguists, place-name specialists, geneticists, and demographers can all bring new light to bear on the story of family names.

PART IV

LITERARY
ONOMASTICS

CHAPTER 20

....

THEORETICAL FOUNDATIONS OF LITERARY ONOMASTICS

....

GRANT W. SMITH

20.1 INTRODUCTION

....

THE study of literature is about how language communicates human experience and gives some aspects of experience a particular significance, and thereby meaning. Naming is a specific and elemental way in which humans use language, and so the function and meaning of names lie at the very heart of literature and of philosophical debates about language. A theoretical view of how names contribute to literary meaning must therefore begin with a look at the philosophy of language and particularly at the debate about name meaning and how language is used in making references.

Plato first raised the issue of reference and meaning in his dialogue *Cratylus*, in which Cratylus argues that there is a *natural*, and hence *descriptive*, relationship between all words (common as well as proper nouns) and their referents. Hermogenes disagrees, arguing that the relationship between words and their referents is instead *arbitrary*, a simple set of social conventions. They appeal to Socrates, but he argues on both sides of the dispute and leaves the question essentially unresolved.

John Stuart Mill (1973 [1843]) set the modern basis for future discussions of names by drawing a categorical distinction between common and proper nouns. Common nouns carry meaning because their definitions specify sets of common attributes among all items in the class of things named—for example, the word *dog* refers to a set of attributes shared by all examples within the class of things so named. Proper nouns, by contrast, such as *Fido*, do not carry meaning in this sense because they refer to specific rather than common attributes, thereby designating individual items within a class. Even though proper names may evoke many specific associations in the minds of individual *address-ees* (see Jakobson 1960), Mill dismisses this aspect of meaning as incidental to the act of reference rather than integral to it: 'By saying: This is York, [the listener may understand] that it contains a Minster. But this [is] by virtue of what he has previously heard concerning York, not by anything implied in the name' (Mill 1973 [1843]: 36). That is to say, the communicative value of any linguistic expression is to be seen strictly in terms of the analytical parameters of its definition, and while common nouns must connote common attributes shared by all members of a group, the essential function of proper nouns is to designate a single individual. That single individual may have recognizable attributes, perhaps Fido's shagginess, but the name itself does not connote those attributes as a part of its definition. That is to say, a specific extralinguistic entity will have attributes that are called to mind when it is referred to, but the name that is used to make the reference is not defined as a word by those attributes. Thus, the name as a feature of language has no meaning beyond its grammatical function, that is, the designation of a specific extralinguistic entity.

Mill's analysis has had profound influence but has not gone unchallenged. In the rest of this chapter, I hope to sketch in very brief form the philosophical debate over the meaning of names, and then to propose that the semiotic theories stemming from the philosophical work of C. S. Peirce (1955) (and others) suggest a better approach to such meaning. Language is a communicative tool, and semiotics considers the possibilities of interpretation to be the most important aspect of meaning—not the attributes in a definition or the analytical essence of the referent, as Mill and others suggest. Rather, the interpretation of every reference arises from a variety of associations, including knowledge addressees may already have of a referent, the context envisioned by the speaker, and, of course, the word (*sign*) itself. In fact, a *sign* usually evokes varied associations simultaneously. Meaningful associations are certainly restrained by social conventions and interaction, but they depend on, and arise from, pre-existing associations in the minds of addressers and especially addressees.

By focusing on the types of associative relationships within a communicative transaction, we can also observe at least three important differences between the ways in which names function in daily speech vis-à-vis imaginative literature. One difference can be seen in the greater degree of prosodic inventiveness in literature. Although we may observe increasing coinages of personal names in recent years, these follow recognizable morphological patterns, but in literature, especially children's literature, we find more play with the sounds of language and fewer restraints—for example *Pooh*. Another difference lies in the rhetorical uses of references, the ways in which authors sometimes manipulate the interpretive associations by delaying or totally withholding the identification of people, places, or things. A third difference is the greater frequency and degree to which names in literature may be interpreted *symbolically*. Our thematic understanding of literature arises largely from the *symbolic* nature of language, including the many associations possibly evoked by names. At the end of this chapter I shall propose that full and complete analyses of names in literature should classify the various types of names found and explain their thematic relevance. Even the most ordinary names carry potential associations from other contexts, and analyses need to show how some associations are more thematically relevant than others. As part of a deliberately crafted sample of language, we may assume that names have thematic relevance and carry more meaning than in common speech because they are, as Aristotle asserted, a part of 'the universal that poetry aims for' (Hutton 1982: 54).

20.2 DESCRIPTIVIST THEORIES OF MEANING

Since the time of Mill, two general types of philosophical theories have emerged about reference and meaning. These are usually referred to as *descriptive* and *causal* theories of reference. *Descriptive* theories arose in direct response to Mill's analysis, which is sometimes referred to as the 'Fido'–Fido theory because it assumes that the meaning of a name is simply embodied in and limited to the analytical attributes of the extralinguistic entity it designates without regard to interpretive associations.

Gottlob Frege (1848–1925) first described a problem with identity statements that can be represented mathematically, that is, if we compare 'a = b' to 'a = a' (Frege 1970: 56). The two signs, 'a' and 'b', may be considered different proper names for the same object. For example, if we say 'Mark Twain is Samuel Clemens' or 'Hesperus is Phosphorus', both terms refer to the same entity. According to Mill's analysis, both statements seem equivalent to saying 'a = a', and their difference is therefore trivial. However, if we assume that both statements are true, there must be more cognitive significance in the names than mere identity. In short, saying that 'a = b' is not the same as saying 'a = a'. It is instead a statement about a relationship in which 'a' and 'b' carry a different *sense* while making the same *reference*. Also, for any 'given reference (an object) there does not belong only a single sign' (Frege 1970: 58). Aristotle, for example, may be referred to as 'the pupil of Plato' and/or as 'the teacher of Alexander'.

The difference may be demonstrated by imagining a psychological relation between a person and a proposition, that is, prefacing a proposition with a relational statement. For example, if we place the statement 'Bob believes' before the proposition 'Mark Twain wrote *Huckleberry Finn*', it does not necessarily follow that 'Bob believes Samuel Clemens wrote *Huckleberry Finn*' even though the names *Mark Twain* and *Samuel Clemens* refer to the same extralinguistic entity. Bob might learn the name *Mark Twain* while reading the novel *Huckleberry Finn*, but he might also learn the name *Samuel Clemens* while reading about nineteenth-century authors without reference to *Huckleberry Finn*. These two names thereby identify the same entity but one name (identifier) cannot always be substituted for the other because they entail different understandings of the same entity in different contexts. In similar fashion, the words *Hesperus* and *Phosphorus* identify the same entity, the planet Venus, but are understood from references to it in different contexts, usually poetic, that is, as the evening star and as the morning star respectively.

Thus, as a part of their meaning, names clearly denote extralinguistic entities as an act of *reference*, but they also carry meaning from contextual associations in terms of *sense*. The names *Mark Twain* and *Samuel Clemens*, or *Hesperus* and *Phosphorus*, carry different cognitive significance that is unaccounted for by the simple act of *reference*, and it is this cognitive significance that Frege calls *sense*.

In describing his concept of *sense*, Frege is careful to exclude a merely subjective interpretation (1970: 59–61). Subjective interpretations of any word vary greatly from person to person 'according to the hints of the poet or the speaker' (1970: 61), and Frege refers to these as 'ideas' based on personal experience. However, the *sense* of a word, according to Frege, varies because different verifiable linguistic contexts may be found in which it has cognitive significance. It is these demonstrable contexts that add descriptive dimensions to name meaning within a verifiable linguistic universe. These differing contexts also account for names that are fictitious or purely conceptual. Even such names as *Santa Claus* carry cognitive significance, that is, *sense*, in the objective realm of *thought*, even though no *reference* is made to a tangible object.

Bertrand Russell (1872–1970) developed a different descriptive theory. In his seminal essay of 1905, 'On Denoting', Russell (1973 [1905]), like Frege, sees logical difficulties in denials of fictitious entities. If names denote existing entities, then statements such as 'Santa Claus does not exist' become simplistic redundancies, and poetic explanations, such as 'Santa Claus does not exist but there is a Santa Claus', become logically contradictory and communicatively worthless.

However, Russell rejects Frege's distinction between meaning and denotation. 'The right phrase, on the view in question, is that some meanings have denotations' (1973 [1905]: 112). To account for names referring to fictitious entities, Russell theorized that proper names function as *abbreviated definite descriptions* of things that we can know either to exist or not to exist. For example, if we know 'Scott was the author of *Waverly*', we can use the name *Scott* when referring to the author of *Waverly*.

To give meaning to denotations, Russell theorizes that names are abbreviated forms of propositions. The statements, 'The present King of France is bald', and 'The present King of France is not bald', are both false because the reference is false. That is to say, the reference, 'the present King of France', is an abbreviation of the proposition, 'This man is the present King of France', and such a proposition is obviously false. There is no man, either bald or not bald, who might be described as the 'present King of France'.

Names therefore 'have no meaning in isolation' (Russell 1973 [1905]: 118) but take on definite descriptive meanings from appropriate contexts of direct or indirect experience. They function very much like the demonstratives 'this' and 'that' in referring to propositions about things with which a speaker is in some way already acquainted.

Furthermore, we can also judge the truth of names that are fictitious (e.g. Santa Claus) or conceptual names (e.g. the Theory of Relativity) because they depend on a context and its formal structure. As Russell (1973 [1905]: 119) says, we can 'know the properties of a thing without having acquaintance with the thing itself, and without, consequently, knowing any single proposition of which the thing itself is a constituent'. That is to say, we can understand a reference insofar as we understand its context.

As in Frege's discussion of names, Russell does not describe meaning as a subjective interpretation that varies from person to person, but as something that can be judged true or false depending on the contexts in which the name has propositional status.

Russell is happy to point out that denials of false propositions are true, such as, 'No man, bald or otherwise, is the present King of France'.

20.3 CAUSAL THEORIES OF NAME MEANING

Causal theories of reference arose in the second half of the twentieth century, propelled primarily by lectures Saul Kripke gave at Princeton University in 1970 and later published as *Naming and Necessity* (1972 and 1980). Kripke argues that you need not be acquainted with a uniquely identifying description of an entity, as posited by Russell, in order to use a name correctly. One only needs to use a name in a way that correctly identifies the entity in question, and in order to do so, one's use of a name need only be a link in a chain of uses following the *cause* of the name.

The *cause* of a name generally amounts to a simple dubbing. For example, when a child is born the parents, hypothetically John and Mary Smith, may say simply, 'we'll call him Jacob', and give no explicit reason, assuming merely the acceptability of the name. The meaning and reasons for the name, even though they exist, are not needed for the name to be used effectively. Everyone at the naming event will, as a courteous formality, henceforth use the name *Jacob* when referring to the child. In addition, many others, including record keepers and casual acquaintances who have never seen the child, will rely on the testimony of the parents and others and still be able to refer to the child accurately with the name *Jacob*. It has also been argued that each time the name is subsequently used in reference to the child, we may say that the reference is 'grounded' in a context that functions as a basis for still more uses of the name (see, e.g., Evans 1982).

Causal theories highlight key weaknesses in *descriptivist* theories, especially Russell's. For example, most people know nothing about Richard Feynman or his contributions to the development of quantum electrodynamics, for which he was awarded the Nobel Prize in 1965, but a few non-specialists would be able to identify him as 'some physicist'. Clearly, the phrase 'some physicist' is not a very *unique* identifier as defined by Russell, and yet the non-specialist is still able to use the name to designate at least one entity within a group (Kripke 1980: 81ff.).

Another problem with Russell's *descriptivist* theory is that people often use names that may refer accurately but are based on false descriptions. Although Einstein can be uniquely identified as the person who discovered the Theory of Relativity, Kripke (1980: 85) notes, 'I often used to hear that Einstein's most famous achievement was the invention of the atomic bomb'. If Einstein's name is used in a way that associates him with the atomic bomb, even though he never worked on the Manhattan Project, the name will nevertheless likely be understood to identify one of the world's most famous physicists. Similarly, neighbours may talk about the new baby 'Jacob' in very uninformed ways.

Kripke (1980: 83–4) also notes that Kurt Gödel may be accurately associated with proving the incompleteness of arithmetic, and yet it is also possible that Gödel might have stolen the proof from his friend Schmidt. In such a case, we must assume that every time the name *Kurt Gödel* is used, the true referent is in fact Schmidt, which distorts intentionality and is obviously a ludicrous assumption.

Similarly, an incorrect name does not necessarily carry its descriptive attributes with its use, and intended referents are not necessarily obscured by the misuse of names. If a quotation is erroneously attributed in a footnote, or if a parent uses the name of one child when addressing another, the reference is not necessarily confused, and a correction is readily made. In fact, a correction confirms the uniqueness of the name as a simple designator because the descriptive attributes supposedly implied by the name are denied. Therefore, the descriptive attributes cannot be part of the name, and the name must be functioning purely as a designator of some entity.

The distinction is reinforced by Kripke's epistemic argument. For example, most of us would associate the name *Richard Nixon* with the descriptive phrase, 'the man who won the 1968 election', but we do not know this to be true a priori; we must go out into the world to know this. The actual winner, had the course of the campaign been different, might have been the loser (Kripke 1980: 41). Therefore, the descriptive phrase states a contingency and is not a necessary component of the *meaning* of the name. What we think we know about a name, its description, is known a posteriori, that is, by checking the facts of this world and of other possible worlds.

However, the name itself, when used, designates a particular entity as a *necessity*, according to Kripke, not as a *contingency*. Unlike any descriptive phrase that might be associated with it, a name designates the same referent no matter what descriptive phrase might be associated with it or in whatever world it might possibly exist. The name *Richard Nixon* would have been used to refer to the same person wherever born and named and whether or not he had been elected President in 1968. The name, once used, is 'a *rigid designator* [because] in every possible world it designates the same object' (Kripke 1980: 48), while the phrase 'the man elected President in 1968' might be associated with someone else in another, different world. Similarly, the new Smith baby will carry the name *Jacob* no matter what he does in life (unless, of course, he changes it, thereby re-dubbing himself). Thus, the concept of *necessity* is a distinguishing feature of Kripke's description of names and in understanding them as '*rigid designators*'.

In a similar manner, Kripke also describes natural kind terms (e.g. *tigers, heat, water, gold*) as *rigid designators*. That is to say, *tigers* can be defined scientifically as a species in a way that excludes other large felines and apparent variations among individual tigers. *Heat* can be defined as 'molecular motion' (Kripke 1980: 131), and *gold* can be defined as an element having the atomic weight of 79. Such references have meanings that are therefore not contingent but necessary. The uses of such natural kind terms differ from names insofar as their original coinage (dubbing) may precede a scientific and non-contingent definition of the referent. Gold may have been originally described as a yellow metal; however, such general attributes are not philosophically referential. 'Fool's gold' has the same general attributes but is not the real thing. Kripke's point is that '[t]he philosophical notion of attribute . . . seems to demand *a priori* (and analytic) coextensiveness as well as necessary coextensiveness' (1980: 138). Gold certainly exists a priori, and the word *gold*, in its philosophical sense, is not an 'abbreviated description' of common attributes but a rigid designation of the element with an atomic weight of 79. In short, the philosophical meaning of *gold* or any other noun is the analytic essence of the thing it designates.

If we consider names and terms of natural kinds as two types of references, Kripke (and other *causal* theorists) differs from both Mill and the descriptivists. Kripke agrees with Mill in denying that proper nouns constitute abbreviated descriptions (as argued by Russell), but he also disagrees with Mill that common nouns refer to a set of general attributes. 'The present view, directly reversing Frege and Russell, (more or less) *endorses* Mill's view of *singular* terms [i.e. names], but *disputes* his view of *general* terms' (Kripke 1980: 135). In short, the philosophical meanings of *all references*, of common nouns as well as of proper nouns, lie in their analytic function as rigid and necessary designations.

Kripke's view of names and references may be summarized in a series of related propositions: (a) names are non-descriptive; (b) names are causally related to their referents; (c) names are directly and necessarily referential; (d) names are rigid designators; and (e) the meaning of a name is the analytic essence of the thing it designates—just as the word *gold* refers to the element with an atomic weight of 79. Thus, the meaning of a reference is restricted to the analytical essence of the entity, physical or conceptual, in the mind of an addresser, regardless of the addresser's analytical understanding. Furthermore, such meaning does not include mental associations possibly intended by the addresser or that might occur to an addressee. The point of view pursued below, and contrary to Kripke's, is that human references are primarily associative rather than analytic, and that understanding the basic types of associations is necessary for understanding the ways in which names and references communicate meaningfully.

20.4 Two Brief Descriptivist Rebuttals

Causal theories now dominate philosophical discussion of names and reference but have not gone unchallenged. John R. Searle has argued that *causal* theories of reference are incomplete without accounting for a speaker's 'Intentional content' within 'the Network and the Background' of a reference (1983: 251). The idea of an 'intentional content' clearly implies a set of interpretive associations attached to a reference, but the difficulty with Searle's approach is his emphasis on the addresser's side of a communicative transaction and on the truth-value of what the addresser intends. We also need to emphasize the interpretive associations of addressees, and the fact that every communicative transaction involves an imperfect negotiation of possible associations by addressers and addressees. In imaginative literature, a successful author will be especially sensitive to the possible associations of a reference in the minds of his audience.

Frederick Kroon (2004) bridges the gap between addressers and addressees by arguing that successful reference depends on the *pretence*, by addressers and addressees, of both the very existence of the referent and a causal chain of the name. For example, even though a reference to *Hamlet* may lack semantic content because no such person exists outside our imaginations, the reference may yet be viewed as a 'pragmatic pretense' (Kroon 2004: 19) assumed by both a speaker and audience for discussion of an imagined entity. Thus, Kroon acknowledges the important role of the addressee and the meaningfulness of references to fictitious entities. However, he maintains a *causal* point of view (much like Kripke's) that all references, even those designating fictitious entities, are presumed to have an analytic essence. He does not explore the ways references may carry varied associative meanings and can be variously interpreted. In the following I hope to show that the analytic essence of a reference is seldom as important to either an addresser or addressee as the associations called to mind by the reference.

20.5 A SEMIOTIC VIEW OF NAMES AND REFERENCE

There can be no doubt that a primary function of names is to refer to specific things within general classes of things, but there are no physical connections between words and the entities to which they might refer. The only connections are in the minds of the interpreters. References may evoke an array of simultaneous associations, and these potential associations include more than the analytic essence of the referents. Thus, the relative success of references depends in an essential way on cognitive associations shared by addressers and addressees.

At the general level, a reference will evoke a range of content and grammar from its prior uses and, at a more specific level, it will evoke the personal associations within a user's experience. For the clerk in a hospital, a baby's name needs to fit a culturally constructed pattern of given name and family name, but relatives might recognize a commemoration and a value placed on family relationships. Similarly, our culture has constructed a wide array of images associated with the name *Obama* that reliably identifies an extralinguistic entity, and when the name is used in different contexts, only some of those images are relevant. At the same time, individuals carry personal associations to their use of the name that vary widely and may have little in common. In specialized work, the meanings of technical terms need to be deliberately restrained for the sake of specificity and education of novices. In such cases, the rigidity of designations is salutary, but socially constructed associations are only a portion of the possible associations that a reference might evoke.

In his formulation of semiotic theory, Charles Sanders Peirce (1955: 99) describes a *sign* as 'something which stands to somebody for something in some respect or capacity. It addresses somebody, that is, creates in the mind of that person an equivalent sign, or perhaps a more developed sign'. That is to say, reference is a cognitive function wherein a *sign* (be it a name, some other word, or a figurine) evokes pre-existent images in the mind. It is always, and in a very literal sense, a re-presentation of something in the human mind, that is, images from previous experience that might, of course, include conceptual models and analytic definitions.

Pierce distinguishes three modes of associative relationships: relationships based on (1) similarity, (2) contiguity/correlation, and (3) arbitrary convention. He also uses the terms *icon, index*, and *symbol* to describe the formal relationship between *signs* and the entities referred to in an act of reference. An *icon* 'is like that thing and used as a sign of it' (Peirce 1955: 102); it is a sign that represents something else on the basis of similarity, as a photograph or map resembles that to which it refers. A photograph of my grand-daughters who live far away reminds me of them. Security forces use camouflage with the hope that they will be interpreted as a continued part of the environment. If a bird looks at a moth that is coloured the same as the bark of the tree on which it sits, the bird will think of bark, and the moth will be safe. By resembling something, an *icon* brings that something to mind in the form of an idea.

An *index*, by contrast, 'is a sign which refers to the Object that it denotes by virtue of being really affected by that Object' (Peirce 1955: 102). In a strict one-to-one relationship, an *index* refers to something on the basis of contiguity or correlation, as smoke indi-cates fire, a thermometer indicates temperature, or the alarm call of an animal indicates a predator. It is clearly different from the thing to which it refers, but 'it necessarily has some Quality in common with the object' (Peirce 1955: 102). An *indexical* interpretation infers a connection between two *iconic* recognitions. If the bird sees movement, it will associate movement with food, and the moth will be eaten.

A *symbol* is the most complex of the three types of signs. It infers a relationship between two or more *indices* and 'refers to the Object that it denotes by virtue of a law, usually an association of general ideas' (Peirce 1955: 102). Birds can be taught to peck for food at the command of an *indexical* sign, possibly a word, but they cannot (we assume) put words into new relationships with one another to express general ideas. *Indexical* interpretations require a tight correlation of time and space between a sign and its refer-ent, and birds are stuck with one-to-one interpretations. *Symbolic* references, by con-trast, are reflected in the relationships of *indices* (words or word parts to nearby words). Because of their combinatorial rules (phonological, morphological, and syntactical) *symbolic* references imply that many things are related by a few attributes, that is, simply by the rules of language, if by nothing else. Thus, *symbolic* references can project an end-less array of implicit knowledge.

If references function *symbolically*, as they commonly do in human language, they may correlate very little, or not at all, with reality, as we can see with such words as *uni-corn, griffin*, and *vampire*. Peirce (1955: 103) describes the realm of *symbolic* reference as 'the possibly imaginary universe', and wild differences in interpretation are easily seen in political discourse as well as artistic expression.

At the same time, the *symbolic* use of language is a great aid to memory. All things can be analysed *indexically*, in terms of one-to-one relationships, as computer languages do, but humans have difficulty remembering such relationships in long series. They have greater difficulty, for example, in remembering names interpreted *indexically*, that is, as simple labels and 'rigid designators', than if the same words are contextualized and interpreted as common nouns. That is to say, people cannot remember proper names nearly so well as they can infer what words might follow other words in any given sentence. Thus, the human mind thrives on *symbolic* references, and language is essentially *symbolic* insofar as it implies a system of higher order relationships 'among an endless array of *indexical* references' (Smith 2006: 20).

20.6 NAMES AS SIGNS

J. S. Mill and the *causal theorists* limit the meaning of names to the analytic essence of a referent. They draw no distinction between names and random labels. However, language functions more as an associative tool than a logical one, and while the associative function of names is primarily *indexical* (designating their referents in one-to-one relationships), other types of associations may add substantial meaning in an act of interpretation. Names are best viewed as types of *signs*, and so the types of associations they evoke, and hence their meaningfulness, may be described as *iconic, indexical,* and *symbolic*.

Iconic associations elicited by names can arise from the phonological and orthographic presentations of words. That is to say, the sensual data, the physical utterance or graphic representations of language, may be interpreted as mimetic of, and therefore appropriate to, the entity designated. If we ask Mary and John Smith why they named their child Jacob, they might give no reason other than, 'It sounds good.' Several researchers, especially Herbert Barry and Stanley Lieberson, have shown distinctive phonological patterns for masculine and feminine names (see e.g. Barry and Harper 1995; Lieberson 2000). Thus, prosody is an important influence in the naming of children, reflected, of course, in the plethora of coinages in recent times. My own research has shown that some phonological patterns are particularly favourable for political candidates (Smith 2007). That is to say, the phonology of names, especially the rhythms of language, seems to be associated with feelings and meaning, in much the same way as the prosody of a poem affects its interpretaion.

In a similar way, the shapes of letters can be associated with a referent on the basis of *iconic* similarity. Such associations are especially obvious in the design of brand names. The letters of *Exxon*, for example, slant forward and combine with the sounds of the word to suggest acceleration. The lettering of *Coca Cola* is rounded to suggest bubbles and flowing liquid. Likewise, the illuminated texts of medieval Europe strove to associate language itself, or at least literacy, with the intricacies of the word of God. Thus, visually as well as aurally, the *iconic* associations sometimes evoked by names may be seen as an important aspect of meaning and interpretation.

C. S. Peirce (1955) describes *indexical* associations as strict one-to-one interpretations, which parallels Kripke's description of names as 'rigid designators', and so designation should be seen as a vital type of association evoked by names, even the most important type. Names refer to individual things and, like function words, are relatively unaffected, semantically, by nearby words.

However, no reference can be understood or have meaning of any sort unless the addressee has prior knowledge of the thing designated. Except for *iconic* (e.g. onomatopoetic) associations, words have no meaning of their own and cannot create an image except by combining pre-existing images. Thus, every act of reference is in fact a re-presentation of an image of the referent in the mind of the addressee (or perhaps a combination of images). In every act of reference, the referent becomes a context that limits our understanding of, and our sense of appropriateness of, the *sign* used; what we know about a referent ineluctably affects our interpretation of the *sign*. Insofar as the word *York* functions as a *sign*, it evokes a pre-existing image in the mind of the addressee, and the fact that it 'contains a Minster' might be necessary for the reference to be accurately interpreted, for example for one *York* to be distinguished from another.

Furthermore, the image conjured in the mind of an addressee by a reference made by an addresser is never exactly the same as the image that is in the mind of the addresser. If I tell my friend that this is my dog *Fido*, my friend will see Fido from a slightly different angle. If I refer to a definable concept such as the Theory of Relativity, my friend will think of details different from my own, and it will take some discussion to determine the relevance of the reference to a particular situation. Thus, as *indices*, names certainly designate individual referents, but our understanding of the reference depends absolutely on our pre-existing knowledge of the referent. Also, a reference is never equally understood by everyone. In the use of a *sign*, an addresser strives to evoke a domain of relevant associations with the referent known by the addressee. However, the communicative process is never perfect because two domains never match perfectly.

Symbolic associations stem from the fact that all names are also words that in turn come from other contexts in which they have, or have had, additional meaning. Just as our understanding of a reference depends on our knowledge of the referent, it is also affected by the word used as a *sign*. Thus, we may say that the interpretation of every reference is *coloured* by the lexical attributes in other contexts of the word used as a name. The idea of *colouring* carries the rhetorical meaning that our interpretations may focus on one type of association, for example, the *indexical*, but also be significantly affected by other types, especially the *symbolic*.

It is useful to see the *symbolic* meaning of names as being relatively transparent or relatively opaque (see Smith 2006: 22). On the opaque end of the scale, we may observe that language, as a system, emphasizes the relationships of words to one another more than their presumed relationships to objective reality, and so every act of interpretaion is affected by the way in which a name might function as another type of word and its potential to combine with other words in describing and classifying human experience. That is to say, the *symbolic* potentiality of all words may colour our interpretation of very opaque names. This *symbolic* potentiality of names is vividly illustrated in brand names and in the use by real estate developers of idyllic names; carefully selected names attract buyers—for example *Avalon Place* and *Emerald Estates*. The lexical attributes of such names are carried over as a part of a *symbolic* interpretation regardless of any literal applicability.

On the transparent end of the scale are clearly descriptive names, specifying attributes that are obvious, intentional, and often thematic. For example, the Golden Gate Bridge spanning San Francisco bay is literally descriptive as well as metaphorical. It spans a gateway to the vast Pacific Ocean and glistens in the golden sun. It is not made of gold, but it certainly has value to the economy of the San Francisco Bay area. More importantly, the name associates the bridge with the state motto and, above all, with state history and the great gold rush of 1849. Thus, the name not only designates a particular bridge, but also associates it with a certain group of other contexts in which the word is used. Of course, descriptive names may also have commercial value.

20.7 NAMES IN LITERATURE

As *signs* names evoke specific domains of *indexical* associations and possibly a wide array of *iconic* and *symbolic* associations. In literature we need to assume a thematic relevance to these associations and such relevance may be judged in terms of artistic unity. However, artistic unity should not be limited to the intentions of an author, but should focus on a range of interpretations. Reasonable interpretations often reach far beyond the intentions of an author, and so analyses of names can be used to support a variety of theoretical approaches to a work of art. For example, a Post-Colonial interpretation of Shakespeare's *Tempest* might argue that the names *Antonio* and *Sebastian* reflect the dark side of a civilized society. Similarly, any other critical approach might be supported so long as the analysis of names assumes the fundamental meaningfulness of semiotic associations and convincingly explains their thematic relevance.

20.7.1 *Iconic* Associations

As noted above, a *sign* is interpreted *iconically* when it brings something to mind as an idea because of its physical similarity to the thing signified. In literature, the sounds of names often suggest ideas that may be thematically relevant. Don Nilsen (2005: 118), for example, argues that the name *Ian Houlihan* suggests the biblical phrase, 'I am who I am', in *The Life of Pi*. Similarly, the first time Othello's name is spoken in Shakespeare's play (and in most subsequent uses), it sounds like a request for an explanation, 'But, Othello, speak. / Did you...' (I.iii.110). In Shakespeare's time, the medial /th/ was pronounced as a simple /t/, and so the name would have been pronounced O-TELL-O. Immediately after this first use of the name, Othello explains that he won the love of Desdemona by telling stories of his life with which she sympathized. Story telling is thus seen as the basis from which love develops and is repeatedly alluded to as an important theme of the play. In such examples, which are more frequent in children's literature, meaning arises from sound alone.

As I have argued earlier (Smith 2005), the sounds of names also reinforce lexical meanings and morphological forms. For example, the names *Ebenezer Scrooge* and *Martin Chuzzelwit* have standard forms but also grating sounds that reinforce their rapacity and miserliness. Among Faulkner's fictive coinages, the crudity of the *Snopes* family is reinforced by the low vowel and the slithering 's' sounds of the name. And *Yoknapatawpha County* looks like (but is not in fact) an Indian derivation (specifically Chickasaw of the Mississippi-Alabama region) typical of many county names in the United States. There is a similarity of onomatopoetic sounds in different languages, and so it may be that the sounds of language have some basis in human physiology, but the *iconic* reinforcement of names can be seen most clearly and concretely in terms of specific cultural and thematic values. And in literature, thematic values matter most.

20.7.2 *Indexical* Associations

As *indices*, names create an expectation that we know something or should know something about the referents, and in literature the *indexical* function of names helps to stimulate our curiosity and lead us forward in our reading. Initially we know very little about the referents (although the *sign* itself may evoke phonetic, morphological, and lexical associations). However, names acquire meaningful associations (what Roland Barthes (1975: 17) calls a 'semic code') as the story or lyric progresses, and prior associations might even be radically altered. For example, in the many plot sources from which Shakespeare drew for *Romeo and Juliet*, the principal characters are viewed primarily as victims of their own lust, but in Shakespeare's play they acquire a different meaning—they become victims of their parents' feud.

An addressee's expectation to know a referent may also be frustrated for thematic purposes. Authors sometimes coin fictive names in order to fictionalize historical events. Marguerite de Navarre, for example, probably refers to her husband, Henri d'Albret, with the name *Hircan* in the *Heptameron*. A name might also be delayed to create a special interest in a character, or characters may function without names, to indicate their unimportance, to create psychological distance, or to emphasize, ironically, the absolute importance of identity in the face of enforced conformity (e.g. the women in Margaret Atwood's *The Handmaid's Tale*). In short, the most dominant type of name associations, the *indexical*, are those most obviously and easily subject to manipulation for artistic ends.

20.7.3 *Symbolic* Associations

As part of an artistic vision, names in literature (vis-à-vis daily speech) are especially apt to evoke *symbolic* associations. They may evoke such associations either because they have potential lexical meanings as other types of words, or because they are borrowed as names from previous contexts and evoke those associations. Their lexical potentialities may be described as direct and obviously descriptive, or as indirect and figurative. Two types of allusions may also be distinguished: (1) the names of the characters and places themselves, and (2) the names of things external to the story but mentioned by the characters or narrator. Whatever the mechanism, *symbolic* associations show the thematic importance of names and enrich their meanings more in literature than in other uses of language.

The most obvious form of names with *symbolic* meaning are those that have potential lexical meaning of their own that is clear, simple, and direct, sometimes called '*redende Namen*', but also referred to as 'tag names' or 'call names'. These might be adjectives turned to nouns (Shakespeare's *Slender*, Arthur Miller's *Willy Lowman*), noun substitutes (*Babe* or *Buck*), or new compounds (*Malvolio*). In a previous article I have referred to such names as 'lexical equivalents' (Smith 2005: 16) and noted that they may contribute to a sense of artifice. For the sake of verisimilitude, some authors deliberately choose names that are from the general onomasticon and are more purely indexical, but doing so sacrifices *symbolic* potential and thematic richness. Art is not just a slice of life but an interpretation, as we can see vividly in the writings of Dickens and many others.

Many names of characters and places, even very common ones, invite figurative interpretations in literature that are rich in *symbolic* associations and thematically important. Basic types of figurative interpretations are *irony, metonymy, metaphor*, and *allegory*. Irony is a dominant feature of modern literature, and much irony may be seen in Shakespeare's *Beatrice* who torments *Benedick* (*Benedictus* = 'he who is blessed') throughout the play, but eventually confesses her true love. Oscar Wilde also develops an entire play around the ironies of being *Earnest*. Metonymic meanings are also obvious in names such as *Goldielocks, Little Red Ridinghood*, and *Devil's Valley* (the title of a novel by André P. Brink). As I pointed out in 2005, metaphoric meanings are common but complex and often laced with irony. It is a type of meaning that 'arises when some attributes normally associated with one entity are transferred to a very different kind of thing' (Smith 2005: 22). In the Bible, the name *Ruth* is for a character associated with patience and loyalty being rewarded with a loving husband, Boaz, but in Morrison's *Song of Solomon*, a similar Ruth is rewarded with brutality and neglect. The term *allegory* may be used for figurative interpretations that are sustained, systematic, and philosophical. There are various types of allegory, but a clear example 'is the medieval play *Everyman*, in which each character is a personification of an abstract concept—*Death, Everyman, Fellowship, Good Deeds, Knowledge*, etc. George Orwell's *Animal Farm* may also be interpreted allegorically, but of a special type called *fable*' (Smith 2005: 22). Of course, the types of figurative interpretations overlap, but the complexities of figurative interpretations merely illustrate the *symbolic* nature of language itself, including the *symbolic* potentialities of names.

Understanding the figurative meanings of names often depends on recognizing intertextual associations, that is, a name as a borrowing from, or an allusion to, previous contexts. The meaning of Ruth's suffering in Morrison's *Song of Solomon* is more poignant when we can draw on our knowledge of the biblical character. James Joyce tells us something about creativity with the name *Stephen Daedalus*, and with the names *Theseus* and *Hippolyta*, Shakespeare casts his entire play, *Midsummer Night's Dream*, in the context of Plutarch's description of a mythical war between the sexes. With other names in the same play, Shakespeare integrates classical mythology with English folklore and the common lives of tradesmen. Character names are also blended with references spoken by the characters themselves to English horticulture, to medieval traditions, and many classical stories. Thus, names in contemporary literature can evoke vast stores of *symbolic* associations from previous literature and cultural history.

20.8 SYSTEMATIC ANALYSIS

As elemental acts of language, names offer us invaluable keys for interpreting literature. All we need do is assume that any particular work has a thematic unity of some sort, some expression about human experience, even if it seems to say that nothing has meaning. It follows that some semiotic associations among the numberless ones possible are more important than others. Every name can evoke many associations and many shades of interpretation, and these interpretations may reach well beyond the intentions of the author. A literary analysis is therefore reasonable insofar as it seeks common themes among the many associations possibly evoked by names in the work analysed.

It follows as a corollary that name analyses should be thorough and systematic. A classification of names should be a starting point because it can help distinguish thematic associations. For example, distinguishing character names (and the allusions they utter) from place-names will help focus on motive and action. Character names might also be sub-divided into borrowings, lexical equivalents, and descriptive labels (e.g. forester, duke), and borrowings can be sub-divided again (e.g. classical, biblical, folkloric). In my analysis of *Midsummer Night's Dream*, the names of *Theseus* and *Hippolyta* appear to be borrowed from a very brief passage in *Plutarch's Lives* describing the settlement of an exhausting war between Athenian warriors and the invading Amazons. Settlement of contention between the sexes is thus an important theme that is reinforced by action and other name associations (mostly classical).

Literary onomastics is not a literary theory of its own, nor does it offer a bias in social values. Onomastic analyses may support differing literary and cultural theories or individualized interpretations. However, names (and some descriptive labels) anchor our analyses to specific information in the texts we are analysing. Thus, literary onomastics is simply a type of analysis that is firmly based on language theory and yet is both specific and systematic.

....

CHAPTER 21

NAMES IN SONGS

A Comparative Analysis of Billy Joel's We Didn't Start The Fire *and Christopher Torr's* Hot Gates

....

BERTIE NEETHLING

21.1 INTRODUCTION

....

THE occurrence of names in songs is common. It is difficult to think of a songwriter who has not at one time or another included the name of a person or a place (the two most likely categories) in a song. Romantic love songs about relationships abound, and the names of those involved in the relationship, whether ongoing or in the past, would be likely to appear in the song lyrics. Place-names are often mentioned in a nostalgic way, often referring to the past when the songwriter lived there and when the naming of that place brings back a myriad of memories. All these names may be the focus point in the songs, but they are nearly always backed up by supporting lyrics, detailing the context in which they are used. There are countless examples of such songs in probably all languages that have a music or songwriting tradition. Bruce Springsteen, for example (see Auxier and Anderson 2008), is singled out for regularly using names in his songs. Many other categories of names may also feature in songs. Names merely in the titles of songs illustrate this profusely.

Onomastics covers a huge variety of name types in various disciplines. Many objects have names, and name scholars tend to focus on one of the many categories, for example, names of people (anthroponymy with many different categories), names of geographical entities (toponyms with many subsections), names of brand or product names, etc. One identified category is the occurrence and study of names in literary works of art that results in the sub-discipline called literary onomastics. Authors of fiction often choose names for characters or places that have great significance in the plot. Readers are often required to have a vast knowledge of names from mythology or history in order to interpret and understand the use of some names in a literary work of art. Literary works of art may cover all the possible variations, from fiction (novel, drama, short story) with a narrative plot, to poetry, which does not always need a narrative.

21.2 NAMES IN SONGS

If one considers names in songs, the question arises: should one consider this phenomenon within one of the broader onomastic categories, or should it be treated separately? It is common knowledge that poetry used to be sung or patterned to music (Simpson 1970: 26). Although poetry and music may have drifted apart, it is probably still valid to refer to songs as lyrical poetry. In this contribution it is argued that there is a resemblance between poetry and song lyrics, and hence the study of names in songs could be considered as part of literary scholarship, that is literary onomastics. There are strong indicators that the lyrics in songs often display many of the literary devices or conventions used in poetry and that the relationship between the two is therefore closer than one may think. Songwriters still employ techniques associated with poetry. Devices such as imagery, simile, metaphor, personification, symbolism, assonance, consonance, alliteration, end rhyme, and internal rhyme are often present in song lyrics. A search on the internet yields many sites illustrating this phenomenon, that is, song lyrics illustrating the use of literary devices. What is particularly interesting is the use of short music clips from songs by various artists (YouTube—Literary devices in songs) where the device is announced and then illustrated. Another website that considers the use of such devices in songs is Literary Devices (n.d.), where each literary device discussed is exemplified by an excerpt from the lyrics of a song.

The argument that one could interpret the study of names in song lyrics as part of literary onomastics is strengthened by looking at the work of some artists who are songwriters/singers as well as poets, and who seemingly accept and realize the connection between the two. Bob Dylan and Leonard Cohen are two such examples. Cohen, who has recently returned to the concert stage despite his age of 77, has, in spite of producing many concert and collective albums, also produced ten poetry albums and two novels. It is not difficult to make the connection between song lyrics and poetry when looking at his work. On a new album released in 2012 with the title *Old Ideas*, the first song, called *Going Home*, is characterized by the following ironical lyrics: *I love to speak with Leonard / He's a sportsman and a shepherd / He's a lazy bastard / Living in a suit.* At the preview of his album in New York, many critics who attended the preview sat with their eyes closed, their heads towards the back, and a small smile as if enjoying the occasion in the sunshine of the melodies (McCrank 2012). The new album is considered a confirmation of life in its fullness, but also its horrors. Cohen does not necessarily provide solutions, he knows better: in the song *Come Healing* he sings: *Behold the gates of mercy / in arbitrary space / and none of us deserving / the cruelty or the grace.* It is quite clear that Cohen is a literary artist when writing his lyrics: he is at the same time a poet. A very recent development is the translation and performance of some of Cohen's songs in Afrikaans, a

South African language. The artist, Koos van der Merwe, had to get the permission from Cohen to translate and to sing his work (Jackson 2013).

That is one of the reasons why the study of song lyrics forms part of literary scholarship, and if there are names involved in the lyrics, it becomes part of literary onomastics.

Bob Dylan is another artist who is generally recognized as an extremely gifted songwriter as well as a poet. Over the past few years he has been nominated for the Nobel Prize in Literature, and that obviously underlines his quality as a poet. Dylan has made some comments about his position, for example 'I'm a poet and I know it'. Another straightforward answer appeared in the liner notes of his second album, *The Freewheelin' Bob Dylan* (1963), where he simply said: 'Anything I can sing, I call a song. Anything I can't sing, I call a poem'.

The connection between lyrics and poetry seems to be recognized. The 'Poetry and Music' page (Poets.org (n.d.)) presents the views of a number of songwriters/poets on this matter. However, for the purposes of this contribution the above is considered adequate in arguing that song lyrics containing names could be studied and considered as part of literary onomastics.

21.3 The Choice of the Two Songs for Comparative Purposes

The choice of songs was determined by an obvious factor: both songs are characterized by an extremely large number of names that essentially constitute the lyrics. There are hardly any other supporting lyrics aside from the refrain.

Billy Joel, the American pop and rock star wrote the lyrics and recorded the song *We Didn't Start The Fire* in 1989. Joel had just turned 40, and being interested in history, took his inspiration from events that had occurred during his lifespan, that is from 1949 to 1989. Being an American, he focused mainly on events involving American people and places. The title suggests that the world was in turmoil, but that Joel's generation, the so-called Baby Boomers, could not be held responsible, and that the world was in a bad state long before they arrived on the scene.

From an onomastic perspective the song is remarkable: it consists mainly of onomastic images in the form of the names of people, places, and other onomastic items like brand names, names from the entertainment world and also book names, that is, literary works of art. A total of 121 such items are chronologically strung along in the verses through the duration of the song which lasts for 4 minutes and 49 seconds. The refrain or chorus that occurs five times is the only part of the song not rendered through these essentially onomastic images while there are only a few other supporting non-onomastic lyrics in a few lines. Where this does appear, it is often used to fit into the rhythmic patterning of the song, while at the same time giving only a hint of the context in which the onomastic item was used. The onomastic items are presented chronologically from 1949 to 1989.

Joel, although including twenty-one toponyms and other onomastic categories, prefers to foreground individuals (fifty-four in total). That might be typical of the role that individuals play in a Western democracy. Not surprisingly, Joel's song is anchored in people and events from the USA, with only a few references to other parts of the world. The one obvious important point to note is that all the names used in the song refer to people who actually lived or might still be alive today, places that still exist, events that really happened in the past, or products that were created by human beings (e.g. literary works of art) and were used (e.g. brands) or enjoyed by society (e.g. films, musicals, TV series, sport, etc.) There is nothing fictional about any of them, and they are firmly based in or connected with reality.

The other song is *Hot Gates*, sung by the South African Laurika Rauch and composed for her by her songwriter-husband, Christopher Torr. During her 1995 concert tour, the well-known local cabaret artist and singer introduced South African audiences to this new song. The song, with the exception of the refrain or chorus and a final chorus verse, consists entirely of place-names or toponyms, strung along a continuum with no other linguistic items present. No fewer than fifty-eight toponyms are used in the song.

The two songs, because of the overwhelming onomastic content, were therefore fairly obvious choices when considering a comparative approach to names featuring in songs. It should also be reasonably clear that the literary devices mentioned earlier, aside from rhythm and rhyme, assonance and alliteration, could not play a role in either song because of the overwhelming presence of names. This immediately raises the question: what then are both songs about, and what do the names tell? A key feature of art is that it has a communicating function in that the artist always has an audience in mind. A work of art could then be considered as semiotic, representing a sign that has an iconic character (Lotman 1972). If we consider these songs as works of art, what is conveyed through the lyrics? One is then challenged by the question as to what proper names, the focus point in the songs, mean. This will follow later.

21.4 RECEPTION OF THE TWO SONGS

Billy Joel, American pop and rock star, was born on 9 May 1949. That assigns him to the generation often referred to as the Baby Boomers—people born after World War II, from 1946 to around 1964. In 1989, when Joel had turned 40, he wrote the lyrics and recorded *We Didn't Start The Fire*. The song was released on his album *Storm Front*. It is characterized by the enumeration of the names of people, places, events, or products that made the headlines in the years 1949–89, the period that covered Joel's lifespan at the time when he wrote the song. The song could be seen as 'a patter song characterised by its moderately fast tempo with rapid succession of rhythmic lyrics' (Wikipedia 2015c). It appears to consist of a series of unrelated images in a rapid-fire, half-spoken, half-sung vocal style.

The reception of the song was mixed. It became a number-one hit song in the USA, and was ranked number seven in the UK at the time. But *Blender Magazine* included the song on its list of the '50 Worst Songs Ever', and in 2004 the song also appeared on VH1's '50 Most Awesomely Bad Songs Ever' in collaboration with Blender. In the USA, however, it was hugely popular and still has a following today. It was also nominated for the Grammy Award for Record of the Year.

The song has been interpreted as 'a rebuttal to criticism of Joel's Baby Boomer generation' by both the preceding and succeeding generations (Wikipedia 2013c). The title *We Didn't Start The Fire* suggests that the frenzied and troubled state of affairs over that period of time had been the state of the world long before the Baby Boomer generation, but the critics did not acknowledge this.

Asked about his inspiration for the song, Joel responded as follows:

> I had turned forty. It was 1989 and I said 'Okay, what's happened in my life?' I wrote down the year 1949. Okay, Harry Truman was president. Popular singer of the day, Doris Day. China went Communist. Another popular singer, Johnny Ray. Big Broadway show, *South Pacific*. Journalist, Walter Winchell. Athlete, Joe DiMaggio. Then I went on to 1950... It's one of the worst melodies I've ever written. I kind of like the lyric though. (DeMain 2004: 119)

Tracy Osborne, from the Teacheroz website (Teacheroz 2009), suggests that the song represents 'a brief history of the United States of America'. On the Sing365.com website, which collects lyrics of many songs and aggregates their reviews, a reviewer by the name of 'Tata' remarks that: 'If every student knew a little something about everyone of these names and events they'd know a "condensed" account of most of the twentieth century' (Sing365.com 2010).

Longrie (1997: 147), a university lecturer, wanted to link his course in literature with a text that would force his students to think historically, a metanarrative that would connect them to the nation's founders. He then decided to use Joel's song as his narrative. Allsop (2009), another history professor, also used the Billy Joel song to uncover the implicit criteria informing someone else's attribution of historical significance to past events. Clearly then some observers are impressed by the structure of the song and how it was composed, or how it can be put to use within a historical context (also see Bordowitz 2006).

Not everybody is impressed. Longrie (1997: 147) refers to a very critical reception of the song by a journalist, Jerry Adler, in *Newsweek*, calling the song 'a way to make history even more boring,... nearly five minute recital of names chosen from the news of the last forty years for no apparent reason than rhyme. Commit this song to memory, kids, and you are guaranteed to have learned absolutely nothing'.

By contrast, *Hot Gates*, judging by its reception in South Africa, was a huge success. Laurika Rauch obviously chose to call her album *Hot Gates*, which was released shortly after she had introduced audiences to the song, because of the immense popularity the song enjoyed. It is clear that the fifty-eight different toponyms in the song cover much of the globe, but there appears to be no immediate logical geographical connection between most of these entities. One's first reaction to some of these names may be positive, evoking images of civilization's strongholds. A closer scrutiny of the toponyms and their roles in history, however, will reveal that they do share one common denominator: an event or events that are best forgotten once took place there. In some cases events affected the lives of only a few (cf. Chappaquiddick), in other cases millions (cf. the World War II references). This then is the binding factor of the song: these place-names represent battlefields that irrevocably shaped and changed the lives of millions of people all over the world.

21.5 Titles/Names of the Songs and Refrains

The first feature of the two songs that suggested comparison, aside from the many names, are their titles/names of the songs. Joel's song is about six years older than Torr's. That suggests that Joel could not in any way have been influenced by *Hot Gates*. The opposite is possible, but also extremely unlikely.

One is struck by the occurrence of the 'heat/hot' concept in both titles. Whereas in Joel's song it is the repetition of the first line of the chorus that serves as the title: *We Didn't Start The Fire*, in Torr's song *Hot Gates* is the title and represents the 'heat/hot' concept. This concept is backed up by the refrain in both songs.

As suggested earlier, the Joel song has been interpreted as 'a rebuttal to criticism of Joel's Baby Boomer generation' by both the preceding and succeeding generations (see Wikipedia 2013c). The title *We Didn't Start The Fire* suggests that the frenzied and troubled state of affairs over that period of time had been the state of the world long before the Baby Boomer generation. One could then seemingly interpret the 'fire' in the title as a metaphor for 'trouble'. This is repeated in the refrain:

> We didn't start the fire
> It was always burning
> Since the world's been turning
> We didn't start the fire
> No we didn't light it
> But we tried to fight it

It is as if Joel, using the personal plural pronoun 'we', is simply suggesting that his generation was not responsible for all the trouble across the world, they did not start it and they were fighting it as best as they could, but with little success.

The title *Hot Gates* of the Torr song is more complex when it comes to interpretation compared to Joel's fairly simple one. The title has its origin in a poem by T. S. Eliot called *Gerontion*. The relevant excerpt is as follows:

> I was neither at the hot gates
> Nor fought in the warm rain
> Nor knee deep in the salt marsh, heaving a cutlass,
> Bitten by flies, fought

Gerontion translates as 'the little old man'. Apparently a former seaman or business man at the end of his tether, the subject reflects upon his possible future and his past, and then realizes with anguish and resentment that he has led a rather non-eventful life. He is blind and lives in 'a decayed house' which is not his own (Salingar 1970: 335–7). Regarding the particular excerpt, Sharpe (1991: 61), a literary critic, has the following to say: 'His sullen negatives obtrude upon a curiously detailed evocation of long-forgotten wars ("hot gates" translates Thermopylae)...'

Eliot then refers specifically to the battle that took place at *Thermopylae*, a pass in Greece famous for the heroic defence by Leonidas and his 300 Spartans against the Persians under Xerxes in 480 BC. *Thermopylae* is the final toponym in the song but then also serves as the title of the song in its translated form. This sets the mood and the tone of the song: all the toponyms appearing in *Hot Gates* represent 'hotspots' where events took place that in some way changed the course of history or gave rise to controversy.

The 'heat/hot' concept in *Hot Gates* is supported by the first two lines of the refrain:

> I can see a fiery fiery glow
> Even as the sun is sinking low

The 'fiery fiery glow' suggests fire, turmoil, and chaos, and this is further backed up by the next two lines:

> I can see a horseman on the run
> O my daughter, o my son

Especially the last line, *O, my daughter, o, my son*, is striking: it may suggest that families were torn apart through the often senseless killings. It is also reminiscent of the lament frequently found in the Old Testament of the Bible. Torr succeeds well in stressing this through the refrain.

Unlike the Joel song that has the same refrain throughout, there is an important change in the Torr song. A corrective, even if an ironic one, comes in the form of the last chorus.

> There's another song that will be sung
> There's another bell that must be rung
> There's another city I've been told
> Where the streets are paved with gold

The other song, the other bell, the other city where the streets are paved with gold, promises a new life, a better life, a life without strife and fighting, where peace will prevail. This is an obvious reference to the biblical *New Jerusalem. Hot Gates* now give way to '*heavenly gates*'. The irony is: is this only possible in the hereafter, in another world? Are we destined never to have peace on earth? The strife torn *Jerusalem* of the first verse, its history extending through more than 4,000 years, is starkly contrasted with the implied *New Jerusalem* of the last chorus. The joyous bell at the end, signalling everlasting peace and joy, is contrasted with the ominous counting down chime right at the beginning that seems to prepare the world for impending doom. Christopher Torr could probably very easily 'update' and rewrite his song using other toponyms with no fear of repeating himself. Humankind will see to that.

The title of Joel's song—*We Didn't Start The Fire*—also seems to suggest that, just as in *Hot Gates*, one would be dealing with 'hotspots' where events took place that made the headlines at the time, and not in a positive way. One could then interpret both 'fire' in the one title and '*Hot (Gates)*' in the other as a metaphor for 'trouble'. In the case of Joel's song, that is by and large true for a large number of entries, notably many toponyms (= 'hotspots' in history) as well as some individuals who were controversial characters and are known and remembered for the wrong reasons. Joel, however, balances the 'negative' entries with 'positive' ones, often referring to individual achievers who have attained iconic status in the USA in their lifetimes, for example authors who wrote good books, performers who became famous, sporting heroes, and other successful entities in the entertainment world such as musicals and films. The title (as well as the refrain) of the Joel song then becomes somewhat inappropriate and irrelevant if these positive portrayals are taken into account. Torr's song does not have this problem: the title and its interpretation (as well as the melancholic refrain) applies to the whole song.

21.6 POETIC QUALITIES OF THE TWO SONGS

In *Hot Gates* one is immediately struck by the fact that every line forms a metrical unit with a seven syllable structure that is meticulously maintained. Only in a few cases was it necessary to improvise in order to support this pattern. By inserting the woeful exclamation 'O' before *Saigon* and *Versailles*, the pattern is maintained. In the case of *Waco*, the toponym is repeated to achieve this pattern although, as will be seen later, the songwriter also had something else in mind here. The last line containing toponyms has *Armageddon* (4 syllables) and *Thermopylae* (also 4 syllables). The rhythm of the line, however, allows Laurika Rauch to accommodate the extra syllable with ease. This particular pattern also forced the songwriter to change his original text. After learning that the correct pronunciation of the village *Lidice* is with three syllables, Torr replaced it with *Auschwitz* (i.e. two syllables). In my opinion that was a gain, because at the level of alliteration, assonance, and rhyme, *Auschwitz* ties in well with the preceding *Austerlitz* and there is a further gain in that the particular line now has considerable cohesion and unity in that all three names (the other two being *Belsen* and *Buchenwald*) refer to German concentration camps during World War II.

As suggested earlier it is still valid to refer to songs as lyrical poetry. Songwriters therefore still employ techniques associated with poetry. This is clear in the rhyming pattern employed. Torr makes use of the simple rhyming couplet whereby the final syllable of every line would rhyme with the final syllable of the next line. What is noticeable though, is the creativity within this seemingly simple pattern in that no fewer than fifteen rhyming patterns are established over thirty-two lines, that is, only one pattern is repeated. This, of course, prevents monotony. It is also true that a singer, in spite of an apparent repetitive and potentially monotonous pattern (on paper), may vary the rhythm of any given line by lengthening or shortening specific syllables, or, as we have seen, by accommodating extra syllables.

Joel uses the same technique but he has more freedom than Torr has with *Hot Gates*: toponyms or place-names have a fixed form, nothing can be added or taken away. Particularly when Joel uses anthroponyms, he at times uses the first name and family name, or just the family name. That allows him to stick to his general rhythm and metrical unit. Occasionally he also adds other lyrical items like *England's got a new queen, Brooklyn's got a winning team, trouble in the Suez, children of thalidomide,* etc. There are a few more. This allows him to play around with the metrical unit and rhyming patterns. This is unlike Torr, who adheres to his seven syllable metrical unit structure.

As mentioned earlier, Joel's song has been described as 'a patter song characterised by its moderately fast tempo with rapid succession of rhythmic lyrics'. It appears to consist of a series of unrelated images in a rapid-fire, half-spoken, half-sung vocal style. This 'fast tempo' allows Joel to create lines varying between 11–14 syllables.

It is also clear that Torr employs alliteration and assonance with great effect. See, for example, the use of the alliterative /S/ in the second verse with Srebrenica, Sebokeng, Sarajevo, and Saigon, as well as the /B/ in the fourth verse with Bucharest, Belfast, Budapest, Bagdad, and Berchtesgaden. It is never overutilized but rather cleverly mixed in so that it does not become too obvious and hence predictable.

The repetition of *Waco* to *Waco Waco* allows Laurika to sing it to sound as *Awake awake, o Bethlehem*. This exceptional creativity provides an ambiguity in the interpretation which is poignantly emphasized by the use of the toponym *Bethlehem* that is also the birthplace of the true Messiah of the Christian faith born from the line of David. The contrast between the two places, *Waco* and *Bethlehem*, as representing the bases of the failed and the true messiah, is then taken further by the alternate reading suggesting that an appeal is made to the true Messiah and/or to His followers to step in and to avert such tragedies or at least to be aware of such false prophets.

Joel's choice of presenting events chronologically makes it a complicated task to effectively use literary qualities like rhyming (internal and end rhyme), alliteration, and assonance. Torr, not bound by chronology although obviously at times exploiting it, was not as bound as Joel. Joel, however, was fairly successful with his internal rhyme in one line, for example *Day/Ray, vaccine/queen, Peron/Dacron, Dean/team, Pasternak/Kerouac, Gaulle/ball*, etc.

21.7 ON THE MEANING OF NAMES

The remaining important question is: what do these names tell? What do they mean? The issue about the meaning of names has been and is still being debated by onomasticians and general linguists, notably semanticists. Raper (1987) summarizes many of the arguments and views in this regard. Some of the most important points of view are, *inter alia*, the following: a name is usually applied to an entity on the basis of some kind of motivation or association. It is probable that most or many of these names originally had lexical meaning, but usually the lexical meaning becomes irrelevant as time goes by and it may even disappear. Name and entity become one, and the referential function—the function of individualizing and distinguishing the entity—becomes primary. Onomasticians and semanticists then seem to agree that, from a purely synchronic point of view, names have reference since they denote identifiable entities in the natural or even imaginary world, but that they do not have lexical meaning or sense (see e.g. Lyons 1977: 219; Hurford and Heasley 1983: 35).

If this should be the final word on the meaning of toponyms in both songs, then they enumerate a great number of places that could be located and identified on a map of the world (with the exception of one imaginary one) and nothing more. Their life as songs would probably have been short lived, because they would essentially fail as works of art that should be conveying information to and communicating with a target audience. Both songs, however, appear to have been popular although Joel's song had a more mixed reception. There obviously has to be more to the meaning of place-names than merely the clinical referential function. How else would one account for the frequent use of place-names in the titles of so many songs, both old and new, not even mentioning the occurrence of place-names within songs? Here are a few titles with place-names from songs in the English language that are well known and popular:

From the Americas: *The old Kentucky home*
New York, New York
Blue Hawaii
Sending postcards from L.A.
California Blues
The girl from Ipanema
Don't cry for me Argentina
Streets of Philadelphia

From Europe and the UK: *Tulips from Amsterdam*
                                           Arrivederci Roma
                                           Galway Bay
                                           The flower of Scotland
                                           Mull of Kintyre

There are obviously many more. Songwriters from the earliest times undoubtedly realized that there is more semantic potential in toponyms besides the function of merely denoting geographical entities. The particular referential function is, of course, of primary importance. Nicolaisen (1974: 105) remarks that such names become convenient localizing devices. But toponyms go far beyond the localizing and referential function: they no doubt evoke specific images (see Ormeling 1993), and it is for this very reason that songwriters (and other creative artists, one might add) often employ toponyms as well as other names. According to Lyons (1977: 220) and Meiring (1993: 274), Strawson and Searle introduced the concept of 'descriptive backing' to account for this characteristic of evoking images. It appears as if this concept can be useful when denoting the type of content associated with names. Meiring (1993) puts it thus:

> This descriptive backing amounts to the collective content of all conventional beliefs and connotations attached to a name. It stands to reason that this descriptive backing also has a subjective content as it is based on individual experience and knowledge about a place, person or object bearing this name. (Meiring 1993: 274)

As the quotation implies, the 'descriptive backing' concept does not only apply to toponyms, but also to anthroponyms and the names of objects. The occurrence of anthroponyms in song titles, is also common. A few well-known ones in English are the following:

Mrs. Robinson
Nikita
Mona Lisa
Wake up little Suzie
Sylvia's mother
Adam's song
Hit the road Jack
Mack the Knife
Me and Bobby McGee

In these cases the 'descriptive backing' is provided in the verses of the song because these names are mostly fictional, unlike the names of persons appearing in Joel's song, who were or are real individuals. Most of them have died, but a few are still living (e.g. *Dylan*, *Bardot*, *Castro*, etc.).

The concept of descriptive backing appears to be synonymous with connotative meaning. According to the semanticist Geoffrey Leech, this type of meaning is open ended since it varies according to each individual's real life experiences (1981: 12–13; see also Meiring's 'subjective content'). Some onomasticians refer to this type of meaning as 'pragmatic' or 'associative' (see Raper 1987: 79, 81).

A name, therefore, having once been applied, gathers connotations that are based on the referent. Nicolaisen wrote an article many years ago (1978) called 'Are there connotative names?', perhaps suggesting that at that time this issue had not been clarified. He contrasts connotation with denotation as follows: connotation is an inclusive, comprehending, embracing process, whereas denotation is an exclusive, isolating, individualizing one (1978: 41; see also Nicolaisen 1976b: 143). He concludes that names can indeed function connotatively and need not have lexical meaning to do so (Nicolaisen 1978: 47).

Louwrens (1994) summarizes the foregoing discussion on the meaning of toponyms (which may also apply to other types of names) as follows:

> What is intended when reference is made to the meaning of such names (= place-names) in a synchronic description, is all the abstract mental concepts which are conjured up by such names in the minds of language users due to different connotations, perceptions, and associations which are attached to these places. (Louwrens 1994: 12)

21.8 Connotative Names in the Two Songs

As mentioned earlier, both songs teem with names, with hardly any other lyrics that might have helped with the interpretation of these names. The 'descriptive backing' concept therefore comes strongly into play as suggested above. This applies to all the name types featuring in both the songs like toponyms, anthroponyms, and even brand names. The huge total makes it impossible to comment on the possible descriptive backing for each name. A selection will be dealt with in this section. It should also be remembered that the connotation or descriptive backing may vary from individual to individual, depending on their exposure or even memory.

Joel's song, from a comparative angle, is also characterized by a fairly strong presence of toponyms or place-names, and most of them refer to places where important events took place that had a profound influence on events at the time. Toponyms like *Red China, North Korea, South Korea, Panmunjom, Dien Bien Phu Falls, Budapest, Suez, Little Rock, Belgians in the Congo, Bay of Pigs, Russians in Afghanistan*, all refer to problematic circumstances or events in those places. Some of them had a more direct effect on the USA, while others were more distant and responsible for worldwide concerns. *Little Rock* and *Bay of Pigs*, for example, would only be considered as geographical entities without the applicable descriptive backing.

Little Rock is the capital of Arkansas in the USA. A decision in 1954 was taken that all laws establishing segregated schools will be unconstitutional, calling on all schools throughout the nation to be desegregated. Little Rock made the headlines when the Arkansas governor joined local whites in resisting integration in the Central High School by dispatching the National Guard to block nine black students from entering the school. They became known as the Little Rock Nine. Eight of the nine students eventually finished the school year although it caused them unspeakable pain, but it was a huge step towards integration in the schooling system. They started attending after the intervention of President Eisenhower.

The *Bay of Pigs* invasion was an unsuccessful military invasion of Cuba undertaken by the paramilitary group Brigade 2506 of the USA on 17 April 1961. The Brigade intended to overthrow the revolutionary leftist government of Fidel Castro. John F. Kennedy gave his consent, and after the main invasion had landed at the *Bay of Pigs*, they finally, however, had to surrender with the majority of troops being publicly interrogated and then sent back to the USA.

Descriptive backing is equally applicable in the case of anthroponyms. Many of these like *Doris Day, Johnny Ray, Joe DiMaggio, Marilyn Monroe, Brando, Marciano, Liberace, James Dean, Elvis Presley, Bardot, Mickey Mantle, Buddy Holly*, and many more became icons in the entertainment and sporting worlds. Americans, even today, still have strong feelings about these individuals, and the connotations may be more positive in some cases but negative in others, like the *Rosenbergs, Stalin, Cohn, Krushchev, Castro, Eichmann*, etc. It is entirely left to the listener to make his or her own judgements or interpretations on the listed items. This interpretation may also differ from Joel's, which is probably 'based on individual experience and knowledge' as suggested by Meiring above. Any other American born at the same time may have opted for different choices. Joel probably had decided ideas (associations, perceptions) about every onomastic item he used, and nobody else will necessarily share those, although it is extremely likely that there will be agreement on many.

It is, at the same time, interesting to carefully observe Joel's choices. Many of the people and events are reasonably well known across the world, but some are intrinsically linked to the USA. It should be reasonably clear that all the people, places, events, products, etc. that feature in the song must have played quite a significant role in American society at the time when they are mentioned, and from a historical perspective impressed Joel enough to include them.

Not unexpectedly toponyms with a South African connection feature strongly in *Hot Gates*. In the fifth verse two South African hotspots are linked up in one line. The *Sharpeville* incident echoed through this country and the world. The township near Vereeniging was the scene of a riot in March 1960, during which a crowd of African demonstrators were fired on by the police and over sixty were killed (*Webster's Family Dictionary* 1992), In more recent times, that is 1992, *Boipatong* which incidentally means 'the place where people hide themselves', was another township rocked by a senseless massacre of many innocent victims at the hands of a number of faceless killers who indiscriminately fired in the dark.

The two South African hotspots are neatly juxtaposed by *My Lai*, a village in Southern Vietnam where a massacre of about 347 civilians by US soldiers took place on 16 March 1968 during the Vietnam War. After the incident had been disclosed by an ex-serviceman in 1969, the investigation resulted in the court martial of several soldiers. Only one, Lt. William Calley, was convicted, but his conviction was eventually overturned (*Webster's Family Dictionary* 1992). The occurrence of these three place-names in one line emphasizes the plight of innocent civilians massacred by forces against which they had no defence. It has been argued that the toponyms all represent 'hotspots' where those events, which in some way changed the course of history or gave rise to controversy, took place (Neethling 1995: 60).

Interestingly enough, Joel also included an event that took place in Vietnam although it did not involve the USA. After World War II France took over its colonial government in Vietnam, then known as Indochina. A Vietnamese independence movement fought the French troops for control of northern Vietnam. The French commanders chose *Dien Bien Phu Falls* as the place to fight the Vietnamese insurgents, but Dien Bien Phu finally fell to the Vietnamese in 1954 which shocked France and brought an end to French Indochina.

In some lines the songwriter of *Hot Gates* has achieved exceptional unity and cohesion, as has already been illustrated. A few other examples from both songs will now be discussed. It will obviously take up too much space should every toponym and its connotations be discussed.

In the second verse of *Hot Gates* the place-name *Waco* is repeated. *Waco* in Texas was the scene of the massacre of children with their parents by the newly acclaimed Messiah of the Order of David, David Koresh. *Newsweek* reported on the events as follows:

> In the end, the anguish was mainly for the children. Altogether, at least 20 of them apparently perished with their parents. Seven had been sired by Koresh, the failed messiah. They were to be the firstborn of a new Davidic line, heirs of his polygamous kingdom. An additional 21 children left the compound during the 51-day siege; most are now orphans. (Anonymous 1993)

The following names from the Second World War—*Dunkirk, Dover, Normandy*—speak for themselves. *Dunkirk*, meaning 'church in the dunes', is so named because it probably developed around a church built in the Dunes of St Eloi in the seventh century. During World War II in 1940 it was the scene of the heroic evacuation of over 300,000 Allied troops hemmed in by German forces. The harbour was completely destroyed during the war, to be partially reopened in 1946. *Dover*, so named after the small river Dour which pierces the famous chalk cliffs here, suffered severely during the war from air raids and long-range bombardments. *Normandy*, so named after the Northmen or Normans that frequently attacked it, was united to England but finally restored to France. During the war in 1944 *Normandy* became a battlefield again when Allied forces landed on its north coast and initiated the campaign leading to the liberation of France, although many of its villages and towns were devastated in the fighting.

In the next line Torr links up *Frankfurt, New York,* and *Lockerbie.* The *Lockerbie* disaster is described by Matthews (1993) as follows:

> The Lockerbie bomb was one of the most bloody and effective acts of terrorism in the history of the 20th Century. At 7:19 pm on 22 December [1988] the citizens of *Lockerbie,* a small town in western Scotland, were horrified to see a massive ball of flame plunging from the sky towards their town. The blazing mass plunged into a suburban street, erupting into an explosion which sent flames 300 feet high before bouncing on into open countryside. As the horrified emergency services raced to the scene it was confirmed the object had been a jetliner. The crash had destroyed 40 houses and gouged a crater 150 feet long and 50 deep. There were no survivors either from the aircraft or the houses. A total of 270 people had died. The aircraft was found to be Pan Am flight 103 bound from *Frankfurt* to *New York,* carrying Americans home for Christmas. (Matthews 1993: 520; emphasis added)

Frankfurt, as the departing point of the ill-fated flight, and *New York,* as the never-to-be-reached destination, are drawn into the horror of the explosion over *Lockerbie.*

The line featuring *Chappaquiddick* and *Waterloo* is significant in that the water image draws together the two seemingly unrelated places and events that occurred there. Did the ambitious Ted Kennedy meet with his political *Waterloo* when he crashed his car off a bridge at *Chappaquiddick* in Massachusetts on 19 July 1969, resulting in the death, by drowning, of his companion Mary Jo Kopechne? (Matthews 1993: 389). That *Chappaquiddick* is still reverberating around the world, albeit in a different context, is nowhere better illustrated than in a newsletter called *Fast Facts* from the South African Institute for Race Relations. Published in 1995, sixteen years after the *Chappaquiddick* incident, Paul Pereira in an article called 'The ANC's Chappaquiddick?' reviews the fatal events of 28 March 1994 when a march by Zulus to the Johannesburg city centre turned into a tragedy when guards at the ANC (African National Congress) headquarters, Shell House, opened fire on the marchers killing a number of Zulus (Anonymous 1995b). This quite clearly demonstrates the connotation a place-name can acquire, even across an ocean. Will the Shell House incident have the same effect on the ANC in years to come?

After the first two verses, some variation from the toponymic content is brought in through the haunting chorus suggesting the destruction, turmoil, and human suffering evoked by merely mentioning these place-names.

The song *Hot Gates* serves as a grim reminder of events best forgotten although the corrective in the last chorus provides a glimmer of hope, in spite of *Armageddon* which is still to follow. The song is an excellent example of the strong connotations linked to toponyms, exploited by a creative songwriter. The 'descriptive backing' connected with each toponym speaks louder than words. If we return to the question raised earlier regarding the meaning of toponyms, one may argue that if ever a single individual has proved that toponyms have meaning far beyond the mere referential meaning, that is, that of denoting a geographical entity, then Christopher Torr has done just that through *Hot Gates*.

Billy Joel in *We Didn't Start The Fire* uses fewer toponyms than Torr but the principle of descriptive backing is also at work here. Although his toponyms are also suggestive of negative events, the style of the 'patter song' as well as the use of other names—anthroponyms and other types alongside the toponyms—seems to take away the gravity of those negative events. Through the emphasis on toponyms in *Hot Gates* as well as the more solemn style of the music, sung by a sole artist (Laurika Rauch) with simple musical arrangement, the song is probably more successful than *We Didn't Start The Fire*, particularly regarding toponyms.

One should, however, not forget that Joel had a somewhat different intention with his song. All events or persons that made an impression on him, good or bad, found a place in his song. That is, of course, acceptable. The title of the song and the refrain, however, are then not so appropriate.

21.9 CONCLUSION

The lyrics of songs are recognized as poetry, and hence a study of names within a song or musical context could be considered as part of literary onomastics. This applies to both songs: despite the dominance of names, poetic qualities such as internal and end rhyme, alliteration, and rhythm do occur. It is, however, also evident that far fewer poetic qualities are used simply because the overwhelming number of names prevent that.

Concerning the comparative angle regarding the two songs, it should be reasonably clear that they share many aspects, but also differ. One may also argue that the economy of expression suggested by only names in a song might be indicative of a songwriter who relies heavily on the 'descriptive backing' every name has, preferring not to expand the lyrical description. Everett (2000) suggests that Joel might have sensed that through these names he was conveying knowledge to the masses via the media. Both songs essentially deal with names, and it should be clear that a name by itself, whether the name of a person, place, product, or event, sets in motion a chain of connotations which are determined by the perceptions of people about these names. These perceptions or connotations may differ in many ways: in their quantitative as well as qualitative nature. They may be skewed, distorted, accurate, or even totally inappropriate. The connotations any individual would have regarding any personal 'entry' in a song referring to actors, sportsmen, singers, authors, etc. would be determined by his or her exposure to the person personally through attending an actual performance, exposure in the media, or perhaps through reading or research.

The important issue is that the names trigger these perceptions. The evocative potential contained in names is well illustrated in the lyrics of songs. If one deals with fictional names, as is often the case, such connotations are only generated by the lyrics of the song, and not beyond that. If, however, a name in a song is based on a person who actually lived or is still living, then the connotations go beyond the actual song. Both songwriters exploited that. Billy Joel realized that that would be the case with his choices, and they were all based on reality: on actual people, places, products, works produced by actual people, etc., whereas Torr simply focused on toponyms, that is existing places (with the exception of one).

The composition and singing styles of the two songs differ quite dramatically. Although this is not the main aim with the comparative purpose, it is worth mentioning. Joel's song is described as 'a patter song' with a fast rhythm. The fact that he included so many onomastic categories in his song probably contributed to that. That also applies to the refrain, in spite of the 'fire' (= trouble) metaphor. Torr's song is very different: it is sung by only one dramatic voice, that of Laurika Rauch, and composed in an equally solemn style that emphasizes all the 'hotspots' the toponyms refer to. It is only in the last refrain that a hopeful desire about the 'New Jerusalem' adds a more positive note to Torr's song. Torr's current standing in the world of music in South Africa is neatly summarized by a columnist as a phenomenal songwriter who draws on inspiration from mythology and classic tales of death, suffering, and deliverance, but who manages to express himself afresh and in a modern idiom. He captures emotions in his lyrics by using few words and striking images and creates timeless melodies (Anonymous 1995a). The phonological and semantic relationship between the songwriter's surname Torr and the German 'das Tor' (= a gate) is probably a mere coincidence but nevertheless interesting when reflecting on *Hot Gates*.

From a reception and impact point of view, *Hot Gates* probably is and was more successful than *We Didn't Start The Fire*. The particular style contributed to that.

It is not surprising that thousands of songwriters have exploited the potential of using names in songs over many years, and will continue to do so in the future. They focus mostly on fictional names, or perhaps on the name of one person or place that actually existed or still exists. The type of song that Billy Joel and Christopher Torr produced is unusual. Both those songwriters are aware of the strong connotations names may evoke, and have exploited it well through the huge number of names they have used.

21.10 ENDNOTE

Websites were mostly consulted regarding Billy Joel and his song. A number of videos of the song are also available on some of the websites. A very interesting one, available from <http://yeli.us?Flash/Fire.html>, does not only provide the lyrics, but every onomastic item is accompanied by a visual image reflecting the specific item. It was seemingly compiled by a Joel enthusiast. A video of Laurika Rauch's performance of *Hot Gates* has also been produced but is not available freely.

21.11 APPENDIX A: *WE DIDN'T START THE FIRE*

Harry Truman, Doris Day, Red China, Johnnie Ray
South Pacific, Walter Winchell, Joe DiMaggio [1949]

Joe McCarthy, Richard Nixon, Studebaker, television
North Korea, South Korea, Marilyn Monroe [1950]

Rosenbergs, H-bomb, Sugar Ray, Panmunjon
Brando, The King and I, and The Catcher in the Rye [1951]

Eisenhower, vaccine, England's got a new queen
Marciano, Liberace, Santayana goodbye [1952]

Chorus
We didn't start the fire
It was always burning
Since the world's been turning
We didn't start the fire
No we didn't light it
But we tried to fight it

Joseph Stalin, Malenkov, Nasser and Prokofiev
Rockefeller, Campanella, Communist Bloc [1953]

Roy Cohn, Juan Peron, Toscanini, Dacron
Dien Bien Phu Falls, Rock Around the Clock [1954]

Einstein, James Dean, Brooklyn's got a winning team
Davy Crockett, Peter Pan, Elvis Presley, Disneyland [1955]

Bardot, Budapest, Alabama, Krushchev
Princess Grace, Peyton Place, trouble in the Suez [1956]

Chorus (as above)

Little Rock, Pasternak, Mickey Mantle, Kerouac
Sputnik, Chou En-Lai, Bridge on the River Kwai [1957]

Lebanon, Charles de Gaulle, California baseball
Starkweather homicide, children of thalidomide [1958]

Buddy Holly, Ben Hur, space monkey, Mafia
Hula hoops, Castro, Edsel is a no-go [1959]

U-2, Syngman Rhee, payola and Kennedy
Chubby Checker, Psycho, Belgians in the Congo [1960]

Chorus (as above)

Hemingway, Eichmann, Stranger in a Strange Land
Dylan, Berlin, Bay of Pigs invasion [1961]

Lawrence of Arabia, British Beatlemania
Ole Miss, John Glenn, Liston beats Patterson [1962]

Pope Paul, Malcolm X, British politician sex
JFK, blown away, what else do I have to say [1963]

Chorus (as above)

Birth control, Ho Chi Minh, Richard Nixon back again [1965–68]
Moonshot, Woodstock, Watergate, punk rock [1969–74]

Begin, Reagan, Palestine, terror on the airline [1976–77]
Ayatollah's in Iran, Russians in Afghanistan [1979]

Wheel of Fortune, Sally Ride, heavy metal, suicide
Foreign debts, homeless vets, AIDS, crack, Bernie Goetz [1983–84]

Hypodermics on the shores, China's under martial law
Rock and Roller cola wars, I can't take it anymore [1988–89]

Chorus

We didn't start the fire
But when we are gone
Will it still burn on, and on, and on, and on . . .

We Didn't Start The Fire
Words and Music by Billy Joel
Copyright © 1989 JOELSONGS
All Rights Administered by ALMO MUSIC CORP
All Rights Reserved. Used by Permission.
Reprinted by Permission of Hal Leonard Corporation

21.12 APPENDIX B: *HOT GATES*

London Paris Rome Berlin
Barcelona Washington
Moscow Beijing Tokyo
Jerusalem Jericho

Waco Waco Bethlehem
Srebrenica Sebokeng
Sarajevo O Saigon
Hiroshima Rubicon

Chorus
I can see a fiery, fiery glow
Even as the sun is sinking low

I can see a horseman on the run
O my daughter, O my son

Dunkirk Dover Normandy
Frankfurt New York Lockerbie
Amajuba Bellevue
Chappaquiddick Waterloo

Bucharest St Petersburg
Heilbron Hobhouse Gettysburg
Belfast Budapest Bagdad
Berchtesgaden Stalingrad

Chorus (as above)

Carthage Dresden Babylon
Sharpeville My Lai Boipatong
Delville Wood El Alamein
St Helena Mitchell's Plain

Balaklava Austerlitz
Belsen Buchenwald Auschwitz
Nagasaki O Versailles
Armageddon Thermopylae

Chorus (as above)
There's another song that will be sung
There's another bell that must be rung
There's another city I've been told
Where the streets are paved with gold

Hot Gates
Copyright © Chris Torr Music
Reproduced by permission

CHAPTER 22

....

GENRE-BASED APPROACHES TO NAMES IN LITERATURE

....

BIRGIT FALCK-KJÄLLQUIST

22.1 INTRODUCTION

....

A fruitful approach to names in literature is to study proper names and their usage in different literary genres and subgenres.

In order to study the names of a literary genre with the aim of mapping the onymic landscape and identifying similarities or differences between different genres, an analysis of proper names in single works by individual authors could—and in fact should—be regarded as a necessity. One approach is to study the functions and typology of names in the works chosen for investigation. In the non-fictional world as in the world of fiction, names primarily function as identifiers. In fiction, names can, however, be created by an author to function as tools for characterizing different entities such as persons, places, landscapes, or artefacts, and thus create the onymic landscape of the work.[1]

Description of the onymic landscape of a literary genre, together with strategies of authorial naming, typology, and so on, in order to faciliate comparison between different characteristics, implies analyses of a fairly large number of names—a difficult and time-consuming task. A digital-statistical approach might make this easier (see further chapter 23).

This chapter will present a selection of investigations focusing on groups of texts related by the genres of prose, drama, cinema films, poetry, and parodies.

---

[1] Debus (1989: 10) observes that regarding names in literature, the author of the literary work is the creator of the names used in his fictional world as well as the name-giver. Debus also emphasizes the fact that the main function of names in the fictional world as well as in the ordinary world is identification. For fictional names, however, the particular function that the author choses to give the names denoting the name-bearers within the fictional world is equally important.

22.2 PROSE

Of the numerous different prose genres only a few have received attention from literary onomasticians. The categories discussed here are thus not to be regarded as representative of all possible prose genres.

As a first step in the analyses of novels that are sometimes seen as part of the genre of regional novels could be regarded Benedicta Windt-Val's 2009 PhD thesis '*Men han het Edvard . . .'. Navn og navnebruk i Sigrid Undsets forfatterskap*.[2] Windt-Val here presents an analysis of personal names used by the Norwegian author Sigrid Undset.

22.2.1 The English Novel of the Nineteenth Century

One of the onomastic scholars who has been working with a genre-based approach to the onymic landscape of the English novel of the nineteenth century is Wilhelm Nicolaisen. A comprehensive survey of his work in this field is Nicolaisen (1995b). Here he presents aspects of the ways in which different authors use the place-names of their fictional worlds to, on the one hand, bind them together against the non-literary world and, on the other, supply plausible links with it. The fictional reality of the two counties described, Thomas Hardy's Wessex (Nicolaisen 1987) and Anthony Trollope's Barsetshire (Nicolaisen 1976a), does not seem to be in doubt. Nicolaisen further exemplifies the importance of the toponymy of literary landscapes, especially in the English regional novel, in his studies on the onymic landscapes of George Eliot's *Middlemarch* and of Anne Bronte's *Agnes Grey*. As Nicolaisen (1995b: 563) observes, 'In both novels, as is true of many others, there are no place-names which do not have something to do with, or are not lingering symbols of, actions, experiences and incidents somehow involving one or more of the characters'. According to this, all place-names within these works are (directly or indirectly) relevant, and sometimes symbolize social and personal relationships. An example is the journey from Tipton to Lowick. In this case, social differences are underlined by the etymological contrast between the two names *Tip-ton* in contrast to *Low-ick*. Another interesting name-pair mentioned by Nicolaisen (1995b: 363) is *Middlemarch–Brassing*, where *Brassing* is considered as a toponymic metaphor, 'the notion of "non-Middlemarch"'. Also discussed is Anne Bronte's *Agnes Grey*. In his analysis of this novel, with its few full place-names, its acronyms as place-names in disguise and its anonyms (a dash instead of a name), Nicolaisen finds that the place nomenclature of the novel helps to structure a secretive world rather than a secret one. Nicolaisen (1995b: 564) suggests that a fuller review would among other things 'reveal the toponymy of the literary landscape, as we find it in nineteenth-century English regional novels, to be a place-nomenclature which records and locates, which responds

---

[2] '"But his Name was Edward . . .". Names and Name Usage in the Works of Sigrid Undset'.

to the environment in traditional human fashion, making habitation out of wilderness through human experience'. He is also of the opinion that the literary landscape in the novels investigated is never mere background symbolism or intended to create a certain atmosphere, but relates to the plot, theme, and characters.

22.2.2 Contemporary Detective Fiction

Also of interest is a study by Gerhard Eis (1970) on names in contemporary detective fiction, first published in 1965 in the periodical *Neophilologus*. Its opening lines are as follows: 'Die Namen sind ein Mittel zur Kennzeichnung von Personen, Orten, Tieren usw. und zur Erzeugung von Stimmung, das von den Schriftstellern meistens mit vollem Bedacht angewendet wird.'[3] Eis, however, emphasizes the importance of bearing in mind that the popularity of names changes according to time and place. This might be considered as especially characteristic of personal names and the names of animals (zoonyms). His corpus consists of a comparatively broad collection of names from about 300 detective stories by German, British, American, French, and Swedish authors. The texts are all in German, which means that a large part of the corpus consists of names from translated publications. The novels are all published in the following pocket book series: Goldmanns Taschen-Krimi, Heyne-Bücher, Mitternachtbücher, RowohltTaschenbücher, Ullstein Bücher (Eis 1970: 61). Eis is of the opinion that in his corpus the authors usually make it clear what kind of person the name-bearer is, as well as whether the name should be regarded as having a pleasant or unpleasant ring, whether comical, droll, attractive, or beautiful, whether regarded as elegant or with a touch of upper or lower social standing. The use of initials for naming certain characters is mentioned but not further developed. Eis (1970: 66–7) also exemplifies that in some cases the author indicates that the personal name of a character has or might have a direct influence on what sort of person she/he is or has become. It seems to be not uncommon to name a character after a well-known (historical) person or after a character from another literary work. Aliases and pseudonyms are analysed and explained. As Eis shows, these are not uncommon in this kind of corpus. He points out that in his corpus, pseudonyms of artists are quite as usual as aliases for criminals, compare the British author Guy Cullingford in the German translation of *Der Zauberer von Soho* (1970: 31) 'Die Künstler, sie haben immer zwei Namen—wie Verbrecher, he?'[4]

Furthermore, it seems from Eis's corpus that different nationalities are differently emotionally charged. In this context, this means that by combining the names of the characters with their parts in the story and the importance thereof, Eis can form an impression of the social standing of a certain name in a certain social environment. Several examples of this are mentioned, for instance from one of the novels by the

---

[3] 'Names are instruments by which to characterize persons, places, animals etc. and to create an atmosphere and are mostly used after careful consideration by the authors.'

[4] 'Artists have two names—like criminals, eh?'

American author Hillary Waugh, where it seems that doctors, judges, magistrates, and so on all have what are considered Anglo-American names, as do most of the policemen. Nevertheless, some of the policemen have German names. The criminals, however, mostly have names from what are considered the German, Romance, and Slavonic or German-Slavonic language areas.

Other questions are how and under what circumstances a character's surname is used, when it is used in combination with the forename, when it is dropped and when a character is mentioned only by the surname.

As to place-names, Eis does not seem to take the same interest in them as in personal names. He focuses mainly on the fact that place-names (with their underlying meaning: as well as personal names) can be beautiful, attractive, and alluring or repellant and unattractive. However, his opinion seems to be that place-names in detective stories are mostly used by authors to give the readers a sense of familiarity with the country, the neighbourhood or the place for the setting. In his opinion, the meaning as well as the sound of a place-name can facilitate a range of interpretations, and different authors exploit this in various ways. As an example of a place-name radiating strong charisma, he mentions *Samarkand* with an example from the Swedish author Stieg Trenter (Eis 1970: 89–90). However, the name *Samarkand* is almost certainly here used with a dual function and meaning (not mentioned by Eis), namely: (a) as the name of a faraway romantic place radiating strong charisma; (b) as the name of a faraway place (and therefore a convenient address for things not to be found).

Names—nicknames—designating entities like cars, an armchair, or a typewriter are mentioned but do not seem to be very frequent in Eis's corpus, with the exception of cars which are mentioned by their nicknames in several of the works investigated. It might be of some interest to note that nicknames designating other objects have been found only in the works of two authors in this corpus: Spencer Dean, in whose works nicknames for precious furs and coats were found; and Stieg Trenter, who in one of his books uses a nickname for an armchair and, in another, one for a typewriter. Eis notes especially that no names designating weapons have been found in his corpus—interesting when considering that names for, for instance, swords are not infrequent in older literature.

Eis's investigation is one of the studies which aims to treat names within a group of texts related by genre. It points forward to what could be achieved with computerized assistance to investigate a still larger corpus of related texts within a particular genre.

An illustration of how far it is possible to go in a specialized analysis of an onymic landscape created by one specific author of detective fiction is provided by the important comprehensive investigation by Ines Sobanski (2000), as well as her shorter presentation of the same work at the 19th ICOS congress in Aberdeen 1996 (Sobanski 1998), on the onymic landscape in detective stories by the well-known British author Gilbert Keith Chesterton, with the priest Father Brown as investigating detective.

The work by Eis discussed here illustrates the advantages as well as the difficulties of presenting an overview of the onymic landscape of a particular genre. It would seem to be almost impossible for a single person to carry out a comprehensive investigation of such an onymic landscape. That must be considered as work for a team of researchers, as Eis notes at the beginning of his very interesting study. Sobanski's work might be said to illustrate this, as well as the advantages of a single researcher concentrating on the output of one author only.

It is, however, interesting to note that Eis and Sobanski have some things in common as to the method of their investigations. As Sobanski (1998) puts it:

> a literary name enters formal and thematic relations with other elements of the story. Therefore, an onomastic study will hardly gain any validity unless it considers the textual environments of a name, which includes other onymic as well as non-onymic elements in the text. (Sobanski 1998: 374)

Eis and Sobanski both use what Sobanski calls 'non-onymic context' in order to show that 'lexical name constituents and their synonyms are taken up in the context to describe characteristics of the person named. In doing so, they serve to confirm semantic associations that the name evokes' (Sobanski 1998: 374). Compare Eis (1970: 64–5), who illustrates his opinion about -en as a social marker of surnames which end in -en: 'Erika Halden (die elegante Kundin)'.[5] Compare also the point made above about Eis combining the names of the characters with their standing in the story and the importance of this for giving his impression of the social standing of a certain name in a certain social environment.

22.2.3 Derivative Literature (Fan Fiction)

Another interesting genre of prose fiction is derivative literature. The term was created by Wilhelm Nicolaisen for a piece of fiction based on—that is derived from—an original work of literature without which it would not exist (Nicolaisen 1987: 50, 1995b: 564–5). It is not easy to find investigations into this very specialized field. Nevertheless Nicolaisen has given his attention to onymic landscapes of this genre in a few short, interesting publications (for references, see Nicolaisen 1995b: 567). Nicolaisen points to the fact that writing derivative literature, such as *Return to Wuthering Heights* by Anna L'Estrange, 'has in recent years become so fashionable that one might almost call it an "industry"'(1995b: 564). As Nicolaisen (1987 [1975]: 51) puts it, 'it seems a fascinating task to search for the ways in which, in addition to other literary means, the evocative bonding of the intertextuality of names has been utilized in order to make derivation a legitimate creative act with plausible results'. One interesting approach for an onomastic research into this genre might be to compare the name system of a later work of fiction with its earlier progenitor. It is, however, not enough to re-use names; they have to be vital parts of the new as well as of the old work.

---

[5] 'Erika Halden (the elegant customer)'.

22.2.4 Comics

Names in comics have been studied by Burelbach (1987 [1978], 1995). His corpus seems to consist of American comics only, which means that, for instance, the Belgian writer Hergé with his Tintin-comics is not represented. Burelbach distinguishes between two major categories of comics: the satiric and the heroic. As examples of the satiric, he mentions comic strips and books such as the *Katzenjammer Kids* and *Donald Duck*, and of the heroic he mentions 'a range from *Smilin' Jack* to *Superman*' (1995: 582). He points to the fact that the American comics of today are written for youthful, relatively naive readers as well as for much more sophisticated ones. Because of this and also because the medium, which consists of brief texts composed of pictures and words, requires that meanings are easily understood, the comics are not particularly subtle either in plot or as to characters. He also stresses that the names of the characters 'obviously evoke easy responses and reveal cultural stereotypes'.

Burelbach limits himself to a study of personal names. In some cases a more or less professional title with a fictitious characterizing purpose functions as part of the name. See further below.

One group of comics, according to Burelbach those of the Disney type, blends beast fable with *commedia dell'arte* to evoke laughter at the misadventures of quasi-human animals. Characters in this group bear 'funny' names created with the help of humorous alliteration, ethnic humour or allusion with a tendency to be ridiculous. Examples of ethnic humour thought demeaning to Europeans are for example *Mickey Mouse* (thought to be anti-Irish), and *Hans* and *Fritz Katzenjammer* (anti-German), etc. Obvious puns occur in for example *Casper Milquetoast, Dagwood Bumstead*, etc. (Burelbach 1995).

Other examples of groups of comics are comics of horror, military action, romantic love, medical melodrama, and super-heroes. In the super-hero comics the problems presented are mostly solved by a super-hero of some kind who is usually equipped with a double identity, one representing a mild-mannered, very ordinary sort of person and the other a super-hero type engaging in all sorts of heroic activities. Each identity is provided with a fitting characterizing name, for example *Peter Parker—Spider-Man, Clark Kent—Superman*. The personal names of the 'ordinary' identity are not analysed by Burelbach, who concentrates on the names of the super-hero identity, the largest group of which is created by inspiration from classical mythology or from the occult. Examples mentioned are *Balder, Goliath, Hercules, Medusa, Odin, Thor*, and *Valkyrie; Ghost Rider, Phantom Girl*, and *Scarlet Witch*. Despite the associations that could be evoked by names like *Medusa* or *Scarlet Witch*, all those characters battle against ultimate evil and chaos—an interesting and provoking thought. The next largest group of characters bear names that emphasize the elemental dichotomy between good and evil, light and dark that is the basis of comic book morality. Names like *Fire Lad, Human Torch, Lightning Lad*, and *Green Lantern* are thought to be associated with light and with the name-bearer's wish and ability to 'light up the world', as Burelbach (1995: 583) puts it. Names like *Aqua Man, Sub-Mariner, Atom, Cosmic Boy, Storm*, and *Ice Man* are supposed to show 'that the very forces of nature are opposed to evil'.

Several of the acting heroes have names containing animal designations like *Batman* (*bat*), *Black Canary* (*canary*), *Black Condor* (*condor*), *Black Panther* (*panther*), *Hellcat* (*cat*), etc.—an interesting fact that might have been more closely analysed from several angles. A small group of names are inspired by designations for several kinds of weapons, for example *Green Arrow* and *Human Bomb*. Another group of heroes bear names containing military titles, heroes such as *Captain America, Captain Marvel*, and *Captain Comet* as well as villains like *Captain Cold* and *Captain Boomerang*. As Burelbach indicates, the military touch is surely due to the fact that a conflict between bad and good is going on in this kind of literature, and that this conflict is imaged in physical battles.

As mentioned above, a title is sometimes included as part of a personal name. Those mentioned in the previous paragraph belong to that group together with three names containing *doctor* + personal name, *Dr Druid, Dr Strange*, and *Dr Fate*. It is an interesting fact that the bearers of those names are all enchanters with occult powers. The explanation offered by Burelbach (1995: 584) for the use of 'Doctor' in these names is that 'the activities of physicians and other scientists must appear decidedly magical to the childlike mind of the reading audience'. However a more adequate explanation might be the use of *doctor* in the meaning 'a medicine man in a primitive culture; any practitioner (e.g. shaman or rainman) of mysterious or magical arts in such a culture' (Webster 1993: 666). Finally, Burelbach points to the fact that name change in the comic universe sometimes reflects certain changes of values in the world outside the world of comics.

Another interesting reflection is that the names of the so-called heroes (mostly extra-terrestrial ones) in this corpus, that is in the American world of comics, are almost all Anglo-Saxon. The names are also short and with trochaic or spondaic rhythms. Burelbach remarks that names of continental European, Arab, and Asian origin 'are notable for their absence'.

An interesting and also intricate reflection by Burelbach is whether—and if so, to what extent—the names of the characters in the world of literature, in this case in the world of comics, evoke positive reactions in the minds of the readers and a wish to resemble the heroes named.

22.2.5 Fantasy Literature

Names in fantasy literature have been the subject of several studies. It seems, however, that investigating the onymic landscape of fantasy literature is at the beginning of a very demanding phase and that interesting studies are underway. The names created by J. R. R. Tolkien have caught the interest of several scholars. In a recently published article, Christopher L. Robinson (2013) discusses the names in some of Tolkien's best-known writings, their genesis and structure as well as their functions. Robinson observes that, according to Tolkien, most of the names in his books are derived from stems and words in a language invented by Tolkien himself. However, referring to a study by T. A. Shippey (1979) Robinson also points to the fact that linguistic material from other sources, such as Old English and Old Norse, is not infrequent in Tolkien's names.

An earlier article by Robinson (2012) is a short study on names in the work of Lord Dunsany, with the inspiring title *The Stuff of Which Names are Made. A Look at the Colorful and Eclectic Namecraft of Lord Dunsany*. Lord Dunsany is a very prolific writer and the names in his works are supposed to contribute much to the special character of his work. However, as Robinson puts it: 'his namecraft is daunting from a critical point of view, due to the sheer quantity of his inventions, together with the heterogeneity of his materials and methods of construction' (2012: 27–8). It would seem that a thorough onomastic study of the names in Lord Dunsay's abundant output would be a demanding undertaking.

In short, fantasy literature is a new, vivid, and interesting branch of the field. As John Algeo (2001: 252) puts it in a short article, 'Fantasy writers are name-givers with no restrictions other than those they choose to observe to make the whole work coherent'. In a way this is probably true of every writer of fiction. Still, it is an interesting idea worth closer study. It seems that investigating the onymic landscape of fantasy literature is at the beginning of an interesting and demanding phase. For this field we are also still waiting for a comprehensive overview.

22.3 DRAMA

Investigations on names in the genre of drama are mostly concerned with personal names rather than the whole onymic landscape. An example of a comprehensive study on the function of personal names in English, American, and German dramas is the work of Henning Thies (1978). In his study Thies does not, however, limit himself to English, American, and German drama but also takes into account Jean Genet (France; *Les Bonnes*), Henrik Ibsen (Norway; *Hedda Gabler*), August Strindberg (Sweden; *Spöksonaten, Till Damaskus*), and classical drama such as *Medea* (Seneca). After a discussion of the theoretical aspects of his subject and of the possibilities that analysis of names in their context opens up, he proceeds to a comprehensive study of the functions of personal names in dramatic texts paying special attention to the context of a dramatic performance. As is pointed out, this 'involves aspects of the socio-cultural background of an author and his audience as well as the different technical conditions of theatre performances' (Thies 1978: 354; cf. Smith 2009, discussed below). Thies exemplifies this by pointing out that 'when a name is uttered on stage in the context of a theatre performance, aspects of sound quality and intonation play a more prominent role for the audience reception of character names than for an individual reading process' (Thies 1978: 354). The time is simply lacking for a spectator to concentrate on a single name because he or she has to follow what is happening on the stage. For this reason, naming in dramatic literature has to be more explicit and obvious than in other genres. According to Thies (1978: 355) this is why the so called 'redende Namen' ('telltale names'), are so common in the comedies and farces of all epoches and nations.

Another function, put forward indeed as the major function of a literary name, is not—as in the non-fictional world—identification, but characterization. This means that the so-called telltale names are not only a means of identification but a definition of the name-bearer—a charactonym. According to Thies (1978: 357), a 'telltale name' can 'perform its characterizing, or rather categorizing, function almost regardless of any textual environment', that is if used as a name and not used ironically; ironic functions can only be understood in context:

> To become meaningful, realistic and neutral names need support of informa-
> tion and situations given in the text, and of audience associations coming from the
> socio-cultural context. When names have acquired a meaning in such a way, they
> can be decoded as charactonyms as well. (Thies 1978: 357)

Several other differences of function between non-literary names and literary names in drama are exemplified. For instance, a name could be used with the purpose of shattering the audience's illusion of the stage performance. The technique is as follows: The real name of an actor on stage is introduced into the play by an author who aims for a detached attitude from the audience. The effect of this is that the audience is constantly reminded of the fact that a theatrical performance is going on. Another way of using names in modern drama is to furnish a character in a play with a number of different names but to see to it that no name stands for a clearly defined identity. The character is thus a collection of different roles and this is symbolized by a collection of names. Further onomastic aspects of modern drama are mentioned, such as the use of certain names to dramatize the unconscious, as in O'Neill's *Mourning becomes Electra* (*Adam* in a scene near the end of the play), or Strindberg with his use of the name *Eva* in *Vägen till Damaskus* (*The Road to Damascus*).

As an illustration of how far it is possible to advance through a specialized analysis of an onymic landscape created by a single author, the investigations by Ines Sobanski (1998, 2000) of the onymic landscape in the detective stories of Gilbert Keith Chesterton were cited in section 22.2.2. Another illustration of this kind is the work of Grant Smith, investigating from different angles names, especially personal names, in Shakespearian drama, thereby throwing light on the close connection between personal names in written drama and stage production (Smith 2009). In the same article, Smith also stresses the fact that several—perhaps most—of the characters within the plays that he has investigated are not furnished with a proper name, but are designated in some other way. Strategies include using indicators of social roles and status, if necessary by adding numbers, such as 'Plebeians 1, 2, 3', or by using an occupational designation such as *Cobbler* or *Messenger* to make identification possible and also to help the director to get the actors on stage in the proper order. As Smith (2009: 910) points out, those designations are also used by Shakespeare for other reasons: 'Shakespeare uses the specific occupational label of *Cobbler* to ridicule the point of view of the tribunes, Murellus and Flavius . . .'. According to Smith (2009: 911–12), Shakespeare viewed (and also used) names as 'social constructs reflecting the social role of a character and espe-cially how that character is viewed by other characters carrying more sense and less ref-erence . . . than we usually see in the meaning of names'. Smith gives us several examples of this, including the name *Borachio*, which as he points out almost certainly derives from Spanish *borracho* 'drunk' or 'drunkard', 'and is therefore a lexical equivalent of how the character has just described himself', namely 'I will, like a true drunkard, utter all to thee' (from *Much Ado about Nothing*, quoted in Smith 2009: 912). Another exam-ple is Smith's interesting explanation of the name *Othello* in the drama *Othello*. As he points out, there is no obvious etymology for the name. However, pronounced on stage as O-TELL-O it would first have sounded like a request for an explanation, as in the first use of the name in the following lines: 'But, Othello, speak . . .'. Smith (2009: 914) stresses the fact that 'in almost all subsequent uses of the name by other characters, the sound of the name again repeats a request for Othello to say something. Thus the name functions as a pun, reminding the audience that Desdemona fell in love with him because of his storytelling'. Smith (2009: 914) argues that Shakespeare's names are con-cretely related to the action on stage and closely tied to individual plays, and therefore open to various interpretations of their significance. His investigation into names in Shakespeare's plays is ongoing. In the short 2009 study, however, he has already indi-cated several significant and striking characteristics in the Shakespearian world of names.

Another group of texts on the genre of drama is the medieval German *Fastnachtspielen*, here represented by the works of Hans Sachs. Hans Blosen (1989) presents the medieval German *Fastnachtspielen* by Hans Sachs from 1510–19 up to 1560–69. He observes that in the older plays especially the different characters do not carry a proper name but are, as in so many other medieval plays, identified by appella-tives like *der Pfaff* (the priest), *der Kremer* (the shopkeeper, tradesman), *der Ziegeuner* (the gypsy), and so on. In most of the later plays, however, the different characters are provided with a proper name. Blosen also emphasizes that some of the above men-tioned appellatives in a number of plays may be used as proper names, so that a fuzzy boundary between a proper name and a kind of no-name may be observed. His inves-tigation is focused on the proper names of the different characters which are analysed in accordance with Birus's (1987, 1989) typology of literary names. He finds that most of the proper names are 'sprechende Namen', transparent names which not only identify a person but also provide information about the name-bearer (such as a certain quality of the name-bearer), or 'characterisierte Namen', characterizing names which resemble the 'sprechende Namen' in many ways, but with the difference that they comprise a well-known name from literature or history, intended to suggest that the name-bearer resembles the literary or historical person in question. Blosen's analysis of proper names may be compared with Birus (1987) and Debus (2002). Blosen throws light upon the onymic landscape of a part of the German drama of the Middle Ages: the naming of characters with regard to the relationship between names and no-names. He also pre-sents a tentative analysis of the proper names of the different characters.

22.4 Cinema Films

Several theoretical as well as practical problems are connected with the investigation of names in cinema films. Hansmartin Siegrist (1995: 576) suggests that one reason why onomastic investigations focusing on cinema films are scarce or lacking may be the difficulty of analysing a work located in a kind of no-mans-land between, for instance, prose fiction in the form of a novel and a cinema film. According to Siegrist (1995: 576), at least 90 per cent of all cinema films must be regarded as adaptions from literary sources, that is they originate from epic prose fiction, from drama and comics, adaptations which mostly show significant differences from the original. So, for instance, names in cinema films differ in that they are created to be more easily remembered and also to be more characterizing. It seems, however, that investigation of the onymic landscape of cinema films is at the beginning of a potentially interesting though demanding phase, and that relevant studies are getting underway.

22.5 Poetry

Names in medieval poetry have been studied by scholars such as Jane Bliss and George T. Gillespie. Gillespie's (1989) work was first presented at the symposium *Namen in deutschen literarischen Texten des Mittelalters* in Kiel 1987. The symposium, initiated by Friedhelm Debus, is—together with the American series of Literary Onomastic Conferences and the publication *Literary Onomastics Studies*—one of the few which aims to initiate and inspire the collection and analysis of names in literature.[6]

22.5.1 Germanic Heroic Poetry

Naming in Germanic heroic poetry has been studied by George Gillespie (1973, 1989), according to whom, about 540 personal names, names of horses, and names of weapons may be found in texts belonging to the genre of Germanic heroic poetry. He points out that many of those names are borne by more than one name-bearer and also that some individuals have different names in different versions of the texts. A comparison is made between personal names in the *Niebelungenlied* and Old English texts such as *Widsith* and *Beowulf*, and also to names in Old Norse literature. Gillespie divides the name-bearers in his corpus into three groups: protagonists (about 136 name-bearers), walkers-on or supernumeraries, and, finally, those

---

[6] One of the papers at this gathering concerned a suitable typology for names in literature, published as Birus (1989). Concerning the typology of names in literature, see Chapter 20.

who are only mentioned by name *en passant* and are never participants in any kind of action: these include biblical characters, saints, and famous literary or historical characters. Of the 136 protagonists, about twenty-five bear names of historical provenence, and around thirty-five bear names of non-historical origin. From this, Gillespie concludes that Germanic heroic poetry can be said to be characterized by a mixture of 'Mythos und Geschichte' (myth and history). He discusses in detail various characteristics of the names in several of the texts. A short summary of what he considers to be the most typical names and naming practices within this genre would have been most interesting.

22.5.2 Naming in Medieval Romance

Naming in medieval romance has been studied by Jane Bliss (2008). After a theoretical discussion of names and their meaning, she observes that several characters in the romances are nameless (sometimes because of being in disguise or incognito). Sometimes those characters are named when the plot so requires (delayed naming). Bliss observes in addition that pseudonyms are freqently used. Total anonymity throughout a romance, however, seems to be less frequent, and Bliss suggests that it is far more common in romances for everyone to have a proper name. She also points out that intertextual references are not infrequent, and that this presupposes an audience familiar with other romances or with folklore as well as (legendary) history, the Bible, and classical stories. Bliss's main interest, however, appears to be connected to the effects of names and their absence on the development of the story in general; names thus, in effect, take an active part and play an important role in the action (consider the title of Bliss 2008: ch. 3, 'The Power of Name'). Furthermore Bliss observes (2008: 11): 'My study explores the significance and the power of name in romance, and suggests that medieval writers were conscious of, if not learned in, theoretical issues'. In her conclusion (2008: 196), Bliss mentions the romance *Amadas et Ydoine*, where the love-story is transmuted by the use of naming as a magic power over life and death. Her approach to the name material of medieval romances points towards an interest in how the names in a romance are used to influence and/or to explain the action. This is an interesting facet of names in works of literature. It is also an aspect that in many ways differs from what has been done hitherto in the field of literary onomastics. Bliss concludes:

> Other, more focused, areas of study would be the examination of all versions of one romance to compare naming-patterns, side-by-side comparison of naming in English texts with their French models (where they are discernibly translated), and examination of a small group of romances (limited by space and time, if not by language) against a background of naming-practices in the rest of life. These topics have been acknowledged in this book, and in the Appendix, and would amply repay further study. (Bliss 2008: 199)

22.5.3 Poetry from Recent Centuries

Comprehensive studies of the onymic landscapes of poetry from recent centuries are scarce, but several interesting studies focus on the work of different authors.

Embodied names[7] in, mainly, American poetry from more recent times are studied by Allen Walker Read (1982), who covers names in several texts, mostly from American poets, with the aim of showing how existing, non-fictional place-names such as Indian place-names, or names of exotic-seeming places far away, can be used to lend an air of mysterious illusion existing only in the author's mind—or dream—about the (fictitious) name-bearer. See also Debus (2002: 76), and Eis's use of the name *Samarkand* mentioned in section 22.2.2.

22.6 PARODIES

Parody may be considered to be a literary genre of its own. All kinds of literature may be parodied, prose fiction of different genres as well as drama and poetry. The names or the onymic landscape of a work can be regarded as one of the most often exploited and also one of the most reliable tools to be used by the parodist, whose aim generally is to distort and to displace. This can be done by 'some form of manipulative reshaping which somehow echoes the name models without striving for accurate duplication' (Nicolaisen 1987: 59), as with the title of the novel *Cold Comfort Farm*, and the names *Graceless* and *Pointless* designating the milchcows belonging to the same farm (Nicolaisen 1987: 60–2). A short overview of names in parodies in English literature is provided by Nicolaisen (1995c: 565), but he limits himself mainly to a single example from prose fiction, the name inventory of Stella Gibbons's novel *Cold Comfort Farm* (1932). A comprehensive overview of names in parodies would also be most welcome.

22.7 CONCLUSION

Literary onomastics is a comparatively new field in the sphere of onomastics. Several genres of literature have been outlined in this chapter, but although many interesting studies are available, in many cases comprehensive overviews are still awaited. Unfortunately these are difficult and time-consuming to produce. A digital approach, however, might facilitate the work, although there is the risk of shallowness if a high

---

[7] For the term *embodied*, see Gardiner (1954: 11); compare also Debus (2002: 70) *verkörperte Namen*.

number of texts are investigated; a great advantage, on the other hand, would be the opportunity to cover large quantities of texts. Another difficulty may be noise (mistakes in the tagging, etc.) when digitizing large text corpora (see chapter 23). It might, however, be possible for a digital approach, in combination with analysis by dedicated scholars specializing in literary onomastics, to produce the most interesting results.

....

CORPUS-BASED APPROACHES TO NAMES IN LITERATURE

....

KARINA VAN DALEN-OSKAM

23.1 INTRODUCTION

....

DURING the last thirty years, name scholars in literary onomastics have increasingly called for the analysis of all proper names in a literary work instead of only one remarkable name or a couple of such names. A clear wish now exists to be able to analyse all the proper names in a collection of works, preferably a digital corpus with texts written by different authors, belonging to different genres and originating from different regions or time periods. Such a digital corpus would have to consist of texts annotated for proper names in all their subdivisions and would be accompanied by tools (computer programs) to search and analyse the corpus, yielding large amounts of results which would need to be approached with quantitative methods leading to new kinds of analysis. We are not quite there yet, but the developments in this area are certainly promising.

This chapter first describes the history and background of the move to a corpus-based approach in research from Germany by Martina Schwanke on several works by Goethe, in Jan-Christian Schwarz's analysis of the Neidhart songs, and in Rosa Kohlheim's and Volker Kohlheim's quantitative analysis of all proper names in one novel by Andreas Maier. Next, the move to more data and larger corpora is described in work done in Sweden and the Netherlands. I will highlight the Swedish development of tools at Gothenburg University, as reported on by Dimitrios Kokkinakis and others; the visualization of names plays an important role in this work. I will also describe Karina van Dalen-Oskam's work on a small pilot-corpus of modern Dutch novels, and describe some aspects of the follow-up project *Namescape* using a much bigger corpus and developing several new tools.

23.2 HISTORY AND BACKGROUND

In her 1992 PhD thesis *Name und Namengebung bei Goethe. Computergestützte Studien zu epischen Werken* ('Names and Naming in Goethe. Computer-Assisted Analysis of Epic Texts'), Martina Schwanke presents the first clearly corpus-based approach to the analysis of literary names. Her research started in the 1980s, during the advent of computers in the humanities, and shows all the challenges and disappointments experienced by scholars in those early days of digital humanities (Schwanke 1992: esp. 127–31). Schwanke's work is based on and builds on the advances made at Christian-Albrechts-Universität in Kiel in the analysis of names in Medieval German literature with a strong focus on lexicography and philology, and making use of new technology.[1] Schwanke's main aim seems to be to convince her readers that the computer is an important new tool that helps the researcher to broaden her scope and deal with more data than ever before, without taking away from the researcher the most important part of scholarly work: interpretation (Schwanke 1992: 92, 489).

Schwanke explains that Goethe often seems to choose proper names in his literary works because of their etymological meaning, thus playing with associations and connotations that were probably also recognized by his contemporary readers. This hypothesis can only be verified, however, by extensive research into Goethe's complete works and by comparing his language with the language of contemporaries and their writings (Schwanke 1992: 85–7, 153). For this, large digital corpora are needed with tools to search for and classify words. And these corpora did not exist when Schwanke began her research. Schwanke herself had to key in Goethe's texts, which cost her many months of hard labour. She therefore limited her digital corpus to five of Goethe's works, *Die Leiden des jungen Werther, Die Wahlverwandtschaften, Hermann und Dorothea, Wilhelm Meisters Lehrjahre*, and *Wilhelm Meisters Wanderjahre*. She used computer tools for lemmatizing, encoding, and concordancing, several of which were developed in Kiel. She enriched her corpus with codes denoting different types of proper names (Schwanke 1992: 144). Before analysing the names in the five chosen works, she looked into the entry 'Name' in several dictionaries from Goethe's time and before, and she analysed the use of the word 'Name' in Goethe's works by using a concordance, showing each occurrence in the texts in its immediate context. This led to several interesting observations which strengthened her hypothesis that Goethe found the meaning of the names he chose important. He may even have checked their meanings in one or more of the dictionaries described before he used them in his own work (Schwanke 1992: 154–91).

---

[1] Pütz (1989) gives a useful overview of the programs developed in Kiel in those years for a lexicon of names in Medieval German literature. The other articles in the same volume also give a clear indication of the state of the art at that time.

To give a better insight into Schwanke's approach, I will describe the chapter about *Die Leiden des jungen Werther* ('The sorrows of young Werther') in more detail. The complete index of names in this novel is an appendix to Schwanke's chapter itself, and gives the names in alphabetical order, the code denoting the name type (personal name, with different subcodes, place-name, or other name), the number of occurrences and the line numbers of all the occurrences. After a short introduction to the text and their names, Schwanke continues with a more detailed description, for practical reasons limiting herself to the personal names. She refers to only one of the place-names in the introductory part of the chapter, *Wahlheim*, a non-existent place-name that could mean 'chosen place of dwelling' to use this as further confirmation of the importance of the etymological meaning of Goethe's names. The personal names are grouped into three subsections: characters only fleetingly connected with the main character Werther, characters who are emotionally important to Werther, and Werther himself and those characters who are connected to him through friendship. The description of the final name in this section ends with the statement that most of the names in *Werther* seem to be of the characterizing type, being names that express aspects of character through their meaning (Schwanke 1992: 215–33).

Schwanke describes the benefit of the computer mainly as a help in viewing and analysing more data than before, thus creating a firmer basis for interpretations by the scholar. She indicates that it is too early to apply a more quantitative approach, because of the lack of sufficiently large corpora at the time of writing. She therefore does not give any percentages, because they certainly would not be representative. She considers her own research to be only a very first pilot study in computer-assisted literary onomastics, specifically into Goethe (Schwanke 1992: 150).

Although Ines Sobanski in her Leipzig thesis about the proper names in the detective stories of G. K. Chesterton (Sobanski 2000) advocates the analysis of all names in a text or a delimited corpus of texts, and their evaluation in the context of their 'onymic landscapes', she does not describe how she processed her own data. It seems that she did not build a digital corpus of the works she studied. Since she gives no statistical information about the names in her (non-digital) corpus either, I will not go any more deeply into her work here. We do find proper name statistics in the PhD thesis of Jan-Christian Schwarz, who, like Schwanke, was based at the Univeristy of Kiel and was also supervised by Friedhelm Debus.

Schwarz's research focuses on the so-called *Neidhart-Lieder*, Medieval German songs written by Neidhart (who died around 1240) and probably several other unknown poets. Schwarz defended his thesis in 2004 and the general advancements in computer hardware and software since the time of Schwanke's research become very clear. Schwarz does not pay explicit attention to the form of his corpus. He carefully describes the selection of the manuscripts and editions he used, and in some cases refers to transcriptions 'that can be consulted' (Schwarz 2005: 44, 46). This could imply that he only used printed and not digital sources, but it could also be that the availability of digital texts from the Medieval German canon was by then so normal that it need not be mentioned. Neither does Schwarz indicate the form of his dataset, but his data are clearly processed digitally, probably in a spreadsheet program such as Excel, enabling sorting of the data, statistical analysis, and visualizations in, for instance, pie-charts with percentage representations of the data. Schwarz prepared a list, supposedly (this is also not described) exhaustive, of all the proper names occurring in the *Neidhart-Lieder*, enriched with different categories of information to be used for several perspectives on the onymic landscape in the poems. His methodology shows the same background as Schwanke's in lexicography and philology.

In the different appendices to the thesis we find all these data, in clear subsections, each of them ending with a pie-chart showing the percentage distribution of the data analysed in that section (Schwarz 2005: 442–568). Schwarz does not usually present percentages in the main part of the study, but each subsection starts with the absolute numbers of the names to be analysed more deeply in that section. Schwarz's point of departure is the established opinion that the *Neidhart-Lieder* are satirical and parodistic in nature. His guiding question is whether the onomastic material in the poems plays a role in these poetic and stylistic strategies and if so, in what form (Schwarz 2005: 15). He limits his research to personal names, in that way describing only a part of the onymic landscape. He divides the personal names into two subsets: compound names built from commonly known name elements (including some names in simplex form such as *Ernst*), and names that are more or less spontaneous compounds of elements from the appellative lexicon (Schwarz 2005: 107–25). In each of these groups, based on the important typological work of Lamping, Debus, and Birus (for the latter two, see chapter 22), Schwarz analyses different kinds of subgroups such as speaking names and 'klangsymbolische Namen' (names with 'speaking sounds'), and 'realistic' names such as the names of heroes, saints, and kings (Schwarz 2005: 225–364).

I will illustrate Schwarz's approach by describing the section on the names of heroes in more detail. After a short discussion of previous research and the selection criteria Schwarz uses, he presents us with some numbers and percentages indicating the distribution of names of heroes throughout the poems. The distribution is not even: in some poems, quite of lot of heroic names occur, while they are completely lacking in many others. He then continues with a more detailed analysis of the names in several poems, again with numbers of names and occurrences to indicate their presence and weight in the texts. He zooms in on names related to two other literary works, *Dietrichs Flucht* and *Rabenschlacht*, where the names seem to enhance certain aggressive elements in the poems, usually surrounding 'simple' people from the countryside in contrast to the courtly elite, thus emphasizing the ironic elements in the poems (Schwarz 2005: 301–29).

Schwarz's interpretations of name usage and name functions are thus backed up by a fairly detailed overview of statistical aspects. Together with the elaborate annexes to the book, this makes it relatively easy for other scholars to verify his data and check his interpretations. The statistics are still relatively basic, being limited to types, tokens, and percentages. The number of names with certain functions is not counted (which cannot be easily done, of course). So the ultimate weighing of the trends in name usage and name functions in the *Neighart-Lieder* is still a mostly qualitative decision by the scholar himself. And this in fact confirms what Schwanke had already stated about the limits of computer-assistance in scholarly work.

In the Netherlands, Karina van Dalen-Oskam's research into literary names was inspired especially by the thesis by Ines Sobanski mentioned above, which analysed the onymic landscape in detective stories by G. K. Chesterton. Van Dalen-Oskam expressed the aim of developing a method for a comparative approach to the 'maps' of different 'onymic landscapes'. After some preliminary ideas (Van Dalen-Oskam and Van Zundert 2004; and Van Dalen-Oskam 2005a: esp. 403–5), she planned her approach in more detail in 2005, calling it 'comparative literary onomastics' (Van Dalen-Oskam 2005b, 2006).[2] Van Dalen-Oskam had a closer look at the names in two Dutch novels, signalling among other things that their use of family names varied: one of the two novels contained only a handful of family names and the other significantly more. Her assumption was that the low number of family names was probably exceptional and that the difference could be explained by the themes and content of both novels.

> In order to put the analyses of the use of family names in these two novels … into perspective and to ascribe a greater value to them, we must compare the onymic landscape in the texts with those in as many other texts as possible. In order to do that we would need to have the following concrete details from the work: how many first names are used in the work, how many family names and what is the ratio of these to each other? All occurrences of the names would also have to be coded with the functions of the name at the particular place in the work, such as identifying, illustrating, etc., so that it might be possible to discover tendencies per work, oeuvre, genre, time or area. The situation in an individual work could then be compared against this. We could then establish what is average or normal in a wide group of texts, but could also compare the usage with that in specific other texts. … Naturally, we also want to be able to cross language borders when doing all this. Only then will it gradually become clear how the use of names functions in their particular landscape, what the constant factors are and how specific authors vary or may even be unique. Constructing such a reference framework requires an enormous effort but I do think that we could make a start in this direction by making optimum use of modern information and communication technology. (Van Dalen-Oskam 2005a: 186–7)

In 2009 Van Dalen-Oskam published an article in which she presented an analysis of the usage and functions of names in one of these two novels, Willem Frederik Hermans's *Nooit meer slapen* (translated into English as *Beyond sleep*).[3] In addition to the article, she published a pdf on her personal website with all the quantitative data that she had gathered from both *Nooit meer slapen* and Karel Glastra van Loon's *Lisa's adem*. In this file, she examined the possibility of drawing up an overview of the

---

[2] The computer program Autonom mentioned in these two publications and in Van Dalen-Oskam and Van Zundert (2004) has not been developed further because of a lack of funding combined with new technological developments that would make a total overhaul of the software necessary.

[3] Some of the topics addressed in this (Dutch) article are described in more detail in English in Van Dalen-Oskam (2012b).

differences in the name functions that seemed to be addressed in both novels. Since establishing name functions is much more subjective than establishing usage of name types, this is an especially sensitive point in the whole approach. Much work still has to be done before we will agree on a trustworthy method to compare name functions in different novels.

In their 2011 article about the names in *Wäldchestag*, the first novel of the German author Andreas Maier, Rosa Kohlheim and Volker Kohlheim also take a quantitative approach. Kohlheim and Kohlheim describe the reception of the novel, which was much lauded and received many prizes, and present an analysis of the personal names as well as the place-names. They provide an inventory of all names in the novel, and begin their article with the observation that the number of name occurrences in the novel is significantly higher than in a corpus of non-literary works. They also compare their calculations with the ones Van Dalen-Oskam made for *Nooit meer slapen*. Here again, *Wäldchestag* proved to have substantially more name occurrences. Additionally, in Maier's novel personal names were much more prevalent than place-names, while in *Nooit meer slapen* place-names are more prominent. Kohlheim and Kohlheim relate this difference to the fact that *Wäldchestag* is a novel about a community of people living in and visiting a small town, while in *Nooit meer slapen*, in which a young academic goes on a geological expedition to the north of Norway, the geography is a structuring element of the novel (Kohlheim and Kohlheim 2011: 275). They go into the geography of *Wäldchestag* more deeply in a separate section of their article, and point out that although place-names are less numerous in novels than personal names, there may be much more to say about this type of literary name. One of their conclusions is that the place-names in *Wäldchestag* also function as a description of the characters in the novel (Kohlheim and Kohlheim 2011: 279–83).

23.3 MORE DATA, LARGER CORPORA

In her publications from 2012 and 2013, Karina van Dalen-Oskam reports on her pilot project on the analysis of all names in a corpus of twenty-two Dutch novels and twenty-two English novels. The small corpus was digitized from her private collection and is not available for other scholars due to issues of intellectual property rights. All the names in the corpus were tagged semi-automatically; after a manual mark-up of a paper copy, the tags for different types of names were put into the digital files using the search and replace option in the text editor used. Several perl scripts were used to count those tags and the results were then statistically analysed in Excel. In her tagset Van Dalen-Oskam, on the one hand, differentiated between personal names, place-names, and other names, with a subdivision for personal names into first names, family names, and nicknames and, on the other hand, between names referring to plot internal entities and names referring to plot external entities. This distinction between for instance *Mordor* as a 'plot internal (place-)name' and *Amsterdam* as a 'plot external (place-)name' was chosen based on the assumption that names referring to completely fictional people, places, or objects have a different stylistic and narrative function than names referring to people, places, or objects that are known to exist in the 'real world'. This assumption can only be tested when the names are marked-up with different tags.

This approach leads to several useful and interesting observations. In most of the novels in the corpus, the number of tokens (word occurrences) that were (part of) a proper name was between 2 per cent and 3.5 per cent. Personal names are clearly most prominent. Place-names occur much less frequently, and the category of other names is usually the smallest. The corpus also contains four Dutch and four English novels for children and young adults and, when ranked from the highest to lowest percentage of names, seven of these novels end up at the top of the list. This higher percentage of names is most probably due to the authors' use of proper names instead of personal pronouns, to make the text more explicit and therefor easier for young(er) readers to understand. Two novels for adults end up in the highest ranks as well, which leads to the assumption that names may have a special function in these novels. Van Dalen-Oskam (2012c) develops the hypothesis that this may have to do with one of the main themes in these novels, that of the stifling family relations of the main character(s). In her analysis of the names in Gerbrand Bakker's novel *Boven is het stil* (translated into English as *The Twin*), Van Dalen-Oskam (2012a) and (2013) describes two interesting functions of place-names that can be identified based on a combination of a corpus-based statistical analysis and *close reading*.

Although the semi-automatic mark-up of proper names in Van Dalen-Oskam's pilot corpus may have a relatively high level of trustworthiness, from a corpus-perspective a set of forty-four novels is still very small. The assumptions based on the analysis of such a pilot corpus need to be tested on a much larger corpus, and then even a semi-manual approach is humanly impossible. So far as I know, two projects have taken steps towards building and/or using digital corpora and tools to enable scholars to analyse more literary onomastic data, one in Sweden and one in the Netherlands.

Lars Borin and Dimitrios Kokkinakis (2010) report on their work into the adaptation of language technology for literary onomastics in Sweden. Named entity recognition (NER) is, as they state, a mature technology that may be of use to scholars in literary onomastics (Borin and Kokkinakis 2010: 54).

> At present, NER systems are geared toward a particular language and genre, and are often fine-tuned to a particular application domain as well. Thus, systems need to be adapted whenever it is to be applied to other languages, genres and/or domains. This adaptation can be automatized to some extent, but it generally involves a fair amount of manual work. This is a one-time effort, however, and having accomplished it, we can then proceed to mark up unlimited amounts of text at virtually no additional cost, as opposed to manual markup, which incurs a cost more or less proportional to the amount of text processed and becomes virtually

impossible when the volume of text grows beyond a certain limit. (Borin and Kokkinakis 2010: 55)

Their NER is written to be used on Swedish fiction from the nineteenth and twentieth centuries as available in the Swedish Literature Bank, *Litteraturbanken* (n.d.). The Swedish Literature Bank is funded by the Swedish Academy as a national cultural heritage project and is a very interesting corpus for large-scale analysis of linguistic and other topics. Their NER system consists of a number of smaller modules that can be applied sequentially (Borin and Kokkinakis 2010: 58). Their system uses several approaches to attain the highest possible results in the automatic recognition and classification of names, such as using gazetteers (lists of single-word or multi-word names), applying animacy recognition (software that can point out speaking characters that may have a name), and lists of first names annotated for gender. They also developed a module that can recognize named entities that are on none of the lists used for training material (Borin and Kokkinakis 2010: 60–1).

   As is common in many NER systems, Borin and Kokkinakis make use of a rather large taxonomy which not only contains people, places, and organizations (the standard main division in NERs, cf. e.g. Sekine and Ranchod 2009) but also artefact names, names of a work or piece of art, event names, and 'measure/numerical' names and 'temporal' names (Borin and Kokkinakis 2010: 62). One of their most interesting approaches is what they call the 'document centered approach'. As they write, 'It is common, at least as a rule of thumb, that if the same entity appears more than once in the same document, such entities tend to have the same labels throughout the document' (Borin and Kokkinakis 2010: 66–7). An NER system usually considers each and every word in a text to decide whether it is a name or not and if so, what type of name. This leads to the counter-intuitive situation that in one and the same novel, an NER tool classifies the name of the main character in different ways, now recognizing it as a personal name, then classifying it as the name of an organization (or some other type of name). This (as I know from personal experience) is extremely annoying for a researcher. In Borin and Kokkinakis's document-centred approach this seemingly erratic behaviour of the NER system is more or less checked.

   When the *Litteraturbanken* (n.d.) corpus was enriched with proper name encoding, the next step was the development of tools to visualize the name usage in a way to help literary name scholars to explore the data. To show their work in this area, Oelke et al. (2012) focus on the personal names in a subcorpus of thirteen novels. Different name variants are linked to a single referent. Each referent (character) is encoded as being female, male, or 'gender-indefinite'. In a network visualization, the characters are the nodes and the number of times certain names occur in the same sentence or paragraph is visualized in the edges, the linking lines between the different nodes being thicker the more the names co-occur. As the authors state, 'network representations can provide interesting insight with respect to the relationship between different persons in the plot' (Oelke et al. 2012: 5). However, these relationships develop throughout a novel. To examine these changes, they develop a visualization to show 'summary plots', which are 'tabular representations in which each column represents a text unit (here: a chapter) and each line corresponds to a person of the novel' (Oelke et al. 2012: 5–6). The colour of the cell is related to the frequency with which the character is mentioned in the text section.

Oelke et al. (2013) present substantial refinements in their visualizations of the developments in the relationships between characters throughout the plot of a novel. Their visualizations are all based on explicit mentions of the proper names of the characters and their adjacency in the text, with the possibility of varying the distance of occurrence. The questions that scholars could then easily answer are, as the authors state: 'When is a certain character introduced to the plot? When do certain characters meet the first time? In which order are the acquaintances made? How intense is a relationship in some part of the novel? What subgroups of characters exist and how do they evolve during the plot?' (Oelke et al. 2013: 373). These visualizations of the 'fingerprint adjacency matrix' are called 'fingerprint glyphs'. The authors demonstrate the usefulness of these glyphs among others for the main characters in J. K. Rowling's *Harry Potter and the Philosopher's Stone*. Repeatedly, they emphasize that analysing the visualizations for the scholar is not a replacement for reading the text.

> Since the relations between characters are determined with a co-occurrence-based measure that does not take the semantics of the text into account, the visual analysis will only be the first step in the literature analysis and is to be followed by closer inspection of interesting passages in the text. We leave it as an issue for future work to develop means to connect the visualization more tightly with the text, potentially also highlighting interesting findings directly in the document. (Oelke et al. 2013: 379)

Although Oelke et al. (2013) were particularly aiming at scholars of literary onomastics with their tools, until now I have not seen any literary onomastics publications describing research in which their tools are used.

The second project to be described here is from the Netherlands and is called *Namescape*; it is being finalized at the time of writing. *Namescape* (2012–13) builds on Karina van Dalen-Oskam's pilot project described at the beginning of this section, with the semi-automatically tagged corpus of forty-four novels of which twenty-two are in Dutch. One of the aims of the project was to annotate a large corpus of Dutch novels (more than 500) for names with a richer tagset than is usual in NERs. We tried to automatically tag first names, family names, and nicknames and group them in 'nyms' per entity, comparable to the grouping of variants as done by Oelke et al. (2012). Another tool added to *Namescape* (2012–13) is called 'entity resolution'. With this, names found in the novels are automatically linked to an entry in Wikipedia, the well-known and very large online encyclopedia. This link is also automatically rated for trustworthiness, based on statistical procedures. The results are far from perfect as yet, but we hope this will in some way lead to an automatic distinction between names referring to plot internal and to plot external entities, something that has never been addressed in existing named entity recognition tools.

Namescape (2012–13) also wanted to foreground the different needs that scholars of literary studies and literary onomastics have compared to linguistic researchers. For certain goals, and from a linguistic perspective, it could be said that, technically, named entity recognition had been resolved and was available as a mature technology. From a literary research perspective, however, the term 'maturity' was a bit too optimistic. This is not only because the NERs first have to be trained on literary materials to work well, but also because the name typology which is relevant to literary onomastic questions was previously not appropriately dealt with in the current NERs.

It is too early to present more concrete findings from *Namescape* (2012–13). Much work still has to be done, including calculations of the level of correctness of the new tools produced when comparing the results to those of the hand-tagged pilot corpus. A first glance shows that the tools still make many mistakes. Quite often, words are marked as names when they are certainly not a name, and in many cases words correctly marked as names are incorrectly classified. What stands out and also invites special attention is that the NER finds many more names (in fact in some cases almost twice as many) than were encoded in the pilot corpus by the scholar. The occurrence of this kind of mistake is called 'noise', suggesting that only a relatively low percentage of all results are incorrect, but that this is not something to worry about too much as long as the amount of correct results is much larger than a scholar would ever have been able to gather manually. It is obvious that the tagging contains a lot of noise. One of the tasks for the near future will be to explore the ways in which literary onomasticians and other literary scholars should deal with this noise. Is it possible to calculate a ratio between the manual results and the automatic ones, and apply that to automatically calculated results from those parts of a large corpus that cannot be compared to a manually-tagged version? And can we then start to answer some of the questions that came up in earlier research with a much larger corpus?

23.4 CONCLUSION: PROSPECTS OF CORPUS-BASED LITERARY ONOMASTICS

The needs of scholars are usually way ahead of the technical and methodological possibilities. Visionary name scholars, such as Martina Schwanke, had to start from scratch, even having to digitize their own corpus. Schwanke had a keen eye in seeing where the computer could be of help in the analysis of large quantities of names. Her 'proof of concept' analysis of the names in five works by Goethe did not go unnoticed; her work is referred to in many publications. Few scholars followed in her footsteps, however. It took a long time before computer tools specific to literary onomastics were developed. Projects coming after Schwanke's, as described in this chapter, each took a small step further. At the time of writing, in 2014, we are on the brink of really being able to apply a large-scale, corpus-based approach to literary onomastics. The reward of digital corpora yielding huge amounts of data to analyse comes with new challenges. The biggest challenge is a methodological one: we will have to find ways to combine results from large corpora, which include a lot of noise (mistakes in the tagging, for instance), with a *close reading* analysis. Only through a combination of these approaches will we be able to increase our knowledge of the usage and functions of proper names in literary texts.

....

CHAPTER 24

LANGUAGE-BASED APPROACHES TO NAMES IN LITERATURE

....

PAUL CAVILL

LITERARY onomastics is a relatively recent discipline, dealing with both personal names and place-names, although there is usually a more specific focus on one or the other depending on the literary work and the interests of the critic. This chapter aims to give a brief historical overview of the deployment of literary onomastics as a linguistic methodology and literary technique, particularly in earlier English literature.

24.1 LITERARY ONOMASTICS

It has been objected that literary onomastics is too little like linguistics because it is 'the analysis of isolates' and '[t]here can be no continuity to literary onomastics, and no meaningful history that appeals to implication'. In short, as T. L. Markey sums up the argument just broached, '[o]ne cannot make a science of sensitivity' (Markey 1982: 134–5). W. F. H. Nicolaisen acknowledges the force of the 'analysis of isolates' point, noting that much early endeavour in the area reduced to 'the meaning of names in literary work X by author Y', without much reference beyond the work or author in question (Nicolaisen 2008: 90).[1] These objections might be countered by remarking that literary study is inescapably the study of isolates, that such

---

[1] A similar point is made by Karina van Dalen-Oskam (2005b) who writes, 'We can only determine the singularity of an author, oeuvre, genre, time or cultural area when we know what is really to be regarded as normal.'

isolates fall into patterns, and that onomastic approaches potentially add another dimension to an understanding of the historical depth of literature and language. As both names and *hapax legomena* are conditioned by the linguistic inventory and imaginative resources of authors, they should also be included in linguistic and literary consideration. Indeed, the six volumes of the Cambridge *History of the English Language* include names as a significant strand of evidence for the study of language; and recent studies of the use of names in literary works are contributing to a greater understanding of the historical context, social conditions, generic expectations, and public reception of writing.

Another question is what a literary name is, and this hangs principally on whether such a name is 'made up' or 'real'. A further issue is whether genre (history, poetry, drama, letter) makes any difference to our perception of the literary effect of toponyms or anthroponyms. The difficulties, however, are more apparent than real. While it is true that some names offer more scope for predicting character and sparking word-play than others, it rarely depends on whether the name is fictitious or in imaginative literature. The disastrous reign of Æthelræd II, king of England 978–1016, was recorded in the Anglo-Saxon Chronicle. Later tradition plays on the meaning of the elements of the king's name, 'noble counsel', in calling him 'Ethelred the Unready', that is, 'ill-advised'. But even in the Chronicle account of his reign in the year 1011 there is a dry comment that 'all these misfortunes came upon us because of *unrædes*, bad counsel' (Plummer 1929 [1892–9]: 141). A historical character's name prompts punning comment in a historical narrative. By the same token, when an author has a degree of freedom in choosing names, these can be used to good effect. Finknottle and Blandings (P. G. Wodehouse) or Maurice Zapp and Euphoric State University (David Lodge) clearly have comic potential even out of context.

One methodological approach which runs through literary onomastics is the division of literary names into 'Cratylic' and 'Hermogenean', from characters in Plato's dialogue *Cratylus*. For Cratylus, names are not merely patterned appellatives, but have meaning in the sense that they represent something important about the person or place. For Hermogenes, names are semantically empty, the conventional application of syllables to identify a person or place. Curtius (1953) analysed the types as 'natural' or 'speaking names' and 'conventional' names, and showed how Cratylic names worked in the Classical and Middle Ages: Odysseus is both the one against whom Zeus is angry (*ōdusao Zeu*) and the 'wrathful one' (*odussomenos*). Curtius sees the pattern develop as far as Dante and others (Curtius 1953: 495–500). Most literary onomastics studies since have used these categories. A sub-category of Cratylic names is bynames: these are given with the specific purpose of identifying characteristics of the person (or place), but bynames are not always transparent, and even when transparent not always felicitous in literature. The byname of a historical character in the Anglo-Saxon Chronicle, Thurcytel *Myran heafod* 'Mare's head' (Plummer 1929 [1892–9]: 140), might be comic, scurrilous, or frightening, if we only knew; and Hardy's Father Time in *Jude the Obscure* seems a little portentous.

24.2 Place-names and Personal Names

The composer of imaginative literature, early and late, has to negotiate the historical realities of naming in English (and in many other languages). The two principal features here are that place-names tend to be resolutely practical and personal names tend to be conventional or aspirational. Place-names tend to designate historically important features of a place, whether of settlement type or topography, ownership or position, although those denotations are quickly lost and overlaid with the accidental associations of history. In their nature place-names tend originally to be Cratylic: they were meaningful and, as associations become attached to particular names over time, remain so. Personal names are Hermogenean: they are apparently random but tend to be given according to recognizable patterns which vary across the generations (Coates 2006d). Certain personal names might be given in hope and 'lived up to',[2] but even the coincidence of surnames and occupation (Baker, Clark) or parentage (Stephenson's father being called Stephen) is relatively rare nowadays and might seem forced in literature. The comic potential of this coincidence is fully realized in the name of Major Major Major Major in *Catch-22*.

The negotiation that imaginative writers make is not infrequently to reverse this pattern of meaning, so that place-names become apparently random and bereft of particular associations attaching to a specific place, and personal names become meaningful and relevant to the character. The result of this is that, so far, literary onomastics has generally focused more on personal names than toponyms. While many a piece of literature will explore and exploit locality, as, for example, Joyce does with Dublin in *Ulysses*, many writers prefer to create rather than exploit existent place associations. Extreme examples of place-name 'dislocation' are Samuel Butler's Erewhon and Dylan Thomas's Llareggub, although Butler uses Erewhon for an unfamiliar, imaginary land and Thomas uses Llareggub to disguise a more immediately familiar and potentially recognizable place. Chaucer's Reeve describes two of the characters in his *Tale* thus:

> Of o toun were they born, that highte Strother,
> Fer in the north; I kan nat telle where.   (Benson 1988: 86, ll. 4014–15)

Chaucer probably knew that *strother* was not so much a 'toun', as a frequent element ('place overgrown with brushwood') in Northumberland and Durham minor place-names, places of no consequence. And while the action of the tale takes place at Trumpington near Cambridge, the young scholars who are the focus of the linguistic

---

[2] Faith, Hope and Charity continue as personal names, for example; Spenser has these characters romantically dressed in *The Faerie Queene* as Fidelia, Speranza and Charissa (Smith 1909: Book 1 Canto X).

and slapstick comedy in the tale are merely 'northern'. Chaucer manages to satirize both the provincial miller of Trumpington with his bungled attempts at chicanery, and the students whose strange speech and place of origin mark them as outsiders, and who are indeed gullible 'northerners', but nevertheless clever enough to get the better of the miller.

24.3 EARLY LITERARY ONOMASTICS

Early English literature inherited from the Bible and its early interpreters a way of understanding names that is essentially literary and Cratylic. The Bible is full of names which were reportedly given on the basis of aetiology, for example, 'And Adam called his wife's name Eve; because she was the mother of all living' (Gen. 3:20); 'And when they came to Marah, they could not drink the waters of Marah, for they were bitter: therefore the name of it was called Marah ("bitter")' (Exo. 15:23). The names of Abram and Sarai are changed, as is Saul's in the New Testament, to reflect changes in status, and in a play on the names, Naomi ('pleasant'), says, 'Call me not Naomi, call me Mara ("bitter"): for the Almighty has dealt very bitterly with me' (Ruth 1:20).

A great wealth of name-lore grew from the Bible. Jerome laid the foundations for much of the literary onomastic invention of the Latin Middle Ages with his *Liber interpretationis hebraicorum nominum* which gave brief definitions of the Hebrew names of Scripture; and this was borrowed with some enthusiasm in Isidore of Seville's encyclopedia, the *Etymologiae*, and augmented by allegorical commentary throughout the medieval period. Jerome's 'Eva calamitas aut uae uel uita' (de Lagarde et al. 1959: 65, 'Eve = calamity or woe or life') is repeated by Isidore 'Eve (*Eva*) means "life" or "calamity" or "woe" (*vae*). Life, because she was the origin of being born; calamity and woe because by her lying she was the cause of death—for "calamity" takes its name from "falling" (*cadere*)' (Barney et al. 2006: 162). Isidore had explained a few lines above this how Hebrew words are differently transliterated and hence susceptible to different interpretations, but took for granted understanding of the anagram that makes *Eva* into *vae* 'woe'. The writer also elides the fact that *calamitas* is etymologically unrelated to the text's *cadendo*. The point is that the names 'were imparted to them prophetically in such a way that they concord with their future or their previous conditions' (Barney et al. 2006: 162); and that concord could be expressed by sound (*ca-*), by letters or syllables (*Eva, vae*), and by association (Eve and The Fall). The Reformation was probably influential in bringing some of the more vividly imaginative linguistic and spiritual interpretations of names into desuetude but it might be noted that the 'Brief table of the interpretation of the propre names which are chiefly found in the olde Testame[n]t' in the Protestant Geneva Bible of 1560, though it omits Eve, includes the essential elements of Jerome's 'Adam homo siue terrenus aut indigena uel terra rubra' in 'Adam man, earthlie, read ("red")' (Berry 2007).

One of the better-known early examples of this kind of linguistic interpretation of names is found in the tradition about Pope Gregory the Great and the English boys in the Roman market. Gregory asked to which race they belonged, the kingdom they came from and the name of their king, and interpreted the replies, 'Angles', 'Deira', and 'Ælle', spiritually as 'angels', *de ira* 'from wrath', and 'Alleluia'. Bede in his *Ecclesiastical History* remarks of Gregory's wit, as he retells the story, *adludens ad nomen*, that Gregory was 'playing on the name' (Colgrave and Mynors 1969: 132–5). Sound and meaning could be manipulated in pleasing punning which nevertheless reveals a deeper spiritual meaning. Anagrams and acrostics were particularly popular in the early modern period (Camden 1605: 182), but solutions to Old English riddles include names of things in runes or Latin letters written in reverse order, for example *Riddles 19* and *23* (Muir 1994). A curious by-way in naming is the ancient and medieval tradition which takes the lack of names in the biblical tradition for various characters such as Noah's wife as licence to invent: Utley (1941) collects 103 names in various languages for Noah's wife.

These modes of interpretation informed the literary practice of early writers. Felix, in his *Life of Saint Guthlac*, the Latin hagiography of an early English saint, confusedly talks of the saint being named from his land or his tribe (respectively Prologue and chapter X, and neither pattern much noted from Anglo-Saxon England), before settling on the notion that the elements of Guthlac's name reflect divine inspiration because it means *belli munus* 'gift [*lac*] of war [*guth*]' and refers to the gift of victory promised to those who spiritually war against vices (Colgrave 1956: 76–9). Later in the *Life*, in chapter XVII, the saint in his secular youth is depicted as raiding and gathering great booty, but then returning a third of it to the victims in a frankly implausible gesture: the story is there to illustrate the interpretation of the name, as Guthlac 'gift of war' gives a gift of war to his victims. Even in the longer of two Old English poems concerning the saint, which does not immediately depend on Felix's *Life*, the thematic recurrence of war and gift has been noted, indicating that this Cratylic understanding of the name was widely known (Robinson 1993: 206–12; Muir 1994, text).

One of the principles of naming in the early Germanic world was that an alliterative theme was carried through from father to sons so that their names could be celebrated in alliterative verse (Stenton 1970 [1924]). *Widsith* is the name of a long poem in Old English that lists the names of lords and tribes of the ancient Germanic world (and more widely), and scholarship has attempted, with some success, to locate and identify the tribes and persons listed (Malone 1962). This has lent credibility to the suggestion that the names represent the essential kernel of stories in the repertoire of the eponymous travelling poet. Another poem in the same manuscript, *Deor* (Muir 1994), is argued to show how this repertoire might come into play. The poem recounts the sufferings endured (or caused by) named men and women, Weland and the victim of his rape, Beaduhild, and others, before the poet tells his own story of suffering. The poet identifies himself, *dryhtne dyre, me wæs Deor noma* 'dear to my lord, my name was Dear' (l. 37). The alliteration of the line picks out the adjectival and nominal forms of *deor* 'dear'; but perhaps the most striking thing is the past tense *wæs*. The poet's name was

Deor: no longer dear to his lord, having been superseded as court poet by another, he has lost his name and some part of his identity. He recalls the names and identifies the stories of those who suffered, but fears that part of his suffering will be that his name will disappear—perhaps, in echo of the refrain of the poem, that his name will pass like the sufferings he records.

Some of the names in *Beowulf* have aroused controversy, especially those of Unferth, who needles Beowulf on his arrival at Heorot, Hygelac, Beowulf's uncle, who dies on a speculative expedition to Frisia, and Grendel, the man-eating attacker of the Danes: their names are interpreted as *unfrið* 'discord', *hygelæc* 'lack of thought', and related to grinding (respectively, among others) by some who see them as being named according to their nature (Fulk et al. 2008: 464–73, and references there cited). Although the details are debated, the Cratylic naming is not implausible, especially as the poet associates names and ideas across the length of the poem. The name of the hero, Beowulf, appears to mean 'bee-wolf' or bear: he fights Grendel without weapons, and late in the poem kills an opposing champion with a bear-hug. The first part of the poem is associated with a type of recurring folk-story known as the 'Bear's son folk-tale'. Heorot 'hart' is the name of Hrothgar's hall, probably because the gables resemble the antlers of the deer; its gables are referred to as *hornas* 'horns', but it provides no defence against Grendel. When describing Grendel's fearsome lake abode, the poet recounts that the 'strong-horned hart' (l. 1369) will face the attacking hounds rather than seek refuge in its waters. The antipathy between Grendel and his human victims is subtly captured by the web of associations around the name and the animal. Another example of this associative play with names is the belated naming of Grendel's victim from Beowulf's party, Hondscio 'glove' (l. 2076). We learn of the man's name within ten lines of the mention of Grendel's *glof* 'glove', in which he carried his victims back to his lair, and repeated reference to hands (*idelhende* 'empty-handed' l. 2081; *gearofolm* 'with ready hand' l. 2085). The poet's audience might have winced as much as the modern reader does.

The other side of the naming coin is non-naming and anonymity. In *Beowulf*, Grendel's mother is described in some detail, but has no name beyond her relationship to her son. The poet muses on, and sometimes almost forgets, her femininity; she is like Grendel, but more complex, more natural, almost more human; she is certainly more nearly successful against Beowulf than her son. The lack of a name hides her identity, and the narrative has to fill out the detail. Another Old English poem, *The Battle of Maldon*, reconstructs the events of a historical confrontation between an English army and a force of Vikings in 991 at Maldon in Essex (Scragg 1991). Many of the English warriors are named, from the nobility to the lowest free man; part of the motivation for one of them, Leofsunu, in fighting on against the odds, is that he knows the gossip that circulates in the village of Sturmer, and does not wish, alive or dead, to be the butt of comments. The Vikings have an unnamed messenger who demands capitulation and tribute, and there is later a reported request for a position of advantage. They are an unindividuated mass like a pack of wolves; they have prowess without honour. The care that the poet takes in naming the English has enabled scholars to locate most of those named in documentary records. The English men who initiated the flight from the battle, Godric, Godwine, and Godwig, the sons of Odda, however, have not been convincingly identified. The intriguing possibility is that the common occurrence of names like Godric makes these men effectively anonymous, or at least unidentifiable (Lockerbie-Cameron 1991: 245–6). Naming can disguise almost as well as non-naming.

In early literary onomastics, it is clear that names are often interpreted as Cratylic, and that onomancy could be directed to both spiritual and secular ends. Etymology (including folk-etymology), name-riddles, anonymity, and association of names and ideas are all deployed with skill and confidence.

24.4 THE MIDDLE ENGLISH PERIOD

Dominant modes in Middle English literary onomastics are personification and allegory. These borrow at least in part from the exegetical traditions of early Christianity mentioned above, but also from two particular literary sources. In Boethius' *Consolation of Philosophy*, the imprisoned sixth-century Roman writer discusses philosophical problems of suffering and free will with the personification of Philosophy in his dreams. The *Consolatio Philosophiae* was freely translated into Old English under King Alfred, and later also by Chaucer, but it was one of the focal philosophical studies of the Middle Ages. Prudentius, somewhat earlier than Boethius, presents in his *Psychomachia* the struggle in the human soul between vice and virtue, with these named, personified, and articulating their individual values, Pride against Humility, Modesty against Lust, and so on. It is a short step from these works to the Morality plays *Everyman* and *Mankind*, to Langland's Lady Meed and Holy Church, and to Bunyan's Christian and Giant Despair in *The Pilgrim's Progress*. Bunyan's naming of characters such as Mr Holy-Man or Mr Valiant-for-Truth coincided with the Puritan adoption of such sententious and biblical names for individuals (Coates 2006d: 322; Valiant-for-Truth is from Jer. 9:3). But equally, Bunyan may have been instrumental in undermining these patterns of naming since the majority of such names in his work relate to negative traits, as in Mr Facing-bothways, Mrs Love-the-flesh and Mr Worldly-Wiseman (Sharrock 1966).

The tendency towards typification in Middle English literature may be briefly illustrated. Alisoun seems to have been the name of the typical attractive woman: the lover's fancy turns from all women to one so named in the lyric-burden 'An hendy hap ich habbe ihent' (Davies 1963: 67); it is also the name of the attractive carpenter's wife in Chaucer's *Miller's Tale*, and of Chaucer's Wife of Bath and her close friend. Its etymology appears to be 'nobility' (Continental Germanic *Adalheidis*) and this, together with its adoption through French, adds a courtly gloss to the name. Part of the humour of its use in Chaucer derives from the rather uncourtly behaviour of the bearers of the name. By contrast, much of the fun in the medieval Morality plays comes from the licence that the names of the Vices permits: in *Mankind*, for example, Mischief, Newguise, Nowadays, Nought, and Titivillus are boisterous and mocking (Lester 2002). The last of these, Titivillus, as a collector of linguistic trifles and bad Latin (Latin *titivillitium* 'trifle, insignificant thing') is ironically the focus of a macaronic lyric (Davies 1963: 198), and is given all kinds of scurrilous and irreverent jests in *Mankind* and in the Towneley play of the *Last Judgement*.

Langland's *Piers Plowman* is populated by various personifications including the Seven Deadly Sins, Wit, Reason, Conscience, and others. Its alliterative verse shows the linguistic pull of typification. In the C-text, Passus XI 211–232 (Skeat 1969 [1888]), there is a brief discussion of the process of transmission of Original Sin by procreation. The name of Cain, the son of Adam and Eve, is mentioned six times, and in four of those cases there is also the adjective *cursed* (ll. 212, 218, 226, 228); two of the examples relate the curse to Cain directly, the other two to humankind and Cain's bloodline. The alliteration in the line associates the name with the curse both directly and indirectly. The A- and B-texts at this point also have the phrase *Caymes kynde* ('Cain's kin', Passus X l. 149, Passus IX l. 119, respectively), and this complex of associations echoes in alliterative verse back to *Beowulf*, where it is reported that Grendel was cursed through his descent from Cain, when the Creator *forscrifen hæfde/in Caines cynne* ('had cursed [him] in the kin of Cain', Fulk et al. 2008: ll. 106b–107a). One of the more subtle developments in *Piers Plowman* is in the nature of the eponymous character. Piers (the name is a variant of Peter) appears initially as an honest working man, but mystically becomes identified with St Peter (the Rock on which the Church is built, Mat. 16:18, an identification that implicitly questioned the authority of the Pope) and even subsequently with Christ himself (Skeat 1969 [1888]: I, xxvi–v) by the common exegesis of I Cor. 10:4 (e.g. in Isidore, Barney et al. 2006: 168).

Cratylic naming is not the only pattern in Middle English literature however. In a recent study, Jane Bliss has analysed medieval romances and discerns a predominantly Hermogenean mode: she writes, 'romance does not, on the whole, want to know what the name means' (Bliss 2008: 26). Indeed, in a playful and knowing fashion, romance writers divest names of significance, as Libeaus Desconus ('The Fair Unkown') becomes a name (Sir Thefair) rather than a description, as does Dégaré ('Lost'), as Bliss shows. In the romance tradition the timing of the disclosure of the name is more important than the name itself. In *Sir Gawain and the Green Knight*, the Green Knight reveals himself as Sir Bertilak de Hautdesert only after Gawain has failed in his test at the end of the story (Andrew and Waldron 2007: line 2445). And while the names might have Cratylic significance, the narrative has been able to maintain the namelessness of the lord of the castle and his lady, and emphasize the greenness of the Green Knight through the text: they are, despite occasional appearances of ordinariness, predominantly 'other', there to test Gawain.

The fourteenth-century poem *Pearl* sits neatly between Boethius and Bunyan, as it is a dream-vision concerned with questions of suffering. In the dream, a beatified girl appears to, and discusses Christian doctrine with, an unnamed man. Most readers interpret the characters in the poem to be a bereaved father whose two-year-old daughter has died, and who now appears to him in her heavenly form (Andrew and Waldron

2007: 14). In the dream she interprets to him gospel parables about salvation and the biblical book of Revelation (the Apocalypse), to teach him about how he may attain to the place where she now is, the New Jerusalem, that visionary place described by John in the New Testament, and to which Christian in the *Pilgrim's Progress* also journeys. The poem is shot through with images and associations of pearls: the girl wears a crown of pearls and a splendid one adorns her breast; she is of pearly whiteness and purity; the value of pearls to princes and jewellers is explored; and biblical references to the parable of the 'pearl of great price' (Mat. 13:45–6) and the 'pearly gates' of the New Jerusalem (Rev. 21:21) are developed. The very structure of the poem, with its 101 stanzas linked by keywords, with the keyword of the last line repeating the first, suggests the endless perfection and roundness of the pearl, or a string of pearls.

A central subtlety of the poem is that it is not entirely clear, but likely, that the girl's name was Pearl or Margaret, and thus the poem engages in name-riddling. The dreamer twice addresses the girl thus:

> 'O perle,' quod I, 'in perleȝ pyȝt,
> Art þou my perle þat I haf playned...'   (ll. 241–2)
> ('O Pearl/pearl,' I said, 'arrayed in pearls:
> Are you my Pearl/pearl, whom I have mourned...?')

and

> 'O perle,' quod I, 'of rych renoun...'   (l. 1182)
> ('O Pearl/pearl,' I said, 'of rich fame...')

The poet also gives the Anglicized Latin term *margary* (and variants, from *margarita* 'pearl') three times, making it possible that Margery or Margaret was the girl's name. Thus the poet plays with almost infinite inventiveness with the Cratylic significance of the name: he makes her, or the pearl, symbolize the Christian, salvation, heaven, treasure, and more, as well as being a child with a childlike didacticism. Most works of the typifying or allegorical kind do not achieve the sense of personality that the poet achieves in this poem in both the dreamer and the maiden. The middle part of the poem is a vehicle for an exposition of the parable of the workers in the vineyard (Mat. 20:1–16), to be sure, but the dreamer and the maiden interact in the rest of the poem in almost natural ways, and neither of them becomes an abstraction.

The tendency towards allegory, personification, and typification in Middle English can be seen in works of the major authors and in figural narrative. The predominant didacticism of the period found extreme Cratylic naming a useful and widely-understood mode of signification. Of course there is literature from this period that may not reflect these patterns: there is Hermogenean realism in naming as well, deployed in the romances and elsewhere. The cases discussed in this section, however, show that skill in characterization and a sensitivity to nuance do not let the meanings of names overpower action and characterization.

24.5 SHAKESPEARE AND THE EARLY MODERN PERIOD

Shakespeare's names have been the subject of much study, and with good reason. Laurie Maguire has a chapter exploring the onomastic background and evidencing the delight that Shakespeare took in playing with names (2007: 10–49). It is progressively harder to generalize about literary onomastic approaches after the Middle Ages, but Shakespeare's names tend to have an intertextual freight. In *Twelfth Night* (c.1600) there are the appropriately-named comic characters, the riotous Sir Toby Belch and the feeble Sir Andrew Aguecheek. The joyous Clown, Feste, is named in the dramatis personae but only once in the play. Like these, Malvolio's name is clearly Cratylic, meaning 'ill-will', but as a character he is more than slightly reminiscent of Malevole in Marston's approximately contemporary *The Malcontent* (published 1604, but probably produced earlier): both characters intend to usurp a higher place than is theirs by right, though Malevole is guileful while Malvolio is both gullible and sententious. In the baiting of Malvolio, Feste pretends to be Sir Topas, a curate: the name might refer to Chaucer's vacuous *Tale of Sir Thopas,* or to the lunatic-healing properties of topaz found in Scot's *Discoverie of Witchcraft* of 1584 (Lothian and Craik 1975: 120–1; Levith 1978: 91); but perhaps additionally in a lapidary tradition evidenced in *The Pearl* (Andrew and Waldron 2007: l. 1012) and Batman's encyclopaedia (Batman 1582: Book XVI ch. 96), the topaz 'hath two coulours', as Feste has two voices and refers repeatedly to light and darkness and various philosophical ambiguities.

Shakespeare looked to Holinshed and Spenser and perhaps Geoffrey of Monmouth for the history, and the old play of *King Leir* for some of the drama, of his *King Lear.* But he added the sub-plot with Edgar and Edmund. Shakespeare popularized the name Cordelia: Holinshed spelt it Cordeilla, and in Spenser it was Cordeill or Cordelia (Smith 1909: Book II Canto X). As Coates notes (2006d: 322), the feminine name type ending <-(i)a> originated in predominantly classical sources and this might have motivated the change Spenser initiated and Shakespeare continued. The theory embraced by Foakes and originating in Anderson was that Cordelia was based on ' "Cor" from Greek for the heart, and "delia" an anagram of ideal' (Foakes 1997: 31, 155).[3] Anderson, with greater linguistic accuracy, suggested Latin *cor, cordis* as the etymon of the first element and proposed that 'If Shakespeare was aware of *Delia* as an anagram for *ideal*, this meaning might further have influenced his choosing of the form' (1987: 7). Although Shakespeare was doubtless aware of the name Delia, for example from the title of Samuel Daniel's 1592 collection of sonnets *Delia*, the posited anagram of *ideal* is unlikely. With the sense 'supremely excellent of its kind', and usually spelt *ideall*, the word is first recorded as a 'hard word' in the second edition of Cawdrey's *Table Alphabeticall* of 1609 (OED: *ideal*,

---

[3] Levith's suggestion for the second element is Greek *delos* 'revealed' (1978: 57).

adj. 2),[4] and it is unlikely that Shakespeare anagrammatized a word not yet widely familiar when he was working on the play in 1605–06. He might have thought of Delia as the
name of a 'sweet maide' with a strong streak of intransigence, such as Daniels addresses
in his verse; but it might have been simply the classical-sounding polysyllable that
appealed.

The sub-plot and its names appear to have been Shakespeare's invention. The historical Edgar (king 959–75), Foakes notes, was 'a famous hero but also noted for cruelty', and Edmund was the name of the 'King of East Anglia from 841, who was reputed
as a hero and as a saint' (1997: 155). It is unclear why the name of the Machiavellian
Edmund in the play should refer to the East Anglian saint. A closer reading of
Holinshed reveals a potentially more plausible reference. King Athelstan (Adelstane
in Holinshed), 925–39, was succeeded by his brother Edmund (king 939–46), whose
son was Edgar (*The Holinshed Project* 2008–13, entry for 1577: 5.92–3). Athelstan was
reputedly a bastard (1557: 5.92); Edmund was a warrior; and Edgar was a peaceable
and judicious king. The essential details that fed Shakespeare's dramatic imagination
can thus be found in two main passages of Holinshed's first volume: the Leir chapters of Book 3 (1577: 5.18) and the chapters relating to the Saxon kings (1577: 5.92–3).
Shakespeare conflated the Saxon brothers to arrive at a bastard Edmund and made
Edgar Edmund's younger brother. Doubtless this conflation of Leir, whose reign
began according to Holinshed in 'the yeare of the world 3105' (approximately 899
BCE), and the reign of Edgar in 'the yeere of our Lord God 959', is as anachronistic as
Gloucester's reference to 'spectacles'. But Shakespeare's imaginative grasp of history
shaped his writing of *King Lear* and it is the names that locate the play in this transhis-
torical and intertextual context.[5]

In *The Winter's Tale*, Perdita 'Lost' is an obvious Cratylic name. Shakespeare changes
the names of the main characters in the play from his source, the romance of *Pandosto*
by Robert Greene (Pafford 1963: 181–225). Greene's Pandosto and Fawnia become
Shakespeare's Leontes and Perdita. Leontes entertains a delusion that his daughter was
conceived in adultery, and in a parody of baptismal naming, the child is handed over
to Antigonus to be disposed of or 'lost', but instead is given a name by curious means.
Hermione appears in a dream to Antigonus and names the child, before he exits 'pursued by a bear' and dies:

> and, for the babe
> Is counted lost for ever, Perdita,
> I prithee call't.   (III.iii.32–4)

The baby Perdita is then found by a shepherd who preserves the name which he could
not know. The choice of the name Perdita, and the implausible way it is given, put a good

---

[4] The only antecedent sense is the Platonic one, 'an idea or archetype', not relevant here.
[5] Fowler (2012: 117–8) suggests that Shakespeare might have been playing on Camden's etymology of
the names, but I think the historical associations are more significant here.

deal of dramatic emphasis on the name. By the mid-point of the play, Leontes believes his daughter and his wife Hermione to be dead. In the dénouement of the final scene years later, both wife and daughter are restored, apparently from death. 'Our Perdita is found' (V.iii.121), says Paulina, and Polixenes remarks (in a cluster of references to life and death) that somehow Hermione has been 'stolen from the dead' (V.iii.115).

The lost is found and the dead is alive again. The contemporary audience would have recognized the echo of the parable of the Prodigal Son from Luke 15:11–32. The Prodigal wastes his inheritance, then returns to his father in desperation; his father welcomes him back, ordering a celebration, 'For,' he says, 'this my son was dead and is alive again; he was lost and is found' (Luke 15:24). This biblical story is mentioned in the play in Act IV scene iii by Autolycus. Using the device of the name Perdita, Shakespeare makes play with the parable: this drama is about a prodigal father, who loses his wife and daughter through his baseless jealousy. But through undeserved grace, the lost is found and the dead restored to life. The themes of sin, repentance, and restoration from the parable are re-focused in the play.[6]

Early Modern literature inherits the literary onomastic devices of earlier traditions and develops its own. There is the persistent echo of the Bible, but in addition there are plausible intertextual references to encyclopaedic and historical literature, to contemporary romance and verse.

24.6 LATER MODERN LITERATURE

In the modern period there have been many studies of names in novels. While the list of Dickens' Cratylic names—amusing, associative, punning—is long, Dickens is perhaps the most extreme example of a trend in the modern period. Thackeray's *Vanity Fair* borrows its title from Bunyan, and its heroine Becky Sharp is indeed sharp. Trollope's Mr Quiverful has, as has been observed, many children. Perhaps more subtly, Jane Austen might be suggesting provinciality with the names Morland ('wasteland') and Thorpe ('minor estate') as against the well-to-do culture of the town of Tilney in Norfolk in *Northanger Abbey*; or the French aristocratic pedigree of Darcy and Lady Catherine de Burgh as against the good fortune of the Bennets (Latin *benedictus* 'blessed') in *Pride and Prejudice*. Certainly in Austen's novels, visitors to Bath are immersed in the maelstrom of society taking the waters, for good or ill: some drown, others emerge cleansed or even healed.

There is space for one final variation on Cratylic naming. Alastair Fowler has discussed the 'georgic' name Hodge, 'which seems to have been the early modern type-name for a rustic or agricultural labourer' (2012: 30), and he cites a range of sixteenth- and seventeenth-century sources. Thomas Hardy, whose character Angel Clare

---

[6] Groves (2007: 186–7) points to the *Noli me tangere* theme in the final scene, also echoing the biblical tradition. The *Winter's Tale* analogy above was proposed in Cavill (2011).

in *Tess of the Durbervilles* finds no trace of 'the pitiable dummy known as Hodge' after a few days living among country people, apparently resented the caricature. This then gives significance to Hardy's choice of the name of 'Drummer Hodge' in his poem about the Boer War (Gibson 1976: 90–1). Hodge, the (onomastic) yokel, becomes detached from his familiar locality and becomes part of a landscape utterly remote: he is buried by a 'kopje-crest' in 'the Bush', presided over by 'strange-eyed constellations'. This Hodge is no localized country bumpkin, but at home in a wide and mysterious universe. The naming in the poem is anti-Cratylic.

24.7 CONCLUSION

As yet no great onomastic imagination has been exercised on the titles of books dealing with literary onomastics: for example, there are two *Names in Literature* (Alvarez-Altman and Burelbach 1987, and Ashley 2003) and one *Literary Names* (Fowler 2012). Yet literary onomastics is a vibrant discipline embracing an enormous range of analytic topics (Alvarez-Altman 1987) and artistic approaches (Smith 2005). The thrust of this essay has not been to enumerate but to illustrate. It has suggested that early English literary onomastics depends linguistically on etymology (including folk- or Isidorean etymology), association, and name-riddling. In the Middle English period we see typification, personification, and allegory as dominant modes. The early Modern period, insofar as generalization is useful, makes extensive use of onomastic echo and borrowing to locate names in an intertextual nexus. And later literary onomastics inherits nearly everything from the earlier periods and uses it in a variety of ways, including the anti-Cratylic.

PART V

SOCIO-ONOMASTICS

<hr style="border: none; border-top: 1px dotted;" />

CHAPTER 25

NAMES IN SOCIETY

<hr style="border: none; border-top: 1px dotted;" />

TERHI AINIALA

25.1 INTRODUCTION

THE emergence of individual names and name categories is always based on the cultural and social context. In other words, names are not only part of language; they are part of society and culture, as well. Names are always born in the interaction between people, the linguistic community, and the environment. People give names to referents they consider worth naming. By giving names, people take control of their environment, leaving their imprint on it, as it were; thus making it part of their own culture.

In socio-onomastics, names in society are examined. Socio-onomastics can be defined, put briefly, as a sociolinguistic study of names. Above all, it explores the use and variation of names. The socio-onomastic research method takes into account the social, cultural, and situational fields in which names are used. (For earlier discussions, see Nicolaisen 1985: 122; Naumann 1989 [1984]: 395; Walther and Schultheis 1989 [1974]: 358; Debus 1995.)

Before discussing the methodology in socio-onomastics in more detail in section 25.3, an overview of the epistemological background will be presented, as well as a brief state of the art. In section 25.4, the major advances in socio-onomastics are presented and discussed.

25.2 ORIGINS

From the late twentieth century onwards, onomastics has aimed strongly at constructing a typological overview of nomenclature. The structure of names and of name systems has been investigated, and name-giving grounds have been classified according to semantic criteria. Research in the field has thus developed from the analysis of individual names towards the investigation of larger entities. (See e.g. Ainiala et al. 2012: 52–5.)

Socio-onomastic research is, in a sense, a natural continuation of typological research. In constructing a structural and semantic picture of nomenclature, questions about name use and variation were asked almost inevitably. This was especially the case in the field of toponomastics and in countries like Finland where the research has been based on place-name collections covering the whole country and through field interviews with local people (Ainiala et al. 2012: 38–42).

The term *socio-onomastics* (or rather *Sozioonomastik* in German) was first used by Hans Walther (1971a) in *Namenforschung heute*. He defined the two main objectives of socio-onomastics to be the following: (1) the study of the social origin and use of different variants of proper names within various situations and contexts, and (2) taking into account the name-giver, name-bearer, and name-user (Walther 1971a: 45).

The socio-onomastic research carried out by Walther and other Eastern German scholars took place within a framework of Marxist linguistics. From the beginning it was meant to be modelled on a structuralist (presumably Labovian) sociolinguistics. It was especially the interaction between names and the society in which they were used that were in focus. Names were seen as undergoing all kinds of formal alterations and thus being in many ways variable. In German, besides 'Sozioonomastik' the term 'Namensoziologie' was also used (see e.g. Witkowski 1964: 60; Seibicke 1982: 11; Naumann 1989 [1984]: 394–5). Usually, no substantial difference was made between these two concepts; the terms were used almost interchangeably.

At the heart of all socio-onomastic endeavour from the beginning were anthroponymic and toponymic variables. Socio-onomastics thus concentrated on the issue of variety (e.g. Nicolaisen 1985: 123). In addition, it was acknowledged that onomastic variables were chiefly created by different societal and cultural registers (Nicolaisen 1985: 123). In other words, socio-onomastics was comparable to sociolinguistics, and thus, name variation was not to be regarded as random, but orderly.

25.3 METHODOLOGY

Name variation is the core concern in socio-onomastics. Research within the field has focused on synchronic variation, although diachronic variation has been studied as well (for more detail see section 25.4). In the following, the synchronic and especially social variation will be looked at in more detail. In addition to social ('sociolect') variation, even situational ('style lect') variation has been examined.

25.3.1 Studying Place-names

The social variation in place-names is a major topic in studying toponymic competence (i.e. people's knowledge of certain names). Everyone's individual toponymic competence includes both names that are in everyday use and names that are used less frequently. In terms of their degree and frequency of use, names can be placed on a con-tinuum ranging from names that are used every day to names that are used only rarely.

When we study people's toponymic competence, we may try to find out how many and what types of place-names people of different ages, professions, and genders know in their home districts (see e.g. Pitkänen 1998, 2010). Or we may examine which names or name variants people of different origin (in particular, natives vs. non-natives) use for specific places (see e.g. Pablé 2009). Moreover, we are interested in studying why people's toponymic competences differ from each other, that is why they use different place-names.

The variables used in studies of toponymic competence are the sociolinguistic ones: age, gender, ethnicity, socio-economic class, nativeness, etc. Studies have mostly focused on the rural village rather than on towns or cities (but see Pablé 2009).

In socio-onomastic studies on place-names, the data have usually been collected through interviews. Since not every member of the community can be interviewed and her or his onomasticon inventoried, the informants have been selected according to the sociolinguistic variables relevant for the study in question. In many cases, individual interviews have been carried out but also some group interviews (see e.g. Ainiala et al. 2012: 56–7.) In a number of studies, questionnaires have been used. Using question-naires, the informants have been asked to list the names they know for particular places and which ones they would use. In some cases, the questionnaires have served as a basis for the interviews (e.g. Pablé 2009: 161).

25.3.2 Studying Personal Names

Socio-onomastic research into personal names comprises, for example, variation in the popularity of names. In particular, the distribution of forename innovations (also referred to as name fashion) has been studied (e.g. Kiviniemi 2006). In addition, research into reasons for name giving is also regarded as part of socio-onomastic study. Statistical data are of major relevance to studies on the popularity of names. But ques-tionnaires and even interviews have also been used in studying criteria for name-giving.

Situational variation also exists in the field of personal names. Various names and name variants are used in different situations. This is particularly true with bynames (nicknames, petnames, etc.) (see e.g. McClure 1981a; Van Langendonck 2007b). For example, Van Langendonck has studied the characteristics of juvenile byname-giving in contrast with adult name-giving (2007b: 317–20).

25.4 Major Advances

Socio-onomastic research has introduced the multifaceted issue of variety in onomas-tics. Names or name systems are not to be understood as static, constant, or stable, but as variable and changing. In studies in toponymic competence it has been shown that very often some names are known to all speakers within the community, while other names are in use only among specific groups of speakers.

25.4.1 Toponymic Competence

25.4.1.1 *Age, Gender, and Profession as Variables*

The role of different variables is a key issue in studying toponymic competence. For example, in a study by Peter Slotte, Kurt Zilliacus, and Gunilla Harling (1973), covering three Swedish-speaking municipalities in Finland, it was claimed that gender affects toponymic competence more than age. Adult males, in fact, knew around 25 per cent more names than women of the same age. These findings can, however, be contested, since in traditional rural cultures men moved about in wider areas than women, for example, in connection with cultivation, hunting, and fishing. But this only means that the difference found cannot therefore be explained as one related to gender; rather, it seems likely that the variable is connected to profession and to the extent people move about.

Accordingly, age definitely affects the use of names and toponymic competence, at least on average. It is natural that the longer people live in an area, the larger their toponymic competence and the greater their need to use different names. In addition, native inhabitants who have spent their childhood and youth in an area often know more names in the area than people who have only moved there as adults. People come to know a region and its names gradually, starting from childhood. A person who has lived in an area for a long time knows and recognizes the various stages of the development and history of the region and she or he may even be using names that have already been abandoned from common use. Native inhabitants may have become emotionally attached to their home district in a different way from that of people who have only moved to the area at a later stage; this adds to the degree and accuracy to which the natives know the region.

Recent studies in toponymic competence have taken a more versatile approach to various variables. For example, a study by Ainiala et al. (2000) established that the names used by young people and women in rural villages focus on cultural names and especially settlement names. Settlement names do, in fact, belong to the central nomenclature of villages, and often nearly all the village people know the names of the most prominent estates and houses. Men know more names of natural features because they have by tradition moved about in the terrain more than women. For example, elk hunting can be considered a significant explanatory factor behind a wide toponymic competence. In such a case, the name territory, that is the range of the area in which people know names, is often extensive. The names of natural features can illustrate a person's toponymic competence—the more names of natural features a village dweller knows, the wider her or his toponymic competence often is. In general, Ainiala et al.'s (2000) findings suggest that occupation and hobbies affect toponymic competence more than age and gender. In addition, the use of names cannot necessarily—at least not in very much detail—be analysed according to user groups. The reason for this is that there are extensive individual differences. Those who move about in the terrain and are more interested in the region as such use and know more names.

When we have looked for the reasons why people know names, we have noticed that place-names are known for many different reasons. Some of the reasons may even be overlapping. Further, there may be several reasons why a person knows a name. The most prominent reasons for knowing the name of a place include at least ownership of the place in question, use of the place (e.g. picking berries, swimming), work at the place (e.g. farming), incident at the place (e.g. a special incident or event that has occurred/occurs at the place), location (e.g. a place very near to one's own home), inhabitant (e.g. a place is known through its inhabitant), conversations (e.g. a place is known through conversations with other inhabitants of a village, not for other reasons), and the form of the name (e.g. the form or the contents of the name are exceptional and thus known). Research has shown that the most common of these are ownership, use, work, and location (Slotte 1976).

Although there may be considerable differences in the use of names among the inhabitants of, for example a rural village, this does not really harm mutual communication. It is easy to talk about central and important places, since their names are well known to all or at least to most. In smaller communities (families, hobby groups), people use names that are only known to the community members.

Family members usually know the same names: young people use mostly the same names as their parents and grandparents. Some places need to be talked about among the family in particular, and everyone needs commonly used nomenclature. Usually the youngest generations do not know all the names the older generations know. It has been noticed that around half of the names used by the oldest generation may be on their way to extinction in rural villages. In this respect, the tendency at the individual level is the same as that of the wider scale of the village—the names especially prone to be extinguished include many names of cultivated lands and terrain names (see also Kepsu 1990).

The degree of knowing and using place-names is associated with the changes in the names: the names that are no longer needed disappear. The number of names in use does not necessarily decrease to the same extent from one generation to the next. Young people give names to new places and invent new names for places that the older generations call by older names. Nevertheless, in studying diachronic variation in place-names, it has been noticed that as many as half of the place-names in rural villages may have disappeared in a relatively short time (in Ainiala's 2010 study during three decades, from the 1960s to 1990s), due to changes in the countryside itself.

Socio-onomastic research in place-names acknowledges that individual differences always exist. It is thus never predictable which names a speaker will know and use, since no two individuals have been confronted with exactly the same linguistic reality. Referencing names is highly context-sensitive, and not simply a matter of name competence. In the latest studies (see e.g. Pablé 2009; Ainiala and Lappalainen 2017) in the field of socio-onomastics, interactional aspects have been taken into account. It has been pointed out, for example, that there are differences between the spontaneous and metalinguistic uses of names. Because of this, data-gathering methods such as interviews have received considerable attention (see e.g. Ainiala and Halonen 2017).

25.4.1.2 *Children as Name-givers*

Children as name-givers and users have only been studied to a very limited degree; however, there are a few studies on this aspect as well. Since the children's world is small and narrow in comparison to the world of adults, appellatives referring to nothing but the type of the place are often enough to serve as names. For a child who knows just one school, shop, and park in her/his surroundings, it is often enough to use the appellatives *School*, *Shop*, and *Park* to refer to the places by name. In fact, names expressing just the type of the place are typical of names used by children, and their share of the entire toponymic competence is generally much larger with children than with adults. As children's worlds gradually widen and begin to cover a larger part of the environment, even their toponymic competences grow and become more versatile.

Naturally, even a small child knows other names than those that express nothing but the type of the place. Children learn names in their environment just as they learn language in general. For instance, they know the names that their parents and siblings use. Further, even very small children learn that there are different written names in their environment, for example on signposts, on walls of buildings, and in advertisements. A child who can read will adopt such names very quickly, if the places are such that they need to be talked about. Children learn to know the familiar shops, kiosks, day-care centres, and other places by their real names—albeit that these places can also be referred to by various names.

Moreover, children often use names of their own invention. Some of these names refer to such playgrounds that do not, in fact, have any other names, whereas some of them are names children have given to places which adults refer to by other names. The names children give are often fairly 'concrete', referring to the activities that take place or the things that are found in the place: people walk dogs on *Koirapolku* 'Dog Path', ducks swim in *Sorsalampi* 'Duck Pond', and you can experience a great echo in *Kaikumetsä* 'Echo Forest'. Children's ideas about places and the world of play are, in turn, reflected in many names, such as *Ihmepuut* 'Wonder Trees', *Kummitustalo* 'Haunted House', *Menninkäismetsä* 'Gnome Forest', and *Taikalampi* 'Magic Pond'. All in all, names given by children reflect the ways in which children perceive and express the world linguistically. Many of these names may be rather short-lived, whereas some of them may be used more permanently and even be transferred to the language used by adults.

Children's place-names are—just like those of other user groups—community-specific, that is, they are names that are only used in a specific community and that help to promote the community's identity. For example, a certain school or class may use their own names for all the places that need to be talked about in connection with the school's activities, school breaks, etc. Children learn these names as they start school and they are often passed on to the next generations of pupils. While some of the names are known throughout the school, others are used in smaller communities, for example among friends and acquaintances (see also Tikka 2006).

25.4.2 Situational Variation in Using Place-names

Situational variation refers to the fact that the use of names varies according to the situational context. Different names and name variants can even be used to refer to the same places. Names need to fulfil different needs in different situations of language use. User-specific and situational variation overlap: one and the same speaker talks about places in various contexts and is a member of different user communities at the same time.

When studying situational variation, it has been noted that the use of different types of names and name variants in different situations is affected at least by the members and the degree of formality of the speech situation. In official situations, people tend to use standard language, whereas communication is freer in a group of familiar people. Furthermore, attention should be paid to what places and what types of places are being talked about. When talking about places that are partly or entirely unknown to speakers in familiar and casual situations, the speakers will, of course, use the 'real', that is, the official or standard-language names of the places. Familiar places can be naturally referred to by 'casual' forms and, for example by forms that have been shortened from longer names. For example, in rural settings people may well use names with just one part and expressing just the type of the place (*Harju* 'Ridge', *Järvi* 'Lake') or other types of names with just one part and without the generic element (*Mäentaus* 'Back of the Hill'), if everybody knows which places the names refer to. Further, when the places are talked about often, the shorter forms are practical. When talking to less familiar people, it is more appropriate to use two-part forms instead (*Kuoppaharju* 'Hole Ridge', *Haukijärvi* 'Pike Lake', *Mäentauspelto* 'Back-of-the-hill Field'). This way, even strangers can recognize the expression as the name of a certain type of place.

In urban environments, people may use official names (*Helsinginkatu* 'Helsinki Street') at times, and their informal variants (*Hesari*) at others. Sometimes people talk about places that do not have official names (*Bägis* 'a staircase behind a library'). Official names are common at least in standard language and formal use. As for unofficial names, some of them belong to standard language and are used very widely, whereas others have very narrow distribution and are used, for example, by a small group as part of the group's own specific language.

Different names and name variants can even be used to refer to one and the same place. Names fulfil different functions in different situations. Many names strengthen the identities of their user community. The group identity is reinforced through using the group's own names as part of the group's own language. In addition, the use of certain name forms may be due to practical reasons. People may use shorter and easier forms rather than longer forms (e.g. *Aleksi* for *Aleksanterinkatu* 'Alexander's Street').

25.4.3 First Name Fashion

In socio-onomastic research into personal names, many intriguing results have been gained. In studying first name fashion and reasons for name-giving, it has been noticed that although parents usually try to find names for their children that are special or rare, their choices often turn out to follow some fashionable trend typical of the period in question. As regards the choice of a name, we can talk about 'an invisible sense' which leads the name-givers to name their children according to fashion subconsciously as it were, with the help of a certain social instinct. All in all, the choice of a first name is based on community values: the name givers' nationality, their mother tongue, religious convictions, and even social status influence the name-giving. For example, in many European countries, highly educated people favour traditional names based on their own language, whereas people with a lower level of education prefer names that are popular and trendy (Vandebosch 1998; Gerhards 2003; Aldrin 2011).

25.4.4 Folk Onomastics

Folk onomastics can be defined as a study of people's beliefs and perceptions about names and name use; thus the term is parallel to folk linguistics and folk dialectology (e.g. Vaattovaara 2009: 32). In onomastics, stances and perceptions towards, for example, place-names have been studied before, but the term folk onomastics has not been used. Nancy Niedzielski and Dennis R. Preston (2000: 302–14) divide people's talk about language into two types: talk about language and talk about language use. The same applies to the analysis of talk about names: people talk about names and name elements (metalanguage 1) and about name use and beliefs connected to name users (metalanguage 2). The following extract illustrates this kind of approach. In it, Abdi (22 years) and Iftin (30 years) present their attitude towards the racist nature of the name *Mogadishu Avenue*. The name is unofficially used for a street in Eastern Helsinki in Finland. The interviewees have Somalian background but have lived in Helsinki since their childhood (Ainiala and Halonen 2017).

(1)   Int[1]:   et se on teille sellai niinku, teit ei haittaa se nimitys.

         so it is for you like it does not bother you that name

---

[1] Int = interviewer.

Abdi: eei.

noo

Int: [et se on nii-]

like it is so

Abdi: [sehän on] [vaan hienoo.] siis, eihän siin o mitään pahaa.

it is just great like surely there is no harm in that

Iftin: [ei haittaa.]

does not bother

Int: ei ni, nii.

no no it doesn't

Abdi: et miks pi- miks se ois haittaa että, se on vaa, Mogadishu Avenue ei

like why sh- why would it bother like, it is just Mogadishu Avenue

si- ei siin mun mielest ei siin o mitää pa- ei silleen et,

there isn't in my opinion there isn't anything ba- in that way like

enkä mä viel kertaakaa oo kuullu semmon kete- kenel- meikäläine

and I haven't yet even once heard any one of us

jolla ois jotain sitä vastaa että miks ne keksi tai

who would have anything against that like why did they invent

mitään sellasta ets kaikkien mielest se on hienoo et on

anything like that everybody thinks it's great that there is

sellanen nimitys siihen et, että jopa suomalaiset käyttää sitä, se

kind of a term to that that even Finns use it that

on viel hienompaa et sit ku muutki käyttää sitä että.

it is even fancier that others too use it like

The extract shows two very important aspects of Abdi's and Iftin's attitude towards the name. First, even though *Mogadishu Avenue* comes from a racist discourse, the name itself is neutral since it is only the name of the capital of Somalia. The men say that they do not know anyone with a Somali background who would be insulted by the usage of the name, and that the name is common property, not linked to names of ethnic origin. Second, the men report that the fact that 'Finns' (the name they themselves use for the majority of people) use it makes it more valuable and not more racist. They even imply that the name was originally used by Somalis living in Helsinki (*jopa suomalaiset* 'even Finns', *muutki* 'others, too'). The origin of the name (whether 'true' or not) also gives the men ownership over it and thus a right to define how to interpret it. In the extract, the interviewees thus express their perceptions of the name *Mogadishu Avenue* and its users.

People's stances and attitudes towards referents of the names may be reflected in the names themselves. This is also regarded as folk onomastic research. For example, unofficial urban place-names may reflect their users' different attitudes. Some of the names may reveal ideas associated with the places and their users (*Peräjunttila* 'Hick Land', *Porvarikoulu* 'Bourgeois School'). In addition, certain slang names may be so strongly associated with particular user groups that many people do not want to use them (see e.g. Ainiala and Lappalainen 2017), or feel that they have the right to use them.

An especially interesting theme in folk onomastics is the attitudes linked to planned nomenclature. This requires analyses of how residents feel about the planned names in their region; what names they regard as good and what names they regard as bad, and why. Many such studies (e.g. Aalto 2002; Ainiala 2004; Johansson 2007) have established that the descriptiveness of the names is considered an important feature. The way the residents of the Finnish town Kouvola see the planned names in their environment has been analysed by Maria Yli-Kojola (2005). Many of the town-dwellers seem to think that it is important that a name tells you something about the place or its residents. From this perspective, one of the respondents regarded, for example *Tietotie* 'Information Road' as a good name, since the respondent's school was located by that road. There was also a clear wish that names in villa districts should be different from those in the block-of-flat districts in the town centre. Further, people paid attention to the fact that names should be consistent with possible future changes in an area. For example, certain street names including agricultural terminology might feel unnatural as names of streets in modern urban shopping centres.

Theme names were generally considered good, since they made it easy to associate a street with a specific part of town. Many respondents wished that such names should reflect the spirit of the town. For example, people felt a suitable theme for the town of Kouvola would be the railway and expressed a wish that more street names belonged under that particular theme. People would argue that 'The town was built around the railway, but the streets are still lacking', and that 'Kouvola is a significant railway junction and famous for it'. In general, the residents of Kouvola wished for simple themes that 'would bring about good memories and nice images'. In addition, the different associations related to a name have an effect on whether people like a name or not. For example, a boy living in Vesakuja ('Sprout Alley'; *Vesa* 'Sprout'; but also a personal name) says he does not like street names containing a personal name. In this case, however, the name belongs to group names of natural features.

In a folk onomastic study of commercial names, attention has been paid to, for example, attitudes towards company names and whether people prefer more transparent and descriptive or arbitrary names (Bergien 2007).

25.5 Conclusion

Socio-onomastic research has been carried out for over forty years now. In spite of the multifaceted research thus far, many areas have still hardly been touched upon. In the socio-onomastic study of place-names, rural names have been in focus for decades, but urban names still lack comprehensive research. So far we know very little about what place-names—both official and unofficial—are used in multi-layered and often multilingual urban environments. The same topic also concerns personal names: How are they used in multilingual contexts? Research into commercial names is still rather scarce due to the young age of the field, and socio-onomastic studies are few. One of the most interesting questions for the future is to investigate the attitudes and stances that people take towards commercial names and how people talk about commercial products and businesses in actual language use.

CHAPTER 26

....

NAMES AND IDENTITY

....

EMILIA ALDRIN

26.1 INTRODUCTION

....

ONE of the main functions of a name is to single out and identify its referent (cf. chapter 3 of this handbook). Therefore, naming is always a question of assigning identity. However, does this necessarily mean that names have an actual impact on the formation or perception of identity? If this is the case, how and why is this effect achieved? Which parts of identity would this concern? Furthermore, what happens when names are changed? These are some of the questions that this chapter will address.

The notion that names and identity are closely intertwined has long been seen as self-evident in onomastic literature. However, although it is often stated as a fact, it is seldom further substantiated, critically examined, or scientifically proved. During recent decades, the identity approach has become increasingly popular in onomastic studies. This development is in line with general linguistics; as well as with other fields, and can be seen as part of a widely spread scientific paradigm of identity (Edwards 2009: 15–18). This calls for a deeper understanding of theories of identity and how they can be put into practice in onomastic studies. Although the topic of name and identity is not new, there are still many questions that are yet to be addressed and areas that need further empirical examination. This chapter will provide an overview of theoretical and methodological tools for the study of names and identity, outline current trends and gaps within the field of research, and give key references for further reading. The focus will be on names in contemporary times, primarily personal names; however, other name categories will also be included to some extent. Due to the expected international group of readers, only research reported in English in internationally available channels (until 2013) will be referred to; although this will limit the scope of attention and likely excludes certain interesting contributions.

The chapter is divided into four sections. This introduction (26.1) will be followed by a theoretical section (26.2), which explores and compares different concepts of identity. The third section (26.3) is more empirical and outlines current research as well as suggesting directions for future research within some major areas. The final section (26.4) provides an overview of methodological approaches, and points out their connections to different theoretical concepts of identity.

26.2 THEORETICAL APPROACHES TO IDENTITY

Theories of identity have been widely used and each scientific field has developed its own understanding of the concept and its significance for different aspects of human behaviour (for a concise overview of the history of the identity-concept, see Bemwell and Stokoe 2006: 18–24). As a result, identity can be defined and used in many different ways. However, a common denominator of most theoretical approaches is the notion that identity is a complex concept, which contains aspects that are to some extent contradictory. Depending on how these contradictions are viewed, different theories tend to emphasize certain aspects of identity over others.

26.2.1 What is Identity?

When we think about our own identity, we often do this in terms of 'who we really are', which is a deep, personal, and sometimes even mystical sense of one's self. But identity is also related to 'identification', that is, how others look upon us and are able to single us out from a group (Joseph 2004: 1–3). These two perspectives, the inside-perspective and the outside-perspective of identity, may overlap, but may also stand in sharp contrast. They may influence one another, but are rarely the same. In onomastic studies, this means that the name-giver, name-carrier, and name-user may hold different views of identities connected to a certain name. It also means that identity seen from the perspective of name-users, and identity seen from the perspective of researchers, are not the same thing. As a consequence, researchers must decide upon whether or not identity should be given prominence in a certain situation in order to be of significance for participants and relevant to analyse (cf. Bemwell and Stokoe 2006: 84–5; Omoniyi and White 2006: 2).

Furthermore, identity contains both an aspect of 'sameness' and an aspect of 'distinction'. We partly identify ourselves (and others) on the basis of the similarities we see in other people, for example female, young, and foreign. However, we also identify ourselves on the basis of what makes us unique and what differentiates us from those whom we do not want to align with, in terms of for example personality traits or group membership. Based on this distinction, researchers sometimes differentiate between personal and social identity. Personal identity signifies an individual's personal and unique experience of his or her own self in terms of all the individual traits he or she possesses

(Edwards 2009: 19). Social identity focuses on how this sense of self is based on the social relations and social groups that the individual engages in.[1] However, most theories see them as co-dependent and intertwined (Joseph 2004: 5; Edwards 2009: 19–20).

Chryssochoou (2003: 229) sees identity as the unified answer to the questions: Who am I? Who are they? and What is our relationship? She concludes that identity research can focus on any one of these questions. First, research can focus on how self-knowledge is constructed, developed, and anchored in previous self-knowledge. Secondly, it can focus on how self-knowledge is communicated to others in dialogue between one´s self and others. Thirdly, it can focus on how self-knowledge is used to create future change in terms of, for example, impact on the actions of others or promoting particular political and social projects or versions of society. Any of these approaches could be applied in studies of names and naming. It has also been observed that identity has further fundamental aspects, including authenticity (in contrast to deceitfulness) and authority (in contrast to powerlessness) (Bucholtz and Hall 2005: 598), which may be of great relevance for the analysis of certain names.

A third complicating factor is that over a life-time and when interacting in different contexts and with different people, our identities tend to change and differentiate. At the same time, it is possible for most of us to perceive ourselves as being one and the same (Edwards 2009: 19; cf. Coupland and Nussbaum 1993). This raises questions of durability and change, which are also relevant for the field of names and identity.

26.2.2 Essentialism and Social Constructionism

Some theories view identity as an essence, a personal property belonging to an individual or a personal dimension within an individual. Identity, therefore, is who we *are*. This understanding implies identity being something given and stable. It is one coherent unity, or includes a core that always remains the same (cf. Krogseth 2012: 162). Most early theories of identity are of this kind, as well as many psychological approaches (for an overview and further references, see Widdicombe 1998: 192–4; Omoniyi and White 2006: 16–18). Other theories view identity as a social construct, something that is socially created and contextually flexible. Identity, therefore, becomes something we *do* (Taylor and Spencer 2004: 4; Bucholtz and Hall 2005: 587) or even a continuous *process* (de Fina et al. 2006: 2). People are seen to have multiple identities and these may even be contradictory (de Fina et al. 2006: 2). Most postmodern and linguistic post-structural theories are of this kind. Within constructionist approaches, there is an ongoing debate regarding to what extent identity is freely chosen by individuals, or rather mediated by varying contextual and societal factors (Omoniyi and White 2006: 2) or a result of negotiation with others in interaction (Widdicombe 1998: 202–3). A different approach altogether is used within ethnomethodology, which disregards the debate regarding

---

[1] Social (collective) identity can also signify norms, values, goals, and ideologies that are common within a group (Krogseth 2012: 163).

what identity is, and instead focuses on how identity is treated by people (Widdicombe 1998: 202–3).

26.2.3 Identity, Language, and Names

Most theoretical approaches acknowledge language as being important for identity creation. Some theories view language primarily as a medium which enables the expression of identity to themselves and to others (Taylor and Spencer 2004: 3). Other theories claim that identity is actually constituted in language (Bemwell and Stokoe 2006: 17). It has even been argued that identity is a major function of language (alongside communication and representation) (Joseph 2004: 20). An important mechanism underlying the relationship between language and identity is indexicality, that is, the creation of semiotic links between linguistic forms and social meanings through making use of cultural, linguistic, and social conventions and norms (Bucholtz and Hall 2005; Eckert 2008).

Regarding name and identity, there is to date no coherent onomastic theory. Some researchers view the relationship between name and identity as primarily symbolic. For example, vom Bruck and Bodenhorn (2006b: 27) see naming as 'the recognition, rather than the imposition of personhood'. Other researchers argue that names have a real impact on identity formation and perception. Alford (1988: 36) describes naming as a way to help shape identity. Longobardi (2006: 190) regards a name as a suit in which people are born: 'a reality in which we emerge, progressively assimilating the characteristics contained in it'. He asks which conditions exist that enable people to accept and reflect themselves in a name that has been chosen by others. From the perspective of the name-giver, naming can be seen as 'a communicative act that serves an identity function' (Laskowski 2010: 84). From this point of view, the question arises of whose identity is communicated and towards whom it is directed. Aldrin (2011: 251) views naming of children as 'a resource for contributing to the creation of different identities' and suggests that they are both identities for themselves and for the child. Fründén (2010: 22–33, 264) has concluded that in cases of name-change, identity is communicated both towards the self, towards groups of which the person is a member (such as an ethnic group), and towards society as a whole (cf. Alford 1988: 51). However, names and identity have also been discussed within other fields such as philosophy, psychology, anthropology, sociology, and economy. Renowned theorists from Plato, Mill, Searle, Kripke to Mead, Freud, Piaget and Levi-Strauss, Bourdieu, Derrida, Lacan, and Butler have approached the topic (for further references and an overview of some of their conclusions, see vom Bruck and Bodenhorn 2006b).

26.3 LINKING NAMES AND IDENTITY

This section will outline some of the major areas within the field of names and identity. However, as anthropologists vom Bruck and Bodenhorn (2006b: 26) have pointed out, it must be remembered that names are part of cultures and specific social contexts, and their meaning and significance for identity must be expected to vary.

26.3.1 Names and Personal Identity

The link between name and personal identity seems to be constructed from early on. Psychological studies show that, as children, we often consider names to be actual parts of objects, carrying the same characteristics. Many children even believe that things cannot exist without their names (Dion 1983: 249). From the point of view of parents, the link between name and identity begins even before the child recognizes it. Layne (2006) has analysed naming practices among parents who lost their child before birth, and found that, in the absence of bodies, names enable parents to talk to and about their babies and hence recognize them as persons. A much investigated topic is the relationship between name and self-esteem. Numerous studies show that people´s assessment of their names is related to how they view themselves. People who like themselves generally also like their names (and vice versa) (Joubert 1993). A recent onomastic study (Wikstrøm 2012) has shown that not only first names, but also surnames, are connected to personal identity, since a common motivation for liking one's surname is that 'it is me'. Furthermore, nicknames are connected to personal identity, in terms of who the name carrier is expected to be within a certain group (Starks et al. 2012).

However, correlation does not prove causation. These studies do not answer whether names actually influence or merely mirror identity. The causation behind the correlation could go either way, or be caused by a third, unknown variable. For example: it has been suggested that the underlying mechanism is a so called mere-ownership effect (Gebauer et al. 2008: 1346), that is a tendency to evaluate objects that are related to oneself (such as a name) more positively than other objects. On the other hand, Wikstrøm (2012: 266) has found that people with uncommon surnames show stronger identification with their names than others, which suggests an impact of name type. Alford (1988: 59) has shown that the etymology of a name also sometimes has an effect on name-bearers. In order to confirm either of these theories, there is a need for further research exploring how different kinds of names (for example: common/unusual, culturally marked/unmarked, etc.) correlate with different degrees of self-esteem and identification, depending on whether they are liked or disliked by the name-bearer.

As identity is created in relation to others, the perception of names may also be of importance for identity formation. This is supported by psychological studies that show people liking their own names more when they believe that others like the name as well (Longobardi 2006). One way to theoretically approach this matter, is through a model of a self-fulfilling prophecy (Erwin 1995: 42–3). Another approach is the name-based interpersonal neglect hypothesis (Gebauer et al. 2011), according to which names influence interpersonal treatment, which in turn influences the identity formation and self-esteem of the name-bearer.

Research on names and personal identity has often been conducted within psychology and through experimental tests that are quantitatively analysed. Therefore, there is a need for complementary qualitative approaches. Furthermore, there has been little investigation into how the relationship between name and identity evolves over time, different situations, and different parts of life (cf. Nicolaisen 1999). There is also a need for further investigation into the relationship of names to other aspects of identity than self-esteem.

26.3.2 Names and Social Identity

A common notion is that personal (individual) identity is primarily expressed through first names; whereas social identity (related to group or family) is primarily expressed through nicknames and surnames (cf. Alford 1988: 144). However, we have already seen that both first names, nicknames, and surnames may express personal identity, and all three name types may also express social identity. Research in this area is often conducted through qualitative approaches; either through interviews or survey questionnaires.

Surnames often constitute an important part of a person's social identity in terms of feeling connectedness to a certain family. According to Finch (2008: 713), surnames can be tools for constituting and managing family relationships. A shared surname can provide a cross-generational linkage with a persons' parents and the previous history of the family, as well as creating a sense of connectedness with partners, spouses, children, and others in a current kin network (Finch 2008: 711, 721). However, as individuals move through different relationships and may have children with different partners, the relationship between a shared (or not shared) surname and a sense of kinship becomes quite complex (Finch 2008: 722; cf. de Stadler 1999: 276–7). This raises questions of the significance of surnames for the construction of family identity in current society. Nevertheless, Davies (2011) has shown that children still view surnames as an important part of the construction of family and kin identities. This is an important area in need of further research.

Nicknames, on the other hand, are connected to a person's social identity within the group where the name is given. The meaning of the nickname may express the position of the name carrier within the group (Harré 1980). Nicknames can also contribute to the social identity of the name giver, expressing who has the status and power to decide how others should be identified (Adams 2009). Since the uses of nicknames vary according to contexts, these names may be more suitable than official names for exploring the flexible nature of identity, which is an interesting area for further studies.

First names may also create or express social identity. This may occur when children are named after relatives (Finch 2008: 719) or are given names to express the cultural background of the family (cf. section 26.3.3 below). According to Longobardi (2006: 91), a child's relationship to its name is a reflection of his or her relationship to the care-givers who chose the name. Aldrin (2011) has shown that, from the parent's point of view, the choice of first name for a child is always part of the creation and display of social identities, including local identities as being, for example, a more or less traditional name-giver, or acting in accordance with certain macro-societal groups.

Regarding social identity in terms of a shared identity within a collective group, it has been noted that the use of specific names within a group can help to provide cohesion and reinforce the sense of a shared identity (Ashley 1996a: 1748; Rymes 1996: 252). According to Ashley, 'the knowledge of those names bespeaks the full-fledged member; failure to follow the rules of names and naming within the group betrays ignorance or signals disrespect' (1996a: 1748). Generally, there is a need for further investigation into naming as part of collective identities and how these processes come into practice in different kinds of groups.

26.3.3 Names and Cultural Identity

It is evident from anthropological studies of naming that the relationship between name and identity can be viewed very differently in different cultures of the world (cf. Alford 1988; vom Bruck and Bodenhorn 2006a). It is also evident that the choice of name can act as an expression or construction of cultural identities. Research in this area is often conducted through surveys and interviews that are analysed using either quantitative or qualitative methods. Several studies have shown that the naming of children among immigrants and couples of 'mixed' cultural backgrounds is often handled through mixing names (or name components) from different cultural spheres in order to create a complex and flexible identity, or through the use of international names (Sue and Telles 2007; Edwards and Caballero 2008; Reisæter 2012).

Naming and name change in minority groups (see de Stadler 1999; Gerritzen 2007b; Fränden 2010) and in former colonies (see Neethling 2007; Reed 2010) have also been studied, in order to provide insights into the handling of multiple cultural identities and identity creation in situations of suppression, stigma, and revitalization. Name changes among recent immigrants, on the other hand, as well as their consequences for cultural identity, have attained very little scientific attention. Many immigrants do change their own names on arrival in the new country, or later; as a result of, for example, misspellings, mispronunciations, or discrimination based on the name, and this is an interesting topic for further investigation.

While it is sometimes taken for granted that name choice in a multicultural environment reflects the degree of cultural assimilation, Bursell (2011: 482–3) argues that it can also serve other functions, such as a pragmatic passing strategy in order to provide anonymity and facilitate public interaction. An important topic that would need further investigation is the observation that the creation of cultural identity through name choice is often intersectionally related to social and gender related issues (cf. Sue and Telles 2007; Becker 2009).

An unexplored topic is the perspective of the named children/adults and their own views on their names as contributing to certain cultural identities (exception,

Thompson 2009: 203). Important questions that are yet to be investigated here include the perceived interplay between the perspectives of the name-giver and name-bearer, as well as the interplay between the inside-perspective of cultural identity and the outside-perspective of cultural identification and their coherence or change throughout different contexts (cf. Bursell 2011: 485).

In an increasingly globalized world, the choice of domestic vs. international names among non-immigrants is another theme that could be fruitfully analysed in terms of how this affects the development of different local or global identities.

26.3.4 Change of Name and Identity

Providing that names and identity are closely linked together, what, then, happens when names are changed? Do name changes reflect changes in identity, or do they bring them about? Alford (1988: 158) considers name change to be a strategy for leaving an old, unwanted identity. It has also been observed that name changes may reflect a wish to declare a new political, religious, or sexual identity (Falk 1975–6: 653–4; Reed 2010). However, in the case of political refugees and others who need to remain invisible in order to survive, a change of name can provide a way to improve one's chances in society without having to change identity (Duchaj and Ntihirageza 2009). Similarly, Emmelheinz (2012: 159) describes the process of name change as a manifestation, not of identity change, but of identity elasticity.

Although voluntary changes of first names among adults are possible in most cultures, they are generally not very common (although in some cultures they are the rule rather than the exception, see Alford 1988: 81). This pattern may be due to the fact that first names are so closely linked to one's identity, so that although one may be dissatisfied with one's name, a change of name would mean too great a cost in terms of identity loss (cf. Humphrey 2006: 166–7). Surprisingly, this matter has hardly been investigated.

Regarding surnames, name changes are much more common and have also been more analysed. Much research has been done on women's change of surname when entering marriage. Early studies of this kind often argue that marital name-change implies defining the self in relation to the husband at an expense to self (see further references in Stafford and Kline 1996: 86). This means that a changed identity is a more or less unavoidable consequence of a changed name. However, later studies have concluded that marital name choice includes negotiations of far more complex identities. It seems to be related to personal identity, including questions of autonomy and professional identity (Laskowski 2010: 81), as well as establishing an identity as a couple (Kerns 2011: 105). It also seems to be related to social identity, including the handling of social values, norms, and social pressure (Mills 2003: 101). There is some disagreement regarding whether the handling of these different identities creates any conflict for the individual (Laskowski 2010), which calls for further investigation. There is also a need for deeper qualitative analyses to complement the available quantitative studies.

Furthermore, men's experiences of different kinds of marital choices (their own as well as those of their spouses) have so far been largely neglected within the field.

Change of name among children is an almost unexplored area. One interesting aspect here is parents' treatment of names of internationally adopted children. As many of these children already carry a name when adopted, parents have a choice: either to keep the full birth culture name or to change it in some way. Suter (2012) has found that identity-concerns are highly important for parents when making this choice, including the handling of both the child's cultural and personal identity as well as a new family identity. Further studies in this area, including studies on adoptees' own views on name-change as a basis for identity construction, would be highly interesting.

26.3.5 Names and Identity in Digital Environments

The growing use of digital environments poses specific questions regarding meanings, constructions, and consequences of identity. According to Gatson (2011: 232), 'selves are constructed, constituted, enacted, and negotiated through multiple mediums, on multiple levels, and with connected and disconnected others' in contemporary society. Since text production is often regarded as being more deliberate than speech production, the creation of online identities may become even more important than offline identities as representations of the self (Gatson 2011: 224, 226).

Names in digital environments enable researchers to explore questions of authenticity vs. deceitfulness, unity vs. multiplicity, and anonymity vs. publicity of identities, as well as the general relationship between online and offline identities. Recent studies show that online names are often self-related and disclose some kind of information about the personal identity of the name-bearer (Bechar-Israeli 1995; Gatson 2011; Hassa 2012). They can further contribute to strengthening solidarity and group identity among participants, as well as attracting contacts (Hagström 2012: 89; Hassa 2012: 206). In some cases, it has been found that they enable people to display a congruent sense of self with a strong link between online and offline identities, rather than fragmentized parts of identity separate from the offline self (Gatson 2011). However, in order to confirm or disregard these initial results, further research is needed where consideration is paid to differences between various digital contexts.

26.3.6 Names and Perceived Identity

Following an outside-perspective on identity, the question of how others perceive identities through names is also important. Existing research related to this area is the topic of name-based stereotypes, that is, the idea that names 'in general arouse widely-held images' in terms of positive or negative generalizations about individuals (Erwin 1995; Lawson 1996a: 1744; cf. Hagström 2012). However, most of this research focuses on stereotype patterns, rather than on the mechanisms behind their creation, or the consequences for individuals' identity formation. Gebauer et al. (2008) have made an interesting attempt to elucidate how the impact of unjust treatment based on name-based stereotypes influences personal identity in terms of self-esteem. Another interesting new topic in this area concerns how people may try to avoid such unjust treatment through selective presentation of identity and to what extent such a strategy may also affect their own sense of identity (Kaplan and Fisher 2009).

Research on names and perceived identity has primarily been conducted through experimental tests. Thus, studies using qualitative approaches would be of benefit to further explore these topics. There is also a need for more studies on the perception of surnames and identity.

26.3.7 Names and Identity in Interaction

During interaction, the choice of name is closely linked to choice of identity, both in terms of how we want to be perceived in a certain situated context, and in terms of how others perceive us. There is a range of possible onomastic appellations (i.e. first name, surname, nickname) as well as non-onymic appellations (i.e. title, pronoun, kinship term) to choose from in order to create various identities. As a result, the use of names in interaction presents an opportunity to explore how identity is negotiated from moment to moment in relation to others (cf. Alford 1988: 97–8, 159–65; Humphrey 2006; McConnel-Ginnet 2006). The study of names in interaction is a rather new area within onomastics (cf. chapter 4 and chapter 29). Further research on names and identity in interaction spreading across cultures, social groups, and varying situations, might illuminate the relationship between flexible identities and the sense of being 'one and the same self' over time, including the issue of possible role conflict. It could also give valuable insights into the relationship between the inside-perspective and outside-perspective of identities.

26.3.8 Identity and Non-anthroponomical Name Categories

Identity theory is naturally most easily applied to anthroponomy, and has also been mostly used in studies of personal names (although see chapter 28). However, studies of other name categories may also benefit from an identity perspective. Since all human actions can constitute part of identity creation, in theory, all names that are chosen by humans could potentially constitute part of the creation, expression, and perception of identities. This is acknowledged by Neethling (2009a), who has studied individualized registration plates of vehicles and found that they express a link to the preferred identity of the vehicle owner in terms of lifestyle, worldview, values, political affiliation, and religious belief. Similarly, it would be possible to study names of pets and horses, as well as nicknames for cars, ships, and other belongings as expressions of identity, with potentially interesting outcomes regarding both personal and social identities of the name-giver; as well as desired or displayed identities of the name-bearers. Object specific and situational variation should also be accounted for. Furthermore, commercial names (cf. chapter 31) could be interesting to explore from an identity perspective. For example: Boerrigter (2007) stresses that the name is a key element of a company's identity and points to the strategic importance of people perceiving the same company identity or image through the name as the one that the company wants to communicate.

26.4 STUDYING NAMES AND IDENTITY—METHODOLOGIES

As should be evident from previous sections of this chapter, there is a multitude of possible methods for studying names in relation to identity. Currently, the most commonly used methods for data collection include written surveys, interviews, and experimental tests. Further methods that are less common, but may have great potential for some topics, include observations and analyses of web-based chat-fora. Every method has benefits as well as disadvantages, and the choice of method should take into consideration factors such as the purpose of the study, name category in focus, theoretical approach to the concept of identity, and, when appropriate, ethical concerns. Regardless of the chosen method, researchers should also consider to what degree the collection of data will enable reliability and generalization.

26.4.1 Interviews

Interviews provide the researcher with in-depth information on participants' own views and experiences of a phenomenon (see for example Laskowski 2010; Aldrin 2011; Suter 2012). As such, they have great value for qualitative studies and approaches to identity from an inside-perspective. Researchers who argue that identity must be prominent in the analysed situation in order to be a relevant theoretical tool might especially consider using this method. It is quite suitable for a constructionist concept of identity, but it is also adequate for research based on a more essentialist concept. Furthermore, interviews can be used to explore a great variety of topics regarding names and identity, including formation, expression, and perception of identities, both personal and social identities, as well as questions of durability and change, unity and multitude, and any name categories. Interviews conducted with groups of people enable analyses of identity negotiation and identity in interaction as well as social identity in terms of a common identity of a group.

A disadvantage of interviews is that they are time-consuming to conduct. If the researcher has an interest in the changing nature of identities in interaction, it is also important to calculate time for careful transcription of the recorded interviews. Another aspect that must be taken into consideration is the so-called observers' paradox. This is the notion that participants may unconsciously alter their answers as a result of, for example, perceptions of what kind of answers are expected, attitudes toward the topic, the behaviour and reactions of the interviewer (and other participants), discomfort with the chosen environment, as well as possible embarrassment at being interviewed by someone of the same or different sex, age, ethnicity, social group, and religion as themselves.

26.4.2 Written Surveys

Written surveys provide the researcher with extensive data and enable an overview over large-scale patterns and conventions, as well as correlations between different intersectional variables (see for example Becker 2009; Aldrin 2011; Kerns 2011; Wikstrøm 2012). They are, therefore, primarily suitable for quantitative analyses; although it is possible to include open-ended questions that can be qualitatively analysed. Furthermore, written surveys are especially appropriate for questions that do not demand long answers. Both personal and social identities can be studied. The method is especially suitable for studies of social identities (in terms of engagement in or a sense of belonging to social groups), correlation between different kinds of identity, and perception of identities and connected norms and values. Written surveys are most easily used when agreeing with an essentialist identity concept. They can be used from a constructionist point of view, but such an attempt needs careful consideration as to what kind of data will be collected in terms of social constructs, how the situational impact can be understood, and to what extent it is possible to regard answers from different respondents as comparable. Negotiation and variability of identities are difficult to capture with this method. A benefit is that written surveys are relatively easy to distribute and collect, but they demand careful planning and testing to ensure that the choice and formulation of questions function satisfactorily. In order to enable proper statistical analysis and measures of signification, researchers also need to master suitable computer programs.

26.4.3 Experimental Tests and Observations

Experimental tests and observations can provide the researcher with information, not only on what people think they do, but on what they actually do in a specific situation (see for example Gebauer et al. 2011; Hagström 2012). Hence, they may be of great value for researchers interested in an outside-perspective of identity. Topics for which these methods are suitable include names and perceived identities, self-assessment in relation to name-assessment, and expressed identities through name use in interaction. While experimental tests are used to study human action in one specific situation that is created and highly controlled by the researcher, observations can be used to compare human action in different situations that are naturally occurring. The methods demand careful planning including consideration of possible ethical issues. As with interviews, the observer's paradox may influence the results. Since neither experimental tests nor observations provide insight into individuals' own view of identity and identification, they cannot be used to study identity formation.

26.4.4 Analysis of Web-based Chat-fora

Web-based chat-fora constitute a new way to collect data (see, e.g., Gatson 2011; Matthews 2011; Hagström 2012; Hassa 2012). Discussions on the internet may provide insights into people's views on names, identity, and identification, without the restraints of a scientific context and a present researcher. Both essentialist and constructionist concepts of identity can be analysed. This method is naturally suitable for studies of names and identity in digital environments, but can also be used to study names in relation to, for example, social and cultural identities, as well as perceived identities, providing that suitable chat-fora are found. It is only possible to analyse name categories that are used or discussed on the internet. A disadvantage of this method is that it is often impossible to gain any background information about the participants. There are also ethical limitations, regarding what kind of analyses it is appropriate to make, considering that people may not always be aware of the fact that what they write in web-based chat-fora is available to a wider public.

CHAPTER 27

LINGUISTIC LANDSCAPES

GUY PUZEY

27.1 INTRODUCTION

In recent years, a steadily growing body of interdisciplinary research has adopted the term *linguistic landscape* (LL) to describe the object of analysis when examining issues of language visibility and the interactions between different languages in public spaces. LL research has largely been carried out in fields such as sociolinguistics, multilingualism, language policy, cultural geography, semiotics, literacy, education, and social psychology, although the findings of these studies are also of relevance to broader disciplinary areas within art and architecture, advertising, tourism, town and rural planning, transport research, and even public health. By investigating the ways in which different languages are rendered visible (or invisible), it is possible to explore the symbolic construction of space and the use of language to mediate social and political relations. With its extensive empirical evidence of the role of names in society, the LL can be an especially compelling object of study in the domain of socio-onomastics. Furthermore, as LL studies essentially focus on the spatial dimension of language use, there is a significant overlap of interests between LL research and toponomastics, which is also reflected in the diverse, cross-disciplinary appeal of both fields.

Extensive research on the LL has really only emerged over the past decade, but a number of studies have already applied the LL approach to investigate specifically onomastic practices, policies, conflicts, identities, attitudes, and attachments. These ventures have shown LL analysis to be a useful new addition to the onomastician's toolkit, while the focus and theoretical framework of onomastics can also offer valuable insights to inform empirical studies of the LL, as this chapter will seek to demonstrate. Before moving on to outline current research directions in the onomastic dimension of LL inquiry, the first sections after this introduction will discuss the expanding definitions of the LL, including the closely related concepts of geosemiotics and semiotic landscapes, as well as key methodological developments in the field.

27.2 THE CONCEPTUALIZATION AND EXPANDING GAZE OF THE LINGUISTIC LANDSCAPE

In sociolinguistics, less empirical attention has traditionally been paid to written language than to spoken language, with proponents of writing and writtenness as objects of study denouncing the apparent assumption in many approaches that writing somehow belongs 'outside the study of the "language proper"' (Lillis and McKinney 2013: 418). The recent proliferation of LL studies is one way in which researchers have sought to redress the balance. Research has been carried out for at least several decades on the use of language in public space, but its emergence and growth as a specialization is largely an innovation of the past decade, encouraged perhaps by the general spatial turn in cultural studies and in the social sciences and more broadly (Jaworski and Thurlow 2010b: 12). The first use of the term *linguistic landscape* in specific, limited reference to language visibility on signs was accompanied by a definition now frequently seen as a point of reference in outlining the basic object of study in the field:

> The language of public road signs, advertising billboards, street names, place names, commercial shop signs, and public signs on government buildings combines to form the linguistic landscape of a given territory, region, or urban agglomeration. (Landry and Bourhis 1997: 25)

As will be discussed shortly, this definition is far from exhaustive in light of the range of material considered in current LL studies, but it is already apparent in Landry and Bourhis' definition that names are a significant component of the LL. Beyond the specific mentions made of place-names and street names, toponyms are also a major component of road signs, while commercial names will appear on most advertising billboards and shop signs, and the main signs on government buildings will also normally include the names of the public institutions or organizations in question.

Since Landry and Bourhis' specific delineation of LL as an object of study in their research on subjective ethnolinguistic vitality in Québec, the LL field has grown through a number of general anthologies (e.g. Gorter 2006a; Shohamy and Gorter 2009; Jaworski and Thurlow 2010a; Hélot et al. 2012), works concentrating on urban multilingualism (Backhaus 2007; Shohamy et al. 2010), an anthology on minority languages (Gorter et al. 2012), a steadily rising number of individual studies, and several special issues and sections of journals, including the selection of articles on 'Toponomastics and Linguistic Landscapes' in *Onoma* 46.[1]

---

[1] Gorter (2013) gives a panoramic account of the emergence of the field, starting from pioneering studies in the 1970s and covering the chronological development of studies in the wake of the definition provided by Landry and Bourhis (1997).

The term *linguistic landscape* is the most widely used umbrella description of the field, hence its use in this overview, but it does also present inherent problems and is not universally accepted. Part of the problematic nature of the term stems from the simple fact that it continues to be used in a general sense to refer to concepts other than language visibility. Alternative terms have been proposed to describe signs in place, such as '*multilingual cityscape*' (Gorter 2006b: 83), although this term seems to exclude the physical presence of text in rural landscapes (see section 27.4.4 below). *Signscape* would also be an appropriate description of the focus of many studies but, unless understood in a semiotic sense, this would exclude text on anything other than signs. A growing number of researchers have expanded the scope of analysis in LL studies to incorporate other elements of linguistic ecology, such as graffiti texts, which can be an important component of the LL (Pennycook 2009, 2010). Although static written texts have been the main focus of the majority of LL studies to date, text in more mobile, ephemeral, or transient forms is also worthy of investigation, such as text on vehicles or clothing (Marten et al. 2012: 4), 'informal' notices (Muth 2014), or the 'detritus zone' comprised of text on discarded packaging or other ephemera (Kallen 2010: 53–5). So perhaps the concept of *language visibility* is closer to the real concerns of many working with the LL approach, but the very notion of visibility presents problems of its own if the scope of the LL is conceived to include a broader range of modes, sensory domains, and perceptual spaces. Some more radical conceptions of the LL see it as an 'ecological arena' (Shohamy and Waksman 2009), encompassing unwritten texts in public spaces, including other visuals, auditory announcements (Diver 2011: 286), and spoken language, but also texts that are not strictly linguistic, such as the body (Milani 2014: 221), clothing, gestures, movement, food, and emotions. Such an extent of performative expression is mirrored in the range of 'languaging' as described by Elana Shohamy (2006: 14–16). These domains might not all be written in the traditional sense, but they can be seen as texts nonetheless by virtue of being readable and capable of being designed or shaped to communicate a message or create a narrative.

While the scope of the LL might usefully be expanded to incorporate texts that are not written and hence less obviously textual in form, some LL studies have investigated language use in spaces that are either not traditionally seen as public, including more restricted indoor spaces such as the wall space of a laboratory (Hanauer 2009) or the interior of a school (Brown 2012). Other studies have sought different conceptions of the very idea of space itself, for instance focusing on the virtual LL of cyberspace (Ivkovic and Lotherington 2009). The methods and insights of the LL approach could also be applied to study the spatial and linguistic attributes of other written matter not necessarily displayed in public spaces, such as the presentation of language within books or on maps, interfacing with the field of literacy studies (Spolsky 2009: 29).

With its expanding analytical gaze, LL research can explore language and space from the perspective of multimodal discourse analysis, necessitating new understandings of the relationship between text and context. From a semiotic point of view, '[w]hile context was previously background, this is no longer the case; context has now become text' (Flowerdew 2014: 17). In terms of discourse in the material world, physical space would previously have been seen as one such background context, but it is now being re-evaluated as part of the text itself. An influential theoretical contribution in this direction has been the elaboration of *geosemiotics*, 'the study of the social meaning of the material placement of signs and discourses and of our actions in the material world' (Scollon and Scollon 2003: 211). Following on from geosemiotics, an alternative term used by some researchers to highlight the multimodal nature of the symbolic construction of space is the *semiotic landscape*, describing 'any (public) space with visible inscription made through deliberate human intervention and meaning making' (Jaworski and Thurlow 2010b: 2), although the 'visible' attribute may be less universally significant than 'deliberate human intervention'. *Geosemiotics* and the *semiotic landscape* do, therefore, appear to suit the more radically wide-ranging conceptions of the LL, and perhaps these alternative umbrella terms will grow in currency over the coming years.

27.3 LINGUISTIC LANDSCAPE METHODOLOGY AND RESEARCH DIRECTIONS

With the LL approach still in an emergent phase, LL investigations have been described as employing an 'eclectic' range of methodologies, while researchers are now facing the challenge of developing more rigorous and controlled methods (Gorter 2013: 205). Indeed, studies in this field have adopted a wide variety of quantitative and qualitative methods, but one element that most LL research has in common—at least among the studies focusing on visual or visible components of the LL—is the technique of photographic data collection. As has been noted above, the rising popularity of the LL as an object of research may be related in part to the increased attention being paid to matters of space and place generally in cultural and social studies, while acting to address the neglect of writing and writtenness in sociolinguistics too, but it has also been prompted by the increased availability and portability of digital photographic equipment. The advent of affordable digital cameras by the early 2000s has been as significant for LL research as portable tape-recorders were to Labovian research in the 1960s (Backhaus 2007: 55). More recently, the proliferation of built-in high-resolution cameras in mobile telephones has meant that many people now carry the key piece of equipment in their pockets wherever they go, so that even the spontaneous capturing of large amounts of LL material can be a relatively straightforward matter.[2] With the accessibility of the

---

[2] Apart from digital photography itself, another technological innovation that has encouraged the growth of the LL approach is the greater availability and searchability of images online. Services such as Google Street View enable users to scout the LL of distant or less accessible areas, viewing panoramic images along routes around the world. As Google updates the Street View images in some areas on a rolling basis, it is now making archived imagery available too. Although these images date back only a few years to the launch of Street View in 2007, they can be expected to build up over time into an impressive historical resource, and the images currently offered already allow for the study of some diachronic changes in the LL.

data collection methodology, 'camera safaris' of the LL can also make rewarding field-work tasks for students engaging with societal multilingualism and language attitudes (Hancock 2012).

Landry and Bourhis (1997) outlined what they saw as the two main functions of the LL. The first function is informational, in the sense that the presence or absence of a given language on signs in a specific territory or locality may provide direct information about linguistic boundaries, while also informing the expectations of the readers of those signs as to which languages are in accepted use for communication in the area. The second function of the LL is symbolic, as the relative visibility of languages in the LL vis-à-vis each other contributes to the shaping of 'subjective ethnolinguistic vitality' (Landry and Bourhis 1997: 27). Many early LL studies began by taking a quantitative approach, systematically investigating primarily the first function in order to probe or map the distribution of text in different languages in a given area, with the quantitative surveys often tied to some further qualitative analysis of the characteristics of multilingual signs (e.g. Cenoz and Gorter 2006; Backhaus 2007). Determining which languages are visible in a given area can in itself sometimes be an indication of the extent of linguistic diversity, as in a survey that identified and mapped traces of twenty-four different languages in the LL of the Esquilino district of Rome (Bagna and Barni 2006: 24).

As these early studies also recognized, it is important to look beyond the basic message that any given LL item might convey to see the complex symbolic nature of the LL. Rarely does the mere presence or absence of text in public spaces represent linguistic hierarchies or the relationships between languages accurately or comprehensively, but the distortions in the 'carnival mirror' of the LL allow for more profound reflections of the way the landscape is constructed (Gorter 2012: 11). The informational function of the LL might attempt to reflect the sociolinguistic situation, but the power of the symbolic function means that the LL can also manipulate an individual's assessment of the relative status of languages in a place. This could in turn influence that individual's linguistic behaviour, so the relationship between LL and sociolinguistic context is bidirectional (Cenoz and Gorter 2006: 67–8).[3] In terms of onomastics, the relationship between LL and socio-onomastic behaviour is also bidirectional (see section 27.4.2 below).

A qualitative approach to the symbolic function of the LL, in order to assess the varying treatment and relative visibility of different languages, might choose to analyse code preference (Scollon and Scollon 2003: 120). When text is displayed in more than one language, it is difficult to avoid giving one language more prominence. This salience could be determined by such factors as the size of text, the positioning of languages within a sign, the relative positioning of one sign to another, choice of colour, or typeface. Sometimes creative solutions can be used to build some compromise

---

[3] If the LL is seen as a living text in its own right, then the bidirectional relationship that exists between LL and its context can be seen in domains other than the purely linguistic, as explored by Jackie Jia Lou (2014) in her geosemiotic study of an advertising campaign related to the gentrification of an area in Washington, DC. Lou (2014: 220) suggests that 'it is the task of the analyst to describe how other forms of capital are transformed into symbolic capital', and that geosemiotics represents one response to this task 'by locating the symbolic power of place in its concrete spatial context'.

FIGURE 27.1 This sign at the entrance to the village of Drumnadrochit, in the Highland council area of Scotland, features the name of the village in both Gaelic and English. It is the intention of the Gaelic Language (Scotland) Act 2005 that Gaelic should have the status of 'an official language of Scotland commanding equal respect to the English language', and the latest design used for official bilingual signage on roads in Scotland incorporates an innovative solution to achieve greater equality of linguistic presentation while also differentiating visually between the two languages. Gaelic text appears above English, in exactly the same typeface, size, and style, but in a slightly less prominent colour (in this case, yellow against a green background, while the English text is in white). Nonetheless, this sign is not completely bilingual: '*Fàilte*' is missing a diacritic mark, there is no reason to capitalize the word '*gu*', and there is no Gaelic version given of 'Please drive carefully'.

Photograph: Guy Puzey, August 2007.

between languages into bilingual sign design, such as with recent Gaelic–English bilingual road signs in Scotland (see Figs. 27.1 and 27.3) and street signs in the Canadian capital Ottawa that use dual French and English generic elements, reading for example 'RUE WELLINGTON ST' (Puzey 2011a: 214–15). The choice and ordering of languages used on signs may correspond to the three simple 'conditions' of language preference proposed by Spolsky and Cooper (1991), in specific relation to signs, before the focus on the LL became widespread. They proposed first that a language chosen will normally be known to the writer (at least to some extent), secondly that a language may be chosen based on the 'presumed reader', and thirdly that the 'symbolic value condition' might play a determining role, implying preference for a language with which the user wishes to be identified, or avoiding a language with which the user does not wish to be identified.

Language policy was described by Spolsky (2004) according to a tripartite model made up of management, practices, and beliefs. The LL can be seen to interface with all three components, often illustrating where there are inconsistencies or discrepancies, and indeed a number of LL studies have focused on policy perspectives (e.g. Dal Negro 2009; Sloboda et al. 2010; Blackwood and Tufi 2012; Puzey 2012). Shohamy (2006) expanded Spolsky's framework to detail the 'mechanisms' of language policy, through which 'real' or 'de facto' policy can be seen. These mechanisms include 'language in the public space', and their close examination can serve to evaluate the extent to which de facto language policy might differ from declared policy or non-policy. In light of the bidirectional relationship between LL and sociolinguistic context, scrutiny of the LL as a language policy mechanism or arena is especially informative in terms of the interconnections between (language) ideology and practice. For instance, the bilingual municipal boundary signs installed by some local authorities in Lombardy, featuring the Lombard forms of place-names alongside those in Italian, are generally perceived as an initiative associated with the Lega Nord (Northern League), a right-wing regionalist political party and movement that has long been carrying out graffiti campaigns to 'dialectize' place-names on road signs. The visibility of this dialect activist campaign has created a situation in which many locals see any organized policy initiative in favour of Lombard dialects as a project of the Lega Nord, irrespective of the identity or affiliation of the actual actors involved (Puzey 2011c: 310).

A key distinction has been made in some LL studies between at least two main 'flows' of agency in the production of the LL, with reference to 'top-down' and 'bottom-up' LL items. The top-down flow was originally defined as 'elements used and exhibited by institutional agencies which in one way or another act under the control of local or central policies', while bottom-up items are 'utilised by individual, associative or corporative actors who enjoy autonomy of action within legal limits' (Ben-Rafael et al. 2006: 10). There are often differences between the linguistic practices of public and private actors, but neither of these flows is monolithic. From the perspective of LL authorship (Malinowski 2009), the processes involved in the construction of the LL can be complex, with a multitude of actors involved in regulating, initiating, owning, designing, and installing LL items (Puzey 2012: 142). As a result, the LL can be used to illustrate how language policy (management, practices, and beliefs) is affected by technocratic and market-driven considerations. Furthermore, the distinction between 'top' and 'bottom' actors can often be blurred or diluted by processes such as privatization, with corporative actors taking over functions previously vested in the state or other public authorities. It can be argued that an approach paying closer attention to the nature and changing distribution of economic, social, cultural, and symbolic capital would provide a more refined understanding of the complex roles of actors. Privatized services, for instance, can arguably be seen as more top-down than those run by the state, if the public has less oversight and direct influence on how the services are run (Puzey 2011c: 31).

Some recent LL research has shown a new methodological focus on 'a more discursive and principled material ethnography of multilingualism', better able to respond to mobility within and between societies (Stroud and Mpendukana 2009: 380). The approach taken by Stroud and Mpendukana, in their ethnographic survey of multilingual landscapes in the township of Khayelitsha in South Africa's Western Cape, considers the material constraints of production in the LL, the social circulation of different languages, and a multiplicity of spaces and semiotic artefacts, including 'signs, newspapers, books, TV channels, music videos, etc.' (Stroud and Mpendukana 2009: 364). A clearer picture emerges from their study of LLs 'as sedimented products of a socially and economically determined articulation of (community) multilingual resources' (Stroud and Mpendukana 2009: 380). These further reflections on the distinctive properties of the LL itself are also related to the previously mentioned conceptualizations of geosemiotics (Scollon and Scollon 2003) and semiotic landscapes (Jaworski and Thurlow 2010b), as well as the established notion of landscape as a 'way of seeing the external world . . . closely bound up with the practical appropriation of space' (Cosgrove 1985: 46).

As well as authorship, another important perspective on the LL is that of its reception or readership. Reader responses to the LL can frequently be found in newspaper letter pages (Puzey 2010), but they can sometimes also be traced in the landscape itself, when objections to LL items are expressed through vandalism (Puzey 2011b). One intriguing comparative study of the public evaluation of the LL adopted an advocacy coalition framework to examine the interactions of bottom-up language activists and top-down language policy actors in the Czech Republic, Hungary, and Wales, with evidence drawn from discourse-based data (Sloboda et al. 2010). Some recent studies have explored the authorship, reading, or habitation of the LL as a lived experience, engaging in participatory fieldwork. In his study of LL authorship in a selection of Korean American businesses in California, Malinowski (2009) took a multimodal analytical approach, drawing on interviews, participant observation and joint visual analysis. Lou (2010) described the planning and design review meetings involved in the use of Chinese on hoardings at a new AT&T shop in the Chinatown district of Washington, DC, as well as using participant-drawn maps as evidence of individual experience of the LL and individual naming practices. One especially stimulating participatory methodology was the 'postmodern "walking tour" interview' used by Garvin (2010) to study cognitive and emotional responses to the LL of Memphis while accompanying participants at the site in question. The video tour method elaborated by Pink (2007) in order to investigate places from a visual ethnographic viewpoint also stands to make an important contribution to future LL research. As increasing attention is paid to the human-interactional aspects of the LL and their role in reading the world, new studies can also be expected to view the LL, and language in general, as part of the 'sensory regime' through which we experience the world (Roth-Gordon 2012).

A contribution to one of the anthologies that marked a turning point in LL studies raised the question as to whether the LL is 'a phenomenon calling for a theory, or simply a collection of somewhat disparate methodologies for studying the nature of public written signs' (Spolsky 2009: 25). The attractiveness, accessibility, and broad scope of the evidence-gathering methodologies are clear, and the sheer volume of data available in the LL has created new opportunities for researchers. Challenges still remain as the methodological and theoretical approaches to the LL steadily continue to develop and mature. The very definition of the LL can be quite elastic, and a more careful separation of umbrella terms may emerge in due course, but the latest developments in agency-focused, ethnographic, material, and participatory research would suggest that there may be some justification for treating the LL—or perhaps more precisely the semiotic landscape—as a distinct phenomenon.

27.4 THE ONOMASTIC DIMENSION OF LINGUISTIC LANDSCAPE RESEARCH

Names occupy a privileged space in the LL, as is clear from the often quoted definition by Landry and Bourhis (1997) (see section 27.2).[4] As a substantial repository of data on observable onomastic practice, the LL is a valuable resource for onomastic research. Furthermore, the new perspectives provided by the LL approach on the social, political, and lived aspects of language in space and place can be valuable contributions to the field of onomastics, but incorporating the specific focus, theoretical and empirical background of onomastics into LL research can also bring benefits to this developing area of study.

A particular synergy would appear to exist between LL studies and the newly formed critical approaches in toponomastic research, which have strengthened the theoretical foundation for investigations into power and place naming. Critical toponomastic studies highlight the effects of unequal power relations on place-names and place-naming processes, shedding light on the 'gloomy side-effect' of the rationalization and standardization of the toponomasticon, which has often led to 'the erasure of the inherited heteroglossia of local names' (Vuolteenaho and Berg 2009: 4). The top-down flow of the LL can, in fact, be a central part of the technocratic-administrative process to establish hegemonic toponymies (Puzey 2011a: 216).

The following subsections will explore some of the areas in which onomastics and the LL approach can be combined to mutual benefit, starting from the LL as a repository of names and observable onomastic practice, moving on to the application of LL research to explore names and language policy, commercial names, and commodification,

---

[4] It is also worth noting that one significant early use of the term 'linguistic landscaping' was by a geographer referring to a specifically onomastic phenomenon: the practice of bestowing aesthetically pleasing names on homes (Lowenthal 1962). This other sense of the term predated the currently widespread definition of the LL by thirty-five years, has had some limited further use in urban architecture studies (Rapoport 1977: 110), and has also appeared in onomastic research (e.g. Vuolteenaho and Ainiala 2009: 227).

before outlining some of the ways in which onomastics might serve to expand the scope of LL studies.

27.4.1 Linguistic Landscapes as Namescapes and Repositories of Names

Before the present general wave of interest in the LL approach, toponomasticians already frequently used place-names as they appear on signs to illustrate descriptive studies. Maps and historical records have been used to a much greater degree than signs as evidence of the written usage of place-names, largely due to the traditionally dominant historical-culturalist orientation of onomastics, but photographs of signs offer the added value of showing the written forms of toponyms displayed in the physical context of the places they denote. This can provide a synchronic dimension to name research by viewing the name in relation to the contemporary landscape, which might, for instance, allow for the relative transparency of the name's meaning to be gauged.

Closely related to the LL is the concept of *namescapes*, occasionally used almost as a synonym of *toponomasticon*, but usually with more of an emphasis on the connotative potential of names and the role of names as components of readable landscapes, as in the comparative reading by Vuolteenaho and Kolamo (2012) of English 'soccer-scapes' and Finnish namescapes tied to the promotion of leisure facilities and commercial businesses. In such studies, the LL can provide empirical evidence of real onomastic practices.

Photographic evidence from the LL can also act as a primary source for the collection of written forms of names, including names that may not appear in maps or gazetteers, perhaps due to their limited range of use or to their relative transience. In his study of the Norf'k-language toponymy of Norfolk Island, Joshua Nash (2011: 100) made use of the LL in this way for the collection of house names and road names.

27.4.2 Linguistic Landscapes, Names, and Language Policy

It was mainly due to experiences of language conflict in minority language contexts that awareness began to spread among onomasticians that 'it does matter in what form a name appears on a sign at the entrance to a village' (Nicolaisen 2011 [1990]: 226). When researchers later started to engage directly with the LL framework and to devote specific attention to place-names as part of the LL, it was also largely in relation to the situation of minority, minoritized, or indigenous languages. Research on Sámi in Norway, Gaelic in Scotland and Nova Scotia, Lombard dialects in Italy and Switzerland (Puzey 2009, 2010, 2011b), indigenous languages in Australia (Kostanski 2011), and Occitan in France (Diver 2011) investigated policies regarding the use of minority place-names in the LL and the societal attitudes towards such practices. Problematizing the onomastic dimension of the LL, these cases all concerned counter-hegemonic acts of naming or renaming.

The forms of names on official signs can be seen as linguistic expressions of 'banal nationalism' (Billig 1995), underlining the position of the LL as 'central to the understanding of individuals' everyday experience of the politics of language' (Puzey 2012: 141).[5] The LL can therefore serve to reinforce the hegemonic narratives of national toponymies. For example, Arabic and Hebrew toponyms are treated differently from each other on official Israeli road signs in the Galilee region, in spite of the officially bilingual policy. While the Hebrew LL is 'clear, accurate, and salient', the Arabic elements in the LL are 'disrupted and spatially suppressed, suffering from nullification, distortion, and designification' (Bigon and Dahamshe 2014: 619). The names of Palestinian settlements in the region are frequently omitted from road signs in favour of the names of Israeli settlements, and many existing Arabic toponyms are replaced with transliterations of the Hebrew names. Some speakers of Arabic have reacted against this, altering signs with spray paint. Indeed, as well as serving 'as a mechanism to affect, manipulate and impose de facto language practices', the LL also operates 'as an arena for protest and negotiations' (Shohamy 2006: 111). This is especially evident in relation to counter-hegemonic toponymic power struggles, often involving minority languages:

> [I]n cases where socio-cultural tensions are paramount, toponymic struggles may surface in a variety of everyday forms: from organized re-naming campaigns to the spontaneous use of alternative names and pronunciations, grouses against the renditions of history in official toponymies, refusals to unlearn marginalized names, and so on. (Vuolteenaho and Berg 2009: 11)

Another example of such a struggle visible in the LL comes from Norway, where the absence of Sámi place-names from most road signs marks a continuation of the long-standing silencing of Sámi names in official use and in the symbolic construction of public space (Rautio Helander 2009). In spite of a legal requirement that, in principle, Sámi place-names should be used alongside Norwegian names wherever these names are in use among local residents, Statens Vegvesen (the Public Roads Administration) has occasionally appeared reluctant to install bilingual signs when these are requested (Pedersen 2009: 42). The issue of bilingual signage has been a sensitive one, not least in the municipality of Gáivuotna-Kåfjord, where the Sámi sections of bilingual signs have in the past been subjected to repeated acts of vandalism (Puzey 2012; see Fig. 27.2).[6]

---

[5] Du Plessis (2013) outlines what can be seen as an interesting example of the LL as a site of banal nationalism, in relation to language choice on car number plates in South Africa.

[6] Road signs, and the threat of road sign vandalism using firearms, are still significant *topoi* in the ongoing debate in Norway about the place of Sámi languages in public spaces (Johansen and Bull 2012; Hiss 2013: 189). The bilingual sign installed in February 2011 at the entrance to the town of Bodø, in Nordland county, had been painted over five times and stolen twice by December 2012 (Guttormsen 2012).

FIGURE 27.2 This municipal boundary sign from Gáivuotna-Kåfjord in Troms county, Norway, is one of the several that were destroyed by vandals. The top panel, featuring the name of the municipality in Sámi, has been erased with shotgun fire. This particular sign is now on display at Tromsø University Museum.

Photograph: Guy Puzey, April 2007.

It is possible to study the LL in terms of the regulatory, planning, and language management approaches to naming and language visibility. For example, Peter Tan (2011) uncovers variations in practice with different categories of names in Singapore's LL, reflecting differences in the application of the officially quadrilingual national language policy. Theodorus du Plessis (2009) discusses the standardization principles currently followed for South African naming, concluding that some of these principles merely reinforce past socio-political hierarchies, in spite of the potential for the LL to legitimize the regime change and help to heal the divisions of apartheid. In Wales, meanwhile, the standardization of Welsh place-names may be seen as part of the construction of a 'more Welsh' LL (Coupland 2010: 84). In terms of restrictive policy, Anastassia Zabrodskaja (2014) points to the changes in Estonian language and toponymic legislation that now require geographical names to be given in Estonian only on signs, as well as requiring registered business names that include key information about the services or location of the business to feature that information in Estonian. Jackie Jia Lou (2013) also considers the use of the name *Chinatown* in urban planning policies in Washington, DC, as part of the place's symbolic construction.

Public reactions to naming controversies in the LL can be examined through discourse-based approaches observing how language beliefs are expressed. For example, Máiréad Moriarty (2012) explored the debate in Ireland over the removal from the official LL of the English place-name *Dingle* for the town known in Irish as *Daingen*

Uí Chúis or *An Daingen* using nexus analysis of language used on the Dingle Wall, a discursive space within the town. In a similar vein, Adrian Koopman (2012b) has used letters printed in local media to explore reactions to the renaming of certain streets in Durban, where some residents painted over signs showing the new street names, objecting to the changes to their local toponymic identities. Identity considerations also came to the fore in relation to name restoration in the Australian state of Victoria, with consequent changes to the LL. Laura Kostanski (2011) describes this debate as a dispute over toponymic identity, revealing a deeply felt individual and societal attachment to place-names, in which LL objects played a major symbolic role.

With the inclusion of minority languages in the LL, the extent of bilingualism or multilingualism is frequently limited to place-names (see Fig. 27.3). Although place-names do have an important identity function, this limited use of minority languages can be seen as tokenism. Indeed, minority languages occasionally appear to be present in the LL primarily for ornamental reasons, as may be the case on the Isle of Man, where Manx text is often presented in a decorative Celtic typeface next to English text in the iconic and supremely legible Transport typeface (Sebba 2010: 68). If any kind of bilingual visual identity is to be successful, it is important that it is backed up by a stronger ethos supportive of plurilingualism (Puzey et al. 2013: 71). Nonetheless, the LL in general,

FIGURE 27.3 A selection of signage at the junction of the A82 and A831 roads in Drumnadrochit, including (on the top centre panel) an unusual instance of a silenced majority language toponym. The Gaelic name *Canaich* is given alone, without the anglicized spelling *Cannich*. This is in accordance with official guidance that 'English place names easily recognisable in Gaelic' can be omitted (Transport Scotland 2006: 44), but it is unclear how the criteria for ease of recognition are applied.

Photograph: Guy Puzey, November 2011.

and place-names in particular, do have the power to shape perceptions of place. This is recognized by Carol Léonard (2009), who suggests that greater knowledge of the French toponomasticon of Saskatchewan among the province's francophone minority could help to counteract LL-derived perceptions of the dominance of English, which is an important example of the two-way relationship between LL and socio-onomastic behaviour (see section 27.3 above).

27.4.3 Commercial Names, Corporate Names, and Commodification

As mentioned above, the LL is a wealth of onomastic source material, especially in terms of more transient naming practices, and there is a particular value of the LL as a start-ing point for research into less established urban names, including commercial names such as those of shops, cafés, and restaurants (Berezkina 2011: 4–5). In her exploration of company names in Turku, Paula Sjöblom (2008c) demonstrates that the meaning of a business name is only partly derived from its linguistic elements. Commercial names draw on a variety of multimodal semiotic resources, with visual, aural, and kinaesthetic modes in addition to the linguistic mode. As studies of geosemiotics and semiotic land-scapes show, the LL is multimodal as a whole, but the business sector is increasingly conscious of the value of these resources and how to use them (Sjöblom 2008c: 351). Multimodality has also become increasingly evident in the multimedia age (Kress and van Leeuwen 1996: 39).

Focusing on the linguistic mode of the LL, and on the choice of languages, Loulou Edelman (2009) points to the particular problem of classifying names according to language. This is especially true of commercial names, although some studies have made use of such classifications, for instance in the diachronic analysis of 1,800 ergo-nyms in the Kazakh capital, Astana (Akzhigitova and Zharkynbekova 2014). When a language choice can be identified, it may 'convey meanings that are not present in the actual words that the name includes' (Sjöblom 2008c: 362). Languages such as French or Italian, for example, may be commodified to suggest fashion or stylishness, while 'global' languages and scripts are frequently used to index notions of cosmo-politanism (Seargeant 2012; Curtin 2014). The names and ephemera associated with businesses can even perform a function related to language learning, as words incor-porated into brands and, for example, restaurant menus, could be among the first that many people learn in other languages (Bagna and Machetti 2012: 228). Generally, however, the characteristics of proper names mean that they cannot always be easily categorized as belonging to any single language, the language of origin is not always obvious, and classification by language can be subjective (Tufi and Blackwood 2010). This is one area in which onomastic perspectives and theories may be able to inform new LL research.

Systems of corporate naming in the public sector are not normally as fluid as in the private sector, but awareness of branding and multimodal resources is also growing among public sector organizations (Hakala and Sjöblom 2013). Multilingualism may be used as a resource in such cases:

> The use of bilingual names for public sector bodies in Scotland is largely part of an effort to demonstrate equal respect for English and Gaelic, but the use of a bilingual corporate identity may also project an image of local or national cultural commitment and socio-cultural responsibility. Since Scotland is the historic base of Gaelic and home to the largest population of Gaelic speakers, the language can also be a valuable resource in place branding or nation branding, contributing to strengthen the sense of place. (Puzey et al. 2013: 21–2).

With the attention paid to place branding and nation branding, even in the public sector, corporate naming in the LL often involves the commodification of names, languages, and the concept of multilingualism itself. This commodification can sometimes be connected to the use of minority languages as well as 'global' languages.

The extent of market pressure in the commodification of the LL is well documented by studying corporate names, advertising, and shop signs (Edelman and Gorter 2010). One intriguing phenomenon exposed by such investigations is the depiction in advertising of secluded holiday landscapes as 'pre-linguistic ... unlabelled, unnamed and "unclaimed"' (Thurlow and Jaworski 2010: 193). This silencing of language and names is intimately linked to the market appropriation and commodification of space, warranting further investigation from an onomastic perspective.

27.4.4 Expanding the Range of LL Studies

Onomastics may have another contribution to make to LL studies by helping to expand the field's spatial gaze. The vast majority of LL studies are concerned with multilingualism in urban areas, and it is true that townscapes and cityscapes exhibit a much higher density of traditionally conceived LL material, which is a consequence of the more concentrated patterns of urban habitation and the form of urban spaces themselves. In LL terms, rural spaces may offer 'a limited class of direction signs and place names, and the roadside billboards often assumed to ruin the landscape' (Spolsky 2009: 33), but this does not mean such spaces should be excluded from analysis.[7] Non-urban spaces are of particular importance in the case of certain minority languages in which the physical presence of public text might be statistically more prevalent in the countryside than in urban agglomerations. Indeed, the exclusion of more geographically peripheral languages from the urban LL—with its connotations of capital, power, and commodity—can be a significant statement of actual language practices. Furthermore,

---

[7] Among research that has expressly sought to focus on rural LLs, there are studies on Austria (Rasinger 2014), Canada (Daveluy and Ferguson 2009), Finland (Laitinen 2014), South Africa (Kotze and du Plessis 2010; du Plessis 2012), and four villages in Norway, Sweden, Finland, and Russia (Salo 2012).

the impact of individual rural LL items may be greater due to their size or relative isolation from other signs.

Many of the studies to date that have combined onomastics and the LL approach have looked at rural contexts (see section 27.4.2 above), and further studies may help to rebalance the dichotomy between urban and rural dimensions. In toponomastics, conversely, the study of urban areas has long been neglected, although there has been a resurgence in recent years, largely due to the influence of other disciplines in the social sciences (Bouvier 2007: 23–4). It can be expected that the interest in urban multilingualism in LL studies and elsewhere will continue to encourage more research on urban toponymy.

27.5 FUTURE DIRECTIONS

LL research is currently served by an annual workshop series, and 2015 saw the launch of *Linguistic Landscape. An International Journal,* so the field can be expected to continue to expand, supported also by the growth of relevant technologies such as Google Street View. Providing evidence of observable onomastic practice, LL fieldwork is a valuable addition to onomastic methodology, and the principal areas of inquiry in the onomastic dimension of LL studies, as discussed in sections 27.4.1–4 above, stand to be further enriched in coming years. Yet the cross-pollination of ideas between LL research and onomastics could also lead in some surprising and productive new directions, as suggested by a recent case study of diving site names that saw this unusual name category as part of an LL ecology (Nash 2013).

The LL can be a useful indicator of synchronic social change as viewed through the onomasticon, but there is also a potential for diachronic study of the LL in tandem with the onomasticon. Although photographic evidence from the past may be more difficult to obtain, archival research may yield some results, as can material evidence of dating within the contemporary LL (Spolsky and Cooper 1991: 5–8). Temporary renaming of people and places in situations of warfare or occupation is a well-known phenomenon (Footitt and Baker 2012: 145–7), but how did this work in practice, and how did it affect the landscape? Within any potential diachronic LL framework, it would be important to avoid the problems of over-emphasizing single moments of production (Lillis and McKinney 2013: 429). This may be achieved by focusing on the LL—and its onomastic dimension—as a series of negotiated, lived experiences with complex flows of authorship and readership. For example, an intriguing phenomenon to examine from an onomastic point of view is the role of translation in the production of names and LL items (Koskinen 2012).

Recent developments in LL research could be applied to provide new insights into the role of names in the material environment (Aronin and Ó Laoire 2013), and as linguistic capital. Furthermore, with the growing use of interviews and participatory fieldwork,

LL research is also finding new ways of exploring attitudes and narratives concerning space, place, and mobility (Stroud and Mpendukana 2009; Stroud and Jegels 2014). For toponomastics, there are significant implications of LL discourse in determining how '*space* is employed as a key material resource in the redefinition of *place*', highlighting 'the role of language as a mediator between space and place' (Lou 2014: 221). As the LL approach matures, it has the potential to instigate a new geosemiotic turn in socio-onomastics, recognizing that multimodality may be intrinsic to the nature of names.

CHAPTER 28

....

TOPONYMIC ATTACHMENT

....

LAURA KOSTANSKI

28.1 WHAT IS TOPONYMIC ATTACHMENT?

WHETHER travelling to a distant land, purchasing an item online, writing their memoires, or discussing plans for the weekend, humans utilize toponyms on a daily basis for a range of communication purposes, needs, and requirements.

Until recently the domain of understanding human identification with, and dependence on, the landscape has tended to focus towards the natural or built environment (Altman and Low 1992a, 1992b). Importantly, modern and postmodern theorists have asserted that natural and built landscapes simultaneously create and reinforce emotional and cultural identities (Hernandez et al. 2007). Since the 1970s there have been analyses and debates centred on the creation of places and their distinction from spaces in the landscape (Tuan 1974, 1977). It is only in recent times that linguists and historians have entered this domain of research and begun to examine how individuals and communities interact in the intangible landscape domain—particularly with the names used to define the places from the spaces.

This chapter explores the theory of *Toponymic Attachment*, developed by Laura Kostanski in 2009, and seeks to explain its intricate nature, structure, and codependencies. Toponymic Attachment is defined as a positive or negative association individuals and groups make with real or imagined toponyms. The theory was founded on the basic principles of Place Attachment, and comparisons are provided between existing geographical-domain-based theories and potential new avenues for exploration. In particular, this chapter explores not only Toponymic Attachment as a potentially expansive subject domain, but also investigates and explains the subdomains of *Toponymic Identity* and *Toponymyic Dependence*. The former is explained as an emotional association formed by and within individuals and groups towards toponyms for historical or cultural purposes. The latter is examined as a functional association with toponyms being utilized for promotional, way finding, or location identification purposes.

Examples are furnished, in the majority, from the original case study which informed the development of the theory—Laura Kostanski's PhD dissertation, *What's in a Name? Toponymic Attachment, Identity and Dependence*, 2009. The study area was that of the Grampians (Gariwerd) National Park, located in Victoria, Australia, which during 1989–90 was the subject of intense public and media scrutiny and debate when the government proposed to reinstate indigenous names for landmarks and areas previously only officially recognized by the government with their non-indigenous or Anglo-Indigenous names. This case study is utilized to provide a focus point for the discussion and context for analysis as the government proposal provoked multiple public expressions of rejection or support, and these examples provide ready illustrations for explaining the theory.

28.1.1 Toponymic Attachment—the Basics

To explore the theory of Toponymic Attachment, we must commence at the very beginning—the point at which toponyms are created. This is necessary as it is the creation of a toponym that is the catalyst for toponymic attachment to be developed, harnessed, utilized, and promoted. It is the making of the name that sets in motion the creation and use of identities and dependencies upon which humans rely to make sense of the landscape around them.

In the literature which explores how toponyms are created, Carter et al. (1993) are among the few who have overtly linked the process of naming to the creation of places from space. Their theoretical cohort include Claude Lévi-Strauss (1962) who noted that place is named space, and Tim Cresswell (2004: 10) who asserted that 'when humans invest meaning in a portion of space and then become attached to it in some way (naming is one such way) it becomes place'. This concept of place positioning human landscape interactions is of integral importance to toponyms which symbolize interaction and identification with the landscape—and these interactions are the predicators and predictors of both Place and Toponymic Attachment. To gather a complete picture of how Place and Toponymic Attachment are formed and what they represent, we need to examine the most basic components of where it all starts—a definition of place.

Relph's (1976: 141) definition of *place* centres on the notion that they are 'profound centres of human existence to which people have deep emotional and psychological ties'. Altman and Low (1992b: 5) note that place 'refers to space that has been given meaning through personal, group, or cultural processes'. Altman and Low argue that in the process of transmogrifying space into place, meanings are attributed to the geographical area. Further to Altman and Low's theory, Eisenhauer et al. (2000: 422) posit that 'the process of transforming spaces into places is influenced by one's culture'. They argue that cultural influence not only controls the processes involved in forming place, but also guides the utilization of this place in all future interactions, 'local community cultures influence sense of place because understandings of the environment are rooted in the cultural network of beliefs of an individual's social group' (Eisenhauer et al. 2000: 422). Thus, the process of creating place influences not only the appearance of the place, but the interactions that occur there. Further to this, the interactions are shaped in part by the locality, and also by the predominant culture of the inhabitants. It is in a sense a symbiotic relationship. How meanings are associated with places is a field of research defined as *sense of place* or *place attachment*.

28.1.2 Place Attachment—the Background

Many geographical and psychological researchers have developed their own *sense of place* theories over the past forty years, and often there is criticism within the literature of the lack of a distinct theory being a hindrance to the progression of the study (Pretty et al. 2003; Patterson and Williams 2005). Nonetheless, to create a structured basis for the theory of place attachment 'sense of place' has been designated as the overarching study of 'place attachment' and 'place interference', with place attachment consisting of 'place identity' and 'place dependence'. This grouping has been determined based on research by various cultural and social geographers (Shamai 1991; Hidalgo and Hernandez 2001; Williams and Vaske 2003; Jorgensen and Stedman 2006).

Shamai (1991) asserts that sense of place is an umbrella concept that includes other concepts such as place attachment, national identity, and regional awareness. Hidalgo and Hernandez (2001: 274) assert that a general description of place attachment defines it as 'an affective bond or link between people and specific places'. They posit that place attachment takes two forms: emotional and physical (Hidalgo and Hernandez 2001). Jorgensen and Stedman (2006) note that place attachment is a concept that can be included under the term 'sense of place', along with the constructs of place identity and place dependence. These two terms, identity and dependence, are similar to Hidalgo and Hernandez's social and physical, and since they are employed by Williams and Vaske (2003) and others (Sharpe and Ewert 2000; White et al. 2008), herein the terms *identity* and *dependence* are utilized. Williams and Vaske (2003) also classify place attachment under the term 'sense of place', but go further than Jorgensen and Stedman and state that identity and dependence are correlated concepts which are sub-constructs of place attachment.

Williams and Vaske (2003) assert that there are two different forms of attachment to place. The first they label 'place dependence' and describe it as a *functional* attachment to place which 'reflects the importance of a place in providing features and conditions that support specific goals or desired activities' and also 'suggests an ongoing relationship with a particular setting'. The second form of attachment to place, Williams and Vaske label 'place identity', which they assert is an *emotional* attachment to place. Further, they posit that place identity 'generally involves a psychological investment with the place that tends to develop over time'. Thus, Williams and Vaske defined place attachment as occurring in two distinguishable forms, that of the emotional and that of the functional.

28.1.3 Place Attachment and Names. An Argument for Toponymic Attachment

Place Attachment is an interesting phenomenon. Stueve et al. (1975) note that attachment can occur or be formed with a place because of a territorial instinct, or a need to develop a psychological stability. The authors also note that the functional explanations of attachment to place attest that the attachments occur because a 'place meets certain social or psychic needs, so that without it people suffer' (Stueve et al. 1975). Riley (1992) asserts that the attachments to place are not to the landscape itself, but to the memories associated with the place. Altman and Low (1992b: 4) note that attachment to a place 'contributes to individual, group and cultural self-definition and integrity' and that the attachment aspect of the term relates to the emotions people experience, whereas the place aspect of the term relates to the environmental settings. Importantly, Altman and Low (1992b) assert that future research into place attachment should concern itself with the 'nature and dynamic of attachment to different types of places and objects' to ascertain whether 'the same principles apply to people's bonding to objects and places of varying scale' or if they can be understood as 'distinct phenomena'. In 2009, the question for Kostanski remained whether it is possible to distinguish attachments made to places from attachments made towards the symbols of places, that is, *is a person's attachment to a place distinguishable from their attachment to a symbol of the place, the toponym?* It is in the data from Kostanski (2009) that a link between a sense of place and a general sense of toponym can be found and a rationale is provided for further investigating what the roles of toponyms are in society.

The general attachments that people can form with toponyms were expressed by many oral history interview participants in Kostanski's (2009) research. The interviewees noted that the attachments they felt towards a toponym were distinguishable, yet intrinsically linked with the places they knew physically or had experienced emotionally. As highlighted earlier, Altman and Low (1992a, 1992b) acknowledge that place attachment can occur towards places that people have never physically experienced. In her interview, one participant in Kostanski's study noted that toponyms might not 'make a place but they give you a vision'. She explained this by stating that 'when you go into a new area, you always get this vision in your mind. You think you know what it's going to be, and when you arrive the first thing that you actually see is something that stays with you, isn't it?' This idea was again iterated by an anonymous interviewee, who stated that the actual linguistic background of a toponym was probably not important to him, rather what he associated with the name was important. He drew a link between how:

> if the Grampians were referred to as *Wilson's Promontory*, it's still like I think, I don't know, it's possibly not important ... And that's not to diminish the importance of referring to something perhaps by its Aboriginal name, but it could be any Aboriginal name the same way it could be any European name.

In the interviews with participants, this idea, that the construct of a toponym was not important but the cultural links and attachments people formed with a toponym were important, often led to confusion. One participant suggested that for people with an association, 'their association is what makes the place rather than the name. But for people that have heard about it second hand or something or read about it in the literature, it's probably reasonably important'. Here they are indicating that a toponym can help to identify an attachment to a place not yet visited.

How toponyms communicate an idea is an interesting concept which requires unravelling. The symbolic nature of names can provide insight into the psychological profile of an area, in that they can identify the cultural mores of the communities that use the names. In the same way that cultural geographers assert that in the cultural formation of places the physical landscape can identify the cultural norms of a society, so can a toponym.

However, we have started this discussion by asserting upfront that names are critical in the interactions people have with the landscape. We should pause here to reflect on whether this is necessarily the case or not. We should ask: *Are we able to create a place with no name? Can it even be a place if it has no name? Importantly, can humans create a sense of place with a feature that is unnamed?* In considering this we must concede that while nameless places might be possible on a small-scale level, they are not possible as a common day occurrence. This is merely because, of all the referencing systems available, across all languages, nouns (including toponyms) are utilized universally for communication purposes and are more effective than coordinates, grid references, or a multitude of other abstract geographical vocabularies to locate places.

Hence, if places need to have names, and a sense of place is created through the interactions of humans with a place, then a sense of toponym should exist when humans interact and utilize toponyms. For, without a sense of toponym linking humans to places, we might not see a need for creating a name to begin with. If humans create an emotional attachment to a place (be it on a small or large scale, in a positive or negative way) then the toponym must, in some form or another, be possible of symbolizing this attachment.

A proposed mathematical formula for these philosophical propositions could be posed as:

(a)

>If, space + name = place
>
>Can we say, place − name = space

(b)

>If, space + interaction = place + name
>
>Can we say, space − interaction = place − name

And,

(c)

>If, place + interaction = sense of place
>
>Does, name + interaction = sense of toponym?

These propositions framed the development of robust examinations into Kostanski's case for why toponymic attachment exists. This exploration commenced with toponymic identity and then toponymic dependence, which are explained in the next section.

28.2 Toponymic Identity

Sharpe and Ewert (2000: 218) define the term *place identity* as a second component of place attachment, which is linked to 'the emotional and symbolic nature of person–place relationships'. Similarly, Williams and Vaske (2003: 5) define place identity as an emotional function of place attachment. Branching the divide between purely geographical literature and psychology literature, Proshansky (1978, 1983) explained place identity as a subconcept of self-identity. Hernandez et al. (2007: 311) concur with this notion of place identity being a component of personal identity and Twigger-Ross and Uzzel (1996: 210) expanded upon Proshansky's notion of place identity to claim that it is 'not a separate part of identity concerned with place, but that all aspects of identity have place-related implications to a greater or lesser extent'. The relationships between physical places and emotional places are symbiotic in the formulation of place identity. From a review of the literature it can be said that the construct of place identity is composed of four key elements: *history/memory, community, emotions*, and *actions/events*. It is important to explore these four key components individually, giving consideration to the discussion of place identity, and noting in each instance similar identifications with toponyms.

28.2.1 History and Memory

Williams and Vaske (2003) assert that 'place identity is not necessarily a direct result of any particular experience with the place' and therefore the formation of place identity through identification with local histories and memories can be similarly developed by both locals and non-locals.

First, we should explore why history and memory are considered to be components of place identity, and by extension toponymic identity. Abrahamson notes that communities occupy their own geographical areas with which they become intimately associated. He argues that through this process of identification 'areas acquire symbolic qualities that include their place names and social histories' (Abrahamson 1996, cited in Ramsay 2003). And whilst not stating explicitly that place-names are linked to place identity, Radley (1990: 47) asserted that 'objects are used to establish a link with the past which helps to sustain identity'.

Tuan (1991: 688) has noted that 'normally only a socio-political revolution would bring about a change of name ... the new name itself has the power to wipe out the past and call forth the new'. As explored by Kostanski (2009), a person protesting the restoration of indigenous toponyms in the Grampians region of Australia remarked that

> there were no Aborigines in the Grampians for Mitchell to name this 'noble range of mountains' as he called them, so he called them the Grampians. This is well entrenched in our history books, and should stay there. It would seem in the minds of some people that our heritage counts for nothing . . . are we not permitted to leave anything for our descendents?

These remarks can be seen in the context of Crane (1997: 1372) theory. Crane posits 'that the future might mourn is the projection of nostalgia; it is also the supposition of historical thinking, which charges itself with the preservation of what would be lost both mentally and materially'. In this manner, where previously it has been argued that it is place identity which helps to connect a population with their history, it can be seen that it is toponymic identity which also connects a population with their history.

Tuan (1991: 685) posits that 'although speech alone cannot materially transform nature, it can direct attention, organize insignificant entities into significant composite wholes, and in so doing, make things formerly overlooked—and hence invisible and non-existent—visible and real'. It can be argued that at the time of the renaming proposal, the suggestion to reinstate indigenous names was a counter-narrative to the mainstream promotion of colonial history which relegated the majority of indigenous histories to pre-1788 status. Geoff Clark, a supporter of the naming proposal, noted in his oral history interview with Kostanski that 'when you come down to the principle, these people [opponents] have to acknowledge that for someone, it is another place, it has another name and another purpose and it has to be acknowledged somewhere'. The proposition is clear here that a toponym can be a symbol of multiple identities, and the use of two toponyms for one place can be a strong reminder of the multiple place histories and cultural identities which exist for a locale. At this point in the discussion, attention needs to be given to notions of how collective or community cultures influence the creation and interpretation of place, and perhaps toponymic, identity.

28.2.2 Community

This component of toponymic attachment explores notions of nationalism, normal, the other, and power and how they relate to the concept of place. George Seddon (1997: 15) theorised that the words of the landscape carry 'cultural baggage' that may 'imply values and endorse power relations'. Jackson (1989: 151) asserts that 'racism in Britain and similar societies is a dominant ideology . . . racism refers to a set of ideas and beliefs that have the weight of authority behind them; they are enshrined in statutes and institutionalised in policy and practice'. The fact that predominantly non-indigenous names were present in the landscape of the Grampians, as shown by the Kostanski's

(2009) case study, served to reinforce these notions of local, and by extension national, identity that was created by colonists and perpetuated by their descendants. This community identity was therefore bound to, and represented by, the toponyms. Penrose and Jackson (1994: 206) assert that 'Aboriginal land claims challenge the apparent "neutrality" of the hegemonic culture' and it should be extended here to assert that the proposal to reinstate indigenous names was a challenge to the mainstream, colonially-defined local and national culture.

The notions of inclusion and exclusion, or insiders and outsiders, are fundamental to an understanding of community and national identity. Babha (1994) notes that 'the processes of "normalising" colonial or western understandings of place and history have sought to confirm the national identities of the colonisers and at the same time has turned the remaining populations into "others"'. One interviewee in Kostanski (2009) asserted that 'since then [1836], everyone has known it as the Grampians, worldwide. Now, why change the name? I mean, its rubbish in my opinion. . . . I'm not a racist but I think what we're doing sometimes is like kow-towing to them and so forth, we're dividing'. They note here that by 'everyone' knowing the area as the Grampians, the normal attitude is to accept that the community identity is that which is represented by the colonial names.

It should be noted, however, that it is not always a national identity which includes and excludes based on notions of race or cultural affiliation. Inclusion and exclusion can also be defined within a culturally homogenous community based on perceptions of connectedness. Research into belonging to a community has indicated that the length of residence in a place can determine the extent of attachment, and by extension identity, a person feels (Hernandez et al. 2007: 311).

There are groups in society which determine who is included as 'normal' and who is perceived as an 'outsider'. In this way place identity is partly formed by community definitions of inclusion and exclusion. Similarly, it can be seen that toponymic identity is partly formed through personal and community identification with particular community understandings of what is condoned as 'normal' and what is condoned as being from 'outside'. People are more likely to form an identity with toponyms which are perceived by them to be 'normal' than those which are considered 'foreign'. The perception of what is worthwhile and should be included in a community's culture, and what is not acceptable, needs to be explored in further detail in relation to names.

28.2.3 Emotions

Altman and Low (1992b: 4) assert that 'one of the hallmarks of place attachment that appears consistently in most analyses is that affect, emotion and feeling are central to the concept'. Therefore, it is important to explore the concept of emotion as a component of both place and toponymic identity. The various emotions that people feel towards and within places has been said to 'embrace an array of places, feelings and experiences' (Manzo 2005: 84).

Various emotional responses were noted in the research data from Kostanski (2009) ranging from expressions of fear, to sentiments of loss and other expressions of jubilation at the thought that the study area toponyms would finally be recognizing indigenous identity.

For some, the time of the proposed renaming was extremely emotional. One participant who has indigenous cultural connections to the case study area, noted that he knew 'the Aboriginal community were very happy about it, about the idea. And it just gives us a bit more recognition that we're not ... a dead culture, which in those times, it was a very big fight we had to fight because [of] some general ignorance I suppose in the wider community'. It was a time acknowledged to be an important step towards the wider community acknowledging and accepting indigenous heritage in the case study area.

It was noted by those who opposed the renaming proposals that they felt emotionally threatened by the proposed renaming. Writers opined that 'As a child I could see the Grampians range from our kitchen window, even had a few days at the Halls Gap school and later had the misfortune to lose my mother as a result of an accident in the Grampians. I could not and will not ever accept any other names for the beauty spots there'. For this respondent, the name 'Grampians' was emotionally connected to the memories held with the area. The possibility of using other names to identify the places in the case study area was impossible for some because the proposed indigenous names would not hold those same emotional connections.

The previous discussion of inclusion and exclusion in relation to place identity leads into an exploration of what is defined as appropriate and inappropriate behaviour in a place. As posited by Manzo (2005: 83) 'the dynamics of exclusion and creating spaces of belonging have a powerful effect on people's emotional relationship to places'. Thus, within the cultural roles defined by community, the emotional effects of feeling included and excluded can play a major role in the formation of identity. Emotions, as a component of identity, assist in determining what is construed as acceptable behaviour in a place.

Recognition of identity is important and can be undertaken through renaming events linked to both non-physical and physical actions. It is at this point in the discussion that the focus on components of place or toponymic identity can be merged into an analysis of place or toponymic dependence. Before a thorough investigation of toponymic dependence can begin, however, it is important to very briefly discuss how events and actions can be considered to be components of both place and toponymic identity.

28.2.4 Events/actions

Jedrej and Nuttal (1996: 123) assert that 'the landscape is a living landscape and place names are mnemonic devices that trigger recollection of particular activities'. Zerubavel (2003: 42) noted that places 'play a major role in identity rhetoric' and he proposed that events such as the hajj to Mecca, or romantic couples visiting the site of their first date, are examples of pilgrimage which bring 'mnemonic communities into closer "contact" with their collective past'. In addition, Zerubavel argued that the protection of old architecture, such as the Chechens defending old stone towers that helped them 'connect' with their ancestors, is a further example of how place evokes identity and memories. Indeed, the contention of Zerubavel's argument is that memories of place imbue a present-day identity on the users or inhabitants of the place. This place identity is almost the glue which holds community groups together through a shared understanding of their collective past.

Chow and Healey (2008: 371) assert that 'place meaning is in part created and confirmed through in-place-experiences' and as such it could be argued following the previous analysis in this chapter that the experiences which create place also create names. Thus, experiences which brought about the original and then subsequent renaming of places could be said to have brought meaning and therefore identity to the people who associate with the area.

The experiences which are deemed to be important by a community are memorialized in various ways. Similarly to the arguments posited by Zerubavel, Lewicka (2008: 214) posits that 'places remember and they do it through their monuments, architectural style of their buildings, inscriptions on walls etc. For people who reside there, the traces play the function of "urban reminders", the "mnemonic aids" to collective memory'. The decision about which monuments are erected and which events are memorialized is a constant battle between those included in the community and those excluded from it. Based on the research data, it appears that events and actions are remembered by place-names, in a way similar to buildings and inscriptions on walls. In this way, in their memorialization of actions and events, communities utilize toponyms as mnemonic devices for their collective identity. The dependence that communities form with toponyms as a result of actions or events is discussed in the next section.

28.3 TOPONYMIC DEPENDENCE

It is evident from the available literature and research data that apart from the reflections upon history, community, and emotions which characterize sentiments of toponymic identity, there are other issues to consider such as wayfinding, addressing services, and emergency service delivery. The attachment that the research data from Kostanski (2009) initially pointed to was a functional attachment which, based on geographical literature on place, is defined as *place dependence*.

As described by Williams and Vaske (2003: 5), place dependence 'reflects the importance of a place in providing features and conditions that support specific goals or desired activities'. They elaborate further and note that the dependence is linked to the physical characteristics of the place, such as a State forest providing a location for legally collecting firewood, or an office providing the location and equipment to run a business. They assert that dependence on a place may increase according to a person's ability to access the site frequently and the concept of place dependence as a functional attachment can be described in its most basic form as a reliance on the physical characteristics of a place to provide recreational, employment, or other required facilities. It is the focus of this section, therefore, to define how just as a dependence on places can be formed, a dependence on a toponym(s) can also be said to occur or exist.

As the research data collected by Kostanski (2009) in the area of functional attachment was expansive, it was thought important to dedicate analysis to the construct of place dependence, and the possible existence of toponymic dependence, as components of place and toponymic attachment distinct from, but correlated to, place identity and toponymic identity. The analysis in this section therefore explores the data themes of *promotion, location*, and *identification* and analyses how the themes can be considered components of place and toponymic dependence. All three themes are intertwined and contain components of each other, but distinctions can be made.

People form functional attachments to toponyms in two ways: by the name fulfilling a need and through the name's comparable attributes. First, the comparable attributes of names will be investigated through discussion of the use of toponyms for promotional purposes. Secondly, the needs that people associate with toponyms will be analysed through discussion of the use of toponyms as locational and identification tools.

28.3.1 Promotion

Among the people who were intimately involved at the government level of the name restoration programme, Kostanski (2009) found that the proposals were underpinned by a strong belief in the traditional indigenous names being useful for promoting indigenous cultural tourism. It could be proposed that in the same way that a place might be compared to others for its attributes, or how a place might be seen to be perfect for certain activities, a toponym might be comparable for its attributes or how it offers certain unique characteristics for promotional purposes.

Previously we have discussed the notion of indigenous and non-indigenous toponyms being identified with certain histories and events. This aspect of toponymic identity also can create a situation whereby a dependency could be formed with a toponym for *promoting* certain histories and events. The promotion of a place's physical attributes and facilities is a fundamental component of tourism marketing strategies. Promotional strategies for all intents and purposes can be linked to capturing and promoting the attributes of a place compared to others. Recent progress in tourism studies has seen the development of a stream of research categorized as *place branding*. This field of studies seeks to explore the ways in which the marketing of places to potential tourists can be undertaken in the most effective manner.

Kotler and Gertner (2002: 41) have asserted that the theories of branding need not be limited to manufactured products alone. Yet, these concepts are not without controversy. Importantly within the academic debate on the concept of place branding has been the argument that theories on the marketing of consumer retail products cannot be likened to marketing a country or places within it (cited in Ollins 2002: 18). The counter argument from pro-place branding theorists asserts that techniques of branding places are similar to those employed in branding companies and their products (Ollins 2002; Hemingway 2007). Ollins (2002: 24) notes particularly that 'people are people whether they work in a company or live in a nation and that means that they can be motivated, inspired and manipulated in the same way, using the same techniques'.

Blain et al. (2005: 328) assert that a place brand is a 'name, symbol, logo, word mark or other graphic that both *identifies* and *differentiates* the destination; furthermore, it conveys the *promise* of a memorable travel *experience* that is uniquely associated with the destination'. They go further and assert that place branding 'requires a unique selling proposition' (Blain et al. 2005: 331). This concept of a brand differentiating one place from another can be likened to the place dependence construct of *comparison*—in similar ways to which a place is depended upon for its comparable characteristics, a place brand could be said to be depended upon for its ability to portray the unique characteristics of a place.

In an oral history interview with Kostanski, one participant asserted that for the restoration of indigenous names to the traditional indigenous rock art sites within the case study area 'I don't have any argument with the rock art sites, I think that that's fine, I think that's probably very appropriate for them . . . [because] they are Aboriginal art sites, why wouldn't they have an Aboriginal name and I mean it's just logical isn't it really?'. This was a sentiment shared by many participants in the oral history interviews; that the utilization of indigenous names for features which were clearly identifiable as being of indigenous cultural heritage was a supportable concept. Thus, it can be stated that the construct of comparison is evident here where participants were supportive of indigenous names being utilized for readily-identifiable indigenous cultural features. It is evident because the participants are stating that the 'uniqueness' of the name captures the characteristics of the place it represents.

Morgan et al. (2002: 11) argue that branding 'can communicate and emphasize the "feel" and "personality" of the place', whilst Fan (2006: 6) notes that the aim of place branding is to 'create a clear, simple, differentiating idea built around emotional qualities which can be symbolised both verbally and visually and understood by diverse audiences in a variety of situations'. Interestingly, Fan (2006: 7) also notes that 'from the marketing perspective, nation branding has the aim of helping the nation to "sell" its products and places'.

Based on the available literature, it would seem that with the growth in cultural heritage tourism, the use of place branding has increased (Hemingway 2007: 332). The questions now are: *Can toponyms be perceived as cultural images, and therefore are they conceivable as brand elements? Are toponyms the symbols of the place product?*

In many of the interviews undertaken by Kostanski (2009), it is apparent that there is a perception of dependence on indigenous and non-indigenous names for tourism purposes. For some, the dependency relates to the promotional aspects attached to the non-indigenous toponyms, and the ability of the toponyms to convey messages of the places' unique characteristics. Importantly, for others, they noted that the dependency is not only for tourism purposes, but also for locational needs. It is hypothesised, as mentioned at the outset of this chapter, that the promotional aspects of the functional attachment on toponyms was only one aspect of the dependency. The locational aspect, whilst similar, can be distinguished in the research data and, although there is scant academic literature on this area, it will now be discussed.

28.3.2 Location

The process of creating place from space requires certain landscape elements to be distinguished from all others and for toponyms to be applied as symbols of the created places. It is posited that to navigate between places the most common method utilized is that of toponymy. Kadmon (1997: 49) refers to toponyms such as *Villarica*, where the name is used by many people, as having connotative or pragmatic meaning. He explained that a name such as Venice, Paris, or Beverly Hills acquires 'meaning beyond the immediate descriptive-lexical meaning embedded in it'. This meaning could be argued to be similar to those meanings explored through toponymic identity, or even compared to the meaning imbued through branding techniques. Importantly though, it was argued by Kadmon that the imbuing of a toponym with connotative meaning makes it 'lose its most salient function, namely its locational value'. Based on the research data from Kostanski (2009), it can be argued otherwise. Namely, that connotative and locational values can be coincident, especially when considered in light of the proposed theory on toponymic dependence.

All of those interviewed during Kostanski's (2009) research programme indicated a strong affiliation with the histories and meanings of both the places and toponyms of the study area. In addition to the affiliations with the connotative meanings of the toponyms, many participants also noted that they were dependent on the toponyms for the purposes of locating themselves within the landscape. For example, one participant asserted that 'names just identify things, help to explain, help in the communication process'. Similarly, another posited that toponyms can simultaneously 'give it [a place] an identity, they give it a location'. In a letter from one case study in Kostanski (2009), the proponent argued that:

> if I was to tell you that I was off to *Budja Budja* for the weekend and also planned to have a look a *Migunang Wirab* you would look more than nonplussed. But if Tourism, Conservation and Environment Minister Steve Crabb gets his way, Budja Budja will be the new name for *Halls Gap* and Migunang Wirab for *McKenzie Falls*.

Toponyms are important for locating places within a landscape, and it is especially important that the names utilized are in common usage and understood by the majority of the population. This reliance on toponyms to assist with or underpin the locational communications process ensures that people form a dependency with toponyms as they allow for ease of spatial communication between two or more people.

In terms of the means of conveying a location, wayfinding is not the only dependency aspect of toponyms. The research data showed that another strongly correlated component of dependency was also at play in the name restoration debate, namely identification. As stated in the introduction to this chapter, identification, whilst sounding similar to the construct of identity, is a distinguishable entity within the proposed theory of toponymic dependence due to its characteristics and these will now be discussed.

28.3.3 Identification

The United Nations Group of Experts on Geographical Names (UNGEGN 2001: 1) assert that consistent use of toponyms is important for a multitude of reasons, among them the purposes of tourism, map and atlas production, automatic navigation, and, importantly for this section of the chapter, communications for postal services and search and rescue operations. Withers (2000: 535) notes that historically, in places such as Ireland 'the mapping process was reliant upon accurate naming: arguably, indeed, mapping depended upon such naming since, however accurate in location and geometric terms maps might be, they were valueless as records of property ownership and guides to taxation without agreed names'. In similar ways in modern times, for the purposes of wayfinding and tourism activities, the use of accurate names on maps is important to allow people to find their way from point a to point b.

Hand in hand with the use of maps is the use of signage to indicate the location of a place. People who are unfamiliar with a place will often use a a map to indicate where they should be navigating to, as well as signage to indicate where they are in relation to their travelling route.

Tim Cresswell (2004: 10) posits that 'in most definitions of landscape the viewer is outside of it. Places are very much things to be inside of'. Hence, if a landscape is something that people can travel through, be outside of, and at once stop and attach a meaning to an area of the landscape, that area of the landscape becomes a place and the landscape can be theorized as a space. Maps and signage can therefore act as a force with which notions of space and definitions of what constitutes a place with worthwhile cultural characteristics are reinforced.

In this way, toponyms act as cultural anchors which guide tourists in their understandings of places in landscapes they are not familiar with. Whether a place is indicated with a signed toponym or not is an important indication of the cultural heritage of an area. Which toponyms are selected to identify and locate a place, indeed which places are selected to be identified through maps and signs, allows insight into the dominant cultural forces at play in the landscape. As asserted by Landry and Bourhis (1997: 25), 'the language of public road signs, advertising billboards, street names, commercial shop signs, and public signs on government buildings combines to form the linguistic landscape of a given territory, region, or urban agglomeration'. Thus, hegemonic discourses can be promoted in tourism, marketing, and promotion campaigns. These discourses can work to 'popularize' indigenous or minority cultures and at once subject them to 'othering' discourses, relegate them as non-existent (i.e. through ignoring/denying/simplifying the history) or relegate them to an outdated 'pre-history' status.

28.4 CONCLUSIONS

Sense of place, as Meinig (1979) suggests, is created by people to make a place distinct or memorable. Indeed, we could do this on a practical plateau by remembering that the kitchen is where we cook food, or that the university is where we work. Emotionally, we can look at our church or synagogue as a place for marriage and the graveyard for death. Each of these places has a memory or feeling attached to them, and this phenomenon is called 'sense of place'. It holds true that toponyms have a memory or feeling attached to them, and we can label this phenomenon a 'sense of toponym'.

Essentially, a toponym acts as a symbol of a place. It can simultaneously hold its own metaphorical, personal, collective, and nationalistic identity separate to those identities held by the place. Whereas the sense of place literature points to the notion that direct physical contact has to have been made with the location, a sense of toponym can occur without direct contact with the location which it represents, it can occur with interaction with the toponym itself.

Place attachment theories posit that people form bonds with places. These places can act as repositories for memories and can create a cultural link within and between communities. Research into the meanings of toponyms for the study area communities has found that people also form bonds with toponyms. The linguistic composition of a toponym is both important because sometimes it identifies cultural heritage, and also unimportant because it is sometimes referenced only symbolically. This distinction between cultural heritage and symbolic nature is interesting, and warrants further investigation. The distinction can be likened to the distinction between place identity and place dependence, the two sub-constructs of place attachment. Heritage can be located within identity and dependence within symbolism.

It is important to note that the elements of identity and dependence are strongly correlated, but are distinguishable from each other. In the same way that a person or community might rely on a toponym to identify cultural heritage, they might also depend on that toponym to provide a unique representation of a place of particular cultural importance. Thus, toponymic identity and dependence are best considered as interrelated constructs of toponymic attachment.

CHAPTER 29

FORMS OF ADDRESS

IRMA TAAVITSAINEN AND ANDREAS H. JUCKER

29.1 INTRODUCTION

ADDRESSING people is one of the most prominent interactive features of language use, and an efficient means of attracting attention or of creating and maintaining interpersonal relations. With terms of address speakers appeal directly to their hearer(s). Two principal kinds can be distinguished: nominal and pronominal address. In onomastics, people's names have reference, but no sense, and 'since names are generally coined in speech rather than in writing, they testify to a colloquial register of language' (Hough 2012: 213). From a pragmatic perspective, nominal terms of address and even people's names often display interpersonal meanings as well. Nicknames and terms of endearment differ very considerably in their pragmatic meaning from terms of abuse on the one hand to formal terms of address on the other (Honegger 2004). There is also a range from colloquial registers to very formal language. Social and attitudinal meanings are embedded into the terms of address with subtle shades of meaning.

In present-day languages it is common to use both nominal and pronominal forms together, for example royalty is addressed with a fixed formula derived from French models: *Your Majesty* (English), *Ers Majestät* (Swedish), *Teidän majesteettinne* (Finnish); *Ihre Majestät* (German). Diplomats are addressed with *Your Excellency*, etc. At the other end of the scale, scolding young rascals, the pattern is the same (Pron + N). In languages where the *tu/vous* (T/V)-distinction has been maintained, the choice of the pronoun can acquire expressive meanings, for example in German, French, Italian, Russian, Polish, and so on (see the articles in Taavitsainen and Jucker 2003). This was also the case in the earlier phases of English, in Middle English and in Early Modern English, but the distinction had virtually disappeared by 1700 (for an overview, see Finkenstaedt 1963; Walker 2007: 63; Mazzon 2010).

Nominal forms of address have also undergone changes. This chapter will focus on nominal terms of address in English, but comparisons with other European languages will be included when relevant. A great deal of research has been devoted to the early phases of English vacillation of T/V pronominal forms, and some of the studies of nominal forms analyse their co-occurrence patterns with pronominal forms. Usage patterns have been studied especially in Shakespeare's plays and in private correspondence, but there is also a fair amount of research on other genres. All periods are not equally well covered, and a great deal remains to be done before a full picture emerges.

29.2 NOMINAL ADDRESS TERMS AND THEIR SEMANTIC TYPES

Most nominal address terms, like people's names, are also used in referring expressions as in the following example taken from the *Corpus of Contemporary American English* (COCA). Mr Wood uses the name *Debby* to refer to his wife, while the interviewer Gangel uses it as a term of address to direct his question directly to her.

(1)   Mr-WOOD: I think I'm a lawyer 24 hours a day with maybe a 10-minute break every once in awhile. But Debby does remind me to sometimes take off the lawyer hat.

GANGEL: Debby, what happens when you get into an argument with him? What's it like?

DEBBY: We don't argue. (COCA, 2000, NBC_Today)

Languages vary in their conventions of adding nominal address to various speech acts. In English vocatives are common, and proper names 'can be freely added to the clause' and are 'especially important in imperative clauses' (Biber et al. 1999: 140). The varying practices of different languages are most conspicuous in the use of professional titles when addressing people.

Nominal terms of address have been placed on various scales of intimacy and politeness, ranging in their semantic types from intimate terms of endearment to more distant expressions with deference, and from polite communication to abuse with derogative name calling. Raumolin-Brunberg (1996) suggests a scale from negative politeness terms to positive politeness terms on the basis of Brown and Levinson's (1987) distinction between negative and positive politeness. On this scale, honorific titles are placed at the negative end of a sliding scale because they represent Brown and Levinson's (1987: 178–87) strategy 'give deference', while terms of endearment and nicknames are placed at the positive end of the scale representing Brown and Levinson's strategies 'use in-group identity markers', 'joke' and 'give gifts' (Raumoling-Brunberg 1996: 171). Professional or occupational titles and kinship terms occupy less extreme positions on this scale (Table 29.1).

Table 29.1 provides a useful way of thinking about the inherent qualities of different types of address terms, but in more recent years politeness theory has moved away from

Table 29.1 The politeness continuum

Negative			Positive
Honorific titles (*lord*)	Other titles (*captain*)	Family (*brother*)	Terms of endearment (*sweetheart*) nicknames (*Will*)

Raumolin-Brunberg (1996: 171), slightly simplified.

Brown and Levinson's essentialist ascription of fixed politeness values to specific expressions (see Locher and Watts 2005; Mills 2011). In specific contexts, for example in ironic, humorous, or reprimanding contexts, address terms may adopt very different politeness, or indeed impoliteness, values.

The shades of meaning are often difficult to catch, particularly in historical texts, but the context helps and allows a discursive interpretation. In some cases we have first-hand textual evidence of the use of *Madam* as a status symbol in late Middle English. According to the *Oxford English Dictionary* (*OED*, s.v. madam), the noun was originally used by servants in speaking to their mistress, and more generally in speaking to a woman of high rank. English *ma dame* was also commonly used by children to their mother, a queen or a lady of very high rank in the extant examples. The desire to enhance one's social esteem by using fine address was regarded as a sin of vanity:

(2) Or ȝe wymmen also, comunly, wulde be kallede 'madame' or 'lady;' Al þys comþ of grete pryde

'Or you women also commonly would like to be called "madam" or "lady". All this comes of great pride.' (Robert Mannyng, *Handlyng Synne* ll. 413–415)

Chaucer makes the same point, and in his time to be addressed as *madame* was one of the advantages for a citizen's wife if her husband was made alderman (*OED*).

(3) It is ful fair to been ycleped 'madame', / And goon to vigilies al before, / And have a mantel roialliche ybore

'It is very nice to be called madam, and go to church before everyone, and carry a cloak like a queen' (*Canterbury Tales*, General Prologue 376–377; our translation).

Madam is used almost exclusively in the address function, but such words are rare. The masculine counterpart *Sir* is not only an address term, but also a title. It is placed before the proper name or a common noun, forming with it a term of address, as *Sir Clerk, Sir King, Sir Knight*. The *OED* records it from the thirteenth century, and contemptuous and ironic uses emerge soon after, for example 'Sir [v.r. Sire] olde lecchour, let thi japes be' (*c.*1386, Chaucer Wife of Bath's Prol. (Harl.) 242). The following passage contains *Sir* both as a title and an address term in polite conversation:

(4)   'Not so, syrs,' seyde sir Gaherys, 'hit was sir Launcelot that slew hym worship-fully with his owne hondys, and he gretys you all well and prayeth you to haste you to the courte. And as unto you, sir Lyonell and sir Ector de Marys, he prayeth you to abyde hym at the courte of kynge Arthure.' (Malory, *Sir Launcelot du Lake*, 268–269)

29.3 RESEARCH ON NOMINAL ADDRESS TERMS: A SHORT REVIEW OF THE LITERATURE

Address terms have been found to be sensitive interpersonal devices in the history of English. They have been studied as indicators of appropriate behaviour between people, and social class distinctions have been discussed. In this section we shall give a short survey of earlier research of the developments in chronological order. In Old English the use of address terms was different from the periods that follow. A great deal of research has focused on the Middle and Early Modern English periods, while Late Modern English practices have not received as much attention.

29.3.1 Old English

The distribution of some central nominal address terms, like *leof, hlaford*, and *ealdor-man*, have been studied by Kohnen (2008) on the basis of the *Dictionary of Old English Corpus*. Address terms are mainly found in sermons and poetry, and kinship terms and religious designations are particularly common in the extant data. Kohnen's focus was on what attitudes these forms conveyed in various communicative situations. According to his study, friendship and affection-invoking family bonds prevail in the data, but authoritative language use based on hierarchical society is also prominent. Politeness in the way it is found in later periods was absent, and Kohnen did not find patterns of courteous behaviour. Instead, the use of address terms in Anglo-Saxon communication reflects mutual obligation and kinship loyalty, and the examples enhanced Christian values of *humilitas* and *caritas*. The following scene from the anonymous *Apollonius of Tyre* contains an address to the King, with native respectful nominal terms:

(5)   ... and eode into þam cynge and cwæð: **Hlaford cyngc**, glada nu and blissa, forðam
      þe Apollonius him ondræt þines rices mægna swa þæt he ne dear ... (ll. 179–81)

      'and went to the king and said: Lord King, be glad and happy now because
      Appolonius is so much afraid of your kingdom's greatness that he dare not...'
      (*Apollonius of Tyre* [0052 (7.17)], our translation)

Chapman's (2008) study on the same materials examines epithets used as insults in connection with second person pronouns. The following example comes from the debate
between the body and the soul; the insult is thrown by the soul as an accusation for getting them both damned:

(6)   La, ðu eorðan lamb & dust & wyrma gifel, & þu wambscyldiga fætels & gealstor &
      fulnes & hræw, hwig forgeate ðu me & þa toweardan tide? (HomU9 (ScraggVerc
      4) 207)

      'Hey, you mud of the earth and dust and food for worms, and you bellyguilty bag
      and pestilence and foulness and corpse, why did you forget me and the future?'
      (translation by Chapman 2008: 2)

Insults were also found in saints' lives and in addresses to devils and sinners. Most
expressions proved conventional and were repeated in various contexts, yet some
showed originality and creativity such as the one above.

29.3.2 Middle English

Research on Middle English address terms has focused on pronominal T/V choices
(Burnley 2003; Knappe and Schümann 2006). In the thirteenth century, English borrowed from French the use of the plural pronoun for single addressees. The usage pattern of choice between the plural or singular pronoun for specific addressees differs
considerably from the patterns in modern languages which still make this distinction, and scholars have tried to establish the precise pattern involving status difference between the speakers (Burnley 2003), but also within more discursive approaches
according to situational factors (Jucker 2006).

   Nominal terms of address have received much less attention, except for Honegger
(2004, 2005). In the first paper he focuses on one specific type of nominal forms of
address in Middle English, on pet names and on terms of endearment between lovers,
and in the second he investigates the influence of the alliterative metre in two Middle
English romances, *Sir Gawain and the Green Knight* and *William of Palerne*, on the
choice of specific nouns in direct address. In dialogues between lovers, Honegger (2004)
argues, forms of address are used that reflect the various stages of courtship. At the initial stages of a love relationship, the typical terms for a woman would be *dame, madame*,

or *lady*, and for a man *sir* or *lord*, often with the qualifying adjective *swete* or *dere*, or the possessive pronoun *my*, and he connects this usage with hierarchy and power and the concern for the negative face of the addressee (Honegger 2004: 44). Beyond the initial stages of a love relationship, the terms of address may change very significantly. They turn to the positive face needs of the addressee. He quotes *hony, sweting, derling, herte,* or *lif* from *William of Palerne* (Honegger 2004: 48), but he also points out that the negatively polite *sire* persists as an address term used by Melior, the female protagonist, for her lover William well beyond the initial stages of their love relationship.

In his second paper, Honegger (2005) investigates the formal constraints of alliterative poetry on the choice of nominal terms of address. He points out that nominal and pronominal forms of address regularly reinforce each other. The T forms of solidarity and affection correlate with nominal terms such as *my leeve brother*, and the T forms of scorn correlate with address terms such as *false Arcite*, while the formal V forms co-occur with more formal nominal terms of address, such as *lord* (in Chaucer's *Knight's Tale*; Honegger 2005: 171), but nominal and pronominal forms may also be used for variation rather than reinforcement. Against this background he argues that the choice in *Sir Gawain and the Green Knight* and *William of Palerne* is often governed by the formal constraints of alliterative poetry rather than by pragmatic considerations.

29.3.3 Early Modern English

Texts of the Early Modern period display a wide range of nominal address terms including kinship terms, titles, rank, and occupational terms in addition to a wide range of terms of endearment and terms of abuse. The most famous instance of verbal abuse in terms of nominal and pronominal address in the early modern period is recorded from a trial. Sir Walter Raleigh, the English aristocrat, explorer and courtier, was accused of high treason in 1603, and an attorney expressed his contempt by throwing an insult at him. He used highly inappropriate language with the pronoun *thou/thee* three times and reinforced its effect by a nominal address of abuse: 'I thou thee, thou Traitor' (*Helsinki Corpus*. E2 XX TRI RALEIGH I, 208). Nominal terms of address used as insults are well known from the Early Modern English period, and in particular Shakespeare's use of them has often been commented on (e.g. Hill and Öttchen 1995; Jucker and Taavitsainen 2000; Busse 2002; Busse 2006).

In Early Modern English, nominal terms of address occur in a large range of dialogic genres where one of their prominent functions is to establish interpersonal relations. The following passage comes from the opening of Izaak Walton's *The Compleat Angler*. The discussants are walking in the countryside on a beautiful sunny morning, in accordance with a literary commonplace. The dialogue has a regular structure with almost every turn opening with a polite address often collocated with discourse markers.

(7) *Venat.*   My friend *Piscator*, you have kept time with my thoughts, for the Sun is just rising, and I my self just now come to this place, and the dogs have just now put down an *Otter*; …

Pisc.   Sir, I am right glad to meet you, and glad to have so fair an entrance into this dayes sport, and glad to see so many dogs …; come honest *Venator*, lets be gone, let us make hast; …

Ven.   Gentleman Huntsman, where found you this *Otter*?

Hunt.   Marry (Sir) we found her a mile from this place a fishing; … I am to have the skin if we kill her.

Ven.   Why, Sir, what's the skin worth?

Hunt.   'Tis worth ten shillings to make gloves; …

Pisc.   I pray, honest Huntsman, let me ask you a pleasant question, do you hunt a beast or a fish? (EEBO 1653, Chapter II)

It is noticeable that the three characters address each other not with their names but with generic titles, such as 'Sir' and with occupational titles, such as 'Piscator' or 'Huntsman'. Often the nouns are modified or combined, as in 'my friend Piscator', 'Gentleman Huntsman' or 'honest Huntsman' in order to signify mutual respect and the focus on their professional activities.

Address is also a compulsory component of both public and private letters. Early letters used patterns such as 'Right trusty and wellbeloved', which could occur with or without a nominal headword (Nevalainen and Raumolin-Brunberg 1995: 545). In general, the repertoire of nominal address forms is fairly limited, with kinship terms, names, and words denoting social and occupational standing forming the stock. This line of study was continued by Nevala (2004), who also explored diachronic changes of address forms in the *Corpus of Early English Correspondence*. She found that address forms in family correspondence manifest interpersonal relations between the writer and the addressee with expressions of positive or negative politeness. In the course of time, positive politeness as expressed in terms of endearment and nicknames increases from the fifteenth to the seventeenth century (Nevala 2004: 143). Among social groups, the gentry lead this change, and royalty lags behind; this was also the case in a follow-up study on the late modern period (Nevala 2004: 248).

Drama and fiction are particularly rich sources for nominal terms of address and their correlation with pronominal ones. Ulrich Busse (2003), for instance, studied the co-occurrence of pronominal and nominal terms of address in Shakespeare's plays. The terms of address that co-occur most often with the pronoun *thou* are terms of endearment (e.g. *bully, chuck, heart, joy, love,* or *wag*), next come terms of abuse (e.g. *devil, dog, fool, knave, rascal, rogue*) and generic terms of address (*boy, friend, gentleman, gentlewoman,* etc.). The terms that co-occur most often with *you*, on the other hand, are titles of courtesy such as *Your Grace, Your (royal) Highness, Your Honour, Your Ladyship, Goodman, goodwife, lady, lord,* or *sir*; then occupational terms of address (such as

Table 29.2 Categories of vocatives in Shakespeare according to B. Busse

Vocative category	Examples (for the sources, see B. Busse 2006: 13)
Conventional terms	'dame', 'dear madam'
Emotion/mind, thought	'my dearest love'
EPITHET	'friend', 'poor Caitiff'
Generic terms	'my boy'
Terms referring to natural phenomena	'O inhuman dog'
Personal names	'barbarous Tamora'
Terms referring to specialised fields	'O limed soul'
Terms of family relationship	'O wonderful son'

Busse (2006: 13), slightly simplified.

captain, doctor, esquire, justice, knight, or *nurse);* and finally terms of family relations (*brother, cousin, coz, daughter, father,* or *husband).*

A similar methodology was applied by Jucker (2012) for a more detailed study of Shakespeare's *Romeo and Juliet.* A combination of a small-scale quantitative study of the correlation of pronominal and nominal terms of address and qualitative micro analysis of selected extracts provides additional insights into the fictional characters of Shakespeare's play. Along the lines of Busse, he does not argue that Shakespeare's carefully constructed language is a direct reflection of the speech of real people at the time, but it does provide a fascinating 'social grammar' of Shakespeare (Busse 2003: 216).

Beatrix Busse's study focused on vocatives, which she defined as 'direct attitudinal adjunct-like forms of address' that can be realized as a nominal group or head alone (Busse 2006: 29). They often occur with the morphological marker 'O', and their position in the clause varies. She found an abundance of 3,111 different types of vocatives in the seventeen plays that formed her corpus (Busse 2006: 9). Her findings fell into eight different categories, as presented in Table 29.2.

29.3.4 Late Modern English

Late Modern English address terms are a fairly neglected area, as only correspondence has received attention. Nevala's (2009) corpus-linguistic assessment deals with the word 'friend' as an address term and reference, and she also discusses third-person nominal reference as an indirect address term. In letters by members of the Lunar Society of Birmingham, 'friend' was used as a device for claiming the speaker's own status as someone authoritative enough to reduce the distance between the interactants and for boosting the addressee's importance as a member of the speaker's in-group (Nevala 2009: 241). The article also discusses how third-person address was used instead of the direct second-person address: on the one hand, as a means of detaching the writer and avoiding personal involvement and, on the other hand, to express intimacy. Agnes Porter (born 1750) was a governess who corresponded with the mother of the children she was responsible for. She reminded the recipient of her dual role as a governess and substitute mother using a type of 'mother-talk' in the third person with a switch from *you* to *her* and nominal address with 'my dear Lady Mary':

(8)   I do indeed take a real concern in your disappointments, having many reasons exclusive of personal ones to wish *you* were here, yet none of them so important as the delight it would give **my dearest Lady Mary** to see **her** loves again . . . I repeat to **my dear Lady Mary** that **her** children are quite well. God bless **her** and them, amen! Po' (Agnes Porter to Lady Mary Talbot, 1809; quoted from Nevala 2009: 249, emphasis original).

29.4 DIVERSIFICATION OF PRESENT-DAY CONVENTIONS

Nominal forms of address have changed over the course of time, and in general the system has become simpler as Present-Day English has a fairly reduced selection of address terms including nouns of kinship like *Daddy* and *Mom*; occupational terms can also be used in the vocative function (*driver, waiter*) in special contexts. The situation is not, however, the same in all Anglophone countries as their histories and intercultural contacts are different and these are reflected in interactional patterns. Interesting developments are emerging, offering material for the variational pragmatic approach that focuses on regional differences in pluricentric languages (Schneider and Barron 2008). Diversification can be verified in pragmatic aspects of language use like nominal address terms, the speech acts of complimenting and thanking, and responses to them. Address terms are sensitive indicators of the degree of formality and politeness in interaction, and different kinds may be required in different countries for communication to flow smoothly. *Sir* is commonly used as an address term for men, but even with this word some differences have been recorded: British English stresses the service aspect as a polite way of addressing the customer and in particular men of authority. American English has a more general definition 'a polite word used to address a man', and in Indian English the word is used after the name of a man who is in position of authority like 'John Sir' (*Cambridge Dictionaries online*). In the following example the situational context is military, a setting which observes hierarchical power relations, here expressed with the frequent use of *sir*. The example is from *Corpus of Contemporary American English*, which together with the *Corpus of Historical American English* (COHA) offers plenty of material for studies like this.

(9) 'You doubt my ability to best a barbarian, soldier?'//The smaller man backed up a pace, hastily sheathing his weapon. 'No, sir. Of course not. My apologies, sir.' (COCA, 2008, Fiction, Bk: DeepMagic)

In recent pragmatic literature, postcolonial forms of address have attracted attention as both Western and native patterns are used in interaction in communication in multilingual and hybrid environments (Anchimbe and Janney 2011: 1451–9). Indian English has an administrative history and its use in legal, educational, military, and media contexts has brought along formal features of language use (see McArthur 2002: 313–26). Its system of address terms is more complex than in most other varieties. Nominal address terms are frequent and include titles alone (*Sir, Madam*), titles (*Doctor, Professor, Inspector*) and honorific suffixes (*Sadhji*), and honorific tags (*Sahib, Huzoor*) in addition to kinship terms and pet names (Dodiya 2006: 210–11). Address terms can be used in different ways, for example the expression 'Your Honour' is a vocative typical of the legal register in face-to-face interaction in the context of a court case, but when used in everyday communication it sounds bookish (Dodiya 2006: 212). The ICE corpus of Indian English gives more than 200 hits of this nominal address term and shows its spread beyond the original context. Anglophone Caribbean practices have been studied by Mühleisen (2011), who found that nominal terms of address and their adaptation to specific conversational situations display special aspects of postcolonial culture as well as linguistic ambiguity (Mühleisen 2011: 1460). Address terms are also used strategically in conflict situations.

29.5 FUTURE RESEARCH

Address terms are a subtle means of conveying different attitudes and indicating the social position and identity of a person in a community. The survey in this chapter on nominal address terms in the history of English shows that not all periods have received equal attention, and there are gaps in our knowledge. Genres are also unevenly covered, and some, for example spoken genres, have hardly been touched upon. A proper contrastive study of address term patterns is still wanting.

In our survey we have tried to focus on non-literary materials, but literary examples were also quoted especially in the Middle English and Early Modern English sections, as these periods with their literary achievements and highly sophisticated address term systems have received a great deal of scholarly attention. Literary examples have no one-to-one fit with natural language use, but authors of fiction exploit real-life practices in their character descriptions to acquire subtle shades of meaning. Irony, or even parody, are often involved as the passage at (10) shows. Address terms in the nineteenth century is a neglected area, but this example from Dickens's *Little Dorrit* proves that attitudes of prestige and social class distinctions (discussed in connection with fourteenth-century examples) continued. Mrs General teaches refined manners to Little

Dorrit including 'proper' address terms. A humorous touch verging on irony is achieved by juxtaposing items of very different semantic values at the end:

(10)   'Papa is a preferable mode of address,' observed Mrs General. 'Father is rather vulgar, my dear. The word Papa, besides, gives a pretty form to the lips. Papa, potatoes, poultry, prunes, and prism are all very good words for the lips . . .' (Book the second, Chapter 5)

CHAPTER 30

··

PSEUDONYMS

··

KATARZYNA ALEKSIEJUK

30.1 Definitions

'Pseudonym' is defined as an onomastic or literary term. Examples of onomastic definitions are: 'a fictitious name of a person usually used by artists, politicians etc. as an alternative to their legal name' (ICOS 2011) and 'a made-up name used by individuals or groups in public or social life alongside or instead of real names' (Podol'skaia 1978: 118). As a literary term pseudonyms are described as 'different from real names' rather than 'fictitious' or 'made-up'. Some authors narrow pseudonyms to signatures in the form of standard names while writings signed by common appellations (as 'A Lady') or initials are considered anonymous. Other categories, such as Hellenized and Latinized names, maiden names, fake names of publishers, or devotional names, might be included, excluded, or classed as 'quasipseudonyms' (Masanov 1969: 285, 316; Świerczyńska 1983: 39–40, 286–7).

30.2 Terminology and Categorization

There is no uniform categorization of pseudonyms, for example Hamst (1867: 47–8) lists thirty-three categories, Courtney (1908: 32–3) has thirty-two, Masanov (1969: 285–7) has ten, and Dmitriev (1977: 276–9) has fifty-seven categories; proposed classifications differ in both terminology and definitions (Figs. 30.1–30.3).

Ján Vladimír Ormis (1944) in *Slovník slovenských pseudonymov* proposed categorization based on five criteria (Świerczyńska 1983: 40–2) (Fig. 30.4). In addition, in terms of structure he divided pseudonyms into:

- Fictonyms—structured like standard names.
- Cryptonyms—letters, words, phrases, or sentences not structured like names.
- Graphonyms—non-alphabetical symbols.

These were further divided into numerous subcategories, which gave 132 categories in total. Świerczyńska (1983: 47) has utilized this idea to compose a simple yet comprehensive classification (Fig. 30.5).

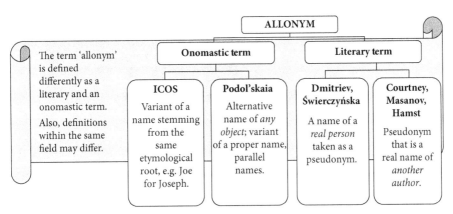

FIGURE 30.1 Allonym: definitions

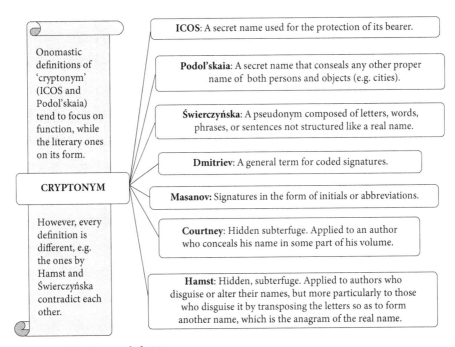

FIGURE 30.2 Cryptonym: definitions

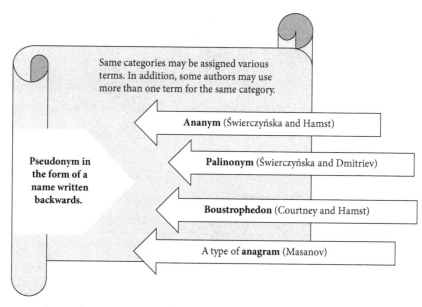

FIGURE 30.3 Terms for a name written backwards

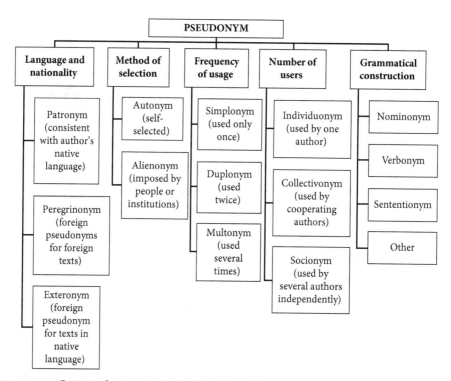

FIGURE 30.4 Criteria of categorization by Ormis (1944)

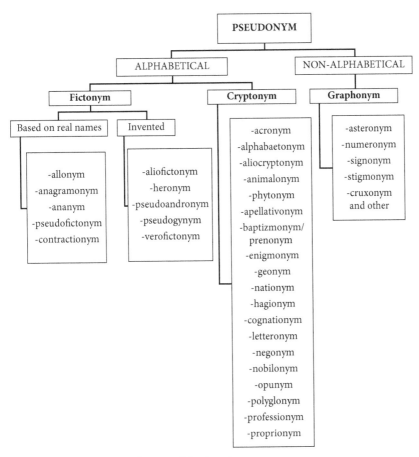

FIGURE 30.5 Categorization by Świerczyńska (1983)

30.2.1 Relevant Literature

Sources of information on pseudonyms include: dictionaries of pseudonyms, bibliographies, catalogues, lists of incipits, biographies, memoirs, correspondence, handbooks of nicknames, the *Who's Who*, relevant journals, bibliographical essays, guides and indices of periodicals' contents, essays on pseudonyms used by a single person. Some exist in inconvenient places, like appendices or rare journals (Taylor and Mosher 1951: 134–95; Masanov 1969: 276–8). Recent works offer fresh perspectives on anonymity and pseudonymity, for example Marcy L. North's (2003) *Anonymous Renaissance*, Catherine Gallagher's (1994) *Nobody's Story*, or Robert J. Griffin's (2003) *The Faces of Anonymity*. Internet resources include Wikipedia's 'List of pseudonyms' (2014b) and other lists arranged by various categories with links to individual biographies, such as 'African writers by country' (Wikipedia 2014c), 'North Korean people by occupation' (Wikipedia 2014d), or 'List of women rhetoricians' (Wikipedia 2014e).

30.2.1.1 *A Note on the History of Pseudonyms*

The first users of assumed names were kings and emperors, popes, soldiers, religious converts, slaves, and prostitutes; later scholars, writers, artists, and politicians adopted this practice. The extent of ancient pseudonymity is unknown due to lack of systematic studies. In the Middle Ages pseudonyms were infrequent. Some authors were known by several names, for example Albertus Magnus, also called Albertus Bolstadius, Albertus de Colonia, Albertus Grotus, Albertus Lavingensis, Albertus Ratisbonensis, and Albertus Teutonicus, but they were not deliberate name alterations. In the sixteenth and seventeenth centuries, the 'Golden Age of pseudonyms', almost every writer (and many artists) used a pseudonym at some point. Another outburst of pseudonyms, the 'Insurrection of pseudonyms', accompanied the outbreak of periodicals in the nineteenth century (Taylor and Mosher 1951: 28, 81–5; Masanov 1969: 123; Świerczyńska 1983: 17).

30.2.1.2 *Reasons for Using Pseudonyms*

Świerczyńska (1983: 21–37) groups the reasons for using pseudonyms into three categories:

- Civil and political—Restricted freedom of speech forces those expressing unaccepted views to conceal their identities. For example, in early modern times, both mutual Inquisition and politics of individual countries put such authors in danger of penalty from ecclesiastical and secular authorities. Also political activists and secret societies such as Freemasonry use pseudonyms for conspiracy (Taylor and Mosher 1951: 162–3).
- Social and conventional—In the seventeenth century female authors started commonly[1] using masculine names to avoid discrimination as writers and ostracism as individuals; also for upper classes writing was found inappropriate. Currently, females writing within supposedly masculine genres may need to conceal their gender to gain credibility—similarly males within feminine genres, such as romantic fiction. Pseudonyms may also be selected to suit a specific genre or a particular text, to separate different fields, or for *infra dig* activities, e.g. by serious authors for lighter writings, by artists for posters, book illustrations, etc., or by composers for music reviews. Pseudonyms also constitute elements of the performer's image; they may replace difficult or plain names (Pola Negri instead of Apolonia Chałupiec), or indicate character of activity: Rob Zombie and Nergal are heavy-metal musicians, while Long Dong Silver and Wilde Oscar are porn actors. Sharing names with others or multiple publishing (several books in a short time, a number of articles in the same issue) might also motivate the use of pseudonyms (Masanov 1969: 256–8; Sharp 1972: v–vii; Wikipedia 2014f).

---

[1] But not exclusively, see e.g. Courtney (1908: 32–70) and Marshall (1985).

- Psychological—Budding writers may conceal their identities due to lack of confidence; conversely, popular authors might wish to avoid reputation-related bias. Some use pseudonyms to separate private life from professional, or to avoid comparison with famous family members. Pseudonyms are also used to claim certain identities: national or ethnic, professional, situational ('Eye Witness'), as well as to indicate views, values, personal qualities, and other individual preferences.

Sometimes a literary mask may obtain autonomy and develop complex relationships with their creators and audiences. 'Koz'ma Prutkov' created by Aleksey Tolstoy and the Zhemchuzhnikov brothers gained a recognition as an existing individual, while 'Piotr Włast', a literary mask of Maria Komornicka, became her/his true identity (Masanov 1969: 227–30; Świerczyńska 1983: 77).

30.2.1.3 *Practices of Using Assumed Names*

Pseudonyms are used in various disciplines: sport (Pelé, Kaká), politics and social activism (Lenin, Trotsky), hacking (Emmanuel Goldstein), and others (Wikipedia 2014b). They might be self-selected or bestowed: by journalists, friends, public opinion, fans etc; group members, like literary circles or gangsters, may name each other. Not all pseudonyms replace the names completely, for example jazz musicians often substitute pseudonyms for their first names: 'Duke' Ellington, 'Bird' Parker, while gangsters tend to incorporate them as middle names: Cornelius 'Needles' Ferry, John 'Dingbat' O'Berta (Masanov 1969: 56–9; Rees and Noble 1985: x, 62–3, 86–7; Rainbolt 2002). Bestowed pseudonyms seem ambiguous as a class: they express familiarity as nicknames do,[2] and they are professional names. Sometimes alternative terms are used for ambiguous varieties of assumed names, especially 'sobriquet'. Other related terms are: byname, alias, moniker, tag, or nom-de-guerre; however they are not unambiguous either, for example 'nom-de-guerre' has been described as (Świerczyńska 1983: 261):

- used by authors in polemics;
- used constantly—in contrast to those used only in public occurrences;
- used by activists, sportspersons, soldiers, etc. in contrast to pen name (nom-de-plume) or stage-name.

Some pseudonyms gradually take over the role of real names, including being placed on the grave, which makes it difficult to assess their legal status, for example 'Gor'kii' ('bitter') is so commonly taken for a surname that it has lost its semantic weight (Dmitriev 1977: 249–50).

---

[2] Podsevatkin (1999: 6–7) suggests that early nicknames, such as 'Valmiki' ('anthill', the ancient Indian poet), are prototypes of pseudonyms.

30.2.2 Reappearing Pseudonyms

Numerous pseudonyms denote more than one individual: for example in the Polish corpus, 70 per cent if single letters and initials are considered, and 40 per cent if these are excluded from calculation. Some are re-used consciously, for example as a family tradition. Others are shared by groups of authors, either in cooperation (collective/joint pseudonyms) or independently, for example standing pseudonyms for columns or book series (Masanov 1969: 59; Sharp 1972: vii; Świerczyńska 1983: 141–6).

30.2.3 Other Related Phenomena

Other types of camouflage might also be considered as some kind of pseudonymity:

- plagiarism;
- buying or otherwise obtaining an author's permission to sign their work;
- imitations—publishing one's own works as someone else's, e.g. false translations or fake texts of popular authors (Masanov 1969: 61, 182–92; Dmitriev 1977: 263–9).

30.2.4 History of Scholarly Interest

Until the eighteenth century anonyma and pseudonyma as well as other phenomena causing authorship-related confusion: pseudepigrapha, homonyms, plagiarism, and Latinized and Hellenized names, were perceived as related and treated together. First works related to name ambiguities appeared in antiquity and addressed figures with the same names (homonyms) in order to differentiate them. In the Renaissance, the interest in homonymy spread when antique writings were discovered. Studying pseudepigrapha, the spurious writings of forged or falsely ascribed authorship, began when the earliest Christian Bible canon was formulated. It pointed the way for students of anonyma and pseudonyma, having devised critical methods for determining the authorship and authenticity assessment. The first substitute names that gained scholarly attention were Latinized and Hellenized names widely used in the Renaissance, either as pseudonyms or new official names, to reflect a fascination with classical antiquity (Taylor and Mosher 1951: 1–78).

Anonyma and pseudonyma first attracted the attention of scholars, especially in theology, philology, philosophy, and literary studies, as well as lawyers. As the role of bibliography evolved, both its scope and character changed: from international to national,[3]

[3] This resulted in lack of international works. Only recently, Michael Peschke has undertaken a gap-bridging project: a sixteen-volume *International Encyclopedia of Pseudonyms* in five languages, published between 2006 and 2009.

from Latin to vernacular, and from in-depth scholarly studies to simple collections for reference use. Although there are older traceable works, the study of anonyma and pseudonyma is often dated from the publication of Friedrich Geissler's (1669) *De nominum mutatione et anonymis scriptoribus* on legal and historical aspects of changes in names. The first true bibliographical reference book was *Theatrum anonymorum et pseudonymorum* by Vincent Placcius (1708). *La Visiera alzata* by Angelico Aprosio (1689), the first collection in a vernacular language limited to a single country, and *Auteurs deguisez* by Adrien Baillet (1690), were the first great contributions by librarians, while *Dictionnaire des ouvrages anonymes et pseudonymes* by Antoine-Alexandre Barbier (1806–8), the first great modern dictionary, combined with Joseph-Marie Quérard's (1845–60) *Les supercheries littéraires dévoilées* revised by Gustave Brunet and Pierre Jannet and compiled by Olivier Barbier and René and Paul Billard (1872–9), constitute the first encyclopaedic work of literary mystifications in a single literature. Important early British works are: *Handbook of Fictitious Names* (Olphar Hamst 1868), *A Dictionary of the Anonymous and Pseudonymous Literature of Great Britain* (Halkett and Laing 1882–8), *Initials and Pseudonyms: a Dictionary of Literary Disguises* (Cushing 1886–8), and *Dictionary of Anonymous and Pseudonymous English Literature* (Kennedy et al. 1926–32). At the beginning of the twentieth century almost every literature in the world had at least one dictionary (Courtney 1908: 8–10; Taylor and Mosher 1951: 80–196; Masanov 1969: 288–315).

30.2.5 Unsolved Pseudonyms

Despite efforts, several literary mysteries remain unsolved. For instance, in the last thirty years of the eighteenth century almost 70 per cent of all British novels were published anonymously or pseudonymously, and nearly 40 per cent of them remain unattributed. Some controversies trigger long-lasting discussions, for example 'Bacon-Shakespeare' or 'Marprelate'. The problem is particularly difficult where great numbers of anonymous and pseudonymous contributions are involved, for example journal articles or Renaissance alchemical writings. Also some contemporary personages successfully conceal their identities, such as street artists ABOVE and Banksy (Taylor and Mosher 1951: 80–7, 163, 177–8; Świerczyńska 1983: 249–51; Griffin 1999: 883; Wikipedia 2014b).

30.2.6 Reception of Pseudonyms

In the Renaissance, Latinized names were criticized as sinful symbols of dedication to pagan culture which the Inquisition may have used to support accusations in trials. Pseudonyms were also pronounced 'devil's devices' facilitating the distribution of 'false doctrine'. In 1616 in Halle a debate on anonymity and pseudonymity in theological controversy was held and in 1715 Gottfried Ludwig requested a state censorship to suppress this practice. All name alterations were also criticized as demonstrating a lack of family pride and causing confusion in genealogies (Taylor and Mosher 1951: 18–28, 89–93).

In the nineteenth century the focus shifted to ethics of anonymity and pseudonymity in journalism, which were criticized for promoting malice and other irresponsible behaviours in writing and publishing, while defended as liberating from political, social, and personal bias (Taylor and Mosher 1951: 178–9; Griffin 1999: 884–5).

Also, the personal attitudes of masked individuals have always been criticized for lack of courage, dishonesty, and not taking writing seriously, as well as for snobbism and poor taste (Świerczyńska 1983: 18–20). Currently, interesting discussions might be found online, for example Proz.com (2012).

30.2.7 Pseudonyms Worldwide

Oriental poets, both classic and modern, might be known by pseudonyms or nicknames. One of the reasons for the popularity of pseudonyms was the tradition of including a pen name (*takhallus*) in the closing verse of a poem (a form of authorship protection), and real names may have not always fitted neatly. In Muslim traditions they may have responded to the high recurrence of personal names. Also social and individual reasons were involved, for example 'Makhfi' ('concealed'), an Indian emperor's daughter, was forced to write secretly. Typical pseudonyms and nicknames are etymologically transparent, referring to appearance, personal traits, biography, literature, views, and important places, such as: Arabic 'al-A'sha' ('weak-sighted') and 'al-Mutanabbi' ('self-nominated prophet'), Persian 'Firdausi' ('heavenly'), Kyrgyz 'Togolok Moldo' ('chubby literate'), Armenian 'Sayat-Nova' ('king-of-songs') and 'Sevak' ('black-eyed'), Uzbek 'Aydyn' ('enlightened') and 'Mahmur' ('drunk'), Turkmen 'Talibi' ('searching'), Tajik 'Bedil' ('heartless'), and Azerbaijani 'Saib Tabrizi' ('from Tabriz'), also called 'Saib Isfahani' as he died in Isfahan. Multiple pseudonyms are not uncommon, for example the Uzbek poetess Mohlaroyim used: 'Nodira' ('unique'), 'Komila' ('whole-hearted'), and 'Maknuna' ('reticent'). Other frequent references cover nationality, literature, and nature: light, fire, moon, wind, names of trees, flowers, and birds (Dmitriev 1977: 100–14, 133, 141–5, 257–8).

Traditional Eastern-Asian naming customs were complex: name-changes accompanying changes in life and tabooing of personal names combined with highly-formalized social relationships generated a sophisticated system of reference and address forms, including a range of alternative names.

In China pseudonyms traditionally were used by writers, artists, bibliophiles, and other distinguished figures. Various formations may be utilized: real names of other persons, names of birthplaces, forename or forenames only, forenames in rearranged order, surnames split into two characters (such as 'Ma-ko' '馬各' used by Lo '駱' Hsüeh-liang), studio names, courtesy names, transliterations of Romanized initials, for example 'Hsi-t'i' used by Chêng Chên-to (C.T.). Recently, the twentieth century's transformation triggered a discussion on a range of social issues that resulted in a wave of pseudonymous publishings (Chu 1977: ix; Shu 1969: ix–x).

In Japan writers, artists, warriors, priests, monks, artisans, peasants, and tradesmen were known by pseudonyms, which often referred to nature: 'Koyo' ('autumn leaves'), 'Ujaku' ('sparrow in the rain'), 'Roka' ('reed flower'), but also to appearance or behaviour, ancient poems, ancestry, places of birth, work, or study; some were modifications of real names, or brainteasers. More recent ones reflect Western influences, for example 'Edogava Rampo' imitating 'Edgar Allan Poe', or 'Oh!great' for 'Ogure Ito' based on similar pronunciation (Dmitriev 1977: 254–6; Frolova 2008: 110).

In colonial Africa, pseudonyms were used to avoid censorship and persecution not only by writers and activists of educated elites, such as South-African Dennis Brutus (John Bruin) or Marcelino dos Santos of Mozambique (Lilinho Micaia, Carlos Kalungano, K. Maala) but also by local readers who contributed to public debates in the form of letters, articles, fiction, and poetry in African-owned newspapers. They used pseudonyms in a playful way to construct their African identities and comment on the colonial regime. By self-naming and renaming they parodied the imperialist practices of labelling Africans, while the name choices, such as 'A Native', 'Overworked', 'Tired', 'Bashful', 'A Man About Town', 'Jim Crow', 'Old Black Joe', 'A Gold Coast Native', 'Rambler', and 'Proud of Name', revealed cultural and political awareness. Pseudonyms often complemented the character of contributions, for example the column 'Home Chat' in *Gold Coast Nation* was composed by 'The Man in the Street' (e.g. Anonymous 1915) or constructed the impression of authenticity in ordinary-looking names, such as 'J. G. Mullen' (Dmitriev 1977: 21; Newell 2010: 10–12, 2013: 6–10).

30.3 Usernames

30.3.1 Terminology and Definitions

Consultation of randomly selected online dictionaries and glossaries of computer and internet terminology in English, Russian, Polish, and Dutch (five in each language) revealed that names on the internet, usually paired with a password, serve to access multiuser environments, such as e-mail, forums, chatrooms, banking, and shopping; some of them are visible to others and may be used for interaction.

In general, English terminology is used: alias, handle, login/login name, nick/nickname, user ID, username, account name, aka, ID/Identifier, and screen name (some Dutch dictionaries included: schuilnaam—'hide-name', gebruikersnaam—'username', and loginnaam) but is not distributed evenly across languages. Also definitions of the same term may vary from one language to another and from one dictionary to another within the same language (Figs. 30.6–30.8).

Terms used by researchers include: 'nick'/'nickname' (Bechar-Israeli 1995; Bays 1998; Scheidt 2001; Swennen 2001; Sidorova 2006; Stommel 2007; Van Langendonck 2007b), 'pseudonym' (Jaffe et al. 1995; Heisler and Crabill 2006) and 'screen name' (Del-Teso-Craviotto 2008).

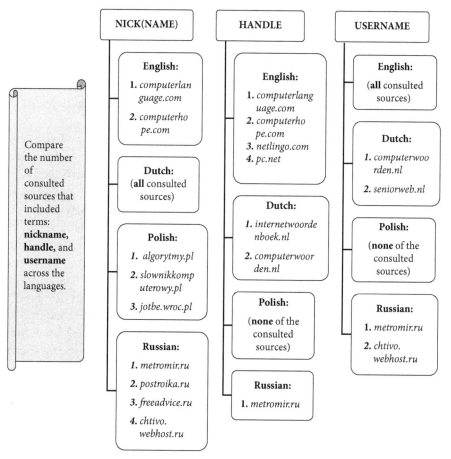

FIGURE 30.6 Distribution of terms: *nick(name)*, *handle*, and *username* across selected sources in Dutch, English, Polish, and Russian

30.3.2 Forms of Username

According to typical rules, usernames must be unique, limited in length, and not all keyboard symbols are allowed. Some domains implement further restrictions, for example filters eliminating offensive vocabulary. Written communication enables using unpronounceable formations (^_^, ^{-_-}^), visual effects (cLoNehEAd, D@rkst@r[Tr]), digits (me33, phRe4k), and sequences of random characters (dddd, ffgghgf) (Bechar-Israeli 1995; Swennen 2001: 100).

30.3.3 Usernames and Pseudonyms

Usernames have been associated with pseudonyms based on self-selection as the key feature (e.g. Van Langendonck 2007b: 300). It should be noted, however, that self-naming

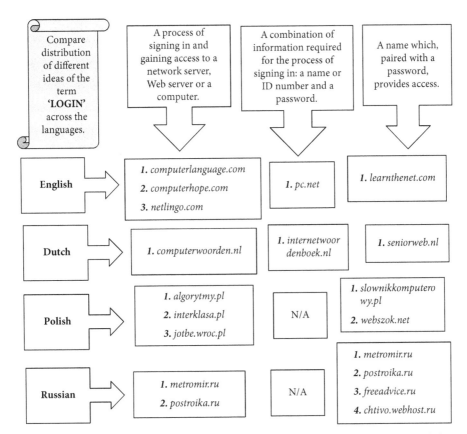

FIGURE 30.7 Definitions of the term *login* in selected sources in Dutch, English, Polish, and Russian

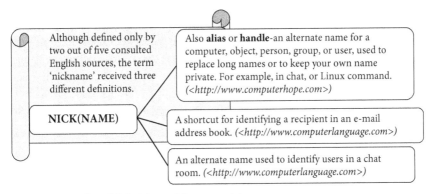

FIGURE 30.8 Examples of definitions of the term *nickname*

and renaming practices are relatively common in official naming (Nikonov 1974: 21–6; Alford 1988: 81–95), and self-ascribed nicknames have also been reported (Mashiri 2004: 40; Adams 2009: 83). Moreover, neither pseudonyms nor usernames have to be self-selected or self-invented. It is common for institutions to set legal names and student or staff numbers as default identifiers; also in unofficial communication real names as well as school or family nicknames are used, thus, self-naming as a feature of recognition might be questioned.

30.3.4 Naming Customs Online and Offline

Official naming is always an institutionalized or conventionalized practice; similarly, usernames are obligatory for members of any virtual environment: the online naming system is a primary, customary means of identification, reference, and address. Also, there are relations between naming and identity that both offline and online naming systems reflect, for example gender specification (Alford 1988: 66; Scheidt 2001; Del-Teso-Craviotto 2008; Herring and Stoerger 2014), expressing aspirations and augmenting self-image (Bechar-Israeli 1995; Nikonov 1974: 30), or name-changes symbolic of identity alterations (Alford 1988: 85–95; Stommel 2007); however, official personal names are never collective whereas online a single entry might indicate multiple users, e.g. Amy & Paul.

30.3.5 Usernames as a Research Subject

Internet naming has received modest interest from onomasticians so far; however, it constitutes an important, although still not sizeable, element of Computer Mediated Communication (CMC) study. Theories designed to study social and linguistic phenomena offline, such as notions of 'frame' and 'face' or dramaturgical perspective (Goffman 1959) and Uncertainty Reduction Theory (Berger and Calabrese 1975), have been successfully applied in researching CMC, including naming practices. Given the reduced access to audio-visual cues and the fact that they are the only obligatory participation indicator, usernames have been demonstrated to function as a 'symbolic locus for presence' that constitutes a reference point for communication, and a primary device of identity performance. Strategies applied to construct virtual personae through both form and content of usernames have also been presented (Bechar-Israeli 1995; Bays 1998; Scheidt 2001; Lev and Lewinsky 2004; Heisler and Crabill 2006; Del-Teso-Craviotto 2008).

30.3.6 Distribution and Categorizations

Research demonstrates a varied semantic distribution of usernames across environments, thus some categorizations are made to fit specific material (Bechar-Israeli 1995; Scheidt 2001). Others attempt to compose comprehensive categorizations (Sidorova 2006: 92–6; Swennen 2001: 97–137; Van Langendonck 2007b: 301–6). Some common references can be observed (Fig. 30.9).

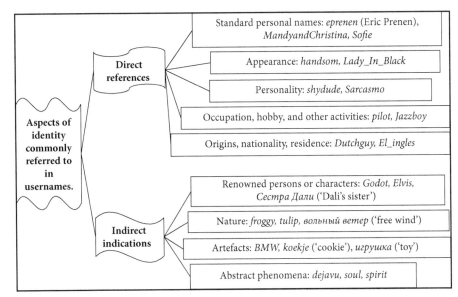

FIGURE 30.9 Examples of popular references in usernames

30.3.7 Anonymity and Authorship Online

The internet puts the notions of authorship, ownership, anonymity, and privacy into a new perspective. Concerns regarding copyrights, data protection, and research ethics are justified, especially that participants' opinions may also vary: some seek publicity within the environments that others perceive as a private space (Hudson and Bruckman 2004: 127–9).

Usernames are usually recognized between the users as a property and when one is shared, typically the senior user would keep it (Bechar-Israeli 1995). However, cases of impersonation (unauthorized adoption of somebody else's username or pretending to be that person) have been recorded (Swennen 2001: 20). Many websites enable protecting usernames by passwords, and some offer their certified registration, for example Nick-NameRegister.com (2015) or Nick-Name.ru (2010–15).[4]

30.3.8 Final Remarks

While usernames share a number of properties with pseudonyms, they retain some unique characteristics.

---

[4] Polish law protects usernames equally to personal names, pseudonyms, and brands (II CSK 539/07).

Both pseudonyms and usernames facilitate a chosen degree of anonymity,[5] selective identity revelation,[6] and creating multiple identities, as well as self-advertising. Resemblance is also observable in both form and semantics as well as in the playful character of certain entities.

Nevertheless, the groups differ in their relation to official naming: pseudonyms differ from legal names by definition, while official names may serve as usernames. Also, unlike usernames, pseudonyms typically apply to the professional activity of renowned figures—hence the research based on attribution, which would not apply to usernames. On this occasion the closest resemblance can perhaps be observed in blogs and personal web pages, reminiscent of traditional publicity in showing a similar dichotomy of producers and audience where the author is a central figure of the discourse.

Given the limited amount of internet data having been researched so far, the presented facts cannot be considered as universally applicable. Internet naming requires more attention for usernames to be introduced into the catalogue of name categories, either as part of a recognized one, or as a new one.

---

[5] 53.2% of users with pseudonymous usernames surveyed by Swennen (2001: 62) reported anonymity as the main reason for not revealing real names.

[6] At the early stage of academic interest, the internet was expected to neutralize social differences and promote equal participation of disadvantaged groups. However, closer examination, especially on gender, has not confirmed these predictions (Jaffe et al. 1995; Scheidt 2001; Swennen 2001: 59; Herring and Stoerger 2014: 577–8).

CHAPTER 31

....

COMMERCIAL NAMES

....

PAULA SJÖBLOM

31.1 INTRODUCTION

....

IN the contemporary globalized world which, in many respects, is controlled by economic and financial factors, names are also affected by an impetus towards commercialism. There is a group of names that are designated by the common term *commercial
names* and that are among the newest subjects of onomastic research. These names differ in many ways from the more traditional areas of onomastics, such as toponyms and
anthroponyms. One of the focal differences is that functionality and semantic features
have a remarkable importance in the study of these names. Furthermore, their linguistic
structure is varied and can be quite complex compared to that of other name types.

It is most practical to define commercial nomenclature from a financial perspective: *commercial names* are names whose function is to steer the choices of consumers
and investors and whose use has economic objectives. An important feature is that there
is usually a juridical owner of a commercial name who outlines its rights and limitations
of use. A typical commercial name refers to a business or to various products, and its
purpose is to help the name owner with marketing and sales. Moreover, commercial
names themselves can be a subject of trade. Thus, these names have monetary value.

There is variation in the terminology of commercial names in different countries
and branches of science. For instance, the convention when speaking about language
and names in marketing research differs from that in linguistics. The varying legislation in different countries also has an impact on terminology. In daily language use,
different commercial name categories often overlap, and it is not always clear what it
really means when we speak of company names, product names, trademarks, or brands.
Some names are officially registered; others are more or less unofficial and are used for
convenience, for practical reasons or for advertising, for instance. There are also names
that are basically not commercial names but which can be given a commercial tone in
some situations (for instance place-names in place branding). The onomastic traditions of speaking about commercial names are different in different countries. All of

these reasons bring about a diverse set of concepts that may complicate familiarity with sources in the field. In this chapter, the main categories of commercial names will be defined (see also Sjöblom 2014).[1]

The term *company name* is an expression which consistently refers to a certain business, identifies a company and its activities, and distinguishes them from other companies. The referent is primarily abstract, an intangible entity, but the name can be used for concrete commercial property as well. A company is a kind of artificial person, and its essence always has legal aspects (see also chapter 39). A typical company is a financial unit whose purpose is to purchase inputs, merge them in the production process and sell acquired assets for the acquisition of income. In this sense, the terms *business name* and *firm name* can also be used. Moreover, non-profit associations of people, such as housing corporations, can be called companies, but the term *company name* is not usually used within onomastics for these kinds of organizations. An enterprise owned by one person is not a company, but a name referring to this kind of business can, however, be called a company name.[2]

Companies make or sell products or services. The ideas of these tangible and intangible products may be individualized and distinguished from other products of the same kind through names that are generally also protected by law. The common term for these types of names is *product name*. A *trademark* is an officially registered or otherwise protected sign referring to a certain product or group of products of a specific manufacturer.[3] It consists primarily of a product name but it can also include non-linguistic elements. The term *brand name* overlaps with company names, product names, and trademarks. A brand name can refer to a product or a group of products (*Smart, Pepsodent*) as well as to a company (*Lumene, Nokia*). It can be defined as a widely known, financially valuable name which includes an image of the surplus value offered by the products. Names of countries, towns and other places, names of celebrities, names of events, etc. can sometimes be brands as well.[4]

In international onomastics, the terminology concerning commercial nomenclature is diverse. In the German tradition, especially, the term *ergonym* proposed by Bauer (1985: 50, 55) is commonly used when speaking about commercial names. Bauer has divided names into five groups based on what relationship the referent has to human beings. Ergonyms are names of objects, that is entities that have been created by humans. The concept is a broad hyperonym, and it does not distinguish any differences between names of commercial entities and non-commercial institutions, such as administrative

[1] Sometimes, the concept *trade name* is also used. However, the meaning of *commercial name* seems to be somewhat broader, also including such names that have not been created primarily for trading but whose sole function is to carry monetary value.

[2] The trailblazer of the onomastic study of company names is Ludger Kremer (1996, 1997). Subsequently, the terminological aspects of company names are widely discussed in Paula Sjöblom's (2006) monograph on Finnish company names, in which legal and marketing points of view are also taken into account.

[3] A full discussion about trademarks can be found in Teutsch (2007: 46–59).

[4] See also Ainiala et al. (2012: 212–13).

fields or churches, nor between different types of commercial names, such as company names and product names. Neither does it distinguish any differences between concrete (e.g. buildings) and abstract (e.g. companies) entities. Terminological questions concerning ergonyms have been broadly discussed by Koss (1996a: 1642, 1996b: 1795–6).

The field of commercial names is broad. It depends on many factors, which names should be regarded as commercial and how these names relate to each other. There is no single answer to the categorization of names. The classification depends, among other aspects, on the language and culture in question, the naming system, and the scholar's own perspective. The researcher always has to define the relation of his or her topic to other nomenclature and place it within a certain naming system (Ainiala et al. 2012: 25). Regarding commercial names, it is also important to take juridical and economic issues into account in order to facilitate discussion between disciplines.

The chapter at hand deals mainly with company, product, and brand names, but it also takes a glance at the commercialization of the Western way of life and its impact on its whole nomenclature.

31.2 THE PAST AND PRESENT OF COMMERCIAL NAMING

There was no need for commercial nomenclature before society began to develop towards free commerce and the mutual competition of merchants. Commerce was strengthened with identifying names given to businesses and products, especially in Great Britain and central Europe in the eighteenth century, and after that also in the Americas and Scandinavia.

Commercial naming is strictly bound to the history of advertising. There has been advertising since there have been goods to sell, but a giant leap forward took place with the appearance of the printed press. The first French newspaper *La Gazette,* founded in 1631, published advertisements, and the first advertising agency was opened in 1786 in London (Tungate 2007: 10). The eighteenth and nineteenth centuries were a time of the rise of the European bourgeoisie. Industry and trade developed along with increasing seafaring. Technological inventions enabled the mass production of goods, and more and more people had enough money to buy items instead of making or just dreaming of them. After the restrictive practices of mercantilism, the Western world began to grow to free commerce. Advertising gave manufacturers visibility and provided information on their products to large audiences (Tungate 2007: 11–12; Ainiala et al. 2012: 226–8; Sjöblom 2012: 424, 426).

One of the primary tasks of advertising is to persuade a target group to buy an advertiser's product instead of other products of the same kind. Therefore, the advertiser—the company—and the product have to be perceived as independent entities with a personality. What could be a more efficient way of making an entity a unique individual than giving it a name?

At first, company names in advertisements were like signatures: shopkeepers or manufacturers guaranteed the availability of their products by having their personal name at the bottom of an advertisement. Little by little, the names of the entrepreneurs moved to a more visible place at the top of the advertisement, and the personal name started to refer to the business itself. Companies were named not only by the personal names of the entrepreneurs but also by names that described the field of business or the original location of the company. Eventually, commercial nomenclature finally reached a stage where companies were named with expressions that did not describe the company directly but were created in a more associative way (Sjöblom 2012: 426–8; Kremer 2012: 131–2).

Product names developed later. At first, products were named after a company. The company name guaranteed the quality of all the products made by the company. The best-known company names grew into brands, and the brand label had a visible position in an advertisement. For example, a sewing machine advertisement that was featured in the Finnish newspaper *Uusi Suometar* in 1880 has an insignia including a stylised image of a needle and thread and the text *The Singer MFC. CO. N.Y.o Trade mark*. The actual advertising text begins with a description of the product (with the name *Singer* in the genitive): *Amerikkalaiset Singerin Alkuperäiset ompelukoneet* 'American original Singer sewing machines' (Sjöblom 2012: 430). The company in 1851 was originally named *I.M. Singer & Co* after the founder's name, and it was renamed fourteen years later as *Singer Manufacturing Company*. The products were sold with the help of the company name, and the tag with the company name on it provided the promise of a certain quality of product. A brand had thus emerged.

The fact that all companies nowadays have names is the result of a historical process driven by industrialization and liberalization, which in many ways changed business activity so that a business could be conceptualized not just as means of earning one's living but also as its own independent being. Changes in company legislation in different countries followed the change in the way of thinking, and formally confirmed the identity of a business. This development took place in the Occident largely in the nineteenth century. Upon entering the twentieth century, many products were also given names which were no longer associated with the name of the manufacturer (Sjöblom 2006: 248–9; Ainiala et al. 2012: 228, 232). Unlike companies, not all products need to have a name, but practically almost all industrial and ready-made products are named, from wide-ranging discount brand names (e.g. *Euro Shopper*) to special names of specific products (e.g. IKEA furniture names: a *Karlstad* chair, a *Songe* mirror, etc.).

In the contemporary world, commercial names are a self-evident part of human culture, and they are legislated by laws and authoritative guidelines. Moreover, many other factors outside the name giver have an impact on naming. Commercial objectives are of course most important when names are being invented. Naming is a part of business communication. With names, a company creates a suitable image of itself and, as is known, images have a strong influence on people's behaviour. A name symbolizes the identity of the company or the product. People tend to buy products which have personality, an image that speaks to them (Bernstein 1985: 40, 233; Dowling 1994: 16,

125; see also Boerrigter 2007: 53–6 on business names and identity). Companies usually also ensure that all names they use will build a unified totality, so that, for example, new product names will fit in to the existing nomenclature.

Name change in a commercial environment is a question that has been discussed to some extent by onomasticians. This is because the governmental guidance of business has decreased gradually, at least in Europe, and corporate mergers and integrated markets have led companies with their new identities to search for new names. Companies may find their previous informative names too restrictive or, in the case of a merger, the name of one company is not approved to represent the whole corporation. In Eastern Europe, there has been an enormous change in the whole ideological environment which has affected commercial names. It is also a question of whether the name should convey associations of the country of origin or a supranational identity. New 'liberating and global' names are often abbreviations or are invented words that are not a part of any language (so-called quasi words) (Fischer 2010; Kremer 2012: 132; Kryukova 2012; Fischer and Wochele 2014).

Commercial names can be an excellent subject for multidisciplinary research. Jurisprudence, cultural geography, cultural studies, psychology, as well as sociology offer interesting viewpoints. There has been a remarkable interest in brands, especially in marketing studies. Because of the different vantage points and objectives of marketing studies and the linguistic examination of names, a multidisciplinary perspective might open up fresh new insights into the subject. While marketing scholars examine commercial names in terms of brand equity and the surplus value that the brand adds to the product, onomasticians emphasize the basic linguistic and cultural significance of names. These two perspectives are certainly present in every name that is employed for commercial purposes (Boerrigter and Nijboer 2012: 6).

31.3 LINGUISTIC STRUCTURE OF COMMERCIAL NAMES

There has been a strong rise in the linguistic analysis of commercial names since the beginning of the 1990s, albeit signs of an increasing interest were already evident from the 1960s (e.g. Borsoi 1967; Praniskas 1968; Gläser 1973; Room 1982; Voigt 1982; Embleton 1990; Koss 1990). From its beginnings up until today, there has been especially illuminating research carried out in German-speaking areas. However, the contemporary onomastic study of commercial names encompasses all continents and numerous languages, including non-Indo-European languages. Evidence of this can be seen in the four publications based on the Names in the Economy symposia series (Kremer and Ronneberger-Sibold 2007; Wochele et al. 2012; Boerrigter and Nijboer 2012; Sjöblom et al. 2013). The last six ICOS conferences show the same tendency: the number of presentations dealing with commercial names all over the world is increasing

(Bergien et al. 2010: 7). Mostly the studies have been published as articles, but there are some onomastic monographs about commercial names as well (Platen 1997; Sjöblom 2006; Teutsch 2007).

There is a great deal of variation in the theories and methods of these studies. Some of them describe the features of a set of materials consisting of a demarcated field of business or product group without paying particular attention to theoretical questions, while others may systematically analyse quite a large set of data of commercial names according to a particular methodology. There have been studies on the linguistic structure of commercial names on all levels of language (i.e. phonology, morphology, syntax, and semantics) as well as the investigation of orthographic features. For the most part, onomasticians have been interested in the lexical elements of commercial names, which have usually been grouped by semantic criteria. This is a natural consequence of the characteristics of commercial names, as meanings seem to play a crucial role in them. The theoretical background of studying the semantics of names has been validated in several studies. Cognitive and functional linguistic viewpoints as well as socio-onomastics and pragmatics have offered a good basis for semantic research (see e.g. Bergien 2007, 2013; Sjöblom 2008a, 2008b; Zilg 2011; Pérez Hernández 2011, 2013). Recently, name use in social interactions has also come up: commercial names could be studied with the methods of text linguistics and conversational analysis (De Stefani 2007, 2009c).

The onymic status of company and product names is thought to be different, the former being undoubtedly proper names, whereas the latter can waver on the sometimes vague line between proper and common nouns (Bergien et al. 2010: 10). There are many studies concerning the propriality of product names (e.g. Platen 1997; Andersson 2004; Van Langendonck 2007a; Lötscher 2010) as well as the genericization of brand names (e.g. Murray 1995; Platen 1997: 121–6; Panic 2003), but these questions are not discussed in this chapter. Instead, we will concentrate on the structure and semantics of both company and product names as well as on their socio-cultural functions.

Structural name analysis cannot be separated from the broader context of commercial names. The structure of these names can be examined on all linguistic levels in connection with their economic functions, and the regularities in naming depend, among other things, on the branch of business. The culture of the country and the particular language affect commercial name giving.[5] Spelling rules may have an influence as well. Since names do not just identify but also draw attention and attract, businesses can benefit from those that deviate from the rules of standard language. For instance, one can write the name with a lowercase initial letter or use capital letters in the middle of the word (*ratiopharm GmbH*, *PayPal*), or there can be grammatical misspellings, such as the avoidance of the genitive or other inflectional cases in Finnish (*Turku Energia* instead of

---

[5] Cultural prospects to commercial naming were discussed at the fourth *Names in the Economy* symposium in 2012. A collection of articles based on papers presented at the symposium has recently been published (Sjöblom et al. 2013).

the standard form *Turun energia* 'Turku+GEN energy'). These kinds of deviations can be called *attractors* (see Kremer 2007: 181–2).

In commercial names, and especially in brand names, language levels are linked with other semiotic systems, such as typography and patterns (cf. Platen 1997: 24–6). As far as graphic elements are concerned, special features are usually deviations from the normal orthography of the language: foreign letters, the use of numbers or special symbols, breaks in writing standards. This applies to company as well as product naming, and the reasons for these typographic peculiarities lie in attractiveness, association, memorability, and the achievement of a unique and legally protectable name (Sjöblom 2006: 103–10; Zilg 2011: 6–7). Graphic elements acquire a quite different meaning in languages that do not use Latin letters. For instance, in ideographic Chinese-language brand naming, one has to take the total number of character strokes into account: an appropriate brand name includes a certain auspicious number of strokes (Li Chang and Li 2008). The combinations of Chinese characters also convey many symbolic meanings in addition to the actual word meaning (Li 2012: 60–1).

Phonological features relate to graphics, but an important additional aspect is the pronunciation of commercial names.[6] Easy pronunciation of a brand or company name helps people to memorize it and, according to marketing studies, is likely to result in brand preference (Bao et al. 2008; Ronneberger-Sibold and Wahl 2013: 233). Commercial names are often loaned from one language to another; therefore, easy syllable structure and widely used phonemes may serve commercial objectives. However, the sound shape of names is language-specific, and what is preferred in one language might not be popular in another. Certain syllable structures and phonological features may signal specific product classes by, for example, being typical for that particular language or awakening associations of some foreign language (Ronneberger-Sibold and Wahl 2013).

Morphological questions concern word formation. Because of severe competition, commercial naming has to be innovative and it has to experiment with normal linguistic boundaries. While, at the same time, names have to be given positive remarks and convey suitable meanings, there is an inevitable need for imaginative word formation. Names are created by means of derivation, composition, blending, and the formation of abbreviations. Many names are created from well-known morphological elements loaned from, for example, Latin, Greek, or English (*lux, neuro, matic, net,* etc.), or parts taken from domestic words like *più* or *issimo* in Italian brand names. These kinds of elements are not necessarily identical with their corresponding free morphemes, but they can be shortened or altered. In a morphologic analysis, the researcher can, for instance, find out which suffixes are most productive in brand naming. Moreover, acronyms (*IKEA < Igvar Kamprad* from *Elmtaryd* in *Agunnaryd*) can be a subject of interest (see e.g. Platen 1997: 84–5; Ronneberger-Sibold 2006: 157, 2007b; Cotticelli Kurras 2007; Zilg 2009: 1092, 2011: 8–18).

---

[6] The speakability of trademarks is discussed quite thoroughly in Teutsch (2012).

The syntactic structure of commercial names cannot be studied by using the same methods as for the syntax of toponyms. Where compound toponyms consist of two meaningful parts, the generic part expressing the topographic type of place, and the specific part identifying the place, company, and product names can be much more complex. Company names—at least official ones—include several separate parts, each having its own function. Some of these parts can be obligatory by law, whereas others are optional. For example, Finnish company names can consist of four parts (boldfaced in the following examples): a corporate identifier (**Oy** Martline **Ab Ltd**[7]), a part expressing the business idea or the branch of business (Tonfisk **Design**), a true identifying part (**Tonfisk** Design), and an explanatory supplementary part that provides additional information (Adidas **Suomi** Oy, 'Adidas Finland Ltd'). According to Finnish legislation, the identifying part is always compulsory, and the corporate identifier is compulsory for limited companies (Sjöblom 2007, 2008b). The syntax of company names in German has correspondingly been studied by Ludger Kremer (1996: 360–1). The results are comparable, but some differences can be observed because of the differences in legislation (Sjöblom 2014).

Product names have an even more multifaceted syntactic structure. Brand names are short and simple because they have to be easy to pronounce and remember. However, if one analyses a long, multi-word product description which identifies a special product, one has to separate several distinctive components of the name. Today, the syntactic structure of product names is becoming more and more complex because a name has to distinguish a certain product from a great mass of other almost similar products (see Fischer 2007: 143). According to Dina Heegen (2013: 322), there can be up to eight different distinctive parts in a product name: umbrella brand, family brand, pseudo-family brand, individual brand, pseudo-individual brand, series, sub-series, and type or flavour. The structure of product names has also been illustrated by Werner Brandl (2007: 88), whose typology is a little more straightforward: a product name consists of brand, product group, product description, and variant (e.g. Müller | Froop | Trinkjoghurt | Erdbeere).[8]

31.4 SEMANTICS AND FUNCTIONS

The perennial problem of the meaning of names has even emerged with the study of commercial naming. There is a need for a theory which accepts the fact that a name

[7] The corporate identifier is usually an abbreviation. Oy stems from the Finnish word osakeyhtiö, and Ab from the Swedish word aktiebolag, both meaning 'limited company'.
[8] A third proposal for analysing the structure of a product description is presented in Ainiala et al. (2012: 247): Unilever Pepsodent® Junior toothpaste Mild Mint comprises five parts, i.e. company name Unilever, trademark Pepsodent®, product name Junior, type of product toothpaste, and qualifier Mild Mint.

can also convey meanings synchronically, and that the meaning of a name is not just the etymological, original meaning in the name-giving situation. Cognitive and functional linguistics as well as communicative viewpoints offer good help. Cognitive theory provides an opportunity to examine brand and company names as linguistic cues, which launch a process of cognitive operations and result in the generation of desirable conceptual associations (Pérez Hernández 2011: 371). The semantic analysis of commercial names is based on considering the relationship between the morpho-phonological structure of the name and cognitive domains evoked by the referent. These relationships can be described as semantic schemes. First, the relationship can be direct, that is, the name directly conveys the meanings related to the referent (*European Medical Network*). Secondly, it can be indirect, that is, the name has a metaphoric (Fin. *Mattogalleria*[9] 'carpet gallery') or metonymic (*Electrolux*[10]) relationship to the referent. Thirdly, the compressed meaning scheme means that the name includes many informative elements compressed into a short form (*Novosat*[11] < Lat. *novus* 'new' + *satellite*). The last scheme is a disconnected relationship, that is, the name form itself does not relate to the referent, but instead, the name gradually acquires associative meanings derived from the referent (*IBM*) (Sjöblom 2008b: 77–9).[12]

There are many other studies which, in one way or another, touch upon the semantics of commercial names (Room 1982; Grüner 1992; Platen 1997: 39–44; Schmitt 1998; Kremer 2007: 183–7; Ronneberger-Sibold 2007a, 2012; Wochele 2007; Neethling 2009b: 282–6; Vincze 2010; Danesi 2011: 182–4; Cotticelli Kurras 2012; Boonpaisarnsatit and Srioutai 2013, etc.). Some of them apply to a diachronic investigation and strive to discover the etymologies of names,[13] and others concentrate on synchrony and the associations awakened by commercial names, albeit not based on the aforementioned theory. Many scholars examine names quite formally by lexically dividing the words included in names into different semantic groups.

One interesting aspect of the semantics of commercial names is word-play. In naming, as in advertising, there are various types of puns including, for example, double meanings. They may prevent boredom but at the same time they convey certain intended meanings in an economical way. While word-plays require more processing effort from the recipient, it can produce special joy when understood (see Djafarova 2008: 267, 269).[14]

---

[9]   The outlets of the company are compared to art exhibition spaces with the word 'gallery'.

[10]   The Latin word in the name meaning 'electric light' is metonymically connected to the line of business, the production of home appliances and appliances for professional use (<http://group. electrolux.com/en/about-electrolux-492/>).

[11]   The company is a data supplier in the telecommunication industry. It specializes in maps, satellite images, aerial photographs, etc. (<www.novosat.com>).

[12]   For more on cognitive operations regarding brand names, see Pérez Hernández (2011).

[13]   Christoph Platen (1997: 95) warns about etymologies that are too imaginative, and suggests using empirical confirmation for interpretations, because many fantasy-like names may be, in reality, very simply motivated. For example, the 'galactic' name of the chocolate bar *Mars* is based on the company founder's surname.

[14]   Puns in naming of casino gaming have been studied for instance by Raento and Douglass (2001: 14–15). Perhaps surprisingly, the casinos in Las Vegas are not likely to have such a name; instead, the majority of the properties have been named with a serious effort.

A functional dimension completes the picture of commercial names.[15] Names are what they are because of what they do. They have a special task in interaction and in business communication. A linguistic sign, such as a brand name, not only refers to an object but also conveys meanings important to the sender (manufacturer, company, etc.), and fulfils interactive functions, such as the persuasion of customers. This is reminiscent of M. A. K. Halliday's (Kress 1976: 25) idea of the three metafunctions of language: textual (= reference), ideational (= meaning), and interpersonal (= interaction).[16] A persuasive function is important, but other socio-cultural, interpersonal functions, such as informative, practical, and integrative functions, can also be present in commercial names (Bergien 2007: 263; Ainiala et al. 2012: 243–4; see also Platen 1997: 45–67).

Communication and the basic function of commercial names, that is reflecting identity, have been prevalent themes in recent studies of commercial names. Names function as a bridge between producers and customers who do not usually have direct interpersonal contact, and they enable people to identify with the denominated products (Zilg 2013: 270). The theoretical background to the research into the communicative features of commercial names has been adapted from Grice's (1975) four communicational maxims in a few studies (Sjöblom 2008a: 422–3; Boonpaisarnsatit and Srioutai 2013: 44–5). The brand name owner wants to convey a certain message to the target audience, which expects the name to bear truth, relevance, information, and clarity, and interprets the name in relation to these maxims. According to Zilg (2013), names can communicate by means of imperative forms (*Mix & Go*), personal pronouns (Span. *Te Cuida* 'he/she/it cares for you'), and possessive forms (Fr. *Ma pause fruit* 'my fruit break'). Such linguistic means create an interpersonal effect. In addition to linguistic elements, other semiotic recourses also act in communication: there has been increasing interest in the subject of the multimodal nature of commercial naming (e.g. Sjöblom 2010; Sorvali 2013).

31.5 GLOBAL ECONOMY AND THE LANGUAGE OF NAMES

One special issue of commercial naming is the question of linguistic origin. While English is the global language of business, it also pervades commercial names throughout the world. This fact can be seen in various onomastic studies (e.g. Ronneberger-Sibold 2007b; Dimova 2008; Sjöblom 2009). Usually, the use of English is explained as being related to qualities such as internationality, attractiveness, modernity, prestige, etc. Some studies show that the popularity of English names is connected

---

[15] The functional dimension of the so called *Fachsprachenonomastik* was highlighted in Gläser (1996: 24).

[16] In the German tradition, onomasticians often refer to Bühler's Organon model (1934), which has some similar ideas about functions of linguistic signs.

to the branch of business or the type of product. Young people seem to have less negative attitudes towards foreign elements in names than older people who think foreign names are less informative (Bergien 2008: 294–5).

However, the language in names provides a much richer picture: not only English loan words but also words from other Western European languages, such as French, Italian, and Spanish,[17] make their way into commercial names in many countries.Latin and ancient Greek have prestige. Furthermore, Western influence can be seen in neologisms in which there is a merge of English elements or those of other Western languages and maybe also elements of the local language or even dialect. It is quite usual for one name to have parts that originate in two or even more languages, not to mention names that consist of quasi-words of no real language (Ainiala et al. 2012: 238–40).

On the one hand, this is the influence of westernization, the cultural influence in all areas of life that pervades other countries and basically comes from North America and the larger countries in Western Europe. Onomasticians in both Eastern Europe and Asia, have indicated that westernization manifests itself in naming in many ways (Stoichiţiou Ichim 2013: 99–101; Wilkerson and Takashi Wilkerson 2013). On the other hand, it is a question of splintered markets. Small enterprises also operating on a local level often choose English or other foreign names. This is partly due to analogy—avoiding the local language has sometimes developed into a trend—but it is partly a result of the contemporary socio-cultural environment: language communities overlap because of accelerating migration in the world. The internet has also brought long distances closer together, bringing about the idea of being local and global almost everywhere at the same time.

31.6 NAMING IN THE COMMERCIAL WORLD

The all-encompassing commercialism of the Western way of life, at least, has an enormous impact on nomenclature. Many name categories, such as the names of housing cooperatives, public organizations, books, television programmes, cruiser ships, and animals (dogs and horses, for instance), have begun to receive commercial tones. New name categories which have a commercial function have emerged: names related to various events, electronic games, music (industry), names of trade centres, etc.[18]

The outer edge of commercial names is an interesting area of research. In some cases, it means a new angle from which it is possible to examine already familiar name types. Toponyms are not commercial names, but in place branding, the place-name is the core of the brand (Hakala and Sjöblom 2013: 157–60). In urban environments,

[17] Interestingly enough, even though Germany is the leading European country economically, German seems not to be very popular in commercial naming outside German-speaking countries—or at least such results have not been reported (cf. Wochele 2007: 326; Rzetelska-Feleszko 2008: 598).
[18] Various articles concerning these themes have been published (see e.g. Vrublevskaya 2012; Hongisto and Sjöblom 2012; Vikstrand 2012; Hämäläinen 2013).

especially in the name planning of new suburban or business areas, marketing orientation is also taken into account (Vuolteenaho et al. 2007: 228–30; Viljamaa-Laakso 2008). Even personal names can carry, if not monetary, at least symbolic and social capital which can indirectly support a person's prosperity. For instance, one may take a new, noble-sounding surname or adopt a name that does not reveal one's ethnic origin (Leibring 2012a), or parents may give their child a name that is unique and is easily memorable, and as such may be a valuable asset to the child (Aldrin 2009).

The political changes at the beginning of the 1990s in Russia and other Eastern European countries have gradually led to socio-cultural changes with the endorsement of globalization and commercialism. The invasion of commercial nomenclature and the enormous changes in company and product names is a reality in post-communist countries. Names of shops, restaurants, and other companies as well as product names are influenced by foreign languages and the function of those names is to rouse positive associations (Rzetelska-Feleszko 2008; Felecan 2008; Dimova 2008; Kryukova 2012; Bugheşiu 2012).

The global wave of changes has influenced commercial names in other parts of the world, as well. After 1994, when South Africa became a full democracy, company and brand names in African languages emerged in addition to previous English and Afrikaans names because there was a need for the black population to raise their economic power (Neethling 2010a). This example shows that in certain political situations, economic objectives can lead to naming models that actually diverge from the universal tendency of using internationally understandable elements in commercial naming.

Another issue to point out is that the modern linguistic landscape is full of commercial names.[19] There has been critical discussion about branded cities—whether companies have the right to display their names all around public spaces: schools, sports stadiums, airports, parks, buses. The unfortunate fact, however, is that cities and other public actors have to lean on sponsors, as other sources of income are not enough; therefore, opposing opinions have also been given (see e.g. Klein 2001; Bacon 2013).

All in all, there is hardly any part of human life which could not be commercialized. The market economy collides with the idealistic notion of independent culture because we are aiming towards global economic growth. For instance, professional artists—writers, musicians, painters, etc.—can also gain power and authority if they succeed in marketing. The non-material benefits that can be achieved by marketing attract most people even if they would not be interested in money. And effective marketing is based on good brands, names that carry plenty of special meanings. Therefore, commercial nomenclature will certainly continue to be of growing interest to scholars for a long time to come.

---

[19] See also Tufi and Blackwood (2010).

PART VI

ONOMASTICS AND OTHER DISCIPLINES

CHAPTER 32

....

NAMES AND ARCHAEOLOGY

....

RICHARD JONES

SOME names, particularly place-names, have long been recognized as carrying archaeo-logical significance. Both in theory and in practice, the potential to combine onomastic and material evidence finds application everywhere (Stuart and Houston 1994; Zadora-Rio 2001; Lape 2002; Whitridge 2004; O'Connor and Kroefges 2008); but here examin-ing this association is restricted to an English context. In what follows, the usefulness of place-names for archaeological prospection, analysis, and interpretation is considered. Emphasis is placed on how the archaeologist's craft has been informed and enriched by an awareness of information communicated through names. The other side of this dia-logue is not neglected; advancing archaeological methods and approaches are radically transforming our understanding of the origins and early development of many forms of settlement as well as the wider landscape, and by so doing, opportunities to re-assess—and at times re-interpret—the names they carry, have begun to open up.

In England place-names have enjoyed an omnipresence in the archaeological con-sciousness from the very dawning of the discipline in the sixteenth century. Early chorographers and antiquarians noted names of archaeological interest in their topo-graphical surveys, often describing relevant artefacts found in their proximity or report-ing stories of discovery circulating locally. At *Cleycester*, a lost name in Warwickshire close to Claybrook, William Camden noted the existence of wall foundations unearthed by the plough and the presence of 'Roman money' (Camden 1610 [1586]). Camden tended to approach place-names uncritically; by contrast, William Dugdale writing a century later was generally more cautious. Thus in the case of nearby Cester-Over, which his predecessor viewed as an unimpeachable 'witness to a site of great antiquity' deriving from *ceaster*, Dugdale's enquiries pointed, erroneously so it happens, to an etymologi-cal root giving the Eastern Over (Over formed from the nearby river Waver (Dugdale 1656: 60)). If somewhat hit and miss in terms of their success, these precocious attempts to use place-names to identify archaeological sites would nevertheless have long-lasting influence. It is against their background that one encounters the rather less well-known nineteenth-century Nottinghamshire antiquarian William Dickinson, whose account of the history of Newark-on-Trent opens with a discussion of the place-name and its loaded meaning:

> It requires little sagacity to discover that New-work (the obvious signification of its name . . .), is a name of reference, of comparison, and of discrimination. If what was then erected was styled the new-work, it is an incontrovertible admission that there was something older, on which the modern establishment was engrafted, and from which it was intended, by this appellation, to be distinguished. (Dickinson 1819: 1–2)

We shall return to these examples at the end, for they offer salutary warnings for those who believe that place-names and archaeology can be easily combined. True, place-names and archaeology should be natural bedfellows, both informing on the past, albeit in different ways. But in reality they often turn out to be false friends. For onomasts the archaeological record is especially frustrating. Not until the Industrial Revolution, when it became commonplace to advertise the geographical origins of particular products on their containers or packaging, have objects acted as good vectors for place-name evidence. With the exception of the few surviving monumental inscriptions (Collingwood and Wright 1965),[1] or the unique tablets found at Vindolanda fort on Hadrian's Wall (Bowman 2004), our knowledge of the names of the small towns and cities of Roman Britain and other military establishments largely derives from official histories and geographical works such as the fifteen itineraries that make up the *Iter Britanniarum* section of the *Antonini Itinerarium* (PNRB). Likewise, it is the written record which provides the earliest attestations for the majority of the place-names still in use, not the archaeological record. No British place-names, for example, feature in runic inscriptions from Britain. It is only very occasionally that individual artefacts reveal otherwise unknown name developments, such as the variant Axport found on coins minted at Axbridge in Somerset, a place otherwise consistently named in the written sources (Carroll 2012). But nothing compares in the archaeological record to the richness of name evidence found in early medieval charters, the Anglo-Saxon Chronicle, Bede's *Historia Ecclesia Gentis Anglorum*, or above all Domesday Book. Onomasts' near total reliance on the written record is captured in Jacquetta Hawkes' observation that in its absence we are deprived of knowing the names of prehistory:

> We can have inherited no single syllable from the names given by Palaeolithic hunters, but never since their day have our landmarks been without them, without some sound to enrich and confirm their personality. (Hawkes 1978: 151–2)

Who does not find it frustrating that we do not know the name given to Stonehenge by its architects and builders? The recorded name we have is less than a thousand years old—less than a fifth of the monument's life (Gover et al. 1939: 360).

---

[1] Examples include Silchester (*Calleva Atrebatum*), Bath (*Aqua Sulis*), Ribchester (*Bremetenacum*), Ilkley (*Verbeia*), and York (*Colonia Eboracensium*).

Such mismatches and lacunae aside, those who study place-names and archaeology are brought together by common methodological approaches to their material. With their long histories, place-names and physical remains are both subject to the twin processes of formation and taphonomic decay. Again, Jacquetta Hawkes offers a more eloquent recognition of this fact than any other:

> Place names are among the things that link men most intimately with their territory. As the generations pass on these names from one to another, successive tongues wear away the syllables just as water and wind smooth the rocks; so closely, indeed that place names outlast the languages that made them, remaining as evidence of the former presence of dispossessed and submerged peoples. A geologist finds proof of the existence of past life in fossils, an archaeologist in objects men have made; an etymologist looks instead to place names which after thousands of years recall the talk of forgotten tribes. (Hawkes 1978: 152)

In establishing robust etymologies for early names, then, scholars are required to work back through variant spellings masking original forms just as an archaeologist must carefully excavate through stratigraphic sequences of soil to reveal what is buried below. Thus, for the American anthropologist, Charles Frake:

> The semantic opacity of a placename is much like the patina on a flint tool. It covers the past of the place, hiding a story and a history. The decipherment of an English placename is rather like an archaeological dig. One strips away the deceptive superficial layers to get at the original meaning. The more stripping required, the more ancient, and thus the more interesting, the past. (Frake 1996: 238)

Many would disagree with the notion that time alone accounts for the multiple layers of meaning which accrete around place-names, certainly to the extent suggested here that opacity can be taken as a proxy for antiquity, but the general point is well made. Nor was this analogy lost on early place-name scholars. Eighty years earlier the Rev. J. B. Johnston wrote:

> In a much-traversed, much-contested territory like England and Wales, the student [of place-names] needs to remove each successive layer of names as carefully, and to scrutinize them as diligently, as a Flinders Petrie when he is digging down into one of Egypt's ancient cemeteries, or as a Macalister exploring one of the great rubbish mounds at Gezer or Lachish. And the place-name student has his own little joys of discovery, his own thrills over a much-tangled skein at last unravelled, as well as a Schliemann at Mycenæ, or a Flinders Petrie at Abydos. (Johnston 1915: 2)

The nineteenth and particularly the early twentieth century was undoubtedly a golden era for archaeology. But as Johnston's list reveals, European archaeologists were more often to be found working in the Near East and on the great centres of civilization than on less spectacular sites closer to home. In England, public interest in archaeology, stimulated in large part by discoveries elsewhere, grew dramatically over this period spawning the county societies which encouraged and coordinated local exploration. Yet the archaeological agenda remained narrow as the early volumes of county journals attest, being largely confined to the investigation of prominent prehistoric monuments such as burial mounds, henges, and hillforts, or exploring the legacies of Roman occupation such as towns, villas, and roads.[2] Scholars interested in later histories or more prosaic places were forced to look to place-names to supplement a meagre historical record in the absence of archaeological investigation. In Germany, for instance, Wihelm Arnold turned to place-names to address what was largely an archaeological question, the identification and delimitation of areas settled by Germanic tribes during the Migration period (Arnold 1875). In France, D'Arbois de Jubainville was the first to attempt to distinguish settlements of Gallo-Roman origin in the use of the place-name suffix -acum (d'Arbois de Jubainville 1890); while in the hands of Longnon, a solid chronology of French place-name elements—pre-Latin, Gallo-Roman, Germanic—had been established by the end of the 1920s (Longnon 1920–9). As this monumental work appeared, so across the Channel, the 1920s saw the establishment of the English Place-Names Survey and with the publication of the *Introduction to English Place-Name Survey* in 1924, the first formal statement regarding the archaeological dimension to place-names contributed by the archaeologist O. G. S. Crawford (1924).

Crawford's survey was restricted almost entirely to place-name elements which appear to refer directly to the antiquities of the Prehistoric, Roman, and pagan post-Roman periods. Consideration of elements which tell of the form and function of early medieval settlements, the very places to which most of the available corpus of names relate, is conspicuous by its absence in his account. As such Crawford's survey was a product of its time. More surprising, however, is that two of the most eminent place-name scholars of the second half of the twentieth century, Ken Cameron (1988: 110–18)[3] and Margaret Gelling (1997: 130–61), should stick so closely to their predecessor's formulation of the topic when they turned to archaeological place-names. Cameron and Gelling wrote at a time when medieval archaeology had become firmly established and the archaeological agenda had moved away from 'monuments' to consideration of 'settlements'; and yet their archaeological parameters appear to have been uninfluenced by these changes. They continued to limit themselves, just as Crawford had done in 1924, to discussion of place-names linked with prehistoric fortifications and linear earthworks; to Roman remains and roads; and to Anglo-Saxon pagan burials and places of worship. Taken together, these three authorities established, consciously or otherwise, an accepted corpus of archaeologically significant place-name elements: *burh, byrig, wear-setl, tōt-ærn*, and *eorth-burh*, terms shown to refer to prehistoric (as well as other period) enclosures; *ceaster, strǣt*, and *flōr* pointing towards significant Roman constructions; *hlāw, hlǣw* as markers of pagan burial mounds; *hearg* and *wēoh, wīh* locating sites of pagan

---

[2] To gain a sense of the archaeological agenda in the mid-nineteenth century, see Blaauw (1848).

[3] The chapter on place-names and archaeology was removed from the 1996 revision of Cameron's book, while Gelling (1997) was essentially a reprint of an edition dating from 1978.

temples or shrines. To these, other terms have been added over the years. Gelling her-self convincingly laid out the case for associating the compound *wīchām* with Roman settlement (Gelling 1967). And there have been notable successes in linking Tunstall/Dunstall-names with abandoned settlements, the most clear being the discovery of a sizeable early medieval rural settlement below fields so named at Pennyland in Milton Keynes (Williams 1993: fig. 53).[4]

If this list, indeed the partially extended list, feels right from a place-name perspec-tive, for archaeologists it now looks extremely odd. First, there is the implication that archaeologically significant place-names are limited only to terms referring to physical features in the English landscape that were already 'archaeological' at the moment of place-name coining. In effect, archaeology is seen to begin (or end depending on your chronological perspective) in the seventh century AD. There is no place in this scheme, it would seem, to acknowledge the archaeological potency of place-names formed at later dates nor those which, while carrying no initial archaeological significance, have become archaeologically interesting over time. Into this category would fall a wide range of habitative generics, place-names in -*cirice* or -*minster*, for example, -*wīc* and -*worth*, -*cot* and -*torp* which imply the presence of certain types of structure, different types of settlement layout, the economic and religious activities taking place within them, or the social status of inhabitants, all of which will have left physical traces for the archaeolo-gist to find.[5] Over and beyond these groups of common place-name generics, it seems preposterous not to include unique names, for example, Faversham (Kent) 'the settle-ment of the smiths' or Battle (Sussex) which are so clearly pregnant with archaeological possibilities.

Secondly, this list implies that names can only be archaeological if they refer directly to the site or feature in question. Yet there are a number of name types which can now be shown to be highly significant archaeologically but which only refer obliquely to the presence of physical remains. Into this category fall names which describe broken or uneven ground. 'Foxholes' is a case in point, attested by the discovery of a multi-period site culminating in a Romano-British rural settlement at Foxholes, Hertfordshire (Partridge 1989).[6] 'Blacklands' is another, where place-namers' appreciation of changes in soil colour point archaeologists to former occupation sites. At least three 'Blacklands'—in Somerset, Wiltshire, and Kent—have produced evidence for Roman settlement, the colour of the soil altered by the addition of organic matter and hearth ashes when occupied (Barber et al. 2013; Wessex Archaeology 2007; Kent Archaeological Field School 2013). Of the eleven known 'Blacklands' field names in Oxfordshire, three are associated with Romano-British settlements (Bond 1982). In Herefordshire, it has been concluded that '44% of *blacklands* sites . . . are on, or near, 67% of known Roman

---

[4] It might be noted that 'Pennyland' itself may be archaeologically significant, although the possibility remains that the name refers to a form of rent or tenure rather than the presence of coins (cf. Field 1989: 163–4). For field names in Staffordshire, see Horovitz (2003: 293).

[5] For references to the relevant literature, see Jones (2013).

[6] Field (1989) records twelve instances of this field name or closely related names in his dictionary.

towns/villages' (Richardson 1996). *Ceastel* 'heap (of stones)' may represent another productive field name element. In Somerset, for example, there are six instances where a correspondence between such names and Roman villas and rural settlements seems probable (Aston and Gerrard 1999: 17).

Thirdly, the traditional list infers that archaeologists are only interested in 'sites', here equated with built structures or occupied spaces. In large part this reflects the state of archaeology up to the end of the 1970s. Since then, however, the archaeological research agenda has moved in several different directions. From the 1980s the advent of landscape archaeology has encouraged 'sites' to be studied within their wider context, shifting emphasis away from the narrow investigation of places of intensive activity towards the broader exploration of the whole cultural environment (Aston 1985). Thus archaeologists have become increasingly interested in how woodland was managed as well as where people lived; they have concerned themselves with agricultural practices—the organization of field systems or animal husbandry for instance—as much as places of worship; their focus has turned to how the landscape was partitioned and administered as much as where people were buried (see Higham and Ryan 2010; Rippon 2012; Jones and Semple 2012a; Williamson et al. 2013). These are fundamental changes and their repercussions for the study of place-names in an archaeological context have yet to be fully appreciated. Against this background, topographical names incorporating, for example *wudu* and *feld*, or quasi-habitative elements such as *lēah* have become just as significant as habitative elements for archaeological fieldwork. As the remit of landscape archaeologists has broadened, so they have increasingly found the traditional division of place-names as habitative or topographical to be a hindrance. Reflecting this, Alexander Rumble has recently proposed the use of a third category of name, the 'man-made landscape feature', as a catch-all for terms used in place-names which appear to describe features and activities that are liable to have left an archaeological trace (Rumble 2011). These include all the terms dealt with by Crawford, Cameron, and Gelling, but are extended to include vocabulary relating to resource management. Cultivation terms such as *æcer* 'plot or strip of cultivated land', *furh* 'furrow (associated with open-field agriculture?)', *hēafod* 'headland', and *land* 'strip in open field' fall into this category; so too terms for enclosures or hedges such as *edisc* 'enclosure', *(ge)hæg* 'fence, enclosure' and *haga* 'hedge, enclosure'; boundary markers; drainage ditches; and pits and quarries. Rumble also identifies a subcategory of names relating to particular manufacturing and processing activities requiring specialized buildings such as *myln* 'mill' and *smiððe* 'smithy' and other structures such as *wer* 'weir'. His final categories cover lines of communication, to include *pæð* 'path or track', *stīg* 'path or narrow road', and *weg* 'way, path, road'; river crossings; and landing places as suggested by *hyð* and *stæð*.

In this new context even mundane, and otherwise overlooked, place-names, such as directional names which embed information about the chronology of settlement formation and inherent hierarchies, as well as pointing to other places in the landscape from which they were named, now find a role in archaeological enquiry alongside the *burh*s, *hearg*s, and *caester*s (Guest and Luke 2005; Semple 2007; Draper 2008, 2012; Baker 2012). What lies north of a Sutton to make it the 'southern farm or estate'? Since the northern settlement must necessarily have already been in place before the name Sutton was coined, how much earlier was it settled? And what was the precise relationship between the northern and southern settlement that ensured that Sutton's name implied or communicated dependency and inferior status (Jones 2012a)?

Importantly too, since the publication of Gelling's last assessment of archaeological place-names, archaeology has undergone a theoretical revolution. The discipline has moved away from empirical studies based on detailed typologies and the classification of inert artefacts to recognize the agency of objects and places and their active role in creating cultures and communities. Archaeologists have become interested in how lives were experienced as much as how they were lived. They now seek to map the mind as much as physical space. Consequently past perceptions of place have become as important as the physical realities of place. Here place-names find a new and important role in archaeological enquiries (Jones and Semple 2012b; Jones 2013: 198–205). Place-names offer windows into how the landscape was visualized, by whom and from where, what mattered to communities, how they defined themselves or were defined by others, how they felt about their home, and a thousand other intangibles. What made Belvoir (Nottinghamshire), Beaulieu (Hampshire), and Bewley (Worcestershire) beautiful to their Norman namers? Why is it that post-conquest names with a French component use subjective assessments of the quality of landscape aesthetics much more readily and with such greater regularity than the Old English names coined by the Anglo-Saxon antecedents? What do misreadings of place-names, such as the folk etymology for Boarstall (Buckinghamshire), associated with the story of a marauding boar, or the renaming of Merdegrave (Leicestershire) as Belgrave, tell us about how people thought about their place-names in the past? Alternatively, what might a case such as Cold Newton (Leicestershire) tell us about the process of naming? Originally simplex Newton, by the thirteenth century it was recorded as both Newton Burdet and Newton Marmion, a reflection of the split lordship under which it was administered. Did these manorial affixes reflect the strength of local lordship? If so, why ultimately did the local vernacular prefix 'Cold', so appropriate to its exposed position in High Leicestershire, oust these names? And how quickly did the memory of Newton's lordly families fade? These are all questions that an archaeologist investigating the medieval history of Cold Newton must consider and correlate against the physical evidence left by this community if they are to gain a better picture of the social dynamics that defined the place, and the sense of belonging it engendered in its residents (Jones 2012b).

In sum, advances in archaeology, bringing in their wake shifts of emphasis and a much extended set of themes to be broached, mean that the vast majority of place-names can now be thought to carry something of archaeological interest. Even purely topographical names inform us, as Gelling and Cole have shown, about how people interacted with their surroundings, bringing them within the ambit of archaeology (Gelling 1984; Gelling and Cole 2000). Any attempt, then, to isolate subgroups that are more archaeologically significant than others must run the risk of appearing either woefully inadequate or poorly conceived, and often both. That said, for most archaeologists the utility of place-names remains their capacity to direct investigators to specific points in the landscape where their name labels imply some form of past activity to be discovered.

The key to using place-names successfully in this way is to recognize that they are not universal panaceas. Over the years perhaps more ink has been split over the relationship between particular types of place-name and pagan Anglo-Saxon cemeteries than any other archaeological question. Working at large scale, early commentators saw a clear correlation between areas of the country containing large numbers of place-names in -ingas, -ingahām, and -inga- and those producing evidence for cemeteries dated from the fifth to seventh centuries AD (Myres 1935; Smith 1956a). Not unreasonably on the basis of the facts in front of them, they drew the conclusion that this spatial correspondence pointed to the idea that 'folk-names' must in some way relate to these burial sites and thus should be dated from the earliest phases of Anglo-Saxon settlement. In his seminal article, John Dodgson (1966: 1) was the first to question this linkage, showing convincingly that 'the communities using that kind of place-name are separate in time, place and burial habit from those using the earliest and those using the latest pagan-burial sites'. The idea persisted, however, that place-names associated with the territorial units within which pagan Anglo-Saxon cemeteries were found, most of which were first recorded long after the conversion period, remained an important resource and worthy of studying in isolation. In what proved to be a painful exercise in futility, Gordon Copley (1986, 1988) carefully catalogued and analysed all names associated with fifth- and sixth-century cemeteries in the Saxon, Jutish, and Anglian areas of southern and eastern England. Forced to concede that territorial divisions underwent considerable reworking in the middle and late Saxon periods, and thus that names associated with the nearest village or the encompassing parish might not have existed at the period of cemetery formation, he cast his net more widely to investigate all names within a ten-mile radius of each cemetery. The results were predictably inconclusive: pagan Anglo-Saxon cemeteries are found associated with a great range of habitative, topographical, and folk-name types, with English place-name elements as well as pre-English. This study is instructive: it reminds us, if we needed reminding, that it is not always possible or indeed appropriate to ask place-names to answer archaeological questions or vice versa when, as in this case, each dataset developed independent of the other. Both in hindsight and by analogy with the examples of Foxholes, Blacklands, and ceastel already cited, a potentially more fruitful line of enquiry may have been to explore field names not major names, for these are far more likely to speak more directly about any archaeological interest (Hills 1977).

One is on much more certain ground when the place-name and archaeological evidence can clearly be shown to relate directly to one another. The investigation of named villages and hamlets is the most obvious example. In the past, combining these two sources of historical information has been hindered by the fact that archaeologists have tended to work outside these settlements. Since the 1990s, however, there has been an explosion in both opportunistic and systematic survey of the historic cores of these towns, villages, and hamlets. There is now a large and growing body of archaeological material available that informs on the earliest phases of these places, and which might be directly related to the names these places bear. In East Anglia and Cambridgeshire, for example, a clear pattern is emerging that suggests that place-names in -*ham* are far more likely to produce pre-ninth-century pottery than settlements in -*tūn*, an outcome which supports the consensus view of place-name scholars that *hams* represent an earlier naming stratum than *tūn* (Lewis 2007).[7]

In the case of places in -*thorp*, more wide-reaching insights into their early life have emerged from the analysis of the artefacts they produce, their general plans, and their landscape setting (Cullen et al. 2011). And there are signs that comparable studies of places in -*wīc* and -*cot* would likewise produce useful results (Jones 2013: 196–7). The early successes of interdisciplinary studies focusing on particular families of names, made possible due to the rapid increase in the amount of archaeological data now available, appear to signal a new way forward and a surer foundation on which to proceed. In these archaeology, often previously the happy recipient of help from place-names, is beginning finally to give something back to its sister discipline.

The story of archaeology and place-names as it has developed over the last century and a half is studded with what-ifs and maybes. One example will suffice. In 1960 two workmen digging a trench for a waterpipe across a field outside the village of Fishbourne near Chichester, Sussex came across a tessellated pavement floor. Evidence for Roman occupation in the vicinity had long been known through chance finds in private gardens. But place-name evidence would play no part in the discovery of what later excavations would reveal to be a very large Roman villa which today is known as Fishbourne Roman Palace. The village name itself, Fishbourne 'fish stream', certainly carries no clue that here would be found the largest Roman domestic building yet discovered north of the Alps. Had archaeologists trawled through the archives, however, they would have discovered, as did Richard Coates (1985), a Tudor field name *Fittenhalle* 'fallen hall' in the parish. The name remains unlocated but it is highly likely that it carries a memory of the ruins of the palace.

This, of course, is symptomatic of the problem: on the one hand, archives are vast making the retrieval of minor names which are proving to be so archaeologically significant an almost unmanageable task; while archaeology is often directed more by serendipitous discovery or the necessity to work in front of destructive development, than guided by careful consideration of the place-name record. If there remains much to do to identify names of archaeological interest, archaeologists have their work cut out too. To return to Cester-Over in Warwickshire where we began: early forms of the name, unknown either to Campden or to Dugdale, provide indisputable proof that this is indeed a *ceaster*-name (Gover et al. 1936: 113). Yet despite the great surge in archaeological investigation that this chapter has sought to emphasize, to what this name refers remains as elusive today as it was in the sixteenth century. No *ceaster*-type settlement has yet been discovered in its vicinity. And as for Newark's 'old work'? Well that too remains a mystery that has yet to be solved.

---

[7] Annual reports were placed in *Medieval Settlements*, the annual report of the Medieval Settlement Research Group between 2005 and 2012.

CHAPTER 33

NAMES AND COGNITIVE PSYCHOLOGY

SERGE BRÉDART

33.1 INTRODUCTION

THE failure to recall someone's name at the right moment can be embarrassing. This difficulty is not rare in everyday life and can be uncomfortable for both the person who is unable to retrieve the searched name and the person whose name cannot be recalled. Personal names can typically be the object of the sometimes irritating experience known as the tip-of-the-tongue (TOT hereafter) state, that is, remaining unable to recall a word that we are absolutely certain to know.

Personal names are a linguistic category that is particularly likely to provoke retrieval difficulties in young and middle-aged adults and that may be especially troublesome for older people. In addition, for some brain-injured patients personal name recall is their only linguistic problem. During the last thirty years, cognitive psychologists and neuropsychologists have attempted to understand why proper names, and more particularly personal names, are so difficult to retrieve. In the present chapter, I will first describe the main empirical evidence demonstrating that persons' names are particularly difficult to recall. Then, different explanations for that particular difficulty will be considered.

33.2 EMPIRICAL EVIDENCE OF THE DIFFICULTY OF RETRIEVING PERSONAL NAMES COMPARED WITH SEMANTIC INFORMATION ABOUT PEOPLE

Personal names are more difficult to recall than semantic information about familiar people such as their occupation or their nationality. In several diary studies, participants kept records for a given period of time (usually one or two months) of any incidents of person identification that they experienced in their everyday life. In such natural settings, participants frequently reported having experienced difficulties in recalling someone's name while remaining able to remember semantic information about the person (e.g. the person's occupation, where the person lives) whom they could not name (e.g. Young et al. 1985). This vulnerability of names to retrieval failures has also been demonstrated in laboratory studies in which the experience of being able to recall a familiar person's occupation or nationality without being able to retrieve that person's name has been reported in many studies (e.g. Hanley and Cowell 1988; Hay et al. 1991). Importantly, these laboratory studies showed a clear asymmetry in incidents: hundreds of incidents were observed during which the participant was able to retrieve semantic information about the target person but not that person's name, whereas no incident was recorded during which a participant recalled the person's name without being able to retrieve any semantic information about the target person (e.g. '*I remember that his name is Richard Jenkins but I do not know what he does, in which context I saw him before, I know nothing else about that man.*')

In addition to studies that recorded the occurrence of retrieval failures, mental chronometry studies are also interesting. In such studies, the time necessary for a participant to retrieve a person's occupation or nationality is compared with the time necessary to retrieve their name. Several studies showed that making binary semantic decisions about people (e.g. pressing a computer key to categorize people as being politicians or singers) is faster than naming them (e.g. Young et al. 1986; Kampf et al. 2002). Such studies may be criticized because response requirements are quite different for making simple binary decisions, on the one hand, and for naming, on the other hand. However, the advantage for the retrieval of semantic information over the retrieval of names remains even when response requirements are equated across tasks. Indeed it appeared that, when two faces were simultaneously presented, participants were faster to judge whether the two people shared the same occupation (or nationality) than to judge whether they had the same first name (e.g. Young et al. 1988; Johnston and Bruce 1990).

In a third category of studies, participants learned to associate occupations and names with unfamiliar faces. These studies demonstrated that it is harder to learn people's names than to learn other information about them (e.g. Cohen and Faulkner 1986; Cohen 1990; Barsics and Brédart 2012). This is observed even when the words to be learned are the same: it is harder to learn that someone is called 'Baker' than to learn that someone is a baker (McWeeny et al. 1987; Rendell et al. 2005). This effect has been called the Baker–baker paradox (Cohen 1990). All the research briefly summarized above showed that retrieving names is more difficult than retrieving other types of biographical information.

33.3 Explaining Why Names Are Harder to Retrieve than Semantic Information about People

Two concurrent hypotheses have been formulated to explain that difference. One hypothesis assumes that access to names is dependent on access to semantic information. The other puts forward the relative uniqueness of personal names.

33.3.1 Names are Retrieved after Semantic Information has been Accessed

Naming a person's face is more difficult than retrieving other biographical information (e.g. occupation or nationality) about the person because name retrieval occurs in a separate and later information processing stage. This explanation is proposed by serial models of familiar face recognition designed in the 1980s, the most famous of them being the seminal model of Bruce and Young (1986). In such models, face recognition requires matching the current representation of the seen face's surface structure with a stored representation in the perceptual long-term memory system devoted to faces. After a face has been recognized, biographical semantic and episodic information about the person (e.g. occupation, nationality, the place where that person was encountered for the first time) may be retrieved. Finally, retrieval of the person's name is dependent upon access to biographical information; it may occur after biographical information has been retrieved. Bruce and Young's (1986) model accounted quite well for empirical data for years. But subsequently a number of studies reported results that could not readily be explained by a serial model.

In an electrophysiological study measuring lateralized readiness potential, Abdel-Rahman et al. (2002) reported that information about famous politicians' nationality (i.e. foreign or domestic) was accessed before information concerning these politicians' names (i.e. 'a' or 'e' being the initial vowel of the surname). However, access to information about their political party (i.e. government or opposition party) was not faster than access to information about their surnames. In addition, Brédart, et al. (2005) showed that participants were faster to name personally familiar people (close work colleagues) than to name their highest degree (e.g. Masters or PhD). In the same study, a second experiment showed that participants were also quicker to name close colleagues than to name their nationality (English, German, or Scottish). In other words, in these two experiments people's names were recalled faster than semantic properties describing them. In another study, Calderwood and Burton (2006) reported that participants who were fans of the TV series *Friends* were able to access the names of the central characters faster than their occupations.

Such empirical results contributed to challenging the serial models of face naming. Several models, designed in the 1990s, proposed that access to biographical information and names may occur in parallel rather than serially (see for instance Burton and Bruce (1992) for the most famous among these models). In such models, the difficulty of name retrieval is explained by their uniqueness.

33.3.2 The Name is a Unique Property

Naming a person is more difficult than retrieving other information because personal names are unique to one person whereas properties like occupation or nationality are shared by many people. For instance, the editor of this book is a British university professor and her name is Carole Hough. I know many British people and many university professors, but I know only one person called Carole Hough, and only a couple of persons named 'Hough'. In parallel models (Interactive Activation and Competition networks) such as the Burton and Bruce model, unique properties are representations that are more 'isolated' (i.e. connected to a relatively small number of other representations in the network) and are consequently harder to activate than more widely shared properties such as occupation or nationality. However, it quickly appeared that the uniqueness hypothesis could not explain some data. If uniqueness is responsible for name vulnerability, then other unique information should be as vulnerable as names. However this does not seem to be the case. Neuropsychologists reported single-case studies of patients with preserved naming of occupations or preserved semantic categorization associated with impaired name retrieval but who remained able to retrieve precise, uniquely specifying, information about famous people such as recalling catchphrases of television presenters or a specific event associated with the target person (e.g. recalling that Magnus Magnusson used to say 'I've started so I'll finish', or explaining why Salman Rushdie was in the news (Harris and Kay 1995; see also Hanley 1995). In addition, in healthy participants, learning a unique semantic property (e.g. learning that someone has a gazelle as a pet) is easier than learning that person's name (Carson 2000). Such results are in contrast with the hypothesis that uniqueness of names makes them harder to recall.

Given the weakness of the uniqueness hypothesis, some researchers recently re-argued for serial models considering that data that were deemed to be inconsistent with the Bruce and Young (1986) model are actually not fatal for that model. For instance, for Hanley (2011a) the fact that in some experiments access to semantic information such as nationality or the academic degree was faster than access to name (i.e. Abdel-Rahman et al. 2002; Brédart et al. 2005; Calderwood and Burton 2006; see above) is not really at odds with serial models. His major argument is that such models do not assume that *all* semantic information known about a person must be accessed before that person's name can be recalled. According to him, only the more salient semantic information should be accessed, and there is no empirical evidence that nationality or academic degree is a salient feature of people. This comment may make sense but it may also lead to circular reasoning: explaining that access to a semantic property is slower than access to a name by the fact that this property is not salient, and explaining that a property is not salient because accessing it is slower than accessing a name. Hanley (2011a) is quite aware of the circularity issue and, to avoid it, he admitted that advocates of serial models must 'provide a convincing account of precisely what semantic information *does* have to be accessed before a name can be retrieved' (Hanley 2011a: 921). Unfortunately, waiting for such evidence, the Bruce and Young (1986) model appears to be currently impossible to falsify (as far as the question of serial access to semantic information and names is concerned).

33.3.3 What Do Studies Comparing Access to Names and Semantic Information Demonstrate?

Even though these studies are often quoted as illustrating that proper names are particularly difficult to retrieve, they did not provide a lot of data that help to demonstrate that personal names are more difficult to retrieve than other kinds of words. Indeed, research comparing the time to choose whether a target person (e.g. Barack Obama) is a politician or a TV presenter by pushing a computer key, with naming latency is not really informative since the categorization task does not require access to phonological forms of the words 'politician' or 'presenter', while the naming task does require such access to the phonology of the surname 'Obama'. Equating response requirements across tasks by simultaneously presenting two faces and asking participants either to judge whether or not the two persons share the same occupation (semantic task) or share the same first name (name task) does not solve this problem. Indeed, under such circumstances, the semantic task does not require access to word forms whereas the name task still does, even if no articulation is required. In contrast, learning tasks are more interesting with respect to the comparison of personal name production *vs* common noun production. Indeed, both the nouns for occupations and the people's names were to be produced. The baker/Baker paradox can be seen as a first piece of evidence that the recall of personal names is harder than the recall of common nouns.

33.4 Empirical Evidence of the Difficulty of Retrieving Personal Names Compared with Common Nouns

In addition to the comparison of access to semantic information and names during the recognition of familiar people, research has demonstrated more widely that the retrieval of personal names is particularly difficult in comparison with other types of words. In a diary study, Burke et al. (1991) observed that participants more frequently reported retrieval incidents involving personal names than object names and abstract words such as non-object nouns, adjectives, verbs, and adverbs. Laboratory studies, in which the number of retrieval attempts across the different categories of words may be more strictly controlled, confirmed this pattern of results. Such studies attempted to provoke retrieval incidents by asking participants to name photographs of famous people and objects (e.g. Evrard 2002) or to answer general knowledge questions that required the retrieval of a personal name (e.g. 'What is the last name of the cosmonaut who was the first person to orbit the earth?'; target: Gagarin) and the retrieval of a common name (e.g. 'What do you call the vessel, usually an ornamental vase on a pedestal, which is used to preserve the ashes of the dead?'; target: urn) or even adjectives and verbs (e.g. Burke et al. 1991). Both studies showed that tip-of-the-tongue experiences occurred more frequently for the retrieval of personal names than for the retrieval of words from other categories (see also Rastle and Burke 1996).

Although the common claim that the retrieval of personal names is disproportionately impaired by normal ageing is not in fact universally accepted, the majority of studies reported that personal names are really more vulnerable to ageing than other categories of words. Studies based on subjective evaluation of memory difficulties will not be considered here because subjective evaluation has proved to be a very weak indicator of actual memory performance (Sunderland et al. 1986; Devolder and Pressley 1991). Diary studies (e.g. Cohen and Faulkner 1986; Burke et al. 1991) and laboratory studies (Burke et al. 1991; Rastle and Burke 1996; Evrard 2002) found that older adults reported more retrieval incidents such as TOTs than did younger adults, and that the age difference was greater for people's names than for common nouns. However, some experimental studies (e.g. Rendell et al. 2005) as well as closer examination of available data (e.g. Maylor 1997) cast doubt on the view that personal names are more adversely affected by ageing than other words. Analysing this discrepancy, James (2006) pointed out that the familiarity of stimuli sets used in some previous studies may not have been equivalent across age. In addition, she argued that the measure used to assess retrieval is critical in drawing conclusions about a disproportionate age deficit and that the discrepancy between studies could have occurred because retrieval performance was evaluated differently. More recent studies attempted to cope with these methodological issues. Using a learning paradigm in order to equate familiarity of stimuli across age groups, James (2004) and Old and Naveh-Benjamin (2012: Experiment 2) found that older participants showed a larger age-related deficit in learning names than in learning semantic information in association with unfamiliar faces. Selecting items well-known to both young and older participants, James (2006) found that older participants showed more TOTs than young participants when recalling famous people's names but there was no age difference for the recall of occupations. Thus, several recent studies support the view that personal names are more vulnerable to ageing than common nouns.

The description of several brain-damaged patients showing an impairment of proper name production (e.g. Semenza and Zettin 1988, 1989), or even more specifically an impairment of personal name production (e.g. Lucchelli and De Renzi 1992; Fery et al. 1995), in the context of preserved production of common nouns has long been seen as a set of data that helped to demonstrate that proper names, and particularly personal names, are more difficult to recall than common nouns. The argument was that no patient convincingly showing the reverse pattern of performance (i.e. an impairment of common noun production associated with an intact production of personal names) had been reported in the literature (e.g. Brédart et al. 1997). However, a double dissociation between two anomic patients who were tested with the same sets of faces and objects has finally been reported (Martins and Farrajota 2007): one patient remained able to name objects but showed a selective impairment at naming faces whereas the other patient had a preserved face naming performance but his object naming performance was impaired. Because of this double dissociation, the occurrence of personal name anomia can no longer be seen as another piece of evidence that personal names are fundamentally harder to recall than common nouns.

33.5 Explanations of Personal Name Vulnerability

Four hypotheses formulated to explain why it is usually harder to retrieve personal names compared with other words such as common nouns will be considered hereafter.

33.5.1 Names have a Particular Semantic Status

Following the work of linguists and philosophers about the semantic status of proper names (e.g. Lyons 1977; Kripke 1980), several (neuro)psychologists (e.g. Semenza and Zettin 1989; Cohen 1990; Burke et al. 1991) hypothesized that personal names are more difficult to retrieve than common nouns because they are meaningless, they lack descriptiveness, they are detached from the semantic network representing conceptual knowledge. Even if names like 'Baker', 'Farmer', or 'Potter' were originally bestowed on people who had such occupations, these personal names are now most frequently borne by people who do not have such occupations. The proper name 'Farmer' has lost the rich meaning of the common noun 'farmer'. Unlike the common noun which is a label for a conceptual category integrated in a rich semantic network, the role of the personal name is usually reduced to designate a given individual. In addition many personal names often correspond to no common noun at all. In Western countries, names (with the exceptions of nicknames) are usually tags that allow their bearers to be identified but, on their own, they describe nothing of their bearers' properties (Lucchelli and De Renzi 1992). From this fact, several authors wrote that proper names are difficult to retrieve because they are arbitrary (e.g. McWeeny et al. 1987; Cohen 1990). However, this could be misleading because, as early as the beginning of the twentieth century, linguists highlighted that the relationship between the meaning of a word in general (except for onomatopoeia) and its phonological word form is arbitrary. There is no necessary reason why people who make and sell bread are called 'bakers'. In French they are called 'boulangers', in Italian 'panettieri', and in Spanish 'panederos'. The relationship between the phonology of a word, even a common noun, and a concept is arbitrary. This relationship is nevertheless conventional, that is, all the people belonging to a linguistic community share the same labels to express a particular concept. But the kind of arbitrariness that Cohen (1990) and McWeeny et al. (1987) considered was different. Imagine that you encounter a man for the first time and you are told that he is a baker. You will automatically infer a number of probable things about him such as he gets up early, kneads dough, or works with an oven wearing an apron. This person, being a member of the 'baker' category, will inherit the properties of this occupational category. Now imagine that you meet a man and you are told that he is called 'Baker', you will not be able infer much information describing him. You will only be able to infer very general things such as that he has a surname which is pretty common in Anglo-Saxon countries and that this surname is the same as some people you know but who probably share no or few semantic properties with him. In short, names are non-descriptive in the sense that they do not provide information about the physical or mental characteristics of their bearers whereas common nouns do (within a linguistic community). To avoid any ambiguity, this property will be referred to as a lack of descriptiveness rather than arbitrariness (see Brédart and Valentine 1998; Fogler and James 2007).

The hypothesis that personal names are hard to retrieve because they tell us little about the characteristics of their bearers has been evaluated by using names of cartoon characters because, in the micro-world of cartoons, characters' names may be non-descriptive as in real life, but they may also be descriptive, that is conveying information regarding their holder's attributes. Brédart and Valentine (1998) compared the retrieval of characters' names that describe a mental attribute (e.g. Grumpy) or a physical attribute (e.g. Snow White) with the retrieval of equally familiar names that conveyed no information about their bearers (e.g. Aladdin or Mary Poppins). They showed that the proportion of correct recall was higher for descriptive names than for names that are not descriptive, and that the proportion of TOTs was lower for descriptive names than for non-descriptive names. This finding was replicated with elderly participants using a different set of characters (Fogler and James 2007). In these two studies, the two types of descriptiveness, mental vs. physical were not compared, simply because it was extremely difficult to build sets of items that would be big enough to allow this comparison. However, Fogler et al. (2010) cleverly bypassed this difficulty by using a learning paradigm in which names were to be associated with new cartoon characters. These pre-experimentally unfamiliar characters were associated with either physically descriptive names (e.g. 'Lengthy' for a giraffe), psychologically descriptive names (e.g. 'Classy'), or non-descriptive names. Results indicated that physically descriptive names were better recalled than psychologically descriptive and non-descriptive names. This study replicated, at least in part, previous studies that showed that descriptive names are easier to recall than non-descriptive names. The failure to show such advantage of psychologically descriptive names over non-descriptive names could simply reflect that the features described by the psychologically descriptive names were less obviously salient than the features described by physically descriptive names. Whatever the case, taken together, the results presented in this section clearly support the view that personal names are difficult to recall because they convey little information about the characteristics of their holders. Yet, this property of personal names does not explain everything about the difficulty of recalling them. Fery, Vincent and Brédart (1995) reported a single-case study that described a patient with a personal name anomia whose performance was no better for cartoon characters with descriptive names than for those with non-descriptive names.

33.5.2 Naming a Person Requires the Retrieval of one Specific Label

Naming a person may be particularly difficult because it requires the retrieval of one particular label whereas common nouns have synonyms or other semantically related alternatives that can be used in case of momentarily impaired lexical access. Cohen and Faulkner (1986: 187) put forward that 'It is probable that retrieval failures for object names are less noticeable since synonyms . . . can be substituted and effectively mask the lapse'. Besides synonyms, in many conversational contexts, labels from different levels of categorization of an object may be used to refer to that object (Brédart 1993). For instance, I may use the words 'pet', 'dog', or 'labrador' to speak of my neighbours' dog. Such diversity of possible labels usually does not exist when naming people. Person naming requires the retrieval of a label associated with one particular level of categorization: the level of individuals. You may use the circumlocution 'the songwriter of Hallelujah' to refer to Leonard Cohen but this would not be naming him. 'The songwriter of Hallelujah' is not Leonard Cohen's name. In contrast, 'pet', 'dog', and 'labrador' are three different nouns that can be used to refer to my neighbours' nice doggie.

In order to evaluate the hypothesis that the retrieval of one specific label is likely to make person naming difficult, faces that have the unusual property of bearing two different names were used (Brédart 1993; Valentine et al. 1999; Stevenage and Lewis 2005). These faces are those of actors who are strongly associated with one nameable character they have played in films or TV series. For instance, 'Harrison Ford' and 'Indiana Jones' may both be used to name the face of the actor playing this character in a photograph. Consistent with the hypothesis, TOTs were less frequent when naming faces that could be named by giving either the actor's name or the character's name than when naming the faces of actors playing characters whose names are not known (e.g. Julia Roberts as Vivian Ward in 'Pretty Women') or when naming the faces of famous characters played by actors whose names are not known (Kojak played by Telly Savalas).[1] Another

---

[1] The advantage of having two names is obvious when the participants are allowed to recall either of the two names associated with a face. However, when the task requires recalling an actor's name, not a character's name, then having two names may be a disadvantage. Then, the two names of a face compete,

study evaluated this hypothesis in a different way. Hanley (2011b) compared the recall of famous faces' names with object naming from pictures. These two sets of items were matched for familiarity. Unsurprisingly, the occurrence of TOTs was more frequent for personal names than for object names. In a second experiment, Hanley selected items to avoid alternatives such as synonyms in both sets of items. Under these circumstances the occurrence of TOTs was not more frequent for face naming than for naming objects.

These two studies support the hypothesis that naming faces elicits more TOTs than naming objects because common nouns can more often be replaced by an acceptable alternative word than personal names can be.

33.5.3 The Set Size of Plausible Phonology is Larger for Personal Names

Brennen (1993) posited that there is a wider variety of phonological forms that are acceptable for personal names than for common nouns. Imagine that a friend introduces you a person and tells you that this person has a job as a *dreaner*, you will probably think that you did not hear well. However, if your friend had told you that the man is called Mr *Dreaner*, you would have found nothing remarkable. For Brennen (1993), we learn at least implicitly that many more phonologies are plausible for personal names than for common nouns because, as adults, we encounter new personal names that consist of unfamiliar phonologies much more frequently than new common nouns. This wider set size of plausible phonology implies that the same amount of retrieved partial phonological information will be more helpful for retrieving the whole phonological form of a common noun than that of a person's name. Griffin (2010) takes the following example: if you have to retrieve the name of an occupation and only the first syllable /bei/ is available to you, only a few occupations are possible (baker and bailiff). If the word to be retrieved is a personal name then the task is less easy because there are many plausible names sharing the first syllable /bei/ (e.g. Bay, Baker, Bale, Baines, Bateman, Bates, and so on). This difference may explain why retrieval difficulties such as in TOT states occur more frequently when retrieving personal names than when retrieving words with more regular forms such as common nouns. This interesting hypothesis has not been formally tested yet.

33.5.4 The Frequency of Personal Name Usage is Relatively Low

Personal names tend to be used less frequently in language than are other words, such as common nouns, making them more difficult to recall. An explanation in terms of the lower

and this competition makes naming slower (Valentine et al. 1999; Stevenage and Lewis 2005; Valentine and Darling 2006); this is known as the *nominal competitor effect*.

frequency of personal name usage could help to explain some data that were unexpected from the Bruce and Young's (1986) model, in particular that the names of highly familiar and personally known people are recalled faster than semantic properties about these people (Brédart et al. 2005; Calderwood and Burton 2006). Indeed, we are more likely to recall the names of our colleagues and classmates than semantic information about them such as their nationalities or occupations. When we encounter personal acquaintances, we produce their names to greet, to call, or we insert the interlocutor's name into the conversation to hold attention (Cohen 1994). In other words, this frequent production of personally familiar people's names would have facilitated access to them. Famous names (i.e. the kind of stimuli that were used in most experimental studies of face naming) do not benefit from such a practice due to the obvious lack of direct interaction with celebrities.

The frequency of usage of personal names is more difficult to estimate than that of other words. There are several available lexical databases that may provide word frequency (e.g. Baayen et al. 1995; New et al. 2004) but there is no corresponding tool for personal name frequency. Sometimes, researchers used the number of entries in the telephone directory as a measure of a surname frequency. The relationship between such estimated surname frequency and face naming is far from clear. High frequency has been reported to make face naming faster or slower depending on the paradigm employed (Valentine and Moore 1995), or to fail to influence it (Brédart and Valentine 1992). However, estimating the frequency of use in such a way is not satisfactory because the frequency of use of a familiar person's surname cannot be assimilated to that surname's frequency in the population. My own surname is not frequent but it is not at all infrequently processed by people who are familiar with me. The frequency of use of a familiar personal name depends both on its frequency in the population and on the degree of familiarity of its bearer (Valentine et al. 1996). Unfortunately, we do not know yet how to combine these two factors to produce a good estimate of frequency of use.

The idea that higher frequency of usage favours successful personal name recall seems to be supported, as least indirectly, by studies showing that more familiar people's faces induce less TOTs than less familiar people's faces when the number of retrieval attempts is carefully controlled (Brédart 1993),[2] and by studies showing that faces' familiarity is positively associated with naming speed (e.g. Moore and Valentine 1998). The findings that names acquired earlier in life elicit fewer TOTs (Bonin et al. 2008) and are recalled faster (Moore and Valentine 1998) than names learned later also support this idea. However, no measure allowing a fair comparison of personal names' frequency of usage

---

[2] Some diary studies reported that retrieval failures occurred more frequently for names of familiar people than for names of people who are not very well known. This effect was labelled the *reversed frequency effect* (e.g. Cohen 1990). However, this effect may just reflect the relative frequency of recall attempts: names of frequently encountered people are likely to be recalled more often than names of less frequently encountered people. Hence, the key measure is not the absolute number of recall failures but the proportion of recall failures among recall attempts. Unfortunately, in these diary studies the number of recall attempts was not controlled. When this point is controlled in the laboratory the reversed frequency effect disappears and a positive relationship emerges (Brédart 1993).

with common nouns' frequency has been found. This precludes evaluating the impact of frequency of usage in carrying out experiments in which the frequency of usage of personal names and common nouns would be carefully manipulated, that is, contrasted or equated.

33.6 CONCLUSION

At the moment, it is widely accepted among cognitive psychologists that there is no one single factor explaining why personal names are more difficult to recall than are other kinds of words such as common nouns. It is likely that a combination of the factors considered above contributes to this difficulty, but the extent of their contribution remains to be determined. In addition to the factors discussed so far, recent studies suggested that the ability to inhibit competing names could play a larger role than previously thought (Ferreira et al. 2014).

Recently, neuroscientists have proposed that proper names (including personal names) and common nouns are, at least in part, processed through different pathways in the brain. The double dissociation between the production of proper names and the production of common nouns (see section 33.4; Martins and Farrajota 2007) as well as findings from neuroimaging studies (e.g. Ross and Olson 2012) support such a view. Naming unique entities, such as people, and naming categories would not recruit exactly the same brain areas. For example, neuroscientists showed that a network comprising the left temporal pole and frontal regions is specifically involved during proper name processing (for reviews see Semenza 2009, 2011; Pisoni et al. 2015). The identification of brain correlates specific to proper name recall is very interesting, but does not per se explain why the recall of proper names is usually harder than the recall of nouns. It remains to uncover the biological factors making the 'proper name' network so vulnerable and to relate those findings with the particularities of personal name processing evidenced by cognitive science.

CHAPTER 34

....

NAMES AND DIALECTOLOGY

....

MARGARET SCOTT

34.1 INTRODUCTION

....

NAMES are relevant to the study of language and society in both the past and the present. The geographical precision with which place-names can be located means that they preserve important evidence for historical dialectology. This is significant in part because of the information they can retain from periods of language for which written evidence is limited, as for example in the case of pre-literary Scots 1100–1375 (CSD 1985: xiii). Fragments of Scots lexis are frequently embedded in personal names and place-names recorded in Latin charters and other legal documents composed during this period. Pre-literary onomastic material exists for many other languages, establishing the onomasticon as a very valuable resource for historical linguistics (see chapter 37). However, names and words are often subject to different processes of change and development and so the onomasticon and lexicon can exhibit quite different behaviours (Hough 2010; Hough 2012: 220–2). Notably for the dialectologist, the comparison of dialect maps with maps of place-name elements frequently reveals a lack of parallelism between the distribution patterns of lexical elements and their onomastic counterparts. An explanatory framework for this phenomenon is provided by the idea of the *onomastic dialect*, originally developed by Nicolaisen (1980) with specific reference to Germanic place-names.

Linguistic analyses of onomastic data may shed light on such philological questions but they can also be politically significant, providing a range of insights into the sociolinguistic and pragmatic functions of non-standard, slang, and dialectal language. A notable example of this approach is found in Paunonen et al.'s (2009) study of Helsinki toponyms. Varieties of language deemed to be regional, minority, or non-standard rarely enjoy the same level of attention and curation as their more powerful counterparts. Furthermore, such marginalised varieties tend to proliferate in spoken rather than written contexts, with the result that evidence may be comparatively ephemeral and difficult for researchers to capture accurately or comprehensively. There may be a local politics of pronunciation, only visible to researchers through close analysis of recorded data, and the oral corpus of local names typically differs from that represented on generic maps (Kearns and Berg 2002). The study of unofficial names is therefore also relevant to the subject of dialectology.

This chapter begins with a discussion of what is meant by *dialect* and why this term (and concept) are complicated by ideas of fixity and subordination. It then considers some of the contexts in which regional words are encoded in official and unofficial onomastica, before moving on to a consideration of the history of the interactions between dialectology and onomastics. The following section examines more recent developments affecting both disciplines, particularly since the 'critical turn' in onomastic research, before examining the evolution and application of Nicolaisen's (1980) concept of the *onomastic dialect*.

34.2 Dialects, Standards, and Linguistic Hegemonies

Dialect is generally understood in linguistics as 'a language variety distinguished from other varieties by difference of grammar and vocabulary', but not necessarily by differences of phonology (Hughes et al. 2012: 3). Standard English grammar and lexis, for example, may be used by a speaker with any accent. However, it is often the case that a local grammar and lexicon will fall together with a local system of pronunciation, so the three are often taken together to constitute a *dialect*. In what follows the term is applied fairly broadly, to take account of the range of materials produced which explore dialect phonology, grammar, and lexis, and to facilitate discussion of language varieties frequently perceived as dialects although their status may be disputed. It is perhaps also necessary to point out that the term *dialect* can be problematic. Some dialectologists have even gone so far as to say that '[t]here are no such things as dialects' in order to emphasize the protean nature of dialects, which vary socially, diachronically, and geographically (Laing and Lass 2009: 417).[1] To some extent it is strange that they should feel the need to make this point so vociferously. It is very difficult to find evidence of scholars actually claiming that dialects have strict boundaries, so the argument is something of a 'straw man'; throughout the history of dialectology, *dialect* has been understood as a convenient shorthand for a *variety* of language, with fuzzy edges. In 1924, Henry Cecil Wyld set out something of a 'manifesto ... for the use of place-name evidence in historical-dialectological research' taking as one of his tenets 'that there are no firm dialect boundaries' (Carroll 2013: xxiv–v). This point has been reiterated frequently by those who came after him, but the argument has resurfaced in

---

[1] Axiomatically, the same is also true of *languages, sociolects, idiolects*, and so forth; it is perhaps possible for any of these constructs to seem like clearly defined structures, but linguists are unlikely to view them as such.

recent years. Integrational linguists have criticized sociolinguists for overemphasizing the idea that language use is dominated by 'fixed codes' and thus perpetuating the myth that dialects have clear boundaries (Harris 1998). Too much focus on linguistic patterns attributed to social groups on the grounds of their ethnic, socio-economic, or gender-based ties can lead to analyses that are based on very narrowly-defined variables or which set out to look for expected codes and ignore findings which contradict theoretical assumptions (Harris 1998). Pablé (2009) invokes onomastic evidence to critique variationist sociolinguistics, arguing that the diverse patterns observable in the use of unofficial toponyms provide evidence of linguistic choices that cannot be accounted for by sociolinguistic paradigms. It is, however, difficult to use onomastic data as a basis for this argument because, as discussed above, the relationship between onomastic and non-onomastic material is complex, and onomastic analyses may not reflect results comparable with other linguistic domains. Rather, Pablé's very interesting collection of data may more helpfully shed light on observable differences between the performative aspects of the lexicon and onomasticon, or suggest that traditional sociolinguistic groupings fail when tested against names specifically.[2]

Perceptions of what constitutes a *language* as opposed to a *dialect* result very much more significantly from historical and political realities than linguistic analysis; all dialects are linguistically equal, including those to which the honorific title 'standard' is prefixed. This is a fundamental point for current formal study of language, frequently stressed in undergraduate textbooks. The 'perceived superiority [of a standard language] is a social fact but not a linguistic fact' (Penhallurick 2010: 185). The word *language* is also used in many different ways: it can denote an individual speaker's understanding of their own linguistic repertoire, or the collective perception of a particular community's repertoire, or a codified variety presented by a linguistic 'authority', and it is worth remembering that '[e]ach of these is the product of some kind of ideology' (Winford 2003: 23).

Extant definitions of the word *dialect* may have the unfortunate side-effect of encouraging the equation of *non-standard* with *substandard*, as for example sense 2 in the *Oxford English Dictionary* (*OED*), which currently appears online unchanged since first drafted in 1895: 'One of the *subordinate* forms or varieties of a language … a *provincial* method of speech' (*OED* s.v. dialect *n.* 2; my italics). 'Subordinate' works against the idea of linguistic equality, and while 'provincial' may literally denote that which is geographically outwith the capital, it simultaneously evokes negative connotations of being 'parochial or narrow-minded; lacking in education, culture, or sophistication' (*OED* s.v. provincial

---

[2] A further complication with Pablé's argument is that variationist sociolinguistics has not tended to concern itself with onomastic material. This has largely remained the purview of data-driven onomasticians with—in many cases, and especially in England—a focus on history and etymology. In recent years, however, ground-breaking socio-onomastic research has been conducted by scholars in the field of human geography, creating a 'critical turn' in onomastics as a whole (Berg and Vuolteenaho 2009). Pablé cites Walther (1989) as evidence that 'the "fixed-code myth" and the "dialect and style myths" constituted the foundation stones for establishing this new discipline [socio-onomastics] in the early 1970s', but makes no reference to the critical toponymic work represented by scholarship such as Pred (1990), Kearns and Berg (2002), Paunonen et al. (2009), where he would perhaps have found more kindred spirits.

adj. 6.). When taking a descriptive approach to language, dictionaries have a duty to represent actual usage faithfully, and *dialect* can indeed be applied with derision. No doubt, when the *OED* entry for *dialect* is revised and updated as part of the ongoing revision programme for the Third Edition, some additional information (such as the meta-label '*depreciative*') will be supplied to assist the reader in separating social prejudice from linguistic fact. The perceived neutrality of the term *variety* has encouraged its use in place of *dialect*, as it allows comparisons to be made between different linguistic entities without the writer having to take a stance on disputes over their political status. One can then discuss the linguistic aspects of *varieties* such as Scots and English, or Catalan and Spanish, without socio-political distractions.

Nevertheless, the social and political status of non-standard varieties is important, and linguists cannot entirely divorce themselves from the underlying problems of linguistic prejudice which often attach to non-standard varieties. Such negative attitudes can all too easily transfer to their speakers, or even arise from or appear to justify wider-reaching forms of prejudice against specific races or cultures. Accusations, voiced by educational psychologists in the 1960s and 1970s, that African American varieties were 'inadequate for learning and logical thinking', a view unilaterally condemned by linguists, provide a stark illustration of the problem (Labov 1972: xvi). Yet echoes of these arguments surface every so often, and public debates about linguistic standards, particularly in educational contexts, are typically visceral and uninformed. Honey's 1983 critique of Bullock's UK government report, *A Language For Life* (1975), discussed by Cameron (1995: 86) was the precursor to an episode of moral panic regarding the teaching of English in England and Wales. According to Bullock, 'the language children brought from home should be accorded value in school' (Cameron 1995: 86). Honey regarded schools as 'failing working-class and ethnic minority children if they did not insist on the *exclusive* use of standard English' (Cameron 1995: 86; my italics). When linguists attempt to contribute to such shouting matches from the viewpoint that 'all varieties are equal', they rarely succeed in challenging the entrenched ideologies that underpin their opponents' arguments. The prevalence and recurrence of negative attitudes to non-standard language may perhaps be best understood by examining the myths on which the primacy of standard languages commonly rests:

> If we take a standard to be a rallying point (a banner around which those fighting for a cause gather), and we apply it to language, then our understanding of language is governed by the myths of **legitimacy** and **greatness**. If we force legitimacy on others, we constrain them to use only one form of language or exclude them from participation in the state. (Watts 2011: 258)

Nevertheless, back in the classroom, tolerance sometimes prevails. Wheeler and Swords (2006, 2010) have devised textbooks that draw deliberate comparisons between African American and American English. Their methodologies facilitate greater understanding of the different linguistic codes and their social function, rather than simply proscribing varieties that challenge existing hegemonies. Matthew Fitt's work with Scottish schoolchildren empowers them to deploy their native voices, writing creatively in Scots, and revealing new routes into learning, hitherto invisible to the linguistically disenfranchised (*Scots Education Resources* 2007).

While such constructive projects exist, they have as yet achieved little recognition, and there is still much evidence for the persecution of dialects. As recently as November 2013, a school in the West Midlands of England proscribed the use of ten words and phrases in the local dialect 'in the context of classroom teaching', according to a BBC report. John White, the head teacher, apparently stated: 'If children are using certain phrases, that can be confusing for them because when they come to spell that word, they are not saying it in standard English and that can hold them back' (Anonymous 2013a). This has not been the experience of Fitt or Wheeler and Swords, who have instead demonstrated that open discussion of language actively promotes educational engagement (Wheeler and Swords 2004; *Scots Education Resources* 2007; Wheeler 2010). As Watts (2011: 258) succinctly puts it, 'speakers will continue to construct differences between standard and non-standard varieties, on the basis of language myths, and sociolinguists should be aware of the need to deconstruct those myths'.[3]

A recent project at the University of Glasgow, *Scots Words and Place-Names* (SWAP; Hough et al. 2011), invited participants to discuss names and lexis through social media, in part to elicit data about the Scots language. Social media may be the gateway for more constructive public discussions about language variation in future, and is particularly useful as a conduit for gathering research data about minority and non-standard varieties (Jones and Uribe-Jongbloed 2013). One of the sidelines of the SWAP project was a competition organized 'with the intention of engaging school children and raising the profile of Scots in schools' (Hough et al. 2011: 7). This proved a successful venture. 'While for some schools the competition provided an impetus to introduce Scots into the classroom, perhaps for the first time, for others, where Scots had already received a good deal of attention, it provided a focus for that work' (Hough et al. 2011: 15). There are arguments for instituting similar projects, across the rest of the UK and internationally, to encourage a more informed debate about modern linguistic realities.

34.3 REGIONAL LANGUAGE IN THE LEXICON AND ONOMASTICON

Place-names occupy an interesting political and social space in relation to arguments about language and dialect. The official, 'top-down' linguistic landscape (see chapter 27)

---

[3] Historians of English can also fall foul of the 'ideology of the standard', encouraging linguistic prejudice by emphasizing the subaltern position of non-standard language. Milroy and Milroy (2012: 169) criticize Henry Cecil Wyld's view that dialects were '"of little importance"', and whose '[c]onventionalised histor[y]' of English 'contribute[d] to what may be called the legitimization of the language, as represented by the standard variety, with concomitant downgrading of non-standard varieties'.

includes a considerable number of dialect terms which have become part of the accepted language of public spaces. In the north of England the dialect term *ginnel* 'narrow passage between houses' occurs in street names such as 'Parkinson's Ginnel' in Southport, Lancashire and 'The Ginnel' in Harrogate, Yorkshire, while its Scots counterpart *vennel* occurs in 'The Boat Vennel' in Ayr and 'The Vennel' in Edinburgh. *Ginnel* is one of the terms noted by Upton for which 'information on the distribution . . . in terms of geographical spread or types of speakers, or indeed their precise meanings for those who use them, is no more than anecdotal' (Upton 2012: 398). Names incorporating these terms may therefore provide a starting point for researchers wishing to shine an academic torch onto vernacular usage.

Official names that reflect local language varieties frequently exist as uncontested names, indicating that regional terms which, as lexical items, would be unknown to (or even actively avoided by) non-regional speakers, are able to exist without prejudice in the onomasticon. For example, the Scots name 'Tam's Brig', in Ayr, South Ayrshire, can be found on the street-sign and in the name of local businesses including the Tam's Brig Post Office. There has never, to the best of my local knowledge, been any suggestion—except perhaps in jest—of the existence of an English parallel, which in translation would be *'Tom's Bridge'. It is noteworthy that local (Scottish) English speakers who would not ordinarily use Scots *brig* to describe a 'bridge' have no reluctance or hesitation in using the place-names in the Scots form. It could be argued that the opacity of names has an impact on users' perceptions, and that the language of origin is of little importance, given that a name's function is largely denotative. However, Tam's Brig and many other Scots street names and minor names can easily be etymologized by speakers with even a minimal knowledge of Scots and Scottish culture, and 'Tam's Brig' would for many be lexically transparent, especially if they know other people called 'Tam'. For both Scots and Northern English, at least, it is apparent that terminology which occurs in the onomasticon has a higher status there than in many other social and linguistic environments.

Local words are also actively employed in commercial contexts, addressing audiences for whom such lexis has positive (or humorous) connotations. As Johnstone (2009) has argued, the use of Pittsburgh dialect on T-shirts both reflects extant pride in this variety, and simultaneously imbues it with value. Similar processes have been observed in Beal's (2009) study of Geordie and Sheffieldish in the north of England. Other areas have yet to be fully examined for commercial parallels, but the representation of Scots is another viable contender, the mouse-mats and mugs produced by Sprint Design displaying dictionary-style accounts of words such as *gallus* 'self-confident, stylish' and *crabbit* 'ill-tempered, grumpy' providing a direct parallel to Johnstone's Pittsburghese examples.

The lexicon and onomasticon of a given location frequently include some areas of overlap, and it is noteworthy that local terms also feature in the names of businesses that seek to emphasize local identity, capitalizing on the marketing advantages this vocabulary affords. Scots illustrations at the time of writing include Fantoosh Fish on Glasgow's Great Western Road and Fantoosh Flooring in Newport-on-Tay, Fife (*fantoosh* 'flashy, ultra-fashionable'), the Wee Blether Tearoom in Kinlochard, Stirlingshire (*wee* 'little', *blether* 'chat'), Tea Jennys Tea Room in Falkirk (*tea jenny* 'a person who drinks a lot of tea') and the childcare provider Weans' World in Johnstone, Renfrewshire (punning on the film title 'Wayne's World' while incorporating the Scots word *wean* 'child').[4]

34.4 Onomastic Data and the History of Dialectology

European dialectology as an academic discipline can best be described as beginning in the nineteenth century, previous interest in dialects being largely restricted to antiquarian scholarship with no cohesive theory or purpose (Shorrocks 2000: 84–5). Victorian researchers were particularly interested in the study of contemporary dialects as repositories of 'archaisms...preserved by [the] rural population' (J. O. Halliwell 1847, in Shorrocks 2000: 85). This line of inquiry was therefore unconcerned with socio-political questions about linguistic hegemony or cultural silencing that have become so important in contexts where minority languages and dialects compete for recognition and legitimization (Helander 2009). Nevertheless, much of the work of the later nineteenth century has yet to be surpassed. In England, for example, the most comprehensive work on dialectal lexis remains Joseph Wright's *English Dialect Dictionary* (1898–1905).

Dialect studies typically progressed through the production of dictionaries and grammars, followed by atlases mapping specific grammatical, lexical, and phonological features (Vieth 2006: 540–1). The main focus of dialectology in the early twentieth century was on dialect geography (Shorrocks 2000: 89). Names were valued in this context because of their clear links to specific places, acting as more trustworthy linguistic anchors than their Old and Middle English textual counterparts whose geographical origins were often in dispute (Carroll 2013: xxiv).[5] Furthermore, name evidence offered a new path forward given that, as Ekwall noted, 'many (or rather most) dialects are not represented in Middle English literature' (1917: 5–6).[6] In 1923 the English Place-Name Society (EPNS) was established and began the painstaking work of gathering and analysing historical toponymic data county by county. In terms of the information collected, there were strengths and weaknesses to the initial approaches adopted by the society, some of which altered as the Survey progressed. In 1925, minor names and field names were not considered to be of particular value in their own right, being made up of commonplace elements, but by 1933 the editors had recognized that such names can 'add substantially to our

---

[4] An extensive collection of photographs detailing examples of Scots in the linguistic landscape is available on the website of the Scots Language Centre (2015) and Michael Hance (2012) delivered a paper entitled 'Scots Place-names in the Linguistic Landscape. Time to Start Talking?' to the day conference of the Scottish Place-Name Society held in Oban on May 5, 2012.

[5] However, the 'lack of temporal specificity' for name evidence can be problematic (Nicolaisen 1995a: 105).

[6] See further Fisiak (1990: 112), and references cited therein.

knowledge of the historical lexicon and of dialectal usage' (Carroll 2013: xiv). Since then, considerable work has been undertaken to identify lexis unattested in literary sources but preserved in the historical onomastic record (Hough 2002), with many collective findings gathered together in Smith's (1956b) dictionary of *English Place-Name Elements* and its successor, the *Vocabulary of English Place Names* (VEPN). The contribution of onomastic evidence to the study of dialectal lexis is also attested by the various uses of names in major historical dictionaries including the *OED* and *A Dictionary of the Older Scottish Tongue* (*DOST*; see further chapter 40).

Smith (1990: 205) remarked that the need for two volumes to house his dictionary was 'a sign of the abundance of the linguistic material, and the introduction to each county survey an indication of its special contribution to historical and dialect studies'. However, not all data were treated with equal regard in the early days of the Survey. When Wyld laid out his plans for the role of onomastics in historical dialectology in the 1920s, he placed tremendous emphasis on phonology, largely ignoring other linguistic applications of onomastic material (Carroll 2013: xxv). While this limited the scope of the work, there was still much to be deduced from the data, names frequently providing very useful evidence for historical sound-changes and phoneme distributions. For example, the <a> spellings of the first elements of East Anglian place-names including Stradsett and Stradbroke illustrate their evolution from West Saxon *strǣt* 'Roman road' rather than its Anglian counterpart *strēt* (Kristensson 2001; Hough 2012: 220). The emphasis on phonology pervaded twentieth-century dialectology, and the focus on rural and historical English meant that urban dialects were largely ignored or dismissed by the academy.[7] The stereotypical 'non-mobile older rural male' or *NORM* was regarded as the ideal source for traditional varieties of language, and there was little academic interest in other non-standard forms. Given that comparative philology as a discipline was in part fuelled by 'a concept of the simplicity and purity of the *Volk* ['folk, people'], who were felt to be closer to nature' (Shorrocks 2000: 87), it is perhaps not surprising that elements of this attitude survived as long as they did. It was not until the advent of sociolinguistics in the 1960s that urban varieties began to receive attention from linguists, notably inspired by Labov's (1966) *The Social Stratification of English in New York City*. Unfortunately, however, dialect geography came to be somewhat marginalized, as sociolinguists were initially more concerned with variables such as economic status, age, and class, rejecting the structural stance of many dialectologists. This bifurcation has been unhelpful to the study of dialect variation, which in more recent work is widely acknowledged to operate along (at least) the three axes of geographical, social, and temporal space (Laing and Lass 2009: 417).

A further problem was that the quest for linguistic universals, emphasized by devotees of Chomsky in the 1960s and 1970s, diverted attention from the vital descriptive

---

[7] For example, the Introduction to the *Scottish National Dictionary* (SND) (1931) stated that 'Owing to the influx of Irish and foreign immigrants in the industrial area near Glasgow the dialect has become hopelessly corrupt' (see further discussion in Scott 2008a: 188).

work necessary for dialect research and encouraged researchers to attempt to fit linguistic information (for any given variety) into the restricted data sets prescribed by transformational-generative grammar, leading Lakoff to warn that linguistic abstractions based on ephemeral theories were of little long-term value (Shorrocks 2000: 91–2). Similarly, Raven McDavid argued that 'the dialectologist's first duty is to present the data in such a way that any reader can replicate the conclusions—or failing to replicate them, can show where the original statement went astray' (McDavid in Shorrocks 2000: 93). Yet while the Chomskyan school was criticized both for the limitations of its method and its ' "intolerant attitude" ' to ' "purely descriptive linguistic work" ' (Sampson in Shorrocks 2000: 93), it was also praised because its focus on the 'inherent systematicity and linguistic logic of *all* languages of the world' was beneficial to the recognition of the intrinsic properties of *all* varieties of language—including, significantly, 'the logic and systematic nature of Black speech' (Smitherman 2006: 10). Shorrocks (2000: 96) goes so far as to say that 'intolerant adherents of dominant paradigms have in some measure controlled university appointments, granting agencies and publishers', but perhaps it is more fair to say that it was ever thus, and that such maladies are in no way restricted to linguistics.

The legacies of the twentieth century with their emphases on phonology and theory have resulted in some considerable gaps in the understanding of English dialect, especially in towns and cities. Nevertheless, it should also be remembered that in the field of historical dialectology at least, such enquiries were diligently continued, notably resulting in a raft of resources including the *Linguistic Atlas of Late Medieval English* (McIntosh et al. 1986; Benskin et al. 2013–) and its two 'daughter' projects, the *Linguistic Atlas of Early Middle English* and the *Linguistic Atlas of Older Scots*. Name evidence continues to inform historical dialectology. Importantly, Kitson (1995: 47–8) has argued that 'the supposed impossibility of Old English dialect mapping is an illusion of scholarship', using onomastic material from charters to demonstrate that such mapping can be achieved. His work has also shown that, when thus mapped, the features of Old English 'relate coherently to modern dialect divisions' (Kitson 1995: 48), challenging previously held notions of a problematic and 'essential' mismatch 'between conventionalised representations of Old English and the dialect divisions of all more recent periods' (Kitson 1995: 47).

34.5 RECENT AND FUTURE DIALECTOLOGY AND ONOMASTICS

Historical dialectology continues, and sociolinguistics has ensured that emergent modern urban varieties such as Multicultural London English are widely studied and valued, overturning the dismissive tendencies of the past (Fox 2012). There has been something of a *rapprochement* between former contending factions in linguistics (Rissanen 2010), although as recently as 2009, Laing and Lass (2009: 417) still felt it necessary to make the point that dialectology is in principle no different from either historical linguistics or sociolinguistics. The advent of new technologies such as corpus analysis, and the growing recognition that diverse forms of dialectal, non-standard, and minority languages are alive and well in social media (see for example Jones 2013; Belling and de Bres 2014), have also facilitated new lines of enquiry into dialectal usage. The Scots word *stooshie* 'quarrel, uproar' looks very twenty-first century when rendered as *s2shi* in social media contexts, and the likes of Facebook and Twitter have the potential to radically alter linguists' relatively limited perceptions of real language in use. An astonishing quantity of material is available for analysis, encouraging a return to a more data-driven linguistics. The Newcastle Corpus of Tyneside English, containing recordings from the 1960s and 1990s, provides one important example of the benefits that corpora can bring to dialectology (see further Beal and Corrigan 2007; Beal et al. 2007).

Nevertheless, dialect collections and corpora have often been produced with a focus on NORMs, from the *Survey of English Dialects*, conducted in the 1950s and 1960s, to the *Freiberg Corpus of English Dialects* (FRED) in the 1970s and 1980s (Szmrecsanyi 2013: 16). Such resources are often interrogated from the standpoint that the traditional dialects they contain are dying out, perpetuating the idea of dialects as odd historical artefacts, bound for the linguistic museum. While there is 'extensive evidence for change leading to loss of distinctiveness in dialects', this does not amount to dialect death (Beal 2010: 2). Scots, for example, has been described as '"dying out" as a spoken language' since at least the early eighteenth century (Aitken 1985: 153). Rather than conceding that dialects are here to stay, some have sought to create an artificial divide between older and more modern varieties, ignoring their existence across a diachronic continuum. According to Wells (1982: 395), 'many would claim that [in Glasgow] authentic Scots, the traditional dialect, has "died out"; yet working-class Glasgow speech includes many features which would normally be considered characteristic of Scots rather than of Standard English'. While it is evident that some words are falling out of use, very often these are terms connected with the fading trades and industries of the NORMs studied so intensively in the twentieth century (Beal 2006: 54), becoming redundant as society changes. Shifts of this kind take place constantly in the wider language, and should not be misunderstood as irrefutable evidence for dialect loss.[8] Furthermore, as Brook pointed out in 1958, 'if dialects are dying, they are ... taking an unconscionable time about it' (1958: 199).

It is still also typically necessary to look outwith England, if not outwith the UK, to find examples of research which takes account of toponymic dialectal material, or indeed the politics of competing names more generally (Scott and Clark 2011: 29–30).[9] As Coates (2013: 158) puts it, '[i]n British, especially English, toponymic work, alternation in place-names is suppressed, or often reduced to a consideration of the relation between a historical pronunciation and a current, often spelling-based, one'.

---

[8] See also Beal's discussion of the findings of Upton and Widdowson (1999), from which 'an optimist could conclude that ... there is no proof of overall erosion of regional variability in the lexicon of English', although the authors conclude that 'there is no doubt that the regional dialect lexicon is being eroded' (Beal 2010: 65).

[9] A notable exception is Pires (2007), who examined the unofficial Birmingham toponym *Pigeon Park*.

Paunonen et al. (2009: 450) examined early twentieth-century toponymic data for Sörnäinen (or Sörkka, in its unofficial form), 'Helsinki's most prominent working-class district'. The language of the 'Sörkka lads' is often characterized as *slang* by the authors, even though it could equally be described as urban dialect.[10] There is considerable scope for similar socio-onomastic research in the UK, particularly because '[m]any places have more than one simultaneously current name, usually one official and at least one unofficial one' (Coates 2013: 153). In the Scottish town of Prestwick in South Ayrshire there is a pathway known locally in Scots as 'The Puddock Sheugh', *puddock sheugh* [pʌdʌkʃʌx] being 'frog (or toad) lane', though the sign on the wall reads: 'Ladykirk Lane'.

There may also exist toponymic contrasts, manifesting as a politics of pronunciation that may be indicative of a speaker's relationship with the local community and their perception of how it is socially structured. Current scholarly research on such questions has tended to look at environments where several names exist in conflict, as for example in Kearns and Berg's (2002) study of the pronunciation of Māori names in New Zealand. Once again, however, there are examples of pronunciation variants in the UK, as Coates (2013: 153) notes, perhaps 'result[ing] from a complex interaction of dialect and accent, modal difference (i.e. speech vs. writing), and sociological factors'. Great Clowes Street in Salford, Greater Manchester, is derived from the name of the Clowes family who were influential landowners in that area (Bullock 2010). Established members of the community (especially those who know its history) typically pronounce Clowes [kluːz], making it homophonic with *clues*, whereas incomers frequently assume the pronunciation to be [klaʊz] by analogy with words like *cows*, or [kləʊz], on analogy with words like *flows*.[11] Pronunciations of local names can be indicators of dialect phonology, but they can also be a marker of historical knowledge and community allegiance.

34.6 ONOMASTIC DIALECTS

As discussed above, onomastic material has often been used as an additional data source for broader questions regarding dialectal research, feeding into prevailing linguistic approaches as and when it was deemed to be useful. However, it is widely acknowledged that names are 'abnormal linguistic objects' when compared with the rest of the language (Coates 2013: 131). This point has been examined in some detail by Nicolaisen with

---

[10] One of the measures often employed to arrive at a distinction between *dialect* and *slang* terms—although these are themselves fuzzy categories at best—is to consider those with demonstrable regional longevity *dialectal*, and those which are comparatively ephemeral, and typically used by only one generation, *slang*. However, if the longevity of a regional term is unknown, as is particularly true for innovations in the lexicon, it is impossible to judge whether or not it will become established in the regional lexicon and it may be 'dismissed' if it is deemed to be *slang* (Beal 2010: 69).

[11] I am grateful to local historian, Roy Bullock, for discussions on this topic, and for granting me access to his unpublished works on Salford street names.

regard to the relationship between lexical items and their corresponding onomastic cousins. In 1980, he invoked the concept of the *onomastic dialect* to describe the area roughly delineated by generic name elements.[12]

Unsurprisingly, the distribution of lexical items is typically more scattered than that of the name evidence, given that 'toponymically applied generics are less easily uprooted than their non-onomastic counterparts in the lexicon' (Nicolaisen 1980: 37). In some instances, considerable similarities exist between lexical isoglosses and their corresponding onomastic isonyms, as in the case of the North American terms *creek*, *brook*, and *lick*, all of which mean 'stream'. Such evidence argues that 'one criterion for toponymic dialects' is 'onomastic variation influenced by [but not identical to] dialectal variation in the lexicon (Nicolaisen 1980: 37–8). In other instances, as in the case of the North American place-name generic *kill*—derived from Dutch *kil* 'stream'—there is no corresponding item in the lexicon (Nicolaisen 1980: 38). A third pattern is observable in the distribution of the term *bayou*—derived from French *bayouc* or *bayouque*, itself from Choctaw *bayuk* 'sluggish water course'—for which 'the present-day lexical use is both more extensive and later than the employment of bayou as a toponymic generic' (Nicolaisen 1980: 38). The historical and present-day influences of different cultures are therefore discernible from the patterns of onomastic dialect variation and the survival of the corresponding terms in the lexicon, whether one is analysing elements derived from French, Dutch, or Spanish in the United States, or elements derived from Celtic, Old Norse, and Old English in England.

Nicolaisen also argues that the transferred use of 'classical names' such as Marathon, Ithaca, Syracuse, Troy, and Rome in the toponymicon of North America represents a further example of an onomastic dialect. The importation of names from other contexts is commonplace, 'but it cannot be linked directly to anything a linguistic atlas will ever show, being closer to transferred non-linguistic cultural traits . . . than to the lexicon of American English' (Nicolaisen 1980: 40). This type of onomastic analysis therefore has the potential to supplement or develop the study of cultural influences and connections both in tandem with and beyond whatever linguistic evidence may emerge for that given context. Furthermore, working on this basis, a vast array of different cultural and linguistic patterns could equally qualify as sub-types of onomastic or toponymic dialect, and could be extended to include anthroponymic dialects.

Nicolaisen further pursued these ideas with a view to determining whether onomastic evidence could be used to identify 'a distinctive Northwest Germanic toponymy that can be said to have close links with the period of the dialectal development of the Germanic languages', at the point where Old English, Old Saxon, Old High German, and other distinctive varieties emerged from Common Germanic (1995a: 112). While his article is essentially exploratory rather than definitive, Nicolaisen notes that the toponymic dialects collectively represented in England by

---

[12] Nicolaisen (1980: 42) also employs the term 'onomastic idiolect' to describe an 'individual name repertoire', which would be 'strongly influenced by its community of name users and name givers, who make up an onomastic dialect area that is also culturally and socially stratified'.

the Old English generic *hlith* 'slope' and its Old Norse cognate *hlíth* 'slope' appear to support the hypothesis:

> If it is fair to assume that two cognate terms with similar pronunciation and identical meaning, one of them Old English, i.e. West Germanic, and the other Old Norse, i.e. North Germanic, reached England as productive toponymic elements and not just as lexical items, then it is more than likely that they were also toponymically productive in their continental areas of origin at the time of their departure and, retrospectively, in early phases of an undifferentiated, or only minimally differentiated, Northwest Germanic toponymic dialect. (Nicolaisen 1995a: 110)

Extending his analysis to other cognate pairs of Old English and Old Norse elements found in English toponyms, Nicolaisen (1995a: 111) argues that these pairings do not simply represent 'lexical items which could be employed in the naming process whenever required', but 'must have been part of a Northwest Germanic onomasticon'. He also calls for a systematic investigation of comparative material across all relevant toponymies, and although this has yet to be carried out, his findings have been generally supported by subsequent research (Hough 2012: 216). Hough (2000) suggests a further pair of onomastic cognates, Old Norse **kíll* 'wedge', found in England, and Swedish *kil* 'tool, wedge' in Sweden, and evidence for an earlier Indo-European onomastic dialect is identified by Kitson (1996) in his analysis of European river names. Insley (2006) has also employed the concept of the onomastic dialect in his analysis of early Germanic and Indo-European personal names, finding anthroponymic isoglosses across an area spanning the British Isles and Continental Europe. While noting that 'name systems are never so simple that they fit into a tidy pattern' (Insley 2006: 123), and that '[a]ll taxonomies are difficult' (Insley 2006: 127), he identifies several recurring anthroponymic elements, one example being **Þrasa-* (found in 'high-status' names including that of the Vandal king, Thrasamund (496–523) (Insley 2006: 125)), which he labels 'Mediterranean Germanic' (Insley 2006: 127).

While much of the extant research relating to onomastic dialects is concerned with early linguistic history, the basic principles have been adapted for what might be termed 'applied onomastic research'. A modern application of anthroponymic dialects is investigated by Tan in his study of the increasing occurrence of English given names within ethnic-Chinese personal names in Singapore, from which he concludes that 'the adoption of English-style personal names through English-based G[iven] N[ame]s is a feature of English dialect development' as it increases its reach as a world language (2004: 382). He also argues that the 'Englishisation of personal names' does not fit neatly into Schneider's 'theory of dialect development' with regard to the spread of World Englishes (2004: 382), thus providing another example of onomastic and non-onomastic data exhibiting different behaviours. The distribution of personal names is also considered by Heeringa and Nerbonne (2006), who examine the relationship between distributions of Dutch surnames and dialects in the Netherlands. Their research shows some of the ways in which modern mapping and genetic technologies may be combined with established onomastic theories to achieve new ends.

34.7 CONCLUSION

From the discussion in this chapter it should be evident that there are a number of different research arenas where onomastic and dialectological studies can benefit one another. Although largely functioning, initially, as a data-source fuelling historical dialectology, onomastics is increasingly emerging as a discipline in its own right. The contribution of onomastics to dialectology is yet to be fully understood and there remains much work to be done to map out, on all available axes, and to examine, through all available theoretical frameworks, the complex relationships between living dialects and onomastic evidence. Shorrocks (2000: 97) includes research on 'local toponyms and personal names' in his list of 'trends in English dialectology . . . largely neglected in the more recent history of the discipline'. It is to be hoped that the 'critical turn' in onomastic research may reinvigorate interest in the relevance of names to the understanding of linguistic politics, which is very often tied to questions of regional and social identity. The answers to these questions define the cultures we live in.

34.8 FURTHER READING

On the history of dialectology in Europe, see Vieth (2006), and for England, Shorrocks (2000). For further information on modern approaches to English historical dialectology, see Dossena and Lass (2004), Laing and Lass (2009), and Williamson (2012). An introduction to English dialect studies is Beal (2010). On the history of onomastic evidence in English historical dialectology, see Fisiak (1990) and references cited therein. Name evidence is used extensively in Kristensson's work on historical English dialectology (1967–2002, 2001); see also Sandred (1997). An introduction to modern socio-onomastics is provided by Berg and Vuolteenaho (2009); see also Paunonen et al. (2009), which is strongly influenced by Pred (1990). See also Kearns and Berg (2002), Rose-Redwood et al. (2010) and Rofe and Szili (2009). For further discussion of Scots see Jones (1997), Corbett et al. (2003), and Unger (2013). For a robust defence of Scots as a complex narrative medium, see Macaulay (2005), a book with wide-ranging implications for the understanding and refutation of the linguistic prejudices frequently attached to regional, minority, and non-standard varieties everywhere.

CHAPTER 35

....

NAMES AND GEOGRAPHY

....

PEDER GAMMELTOFT

Just as all phenomena exist in time and thus have a history, they also exist in space and have a geography.

(United States National Research Council, 1997)

35.1 INTRODUCTION

PLACE-NAMES and geography are closely interlinked—understanding of either discipline cannot be carried out without some knowledge and use of both. In many cases, place-names can be seen to be the spoken expression of Man's view of the surrounding landscape. Although many geographers are trained in toponymy, this is not necessarily a focal preoccupation. Geographers study spatial and temporal distribution of phenomena, processes, and features. In addition, the interaction of humans with their environment is also a main study area. Because the study of geography concerns a number of disciplines—such as economics, health, climate, plants, and animals—geography is a very interdisciplinary science, with close attention to the relationship between physical and human phenomena and its spatial patterns.

Geography as a discipline can be split broadly into two main subsidiary fields: human geography and physical geography. Human geography largely focuses on how humans create, view, manage, and influence space. It is a branch of geography that focuses on the study of patterns and processes that shape human society. It encompasses the human, political, cultural, social, and economic aspects. Physical geography, on the other hand, examines the natural environment, and how organisms, climate, soil, water, and landforms produce and interact. The focus is on geography as an Earth science. It aims to understand the physical problems and the issues of lithosphere, hydrosphere, atmosphere, pedosphere, and global flora and fauna patterns (biosphere).

The combination of both fields is known as environmental geography—focusing on interactions between the environment and humans. This brand describes the spatial aspects of interactions between humans and the natural world. It requires an understanding of the traditional aspects of physical and human geography, as well as the ways in which human societies conceptualize the environment.

Environmental geography has bridged human and physical geography, and has partly arisen as a result of the change in human relationship with the environment—as a result of globalization and technological change. Thus, a new approach was needed to understand the changing and dynamic relationship between Man and the natural world. Examples of areas of research in environmental geography include emergency management, environmental management, sustainability, and political ecology. Further subdivisions exist, including urban planning, regional planning, and spatial planning. These branches use the science of geography to determine how to develop (or not develop) a region in order to meet particular criteria, such as safety, beauty, economic opportunities, the preservation of the built or natural heritage, and so on.

35.2 PLACE-NAMES AS EXPRESSIONS OF GEOGRAPHY

Place-names act within both physical and human geography, in as much as they describe aspects of both the natural world and human created space at around the time of naming. One of the challenges in using place-names in connection with geography are to establish when a name was coined and the significance of the naming focus. Another main challenge lies in later onomastic developments, which, through metonymical processes—for example a place-name comes to signify a different type of locality from the one it originally did—create a mismatch between the current denotation and the original place-name meaning. In the case of metonymy, it can often be difficult to single out the original name bearing or name originating locality, and a certain amount of qualified guesswork frequently has to be applied in singling out the original name bearer.

The geographical aspect is usually most clearly expressed in the generic element of place-names, as their function within the name is to state what type of locality the name concerns. Thus, any place-name with a generic in *-grad*, *-stadt*, *-ville*, and *Baille-* will normally denote some kind of conglomerated settlement ranging from a group of buildings to a village or town. In the same way, a name in *-bosch*, *-skov*, or *-wood* would originally have denoted a coherent area consisting almost exclusively of trees. In this respect place-names act as an intermediary between present and past geographical realities. Place-names usually denote localities of today, which may or may not be the same as the original denotation. However, in terms of the meaning carried in the place-name expression, the place-name describes a perceived state of geography at the time of naming—a situation which may be radically different from what can be observed today. For instance, the name *Werningerode* (1122 *Werniggerode, Werningerode*) in Harzen,

Germany, originally denoted a clearing (Middle High German *rot* 'clearing') (Eichler and Walther 1986: 20), that is, a brief geographical state of pointing to an area affected by the human activity of tree-felling (Eichler and Walther 1986: 292–3). Here we have embedded in the name an instance of human intervention with physical geography. In relation to the current denotation of *Werningerode* as a town situated between Harzen and Magdeburg, there is no correspondence whatsoever. Nonetheless, it can be speculated, through the place-name's original denotation, that this town was established as a result of woodland having been cleared.

It should be mentioned, however, that some types of place-names are not capable of expressing geographical content. The most common type of place-names in this category are derivations, that is, place-names formed by adding a suffix to a word in existence at the time of naming. To the north-east of the above-mentioned *Werningerode*, we find the name of *Gröningen* (905 *Gronigge*, 934 *Groninga*, 961 *Gruoningi*) which is an -*ingi*/-*inga* derivation of Old Saxon *grōni* 'green' (Eichler and Walther 1986: 24–5, 120). In this case, the name is only capable of conveying that something is akin to 'green', but not what it is, be it landscape, people, or perceived qualities. In addition, a few generic elements do not relate to geography but to societal factors, particularly aspects of ownership, purchase, or inheritance. This is the case for instance with *Gröningen*'s neighbouring town, *Hadmersleben* (963 *Hathumereslevu*, 994 *Hadumereslevu*) (Eichler and Walther 1986: 127), a place-name in German -*leben*, which, like its Danish and Swedish counterparts in -*lev* and -*löv* (Søndergaard 1972: 158–80), derive from Common Germanic *laiba* 'inheritance' (Eichler and Walther 1986: 19). The naming thus concerns an act between people, the act of leaving something to another person or receiving something from someone else. It is very telling that the vast majority of this name type features late Iron Age personal names and titles as specifics, something which is also seen in later names in -*køb*/-*köp* 'purchase' in Southern Scandinavia. Here names such as *Basseköp* (1499 *Bassekøp*), *Høsterkøb* (1185–87 *Husfrecop*, 1193 *Husfrekop*, c.1370 *Husfrwkøp*), and *Svenskøp* (1377 *Swensskip*, 1390 *Suenskøb*), describe how they were purchased by *Bassi*, the wife (< Danish *hustru* 'wife, spouse') and *Svend*, respectively. Again, central to the naming is a transaction between people, a purchase.

How precise then is the geographical aspect in names? Many of the words used in place-names have a general meaning in language, but several studies have indicated that place-name elements can have a more specific meaning than they have as ordinary words. For instance, Gelling and Cole (2000: 145–8) have shown that the Old English word *beorg* 'hill, mountain' in place-names carries the meaning 'rounded hill, tumulus', occasionally 'a rounded knob at the end of a ridge', where the central characteristic element is a continuously rounded profile and a smallish size, see Fig. 35.1. Gelling and Cole (2000) admit that it has not been possible to fit this appearance to all places with *beorg* as the generic element. And, indeed, it is possible that the meaning may differ geographically. This is what Mølgaard (2012: 73–81) has shown in her study of the Danish cognate *bjerg* in central Jutland. In Danish, the word connotes an

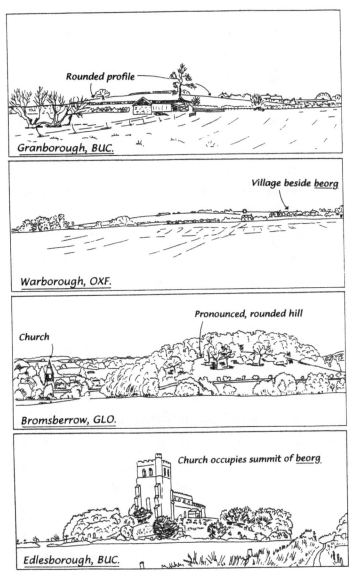

FIGURE 35.1 Sketch map from Gelling and Cole (2000: 248), showing landscape representations of OE *beorg*.

Reproduced by kind permission of the author.

'elevation' in general, but in Mølgaard's (2012) study, the place-name element *bjerg* tended to denote either: (a) a 'rounded or cone-shaped elevation', prevalent in the western and central parts of central Jutland, a meaning akin to Gelling and Cole's central meaning, (b) 'an elevation of ness-like character', predominant in the western parts of the research area, or (c) an 'elevation on the edge of a plateau', found throughout the research area and relatively similar to Gelling and Cole's (2000) second definition of 'a rounded knob at the end of a ridge'. In addition, there was also a small number of names in -*bjerg* which could not be classified. The unexpected result of Mølgaard's (2012) research was that the element *bjerg* was predominant in the western parts of her study area, central Jutland. This is surprising, as this part of the country is known to be the least elevated in Denmark. In addition, the fact that several types of denotations could be singled out in, partly, differing areas also shows how place-names tend to merge with local landscape and take on meanings found in the local geography. Thus semantics and landscape morphology become closely interlinked in such a way that an element like Danish *bjerg*, whose Common Germanic meaning is that of 'mountain', may end up denoting smallish elevations in a landscape barely rising 30–40 metres above sea level.

35.3 PLACE-NAMES AS INDICATORS OF FORMER LANDSCAPE

Man has had a profound effect on geography. For instance, most of the acreage of Western Europe has over the centuries been transformed into arable land at the cost of forests, meadows, and the reclamation of land from seas and fjords. Again, a lot of the arable land has later been given over to urbanization as the world's population has grown at ever increasing rates at the same time as billions of people have migrated from rural areas to urban centres in the latest century or so, a tendency which is forecast to increase over the next decades.

Greater London, as an example, now covers 1,579 km², and houses in the region of 8 million people. It goes without saying that the geographical transformations in terms of housing and infrastructural developments are enormous and the current geographical reality in Greater London is completely different from a century, let alone a millennium, ago.

In many cases, place-names can give an indication of the earlier geographical states of areas that have undergone substantial human geographical changes. In that respect, the Greater London District of *Wandsworth* (eleventh-century *Wendleswurthe*), whose generic derives from Old English (OE) *worþ* 'homestead' (Ekwall 1947: 510–11; Mills 2001: 239), shows that this area was once home to an Anglo-Saxon settlement. In fact, when including the other places within this district, we get a picture of an area overwhelmingly Anglo-Saxon in character. Not only do we have original landscape denoting names such as *Battersea* (693 *Badrices ege, Batrices ege*), sporting a generic in OE *ēg, iēg* 'island' (Mills 2001: 14–15), but also human geography related names such as *Balham* (957 *Bælgenham*, from OE *hām* 'village, estate, manor, homestead'), *Putney* (1086 *Putelei*, 1279 *Puttenhuthe*, from OE *hȳþ* 'landing place'), and *Roehampton* (1350

Rokehampton, from OE *hāmtūn* 'home farm, central estate') (Ekwall 1947: 203, 206; Mills 2001: 9, 184, 192). In general the place-names of *Wandsworth*, in terms of etymology, convey a picture of a rural, agricultural area, reflecting a geographical situation from, possibly, as early as the fifth–sixth centuries and onwards. The current associations of the district, with its former wharf area on the river-front now lined with new apartment blocks, bars and, restaurants, its recently regenerated Southside shopping centre, and housing developed over the centuries for immigrants seeking their luck in London, could not be much further removed from this. Instead, the place-names of *Wandsworth* have now come to signify urbanism and aspects of London life.

Even in less changed environments, place-names may help to reconstruct former geographical realities. In a study from 2006, Gammeltoft and Egeberg have shown how field names may help to pinpoint lost burial mounds and, thus, reconstruct ancient communication routes (Gammeltoft and Egeberg 2006). It has long been observed that burial mounds in Denmark often follow ancient roads and tracks (Müller 1904: 1–64; Egeberg 2004: 44–51), something which is most clearly observable in West Jutland where extensive farming is a relatively recent phenomenon. Thus, a significant number of burial mounds have avoided being removed to make way for farming, and those which have been removed are to a large extent still localizable in the surface soil or on cadastral maps from the turn of the nineteenth century, see Fig. 35.2.

In the early 2000s a project, *Høj og Vad Projektet* (the Mound and Ford Project), registering grave mounds and ancient fords in West Jutland, had localized several thousand mounds and a significant number of fords in an area of 25 × 40 km^2 (Gammeltoft and Egeberg 2006: 15). In this way, a number of hitherto unknown ancient roads were uncovered, as mounds lining the roads made it possible to reconstruct the routes exactly and fords showed where the routes crossed watercourses. One problem was, however, to connect the routes visible by means of lines of mounds to the registered ancient fords, as there was often an area of 'blank' land between mounds and fords. It was discovered that the areas void of mounds constituted areas of longstanding cultivation where mounds would have been removed much earlier.

However, by consulting local place-names, particularly field names, it was possible to locate a significant number of lost mounds. These were identified through the form *-høj* 'mound, hill'. In addition, some names indicating roads and paths were also located. In this way, it was possible to reconstruct the missing stretches of roads in the arable between the less intensively cultivated land and fords. The localization of ancient roads will naturally be less precise when dealing with field names alone, as the field names themselves define a much looser localization in as much as they state that a piece of land is related to a mound—either by having a mound in the field or by being situated next to a mound. In reality, however, the localization proved precise enough to provide a general impression of the ancient route, see Fig. 35.3.

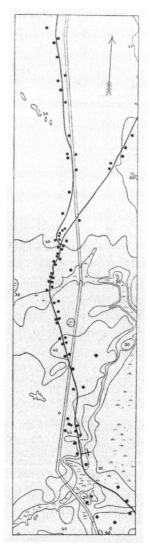

FIGURE 35.2 Map from Müller (1904: 18), showing the distribution of Bronze Age mounds running along ancient roads

35.4 GEOSPATIAL TECHNOLOGY AND PLACE-NAMES

With the increasing digitization of geospatial data, place-names are being looked upon with increasing interest from geospatial management organization.[1] The interests span

[1] An early example of widely available geospatial data put in use in online applications is postal information (usually post codes and addresses). The availability of such datasets has meant that it is often

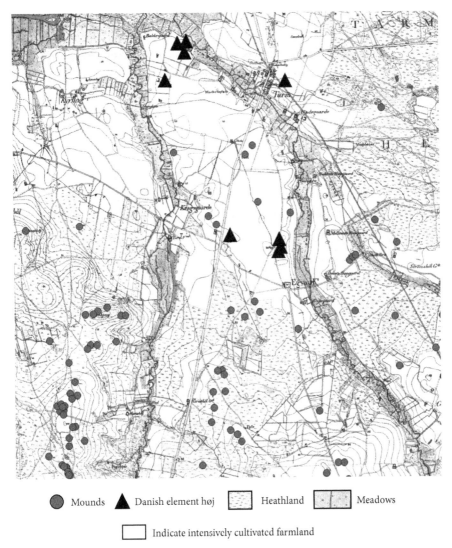

FIGURE 35.3 Map of northern Egvad parish from 1871. The map is marked with black circles indicating known mounds; black triangles indicating place-names containing the Danish element *-høj*

from creating reliable transnational place-name data, through making such data publicly available, to ensuring regional or universal standards. The rise in focus on high quality place-name data is mainly technology-driven—it has simply become much easier to utilize online geospatial data for private and public users over the last few years. Geospatial data is no longer solely of national interest but of international importance.

easier to find a location by means of a post code or a specific address than by means of a place-name. However, from a user's point of view, place-names are much more usable than specific addresses, and

With the rise of Geographic Information Systems (GIS) in the 1980s, desktop analyses of geospatial data became available for a wider audience and complex modelling of geography, geology, and social and cultural conditions has grown explosively since the 1990s. However, the use of GIS in place-name research has often been little but distribution maps of specific place-name types, sometimes in combination with analyses of soil conditions, surface geology, and the like.[2] Spatial data exist either as licensed data or open source, as download or online via web services.[3] Place-name data has traditionally, bar a couple of notable exceptions,[4] been licensed products—although more and more countries are releasing place-name datasets as open source.

The major problem with GIS datasets is that it has not been easy to publish point, line, or polygon data on the internet. This has to some extent been remedied by the establishment of the KML-data standard which allows the viewing of geospatial data directly online on GoogleEarth, GoogleMaps, Open Street Map, etc. So far, this technology is somewhat restricted in comparison with GIS software but works well for displaying place-name data in the form of places, lines (e.g. roads and rivers), and areas (e.g. administrative or historical divisions). However, the development of browser-based GIS software is currently exploding, with numerous solutions available (at cost) already. These products are generally still lacking somewhat in features in comparison to desktop GIS programs.

35.4.1 Place-name Databases

Place-name datasets have become a central component of GPS navigation systems and online maps,[5] and are widely used in scientific research. There are, however, often notable differences between geospatial place-name datasets and scientific place-name datasets—the former often being single-table datasets with coordinate information,[6] in addition to place-name, feature type, and administrative information. Scientific

---

particularly post codes. After all, how many would actively search for the postal code 6240 and not Løgumkloster (Denmark) in order to seek out the location of this town?

[2] The most common GIS systems are licence-only ArcGis and MapInfo. Lately, however, initiatives like the Open Geospatial consortium, with resulting open GIS standards, have resulted in an array of free or low-cost GIS software.

[3] Normally in the form of a either (1) a Web Map Service (WMS), a standard protocol for serving georeferenced map images over the internet generated by a map server using data from a GIS database, or (2) a Web Feature Service Interface Standard (WFS) providing an interface allowing requests for geographical features across the web using platform-independent calls. The WMS/WFS specifications is developed and published by the Open Geospatial Consortium.

[4] Such as the US based GeoNames.

[5] Such as GoogleEarth, GoogleMaps, Bing Maps, Open Street Map, and national versions, e.g. the British OS VectorMaps, etc. Place-name datasets also have potential interest for the so-called Augmented Reality technology, currently pioneered by smartphone-applications such as Layar and Wikitude.

[6] Normally either in latitude/longitude or the international WGS 84 system. The open KML-standards as promoted by Google use latitude and longitude coordinates, whereas GeoNames feature both standards. GIS software is usually capable of working with a wide array of coordinate systems.

(a)

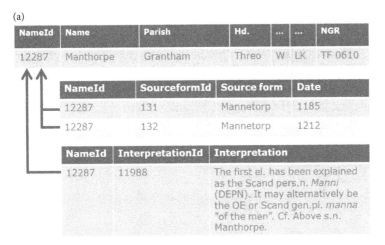

NameId	Name	Parish	Hd.	...	...	NGR
12287	Manthorpe	Grantham	Threo	W	LK	TF 0610

NameId	SourceformId	Source form	Date
12287	131	Mannetorp	1185
12287	132	Mannetorp	1212

NameId	InterpretationId	Interpretation
12287	11988	The first el. has been explained as the Scand pers.n. *Manni* (DEPN). It may alternatively be the OE or Scand gen.pl. *manna* "of the men". Cf. Above s.n. Manthorpe.

FIGURE 35.4A Relational database structure

(b)
```xml
<xml>
 <Place-name>
  <Id>12287</Id>
   <Name>Manthorpe</Name>
    <Localisation>Grantham, Threo, W, LK</Localisation>
   <NGR>TF 0616</NGR>
       <Historical forms>
           <Historical form>
               <Form>Mannetorp</Form>
               <Date>1185</Date>
           </Historical form>
           < Historical form>
               <Form>Mannetorp</Form>
               <Date>1212</Date>
           </Historical form>
       </Historical forms>
    <Interpretation> The first el. has been explained as the
    Scand pers.n. <i>Manni</i> (DEPN). It may alternatively
    be the OE or Scand gen.pl. <i>manna</i> "of the men".
    Cf. Above s.n. Manthorpe. </Interpretation>
 </Place-name>
</xml>
```

FIGURE 35.4B Hierarchical database structure

place-name datasets are often multi-tabular,[7] displaying current and historical name forms as well as interpretations and etymology for individual place-names, but not necessarily coordinate information, see Fig. 35.4.[8] A combination—or merger—of the two data types will yield considerable benefits for both usages, though.

---

[7] Normally in the form of relational databases in SQL formats or in semi-structured datasets based on the XML standard or the like.

[8] The latest in database development is the so-called *open structure* databases, usually in xml or JSON format where data are not stored in individual and specially designated data fields but more or

35.4.2 International Onomastic-geospatial Initiatives

With more and more place-name data becoming available to single users and data use becoming international and universal, the need for international standards is growing. Several initiatives exist for the management of geospatial data, including place-name data, such as the EU-initiated EuroGeoNames[9] and the INSPIRE Directive.[10] At an international level, the United Nations has two initiatives: UNGEGN[11] and GGIM.[12] Of these, UNGEGN is a place-name specific initiative, such as EuroGeoNames, whereas the GGIM and INSPIRE span all aspects of geospatial data.

less as text as in a word-processing document. Although heralded as the next big thing, for place-name purposes—where we often operate with several names of exactly the same form—the immediate benefits of non-tabular data aggregation is easily lost to the need for tagging of data in order to assure correctness.

[9] EuroGeoNames is a branch of EuroGeographics (<http://www.eurogeographics.org/>, whose activities focus on underpinning the European Spatial Data Infrastructure INSPIRE). EuroGeoNames combines Geographic Names from the National Mapping and Cadastral Agencies across Europe to create a unique open-access service and data set. EuroGeonames aims to provide significant benefits for public, private, and personal use by enabling place-name data suppliers to provide geo-referenced location information by providing: (1) reliable, high quality, comprehensive geographic names from official sources; (2) translation for place-name data into 25 languages; (3) easy access to updates; (4) a service-based infrastructure for collection and delivery of data; (5) a web interface that allows simple, live search and reference in all languages.

[10] INSPIRE (1995–2015) = Infrastructure for Spatial Information in the European Community. The INSPIRE directive aims to create a European Union spatial data infrastructure to enable the sharing of spatial information among public sector organizations and secure public access to spatial information across Europe. The spatial information under the directive is extensive with a great variety of topical and technical themes. INSPIRE is based on a number of common principles: (1) data should be collected only once and kept where it can be maintained most effectively; (2) spatial information must be possible to combine seamlessly from different sources across Europe and be used by many users and applications; (3) data should be available at all levels or scales irrespective of level/scale of collection; (4) geographic information needed for good, all-level governance should be readily and transparently available, and (5) easy to find what geographic information is available, how it can be used to meet a particular need, and under which conditions it can be acquired and used.

[11] UNGEGN = United Nations Group of Experts on Geographical Names, is one of seven expert-groups under the UN's Economic and Social Council (ECOSOC) which provide technical recommendations on standardizing geographical names at national and international levels. Conferences are held every five years under United Nations Conferences on the Standardization of Geographical Names (UNCSGN), whereas UNGEGN meets bi-annually between the Conferences to follow up the implementation of resolutions adopted by the Conferences and to ensure continuity of activities between Conferences. Today, UNGEGN has more than 400 members from over 100 countries. Outside its meetings, UNGEGN functions through 23 geographical/linguistic divisions and through working groups, currently addressing issues of training courses, digital data files and gazetteers, romanization systems, country names, terminology, publicity and funding, and toponymic guidelines.

[12] GGIM = United Nations initiative on Global Geospatial Information Management, a geospatial initiative which aims to play a leading role in setting the agenda for the development of global geospatial information and promoting its use to address key global challenges. It provides a forum to liaise and coordinate among Member States, and between Member States and international organizations.

CHAPTER 36

....

NAMES AND HISTORY

....

GILLIAN FELLOWS-JENSEN

36.1 INTRODUCTION

THE accumulated strata of place-names have sometimes been compared with the strata shown on geological maps and it can be tempting to follow this practice. Since the history of recorded place-names in England, the focus of this chapter, falls entirely within the last two and a half millennia, however, the actual geological strata have little relevance for the progress of settlement. A more satisfactory metaphor would seem to be to look upon the process as similar to the fate of a medieval palimpsest, a parchment text that has been wholly or partly scraped, rubbed, or washed away so that new material can supersede whatever may have stood there before. With the aid of modern techniques it has recently become possible for philologists to read what has hitherto been considered unreadable and to decipher the content of texts that had formerly been thought to be lost for ever. While some of the names that we find on a modern map can be traced back for two millennia and their meaning understood, some old names have undoubtedly been replaced in part or whole by younger ones. It can therefore be necessary to strip off any covering material before we can find our way back to the oldest name, often with the aid of sophisticated philological techniques. The effect is rather like peeling the skins off a grubby onion to find not the writing material in the condition it had when the first scribe committed his information to posterity but one or more older texts. My aim here is to remove these skins one by one to show the layers of names left by progressively older waves of namers.

36.2 THE POST-NORMAN PERIOD

The place-name creations of the last eight centuries of English history have not had a great effect on the pre-existing names. Most of the areas betraying recent settlement are found within or around earlier settled areas. New Costessey in Norfolk, for example, is a settlement that grew up gradually between the two world wars and later developed into a suburb on the north-eastern outskirts of Norwich, while Old Costessey, a short distance away, is the name of an old settlement that was established on an island of raised ground in a bend of the river Wensum and its English name 'Cost's island' is recorded as *Costeseia* in Domesday Book (CDEPN: 159–60).

With the introduction of improved methods of transport, however, there has been an increased dispersal of settlement. Railways began to spread their tentacles out from the major urban centres in the nineteenth century, while urbanization tended to obliterate some names. The construction of the railways had given work to many Irish labourers and the immigrant classes everywhere tended to settle in the poorer areas in booming cities. One of the few place-names to mark this unplanned influx into the country by an appearance on a map is *Little Ireland* close to Oxford Road Station in Manchester, which is marked on the Ordnance Survey five-foot plan from 1849 (Busteed 2012). The residential housing here was, however, short-lived. Built in about 1827, it was demolished in about 1877. The name reflects the fact that in 1841 over 75 per cent of the population here was Irish. The reason why a blue plaque marks the site is that the appalling conditions there, although by no means unique in Manchester or other cities, were empathetically treated by the eminent German socialist philosopher Friedrich Engels (1845) in his influential *Die Lage der arbeitenden Klasse in England*, first published in English in 1887. Similar names given to areas in industrial cities with a substantial immigrant population, at first Irish, Italians, and Jews, and after the Second World War even greater numbers of colonial and foreign immigrants, have certainly given rise to many names, most of which have been unofficial and transient.

Of more permanent relevance for the history of naming are the official names given in recent centuries to what may be called 'New towns'. *New Brighton* in Cheshire was a district which was developed by a retired merchant from Liverpool, who purchased about 170 acres of sandhills and heathland in 1830 and named the area after the resort in Sussex which had become famous in the late eighteenth century. New Brighton was described in an advertisement as an eligible investment as a watering-place for the gentry of Liverpool (Room 1985: 76). By the end of the century New Brighton was a thriving seaside resort and, with the innovative composer Granville Bantock as its Director of Music from 1897 to 1900, it had become a focal point for classical music performance in northern England. Elgar conducted its orchestra on several occasions, once at only the second public performance of the Enigma variations in July 1899 (Kelly 2013: 46–52, 58). I visited the resort in my childhood in the 1940s but its popularity declined after the war. The name New Brighton is a transferred name of the type particularly familiar from the United States. It is important to distinguish transferred names of this type from names in which the prefix 'New' has been attached to an older place-name to denote a newer neighbouring settlement, as in the case of New Costessey.

Welwyn Garden City in Hertfordshire was designated a planned town in 1948. It was only the second 'garden city' and had been planned from the 1920s to promote health, industry, and community living. It was laid out along tree-lined boulevards but it was symbolized for me in my childhood by the picture of the Shredded Wheat factory on the packet holding breakfast cereal, even though I later visited the garden city frequently. The name of the original settlement at *Welwyn*, a fording-point on a river, is recorded in a tenth-century charter and is a so-called dative-plural name meaning 'at the willows' (CDEPN: 661). It survives as a parish village, sometimes referred to as *Old Welwyn*.

Milton Keynes in Buckinghamshire has a different history. The original estate is mentioned as *Mid(d)eltone* in Domesday Book and the manorial affix reflects the fact that this had passed in the twelfth century into the hands of a Norman family from either Cahaignes in Eure or Cahagnes in Calvados (CDEPN: 415). The new town, designated in 1967, now embraces several earlier settlements and took its name from just one of these. It is uncertain what effect the development will have on the names borne by all the older settlements but it seems that most of the historic settlements with an ancient church will at least survive as the names of suburbs.

36.3   THE NORMAN PERIOD

The Normans, whose influence on the personal nomenclature of the English was so great that forenames of pre-Norman origin had dropped almost completely out of use by the early years of the thirteenth century, made singularly little impression on the place-names of England. In general the Normans after the Conquest in 1066 seem to have been content to employ the settlement names they found on their arrival. The importance of castle-building was, of course, of great significance for the lasting success of the Conquest and several of the fortified castles received French names. They occur particularly frequently in the frontier areas. The naming of one new Norman castle resulted in the disappearance of a neighbouring settlement. The first holder of the Earldom of Richmond was Alan Rufus, a second cousin of William the Conqueror. He laid the foundations of his great castle overlooking the Swale at a site that had earlier been referred to as *Hindrelaghe* (< *hindarlēah*) 'hind's clearing'. The name given to the great defensive castle when completed early in the twelfth century was *Richmond* (< French *Richemund(e)* 'strong hill'), transferred from one of the places of that name in France (CDEPN: 499). Interestingly enough, this Yorkshire castle was later the inspiration behind the re-naming of the royal palace in Surrey called *Shene* (whose English name probably meant 'at the shelters'), when Henry VII had it rebuilt after a fire. Robert de Todenei, the Conqueror's standard-bearer, founded his castle *Belvoir* (< French *Belveder* 'beautiful view') on a commanding headland in the Leicestershire Wolds (CDEPN: 50). *Malpas* in Cheshire lies on the border with Shropshire and Wales. The French name means 'difficult passage' and has replaced English *Depenbech* 'deep valley'. Robert son of Hugh had been given the land by the Conqueror and the arrangements at his castle here point to an estate organized for border warfare (Higham 2004: 53–5, 142–6). It must have served as a frontier fortress in the Norman period. Another

castle associated with the Conqueror received a name in which the word meaning 'castle' could follow or precede a Norman personal name. The forms *Castellum
Bern'* c.1150 and *Castrum Bernardi* 1235 refer to *Barnard Castle* in Durham, which
was built by Bernard Balliol I († 1165) on a site overlooking the Tees (CDEPN: 36).
Bernard was the son of Guy de Baliol from Picardy, to whom William Rufus had
granted a large estate in this area.

    Newly founded religious houses were also frequently given names of French origin.
This was because great French churches had received huge benefits as a result of the
Conquest and invested the revenue in new houses, often in remote areas, that were
placed under the leadership of, and colonized from, French monasteries. Monasteries
with French names are found particularly frequently in Yorkshire. The abbey of
Fountains was established in 1132 and called *Fontibus* with a Latin dative plural form
meaning 'at the springs' (CDEPN: 238). *Jervaulx* and *Rievaulx* both have hybrid names
in which the old river-names *Ure* and *Rye* precede Old French *vals* 'valley'. Jervaulx was
originally founded in 1145 at the place earlier called by the Nordic name *Fors* 'waterfall'
but it was evacuated in 1156 to its present site on the banks of the Ure (CDEPN: 336).
Rievaulx was founded in 1131 in the valley of the Rye (CDEPN: 500). *Meaux* abbey was
founded in 1150 south of the settlement in the carrs still known by the Nordic name
Melse < *mel+sæ* 'sand-bank by the pool') at the time of Domesday Book but destroyed
in the twelfth century to make room for the abbey's north grange. This name was
mistakenly associated with that of Meaux Abbey in France, where the abbey chronicle interprets it as coming from Latin *sapor mellis* 'flavour of honey' (CDEPN: 405).
French laudatory names were accorded to some of the monastic foundations established as late as in the fourteenth century. *Haltemprice* meaning 'high enterprise' is
the name bestowed upon a priory of Augustinian canons established at Cottingham
in 1322 but soon moved to a nearby site whose name *Neweton* was then lost (Smith
1937: 208). *Mount Grace* meaning 'hill of grace' is the name of a Carthusian priory that
in 1396 occupied the site of a settlement on the edge of the moors that at the time of
Domesday Book bore the Nordic name *Bordelby* but was later displaced by the priory
(CDEPN: 424).

36.4 THE NORDIC PERIOD

The arrival of the Vikings in the ninth century brings us to a period when the giving of
new or modified names on a large scale to older settlements can be dated to between the
late ninth century, when the Danes first began to partition the land between themselves,
and the late eleventh century when the majority of the relevant names were recorded
in Domesday Book. A few of these Nordic names can be dated more closely linguistically because they contain archaic forms of Nordic personal names. The names Anlaby
in Yorkshire, Anglezark in Lancashire, and a lost *Anlafestun* in Northamptonshire, for

example, all contain an archaic form of the Old Scandinavian name *Anu-laiƀar which had developed into Óláf by about the year 1000 (Fellows-Jensen 1990: 150–2).

An influential map entitled 'The Scandinavian Settlement' (Smith 1956b: map 10) seemed to confirm the effectiveness of the southern boundary between Danish and English territory that had been drawn up between King Alfred and the Danish king Guthrum in the 880s (Whitelock 1955: 380–1) for it suggests that with few exceptions the Danish settlement was confined to the north and the east of this boundary. More sophisticated analyses of the place-name evidence, however, have since shown the situation to be less straightforward.

Some Nordic hybrid names are compounds of the Old English generic tūn, a very general word for 'settlement', with a personal name of Nordic origin. Their distribution is shown by Fellows-Jensen (2012: fig. 21.1). While the majority of the actual settlements involved may have been established much earlier, the presence of the Nordic personal names shows that the dues and rights owing to the settlement must first have been transferred to a man with a Nordic name at some time after the three known partitions of land between the Danes in 876, 877, and 880. The earliest written references to such names are in four land transactions described in charters from the tenth century. The most significant features about the distribution of this type of name in the Danelaw are their comparative rarity in Lincolnshire, perhaps because the element tūn did not have time to become frequent there, while the high degree of anglicization of the Nordic personal names occurring in the names in East Anglia, for example Kitelbeorn in Kettlebaston and Thurstan in Thurston, suggests that there must have been close linguistic contact between the Danes and the English before the Danes lost control of that region in 917.

The hybrid tūn-names found in southern and western England, many of which are not recorded in Domesday Book, must bear names borne by Danish followers of King Cnut and his successors in the eleventh century. Many of these men have names containing the first element Thór- (from the name of the heathen god), for example Thorth in Durstone and Thorkel in Thruxton in Herefordshire, Thorferth in Thorverton in Devon and Thorlak in Thurloxton in Somerset. Hybrid names also spread north-west away from the Danelaw, for example Flík in Flixton in Lancashire. More striking are the sixty hybrid tūn-names in south-eastern Scotland, where there are no fewer than four names containing Orm and four containing Dolgfin (Nicolaisen 1967: 228, 231). The names in Scotland are analogical Scots-English formations reflecting an outwards movement from the Danelaw.

The Nordic element that occurs most frequently in Britain is bý, which can denote a settlement of almost any size or status but probably one which resulted from a re-naming after a redistribution of settlement (Fellows-Jensen 2006:101–3). The specifics of many of these names are Nordic personal names, presumably the names of the new holders of the rights and dues. There are at least 880 býs in England, Scotland, and the Isle of Man. There is, however, only one absolutely certain instance of such a re-naming, that noted in Æthelweard's comment in his tenth-century Chronicle that in 871 the town of Derby was called *Deoraby* by the Danes in replacement for its earlier English name *Northuuorthige* (Campbell 1962: 37; CDEPN: 184).

Most of the *bý*s are found where Danish settlement is to be expected, to the north and east of the Danelaw boundary. They are of particularly frequent occurrence in Leicestershire, Lincolnshire, and the North Riding of Yorkshire but are rare in East Anglia, which had come early under English control, with the exception of the marked cluster on the island of Flegg in Norfolk, which may have survived as a fortified Viking base with a strategic role in protecting commercial traffic between Norwich and the continental markets (Campbell 2001: 18–21; Abrams and Parsons 2004: 418). Most of the *bý*-names in the Danelaw proper were formed at the latest before the time of Domesday Book. Later the *bý*s penetrated across the Pennines, moving along the Eden valley towards Carlisle and spreading north from the Carlisle plain into Scotland and south from Carlisle along the coastal plain and then across the sea to the Isle of Man and perhaps back from there to southern Lancashire and Cheshire (Fellows-Jensen 1983: 54–5). In these areas they must be analogical formations coined at later dates. Since many of the *bý*-names in Scotland have exact parallels in the Danelaw, it also seems likely that such names were brought from there to Scotland by great landowners at one period or another (Fellows-Jensen 1989–90: 54–5; Taylor 2004: 72).

The second most common Nordic element to occur in England is *thorp*, which denotes a secondary settlement. There are at least 570 *thorp*s and these occur in roughly the same areas as the *bý*s in the Danelaw proper but the element has made little impression outside of it (Fellows-Jensen 2009: 43–5, fig. 1). There are, however, at least fifty-four names containing the cognate English element *throp* which form an attenuated tail running south-west from the Danelaw as far as Dorset. It has therefore been thought that *throp*-names in England may once have been more widespread and that the *thorp*-names simply reflect an adaptation of English names to fit the Danish pattern. I am, however, convinced that the *thorp*-names in the Danelaw are largely the result of Danish influence.

The last Nordic element I want to discuss is *thveit*, which originally denoted a clearing produced by cutting down trees or shrubland but was subsequently used of the settlement established on the sites. It is found in at least 267 names in England and Scotland (Fellows-Jensen 2014: fig. 10.4). The generic is certainly of Nordic origin but its distribution pattern is noticeably different from that of the Nordic elements discussed above. The only parts of the Danelaw where it is of frequent occurrence are the West Riding of Yorkshire and the well-wooded parts on the border between Derbyshire and Nottinghamshire. Although it must have been more widespread in the early Viking period, it would seem to have dropped out of use at an early date in East Anglia. In the Furness Fells in northern Lancashire there are several *thveit*-names which have Nordic specifics, for example *íkorni* 'squirrel' in Ickenthwaite, and although these names are first recorded after 1500, it seems likely that it was the Vikings or their descendants who first established the clearings to increase the area of arable land available (Fellows-Jensen 1985: 348–57). On the other hand, many of the *thveit*-names in northern England probably reflect the fact that after Danish had ceased to be spoken in the Danelaw, the language continued to be used in more isolated areas, enabling it to be absorbed into the local English dialects.

36.5 THE OLD ENGLISH PERIOD

The best map to reveal the early spread of English settlement is that published by Kenneth Jackson (1953: 220) showing the survival of Celtic river names, where Area I, including everything east of a line which runs from the Yorkshire Wolds to Salisbury Plain and the New Forest, is taken to show the approximate extent of English settlement in about 600 AD. This is because the only British river-names to survive there are those of large or medium-sized watercourses.

John Dodgson (1966: 5) was the first to note that names denoting natural features might well belong to the earliest period of English settlement and a study of the names recorded down to 731 confirms that such names are the ones of most frequent occurrence (Cox 1975–6). Margaret Gelling (1976: 835) has demonstrated that settlement names in areas of early Saxon occupation in Berkshire are topographical names in *ford*, *īeg*, *wella*, and *hamm*, and names originally denoting watercourses. All these names probably had a quasi-habitative significance and Gelling considers that they probably represent the take-over by the English of pre-existing British settlements.

The element *hām* meaning 'home(stead)' belongs to an early stratum of names in England, occurring twenty-one times in early records (Cox 1975–6). In south-east England place-names in *-hām* tend to be borne by settlements on the edges of areas of Romano-British settlement but while they sometimes seem to be contemporary with pagan burial sites, they also occur in areas where the pagan burial fashion had become obsolete (Dodgson 1973: 19). Barrie Cox (1972–3: 45–7) has confirmed that the names in *-hām* in the East Midlands and East Anglia can belong to the pagan Anglo-Saxon period, while Dodgson points out that further north such names in Cheshire probably reflect an English 'take-over' as late as in the seventh century.

Probably starting at a slightly later date than most of the names in *-hām* are those whose specifics are names in *-ingas* of English tribes or families, for example Nottingham, while tribal names standing alone, for example Hastings, which probably originally denoted districts rather than individual settlements, may point to an even later stage of fixed settlement. The groups involved were not uniform in size. Some gave names to very large territories that came to form significant economic units, for example the wapentake of Gilling, named from the *Gētlingas* in Yorkshire (CDEPN: 250), or the two areas in Essex which reflect the presence of the *Gingas* and the *Hrōthingas* (Bassett 1989: 22). In the territory of the Middle Saxons near London, however, the lands of the *Gillingas* in Ealing and the *Geddingas* in Yeading are quite small (Bailey 1989: 116–18). Perhaps the survival of these small groups long enough to ensure that their names became fossilized as place-names may reflect the fact that the presence of London hindered their consolidation into a kingdom.

Some of the other habitation names recorded in the early sources, namely those containing the generics *burh, ceaster*, and *wīc*, denote settlements established before the arrival of the English and will be discussed in later paragraphs, while the very few early names in *-tūn* are harbingers of the name-type that later became the dominant one in England. Map 12 in CDEPN (lxii), showing the *tūn*-names in 1086, and Map 52 in Udolph (1994: 699) combine to give some indication of the spread of this element. It is found in considerable numbers in most of England, although less frequently in the Saxon areas where other types of names had established themselves, and it even penetrated into Cornwall in the south-west and the Lake District in the north-west. A few of the many sub-groups of the names in *-tūn* deserve further comment.

The largest of these consists of the at least 823 names in *-ingtūn* (Fellows-Jensen 1996: 63). Most of these names seem to contain an earlier place-name in singular *-ing* based either on a personal name or an appellative or adjective (Arngart 1972), although other scholars prefer to look upon the *ing* in these names simply as a connective particle, possibly alternating with a genitive ending (Smith 1956b: 1, 291–3). While a few of the singular names in *-ing* in the south-west did not find their final form until after the Norman Conquest, most of the names would seem to have been coined well before that time, for 29 per cent of them are found in pre-Conquest sources and the personal names involved are often monothematic or hypocoristic names of the same type as are found in the older names in *-hām* and *-ingahām*. Many of the *-ingtūn* names are probably from the eighth century, while others must derive from the later period when the Anglo-Saxons were extending their boundaries westwards. It is interesting that there are also a number of *-ingtūn* names in the Pas de Calais in France which must have been coined by the beginning of the ninth century at the latest, since they are recorded in sources from the first decade of that century. They closely resemble the names in England and may well have been coined by settlers from Anglo-Saxon England on analogy with the names from south-east England. Another extension of the names in *-ingtūn* is to be seen in the north where they push out from Northumberland into Berwickshire and the Lothians, suggesting a date as late as the seventh century (Nicolaisen 2001: 95–6).

A significant group of *tūn*-names is that containing the *Kingstons* and related forms, sixty-eight in all (Bourne 2012: 264). The most frequently occurring form is *Kingston*, containing the Old English word *cyn(in)g* 'king'. Some forms contain the adjective *cyne* 'royal', while others such as *Conington* or *Coniston(e)* contain Nordic versions of the word for 'king'. Most of the settlements bearing the names are of a comparatively modest status and are hardly to be looked upon as royal residences. They became increasingly common in the course of the eighth century and were once thought to be of late coinage because they were likely to reflect a sophisticated social infrastructure, but since the term *cyninges tūn* occurs as early as in the seventh-century laws of Æthelberht and the ninth-century laws of Alfred denoting places where fines may be imposed, it has been argued convincingly that the distribution of such places at comparatively regular intervals along major highways suggests that they must have had a strategic significance as mustering points, sites of a local lock-up, or places where fresh horses, messengers, and escorts could be acquired (Hough 1997a: 55; Bourne 2012: 271).

36.6 The Roman Period

The Romans in Britain showed little interest in imposing new Latin names on existing localities. Most of the existing Celtic names that were of interest to them were employed in semi-latinized forms. That these forms can sometimes still be identified in the modern names suggests that the ruins of the settlements in question must have been sufficiently substantial for the English arrivals to have allowed the sites to develop into their future greatness. Only four Latin names survive for the over 600 villas the Romans are known to have constructed in Britain and the location of only one of these has been identified (*Sulloniacis* 'Sullonius' estate') at Brockley Hill in Middlesex (PNRB: 463). When the Roman army established forts in Britain, they regularly referred to them by the name of the unit in garrison. Sometimes, however, a fort might be referred to by a Latin descriptive name such as *Castra Exploratorum* 'camp of the scouts' at the place later called Netherby in Cumberland (PNRB: 302). Occasionally other types of building were referred to by a Latin name, for example the two places called *Salinis* 'at the salt-works' (PNRB: 451). The honorific title *Augusta* was conferred on the city of London in the fourth century for official use and the mint-mark AVG occurs on contemporary coins but the name dropped out of use in the post-Imperial period (PNRB: 260).

There are also a number of place-names which contain words of Latin origin that would seem to have been borrowed into English while spoken Latin was still current in Britain. There is a very useful summary by Margaret Gelling (1997: 63–86) of the most significant of these words. Particularly striking are the instances of the employment of the English word *wīc*, a loanword from Latin *vicus*, denoting the smallest unit of self-government in the Roman province, when compounded with Old English *hām*. Gelling argues convincingly that these compounds, which are found in Lowland Britain and generally close to a Roman road but avoiding the immediate vicinity of the most important towns, probably signified the centre of a land-unit, perhaps 'a small town'. Examples of other Latin loanwords borrowed in southern England are: *funta* 'spring, fountain' in Chalfont; *camp* < *campus* 'field, open space' in Campsey; *port* < *portus* 'harbour, port' in Portsmouth; as well as *ecles* < *ecclesia* 'church' in three instances of Eccles, one in Kent and two in East Anglia. The occurrence of this word for 'church' in the north-west, however, is more likely to reflect the influence of British Christianity (Cameron 1968: 87–92). Names containing the Latin word *castra* will be discussed below.

36.7 The Celtic Period

Since the surviving names of Celtic origin in England are comparatively few in number, it is useful to look at the place-names of English origin that contain an element that seems to point to Celtic settlements, namely those containing *w(e)alh* 'Welshman', genitive singular and nominative plural *w(e)ales* and genitive plural *w(e)ale*. Detailed research by Kenneth Cameron (1979–80: 1–46 with map) and Margaret Faull (1975: 20–44) has shown that in place-names this element normally denotes 'a Welshman' or 'a foreigner speaking a Celtic language' and not as in some literary sources 'a slave or servant'. The relevant names are fairly widely distributed over England with the exception of the extreme north of the country, where subsequent Nordic settlement may have eradicated such names. In southern England the habitation names containing *w(e)alh* seemed to Cameron to be outliers of English settlements and often to have correlations with Romano-British sites. In western areas from Devon in the south through to southern Lancashire in the north the settlements can hardly be earlier than from the eighth century and must simply reflect a longer survival of Celtic speakers there. The township of *Wales* in the south of the West Riding of Yorkshire, on the other hand, its name simply meaning 'the Welshmen', lies on an important boundary between Yorkshire and Derbyshire and must have denoted a surviving British presence here as late as the seventh century (Smith 1961a: 155). The survival of this name is perhaps to be compared with that of the name *Leeds* (< *Loidis*), earlier a district name, probably originally a folk-name denoting a Celtic tribe in the ancient British kingdom of Elmet (Smith 1961b: 124–5).

The fact that place-names denoting the presence of men of Celtic origin are so widespread in England hardly suggests that the Anglo-Saxons exterminated the British in the modern sense of that word, namely utter destruction, or even in the etymological sense of expulsion from the limits of a country. It seems more likely that while the invading Anglo-Saxons took over the running of existing estates and gave them new names, such of the British inhabitants as were willing to accept servile status as labourers or servants were allowed to stay put, while others may have established themselves in modest smallholdings on vacant land, some of which could well have received names such as *Walton* or *Walcroft*. Yet other Britons must have ventured further afield to the Celtic territories in the west.

Some major place-names pointing clearly to Roman settlements are those which later received the Old English element *c(e)aster* < Latin *castra* in final position. Strictly speaking these names are Old English formations but they are treated here because the English element seems to have acquired the meaning 'Roman town'. Since this word is not found in any other Germanic language, it must have been borrowed by the Anglo-Saxons after their arrival in England. The specific element in many of these names is a form of the Celtic name of either the town itself, for example *Mamucium* in Manchester, or the neighbouring river, for example *Danum* 'Don' in Doncaster (CDEPN: 395, 190). The names suggest the survival of visible remains of urban settlement.

The name of the capital city, London, however, is one of the few place-names from the Celtic period to survive in recognizable form. In its Latin locative form *Londinio* it is recorded not only in the Roman geographical sources but also in a graffito scratched on a second-century jug, probably as part of the address of a local wine-merchant.

The etymology of the name, however, remains uncertain in spite of much research (CDEPN: 379). The name of another great city, York, can hardly be said to survive in recognizable form but its development from Celtic times to the present day can be traced thanks to the abundant written sources (Fellows-Jensen 1998: 226–37). The Latin forms *Eburacum, Eboracum* reflect a British name in which the adjectival suffix *-āco* has been added to a British plant-term **Ebŭro* of uncertain meaning, perhaps 'yew-tree', to form a place-name with a collective sense 'place abounding in **ebŭr*'. This name was taken over by the military fortress built on the left bank of the Ouse but had probably originally denoted a pre-existing settlement. Subsequently the name was reinterpreted first by the Anglo-Saxons as a place-name *Eoforwīc* incorporating Old English *efor* 'wild boar' and *wīc* 'settlement' and then by the Vikings who substituted their own East Scandinavian form of the word for 'wild boar' **iūr* and later contracted the name to the form *York*.

In general it will be noted that Celtic place-names had a better chance of surviving in western parts of England closer to regions of Welsh settlement. In Lancashire, for example, we find *Wigan* and *Darwen*, in Cheshire *Tarvin* and *Macefen*, and in Devon *Trebick* and *Landkey*. Further to the east very few major place-names still reflect a Celtic presence. *Dover* is recorded in a Latin locative plural form *Dubris*, probably reflecting a British **Dŭbrās* meaning 'the waters' and referring to the stream here (CDEPN: 192). It has been noted that there are several places called Douvres in France. The survival of the name in Kent to the present-day, however, must reflect that it was the name of the Roman camp at this the closest crossing place to the Continent.

What do tend to survive in England are a number of Celtic words denoting topographical features which have been borrowed into English as loanwords and subsequently employed to coin place-names that were appropriate to the specific site. The British word *cumb*, for example, is used in its highly specialized sense of 'a short, broad valley with three steeply rising sides' all over England (Gelling and Cole 2000: 103–9). In Herefordshire and the south-west it is even frequent in the names of major places. The British word *crūg* is used in Old English of a 'hill, mound, tumulus'. It is of frequent occurrence in the south-west and also noted in Derbyshire as *Crich*, in Cheshire as *Critch*, and in Lancashire in *Croichlow* with the addition of an explanatory or tautological Old English *hlāw* 'mound' (Gelling and Cole 2000: 159–63). The element *cęd* 'wood, forest' is one of the commonest Celtic words in English place-names and rather widespread there, occurring in a Romano-British compound *Letocetum* (*Lichfeld* in Staffordshire), together with English elements in place-names such as *Cheadle* in Cheshire and *Cheetham* in Lancashire, and once exceptionally compounded with the Nordic element *stefna* 'administrative district' in *Kesteven* in Lincolnshire (Gelling and Cole 2000: 223–34). The element *penn* 'head, top, end' is also common in English place-names, occurring in the British compound **penn-cęd* 'wood's end' in *Penketh* in Lancashire, *Penkridge* in Cheshire, Shropshire, and Staffordshire and *Penge* in London, as well as in hybrid names such as *Pendle* and *Pendlebury* in Lancashire (Gelling and Cole 2000: 210–13).

36.8 The Old European Period

The Celts were not the indigenous population of England but an immigrant people who imposed themselves at some time in the first millennium on a sedentary population about whom we know very little. Bill Nicolaisen has compiled lists of the river-names of the British mainland that he considers are probably or possibly names that belong to what might be referred to as the Old European network (1957, 1971, 1982). These include the *Aire*, the *Ure*, the *Rye*, and the *Nidd* in Yorkshire, the *Wyre* in Lancashire, the *Carrant* in Gloucestershire, the *Carey* in Devon, and perhaps some of the extensive group of river names derived from the Indo-European root *tâ-/*tə-* 'to flow', for example *Team, Tame, Thames, Tone*, etc. With the present state of our knowledge there is little we can learn about the history of the period.

36.9 Conclusion

Some river names which do not seem to be of Celtic or Germanic origin may have been coined by the Old Europeans. Many more river names are certainly of Celtic origin. These occur most frequently in western England. The names of *London* and *York* seem to be of Celtic origin and earlier forms of the names of many of the settlements that developed into Romano-British towns are found in compounds with *-c(e)aster*. The frequency of occurrence of names of Celtic linguistic origin increases as we move westwards towards the areas where a Celtic population survived rather longer, in Wales even until the present day. None of the Latin name-forms coined by the Romans survive today with the exception perhaps of *Britannia* as the ceremonial name of the island of Britain. Two names found with classical forms in daily use have no direct link with the Romans. The modern name of *Pontefract* in Yorkshire is based on the Latin form *Pontefracto* 'broken bridge' of the stronghold built by the Norman lord who was entrusted by William the Conqueror with the task of quelling the English insurrection after the Conquest (CDEPN: 477), while *Morecambe*, a holiday resort in Lancashire, received this name in 1870 as an antiquarian revival of a name recorded on Ptolemy's map *c.*150 (PNRB: 420). The vast majority of the settlement names recorded in England are of English origin, although the distribution pattern of these is less dense in the areas in the east, where the Vikings settled in the Danelaw and displaced English names with Nordic ones, and in the west where the Celts withstood the English advance. The Normans established and named castles, particularly in frontier areas, and religious houses. Post-Norman names are comparatively rare but quite widespread and seem to result from efforts in the modern period to house a constantly increasing population.

....

CHAPTER 37

NAMES AND HISTORICAL LINGUISTICS

....

RICHARD COATES

37.1 NAMES AS LINGUISTIC DATA

....

THE status of proper names (henceforth just *names*) as data in historical linguistics has often been considered problematic, for distinct but intersecting reasons. First, at one level, names are linguistic objects; they can be simple words, compound and complex words, phrases, all with a particular phonological and orthographic shape dependent to a large degree on the language with which they are primarily associated.[1] In these respects they are just like their counterparts in a language's ordinary vocabulary and grammar. They can therefore be explained etymologically to the same extent as their counterparts, and (with reservations to be noted) used as evidence for linguistic changes to the same extent, especially for phonological changes, for the loss of vocabulary which formerly existed, and for changes in the meanings of words. But because of the haphazard survival of texts, or indeed any written material, from remote periods of time, it is not unusual for names to be the sole or principal evidence for some otherwise lost language, or for an earlier state of an existing one. In such cases a methodological decision needs to be made about whether names can be assumed to be representative of the language in question, and, where the historical background is particularly obscure, about whether they can permit that language to be identified. Names which constitute the only evidence for some language can only be interpreted through comparative study of the vocabulary of another language. Secondly, it is widely acknowledged that using names for these purposes can be contentious because, in addition to linguistic change of the sorts which affect ordinary vocabulary, names may undergo other changes which have to do with the special nature of names. The idea of such special changes is explored below, and their position in

---

[1] Not necessarily their language of origin: consider the 'English' name *London*, of pre-English origin.

historical argumentation evaluated. Thirdly, any study of this topic needs to acknowledge that the notion *name* itself is in one sense essentially historical. Names are what they are because they are produced from linguistic material either by a kind of semantic bleaching arising through usage in context (name *evolution*, evolution into a name), reinforced by phonetic attrition which is in part due to their special status; or by deliberate cancellation, at a point in time, of some aspects of the meaning of the lexis and grammar involved in their construction through being applied to an individual (name *bestowal*). Both sorts of *onymization* or becoming a name (bleaching of sense in and through usage, and deliberate cancellation of sense) are historical occurrences. Onymization can be viewed as a category of historical change on a par with *grammaticalization*, both profoundly affecting the way linguistic expressions perform the task of meaning in some context. Both, in their different ways, take lexical items out of what might be viewed as the core lexicon. Fourthly, while the relation between onomastics and general historical linguistics is necessary and intimate because names and vocabulary share properties, names may have a historical cyclicity of their own, from onymization of lexical expressions to settled name status to possible deonymization ((re)lexicalization) through tropes such as metaphor (*that was his personal Rubicon*) and the presentation of salient named individuals or their attributes as types as opposed to individuals (*this place could be an embryonic New York*; there are types of hat called *trilby, bowler,* and *stetson*, the first from the surname of a fictional character and the latter two from the surnames of men involved in their manufacture). A further historical consideration is that naming systems appear to evolve from favouring descriptively true labels for individual persons, places, or things to favouring arbitrary labels; on this, see further below.

The vast majority of names originate as referring expressions formed from ordinary vocabulary and therefore, in principle, have a discoverable etymology. But a distinction should be maintained between their *etymology*, the product of the purely linguistic business of identifying the elements and structures out of which they were formed, and their *motivation*, or the historical reason(s) for the application of a name to a particular contextualized person, place, or other individual of whatever category.

37.2 Names as Historical Evidence

Let us rehearse first of all the relationship that has evolved between name-study and historical linguistics. The main issues can be distinguished as the *microlinguistic* and the *macrolinguistic*.

37.2.1 Microlinguistics

The principal microlinguistic issue has been the status of names as evidence in reasoning about language change. The *Junggrammatiker* or *Neogrammarian* doctrine (following Osthoff and Brugmann 1878) was that each sound-change operates regularly. That means first that it proceeds without excepting any words containing the affected sounds in the relevant phonetic environment, subject to well-understood but relatively minor qualifications such as the intervention of analogy or of potentially troublesome homophony to reverse or prevent its application; and secondly that it must be understood as proceeding more or less simultaneously across the entire vocabulary of a language, and therefore below the level of perceptibility by its speakers. This doctrine immediately calls into question the status of names as evidence. It has always been known that names are semantically, that is synchronically, different from regular vocabulary to some extent, a point which will be developed in full in section 37.4. Since they are therefore abnormal linguistic objects, what kind of light can they shed on the behaviour of normal ones? Should evidence for linguistic change derived from names be discarded, or at least treated with caution? The issue which has been thought troublesome is that names often seem to show evidence for particular changes appreciably before those changes are observable in the general vocabulary, and that perhaps there are even changes which are restricted to names (Colman 1992: 59–67; Clark 1995 [1991]: 150–2). A change operating under such conditions, which are not purely phonological because being a name is stipulated as a condition, would run counter to the Neogrammarian hypothesis of exceptionless sound-change.

As an example of the application of such a condition, Fran Colman (1992: 15) notes the possibility that a personal name element can be exempt from a sound-change. She reminds us of Alistair Campbell's (1959: §200.1, note 4) observation that the name-element Ælf- in the West Saxon dialect of Old English seems to be systematically excepted from the general change [æ] > [ie] before [l] followed by another consonant; it is presumably preserved by being identified with the [æ] which is preserved in other phonetic environments, for example in æppel 'apple'. But this idea is strange because it suggests that a pronunciation which has become 'impossible' is preserved only in names. Imagine the regular disappearance of preconsonantal [r] in some accent except in place-names; it would vanish in barking but not in Barking. If the phenomenon Colman describes is real, we can perhaps interpret it as an attempt to maintain or mimic a conservative local pronunciation at the place so named. Such things do really happen, but the problem is not whether names preserve sounds which are historically out of place and out of time, but whether they are preserved in certain names: the exceptions lack systematicity, and in any case they are constrained by the phonology of the accent which is receiving the problematic pronunciation.

Recognizing that sound-change is a matter of geographical ebb and flow, it is possible to use place-name material in support of claims about the former geographical distribution of certain phonological features. The conspicuous voicing of initial fricatives of the English south and west all but disappeared in the living language in the twentieth century, but the persistence of such place-names as Yellow (Somerset) and Zeal (Devon) gives a clue to its former extent, which has also been perseveringly traced in personal name and place-name data by Gillis Kristensson, whose survey was published between 1967 and 2002. Phonological survivals of the Yellow kind appear to exemplify onomastic exceptions to sound-changes, but they can readily be seen for what they are: they are accidentals, that is, features of individual names, as seen from the fact that other names in south-western counties of England now have 'standard' initial /f/: *Frome, Foxcombe, Fiddington, Farway*. Examples such as these also make it clear that the retention process is more a sociolinguistic one than a psycholinguistic one. Regional initial /v/ and /z/ can be preserved by any speaker who already has both /f/ and /v/, /s/ and /z/, contrasting in initial position: that is, a speaker of any English accent whose vocabulary includes words of for example French (*value, village, zest*), Latin (*valid, vast*), or Greek (*zone, zeal*) origin. Any south-western speaker who acquired a non-regional pronunciation, that is who pronounced *fast* as /faːst/ instead of /vaːst/ would also have such initial contrasts and therefore be able to retain archaic pronunciations such as *Vellow*.

37.2.2 Macrolinguistics

The historical macrolinguistic importance of names resides in the fact that names may provide the only evidence for the previous existence of some language, or for the existence of a known language in a previously unsuspected area. In the British Isles, for example, it is clear that there are long-established names which cannot at present be explained from the known vocabulary of the local historically attested Celtic and Germanic languages, or Latin, or French. They include, for example, the place-name *Rame* in Cornwall, the hill name *The Cheviot*, the island name *Islay*. and the river name *Humber*. What is it reasonable to do with them? They may be examined to see whether they share features which might lead to the conclusion that they were formulated in one or more languages whose characteristics can be defined by the onomastic evidence. Such a language may or may not be identifiable. It may be possible to ascribe it to some historically or prehistorically known group of people, or to a known linguistic lineage; thus some names in the British Isles have been ascribed to Pictish (Sutherland 1994: 200–3; Nicolaisen 1996) or to North-West Semitic (Coates 2012b), both of which ideas are controversial, at least to some degree.

The same sorts of reasoning can be applied in the case of names which, although formulated in a relevant language whose characteristics are well known, appear to be out of place. For example, the very small scatter of apparently Cornish place-names in Devon can be taken as evidence that Cornish (or its ancestor) was once spoken east of the river Tamar; more broadly, it is universally accepted on the basis of place-name evidence that present-day England was once an area where British Celtic (the ancestor of Cornish and Welsh) was spoken, and fortunately that chimes with everything which is known from works of history from the most ancient times onwards. The important methodological point here is that there is no textual, that is non-onomastic, evidence for British Celtic at the relevant period except in a few inscriptions discovered in recent decades in Bath and Uley (Tomlin 1988, 1993); names otherwise constitute all the evidence. On a similar basis, and with varying amounts of other historical evidence in support, we know that Welsh was once spoken in western Herefordshire and Shropshire (see Coates and Breeze 2000: maps) and a language very closely related to it (generally distinguished as *Cumbric*) in southern Scotland and northern England (Jackson 1953: 9–10, 219), and that Irish was spoken in Wirral, alongside Scandinavian (e.g. Coates 2011). It is remarkable also that there is not much textual evidence for the use of Old Scandinavian (Old Danish and Norwegian) in England; apart from works of historical report, much of the very considerable amount of evidence derives from names, and largely from place-names, although there is also dialect vocabulary from this source recorded during the modern period. Elsewhere, much has been made of the Roman-period place-name *Iliberris* near Granada (represented by modern *Elvira*). Basque scholars have pointed out that, taking into account the effects of known phonetic changes, this is the ancestral form of Basque *hiri berri* 'new city' (Trask 1997: 38–9), and that it must have been available during the existence of the Roman empire. We must either conclude that Basque was once spoken or written at Elvira, far from anywhere where it is known to have been used, or that we are staring at a remarkable coincidence.

Such matters are part of the staple diet of historical onomastics in continental Europe. The historical extent of Celtic in central and southern Europe and western Asia, as revealed by its place-name residue, has been thoroughly re-examined recently by Patrick Sims-Williams (2006); the position and movement through the centuries of the great linguistic boundaries, for example between the Slavic and Germanic families, between Germanic and Romance, and between Romance and Basque, remain subject to lively study.

Onomastic evidence may be used in the same way at the level of dialect. It has recently been pointed out (Coates 2006c: 9–10) that the English generic place-name element *chester*, meaning '[remains of a] Roman walled town' (later also applied to other structures), is phonologically anomalous because it occurs in place-names throughout England even though its form is appropriate only to an origin in strict West Saxon Old English and is therefore not expected to occur in the Midlands or North. But it does, for example in *Chester*-le-Street (Co. Durham) and *Manchester* (Lancashire). It is clear from such examples that understanding the geographical spread of some microlinguistic feature may require an element of cultural interpretation. Some genuinely highly localized linguistic features found (or so far found) only in place names in the south-east of England, some phonological, some lexical, have been plotted in Coates (2007). These matters mean that names can be understood as the footprints of a dialect, preserved as if archaeologically. They can be taken as proxies for the excavated artefacts of particular cultures to the extent that bearers of a culture and users of a language may be equated: a problematic issue.

37.3 Names as Linguistically Special in Relation to Change

An issue alluded to above is whether there can be sound-changes whose operation is limited to names, or which operate in names earlier, or more radically, than in other words (Colman 1992: 59–67; Clark 1995 [1991]: 150–2). As far as place-names are concerned, it seems inescapable that changes of a reductive kind are more frequent and more radical in names than in the common vocabulary. The record includes such notorious examples as /ˈʊlzəri/ Woolfardisworthy (Devon), /ˈheɪzbrə/ Happisburgh (Norfolk), /ˈemzlə/ Helmsley (North Riding of Yorkshire), /ˈɪlsn/ Ilkeston (Derbyshire) and /ˈaːrnɪʃ/ Hardenhuish (Wiltshire), some now obsolete (Forster 1986). Strictly speaking, these have evidential value only if it can be shown that phonologically parallel expressions in the relevant local dialect which are *not* names do not reduce to the same extent, and such comparative evidence is by no means easy to acquire because names are not necessarily structured like ordinary words and phrases. Nevertheless the notion is widely believed to be true, on the basis of an argument from first principles, which is presented here in a simplified form but overlooking some difficulties. Consider the word *pen*. As an English lexical item, it needs to be kept distinct from *pan, pin, pun, pain, pawn, pine*, etc. Precision as regards the articulation of its vowel is therefore crucial. Now take the place-name *Penn* (Staffordshire; Horovitz 2005: 433). No such precision is required since there are no phonologically similar English place-names (and such as there are are overseas, far distant from Penn and probably unknown to many of the conversational participants who mention Penn, such as for instance the village in Greece called *Pan*, or *Pernes* in the Pas-de-Calais as spoken by an English-speaker). Therefore, in principle, the articulation of the vowel is free to wander into the space of other vowels without compromising successful communication. Something like this may account for orthographic developments such as that seen in the name *Wilmington* (Sussex; Mawer and Stenton 1930: 412–13), which appears in the documentary record with <i>, <e>, and <u> in the first syllable[2] before the period during which the administrative standardization of names became effective. The development of names may also be affected by the principle of phonological sufficiency. In a historically complex name such as most English ones are, the job of identifying a place unambiguously in some context is likely to be done before the utterance of the full name is complete. If the speaker says *I'm going to Leintwardine*, the hearer will have probably established where the speaker is going with reasonable probability by the time s/he hears the first /n/, especially if they are conversing in Herefordshire where the village of this name lies, and with certainty by the /w/. Any material after what psycholinguists call the *decision point* (Marslen-Wilson 1987), which will usually be unstressed in English names (including *Leintwardine*), can be articulated indistinctly or even lost without seriously affecting the success of communication unless the hearer is a tiresome pedant (allowing deafness as an excuse). The local alternant 'Hunston' for the town of *Hunstanton* (Norfolk) shows the theory in action, as does, even more radically, the deliberate abbreviation exemplified in /brɪz/ for *Brislington* in Bristol.

However, it is hard to sustain the idea that there are really sound-changes whose operation is literally restricted to names. Clark (1995 [1991]: 152) prefers the formulation

---

[2] This distribution of letters is often evidence for etymological /y/, but the first element of this name is believed to be the Old English male given name *Wilma*.

that names may be subject to what she calls 'the unchecked operation of general native tendencies', that is processes (usually the consequences of rapid speech, the attempt to achieve 'high speed performance with low speed machinery', as Alvin Liberman and his collaborators put it in 1967: 446) that play out less vigorously in expressions other than names. Clark uses this to account for the radical consonant cluster reductions seen after the first, stressed, vowel (and no doubt after the decision point) in certain place-names like *Exeter* (from recorded Old English *Exanceaster* 'Exe *ceaster, ceaster* on the [river] Exe') and formerly also in another *ceaster* name, *Cirencester* (once pronounced /ˌsɪsɪtə(r)/ 'Sissiter'). In these names, a process of consonantal dissimilatory loss affecting a succession of [s] (in combination with other processes) takes place, but with more drastic effects than are seen in English words where, for example, a succession of [r] may be dissimilated by the simple loss of the first one (*library, February*).

Some unexpected developments may be ascribed, as with exceptional cases in ordinary vocabulary, to analogy with other lexical items. An original Old English *Herebeorhtingas* in Sussex (Mawer and Stenton 1930: 325) seems to have been influenced by *harp* as early as the thirteenth century to yield Early Modern English forms like *Harpings*. In addition to arbitrary influence from often irrelevant words, place-names may be affected by names of nearby places, as in the case of the convergence of *Misterton* (Somerset), from Old English **mynster-tūn*, and *Mosterton* (Dorset), from Old English **Mortes þorn*, two miles apart, and a collection of other pairs discussed in Coates (1987).

37.4 BECOMING A NAME—NAMES AS HISTORICAL OBJECTS

An important fact is that ordinary referring expressions may become proper names. That is, they may evolve through repeated usage in such a way that users no longer access their lexical and grammatical content in order to achieve successful reference. This must be true, otherwise traditional historical onomastics, which seeks to explain obscure names by relating them to their etymological (lexical and grammatical) source, would be impossible and unthinkable. Expressions such as *The Rocky Mountains* or *The Dead Sea* or *The Russian Revolution* or *The English National Opera* might be names for some users (those who do not access their lexical content in order to achieve successful reference in some context), arguably not names for others (those who do access their lexical content in order to achieve it), and variably names for yet others (those who sometimes access their lexical content). Such expressions may be on the way to becoming names, if they are not names already. But it may really be an either–or matter. It has been argued elsewhere (e.g. Coates 2005) that once a user has used an expression as a name (i.e. has used it to refer *onymically*), it is improbable that, under normal circumstances, that user will ever again use it *semantically* (i.e. with its full etymological source expression dictating the manner in which it refers), allowing perhaps for a brief transitional period. This is because semantic reference is mediated by lexical and grammatical meaning, and its processing costs must therefore be higher. Zipf's Law (Zipf 1949), or an analogue of it, requires us to believe that the processing systems of language-users will apply the least effort required to achieve their communicative goal of successful reference in context. There is a hypothetical neurophysiological consequence: if onymic reference involves bypassing lexical meaning, there must be a physical neural route which is in some sense less costly to use.

These considerations indicate that names as terms conventionally used to refer to, and therefore denoting, individuals may arise by *evolution* amounting to semantic bleaching. But they can also arise by *bestowal*, that is the deliberate creation, at a point in time, of a relation between an individual and a name. The crucial factor in both cases is that the process cancels or renders inapplicable any sense that the expression previously had, gradually in the case of evolution or instantly in the case of bestowal. Proper names thus belong to a category distinct from other linguistic objects because they have undergone a historical process of semantic evisceration of one of these two types. It is important to note that this does not mean the sense cannot ever be recovered during conversational processing, for a range of possible purposes, and this matter will be returned to below.

Names may belong to an existing culturally sanctioned name-stock and be bestowed on new individuals. The name *Richard* had already long been in existence when it was bestowed on its many living bearers. Names may also be created afresh for an individual. The name *Beyoncé* was apparently novel when bestowed on the well-known singer, although altered from her mother's pre-marriage surname.

Names may, then, evolve from non-onymic expressions (as explored and exemplified in Coates 2000, 2012a). They may also be coined directly with no lexical antecedents or out of existing lexical material and bestowed upon an individual. Bestowal is always a culturally significant act—consider the care which parents typically deploy when choosing names for their children, and the reasonings they may use to justify that choice—and can be especially loaded or contentious when existing linguistic material is re-used. An instructive, if extreme, recent case involves the designation *the former Yugoslav Republic of Macedonia*, which was agreed internationally for certain official purposes in 1993 as a way of referring to the newly independent European state. The ponderous expression was created with the intention of defusing the diplomatic tensions surrounding the proposal that the state should simply be called *Macedonia*. An international understanding required that the state name did not consist of the historic region name *Macedonia*, because Greece objected to this simple designation on historical-political grounds, and that *the former Yugoslav Republic of Macedonia* should be officially understood as a 'provisional designator' rather than in any diplomatic sense the name of the state. This point was symbolized by the painstakingly chosen lower-case <f> in *former*. There is a further issue. *The former Yugoslav Republic of Macedonia* looks meaningful with the exception of the embedded region name which occupies final position in the expression, to interpret which requires philological knowledge. The fact that it otherwise consists of ordinary words carrying their normal senses ought to mean that from the linguistic point of view, too, the full expression is not a name, and viewed from that perspective the capital <R> in *Republic* might be judged misleading. The expression was evidently translatable in every detail (compare the Macedonian поранешна Југословенска Република Македонија, *poranešna Jugoslovenska Republika Makedonija*, equally with a lower-case <п>, <*p*>, in the word meaning 'former'). But the state was often referred to by the (English) acronym *FYROM* (note, not *fYRoM* or *fYroM*), which was used as if a name alongside *Macedonia*, for example on maps such as Google Earth. So there was unclarity, from the linguistic perspective, about the properhood or otherwise of the expression.

The discussion of *Macedonia/FYROM* focuses the idea that fully transparent and translatable expressions are not names in the strictest sense. It may seem perverse to claim that names as such lack sense in those cases where they remain lexically and grammatically transparent. But this claim is obviously true. The village of Humberstone (Lincolnshire, England) was transparently named from a historically attested stone marking by convention the mouth of the river Humber. Its usefulness as a name for the village has not been compromised by the disappearance of the stone, and would not be compromised if the mouth of the river Humber shifted under changing tidal conditions. Knowledge of the stone or the river is not crucial to refer to the place successfully or to understand such a reference. Historical knowledge about the place-name counts for nothing conversationally or logically; so also for the inhabited places called *Newbridge*, *Stonehouse*, *Blackwood*, and so on. A Spanish woman named *(María de los) Dolores* '(Mary of the) sorrows' is not required literally to bear a burden of sorrow, whether her own or the Virgin Mary's; the relationship between the woman and her name is more complex than that, and, of course, culturally loaded and set about with historically contingent doctrines about the relationship between human beings and the supernatural. The name's meaning of 'sorrows' is historical, that is etymological, but as a linguistic entity the name carries no such sense; if it did, *Dolores is happy* would be both grammatically and semantically contradictory, whether in English or Spanish. In the face of this kind of evidence, we must conclude that any apparent sense in names is not really sense but (correct or incorrect) etymological understanding, which is not the same. Sense and etymology are kept apart by the logical security or insecurity of the inferences which they allow. *A stone* or *the stone* is what is perceived by the senses, whilst a name including -*stone* does not necessarily reveal anything comparable; today's Humberstone is not a stone. In names, a transparent etymology amounts in linguistic terms to a conveyed meaning, not an asserted one: that is, it is a meaning with no secure logical status, but one which is merely suggested, and therefore *available* in principle for translation or other sorts of manipulation whilst not being *required* for the primary task of referring.

On the basis of examples like this, 'What does a name mean?' proves to be a misleading question, if it is intended to be understood synchronically. A name *means* in that it denotes whatever it is used to refer to, but it and its constituents lack sense. 'How does a name mean?' is a better question, and that is the only question of synchronic linguistic importance: it means through establishing reference to an individual in a context, and making that link permanent through repeated use. The 'How?' question is thus to be understood as 'How does a name identify a referent in a context of use?' The answer is 'Through shared knowledge of an arbitrary but stable and rigid association of a linguistic form with an individual'. The corresponding diachronic question is: 'What did a name mean?' (i.e. 'What sense did it have?')—note that, crucially, the verb is in the past tense, which acknowledges the disappearance of sense as definitional in onymization, the transition to being a name.

Where does this position regarding transparent names leave expressions such as *The United Nations*, or *The Houses of Parliament*, or *The Big Friendly Giant*, a character in a story by Roald Dahl (1982)? They are lexically and grammatically transparent, but are they names in any sense, as the use of capital letters seems, by convention, to suggest? They have become names if they achieve reference successfully through some means other than the literal, compositional, interpretation of their lexis and grammar. If they do this, it is through the historical process of semantic bleaching referred to above. It is hard to say to what extent they do, but that they MAY do is guaranteed in at least some cases by the alternative use of acronyms (*The UN, The BFG*) which obscure access to the lexical content without permanently closing it off. In *The Houses of Parliament*, it would not be difficult to argue that *house* is being used with a lexically abnormal denotation specific to this and similar namelike expressions such as *The White House*, that is, here it does not denote a building whose major purpose is a dwelling. These are considerations which would support the idea that transparent expressions with apparently normal structures may become names, and allow the same privilege to apparently general but in fact monodenotational expressions such as the institutional designations *The Eat & Drink Company* or *The Open University*, and to expressions which are normally pragmatically monoreferential in the context in which they are uttered, such as the designations *Faculty Board* or *Finance and General Purposes Committee*, whose properhood is symbolized in English not only by capitalization but also by the same historical ellipsis of the definite article as is found in other expressions which are indisputably names in English, such as *(The) Gambia* and *(The) Ukraine*.

37.5 EVOLUTION OF NAMING SYSTEMS

Many individuals fall into categories of nameable (persons, places, geographical features, institutions, and so on), and the range of nameables is to some extent culturally variable. It is possible to suggest a general principle guiding the evolution of naming systems for nameables. Whenever a new category of nameables is created, naming strategies for members of that category are likely to develop in the same way, a point illustrated in chapter 46 in this handbook 'Railway Locomotive Names and Train Names'. The names of the prototypes of such new nameables will tend to play on the *essential* characteristics of the individuals in question. In the case of steam-powered locomotives, this involved first names including words for fire, steam, coal, and the like, or words alluding to these in some more oblique way, permitting the policy of transferring names from other categories of nameable which offered analogies in the shape of tropes such as metaphors and metonyms. If a prototype is successful, it will give rise to mass-produced copies, as a result of which the essential features of the prototype individuals are no longer remarkable. If naming is maintained as a policy, individualization according to less well-defined criteria becomes necessary in order to maximize the possibility of successful reference. For locomotives, at least, new name-types were created by switching from essential features to other salient features of the name-sources (e.g. from allusive reference to supernatural beings associated with fire to supernatural beings of any description). A consistent development of this new policy direction permits class-naming with no allusions at all to essential features of the machines. This does not create problems of reference, however, because, as established above, in order to be successful as a name a name-form does not need to be interpretable, that is to have sense: an expression which is free of sense and/or arbitrary in form works perfectly well as a name. Names can therefore arise which are examples of types having little, or nothing at all, to do with essential attributes of the relevant objects, and this has often been achieved by transfer from other types of nameable. Locomotives came to be named after planets, directors of railway companies, national heroes, RAF airfields, and so on, and also adopted taxonyms (e.g. the species-'names' of natural kinds, like wild birds, which are really ordinary lexical items, not names). Development stopped at this point, however; there is no trace of the linguistically random naming which is a perfectly conceivable next step: that is the creation of names which are grounded neither in the onomastic practices used for other nameables (persons, places, etc.), nor in taxonyms.

This whole development schema can be illustrated, somewhat speculatively in part, using place-names. It might be thought that the earliest names for places (in the broadest sense, including those of geographical features as well as inhabited places) were descriptions of the places in question, for example of their appearance or their ownership; or were transferred by an obvious metonymy from some adjacent feature, as when an inhabited place is named from an adjacent river or hill. The passage of time allows for the persistence of a name beyond the moment when it rests on an essential characteristic such as an assertion of ownership: for instance after an owner's death. At such a point it becomes essential only in a historical way, and since history may well be forgotten, the name is from then on synchronically unmotivated, and, for a new generations of oblivious users, arbitrary, although perhaps retaining some of the characteristic lexical and grammatical shape of a place-name in their language. Equally, phonological change may distort the linguistic characteristics of a name beyond recognition. At one or other of these points, and as places proliferate, any overriding requirement that a place-name should convey information about a place's essence has vanished, and places may be named in one of several increasingly arbitrary ways: by the commemoration of other places by name-transfer, by the commemoration of other nameables such as people by simple application of their names as place-names (i.e. rather than by building a person's name into a place-name template, for example *Lafayette* (Louisiana, USA) as compared with *Fayetteville* (North Carolina, USA) with the place-name forming element -*ville*), or by the application of a name which is on a spectrum of arbitrariness stretching from an incident name to a name which is a pure invention. All of the latter stages of such a development can be illustrated easily from a consideration of the place-names of North America. The oldest and most essential types of naming do not disappear, but reduce as a proportion of the names which are newly given. In the English-speaking world, similar patterns of development can be discerned in the history of naming from surnames to rock music band names to commercial business names.

37.6   THE ETYMOLOGY OF NAMES

Regardless of the route by which a name came to denote an individual, one of the central tasks of historical onomastics is to recover the original form and sense of the name as a linguistic object, and another is, where possible, to establish the motivation for its application in individual cases. This widely practised discipline leads to the creation of, for example, academically respectable historical place-name surveys like the Survey of English Place-Names (1924–) and dictionaries of names of all kinds, such as the *Cambridge Dictionary of English Place-Names* (Watts 2004), the *Dictionary of Football Club Nicknames in Britain and Ireland* (Tyas 2013), the *Dictionary of American Family Names* (DAFN), or the book which includes a dictionary of attested Austrian cow-names (Reichmayr 2005), right through to the many books and web-sites purporting to explain 'baby-names'. Place-name studies tend towards an ideal of explaining both the etymology and the motivation of a name. In works dealing with personal names, especially given names, the point of the enterprise is to give an etymological explanation of individual names as types or *proprial lemmas* (in the sense introduced by Van Langendonck 2007b: 84–102), irrespective of their culturally guided, but tending towards arbitrary, application to individuals.

The most widespread use of historical linguistics in onomastics, then, is the use of knowledge of past states of a language to establish the etymology of a name. The best developed branch of this endeavour is historical *toponomastics* or the scientific study of place-names, although it applies also to personal names, and in principle to any other nameables. The difficulty of this task depends on the complexity of the linguistic heritage of the region in question. Before the arrival of Europeans, New Zealand was exclusively Māori-speaking, and even though this language has only been recorded for the past 200 years or so, it is relatively easy to establish the etymology of, for example, most Māori place-names, even if they might go back 1,000 years to the original Māori landtaking.[3] Much of Western Europe, by contrast, has a heavily layered history involving as we dig down, in some places, successively Romance, Germanic, Celtic, and pre-Celtic languages, and it may sometimes be hard to establish in what language a name was formulated, let alone what it originally meant. For example, the name of the city of Toulouse in France remains unexplained, and of uncertain relation to that of Tolosa in the Basque Country. It has only recently been reasserted with relative certainty that the name of Bern, the capital of Switzerland, is a transferred and

---

[3] See for example New Zealand History (n.d.), which lists 1,000 Māori place-names.

germanized form of that of Verona in Italy (Schneider and Blatter 2011: 87–90), rather than a name formed locally in a Celtic or Germanic language, and even now there are reasons inspired by a local archaeological find for a niggling doubt.[4] An overlay of Scandinavian or English has often made the interpretation of certain Scottish and Irish names dependent on the survival of particular local pronunciations or on historical evidence preserved in manuscripts written in languages other than that of a name's probable origin. Such a situation is repeated in any country affected by the immigration of colonists.

A consistent methodology for place-name study has been established, however difficult it may be to implement in such circumstances. It is necessary to make a collection of a representative sample of the recorded spellings of a name, especially the oldest available, and to apply knowledge of languages known or suspected of having been spoken in the relevant area, taking into account what is known of that language's lexical, morphological, and phonological history, the relation of its phonology to the history of its orthography, and, where relevant, the way it has treated material copied ('borrowed') from other languages.

Some solutions are quite straightforward.[5] The name of Lincoln (England) is a transparent continuation of the recorded Roman-period name *Lindum Colonia*, consisting of the Latin word *colonia* 'veterans' settlement' coupled with a latinized version of British Celtic **lindon* 'lake', with some mild phonetic reduction which took place in the post-Roman and Anglo-Saxon period. Good motivation for this is provided by the large lake at the place. Oxford is recorded as *Oxnaforda* in about 925 AD. This is a good match for an Old English *ox(e)na ford* 'oxen (genitive plural) ford' in the dative singular required after the preposition *to*. The dative singular of nouns in the relevant class has the normalized early form *-æ*, and *-a* is generally reckoned to be acceptably close to this. Other early spellings are consistent with this. That is the etymology; its motivation may be less clear. The analyst's view of how the two words are to be understood together may lead to the decision to offer the gloss 'ford of the oxen' (whatever that might imply) or the even vaguer 'oxen ford', where the nature of the link is left inexplicit. There may be irresolvable ambiguities. Coventry is *Cofentreo* in about 1060, indicating derivation from the words *cofa*, a weak noun (here in the genitive singular) meaning 'inner chamber; recess in a hillside', or a male personal name of the same form, and *trēo(w)* 'tree'. There may be a need to resort to speculative hypotheses which are even less testable. The early spellings for Ipswich, such as *Gipeswic* in 1086, show that the second element is Old English *wīc* 'specialized place, trading station'. The first does not match any recorded Old English words, but tentative progress can be made: it is left to the analyst's ingenuity to suggest a possible, but unrecorded, relative of the verb *gipian* 'to gape, yawn', with reference to the wide estuary here, or an element consistent with the apparent genitive

---

[4] An artefact was recovered in 1984 bearing an inscription partly resembling the name of Bern, *Brenodor*, from a context long predating the historical relevance of Verona to the area of Bern (Schneider and Blatter 2011: 280), but the similarity may well be coincidental.

[5] In what follows, the documentary evidence is taken from the relevant volumes of SEPN (1924–) or from Watts (2004).

singular of a noun of a strong declension, such as an unrecorded personal name *Gip* or *Gipi*. At the far end of the scale of difficulty is a name like the extensively recorded *Worcester*, which is found in such morphologically inconsistent forms as *Uegorna cestre*, *Wigranceastre*, and *Uuegrinancæstir* in eleventh- and twelfth-century copies of Anglo-Saxon period documents. The parallel records of a Latin name, *Uueogorna civitate* and similar, confirm that the second English element must be *ceaster* '[remains of a] Roman walled town', rendered by *civitas* in Latin. The first has been interpreted as an earlier, pre-English, name for the town, or for some nearby geographical feature like the Wyre Forest, which may be etymologically identical with it, but the forest does not in modern times stretch as far as Worcester, and that fact weakens the case for one possible motivation of the name. It has also been taken as a folk-name, that is a tribal name, possibly deriving from the supposed geographical name. The nearest parallel appears to be the name of at least one river in ancient Gaul, *Vigora*, which has no obvious Celtic origin. However, this does not appear to relate to the Roman name of Worcester, believed to be *Vertis*, and the meaning, and even the source language, of *Vigora* is unknown. No further speculation about *Worcester* can ignore these carefully assembled linguistic hints; something constructive can be said about it, but for the present, the trail has a dead end.

Over and above considerations of etymology, place-names may change for reasons other than normal phonetic evolution. The substitution of one name for another may be a matter of politics, demography, and sociolinguistics, as with the interchange between Lithuanian *Vilnius* and the related Polish *Wilno*. But substitution is often not a matter of linguistics at all, but of culture and politics, as for example with the replacement of native names in North America by European ones, or the replacement of historic names in Russia after the revolution of 1917 and their partial restoration after the political changes of 1989.

The etymology of personal names, both given names and surnames, may also be investigated, using broadly similar methodology to the one outlined for place-names. With these, the motivation for their application to a particular individual also becomes a pressing matter. The etymology of *Miriam, Mary, Marie, Maria, Mari*, and *Moira* can be ultimately traced to a Hebrew source. But each is a name formulated in a particular language, and each carries different cultural baggage. They may cross cultural boundaries, and within some receptive culture these are not variants but synchronically distinct names, applicable according to the choice of those privileged to name children. As with other categories of nameable, an evolution may be traced in some cultures, including English, from more transparent to more arbitrary given names, let us say from *Lēofwine* 'dear' + 'friend' in Old English to the synchronically obscure *Lola*.

37.7 CONCLUSION

Names are linguistic objects which can play a large role in elucidating history, for example ancient folk-presences and folk-movements. They are one source of primary evidence for earlier phases of known languages, and may represent the only evidence for otherwise unknown ones. They have a strongly historical nature, in that the creation or the application of a name to an individual is an act rooted in a particular moment in time, and that name may carry a load of cultural and historic meanings which may be called up for a range of purposes, including justifying labelling an individual with that name. At the same time, names are detached from history in their primary role as referring expressions, but in that role they are subjected, through conversational usage, to the normal pressures of linguistic, especially phonetic, change.

CHAPTER 38

··

NAMES AND LANGUAGE CONTACT

··

BERIT SANDNES

38.1 INTRODUCTION

··

NAMES offer interesting insights into linguistic processes in language contact areas. Place-names are likely to be among the first items to be borrowed when people speaking different languages meet, since they do not need to be understood. The names function as labels for places which can be singled out by pointing at them, meaning that only a minimum of communication is needed. The widely-travelled Vikings adopted such names as *Apardjon* (Aberdeen), *Marselia* (Marseille), and *Dyrakksborg* (Durazzo). This does not by any means imply that place-names are always borrowed in contact situations. In principle, any group faced with the place-names of another group may choose either to ignore the names or to adopt them, with varying degrees of linguistic adaptation.

Personal names tend to follow broader cultural influences and the exchange of personal names is not restricted to direct contact situations. One example is the rapid spread of Christian names in areas converting to Christianity. In more recent times, English names have spread around the world as a result of colonization and the later impact of English-language popular culture. All names may function as indications of contact, although there is a certain chronological difference. Place-names give a diachronic picture, indicating which cultures have actually been present in an area through time. Personal names are less dependent on direct contact or presence, and although the personal names of a people reflect historical influences, trends in personal names also reflect which cultures are dominant at the moment.

The aim of this chapter is to give a background to contact linguistics and contact onomastics, focusing on place-names. It should be pointed out that contact onomastics is not an established discipline with an accepted method of approach. Rather, it started out as individual studies of place-names in contact situations, such as Scandinavian names in Britain or Slavic names in Germany. Weinreich's (1953) influential work *Languages in Contact* formed the basis for contact linguistics as well as sociolinguistics, and modern studies of place-names in contact areas often include ideas from contact linguistics.

38.2 DEFINING CONTACT ONOMASTICS

Studies of place-names in contact areas may be monolingual or bilingual in their approach. An early example of the former is Jakobsen's (1901) work on Norse place-names in Shetland. He identifies and interprets loan names of Old Norse origin with little regard to the Scots English dialect in which the names are transmitted. Modern collections of minority place-names, for example indigenous names in Australia, may also be basically monolingual in approach. Other studies are interested in both contact languages and how features from both (or all) languages involved appear in the place-name material. Some of the early studies of Scandinavian influence on English names describe the setting in which the names were coined and transmitted as well as the actual indicators of contact in names (e.g. Lindkvist 1912; Björkman 1913). In this way, they pre-empt contact linguistics.

A fundamental assumption of contact linguistics is that linguistic development cannot be attributed solely to language internal processes. The same applies to names in contact. The developments observed in borrowed names can be described in linguistic terms such as translations and adaptations, but these processes cannot be reduced to a matter of regular linguistic change in one language. To understand the processes, the speakers who translate or adapt the names have to be taken into consideration. Finally, an outline of the socio-cultural setting is necessary to understand why place-names are adapted in certain ways and why they are borrowed or rejected in the first place. Contact onomastics thus has to address the socio-cultural setting and the language users as well as the relevant languages, a tripartite approach familiar from contact linguistics.

38.3 THE CONTACT SITUATION

Every contact situation is unique in terms of the languages that meet and how they relate. A number of general factors that have a bearing on the borrowing and adaptation of names can be identified, however. A prolonged period of contact may generate more borrowing and interference than short-time contact, but as noted initially, the exchange of names (and words) only requires casual contact (cf. Thomason and Kaufman 1991: 50). Borrowing is possible whether the languages are related or not, but the way borrowed elements are adapted is influenced by factors such as the proximity of the contact languages and the bilingual competence of the speakers. First of all, a fundamental distinction can be drawn between synchronous and historical language contact.

38.3.1 Living Contact

In bi- or multilingual settings, mutual influence between the languages is still possible. A striking, though rather unusual, example of mutual name borrowing is a village in Swedish Lapland called *Kvikkjokk* in Swedish and *Húhttán* in Sámi. The Swedish name is an adaptation of a Sámi river name *Guojkkajåhka*, whereas the Sámi name is an adaptation of Swedish *hyttan*, referring to a melting hut (Frändén 2013: 93). More than two contact languages mean more potential variant forms. One example is the Northern German town called *Eckernförde* in High German, *Eckernföör* in Low German, and *Egernførde* in standard Danish, and which also has a local Danish form *Nysted*. In South Tyrol, most names have a German and an Italian form and some have a Ladin form as well, for example *Brixen—Bressanone—Porsenù*.

The choice of name-form is normally regulated by the linguistic context. In Finland, for instance, Finnish name forms such as *Tornio* and *Turku* appear in Finnish contexts whereas the Swedish forms *Torneå* and *Åbo* should be used in Swedish communication. There are exceptions, however. The famous Australian red mountain is officially gazetted as *Ayers Rock/Uluru*. The latter form is from the Pitjantjatjara language, but may also be used by English speakers. Further discussion of the status of variant forms is discussed in section 38.3.3.

Alternative names may or may not be linguistically related. The relation between name pairs has been studied in various areas since the pioneer work of Kranzmayer (1934). Based on studies of place-names in German-Slavic contact areas, he identifies three kinds of name pairs. Semantically bound pairs share the same meaning, for example Sorbian *Nowa Wjes* and German *Neudorf* 'the new settlement'. Phonologically bound pairs are related by sound, for example Sorbian *Budyšin* > Germ. *Bautzen*. In addition, there are free name pairs, that is, the two names are independent formations. Subsequent studies have added a fourth group, hybrid forms or partial translations. In most cases, the generic is translated, whereas the specific is phonetically adapted (section 38.3.1).

38.3.2 Historical Contact

In many cases, the linguistic contact is historical, that is one of the contact languages is no longer spoken in the area. Although Jakobsen (1901, see section 38.1) did not explicitly state so, the Norse language was dead in Shetland when he undertook his studies there in the late nineteenth century. The only living language was a Scots English dialect, which included a large number of names and dialect words borrowed from Old Norse.

It is quite common for place-names to be the most visible or in fact the only legacy of a lost language. In Scotland, over 300 names with the generic *Pit-* 'a piece of land' are the most tangible remains of the language of the Pictish people. In other parts of Britain names in *Pen-* < *penn* 'head, top end' are testimony to the Brittonic tribes who lived there before the Anglo-Saxon settlement. Place-names may even testify to subsequent groups of settlers. The oldest part of Scottish *Ardtornish Point* is OScand *Tornes* (generic *nes* 'headland'). This enters into a Gaelic formation with the generic *árd* 'headland' and finally *point* is added for clarity for speakers of Scots English (Nicolaisen 2001: 72).

Historical contact does not normally generate name pairs; only one name-form survives as part of the surviving language. From a synchronic point of view, this name-form is part of the living language, even if the original formation took place in another language. On a synchronous level, *Pitlochry* is a Scots English name, though it was coined by the Picts. It should not, and in fact cannot, be labelled a Pictish name, as the language is long dead. *Pitlochry* or *Woolongong* may betray their non-English origin by their form, whereas other names are adapted to the extent that no trace of non-native origin is indicated (cf. 38.4).

38.3.3 Status and Symbolic Value of Place-names in Bilingual Contexts

Few bilingual situations are completely symmetrical. For instance, all speakers of Sámi also speak a majority language that is used in communication outside the group. This affects the choice between variant name-forms. Sámi speakers are likely to use the Norwegian form *Tana* instead of the Sámi original form *Deatnu* when talking to Norwegians, for instance.

The place-names of minorities obviously run the risk of being marginalized if they are restricted to communication within their own group. The position of such names also depends on political decisions and regulations, however. Regulations of the young Norwegian state in the early twentieth century required that every holding bought from the government in the linguistically mixed North should have a Norwegian name. This meant that a lot of existing Sámi and Finnish names were excluded from official records and the owners were sometimes unaware of the official name of their estate (Andersen 2013). The situation was fundamentally altered by the current place-name law from 1991, which states that Sámi and Finnish forms in common use should be used on maps, signs, registers, etc. (Fig. 38.1), and that a Norwegian form is not mandatory. In areas of Sámi administration, the Sámi name-forms should come first. A similar initiative was taken by the German federal state Schleswig-Holstein in 2007. Road signs should also give the place-names in the minority languages Danish, Frisian, and Low German. Although such initiatives are positive, it should be added that the presence of a law or a road sign does not automatically generate respect for minority names in all groups.

A minority language may be dominant in certain regions, such as the Faeroes and Greenland within the kingdom of Denmark or in colonies. Naming or renaming places is one way of expressing a new order in colonial situations. When the Dutch settlement of *Nieuw Amsterdam* on Manhattan was conquered by English forces, it was renamed *New York* in honour of the Duke of York, later King James II. Not surprisingly,

FIGURE 38.1 Road sign in Norwegian, North Sámi, and local Finnish (Kvænsk).

Photograph: Kurt Johnsen.

independence or home rule regularly leads to replacement of the names of former colonies, for example *Rhodesia > Zimbabwe, Godthåb > Nuuk* in Greenland. The symbolic value is obvious; renaming is a way of claiming ownership of the land.

Rather extreme examples of political naming are found in Eastern Europe. In Belgrade, for instance, some streets have changed names half a dozen times since the late nineteenth century, to reflect the current ethnic or political orientation: the south Slavic movement, the establishment of Yugoslavia, the Nazi occupation during the Second World War, pro-Soviet and subsequent anti-Soviet orientation, and finally the breakdown of Yugoslavia all resulted in new names (Rajić 2007).

38.4 Language Contact in Place-names

Place-names borrowed into another language are unlikely to be adopted without changes, and the vast majority of borrowed names actually show traces of adaptation to the recipient language. These range from phonetic adaptations, such as in *Mississippi* borrowed from Ojibwe *misi-ziibi* 'Great River', to transformations that render the borrowed names indistinguishable from native names, for example Old Norse <u>*Orkneyjar*</u> 'seal island' (now Orkney) which we know to be an adaptation only because a pre-Norse source gives the form <u>*Orchades*</u>.

To analyse the adaptation processes in contact place-names, we clearly need to consider both (all) languages involved, as the names are likely to display features from both (all). Contact linguists have pointed out that the languages in contact are usually dialectal variants rather than standard language. In cases of historical contact, earlier stages of languages and even more or less unrecorded languages may be involved. A proper analysis of the adaptation process requires a description of each of the contact languages to the extent this is possible. The contact languages are unique in each contact situation and have to be surveyed individually, but it is interesting to note that the same adaptation processes can be observed in linguistically very diverse areas.

38.4.1 Phonological Adaptation

Phonological adaptation means the replacement of unfamiliar sounds and sound combinations by sounds and sound sequences that are acceptable in the recipient language. The initial palatal lateral [ʎ] in the Gaelic name *Leòdhas* is foreign to English speakers and is replaced by its alveolar counterpart in the English form *Lewis*, and the velar fricative [x] in the last syllable of the Brittonic name *Glaschu* is replaced in the form *Glasgow*. Foreign sound combinations are also regularly replaced. For instance, Standard Finnish does not accept initial consonant clusters, and adopts *Stockholm* in the form *Tukholma*. Phonological substitution can be observed in all contact situations, and for many borrowed names, this is as far as adaptation extends.

Phonological adaptation differs from all other types of adaptation by being, as it seems, mandatory. All borrowed names have to adapt to the phonology of the recipient language in the sense that all unacceptable sounds and sound combinations have to be replaced. This appears to be natural, as a loan name can only become part of a new language if speakers are able to pronounce the name in their own sound system.

Fundamentally, phonological adaptation seems to demonstrate the resistance of phonological structures, but even these may undergo changes in areas of intense contact. In southern Finnish dialects, initial consonant clusters have become acceptable under the influence of Swedish, and Swedish *Kronoby* is adapted as *Kruunupyy*. In such cases, the contact-induced system-change probably comes first. Another example is the sound sequence *sk-* in English names and words like *Skegness* and *skin*. It was introduced by Scandinavian incomers, who adapted existing names (Fellows-Jensen 1985: 196) as well as coining their own. Their linguistic presence was strong enough to influence the English phonotax.

38.4.2 Morphological Adaptation

Grammatical features of the original form may be translated into the recipient language, for example *The Trossachs* reflecting the plurality of *Na Trosaichean* 'the cross-hills', or the definiteness of the river names *The Thames* and *Der Rhein* retained in the Scandinavian forms *Themsen, Rhinen*. The final -*en* is the definite article, suffixed according to Scandinavian grammar. In other cases, morphemes are added to the original names. *Syllingar* for *The Scilly Isles* in Old Norse Sagas can be compared with *Sully* recorded in the twelfth century. The Old Norse form contains a derivational morpheme *ing* as well as a plural morpheme *ar*. Whereas the plural morpheme conveys a meaning 'several islands', the *ing*-morpheme seems to be added solely for the benefit of integration into the Old Norse onomasticon, where names ending in *ing* are quite common.

Translating or adding morphemes is not a necessary part of the adaptation process, but, as we see, it may convey meaning on a grammatical level as well as contribute to the integration of a borrowed name in the recipient language.

38.4.3 Syntactic Adaptation

We have already seen how the definite article of *The Thames* is suffixed in the Scandinavian form *Themsen*, according to Scandinavian morphosyntax. Most place-names are compounds, consisting of a generic and a specific. In Celtic languages, the generic comes first and in modern Germanic languages, the generic is final. This means that a syntactic adaptation may take place when names are borrowed from a Germanic to a Celtic language or vice versa. In British *Din Eydin* 'stronghold of Eydin' and modern Gaelic *Dùn Eideann* the generic comes first. In the Scots English form *Edinburgh*, the generic has been moved to final position in accordance with common syntax. In South Tyrol the parallel forms *Pustertal* (German) and *Val Pusteria* (Italian) demonstrate the same syntactic difference. The generics *tal* and *Val* both mean 'valley'.

Syntactic adaptation requires some degree of bilingual competence: a speaker who identifies at least one of the elements and puts it in the right place.

38.4.4 Semantic Adaptation—Translation

Semantic adaptation implies the translation of one or both elements of a name. Partial translations are fairly common and normally affect the generic, compare *Edinburgh* above. In the English name-form *The Pacific Ocean*, the generic is a translation of Portuguese *mar* in the name *Mar Pacifico* given by Magellan. Considering the restricted usage of the word *pacific* in English, the specific could be a phonological adaptation. This can be compared to the form in Scandinavian languages, in which *pacific* is replaced by the unmarked word *stille, stilla* 'quiet, calm, silent, tranquil'. The forms *Stillehavet* (Danish, Norwegian) and *Stilla havet* (Swedish) 'tranquil/calm ocean' can only be interpreted as full translations.

Translation requires some bilingual competence, and may be easier in closely related languages. A study of place-names in Sámi–Finnish–Swedish contact areas in

Northern Sweden (Pellijeff 1980) shows that translation of elements is more common between the related languages Sámi and Finnish, whereas phonological adaptation is the rule for names borrowed into Swedish. The term semi-communication has been used to describe immediate understanding between closely related languages. For instance, the translation from Dutch *Voegle Sant* to Swedish *Fogle sand* in Nova Suecia does not really require a bilingual speaker (compare section 38.6).

Surveys from different contact areas seem to agree that generics are translated more often than specifics. This is partly due to the fact that generics are more stereotypical; generics such as *hill*, *ton*, and *wich* enter into many English place-names for instance. A number of generics also refer to features that both groups observe. The former regulations for place-names in Northern Norway, designed to create a Norwegian nomenclature (section 38.3.3), list some common Sámi generics that are to be translated: *varre*, *javrre*, *jokka* 'mountain lake, river'. These are typical examples of generics referring to visible features, which are familiar to anyone with a minimum of knowledge of a contact language.

38.4.5 Lexical Adaptation

Finally, place-name elements may be replaced by words in the recipient language that are phonetically similar but semantically unrelated, that is words that sound similar. Even if such adaptations are quite rare, they may be very conspicuous if the compound form makes no sense whatsoever as a place-name. Old Norse *Kirkjuvág* 'church inlet' in Orkney is adapted as *Kirkwall*. The specific is translated correctly, whereas the generic has been replaced by the Scots English word *wall*. The final consonants of both *vág* and *wall* are vocalized, causing phonological similarity. 'Church-wall' makes sense lexically, although perhaps not as a place-name. The Old Norse element *tjörn* 'pond, small lake' causes more problems. It has been adapted as *shun*, *chin*, *gin*, and *Jenny*, and old local maps show name forms such as *Loch of Jenny* and the rather unlikely *Loch of Gin* (Sandnes 2010: 363ff.).

Examples can be given from different areas. Norwegian *luft* 'air' replaces Sámi dialect *loufta* 'bay' in some Norwegian names. One rather peculiar adaptation is *Hjemmeluft* 'home air' from Sámi *Jiemmaluofta*. Tasty German examples include *Roßwein* 'horse wine' < *Rusavin* as well as *Kuhbier* 'cow beer' and *Wassersuppe* 'water soup', all clearly adaptations of unidentified Slavic names (Walther 1980: 1949–50).

As the examples demonstrate, different adaptation strategies can be observed within one name. A combination of translated generics and phonetically or lexically adapted specifics is quite common. One example is *Din Eidyn > Edinburgh*, which also shows an additional adaptation to Scots syntax. Sorbian *Stare sedło* 'old village' has been adapted into German in the form *Starsiedel*, in which the generic relates to the verb *siedeln* 'settle' and the specific is unanalysed. A translation of both elements could render the name in a purely German form *Altendorf*, and without records of the original form, there is no way of telling that translation has taken place (Walther 1980: 1949–50).

38.5 Mixed Names—Hybrid Names?

Place-names containing elements from more than one language are of special interest to contact onomastic studies. Some of these may be the result of the adaptation processes described above, but adaptation alone cannot explain these seemingly mixed names.

Many mixed names are coined with borrowed words. In contact areas, words are borrowed as well as place-names and once established, loan-words may enter into place-names. After the Anglo-Saxons had borrowed the Brittonic word *cumb* 'combe, valley', it could be used in Old English place-name formation. Further north, the Old Norse word *sker* 'rocky islet' was borrowed into Scots English in the form *skerry*, and into Gaelic as *sgeir*. Formations such as *Castle Skerry* or *Sgeir Bheag* 'small rocky islet' should be seen as regular Scots and Gaelic formations containing a loan-word and not as hybrids from a formation point of view. In rare cases, loans are restricted to place-name formation. In former Slavic-speaking areas in Germany, the Slavic elements *-witz*, *-litz* and *-nitz* entered into the German language as place-name forming elements (Walther 1980: 147).

Existing place-names often enter into new formations, and these may be of a different linguistic origin. Many American places take their names from the languages of the Native American tribes. Once these have been adopted, they may serve as the basis for secondary formations, for example *Tampa—Tampa Bay*, *Chattanooga—Chattanooga Valley*. Such names also exemplify the different role of the generic and the specific in a name. The specific actually carries the primary function of a name, that is to single out a certain location. A name of Native American origin such as *Chattanooga* serves this purpose perfectly well. In fact, the re-use of existing place-names makes perfect sense, as anyone familiar with *Chattanooga* can figure out the approximate location of *Chattanooga Valley*. The generic, on the other hand, typically defines the location. Since one can only describe a locality in the living language, the generic is a good indication of the formation language (Sandnes 2010: 266).

A classifying element can be added to place-names lacking an explicit generic, as exemplified by *Ardtornish Point* in section 38.3.2. This is called epexegesis, or somewhat misleadingly, tautological addition. It is unlikely that the Gaelic speakers who coined the name *Ardtornish* recognized the Old Norse element *nes* 'headland, point'. They probably regarded *Tornish* as a unit and added a Gaelic element *ard* 'headland' to identify the locality. The process was repeated by the English speakers who added a new explicit generic, *point*. Although it is often maintained that names function as labels and do not need to mean anything, a meaningful generic seems to be desirable in certain contexts. Moreover, a classifying generic may be added to distinguish between different localities bearing the same name. *Mississippi* primarily refers to the river (section 38.3), but now also denotes a state. Thus, the form *Mississippi River* is used to refer specifically to the river.

So far, we have seen that place-names may contain elements from more than one language as a result of adaptation, lexical borrowing or addition of a generic. The question remains whether formations can be bilingual from the outset, that is coined with a specific from one language and the generic from another. This is actually a matter of debate. Whereas Scandinavian scholars reject the possibility of hybrid formations, this option is not fully ruled out in the British tradition. This means that *Conesford* is initially interpreted as a compound of Old Danish *kunung* + Old English *ford*, though a note is added that '*kunung* "king" may possibly have replaced an earlier OE *cynung*' (Sandred and Lindström 1989: 114).

A special kind of hybrid formation is suggested for the so-called *Grimston-hybrids* in the Danelaw, compounded of Old English *tūn* and Old Norse specifics. According to British scholars, the class evolved because Danish settlers kept the Old English generic *tūn* and replaced the specific with Old Danish elements (Fellows-Jensen 1972: 110). This could be labelled partial re-naming. Alternatively, the Grimston-hybrids could be interpreted as regular monolingual coinages. Even if *tūn* does not appear to be productive in place-name formation in Denmark when the Vikings came to Britain, Scandinavians were familiar with the word *tún*. Moreover, the settlers would certainly become familiar with the place-name element in England, where *tūn*-names are frequent. We may compare the Germans who borrowed Slavic -*witz* and -*nitz* as place-formation suffixes (section 38.5).

It is hard to find proof of hybrid formation, and as several scholars have pointed out, monolingual formation should definitely be looked upon as the rule. The reason is rarely explicitly expressed, but rests on the general assumption that bilingual individuals use one language in a specific context. A place-name is coined in a certain linguistic context and even if the speakers are bilingual, a code shift is not to be expected in a very limited linguistic unit such as a name.

38.6 THE SPEAKER

All place-names are coined and transmitted by speakers, and the role of speakers becomes particularly visible in contact onomastics. On the most fundamental level, the acceptance or rejection of existing names is a matter of choice for the incomers. Britain with its successive waves of immigration may serve as an example, as the settling groups had rather different attitudes to existing place-names. Both the Romans and the Normans generally accepted established names and coined relatively few new names. The Anglo-Saxons borrowed quite a number of existing names, especially for important topographical features, which survive as part of the English onomasticon (Gelling 1997: 90). The Scandinavian settlers in the Danelaw also adopted existing names, adapting them phonetically and lexically (Fellows-Jensen 1985: 193ff.). The Scandinavian settlers in Shetland and Orkney had a totally different attitude to existing place-names, however. Virtually no pre-Viking names survive (section 38.3). The Norse settlers have either rejected all pre-existing names, or made such radical adaptations that the pre-Norse forms are unrecognizable. This is sometimes taken as evidence that the Norse wiped out the natives from the isles.

Many changes in place-names and other words cannot be explained as systemic changes and have to relate to speakers. As for the adaptation processes discussed above, only phonological substitution can be interpreted as generated by the language system. All other adaptations presuppose speakers who analyse the names and make adjustments. The proficiency of the speaker may influence the process. Translation depends on bilingual competence, although understanding frequent generics requires a minimal amount of bilingual competence. For instance, English speakers may know the meaning of Welsh *llan* 'church' or Gaelic *beinn* 'mountain'. If speakers are able to identify elements, they may translate them. They may also choose not to translate *Beinn Nibheis* into *Nevis Mountain. Most borrowed names, like *Ben Nevis*, merely undergo phonological adaptation. Translations, especially full translations, are relatively rare. Perhaps bilingual speakers see no reason to translate elements they understand. However, a generic may be translated or an epexegetic element added if an explicit generic is desired (cf. *Ardtornish Point* above). It has been maintained that explicit generics are favoured by mapmakers. We may conclude, then, that the development of a place-name is dependent on individual choices as well as the speaker's proficiency.

The term analysis is perhaps somewhat misleading. It is impossible to determine to what extent the process is conscious, and the speakers' interpretations of the place-name elements do not necessarily agree with the original elements. Reanalysis may be a better term. We saw above (section 38.4.5) that elements in opaque place-names can be substituted by similar-sounding words, for example *wall* for *vágr* 'bay' in the name *Kirkwall*. It should be pointed out that such substitutions occur in monolingual areas when names are no longer understood, but are more likely to happen when names are borrowed into other languages and the connection with the living language is effectively broken. The role of the speaker is obvious in these cases, where the framework for interpretation and substitution is the living language rather than the coining language.

38.7 CASE STUDY: NOVA SUECIA

The short-lived colony Nova Suecia (1638–55) illustrates a wide range of contact-onomastic matters. A Swedish colony was founded at the mouth of Delaware River, following the pattern of the Dutch colony on Manhattan. Nova Suecia was actually initiated by a Dutchman, Peter Minuit, who negotiated the 'purchase' of Manhattan. At that time, Finland was under Swedish rule and quite a few of the colonists were Finns. Their neighbours in America were Native Americans, but also Dutchmen from the Nieuw Amsterdam colony to the north and English speakers from the Virginia colony to the south. The colonists managed to establish fairly peaceful relations with the native tribes, whereas relations with the Dutch were tense. The late phase of the colony, including a large number of place-names, is well recorded on maps and in text by the engineer Per Lindeström (Lindeström 1692; Utterström 1998).

Interestingly, Peter Minuit received certain instructions pertaining to the place-names of the colony: the queen and the capital were to be commemorated and the best harbours should be named after famous Swedes. A small fort was in fact named (*Fort*) *Christina* after the queen. Most other forts and settlements were named after locations in Sweden and Finland, often with the addition of *Nya* 'new': *Elfsborg, Nya Göteborg, Nya Vasa, Nya Korsholm*. There is a personal connection for the latter two, since the governor had served at Korsholm castle near Vasa. *Elfsborg* was infested with mosquitoes and later abandoned. It was aptly renamed *Myggenborg* 'mosquito castle'. Most Finns lived in a settlement called *Finland* or *Chamassung*. The residence of governor *Printz* was called *Printzhov*, and the first freeman's settlement was named *Stillens land* after its owner, Olof *Stille*. Both have alternative Indian names, *Tenakong* and *Techoherassi*. Personal names are otherwise rare, so *Naamans Kijl* and *Naamans Fallet* deserve special mention. The specific is the name of a sachem (paramount chief) with whom the colonists were negotiating a land transaction, and the gesture of naming places in his honour could be part of an acquisition strategy.

Most Swedish names are found near the mouth of the river. Some may be translations of Indian names. Utterström gives only one example, Swedish *Hwitlerskil* 'white clay

FIGURE 38.2 Copperplate copy of Lindeström's map of Nova Suecia, published by Th. Campanius Holm 1702 (Kort beskrifning om provincien Nya Swerige uti America: som nu foertjden af the Engelske kallas Pensylvania. Stockholm.)

Held in the General Collection, Beinecke Rare Book and Manuscript Library, Yale University.

creek' or *Swapecksisko*, which appears to contain *wopæk sisko* 'white clay'. Other translations are difficult to establish as long as we do not have access to the native names and their etymology (see section 38.4.5). Some names contain elements from both languages, for example *Mechansio Berg*. The Swedish generic means 'hill'. This seems to be an epexegetic form, for in his diary Lindeström also refers to the mountain as *Meckansio*. If so, the island name *Mechansio Eijlandh* is likely to be a secondary formation, 'the island near Mechansio'. *Mechansio Berg* and *Mechansio Eijlandh* should be analysed as Swedish formations with a borrowed name as their specifics (section 38.4). The number of purely Indian names increases further up the river and makes up the majority of the recorded names. As the above examples show, alternative names are common. Even personal names may be translated. Lindeström remarks that the natives' name for Governor Printz is *Meschatz*, which means 'big belly'. To sum up, the recorded place-name material is proof of linguistic interchange between Indians and Swedes. The adoption of native names seems to indicate a rather respectful attitude from the colonists towards the original inhabitants, which is corroborated by Linderstöm's diary.

The relation to the Dutch neighbours was more hostile. This is expressed in linguistic terms when a Dutch stronghold called *Fort Casimir* was conquered on Trinity Sunday and renamed *Trefaldighet* 'Trinity' (section 38.3.3). On the other hand, the colonists adopted Dutch place-names such as *Cap Hinlopen* and *Sandhoecken* (with the Swedish definite article added). Interestingly, the Swedes also borrowed place-name elements, most importantly the generics *kil* in the sense 'river, creek' and *eiland* 'island'. The latter is recorded in the plural form *eiländer* 'islands', proving that the word was an integrated loan. A seemingly mixed name such as *Plommon Eiland* is thus a purely Swedish formation, compounded of Swedish *plommon* 'plum' and a loan-word meaning 'island'. Since Dutch and Swedish are relatively closely related languages, translation can be more or less automatic in some cases, for example *Voegle Sant* > *Fogle sand*. Examples of lexical adaptation include the rendering of Dutch *Schuyl kijl* 'hide or hidden creek' as *Skiörkil*, literally 'fragile creek'. The same name is also written *Skylekilen* in the diary, showing phonological and morphological adaptation.

The Swedish colony was short-lived, and nearly all the names created by the Swedes were replaced by later settlers. Many may have been map forms that never had time to become established. The Dutch, who held Christina for nine years, renamed it *Altena*, but the name was soon changed to its present form *Wilmington* by the English. The only Swedish element to survive may be the queen's name in the river name *Christina River*.

38.8 CONCLUSIONS

Examples drawn from various areas and different periods demonstrate that names are easily borrowed between languages. To function in a new linguistic setting, borrowed names are adapted to the sound system of the recipient language, for example *Guojkkajåhka* > *Kvikkjokk*. No further adjustment is needed, but adaptation is still possible on all linguistic levels. Syntax and morphology may be adjusted. The elements of the name may be translated or substituted by similar-sounding words in the new language, for example *Rusavin > Roßwein*. Translation is probably easier if the contact languages are closely related. If the contact languages are close, certain elements will be immediately intelligible and phonological adaptations may in fact produce correct translations, such as the substitution of English *Ash-* for Scandinavian *Ask-* in English place-names and vice versa.

The importance of the speaker is particularly obvious in contact onomastics, since so many of the changes observed cannot be explained as a result of regular linguistic change. Processes such as translations, replacement of elements, and syntactic adaptation such as *Pustertal > Val Pusteria* can only be explained as a result of a speaker's interpretation and adaptation.

CHAPTER 39

....

NAMES AND LAW

....

ANDREAS TEUTSCH

39.1 INTRODUCTION

INTUITIVELY we might state that there is a close and reciprocal relationship between names and law. However, when it comes to a closer look at names and law, their correlation seems less obvious or intentional. As a matter of fact, the following questions reveal legal problems covered by name issues:

- Why was *Michael Herbert Dengler's* application to change his name to *1069* in the USA rejected (Kushner 2009: 315), although as a matter of rule any desired name can be adopted?
- Why did the Appellant Court of Bremen in Germany finally allow the name *Frieden Mit Gott Allein Durch Jesus Christus* ('*Peace With God Only Through Jesus Christ*'), although the name does not comply with German civil law on naming?
- Why did the Heal the World foundation file dozens of trademark applications for *Michael Jackson* for a large variety of goods and services immediately after his death (Vassallo and Hiney 2009: 42)?
- Why did the neighbouring states of Greece and the Republic of Macedonia need an international arbitration commission in order to settle on the name of the former Yugoslav Republic of Macedonia (United Nations Security Council Resolution 817)?

This listing of a couple of individual cases shows how the law is related to names or how it is implemented during the process of naming. Of course, the above series of examples does not cover all possible occurrences in which naming processes or names are legally affected, that is where a name or naming issue is affected by law or, vice versa, where the law has to find a solution for a name or naming conflict. Furthermore, this introductory list of questions does not seem to be systematic.

Nonetheless, answering those questions can help to group legal name issues according to their occurrences. However, single (national/regional) legal usage will—apart from providing examples—not be an issue and can always vary from what is generally stated here. Rather I will try to put the interdisciplinary topic into the Procrustean bed of giving an overview on how a name type can be affected by law.

All the above questions concern names in a possible conflict situation; and all these situations concern the law, statutes, legal rulings, or legal action. Those regulations are embedded in two major legal systems: common law and civil law. Although this general division is valid for any legal aspect, the different impact of these respective systems on name conflicts will here only be discussed in relation to people's names, as differences are most apparent in this area.

The objective of the following considerations is to carve out the points where names and the law converge. Thus, it doesn not emanate from an empirical viewpoint on names and naming but in fact will demonstrate to the onomastic scholar some of the legal considerations on names. For this reason, I will first discuss the interdisciplinary relationship between names and the law. As this approach will restrict the view both of names and of the law I will define three groups of names and propose a legally adapted terminology. The main part of the chapter consists of a discussion of the particular features of each of the defined groups.

Last but not least I would like to point out that this chapter takes a purely synchronic view of names and the law.

39.2 LEGAL PERSPECTIVE VS. ONOMASTIC PERSPECTIVE

Names are regarded, *inter alia*, as social phenomena (e.g. Ernst 2010: 61). The same applies to the law since it is 'the enforceable body of rules that govern any society' (ODL 2009: 316). This definition reduces the totality of legal norms to behavioural codes which have the aim of guaranteeing social orderliness (Seelmann 2007: 51). Therefore, the above-mentioned consideration paves the way for a potential legal conflict as names are markers for individuals, since especially under legal aspects, names serve to fulfil the dual function of distinguishing people and fixing their identity (Koss 2002: 134).

There is of course a vast number of other, broader, or even more detailed definitions of law and names. Yet, given that the present point of view merely concerns the issue of identity, the following reflections only need to be based on the social definition of law and names. Lastly, the setting of 'names and the law' in a social environment already engenders one point in common. Nevertheless, there are also contrasting elements to be considered.

On the one hand, any implementation of the law is always prescriptive. But the law goes nowhere towards answering the question of what a name is, nor does the law make statements about the question of how a name functions—this is the remit of onomastics (Nübling et al. 2012: 12ff.). In most legal systems there is a general law in the field of personality rights which in one way or another stipulates that a person has to be given a name. With this in mind, a very important principle of jurisdiction has to be stressed: no legal action can be taken without a legal base. This might seem trivial, especially to non-jurists, but the impact has to be considered carefully to understand the role of the law in name and naming issues. Any legal statement whatsoever needs a legal base—not a moral, cultural, economic, or political base; the latter can only be related to the legal base, they cannot substitute for it. Furthermore, the legal principle of *nullo actore, nullus iudex*, which was extended into standard language by means of the English proverb '*The squeaky wheel gets the grease*', is of vital importance as well. Name conflicts not only need a legal basis but also a nominal plaintiff, who can be an authority, a name-giver, a named person, etc.

On the other hand, onomastics is purely descriptive and deals directly with issues describing anything in relation to names (Handschuck and Schröer 2010: 15), whereas law deals with the application and setting of legal rules within a conflict situation. Consequently, an interdisciplinary approach does not reveal mutual consent—rather such an approach can only invite taking on the respective viewpoints.

From this perspective it becomes clear that law only deals with names or naming processes as far as there is an actionable conflict. This also means that the two disciplines involved do not have a natural contact point, as perhaps onomastics and sociolinguistics do. In fact, law deals with any legally ascertainable issue, whereas onomastics has a consistently defined object of study. It does not matter for jurisprudence whether a regulating decision is requested regarding the appropriateness of a forename or regarding the question of whether followers of the Flying Spaghetti Monster may wear a colander on ID-photographs (Anonymous 2013b), jurisprudence has to apply the same methodology and the same legal considerations to any case. In contrast, onomastics describes names in the light of their empirical or epistemic objectives.

39.3 TYPES OF NAMES FROM A LEGAL PERSPECTIVE

Since names are clearly defined by onomastics but not by jurisprudence, it has to be ensured that both disciplines have the same understanding of the object of study.

In order to transfer names and naming into the realm of the law, the different name types, defined by onomastics, have to be linked to legal issues, that is to conflict situations. This juridical prerequisite excludes several name types since conflict situations that are not based on legal grounds can reasonably be ignored. Therefore, in the present interdisciplinary environment the question of the name types has to be grouped according to the different fields of legal conflicts related to names.

In the present social setting—as this is the specified common point within the interdisciplinary approach—the grouping of name types for legal reason seems obvious: There is the large field of commercial names (with its own well-developed legal field), and there are individuals (people) and their environment (places). With this in mind I propose the following groups:

- The first group contains legal conflicts in relation to competition and business law. These conflicts focus on economic values. Commercial names are product names, company names, celebrity names used in commercials, protected geographical indications, etc. Commercial names have developed their own case law based on *leges speciales* in the field of competition and business law, such as trademark protection law.
- The second group concerns toponyms. Legal considerations are only applied indirectly, whereas aspects of tradition, politics and language policies are more important. Although legal involvement within toponymic conflicts is only ancillary, it seems appropriate that toponyms constitute a separate group.
- The third group contains legal conflicts in relation to people's names (except for commercial use). Conflicts due to name changing or name giving have to be considered. The focus is the individual to be or wanting to be identified.

The three groups will be discussed in the following, but the structure and the extent of each discussion will be different. In fact, the first group has a well-developed case law framework and it is a well-developed field within jurisprudence. In order to link the subject to onomastics, I will thus primarily discuss the use of different name type functions deviating from those usually set by onomastics. The second group will be dealt with rather briefly because the legal impact is more or less indirect. The third group is the largest group since it deals with names as personal identifiers within the setting of many different legal systems in combination with a large variety of conflicts.

Finally, I would like to point out that there are other possibilities for classifying the conflict potential of names (e.g. Fritzsche 2008: 309). These approaches, however, put legal aspects clearly ahead of onomastic considerations.

39.4 COMMERCIAL NAME TYPES AND THEIR CONFLICT POTENTIAL

The particular feature of this group is the lack of consistent use of onomastic name types. From the legal point of view it is important that the conflict potential is foreseeable as the legal bases are clearly defined. The legal statutes and case law in question contain trademark law, copyright law, company law, international treaties, miscellaneous commercial regulations, publicity rights, and personal rights—all within the field of anti-trust law, business law, competition law, and so on. Those laws all have one issue in common, which is the protection of immaterial economic values. Although it is a fairly harmonized set of laws internationally, there are, of course, differences in the respective national application and interpretation of statutes and case law (Teutsch 2007: 25 et *passim*).

The economic value relating to names can apply to any name type: it can concern company names (Bergien 2007: 264), place-names, or personal names as far as they contain a commercial value (Teutsch 2007, 2013: 600). Therefore, names are to be found within a conflict potential that is based on economic values of language signs due to their mere sound or image (Teutsch 2012: 88).

Some legal scholars include any language sign in this group due to their communicative function and speak about 'commercial communication signs' (Fezer 2005: 10). Others distinguish 'names' from other '(language) commercial signs', as, for example, fancy words or generic terms (Fritzsche 2008: 309).

But which types of names with economic value are likely to be at the centre of legal conflicts? An analysis of legal name types in the field of commercial law conflicts based on findings by Ballon (2007: 61ff.) and Fritzsche (2008: 311ff.) yields the following groups:

- proper names, names of historical people:
  - *name type: can only be anthroponyms,*
  - *legal base: trademark law, personal rights;*

- denominations of geographical origin and indications of provenance:
  - *name type: can only be toponyms,*
  - *legal base: trademark law, international treaties, and regulations;*

- names of organizations, company names, domain names:
  - *name type: can contain any onomastic name type,*
  - *legal base: trademark law, company law, domain name regulations;*

- brand names, trademarks, trade denominations:
  - *name type: can contain any onomastic name type,*
  - *legal base: trademark law, international treaties, copyright law, company law.*

Moreover, there is a legal distinction with regard to the conflict potential in the field of business or competition law, namely legal conflicts based on 'absolute' grounds and 'relative' grounds for conflicts which concern non-registrations and infringements of any kind (Fritzsche 2008: 311 et seq.). This distinction is basic and will only be extended by 'publicity right' (Vassallo and Hiney 2009), which concerns the economic value of celebrities' names and image.

From the interdisciplinary viewpoint, these subgroups show that legal conflicts, especially with regard to economic value, are formal and procedural issues, which means that onomastic considerations are hardly relevant.

39.4.1 Absolute Grounds

Conflicts based on absolute grounds refer to commercial names that cannot be assigned legal protection. This happens often in the case of trademarks consisting of descriptive appellatives (due to their descriptive sense). Nevertheless, given that names normally are devoid of sense, they are hardly subject to being refused legal protection (Teutsch 2007: 125, 130 et seq.). There are exceptions, namely where a proper name can be seen as a generic indication for a genre, like *Mozart* for sound carriers or where a toponym serves to indicate thematic content, like *Costa Blanca* for a holiday guide (Teutsch 2007: 79, fn. 50). In these cases the names can be refused protection, unless protection has already been granted. This is the reason why the Heal the World foundation registered the name *Michael Jackson* after his death and before finally becoming an icon of the pop music world and with this, a mere token for a certain genre of music.

Another important exception is geographical indications that are protected through particular treaties, mostly for agricultural products such as wines, liquors, honeys, fruits, cheeses, sausages, etc. There are several varieties of protected geographical indications (PGI) including protected designations of origin (PDO) and traditional specialities guaranteed (TSG) (Wikipedia n.d.).

39.4.2 Relative Grounds

Relative grounds are assessed depending on or in comparison with another sign or other circumstances. From the onomastic perspective, only the case of proper names is of any interest. The courts sometimes make intuitive statements about names, without reference to any onomastic expertise. For example, the European General Court[1] states in the case *McKenzie* against *McKinley*:

> The intervener has proved the existence of several marks containing, inter alia, the prefix 'Mc' which are present on the national and Community markets. In addition, the relevant public is accustomed to the presence of Scottish or Irish family names in daily life and is able to distinguish between the marks at issue.[2]

Furthermore, the terminology of the courts is less detailed than in onomastics, as shown by the following example where the European General Court states:

> The word sign PICASSO has a clear and specific semantic content for the relevant public.... The reputation of the painter Pablo Picasso is such that it is not plausible to consider, in the absence of specific evidence to the contrary, that the sign PICASSO as a mark for motor vehicles may, in the perception of the average consumer, override

[1] Please note: citation references of judgments will appear in footnotes with the original reference number.
[2] Judgment of 18/05/2011, case T-502/07, para. 44.

the name of the painter so that that consumer, confronted with the sign PICASSO in the context of the goods concerned, will henceforth disregard the meaning of the sign as the name of the painter and perceive it principally as a mark, among other marks, of motor vehicles.[3]

It is clear that the court is determining rules how to handle proper names only in a legal environment. Onomastic considerations are thus marginal.

39.4.3 Publicity Rights

Another important issue for onomastic and legal interference is the field of publicity right claims. Vassallo and Hiney (2009) warn in their introduction to their article about publicity rights that:

> using a famous person's identity to promote a product or service can be very tempting for marketers, but if handled incorrectly it can lead to publicity right claims that may extend beyond the celebrity's lifetime. (Vassallo and Hiney 2009: 42)

Note that by 'incorrect handling' the authors are referring to incorrect legal handling. Furthermore, it is interesting to see that protection of the commercial value of famous people's names can go beyond their death, other than legal issues concerning individual names (see section 39.6 below).

The right of publicity is defined as the 'inherent right of every human being to control the commercial use of his or her identity' (Vassallo and Hiney 2009: 42ff.). In order to claim publicity rights, the infringement has to be made on purpose as an ' "insignificant" or "incidental" use of a person's identity will not violate a right of publicity' (Vassallo and Hiney 2009: 44).

39.4.4 Further Reading

For further reading, see Kremer and Ronneberger-Sibold (2007), Wochele et al. (2012), and Sjöblom et al. (2013).

39.5 Disagreements in the Field of Toponyms

Šrámek defines the toponymic conflict potential as 'conflict and rivalry of names expressing an ideologically definable feature' (2008: 15, my translation).[4] This gives

---

[3] Judgment of 22/06/2004, case T-185/02, para. 57.
[4] Text in original: 'Konflikt und Konkurrenz von Namen als Ausdruck eines ideologisch definierbaren Merkmals'.

a first impression of conflicts based on place-names as being a source of ideological issues rather than legal ones. Nevertheless, there is a broader need for regulation of place-naming due to globalization and international standardization. Conversely, this generates an enhancement of ideological issues due to the subsidiary requirements of minorities.

Language policy is the major source of both conflicts and conflict clearing in the field of place-names. Naming can be forced in order to suppress one community and show the dominance of another, for example the Germanization of place-names in the Lorraine region in France during the Nazi regime (Pitz 2008). On the other hand, naming policy can be established in order to conserve the integrity and identity of an ethnic minority within a country, for example the naming policy due to Māori place-names in New Zealand (Matthews 2011). Furthermore, it can concern the language policy within a uniform bilingual community, for example official place-naming regulations as a balancing act between vernacular and standard German in Switzerland (Garovi 2010). These language policies—be they with negative or positive objectives—are driven by socio-political forces on a national or regional level.

On an international level there are also efforts to harmonize place-naming regulations that nowadays find their way into national regulations. In 1948, the United Nations Economic and Social Council became aware of the need to set up rules for the standardization of geographical names. Out of this need arose the United Nations Group of Experts on Geographical Names. This group developed a set of proposals that have been (more or less) implemented in national or regional naming regulations.

New Zealand is a typical example of a country finding a solution in place-name legislation due to a social conflict situation.[5] The geographic board fixes rules on place-naming for the following reasons:

- for statutory compliance;
- to follow established local usage;
- where there is an awareness that the current name is culturally inappropriate;
- where the name is confusing to a local community;
- where other issues, e.g. safety, are a compelling reason to consider change. (Land Information New Zealand n.d.)

Another example from Estonia shows that a place-name law can be passed in order to come to terms with national history. The Estonian Place Name Act (2003) defines its scope of application in its first paragraph, thus:

(1) This Act regulates the establishment and use of Estonian place names and the exercise of supervision thereover.
(2) The purpose of this Act is to ensure the harmonised use of Estonian place names and the protection of place names of cultural and historical value.

---

[5] The case which led to this regulation is discussed by Matthews (2011: 16ff.).

A final example of regional place-name legislation comes from the district of Buenos Aires. After six years of planning and working to extend the underground line A, the moment of its grand opening finally arrived in September 2013. Line A was 9.8 km longer and gave access to eighteen new stations. The plan was to give the new station at the end of the line the name 'Flores y San Pedrito'. However, a couple of days before its inauguration the district governor launched the idea of naming the station 'Papa Francisco' in honour of the former archbishop of Buenos Aires and then Pope. The district governor was, however, obstructed by his political opponents who invoked a district regulation that allows people's names for public spaces only for people who have been deceased for at least ten years. On the day of the inauguration the district governor said in his speech that he considered the name 'Flores y San Pedrito' as being provisional and pointed to a project to change the legal obstacle and give 'Papa Francisco' his station at the end of the line even in his lifetime.[6]

These few examples show that the scope of place-name legislation covers administrative purposes and protection of minorities as well as consistency and conservation of traditions. As a rule the individual is not directly affected by place-naming or changes of place-names, although it is possible that communities are concerned. It is thus a more ideological or supra-social source for conflict and not an individual one. It can, however, have repercussions for the individual living in a region with a conflictive place-name.

This effect is particularly visible where a place-name clashes with territorial claims, for example the well-known dispute between Argentina and the UK about the archipelago *Islas Malvinas* or *Falkland Islands*. There are many such cases, just as well-known, like the dispute about the *Japanese Sea* or the disaccord between Greece and the Republic of Macedonia. Luckily, most of these conflicts are settled by international mediation.

Legally, place-names are a collective phenomenon subject to language policy and political conflicts. Therefore, legally fought conflicts in the field of toponyms (excepting those in commercial use) are relatively rare because their conflict potential has little legal foundation and is instead a matter of cultural, historical, and political issues.

39.5.1 Further Reading

For further reading, see Eller et al. (2008), Diver (2011), Kostanski (2011), Puzey (2011a), Tan (2011), and UNGEGN (2014).

39.6 PROPER NAMES AND PERSONAL RIGHTS IN THE LIGHT OF PUBLIC LAW

Apart from commercial names and their conflict potential based on economic value, and toponyms which follow their own supra-social rules, there is the large field of people's names that gives way to legal dispute.

---

[6] The whole occurrence can be traced in the internet news portal: <http://tn.com.ar/envivo/24hs>.

The core of conflicts over people's names also reflects a conflict between personal desires and the obligation of governmental authority. The administrative control function complies with the mere identification of people and disregards individualizing factors. As a result of this disregard, the particular relation between the individual and their name remains legally unattended (Pintens 2009: 1094). The individualizing motive of names cannot be totally neglected, which is the reason why names are subject to personal rights.

39.6.1 Why Does it Come to Legal Conflicts?

The obligation as well as the will to give a name to a (newborn) person is universal. As a rule, this lies in the hands of the parents, and in so doing the naming motivation can be diverse: tradition, fashion, personal preference, etc. (Handschuck and Schröer 2010: 17, 18). It can thus be assumed that in societies with legal systems that result in people sticking to a strict traditional naming system there are few if any legal name conflicts. Moreover, in societies where naming represents the personal preference of the name-giver (Koss 2002: 130), there is no conflict as long as the legally outstanding identification function of names remains within the framework of legal boundaries. Hence, three main reasons for recent name conflicts can be detected (Koss 2002: 130; Goldin and Shim 2004):

- internationalization of naming, i.e. names that do not fit in a given legal system—this applies to given names and surnames;
- creation of fancy names, i.e. names without (etymological) tradition—this applies primarily to given names;
- modern family model, i.e. the role of women in society and family—this applies primarily to surnames.

Another sub-categorization has to be considered concerning the naming process. Conflicts arise, on the one hand, during the process of giving a name and, on the other hand, due to changing a name. This can account for both given names and surnames. Jurisdiction is aware that the rough division of given names and surnames seems blurred from a cultural viewpoint:

> There are . . . given names, which are seen (however common they may be) as a personal, intimate and individual identification, and there are surnames . . ., which almost always identify a person by reference to his or her family or lineage and are in that connection often viewed as an essential part of an inalienable birthright. Yet beyond that basic categorisation, there is considerable variety.[7]

---

[7] European Court of Justice, opinion of Advocate General of 22/05/2003, C-148/02.

Finally, the conflict potential depends on the legal system. Common law systems usually have less strict regulations than systems with statutory law (Kushner 2009: 318; Pintens 2009: 1095).

39.6.2 Name Changes in General Legal Systems

Strictly speaking, common law does not apply jurisdiction on the basis of statutes emanating from a formal governmental law-giving act, but rather on the basis of legal custom and precedent law cases, whereas civil law systems act legally within the framework of a corpus of formally given statutes and regulations. It is important to point out that neither of the two systems exists in its pure form. In common law systems there are (more and more) formally set statutes by governments just as much as in civil systems where customary law and case law play an important subsidiary role beside the corpus of statutes (Seiler 2009: 42).

In order to show how the systems influence name regulations, I suggest considering the following example texts. The first is an explanatory note published by the Californian Courts on name changes (California Court 2015):

> (i)   In California, you generally have the legal right to change your name simply by using a new name in all aspects of your life, also known as the 'usage method'. BUT, with few exceptions, government agencies require a court order as official proof of a name change so getting a court order is the best way to make sure you legally change your name.

The second text is an excerpt from article 30 of the Swiss Civil Law concerning name changes:

> (ii)   Art. 30 para. 1: The government of the canton of residence may permit a person to change his or her name for good cause (Swiss Civil Code 2014).

Apart from their different binding effect—as the one is a piece of authority information and the other is a legal norm—there are further differences. Text (i) from a common law system grants the general right to a new name simply by use and states that for some official uses the new name might entail a court order (in the UK the equivalent would be a deed poll). Text (ii) from a civil system determines a deciding authority and requires a 'good cause'. Of course, the 'good cause' is a matter of legal interpretation. Some courts see, for instance, religious motives or traumatic occurrences like sexual abuse as being sufficient reason to change a name.

In other words, name changes in common law systems are entirely in the hands of the individual, while authorities are merely issuing offices for evidence if so required. Only the likelihood of fraud can be an obstacle to a name change under a common law system (Pintens 2009: 1095). In legal systems where name changes are regulated by statutory laws or regulations, the applicant needs the full consent of an authority and the change has to be justified, which implies that a simple 'change' is excluded; the mere use of another name has no binding effect. The final decision about a name change lies in the hands of an authority.

39.6.3 Which Conflicts Can Occur?

Conflicts can occur when a person does not yet have a name but should receive one. Moreover, conflicts can occur where an existing name is changed. There are different regulations that can differ from one authority to another or from one country or region to another—this implies an enormous amount of different regulations. Therefore, in the following there will be a set of typical conflict potentials that certainly do not apply to every country.

The responsibility to give a newborn a name remains in the hands of the parents (Koss 2002: 130) and is a matter of personal right. Of course, in legal systems with little constraint for name changes, the freedom for naming is generally large. In contrast, legal systems with more restrictions and decision taking authorities show more potential to eke out consent in naming conflicts.

39.6.3.1 *The Problem of Identifying Gender*

It has already been said that identifying an individual is one of the major functions of naming. Nothing is more obvious than identifying a person with manifest features such as gender. In many countries there is a legal obligation to choose a name that allows a clear gender assignment. As a matter of fact, gender marking is one of the major cross-cultural characteristics as it is the main feature in many cultures with different naming systems (Nübling et al. 2012: 185).

It is, however, not universal and, recently, gender identification by given name has been the subject of heated debate (Nübling et al. 2012: 127). Gender identification can be required to fulfil a social need for equivalent opportunities but can be complicated by an increasing mixture of names from other cultures with gender markers that are not compatible with traditional, national ones. More and more, gender neutral names are being given. On the one hand, names are chosen that do not have a linguistic gender marker, particularly names from 'genderless' languages such as English (Brylla 2001a: 43). On the other hand, mixed cultural societies are aware that gender marking differs significantly from language to language, as was shown in the judgment of the regional appellant court in Frankfurt (Germany).[8] In this case, it was stated that the Italian male first names *Nicola* and *Andrea* are acceptable as boys' names for the German birth register although they are perceived in the German language as being female and despite the names existing as female names in German.

A third possibility is that the hosting culture does not associate any gender with the name although for the migrant culture the gender is clear, as in the case of a Sri Lankan

---

[8] OLG Frankfurt am Main 20 W 411/93.

couple in Germany who gave their daughter the name *Mienaatchi* ('The Bride of Shiva').
After initial doubts from the civil registrar, the regional appellant court in Stuttgart[9]
accepted the name by taking into account the cultural background of the parents.

39.6.3.2 *The Problem with Different Naming Traditions*

According to national naming traditions, some civil registers cope with possible changes
due to gender and marital status while others do not. There is a tendency for even strict
civil registers to take on the traditional habits of other countries. This was the case in
Switzerland, where in 1980 the Supreme Court confirmed the immutability of family
names in the civil register, which is why one female complainant had to carry the family
name *Temelkov* and not *Temelkova*,[10] but in 2004 the court accepted that the son of a single mother with the family name *Dzieglawska* was not registered with the female version
of her family name but with the appropriate male form *Dzieglawski*.[11]

National naming traditions do not only concern the gender of the carrier of a surname
but also the composition of family names, bynames, and so on. The litigation of a Spanish-
Belgian couple about their offspring's family name can serve as an example. This case is
interesting insofar as it resulted in a European Court of Justice (ECJ) preliminary ruling and
thus has a binding effect on national legislation of the EU member states. At the time of the
litigation the Belgian legal regulation stipulated that children of a married couple received
the family name of the father, such that the children's Belgian birth certificates would
carry the surname of the father: *Garcia Avello*. In contrast, their registration at the Spanish
Embassy was done according to the Spanish family naming tradition that creates children's
family names from the respective first part of the family names of the parents (in this case the
maiden name of the mother), which would give *Garcia Weber*. In order to resolve this con-
tradiction of two differing family names for the children, the Belgian authorities proposed
to reduce the family name to the common element *Garcia*. The parents disagreed and filed
a law suit. The ECJ ruled that the naming traditions of other member states had to be taken
into account and the Belgian authorities had to accept *Garcia Weber*.[12]

The ECJ acknowledged the function of surnames in family bonds and lineage as well
as the incompatibility of many naming systems,[13] with the Advocate General stating that
if the family name were composed according to the Belgian system, 'Mr. Garcia Avello's
children appear to be his siblings'.[14] And he went on to explain that:

> An even more striking example ... would be the daughter, born in Belgium, of an
> Icelandic father and a Belgian mother. If the Belgian rule were applied, she would
> appear to an Icelander to be her grandfather's son rather than her father's daughter.[15]

---

[9] OLG Stuttgart 8 W 380/02.
[10] BGE 106 II 103.
[11] BGE 131 III 201.
[12] ECJ judgment of 02/10/2003, C-148/02.
[13] ECJ, opinion of Advocate General of 22/05/2003, C-148/02, para. 5.
[14] ECJ, opinion of Advocate General of 22/05/2003, C-148/02, para. 55.
[15] ECJ, opinion of Advocate General of 22/05/2003, C-148/02, Fn. 25.

Finally, cultural exchange and mobility leads not only to names with a different conception but also with a different form. This concerns above all foreign languages and writing systems. In 1984 the Supreme Court in Switzerland[16] ordered the civil register of the city of Zurich to accept the correct spelling of an original Hungarian family name *Széchényi* instead of *Szechenyi*. The regulation of the civil register in Zurich foresaw that names deriving from a non-Swiss national language had to be adapted to the canton language, in this case German. The court found that even though the name was originally Hungarian, it used the same diacritics as French which is a national language of Switzerland. Therefore, the correct Hungarian spelling had to be accepted.

Moreover, the personal opinion of the name carrier has to be taken into account even if it differs from authority rules. This is particularly noticeable when names are transcribed from other writing systems. One landmark case was a Greek plaintiff before the ECJ.[17] The plaintiff did not agree to the phonetic transcription of this name Χρήστος Κωνσταντινίδης on his marriage certificate to *Christos Konstadinidis* but demanded the transcription *Konstantinidis*. Given that the name on the marriage certificate had to correspond to the birth certificate, the responsible district court required a translation of his birth certificate. The translator used the ISO-Norm 18, according to which the transcription read *Hréstos Kónstantinidés*. The plaintiff disagreed with this transcription as it would distort the pronunciation of his name. In its preliminary ruling the ECJ found that it is unacceptable for a person to have to use a transcription of a name that does not reflect its usual pronunciation.

Naming traditions can also create a potential conflict in relation to moral concept changes, as Kushner (2009: 317) notes:

> More recently courts have struggled with the public policy implications of allowing transgender petitioners to change their names, and of allowing same-sex couples to change their surnames to match one another's.

The same struggle can have a political source, for example Kurdish names in Turkey (Akin 2004: 33). However, the intervention of legal action is always bound by a plaintiff's effort to claim a right or an infringement. Keep in mind: *The squeaky wheel gets the grease.*

39.6.3.3 *Traditional Functions of Family Names and Conflict of Laws*

With regards to a large variety of naming traditions, it must not be forgotten that one of the basic principles in jurisprudence is that any action, judgment, ruling, and so on is based on an effective law (statute, rule, etc.). Although jurisprudence takes more and more account of modern cross-cultural social settings, this legal principle must be born in mind. A ruling cannot be made for the sake of cultural acceptance and tolerance.

---

[16] BGE 110 II 324.
[17] ECJ judgment of 30/03/1993, C-168/91.

Therefore, it is imperative not only to point to social or moral changes in modern societies but also to an internationalization of laws. There is an increasing number of international treaties and laws that have an impact on naming or name changes (such as the above-mentioned preliminary rulings of the ECJ). Furthermore, it is important (although trivial) to stress that any sovereign state and its government have their own sovereign legal system. Any international exchange is thus regulated by a multitude of different laws deriving from different legal systems. The technical term for this is 'conflict of laws'.[18]

This is why legal decision takers confronted with conflicting naming cultures are also confronted with conflicting legal systems. Due to different naming policies, the outcome of a legal decision on names can vary enormously, even within a clear cut national system. It all depends on the question of which legal norm a court sets ahead of another.

A good example is the unusual given name *Frieden Mit Gott Allein Durch Jesus Christus* ('*Peace With God Only Through Jesus Christ*'). The bearer of this name was born in South Africa where his name was registered. At the age of fifteen *Frieden Mit Gott Allein Durch Jesus Christus* moved to Germany and demanded his name be registered by the registry office. The authorities were helpless because according to the German legal system the name was unacceptable. The court ruled that although the given name itself did not comply with the principles of the German name law, the name had to be registered on the basis of the fundamental right of the bearer to have a name. The name bearer did not have another name and it would be unacceptable to ask him to change his name after fifteen years.[19] In this case the fundamental personal rights stood above the administrative regulation.

In a case of a Swiss-Sri Lankan couple in Switzerland, the woman demanded that she be allowed to take the first name of her husband to be her and her later children's surname (as is the tradition in Sri Lanka) and not his last name (which would imply that her 'father-in-law' were her husband). Furthermore, the plaintiff claimed as well that Conflict of Laws (Private International Law) stipulated a guarantee of maintaining different name systems in Switzerland. However, the court ruled that the Sri Lankan marital name tradition did not comply with the constitutional equal rights principle in Switzerland. The constitutional principle of gender equality was set over the guarantee of maintaining foreign naming patterns.[20]

39.6.3.4 *The Problem of a Child's Best Interest*

With given names in particular, equal opportunities and cross-cultural parameters are closely related to another legal constraint which is a child's best interest. For commercial names the challenge may be to be outstanding, whereas for a child's name the parents' attempt to confer an outstanding name may be inconsiderate and selfish. Examples of

---

[18] Here the word 'conflict' does not refer to a dispute on a legal basis but rather to several laws that collide with each other or that 'stand' in a conflict to each other.

[19] OLG Bremen 1 W 49/95.

[20] BGE 136 III 168.

such name disputes frequently achieve coverage in the popular media. Therefore, I will only discuss the legal institution of 'the child's best interest'.

A spontaneous, inconsiderate name choice can harm a child so that a legal, protective intervention is necessary, as can be illustrated by a case from New Zealand. A family court judge removed a 9-year-old girl from the custody from her parents due to her name *Talula Does The Hula From Hawaii*. According to the child's lawyer, she was embarrassed about her name and avoided contact with others out of the fear of having to reveal her name. The judge stated:

> The court is profoundly concerned about the very poor judgment that this child's parents have shown in choosing this name. It makes a fool of the child and sets her up with a social disability and handicap, unnecessarily (as cited in McMahon 2008).

Clearly the girl herself was looking for legal help to change her name, even as a minor. In countries with authority consent for registering a name, the child's best interest is more frequently observed and creates a large number of court cases. The name must not be offensive and must be suitable to be worn as a name, for example the name *Störenfried* ('*Troublemaker*') is inappropriate for a child (Hess 1996).

Of course, the question of the child's best interest depends on the cultural setting of the child. This becomes particularly clear if we look at naming cultures that do not follow common lines, for example the naming tradition of the Akan in Ghana. Guerini (2005: 7) states:

> Naming practices in African societies represent a form of indirect and implicit communication with the community at large, which allows the expression of potentially embarrassing surrounding feelings and thought avoiding direct confrontation, which may compromise the relationship among members in a group or in a speech community.

The Akan give offending and disrespectful names to their children in order to deter bad influence through malicious spirits. Guerini (2005: 22) calls these names 'survival names'. According to the Akan it is in the child's best interest to receive an inappropriate name to prevent the child from being harmed.

Therefore, the legal institute of the child's best interest is of course a matter of interpretation and its exceeding construct could rapidly change to (legal, governmental) totalitarianism, as a child's welfare lies principally in the hands of the parents.

Given that the margin of the construction of the child's best interest is large, there can sometimes be protest reactions by parents against the naming policy of authorities. This happened in a well-known Swedish case with the protest name *Brfxxccxxmnpcccclllmmnprxvclmnckssqlbb11116* (pronounced Albin). Due to Swedish law a child's name must be registered with the appropriate authority at least by the age of five. The parents in this case failed to meet the deadline and were fined. As a protest against the fine, the parents chose the name *Brfxxccxxmnpcccclllmmnprxvclmnckssqlbb11116*.

The authority, of course, did not accept this name and the parents changed it to *A* (also pronounced Albin), which again was declined (Wikipedia 2014g).

Furthermore, a given name should have the function of a 'name' in contrast to a generic term. This onomastic core question is not satisfactorily answered by the law. In Germany for example, the names *Sonne*[21] (*'Sun'*) and *Pfefferminze*[22] (*'Peppermint'*) have been refused as forenames whereas *Sundance*[23] and *Biene*[24] (*'Bee'*) have been accepted. Legally, this can only be interpreted in the sense of judicial independence. It has to be mentioned that the issue of whether a sign can have the function of a name is (in a much looser extent of course) also discussed in common law systems. A name change from *Michael Herbert Dengler* to *1069* was refused by the Supreme Courts in Minnesota and North Dakota, although with the reasoning that the desired name was composed of only non-alphabetical characters. The Minnesota courts, however, announced that a phonetic spelling of *1069* might be acceptable (Kushner 2009: 315 and fn. 9).

39.6.3.5 *Laws Enforcing a Change of Name*

Finally, I would like to point to a small number of laws that (in some cases) foresee the explicit change of a name or explicitly prohibit a name. There is, for example, an Austrian Law concerning the inadmissability of nobility. Paragraph 2 stipulates that 'carrying titles of nobility and dignities is prohibited [for Austrian citizens]'.[25]

Moreover, many countries have laws about transgender issues. These laws regulate the far-reaching change from one sex to another and all the accompanying circumstances like the change of name. The transgender legislation facilitates the name change for authorities.

The same applies for adoption laws. Not only are the conditions and proceedings of adoption regulated but so too is the change of name or the taking over of the new family name. Again, this law facilitates the name change for authorities.

The issue of name changes in these statutes is, of course, obsolete in common law countries where only fraud prevention is held as an obstacle to changing a name.

39.6.4 Further Reading

For further reading see vol. 47 of the *Onoma* journal, and Kushner (2009) and Sperling (2012).

---

[21] AG Nürnberg UR III 90/93.
[22] AG Traunstein 3 UR III 2334/95.
[23] LG Saarbrücken 5 T 789/00.
[24] AG Nürnberg UR III, 283/1999.
[25] <http://www.ris.bka.gv.at/Bund/> (StGB1. Nr. 211/1919).

39.7 CONCLUSION AND OUTLOOK

It is not our cultural, traditional, political, moral, etc. awareness of adverse naming that is decisive for legal action but rather a concrete element of offence or a concrete legal fact. Therefore, a legal name conflict always demands a plaintiff and a legal cause of action. This is the legal framework in which onomastic considerations can gain ground. On this basis, three groups of name types can be defined as having a certain legal conflict potential: commercial names, toponyms, and anthroponyms.

It can be summarized that commercial names follow their own legal rules and form their own specific field of law. This is why they have to stand apart in the 'names and law' discussion as a particular group. The core issue from a legal point of view is to protect the commercial value which can also cover the personal rights.

The legal environment of toponyms is one of the matters dealt with by the UN. There is a strong international need for standardization. Disputes have a highly political significance but are rarely judged in a legal process. National tendencies show that toponym issues lead to the protection of minorities. Cultural traditions play a major role in the field of place-names and thus play a superior role to legal aspects.

Regarding anthroponyms, legal tendencies (in strict countries) show a dissolution of strict gender identification and more flexibility due to modern culturally mixed societies. However, people's names are still recognized as being a very personal identifier, a reason why legal rulings need other parameters to judge against a name, such as basic rights: personal rights, child welfare, and gender equality. The personalization of names is much easier in common law countries since the mere use of another name can be sufficient. Conflicts of law may develop more often in the future as societies with different naming systems and different legal systems move closer together.

....

CHAPTER 40

NAMES AND LEXICOGRAPHY

....

ALISON GRANT

40.1 INTRODUCTION

40.1.1 A Brief History of the Use of Onomastic Material in Lexicography

The benefit of lexicographical material to those working in the field of onomastic study is well established. Writing in 2005, W. F. H. Nicolaisen remarked upon the frequency with which name scholars consult dictionaries 'in an attempt to convert retrospectively the names under scrutiny into the words they once were'. The purpose of his article, however, was to highlight the benefits of the reciprocal process, that is 'the ways in which toponymic evidence can assist the historian of the lexicon' (Nicolaisen 2005: 112).

Historically, lexicographers have tended to consider onomastic material as beyond the scope of their dictionaries. In the eighteenth century, Samuel Johnson (1755) explained in the preface to his *A Dictionary of the English Language* that:

> As my design was a dictionary, common or appellative, I have omitted all words which have relation to proper names; such as *Arian, Socinian, Calvinist, Benedictine, Mahometan*; but have retained those of a more general nature, as *Heathen, Pagan*. (Johnson 1755)

A similar approach was taken more than a century later by James Murray, the first editor of the original edition of the *Oxford English Dictionary* (hereafter *OED*), who explained in his introduction to the first volume that:

In addition to, and behind, the common vocabulary, in all its diverging lines, lies an infinite number of *Proper* or merely *denotative* names, outside the province of lexicography, yet touching it in thousands of points. (Murray *et al.* 1888–1928: 1, xvii)

Regardless of whether or not 'proper' names ought be included in dictionaries, a major disadvantage of this general trend towards the exclusion of onomastic material from consideration is the loss of much valuable information which could be gleaned from these 'thousands of points'.

Writing just after the completion of the first edition of the *OED*, Allen Mawer (1930) reflected on how much work in the field of English lexicography still remained to be done.

Quite apart from the likelihood of new words or earlier examples of words already known being found in texts as yet unprinted or even unknown, there are a large number of known sources which remain as yet almost entirely untapped. One of those sources it to be found in place-names . . . Another rich mine which is as yet almost entirely unworked is that of personal names. (Mawer 1930: 11)

Mawer's article explored the various ways in which onomastic sources could augment the lexis, concluding that 'it is to be hoped that students of the history of our language may soon turn their attention to the systematic analysis of this material' (1930: 16).

As Mawer himself was only too well aware, one of the main drawbacks to the incorporation of onomastic material in dictionaries was a lack of availability of reliable data. A few years earlier, he had been instrumental in the founding of the English Place-Name Society, whose primary goal was a systematic and comprehensive survey of the place-names of each English county. Work on this invaluable project continues into the twenty-first century, but the completed county volumes and stand-alone dictionaries now offer a wealth of toponymic material which was unavailable to the editors of the first edition of the *OED*.

Although a second edition of the *OED* was completed in 1989, the focus of this work was the integration of the ancillary material contained in the First and Second Supplements (published in 1933 and 1972–86 respectively). Many of the original entries remained substantially unchanged. It is only with the advent of a new third edition of the *OED* (2000–) that a complete revision is being undertaken, with a much more inclusive policy regarding onomastic evidence.[1]

The lexicographical position in Scotland is somewhat different. Whereas the *OED* covers the whole of the English language from its inception to the present day, the equivalent Scots material is divided between two multi-volume works. The first of these is *A Dictionary of the Older Scottish Tongue* (hereafter *DOST*). This

---

[1] For more information on the *OED*'s current policy regarding onomastic material, see Scott (2004).

twelve-volume work was published between 1931 and 2002, covering the language of the Older Scots period (1100–1700). The Modern Scots material (from 1700 onwards) is encompassed by the ten-volume *Scottish National Dictionary* (hereafter *SND*), which was completed between 1931 and 1976.[2] As is the case with the *OED*, the use of onomastic evidence is minimal and unsystematic in both of these works, particularly in the early volumes. However, although the editors of *SND* have published two Supplements (in 1976 and 2005 respectively), there are no immediate plans to revise and update either *DOST* or *SND* in the manner currently being undertaken by the editors of the *OED* in England.

Reliable onomastic source material is also less readily available in Scotland. Although a Scottish Place-Name Survey was established along the lines of its English counterpart in the School of Scottish Studies at the University of Edinburgh in the early 1950s by Winifred Temple, much of the resulting research remains unpublished. Likewise, two valuable PhD theses undertaken at the university in the 1940s, May Williamson's *The Non-Celtic Place-Names of the Scottish Border Counties* and Norman Dixon's *The Place-Names of Midlothian*, remained unpublished until relatively recently, and thus were unavailable to the editors of either *SND* or *DOST*.[3] A third PhD thesis, *The Place-Names of West Lothian*, had been completed in 1937 by Angus Macdonald, who also worked as an editor on *SND*.[4] This slim volume, published in 1941, was one of the few toponymic sources used by the subsequent editors of both dictionaries.

In recent years, however, work has finally begun on a toponymic corpus for Scotland. Simon Taylor's five-volume *The Place-Names of Fife*, published between 2006 and 2012 (Taylor with Márkus 2006–12), forms the beginnings of an authoritative county survey in line with the English model, with further volumes planned as part of an ongoing STIT Project (Scottish Toponymy in Transition) based at the University of Glasgow. Also, despite the lack of firm plans for a revision of either of the multi-volume dictionaries of Scots, work is currently underway on a new edition of the *Concise Scots Dictionary*. This single-volume work, originally compiled between 1975 and 1985, contains material from both *DOST* and *SND* in condensed form, and the revised edition will incorporate both place-name and surname evidence to augment the lexical material. Some of the toponymic material currently being incorporated into the new *Concise Scots Dictionary* was collected during the 2011 SWAP Project (Scottish Words and Place-names), which was a joint undertaking by the University of Glasgow, Scottish Language Dictionaries Ltd, and the Scottish Place-Name Society.

---

[2] For a useful introduction to the history and development of these two dictionaries, see Dareau and Macleod (2009).

[3] E-editions of these theses have now been made available on the Scottish Place-Name Society's website (SPNS 1995–2009).

[4] For a recent study on the history and development of SND, see Macleod (2011).

40.1.2 The Problematic Relationship between the Lexicon and the Onomasticon

The lack of reliable source material is only one of the problems faced by lexicographers. As Mawer (1930: 12) noted, there is also 'the difficulty of interpreting much of this material'. The exact nature of the relationship between words and names has been the subject of much scholarly discussion over the years. There is clearly a strong connection between the two phenomena, as Nicolaisen (2011 [1980]) details:

> Names are initially, one might even say primarily, linguistic terms. When first given they usually mean in the way in which words mean, and when used they are embedded in linguistic contexts—phonologically, morphologically, syntactically. It is therefore fair to expect them to yield, when studied, chiefly linguistic information. (Nicolaisen 2011 [1980]: 81)

However, Nicolaisen (1980: 100) was already exploring the way in which names function differently from lexical items, conceptualizing the new idea of 'an onomasticon, as separate from though related to a lexicon'. Since then, scholars including Colman (1996), Kitson (2002), Fellows-Jensen (2007), and Scott (2008b) have explored the ways in which names evolve within their own *onomastic dialect* independently of the lexis, following different rules from those of their lexical counterparts, with differing geographic boundaries, encompassing differing phonological and semantic developments, and with the capacity to pass into the lexicon as well as evolving out of it. As Hough (2010: 2) recently concluded, the language of names can no longer be regarded as a subset of everyday, spoken language, but instead 'represents a toponymic register distinct from both demotic and literary lexis'.

This must be borne in mind by the lexicographer. Onomastic material has limitations which do not apply to purely lexical items, and names are arguably at their most linguistically useful at their point of inception. Thus, whilst a historical record of a place-name can provide evidence that a word was in use earlier than is attested in the lexicon, it does not provide evidence that the word was ever in use in everyday speech. Likewise, such records offer no evidence for the continuing use of a word in the language, as a toponym can continue to be transmitted on a purely onomastic level long after its component words have ceased to be used or understood.

Similarly, certain types of surname, such as those given as nicknames and those derived from occupations, will have a narrow window of lexical force which will apply at the time the name is coined, but will not necessarily persist. Nicolaisen (2011 [1980]): 91) notes that the point at which a surname becomes hereditary is also the point at which it becomes detached from its lexical etymon, and thereafter its evidential value is greatly diminished. There are further limitations to be borne in mind when dealing with surname evidence. For example, as Hough (2003: 41) notes, 'it would be misleading to assume . . . that an occupational surname necessarily designated the sole, or even primary, employment of its bearer'.

However, whilst the onomasticon and the lexicon clearly function and develop very differently from one another, the points at which they intersect can still furnish the lexicographer with much useful data, provided that it is treated with care. The rest of this chapter will explore the ways in which onomastic material can augment and elucidate lexical material to enhance our understanding of language as a whole.

40.2 THE EVIDENTIAL VALUE OF PLACE-NAMES

40.2.1 Ante-dating Lexical Material

One of the most important contributions that place-names make to the study of language is to provide ante-datings for lexical items. A useful case study here is the word *dod*.

The second edition of the *OED* defines *dod* as meaning 'a rounded summit or eminence, either as a separate hill, or more frequently a lower summit or distinct shoulder or boss of a hill'. The earliest example of *dod* recorded in *OED* is from the *Penny Cyclopedia* of 1843, in which an article on the (now former) county of Westmorland lists *Dod Hill* among the various significant local peaks.[5]

However, a search of the *SEPN* county volumes for northern England reveals that *dod* is first recorded in place-name sources more than six centuries earlier. Smith's (1964–6: 2, 217) survey of Westmorland indicates that the name Rest Dodd is attested as *Restdode* in the late twelfth century and as *Rostdode* in the thirteenth century. Similarly, Armstrong et al.'s (1950–2: 1, 411) survey of Cumberland records that *le Dod de Gillefinchor* and *the other high Dod of Gillefinchor* are mentioned in the Loweswater bounds of 1230. Other examples from the Cumberland volumes which ante-date the lexical evidence include Brown Dodd, which is *Broundodde* in 1272, The Dod, recorded as *Dod* in 1599, Dodd Crag which is *dodcrage* in 1615, Dodbury, which is *Doddburye* in 1631, and Great Dod, which is on record as *Dod Fell* in 1783. Additional examples from the Westmorland volumes include Middle Dod, which is *Midledod syde* in 1588 and Great Dod, which is recorded as *Mickledod* in 1687.

The situation is mirrored in Scotland (see Grant 2012b). *SND* has only a stub article for *dod*, 'a bare hill with a rounded top', containing a single quotation from 1715, which states that '*Hills* are variously named, according to their magnitude as Law . . . Dod'. There is no equivalent entry in *DOST*. However, there are dozens of hill names containing this element across southern, central, and eastern Scotland, many of which have historical forms on record throughout the Older Scots period.

---

[5] All of the county names used in this chapter for both England and Scotland refer to the pre-1975 system.

The earliest of these is found in Williamson's (1942: 255) thesis, where *Brunemore super dod* is on record in 1165–75, referring to a moor near Dod in Roxburghshire. Other early records include the now lost Midlothian name *Broundod* 1336–37, identified by Dixon (1947: 227), and *PNF* 4 has located another lost *Broundod* name in Fife which was recorded as *Brountod* 1529 and *Broundod* 1540. Two further examples from Williamson (1942: 244, 264) are Dodrig and Dod Burn in Roxburghshire, first recorded as *Dodburne* in 1569 and *Dodrig* in 1574 respectively. The evidence available in published studies can be supplemented by direct recourse to the historical records themselves. For example, an examination of the Register of the Great Seal of Scotland (hereafter *RMS*) reveals that Dodhouse in Berwickshire was recorded as *Dodhous* in 1509, and Dods in the same county was *Dodis* in 1525–26 and *Doddis* in 1558. In Angus, *the lands of Dods* are recorded in 1653, and *the Dod* is recorded in 1580–81, whilst in Roxburghshire, there are records of *Dodhill* in 1587, and in the East Lothian, *the four acres called Dod* are recorded in 1658, and Bentydod is on record as '*Beltoun Dod* alias *Bentidod*' in 1660. Another useful source here is the Blaeu Atlas, published in 1654, which records various *dod* names, including *Dodhead* in Selkirkshire, and *Dodhouse, Dods*, and *Dodds* in Berwickshire. Together, these toponymic records provide evidence that the word can be ante-dated in Scots by more than 500 years.

The latter part of the *OED* definition 'a lower summit or distinct shoulder or boss of a hill' is pertinent when reevaluating the interpretation of the word within a Scots context. Not all of the Scottish instances refer to distinct hills with rounded tops, and it seems that a secondary meaning of 'a (rounded) lump or shoulder on a larger hill' ought to be added alongside the original definition given by the *SND* in any future revision of this entry.

There are many other lexical items which can be ante-dated in this way. The toponymic research of the editors of the ongoing *SEPN* (1924–) has provided numerous instances of words which are recorded in place-names much earlier than they are recorded in lexicographical sources. Hough (2002) offers a useful catalogue of these early attestations, with examples including *sinke* 'a cesspool, a cesspit' which is attested in the Middle English Dictionary (hereafter *MED*) from 1413–14, but is found in the field name *Suinwrosinc* in the early thirteenth century, and in the place-name Sink Moss in 1336. Likewise, *houshold* 'a landholding able to support one household' is in record in the *MED* from a.1387, but is found in the field names *le Houshold* in 1300 and *Houshald* in 1314–19. Similarly, *wrinkel* 'a winding or curving' is attested in the *OED* from 1430–40, but is found in the field name *Wrynkilsiche* 1272–1307, and *yoking* 'the harnessing of an ox-team' is attested in the *OED* from 1580, but is found in the field name *Yokkynge Feld Wodeles* over a century earlier in 1468.

The Scots toponymicon offers similar ante-datings. Scott (2007: 6) notes that *howlet* 'an owl' is first attested in *DOST* from *c.*1450, but is found in the place-name *Howelotestone* in 1336–7. Scott also notes (2008b: 93) that the lost name *les Sanctuary-croftis* first recorded in 1451 predates the earliest lexical instance of *sanctuary* in *DOST* by approximately sixty years. Further examples identified during the SWAP project include *berry*, which is attested in *DOST* from 1490 onwards, but is found as

Berybus in 1455 and as *Berybusk* in 1474 in Williamson's (1942: 216) early forms of the Selkirkshire place-name Berrybush. Williamson (1942: 72) also has a 1288 form *Hardley* for Hardlee in Roxburghshire, whereas the earliest record in *DOST* for the adjective *hard* is from the late-fourteenth-century text *Legends of the Saints*. Additionally, *PNF* 1 identifies a burn named *Yhalwleche* in a boundary record of *c*.1335, ante-dating the earliest lexical record for the word *yellow* in *DOST* by more than forty years.

40.2.2 Toponymic Evidence for Otherwise Unattested Lexical Material

In addition to providing ante-datings for many items of the lexis, the toponymicon also provides instances of otherwise-unattested vocabulary items. For example, on the basis of a small group of English place-names including Poughley Farm in Berkshire, Hough (2001b) demonstrates the likely existence of an Old English word **pohha/*pocca* 'a fallow deer', connected with OE *pocc* 'spot', which may have been replaced by the Old French word *fawn* in the aftermath of the Norman Conquest. There are numerous other instances of animal names otherwise unattested in the corpus of Old English, including **ean* 'lamb', **gæten* 'kid', **galt* 'pig, boar', **padduc* 'frog', **tacca* 'young sheep', **tige* 'goat', and **wearg* 'wolf'.[6]

Place-names have also provided a substantial corpus of words otherwise unattested in Middle English. A catalogue of examples compiled by Hough (2002) include **big* 'a building' attested in the names *Canonbig* (1372) and *Newbig* (mid-thirteenth century), **cut(t)el* 'an artificial water-channel' evidenced in the field name *Cuttelhulle* (*c*.1270–80) and the place-name *Cuttele mill* (1278), **dey* 'a dairy' attested in field names including *Deylese* (1365) and *the deyhous* (1442), and **sty-way* 'a pathway, a narrow road, a footpath' attested in field names such as *le Stiyweylandis* (1280) and *Stywaystrete* (1432). One further example from this list is **flodder* 'a mire, a boggy place', recorded in the field names *Floddreacre* (1201) and *Floderforlong* (1311). Although this element remains absent from the *OED* at the time of writing, supporting evidence is found in the form of a Scots cognate, recorded in the *DOST* entry *fludder* (n) 'a bog or mire' recorded from 1611 and in the *SND* entry *fluther* (n2) 'a boggy piece of ground, a marsh'. A Scots ante-dating to this lexical evidence can be found in the lost West Lothian place-name **Fludders*, for which Macdonald (1941: 21) has the historical forms *Flod(d)eris* 1540–1 and *Flud(d)eris* 1558–9. Material of this kind is being carefully collated by the editors of Scottish Language Dictionaries to be used in any future revision of *DOST*.

Similar examples of otherwise unattested material can be identified for the Scots language. Scott (2004: 216) notes that Macdonald's historical forms of the name Priest Mill in West Lothian (including *Breistmyln(e)* 1534 and *Brestmyln* 1538) provide evidence of an otherwise-unattested compound **breist-mill* 'a mill driven by a breast water-wheel' which

---

[6] For a more comprehensive list, see Hough (2001b: 1).

ante-dates the earliest English lexical attestation (1674 in *OED*) by nearly a century and a half. Similarly, whilst the *OED* has an entry for the adjective *oaky* (meaning 'characterized by or consisting of oak') with lexical records dating back to the early seventeenth century, there is no lexicographical record of a Scots cognate. However, *PNF* 5 has identified a potential Scots form **aiky* on the basis of a Fife name, Aiky Hill, first recorded in 1855 in the first edition of the six-inch OS map. To this can be added the East Lothian name Aikeyside, which was recorded as *Akkiesyde* 1597–8 [*RMS*] and *Aikiesyde* 1635 [*RMS*] and Aikie Bush in Kirkcudbrightshire, which was recorded as *Aikybuss* on a late-sixteenth-century Timothy Pont map. In the same county, another Aiky Hill name was recorded as *Aikiehill* in 1673 [*Kirkcudbright Sheriff Court Deeds*], and Aikieslack is on record as *Akyslack* in 1797 [*Ainslie Map of Kirkcudbright*]. Additionally, Aikey Brae in Aberdeenshire was recorded as *Aikie-Brae* in 1732 [*Antiquities*], noteworthy for being the site of the old Aikey Fair. As well as providing evidence for the existence of this term in the Scots toponymicon, the earliest of these records also ante-dates the English evidence by more than seventy years.

An additional example of an otherwise-unattested Scots word is identified by Williamson (1942: 251), who postulates an element **eschy* 'overgrown with ash-trees' on the basis of the Selkirkshire place-name Ashiesteel which was recorded as *Eschesteile* 1455. Supporting evidence is found in Ashybank in Roxburghshire, which was *Eschebank* 1511 [*RMS*], and in the same county there is the lost **Ashyhaugh*, recorded as *Eschehauch* 1569 [*RMS*] and *Eschiehauch* 1607 [*RMS*]. Ashy Holm on the border between Kirkcudbrightshire and Dumfriesshire was recorded as *Escheholme* in 1577 [*RMS*]. Another Ashyhaugh in East Lothian was recorded on the first edition of the six-inch OS map as *Ashyhaugh* in 1855. As is the case with **aiky*, this element does not feature in either *DOST* or *SND*, but both were clearly being utilized in the toponymic register of Scots speakers across the southern part of the country.

40.2.3 Evidence for the Reinterpretation of Lexical Material

Place-name evidence can also be useful in the reinterpretation of existing lexical items, offering both revisions of meaning and expansion of semantic range. For example, Hough (1999) has argued that the occurrence of Anglian *bēmere* 'a trumpeter' in place-names such as Bemersyde in Berwickshire is unlikely to commemorate a musician, but is instead more likely to reflect a transferred use of the term for a bird with a trumpet-like call, such as the bittern.

Similarly, colour terms are commonly found as the specific element in place-names, but recent scholarship reveals that some apparent instances lack the expected adjectival endings and prove contextually problematic, pointing instead to their transferred use as animal names.[7] For example, Hough (1995) has argued that names such as Grazeley

---

[7] For a useful discussion, see Hough (2006).

in Berkshire (containing *sol* 'wallowing place') points to an otherwise-unattested *græg '(grey) wolf' rather than the colour *grey*. Likewise Hough (1998) suggests that names such as Brownsall in Dorset may offer evidence of an otherwise-unattested *brūn '(brown) pig', rather than the colour *brown*. Scott (2007) has identified further Scots place-names including the lost *Brunecnolh* in Roxburghshire and the similarly lost *Brownlaw(s)* in West Lothian, whose historical forms may show reflexes of an OE genitive plural *brūna 'of the pigs' rather than reflecting adjectival formations containing a colour term.

Additionally, some lexical items are marked in dictionaries as occurring only within a poetic or literary register. For example, in Scots, the word *firth* is represented by two dictionary entries. *DOST firth, fyrth* (n1) defines the term as 'a wood', and notes that it occurs 'only in poetry'.[8] The earliest recorded usage is in the late-fourteenth-century text *Legends of the Saints*. The related *SND* entry *firth* (n2) confirms the meaning of 'a wood, wooded country' and also that the word is only found in poetry. However, this narrow semantic context is brought into question by the existence of a group of Scots place-names which appear to contain this element. Williamson (1942) identified two examples in Roxburghshire: the lost *Firthhouse*, recorded as such in 1662, and Firth, which was recorded as *Firth* in 1588 and 1662. It is perhaps worth noting that as Roxburghshire is a land-locked county, there is little chance of the names referring to the other kind of *firth*, 'an estuary or inlet of the sea', which is also evidenced in the Scots language. Similarly, Dixon (1947) recorded another Firth in the inland parish of Lasswade in Midlothian, with early forms including *Frythe* in 1336–7 and *Firth* in 1609. More recently, *PNF* 3 has identified a small group of *firth* names in Fife. These include a lost name *Oxfriht*, which was recorded in the Caiplie Charter of 1235, a similarly lost *Firth Muir, recorded as *Firthmure* 1592 and *Firthmur* 1594, and Frithfield, whose early forms include *Furthfield* c.1560 and *Firthfeild* 1578 x 1591. Additionally, there are two Firth names in Angus, one of which was recorded as *Firth of Bellishane* in 1663 [*RMS*].

This small corpus of place-names has implications for any future revision of the Scots dictionaries. First, the 'verse only' labels will need to be reconsidered as the word must have, at least originally, encompassed a wider register. Secondly, the *DOST* entry can be ante-dated by nearly a century and a half because of the *Oxfriht* form on record in Fife in 1235. Finally, the definition of *firth* in both *DOST* and *SND* will also need to be re-examined, in the light of both the toponymic evidence and the English cognate form. The *OED* entry *firth* (n1) records a wider range of meanings for the term than simply a wood or wooded country, including 'a piece of ground covered with brushwood'. Similarly, in their study of this element, Gelling and Cole (2000: 224–6) have concluded that in English place-names *firth* can frequently signify 'land overgrown with brushwood, scrubland on the edge of a forest' rather than referring specifically to 'a wood', and *PNF* 5 argues that this interpretation should be taken into consideration for the Scottish examples as well. The fact that *firth* is found in Scots place-names in combination with

---

[8] See Grant (2012a) for a full discussion of this element.

generics such as *field* and *muir*, with their apparent implication of open space, would appear to lend credence to the additional sense of 'scrubland, brushland', and this ought to be reflected in any revision of the definition of the term in the Scots dictionaries.

40.3 THE EVIDENTIAL VALUE OF SURNAMES

40.3.1 Ante-dating Lexical Material

As with place-names, one of the most important contributions made to lexicography by surname evidence is the ante-dating of lexical material. Mawer's 1930 article included some initial examples of occupational surnames drawn from the Sussex subsidy rolls which significantly ante-dated the earliest lexical attestation of these terms in the *OED*. Five years later, Fransson's 1935 PhD thesis *Middle English Surnames of Occupation: 1100–1350* identified a substantial corpus of these names. For example, 'candle-maker' was first attested in 1611 in the *OED*, but Fransson's earliest record is of an *Alan. le. Candelmakere* more than three centuries earlier in 1289. Similarly, 'knife-smith' was first attested in 1738 in the *OED*, but Fransson records a *Will. Knysmyt* in 1326; 'herring-monger' was first attested in 1614 in the *OED*, whereas Fransson has an *Is' Relicta Heryngmongere* in 1296; and 'flaxman' was first attested in 1509 in the OED, but Fransson records a *Walt. Flexman* in 1327.

Thuresson's *Middle English Occupational Terms* (1950) expanded on the work begun by Fransson, identifying many further instances of occupational surnames which ante-dated the lexical material in *OED*. Examples include *Rob. Ploghmaystre* recorded in 1297, where the earliest record of a 'ploughmaster' in *OED* dates from 1642. *Margaret Fisshwf* is on record in 1381, well before the earliest lexical record in OED, which dates from 1523. Additionally, *Matth. Clogmaker* is recorded in 1367 (1723 in *OED*), *Rog. le Harpemaker* is recorded in 1380 (*c.*1515 in *OED*) and *Rog. le Lacemaker* is recorded in 1305 (1589 in *OED*), offering substantial ante-datings for the existence of these types of craftsmen.

None of the above entries has yet been revised in the *OED* at the time of writing, but the current editorial team are making good use of onomastic sources in their preparation of a third edition. As McClure (2011a) notes, the entry for *mould-maker* in the second edition of the *OED* had lexical attestations from 1780 onwards, but the new entry in the third edition has been ante-dated by more than 400 years using surname evidence gleaned from the *MED*, and now *Gilbertus le moldemaker*, who was living in York in 1337, has the honour of being the earliest attestation of this compound in the dictionary.

There are no comparative studies of Scots surnames of occupation. However, many examples can be found in Black's (1946) dictionary of Scottish Surnames,[9] and the

---

[9] The introduction to Black's dictionary offers a useful outline of occupational surnames in Scots; see also Nicolaisen 2011 [1980]).

editors of the new edition of the *Concise Scots Dictionary* are currently making use of this material to find ante-datings for existing dictionary entries.[10] For example, the occupational term *dyker* 'a builder of dykes' is evidenced in two *DOST* entries: *(dykar)*, *dikar* (n) which has a single quotation dated 1497, and *dyker, dycker* (n) containing three seventeenth-century quotations. Yet Black identifies a *Robert Diker de Elgin* who served as a juror in 1261, ante-dating the term by more than two centuries. Similarly, the DOST entry *barkar, barker* (n) 'a tanner' has lexical evidence from the fifteenth century onwards, but Black records an *Alisaundre le Barker*, Provost of Haddington, who rendered homage to King Edward I of England in 1296. Finally, the DOST entry for *bellman, belman* (n) 'a bell-ringer, a town crier' has lexical records dating from 1471, whereas Black records a *Gilbert Belman* more than seventy years earlier in 1398.

40.3.2 Evidence for Otherwise Unattested Lexical Material

As well as providing a substantial corpus of ante-datings for existing lexical items, Fransson's (1935) study of Middle English surnames also revealed 252 occupational terms which were otherwise unattested in the lexicon. Records of early bearers including *John Boltsmith* (1346), *Joh. le Gosmanger* (1344), *Jacobus le Ledsmyth* (1329), *Rob. Silverhewer* (1212), *Joh. Le Skynwassere* (1281), and *Rich. le Wolbetere* (1271) provide evidence for the occupations of 'bolt-smith', 'goose-monger', 'lead-smith' 'silver-hewer', 'skin-washer', and 'wool-beater' respectively. These were not recorded in the first (or indeed the second) edition of the *OED*, and have not been added to the dictionary at the time of writing. Thuresson (1950) also has a large collection of occupational terms which were not included in the original *OED*, including *Warin. the Calfehirde* (1269), *Rog. le Heyberare* (1306), *Will. Qwsshynmaker* (1367), *Will. Stirkhyrd* (1281), *Ric. Straumongere* (1294), and *Will. le Swyndriuere* (1317), providing evidence for the occupations of 'calf-herd', 'hay-bearer', 'cushion-maker', 'stirk-herd', 'straw-monger', and 'swine-driver' respectively. Likewise, these terms remain absent from the *OED* at the time of writing.

Material of this kind can also be identified in the Scots language. For example, there is no entry in either *DOST* or *SND* for *beltmaker, but Black's (1946) dictionary reveals that *Walter Beltmakare* was a burgess of Edinburgh in 1477 and *Agnes Beltmakar* was a 'cake-baxter' in Stirling in 1525.[11] A full-entry search of the online version of *DOST* reveals that further evidence of beltmaking is found within other entries.[12] *DOST*

---

[10] The editors of *DOST* did make use of Black's *Surnames of Scotland* for the later volumes, but Black's work was not published until 1946.

[11] As Nicolaisen (2011 [1980]: 90) notes, the fact that Agnes Beltmakar's occupation was given as 'cake-baxter' reveals that in this case the compound had already developed from an occupational designation into a hereditary surname.

[12] Online versions of both *DOST* and *SND* can be accessed for free at the Dictionary of the Scots Language: <www.dsl.ac.uk>.

ham(m)erman (n) has mention of a *John Henry, beltmaker,* who *aucht properlie to enter with the hammermen* in 1630, and *DOST pendicle* (n) reveals that *James Henrye belt-maker* was *to enter with the said hammermen* in the same year. Black also has a record of a *Nevin Watirleder* who held a tenement in Edinburgh c.1426. The compound **water-leader* 'a water-carrier' is otherwise unattested in *DOST*, although there are two similar compounds *burne-ledar* (n) and *wattirman* (n) which share this meaning, with records dating from the sixteenth and seventeenth centuries respectively. Finally, Black notes that a *Johannes Dubber* witnessed a charter in Glasgow c.1290, and a *John Dubber* was listed in the Exchequer Rolls of 1329. He gives the etymology of the name as Old French *doubeur* 'repairer'. The term **dubber* does not appear in *DOST*, but there are two apparently-related verbs, *redubbre* and *redub* 'to put right, correct, amend' with lexical attestations from the early sixteenth century. Surname evidence of this kind preserves valuable snippets of vocabulary which would be otherwise unknown.

40.4 THE EVIDENTIAL VALUE OF PERSONAL NAMES

Personal names are arguably less useful to the lexicographer than either place-names or surnames. As Kitson (2002: 99) notes, even as far back as the Anglo-Saxon period, such names often lacked lexical meaning, and when 'combining elements to make whole names, associations of elements were far more important than any idea of through-composed meaning'. He also notes (Kitson 2002: 100) that 'there are names which understood as a whole would make nonsense', citing *Friþuwulf* 'peace-wolf' as an example.

In the modern era, personal names are usually semantically opaque, and hold no intrinsic information about their bearers. However, one area in which personal names are of interest to the lexicographer is where they are used in the generation of new lexical items. McClure (2011b) notes that English personal names are frequently used to form names for plants, such as *sweet william*, animals such as *tomcat, billy goat,* and *nanny goat,* and machines such as the *spinning jenny.*

Names of this nature also proliferate in Scots. *SND* records that *Meggie-mony-feet* refers to a centipede, whereas *Meggie-spinnie* is a spider. *Robbie-cuddie* is a wren, *jenny-lang-legs* is a cranefly, and *gabblin' Tam* is an Ayrshire term for a willow-warbler. *Lizzie-run-the-hedge* is a name for goosegrass in the Scottish Borders, and *William-and-Mary* is a Banffshire name for the lungwort. A *Handy Betty* is a Dumfries-shire word for a plate-warmer, whereas a *Tidy Betty* is an ash-pan.

McClure (2011b) also notes that *jack* and *jill* have been in use as prototypical names for ordinary men and women since at least the fifteenth century, with the former being found in phrases such as *jack-of-all-trades* and compounds such as *jack-tar. DOST* records that *ja(c)k* (together with *jo(c)k*) and *jennie* were also used as prototypical names for ordinary people in Scots from the sixteenth century, with *jo(c)k* first being used to refer to a 'typical' Scotsman in 1641.

SND includes more contentious entries for personal names such as *Billy* and *Dan*, which were lexicalized in West Central Scotland to refer to Protestants and Catholics respectively, due to the perceived popularity of the names within each religious group, as illustrated by the once-infamous question 'Are you a billy or a dan?' The lexicalization of such names, particularly in a negative context, will have an impact on their subsequent perception and use within the anthroponymicon.

40.5 CONCLUSION

It is clear that the lexicon and the onomasticon are connected and interdependent, and that one cannot be fully understood without reference to the other. Place-names and surnames are exceptionally useful to the lexicographer, and have tremendous potential to fill in the gaps for the earliest stages of language, particularly in the case of the Old and Middle English periods in the English language, and the pre-literary period (up to 1375) in the Scots language. Such names can provide evidence for an earlier presence of a word than is indicated by the lexical material, in addition to offering evidence for the existence of words which would otherwise be unknown. Names enhance our understanding of language origin and development, and allow us to locate additional registers and semantic functions.

However, despite the substantial amount of work which has been undertaken in this area over the last eighty years, Mawer's desire for a systematic analysis of onomastic material remains only partially fulfilled, with many more veins in his 'rich mine' of onomastic sources remaining as yet unexcavated. There is still much work to be done by the editors of the ongoing revision of the *OED* in England and by the editors of the *Concise Scots Dictionary* in Scotland, both in the gathering of new onomastic source material, and in the analysis of the material which has already been gathered.

CHAPTER 41

....

PLACE-NAMES
AND RELIGION

A Study of Early Christian Ireland

....

KAY MUHR

41.1 INTRODUCTION

....

RELIGION ('binding') is a human construct of pattern and structure, a way of understanding the world and the place of human beings in it. Religion is now often viewed as an aspect of human life rather than relating to the whole of it, 'binding' it all together. As a community ethos or view of right behaviour, religion can result in outcomes which could be categorized as legal, medical, scholarly, recreational, artistic, and customary, and actions other than ritual, worship, and prayer inspired by something divine, supernatural, or beyond ourselves. The connections can be shown in the pervasive religious belief that acting in accordance with the divine plan promotes the fertility of nature and thus human prosperity, as expressed for example in the Bible (Ezekiel 34:26; Leviticus 25:18), or in Ancient Greece, where dramatic and severe funeral rituals not only expressed hopes for the deceased but demonstrated entitlement to an inheritance (Alexiou 1974: 20–1).

Many aspects of religious expression do not result in place-names. However, natural landscape features inspiring awe, sites and buildings of individual pilgrimage or communal gathering for prayer, ritual, and worship, and burial places for the dead and memorials to famous people often bear place-names attesting to religious belief. Although the word-elements in such place-names differ over time, especially with the change from pagan to Christian religion, it is clear that many of the concepts endure.

Irish Gaels clearly had a religion, a structure defining the world and their place in it, before accepting Christianity in or from the early fifth century. Classical writers attest belief in an afterlife among the continental Celts.[1] Although anything we know about

---

[1] Lucan, Pharsalia 1.450–8: l.458 *longae, canitis si cognita, uitae mors media est* 'death, if what you sing is true, is but the mid-point of [a] long life'.

Ireland was written by those who had become Christian, earlier tradition partly survives in the words of the language and in mythical narratives in early Irish, which 'affirm the coexistence of parallel worlds in which human conduct finds its counterpart in the world of the gods' (Deane 2011: 5). A major part of the religious structuring throughout concerns the permeable boundary between the ordinary and the sacred, special places, or times, or events, where the human and this divine world came closer together. Place-names cannot reveal the moral code, the prickly sense of honour and *fír flatha* or 'prince's truth' evident in the stories of warriors and kings, but they often describe the features of the landscape that linked the natural and visible with the unseen world:

> All that survives in the historical and literary record can only be fully understood by relating it to actual places within the landscape. Places are portals to history and identity and it is within the landscape itself, among the monuments and other significant places, that archaeology, history, onomastics and literature meet, for it is here that all human beliefs, aspirations and endeavours are forged. (Schot et al. 2011: xvi)

Margaret Gelling's comment (2009: 7) that, 'In Celtic-speaking areas there must have been wholesale replacement of earlier names by new names referring to churches, enclosed graveyards, church dedications, and the shrines where saints' relics were preserved' is admittedly mainly talking about P-Celtic areas, but is certainly not true for Ireland, as many Christian sites in early Ireland do retain the place-names they bore before conversion. This chapter will focus on place-names in Ireland, some natural feature names of pre-Christian religious significance, and burial monuments pagan to Christian, including some of the place-name terminology borrowed from Christian Latin. It will offer a particular study of two first-millennium Irish-language place-name terms, *findabair* and *tamlacht[ae]*, in their cultural background in Early Christian Ireland.

41.2 *FINDABAIR*

Findabair, so spelled in an early instance, is a recurring place-name in Ireland, most often used alone and attested in about twenty-five current townland names, anglicized as Fennor, Finner, and the like.[2] The same form also occurs as a female personal name, which has been equated with Welsh *Gwenhwyfar* 'Guinevere', the wife of King Arthur, although the etymology, most plausibly *find* + *siabair* 'white spectre', is unlikely to be the same as the place-name (Mac an Bhaird 1991–3: 11). The Irish woman's name notably

---

[2] The typically Irish small administrative divisions now known as townlands, an economic unit averaging 300 acres, are recorded with their civil parishes, baronies, and counties in the *Townland Index* for Ireland, first published in 1861. Transcribed by John Broderick (aka SeanRuad), it is now available online (*Townland Index* 1861).

refers to the daughter of Queen Medb in the Irish epic *Táin Bó Cuailnge*, where a place *Finnabair Slébe* 'Finnabair of the mountain' is named after her (O'Rahilly 1976: ll. 3349, 3365). A personal name interpretation has occasionally been used by later scholars for place-names where Findabair is the specific, such as Kilfenora, Clare, and Knockfenora, Limerick (generic 'church' and 'hill'; Joyce 1869–1913: II, 275; cf. Kilfenora Ordnance Survey Name-book FIONTAR (2008–14b). The declension was the same in both personal and place-names, the genitive being a *k*-stem, in early Irish *Findabrach*. In Modern Irish the place-name is spelled *Fionnúir*, genitive *Fionnúrach*.

The term is an early compound, of an adjective (normally following its noun in Irish) and a noun, and there are several further place-name examples which have not survived to the present in Ireland.[3] The coinage of noun-plus-noun compound names is generally datable to before AD 600, although adjective-plus-noun may have a longer time-span, up to AD 1200 (Mac Giolla Easpaig 1981: 152, 163; Tempan 2009: 65). However *Findabair/Finnabair* is attested early.

The etymology of the place-name was discussed by T. F. O'Rahilly, who derived it from Celtic **Vindo-dubris* 'White water', and compared Gwenndwr in Brecon, Wendover in Buckinghamshire; French Vendeuvre, Vendoeuvre, Vendoeuvres, Vandoeuvre; and Vendoeuvres in the canton of Geneva, Switzerland. He pointed out that it is 'of frequent occurrence' in Ireland, but explained its *k*-declension in Irish as a 'later analogous development' (O'Rahilly 1933: 210–12).

Dobhar 'water' is a masculine *o*-stem in Irish (Dinneen 1927: 349; and earlier Irish DIL: 218). The example of this compound found in Wendover, Buckinghamshire was referred to in Anglo-Saxon as *æt Wændofron* (plural). There is no suggestion of velar inflection in this (Mawer and Stenton 1929: 24; Jackson 1953: 629–30). W. J. Watson (1926: 456) found one clear Scottish example, Findourie 'white stream', in Careston parish, Forfar, also deriving it from *dobhar* 'water'.

Eoin MacNeill and more recently Alan Mac an Bhaird explained the velar ending as reflecting a compound of *vindo-*, modern Irish *fionn*, with *brí, breg* 'hill, high place' (MacNeill 1930: 12 n1; Mac an Bhaird 1991–3: 11). *Brí* is another familiar Celtic element as in the names of the tribe *Brigantii*, and St *Brigit* (Wagner 1981: 7).

There is no text that plainly tells us that *Findabair* was a pagan religious place-name. The likelihood that it was so comes from etymology, distribution—many of the places were important—and sometimes archaeology. In many Irish examples the places contain Christian churches. The possible etymology brings in whiteness of colour, water, and hills, all sacred in other contexts.

---

[3] Current place-names in Ireland are usually best known in an anglicized spelling created by non-Gaelic administrators during the second millennium. Notable landmarks, fortifications and churches, and also battle-sites, may be referred to early, but, unless named from these, townlands may not have their names recorded before the thirteenth (church lands) or even seventeenth century. See Hogan (1910), its successor *HDGP* in progress and being published by ITS, Murray (2010), and the *Townland Index* (1861). Spelling in Irish also changed through time.

In Irish the earliest certain instance is found in the seventh-century Life of St Patrick by *Muirchú*, where, as in the Bible story of the sending of the Ark of the Covenant to Shiloh (2 Samuel 6; 1 Chronicles 13.5) the place where Patrick's body should be buried is discerned by entrusting it to a cart drawn by untamed cattle. The sacred wagon-team was obtained *a loco qui Clocher vocatur ab oriente Findubrec de pecoribus Conail* 'from a place called Clocher east of Findabair, from the cattle of Conal' (Bieler 1979: 120, Muirchú §II 11.2).

Many people have identified this Findabair with the townland of Finnabrogue near Downpatrick, Co. Down (Bieler 1979: 258, fn. by de hÓir; Hamlin 2000: 120 n.17). *Finnabair* near Downpatrick was clearly a significant place, being mentioned in an annal reference in AD 1010 (Mac Airt and Mac Niocaill 1983), and the place-name legend of the Ulster royal site *Emain Macha*, which refers to three Ulster kings in joint rule over Ireland, the third being *Cimbaeth* son of *Finntan* in *Finnabair Maige hInis* 'Finnabair of Lecale', the area of Downpatrick (Van Hamel 1933: 33, §30). Finnabrogue townland has a low hill, but is also close to water, as shown on early maps before the Quoile marshes were drained much closer than it is now (R. Warner, pers. comm.).

The place-name may also appear in the Greek geographer Ptolemy's coordinates for a map of Ireland *c.*AD 150 as a river mouth in the north-east (between the rivers Boyne and Lagan) called *OUINDERIOS*. 'Ptolemy's ultimate source evidently asked for the name of the river and received the name of a place at the rivermouth...' (Mac an Bhaird 1993: 11, §10.5). Mac an Bhaird believes these references are to a *windobrigs* gen. *windobrigos* (reading *OUINDOBRIOS*) identified by him as Finnabrogue.

Historical texts contain further examples. Muirchú's story of the burial of St Patrick, repeated in the later *Tripartite Life* (Stokes 1887: 252), could refer to the Downpatrick Finnabrogue, or to the townland of Findermore at Clogher in Tyrone. The Tripartite Life contains two more references to places called Findabair, of which one definitely is a hill in the Clogher valley (*Lemuin*): *Luid Patric iarsin hiLemuin .i. Findabair ainm in tailcha inro pritchad Patraic.* 'Patrick went then to the Clogher valley, and Findabair is the name of the hillock where he preached'. This is also the place where the Life says St Brigit had a dream of two stones, one big, and one small: *Atchonarc íar sin dí chloich, indara cloich becc 7 alaili mór* (Stokes 1887: 176). From a surviving cross-inscribed standing stone on a hill of 300 feet at the townland of Findermore 'great *Findabair*', another stone is visible (Hamlin 2008: 386). The description of the site convinced Richard Warner that Findermore is the correct location (Warner 2006: 172). Moreover, Findermore seems likely for the burial story, since the ruling family at Clogher, descended from Conall *mac Daimíne mac Daim Argait* 'son of little ox son of silver ox', were closely linked with cattle. In later place-name tradition, Devenish monastery in Fermanagh got its name *Daimhinis* 'ox island' because Conall mac Daimíne kept his cattle there (Stokes 1905: 206n; O'Brien 1962: 140 §141a27).

The other story in the *Tripartite Life* involves Patrick staying forty nights at a place called *Findobuir*, apparently a royal residence, between *Collunt*, now Slieve Gallion, and Lough Neagh, with the intention of establishing a monastic city (*cathraig*) there (Stokes 1887: 168). The visit to *Collunt*, named *Collunt Patricii*, is given briefly by Tírechán (Bieler

1979: 163, 255n). The name *Findobuir* does not survive, but a later inquisition in 1633 recorded a subdivision called *Fynworre*, possibly the elevation now bearing the name Silver Hill, in Ballydawley or Crospatrick townlands, parish of Tamlaght, a suitable location in south-east Co. Derry (Ó Doibhlin 1971: 145–6). The area remained church land associated with St Patrick.

Further places of the name definitely became sites of churches. *Findabair Abae* 'Findabair of the river' was mentioned from the ninth century in the *Annals of Ulster*: a steward in AD 829, abbots in 809, 838, 845, a bishop in 907, a Viking attack on the church in 834, and another attack in 939 in which a priest was killed (Mac Airt and Mac Niocaill 1983). A church site survives in the townland of Fennor, on a height on the southern bank of the Boyne in Co. Meath. The patron saint was called Nechtan, described as a nephew of St Patrick, son of his sister Liamain. *Findabair Aba* 'Findabair of the river' is named in all the Irish Martyrologies or Saints' Calendars, among which Óengus gives most information 'Findabair of the river on the bank of the Boyne in Brega' (Stokes 1905: 128; CGSH: §722.75). The parallel of the name Nechtan with 'Neptune', and an Otherworld Nechtan, dweller in a *síd* or 'Otherworld hill' at the source of the Boyne, and husband of the river-goddess Boyne, has been noted (Wagner 1981: 17; Ó Riain 2011: 512).

The Irish Annals record another example on the river Boyne, *Finnabair-na-ningen* 'Findabair of the maidens', an old name for Drogheda townland, which was given to the clergy by Muirchertach Ó Lochlainn when Mellifont abbey (*Teampall na manach*) was consecrated in 1157 (O'Donovan 1990 [1856]).

There are three examples of places called *Cill Fhionnabhrach* 'the church of Fionnabhair', apparently based on an earlier place-name, as no known saint was so called. The most important is Kilfenora townland in the parish and diocese of Kilfenora in Co. Clare, referred to as *Cill Finnabrach* from the Annals of Innisfallen in AD 1055 to the Four Masters in AD 1599 (O'Donovan [1990] 1856: 5, 1288; Hogan 1910: 192; Mac Airt 1951). The church is on a low plateau, but there is no notable water: an oral legend says there was none until saint Fachnan discovered a well at Bullan, north-east of the church (Evans 1966: 70; Power 2012: 22).

In AD 1228 the Abbey of Killenny owned the 'manor of *Fynnore*' (with variant spellings *Fynhawere* 54, *Fynower* 55, both 1228), now the townland of Killenora, parish of Kellistown Co. Carlow (Butler and Bernard 1918: 53–5, map 188). This example has anglicized the lenited form, rather than the basic initial *F* of *Findabair*. There is also Kilfenora townland in the parish of Ardfert, Co. Kerry, a parish which has a cluster of ecclesiastical names.

Finner in the parish of Inishmacsaint, Co. Donegal, is a large townland of 1,582 acres, containing an old burying ground, on the low-lying south bank of the river Erne where it flows into the sea (1:50,000 sh.16). According to the *Archaeological Survey of Co. Donegal*, as well as a seventeenth-century church, there are many archaeological remains, including passage tombs, ringforts, and a now-destroyed 'important early ecclesiastical site' with 'substantial banks and the foundations of a church' (Lacy et al. 1983: 37, 43, 173, 176–7, 266). George Eogan gave Finner as an example of a group of megalithic tombs (Eogan 1986: 93).

Fennor townland in Rathconnell parish, Co. Westmeath, has been described as: 'Glebe, containing a church in ruin and a burying ground' (Walsh 1957: 237). It is likely in AD 799 to have been a battle site also: *bellum Finnubrach hi Tethbai, ubi reges multi occisi sunt* 'the battle of Fennor in Tethba, where many kings were killed' (Mac Airt and Mac Niocaill 1983).

Some other Fennors are referred to as battle sites, while battles were often fought on boundaries (Ó Riain 1972). Fennor townland in Duneany parish, Co. Kildare, is the likely site of *Flannchath Fionnabhrach* 'the blood-red battle of Fennor' in AD 506, by the Laighin 'Leinstermen' against the Uí Néill (O'Donovan 1990 [1856]), and of another *bellum Finnubrach* in AD 719, an 'encounter' between Leinstermen (Mac Airt and Mac Niocaill 1983). Battles recorded in the *Annals of Tigernach* in AD 524 and 718 probably took place here (Ó Murchadha 1997: 145). An Ulster reference to *Cath Fersde agus Cath Fionnabhrach* 'the battle of Fersat and the battle of Fionnabhair', is probably to be understood as referring to the ford at Belfast and to Finnabrogue (*LCAB*: 18–19).

Some other *Finnabair* references in Ulster provide further information on topography. The final *-d* of Finnard townland in Newry parish is a nineteenth-century addition to the anglicized spelling (Toner and Ó Mainnín 1992: 26–7). The Clanrye River goes round the west and north of this *Finnabair*, while the townland is centred on a small hill 345 feet high with a ringfort on top. Another Co. Down example, on the Ards peninsula, is Ballyfinragh ('townland of Finnabair', *Baile Fionnúrach*, still pronounced with five syllables) in the parish of Witter (Hughes and Hannan 1992: 124–5). This is a low hill rising to *c*.100 feet, with Ballyfinragh Lough to the north-east. There are three examples in Co. Fermanagh, including the island of Inishfendra, and Finner townland (with a division called Knocknashee) above the river Erne at Belleek (Muhr 2014: 38–9).

There is also the name *Mag Finnabrach* 'plain of Finnabair', now the baronies of Moyfenrath Lower and Upper in Meath, explained as named from a woman (Gwynn 1903–35: IV, 216, 484n), and *Sídh Finnabrach*, 'Otherworld dwelling of Finnabair' (Gwynn 1903–35: III, 483). *Sídh Finnabrach* was allocated by Manannán to an Otherworld chieftain called Faghartach, and its location near the Boyne tombs suggest it was the same place as the church site called Fennor over the south bank of the Boyne (Hogan 1910: 599; Duncan 1932: 185, 188, 207). Most places called *síd/sídh* are in fact hills, and the element will be discussed under hill names shortly.

41.2.1 Etymology

Taking the initial element of the compound Finnabair first, the adjective *finn* is one of three words meaning 'white' in Irish, but where *bán* has connotations of paleness, and *gel* of brightness, *finn* may connote 'blessed' ('frequent in (Christian) religious poetry'), and in the moral sense 'fair, just, true' (DIL: 141–2 sense d; *fionn* 'white, holy' in Watson 1926: 307), an etymology which Wagner associated with knowledge and understanding (Wagner 1971: 23 n.27). The second element may refer to water or to a hill.

41.3 WATER

Despite the abundance of water in Ireland, it is not hard to find evidence for its sanctity, in the names of rivers which were considered as goddesses, the celebration of wells, and examples of other divine names in place-names. In one seventh-century life, St Patrick was accused of worshipping water, used by him in the rite of baptism. A druid objected to a water-test with Patrick 'for water is a god of his' *aquam enim deum habet*; and in alternate years, *nunc aquam nunc ignem deum venerator*, 'he worships...now water now fire as his god' (Bieler 1979: 94, Muirchú §I 20).

Rivers were represented in early Irish as goddesses. Patrick's other early biographer Tírechán refers to the river Shannon *quae dicitur bandea* 'which is called a goddess' (Bieler 1979: 138, Tírechán §19.5) and demonstrates the origin of another river name, *An Bhanna*, the Bann, as *ban-dea* meaning 'goddess' (*Flumen Bandae*, Bieler 1979: 160, Tírechán §48.2; Ó Mainnín 1993: 175–7). The early form *bouvinda* recorded by Ptolemy for *An Bhóinn*, the river Boyne, means either 'white cow' or 'she who has white cows' (O'Rahilly 1946: 3; Wagner 1981: 5). The Boyne appears as a mythological character in early tales, wife of Nechtan, and by the Dagdae 'the good god' mother of Óengus of the Boyne tombs (Gwynn 1903–35: III, 36–7; Wagner 1981: 5). Wagner (1981: 5) gives *Loígde* 'calf goddess' as an early name for the river Bandon. In Adamnán's *Life of St Columba*, the river Lochy in Scotland was explained as *nigra dea* 'black goddess' '*in fluvio qui Latine dici potest Nigra Dea*'. The reference to a river *Fendae* in Donegal shows that the river Finn was also a 'white goddess' (Anderson and Anderson 1961: 142, 414n, 535n).

Another supernatural being in place-names was *Manannán*, according to the account in *Cormac's Glossary* the eponym of the Isle of Man, and called 'god of the sea' (Stokes 1862: 31) and later Otherworld 'high-king' in Ireland (Duncan 1932: 184, 188, 206). It is likely that John O'Donovan's interpretations of the dangerous underwater reef called Carrickmannon, off Kinbane headland on the north coast in the parish of Ramoan (Mac Gabhann 1997: 268), and the townland of Carrickmannan (containing Carrickmannan Lake), parish of Killinchy Co. Down, as *Carraig Mhanainn* 'Manannán's rock' (*Ballycarickmanan* 1605) are correct, and that the second element is *Manainn*, a short form of *Manannán*. Máire MacNeill has collected some recurring supernatural stories of watery places, such as Mannin Lake, Co. Mayo (MacNeill 1962: 614) and Manann Castle, Monaghan (MacNeill 1962: 163–9, 500–2). Dónall Mac Giolla Easpaig (pers. comm.) has made a study of all the *–Mannan* place-names in Ireland, and found that most of them contain water features.

41.3.1 Wells

As with the rivers, the mysterious first appearance of water from the ground was held sacred. Supernatural knowledge or inspiration floated down the rivers Boyne and Shannon in nuts or bubbles from the mysterious spring of Segais (Gwynn 1903–35: III,

26, 292–5; Muhr 1999: 196, 199–200). *Tobar Nechtain* 'the well of Nechtan' the husband of Boann, was the source of the river Boyne at Carbury hill, which was also called *Síd Nechtain* 'Nechtan's Otherworld dwelling' (Gwynn 1903–35: III, 28 l.43). Tírechán described St Patrick's visit to the well of *Findmag* 'the white plain', which he says was then worshipped *in modum dii* 'as a god' (Bieler 1979: 153, Tírechán §39.2). Many wells now dedicated to saints rather than deities appear in townland names.

41.4 HILLS

As watery places recur in Irish mythology, so also do hills. Uplands as well as rivers regularly marked the boundaries between territories, while hills with a view of the territories around were favoured as a focal point for assembly sites. Distinctive hills, often with mythological associations, were used as landmarks for route-finding. The Irish literary genre of *dindsenchas*, the 'lore of high places', celebrated a basic 'triangulation' of Ireland; for the learned and for travellers who needed to know routeways and also where the boundaries of the local kingdoms or *tuatha* ran, since ordinary people (unlike poets, lawyers, and clerics) lost status and thus legal protection in another's territory (Kelly 1988: 4). The view from a hill was used by poet seers not only for consolidating their knowledge of the landscape, but also for the ritual of damaging an enemy by satire (Muhr 2006).

41.4.1 *Temair*

Another sacred hill-word is *Teamair*, Tara, used not only of the legendary assembly site in Meath including a cursus, other ancient earthworks and burial mounds, but of about twenty-seven surviving other places throughout Ireland, as well as some in medieval records but unidentified (Evans 1966: 174–6; Ó Muraíle 2005). However, rather than meaning a place with a view (see Joyce 1869–1913: I, 294–6; Watson 1926: 505; Mac Giolla Easpaig 2005: 423–9; Ó Muraíle 2005: 474–6) the latest study derives it from the root *tem* 'cut', meaning 'an area cut off', 'demarcated for sacred purposes' (Mac Giolla Easpaig 2005: 446–7).

41.5 *SÍD*

Hills also linked to the Irish 'Otherworld', a pagan concept, originally of the world of the gods, which endured alongside Christianity. Early Irish literature maintained that the Otherworld people occupied a parallel world in the 'underneath half of Ireland' (*in leth ro boí sís d'Hérind*, Watson 1926: 1 l.5). High ground was typically wild and untamed, not regularly frequented by humans, the place of magic and adventure, while distinctive summits were the home of the supernatural beings, the *aos sídhe* sometimes translated as 'people of the mounds'. Their parallel world was never far away, but only accessible at particular times via particular entrances, usually leading inside hills, although sometimes through caves on lower ground, under lakes, or across the sea. The element *Síd* 'Otherworld dwelling' features in many early place-names, with about 150 sites called *Síd* or its diminutive *Sídán* recorded in Hogan's *Onomasticon* (Hogan 1910: 597–600; place-name class discussed in Muhr 2011: 239–40).

The Irish word *síd* 'mound, hollow hill, otherworld dwelling' has a homonym in the word *síd* meaning 'peace', one of the features of the reign of a good king, when the parallel worlds are in harmony. The etymology and relationship has been much discussed, but a fruitful approach links the two concepts via the idea of 'settlement', akin mythologically to Norse *saetr*, the summer hill dwelling connected to the more permanent dwelling in the valley (Wagner 1981: 3).

Many of the early *síd* names include the personal name of an Otherworld, originally divine, chieftain, and about forty different Otherworld people are named. Often the same site may also be described by a place-name location, for example *Síd al/ar Femen* 'the Otherworld hill beyond or at Femen (located using a plain in Munster), or *Síd Buidb (Síd mBuidb)* identified by the name of its Otherworld king, Bodb. The location is sometimes ambiguous, as with *Síd Nenta*, either *al uisce* 'beyond' or *fo uisce* 'under' the water of Lough Ree. Knockmany hill and townland in Tyrone, looking down on the routeway of the Clogher valley, may be suggested as a typical identifiable *síd*: a small but prominent hill with a wide view, with a distinctive rock feature on top, natural or man-made. It was *Síd Chnuic Báine* 'the Otherworld dwelling of Báine's hill', named after an Otherworld woman (Muhr 2011: 244–5).

Some of these *Síd* sites are places referred to many times in Irish literature, while many others are mentioned only once. The specific elements of their names reveal distribution of a *sídh* in twenty different named regional locations across Ireland. Although there is not enough information to establish any hierarchy, for example into provincial *sída*, it is clear that every human settlement could be visualized as having its parallel in the other world.

Early texts acknowledged the previous divine role of the *aes síde* 'people of the Otherworld'. In Tírechán's seventh-century account of St Patrick's arrival at the royal site of Rathcroghan in Connaught, people thought these strangers were:

uiros side aut deorum terrenorum aut fantassiam,
'men of the otherworld or earth-gods or a phantom,'
(Bieler 1979: 142, Tírechán §26)

Fiacc's Hymn in the Irish *Liber Hymnorum*, states that:

for túaith Hérenn bái temel | túatha adortais síde,
'On the folk of Ireland there was darkness: the peoples used to worship síde'.
(Stokes 1887: 414–15)

However there is little record of Otherworld worship, only literary texts which portray its parallel world as a place where time moves differently, of physical beauty, supernatural riches, and fertility (Muhr 1999: 197; Ó Cadhla 2014: 128, 132–7).

41.6 *FINDABAIR*: LINKING CONCEPTS OF NAMING THE SACRED LANDSCAPE

Earlier than the etymologists, the Irish place-name scholar P. W. Joyce had collected the Irish instances of *Fionnabhair*, and decided that whatever the exact meaning it was 'locally applied to a "whitish spot"' (Joyce 1869–1913: II, 273–5). In 1839, from his toponymic experience on the first Ordnance Survey, Eugene O'Curry had written of the second part of Kilfenora, 'a name given to several localities in Ireland, and which are generally found to be pretty fertile elevations' (FIONTAR 2008–14b; Clare County Library n.d.). The meaning *Fionnchnoc* 'white hill' has been used by the Dublin place-name office for the latter part of Knockfenora in Co. Limerick (FIONTAR 2008–14c). However, a 'fertile hill' also needs water, and the problem of etymology may be resolved by postulating that a wider Celtic compound *find + dobur* 'white hill' may have existed in Irish, like a compound *find + siabair* 'white spectre' but that both have become *k*-stems by falling together by analogy with a dominant *find + breg* 'white hill'.

Otherworld *síd* 'peace' and Biblical descriptions of the beauty of heaven (Ezekiel 47: 1–12; Revelation 21: 15–22, 2) meant that for a while there was a certain Christian rapprochement with the acceptable aspects of the pagan otherworld. In the poems of Bláthmhac (Carney 1964: 62, ll. 731–2) the host of heaven *muinter* [*nime*] give welcome: *fri mac a flatho fire | fri loegán a slánside* 'to the son of their true chief, the darling [lit. 'little calf'] of their safe Otherworld dwelling'. There is no editor's note on the word *síd*, which must bear a double meaning as heavenly 'peace', as in the prose tale *Echtrae Chondlai* 'Connlae's otherworld adventure' (McCone 2000: 56, 136). The saints' calendar of Oengus also refers to heaven as *Sídflaith* 'realm of peace' (Stokes 1905: 123, 162).

However the Christian parallel was not maintained, and the word was not used to name churches. The divine personal names have been lost but many surviving place-names containing the element *síd[h]* are now townland names, mostly with 'shee' in second place as a specific (27 examples), or based on the diminutive *sídheán* (44 examples), usually simplex, in various spellings: Shean, Sheean, Sheeaun, Sheehaun (*Townland Index*, 821–3). A common translation in Irish place-names has been the apparently whimsical Fairymount (Muhr 2011: 240). Later the Otherworld dwellings were often located in old human habitation sites or 'fairy forts', and the idea that these are sacred places, not to be meddled with without supernatural consequences, has been maintained in oral tradition till recent times.

Not all the *síd* names include the word every time: other first elements include various hill words: *benn* 'crag, pinnacle', *brí* 'height', *carn* 'rock heap', *carraig* 'rock', *cnoc* 'hill', *cruach* 'stack-shaped hill', *duma* 'mound', *sliab* 'mountain', as well as *tech* 'house', the word for an ordinary human dwelling.

41.7 *Tech*

In contrast to síd and hill and water words, *tech*, the ordinary word for 'house', was also used to name supernatural dwellings. Sites of a divine being's house are listed in Hogan (1910: 622–7): *Tech Aengusa an Broga; Tech Elcmaire in Brogha*, the 'house of Aengus, or 'of Elcmar, of the Brugh' being the same as *Síd in Brogha*, the burial mound of New Grange on the Boyne; 'Cermna's house' or *Tech Cermnai* being the same as *Síd Cuillind*, Slieve Gullion with its summit cairns; *Tech Nectain* in the tale *Togáil Tigi Nechtain*, 'the destruction of Nechtan's house' being the same as *Síd Nechtain*, the hill above the well called *Tobar Nechtain* at the source of the Boyne. Research on *tech* in place-names has shown it used for other archaeological sites, and the townland name Drumintee Co. Armagh, 'ridge of the house' possibly continues the earlier name *Tech Cermnai* for Slieve Gullion, where the cairn was later called 'the Cailleach Bhéara's house' from another supernatural resident (MacNeill 1962: 161; Muhr 2008: 225, 2011: 238, 240).

The most famous Otherworld site called *tech* was out in the sea: *Tech nDuinn* 'Donn's house', being the Irish name for the Bull Island off Kenmare in Kerry. According to legend, Donn died before he could invade Ireland and his body was left on the high rock or island now bearing his name, since when, *do rreir na ngennti* ... 'according to the heathen':

Adellad na hanmanda peacacha co teach n[D]uind ria techt a n-ifearn, . . co tabraid a mbendachtain for anmain Duinn.

'the souls of sinners visit Tech Duinn before they go to hell, and give their blessing, ere they go, to the soul of Donn'. (Gwynn 1903–35: IV, 310–11, quoting from the Prose Dindsenchas)

Earlier tradition was thus transmuted to a kind of purgatory, but various references make clear that Donn was originally god of the dead (Müller-Lisowski 1948: 148).

Deirdre Flanagan (1984: 38) saw this mythological usage as the antecedent of *tech* as an ecclesiastical place-name in the pre-twelfth-century period, where it is quite frequent and usually followed by the name of the saint. She collected a number of these and wondered if 'the Christian deployment of the generic *tech* might suggest the site of a saint's grave or relics' (Flanagan 1981–2: 74).

When the *Síd* sites of the early literature are explored, many of them refer to hilltop cairns, or burial mounds, and up to recent times a recurring story tells how a human visitor to the fairy hill recognized there people he had thought were dead (Evans-Wentz 1911: 39–40; Ó Suilleabháin 1942: 450; Bhreathnach 2010: 25). *Síd in Broga* 'Otherworld hill of the palace' or *Brug na Bóinne* 'the palace of the Boyne' is the chambered tomb of New Grange, with decorated stones, in the extensive megalithic cemetery at the Bend of the Boyne (Evans 1966: 165–6, 172–4). *Sídh Cruachain* was a low hill with a small summit mound in the extensive archaeological landscape at Rathcroghan, Roscommon (Evans 1966: 184). *Sídh Cuillinn* was on Slieve Gullion, 1,894 feet (573 m), which has two hill-top cairns and a chambered tomb (Evans 1966: 61–2; Neill 2009: 128–30, 145–7; Muhr 2011: 238). *Síd ar Femen* or *Síd Ban Finn*, the 'Otherworld hill of Femen', or 'of the fair women', is a round hill-top cairn even higher on Slievenamon (*Sliabh na mBan* 'mountain of the women') in Tipperary (Evans 1966: 196). Knockmany, already mentioned, has a hilltop cairn and chambered tomb with elaborately carved stones (Evans 1966: 202). Knockfierna (MacNeill 1962: 202) or Knockfeerina (Evans 1966: 145) in Co. Limerick has a hill-top cairn (950 feet; 288 m), and its name comes from *cnoc* 'hill' of the early district name *Frigriu, Frigrenn*, later re-interpreted as *fírinne* 'truth' as an epithet of its Otherworld chieftain, Donn.

41.8 *FERT[AE]*

The significance of graves in early Irish law shows them to be another type of religious place-name. The gravemound or *fert* of the landowner marked the boundary of his family's land, while standing stones or gravestones are also possible boundary markers (Kelly 1988: 186–189; 1997: 409). There are two *ferta* named in actual boundary descriptions, *Fert Moraind* in the border of the territory of *Uí Chathbad Tíre*; and *Fert Sceinde* in the border of the share of Cormac Cas (O'Brien 1962: 206, 222; Charles-Edwards 1993: 262; Bhreathnach 2010: 27–8). Moreover, the presence of a *fert* rendered the land in which it was sited *nemed* or sacred, as with land made sacred by being 'owned by the Church or by a lay dignitary' (Kelly 1997: 436 n.248, *nemed cille no dúin no a maigen firt*). The pre-Christian legal term *nemed* 'sacred' was transferred for Christian use, and used in referring to churches (and their sheltering trees), although unlike Scotland it rarely appears in Irish place-names (Muhr 1996: 217; 2002: 27, 43; Barrow 1998: 56, 58–9; Boyle 2005).

In heroic tales a grave called *fert* appears in conventional use as the grave of a pagan hero:

Ro lád trá a gáir gubai et a fert et a liae

'The cry of lamentation for him, and his gravemound, and gravestone, were made'. (Van Hamel 1933: 15)

Fergus Kelly gives another example: 'his funeral mound (*fert*) is dug, lamentation (*gubae*) is raised for him, and his cattle slaughtered' (Kelly 1997: 52).

Many examples of *fert* followed by the genitive of a personal name appear in the texts. William Reeves first collected place-names containing the word *fert[ae]*, noting from examples such as *Fert mBoinne, Fert Echtra, Fert Neimhidh, Fert Scota*, that it was 'almost always found in pagan association'. He considered it 'originally denoted a pagan grave of a peculiar form' (Reeves 1900 [1860]: 27–9). That form is actually described in Tírechán's Life of Patrick, in Latin *c.*AD 670, which contains a description of the burial of two young female converts. The daughters of King Loegaire at *Cruachain* (Rathcroghan, Co. Roscommon) were baptized by Patrick, and chose to die immediately so as to see Christ. They were buried then beside the well of Clebach where Patrick met them first, and their people made *fossam rotundam in similitudinem fertae* 'a round ditch after the manner of a *ferta*, because this is what the heathen Irish (*Scotice homines et gentiles*) used to do, but we call it *relic*, that is, the remains (*residuae*) of the maidens. And the *ferta* was made over to Patrick with the bones of the holy virgins, and to his heirs after him for ever, and he made an earthen church (*ecclesiam terrenam*) in that place' (Bieler 1979: 144–5, Tírechán §26:).

Fert is used of Christians in some further early instances. The place-name *Ferta* in an annal for AD 504 appears to be where the person of the name was buried:

Cerpán mortuus est, episcopus o Ferti Cherpain oc Temuir.

'Cerpán died, a bishop from Ferta Cerpáin at Tara'. (Mac Airt and Mac Niocaill 1983)

Cerpán's grave could be the same person or place as his 'house', *Tech Cerpáin* (Bieler 1979: 163, Tírechán §51; 132, Cerpanus §13). *Fert Scéithe*, the grave of the woman saint Sciath (*Sciath ingen Mechair ic Firt Scethi i mMúscraige*, CGSH: 109 §665.2, 180 §722.98) is the only example in the genealogies of the saints, and has been identified with Ardskeagh townland, parish of Buttevant, Co. Cork.

Fert[a] also occurs in the names of churches. A church at Armagh called *Fertae Martyrum* in Muirchú's Life of Patrick was translated by Bieler as 'the Burial-Ground of the Martyrs' (Bieler 1979: 24, 108). Later, from AD 1179, it was known as *Teampall na Ferta* 'church of the burial mound' (Muhr 2002: 38–9).

There are three churches called *cluain ferta* 'meadow of the grave-mound' in the Saints Calendar of Oengus (Stokes 1905: 379). These are *Cluain Ferta Brénainn*, now Clonfert, Co. Galway (Stokes 1905: 76, 86, 112, 242; Evans 1966: 118–19); *Cluain Ferta Molua*, now Clonfertmulloe al. Kyle, in Co. Laois (Stokes 1905: 42, 180, 260). Dónall Mac Giolla Easpaig (1996: 799–800) considers the saint's name was added to the place-name later, after the saint had been 'granted the pagan burial mound as the site for a fairly simply constructed church'. The third example is *Cluain Ferta Mongáin*, now Kilclonfert, Co. Offaly (Stokes 1905: 198; Mac Airt and Mac Niocaill 1983: 788; O'Donovan 1990 [1856]: AD 789.). There is also Ardfert 'height of the grave', diocesan church of Kerry, said to have been founded by St Brendan 'the Navigator' before his chief church of Clonfert in Co. Galway.

The transfer in Early Ireland of pagan to recognizably Christian burial practices has been studied from an archaeological perspective by Elizabeth O'Brien. Far from immediate change, she considers that 'by the end of the eighth century secondary burial in prehistoric ancestral burial mounds or ferta had ceased', and 'as a general rule, from the eighth century onwards, burial close to the saints gradually became an acceptable substitute for burial among the ancestors' (O'Brien 2009: 150). Charles-Edwards (1993: 264) discussed the significance of burial places to Christians, where burial in the monastery means being or becoming a kinsman of the monks.

41.9 Borrowings from Latin

A new terminology for Christian churches was also borrowed from Latin: *domnach, cell, dísert, aireagal, martar,* and *reilic:* usually with some change of meaning reflecting local conditions. *Domnach* from *Dominicum* 'belonging to the Lord' is the earliest term, by the eighth century firmly associated with St Patrick's mission (Flanagan 1984: 25–31). *Cell* later *cill,* from *cella,* is the most pervasive term, but already from its time of first adoption meaning not a 'cell' or individual church building but an entire monastic establishment, with church and living quarters (Flanagan 1984: 31–3). *Cill* was eventually, in the second millennium, replaced by the term *teampall,* from *templum* (Flanagan 1984: 40), but the meaning 'graveyard' continued, and was extended by the derivatives *cillín* and *cealltrach* for unofficial graveyards, used for the burial of strangers and the unbaptized, including babies (*cillín,* DIL: 186; Joyce 1869: I, 316–17; *cealltrach,* Dinneen 1927 'a churchyard; a burying place for unbaptised infants (Con[nacht])'; Muhr 2014: 42). *Dísert* from *desertum* meant 'place apart, hermitage' and has been considered typical of foundations during the eighth-century *Céli Dé* 'client of God' devotional movement (Flanagan 1981–2: 72, 1984: 34–5; Flanagan and Flanagan 1994: map 69–70; Toner 1996: 18, 83–5). *Airegal* from *oraculum* seems to have meant 'oratory' in place-names (Flanagan and Flanagan 1994: 82; DIL: 193). *Martar* or *martrae,* from *martyrium,* was used to mean 'relics' (Reeves 1857, 314; Bieler 1979: 233 note to Tírechán §51; Bhreathnach 2010: 26), and the early compound *martarthech* 'relic house' is one of the reasons why Deirdre Flanagan (1981–2: 74, 1984: 38 fn. 53) drew parallels between *tech* as a term for a church and as a 'supernatural' dwelling. Finally, *reilic* from *reliquiae* becomes the ordinary word for 'graveyard' rather than 'relics' (Reeves 1857: 452; Joyce 1869: I, 346; Bhreathnach 2010: 26).

41.10 *Tamlacht[ae]*

A word borrowed from Latin *lectus* 'couch', *lecht,* has been used for grave monuments including megalithic tombs up to recent times (Stokes 1862: 27; DIL: 69–70 'grave, tomb, sepulchral monument, resting place'). A compound *tamlachtae* 'burial place' is also attested early in place-name use, usually as a simplex, as with *findabair* (DIL: 66–7). Although its etymology has been confused, not least in the text known as Cormac's

Glossary, with *tám* 'plague, stupor' and *slecht* 'slaying' (DIL: 29, 65; Stokes 1862: 43, 45 *táimhshlechta*) it seems more likely that the first element, with a short vowel, is *tem* 'cut off, set apart' as in the sacred assembly-hill of Tara, and that the second is *lecht* 'grave' (*tem* 'an area cut off', 'demarcated for sacred purposes'; Mac Giolla Easpaig 2005: 446–7). Dónall Mac Giolla Easpaig did not mention *tamlacht* in his collection of noun + noun compounds (1981), but said further in his article on the Tara names that he hoped to publish a detailed study (2005: 446–7, n129).

Paul Tempan calls *tamlacht* one of the compounds which are 'clearly more modern' since it denotes an 'ecclesiastical structure', and gives for it the meaning 'graveyard' (Tempan 2009: 71). Deirdre Flanagan had considered,

> To all appearances *tamlacht* denoted a 'burial place', of pagan rather than Christian association. It is an early word, attested mainly in place-names, with little significant documentation as a lexical item in Irish writings. As a place-name element, it appears sufficiently often in the name of early ecclesiastical sites. . . . Most instances are in the north of the country, with the highest county incidence in Derry. (Flanagan 1981–2: 74–5)

To Flanagan, 'the outstanding instance of *tamlacht* as an ecclesiastical name is Tallaght near Dublin, earlier *Tamlacht Maolruain*, founded by Maolruain in 769 AD in a place where there is known to have been an early bronze age cemetery' (Flanagan and Flanagan 1994: 146). Estyn Evans said of Tallaght monastery, 'Very little remains of the original structures'. The modern parish church occupies the site, and in the graveyard is 'a large granite basin known as St Mulroon's fosset' (Evans 1966: 111).

In the account of Irish prehistory in the *Annals of the Four Masters* ('Age of the World' 2820), the death of 9,000 of the followers of the legendary invader Parthalón is given as the reason for the place-name, *Taimhleacht Muintire Pharthalóin* 'the burial place of Parthalón's people'. John O'Donovan identified the place with Tallaght near Dublin, site of the later monastery, citing Cormac's Glossary and noting that, 'some very ancient tumuli are still to be seen on the hill there. The word . . . signifies a place, where a number of persons, cut off by the plague, were interred together' (O'Donovan 1990 [1856]: I, 8). The place is not named in the other texts of *Lebor Gabála*, the legendary 'Book of Invasions' (Ó Riain 2009), although plague is mentioned, as *taimlecht* (Macalister 1938– 56: II, 265; III, 8). Keating's seventeenth-century history locates the death from plague (*pláigh*) of Parthalón's 9,000 followers at *Binn Éadair*, Howth (Keating 1902: I, 162).

However, the earliest instance of the term is in early eighth-century land bounds in the Additamenta to Tírechán's Life of St Patrick, which Fergus Kelly dates to about AD 700 (Bieler 1979: 172–3, 246). Two men Caechán and Macc Cairthinn were baptized and offered to God and Patrick *quintam partem Caichain* 'Caechán's fifth part'. The boundaries of the land-unit are given in detail, including (place-names in italics):

> Hae sunt fines quintae partis. i. *Coicid Caicháin*: . . . Otha glais *Conacolto* cu r*Reiriu* 7 ótha crich *Drommo Nit* cu glais *Tamlachtae Dublocho* la gglais cu *Grenlaich Fote*,

The text was put into English by Bieler (1979: 173) with the names partly translated: for example interpreting *glais* as 'stream', *Conacolto* as the genitive of *Conaclid*:

> These are the boundaries of the fifth part, that is Caíchán's Fifth: . . . From the stream of *Conaclid* to *Reiri* and from the border of *Druimm Nit* to the stream of *Tamlacht Dublocho*, along the stream to *Grenlach Fote*

Tamlacht Dublocho means 'grave of the black lake', and like instances of *fert* 'grave-mound' as discussed above, it is used to mark a boundary. Other marker-elements that can be translated are forms of *druimm* 'ridge', and *grellach* 'marsh'.

In the Irish epic *Táin Bó Cuailnge* (O'Rahilly 1976: 27, l. 871), the famous warrior Cú Chulainn came across Órlám's charioteer at a place called *Tamlachta Órláim* to the north of *Dísert Lochait*, killed Órlám, and sent the charioteer back to Ailill and Medb of Connacht with his head. Nothing is said explicitly about the burial of Órlám's body, but it looks as if *Tamlachta Órláim* must be Órlám's grave, despite the lack of explanation for *tamlachta*. With the other early 'religious' borrowed place-name element, *dísert*, in a place-name nearby, this seems likely to be a rare example of place-names being used 'out of register', with Christian connotations in a secular tale (Flanagan and Flanagan 1994: 145; Muhr 2002: 44).

Dáire's daughter Ercnat's church at *Tamlachta Bó* 'burial-place of the cow[s]' is named in the Tripartite Life of St Patrick immediately after the founding of Armagh: *Ercnat ingen Dáre fil aTamlachtau Bó* 'Ercnat Dáre's daughter who is in *Tamlachta Bó* (Stokes 1887: 232). This is now the townland of Tamlaght in Eglish parish, Armagh, no longer with an evident church site. The Tyrone townland in Clonfeacle parish called in 1643 *Gort Tamhlacht na Muc* 'field of the burial-place of the pigs' is now simply Gort (Ó Donnchadha 1931: 21; Muhr 2001: 304; 2002: 36n; Hamlin 2008: 174).

Apart from Tallaght parish outside Dublin, and Tawlaght townland next to Kilfenora townland in Ardfert, Kerry, as mapped by the Flanagans, and Taulaght townland in Co. Waterford (with memory of a church site) plus an old name for Donaghmore in Co. Laois, the distribution is northern (Flanagan and Flanagan 1994: 146). *Tamlacht* was used to name a number of Ulster church sites, including four parishes in Co. Derry, and several others in the past. As a townland name, there are four in Derry, four in Monaghan (anglicized Tamlat), four in Antrim, three in Tyrone, two in Armagh, one in Fermanagh.

'Of the six Derry *tamlacht* names, four are documented early church-sites' (Flanagan and Flanagan 1994: 146). In the north-west, Tamlaghtard or Magilligan, *Tamlacht Arda*, 'Tamlacht of the peninsula', was a parish entirely of church land, with the early site in a townland of the name (Hamlin 2008: 280; possibly Stokes 1887: 161). Tamlaght Finlagan is named after its patron Fionnlugh (Flanagan and Flanagan 1994: 145–6). The site of the ancient parish church lies just outside the townland called Tamlaght. Tamlaght O'Crilly, named after its erenagh family, has no townland of the name, only a village (Hamlin 2008: 281). The fourth parish called Tamlaght was formerly named topographically Tamlaght Killetra 'of the lower wood', and has its church site, with a megalithic tomb across the road, in the townland of Tamlaght near Coagh (Hamlin 2008: 279–80).

Other significant examples are in Co. Down. The small graveyard of Tamlaght in Lisnacree townland in Kilkeel parish, in the Mournes, was the site of a medieval chapel in ruins by 1622, but can be identified with *Tamlacht Boirche* 'Tamlaght of the Mournes' mentioned in all of the Saints' Calendars (Ó Mainnín 1993: 64–5; Hamlin 2008: 20, 325). It was associated with a saint called Tuán, who was cousin to St Domangart, of the Dal Fiatach ruling family, and had survived the Flood according to the text in which he told his life-story to St Finnian of Movilla (Carey 1984).

Magherahamlet, now a parish in Co. Down, was *Machaire Thamhlachta* '(church-) plain' or 'field of the burial place' (Reeves 1847: 315n). Although there is no townland of the name, it was attested as the 'rectory of *Magherhamlaght*' about 1610, and made a parish about 1847 after separation from Dromara, of which it had been a chapel (Reeves 1847: 105). Aghaderg parish in western Co. Down had two *tamlachta* sites, of Menan and Umhal, mentioned in the Saints' Calendars. *Tamlachta Mennain* (Stokes 1905: 228) has been generally identified as the townland of Meenan in the parish of Aghaderg, although Greenan and Drumsallagh were the traditional church sites locally (Muhr 1996: 17, 19, 49–50; Hamlin 2008: 299).

In Co. Armagh, until the mid-seventeenth century, the parish of Ballymore bore the name *Tamlacht Gliad* 'burial ground of strife' in various anglicized forms (*Tawnatlee* etc., Muhr 2001: 303). The earlier church site is in the east of the parish bordering Co. Down, near another graveyard called Relicarn, at which a ninth-century bell was found (Muhr 2001: 303; Hamlin 2008: 232; Neill 2009: 482). There is an archaeological mound called Doonan in Tamlaght townland in Derrynoose (Neill 2009: 147–8). Tamlaght townland in Derryvullan, Fermanagh, is adjacent to the early church site of the parish. Investigation of all instances is ongoing, but in several *tamlacht* has been confused with *tamhnach* 'a green patch', probably containing the same first element (Mac Giolla Easpaig 2005: 447; McKay and Muhr 2007: 88).

Gene Haley (2008) has taken seriously the idea that *tamlacht* is a plague burial site (the historical plague of AD 664), but Ann Hamlin (2008: 13, 174–5), quoting Deirdre Flanagan, suggests that it might be a term for a prehistoric megalithic grave.

Megalithic remains are in the parish of Tallaght (i.e. Tallaght, Dublin) rather than in the townland of the same name. There are ancient remains in some other instances of the term: for instance the megalith in Tamlaght townland, Co. Derry, across the road from the site of Tamlaght parish church (Hamlin 2008: 279–80), while Tawlaght townland in Templecarn parish, Donegal H 1071 also contains two megalithic tombs (Lacy et al. 1983: 29).

However the link with ancient monuments (also found in church sites with other names) is not strong, and Tempan (2009) translates *tamlacht* simply as 'graveyard'. I suspect the set-apart designation may represent a new term coined for a new type of Christian burial, no longer in the ancestral *ferta*, but with the Christian community. Deirdre Flanagan saw a possible specialization in the Latin borrowing *dísert* 'hermitage', dateable to around AD 800 (Flanagan 1984: 34–6), and it is notable that two native words that come into use for early churches, *lann* and *beannchor*, both indicate some sort of marking-off of land for Christian purposes (Flanagan 1981–2: 74; Jones 1991–3; Toner 1996: 10; Mac Mathúna 1997). The Latinate etymology and ecclesiastical associations of *tamlacht* suggest that, far from being a new word for a pagan grave-type, it was coined for a new type of Christian burial. The restricted northern distribution (there is probably one example in Scotland, Garthamlock near Glasgow, Taylor 2007b: 15) may indicate that this was an obscure term that never gained wide currency, leading to its literary association with ancient history and death from plague (DIL: 29).

41.11 CONCLUSION

'We are confronted with a constant re-composition of landscapes, sacralised under different canons' (Schot et al. 2011: xvii). This chapter has discussed some place-name types that may be considered religious in Ireland, from those like *finnabair*, numinous in meaning (although often the site of churches) to the more precise like *tech* 'house' and *fert* 'grave-mound'. In some cases (*síd* 'Otherworld dwelling'), the record regards the words and places as more pagan than Christian, although there is evidence of attempts to incorporate some of their old pagan significance into Christian belief. In other cases words borrowed or partly borrowed from Christian Latin (*tamlacht* 'set-apart grave') have been adapted in meaning to suit the development of Christianity in early Ireland.

PART VII

OTHER TYPES
OF NAMES

CHAPTER 42

....

AIRCRAFT NAMES

....

GUY PUZEY

42.1 INTRODUCTION

HUMANKIND has developed a great variety of machines in its quest to venture skywards. The rapid development of controlled flight since the beginning of the twentieth century has seen technology progress from gliders to propeller-driven and later jet-powered fixed-wing aircraft, not to mention airships, rotary-wing aircraft, rockets, and hovercraft. This proliferation of different machines has, as a matter of course, led to the emergence of vast domains of specialist terminology, including the names of aircraft themselves.[1]

42.2 BRITISH MILITARY AIRCRAFT

The first official system for naming heavier-than-air military aircraft in British service was developed in 1911 by what was then called the Army Balloon Factory, later known as the Royal Aircraft Factory. The initial system described three main types of aircraft: the Blériot Type (with a propeller mounted forward of the engine), the Farman Type (with a propeller mounted aft of the engine), and the Santos-Dumont Type (with a smaller horizontal surface mounted forward of the main wing, in a so-called canard configuration) (Wansbrough-White 1995: 20). Aircraft produced by the Factory would be named with initials indicating their type followed by a number, for instance the *Royal Aircraft Factory S.E.1*,[2] with the abbreviation standing for 'Santos Experimental 1'. Further

---

[1] This chapter is concerned with the names of manned objects intended to fly solely through our planet's atmosphere, but humankind has of course ventured further with other flying machines. For a discussion of the names of early rockets, ballistic missiles, and satellites, see Pearce (1962).

[2] For the purposes of this chapter, italics will be used for aircraft names. Aircraft will normally be named in full upon their first mention: in formal technical contexts, aircraft are usually referred to

abbreviations were later added, and some of the original abbreviations acquired new meanings, with the name of the *Royal Aircraft Factory S.E.5* referring to its role as 'Scout Experimental', although this type went well beyond the experimental stage, with over 5,000 built. These alphanumeric designations were used in common parlance by aircrews and groundcrews, as demonstrated in service song lyrics of World War I such as 'The B.E.2C is my bus' or 'It was an old F.E.2B' (cited in Ward-Jackson 1945: 10, 29), although the designations themselves were frequently shortened, as in 'Keep the 2Cs turning' (Ward-Jackson 1945: 12).

Although the Royal Aircraft Factory was an official establishment, it was only one of a number of design bureaux and manufacturers active at that time, most of which established their own naming practices. The company founded by Thomas Sopwith became known for the zoological names of its aircraft, such as the *Sopwith Dolphin*, the *Sopwith Salamander*, and the *Sopwith Camel*, the latter name stemming either from the hump on the fuselage forward of the cockpit or from the visual effect produced by the relative angles of the upper and lower wings (Wansbrough-White 1995: 97). The *Camel*'s name started as a nickname, and indeed aircraft are often better known by their unofficial names, which are bestowed on most aircraft by their aircrew, ground crew, or passengers. One exception seems to have been the aforementioned *S.E.5*, with the nickname *Sepha* apparently only used within the Royal Aircraft Factory itself, a most unusual situation for such a prolific aircraft (Wansbrough-White 1995: 81).

When a unified official naming system for service aircraft was introduced by the Ministry of Munitions in February 1918, it put forward classes of standardized 'nicknames' instead of designation numbers. The 'class' of name identified the purpose of the aircraft, so fighter aircraft would be given names of animals, plants, or minerals; bomber aircraft would be given geographical names; and heavy armoured machines would be given personal names from mythology. Subclasses of names would indicate the size of aircraft or whether it was land-based or sea-based. For example, three-seater sea-based fighters would be named after shellfish, single-seater land-based bombers would be named after inland Italian towns, and a hypothetical heavy armoured sea-based machine weighing between 10 and 20 tons would be named after a mythological Northern European female. Furthermore, the initial letters of the name would denote the manufacturer, so the 'SN' in *Snipe* identified it as a Sopwith-designed aircraft. Names to be chosen had to be both 'suitable' and 'novel'. This system presented a number of problems in its detail, and it was modified one month later, removing categories such as flowers and rocks, as well as eliminating, for example, the need to distinguish between

by their full name including the name of the manufacturer as well as the name of the type, which may include an alphanumeric type designation, e.g. the *Lockheed C-130 Hercules*. Sub-type variants may feature an updated mark number or modified designation (*Lockheed C-130H Hercules*), a modified name, often descriptive of an update or new function (*Lockheed C-130J Super Hercules*), or a completely new type name (*Lockheed EC-130H Compass Call*). Some may be known by different names or designations depending on the user, for instance the *Lockheed C-130J Super Hercules* is named the *Lockheed Hercules C.5* when in British service. In normal speech, aircraft are often referred to by their type name only (*Hercules*).

different types of fish depending on the size of aircraft when naming single-engined sea-planes or flying boats (Wansbrough-White 1995: 23–5).

A significant development in air power came with the establishment of the world's first independent air arm on 1 April 1918, when the Royal Air Force (RAF) was formed by the amalgamation of the army's Royal Flying Corps and the Royal Naval Air Service. With the birth of the new service, the Ministry of Munitions introduced another aircraft nomenclature system in July 1918 in the form of its Technical Department Instruction 538. This system provided the basic format for all future British military aircraft naming, decreeing that aircraft names would consist of two main elements, the first being a name chosen by the aircraft's design firm 'to indicate the origin of the design' and the second being a 'nickname' (cited in Wansbrough-White 1995: 26). By making the constructor's name itself an integral part of aircraft names, this system responded to criticism from the Society of British Aircraft Constructors that the origins of a design were not immediately apparent in names deriving from the February and March 1918 systems. The new system also updated the categories of nicknames to be given to aircraft, which included zoological names, geographical names, personal names from mythology, and attributes, all divided according to the size of aircraft and whether they were land-based or sea-based. Certain categories of name were explicitly excluded by this scheme owing to their use for naming aero-engines, including birds of prey, used at that time for engines designed by Rolls-Royce.

The naming categories based on zoology, geography, mythology, and attributes were discontinued in 1927, when the Air Ministry began naming aircraft with initial letters referring to roles (e.g. with 'C' allocated to troop carriers such as the *Handley Page Clive*). This mnemonic scheme represented a compromise between the British approach to naming aircraft and the American system of alphanumeric type designations, but it soon proved impractical.

New type-based categories were introduced in 1932 and slightly updated in 1939, in an effort to improve relations between officialdom and industry and to produce more appropriate names. For example, fighters were to be named with 'general words indicating speed, activity or aggressiveness', while trainers would be named after 'words indicating tuition and places of education' (cited in Wansbrough-White 1995: 135). This led to fighter names such as the *Gloster Gladiator, Hawker Tempest*, and *Supermarine Spitfire*, and trainers such as the *de Havilland Dominie, Miles Magister*, and *Airspeed Oxford*. Most bombers were to be named after inland towns in the British Empire or places with British historical associations, hence the *Avro Lancaster, Handley Page Halifax, Short Stirling*, and *Fairey Battle*, named after the town in East Sussex. Some names straddled several categories. The *Bristol Beaufort* torpedo bomber was, for instance, possibly named after the Duke of Beaufort, but it may also have been named after the Beaufort Sea, thus satisfying the 1932 requirements for torpedo bombers to be named after oceans, seas, or estuaries.

During the Cold War, the same system largely continued but with a new category introduced in 1949 for helicopters. These were to be named after trees, but the *Bristol Sycamore* seems to be the only one named in such a fashion. Although there had been divergences from the official system before, the profile of exceptions grew from the 1950s onwards, notably with the so-called V-bombers. The established pattern for naming bombers was after inland towns in what had by then become the Commonwealth, and this continued in the immediate post-war period with the *English Electric Canberra*. Some felt that the new generation of strategic nuclear bombers called for more dynamic-sounding names, and the first of the three aircraft in this class was named the *Vickers Valiant*.[3] It was eventually decided to name the three bombers as a family, so the other two became the *Avro Vulcan* and the *Handley Page Victor*, described from October 1952 as a 'V' class (Wynn 1994: 56). Apart from the alliterative attraction of the name of the *Valiant*, the letter 'V' was perhaps reminiscent of the 'V for Victory' slogan of the previous decade, while also evoking the swept wings of all three bombers, especially the delta wing of the *Vulcan*.

The apparent departure in more recent decades from the earlier nomenclature systems might be explained by the fact that newer types of aircraft tend to be introduced less frequently, have longer development periods, and remain in service for longer. Furthermore, while the marketing role of aircraft names has been recognized since before World War I, it is now a paramount concern for manufacturers. Many aircraft in recent British service have been international ventures or imported aircraft, some of which, such as the *Lockheed Hercules*, come with well-established names.

42.3 US MILITARY AIRCRAFT

In the United States, the alphanumeric designations of military aircraft types are frequently used alone. These codes are known as Mission Design Series designators and include information on an aircraft's basic mission by use of a letter code, so the *[Northrop Grumman] B-2* is a bomber, while the *[Boeing] P-8* is a maritime patrol aircraft. Most US military aircraft also have 'popular names', for example the *B-2 Spirit* and the *P-8 Poseidon*. The Mission Design Series codes are the official designations, but the Pentagon has an approval process for popular names, with current guidelines stating that a suitable name is short and 'characterizes the mission and operational capabilities of the vehicle' (US Air Force 2005: 6). Not all aircraft have officially recognized popular names, for instance the *Lockheed SR-71*, a retired reconnaissance aircraft which only had unofficial nicknames, such as the *Blackbird*.

While in development, the *General Dynamics F-16* had been unofficially known for some time as the *Falcon*, which led to the official selection of the popular name *Fighting Falcon*. The addition of the word 'Fighting' was necessitated by the existence of *Falcon* as

[3] Although the July 1918 system discontinued the practice established earlier that year of allocating initial letters to constructors, numerous future aircraft names would feature alliteration between constructors' names and type names, as illustrated by the *Vickers Valiant* and many others such as the *Bristol Blenheim*, *Hawker Hurricane*, and *Blackburn Buccaneer*.

a copyrighted name for a range of aircraft produced by the French company Dassault-Breguet (*Flight International* 1980). Indeed, the current Pentagon approval process includes a trademark search by the Air Force Legal Services Agency (Judge Advocate General Patent Division) (US Air Force 2005: 4).

42.4 REPORTING NAMES

During World War II, Allied forces in the Pacific theatre developed codenames in order to facilitate communications when reporting on Japanese aircraft, the official names of which might either follow naming patterns based on the Japanese Imperial calendar or might be unknown to the Allies. The codenames used were short, easily remembered words, including tree names for trainers (e.g. *Oak* or *Willow*), female first names beginning with 'T' for transports (*Tabby*) and male first names for fighters (*Clint* or *Frank*). Among these names were a number of in-jokes planted by intelligence staff (Horton 1994: 153).

In 1954, the Air Standards Coordinating Committee (a joint initiative of Australia, Canada, New Zealand, the UK, and the USA) revived the use of reporting names to refer to Soviet, Chinese, and, later, Russian equipment. These codenames are widely used by NATO members and their allies. The initial letter indicates the type of aircraft: 'B' for bombers (e.g. *Badger, Blowlamp*, or *Bull*), 'C' for transports (*Camber, Coaler*, or *Coot*), 'F' for fighters (*Fishbed, Foxbat*, or *Fritz*), 'H' for helicopters (*Helix, Hind*, or *Hippo*) and 'M' for miscellaneous (*Mainstay, Midas*, or *Mote*). The names chosen are all recognizably English, but there is a considerable mixture of common and less common words. Many of the names have a vaguely insulting or absurd tone (*Careless, Flatpack, Hoodlum, Mug*), while some are perhaps more complimentary and are even adopted by the aircraft's users themselves. For example, the *Mikoyan MiG-29 'Fulcrum'* was indeed a key part of the Warsaw Pact's air defence, and the *Tupolev Tu-95 'Bear'* is still seen as a symbol of Russian power when on long-range patrols.

42.5 CIVIL AIRCRAFT

There is some overlap between civil and military naming when an aircraft is used in both domains, but the choice of name for civil aircraft is usually the prerogative of the manufacturer alone. As many civil aircraft perform broadly similar transportation functions, and certain manufacturers specialize in particular sizes or configurations, civil aircraft are often popularly identified by the brand name of their manufacturer alone, for example 'an Airbus', 'a Boeing', or 'a Cessna'.

The Boeing Company's successful series of commercial airliners are well known by their numerical codes. The company allocated its '700-series' of model numbers to its jet transport ventures, but it was not convinced that 'Model 700' sounded ambitious enough for its first jet airliner, so it resolved to name it the *Boeing 707* instead (Lombardi 2004). The *Boeing 707* did originally have a name as well as a number, the *Jet Stratoliner*, but it was the model number that caught on (Horton 1994: 73). A pattern was thereby established, and there followed the *Boeing 727, 737, 747* (most widely known by its *Jumbo Jet* nickname), *757, 767,* and *777*.[4] For the company's latest addition to the series, it took the rare step of adding an official name to the model number, to be chosen by a global public vote from the shortlist of *Dreamliner, eLiner, Global Cruiser,* and *Stratoclimber*. The eventual name selected was the *Boeing 787 Dreamliner*, although *Global Cruiser* won the most votes within the USA (Tinseth 2011).

In spite of the earlier British penchant for naming aircraft, some British-produced airliners have only alphanumeric model numbers, such as the *Vickers VC10*, with the initials standing for Vickers Commercial. The lack of any further name may have been an attempt to choose a more neutral designation better suited to international exports than nationalistic names such as the *Bristol Britannia*, but Sir George Edwards, the then chief designer at Vickers, also claimed the company had simply grown 'tired' of choosing names (Wansbrough-White 1995: 82).[5]

42.6 INTERNATIONAL PROJECTS

International aircraft projects present interesting problems in terms of naming. The meaning of an aircraft name does not have to be immediately obvious, but it is advantageous if it is at least easily pronounceable in the languages of relevant partners. It can also be a challenge to find an internationally suitable name that does not cause embarrassment or harm cultural sensitivities. Furthermore, the political complications of such projects mean that some motivations for name choices are occasionally made public.

One of the most high-profile international projects in civil aviation was the co-operation on supersonic passenger transport that resulted in the *Aérospatiale-BAC Concorde*. The name was said to have been coined by the child of a British Aircraft Corporation official (Costello and Hughes 1976: 57) and was intended to be indicative of the good British–French industrial and political relations that enabled the project to go ahead. Although the official name featured the French spelling from the outset, the British government discouraged the use of the 'e' for a period in the 1960s following an

---

[4] The 717 code was originally given as the internal model number of the military refuelling aircraft now officially known as the *Boeing KC-135 Stratotanker*, but, as that earlier use was not widely known, the name *Boeing 717* was later used to rebrand the *McDonnell Douglas MD-95* after the two companies merged in 1997.

[5] In 1962, when the type was entering service with the RAF, new names were suggested, but the existing name remained (Wansbrough-White 1995: 46). One of the proposed type names from 1962, *Voyager*, has recently resurfaced as the chosen name for the VC10's replacement as the RAF's main tanker and transport aircraft, the *Airbus Voyager*.

unrelated disagreement between British Prime Minister Harold Macmillan and French President Charles de Gaulle. Apparently unaware of the reasons behind this, British Minister of Technology Tony Benn reinstated the 'e' during a visit to Toulouse in 1967, proclaiming: 'That is "e" for excellence; "E" for England and "e" for "*entente cordiale*" ' (Benn 1996: 175). Upon receiving a letter from a man who pointed out that some components were made in Scotland too, Benn (1996: 175) replied that it was 'also "E" for "*Écosse*" '.

In 1976, the air forces of Germany, Italy, and the UK chose *Panavia Tornado* as the name for the combat aircraft developed by the tri-national Panavia consortium (*Flight International* 1976). The meteorological phenomenon the aircraft was named after is known by the same word in English, German, and Italian, albeit with slightly different pronunciations.

In later years, multinational consortia themselves would be more closely involved in naming international military aircraft. In 1998, the Eurofighter consortium from Germany, Italy, Spain, and the UK were due to name their jointly produced combat aircraft, which had until then been known as the *Eurofighter 2000* or *EF2000*. This project name was appropriate for the geographical base of the partner companies and governments and for the timing of the project, with the prototypes taking to the air in the 1990s, but perhaps a need for a more evocative name was felt. Furthermore, the formal delivery and entry into service of the aircraft would come after the beginning of the third millennium. The potential export market for an aircraft design is often an important consideration in choosing a name, and the name Eurofighter only served to stress the aircraft's genesis as a design for European military operators, possibly discouraging customers outside of Europe. The frontrunner among suggested names was *Eurofighter Typhoon*, which suggested a clear association with the earlier *Tornado* project. A naming announcement was expected in March 1998 pending checks on the linguistic appropriateness of the name for the global market (Jeziorski 1998: 35). This announcement was not forthcoming, however, and the naming ceremony was postponed until September of that year, reportedly due to objections from German partners over the name's previous use with the *Hawker Typhoon*, a British fighter-bomber of World War II.[6]

Any objections were downplayed by the consortium's managing director, Brian Phillipson, who pointed to the history of the *Messerschmitt Bf 108*, a German recreational aircraft nicknamed *Taifun*. Significantly, though, Phillipson stressed that 'you can say Typhoon in all four [Eurofighter partner] countries' languages and you can say it in Japanese and it is not rude' (cited in Ripley 1998). While the name may be well suited as a brand for the Asian export market, its spelling is clearly English, not the German *taifun*, Italian *tifone*, or Spanish *tifón*.

This was not the first time that this project's name had caused controversy. When the forerunner project was renamed from *Future European Fighter Aircraft* to *European Fighter Aircraft*, this was said to be due to the acronym FEFA having 'unfortunately rude

---

[6] The name *Tornado* had also been used for several earlier aircraft, including a British fighter design of World War II, but the *Hawker Typhoon* was better known.

connotations in Italian' (*Flight International* 1984). Maybe this alluded to a homophone of this English acronym, the Italian noun *fifa*, 'fright' or 'jitters'.

Perhaps due to the name *Typhoon* highlighting the fact that the partner nations were former adversaries, it was originally stated that this name was only for export marketing purposes. As the name's use spread, though, it was officially adopted as the in-service name in all partner nations in 2002, according to British sources (House of Commons Committee of Public Accounts 2011: Ev 38). Nevertheless, the German Air Force most frequently uses the name *Eurofighter* alone.

The US-led multi-national Joint Strike Fighter project has led to the *Lockheed Martin F-35 Lightning II*. The name of this aircraft was intended to be commemorative, as suggested by the Roman numerals, but it recognizes the international nature of the project by referring to two different historic aircraft: the US *Lockheed P-38 Lightning* and the British *English Electric Lightning* (Lockheed Martin 2006). A US Air Force press release fails to mention the British precedent for the name but expands on the name's metaphorical implications: 'Like lightning, the F-35 Lightning II will strike with destructive force. The stealth characteristics of the jet will allow the F-35 to strike the enemy with accuracy and unpredictability; when the enemy finally hears the thunder, the F-35 is long gone' (US Air Force 2006).

42.7 INDIVIDUAL AIRCRAFT

Individual aircraft are designated by civil registrations or military serial numbers. While aviation has drawn much of its terminology from the maritime world, and some ways of naming aircraft would appear to be inspired by maritime practices, the use of registrations points to one key difference: individual maritime vessels are almost always named but not always registered, while aircraft are almost always registered but not always named (Embleton and Lapierre 1997: 232). In some cases, though, registrations are also used as names. Civil aircraft worldwide use a prefix denoting the country in which they are registered (e.g. 'G' for the UK) followed by a combination of letters and/ or numbers. The seven aircraft of British Airways' *Concorde* fleet had registrations ranging from G-BOAA to G-BOAG, and staff knew them colloquially by the last two letters (e.g. *Alpha Alpha*). The flagship of the fleet was *Alpha Charlie*, as the acronym 'BOAC' belonged to the predecessor company that ordered the aircraft, the British Overseas Airways Corporation. Another example of an aircraft with a bespoke registration is the last airworthy *Avro Vulcan*, which bears the civil registration G-VLCN. It has been given the nickname *The Spirit of Great Britain* by its civilian operators, but it is better known by its old military serial, XH558.

The unofficial naming of individual military aircraft was widespread in the US Army Air Force of World War II, and names were often emblazoned on the aircraft themselves together with 'nose art', which might feature heraldry or, more commonly, cartoon characters and pin-ups. One of the best known examples of a nicknamed individual aircraft is *Enola Gay*, the *Boeing B-29 Superfortress* that dropped the atomic bomb on Hiroshima and that was named after the pilot's mother (Wood 1992: 42). The nicknaming practice was emulated by British and Commonwealth aircrews, especially in Bomber Command, with names often derived from the large squadron code letters painted on the rear fuselage. For example, *Avro Lancaster* RF141, bearing the squadron code 'JO-U', was given the name *Uncle Joe Again* (Wood 1992: 20). Names and nose art were apparently more common among Canadian than British crews. One of the longest names given to an individual aircraft in World War II might be *Chinawattakamapoosekinapee*, a *Supermarine Spitfire* of 421 Squadron Royal Canadian Air Force, which also bore nose art in the form of the profile of a Native Canadian in headdress, the logo of the Squadron's sponsor, the McColl-Frontenac Oil Company. The name was the invention of pilots Mac Gordon and Bill Marshall and is said to have been coined over some beers (Fochuk 1999: 48). It has been suggested that such names enabled crews to identify more closely with their aircraft and to bond together more cohesively as a crew (Klare 1991: 14). In many cases, however, aircraft were pooled, so crews could be unaware of the background to names (Fochuk 1999: xi).

Official names were sometimes given to individual aircraft (see Fig. 42.1 for a modern example), often in recognition of sponsorship from savings drives such as the 1943 'Wings for Victory' campaign, with 'presentation aircraft' named in honour of towns or companies that had donated large sums towards production. One unusual

FIGURE 42.1 Two black-painted *Dassault DA-20 Jet Falcon* aircraft are operated by 717 Squadron of the Royal Norwegian Air Force, covering electronic warfare and VIP transport roles. Appropriately, the pair have been named *Hugin* and *Munin* after the two ravens of Norse mythology (Old Norse *Huginn* and *Muninn*, 'thought' and 'memory' or 'mind') that flew across the world, bringing information back to the god Odin.

Photograph: Guy Puzey, September 2011.

case was that of 427 Squadron Royal Canadian Air Force, which was sponsored by the Metro-Goldwyn-Mayer film company and named each of its *Handley Page Halifax* aircraft after MGM stars (Armstrong 1999: 48–9). Official names might also be given to individual aircraft that represented production milestones, such as *Hawker Hurricane* PZ865, named *The Last of the Many* as the last of the 14,533 aircraft of the type to be produced.

The title of Charles Lindbergh's 1927 account of his solo transatlantic flight, *We—Pilot and Plane*, is a particularly succinct expression of the significant bond between Lindbergh and his mount, *The Spirit of St. Louis*. Names beginning with 'The Spirit of' remain popular for individual aircraft in both military and civilian service. For instance, nineteen of the twenty-one *Northrop Grumman B-2 Spirit* stealth bomber aircraft have been named after the 'spirit of' various US states (e.g. *Spirit of Alaska* or *Spirit of Ohio*), with the remaining two named *Spirit of America* and *Spirit of Kitty Hawk*. These names are officially recognized and many were bestowed at naming ceremonies in the relevant states. Other examples can be found among the *ATR 42* aircraft once operated by Ryanair, three of which were given 'spirit of' names, such as *The Spirit of Waterford*. The British airline easyJet currently operates an *Airbus A319* named *Spirit of easyJet*, which also carries displayed on the fuselage the names of employees who have won the company's 'Spirit Award'.

Other airlines often name their aircraft in thematic groups. British Airways used to name much of its *Boeing 737* fleet after British rivers (e.g. *River Glass*), *747*s after British cities (*City of Cardiff/Dinas Caerdydd*), *757*s after British castles (*Glamis Castle*), *767*s after European cities (*City of Milan*), and *777*s after aviation pioneers (*Sir Frank Whittle*). These names were once painted on the fuselage, although they have disappeared with rebranding in the last decade.

CHAPTER 43

ANIMAL NAMES

KATHARINA LEIBRING

43.1 INTRODUCTION

ANIMAL names have probably existed for as long as humans have tamed and utilized animals. The names of mythological animals found in many ancient religions and cultures can testify to this.[1] Some very early examples of names of real animals are the names preserved for Egyptian dogs, cats, and horses from the Old Kingdom, that is over 4,500 years ago.[2] Some 1,500 years later, names of draught oxen from Crete are preserved on clay tablets written in Linear B (Chadwick 1958: 119). Some of their names, based on characteristics of their bearers (in English translation *Dapple, Darkie, Whitefoot*), are similar to cattle names found up to the present day in many places round the world.

Scholarly research on animal names has been carried out for decades in many countries, especially in Eastern Europe and Scandinavia, but there are still few syntheses. During recent years, interest in this name category has grown, and animal names have been allocated regular chapters in onomastic handbooks from several countries, chapters written by, for example Warchoł (2004), Nübling (2012), Saarelma (2012a), Leibring (2013). With the exception of Warchoł, these are all focused on names in a specific country. Warchoł gives a very valuable overview of animal names in Slavic-speaking countries, but, in general, very little research has been undertaken on comparing, for example, the semantic content of animal names from different language groups. However, in the proceedings from the Mainz symposium on zoonyms held in 2013 (Dammel et al. 2015), new insights and perspectives on zoonymics in several countries are presented.

My aim here is to present an overview of animal names in history and at the present day, not limiting myself to one country. The focus is on Europe, and many examples are

---

[1] There are e.g. names of mythological cows in Rigveda (Gubernatis 1874: 20) and of several mythological animals in ancient Egypt (Helck and Otto 1989: 589–90). In more recent times, we find in Norse mythology Sleipnir, the eight-legged horse, and the cow Auðhumbla whose milk never ends.

[2] For more information on these names, see Fischer (1977: 173–8) and Helck and Otto (1989: 589–90).

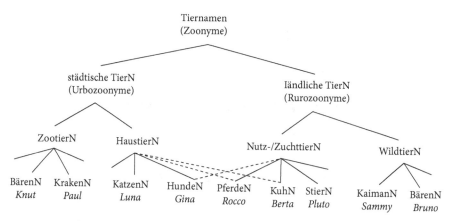

FIGURE 43.1 Different categories of contemporary animal names based on an urban–rural division.

From Nübling (2012: 192).

taken from Scandinavia, as that area is relatively well researched, although some references to name-giving in Africa and the Arctic will be included.

This chapter deals mainly with the names used by owners or carers in the daily handling of the animal, the *call name*, which in German is called *Rufname*. Many animals, especially those belonging to specific breeds (of dogs, cats, and horses) are also given *register names*. These names often contain the breeder's or kennel's name combined with an individual name, for example *Welcop's Lollos-Leika*. The individual part (here, *Lollos-Leika*) is sometimes given to harmonize with certain prerequisites, such as that all puppies in a litter should have names beginning with a certain letter. The register names are registered in stud books and are normally not used for communication, although the call name can be based on parts of the register name.[3] In addition to their call name, many animals, especially companion animals, can have *informal names*, sometimes several, used only in small circles, for example within the owner-family.

The chapter begins with a discussion of why we give (or do not give) names to animals, and which animals are most likely to receive names. In the recently published German handbook *Namen* (Nübling 2012: 192), an illuminating scheme of contemporary animal names is presented, which takes its roots in the division between urban and rural animals (see Fig. 43.1). In general, the sectors where most animal names are found are among farm or production animals (German *Nutz-* or *Zuchttiere*) and pet or companion animals (German *Haustiere*), so the two main parts of this chapter will be devoted to the names of (a) farm/production animals and (b) companion animals from historical times until the present day. Horses have of old occupied an in-between

---

[3] In this example, the dog Welcop's Lollos-Leika has the call name *Lollo*.

position, but they will be discussed under the section of farm animals, including the names of race-horses, even though these are on the border area of commercial names.

A third category of potentially named animals are zoo animals, and a short section is devoted to their names.

43.2 REASONS FOR NAMING ANIMALS

Why we choose to give a name to an individual, a place, or a thing can, according to the Norwegian ethnologist Bjarne Rogan, be for one of three main reasons, all also valid for the naming of animals. Rogan (1994) refers to the singularizing function, the expressive function, and the ritual function. Regarding animals, the singularizing function is most important, although the expressive function can be used, for example, for statements of power when we give a fierce dog the name *Attila*. The ritual function is used for instance when we recycle names of former animals.

Not all animals living close to humans are given an individual name, but there are several requisites that can make naming more probable.[4] Some important features are:

- the animal is regarded as an individual by the carer/handler/owner;
- the animal is treated as an individual (being milked, ridden, etc. or lives in the family home);
- there is a need for identification of the animal—or for communication with it;
- the animal is expected to live for several years, i.e. is not regarded only as food;
- the animal is one of several in a herd or flock;
- the animal is in some way distinctive in its outer appearance (e.g. by colour, markings etc.).

The relative significance of these reasons varies over time and between societies and occasions, but some of them are usually present in the background of the name giver's mind when an animal is given a name. Which species of animals will be named is also dependent on the agricultural and social structure of each society; in Sámi cultures reindeer play an important role, and some will be named, while in other cultures horses and camels are utilized and given names.[5] The varying functions of an animal species can also influence the naming potential, so that for example milking sheep have names, as in Iceland (Jónsson 1912), but most sheep do not have names in cultures where they are kept primarily as wool and meat producers.

---

[4] This discussion is inspired by Dobnig-Jülch (1996: 1584).
[5] On names of camels, see Drouin (1990).

43.3 NAMES OF HORSES AND FARM/ PRODUCTION ANIMALS

43.3.1 Names of Horses

Horses have over time occupied different positions, as they have been used as riding animals in both war and peacetime, and as draught horses in both urban and rural settings. In Western countries today they are mostly used either as competition horses or for leisure and recreation. The names of horses have undergone several transformations, and for some horse categories and many breeds the names are also regularized, as Judith Schwerdt (2007) shows in her paper on German horse names. An example where the language of the name is regulated is Icelandic horses, which are obliged to have names in the Icelandic language to be registered in the international stud book for Icelandic horses (Leibring 2009: 659).

Another example of name regulation is the naming of American and British race-horses, where two horses alive at the same time cannot have the same name. Names can, however, be recycled after a transition period (Ashley 1996b: 1589–90) These regulations are made partly on commercial grounds with the intention of avoiding mix-ups among competing horses. Many names of racehorses in Scandinavia are constructed of two parts, where one tells of the animal's blood-line, and the other is the individual name. Examples are *Ina Scot* and *Gidde Paloma*, where *Scot* and *Paloma* are the names of the respective horse's sire (or, even, grandsire), while *Ina* and *Gidde* are the individual name parts.

From a historical viewpoint, names of horses are found in medieval and early modern sources, for example wills, both in the British Isles and in Germany. George Redmonds (2004b: 139–142) shows that medieval horse names are often descriptive of the animal (colour, origin) and that the description could be combined with the owner's or breeder's surname. These early horse names mostly represent names given by the higher classes (Bentzien 1968). A good overview of older horse names in Germany is given by Schwerdt (2007). As her paper and as research from several countries illustrates, many horse names from early modern times were based on the bearer's characteristics, like colour, marking, or place of origin.[6] Some of these names are on the verge of being appellatives, as the German *Stutzohr*, meaning 'short ear' (Schwerdt 2007: 8) or the English *Long legs* (Redmonds 2004b: 142). Complimentary adjectives or appellatives were also used, like *Aimable* and *Brillant*, the latter the name of King Charles XI of Sweden's favourite horse (Karlsson 2004: 49).

In the eighteenth and nineteenth centuries, names of riding-horses and war-horses could also be named after mythological deities. Ordinary personal names were also

---

[6] See e.g. Schwerdt (2007, with references) from Germany; Karlsson (2004) from Sweden; Redmonds (2004b) from Britain.

becoming more common, especially for mares (Karlsson 2004). The naming of farm horses after their colour or markings continued well into the nineteenth century, although even among them personal names became more common, as they are today.

Little information is collected on the names of today's leisure horses, but recent research from Germany indicates three name groups of roughly the same size: horse names based on other names where anthroponyms and ergonyms are the most common, names based on appellatives, and opaque names.[7] Call names are thus sometimes created from parts of the register names, sometimes taken from other onymic areas, and have in many cases no lexical meaning.

43.3.2 Names of Cattle

43.3.2.1 *Names in Europe's Traditional Agricultural Societies*

The usage of animal names in cultures or times of traditional small-scale husbandry is common, as many animals will be regarded as individuals. Cows and goats will be milked daily, and the oxen are harnessed and given instructions where names are used. This close relationship between man and animal[8] is visible in the abundance of cattle names, especially cow names, preserved from large areas of Europe in documents from the sixteenth to nineteenth centuries. There are many similarities between the name-giving grounds in different countries and languages (Leibring 2000: 343). Many of these names may well have existed orally for a long time before they first were written down.

From Scandinavia, large sources of cattle names are documented from the early eighteenth century onwards.[9] Over 1,500 different cow names and more than 300 different names for bulls and oxen can be compiled by combining the name-stock in different works on Scandinavian cattle names.[10] A large common onomasticon of names and name elements for cows, bulls, and oxen was well established in the mid-eighteenth century. Many of these names are compounds, where the first part describes and the second part is a generic, denoting 'cow' or 'ox'.[11] A majority of these names do in some ways allude to the bearer's physical or mental characteristics. Colour and markings are the most common specifying categories, with names indicating time (season, month, day of the week, time of day) as another large group. Those names usually allude to the time

---

[7] See Nübling (2012: 200), who has compiled the results given in Schwerdt (2007).

[8] Not to be confused with the modern way of anthropomorphizing companion animals. The farm animals were always regarded as different from, and inferior to, humans.

[9] Many names are found in estate inventories from ordinary farms, thus giving us access to animal names from people not belonging to the upper classes.

[10] See Leibring (2000) for a more detailed overview on the development of Scandinavian cattle names from 1750 onwards.

[11] Some frequent elements denoting 'cow' in Scandinavian cow names are *-gås*, *-linna*, *-ros*, and for bulls and oxen *-berg*, *-dräng* and *-man* (Leibring 2000).

of the bearer's birth, or sometimes to the time of its purchase (Leibring 2000: 356–7). Animal names indicating time are also found in several countries in Eastern Europe.[12]

Many Scandinavian cattle names are also derived from positive adjectives, for example 'beautiful', 'gentle', etc., or express praise. They can be regarded as wish names. Few personal names are found among the older Scandinavian cow names, and those used are sometimes taken from the Almanac, mostly names not common among the local farming community. The same phenomenon is observed from, for example, Poland (Górnowicz 1959: 457). The custom of not using local personal names could be attributed to the perceived divide between mankind and animal. However, many Swedish ox and bull names are identical with existing surnames, especially soldier's names that often ended in *-berg* or *-man*. It should be noted that such names were not used among the farmers, who used the patronymic system.[13]

In some Slavonic-speaking countries, cow names containing suffixes were common, as is shown for example by Piotr Galas (1968) from Poland, Michael Reichmayr (2005) from Slovenia and Milan Majtán (2009) from Slovakia. The traditional cow names in those countries were, as in Scandinavia, often created from adjectives denoting colour or markings.

Names denoting or describing the animal's physical traits are also found from the north of England in the seventeenth century (Redmonds 2004b: 148). Some examples of praise names and wish names are *Gentle*, *Lovely*, and *Welcome Home* (Thomas 1983: 96). Specific cow name elements or suffixes are not found in the English literature on cattle names. However, some names from Yorkshire bear strong resemblances to cattle names in Scandinavia, for example *Motherlike* (Thomas 1983: 96) and *Whitehorn* (Redmonds 2004b: 148).

43.3.2.2 *Cattle Names in Southern Africa*

Cattle, both cows and oxen, have for a long time been very important in the local economy, and there is a rich corpus of names. In southern Africa, many cattle names have the same semantic content as animals in Europe, that is their colours, markings, or other characteristics are used in naming (Koopman 2002b: 212–19). Also concrete appellatives, such as musical instruments, are adapted as cow names, for example *uVavulini* ('violin') Among the Zulu, many names of oxen are loans from Afrikaans (e.g. *Blauwberg* > *uBhulobehe* for an ox of blue-grey colour). The elements *-berg* and *-man* are, as we can see, identical to common name elements in Swedish names for oxen, and they both symbolize strength, an important component for a draught-animal. In both Swedish and Afrikaans, many of these ox names are identical to surnames.

Cattle names in southern Africa (and dog names—see below) are also sometimes used as ways of communicating thoughts or statements that otherwise could not be uttered, especially to express discontent or criticism. Koopman (2002b: 221) gives

---

[12]   According to Genowefa Surma (1988: 179) such names were also found in Bulgaria, Romania, and parts of Poland.

[13]   For a discussion of this, see Leibring (2000: 370–1).

several examples of ox names directed at the ox-driver's neighbours: *uBayangizonda* 'they hate me' (meaning that the driver knows his neighbours' feelings about him) and *uSiyempini* 'we are going to war', the latter being a warning to them. This use of cattle names for social comments is not, as far as I am aware, discussed in any European literature.

43.3.2.3 *Cattle Names in Transition and Today*

As organized cattle breeding began in earnest in many European countries during the nineteenth century, followed by mechanization and more large-scale husbandry, the name stock as well as the motivations for naming cattle changed. The bigger herds meant that the individual animal played a less important role to the name-giver. One aim of organized breeding was to standardize the breeds, which meant that more animals had a similar appearance, so it became difficult to give identifying names according to colour or marking. In Scandinavia, many of the old compound names were first shortened and later forgotten. The size of the cow onomasticon was reduced.

Different strategies for revealing breeding lines were used, for example using the same first letter as the mother's name for the names of all her offspring, or giving names starting with the same letter to all calves born in a certain year.[14] As a consequence of these new name-giving strategies, more women's names were taken into use for cows, both names used among the local people and names of well-known women, real or fictive. This structural change is shown in research concerning cattle names from different countries.[15] These more modern cow names had in many cases two syllables and ended in -*a*, which made their morphological structure quite similar to women's names.

In many European countries during the last few decades, the rise of large-scale 'milk factories' or 'meat factories' where animals have a shorter life-span and are regarded almost exclusively as a production line, together with increased demands for documentation, has led to cattle names in many instances being replaced by numbers as the basis for identification. Among countries in the European Union, these numbers, put in the ears of the animal, contain the number of the country, the number of the farm, and the specific animal's identity number. In the local farm's register, a name can sometimes be given, which in many cases is the same as the cow's mother, quite often a female first name. This custom can have been ongoing for many generations, so that the name will be reminiscent of a bovine ancestress perhaps born a hundred years ago. In regions where small-scale farming is still alive, the more traditional individual naming of cows lives on, although names of women are frequently used.[16]

[14] This system was implemented among Finnish milk cows in the 1950s (Saarelma 2012a: 205).
[15] On this, see Leibring (2000); Reichmayr (2005); Saarelma (2012a).
[16] On this, see Leibring (2000); Warchoł (2004); and Reichmayr (2005).

43.3.3 Goat Names

From the sparse literature on goat names, we find that, at least in Scandinavia, there was a broad spectrum of names, especially for she-goats, during the eighteenth and nineteenth centuries. Like cows, goats were named from their colour, markings, and other physical traits. Some popular Swedish goat names were *Blacka*, *Grimma*, and *Glosa*, alluding to pale colour and different kinds of face markings (Leibring 2001: 20–1). The goat's capricious and lively nature is also reflected in some names. One Swedish example is *Dansdocka* 'dancing doll', and there are also certain pejorative names, something that is not common among cow names. There are also some Bulgarian goat names that allude to negative traits, for example *G'ávol* 'devil', writes Budziszewska (1993: 248). The largest groups of goat names in her collection from the 1900s denote physical characteristics, as do the older Scandinavian names. According to a Norwegian study, during the last century, the traditional goat names have become less frequent, and the use of women's names and opaque names has increased. This is partly due to bigger herds and the fact that, in the milk control register, names are not compulsory (Karbø and Kruken 1994).

43.3.4 Names of Other Farm Animals

Milking sheep have sometimes been named, as is shown by the many examples from Iceland (Jónsson 1912) and Bulgaria (Budziszewska 1993). These names, like goat names, are often derived from colour, markings, or behaviour. Names denoting the time of birth are also found. The ordinary pastoral care of sheep in large herds has, however, in many cultures hindered them from being given individual names. Pigs and poultry have not normally been named on a regular basis, although certain individuals might have been named. A well-known pastime for many country-bred children has been to single out a favourite chicken or a suckling-pig by giving it a name. Name-giving of this kind has not yet been studied.

43.4 NAMES OF COMPANION ANIMALS

43.4.1 Dog Names

It is difficult to draw a line between production/utility animals and companion animals, especially regarding dogs. Both working dogs and companion dogs have existed for a long time, as dogs are the oldest known domesticated animals in the world.

Many dogs today perform important duties as guard dogs, hunting dogs, sled dogs, herding dogs, police dogs, etc., duties that in many cases have been carried out for a long time. These working dogs have had names as well as the companion dogs, as we can see from lists of hunting dogs from medieval England (Redmonds 2004b; Walker-Meikle

2012), and from the diaries and correspondence of royal personages where dogs of all kinds, both working dogs and companion dogs, feature (Karlsson 1987).

Before discussing dog names in Europe, I will give a couple of examples of the usage of dog names from other cultures.

Among the Inuits in the Arctic, sled dogs have been, and are, important as working animals, and they have occupied a special position that set them apart from other animals in the local society. Each dog, write Laugrand and Oosten (2002: 91), has a social identity. The dog names could be of several types, either taken from the animal's characteristics, for example colour or temperament, or its place of origin, or the dog could be called after a dead relative, as a kind of remembrance act. In some communities, dogs could also get the same names as living friends or members of the family, which was a way of honouring the namesakes.

In many traditional African cultures, dog names are used as a means of communication, especially for expressing criticism, partly in the same way as the names of oxen are used among the Zulu (see section 43.3.2.2). Batoma (2009) gives a comprehensive overview of the different strategies and reasons for this custom, concluding with three main explanatory models or perspectives. The names can be used for a humorous solution of a conflict, as a polite way of addressing a conflict, and as a way for a low-status person to take revenge on a person with higher status. Elaborate names of this type are not found in the European literature, although simpler ways of expressing humour or ridicule are known.[17]

Dog names of old were often related to the animal's looks, but personal names have also been used in many cultures. We find examples of both these categories even among the Egyptian names from over 5,000 years ago (Fischer 1977). One important factor concerning dog names, that Xenophon wrote about, is that a dog name should be easy to say and call out.[18] A dog name that contains two spoken syllables was the preferred phonological structure, and is so even today.

Little research has been carried out on the names of dogs on farms before the late nineteenth century, but the few sources preserved show that sometimes personal names, but more often colours, temperament, occupation, function, human titles, etc. were used as inspirations for names. The Swedish scholar Johan Nordlander (1880) gives examples of all these categories in his collections of dog names in rural areas.[19] Many of these names are concerned with the dog's functions, but there are also names of Greek and Roman deities as well as names containing noble titles in different languages (*Baron, Lady, Kaiser*), similar to dog names from different countries.

---

[17] Some examples are the custom of giving dogs (and other animals) names of disliked politicians, and the Scandinavian 'question–answer' names. A person asks about a dog's name and gets the answers 'Guess!' or 'Ask-him', thus confusing the person who puts the question (Nordlander 1880: 421).

[18] Xenophon: Cynegeticus, chapter 7.

[19] This is one of the very first collections of animal names with a scientific view of analysing both the names and their functions.

Keeping dogs for company has been a well-known pastime for several centuries at least among the higher classes in society.[20] During the last hundred years, the position of many dogs and cats has changed, so that nowadays, most dogs (and cats, as will be discussed below) in many of the post-industrial and urbanized societies are treated as companions or members of the family, sometimes being anthropomorphized. This is shown, among other things, in the way the animals are named. The more traditional dog names live on especially for utility dogs (hunting and herding dogs, etc.).

Even though dogs and other companion animals can in theory be given call names of any kind (and many will receive a unique name), there are certain recurring name categories. Personal names, either taken from popular first names or from the names of well-known personalities (real or fictive) make up the largest parts of the dog onomasticon in several countries. Research by Eva Schaab in Germany shows that almost 60 per cent of the names of 1,000 dogs collected in 2011 were anthroponyms,[21] and in my study of the 500 most popular Swedish dog names, slightly over 60 per cent can be categorized as anthroponyms.[22] Certain personal names are very popular as dog names; almost 6,000 Swedish dogs bear the girl's name *Molly* today.

Other important name groups are names derived from appellatives denoting people or personal titles (*Lady, Baron*), and names made up of commercial names, not least names of liquor and spirits (*Tequila, Whisky*, etc.). Names containing English adjectives (*Happy, Lucky*) are also common in several countries.

A family dog today will often receive the same name as a contemporary baby. This tendency is most striking for female dogs. Among the twenty most popular names for female dogs in Sweden in 2012, twelve were also found on the list of the top 100 names given to baby girls that year, and five more were given to at least fifty girls (Leibring 2014). The two most popular dog names, *Molly* and *Wilma*, were number 9 and 11 on the list of popular girls' names. However, only seven of the most popular male dog names were found on the top 100 list for boys. Schaab (2012: 147) found similar results in Germany—more popular female baby names than male are used for dogs. This can be explained by several reasons: one being that many masculine names are borrowed from heroes in popular culture; the names of fictional characters like *Zorro* and *Rocky* are popular dog names, as are the names *Tyson* and *Elvis*. Also, there are more fictional male animals than female to serve as name inspirers. Not least have the names of animals (not just dogs) in Disney films played an important role: *Pluto*, the *Tramp, Balto, Simba, Baloo*, etc. For further discussion of gender differences in animal names, see section 43.6.

---

[20] See e.g. Walker-Meikle (2012) on medieval pets.

[21] Schaab (2012: 146). In this, she includes first names, nicknames, and surnames. Names of gods and fictional persons make up a further 10%.

[22] For this section, I have used material from the Swedish Dog Register, which at the moment has over 750,000 entries. The 500 most frequent names are borne by approximately 278,000 dogs.

43.4.2 Cat Names

There are great similarities between contemporary cat names and dog names, not least that the cat's physical and spiritual features are important as motivations for names. A characteristic not found as often in dog names is that many cat names are related to the different sounds (meowing, purring, etc.) that cats can make (Saarelma 2012a: 205). As among dogs, many anthroponyms are used, especially for female cats (Leibring 2012b: 142). However, the feline onomasticon is fairly well-developed, as many popular cat names are used only for animals. On the names of contemporary cats from Finland and Denmark, Meldgaard (1993) and Blomqvist (2011) both state that names denoting colour or fur structure, as well as diminutive names, are common.[23] These names can also be metaphorical, as for example some names containing the names of strong liquor (*Whisky, Cognac*) are given to animals of that colour. Little research has been done on historical cat names, and the source situation is not very good, as cats have only quite recently been accepted as really domesticated animals.[24] In general, one can sense a greater freedom to give cats names with more variability both phonologically and morphologically. One reason for this is probably that cats in general do not respond to their names as willingly as dogs do, thus reducing the need for giving one's cat a name that is easy to call out.

43.4.3 Names of Other Companion Animals

Very little research has so far been done on the names of rabbits, guinea pigs, canaries, snakes, etc.[25] Lists of suitable names for rabbits and guinea pigs on the internet show that, apart from anthroponyms, there are many names denoting colour, small size, soft fur, and, in general bestowing endearments. Many of these names are also found as cat names. As many animal owners are children, names from children's literature, films, television programmes, and computer games also play an important role. A common rabbit name in different translations seems to be *Thumper* (from the Disney film *Bambi*)—in Swedish *Stampe*, in German *Klopfer*.

43.5 Names of Zoo Animals

Many animals, especially mammals, living in zoological gardens have names, mostly used by the handlers. Some of these names can, however, reach the public, if the animal

---

[23] See Meldgaard (1993) and Blomqvist (2011). In both these works, large collections of contemporary cat names are discussed.

[24] Gunnar Broberg (2004: 260ff.) gives many examples of the variance among older cat names, both Swedish and from other countries.

[25] See Leibring (2009) for a short introduction on names given to jumping rabbits. In the proceedings from the symposium on animal names in Mainz, 2013 (Dammel et al. 2015), rabbit names, cat names, and children as name-givers are discussed.

is in some way special or singled out. One well-known example is the polar bear Knut, whose life and death in the zoo of Berlin was closely followed in the mass media. In some zoos, the general public are also invited to name bear cubs, elk calves, or other newborn animals. Not much research has yet been done on these names, but a majority of them seem to be taken from the anthroponomasticon, as Ewald and Klager (2007) show from Germany. The genuine habitat of the animal can also inspire names, as can major events in society.

43.6 GENDER DIFFERENCES IN ANIMAL NAMES

The name-giving to animals tends in many cases to be fairly gender-specific. The morphological dissimilarities between male and female anthroponyms in several languages are also reproduced among animal names. Some examples of the same names used for animals, especially dogs, of both sexes are, however, found.[26] For all animal species, with the exception of cows and goats in the European traditional agricultural societies, more personal first names are used for female animals than for male. One explanation for the overwhelming use of women's first names could be that the tendency to borrow existing surnames for animals (as far as is known) is more or less restricted to male animals, meaning that the anthroponymic name pool is larger for male animals. This structure is known from the names of bulls and oxen in the traditional agricultural society (see section 4.3), as well as from contemporary names of dogs and cats. Less is known of female horses' names than of male horses in historical sources, as the mares seem to have been of less interest.[27] There are also more male animals featured in popular culture, thus producing more male role models and name inspiration and increasing the discrepancy in name-giving between the sexes.

43.7 SUMMING UP

The zoonomastica for different animals have changed over time and between cultures and societies. One or two centuries ago, most people, both rural and urban, had daily contact both with production animals and with companion animals. The names of these

[26] Few studies have been carried out into this subject, but the practice is known from both Swedish-Estonia and the Faroe Islands (Leibring 2014: 134). The names used for both sexes seem to be of more masculine rather than feminine origin.
[27] Cf. Karlsson (2004) where he shows that the first lists of mares with proper names from the royal stables are as late as from the early 1800s. The names of stallions are already recorded in the 1680s. The mares at that time are identified by descriptions and not proper names.

animals were often given according to the specific name-bearer's appearance or circumstances. The use of anthroponyms was not as widespread as today. Instead, specific onomastica for different animal species existed. Many of these traditional names fell out of fashion and even disappeared with agricultural structural changes.

Most people in today's modern and urbanized societies come into contact only with companion animals. Dogs and cats especially have been given full access to our homes, and they are in many cases treated as family members, being given the same names as our children. The anthropomorphization is obvious. In several countries, popular baby names coincide with the popular names for dogs and cats. This is most noticeable among female animals, as there are larger pools of names for male animals from other sources. Today, in general, many animal names are borrowed from other parts of the onomasticon, not only from the anthroponomasticon, but also from toponyms and commercial names.

Because of the contemporary strong tendency to give popular anthroponyms to animals, many identical names are given to animals of different species. Some names are also used internationally, for example *Simba* and *Lucky*, names that can be given to animals of all kinds. However, name pools for certain species do still exist, especially specific characterizing names. Some names have also reached such a level of popularity for a certain animal species that they can even be regarded as archetypical, like the dog name *Fido* and, in Sweden, the cow name *Majros*.

No small amount of research has been devoted to animal names, but much remains to be done. Not least is the question of how the names are (or have been) motivated. Deep and systematic studies of animal names all over the world are a challenge to any student and scholar of onomastics as ways of finding new perspectives on name-creation and name-giving.

CHAPTER 44

··

ASTRONOMICAL NAMES

··

MARC ALEXANDER

44.1 INTRODUCTION

IT can be difficult for modern city-dwellers to fully comprehend the impact of the night sky on the history of human culture. At a time before artificial light and pollution, the striking firmament inspired awe and curiosity; in the modern era, astronomical phenomena offer an insight into the nature and origin of the universe. This chapter overviews the naming practices associated in the past and in the present with a range of astronomical phenomena, linking them to the cultures and worldviews of both times.

44.2 HISTORICAL NAMING PRACTICES

44.2.1 Constellations

Stars, points of light against the night sky, were first given names as part of constellations, the grouping of stars into recognizable patterns, themselves given names based on what these patterns resembled. These patterns could then be used as reference mechanisms to sort the wide and complex sky into identifiable regions and arrangements, enabling a recognition of the regular and predictable features of the heavens and the use of this for the purposes of religion, agricultural calendars, and navigation. It has been argued that the prehistoric cave paintings at Lascaux in France contain the earliest representations of constellations, namely what are now known as the Pleiades and Taurus (Rappenglück 1996; the Lascaux paintings are dated at approximately 15,000 BC), while Owen Gingerich (1992: 10) argues that the name of the Great Bear constellation (also often known as Ursa Major) could have been the first named star grouping, as the identification of this star grouping with a bear is found simultaneously across areas in Siberia, North America, and Europe. Gibbon (1964: 241), however, provides folkloric evidence that the identification of these stars as a bear falls into three distinct groups (each of which do not agree on which part of the constellation represents a bear, with the top rump of one interpretation being the entire bear in another). Nonetheless, the prehistoric identification of one particular region of sky with a bear across three continents can either be a substantial coincidence or an indication of a name and mythology dating back to the last Ice Age, when land travel was possible from Eurasia to North America. Aside from such speculations, a Babylonian prayer tablet from 1,300 BC is the earliest surviving mention of constellations, mentioning four in total, and the descent of these Mesopotamian star groupings were then known to the Greeks, who added a further eighteen to get the forty-eight codified by Ptolemy's second-century *Almagest* (Schaefer 2006). Others were added piecemeal in the following centuries, particularly from regions remote to Greece and the Middle East, and generally depicted animals or humans (including mythological characters). Notably, fourteen southern hemisphere constellations were named in 1763 in the *Coelum Australe Stelliferum* by the Abbé Nicolas Louis de La Caille, in areas where stars were previously too faint to be seen. These constellations, still in use today, are exceptional as thirteen of them do not use mythological names but instead those of scientific equipment (such as Antlia, the air pump, Horologium, the clock, Microscopium, the microscope, Pyxis, the compass, and Telescopium, the telescope), and the other, Mensa (originally Mons Mensa), was named after Table Mountain in South Africa.

Modern astronomers therefore recognize eighty-eight constellations, as confirmed at the first meeting of the International Astronomical Union in 1922—each region of the sky therefore belongs to one constellation or another due to the boundaries set around each in order to completely divide up the sky. (Star patterns other than these eighty-eight are generally known as *asterisms*; the constellations collectively known as the Zodiac are simply those through which, from the perspective of the Earth, the Sun appears to pass.)

44.2.2 Stars

Before the existence of modern star catalogues, stars have primarily been given one of two different names; one based on the constellation it belongs to (either as part of the constellation's pattern itself, or just within the region of the sky bounded by the constellation), or—for 300 or so prominent stars—a unique, so-called 'traditional' name.

44.2.2.1 *Traditional Names*

Many star names are, in their etymology, related to constellations. For example, in Ursa Major, there are the stars Dubhe (Arabic, 'the bear'), Merak (an abbreviation of the Arabic for 'the flank of the greater bear'), Phecda (abbreviated Arabic, 'the thigh of the greater bear'), and Megrez (abbreviated Arabic, 'the base of the greater bear['s tail]'), among others; the Eridanus constellation, resembling a river being poured from Aquarius, has Acamar/Achernar (Arabic, 'the river's end'), Zaurak (Arabic, 'the boat'), Rana (Latin, 'the frog'); the nearest bright star to the bear constellations, Ursa Major and

Minor, is Arcturus (Greek, 'guardian of the bear'). The majority of these names come from Greek, Arabic, and Latin, with the Greek often influenced by Babylonian names, and with inter-language borrowings meaning many star names have convoluted etymologies to rival any other words in the major languages. For example, Kunitzsch and Smart (2006) in their excellent *Dictionary of Modern Star Names*, describe the etymology of the star Theemin, in Eridanus, as:

> The formation of this name begins with one of the words used by Ptolemy to describe this star in the Almagest: ἡ καμπή, 'the bend [of the river].' This was misread by the sci-Arabs [scientifically-focused Arabs], who transliterated the word as *bhmn*. This, in turn, was transliterated as *beemun* in the Medieval Latin *Almagest*, which was corrupted to *beemin, beemim*, etc. Then in Renaissance times, the derivation of the form *beemim* was erroneously attributed to the Hebrew word t$^{e)}$ōmīm 'twins.' Subsequently this erroneous word, written as *Theemim*, then 'Theemin,' was applied as a star name to any of the various dim stars running from υ1 to h Eri[danus]. (Kunitzsch and Smart 2006: 37)

While many names are in some sense transparent (once their etymology is determined) with regards to their relation to their constellation, there are other traditionally-named stars which do not follow this pattern. These have individual reasons for their names, such as Polaris (Latin, 'of the [north] pole'), Barnard's Star (one of a very few stars named after persons, a star not visible to the naked eye but named in the twentieth century for Edward E. Barnard, who worked on it in 1916, and named because it is the focus of much astronomical work as it is very close to our own solar system), Cor Caroli (Latin, 'Charles' Heart', named in 1660 in honour of either Charles I or Charles II of England). Other than these bright, prominent stars, the majority of star names are given through catalogue systems.

44.2.2.2 *Catalogue Names*

The two late modern star cataloguing systems still in use are known as the Bayer and Flamsteed systems. The Bayer system, published in 1603 by Johann Bayer in his *Uranometria*, labels stars based generally on their relative brightness within a constellation, using Greek letters to identify these—so, for example, the brightest star in the constellation Lyra (named after Orpheus' lyre) is called Alpha Lyrae, or α Lyrae (traditional name Vega). When constellations require more Greek letters than there are available, Bayer used Latin letters. The Flamsteed system, from John Flamsteed's 1712 *Historia Coelestis Britannica* (published without Flamsteed's consent), is similar, but assigns numbers to stars working from the right to the left of the sky, giving the same star the designation 3 Lyrae. As can be seen from the title of Flamsteed's catalogue, these numbers are only available for stars visible from Great Britain, but they retain some use in modern designations for stars without a Bayer number—51 Pegasi, for example, which was the first star similar to our own Sun to be found with a planet orbiting it (Mayor and Queloz 1995). Some problems for modern users are occasionally encountered here by the use of the Latin genitive, which can be confusing for those unaccustomed to it (for example, Apus/Apodis, Aquarius/Aquarii, Cancer/Cancri, Canes Venatici/Canum Venaticorum, Crux/Crucis, Vela/Velorum).

Many stars labeled this way also have traditional names (in particular, Bayer alpha and beta stars, being the brightest in a constellation, often do): for example, in the 175 stars we know to be in the Perseus constellation, eight have traditional names (Alpha, Beta, Gamma, Rho, Eta, Kappa, Omicron, and Xi), 41 have Bayer designations, and 63 have Flamsteed designations. Some new constellations created after Bayer have been allocated Bayer-style star names—so that, for example, the brightest star in La Caille's Telescopium constellation is Alpha Telescopii.

44.2.3 Wandering Stars: The Planets

The major planets took some time to be identified as planets as we understand them, as they appeared to be stars which moved independently of the general wheel of the constellations; our modern term planet comes from the Greek *planetes asteres*, 'wandering stars'. The seven wandering stars are therefore the Sun, Moon, Mercury, Venus, Mars, Jupiter, and Saturn, with the last five being the *classical planets*. Our records of the naming of planets generally begins in the cultures of Mesopotamia and the belief that 'the planets were not themselves divine, but were manipulated by the gods' (Campion 2008: 254); the pattern of naming approximates the features found in the later gods, meaning that the associations drawn between the members of the various Mesopotamian pantheon were translated into later cultures. We therefore find the planet known as Venus associated with the Sumerian Inanna and Akkadian Ishtar, a female fertility god; Mars with Nergal, god of the underworld and war, amongst other things; Jupiter with Marduk, head of the pantheon; and Mercury with Nabu, the scribe of the gods (Campion 2008: 255). These were translated into the pantheons of Greece and then Rome, although it would be a mistake to believe that they were in any way fixed, as is made clear in the Roman *Hygini Fabulae,* from the first century AD:

> The second star is that of Sol; others say of Saturnus. Eratosthenes claim that it is called Phaethon, from the son of Sol. . . . The third star is that of Mars, though others say it belongs to Hercules. . . . Since [Aphrodite] inflamed him violently with love, she called the star Pyroeis, indicating this fact. The fourth star is that of Venus, Luciferus by name. Some say it is Juno's. In many tales it is recorded that it is called Hesperus, too. It seems to be the largest of all stars. (Grant 1960: 228)

With some of this confusion allowed for, it is nonetheless undoubted that the Roman names now known widely throughout the West originated with neither the Greeks nor the Romans, although many astronomical sources incorrectly say they do. By contrast, Chinese names for these planets are based around their literal descriptions and purposes—for example, Jupiter is the 'year star', whose movement can be used to establish a calendar, Mars the 'glitterer', Venus the 'great white' star, and Mercury the 'hour star' (Kelley and Milone 2005: 328) as well as names based on elements; later discoveries are direct translations from the Western names, with Neptune's name, *haĭwáng-xīng*, meaning 'god [or king] of the sea'.

44.3 MODERN NAMING PRACTICES

Modern astronomical naming is controlled primarily by the International Astronomical Union (IAU), the main association of professional astronomers, and its Divisions, Commissions, and Working Groups (particularly those for Planetary System Nomenclature, Small Bodies Nomenclature, Meteor Shower Nomenclature, Public Naming of Planets and Planetary Satellites, and that on Designations, meaning the names of astronomical sources of radiation outside the solar system). The general principle for naming followed by the IAU is that the discoverers of a new object or feature have the right to submit a proposed name to the relevant working group, which will then approve or deny the proposal following consideration of certain requirements, outlined below. Until a name is confirmed, objects and features are generally given a provisional name code based on an established formula.

44.3.1 Stars

Most astronomers continue to use Bayer or Flamsteed numbers, if available, for stars. Modern catalogues, however, refer to stars using numerical references; Vega, referred to above as Alpha Lyrae in the Bayer system and 3 Lyrae in Flamsteed, is BD +38°3238 in the Bonner Durchmusterung (BD; Bonn Survey), HD 172167 in the Henry Draper Catalogue, HR 7001 in the Yale Bright Star Catalogue, SAO 67174 in the Smithsonian Astrophysical Observatory Star Catalog, and HIP 91262 in the Hipparcos Catalogue. The most commonly used of these are the Smithsonian and Hipparcos Catalogues, and (for fainter stars) the Hubble Space Telescope Star Guide Catalog, although yet newer and more comprehensive catalogues are still being released. The IAU does not recognize any one catalogue over another.

44.3.1.1 *Commercial Star 'Naming'*

As the IAU is the only internationally recognized naming body for astronomical phenomena, and as it does not name stars (as star names are not useful for scientists) or accept commercial requests to name astronomical phenomena, it should go without saying that commercial companies which offer to name stars (for example, as birthday presents) in return for a fee are not doing so with any authority. A planetarium worker comments in Bishop (2004) that:

My boss . . . likes to tell his classes that they can achieve the same effect by walking into the back yard, pointing to a star, and saying, 'I hereby name you Aunt Betty.' You then complete the ceremony by removing from your wallet $45 and setting it on fire. (Bishop 2004: 1)

Often denigrated by astronomers, these commercial companies—at best engaged in some harmless fun, at worst deeply deceptive—nonetheless show the fascination with stars and their names which continues to the present day.

44.3.2 Planets and Moons

The first planet to be discovered in the post-classical period was Uranus, in 1781, and its discoverer, William Herschel, originally proposed to name it after the then King, George III. This was not a popular choice internationally, and the German astronomer Johann Elert Bode instead proposed the unpolitical Uranus, who was the father of Saturn and grandfather of Jupiter (Miner 1998: 12). This was, it should be noted, not the first sighting of Uranus, but rather was the first to lead to its identification as a planet; amongst others Flamsteed in 1690, observed Uranus and catalogued it as the star 34 Tauri, in the constellation Taurus. Neptune followed in 1846, with a similar controversy after its French discoverer wished to name it after himself (Kollerstrom 2009). As Pluto (named for the god of the underworld) is no longer considered a major planet, due to its marginal inclusion in that category and the discovery of many items just like it in the solar system, there will likely be no more major planets named in this solar system. Dwarf planets (of which there are currently five—Ceres, Pluto, Eris, Haumea, and Makemake—with more discovered but unconfirmed) are named after fertility or creation deities, with the exceptions of Pluto and Eris. Planets found outwith the solar system are named after their parent star, consisting of that star's name suffixed with a lower-case Latin letter, starting with b for the first-discovered planet orbiting that star and continuing onwards (such as 51 Pegasi b, which is the first planet discovered orbiting the star 51 Pegasi, which is itself known by its Flamsteed designation; Mayor and Queloz 1995).

Moons of planets (also known as satellites) are given designations using their parent planet's name followed by capital Roman numerals depending on the order of discovery, and are also allocated proper names in a consistent fashion, drawn from IAU-approved naming practices. Moons of Jupiter, for example, are named after the lovers of Jupiter in mythology, beginning with the four moons discovered in 1610 by Galileo (Ganymede, Callisto, Io, and Europa, also known as Jupiter I to Jupiter IV). These moons also have a further restriction in that they are named with names ending in -a or -o if the moon's orbit is prograde (in the same direction as Jupiter's orbit of the sun), and in -e if the orbit is retrograde (the converse direction). Recent advances in technology means that even the list of lovers of Jupiter has been exhausted, and now the descendants of Jupiter are permitted names for Jovian satellites. Saturn's satellites are named after mythological giants, originally only the Greco-Roman titans, but now extended to giants in any mythology (for example, Saturn XXVI is Aegir, a Norse giant, XXVII Bebhionn, a Celtic giantess, and XXIX Siarnaq, an Inuit giant); rules also govern which origin language should be used for newly-discovered Saturnian satellites based on the angle of the moon's orbit. The moons of Uranus are named after characters in Shakespeare (such as Uranus X, Desdemona, or XVIII, Prospero). These structures can seem playful in their systematicity, but also have a mnemonic-like basis: rather like the designations which include the parent planet's name, the names of these moons identify themselves as part of a pattern which assists with recognition of where a given satellite originates. Should someone familiar with the general principles behind each system encounter moon names such as Portia, Cressida, Titan, Hyperion, Pasiphae, or Leda, then they have a good chance of working out which planet they orbit (given, of course, a certain amount of background cultural knowledge—knowledge, it should be noted, which was much more prevalent in previous centuries than now).

Planetary features are similarly named in pre-defined groups. Venus, for example, has all its surface features named after women (real or mythological), with canyons named after goddesses of the hunt, large craters after famous real women, small craters after female first names, low plains after mythological heroines, continents after goddesses of love, high plains after goddesses of prosperity, ridges after sky goddesses, and so on. Only one feature, a mountain named after physicist James Clark Maxwell, is named after a male, and this only because the name was accepted before the current system was established. Similarly, Mercury has features named after deceased artists or musicians, works of architecture, ships of discovery, and so on, and Mars has areas named for small Earth villages or rivers. Similar principles apply here to the mnemonic devices, but these also bring home the IAU urge to make sure all naming is systematic, and so less open to frivolous or commercial pressure (such as naming a continent or crater after a company, or a living person).

44.3.3 Comets

Comets, once named haphazardly and often with a possessive (such as Halley's Comet), are now systematically named with the word Comet followed by the sur-names of its discoverers (usually no more than two names); thus Comet Halley, or Comet Hale-Bopp (discovered in 1995 by Alan Hale and Thomas Bopp). This leads to some interesting rule-bending; a person with a hyphenated surname (the astrono-mer Stephen Singer-Brewster) discovered a comet in 1986 which could not be known as Comet Singer-Brewster, as this would suggest discovery by one person called Singer and another Brewster; the comet was eventually called Comet Singer Brewster, with no hyphen, to indicate these circumstances; similarly, the husband-and-wife team of Carolyn and Eugene Shoemaker had their names merged into one (their discoveries being Comet Shoemaker 1, 2, 3, etc.), rather than Shoemaker-Shoemaker (Machholz 1989: 26). Comets are also given a complex coded designation depending on what type of comet they are and at what point in the year they were discovered.

44.4 CONCLUSION

The number of names of all the items, people, and places which currently are or have ever been on the Earth are dwarfed in magnitude by the number of items in the deep reaches of space. As technology gets ever more precise, and we discover more and more of the stars and planets which surround us, more and more items are given designations and, if necessary, given a name to act as a more comprehensible replacement for that designation. In a pointed demonstration of the importance of names and naming to our sense of place and identity in the world, the ever-growing number of such features—from a handful of constellations in the distant past, to the member stars of those constellations, to the planets either orbiting those stars or acting as companions to our own Earth, to the individual valleys and craters and mountains on each moon and satellite and planet we discover—continue to be linked now as they were in the past to our culture and history by those naming practices which bind our mythologies, stories, researchers, and heroes to the bright lights of the stars and planets which surround us.

CHAPTER 45

NAMES OF DWELLINGS

ADRIAN KOOPMAN

45.1 INTRODUCTION

I have known the Frenzel family for twenty-five years. For twenty-four of those twenty-five years they have been content to live at No. 20 Grimthorpe Avenue, just a few houses along from where I live at No. 37. In 2010 the family (mother, father, and three sons), all devout Christians, decided to visit Israel, and during that visit, came across the oasis and gorge named Ein Gedi, where a considerable amount of water issues from the desert floor, sustains a hidden, flourishing ribbon of vegetation for a kilometre or so, and then disappears again into the desert near the Dead Sea. Marvelling at God's munificence, on their return to No. 20 Grimthorpe Avenue, the family felt they had received a direct message from God 'to be fruitful in their community', and named their house *Ein Gedi*. The signboard erected outside the front gate (see Figs. 45.1–45.2) has an abstract image of the oasis on one side, and on the other the name and the words 'Frenzel Family Home', surrounded by brightly-coloured flowers all enclosed in a blue river. The colours selected, says Mrs Noleen Frenzel, are all symbolic: the red represents the blood of Christ, the yellow the glory of God, and so on.

We will return to the name *Ein Gedi* in the course of this chapter.

45.2 RANGE OF NAMED ENTITIES TO BE COVERED IN THIS CHAPTER

The names that are discussed in this chapter are those of dwellings where the resident or a previous resident is/was responsible for the name. The focus is on the names of

FIGURE 45.1 *Ein Gedi*: the name of the Frenzel family's house

FIGURE 45.2 The reverse side: the name *Ein Gedi* repeated, with the family identity and the symbolic flowers and river

private residences, including the names of 'country houses' and castles, thus excluding the names of flats and other multiple residential complexes, and other places where people might live (albeit temporarily), such as boarding houses and hotels. These have been discussed by various scholars, often with an eye on how names are chosen for their marketing value.[1] Although the names of 'pubs' (public houses, inns, taverns) have attracted much attention,[2] they are not covered here. On the other hand the names of privately-owned beach cottages and other holiday homes are discussed. The naming of Zulu homesteads will be looked at in some detail to provide a comparative framework for the material, which is otherwise mainly of European origin.

As regards approaches to the study of house names, again lack of space means only certain areas can be covered. This chapter looks at the function of house names, semantic issues including semantic categorization, and the dynamics between house name, house number, and signboard. The syntax and morphology of house names, in themselves interesting topics, must be left out, as must the issue of changing patterns in house names.[3]

45.3 THE FUNCTION OF A HOUSE NAME

It is generally accepted that the function of any name, whether an anthroponym, a toponym, a brand name, or any other type, is referential. That is to say, the name functions to identify, to single out any entity from others of the same kind. This function is often referred to as the denotative function. It could be argued that in many cases of house names, this function is superfluous, in that most named house names also have a numbered street address. De Bruyn (1997) points out that:

> ... met die gee van name aan strandhuise die doel van naamgewing om te identifiseer, vervaag het. Dit gaan nie suiwer daaroor om huis A van huis B, D, E, ensovoorts te onderskei nie, omdat daarvoor elkeen immers 'n adres het en daarvolgens gevind kan word.

> [... with the giving of names to beach cottages, the aim of name-giving to identify has fallen away. It is no longer purely about differentiating between house, A, B, D, E, etc., because each has its own [street] address and can be found by it.] (De Bruyn 1997: 70)

On the other hand, houses have not always had street numbers. Miles (1973: 10) tells us that the history of numbering houses began in France in 1463 on the Pont Notre Dame in France, but that 'the naming of houses is a much older habit'. And for houses set in open country, where there is neither number nor street, the primary function of the name will be referential.

---

[1] See for examples Neethling (2000) and Koopman (2002a).
[2] See for examples Dunkling and Wright (1987) and Cox (1994).
[3] Miles (1973: 38ff.) gives details of both of these, showing how earlier house names in Great Britain almost always included generics like 'house', 'hall', 'lodge', and 'villa', which started disappearing in the first half of the twentieth century.

In rural Zululand, the name of a homestead has a very definite referential function. Homesteads, consisting normally of several huts clustered around a central cattle byre, are scattered at intervals around the countryside, and many are reached only by a foot-path. The surname (or clan name) of the owner cannot be used to identify a particular homestead as most parts of rural Zululand are settled by clans with the same clan name. It is no good identifying a particular homestead as *KwaKhanyile* ('Khanyile's place') if over 60 per cent of the families in the neighbourhood have the clan name Khanyile.

As with most names, if the denotative (referential) function is primary, then the lexical (or underlying) meaning of the name becomes irrelevant. Even a name which is lexically totally opaque can still denote. When the denotative function is unnecessary, as in the case of named houses which also have a numbered street address, then the lexical meaning is invariably associated with the intention of the owner in the naming of the house, and what we might term 'secondary' functions. Such secondary functions can include the following:

- referring to the physical appearance of the house and/or its surroundings, as in *The Cottage, The Pines, Windy Gap*, and *Seaview*;
- expressing nostalgia, by transferring to the house a name originally the name of the place where one was born, or where one spent a wonderful holiday;
- expressing a worldview, especially one which sees the house as a home, a haven, and a place to rest after a life's work (the *Dunromin* type)
- exhibiting one's linguistic skill and offering the passer-by an onomastic joke, such as the reversed name *Emahroo* (< 'oor hame');
- sending a message to neighbours and the wider world;
- referring to the people who live in the house.

Further examples of all these are given below.

45.4 SEMANTICS AND SEMANTIC CATEGORIES

This section can be divided into (a) the notion of meaning generally in house names, and levels of meaning; and (b) semantic categories.

The meaning of the house name (or, rather, the reason behind the name) depends on knowing the story behind the name. When a house with two chimneys is named *Twinstax*, the immediate assumption is that the name is a variant of 'twin stacks', that is two chimneys. However, Miles (1982: 19) says that in this particular case the name was given because the down-payment on the house was made possible by a tax refund and an insurance payout following the birth of twins. Dunkling (1971: 15) points out that the same house name may have a wide range of different reasons behind it and that only the person or persons who chose the name can explain the reason for its choice. With such names, she says, the 'meaning' of the name is perhaps best thought of as precisely those reasons for choice. For the Frenzel family whose story begins this chapter, the lexical meaning of *Ein Gedi*—'Kid Spring' (< Hebrew *ein* 'spring' + *gedi* 'goat kid') is not relevant. For them, the meaning of the name is more like 'Fountain of God'.

When it comes to semantic categorization of house names, different writers on house names have, as may be expected, different systems of categorization. Dunkling's (1971) categories are fairly typical. She divides English house names into the following five categories:

- *Transferred Names*, which are the 'countless house names which are simply place names, hotel names, street names, ship names, pub names, etc. which have been borrowed and used for a house' (1971: 14). Dunkling calls these 'linguistic souvenirs', and says '[s]ometimes they are chosen because they sound attractive in themselves, but their main function is to evoke memories.' The Frenzels' *Ein Gedi* belongs to this category.

- *Descriptive Names*: from the evidence of other collectors and scholars of house names, this is certainly the most common type of house name. Such names can describe the house itself (*Five Gables, Crazy Chimneys, The Thatch*), its setting (*Hilltop, High Corner, Bayview, Harbour Winds*), fauna associated with the house (*The Sparrows, Kestrel Grange, Beaver's Holt*), and—very commonly—dominant plant life (*The Laurels, Acacia Villa, Baytree Cottage, Rosemead*).

- *Blended Names*, where parts of the names of the husband and wife and/or the children are combined into a house name. There are various ways of doing this: simple combinations such as *Alaneileen, Dorsyd* (< Doris and Sydney), and *Rosedene* (< Rose and Denise), anagrams, as in *Ferndean* (< Fred and Anne), and adding some sort of generic to an anthroponym, as in *Alanholme, Bryanville*, and *Smithfield*. Dunkling notes (1971: 31) that Mr and Mrs Wood, whose house is named *Woodsland* find that most people insist on 'correcting' this to 'Woodlands'.

- *Foreign names*:[4] Dunkling gives examples of names taken from Welsh, Cornish, Scottish Gaelic, Australian aboriginal languages, French and Spanish, among others. Examples include *Ty Newydd* (Welsh: 'new house'), *Wahroonga* (Australian aborigine: 'our house'), and well-worn names like *Dulce Domum, Nil Desperandum, Bienvenu, Chez Nous, Pied-A-Terre*, and *Sans Souci*, which hardly need translating.

- *Other Names*: Dunkling's examples under this 'miscellaneous' category cover a very wide range of names. One well-known type is the *Dunromin* (< done with roaming') type, where house-owners see their new home as a final resting place after years of toil. Such names often come with unorthodox spelling, as in *Ersanmine*,

---

[4] Dunkling uses the term 'foreign' to mean 'non-English'.

Weetew, Uanme, Rominova, and *Dunmovin*. The cost of a house is often referred to as in *Overdraft* and *On The Rocks, Costalotta*, and *Costa Pyle*. Adam Edwards (2008) gives the examples of people who moved into houses with already existing names, and changed them slightly to refer to their financial circumstances: *Millstone* became *Milestone* when the new owner had finished paying off his mortgage and *Stonybrook* became *Stonybroke*. One of Dunkling's 'other' names certainly defies classification: the name *Buntsarnglo* was the result of someone at a house-warming party trying to say 'Aunt's bungalow', and not succeeding because of the effects of alcohol.

Shabalala (1999)[5] subdivided Zulu homestead names into seven semantic categories, while Ntuli (1992a, 1992b) found that six categories would suffice. Koopman (2002b: 183–95), after adding historical data to the data collected,[6] found that Zulu homestead names could be divided into two basic categories: those that refer to the homestead itself, and those that relate to the inhabitants. The names referring to the homes themselves are very similar to the descriptive names mentioned above for English house names, for example *eLangeni* ('in the sun'), *eNkungwini* ('in the mist'), *oNdini* ('on the heights'), and *eZimfabeni* ('place of mimosa trees'). Zulu house names are not based on the personal names or surnames of the inhabitants, and there are no linguistic jokes. Unorthodox spelling is obviously not an issue when the names occur only in an oral format.

Zulu homestead names that refer to the inhabitants may refer to a certain incident, as in *Phumphele* ('get out right now') and *kwaDeqheluka* ('keep on shifting'), and may reflect the inhabitants' wishes for peace, good health, and happiness, as in *eKuthuleni* ('place of peace'), *eKuphumeleni* ('place of rest'), and *eKujabuleni* ('place of happiness'). These are the direct equivalents of English house names like *Friendlea, Seventh Heaven*, and *Merriedean* (Dunkling 1971: 44).

One particularly interesting type of homestead name, one for which I can find no equivalents in the English data, is that which carries a message to kin and neighbours, usually a name which refers to tensions, friction, witchcraft, and jealousy. Dog names, ox names, and even personal names are used in this fashion in Zulu society (see Koopman 1992, 2002b: 211–28) and indeed in many African societies (see Batoma 2009), so homestead names are not unique. Examples are *kwaMuntungifunani* ('what does [that] person want from me?'), *kwaPhumuzumlomo* ('give the mouth a rest'— a reference to gossiping neighbours), *kwaBhekomzondayo* ('looking at the one you hate'), and *eMbangweni* ('place of strife and dispute').

---

[5] Part of this dissertation was later published under Shabalala's married surname. See Machaba (2000).

[6] Taken from the six volumes of the James Stuart Archive, edited by Webb and Wright (1976–2014).

45.5 The House Name, the House Number, and the Signboard

Occasionally the name given to a house is based on the already existing street number. The literature gives a number of examples of this type of name, including *Gross House* (No. 144 in street). *Wuntun* (i.e. 'one ton' or 100), and verbalized numbers, almost invariably with contorted spellings, like *Nyneteign, Thir-T-Nyne, Numbawun,* and *Tootoothree* (Dunkling 1971: 11). What appears to be becoming popular in the twenty-first century, is a 'name' consisting of the number and/or the street name, in the form *183 on Main* or *Palms on Alex* (see Fig. 45.3 and Fig. 45.4).

Miles (1973) makes an interesting point about the relationship between name and number: when larger properties in an already numbered road are subdivided and new houses built, they will

> . . . have to carry an A or a B after the number of the original house. This immediately suggests that the house is merely an appendage, or else that you live in the upstairs flat. A name on such a house becomes essential. (Miles 1973: 31)

Dunkling (1971: 11) gives an interesting example of such a case: when a house in a subdivision was numbered '2b', the new owners named it *Ornot*, a reference to Shakespeare's famous phrase 'To be or not to be'.

It seems axiomatic that named houses will have a board or some other visual version of the name outside, where passers-by, visitors, and postmen can see it, but this has not always been the case. Miles points out that:

> [These older] names . . . would have become attached to a house by popular repute, recorded more or less accurately in deeds and correspondence at fairly wide intervals of time, but most of the people who used the names must have carried them in their heads—the ordinary passer-by could not have read the name, and the penny post was many years in the future. (Miles 1973: 20)

In preliterate times in rural Zululand,[7] written forms of homestead names obviously could not have existed. What is perhaps curious is that even now, in the twenty-first century, when by far the majority of Zulu-speakers, even in rural areas, are literate, signboards for the names of homesteads are nowhere to be found.

Finally, names and their signboards often interact in curious ways. Dunkling (1971: 16) gives the example of a house in England named *Arden*. The immediate assumption is that this is one of a considerable number of houses named Arden or Arden House

---

[7] The earliest forms of written Zulu were devised by missionaries from approximately the 1840s onwards.

FIGURE 45.3 AND FIGURE 45.4 This house could easily have been simply named *The Palms*, as there are several large palm trees in the garden. They chose, however, a name that links these trees to the name of the road. There is a double meaning here, as Alexandra Road itself is lined with palms (see lower photo), so the name means both '*The Palms* on Alex[andra Road]' as well as 'the palms on Alexandra Road'.

(originally from Shakespeare).[8] Dunkling's example 'turned out to be the remains of a wartime sign which had originally said WARDEN'. In another example, one of my own onomastic colleagues in the 1980s bought an old farmhouse in the tellingly-named district of Balgowan some fifty kilometres west of Pietermaritzburg, where by far the majority of names for farms and houses in the district are of Scottish origin. Their farmhouse carried the name *Tirlings* in large individual wooden letters on the front gate. Research suggested that originally the farmhouse had been called *Stirling*, which would have fitted the onomastic profile of the area, but that the 'S' had fallen off at some time in the past, and was later put back on the 'wrong' end of the name by someone who did not recognize the name *Stirling*.

In the case of the Frenzel family, it is clear that the signboard, together with its images, words, and colours, is an integral part of the name.

---

[8] Miles (1973: 24): 'Shakespeare's *Anne Hathaway's Cottage, Hall's Croft, Mary Arden's House,* and *New Place* are well enough known . . .'.

CHAPTER 46

RAILWAY LOCOMOTIVE NAMES AND TRAIN NAMES

RICHARD COATES

46.1 INTRODUCTION

THE names of railway locomotives, as illustrated by British examples, are a problematic topic, synchronically speaking. As with many other categories of names, for instance those of racehorses, businesses, or personal identifiers in the virtual world (e.g. Facebook usernames), any linguistic object—word, phrase, or arbitrary string—may serve as a name. In fact this liberal formulation is not liberal enough, because even primary names (personal and place-names) have been created consisting of non-linguistic objects, of which ♀, representing a legally protected assumed name of the singer also calling himself The Artist Formerly Known As Prince, is only the most famous. That being so, it makes sense to approach locomotive names from a historical perspective, because a historical development in their nature is clearly discernible, from which a principle of historical onomastics may be inferred underpinning the development of naming systems in general.[1]

The early history of railway locomotives powered by steam is marked by two striking facts. The first is that many received names, even where there was no practical need to distinguish them in such a way because they were isolated individuals. The second is that those names tended strongly to express essential attributes of the machines themselves. *Essential names* are or contain descriptions of, or more usually allusions to, characteristics of the individual thing named. For instance, the

---

[1] The main sources used for name material are Cleland (1825), De Quincey (1849), 'Sekon' (1899), Dendy Marshall (1928, esp. Part I, 'The first hundred railway engines'; 1953, esp. valuable on early manufacturers), Casserley (1967), Talbot (*c*.1982), Goodman (1994, 2002), Pike (2000), Green (2003–15), Hunt (*c*.2005; especially on manufacturer Fairbairn), Walton (2005), Baldwin (2008), Jones (2008), and the *Great Western Archive*.

first named English railway locomotive was *Catch me who can* (1808), with an obvious allusion to its speed. Another early one was *Puffing Billy* (1813), with its allusion to the sight and sound of the exhaust high-pressure steam. There may be more than one such allusion in a single name. *The Steam Horse* was a contraption which achieved forward motion not using steam-driven wheels but with the steam driving two mechanical devices like horses' legs. Its name enshrines the source of power, steam, an allusion to the action of the leg-like objects, and an allusion to the horse as the standard of comparison for its role as motive power (compare *horsepower* as a long-lived unit for measuring workrate). Some such allusions were fully metaphorical or mythological, as in the cases of *Rocket* (1829) and *Vulcan* (1831–2), with their allusions to speed and fire. Essential names, so defined, are common during the early years of railway development in England.

However, locomotives soon came to be produced not as individual machines but to standard types or classes. Name-giving remained the norm for at least some types, but the names themselves tended to be typed, and typed in a less constrained way than earlier ones. The later onymic types veered sharply away from being literally or allusively descriptive. This trend, and the sources of these developed onymic types, are of cultural interest, and some types have had a very long currency in Britain.

46.2 GROUNDWORK: THE NAMES OF PRE-1846 LOCOMOTIVES

There is no compelling reason why locomotives should be named at all. Quite a few early colliery engines, including the very first in 1803–04, were nameless. As they multiplied, they could simply have been distinguished by numbers. Whilst that often happened, many were given both a number and a name. This situation remained common for at least passenger locomotives, and many early goods (freight) locomotives were named too. Such an onomastic impulse makes sense in the light of other naming practices current at the beginning of the Industrial Revolution. Machines as such (pumps, spinning frames, looms, drills) did not generally bear individual proper names. But modes of transport did. The practice of naming locomotives seems to have followed the naming of horse-drawn coaches operating scheduled services between towns, especially mail-coaches. Most such services came to bear a name, and this name generally attached also to the vehicle which performed the service because it was painted on it. In France, the famous *Diligence* ran between Paris and Lyon from 1623. By 1669, there was a service between London and Oxford called the *Flying Coach*. Passenger-carrying mail-coaches first operated in Britain in 1784. They were the main competitor and the most obvious analogue of the early railway passenger services, until the expansion of the railway network killed off almost all the coaches by the 1850s. The source of motive power which the steam locomotive replaced was the horse, and it was normal (but not universal) practice for horses to bear names. The horse, in one way or another, has had a large influence on naming practices for locomotives in Britain.

The essential names of these early machines fall into five categories which form a nexus of related ideas: *new; powerful; quick; mechanical;* and *excellent.* This set overlaps substantially with the concepts most often deployed in consumer advertising, as established long ago by Leech (1966: 52). The detail of this typology might be queried, but the broad outlines seem beyond dispute.

46.2.1 New

This section looks at names which designate a clever device, created by technological advance, producing *novelty* and (therefore) *progress* and *superiority*. By allusion to innovation:

Experiment (1828 and 1833), *Novelty* (1829), *Pioneer* (1837), *Surprise* (1838)

By allusion to physical and perceptual characteristics:

The Steam Horse (1813) and *Steam Elephant* (1815) where the novelty is expressed by the surprising collocations rather than the vocabulary; *Chittapratt* (1826; unusually, onomatopoeic from the noise it made), *Twin Sisters* (1829; unusually having two vertical boilers), *Mountaineer* (1834; a rack-and-pinion locomotive, i.e. one designed to be capable of climbing steeply)

By metonymic allusion to industry in the widest sense:

Perseverance (1829), *Industry* (1832), *Yn Barod Etto* (1832—Welsh translation of familiar tag *Semper paratus/Ever Ready*)

By allusion to the idea that novelty or mystery can be produced by sorcery:

Lancashire Witch (1828), *Hecate* (1829)

46.2.2 Powerful

A selection of names designate a device which is *powerful*. The prototypes of power were *natural* and *dangerous*: meteorological and animal. Locomotives were named metaphorically after the things which they recalled by the noises they made (e.g. by roaring, thundering, hissing) but which they outperformed in power. Names in this category suggested the harnessing of danger and claimed steam as the new prototype of power.

By allusion to natural power and its implicit danger:

Stourbridge Lion (1828), *Elephant* (1834), *L'Éléphant* (1836), *Shark* (1837), *Lightning* (1837), *Lion* (1838), *Eagle* (1838), *Viper* (1838)

By classical or biblical allusion to characters with human strength or divine power:

Hecate (1829), *Fury* (1831 and 1838), *Vulcan* (1831-2), *Ajax* (1832), *Goliath* (1833), *Atlas* (1833/4), *Hector* (1834), *Samson* (1837), *Cyclops* (*c*.1837), *Hercules* (*c*.1838)

46.2.3 Quick

Another category of names are chosen for a device which *moves rapidly*. The prototype of speed was flight, and the available prototypes of speedy transport were the (race)horse and the mail-coach, themselves often named after speedy things. Locomotives were named after the things they outperformed in speed, and such naming represented a claim for steam as the new prototype of speed. This category is not just a matter of naming, but something built into the perceptions and discourse of the period. Early commentators tended to compare locomotives with animals, and the experience of travel with flying. For many years trains (as opposed to locomotives) could bear such names as *The Cheltenham Flyer* or *The Flying Scotsman*. Early locomotives whose names are not otherwise easily classifiable were *Bee* (1841) and *Hornet* (1840), recalling flying creatures directly:

Catch me who can (1808), *Active* (1825), *Alert* (1837)

Other names were indirect, employing a metaphorical allusion to speedy objects, including the wind (cf. 'run like the wind') and the mail-coach:

Wylam Dilly (recalling *Diligence*; 1813-14), **Dart** (1822), **Star** (1822), **Tallyho** (1822), *Diligence* (1826), *Wildfire* (1829), *Meteor* (1829), *Arrow* (1829), *Rocket* (1829), *Red Rover* (1833—from the Bristol–Brighton stagecoach), *Hurricane* (1837 and 1845), *Lightning* (1837), *Sirocco* (1841-2), *Swallow* (1841)

The **emboldened** names are interesting because they were actually given to commemorate racehorses famous in 1822, but they might equally have been given following other principles, such as the perpetuation of mail-coach names or the use of names which themselves conveyed speed or excellence.

46.2.4 Mechanical

Mechanical names allude to the literal outward signs of the new *mechanical* motive power, *fire* and *steam*, with *coal* as the source of the power. Names which derive from such signs directly are:

Puffing Billy (1813–14), *Steam Elephant* (1815), *Black Diamond* (1826; an epithet of coal), *Firefly*

Names which derive by metaphorical allusion to generators of heat, fire or noise, whether natural phenomena or a supposed supernatural cause of these are:

Wildfire (1829), *Vulcan* (1831), *Lightning* (1837), *Vesuvius* (*c*.1837), *Thunderer* (1837)—as an epithet of Jupiter, *Sun* (*c*.1837)

46.2.5 Excellent

A further category of names designate a device which is *excellent*. Excellence permits pride, the conventional sources of which were in the family pride deriving from nobility and royalty (their wealth allowing industrial patronage), and, in the context of the time, from national military heroics. Other excellence names reflected the newer notion of local civic pride, and also pride in individual foundries and engineers, which may also be viewed as a simple form of advertising.

Excellence names which are by description or allusion to accepted standards, including moral ones:

Sans Pareil (1829), *Perseverance* (1829), *Success* (1832), *Alpha* (1835)

Some are by allusion to royalty and nobility, including exotics:

Prince Regent (1812), *Lady Mary* (1813–14), *Royal George* (1827), *Earl of Airlie* (1833), *Victoria* (1838, that is, in the year of the queen's accession), *Vizier* and *Sultan* (1841)

Others by allusion to military power, prowess, and success:

Salamanca (1812; after Wellington's victory in the Peninsular War), *Lord Wellington* (1813–14), *Blücher* (1814), *Victory* (1828; or after the flagship of Trafalgar?), *Dreadnought* (1830; after an early-nineteenth-century ship of the line involved at Trafalgar, but also a literal allusion to heroism)

A group by allusion to the place of manufacture (or to their engineers or foundries) or to the place of deployment, expressing local pride:

Wylam Dilly (1813–14), *Killingworth* (1816), *Pride of Newcastle* (1827), *Stourbridge Lion* (1828), *Liverpool* (1830), *Northumbrian* (1830), *Stephenson* (1832), *Warrington* (1832), *Newton* (1832), *Vulcan* (1832), *Caledonian* (1832), *Jacob Perkins* (?1836), *Trevithick* (1841); this type was extended to symbols of national pride with *Britannia* (1829) and *John Bull* (1831; the personification of English resilience)

And lastly by use of the topos *star*; in the 1820s this word acquired its metaphorical theatrical application, and the many locomotives named after literal stars may play on this new sense:

North Star (1830), and many others (1838 onwards), where the allusion is to accurate direction-finding through magnetism, a theme continued by *Lode Star* and *Polar Star*; then *Dog Star, Bright Star, Evening Star, Shooting Star, Western Star* (1839–41)

The fifth category, *excellent*, could be viewed as including the content of the others. Some names in this category literally claim the locomotive to be excellent, e.g. *Sans Pareil* (1829), French for 'unmatched', whereas most of them claim excellence for the locomotive by metonymy: by association with, for example, royalty or military achievements. Literal claims for excellence are essential, but the sub-type of metonymic naming is not; it is a bridge by which *commemorative* naming eventually becomes the norm for locomotives in Britain.

These categories are sets of positive attributes for locomotives when viewed (a) functionally, as enabling rapid movement between places, and (b) aesthetically, as doing so in an impressive way. Early names are grounded literally in the features of the new technology; also metaphorically via the best exemplars of older standards of speed and power, and (arguably) metonymically by relation to certain exemplars of excellence.

46.3 LATER NAMING POLICIES

If the dominant early policy was to give essential names, new strategies emerge from seeds in the old one, and these new policies can be seen to result in the *commemorative* class-naming, or naming-after other nameables, which later became dominant. The process involved is one of *refocusing*, that is allowing new name-sources through taking a salient essential feature and naming locomotives after other nameables which share that feature but also have others. For instance, FIRE is essential for every steam locomotive. This may give rise to a metonymic fire-related name, such as *Vulcan* (1832), from the Roman smith-god. However *Vulcan* is also representative of another class, namely SUPERNATURAL POWER, and refocusing or switching attention from an attribute of Vulcan to his person permits the exploitation of the names of other (demi-)gods not primarily associated with fire, such as *Hecate* and *Fury*. Charles Tayleur's foundry exploited the overlap between astronomy and classical mythology with its *Vulcan, Apollo*, and *Venus* (1838). Another example is the early use of *Star* in locomotive names. The first is *North Star* (1830 and 1838), using a current name of the star Polaris (α Ursae Minoris), and therefore alluding to accurate direction-finding and so indirectly to SPEED. But the North Star is also just a STAR, and refocusing or a shift in salience to the more general attribute allows the use of other star names which have nothing to do with speed (*Red Star, Evening Star*, etc.), and a further generalization to HEAVENLY BODY allows *Planet, Globe, Comet*, etc.

Some of the salience switches just illustrated are 'bridges' to the systematic naming which typifies commemoration.[2] As noted, the arrival of *North Star* (1830) on the GWR[3] opened up the use of other star names on locomotives built to the chief engineer I. K. Brunel's own specifications (1838–41) in an unmistakably strategic way: *Dog Star, Bright Star, Evening Star, Lode Star, Polar Star, Red Star, Shooting Star*. Here can be seen the germ of the idea that sets of labels for classes of objects, places, or persons (generally proper names, sometimes taxonyms, i.e. labels for natural kinds or species) can be reapplied to locomotives, and this *commemorative* naming became the dominant strategy of later years.

Many modern (post-1846) steam locomotives received names which are most often appropriated from, or commemorate, something or someone else. Often that original name has no obvious connection with the nature of locomotive power at all. For example, we can find classes of engine named with the names of Scottish lochs, English country houses, squadrons of the Royal Air Force, Britain's counties and imperial possessions, shipping lines of the Merchant Navy, characters in the novels of Sir Walter Scott, English public schools, and football clubs; and also from the taxonyms of deer and antelopes, and, for very small locomotives, of very small creatures.[4] The express passenger locomotives of the LNER, from 1923, especially classes A3 and A2, were typically named after famous speedy racehorses of the nineteenth and early twentieth centuries (e.g. *Brown Jack, Hermit, Victor Wild, Pretty Polly, Tagalie, Hyperion, Airborne*), a relatively unusual case of continuing a tradition of commemoration grounded in essential metonyms which continued into the British Railways diesel era.[5] By contrast, among the oldest names, we find a much larger proportion of essential (descriptive) names, that is names whose motivation can be found in the nature of the locomotive itself and the technological development which it embodies. For more on the question of the relation between these two broad types, *essential* and *commemorative*, see section 46.5.

Whilst some of the later sets may be viewed as having loose connections with earlier themes such as the excellence of heroism (knights of the Round Table, English admirals, warships, recipients of the Victoria Cross in the Great War[6]) or the excellence of

---

[2] For recent works on systematic naming in general, see Andersson (1994) and Wahlberg (2006), and other works referenced in the latter. For locomotive names in academic literature, see Karlsson (1994). This article is founded on the conference paper published as Coates (2009a).

[3] In this article, modern locomotives and trains are assigned to the relevant mid-twentieth century, pre-nationalization, railway companies: GWR, Great Western Railway; LMSR, London, Midland and Scottish Railway; LNER, London and North-Eastern Railway; SR, Southern Railway; or to BR, the nationalized British Railways.

[4] Respectively: (some of) LNER class K2; GWR 'Hall', 'Grange' and 'Manor' classes; (many of) SR 'Battle of Britain' class; GWR 'County' class and (some of) LNER class D49, and (some of) LMSR 'Jubilee' class; SR 'Merchant Navy' class; LNER class D30; SR 'Schools' class; (some of) LNER class B17; antelopes, (some of) LNER class B1; and small creatures, certain LMSR narrow-gauge works locomotives.

[5] British Railways 'Deltic' class.

[6] Respectively: (most of) SR 'King Arthur' class; SR 'Lord Nelson' class; (some of) LMSR 'Patriot' class.

family (kings, dukes[7]), they typically lack the direct connections of literal appropriateness, topicality or local pride. Some sets have only the faintest connection, or none at all, with earlier themes (packs of foxhounds; bird and flower taxonyms; World War I battles, few of which were glorious decisive victories; and English country houses, by no means all of which were in the territory served by the relevant railway company[8]). Only very rarely were essential names applied in the twentieth century; one instance is the names containing the word *silver* to LNER locomotives which were at first actually painted silver, and this, in the 1930s, is arguably a different kind of essentiality from the earlier sorts, amounting to an advertising gimmick, though still trading on the symbolic excellence of precious metal.

These observations suggest the testable general principle of onomastics that, whenever a new category of nameables is created, naming strategies for members of that category are likely to develop in the same way. The names of the prototypes will tend to have names playing on their essential characteristics. Often this will involve transferring names from other categories of nameables offering analogies in the shape of metaphors and metonyms. Notably, later prototype steam locomotives often carried essential names, like the oil-fired *Petrolea* (1886), and *Decapod* (1902) with its ten driving-wheels; likewise the early diesel passenger locomotives *Lion* and *Falcon* (1962), both exploiting traditional categories, and *Deltic* (referring to a feature of its engine, the opposed-piston system; 1955), although the first two may also recall classic early steam locomotives. The prototype gas turbine 'tilting train' was simply called *the Advanced Passenger Train—Experimental* (1972). Successful prototypes give way to mass-produced instances, as a result of which their historic essential features are no longer remarkable. Then, individualization is necessary for successful reference, but there can be advantages in thematic naming, including for public relations; as a result, name-classes emerge which are permitted by switching from essential features to other salient features of the name-sources. This opens the floodgates to class-naming with no essential allusions, in keeping with the securely established idea that, to be a successful name, a name-form does not need to be interpretable: a name which is arbitrary in form works perfectly well as a name. Names can arise which are examples of types having little, or nothing at all, to do with essential attributes of the relevant objects. Locomotives came to be named after country houses, football clubs, antelopes, and so on. The more obscure antelope names applied to Thompson's B1 class steam locomotives of the LNER probably seemed just arbitrary labels for most English-speakers (*Bongo, Oribi, Sassaby, Inyala, Puku, Hirola*), and some of the antelopes whose taxonyms were appropriated are not notably speedy (e.g. the eland), so allusion to this essential feature was not crucial for this class. Development has stopped at this point, however; there is no trace of linguistically completely random naming, and the most modern trend of all has been the naming of freight locomotives after commercial firms who have presumably paid for the privilege.

[7] GWR 'King' and 'Duke' classes.
[8] Respectively: (some of) LNER class D49; (some of) LNER class A4 and (some of) GWR 4100 class; (some of) LNER class D11; several GWR classes (as in note 4).

46.4 NAMES OF TRAINS

The names of trains are a matter which the casual observer confuses with that of loco-motive names. Locomotives are the engineered machines used to pull trains (chains of carriages, vans, or wagons). The possible confusion is not helped by the fact that the most famous steam locomotive of all, the LNER's *Flying Scotsman*, was named to publi-cize, and to pull, the equally famous 1920s London–Edinburgh timetabled express train called *The Flying Scotsman* (which can however be traced back as far as 1862). Along with the *Irish Mail*, the oldest traceable named train is the GWR's *Flying Dutchman* (London–Exeter), apparently Gothickly named in 1849 from the ill-omened ghost ship, but in fact named after a racehorse famous in that year. Trains in Britain have gener-ally borne more or less transparent destination names such as the GWR's *Bristolian* and *Cornish Riviera Express* and the SR's *Brighton Belle*, allusive ones like the LNER's *Master Cutler* which served Sheffield, or less transparently allusive ones such as the SR/LMSR's Manchester–Bournemouth *Pines Express*. Occasional examples of other types can be found, such as the SR's *Golden Arrow*, which provides a hint of essentialist nam-ing through speed and symbolic excellence, and British Railways's *Talisman*, which, like many of the LNER's locomotive names, is rooted in the novels of Sir Walter Scott, and obliquely suggests its Edinburgh destination.

46.5 GENERAL LINGUISTIC CONSIDERATIONS: A 'LAW' OF NAME DEVELOPMENT OR ONOMASTIC TRAJECTORY

The idea of historical development from essential to commemorative to fully arbitrary naming can be tested on other nameables. The names of rock music bands have under-gone a partly similar evolution. The earliest ones had names which were grammati-cally plural or collective definite noun phrases suitable to a plurality of musicians, and they often had musically relevant lexical content, in the case of the emboldened names (The Crickets, The Shadows, The Rolling Stones, The Four Tops, The Doors, The Herd; **The Blue Notes, The Yardbirds**), but rapidly towards the end of the 1960s evolved in the direction of grammatically and lexically arbitrary labels (Humble Pie, The Lovin' Spoonful, The Who, Mott the Hoople, Procol Harum), and this has remained the norm into the twenty-first century. Many such names were appropriated from other things or persons (The Ivy League, Amen Corner, Jethro Tull, Mungo Jerry). It appears that business names have a similar history. The majority of high-street retail businesses were once small, and were named either from their founder or proprietor, and/or in a way which evoked directly the kind of trade they were engaged in (Marks and Spencer,

Boot's the Chemist, The Great Grimsby Coal, Salt and Tanning Company). More recent business names—especially the supermarkets which have displaced the smaller businesses—have had names which, viewed synchronically, are arbitrary: Waitrose, Wavy Line, Asda, Tesco, Aldi, and the Cosalt which continues the Grimsby firm, which now makes caravans. It might be suggested that, in the anglophone world at large, place-names have evolved similarly.

These examples suggest that there is a general 'law' of naming development, an 'onomastic trajectory':

> As examples of similar nameable entities multiply, the strategy of name-bestowal shifts from *essential (descriptive)* to *commemorative,* and therefore bestowed names become increasingly arbitrary for that category of nameables.

This can be shown clearly to apply to the names of locomotives, but is not applicable to the names of trains, which never proliferated to any comparable extent.

CHAPTER 47

···

SHIP NAMES

···

MALCOLM JONES

In this chapter we consider the names given to ships from the earliest times to the present day. By *ships* are to be understood ocean-going vessels, for the most part, as opposed to *boats* which tend to be smaller 'pleasure-craft' with names more personally motivated, not usually accorded the dignity of a name in earlier times, and in modern times often whimsically named. Like other specialized areas of nomenclature, the study of ships' names, while interesting in itself, can also shed valuable light on the history of the lexicon.[1]

Significantly, it is from a nautical dictionary, published in 1711, that the *Oxford English Dictionary* (*OED*) quotes for its earliest citation of *lop-sided*, 'disproportionately heavy on one side', and yet a Patent Roll of 1291 refers to a ship named the *Lopside* some four centuries earlier. Such spectacular instances are rare, but more modest ante-datings—decades rather than centuries—are not uncommon amongst the corpus of earlier ship names. The Jacobean *Loblollypot* is a case in point (taken from Marsden 1905), although only ante-dating *OED*'s first record of the compound by a decade or so, but in the present context it is the semantic implication, that is rather more significant—if we make the onomastician's assumption just mentioned.

What is/was a *loblollypot*? One might guess it was a *pot* for *loblolly*—but what is *loblolly*? The *OED* informs us it is a 'Thick gruel or spoon-meat' (I compare *lob-scouse* and *lobby*), but more significantly the entry continues, 'frequently referred to as a rustic or nautical dish or simple medicinal remedy', and quotes from a text of 1620 which states that wheat 'makes an excellent grewell, or lob-lolly which is very soueraigne at Sea'. So *loblollypot* means something like 'porridge-pot'—and therefore, perhaps, we should envisage a large circular or cauldron-type vessel which would bob about uncomfortably in water (cf. the colloquial use of *tub* and *bucket* in the same way). Or was the sobriquet

---

[1] The only book-length treatment of our subject is Kennedy (1974). In 1572 Thomas Colshill, who styles himself Surveyor of the Port of London, compiled a list of almost 1400 merchant ships, an invaluable manuscript record now in The National Archive [SP 15/22], and a document which still awaits proper study.

given not for reasons of the vessel's instability at all, but for some other resonance of the loblolly-pot? Was it perhaps a well-stocked vessel renowned for feeding its crew well—surely a noteworthy exception in this era? It is difficult to believe that the ship when built was given that name—it sounds more like a nickname bestowed later in her life. The contemporary *Horse Turd* is similarly mysterious at this distance, but again was presumably a nickname applied to the early seventeenth-century ship in question—at least, it is difficult to believe she was named this from her launching.

Analysis of almost 350 English ships' names from a listing made in 1338 (Jones 2000) shows the motivation behind their naming to be overwhelmingly 'religious': just over 10 per cent were named after the Virgin Mary, while a third of the fleet were named after various saints, with Margaret being the most popular—perhaps based on the fact that she could not be drowned, according to her medieval *Life*. Interestingly, Christ is only alluded to somewhat indirectly—one example of the *Seint Savour* [Holy Saviour]— but there are thirteen examples of the *Trinity* and three of the *Seint Spirit*. The *Godbefore*, a pious ejaculation invoking God's protection, might be compared with the contemporary French vessel *Dieu la garde* (1349). The hopeful *Blithe* was the most popular secular name, closely followed by *Godyer*, that is 'good year'—compare the French *Bonan* (1340), and *Welfare*, to be interpreted optatively, as 'wishful naming', meaning something like 'may she (and all who sail in her) fare well'. This last is of course a common motivation (and implicit in all the religious names), the hope to prosper and return home safely, charmingly exemplified by the late fifteenth century *Cumwelltohous* (Childs 1986: 212). A vessel named *Smotheweder* [smooth weather] in the 1338 fleet provides an ante-dating of about half a century for this sense of *smooth*—semantically, cf. the *Fairewedere* (1326), and the *Sconeweder* (1381; out of Sluys)—again, I suggest, an optative formation and intention. Ironically, a 1682 list of English ships captured by corsairs is typical in its inclusion of many such would-be auspicious names, including *Fortune, Prosperous, Return* and *Happy Return, Blessing* (2), *Speedwell* (2), and *Hopewell* (4).[2]

The 1338 fleet included a *Messenger*, as well as a ship incongruously named the *Lightfot*—but that is also attested at this period as a nickname for a (human) messenger, who should, of course, be light-footed. The *Snellard* of 1257 must have been similarly fast, but the word has been lost from the vocabulary, only its opposite, *sluggard*, surviving.

If we compare the 1338 English fleet with a somewhat larger and later corpus of Spanish vessels, the Virgin is again the most popular name, accounting for a full third of all names, whereas St Margaret is entirely absent, and the proportion of non-religious names tiny (Hadziiossif 1989). If we move forward in time to the *Armada* of 1588, we have another set of comparable English and Spanish data: 210 and 136 names, respectively.[3] But as we are now in post-Reformation Protestant England, the only saint's name present is that of the national warrior patron, a single example of the *St. George*. There

---

[2] *A List of Ships Taken Since July 1677* (1682) [Wing L2405B].

[3] A convenient listing of the names of the ships of both fleets is to be found in Rodríguez-Salgado et al. (1988: 154–8).

is a *Grace of God*, two *Gift of God*, and an *Ascension*, but the *Virgin God Save Her* will, of course, allude to the Virgin Queen, Elizabeth, commander of the fleet. Much as in earlier times, a quarter of the Spanish Armada ships are named after the Virgin Mary, the rest after various local and international saints, with hardly any non-religious names.

The English Armada fleet included eight vessels 'surnamed' *Bonaventure*, for example the *Elizabeth Bonaventure*, but there was also a *Buena Ventura* on the Spanish side. By this date *Bonaventure* had evidently become something of a generic tag in ship-naming.[4] Already a century earlier, one of the fighting ships in Henry VII's navy was called the *Bonaventure* (1489), but an Italian vessel of that name, the *Bonaventura*, was plying the Mediterranean in the late thirteenth century. The name by itself means 'good luck', another optative formation. A further category represented in the English fleet is the type name, the name that is really a generic, and describes a particular class of ship or its function: the *Advice* (a light fast vessel used to carry dispatches[5]), the *Brigantine*, *Caravel*, *Frigate*, *Galleon*, *Gallego*, *Scout* (ante-dating *OED* by over a century), and *Spy* (ante-dating *OED spy-boat* by half a century).

Another ante-dating is provided by the name of the *Nonpareil* ('having no peer'), when applied to a thing rather than a person, but more significantly, it is an example of a change of name for political reasons, having been formerly known as the *Philip and Mary*, that is the Catholic Queen and her Spanish consort who reigned in England jointly from 1553 to 1558. The name was doubtless changed long before the date of the Armada, and probably very shortly after the accession of Elizabeth in 1558, for ships' names are inevitably signs of their times, and move with the times. After the execution of Charles in 1649 the Commonwealth government renamed the *Charles* the *Liberty*, and the *Henrietta Maria* the *Paragon*, and in keeping with the new stress on the sovereignty of Parliament, another of the state's warships was even named the *Speaker*. Conversely, at the Restoration, when selected as the ship to bring home the exiled king, the *Naseby*, so named by Cromwell after a famous Parliamentary victory, was instantly renamed the *Royal Charles*. The French Revolution led to similar wholesale name-changes, the *Royal Louis* becoming the *Républicain*, the *Dauphin Royal* the *Sans-culotte* (nickname denoting an extreme republican), and one of the revolutionary government's new warships was named the *Droits de l'Homme* (Rights of Man). Similarly, the Communist victors of the Russian Revolution of 1917 objected even to names recalling earlier (tsarist) victories, so that the battleship *Sevastopol* was renamed the *Paris Commune*, only to revert to its earlier name during the more patriotic World War II era, and with the subsequent demise of the Soviet Union, the battleship *Yuri Andropov* (president, 1982–84) was renamed after Tsar *Peter the Great*.

From the earliest times, the majority of ship names have been drawn from a relatively small number of categories. One of the earliest lists of names that has come down to us is

[4] It seems to me that *Constance* is another such, e.g. *Elizabeth Constance, Mary Constance, Susan Constance* in Marsden (1905).

[5] cf. from an account of Drake's voyage (*c.*1595): *We took a frygotte which was an advice of the kinge's [of Spain].*

a fourth-century BC inventory from the Athenian shipyard at Piraeus. Over 260 vessels are named: there are plenty of 'religious' names (especially of female deities), warlike names (*Audacious* (7), *Courage, Power, Victory* (39), *Glory, Battle Order, War Glory, War Spirit*), abstract principles (*Excellence* (3), *Friendliness* (16), *Liberty, Democracy* (3), *Good Government, Happiness, Peace* (3), *Sufficiency*), and a few names of animals regarded as either swift (*Gazelle*) or fierce (*She-Wolf*), as well as the optative names we have already encountered (*Auspicious, Good Luck* (3), *Health, Safe Passage*).

The Armada fleet also, and typically, included a number of animal and bird names—by this date some of the animals are presumably heraldic, however, like Sir Francis Drake's *Golden Hind*—which had circumnavigated the globe a decade earlier. Formerly the *Pelican*, the ship was renamed by Drake on his celebrated voyage as a compliment to his patron, Sir Christopher Hatton, whose badge it was. In the same 'herd' were also a *White Hind*, a *Roebuck*, a *Hart*, and two *Antelope*, and similarly fleet of foot, the *Little Hare* and the *Greyhound*. The *Black Dog* might also be heraldic, perhaps, although was already by this date the name given to a predatory spectral hound of menacing reputation, and perhaps those associations are present here. Real animals renowned for their fierceness are also represented; there were three *Tiger*, four *Lion* of various colours (and thus probably heraldic badges), two *Bear*, and a *Bull*. The *Rat* seems a somewhat odd choice, but the *Dolphin*, being a fast-moving agile marine animal, is an entirely appropriate name. Avowedly legendary animals are present too: the *Unicorn*, the *Phoenix* (also one of the Queen's badges), and two *Griffin*. Of those vessels named after birds, only the *Pelican* might qualify as a sea-bird, but is more likely present in its role as the traditional symbol of Christ's sacrifice. The *Lark* and the two *Nightingale*, both renowned for their song, also seem rather out of place here, whereas the *Swallow* is clearly appropriate for its speed and agility, as is the *Merlin*, surprisingly the sole representative of the popularity of birds of prey in the naming of warships. (The slightly later Jacobean listing, for example, includes the *Eagle, Falcon, Hawk, Jerfalcon, Lanneret, Osprey, Peregrine*, and *Saker*.)

There is also a small group of flower names in the English Armada fleet, some of which may again be heraldic: the *Rose*, the *Heartsease*, the *Pansy*, the *Violet*, the *Primrose* (2), the *Mayflower* (2), and the *Marigold* (3). The last-named flower was particularly associated in pre-Reformation tradition with the Virgin, whose name it bears, and it may be that such covert symbolism was a deliberate choice by a Catholic owner anxious not to draw unnecessary attention from the Protestant authorities. The *Mayflower* was a very popular name at this period—though quite what species was intended by the name is uncertain, cowslip, primrose, ladysmock, and marsh marigold all being known by this name at that date. The Jacobean listing adds the *Carnation, Daisy, Gilliflower*, and *Lily*. If we discount the generic *Blome* [bloom], however, the only flower name in the 1338 fleet was the *Rose* (7 ships so named).

Whereas we have imposed such categories retrospectively on these lists, as a mere taxonomic tool for the purpose of convenient statistical analysis, not much later we witness the deliberate use of names from a specific category allotted to vessels of a particular 'class'—a practice widely evidenced in modern navies, cruise-lines, etc. What looks like an early example of this practice is to be found in the list of ships belonging to the new Commonwealth drawn up by Samuel Pepys in 1651, in which the *Ruby, Diamond*, and *Sapphire* appear together, and the accompanying statistics show them to be all of the same size (Bruzelius 2000). In the twentieth century, William Robertson, a Glasgow shipping company, named all its steamers after gemstones, from *Amber* to *Tourmaline*, the fleet becoming known as the 'Gem Line'. One modern commercial operator has a fleet of four cruise-liners all with names beginning with *B-*, three of them alluding to the Scottish Highlands—*Boudicca* being the odd one out. The British navy had a fleet of eight *Porpoise*-class non-nuclear submarines launched in the late 1950s which included the *Rorqual, Narwhal, Cachalot*, and *Grampus*, while the US navy's modern *Ohio*-class nuclear submarines are all named after American states.

Of course, another enduring motivation for naming a ship is to give it the name of the owner or his spouse. This practice was certainly in evidence in the late Middle Ages: the *Blasius Alberegno* and the *Giovanni Contareno* are two Venetian ships of the early fifteenth century named after their owners, and in England the late-fifteenth-century London Petty Customs accounts name, for example, the *Thomas Basset*, the *Martyn Baldry*, the *John Remyngton*, and the *Mary Dawbeney* (Cobb 1990). As ever, caution is necessary in interpreting such apparent owners' names, however: the *Mary Boston*, for example, is elsewhere named as the *Mary of Boston*, the port in Lincolnshire.

What we may perhaps term 'whimsical naming' is largely a modern fashion in ship-naming, but the Jacobean listing includes several names which may well be facetious. Names which fall into this category include the *Diligent Bee, Flying Cow, Horse Turd, Little Profit, Peppercorn, Poor Man's Plough, Rotten Apple, Saucy Jack*, and the phrasal *Why not I*.

The *Diligent Bee* is presumably named in tribute to the proverbially industrious insect, here a merchantman plying busily between trading ports—but the *Flying Cow*? The *Peppercorn* was presumably either tiny, or acquired for a nominal sum—perhaps because barely seaworthy (and provides a slight ante-dating of the transferred, non-rental, sense, 'a thing of very small value'). *Poor Man's Plough* is a late-attested facetious euphemism for a plough not drawn by animals, such as a breast-plough, or even sometimes, for a hoe or spade, but—unlike the *Water Plough* from the same list, which illustrates the ancient metaphor of a ship ploughing the waves—does not seem immediately meaningful. *Why not I* is perhaps some kind of a catch-question name—like the pet dog belonging to Lady Lisle in Tudor times when Calais was still in English hands, mischievously named *Pourquoi* (why).[6] Still other names may not be quite what they seem: when trying to understand names given to ships in earlier eras we must be careful not to think anachronistically. There have been several ships named the *Truelove*, for instance, including one built in London in 1595, but *truelove* is the name of a flower too, also known as *herb paris*. Another of its names, *four-leaved grass*, perhaps implies that like the better-known clover, when that plant is found in a four-leaved variety, the truelove too was regarded as an emblem of good luck. It will certainly have been the

---

[6] For this and discussion of other facetiously bestowed dogs' names, see Jones (2002: 183–4).

superstitious belief in the luck-bringing properties of the four-leaved variety of clover that was responsible for the naming of the *Klaverbladt* [Cloverleaf] plying out of Amsterdam in the 1560s.

The *OED* defines one sense of the word *cockleshell* as 'a small frail boat . . ', but three centuries before the *OED*'s first citation we know of a Jacobean ship bearing that very name. It is not difficult to imagine how fragile even the most hardened of Columbus's mariners must have felt, trapped in a tiny wooden vessel in a tempest in mid-ocean, how he might bless the fact that his ship was named after the Blessed Virgin herself, the *Santa Maria*, and call on her to intercede with the God of the storm, that He might yet *bring them unto their desired haven*. Such protective naming has always played an important role in the naming of ships, and even today continues to give some comfort to those *that goe downe to the sea in shippes: that doe businesse in great waters.*[7]

---

[7] Psalm 107:23 (*AV*).

BIBLIOGRAPHY

Aalto, Tiina (2002). 'Osoitteena Osmankäämintie: tutkimus eräästä ryhmänimistöstä', *Virittäjä* 106: 208–22.

Abbott, Barbara (2002). 'Definiteness and Proper Names. Some Bad News for the Description Theory', *Journal of Semantics* 19: 191–201.

Abdel-Rahman, Rasha, Sommer, Werner, and Schweinberger, Stefan R. (2002). 'Brain-Potential Evidence for the Time Course of Access to Biographical Facts and Names of Familiar Persons', *Journal of Experimental Psychology. Learning, Memory, and Cognition* 28: 366–73.

Abrams, Lesley, and Parsons, David N. (2004). 'Place-Names and the History of Scandinavian Settlement in England', in John Hines, Alan Lane, and Mark Redknap (eds.), *Land, Sea and Home*. Leeds: Maney Publishing, 379–431.

Aceto, Michael (2002). 'Ethnic Personal Names and Multiple Identities in Anglophone Caribbean Speech Communities in Latin America', *Language in Society* 31: 577–608.

Adams, Michael (2009). 'Power, Politeness, and the Pragmatics of Nicknames', *Names* 57.2: 81–91.

Ageeva, P. A. (1985). *Proischoždenie imen rek i ozer*. Moskva: Nauka.

Agyekum, Kofi (2006). 'The Sociolinguistics of Akan Personal Names', *Nordic Journal of African Studies* 15: 206–35.

Ahmed, Salahuddin (1999). *A Dictionary of Muslim Names*. New York: New York University Press.

Ahrens, Wolfgang, Embleton, Sheila, and Lapierre, André (eds.) (2009). *Names in Multi-Lingual, Multi-Cultural and Multi-Ethnic Contact. Proceedings of the 23rd International Congress of Onomastic Sciences, August 17–22, 2008, York University, Toronto, Canada*. Toronto: York University. Available online at: <http://yorkspace.library.yorku.ca/xmlui/handle/10315/2901>.

Ainiala, Terhi (2004). 'Kadunnimet opastajina ja sivistäjinä: kesän 2002 keskustelun tarkastelua', *Virittäjä* 108: 106–15.

Ainiala, Terhi (2010). 'Place Names—Changes and Losses', in Eva Brylla and Mats Wahlberg (eds.), *Proceedings of the 21st International Congress of Onomastic Sciences, Uppsala, 19–24 August 2002*, vol. 5. Uppsala: Institutet för Språk och folkminnen, 297–304.

Ainiala, Terhi and Halonen, Mia (2017). 'The Perception of Somali Place Names among Immigrant Somali Youth in Helsinki', in Terhi Ainiala and Jan-Ola Östman (eds.), *Socio-onomastics. The Pragmatics of Names*, 203–226. Amsterdam: John Benjamins.

Ainiala, Terhi and Lappalainen, Hanna (2017). 'Orienting to Norms: Variability in the Use of Names for Helsinki', in Terhi Ainiala and Jan-Ola Östman (eds.), *Socio-onomastics. The Pragmatics of Names*, 129–153. Amsterdam: John Benjamins.

Ainiala, Terhi, and Vuolteenaho, Jani (2006). 'How to Study Urban Onomastic Landscape?' *Acta Onomastica* 47: 58–63.

Ainiala, Terhi, Komppa, Johanna, Mallat, Kaija, and Pitkänen, Ritva Liisa (2000). 'Paikannimien käyttö ja osaaminen—nimitaito Pälkäneen Laitikkalassa', *Virittäjä* 104: 330–54.

Ainiala, Terhi, Saarelma, Minna, and Sjöblom, Paula (2012). *Names in Focus. An Introduction to Finnish Onomastics.* trans by Leonard Pearl. Studia Fennica Linguistica 17. Helsinki: Finnish Literature Society.

Aitchison, Jean (2012). *Words in the Mind. An Introduction to the Mental Lexicon.* 4th edn. Chichester: Wiley-Blackwell.

Aitken, Adam J. (1985). 'Introduction', in Mairi Robinson (ed.), *The Concise Scots Dictionary.* Aberdeen: Aberdeen University Press, ix–xli.

Akin, Salih (2004). 'La dénomination des personne et la construction identitaire: le cas des prénoms kurdes en Turquie', *bulletin vals-asla* 80: 27–38.

Akinnaso, F. Niyi (1980). 'The Sociolinguistic Basis of Yoruba Personal Names', *Anthropological Linguistics* 22: 275–304.

Akinnaso, F. Niyi (1981). 'Names and Naming Principles in Cross-Cultural Perspective', *Names* 29: 37–63.

Akzhigitova, Assel, and Zharkynbekova, Sholpan (2014). 'Language Planning in Kazakhstan. The Case of Ergonyms as Another Scene of Linguistic Landscape of Astana', *Language Problems and Language Planning* 38.1: 42–57.

Albøge, Gordon, Villarsen Meldgaard, Eva, and Weise, Lis (eds.) (1991). *Analogi i navngivning. Tiende Nordiske Navneforskerkongres, Brandbjerg 20.–24. maj 1989.* Uppsala: NORNA-förlaget.

Alderman, Derek H. (2008). 'Place, Naming and the Interpretation of Cultural Landscapes', in Brian Graham and Peter Howard (eds.), *The Ashgate Research Companion to Heritage and Identity.* Aldershop: Ashgate, 195–214.

Aldrin, Emilia (2009). 'The Choice of First Names as a Social Resource and Act of Identity Among Multilingual Families in Contemporary Sweden', in Wolfgang Ahrens, Sheila Embleton, and André Lapierre (eds.), *Names in Multi-Lingual, Multi-Cultural and Multi-Ethnic Contact. Proceedings of the 23rd International Congress of Onomastic Sciences, August 17–22, 2008, York University, Toronto, Canada.* Toronto: York University, 86–92. Available online at: <http://yorkspace.library.yorku.ca/xmlui/bitstream/handle/10315/2926/icos23_86.pdf?sequence=1>.

Aldrin, Emilia (2011). *Namnval som social handling. Val av förnamn och samtal om förnamn bland föräldrar i Göteborg 2007–2009.* Namn och samhälle 24. Uppsala: Uppsala universitet.

Alexiou, Margaret (1974). *The Ritual Lament in Greek Tradition.* Cambridge: Cambridge University Press.

Alford, Richard D. (1988). *Naming and Identity. A Cross-Cultural Study of Personal Naming Practices.* New Haven, CT: HRAF.

Algeo, John (1985, 2010). 'Is a Theory of Names Possible?', *Names* 33: 136–44. Reprinted in *Names* 58: 90–6.

Algeo, John (2001). 'A Fancy for the Fantastic. Reflections on Names in Fantasy Literature', *Names* 49: 248–53.

Alia, Valerie (2007). *Names and Nunavut. Culture and Identity in Arctic Canada.* New York: Berghahn Books.

Allerton, David J. (1987). 'The Linguistic and Sociolinguistic Status of Proper Names', *Journal of Pragmatics* 11: 61–92.

Allsop, Scott (2009). 'We Didn't Start The Fire. Using 1980s Popular Music to Explore Historical Significance by Stealth', *Teaching History* 137: 52–9.

Altman, Irwin, and Low, Setha (eds.) (1992a). *Place Attachment*. New York: Plenum Press.

Altman, Irwin, and Low, Setha (1992b). 'Place Attachment. A Conceptual Inquiry', in Irwin Altman and Setha Low (eds.), *Place Attachment*. New York: Plenum Press, 1–12.

Alvarez-Altman, Grace (1987). 'A Methodology for Literary Onomastics. An Analytical Guide for Studying Names in Literature', in Grace Alvarez-Altman and Frederick M. Burelbach (eds.), *Names in Literature. Essays from Literary Onomastics Studies*. Lanham, MD: University Press of America, 1–9.

Alvarez-Altman, Grace, and. Burelbach, Frederick M (eds.) (1987). *Names in Literature. Essays from Literary Onomastics Studies*. Lanham, MD: University Press of America.

Anchimbe, Eric A. (2011). 'On Not Calling People by Their Names. Pragmatic Undertones of Sociocultural Relationships in a Postcolony', *Journal of Pragmatics* 43: 1472–83.

Anchimbe, Eric A., and Janney, Richard W. (2011). 'Postcolonial Pragmatics. An Introduction', *Journal of Pragmatics* 43: 1451–9.

Andersen, Johnny (2013). 'Navnsetting på kart—overgangen fra fornorskingstid til ny tid', in *Nytt om namn* 57: 27–32.

Anderson, Alan O. and Anderson, Marjorie O. (eds.) (1961). *Adomnán's Life of Columba*, Edinburgh: Thomas Nelson and Son.

Anderson, John M. (2003). 'On the Structure of Names', *Folia Linguistica* 37: 347–98.

Anderson, John M. (2004). 'On the Grammatical Status of Names', *Language* 80: 435–74.

Anderson, John M. (2007). *The Grammar of Names*. Oxford: Oxford University Press.

Anderson, Judith H. (1987). 'The Conspiracy of Realism. Impasse and Vision in *King Lear*', *Studies in Philology* 84: 1–23.

Andersson, Thorsten (1965). *Svenska häradsnamn*. Nomina Germanica 14. Uppsala: Nomina Germanica.

Andersson, Thorsten (1972). 'Norden och det forna Europa. Några synpunkter på ortnamnens ålder och samband', *Namn och Bygd* 60: 5–53.

Andersson, Thorsten (1980). 'Ord eller suffixbildning? Till frågan om rekonstruktion av ord ur ortnamn', in Vibeke Dalberg, Bente Holmberg, and John Kousgård Sørensen (eds.), *Sprogvidenskabelig udnyttelse af stednavnematerialet. NORNAs syvende symposiun i København, 18–20 maj 1979*. NORNA-rapporter 18. Uppsala: Nordiska samarbetskommittén för namnforskning, 9–39.

Andersson, Thorsten (1983). 'Personnamn. Till begreppets avgränsning', in Goran Hallberg, Stig Isaksson, and Bengt Pamp (eds.), *Personnamnsterminologi. NORNAs åttonde symposium i Lund 10–12 oktober 1981*. NORNA-rapporter 23. Uppsala: NORNA-förlaget, 9–22.

Andersson, Thorsten (1988). 'Zur Geschichte der Theorie einer alteuropäischen Hydronymie', in Thorsten Andersson (ed.), *Probleme der Namenbildung. Rekonstruktion von Eigennamen und der ihnen zugrundeliegenden Appellative. Akten eines internationalen Symposiums in Uppsala 1.–4. September 1986*. Acta Universitatis Upsaliensis. Nomina Germanica 18. Uppsala: Uppsala universitet, 59–90.

Andersson, Thorsten (1994). 'Olika egennamnskategorier—förenade och särskiljande drag', in Kristinn Jóhanesson, Hugo Karlsson, and Bo Ralph (eds.), *Övriga namn. Handlingar från NORNA:s nittonde symposium i Göteborg, 4–6 december 1991*. NORNA-rapporter 56. Uppsala: NORNA-förlaget, 141–7.

Andersson, Thorsten (1997). 'Rörelser inom onomastikonet', in *Ord och några visor tillägnade Kurt Zilliacus 21.7.1997*. Helsingfors: Institutionen för nordiska språk, 13–19.

Andersson, Thorsten (1998). 'Germanskt personnamnsskick i indoeuropeiskt perspektiv', in Thorsten Andersson, et al. (ed.), *Personnamn och social identitet*. Stockholm: KVHAA, 13–35.

Andersson, Thorsten (2003). 'Personennamen', in Heinrich Beck, Dieter Geuenich, and Heiko Steuer (eds.), *Reallexikon der Germanischen Altertumskunde*. Berlin/New York: Walter de Gruyter, 589–614.

Andersson, Thorsten (2004). 'Varumärkens grammatiska status', in Svante Strandberg, Mats Wahlberg, and Björn Heinrici (eds.), *Namn. Hyllningsskrift till Eva Brylla den 1 mars 2004*. Namn och samhälle 15. Uppsala: Uppsala universitet, 7–14.

Andersson, Thorsten (2004). 'Die Suffixbildungen in der altgermanischen Toponymie', in Thorsten Andersson and Eva Nyman (eds.), *Suffixbildungen in alten Ortsnamen. Akten eines internationalen Symposiums in Uppsala 14.–16. Mai 2004*. Acta Academiae Regiae Gustavi Adolphi 88. Uppsala: Kungl. Gustav Adolfs Akademien för Svensk Folkkultur, 13–26.

Andersson, Thorsten (2011). 'Skandinavische Familiennamengeographie. Westskandinavien', in Rita Heuser, Damaris Nübling, and Mirjam Schmuck (eds.), *Familiennamengeographie. Ergebnisse und Perspektiven europäischer Forschung*. Berlin/New York: de Gruyter, 1–12.

Andersson, Thorsten (2012). 'Onomastik—Überlegungen im Anschluss an eine neue Einführung', *Studia anthroponymica Scandinavica* 30: 123–60.

Andersson, Thorsten, and Nyman, Eva (eds.) (2004). *Suffixbildungen in alten Ortsnamen. Akten eines internationalen Symposiums in Uppsala 14.–16. Mai 2004*. Acta Academiae Regiae Gustavi Adolphi 88. Uppsala: Kungl. Gustav Adolfs Akademien för Svensk Folkkultur.

Andrew, Malcolm, and Waldron, Ronald (eds.) (2007). *The Poems of the Pearl Manuscript*. 5th edn. Exeter: University of Exeter Press.

Anonymous (1915). 'Home Chat', *Gold Coast Nation*, 11 March: 861.

Anonymous (1966). 'Cook, James', *Australian Dictionary of Biography*, vol. 1. Melbourne: Melbourne University Press. Available in electronic format at: <http://adb.anu.edu.au/biography/cook-james-1917>.

Anonymous (1993). *Newsweek*, May 3.

Anonymous (1995a). 'Gauteng Afrikaans Daily', *Beeld*, 6 September.

Anonymous (1995b). 'Cape Afrikaans Daily', *Die Burger*, 20 September.

Anonymous (2008). 'New DNA Evidence Overturns Population Migration Theory in Island Southeast Asia', *Phys.Org*, 23 May. Available online at: <http://phys.org/news130761648.html>.

Anonymous (2011). 'Welcome to Giro Bay. Fed-up Rangers Rubbish Loch Lomond's Litter Louts', *The Scotsman*, 9 March. Available online at: <http://www.scotsman.com/news/welcome-to-giro-bay-fed-up-rangers-rubbish-loch-lomond-s-litter-louts-1-1530937> [accessed July 2014].

Anonymous (2013a). 'Colley Lane School in Halesowen Bans Black Country Dialect'. BBC News, 14 November. Available online at: <http://www.bbc.co.uk/news/uk-england-birmingham-24941692> [accessed 15 November 2013].

Anonymous (2013b). 'Tschechischer Politiker. Nudelsieb im Personalausweis', *Spiegel Online. Panorama*, 13 August. Available online at: <http://www.spiegel.de/panorama/tschechien-politiker-posiert-fuer-personalausweis-mit-nudelsieb-a-916275.html>.

Antoun, Richard T. (1968). 'On the Significance of Names in an Arab Village', *Ethnology* 7: 158–70.

Aprosio, Angelico (1689). *La Visiera alzata, hecatoste di scrittori, che vaghi d'andare in maschera fuor del tempo di Carnovale, sono scoperti da Gio*. Parma: Heredi del Vigna.

Archer, Steve (2011). *British 19th Century Surname Atlas*. Version 1.1. CD Rom. Archer Software.

Archif Melville Richards (n.d.) Available online at: <http://www.e-gymraeg.co.uk/enwaulleoedd/amr/cronfa_en.aspx>.

Armstrong, A. M., Mawer, Allen, Stenton, Frank M., Dickins, Bruce (1950–2). *The Place-Names of Cumberland. Parts 1–3.* English Place-Name Society 20–22. Cambridge: Cambridge University Press.

Armstrong, John G. (1999). 'RCAF Identity in Bomber Command. Squadron Names and Sponsors', *Canadian Military History* 8.2: 43–52.

Armstrong, Mostyn John (1775). *A Companion to the Map of the County of Peebles or Tweedale.* Edinburgh: W. Creech.

Arngart, O. (1972). 'On the *ingtūn* Type of English Place-Name', *Studia Neophilologica* 44: 263–73.

Arnold, Wilhelm (1875). *Ansiedlungen und Wanderungen deutscher Stämme. Zumeist nach hessischen Ortsnamen.* Marburg: N.G. Elwert.

Aronin, Larissa, and Ó Laoire, Muiris (2013). 'The Material Culture of Multilingualism: Moving Beyond the Linguistic Landscape', *International Journal of Multilingualism* 10.3: 225–35.

Ashley, Leonard R. N. (1996a). 'Internal Names', in Ernst Eichler, et al. (eds.), *Namenforschung/Name Studies/Les noms propres. Ein internationals Handbuch zur Onomastik/International Handbook of Onomastics/Manuel international d'onomastique*, vol. 2. Berlin/New York: de Gruyter, 1745–50.

Ashley, Leonard R. N. (1996b). 'Names of Racehorses in the United Kingdom and the United States', in Ernst Eichler, et al. (eds.), *Namenforschung/Name Studies/Les noms propres. Ein internationals Handbuch zur Onomastik/International Handbook of Onomastics/Manuel international d'onomastique*, vol. 2. Berlin/New York: de Gruyter, 1589–90.

Ashley, Leonard R. N. (2003). *Names in Literature.* Bloomington, IN: Authorhouse.

Ashworth, Gregory, and Kavaratzis, Mihalis (eds.) (2010). *Towards Effective Place Brand Management. Branding European Cities and Regions.* Cheltenham: Edward Elgar.

Aston, Michael (1985). *Interpreting the Landscape. Landscape Archaeology in Local Studies.* London: Batsford.

Aston, Micheal, and Gerrard, Chistopher (1999). ' "Unique, Traditional and Charming". The Shapwick Project', *The Antiquaries Journal* 79: 1–58.

Astor, Jacques (2002). *Dictionnaire des noms de famille et noms de lieux du midi de la France.* Paris: Beffroi.

Auxier, Randall E., and Anderson, Doug (eds.) (2008). *Bruce Springsteen and Philosophy. Darkness on the Edge of Truth.* Chicago/La Salle, IL: Open Court.

Azaryahu, Maoz (1996). 'The Power of Commemorative Street Names', *Environment and Planning D. Society and Space* 14.3: 311–30.

Azaryahu, Maoz (1997). 'German Re-Unification and the Politics of Street Re-Naming. The Case of East Berlin', *Political Geography* 16.6: 479–93.

Azaryahu, Maoz, and Kook, Rebecca (2002). 'Mapping the Nation. Street Names and Arab-Palestinian Identity. Three Case Studies', *Nations and Nationalism* 8.2: 195–213.

Baayen, R. Harald, Piepenbrock, Richard, and Gulikers, Leon (1995). *The CELEX Lexical Database.* CD Rom. Philadelphia, PA: Linguistic Data Consortium, University of Pennsylvania.

Babha, Homi (1994). *The Location of Culture.* London: Routledge.

Bach, Adolf (1953–4). *Deutsche Namenkunde 2: 1–2. Die deutschen Ortsnamen 1–2.* Heidelberg: Carl Winter.

Backhaus, Peter (2007). *Linguistic Landscapes. A Comparative Study of Urban Multilingualism in Tokyo.* Clevedon: Multilingual Matters.

Bacon, Gareth (2013). *Untapped Resource. Bearing Down on Fares Through Sponsorship*. London: GLA Conservatives.

Bagna, Carla, and Barni, Monica (2006). 'Per una mappatura dei repertori linguistici urbani: nuovi strumenti e metodologie', in Nicola De Blasi and Carla Marcato (eds.), *La città e le sue lingue: Repertori linguistici urbani*. Naples: Liguori, 1–43.

Bagna, Carla, and Machetti, Sabrina (2012). 'LL and (Italian) Menus and Brand Names. A Survey Around the World', in Christine Hélot, et al. (eds.), *Linguistic Landscapes, Multilingualism and Social Change*. Frankfurt: Peter Lang, 217–30.

Bahlow, Hans (1967). *Deutsches Namenlexikon*. Munich: Keyersche Verlagsbuchhandlung.

Bahlow, Hans (1993). *Dictionary of German Names*. trans. by Edda Gentry. Madison, WI: University of Wisconsin Press.

Bailey, Keith (1989). 'The Middle Saxons', in Steven Bassett (ed.), *The Origins of Anglo-Saxon Kingdoms*. Leicester: University Press, 108–22.

Baillet, Adrien (1690). *Auteurs déguisez sous des noms étrangées*. Paris: Chez Antoine Dezallier.

Baker, John (2012). 'What Makes a Stronghold? Reference to Construction Materials in Place-Names in OE *fæsten, burh*, and *(ge)weorc*', in Richard Jones and Sarah Semple (eds.), *Sense of Place in Anglo-Saxon England*. Donington: Shaun Tyas, 316–33.

Baldwin, David H. (2008). *What's in a Name? The Origins, Meanings and Significance of Steam Locomotive Names in the British Railways Era. Part 1: LNER*. Trafford.

Baldwin, John, and Drummond, Peter (2011). *Pentland Place-Names. An Introductory Guide*. Edinburgh: The Friends of the Pentlands.

Ballon, Gabriël-Luc (2007). 'La protection des noms choisis pour exercer une activité économique: l'approche juridique', in Ludger Kremer and Elke Ronneberger-Sibold (eds.), *Names in Commerce and Industry. Past and Present*. Berlin: Logos, 61–8.

Bamberger, Joan (1974). 'Naming and the Transmission of Status in a Central Brazilian Society', *Ethnology* 13: 363–78.

Bandle, Oskar (1984). 'Zur Typologie der germanischen Flussnamen', in Birger Liljestrand, et al. (eds.), *Florilegium Nordicum. En bukett nordiska språk- och namnstudier tillägnade Sigurd Fries den 22 april 1984*. Acta Universitatis Umensis. Umeå Studies in the Humanities 61. Umeå: Umeå universitet, 18–29.

Bandle, Oskar (2005). 'Seenamen 1–2', *Reallexikon der Germanischen Altertumskunde*. 2nd edn, vol. 28: 41–5.

Bangs, Jeremy D. (ed.) (1997). *The Seventeenth-Century Town Records of Scituate, Massachusetts*, vol. 1. Boston, MA: New England Historic Genealogical Society.

Bao, Y., Shao, A. T., and Rivers, D. (2008). 'Creating New Brand Names. Effects of Relevance, Connotation, and Pronunciation', *Journal of Advertising Research* 48: 148–62.

Barber, Alistair, Schuster Jörn, and Holbrook, Neil (2013). 'Prehistoric Activity and Roman Rural Settlement at Blacklands, Staverton. Excavations in 2007', *Wiltshire Archaeological and Natural History Magazine* 106: 16–51.

Barbier, Antoine Alexandre (1806–8). *Dictionnaire des ouvrages anonymes et pseudonymes*. 4 vols. Paris: Imprimerie Bibliographique.

Bardsley, Charles W. (1875). *English Surnames. Their Sources and Significations*. London: Chatto and Windus.

Bardsley, Charles W. (1901). *A Dictionary of English and Welsh Surnames*. London: Henry Frowde.

Barker, Stephanie, Spoerlein, Stefankai, Vetter, Tobias, and Viereck, Wolfgang (2007). *An Atlas of English Surnames*. University of Bamberg Studies in English Linguistics 52. Oxford: Peter Lang.

Barnard, Alan (2000). *History and Theory in Anthropology*. Cambridge: Cambridge University Press.

Barney, Stephen, et al. (trans.) (2006). *Etymologies of Isidore of Seville*. Cambridge: Cambridge University Press.

Barrow, Geoffrey W. S. (1998). 'The Uses of Place-Names and Scottish History. Pointers and Pitfalls', in Simon Taylor (ed.), *The Uses of Place-Names. Language, Landscape, Archaeology, Environment, Literature and History*. Edinburgh: Scottish Cultural Press, 54–74.

Barry, Herbert III, and Harper, Aylene S. (1995). 'Increased Choice of Female Phonetic Attributes in First Names', *Sexroles. A Journal of Research* 32: 809–19.

Barsics, Catherine, and Brédart, Serge (2012). 'Recalling Semantic Information about Newly Learned Faces and Voices', *Memory* 20: 527–34.

Barth, Fredrik, Gingrich, Andre, Parkin Robert, and Silverman, Sydel (2005). *One Discipline, Four Ways. British, German, French and American Anthropology*. Chicago: University of Chicago Press.

Barthes, Roland (1975). *S/Z, An Essay*. transl. by Richard Miller. Preface by Richard Howard. New York: Macmillan.

Bartholomew's CLAN MAP: Scotland of Old (n.d.). Edinburgh: Bartholomew and Son.

Bassett, Steven (1989). 'In Search of the Origins of Anglo-Saxon Kingdoms', in Steven Bassett (ed.), *The Origins of Anglo-Saxon Kingdoms*. Leicester: Leicester University Press, 3–27.

Basso, Keith H. (1980). 'Western Apache Place-Name Hierarchies', in Elisabeth Tooker (ed.), *Naming Systems. 1980 Proceedings of The American Ethnological Society*. Washington: American Ethnological Society, 78–94.

Basso, Keith H. (1984). 'Stalking With Stories. Names, Places, and Moral Narratives Among the Western Apache', in Edward M. Bruner (ed.), *Text, Play, and Story*. Washington, DC: American Ethnological Society, 19–55.

Batman, Stephen (1582). *Batman vppon Bartholome, his Booke* De Proprietatibus Rerum. London: Thomas East.

Batoma, Atoma (2009). 'Talking through One's Dog. Zoonomy and Polemical Communication in Traditional Africa', *Onoma* 44: 15–34.

Bauer, Gerhard (1985). *Namenkunde des Deutschen*. Bern/Frankfurt/New York: Peter Lang.

Bayer, Johann (1603). *Uranometria, omnium asterismorum continens schemata, nova methodo delineata, aereis laminis expressa*. Augsburg: Christophorus Mangus.

Bayer, Joseph (1991). 'Representatie van algemene namen en eigennamen in het mentale lexicon: neurolinguistische evidentie', *Tabu* 21.2: 53–66.

Bays, Hillary (1998). 'Framing and Face in Internet Exchanges. A Socio-Cognitive Approach', *Linguistik online* 1.1. Available online at: <https://bop.unibe.ch/linguistik-online/article/view/1080/1769>.

Beal, Joan C. (2006). *Language and Region*. London: Routledge.

Beal, Joan C. (2009). 'Enregisterment, Commodification and Historical Context. "Geordie" versus "Sheffieldish"', *American Speech* 84.2: 138–56.

Beal, Joan C. (2010). *An Introduction to Regional Englishes*. Edinburgh: Edinburgh University Press.

Beal, Joan C., and Corrigan, Karen P. (2007), 'Time and Tyne. A Corpus Based Study of Variation and Change in Relativization Strategies in Tyneside English', in Stephan Elspass (ed.), *Language History from Below-Linguistic Variation in the Germanic Languages from 1700–2000. Proceedings*. Berlin: Walter de Gruyter, 1–16.

Beal, Joan C., Corrigan, Karen P., and Moisl, Herman L. (2007), 'Taming Digital Voices and Texts. Models and Methods for Handling Unconventional Synchronic Corpora', in Joan C. Beal, Karen P. Corrigan, and Hermann L. Moisl (eds.), *Creating and Digitizing Language Corpora*, vol. 1. Houndmills: Palgrave Macmillan, 1–15.

Bean, Susan S. (1980). 'Ethnology and the Study of Proper Names', *Anthropological Linguistics* 22: 305–16.

Bechar-Israeli, Haya (1995). 'From "Bonehead" to "cLoNehEAd". Nicknames, Play and Identity on Internet Relay Chat', *Journal of Computer-Mediated Communication* 1.2. Available online at: <http://onlinelibrary.wiley.com/doi/10.1111/j.1083-6101.1995.tb00325.x/full>.

Becker, Birgit (2009). 'Immigrants' Emotional Identification with the Host Society. The Example of Turkish Parents' Naming Practices in Germany', *Ethnicities* 9: 200–25.

Beidelman, Thomas O. (1974). 'Kaguru Names and Naming', *Journal of Anthropological Research* 30: 281–93.

Beider, Alexander (1993). *A Dictionary of Jewish Surnames from the Russian Empire*. Teaneck, NJ: Avotaynu.

Beider, Alexander (1995). *Jewish Surnames in Prague. 15th to 18th Centuries*. Teaneck, NJ: Avotaynu.

Beider, Alexander (1996). *A Dictionary of Jewish Surnames from the Kingdom of Poland*. Teaneck, NJ: Avotaynu.

Belling, Luc, and de Bres, Julia (2014). 'Digital Superdiversity in Luxembourg. The Role of Luxembourgish in a Multilingual Facebook Group', *Discourse, Context and Media* 4–5: 74–86. Available online at: <http://dx.doi.org/10.1016/j.dcm.2014.03.002>.

Bemwell, Bethan, and Stokoe, Elizabeth (2006). *Discourse and Identity*. Edinburgh: Edinburgh University Press.

Bender, Byron (1970). 'An Oceanic Place-name Study', in Stephen A. Wurm and Donald C. Laycock (eds.), *Pacific Linguistic Studies in Honour of Arthur Capell*. Pacific Linguistic Series C 13. Canberra: Linguistic Circle of Canberra, 165–88.

Beneš, Josef (1998). *Německá Príjmení Čechu*. Ustí nad Labem: Univerzita J.E. Purkyně.

Benn, Tony (1996). *The Benn Diaries. 1940–1990*. London: Arrow.

Ben-Rafael, Eliezer, et al. (2006). 'Linguistic Landscape as Symbolic Construction of the Public Space. The Case of Israel', in Durk Gorter (ed.), *Linguistic Landscape. A New Approach to Multilingualism*. Clevedon: Multilingual Matters, 7–30.

Benskin, Michael, Laing, Margaret, Karaiskos, Vasilis, and Williamson, Keith (2013–). *An Electronic Version of a Linguistic Atlas of Late Mediaeval English*. Edinburgh: Edinburgh University Press. Available online at: <http://www.lel.ed.ac.uk/ihd/elalme/elalme.html>.

Benson, Larry D. (ed.) (1988). *The Riverside Chaucer*. Oxford: Oxford University Press.

Benson, Sven (1972). 'Namngivning och namntypologi', *Sydsvenska ortnamnssällskapets årsskrift*: 34–40.

Bentley, Trevor (1999). *Pakeha Maori*. Auckland: Penguin.

Bentzien, Ulrich (1968). 'Tiereigennamen. Untersucht an einem Quellenfund aus Mecklenburg', *Deutsches Jahrbuch für Volkskunde* 14: 39–55.

Berezkina, Maimu (2011). 'Holdninger til stedsnavn i Oslo: En studie basert på opplysninger fra tre ulike etniske grupper'. Unpublished Master's dissertation, University of Oslo.

Berg, Lawrence D., and Vuolteenaho, Jani (eds.) (2009). *Critical Toponymies. The Contested Politics of Place-Naming.* Farnham: Ashgate.

Berger, Charles, and Calabrese, Richard (1975). 'Some Explorations in Initial Interaction and Beyond', *Human Communication* 1: 99–112.

Berger, Dieter (1999). *Duden. Geographische Namen in Deutschland. Herkunft und Bedeutung der Namen von Ländern, Städten, Bergen und Gewässern.* 2nd rev. edn. Mannheim/Leipzig/Wien/Zürich: Duden.

Bergermayer, Angela (2005). *Glossar der Etyma der eingedeutschten Namen slavischer Herkunft in Niederösterreich.* Wien: Verlag der Akademie der Wissenschaften.

Bergien, Angelika (2007). 'In Search of the Perfect Name. Prototypical and Iconic Effects of Linguistic Patterns in Company Names', in Ludger Kremer and Elke Ronneberger-Sibold (eds.), *Names in Commerce and Industry. Past and Present.* Berlin: Logos, 259–72.

Bergien, Angelika (2008). 'Global and Regional Considerations in the Formation of Company Names', in Donatella Bremer, Michele Bani, Franco Belli, and Matteo Paolini (eds.), *I Nomi Nel Tempo e Nello Spazio. Atti del XXII Congresso Internazionale di Scienze Onomastiche. Pisa, 28 agosto–4 settembre 2005,* vol. 2. Pisa: Edizioni ETS, 289–97.

Bergien, Angelika (2013). 'The Lady Gaga Economy. How Paragons Conquer Today's Business Discourse', in Paula Sjöblom, Terhi Ainiala, and Ulla Hakala (eds.), *Names in the Economy. Cultural Prospects.* Newcastle: Cambridge Scholars, 332–44.

Bergien, Angelika, Kremer, Ludger, and Zilg, Antje (2010). 'Commercial Names as Indicators of Innovation and Change. New Reflections and Challenges', *Onoma* 43: 7–23.

Bernard, H. Russell (2011). *Research Methods in Anthropology.* 5th edn. Plymouth: AltaMira.

Bernstein, David (1985). *Company Image and Reality. A Critique of Corporate Communications.* Eastbourne: Holt, Rinehart and Winston.

Berry, Lloyd E. (ed.) (2007). *The Geneva Bible. A Facsimile of the 1560 Edition.* Peabody, MA: Hendrickson.

Bertrand, Melanie (2010). 'Differing Functions of Deracialized Speech. The Use of Place Names to Index Race in Focus Groups With African American and White Patients', *Text and Talk* 30.5: 485–505.

Bessat, Hubert, and Germi, Claudette (2001). *Les noms du paysage alpin. Atlas toponymique, Savoie, Vallée d'Aoste, Dauphiné, Provence.* Grenoble: Ellug.

Bezlaj, France (1956–61). *Slovenska vodna imena.* 2 vols. Ljubljana: SAZU.

Bezlaj, France (1976–95). *Etimološki slovar slovenskega jezika.* 3 vols. Ljubljana: SAZU.

Bhreathnach, Edel (ed.) (2005). *The Kingship and Landscape of Tara.* Dublin: Four Courts.

Bhreathnach, Edel (2010). 'From *fert[ae]* to *relic.* Mapping Death in Early Sources', in Christiaan Corlett and Michael Potterton (eds.), *Death and Burial in Early Medieval Ireland.* Dublin: Wordwell, 23–31.

Bhulbh, Seán de (1997). *Irish Surnames.* Faing: Comhar-Chumann Íde Naofa.

Biber, Douglas, et al. (1999). *Longman Grammar of Spoken and Written English.* London: Longman.

Bieler, Ludwig (ed. and trans.) (1979). *The Patrician Texts in the Book of Armagh.* Dublin: The Dublin Institute for Advanced Studies.

Bigon, Liora, and Dahamshe, Amer (2014). 'An Anatomy of Symbolic Power. Israeli Road-Sign Policy and the Palestinian Minority', *Environment and Planning D: Society and Space* 32: 606–21.

Billig, Michael (1995). *Banal Nationalism.* London: Sage.

Birus, Hendrik (1987). 'Vorschlag zu einer Typologie literarischer Namen', *LiLi Zeitschrift für Litteraturwissenschaft und Linguistik,* 17: 38–51.

Birus, Hendrik (1989). 'Vorschlag zu einer Typologie literarische Namen. Exemplifiert an Heissenbüttels Namenspektrum', in Friedrich Debus and Horst Pütz (eds.), *Namen in deutschen literarischen Texten des Mittelalters. Vorträge, Symposion Kiel, 9.–12.9.1987.* Kieler Beiträge zur deutschen Sprachgeschichte 12. Neumünster: Wachholtz, 17–41.

Bishop, Jeanne E. (2004). 'How Astronomical Objects Are Named', *The Planetarian* 33.3: 6–24.

Björkman, Erik (1913). 'Nordiska ortnamn i England', *Namn och Bygd* 1: 80–95.

Blaauw, William H. (1848). 'On Sussex Archaeology', *Sussex Archaeological Collections* 1: 1–13.

Black, George F. (1946). *The Surnames of Scotland. Their Origin, Meaning, and History.* New York: The New York Public Library.

Blackwood, Robert, and Tufi, Stefania (2012). 'Policies vs Non-Policies. Analysing Regional Languages and the National Standard in the Linguistic Landscape of French and Italian Mediterranean Cities', in Durk Gorter, Heiko F. Marten, and Luk Van Mensel (eds.), *Minority Languages in the Linguistic Landscape.* Basingstoke: Palgrave Macmillan, 109–26.

Blaeu, Joan (1654). *Theatrum Orbis Terrarum Sive Atlas Novus.* Amsterdam.

Blain, Carmen, Levy, Stuart, and Brent, Ritchie (2005). 'Destination Branding. Insights and Practices from Destination Management Organisations', *Journal of Travel Research* 43: 328–38.

Bliss, Jane (2008). *Naming and Namelessness in Medieval Romance.* Cambridge: D. S. Brewer.

Bloch, Maurice (2006). 'Teknonymy and the Evocation of the "Social" Among the Zafimaniry of Madagascar', Gabriele Vom Bruck and Barbara Bodenhorn (eds.), *An Anthropology of Names and Naming.* Cambridge: Cambridge University Press, 97–114.

Blok, Dirk P. (1965). 'Probleme der Flußnamenforschung in den alluvialen Gebieten der Niederlande', in Rudolf Schützeichel and Matthias Zender (eds.), *Namenforschung. Festschrift für Adolf Bach zum 75. Geburtstag am 31. Januar 1965.* Heidelberg: Carl Winter, 212–27.

Blomqvist, Marianne (2011). *Våra fyrfota vänner har också namn.* Helsingfors: Svenska folkskolans vänner.

Blosen, Hans (1989). 'Name und Rolle in den Fastnachtsspielen des Hans Sachs', in Friedrich Debus and Horst Pütz (eds.), *Namen in deutschen literarischen Texten des Mittelalters. Vorträge, Symposion Kiel, 9.–12.9.1987.* Kieler Beiträge zur deutschen Sprachgeschichte 12. Neumünster: Wachholtz, 241–70.

Blum, Susan D. (1997). 'Naming Practices and the Power of Words in China', *Language in Society* 26: 357–79.

Boas, Franz (1901–7). *The Eskimo of Baffin Land and Hudson Bay.* Bulletin of the American Museum of Natural History 15, New York.

Boas, Franz (1934). *Geographical Names of the Kwakiutl Indians.* New York: Columbia University Press.

Bodenhorn, Barbara, and Vom Bruck, Gabriele (2006). '"Entangled in Histories". An Introduction to the Anthropology of Names and Naming', in Gabriele Vom Bruck and Barbara Bodenhorn (eds.), *The Anthropology of Names and Naming.* Cambridge, Cambridge University Press, 1–30.

Boerrigter, Reina (2007). 'Identity Reflecting Business Names', in Eva Brylla and Mats Wahlberg (eds.), *Proceedings of the 21st International Congress of Onomastic Sciences, Uppsala, 19–24 August 2002,* vol. 3. Uppsala: Institutet för språk och folkminnen, 53–61.

Boerrigter, Reina, and Nijboer, Harm (eds.) (2012). *Names as Language and Capital. Proceedings Names in the Economy III, Amsterdam, 11–13 June 2009.* Amsterdam: Meertens Instituut. Available online at: <http://depot.knaw.nl/12899/>.

Boesch, Bruno (1957). 'Die Eigennamen in ihrer geistigen und seelischen Bedeutung für den Menschen', *Der Deutschunterricht* 9.5: 32–50.

Boesch, Bruno (1981). 'Die Gewässernamen des Bodenseeraumes', *Beiträge zur Namenforschung (Neue Folge)* 16: 13–39.

Bölcskei, Andrea (2010). 'Distinctive Additions in English Settlement Names: A Cognitive Linguistic Approach', *Nomina* 33: 101–20.

Bollaert, William (1850). 'Observations on the Indian Tribes in Texas', *Journal of the Ethnological Society of London* 2: 262–83.

Bond, James (1982). 'Oxfordshire Field-Names', *Oxfordshire Local History* 1.4: 2–15.

Bonin, Patrick, Perret, Cyril, Méot, Alain, Ferrand, Ludovic, and Mermillod, Martial (2008). 'Psycholinguistic Norms and Face Naming Times for Photographs of Celebrities in French', *Behavior Research Methods* 40: 137–46.

Boonpaisarnsatit, Nithat, and Srioutai, Jiranthara (2013). 'Thailand's Exported Food Product Brand Naming. Semantic and Pragmatic Perspectives', in Paula Sjöblom, Terhi Ainiala, and Ulla Hakala (eds.), *Names in the Economy. Cultural Prospects*. Newcastle: Cambridge Scholars, 26–54.

Bordowitz, Hank (2006). *Billy Joel. The Life and Times of an Angry Young Man.* New York: Billboard Books.

Borg, Alexander, and Kressel, Gideon M. (2001). 'Bedouin Personal Names in the Negev and Sinai', *Journal of Arabic Linguistics* 40: 32–70.

Borin, Lars, and Kokkinakis, Dimitrios (2010). 'Literary Onomastics and Language Technology', in Willie van Peer, Sonia Zyngier, and Vander Viana (eds.), *Literary Education and Digital Learning: Methods and Technologies for Humanities Studies.* IGI GLobal, 53–78. doi: 10.4018/978-1-60566-932-8.ch003.

Borsoi, Edward E. (1967). 'A Linguistic Analysis of Trade Names in American-Spanish'. PhD dissertation, University of Illinois.

Bourdieu, Pierre (1991). *Language and Symbolic Power.* trans. by Gino Raymond and Matthew Adamson. Cambridge: Harvard University Press.

Bourne, Jill (2012). 'Kingston. The Place-Name and Its Content', in Richard Jones and Sarah Semple (eds.), *Sense of Place in Anglo-Saxon England.* Donington: Shaun Tyas, 260–83.

Bouvier, Jean-Claude (2007). 'Le Langage de la toponymie urbaine—Approche méthodologique', *Onoma* 42: 23–38.

Bowden, Georgina R., et al. (2008). 'Excavating Past Population Structures by Surname-Based Sampling. The Genetic Legacy of the Vikings in Northwest England', *Molecular Biology and Evolution* 25: 301–9.

Bowman, Alan K. (2004). *Life and Letters on the Roman Frontier.* Rev. edn. London: British Museum.

Boyle, Paddy (2005). 'A Townland Called Nevitt', *Archaeology Ireland* 19.2: 26–30.

Bramwell, Ellen (2007). 'Community Bynames in the Western Isles', *Nomina* 30: 35–56.

Bramwell, Ellen S. (2012). 'Naming in Society. A Cross-Cultural Study of Five Communities in Scotland'. PhD dissertation, University of Glasgow.

Brandes, Stanley H. (1975). 'The Structural and Demographic Implications of Nicknames in Navanogal, Spain', *American Ethnologist* 2: 139–48.

Brandl, Werner (2007). 'Buy English? Changes in German Product Naming', in Ludger Kremer and Elke Ronneberger-Sibold (eds.), *Names in Commerce and Industry. Past and Present.* Berlin: Logos, 87–98.

Branford, Jean (1980). *A Dictionary of South African English*. Cape Town: Oxford University Press.

Brechenmacher, Josef K. (1936). *Deutsche Sippennamen*. Görlitz: C.A. Starke.

Brechenmacher, Josef K. (1957). *Etymologisches Worterbuch der Deutschen Familiennamen*. Limburg: C.A. Starke.

Brédart, Serge (1993). 'Retrieval Failures in Face Naming', *Memory* 1: 351–66.

Brédart, Serge, and Valentine, Tim (1992). 'From Monroe to Moreau. An Analysis of Face Naming Errors', *Cognition* 45: 187–227.

Brédart, Serge, and Valentine, Tim (1998). 'Descriptiveness and Proper Name Retrieval', *Memory* 6: 199–206.

Brédart, Serge, Brennen, Tim, and Valentine, Tim (1997). 'Dissociations Between the Processing of Proper and Common Names', *Cognitive Neuropsychology* 14: 209–17.

Brédart, Serge, Brennen, Tim, Delchambre, Marie, McNeill, Alan, and Burton, A. Mike (2005). 'Naming Very Familiar People. When Retrieving Names is Faster Than Retrieving Semantic Biographical Information', *British Journal of Psychology* 96: 205–14.

Breen, Richard (1982). 'Naming Practices in Western Ireland', *Man (New Series)* 17: 701–13.

Bregenzer, John (1968). 'Naming Practices in South America', *Journal of the Minnesota Academy of Sciences* 35: 47–50.

Brendler, Andrea, and Brendler, Silvio (eds.) (2007). *Europäische Personennamensysteme. Ein Handbuch von Abasisch bis Zentralladinisch*. Hamburg: Baar.

Brendler, Silvio (2005). 'Über den gerechten Tod der Auffassung vom Namen als bilaterales Zeichen', in Eva Brylla and Mats Wahlberg (eds.), *Proceedings of the XXIst International Congress of Onomastic Sciences* (Uppsala 2002), vol. I. Uppsala: SOFI, 98–117.

Brendler, Silvio (2008). *Nomematik. Identitätstheoretische Grundlagen der Namenforschung (Insbesondere der Namengeschichte, Namenlexikographie, Namengeographie, Namenstatistik und Namenstheorie)*. Hamburg: Baar.

Brennen, Tim (1993). 'The Difficulty with Recalling People's Names. The Plausible Phonology Hypothesis', *Memory* 1: 409–31.

Brink, Stefan (1988). 'Denotationsförändringar bland våra äldsta bebyggelsenamn-styper', in Peter Slotte (ed.), *Denotationsbyte i ortnamn*. NORNA-rapporter 37. Uppsala: NORNA-förlaget, 63–88.

Brink, Stefan (1996). 'The Onomasticon and the Role of Analogy in Name Formation', *Namn och bygd* 84: 61–84.

Brink, Stefan (2012). 'De nordiska språkens påverkan på ortnamnsskicket i Storbritannien', in Björn Bihl, Peter Andersson, and Lena Lötmarker (eds.), *Svenskans beskrivning 32. Förhandlingar vid trettioandra sammankonsten för svenskans beskrivning Karlstad den 13–14 oktober 2011*. Nordsvenska 19. Karlstad: University of Karlstad, 38–51.

Broberg, Gunnar (2004). *Kattens historia*. Stockholm: Atlantis.

Broderick, George (1994). *Placenames of the Isle of Man*, vol. 1. Tübingen: Niemeyer.

Broderick, George (2000). *Placenames of the Isle of Man*, vol. 5. Tübingen: Niemeyer.

Bromberger, Christian (1982). 'Pour une analyse anthropologique des noms de personnes', *Langages* 66: 103–24.

Brook, George L. (1958). *A History of the English Language*. London: André Deutsch.

Broun, Davit (2008). 'The Property Records in the Book of Deer as a Source for Early Scottish Society', in Katherine Forsyth (ed.), *Studies on the Book of Deer*. Dublin: Four Courts Press, 313–60.

Brown, Donald E. (1991). *Human Universals*. London: McGraw-Hill.

Brown, Kara D. (2012). 'The Linguistic Landscape of Educational Spaces. Language Revitalization and Schools in Southeastern Estonia', in Durk Gorter, Heiko F. Marten, and Luk Van Mensel (eds.), *Minority Languages in the Linguistic Landscape*. Basingstoke: Palgrave Macmillan, 281–98.

Brown, Penelope, and Levinson, Stephen C. (1987). *Politeness. Some Universals in Language Usage*. Studies in Interactional Sociolinguistics 4. Cambridge: Cambridge University Press.

Brown, William (ed.) (1892). *Yorkshire Inquisitions of the Reigns of Henry III and Edward I*. Yorkshire Archaeological and Topographical Association, Record Series, vol. 12.

Bruce, Vicki, and Young, Andy (1986). 'Understanding Face Recognition', *British Journal of Psychology* 77: 305–27.

Brunt, Lodewijk (2001). 'Into the Community', in Paul Atkinson, Amanda Coffey, Sara Delamont, John Loflandand, and Lyn Lofland (eds.), *Handbook of Ethnography*. London: Sage, 80–91.

Bruzelius, Lars (transc.) (2000). 'A List of all the Ships, Frigates, and other Vessels belonging to the State's Navy, on 1st March, 1651', from Charles Derrick (1806), *Memoirs of the Rise and Progress of the Royal Navy*. London: H. Teape, 69–74. Available online at: <http://www.bruzelius.info/Nautica/Naval_History/GB/Derrick%281806%29_p69.html>.

Bryant. Alfred T. (1929). *Olden Times in Zululand and Natal*. London: Longmans, Green and Co.

Brylla, Eva (1990). 'Morphological Types of Old Swedish Personal By-names', in Eeva M. Närhi (ed.), *Proceedings of the XVIIth International Congress of Onomastic Sciences. Helsinki 13–18 August 1990*, vol. 1. Helsinki: The University of Helsinki and the Finnish Research Centre for Domestic Languages, 224–31.

Brylla, Eva (1999). '*Anna Mædh inga hænder, Karl Dængenæf* and *Ingridh Thiuvafinger*. Några exempel på medeltida binamn', in Lennart Elmevik, Svante Strandberg, Eva Brylla, Mats Wahlberg, and Henrik Williams (eds.), *Runor och namn, Hyllningsskrift till Lena Peterson den 27 januari 1999*. Namn och samhälle 10. Uppsala: Uppsala universitetet, 11–19.

Brylla, Eva (2001a). 'Personnamn och genus. Manligt och kvinnligt i namnen', in Gunilla Harling-Kranck (ed.), *Namn i en föränderlig värld*. Helsinki: Svenska litteratursällskapet i Finland, 36–44.

Brylla, Eva (2001b). 'Personnamn och genus', *Studia anthroponymica Scandinavica* 19: 11–29.

Brylla, Eva (2004). *Förnamn i Sverige. Kortfattat namnlexikon*. Stockholm: Liber.

Brylla, Eva (2012). 'Binamn i Norden', in Staffan Nyström, Eva Brylla, Katharina Leibring, Lennart Ryman, and Per Vikstrand (eds.), *Binamn. Uppkomst, bildning, terminologi och bruk. Handlingar från NORNA:s 40:e symposium i Älvkarleö, Uppland, 29/9–1/10 2010*. NORNA-rapporter 88. Uppsala: NORNA-förlaget, 9–22.

Brylla, Eva (2013). 'Binamn', in Staffan Nyström, et al. (eds.), *Namn och namnforskning. Ett levande läromedel om ortnamn, personnamn och andra namn*. Uppsala: Uppsala universitetet, 114–18. Available online at: <http://uu.diva-portal.org/smash/get/diva2:606610/FULLTEXT01.pdf>.

Brylla, Eva, and Wahlberg, Mats (2005–10). *Proceedings of the 21st International Congress of Onomastic Sciences, Uppsala, 19–24 August 2002*. 5 vols. Uppsala: Institutet för språk och folkminnen.

Bryson, Bill. (1994). *Made in America*. London: Black Swan.

Bucholtz, Mary, and Hall, Kira (2005). 'Identity and Interaction. A Sociocultural Linguistic Approach', *Discourse Studies. An Interdisciplinary Journal for the Study of Text and Talk* 7.4–5: 585–614.

Budziszewska, Wanda (1993). 'Imiona bułgarskich zwierząt domowych', *Onomastica* 38: 235–59.

Bugge, Alexander (1905). *Vesterlandenes indflydelse paa nordboernes og særlig nordmændenes ydre kultur, levesæt og samfundsforhold i vikingetiden*. Christiania: Jacob Dybwad.

Bugheșiu, Alina (2012). 'On Brands and Branding in the Romanian Space', in Oliviu Felecan (ed.), *Name and Naming. Synchronic and Diachronic Perspectives*. Newcastle: Cambridge Scholars, 388–400.

Bühler, Karl (1934). *Sprachtheorie: Die Darstellungsfunktion der Sprache*. 3. Stuttgart: Auflage. G. Fischer.

Bullock, Roy (2010). *The Origins of Salford Street Names*. Unpublished typescript.

Burelbach, Frederick M. (1987 [1978]). 'Look! Up in the Sky! It's What's His Name!', *Literary Onomastics Studies* 5: 34–55 [reprinted in Alvarez-Altman and Burelbach (1987): 105–117].

Burelbach, Frederick M. (1995). 'The Stylistic Function of Names in Comics', in Ernst Eichler, et al. (eds.), *Namenforschung/Name Studies/Les noms propres. Ein internationals Handbuch zur Onomastik/International Handbook of Onomastics/Manuel international d'onomastique*, vol 1. Berlin/New York: de Gruyter, 582–5.

Burke, Deborah M., MacKay, Donald G., Worthley, Joanna S., and Wade, Elizabeth (1991). 'On the Tip of the Tongue. What Causes Word Finding Failures in Young and Older Adults?', *Journal of Memory and Language* 30: 542–79.

Burnley, David (2003). 'The T/V Pronouns in Later Middle English Literature', in Irma Taavitsainen and Andreas H. Jucker (eds.), *Diachronic Perspectives on Address Term Systems. Pragmatics and Beyond New Series* 107. Amsterdam/Philadelphia: John Benjamins, 27–45.

Bursell, Moa (2011). 'Name Change and Destigmatization among Middle Eastern Immigrants in Sweden', *Ethnic and Racial Studies* 35.3: 471–87.

Burton, A. Mike, and Bruce, Vicki (1992). 'I Recognize Your Face But I Can't Remember Your Name. A Simple Explanation?', *British Journal of Psychology* 83: 45–60.

Burton, A. Mike, Bruce, Vicki, and Johnston, Robert A. (1990). 'Understanding Face Recognition with an Interactive Activation Model', *British Journal of Psychology* 81: 361–80.

Busse, Beatrix (2006). *Vocative Constructions in the Language of Shakespeare*. Pragmatics and Beyond New Series 150. Amsterdam/Philadelphia: John Benjamins.

Busse, Ulrich (2002). *Linguistic Variation in the Shakespeare Corpus. Morpho-Syntactic Variability of Second Person Pronouns*. Pragmatics and Beyond New Series 106. Amsterdam/Philadelphia: John Benjamins.

Busse, Ulrich (2003). 'The Co-occurrence of Nominal and Pronominal Address Forms in the Shakespeare Corpus. Who Says Thou or You to Whom?', in Irma Taavitsainen and Andreas H. Jucker (eds.), *Diachronic Perspectives on Address Term Systems*. Pragmatics and Beyond New Series 107. Amsterdam/Philadelphia: John Benjamins, 193–221.

Busteed, Mervyn (2012). 'Little Ireland', in Paul Hindle (ed.), *Exploring Greater Manchester*. Manchester Geographical Society. Available online at: <http://www.mangeogsoc.org.uk/egm/3_1_Little_Ireland.pdf>.

Butler, Constance Mary, and Bernard, John H. (1918). 'Charters of the Abbey of Duiske', *PRIA* 35: 1–188.

Butler, Judith (1997). *Excitable Speech. A Politics of the Performative*. New York: Routledge.

Caffarelli, Enzo, and Gerritzen, Doreen (2002). 'Frequenze onomastiche. I prenomi più frequenti nel mondo alla fine del secondo millennio', *Rivista Italiana di Onomastica* 8: 631–709.

Calderwood, Lesley, and Burton, A. Mike (2006). 'Children and Adults Recall the Names of Highly Familiar Faces Faster than Semantic Information', *British Journal of Psychology* 97: 441–54.

California Court (2015). 'Change an Adult's Name'. Available online at: <http://www.courts. ca.gov/1051.htm>.

Camb. Reg. = Registrum Monasterii S. Marie de Cambuskenneth (1872). Grampian Club.

Cambridge Dictionaries Online (2015). Cambridge University Press. Available online at: <http:// dictionary.cambridge.org/>.

Camden, William (1605). Remains Concerning Britain. London: Charles Harper.

Camden, William (1610 [1586]). Britannia. trans. by Philemon Holland.

Cameron, Deborah (1995). Verbal Hygiene. London: Routledge.

Cameron, Kenneth (1965). Scandinavian Settlement in the Territory of the Five Boroughs: The Place-name Evidence. Nottingham: University of Nottingham. [reprinted in Cameron 1975, 115–38.]

Cameron, Kenneth (1968). 'Eccles in English Place Names', in Maurice W. Barley and Richard P. C. Hanson (eds.), Christianity in Britain, 300–700. Leicester: Leicester University Press, 87–92.

Cameron, Kenneth (1970). 'Scandinavian Settlement in the Territory of the Five Boroughs: The Place-Name Evidence. Part II: Place-Names in thorp', Mediaeval Scandinavia 3: 35–49. [reprinted in Cameron 1975, 139–56.]

Cameron, Kenneth (1971). 'Scandinavian Settlement in the Territory of the Five Boroughs: The Place-Name Evidence. Part III: The Grimston-Hybrids', in Peter Clemoes and Kathleen Hughes (eds.), England Before the Conquest: Studies in primary sources presented to Dorothy Whitelock. Cambridge: Cambridge University Press, 147–63. [reprinted in Cameron 1975, 157–71.]

Cameron, Kenneth (ed.) (1975). Place-Name Evidence for the Anglo-Saxon Invasion and Scandinavian Settlements. Nottingham: English Place-Name Society.

Cameron, Kenneth (1979–80). 'The Meaning and Significance of Old English walh in English Place-Names', Journal of the English Place-Name Society 12: 1–34.

Cameron, Kenneth (1985). The Place-Names of Lincolnshire. Part 1. English Place-Name Society 58. Nottingham: English Place-Name Society.

Cameron, Kenneth (1988). English Place-Names. London: Batsford.

Cameron, Kenneth (1996). English Place Names. New edn. London: Batsford.

Campbell, Alistair (1959). Old English Grammar. Oxford: Clarendon Press.

Campbell, Alistair (ed. and trans.) (1962). The Chronicle of Æthelweard. London/ Edinburgh: Thomas Nelson.

Campbell, James (2001). 'What Is Not Known About the Reign of Edward the Elder?', in Nicholas J. Higham and David H. Hill (eds.), Edward the Elder, 899–924. London/ New York: Routledge, 12–24.

Campion, Nicholas (2008). 'Astrology in Babylonia', in Helaine Selin (ed.), Encyclopaedia of the History of Science, Technology, and Medicine in Non-Western Cultures. 2nd rev. ed. Berlin: Springer, 248–62.

Caprini, Rita (2001). Nomi propri. Alessandria: Edizioni dell'Orso.

Carey, John (ed. and trans.) (1984). 'Scél Tuáin meic Chairill', Ériu 35: 93–111.

Carlquist, Jonas (2005). 'Internetnamn som socialt fenomen', in Staffan Nyström (ed.), Namnens dynamik. Utvecklingstendenser och drivkrafter inom nordiskt namnskick. Handlingar från den trettonde nordiska namnforskarkongressen i Tällberg 15–18 augusti 2003. NORNA-rapporter 80. Uppsala: NORNA-förlaget, 89–100.

Carlquist, Jonas (2012). 'Namn bruk på nätet', in Staffan Nyström, et al. (eds.), Namn och namnforskning. Ett levande läromedel om ortnamn, personnamn och andra namn.

Uppsala: Uppsala universitetet, 164–7. Available online at <http://uu.diva-portal.org/smash/get/diva2:606610/FULLTEXT01.pdf>.

Carney, James (ed.) (1964). *The Poems of Bláthmhac, Son of Cú Brettan, Together with the Irish Gospel of Thomas and a Poem on the Virgin Mary.* Irish Texts Society 47. London: Irish Text Society.

Carroll, Jayne (2012). 'Changing Names, Changing Functions?', in Richard Jones and Sarah Semple (eds.), *Sense of Place in Anglo-Saxon England.* Donington: Shaun Tyas, 168–79.

Carroll, Jayne (2013). 'Perceiving Place Through Time. English Place-Name Studies, 1924–2013', in Jayne Carroll and David Parsons (eds.), *Perceptions of Place. Twenty-First Century Interpretations of English Place-Name Studies.* Nottingham: English Place-Name Society, xiii–xxxvii.

Carroll, Jayne, and Parsons, David N. (eds.) (2013). *Perceptions of Place. Twenty-First Century Interpretations of English Place-Name Studies.* Nottingham: English Place-Name Society.

Carson, Derek, Burton, A. Mike, and Bruce, Vicki (2000). 'Putting Names to Faces. A Review and Tests of the Models', *Pragmatics and Cognition* 8: 9–62.

Carter, Erica, Donald, James and Squires, Judith (eds.) (1993). *Space and Place. Theories of Identity and Location.* London: Lawrence and Wishart.

Casserley, Henry C. (1967). *British Locomotive Names of the Twentieth Century.* London: Ian Allan.

Cavill, Paul (2011). 'Exploring Spirituality in Schools Outreach', in Geoff Baker and Andrew Fisher (eds.), *Arts and Humanities Academics in Schools. Mapping the Pedagogical Interface.* London: Continuum, 151–64.

CDEPN = Watts, Victor, with Insley, John, and Gelling, Margaret (eds.) (2004). *The Cambridge Dictionary of English Place-Names.* Cambridge: Cambridge University Press.

Cenoz, Jasone, and Gorter, Durk (2006). 'Linguistic Landscape and Minority Languages', in Durk Gorter (ed.), *Linguistic Landscape. A New Approach to Multilingualism.* Clevedon: Multilingual Matters, 67–80.

Centraal Bureau voor Genealogie (2000–). *Nederlandse Familienamenbank.* [online] Available at: <https://www.meertens.knaw.nl/nfb/> [accessed 30 March 2014].

CGSH = Ó Riain, Padraig (ed.) (1985). *Corpus Genealogiarum Sanctorum Hiberniae,* Dublin: Dublin Institute for Advanced Studies.

Chadwick, John (1958). *The Decipherment of Linear B.* Cambridge: Cambridge University Press.

Chao, Sheau-yueh J. (2000). *In Search of your Asian Roots. Genealogical Research on Chinese Surnames.* Baltimore, MD: Clearfield.

Chapman, Don (2008). '"You Belly-Guilty Bag". Insulting Epithets in Old English', *Journal of Historical Pragmatics* 9.1: 1–19.

Charles, Lucile H. (1951). 'Drama in First-Naming Ceremonies', *Journal of American Folklore* 64: 11–35.

Charles-Edwards, T. M. (1993). *Irish and Welsh Kinship.* Oxford: Clarendon Press.

The Charters of William II and Henry I (n.d.). Available online at: <https://actswilliam2henry1.wordpress.com/>.

Chelliah, Shobhana L. (2005). 'Asserting Nationhood through Personal Name Choice: The Case of the Meithei of Northeast India', *Anthropological Linguistics* 47: 169–216.

Childs, Wendy R. (ed.) (1986). *The Customs Accounts of Hull 1453–1490.* Leeds: The Yorkshire Archaeological Society.

Chow, Kenny, and Healey, Mick (2008). 'Place Attachment and Place Identity. First-Year University Undergraduates Making the Transition from Home to University', *Journal of Environmental Psychology* 28: 362–72.

Chryssochoou, Xenia (2003). 'Studying Identity in Social Psychology. Some Thoughts on the Definition of Identity and its Relation to Action', *Journal of Language and Politics* 3.3: 225–41.

Chu, Pao-Liang (1977). *Twentieth-Century Chinese Writers and Their Pen Names*. Boston, MA: G.K. Hallandco.

Cislaru, Georgeta (2006). 'Propriétés catégorielles des noms de pays', *Onoma* 41: 83–113.

Cislaru, Georgeta (2012). 'Les facettes des toponymes: des données contextuelles aux modèles sémantiques', in *Colloque international: Défis de la toponymie synchronique. Structures, contextes et usages*. Université Rennes, 22–23 March 2012.

City of Cape Town (2007). 'Positive Response to City's Renaming Process'. Media release 277, 30 July. Available online at: <http://www.capetown.gov.za/en/MediaReleases/Pages/PositiveresponseToCitysRenamingProcess.aspx>.

Clankie, Shawn Michael (2000). 'On Brand Name Change. A Theory of Genericization'. *Dissertation Abstracts International, A: The Humanities and Social Sciences*, 2890-A. Available online at: <http://search.proquest.com/docview/85530924?accountid=14774>.

Clare County Library (n.d.). 'Parish of Kilfenora (a)'. *Ordnance Survey Letters by John O'Donovan and Eugene Curry,1839*. Available online at: <http://www.clarelibrary.ie/eolas/coclare/history/osl/kilfenora1_situation.htm>.

Clark, Cecily (1995 [1991]). 'Towards a Reassessment of Anglo-Norman Influence on English Place-Names', in P. Sture Ureland and George Broderick (eds.), *Language Contact in the British Isles. Proceedings of the 8th International Symposium on Language Contact in Europe, Douglas, Isle of Man, 1988*. Tübingen: Niemeyer, 275–95. [reprinted in Jackson (1995): 144–55].

Clark, Cecily (1995). 'REVIEW. Richard McKinley, *The Surnames of Sussex* (Oxford, 1988)', in Peter Jackson (ed.), *Words, Names, and History. Selected Papers of Cecily Clark*. Cambridge: Boydell and Brewer, 381–4.

Clark, Cecily (2002). 'Socio-Economic Status and Individual Identity: Essential Factors in the Analysis of Middle English Personal-Naming', in David Postles (ed.), *Naming, Society and Regional Identity*. Oxford: Leopard's Head Press, 101–21.

Clayman, Steven E. (2010). 'Address Terms in the Service of Other Actions. The Case of News Interview Talk', *Discourse and Communication* 4: 161–83.

Clayman, Steven E., and Heritage, John (2002). *The News Interview. Journalists and Public Figures on the Air*. Cambridge: Cambridge University Press.

Cleland, James (1825). *A Historical Account of the Steam Engine, and Its Application in Propelling Vessels*, [etc.]. Glasgow: publisher unknown.

Clifton, Jonathan (2013). 'What's in a Name? Names, National Identity, Assimilation, and the New Racist Discourse of Marine Le Pen', *Pragmatics* 23.3: 403–20.

Coates, Richard (1985). 'The Possible Significance of the Tudor f.n. Fittenhall (New Fishbourne)', *Sussex History* 2.9: 23–5.

Coates, Richard (1987). 'Pragmatic Sources of Analogical Reformation', *Journal of Linguistics* 23: 319–40.

Coates, Richard (2000). 'Singular Definite Expressions with a Unique Denotatum and the Limits of Properhood', *Linguistics* 38.6: 1161–74.

Coates, Richard (2005). 'A Speculative Psycholinguistic Model of Onymization', in Dunja Brozović-Rončević and Enzo Caffarelli (eds.), *Denominando il mondo. Dal nome comune al nome proprio. Atti del simposio internazionale, Zara, 1–4 Settembre 2004./Naming the World. From Common Nouns to Proper Names. Proceedings from the International Symposium, Zadar, September 1st–4th, 2004*. Rome: Società Editrice Romana, 3–13.

Coates, Richard (2006a). 'Properhood', *Language* 82.2: 356–82.

Coates, Richard (2006b). 'Some Consequences and Critiques of the Pragmatic Theory of Properhood', *Onoma* 41: 27–44.

Coates, Richard (2006c). 'Chesterblade, Somerset, with a Reflection on the Element *chester*', *Journal of the English Place-Name Society* 38: 5–12.

Coates, Richard (2006d). 'Names', in Richard Hogg and David Denison (eds.), *A History of the English Language*. Cambridge: Cambridge University Press, 312–51.

Coates, Richard (2006e). 'Introduction', *Onoma* 41: 7–13.

Coates, Richard (2007). 'Microdialectological Investigations in the English South-East', *Locus Focus. Forum of the Sussex Place-Names Net* 7.1–2: 62–80.

Coates, Richard (2009a). 'A Natural History of Proper Naming in the Context of Emerging Mass Production. The Case of British Railway Locomotives', in Wolfgang Ahrens, Sheila Embleton, and André Lapierre (eds.), *Names in Multi-Lingual, Multi-Cultural and Multi-Ethnic Contact. Proceedings of the 23rd International Congress of Onomastic Sciences, August 17–22, 2008, York University, Toronto, Canada*. Toronto: York University, 209–27. Available online at: <http://yorkspace.library.yorku.ca/xmlui/bitstream/handle/10315/3641/icos23_209.pdf?sequence=1>.

Coates, Richard (2009b). 'A Strictly Millian Approach to the Definition of the Proper Name', *Mind and Language* 24.4: 433–44.

Coates, Richard (2011). 'The Sociolinguistic Context of Brunanburh', in Michael D. Livingston (ed.), *The Battle of Brunanburh. A Casebook*. Exeter: University of Exeter Press, 283–302.

Coates, Richard (2012a). 'To *þære fulan flóde. óf þære fulan flode*. On Becoming a Name in Easton and Winchester, Hampshire', in David Denison, Ricardo Bermúdez-Otero, Chris McCully, and Emma Moore (eds.), *Analysing Older English*. Cambridge: Cambridge University Press, 28–34.

Coates, Richard (2012b). 'A Toponomastic Contribution to the Linguistic Prehistory of the British Isles', *Nomina* 35: 49–102.

Coates, Richard (2012c). 'Eight Issues in the Pragmatic Theory of Properhood', *Acta Linguistica Lithuanica* 66: 119–40.

Coates, Richard (2013). 'Place-Names and Linguistics', in Jayne Carroll and David N. Parsons (eds.), *Perceptions of Place. Twenty-First Century Interpretations of English Place-Name Studies*. Nottingham: English Place-Name Society, 129–60.

Coates, Richard, and Breeze, Andrew, with a contribution by David Horovitz (2000). *Celtic Voices, English Places. Studies of the Celtic Impact on Place-Names in England*. Stamford: Shaun Tyas.

Cobb, H. S. (ed.) (1990). *The Overseas Trade of London, Exchequer Customs Accounts 1480–1*. London: London Record Society.

Cohen, Gillian (1990). 'Why is it Difficult to Put Names to Faces?', *British Journal of Psychology* 81: 287–97.

Cohen, Gillian (1994). 'Age-Related Problems in the Use of Proper Names in Communication', in Mary L. Hummert, John M. Wiemann, and John F. Nussbaum (eds.), *Interpersonal Communication in Older Adulthood*. London: Sage, 40–57.

Cohen, Gillian, and Burke, Deborah M. (1993). 'Memory for Proper Names. A Review', *Memory* 1: 249–63.

Cohen, Gillian, and Faulkner, Dorothy (1986). 'Memory for Proper Names. Age Difference in Retrieval', *British Journal of Developmental Psychology* 4: 187–97.

Cole, Peter (1974). 'Indefiniteness and Anaphoricity', *Language* 50.4: 665–74.

Colgrave, Bertram (ed. and trans.) (1956). *Felix's Life of Saint Guthlac*. Cambridge: Cambridge University Press.

Colgrave, Bertram, and Mynors, R. A. B. (eds.) (1969). *Bede's Ecclesiastical History of the English People*. Oxford: Clarendon Press.

Collier, George A., and Bricker, Victoria R. (1970). 'Nicknames and Social Structure in Zinacantan', *American Anthropologist* 72: 289–302.

Collingwood, R. G., and Wright, R. P. (1965). *The Roman Inscriptions of Britain*. Oxford: Clarendon Press.

Colman, Fran (1992). *Money Talks. Reconstructing Old English*. Trends in Linguistics. Studies and Monographs 56. The Hague: Mouton de Gruyter.

Colman, Fran (1996). 'Names Will Never Hurt Me', in M. J. Toswell and Elizabeth M. Tyler (eds.), *Studies in English Language and Literature. 'Doubt Wisely'. Papers in Honour of E. G. Stanley*. London and New York: Routledge, 13–28.

Commemorations of Saints in Scottish Place-Names (2010–13). Available online at: <http://www.saintsplaces.gla.ac.uk/>.

Copley, Gordon J. (1986). *Archaeology and Place-Names in the Fifth and Sixth Centuries*, BAR British Series 147. Oxford: British Archaeological Reports.

Copley, Gordon J. (1988). *Early Place-Names of the Anglian Regions of England*, BAR British Series 185. Oxford: British Archaeological Reports.

Corbett, John, McClure, J. Derrick, and Stuart-Smith, Jane (eds.) (2003). *The Edinburgh Companion to Scots*. Edinburgh: Edinburgh University Press.

Coromines, Joan (1989–97). *Onomasticon Cataloniae. Els noms De lloc i Noms de Persona de totes les Terres de Llengua Catalana*. 8 vols. Barcelona: Curia, Caixa d'Estalvis i Pensions de Barcelona, La Caixa.

Cosgrove, Denis (1985). 'Prospect, Perspective and the Evolution of the Landscape Idea', *Transactions of the Institute of British Geographers* 10.1: 45–62.

Costello, John, and Hughes, Terry (1976). *Concorde. The International Race for a Supersonic Passenger Transport*. London: Angus and Robertson.

Cotticelli Kurras, Paola (2007). 'Die Entwicklung der hybriden Wortschöpfungen bei den italienischen Markennamen', in Ludger Kremer and Elke Ronneberger-Sibold (eds.), *Names in Commerce and Industry. Past and Present*. Berlin: Logos, 167–85.

Cotticelli Kurras, Paola (2012). 'Assoziationen italienischer Markennamen im 20. Jahrhundert', in Holger Wochele, Julia Kuhn, and Martin Stegu (eds.), *Onomastics Goes Business. Role and Relevance of Brands, Company and Other Names in Economic Contexts*. Berlin: Logos, 53–67.

Cottle, Basil (1967). *The Penguin Dictionary of Surnames*. London: Penguin.

Coupland, Nikolas (2010). 'Welsh Linguistic Landscapes "From Above" and "From Below"', in Adam Jaworski and Crispin Thurlow (eds.), *Semiotic Landscapes. Language, Image, Space*. London: Continuum, 77–101.

Coupland, Nikolas, and Nussbaum, Jon F. (eds.) (1993). *Discourse and Lifespan Identity*. Newbury Park: Sage Publications.

Courtney, William Prideaux (1908). *The Secrets of our National Literature*. London: Archibald Constable.

Cox, Anna (2004). 'New Newtown Street Names Honour Artists', *The Star*, 6 February: 10.

Cox, Anna (2006). 'More Name Changes Soon', *Saturday Star*, 11 February: 2.

Cox, Anna (2008). 'Council to Rename 18 Joburg Streets After Stalwart', *The Star*, 10 September: 6.

Cox, Barrie (1972–3). 'The Significance of the Distribution of English Place-Names in -hām in the Midlands and East Anglia', *Journal of the English Place-Name Society* 5: 15–73. [reprinted in Cameron 1975, 55–98].

Cox, Barrie (1975–6). 'The Place-Names of the Earliest English Records', *Journal of the English Place-Name Society* 8: 12–66.

Cox, Barrie (1989). 'Rutland and the Scandinavian Settlements. The Place-Name Evidence', *Anglo-Saxon England* 18: 135–47.

Cox, Barrie (1989–90). 'Rutland in the Danelaw. A Field-Names Perspective', *Journal of the English Place-Name Society* 22: 7–22.

Cox, Barrie (1994). *English Inn and Tavern Names*. Nottingham: Centre for English Name Studies, University of Nottingham.

Cox, Barrie (2014). *The Place-Names of Leicestershire. Part 6*. English Place-Name Society 90. Nottingham: English Place-Name Society.

Cox, Richard A. V. (1997). 'Modern Scottish Gaelic Reflexes of Two Pictish Words: **pett* and **lannerc*', *Nomina* 20: 47–58.

Cox, Richard A. V. (2008). 'The Syntax of the Place-Names', in Katherine Forsyth (ed.), *Studies on the Book of Deer*. Dublin: Four Courts, 309–12.

Craigie, William A. (1897). 'Gaelic Words and Names in the Icelandic Sagas', *Zeitschrift für Celtische Philologie* 1: 439–54.

Crane, Susan (1997). 'Writing the Individual Back into Collective Memory', *The American Historical Review* 102.5: 1372–85.

Crawford, Osbert G. S. (1924). 'Place-Names and Archaeology', in Allen Mawer and Frank M. Stenton, *Introduction to the Survey of English Place-Names*. English Place-Name Society 1. Cambridge: Cambridge University Press, 143–64.

Cresswell, Tim (2004). *Place. A Short Introduction*. Melbourne: Blackwell.

Croft, William (1990). *Typology and Universals*. Cambridge: Cambridge University Press.

Croft, William (2001). *Radical Construction Grammar. Syntactic Theory in Typological Perspective*. Oxford: Oxford University Press.

CSD = Robinson, Mairi (ed.) (1985). *Concise Scots Dictionary*. Aberdeen: Aberdeen University Press.

Cullen, Paul (2013). 'Place-Names and Landscape Terminology', in Jayne Carroll and David N. Parsons (eds.) *Perceptions of Place. Twenty-First-Century Interpretations of English Place-Name Studies*. Nottingham: English Place-Name Society, 161–79.

Cullen, Paul, Jones, Richard, and Parsons, David N. (2011). *Thorps in a Changing Landscape*. Hatfield: University of Hertfordshire Press.

Curtin, Melissa (2014). 'Mapping Cosmopolitanisms in Taipei. Toward a Theorisation of Cosmopolitanism in Linguistic Landscape Research', *International Journal of the Sociology of Language* 228: 153–77.

Curtius, Ernst Robert (1953). *European Literature and the Latin Middle Ages*. London: Routledge and Kegan Paul.

Cushing, William (1886–8). *Initials and Pseudonyms. A Dictionary of Literary Disguises*. 2 vols. New York: T.Y. Crowell.

D'Anglure, Bernard Saladin (2010). 'Names and Naming', in Alan Barnard and Jonathan Spencer (eds.), *The Routledge Encyclopedia of Social and Cultural Anthropology*. 2nd edn. London: Routledge, 496–7.

d'Arbois de Jubainville, Henry (1890). *Recherches sur l'origine de la propriété foncière et des noms de lieux habités en France*. Paris: E. Thorin.

DAFN = Hanks, Patrick (ed.) (2003). *Dictionary of American Family Names*. 3 vols. New York: Oxford University Press.

Dahl, Roald (1982). *The BFG*. London: Jonathan Cape.

Dal Negro, Silvia (2009). 'Local Policy Modeling the Linguistic Landscape', in Elana Shohamy and Durk Gorter (eds.), *Linguistic Landscape. Expanding the Scenery*. Abingdon: Routledge, 206–18.

Dalberg, Vibeke (1985). 'On Homonymy Between Proper Name and Appellative', *Names* 33.3: 127–37.

Dalberg, Vibeke (2000). 'Apparently Identical Terms for "Personal By-name"', in Dieter Kremer and Rudolf Šrámek (eds.), *Onomastik. Akten des 18. Internationalen Kongresses für Namenforschung. Trier, 12.–17. April 1993*, vol. 2. Patronymica Romanica 15. Tübingen: Niemeyer, 36–40.

Dalberg, Vibeke (2008). 'The Role of Toponymic Analogy in the Reshaping of Place-Names', in Gillian Fellows-Jensen, et al. (eds.), *Vibeke Dalberg. Name and Place. Ten Essays on the Dynamics of Place-Names*. Copenhagen: Department of Scandinavian Research, University of Copenhagen, 68–78.

Dammel, Antje, Nübling, Damaris, and Schmuck, Mirjam (eds.) (2015). *Tiernamen—Zoonyme. Band 1. Haustiere* (Beiträge zur Namenforschung 50:1). Heidelberg: Winter.

Danesi, Marcel (2011). 'What's in a Brand Name? A Note on the Onomastics of Brand Naming', *Names* 59.3: 175–85.

Daniel, Samuel (1592). *Delia. Contayning certayne Sonnets: vvith the complaint of Rosamond*. London: Simon Waterson.

Daniell, William F. (1856). 'On the Ethnography of Akkrah and Adampe, Gold Coast, Western Africa', *Journal of the Ethnological Society of London* 4: 1–32.

Dareau, Margaret, and Macleod, Iseabail (2009). 'Dictionaries of Scots', in Anthony Paul Cowie (ed.), *The Oxford History of English Lexicography*, vol. 1. Oxford: Clarendon Press, 302–25.

Dauzat, Albert (1945). *Le Noms de Famille de France*. Paris: Payot.

Dauzat, Albert (1951). *Dictionnaire Étymologique de Noms de Famille et de Prénoms de France*. Paris: Larousse.

Dauzat, Albert, Deslandes, Gaston, and Rostaing, Charles (eds.) (1978). *Dictionnaire étymologique des noms de rivières et de montagnes en France*. Paris: Éditions Klincksieck.

Daveluy, Michelle, and Ferguson, Jenanne (2009). 'Scripted Urbanity in the Canadian North', *Journal of Linguistic Anthropology* 19.1: 78–100.

David I Chrs. = Barrow, Geoffrey W. S. (ed.) (1999). *The Charters of David I. The Written Acts of David I King of Scots, 1124-53, and of his son Henry, Earl of Northumberland, 1139-52*. Woodbridge: Boydell.

Davies, Hayley (2011). 'Sharing Surnames. Children, Family and Kinship', *Sociology* 45: 554–69.

Davies, Reginald T. (ed.) (1963). *Medieval English Lyrics. A Critical Anthology*. London: Faber.

Davis, P. (1999). 'What's the Fuss About?', *Sunday Tribune*, 4 April: 17.

Dawkins, Richard (2006). *The God Delusion*. London: The Bantam Press.

De Bruyn, P. S. (1997). 'Kommunikatiewe elemente in die name van strandhuise', *Nomina Africana* 11.1: 67–86.

de Fina, Anna, Schiffrin, Deborah, and Bamberg, Michael (eds.) (2006). *Discourse and Identity*. Cambridge: Cambridge University Press.

De Grave, Jean-Marc (2011). 'Naming as a Dynamic Process', *Indonesia and the Malay World* 39: 69–88.

de la Caille, Nicolas-Louis (1763). *Coelum Australe Stelliferum; seu observationes ad construendum stellarum Australium catalogum institutae*. Paris: Hipp, Guerin, et Delatour.

de Lagarde, Paul, Morin, Germain, and Adriaen, Marc (eds.) (1959). *S. Hieronymi presbyteri opera. Pars I: Opera exegetica 1. Hebraicae quaestiones in libro Geneseos; Liber interpretationis hebraicorum nominum; in Psalmos; Commentarius in Ecclesiasten.* Corpus Christianorum Series Latina 72. Turnhout: Brepols.

de Laguna, Federica (1972). *Under Mount St. Elias. The History and Culture of the Yakutat Tlingit.* Washington, DC: Smithsonian Institution Press.

De Quincey, Thomas (1849). 'The English Mail-Coach, or the Glory of Motion', *Blackwood's Magazine* (October). ed. Milton Haight Turk (2004). Available online at: <http://online-books.library.upenn.edu/webbin/gutbook/lookup?num=6359>. [accessed 31 July 2008].

de Stadler, Leon G. (1999). 'Changing your Name in South Africa. A Socio-Onomastic Perspective on a Troubled Society', in Dieter Kremer and Friedhelm Debus (eds.), *Onomastik. Akten des 18. Internationalen Kongresses für Namenforschung, Trier, 12.–17. April 1993*, vol. 3. Patronymica Romanica 16. Tübingen: Niemeyer.

De Stefani, Elwys (2004). 'I nomi propri nel parlati spontaneo. Aspetti interazionali', *Bulletin Suisse de Linguistique Appliquée* 80: 95–108.

De Stefani, Elwys (2007). 'Asphalttiger und Grossssstadt-Gazellen. Handelsnamen als sprachliche Ressourcen in Zeitungsberichten und im Gespräch', in Ludger Kremer and Elke Ronneberger-Sibold (eds.), *Names in Commerce and Industry. Past and Present.* Berlin: Logos, 233–57.

De Stefani, Elwys (2009a). 'Per un'onomastica interazionale. I nomi propri nella conversazione', *Rivista Italiana di Onomastica* 15.1: 9–40.

De Stefani, Elwys (2009b). 'Ortsnamen und Ortsbeschreibungen im Gespräch und deren Relevanz für die soziale Strukturierung einer alpinen Gemeinschaft', in Wolfgang Ahrens, Sheila Embleton, and André Lapierre (eds.), *Names in Multi-Lingual, Multi-Cultural and Multi-Ethnic Contact. Proceedings of the 23rd International Congress of Onomastic Sciences, August 17–22, 2008, York University, Toronto, Canada.* Toronto: York University, 298–310. Available online at: <http://yorkspace.library.yorku.ca/xmlui/bitstream/handle/10315/3959/icos23_298.pdf?sequence=1>.

De Stefani, Elwys (2009c). 'Spielen Warennamen bei der Kaufentscheidung eine Rolle? Eine Untersuchung spontaner Kundeninteraktion', in Eva Lavric, Fiorenza Fischer, Carmen Konzett, Julia Kuhn, and Holger Wochele (eds.), *People, Products, and Professions. Choosing a Name, Choosing a Language.* Frankfurt am Main: Peter Lang, 239–53.

De Stefani, Elwys, and Pepin, Nicolas (2006). 'Une approche interactionniste de l'étude des noms propres. Les surnoms de famille', *Onoma* 41: 131–62.

De Stefani, Elwys, and Pepin, Nicolas (2010). 'Eigennamen in der gesprochenen Sprache. Eine Einführung', in Nicolas Pepin and Elwys De Stefani (eds.), *Eigennamen in der gesprochenen Sprache.* Tübingen: Francke, 1–34.

De Stefani, Elwys, and Ticca, Anna Claudia (2011). 'Endonimi, esonimi e altre forme onimiche. Una verifica empirica', *Rivista Italiana di Onomastica* 17.2: 477–501.

Deane, Marion (2011). 'From Sacred Marriage to Clientship. A Mythical Account of the Establishment of Kingship as an Institution', in Roseanne Schot, Conor Newman, and Edel Bhreathnach (eds.), *Landscapes of Cult and Kingship.* Dublin: Four Courts, 1–21.

Debrabandere, Frans (1993). *Verklarend Woordenboek van de Familienamen in België en Noord-Frankrijk.* Brussels: Gemeentekrediet.

Debus, Friedhelm (1980). 'Onomastik', in Hans P. Althaus, Helmut Henne, and Herbert E. Wiegand (eds.), *Lexikon der germanistischen Linguistik*, vol. 2, rev. and enlarged ed. vollständig neu bearbeitete und erweiterte Aufl. Studienausgabe 1. Tübingen: Niemeyer, 187–98.

Debus, Friedhelm (1989). 'Namen in deutschen literarischen Texten des Mittelalters. Einführung in die Thematik', in Friedrich Debus and Horst Pütz (eds.), *Namen in deutschen literarischen Texten des Mittelalters. Vorträge, Symposion Kiel, 9.–12.9.1987.* Kieler Beiträge zur deutschen Sprachgeschichte 12. Neumünster: Wachholtz, 9–15.

Debus, Friedhelm (1995). 'Soziolinguistik der Eigennamen. Name und Gesellschaft (Sozio-Onomastik)', in Ernst Eichler, et al. (eds.), *Namenforschung/Name Studies/Les noms propres. Ein internationals Handbuch zur Onomastik/International Handbook of Onomastics/ Manuel international d'onomastique*, vol. 1. Berlin/New York: de Gruyter, 393–9.

Debus, Friedhelm (2002). *Namen in literarischen Werken. (Er–)Findung—Form—Funktion.* Akademie der Wissenschaften und der Literatur. Mainz/Stuttgart: Franz Steiner.

Debus, Friedhelm (2010). 'Zur Klassifikation und Terminologie der Namenarten', *Beiträge zur Namenforschung. Neue Folge* 45: 359–69.

Debus, Friedhelm (2012). *Namenkunde und Namengeschichte. Eine Einführung.* Grundlagen der Germanistik 51. Berlin: Erich Schmidt.

Debus, Friedhelm, and Seibicke, Wilfried (eds.) (1989). *Reader zur Namenkunde*, vol. 1. Hildesheim: Georg Olms.

DeFelice, Emidio (1978). *Dizionaro dei Cognomi Italiani.* Milan: Arnoldo Mondadori.

DeFelice, Emidio (1980). *I Cognomi Italiani.* Bologna: Il Mulino.

Del-Teso-Craviotto, Marisol (2008). 'Gender and Sexual Identity Authentication in Language Use. The Case of Chat Rooms', *Discourse Studies* 10: 251–70.

DeMain, Bill (2004). *In Their Own Words. Songwriters Talk about the Creative Process.* Westport, CT: Praeger.

Dendy Marshall, C. F. (1928). *Two Essays in Early Locomotive History.* London: Locomotive Publishing Co. Available online at: <http://www.steamindex.com/library/dendymar. htm#essays>.

Dendy Marshall, C. F. (1953). *History of the Railway Locomotive Down to the End of the Year 1831.* London: Locomotive Publishing Co.

Devolder, Patricia A., and Pressley, Michael (1991). 'Memory Complaints in Younger and Older Adults', *Applied Cognitive Psychology* 5: 443–54.

DFA = *Der Deutsche Familiennamenatlas* (n.d.). Namenforschung.net. Available online at: <http://www.namenforschung.net/dfa>.

Dickinson, Jennifer A. (2007). 'How Do You Write Yourself? How Do You Call Yourself?: Official and Unofficial Naming Practices in a Transcarpathian Ukrainian Village', *Anthropological Linguistics* 49: 118–41.

Dickinson, William (1819). *The History and Antiquities of The Town of Newark, in The County of Nottingham.* London: Holt and Hage.

DIL = Quinn, E. G., et al. (1913–76). *Dictionary of Irish Language Based Mainly on Old and Middle Irish Materials.* Dublin: Royal Irish Academy. Available online at: <http://edil.qub. ac.uk/dictionary/search.php>.

Dillon, Charles, and Jefferies, Henry A. (eds.). *Tyrone History and Society.* Dublin: Geography Publications.

Dimova, Slobodanka (2008). 'English in Macedonian Commercial Nomenclature', *World Englishes* 27.1: 83–100.

Dinneen, Patrick S. (1927). *Foclóir Gaedhilge agus Béarla. An Irish-English Dictionary,* Dublin: M. H. Gill and Son.

Dion, Kenneth L. (1983). 'Names, Identity, and Self', *Names* 31.4: 245–57.

Dittmaier, Heinrich (1963). *Rheinische Flurnamen.* Bonn: Roehrscheid.

Diver, Laura Carmel (2011). 'Bilingual Occitan Signage in Conflict. The Curious Case of Villeneuve-lès-Maguelone', *Onoma* 46: 275–99.

Dixon, Norman (1947). 'The Place-Names of Midlothian'. PhD dissertation, University of Edinburgh.

Djafarova, Elmira (2008). 'Why do Advertisers Use Puns? A Linguistic Perspective', *Journal of Advertising Research* 48.2: 267–75.

Djurberg, Daniel (1776). *Karta över Polynesien eller Femte Delen af Jordklotet af Daniel Djurberg, Ledamot af Cosmografiska Sällsk. I Upsala*. Stockholm: Säljes hos Bokhandlar en Holmberg.

Djurberg, Daniel, and Åkerman, Anders (1780). *Atlas Juvenilis eller Geographiska Chartor*. Stockholm.

Dmitriev, Valentin Grigorievich (1977). *Skryvshie svoie imia*. Moskva: Nauka.

Dobnig-Jülch, Edeltraud (1977). *Pragmatik und Eigennamen. Untersuchungen zur Theorie und Praxis der Kommunikation mit Eigennamen, besonders von Zuchttieren*. Reihe Germanistische Linguistik 9. Tübingen: Niemeyer.

Dobnig-Jülch, Edeltraud (1996). 'Namen von Haustieren und Zuchttieren', in Ernst Eichler, et al. (eds.) *Namenforschung/Name Studies/Les noms propres. Ein internationals Handbuch zur Onomastik/International Handbook of Onomastics/Manuel international d'onomastique*, vol. 2. Berlin/New York: de Gruyter, 1583–9.

Dodgson, John McNeal (1966). 'The Significance of the Distribution of the English Place-Name in -*ingas*, -*inga*- in South-East England', *Medieval Archaeology* 10: 1–29.

Dodgson, John McNeal (1970). *The Place-Names of Cheshire. Part 1*. English Place-Name Society 44. Cambridge: Cambridge University Press.

Dodgson, John McNeal (1973). 'Place-Names from *hām*, Distinguished from *hamm* Names, in Relation to the Settlement of Kent, Surrey and Sussex', *Anglo-Saxon England* 2: 1–50.

Dodiya, Jaydipsinh (2006). *Perspectives on Indian English Fiction*. New Delhi: Sarup and Sons.

Donne, John (1624). 'Devotions upon emergent occasions and seuerall steps in my sicknes', in *Meditation XVII*. London: Thomas Jones.

Donnellan, Keith (1972). 'Proper Names and Identifying Descriptions', in David Davidson and Gilbert Harman (eds.), *Semantics of Natural Language*. 2nd edn. Dordrecht/Boston: Reidel, 356–79.

Donnellan, Keith (1974). 'Speaking of Nothing', *The Philosophical Review* 83: 3–31.

Dorian, Nancy C. (1970). 'A Substitute Name System in the Scottish Highlands', *American Anthropologist. New Series* 72: 303–19.

Dorward, David (1978). *Scottish Surnames*. Edinburgh: Blackwood.

Dossena, Marina, and Lass, Roger (eds.) (2004). *Methods and Data in English Historical Dialectology*. Linguistic Insights: Studies in Language and Communication 16. Bern: Peter Lang.

DOST = Craigie, William, et al. (eds.) (1931–2002). *A Dictionary of the Older Scottish Tongue*. 12 vols. Oxford: Oxford University Press. Available online at: <http://www.dsl.ac.uk>.

Dowling, Grahame R. (1994). *Corporate Reputations. Strategies for Developing the Corporate Brand*. London: Kogan Page.

Downing, Pamela (1996). 'Proper Names as a Referential Option in English Conversation', in Barbara A. Fox (ed.), *Studies in Anaphora*. Amsterdam/Philadelphia: John Benjamins, 95–143.

Draper, Simon (2008). 'The Significance of OE *burh* in Anglo-Saxon England', *Anglo-Saxon Studies in Archaeology and History* 15: 240–53.

Draper, Simon (2011). 'Language and the Anglo-Saxon Landscape', in Nicholas J. Higham and Martin J. Ryan (eds.), *Place-Names, Language and the Anglo-Saxon Landscape.* Manchester: Manchester University Press, 85–104.

Draper, Simon (2012). '*Burh* Enclosures in Anglo-Saxon Settlements. Case-Studies in Wiltshire', in Richard Jones and Sarah Semple (eds.), *Sense of Place in Anglo-Saxon England.* Donington: Shaun Tyas, 334–51.

Drouin, Jeannine (1990). 'Variations sur les noms de chameaux dans la société touaregue (Niger)', in Eeva M. Närhi (ed.), *Proceedings of the XVIIth International Congress of Onomastic Sciences. Helsinki 13–18 August 1990*, vol. 1. Helsinki: University of Helsinki and The Finnish Research Centre for Domestic Languages, 276–83.

Drummond, Peter (2007a). *Scottish Hill Names. The Origin and Meaning of the Names of Scotland's Hills and Mountains.* Glasgow: Scottish Mountaineering Trust.

Drummond, Peter (2007b). 'Southern Scottish Hill Generics. Testing the Gelling and Cole Hypothesis', *Nomina* 30: 85–100.

Drummond, Peter (2009). 'Place-Name Losses and Changes—A Study in Peeblesshire. A Comparative Study of Hill-Names and Other Toponyms', *Nomina* 32: 5–17.

DSÅ = Kousgård Sørensen, John (1968–96). *Danske sø- og ånavne.* 8 vols. Navnestudier udg. af Institut for Navneforskning 6, 12, 15, 21, 24, 28, 29, 35. København: C.A. Reitzels.

DSL = Dictionary of the Scots Language (n.d.). Available online at: <http://www.dsl.ac.uk/>.

Du Plessis, Theodorus (2009). 'Language Visibility and the Transformation of Geographical Names in South Africa', *Language Matters. Studies in the Languages of Africa* 40.2: 215–38.

Du Plessis, Theodorus (2012). 'The Role of Language Policy in Linguistic Landscape Changes in a Rural Area of the Free State Province of South Africa', *Language Matters. Studies in the Languages of Africa* 43.2: 263–82.

Du Plessis, Theodorus (2013). 'Language Conflict and Change in Language Visibility in South Africa's Free State Province Number Plate Case', *Language Matters. Studies in the Languages of Africa* 44.3: 126–48.

Du Rietz, Rolf (1961). 'Daniel Djurbergs namn på Australien', *Ymer* 2: 81–100.

Duchaj, Karen A., and Ntihirageza, Jeanine (2009). 'The Power of Names among Burundian Refugees in Tanzania', in Wolfgang Ahrens, Sheila Embleton, and André Lapierre (eds.), *Names in Multi-Lingual, Multi-Cultural and Multi-Ethnic Contact. Proceedings of the 23rd International Congress of Onomastic Sciences, August 17–22, 2008, York University, Toronto, Canada.* Toronto: York University, 337–45. Available online at: <http://yorkspace.library.yorku.ca/xmlui/bitstream/handle/10315/3962/icos23_337.pdf?sequence=1>.

Dugdale, William (1656). *The Antiquities of Warwickshire.* London: Thomas Warren.

Duncan, Lilian (ed. and trans.) (1932). 'Altram Tige Dá Medar', *Ériu* 11: 184–225.

Dunkling, Leslie (1971). *English House Names.* Woking: The Gresham Press.

Dunkling, Leslie, and Wright, Gordon (1987). *A Dictionary of Pub Names.* London: Routledge and Keegan Paul.

Duranti, Alessandro (1997). *Linguistic Anthropology.* Cambridge: Cambridge University Press.

Eckert, Penelope (2008). 'Variation and the Indexical Field', *Journal of Sociolinguistics* 12.4: 453–76.

Eckert, Penelope, and McConnell-Ginet, Sally (1992). 'Think Practically and Look Locally. Language and Gender as Community-Based Practice', *Annual Review of Anthropology* 21: 461–90.

Edelman, Loulou (2009). 'What's in a Name? Classification of Proper Names by Language', in Elana Shohamy and Durk Gorter (eds.), *Linguistic Landscape. Expanding the Scenery*. Abingdon: Routledge, 141–54.

Edelman, Loulou, and Gorter, Durk (2010). 'Linguistic Landscapes and the Market', in Helen Kelly-Holmes and Gerlinde Mautner (eds.), *Language and the Market*. Basingstoke: Palgrave Macmillan, 96–108.

Edwards, Adam (2008). 'House Names. Playing the Naming Game', *The Telegraph*, 12 November. Availale online at: <http://www.telegraph.co.uk/finance/property/3446023/House-names-Playing-the-naming-game.html> [accessed 12 Feb 2012].

Edwards, John (2009). *Language and Identity*. Cambridge: Cambridge University Press.

Edwards, Rosalind, and Caballero, Chamion (2008). 'What's in a Name? An Exploration of the Significance of Personal Naming of "mixed" Children for Parents from Different Racial, Ethnic and Faith Backgrounds', *The Sociological Review* 56.1: 39–60.

Egeberg, Torben (2004). 'Høje og hjulspor i tusindvis. Færdsel i det jyske landskab', *FRAM* 2004: 44–51.

Egli, Johann Jacob (1876). *Nomina geographica*. Leipzig: Friedrich Brandstetter.

Eichler, Ernst (1981). 'Alte Gewässernamen zwischen Ostsee und Erzgebirge. Mit einem Anhang', *Beiträge zur Namenforschung (Neue Folge)* 16: 40–54.

Eichler, Ernst, and Walther, Hans (1986). *Städtenamenbuch der DDR*. Leipzig: VEB Bibliographisches Institut.

Eichler, Ernst, Hilty, Gerold, Löffler, Heinrich, Steger, Hugo, and Zgusta, Ladislav (eds.) (1995–6). *Namenforschung/Name Studies/Les noms propres. Ein internationals Handbuch zur Onomastik/International Handbook of Onomastics/Manuel international d'onomastique*. 3 vols. Berlin/New York: de Gruyter.

EIHM = O'Rahilly, Thomas F. (1946). *Early Irish History and Mythology*. Dublin: Dublin Institute for Advanced Studies.

Eis, Gerhard (1970). 'Über die Namen im Kriminalroman der Gegenwart', in Gerhard Eis (ed.), *Vom Zauber der Namen. Vier Essays*. Berlin: Erich Schmidt, 59–92.

Eisenhauer, Brian, Krannich, Richard, and Blahna, Dale (2000). 'Attachments to Special Places on Public Lands: An Analysis of Activities, Reason for Attachments and Community Connections', *Society and Natural Resources* 13: 421–41.

Ejder, Bertil (1950). 'Något om namnen på våra slott och herrgårdar', *Ortnamnssällskapets i Uppsala årsskrift*: 19–34.

Ekre, Lars (1960). *Opplysningar til stadnamn frå Midt-Jotunheimen og tilgrensande bygder*. Skrifter frå Norsk stadnamnarkiv 1. Oslo/Bergen: Universitetsforlaget.

Ekwall, Eilert (1917). *Contributions to the History of Old English Dialects*. Lund: C.W.K. Gleerup.

Ekwall, Eilert (1928). *English River-Names*. Oxford: Clarendon Press.

Ekwall, Eilert (1947). *The Concise Oxford Dictionary of English Place-Names*. Oxford: Oxford University Press.

Ekwall, Eilert (1960). *The Concise Oxford Dictionary of English Place-Names*. 4th edn. Oxford: Clarendon Press.

Ellen, R. F. (1983). 'Semantic Anarchy and Ordered Social Practice in Nuaulu Personal Naming', *Bijdragen tot de Taal-, Land- en Volkenkunde* 139: 18–45.

Eller, Nicole, Hackl, Stefan, and L'upták, Marek (eds.) (2008). *Namen und ihr Konfliktpotential im europäischen Kontext*. Regensburg: Edition Vulpes.

Elmevik, Lennart (2004). 'Über die *-n-* und *-sn-* Suffixe in nordischen Appellativen und Ortsnamen', in Thorsten Andersson and Eva Nyman (eds.), *Suffixbildungen in alten*

Ortsnamen. Akten eines internationalen Symposiums in Uppsala 14.–16. Mai 2004. Acta Academiae Regiae Gustavi Adolphi 88. Uppsala: Kungl. Gustav Adolfs Akademien för Svensk Folkkultur, 45–59.

Elmevik, Lennart (2010). 'Rekonstruktion von Wörtern aus Ortsnamen. Einige Bemerkungen zur Beleuchtung eines Problemkomplexes', in Lennart Elmevik and Svante Strandberg (eds.), *Probleme der Rekonstruktion untergegangener Wörter aus alten Eigennamen. Akten eines internationalen Symposiums in Uppsala 7.–9. April 2010.* Acta Academiae Regiae Gustavi Adolphi 112. Uppsala: Kungl. Gustav Adolfs Akademien för Svensk Folkkultur, 25–35.

Elmevik, Lennart, and Strandberg, Svante (eds.) (2010). *Probleme der Rekonstruktion untergegangener Wörter aus alten Eigennamen. Akten eines internationalen Symposiums in Uppsala 7.–9. April 2010.* Acta Academiae Regiae Gustavi Adolphi 112. Uppsala: Kungl. Gustav Adolfs Akademien för Svensk Folkkultur.

Embleton, Sheila (1990). 'The Use of Titles in Business Names', in Eeva M. Närhi (ed.), *Proceedings of the XVIIth International Congress of Onomastic Sciences. Helsinki 13–18 August 1990*, vol. 2. Helsinki: University of Helsinki and The Finnish Research Centre for Domestic Languages, 300–6.

Embleton, Sheila, and Lapierre, André (1997). 'Commercial Aircraft Naming. History of Naming of Means of Transport', in Ritva Liisa Pitkänen and Kaija Mallat (eds.), *You Name It. Perspectives on Onomastic Research*. Helsinki: Finnish Literature Society, 217–36.

Emmelheinz, Celia (2012). 'Naming a New Self. Identity Elasticity and Self-Definition in Voluntary Name Changes', *Names* 60.3: 156–65.

Enfield, Nicholas J., and Stivers, Tanya (eds.) (2007). *Person Reference in Interaction. Linguistic, Cultural and Social Perspectives*. Cambridge: Cambridge University Press.

Engels, Friedrich (1945). *Die Lage der arbeitenden Klasse in England*. Leipzig: Otto Wigand.

Entrikin, J. Nicholas (1991). *The Betweenness of Place. Towards a Geography of Modernity*. Baltimore: Johns Hopkins University Press.

Eogan, George (1986). *Knowth and the Passage-Tombs of Ireland*. London: Thames and Hudson.

Erickson, Paul A., and Murphy, Liam D. (2013). *A History of Anthropological Theory*. 4th edn. Toronto: University of Toronto Press.

Eriksen, Thomas Hylland (2004). *What Is Anthropology?* London: Pluto Press.

Eriksen, Thomas Hylland (2010). *Small Places, Large Issues*. 3rd edn. London: Pluto Press.

Ernst, Peter (2010). 'Onomastische Motivationsforschung. Vom Beschreiben zum Erklären', *Onoma* 45: 61–78.

Erskine, David (ed.) (1953). *Augustus Hervey's Journal*. London: William Kimber.

Erwin, Philip (1995). 'A Review of the Effects of Personal Name Stereotypes', *Representative Research in Social Psychology* 20.7: 41–52.

Estonian Place Names Act (2003). Transl. Estonian Legal Language Centre (Eesti Õiguskeele Keskus, <http://www.legaltext.ee>). Available online at: <https://unstats.un.org/unsd/geo-info/UNGEGN/docs/NNA/Estonia_Place%20Names%20Act_English.pdf>.

Evans, Estyn (1966). *Prehistoric and Early Christian Ireland. A Guide*. London: Batsford.

Evans, Gareth (1982). *The Varieties of Reference*. New York: Oxford University Press.

Evans, G. Blakemore (ed.) (1997). *The Riverside Shakespeare*. 2nd edn. Boston: Houghton Mifflin.

Evans, Ivor H. (rev.) (1993). *The Wordsworth Dictionary of Phrase and Fable*. Hertfordshire: Wordsworth Editions.

Evans-Pritchard, E. E. (1946). 'Topographical Terms in Common Use among the Bedouin of Cyrenaica', *The Journal of the Royal Anthropological Institute of Great Britain and Ireland* 76: 177–88.

Evans-Wentz, W. Y. (1911). *The Fairy Faith in Celtic Countries*. London/New York: H. Frowde.

Everett, Walter (2000). 'The Learned vs. the Vernacular in the Songs of Billy Joel', *Contemporary Music Review* 18.4: 105–29.

Everett-Heath, John (2005). *The Concise Dictionary of World Place-Names*. Oxford: Oxford University Press.

Evrard, Muriel (2002). 'Ageing and Lexical Access to Common and Proper Names in Picture Naming', *Brain and Language* 81: 174–9.

Ewald, Petra, and Klager, Christian (2007). 'Namen von Zootieren. Zum Wesen und Gebrauch einer vernachlässigten Namenklasse', *Beiträge zur Namenforschung* 42: 325–45.

Ewen, Cecil L'Estrange (1931). *A History of Surnames in the British Isles*. London: Kegan Paul.

Ewen, Cecil L'Estrange (1938). *A Guide to the Origin of British Surnames*. London: Kegan Paul.

Fairclough, Norman (1995). *Critical Discourse Analysis. The Critical Study of Language*. London/New York: Longman.

Falk, Avner (1975–6). 'Identity and Name Changes', *The Psychoanalytic Review* 62.4: 647–57.

FamilySearch (2012). 'International Genealogical Index'. Available online at: <https://family-search.org/search/collection/igi> [accessed from 1 November 2010–30 March 2014].

Fan, Ying (2006). 'Branding the Nation. What is Being Branded?', *Journal of Vacation Marketing* 12.1: 5–14.

Faraco, J. Carlos González, and Murphy, Michael D. (1997). 'Street Names and Political Regimes in an Andalusian Town', *Ethnology* 36: 123–48.

Farø, Ken (2005). 'Hvem er egentlig Hade Hanne? Mediale tilnavne i dansk', *Studia anthroponymica Scandinavica* 23: 53–70.

Faull, Margaret L. (1975). 'The Semantic Development of Old English *Wealh*', *Leeds Studies in English (New Series)* 8: 20–44.

Felecan, Oliviu (2008). 'I nomi delle istituzioni Romene dopo il 1989', in Donatella Bremer, Michele Bani, Franco Belli, and Matteo Paolini (eds.), *I Nomi Nel Tempo e Nello Spazio. Atti del XXII Congresso Internazionale di Scienze Onomastiche. Pisa, 28 agosto–4 settembre 2005*, vol. 2. Pisa: Edizioni ETS, 579–93.

Fellows Jensen, Gillian (1972). *Scandinavian Settlement Names in Yorkshire*. Copenhagen: Akademisk Forlag.

Fellows-Jensen, Gillian (1983). 'Anthroponymical Specifics in Place-Names in -*bý* in the British Isles'. *Studia Anthroponymica Scandinavica* 1: 45–60.

Fellows-Jensen, Gillian (1985). *Scandinavian Settlement Names in the North-West*. Copenhagen: C.A. Reitzels.

Fellows-Jensen, Gillian (1989–90). 'Scandinavians in Southern Scotland?', *Nomina* 13: 41–60.

Fellows-Jensen, Gillian (1990). 'Scandinavian Personal Names in Foreign Fields', in Pierre Chaunu (ed.), *Recueil d'études en homage à Lucien Musset*. Cahier des Annales de Normandie 23. Caen: Musée de Normandie, 149–59.

Fellows-Jensen, Gillian (1995). 'The Light Thrown by the Early Place-Names of Southern Scandinavia and England on Population Movement in the Migration Period', in Edith Marold and Christiane Zimmermann (eds.), *Nordwestgermanisch*. Ergänzungsbände zum Reallexikon der Germanischen Altertumskunde 13. Berlin/New York: de Gruyter, 57–76.

Fellows-Jensen, Gillian (1996). 'Doddington Revisited', *NOWELE* 28/29: 361–76.

Fellows-Jensen, Gillian (1998). 'The Origin and Development of the Name York', in D. W. Rollason, with Derek Gore and Gillian Fellows-Jensen (eds.), *Sources for York History to AD 1100*. The Archaeology of York 1. York: York Archaeological Trust, 226–37.

Fellows-Jensen, Gillian (2006). 'On the Dating of Place-Names in -bý in England and Scotland and of the Settlements Bearing These Names', in Eva Brylla and Mats Wahlberg (eds.), *Proceedings of the 21st International Congress of Onomastic Sciences Uppsala, 19–24 August 2002*, vol. 2. Uppsala: Språk- och folkminnesinstitutet, 96–104.

Fellows-Jensen, Gillian (2007). 'The Scandinavian Element *gata* Outside the Urbanised Settlements of the Danelaw', in Beverley Ballin Smith, Simon Taylor, and Gareth Williams (eds.), *West Over Sea. Studies in Scandinavian Sea-Borne Expansion and Settlement Before 1300. A Festschrift in Honour of Dr Barbara E. Crawford*. Leiden: Brill, 445–59.

Fellows-Jensen, Gillian (2008). 'Scandinavian Place Names in the British Isles', in Stefan Brink (ed.), *The Viking World*. Abingdon: Routledge, 391–400.

Fellows-Jensen, Gillian (2009). 'A Few More Words on Place-Names in *thorp* in England', in Peder Dam, et al. (eds.), *Torp som ortnamn och bebyggelse*. Skrifter utgivna av Dialekt- och ortnamnsarkivet i Lund 11. Lund: Institutet för språk och folkminnen, Dialekt- och ortnamnsarkivet i Lund, 43–53.

Fellows-Jensen, Gillian (2012). 'Grimston and Grimsby. The Danes as Re-Namers', in Richard Jones and Sarah Semple (eds.), *Sense of Place in Anglo-Saxon England*. Donington: Shaun Tyas, 352–63.

Fellows-Jensen, Gillian (2014). 'Bursting the Bounds of the Danelaw', in Gale Owen-Crocker and Susan D. Thomson (eds.), *Towns and Topography. Essays in Memory of David Hill*. Oxford: Oxbow Books.

Fenwick, Carolyn C. (ed.) (1998–2005). *The Poll Taxes of 1377, 1379 and 1381*. Parts 1–3. Oxford: Oxford University Press.

Ferreira, Catarina S., Marful, Alejandra, and Bajo, Teresa (2014). 'Interference Resolution in Face Perception and Name Retrieval', *Acta Psychologica* 153: 120–8.

Fery, Patrick, Vincent, Eric, and Brédart, Serge (1995). 'Personal Name Anomia. A Single-Case Study', *Cortex* 31: 191–8.

Fezer, Karl-Heinz (2005). 'Die Marke als Markenformat—Baustein einer Theorie der variablen Marke', *sic!* Sondernummer: 9–16.

Field, John (1989). *A Dictionary of English Field Names*. Gloucester: Sutton.

Fillitz, Thomas (2002). 'The Notion of Art. From Regional to Distant Comparison', in André Gingrich and Richard G.Fox (eds.), *Anthropology, by Comparison*. London: Routledge, 204–24.

Finch, Janet (2008). 'Naming Names. Kinship, Individuality and Personal Names', *Sociology* 42: 709–25.

Finkenstaedt, Thomas (1963). You *and thou. Studien zur Anrede im Englischen*. Berlin: Walter de Gruyter.

Finsterwalder, Karl (1978). *Tiroler Namenkunde*. Innsbruck: Institut für Deutsche Philologie.

Finsterwalder, Karl (1990–5). *Tiroler Ortsnamenkunde*. 3 vols. Innsbruck: Wagner.

FIONTAR (2008–14a). = *Logainm.ie. Place-Names Database of Ireland*. Available online at: <http://www.logainm.ie>.

FIONTAR (2008–14b). = 'Cill Fhionnúrach'. *Logainm.ie. Place-Names Database of Ireland*. Available online at: <www.logainm.ie/1416513.aspx>.

FIONTAR (2008–14c). = 'Cnoc Fhionnúrach'. *Logainm.ie. Place-Names Database of Ireland*. Available online at: <http://www.logainm.ie/30840.aspx>.

Fischer, Fiorenza (2007). 'Produktnamen und Information—cui prodest nomen?', in Ludger Kremer and Elke Ronneberger-Sibold (eds.), *Names in Commerce and Industry. Past and Present*. Berlin: Logos, 141–52.

Fischer, Fiorenza (2010). 'Mergers and Acquisitions und Unternehmensnamen', *Onoma* 43: 231–350.

Fischer, Fiorenza, and Wochele, Holger (2014). 'Namenwahrnehmung im Alltagsleben: Unternehmensnamen im Spannungsfeld zwischen nationaler und europäischer Identität', in Joan Tort i Donada and Montserrat Montagut i Montagut (eds.), *Els noms en la vida quotidiana. Actes del XXIV Congrés Internacional d'ICOS sobre Ciències Onomàstiques. Names in Daily Life. Proceedings of the XXIV ICOS International Congress of Onomastic Sciences.* Generalitat de Catalunya, Departament de Cultura. Available online at: <http://llengua.gencat.cat/ca/serveis/informacio_i_difusio/publicacions_en_linia/btpl_col/actes_icos>.

Fischer, Henry G. (1977). 'More Ancient Egyptian Names of Dogs and Other Animals', *Metropolitan Museum Journal* 12: 173–8.

Fisiak, Jacek (1990). '*Domesday Book* and Late Old English Dialects', in Henning Andersen and Konrad Koerner (eds.), *Historical Linguistics, 1987. Papers from the 8th International Conference on Historical Linguistics (8 ICHL): Lille, 31 August–4 September 1987.* Amsterdam: John Benjamins, 107–28.

Flamsteed, John (1725 [1712]). *Historia celestis Britannica tribus voluminibus contenta.* London: H. Meere.

Flanagan, Deirdre (1981–2). 'A Summary Guide to the More Commonly Attested Ecclesiastical Elements in Place-Names', *The Bulletin of the Ulster Place-Name Society* 4: 69–75.

Flanagan, Deirdre (1984). 'The Christian Impact on Early Ireland. Place-Names Evidence', in Próinséas Ní Chatháin and Michael Richter (eds.), *Ireland and Europe. The Early Church*, Stuttgart: Klett-Cotta, 25–42.

Flanagan, Deirdre, and Flanagan, Laurence (1994). *Irish Place Names.* Dublin: Gill and Macmillan.

Flight International (1976). 'Tornado Production Go-Ahead?', *Flight International*, 20 March: 682.

Flight International (1980). 'F-16 Named', *Flight International*, 2 August: 406.

Flight International (1984). 'Fefa is Efa', *Flight International*, 17 March: 668.

Flowerdew, John (2014). 'Introduction. Discourse in Context', in John Flowerdew (ed.), *Discourse in Context.* London: Bloomsbury, 1–25.

Foakes, Reginald A. (ed.) (1997). *King Lear.* The Arden Shakespeare Third Series. London: Bloomsbury.

Fochuk, Stephen M. (1999). *Metal Canvas. Canadians and World War II Nose Art.* St. Catharines, ON: Vanwell.

Fogler, Kethera A., and James, Lori E. (2007). 'Charlie Brown versus Snow White. The Effects of Descriptiveness on Young and Older Adults' Retrieval of Proper Names', *Journal of Gerontology Series B (Psychological Sciences)* 62: 201–7.

Fogler, Kethera A., James, Lori E., and Crandall, Elizabeth A. (2010). 'How Name Descriptiveness Impacts Proper Name Learning in Young and Older Adults', *Aging, Neuropsychology and Cognition* 17: 505–18.

Foley, Claire, and McHugh, Ronan (eds.) (2014). *An Archaeological Survey of County Fermanagh.* 2 vols. Belfast: NIEA.

Footitt, Hilary, and Baker, Catherine (2012). 'Fraternization', in Hilary Footitt and Michael Kelly (eds.), *Languages at War. Policies and Practices of Language Contacts in Conflict.* Basingstoke: Palgrave Macmillan, 139–62.

Ford, Boris (ed.) (1970). *The Modern Age, James to Eliot.* The Pelican Guide to English Literature 7. Harmondsworth: Penguin.

Förstemann, Ernst (1967). *Altdeutsches Namenbuch*, vol. 2. München: Fink.

Forster, Klaus (1986). *A Pronouncing Dictionary of English Place-Names Including Standard Local and Archaic Variants*. London: Routledge and Kegan Paul.

Forsyth, J. W. (1967). 'Tasman, Abel Janszoon (1603–1659)'. *Australian Dictionary of Biography*, vol. 2. Melbourne: Melbourne University Press. Available in an electronic format at: <http://adb.anu.edu.au/biography/tasman-abel-janszoon-2716>.

Forsyth, Katherine (ed.) (2008). *Studies on the Book of Deer*. Dublin: Four Courts.

Fowler, Alastair (2012). *Literary Names. Personal Names in English Literature*. Oxford: Oxford University Press.

Fox, J. R. (1963). 'Structure of Personal Names on Tory Island', *Man* 63: 153–5.

Fox, Sue (2012). 'Cockney', in Alexander Bergs and Laurel Brinton (eds.), *English Historical Linguistics. An International Handbook*, vol. 2. Berlin: Mouton de Gruyter, 2013–31.

Frake, Charles O. (1996). 'Pleasant Places, Past Times, and Sheltered Identity in Rural East Anglia', in Steven Feld and Keith H. Basso (eds.), *Senses of Place*. Santa Fe, CA: School of American Research Press, 229–57.

Fründén, Märit (2010). *'Att blotta vem jag är' Släktnamnsskick och släktnamnsbyten hos samer i Sverige 1920–2009*. Uppsala: Uppsala University.

Fründén, Marit (2013). 'Samiska ortnamn', in Staffan Nyström, et al. (eds.), *Namn och namnforskning. Ett levande läromedel om ortnamn, personnamn och andra namn*. Uppsala: Uppsala universitetet, 92–4. Available online at: <http://www.diva-portal.org/smash/get/diva2:606610/FULLTEXT01.pdf>.

Fransson, Gustav (1935). *Middle English Surnames of Occupation 1100–1350*. Lund: C.W.K. Gleerup.

Franzén, Gösta (1964). *Laxdœlabygdens ortnamn*. Acta Academiae Regiae Gustavi Adolphi 42. Uppsala: Kungl. Gustav Adolfs Akademien för Svensk Folkkultur.

Fraser, C. M. (ed.) (1991). *Durham Quarter Sessions Rolls 1471–1625*, vol. 119. Newcastle upon Tyne: Surtees Society.

Fraser, George MacDonald (1971). *The Steel Bonnets. Story of the Anglo-Scottish Border Reivers*. London: Barrie and Jenkins.

Fraser, Ian (1970). 'Place-Names from Oral Tradition—An Informant's Repertoire', *Scottish Studies* 14: 192–7.

Fraser, Ian (1977). 'The Onomastician Afield', *Nomina* 1: 37–43.

Fraser, Ian (1980). 'The Scottish Place-Name Survey. Recording Place-Names from Oral Tradition', *Scottish Literary Journal*, Supplement 10: 19–24.

Frazer, J. G. (2004 [1890]). *The Golden Bough*. Edinburgh: Canongate.

Frege, Gottlob (1892). 'Über Sinn und Bedeutung', *Zeitschrift für Philosophie und philosophische Kritik (Neue Folge)* 100: 25–50.

Frege, Gottlob (1970). 'On Sense and Reference', trans. by Max Black, in Peter Geach and Max Black (eds. and trans.), *Translations from the Philosophical Writings of Gottlob Frege*. 2nd edn. Oxford: Blackwell, 56–78.

Fridell, Staffan (1998). '*Hulundsfarahult, Hulingsryd* och *Hultsfred*', *Namn och bygd* 86: 17–24.

Fritzsche, Jörg (2008). 'Namenkonflikte im europäischen Kennzeichenrecht', in Nicole Eller, Stefan Hackl, and Marek Ľupták (eds.), *Namen und ihr Konfliktpotential im europäischen Kontext*. Regensburg: Edition Vulpes, 309–32.

Frolova, E. L. (2008). 'Ethnic and Cultural Functions of Name in Traditional Japanese Society', *Archaeology Ethnology and Anthropology of Eurasia* 35: 105–12.

Fulk, R. D., Robert E. Bjork and John D. Niles (eds.) (2008). *Klaeber's Beowulf and the Fight at Finnsburg*. 4th edn. Toronto: University of Toronto Press.

Gaelic Language (Scotland) Act 2005 asp 7 (2005). Available online at: <http://www.legislation. gov.uk/asp/2005/7/contents>.

Galas, Piotr (1968). 'Nazwy krów z przyrostkiem –ula w powiecie Bocheńskim', in Stefan Hrabec (ed.), *Symbolae philologicae in honorem Vitoldi Taszycki*. Wrocław: Polska Akademia Nauk, 85–90.

Galasiński, Dariusz, and Skowronek, Katarzyna (2001). 'Naming the Nation. A Critical Analysis of Names in Polish Political Discourse', *Political Communication* 18: 51–66.

Gallagher, Catherine (1994). *Nobody's Story. The Vanishing Acts of Women Writers in the Marketplace 1670–1820*. Oxford: Clarendon Press.

Gammeltoft, Peder (2005). '"Look Now, Stranger, at this Island". A Brief Survey of the Island-Names of Shetland and Orkney', in Andras Mortensen and Símun V. Arge (eds.), *Viking and Norse in the North Atlantic. Selected Papers from the Proceedings of the Fourteenth Viking Congress, Tórshavn, 19–30 July 2001*. Tórshavn: Føroya Fróðskaparfelag, 257–63.

Gammeltoft, Peder, and Egeberg, Torben (2006). *Stednavne i Egvad Sogn—en forsknings- og forvaltningsrapport*. Skjern/Copenhagen. Available online at: <http://nfi.ku.dk/ publikationer/webpublikationer/egvad>.

Gardiner, Alan (1954). *The Theory of Proper Names*. 2nd edn. London: Oxford University Press.

Garfinkel, Harvey (1967). *Studies in Ethnomethodology*. Englewood Cliffs, NJ: Prentice-Hall.

Garovi, Angelo (2010). 'Probleme bei der Festlegung der Schreibweise von Lokalnamen auf amtlichen Karten der Schweiz', *Onoma* 45: 79–86.

Garvin, Rebecca Todd (2010). 'Responses to the Linguistic Landscape in Memphis, Tennessee. An Urban Space in Transition', in Elana Shohamy, Eliezer Ben-Rafael, and Monica Barni (eds.), *Linguistic Landscape in the City*. Bristol: Multilingual Matters, 252–71.

Gary-Prieur, Marie-Noëlle (1994). *Grammaire du Nom Propre*. Paris: Presses Universitaires de France.

Gatson, Sarah N. (2011). 'Self-Naming Practices on the Internet. Identity, Authenticity, and Community', *Cultural Studies <=> Critical Methodologies* 11: 224–35.

Geach, Peter (1957). *Mental Acts*. London: Routledge and Kegan Paul.

Gebauer, Jochen E., Riketta, Michael, Broemer, Philip, and Maio, Gregory R. (2008). '"How Much do you Like your Name?" An Implicit Measure of Global Self-Esteem', *Journal of Experimental Social Psychology* 44: 1346–54.

Gebauer, Jochen E., Leary, Mark R., and Neberich, Wiebke (2011). 'Unfortunate First Names. Effects of Name-Based Relational Devaluation and Interpersonal Neglect', *Social Psychological and Personality Science* 3.5: 590–6.

Geertz, Clifford (1973). 'Person, Time and Conduct in Bali', in Clifford Geertz (ed.), *The Interpretation of Cultures*. New York: Basic Books, 360–411.

Geertz, Hildred, and Geertz, Clifford (1964). 'Teknonymy in Bali. Parenthood, Age-Grading and Genealogical Amnesia', *Man* 94.2: 94–108.

Gehweiler, Elke (2008). 'From Proper Name to Primary Interjection. The Case of Gee!', *Journal of Historical Pragmatics* 9.1: 71–93.

Geissler, Friedrich (1669). *De nominum mutatione et anonymis scriptoribus*. Leipzig: J.E. Hahn.

Gelling, Margaret (1953–4). *The Place-Names of Oxfordshire. Parts 1–2*. English Place-Name Society 23–24. Cambridge: Cambridge University Press.

Gelling, Margaret (1967). 'English Place-Names Derived from the Compound *wīchām*', *Medieval Archaeology* 11: 87–104.

Gelling, Margaret (1976). *The Place-Names of Berkshire. Part 3*. English Place-Name Society 51. Cambridge: Cambridge University Press.

Gelling, Margaret (1997). *Signposts to the Past.* 3rd edn. Chichester: Phillimore.

Gelling, Margaret (1984). *Place-Names in the Landscape. The Geographical Roots of Britain's Place-Names.* London: Dent.

Gelling, Margaret (2005). 'Seenamen 3a', *Reallexikon der Germanischen Altertumskunde.* 2nd edn, vol. 28: 45–47.

Gelling, Margaret (2009). 'The Word *church* in English Place-Names', in Eleanor Quinton (ed.), *The Church in English Place-Names.* Nottingham: English Place-Name Society, 7–14.

Gelling, Margaret, and Cole, Ann (2000). *The Landscape of Place-Names.* Stamford: Shaun Tyas.

General Register Office for Scotland (2015). National Records of Scotland. Available online at: <http://www.gro-scotland.gov.uk/>.

Geraghty, Paul (1993). 'Pulotu, Polynesian Homeland', *Journal of the Polynesian Society* 120: 343–84.

Geraghty, Paul (2005a). 'Placenames of Fiji 1', *Placenames Australia. Newsletter of the Australian National Placename Survey*, June 2005: 6–7. Available online at: <http://www.anps.org.au/documents/June_2005.pdf>.

Geraghty, Paul (2005b). 'Placenames of Fiji 3', *Placenames Australia. Newsletter of the Australian National Placename Survey*, December 2005: 10. Available online at: <http://www.anps.org.au/documents/December_2005.pdf>.

Geraghty, Paul, and Tent, Jan (2010). 'Two Unusual Names for the Australian Continent, Part 2', *Placenames Australia. Newsletter of the Australian National Placename Survey*, June 2010: 4–7. Available online at: <http://www.anps.org.au/documents/June_2010.pdf>.

Gerhards, Jürgen (2003). *Die Moderne und ihre Vornamen. Eine Einladung in die Kultursoziologie.* Wiesbaden: Westdeutscher Verlag.

Gerritzen, Doreen (2007a) 'Das niederländische Personennamensystem', in Silvio Brendler (ed.), *Europäische Personennamensysteme. Ein Handbuch.* Hamburg: Baar, 534–43.

Gerritzen, Doreen (2007b). 'First Names of Moroccan and Turkish Immigrants in the Netherlands', in Eva Brylla and Mats Wahlberg (eds.), *Proceedings of the 21st International Congress of Onomastic Sciences, Uppsala 19–24 August 2002*, vol. 3. Uppsala: Uppsala University, 120–9.

Gibbon, William B. (1964). 'Asiatic Parallels in North American Star Lore. Ursa Major', *The Journal of American Folklore* 77.305: 236–50.

Gibson, James (ed.) (1976). *The Complete Poems of Thomas Hardy.* London: Macmillan.

Gillespie, George T. (1973). *A Catalogue of Persons Named in German Heroic Literature (700–1600). Including Named Animals and Objects and Ethnic Names.* Oxford: Clarendon.

Gillespie, George T. (1989). 'Die Namengebung der deutschen Heldendichtung', in Friedrich Debus and Horst Pütz (eds.), *Namen in deutschen literarischen Texten des Mittelalters. Vorträge, Symposion Kiel, 9.–12.9.1987.* Kieler Beiträge zur deutschen Sprachgeschichte 12. Neumünster: Wachholtz, 115–45.

Gilmore, David D. (1982). 'Some Notes on Community Nicknaming in Spain', *Man (New Series)* 17: 686–700.

Gingerich, Owen (1992). *The Great Copernicus Chase and Other Adventures in Astronomical History.* Cambridge: Cambridge University Press.

Gläser, Rosemarie (1973). 'Zur Namengebung in der Wirtschaftswerbung: Warenzeichen im britischen und amerikanischen Englisch', in Hans Walther (ed.), *Der Name in Sprache und Gesellschaft. Beiträge zur Theorie der Onomastik.* Deutsch-slawische Forschungen zur Namenkunde und Siedlungsgeschichte 27. Berlin: Akademie-Verlag, 220–38.

Gläser, Rosemarie (1996). 'Gegenstand, Ziel und Methoden der Fachsprachenonomastik', in Rosemarie Gläser (ed.), *Eigennamen in der Fachkommunikation*. Frankfurt am Main: Peter Lang, 15–33.

Glasse, R. M. (1987). 'Huli Names and Naming', *Ethnology* 26: 201–8.

Goffman, Erving (1959). *Presentation of Self in Everyday Life*. Garden City, NY: Doubleday Anchor Books.

Goldin, Claudia, and Shim, Maria (2004). 'Making a Name. Women's Surnames at Marriage and Beyond', *Journal of Economic Perspectives* 18: 143–60.

Goodenough, Ward H. (1965). 'Personal Names and Modes of Address in Two Oceanic Communities', in Melford E. Spiro (ed.), *Context and Meaning in Cultural Anthropology*. New York: Free Press, 265–76.

Goodman, John (1994). *LMS Locomotive Names. The Named Locomotives of the London Midland and Scottish Railway and Its Constituent Companies*. Lincoln: Railway Correspondence and Travel Society.

Goodman, John (2002). *LandNWR Locomotive Names. The Named Locomotives of the London and North Western Railway and Its Amalgamated Companies*. Peterborough: Railway Correspondence and Travel Society.

Górnowicz, Hubert (1959). 'Zawołania zwierząt domowych w Sztumskiem', *Onomastica* 5: 451–62.

Gorter, Durk (ed.) (2006a). *Linguistic Landscape. A New Approach to Multilingualism*. Clevedon: Multilingual Matters.

Gorter, Durk (2006b). 'Further Possibilities for Linguistic Landscape Research', in Durk Gorter (ed.), *Linguistic Landscape. A New Approach to Multilingualism*. Clevedon: Multilingual Matters, 81–9.

Gorter, Durk (2012). 'Signposts in the Linguistic Landscape', in Christine Hélot, et al. (eds.), *Linguistic Landscapes, Multilingualism and Social Change*. Frankfurt: Peter Lang, 9–12.

Gorter, Durk (2013). 'Linguistic Landscapes in a Multilingual World', *Annual Review of Applied Linguistics* 33: 190–212.

Gorter, Durk, Marten, Heiko F., and Van Mensel, Luk (eds.) (2012). *Minority Languages in the Linguistic Landscape*. Basingstoke: Palgrave Macmillan.

Gottschald, Max (1932). *Deutsche Namenkunde*. Munich: J.F. Lehmann.

Gover, J. E. B., Mawer, Allen, and Stenton, Frank M., with Houghton, F. T. S. (1936). *The Place-Names of Warwickshire*. English Place-Name Society 13. Cambridge: Cambridge University Press.

Gover, J. E. B., Mawer, Allen, and Stenton, Frank M. (1939). *The Place-Names of Wiltshire*. English Place-Name Society 16. Cambridge: Cambridge University Press.

Grant, Alison (2012a). 'Scottish Place-Names. Firth', *Scottish Language Dictionaries Newsletter*, Autumn 2012.

Grant, Alison (2012b). 'Scottish Place-Names. Dod', *Scottish Language Dictionaries Newsletter*, Spring 2012.

Grant, Mary (ed. and trans.) (1960). *The Myths of Hyginus*. University of Kansas Publications in Humanistic Studies 34. Lawrence: University of Kansas Press.

Great Western Archive (2013). 'Great Western Standard Gauge Locomotive Name Database'. Available online at: <http://www.greatwestern.org.uk/names.htm>. [accessed July 2008].

Green, Richard (2003–15). *Locos in Profile*. Available online at: <http://www.locos-in-profile.co.uk>. [accessed July 2008].

Greenwell, W. Rev. (ed.) (1967 [1860]). *Wills and Inventories from the Registry at Durham*, vol. 38. Durham: Surtees Society.

Grenham, John (2003). *Grenham's Irish Surnames*. CD Rom. Eneclann.

Greule, Albrecht (1973). *Vor- und frühgermanische Flußnamen am Oberrhein. Ein Beitrag zur Gewässernamengebung des Elsaß, der Nordschweiz und Südbadens*. Beiträge zur Namenforschung (Neue Folge) 10. Heidelberg: Carl Winter.

Greule, Albrecht (1996a). 'Gewässernamen: Morphologie, Benennungsmotive, Schichten', in Ernst Eichler, et al. (eds.), *Namenforschung/Name Studies/Les noms propres. Ein internationals Handbuch zur Onomastik/International Handbook of Onomastics/Manuel international d'onomastique*, vol. 2. Berlin/New York: de Gruyter, 1534–9.

Greule, Albrecht (1996b). 'Namen von Flußsystemen am Beispiel des Mains', in Ernst Eichler, et al. (eds.), *Namenforschung/Name Studies/Les noms propres. Ein internationals Handbuch zur Onomastik/International Handbook of Onomastics/Manuel international d'onomastique*, vol 2. Berlin/New York: de Gruyter, 1548–53.

Greule, Albrecht (2004). 'Die Rolle der Derivation in der altgermanischen Hydronymie', in Thorsten Andersson and Eva Nyman (eds.), *Suffixbildungen in alten Ortsnamen. Akten eines internationalen Symposiums in Uppsala 14.–16. Mai 2004*. Acta Academiae Regiae Gustavi Adolphi 88. Uppsala: Kungl. Gustav Adolfs Akademien för Svensk Folkkultur, 199–213.

Greule, Albrecht (2007). *Etymologische Studien zu geographischen Namen in Europa. Ausgewählte Beiträge 1998–2006*. ed. by Wolfgang Janka and Michael Prinz. Regensburger Studien zur Namenforschung 2. Regensburg: Edition Vulpes.

Greule, Albrecht (2009a). 'Donau, Rhein, Moldau und die Indogermanisierung Europas. Danube, Rhine, Moldau and the Indo-Germanisation of Europe', in Milan Harvalík, Eva Mináŕová, and Jana M. Tušková (eds.), *Teoretické a komunikační aspekty proprií. Prof. Rudolfu Šrámkovi k životnímu jubileu*. Brno: Masarykova univerzita, 205–10.

Greule, Albrecht (2009b). 'Spuren der Vorzeit. Die Flussnamen Sachsen-Anhalts und andere Namengeschichten', in Albrecht Greule and Matthias Springer (eds.), *Namen des Frühmittelalters als sprachliche Zeugnisse und als Geschichtsquellen*. Ergänzungsbände zum Reallexikon der Germanischen Altertumskunde 66. Berlin/New York: Walter de Gruyter, 145–57.

Grice, H. Paul (1975). 'Logic and Conversation', in Peter Cole and Jerry L. Morgan (eds.), *Syntax and Semantics*, vol. 3. New York: Academic Press, 41–58.

Griffin, Robert J. (1999). 'Anonymity and Authorship', *New Literary History* 30: 877–95.

Griffin, Robert J. (ed.) (2003). *The Faces of Anonymity: Anonymous and Pseudonymous Publication from the Sixteenth to the Twentieth Century*. New York and Basingstoke: Palgrave Macmillan.

Griffin, Zenzi M. (2010). 'Retrieving Personal Names, Referring Expressions, and Terms of Address', *Psychology of Learning and Motivation* 53: 345–87.

Groves, Beatrice (2007). *Texts and Traditions. Religion in Shakespeare 1592–1604*. Oxford: Clarendon Press.

Grüner, Rolf W. (1992). 'Firmaname in Bloemfontein uit'n Onomastiese Perspektief', *Nomina Africana* 6.1: 24–31.

Gubernatis, Angelo de (1874). *Die Thiere in der indogermanischen Mythologie*. Leipzig: F.W. Grunow.

Guerini, Federica (2005). 'Akan Traditional Personal Name System in Ghana. A Semantic and Functional Perspective', *Nomina Africana* 19.2: 5–38.

Guest, Peter, and Luke, Mike (2005). 'Geophysical Survey at the Chesters Near Moorcourt Farm, Lyonshall. Some Observations on Field Names with Possible Roman Connections', *Transactions of the Woolhope Naturalists' Field Club* 53: 77–80.

Guillén Calvo, Juan José (1981). *Toponimia del Valle de Tena*. Zaragoza: Fernando el Católico.

Guppy, Henry B. (1890). *The Homes of Family Names in Great Britain*. London: Harrison and Sons.

Guttormsen, Pål (2012). 'Nå har det skjedd igjen!', *Avisa Nordland*, 11 December 2012. Available online at: <http://www.an.no/nyheter/article6389708.ece> [accessed 28 October 2013].

Gwynn, Edward (ed. and trans.) (1903–35). *The Metrical Dindshenchas*. 5 vols. Dublin: Royal Irish Academy.

Hadziiossif, Jacqueline (1989). 'La piété des gens de mer en Méditerrannée et en Atlantique d'après les vocables de navires aux XVe et XVIe siècles', in Alain Cabantous and Françoise Hildesheimer (eds.), *Foi chrétienne et milieux maritimes (XVe–XXe siècles)*. Paris: Publisud, 169–87.

Hagström, Charlotte (2012). 'Naming Me, Naming You. Personal Names, Online Signatures and Cultural Meaning', in Botolv Helleland, Christian-Emil Ore, and Solveig Wikstrøm (eds.), *Names and Identities*. Oslo Studies in Language 4.2. Oslo: University of Oslo, 81–93. Available online at: <https://www.journals.uio.no/index.php/osla/article/view/312/437>.

Hakala, Ulla, and Sjöblom, Paula (2013). 'The Touchy Subject of the Place Name. Contemplating Municipality Names and Branding in Merging Situations', in Paula Sjöblom, Terhi Ainiala, and Ulla Hakala (eds.), *Names in the Economy. Cultural Prospects*. Newcastle: Cambridge Scholars, 152–72.

Haley, Gene C. (2008). '*Tamlachta*. The Map of Plague Burials and Some Implications for Early Irish History', *Proceedings of the Harvard Celtic Colloquium* 22: 96–140.

Halkett, Samuel, and Laing, John (1882–8). *A Dictionary of the Anonymous and Pseudonymous Literature of Great Britain*. 4 vols. Edinburgh: William Paterson.

Hall, T. Walter (ed.) (1914). *Descriptive Catalogue of the Jackson Collection*. Sheffield: Northend.

Hallberg, Göran (1976). 'Kring bebyggelsenamnen i Rönnebergs härad', *Sydsvenska ortnamns-sällskapets årsskrift*: 3–42.

Hämäläinen, Lasse (2013). 'User Names in the Online Gaming Community Playforia', in Paula Sjöblom, Terhi Ainiala, and Ulla Hakala (eds.), *Names in the Economy. Cultural Prospects*. Newcastle: Cambridge Scholars, 214–29.

Hamlin, Ann (2000). 'The Early Church in Tyrone to the Twelfth Century', in Charles Dillon and Henry A. Jefferies (eds.), *Tyrone History and Society*. Dublin: Geography Publications, 85–126.

Hamlin, Ann (2008). *The Archaeology of Early Christianity in the North of Ireland*. ed. by Thomas Kerr, with contributions from Janet Bell, Alison Kyle, Marion Meek, and Brian Sloan. BAR British series 460. Oxford: Archaeopress.

Hamst, Olphar [Ralph Thomas] (1867). *A Martyr to Bibliography*. London: J.R. Smith.

Hamst, Olphar [Ralph Thomas] (1868). *Handbook of Fictitious Names*. London: J.R. Smith.

Hanauer, David I. (2009). 'Science and the Linguistic Landscape. A Genre Analysis of Representational Wall Space in a Microbiology Laboratory', in Elana Shohamy and Durk Gorter (eds.), *Linguistic Landscape. Expanding the Scenery*. Abingdon: Routledge, 287–301.

Hance, Michael (2012). 'Scots Place-names in the Linguistic Landscape. Time to Start Talking?' Paper presented at the Scottish Place-Name Society Conference, Oban, 5 May 2012.

Hancock, Andy (2012). 'Capturing the Linguistic Landscape of Edinburgh. A Pedagogical Tool to Investigate Student Teachers' Understandings of Cultural and Linguistic Diversity', in Christine Hélot, et al. (eds.), *Linguistic Landscapes, Multilingualism and Social Change*. Frankfurt: Peter Lang, 249–66.

Handschuck, Sabine, and Schröer, Hubertus (2010). *Eigennamen in der interkulturellen Verständigung*. Augsburg: ZIEL.

Hanks, Patrick (2009). 'Dictionaries of Personal Names', in A. P. Cowie (ed.), *The Oxford History of English Lexicography*, vol. 2. Oxford: Oxford University Press, 122–48.

Hanks, Patrick, and Hodges, Flavia (1988). *A Dictionary of Surnames*. Oxford: Oxford University Press.

Hanks, Patrick, and Hodges, Flavia (2001). *A Concise Dictionary of First Names*. 3rd edn. Oxford: Oxford University Press.

Hanks, Patrick, and Muhr, Kay (2012). 'Exchanging Names. Population Movements and the Forms of Family Names in Ireland and Britain'. Paper presented at annual conference, Society for Name Studies in Britain and Ireland, Athenry, 30 March–1 April 2012. Available online at: <http://www1.uwe.ac.uk/cahe/research/bristolcentreforlinguistics/fanuk.aspx>.

Hanks, Patrick, Coates, Richard, and McClure, Peter (2012). 'Methods for Studying the Origins and History of Family Names in Britain. Philology Meets Statistics in a Multicultural Context', in Lars-Gunnar Larsson and Staffan Nyström (eds.), *Facts and Findings on Personal Names. Some European Examples. Proceedings of an International Symposium in Uppsala, October 20–21, 2011*. Uppsala: Kungliga Vetenskapssamhället, 37–58.

Hanley, J. Richard (1995). 'Are Names Difficult to Recall Because They Are Unique? A Case Study of a Patient with Anomia', *The Quarterly Journal of Experimental Psychology* 48A: 487–506.

Hanley, J. Richard (2011a). 'An Appreciation of Bruce and Young's (1986) Serial Stage Model of Face Naming after 25 years', *British Journal of Psychology* 102: 915–30.

Hanley, J. Richard (2011b). 'Why are Names of People Associated with So Many Phonological Retrieval Failures?', *Psychonomic Bulletin and Review* 18: 612–17.

Hanley, J. Richard, and Cowell, Elaine S. (1988). 'The Effects of Different Types of Retrieval Cues on the Recall of Names of Famous Faces', *Memory and Cognition* 16: 545–55.

Hansack, Ernst (2004). 'Das Wesen des Namens', in Andrea Brendler and Silvio Brendler (eds.), *Namenarten und ihre Erforschung. Ein Lehrbuch für das Studium der Onomastik*. Hamburg: Baar, 51–65.

Harré, Rom (1980). 'What's in a nickname?' *Psychology Today*: 78–84.

Harrington, John P. (1916). *The Ethnography of the Tewa Indians*. Washington, DC: Government Printing Office.

Harris, Darryl M., and Kay, Janice (1995). 'I Know Your Face But I Can't Remember Your Name. Is it Because Names are Unique?', *British Journal of Psychology* 86: 345–58.

Harris, Roy (1998). 'The Dialect Myth', in Roy Harris and George Wolf (eds.), *Integrational Linguistics. A First Reader*. Oxford: Pergamon, 83–95.

Haspelmath, Martin (2010). 'Comparative Concepts and Descriptive Categories in Crosslinguistic Studies', *Language* 86.3: 663–87.

Hassa, Samira (2012). 'Projecting, Exposing, Revealing Self in the Digital World. Usernames as a Social Practice in a Moroccan Chatroom', *Names* 60.4: 201–9.

Hattingh, P. S., Kadmon, Naftali, Raper, Peter E., and Booysen, Ingrid (eds.) (1993). *Training Course in Toponomy for Southern Africa*. Pretoria: University of Pretoria.

Hausner, Isolde, and Schuster, Elisabeth (1999). *Altdeutsches Namenbuch. Die Überlieferung der Ortsnamen in Österreich und Südtirol von den Anfängen bis 1200 (ANB)*, vol. 1: A–M. Wien: Verlag der Akademie der Wissenschaften.

Hawkes, Jacquetta (1978). *A Land*. Newton Abbot: David and Charles.

Hawkesworth, John (1773). *An Account of the Voyages Undertaken by the Order of His Present Majesty for Making Discoveries in the Southern Hemisphere, and Successfully Performed by Commodore Byron, Captain Carteret, Captain Wallis, and Captain Cook, in the Dolphin, the Swallow, and the Endeavour. Drawn up from the Journals which were Kept by the Several Commanders, and from the papers of Joseph Banks Esq.* vol. 2. London: W. Strahan and T. Cadell. Available online at: <http://southseas.nla.gov.au/index_voyaging.html>.

Hay, Dennis C., Young, Andrew W., and Ellis, Andrew W. (1991). 'Routes Through The Face Recognition System', *The Quarterly Journal of Experimental Psychology* 43A: 761–91.

Heberle, Rudolph (1973). 'The Sociological System of Ferdinand Tönnies. An Introduction', in W. J. Cahnman (ed.), *Ferdinand Tönnies. A New Evaluation*. Leiden: Brill, 47–61.

Heegen, Dina (2013). 'An Extended Typology for Product Names. Examples of the Yoghurt Names of the German and Swedish Market', in Paula Sjöblom, Terhi Ainiala, and Ulla Hakala (eds.), *Names in the Economy. Cultural Prospects*. Newcastle: Cambridge Scholars, 311–31.

Heeringa, Wilbert, and Nerbonne, John (2006). 'To What Extent are Surnames Words? Comparing Geographic Patterns of Surname and Dialect Variation in the Netherlands', *Literary and Linguistic Computing* 21.4: 507–27.

Heisler, Jennifer M., and Crabill, Scott L. (2006). 'Who are "stinkybug" and "Packerfan4"? Email Pseudonyms and Participants' Perceptions of Demography, Productivity, and Personality', *Journal of Computer-Mediated Communication* 12: 114–35.

Helander, Kaisa R. (2009). 'Toponymic Silence and Sámi Place Names During the Growth of the Norwegian State', in Lawrence D. Berg and Jani Vuolteenaho (eds.), *Critical Toponymies. The Contested Politics of Place-Naming*. Farnham: Ashgate, 253–66.

Helck, Wolfgang, and Eberhard, Otto (eds.) (1989). *Lexikon der Ägyptologie*, vol. 6. Harrassowitz: Wiesbaden.

Helleland, Botolv (1991). 'Typen Lien i høve til Lia. Analogi i form og funksjon', in Gordon Albøge, et al. (eds.), *Analogi i navngivning. Tiende Nordiske Navneforskerkongres, Brandbjerg 20.–24. maj 1989*. Uppsala: NORNA-förlaget, 83–99.

Helleland, Botolv (1997). 'Slektsnamn av stadnamn', in *Årsmelding for namnegransking 1996*. Oslo: Universitetet i Oslo. Institutt for nordistikk og litteraturvitskap, 51–61.

Helleland, Botolv (1999). 'Ortsnamen als Ursprung von Familiennamen in Norwegen', in Dieter Kremer and Thorsten Andersson (eds.), *Onomastik. Akten des 18. internationales Kongresses für Namenforschung. Trier, 12.–17. April 1993*, vol. 4. Patronymica Romanica 17. Tübingen: Niemeyer, 159–68.

Helleland, Botolv (2004). 'Ableitungstypen in Flussnamen Westnorwegens', in Thorsten Andersson and Eva Nyman (eds.), *Suffixbildungen in alten Ortsnamen. Akten eines internationalen Symposiums in Uppsala 14.–16. Mai 2004*. Acta Academiae Regiae Gustavi Adolphi 88. Uppsala: Kungl. Gustav Adolfs Akademien för Svensk Folkkultur, 177–97.

Hellquist, Elof (1903–6). *Studier öfver de svenska sjönamnen, deras härledning ock historia*. Bidrag till kännedom om de svenska landsmålen ock svenskt folkliv 20. 6 vols. Stockholm: P.A. Norstedt & Söner.

Hellquist, Elof (1912). 'Fornsvenska tillnamn', in *Xenia Lideniana. Festskrift tillägnad professor Evald Lidén på hans femtioårsdag den 3 oktober 1912*. Stockholm: P.A. Norstedt & Söner, 84–115.

Hélot, Christine, et al. (eds.) (2012). *Linguistic Landscapes, Multilingualism and Social Change*. Frankfurt: Peter Lang.

Hemingway, Wayne (2007). 'Placemaking—Cultural Branding', *Place Branding and Public Diplomacy* 3.4: 332–6.

Henzen, Walter (1965). *Deutsche Wortbildung*. 3rd edn. Tübingen: Niemeyer.

Hernandez, Bernardo, Hidalgo, Carmen, Salazar-Laplace, M. Esther, and Hess, Stephany (2007). 'Place Attachment and Identity in Natives and Non-Natives', *Journal of Environmental Psychology* 27: 310–19.

Herring, Susan C., and Stoerger, Sharon (2014). 'Gender and (A)nonymity in Computer-Mediated Communication', in Susan Ehrlich, Miriam Meyerhoff, Janet Holmes (eds.), *The Handbook of Language, Gender, and Sexuality*. 2nd edn. Chichester: Wiley Blackwell, 567–86.

Hess, Elke (1996). 'Störenfried fand vor Gericht keine Gnade', *Berliner Zeitung*, 25 January. Available online at: <http://www.berliner-zeitung.de/archiv>.

Hey, David (ed.) (1992). *The Origins of One Hundred Sheffield Surnames*. Sheffield: University of Sheffield.

Hey, David (2000). *Family Names and Family History*. London: Hambledon and London.

Hickerson, Nancy Parrott (2000). *Linguistic Anthropology*. 2nd edn. London: Harcourt.

Hidalgo, Carmen, and Hernandez, Bernardo (2001). 'Place Attachment. Conceptual and Empirical Questions', *Journal of Environmental Psychology* 21: 273–81.

Higham, Nicholas J. (2004). *A Frontier Landscape. The North West in the Middle Ages*. Bollington: Windgather Press.

Higham, Nicholas J., and Ryan, Martin J. (eds.) (2010). *Landscape Archaeology of Anglo-Saxon England*. Woodbridge: Boydell.

Hill, Wane F., and Öttchen, Cynthia J. (1995). *Shakespeare's Insults. Educating Your Wit*. New York: Crown Trade.

Hills, Catherine (1977). *The Anglo-Saxon Cemetery at Spong Hill, North Elmham, Part I: Catalogue of Cremations*. East Anglian Archaeology Report 6. Gressenhall: Norfolk Archaeological Unit.

Hilterman, Tracy, and Koopman, Adrian (2003). 'A High Degree of Wayward Folly . . . —An Analysis of Public Response to a Proposal To Rename Streets in Central Pietermaritzburg', *Nomina Africana* 17.2: 1–36.

Hiss, Florian (2013). 'Tromsø as a "Sámi Town"? Language Ideologies, Attitudes, and Debates Surrounding Bilingual Language Policies', *Language Policy* 12: 177–96.

Hlahla, Patrick (2013). 'Public Get Another Say on Street Names', *Iol News*, 28 June. Available online at: <http://www.iol.co.za/news/crime-courts/public-get-another-say-on-street-names-1.1539206#.VOMVM_mDlcY>.

Hoffmann, Ludger (1999). 'Eigennamen im sprachlichen Handeln', in Kristin Bührig and Yaron Matras (eds.), *Sprachtheorie und sprachliches Handeln*. Tübingen: Stauffenburg, 213–34.

Hogan, Edmund (1910). *Onomasticon Goedelicum locorum et tribuum Hiberniae et Scotiae*, Dublin: Hodges Figgis. Electronic version available at: <http://publish.ucc.ie/doi/locus>.

The Holinshed Project (2008–13). Available online at: <http://www.cems.ox.ac.uk/holinshed>. [accessed October 2013].

Hollis, Jarrod, and Valentine, Tim (2001). 'Proper-Name Processing. Are Proper Names Pure Referencing Expressions?', *Journal of Experimental Psychology. Learning, Memory, and Cognition* 27.1: 99–116.

Honegger, Thomas (2004). 'Nominal Forms of Address in Middle English. Pet Names and Terms of Endearment Between Lovers', in Christoph Bode, Sebastian Domsch, and Hans Sauer (eds.), *Anglistentag 2003. Proceedings*. Trier: Wissenschaftlicher Verlag, 39–55.

Honegger, Thomas (2005). '"Wyȝe welcum iwys to this place"—and Never Mind the Alliteration. An Inquiry into the Use of Forms of Address in Two Alliterative ME Romances', in Nikolaus Ritt and Herbert Schendl (eds.). *Rethinking Middle English. Linguistic and Literary Approaches*. Frankfurt am Main: Peter Lang, 169–78.

Hongisto, Ilari, and Sjöblom, Paula (2012). 'Names as Valuable Resources in the Music Market', in Reina Boerrigter and Harm Nijboer (eds.), *Names as Language and Capital. Proceedings Names in the Economy III, Amsterdam, 11–13 June 2009*. Amsterdam: Meertens Instituut, 32–40. Available online at: <http://depot.knaw.nl/12899/>.

Hooker, R. A. (1990). *Pathfinder Gazetteer. Essential Companion to the Ordnance Survey Pathfinder Series Map*. Hawick: Gazetteer Systems.

Hopper, Paul (1990). 'The Emergence of the Category Proper Name in Discourse', in Hayley G. Davis and Talbot J. Taylor (eds.), *Redefining Linguistics*. London: Routledge, 149–67.

Hornung, Maria (1989). *Lexikon Österreichischer Familiennamen*. Vienna: Niederösterreichisches Pressehaus.

Hornung, Maria (1994). 'Die Flurnamenforschung in Niederösterreich. Neue Perspektiven durch die Vorarbeiten im Niederösterreichischen Flurnamenbuch', in Friedhelm Debus (ed.), *Zu Ergebnissen und Perspektiven in der Namenforschung in Österreich*. Heidelberg: Winter, 35–50.

Horovitz, David (2003). 'A Survey and Analysis of the Place-Names of Staffordshire'. Unpublished PhD dissertation, University of Nottingham.

Horovitz, David (2005). *The Place-Names of Staffordshire*. Brewood: privately published.

Horton, John (1994). *The Grub Street Dictionary of International Aircraft Nicknames, Variants and Colloquial Terms*. London: Grub Street.

Hosák, Ladislav, and Šramek, Rudolf (1970–80). *Místní jména na Moravě a ve Slezsku*. 2 vols. Praha: Acad. Nakl. Československé Akad Věd.

Hough, Carole (1995). 'OE *græg* in Place-Names', *Neuphilologische Mitteilungen* 96: 361–5.

Hough, Carole (1997a). 'The Place-Name Kingston and the Laws of Æthelberht', *Studia Neophilologica* 69: 55–7.

Hough, Carole (1997b). 'The Earliest Old English Place-Names in Scotland', *Notes and Queries* 44: 148–50.

Hough, Carole (1998). 'OE *brūn* in Place-Names', *English Studies* 79: 512–21.

Hough, Carole (1999). 'The Trumpeters of Bemersyde. A Scottish Place-Name Reconsidered', *Names* 47: 257–68.

Hough, Carole (2000). 'ON *kíll* in English Place-Names', *Studia Neophilologica* 72: 1–5.

Hough, Carole (2001a). 'P-Celtic *tref* in Scottish Place-Names', *Notes and Queries* 48: 213–15.

Hough, Carole (2001b). 'Place-Name Evidence for an Anglo-Saxon Animal Name: OE *pohha/*pocca* "fallow deer" ', *Anglo-Saxon England* 30: 1–14.

Hough, Carole (2002). 'Onomastic Evidence for Middle English Vocabulary', in Peter J. Lucas and Angela M. Lucas (eds.), *Middle English from Tongue to Text. Selected Papers from the Third International Conference on Middle English: Language and Text, held at Dublin, Ireland, 1–4 July 1999*. Bern/Frankfurt: Peter Lang, 155–67.

Hough, Carole (2003). 'Scottish Surnames', in John Corbett, J. Derrick McClure, and Jane Stuart-Smith (eds.), *The Edinburgh Companion to Scots*. Edinburgh: Edinburgh University Press, 31–49.

Hough, Carole (2006). 'Colours of the Landscape. Old English Colour Terms in Place-Names', in Carole P. Biggam and Christian J. Kay (eds.), *Progress in Colour Studies. Volume 1: Language and Culture*. Amsterdam/Philadelphia: John Benjamins, 181–98.

Hough, Carole (2009). 'The Role of Onomastics in Historical Linguistics', *Journal of Scottish Name Studies* 3: 29–46.

Hough, Carole (2010). *Toponymicon and Lexicon in North-West Europe. 'Ever-Changing Connection'*. E.C. Quiggin Memorial Lectures 12. Cambridge: University of Cambridge, Department of Anglo-Saxon, Norse and Celtic.

Hough, Carole (2012). 'Linguistic Levels. Onomastics', in Alexander Bergs and Laurel J. Brinton (eds.), *English Historical Linguistics. An International Handbook*, vol. 1. Berlin: Mouton de Gruyter, 212–23.

Hough, Carole (2015). 'Place and Other Names', in John Taylor (ed.), *The Oxford Handbook of the Word*. Oxford: Oxford University Press, 634–49.

Hough, Carole, Bramwell, Ellen, and Grieve, Dorian (2011). *JISC Final Report. Scots Words and Place-Names*. JISC. Available online at: <http://www.jisc.ac.uk/media/documents/programmes/digitisation/swapfinalreport.pdf>.

House of Commons Committee of Public Accounts (2011). *Management of the Typhoon Project: Thirtieth Report of Session 2010-12*. London: The Stationery Office.

Hovda, Per (1945). 'Fossenamn', *Maal og minne*: 97–115.

Hovda, Per (1966). *Norske elvenamn. Eit tillegg til O. Rygh «Norske Elvenavne»*. Oslo: Universitetsforlaget.

Hovda, Per (1971). 'Til norske elvenamn', *Namn och Bygd* 59: 124–48.

HRAF (2015). *HRAF—Human Relations Area Files*. Yale University. Available online at: <http://hraf.yale.edu/>.

Hudson, James M., and Bruckman, Amy (2004). '"Go Away". Participant Objections to Being Studied and the Ethics of Chatroom Research', *The Information Society* 20: 127–39.

Hudson, Richard (1990). *English Word Grammar*. Oxford: Blackwell.

Hughes, A. J. and Hannan, R. (1992). *Place-Names of Northern Ireland*, vol. 2. *County Down II: The Ards*, Belfast: The Institute of Irish Studies.

Hughes, Arthur, Trudgill, Peter, and Watt, Dominic (2012). *English Accents and Dialects*. 5th edn. London: Routledge.

Hugh-Jones, Stephen (2006). 'The Substance of Northwest Amazonian Names', in Gabriele Vom Bruck and Barbara Bodenhorn (eds.), *An Anthropology of Names and Naming*. Cambridge: Cambridge University Press, 73–96.

Humphrey, Caroline (2006). 'On Being Named and Not Named. Authority, Persons, and their Names in Mongolia', in Gabriele Vom Bruck and Barbara Bodenhorn (eds.), *The Anthropology of Names and Naming*. Cambridge: Cambridge University Press, 157–76.

Hunt, David (*c*.2005) 'Locomotive Builders to the Midland Railway', *Midland Record* 21: 111–26.

Hurford, James R., and Heasley, Brendan (1983). *Semantics. A Coursebook*. Cambridge: Cambridge University Press.

Hutton, James (ed. and trans.) (1982). *Aristotle's Poetics*. New York: W.W. Norton and Co.

Hymes, Dell (1963). 'A Perspective for Linguistic Anthropology', *The Voice of America Lectures. Anthropology Series* 17: 1–11.

Hymes, Dell (1996). *Ethnography, Linguistics, Narrative Inequality. Toward an Understanding of Voice*. London: Taylor and Francis.

ICOS (2011). 'List of Key Onomastic Terms'. Available online at: <http://icosweb.net/drupal/sites/default/files/ICOS-Terms-en.pdf>.

Idiatov, Dmitry (2007). 'A Typology of Non-Selective Interrogative Pronominals'. PhD dissertation, University of Antwerp.

Idiatov, Dmitry (2010). 'Non-Selective Interrogative Pronominals, Categorical Presuppositional Meanings of Proper Names and Propriality'. Paper presented at *The Grammar of Proper Names—A Typological Perspective*, University of Regensburg.

II CSK 539/07. Available online at: <http://www.sn.pl/Sites/orzecznictwo/Orzeczenia2/II%20CSK%20539-07-1.pdf>.

Insley, John (2006). 'Early Germanic Personal Names and Onomastic Dialects', in Andrew J. Johnston, Ferdinand von Mengden, and Stefan Thim (eds.), *Language and Text*.

Current Perspectives on English and Germanic Historical Linguistics and Philology. Heidelberg: Winter, 113–31.

Insley, John (2007). 'Das englische Personennamensystem', in Andrea Brendler and Silvio Brendler, *Europäische Personennamensysteme. Ein Handbuch von Abasisch bis Zentralladinisch. Anlässlich der 65. Geburtstage von Rosa Kohlheim und Volker Kohlheim.* Hamburg: Baar, 159–69.

INSPIRE (1995–2015). Infrastructure for Spatial Information in the European Community. Available online at: <http://inspire.jrc.ec.europa.eu/>.

International Astronomical Union (n.d.). 'Naming Astronomical Objects'. Available online at: <http://www.iau.org/public/themes/naming/>.

Iteanu, André (2000). 'Processing of Naming, Cambridge, 14–15 September 1999', *Anthropology Today* 16.3: 24–5.

Iteanu, André (2006). 'Why the Dead Do Not Bear Names. The Orokaiva Name System', in Gabriele Vom Bruck and Barbara Bodenhorn (eds.), *An Anthropology of Names and Naming.* Cambridge: Cambridge University Press, 51–72.

Ivkovic, Dejan, and Lotherington, Heather (2009). 'Multilingualism in Cyberspace: Conceptualising the Virtual Linguistic Landscape', *International Journal of Multilingualism* 6.1: 17–36.

Jackson, Kenneth H. (1953). *Language and History in Early Britain.* Edinburgh: Edinburgh University Press.

Jackson, Kenneth H. (1972). *The Gaelic Notes in the Book of Deer.* Cambridge: Cambridge University Press.

Jackson, Neels (2001). 'D.F. Malanrylaan Sondag amptelik hernoem', *Beeld*, 26 September: 4.

Jackson, Neels (2013). 'Cohen lig sy hoed in Afrikaans', *Die Burger*, 7 June.

Jackson, Peter (1989). *Maps of Meaning. An Introduction to Cultural Geography.* London: Unwin Hyman.

Jackson, Peter (ed.) (1995), *Words, Names and History. Selected Papers of Cecily Clark.* Cambridge: D.S. Brewer.

Jacobsson, Stefan (2012). 'Personbinamn på vikingatida runstenar. Hur vanliga är de och varför finns de där?', in Staffan Nyström, Eva Brylla, Katharina Leibring, Lennart Ryman, and Per Vikstrand (eds.), *Binamn. Uppkomst, bildning, terminologi och bruk. Handlingar från NORNA:s 40:e symposium i Älvkarleö, Uppland, 29/9–1/10 2010.* NORNA-rapporter 88. Uppsala: NORNA-förlaget, 49–64.

Jaffe, J. Michael, Lee, Young-Eum, Huang, LiNing, and Oshagan, Hayg (1995). *Gender, Pseudonyms and CMC. Masking Identities and Baring Souls.* Available online at: <http://smg.media.mit.edu/library/jaffe1995.html> [accessed 30 January 2013].

Jahoda, Gustav (1954). 'A Note on Ashanti Names and Their Relationships to Personality', *British Journal of Psychology* 45: 192–5.

Jakobsen, Jakob (1901). *Shetlandsøernes Stednavne.* Copenhagen: Thiele.

Jakobsen, Jakob (1957). *Greinir og ritgerðir.* Thórshavn: Jacobsens.

Jakobson, Roman (1960). 'Closing Statements. Linguistics and Poetics', in Thomas A. Sebeok (ed.), *Style in Language.* Cambridge, MA: MIT Press, 350–77.

James, Lori E. (2004). 'Meeting Mister Farmer versus Meeting a Farmer. Specific Effects of Aging on Learning Proper Names', *Psychology and Aging* 19: 515–22.

James, Lori E. (2006). 'Specific Effects of Aging on Proper Name Retrieval. Now You See Them, Now You Don't', *Journal of Gerontology, Series B (Psychological Sciences)* 61: 180–3.

Janner, Maria Chiara (2013). 'Notes on the Syntax of Commercial Names in Italian', in Paula Sjöblom, Terhi Ainiala, and Ulla Hakala (eds.), *Names in the Economy. Cultural Prospects*. Newcastle: Cambridge Scholars, 250–68.

Jaworski, Adam, and Thurlow, Crispin (eds.) (2010a). *Semiotic Landscapes. Language, Image, Space*. London: Continuum.

Jaworski, Adam, and Thurlow, Crispin (2010b). 'Introducing Semiotic Landscapes', in Adam Jaworski and Crispin Thurlow (eds.), *Semiotic Landscapes: Language, Image, Space*. London: Continuum, 1–40.

Jedrej, Charles, and Nuttall, Mark (1996). *White Settlers. The Impact of Rural Repopulation in Scotland*. Luxembourg: Harwood Academic.

Jefferson, Gail (2004). 'Glossary of Transcript Symbols with an Introduction', in Gene Lerner (ed.), *Conversation Analysis. Studies from the First Generation*. Amsterdam/Philadelphia: John Benjamins, 13–31.

Jespersen, Otto (1924). *The Philosophy of Grammar*. With a new Introduction and Index by James D. McCawley. Chicago/London: The University of Chicago Press.

Jeziorski, Andrzej (1998). 'Preparing for Production', *Flight International*, 25 February: 34–5.

Jisc (2011–13). 'Digital Exposure of English Place-Names (DEEP)'. Available online at: <http://www.webarchive.org.uk/wayback/archive/20140614055054/> <http://www.jisc.ac.uk/what-wedo/programmes/digitisation/content2011_2013/deep.aspx>.

Jobling, Mark A. (2001). 'In the Name of the Father. Surnames and Genetics', *Trends in Genetics* 17.6: 353–7.

Johansen, Åse Mette, and Bull, Tove (2012). 'Språkpolitikk og (u)synleggjering i det semiotiske landskapet på Universitetet i Tromsø', *Nordlyd* 39.2: 17–45.

Johansson, Carina (2007). *I gatuplanet. Namnbrukarperspektiv på gatunamn i Stockholm*. Uppsala: Uppsala University.

Johnson, Samuel (1755). *A Dictionary of the English Language*. 2 vols. London: J. & P. Knapton.

Johnston, James B. (1915). *The Place-Names of England and Wales*. London: John Murray.

Johnston, Robert A., and Bruce, Vicki (1990). 'Lost Properties? Retrieval Differences Between Name Codes and Semantic Codes for Familiar People', *Psychological Research* 52: 62–7.

Johnstone, Barbara (2009). 'Pittsburghese Shirts. Commodification and the Enregisterment of an Urban Dialect', *American Speech* 84.2: 157–75. Available online at: <http://works.bepress.com/barbara_johnstone/45>.

Jones, Bedwyr L. (1991–3). 'Why *Bangor*?', *Ainm* 5: 58–65.

Jones, Charles (ed.) (1997). *The Edinburgh History of the Scots Language*. Edinburgh: Edinburgh University Press.

Jones, Enrique H. G., and Uribe-Jongbloed, Elin (eds.) (2013). *Social Media and Minority Languages. Convergence and the Creative Industries*. Bristol: Multilingual Matters.

Jones, Kevin P. (2008). *Steam Index*. Available online at: <http://www.steamindex.com> [accessed July 2008].

Jones, Malcolm (2000). 'The Names Given to Ships in Fourteenth- and Fifteenth-Century England', *Nomina* 23: 23–36.

Jones, Malcolm (2002). *The Secret Middle Ages. Discovering the Real Medieval World*. Stroud: Sutton.

Jones, Richard (2012a). 'Directional Names in the Early Medieval Landscape', in Richard Jones and Sarah Semple (eds.), *Sense of Place in Anglo-Saxon England*. Donington: Shaun Tyas, 196–210.

Jones, Richard (2012b). 'Thinking Through the Manorial Affix. People and Place in Medieval England', in Sam Turner and Bob Silvester (eds.), *Life in Medieval Landscapes. People and Places in the Middle Ages*. Oxford: Windgather, 251–67.

Jones, Richard (2013). 'Settlement Archaeology and Place-Names', in Jayne Carroll and David N. Parsons (eds.), *Perceptions of Place*. Nottingham: English Place-Name Society, 181–208.

Jones, Richard, and Semple, Sarah (eds.) (2012a). *Sense of Place in Anglo-Saxon England*. Donington: Shaun Tyas.

Jones, Richard, and Semple, Sarah (2012b). 'Making Sense of Place in Anglo-Saxon England', in Richard Jones and Sarah Semple (eds.), *Sense of Place in Anglo-Saxon England*. Donington: Shaun Tyas, 1–15.

Jönsjö, Jan (1979). *Studies on Middle English Nicknames*, vol. 1. Lund: Gleerup.

Jónsson, Finnur (1912), 'Dyrenavne', *Arkiv för nordisk filologi* 28: 325–40.

Jørgensen, Bent (2008). *Danske stednavne*. Copenhagen: Gyldendal.

Jorgensen, Bradley, and Stedman, Richard (2006), 'A Comparative Analysis of Predictors of Sense of Place Dimensions. Attachment to, Dependence on, and Identification with Lakeshore Properties', *Journal of Environmental Management* 79: 316–27.

Joseph, John E. (2004). *Language and Identity. National, Ethnic, Religious*. Basingstoke: Palgrave Macmillan.

Joubert, Charles E. (1993). 'Personal Name as a Psychological Variable', *Missoula Psychological Reports* 73: 1123–45.

Joyce, Patrick W. (1869–1913). *The Origin and History of Irish Names of Places*. 3 vols. Dublin: M.H. Gill and Son.

Jowett, Benjamin (trans.) (1892). *The Dialogues of Plato*. 3rd edn, 5 vols. Oxford: Oxford University Press. Available at: <http://ebooks.adelaide.edu.au/p/plato/p71cra/index.html>.

Jucker, Andreas H. (2006). '"Thou Art So Loothly and So Oold Also". The Use of *Ye* and *Thou* in Chaucer's *Canterbury Tales*', *Anglistik* 17.2: 57–72.

Jucker, Andreas H. (2012). '"What's in a Name?". Names and Terms of Address in Shakespeare's *Romeo and Juliet*', in Sarah Chevalier and Thomas Honegger (eds.), *Words, Words, Words. Philology and Beyond. Festschrift for Andreas Fischer on the Occasion of his 65th Birthday*. Tübingen: Narr, 77–97.

Jucker, Andreas H., and Taavitsainen, Irma (2000). 'Diachronic Speech Act Analysis. Insults From Flyting to Flaming', *Journal of Historical Pragmatics* 1.1: 67–95.

Julyan, Robert H. (1984). *Mountain Names*. Seattle: The Mountaineers.

Julyan, Robert H., and Julyan, Mary (1993). *Place Names of the White Mountains*. 2nd edn. Hanover, NH: University Press of New England.

Kadmon, Naftali (1997). *Toponymy. The Lore, Laws and Language of Geographical Names*. New York, NY: Vantage.

Kallen, Jeffrey L. (2010). 'Changing Landscapes. Language, Space and Policy in the Dublin Linguistic Landscape', in Adam Jaworski and Crispin Thurlow (eds.), *Semiotic Landscapes. Language, Image, Space*. London: Continuum, 41–58.

Källström, Magnus (2012). 'Binamn på vikingatida runstenar. Hur vanliga är de och varför finns de där?', in Staffan Nyström, Eva Brylla, Katharina Leibring, Lennart Ryman, and Per Vikstrand (eds.), *Binamn. Uppkomst, bildning, terminologi och bruk. Handlingar från NORNA:s 40:e symposium i Älvkarleö, Uppland, 29/9–1/10 2010*. NORNA-rapporter 88. Uppsala: NORNA-förlaget, 65–88.

Kálmán, Béla (1978). *The World of Names. A Study in Hungarian Onomatology*. Budapest: Akadémiai Kiadó.

Kalverkämper, Hartwig (1977). *Textlinguistik der Eigennamen*. Stuttgart: Klett-Cotta.

Kampf, Michal, Nachson, Israel, and Babkoff, Harvey (2002). 'A Serial Test of the Laterality of Familiar Face Recognition', *Brain and Cognition* 50: 35–50.

Kaplan, David M., and Fisher, James E. (2009). 'A Rose by Any Other Name. Identity and Impression Management in Résumés', *Employee Responsibilities and Rights Journal* 21: 319–32.

Karbø, Asbjörn, and Kruken, Kristoffer (1994). *Blåmann og Lykle. Norske geitenamn*. Oslo: Landbruksforlaget.

Karlsson, Hugo (1987). 'Hundnamn i Sverige ca 1650–1800', in Göran Hallberg, Stig Isaksson, Bengt Pamp, and Eero Kiviniemi (eds.), *Nionde nordiska namnforskarkongressen, Lund, 4–8 augusti 1985*. Uppsala: NORNA-förlaget, 81–93.

Karlsson, Hugo (1994). 'Namn på ånglokomotiv', in Kristinn Jóhanesson, Hugo Karlsson, and Bo Ralph (eds.), *Övriga namn. Handlingar från NORNA:s nittonde symposium i Göteborg, 4–6 december 1991*. NORNA-rapporter 56. Uppsala: NORNA-förlaget, 203–15.

Karlsson, Hugo (2004). *Namn på Kungl. Maj:ts hästar 1628–1815. En ord- och namnstudie*. Uppsala: Uppsala universitet.

Karmiloff-Smith, Annette (1979). *A Functional Approach to Child Language. A Study of Determiners and Reference*. Cambridge: Cambridge University Press.

Kearns, Robin A., and Berg, Lawrence D. (2002). 'Proclaiming Place. Towards a Geography of Place Name Pronunciation', *Social and Cultural Geography* 3.3: 283–302.

Keating, Geoffrey (1902). *Foras feasa ar Éirinn: the history of Ireland*, vol. 1. trans. by Edward Comyn and Patrik S Dinneen. Dublin: Irish Texts Society.

Kelley, David H., and Milone, Eugene F. (2005). *Exploring Ancient Skies. An Encyclopedic Survey of Archaeoastronomy*. Berlin: Springer.

Kelly, Fergus (1988). *A Guide to Early Irish Law*. Dublin: Dublin Institute for Advanced Studies.

Kelly, Fergus (1997). *Early Irish Farming*. Dublin: Dublin Institute for Advanced Studies.

Kelly, John E. (2013). *Elgar's Best Friend. Alfred Rodewald of Liverpool*. Lancaster: Carnegie Publishing.

Kennedy, Don H. (1974). *Ship Names Origins and Usages during 45 Centuries*. Charlottesville, VA: University Press of Virginia.

Kennedy, James, Smith, W. A., and Johnson, A. F. (rev.) (1926–32). *Dictionary of Anonymous and Pseudonymous English Literature*. 4 vols. Edinburgh: Oliver and Boyd.

Kent Archaeological Field School (2013). *The Roman Religious Sanctuary at 'Blacklands', School Farm, Graveney Road, Faversham, Kent*. Unpublished report.

Kepsu, Saulo (1990). 'Toponymie des Dorfes Kepsu', in Heikki Leskinen and Eero Kiviniemi (eds.), *Finnish Onomastics. Namenkunde in Finnland*. Helsinki: Suomalaisen Kirjallisuuden Seura, 61–83.

Kerns, Myleah Y. (2011). 'North American Women's Surname Choice Based on Ethnicity and Self-Identification as Feminists', *Names* 59.2: 104–17.

Kettner, Bernd-Ulrich (1972). *Flußnamen im Stromgebiet der oberen und mittleren Leine*. Name und Wort. Göttinger Arbeiten zur niederdeutschen Philologie 6. Rinteln: C. Bösendahl.

Key to English Place-Names (2015). Available online at: <http://kepn.nottingham.ac.uk>.

King, Jacob (2008). 'Analytical Tools for Toponymy. Their Application to Scottish Hydronymy'. PhD dissertation, University of Edinburgh. Available online at: <http://www.era.lib.ed.ac.uk/handle/1842/3020>.

King, Turi E., and Jobling, Mark A. (2009). 'What's in a Name? Y Chromosomes, Surnames and the Genetic Genealogy Revolution', *Trends in Genetics* 25.8: 351–60.

Kitson, Peter R. (1995). 'The Nature of Old English Dialect Distributions, Mainly as Exhibited in Charter Boundaries', in Jacek Fisiak (ed.), *Medieval Dialectology*. Berlin: Mouton de Gruyter, 43–153.

Kitson, Peter R. (1996). 'British and European River-Names', *Transactions of the Philological Society* 94: 73–118.

Kitson, Peter (2002). 'How Anglo-Saxon Personal Names Work', *Nomina* 25: 91–132.

Kiviniemi, Eero (1973). 'Om "uppkallelse och namnmode" i namngivningen'. Unpublished paper.

Kiviniemi, Eero (1974). '*Kyynärjärvi* i Askola—ett exempel på analogi vid namngivningen och dess konsekvenser för namnanalysen'. Unpublished paper.

Kiviniemi, Eero (1991). 'Analogisk namngivning och den toponomastiska teorin', in Gordon Albøge, et al. (eds.), *Analogi i navngivning. Tiende Nordiske Navneforskerkongres, Brandbjerg 20.-24. maj 1989.* Uppsala: NORNA-förlaget, 111–20.

Kiviniemi, Eero (2006). *Suomalaisten etunimet*. Helsinki: Suomalaisen Kirjallisuuden Seura.

Klare, George R. (1991). 'Why Nose Art? A Psychologist's View', in Jeffrey L. Ethell and Clarence Simonsen (eds.), *The History of Aircraft Nose Art. WWI to Today*. Sparkford: Haynes, 11–16.

Kleiber, Georges (1992). 'Article défini, unicité et pertinence', *Revue Romane* (DK) 27.1: 61–89.

Kleiber, Wolfgang (1985). 'Die Flurnamen. Voraussetzungen, Methoden und Ergebnisse sprach- und kulturhistorischer Auswertung', in Werner Besch, Oskar Reichmann, and Stefan Sonderegger (eds.), *Sprachgeschichte. Ein Handbuch zur Geschichte der deutschen Sprache und ihrer Erforschung*, vol. 2. Berlin: de Gruyter, 2130–41.

Klein, Naomi (2001). *No Logo*. London: Flamingo.

Kloosterman, Alphons M. J. (1976). *Discoverers of The Cook Islands and the Names They Gave*. Cook Islands Library and Museum. Available online at: <http://nzetc.victoria.ac.nz/tm/scholarly/tei-KloDisc-t1-body-d10.html>.

Knappe, Gabriele, and Schümann, Michael (2006). 'Thou and Ye. A Collocational-Phraseological Approach to Pronoun Change in Chaucer's *Canterbury Tales*', *Studia Anglica Posnaniensia* 42: 213–38.

Knudsen, Gunnar, Kristiansen, Marius, and Hornby, Rikard (1936–64). *Danmarks Gamle Personnavne*. 2 vols. Copenhagen: Gad.

Koch, John T. (ed.) (2006). *Celtic Culture. A Historical Encyclopedia*. 5 vols. Santa Barbara/Denver/Oxford: ABC-Clio.

Kohlheim, Rosa (1996). 'Personennamen II: Familiennamen. Typologie und Benennungssysteme bei Familiennamen: principiell und kulturvergleichend', in Ernst Eichler, et al. (eds.), *Namenforschung/Name Studies/Les noms propres. Ein internationals Handbuch zur Onomastik/International Handbook of Onomastics/Manuel international d'onomastique*, vol. 1. Berlin/New York: de Gruyter, 1247–59.

Kohlheim, Rosa, and Kohlheim, Volker (2008). *Duden. Lexikon der Familiennamen*. Mannheim/Leipzig/Wien/Zürich: Duden.

Kohlheim, Rosa, and Kohlheim, Volker (2011). 'Der literarische Name zur Jahrtausendwende: Andreas Maiers Roman *Wäldchestag* als Beispiel', *Beiträge zur Namenforschung (Neue Folge)* 46.3: 269–85.

Kohlheim, Rosa, and Kohlheim, Volker (2013). *Duden Namenbuch*. 6th edn. Mannheim: Duden.

Kohlheim, Volker (1977). *Regensburger Rofnamen des 13. und 14. Jahrhunderts. Linguistische und sozio-onomastische Untersuchungen zur Struktur und Motivik spätmittelalterlicher Rufnamen*. Wiesbaden: Steiner.

Kohnen, Thomas (2008). 'Linguistic Politeness in Anglo-Saxon England? A Study of Old English Address Terms', *Journal of Historical Pragmatics* 9.1: 140–58.

Kollerstrom, Nicholas (2009). 'The Naming of Neptune', *Journal of Astronomical History and Heritage* 12.1: 66–71.

Koopman, Adrian (1992). 'The Socio-Cultural Aspects of Zulu Ox- and Dog-Names'. *Nomina Africana* 6.1: 1–13.

Koopman, Adrian (2002a). 'Naming as a Marketing Strategy in a Coastal Resort. The Case of St. Lucia', *Nomina Africana* 16.1–2: 42–55.

Koopman, Adrian (2002b). *Zulu Names*. Pietermaritzburg: University of Natal Press.

Koopman, Adrian (2008). 'Zulu Names', in Benedict Carton, John Laband, and Jabulani Sithole (eds.), *Zulu Identities. Being Zulu, Past and Present*, Pietermaritzburg: University of KwaZulu-Natal Press, 439–48.

Koopman, Adrian (2012a). 'Street-Name Changes in Pietermaritzburg and Durban Within Their Historical and Global Contexts', *Nomina Africana* 26.1: 95–112.

Koopman, Adrian (2012b). 'The Post-Colonial Identity of Durban', in Botolv Helleland, Christian-Emil Ore, and Solveig Wikstrøm (eds.), *Names and Identities*. Oslo Studies in Language 4.2. Oslo: University of Oslo, 133–59. Available online at: <https://www.journals.uio.no/index.php/osla/article/view/315/440>.

Koskinen, Kaisa (2012). 'Linguistic Landscape as a Translational Space. The Case of Hervanta, Tampere', *COLLeGIUM. Studies Across Disciplines in the Humanities and Social Sciences* 13: 73–92.

Koss, Gerhard (1990). 'Warennamen: Information—Assoziation—Suggestion', in Eeva M. Närhi (ed.), *Proceedings of the XVIIth International Congress of Onomastic Sciences. Helsinki 13–18 August 1990*, vol 2. Helsinki: University of Helsinki and the Finnish Research Centre for Domestic Languages, 38–45.

Koss, Gerhard (1996a). 'Warennamen', in Ernst Eichler, et al. (eds.), *Namenforschung/Name Studies/Les noms propres. Ein internationals Handbuch zur Onomastik/International Handbook of Onomastics/Manuel international d'onomastique*, vol. 2. Berlin/New York: de Gruyter, 1642–8.

Koss, Gerhard (1996b). 'Warennamen-, Firmennamenrecht', in Ernst Eichler, et al. (eds.), *Namenforschung/Name Studies/Les noms propres. Ein internationals Handbuch zur Onomastik/International Handbook of Onomastics/Manuel international d'onomastique*, vol. 2. Berlin/New York: de Gruyter, 1795–1802.

Koss, Gerhard (2002). *Namenforschung*. Tübingen: Max Niemeyer.

Kostanski, Laura (2009). ' "What's in a Name?". Place and Toponymic Attachment, Identity and Dependence. A case study of the Grampians (Gariwerd) National Park Name Restoration Process'. PhD dissertation, University of Ballarat.

Kostanski, Laura (2011). 'Signs of the Times. Changing Names and Cultural Values in Australia', *Onoma* 46: 251–74.

Kostanski, Laura, and Clark, Ian D. (2009). 'Reviving Old Indigenous Names for New Purposes', in Harold Koch and Luisa Hercus (eds.), *Aboriginal Place-Names. Naming and Re-Naming the Australian Landscape*. Canberra: ANU E, 189–206.

Kotler, Philip, and Gertner, David (2002). 'Country as Brand, Product and Beyond. A Place Marketing and Brand Management Perspective', in Nigel Morgan, Annette Pritchard, and Roger Pride (eds.), *Destination Branding. Creating the Unique Destination Proposition*. Oxford: Elsevier Butterworth-Heinemann, 40–56.

Kotze, Chrismi-Rinda, and du Plessis, Theoorus (2010). 'Language Visibility in the Xhariep. A Comparison of the Linguistic Landscape of Three Neighbouring Towns', *Language Matters. Studies in the Languages of Africa* 41.1: 72–96.

Kousgård Sørensen, John (1972). 'Danmark og Gammeleuropa', *Namn och Bygd* 60: 59–77.

Kousgård Sørensen, John (1984). 'Navn og bebyggelse. Om -*rød* i Nordsjælland', in Vibeke Dalberg, et al. (eds.), *Bebyggelsers of bebyggelsenavnes alder*. NORNA-rapporter 26. Uppsala: NORNA-förlaget, 215–28.

Kowaleski, Maryanne (1995). *Local Markets and Regional Trade in Medieval Exeter*. Cambridge: Cambridge University Press.

Krahe, Hans (1963). *Die Struktur der alteuropäischen Hydronymie*. Akademie der Wissenschaften und der Literatur. Abhandlungen der geistes- und sozialwissenschaftlichen Klasse. Jahrgang 1962:5. Mainz: Verlag der Akademie der Wissenschaften und der Literatur in Mainz.

Krahe, Hans (1964). *Unsere ältesten Flußnamen*. Wiesbaden: Otto Harrassowitz.

Krahe, Hans (1965). 'Vorgermanische und frühgermanische Flußnamen-schichten. Mittel zu ihrer Unterscheidung', in Rudolf Schützeichel and Matthias Zender (eds.), *Namenforschung. Festschrift für Adolf Bach zum 75. Geburtstag am 31. Januar 1965*. Heidelberg: Carl Winter, 192–8.

Kranzmayer, Eberhard (1934): 'Zur Ortsnamenforschung im Grenzland', *Zeitschrift für Ortsnamenforschung* 10: 105–48.

Kremer, Ludger (1996). 'Die Firma. Einige Beobachtungen zur Unternehmens-Namengebung', in Jörg Hennig and Jürgen Meier (eds.), *Varietäten der deutsche Sprache. Festschrift für Dieter Möhn*. Frankfurt am Main/Bern/Paris: Peter Lang, 357–70.

Kremer, Ludger (1997). 'Sind Namen "Schall und Rauch"? Zur Werbewirkung von Unternehmensnamen', in Lita Lundquist, Herbiert Picht, and Jacques Qvistgaard (eds.), *LSP, Identity and Interface. Research, Knowledge and Society. Proceedings of the 11th European Symposium on Language for Special Purposes*, vol. 2. Copenhagen: Copenhagen Business School, 572–81.

Kremer, Ludger (2007). 'Tendenzen der Namengebung bei deutschen Unternehmen', in Eva Brylla and Mats Wahlberg (eds.), *Proceedings of the 21st International Congress of Onomastic Sciences. Uppsala 19–24 August 2002*, vol. 3. Uppsala: Institutet för spark- och folkminnen, 177–92.

Kremer, Ludger (2012). 'Von der *Vereinsbank in Hamburg* zur *HVB*. Zur Diachronie deutscher Unternehmensnamen', in Holger Wochele, Julia Kuhn, and Martin Stegu (eds.), *Onomastics Goes Business. Role and Relevance of Brands, Company and Other Names in Economic Contexts*. Berlin: Logos, 129–40.

Kremer, Ludger, and Ronneberger-Sibold, Elke (eds.) (2007). *Names in Commerce and Industry. Past and Present*. Berlin: Logos.

Kress, Günther R. (ed.) (1976). *Halliday. System and Function of Language. Selected Papers*. London: Oxford University Press.

Kress, Gunther, and van Leeuwen, Theo (1996). *Reading Images. The Grammar of Visual Design*. London: Routledge.

Kripke, Saul (1972). 'Naming and Necessity', in David Davidson and Gilbert Harman (eds.), *Semantics of Natural Language*. 2nd edn. Dordrecht/Boston: Reidel, 253–355.

Kripke, Saul (1980). *Naming and Necessity*. Cambridge, MA: Harvard University Press.

Kristensson, Gillis (1967–2002). *A Survey of Middle English Dialects, 1290–1350*. 5 vols. Lund: Lund University Press.

Kristensson, Gillis (2001). 'Language in Contact. Old East Saxon and East Anglian', in Jacek Fisiak and Peter Trudgill (eds.), *East Anglian English*. Cambridge: D.S. Brewer, 63–70.

Kristol, Andres (ed.) (2005). *Dictionnaire toponymique des communes suisses—Lexikon der schweizerischen Gemeindenamen—Dizionario toponomastico dei comuni svizzeri*. Frauenfeld/Stuttgart/Wien: Huber.

Krogseth, Otto (2012). 'Names and Collective Identity', in Botolv Helleland, Christian-Emil Ore and Solveig Wikstrøm (eds.), *Names and Identities*. Oslo Studies in Language 4.2. Oslo: University of Oslo, 162–66. Available online at: <https://www.journals.uio.no/index.php/osla/article/view/316/441>.

Kronsteiner, Otto (1967–8). 'Der slawische Flußname "Bystrica" und seine Bedeutung', *Wiener Slavistisches Jahrbuch* 14: 83–7.

Kroon, Frederick (2004). 'Descriptivism, Pretense, and the Frege-Russell Problems', *The Philosophical Review* 113: 1–30.

Kruken, Kristoffer (2013). *Norsk personnamnleksikon*. 3rd edn. Oslo: Det Norske Samlaget.

Kryukova, Irina (2012). 'Rebranding in Russian Ergonymy as a Matter of Sociolinguistics', in Reina Boerrigter and Harm Nijboer (eds.), *Names as Language and Capital. Proceedings Names in the Economy III, Amsterdam, 11–13 June 2009*, 41–47. Amsterdam: Meertens Instituut. Available online at: <http://depot.knaw.nl/12899/>.

Kuhn, Julia (2001). 'Romanische Orts- und Flurnamen im Raum *Tscherlach*', in Peter Wunderli, Iwar Werlen, and Matthias Grünert (eds.), *Italica—Raetica—Gallica*. Tübingen/Basel: Francke, 43–58.

Kuhn, Julia (2002). *Die romanischen Orts- und Flurnamen von Walenstadt und Quarten/St. Gallen/Schweiz*. Innsbruck: AMOE.

Kuhn, Julia (2005). 'Anthropology and Etymology—*Murg*. An Example of the Relation Between Toponomastics and the Language Spoken by the Inhabitants', in Graesimos Chatzidamianos, G. Chi, L. Frey, K. Hargreaves, T. Kras, N. Noakovic, and E. Vilar Beltrán (eds.), *CamLing 2005. Proceedings of the University of Cambridge Third Postgraduate Conference in Language Research in Association with the Cambridge Institute of Language Research, Held on 18 March 2005*. Cambridge: Cambridge Institute of Language Research, 54–63.

Kunitzsch, Paul, and Smart, Tim (2006). *A Dictionary of Modern Star Names*. 2nd rev. edn. Cambridge, MA: Sky Publishing.

Kunze, Konrad (2004). *dtv-Atlas Namenkunde, Vor- und Familiennamen im deutschen Sprachgebiet*. 5th rev. and corrected edn. München: Deutscher Taschenbuch.

Kuryłowicz, Jerzy (1980). 'The Linguistic Status of Proper Nouns (Names)', *Onomastica* 25: 5–8.

Kushida, Shuya (2015). 'Using Names for Referring without Claiming Shared Knowledge: Name-quoting Descriptors in Japanese', *Research on Language and Social Interaction* 48.2: 230–51.

Kushner, Julia Shear (2009). 'The Right To Control One's Name', *UCLA Law Review* 57.313: 313–64.

La Palme Reyes, Marie, MacNamara, John, Reyes, G. E., and Zolfaghari, H. (1993). 'Proper Names and How They Are Learned', *Memory* 1.4: 433–55.

Laansalu, Tiina, and Alas, Marit (2013). 'Intercultural Influences in Contemporary Estonian Settlement Names', in Oliviu Felecan (ed.), *Name and Naming. Proceedings of the Second International Conference on Onomastics. Onomastics in Contemporary Public Space, Baia Mare, May 9–11, 2013*. Cluj-Napoca: Editura Mega / Editura Argonaut, 339–54.

Labov, William (1966). *The Social Stratification of English in New York City*. Washington, DC: Center for Applied Linguistics.

Labov, William (1972). *Language in the Inner City. Studies in the Black English Vernacular*. Philadelphia: University of Pennsylvania Press.

Lackey, Douglas (ed.) (1973). *Bertrand Russell. Essays in Analysis*. New York: George Braziller.

Lacy, Brian, with Cody, Eamon, Cotter, Claire, Cuppage, Judy, Dunne, Noel, Hurley, Vincent, O'Rahilly, Celie, Walsh, Paul, and Ó Nualláin, Seán (eds.) (1983). *Archaeological Survey of County Donegal*. Lifford: Donegal County Council.

Laing, Margaret, and Lass, Roger (2009). 'Early Middle English Dialectology. Problems and Prospects', in Ans van Kemenade and Bettelou Los (eds.), *The Handbook of the History of English*. Oxford: Blackwell, 417–51.

Laitinen, Mikko (2014). '630 Kilometres by Bicycle. Observations of English in Urban and Rural Finland', *International Journal of the Sociology of Language* 228: 55–77.

Lakoff, George (1968). *Pronouns and Reference. Parts I and II*. Reproduced by the Linguistics Club, Indiana University.

Lambek, Michael (2006). 'What's in a Name? Name Bestowal and the Identity of Spirits in Mayotte and Northwest Madagascar', in Gabriele Vom Bruck and Barbara Bodenhorn (eds.), *The Anthropology of Names and Naming*. Cambridge: Cambridge University Press, 115–38.

Land Information New Zealand (n.d.). 'Whanganui Place Name Report—Board Policies and Relevant Legislation'. Available online at: <http://www.linz.govt.nz/regulatory/place-names/place-name-consultation/7410>.

Landry, Rodrigue, and Bourhis, Richard Y. (1997). 'Linguistic Landscape and Ethnolinguistic Vitality. An Empirical Study', *Journal of Language and Social Psychology* 16: 23–49.

Langacker, Ronald W. (1987). *Foundations of Cognitive Grammar, vol. I: Theoretical Prerequisites*. Stanford: Stanford University Press.

Langacker, Ronald W. (1991). *Foundations of Cognitive Grammar, vol. II: Descriptive Application*. Stanford: Stanford University Press.

Lape, Peter V. (2002). 'Historic Maps and Archaeology as a Means of Understanding Late Precolonial Settlement in the Banda Islands, Indonesia', *Asian Perspectives* 41.1: 43–70.

Laskowski, Kara A. (2010). 'Women's Post-Marital Name Retention and the Communication of Identity', *Names* 58.2: 75–89.

Laugrand, Frédéric, and Oosten, Jarich (2002). 'Canicide and Healing. The Position of the Dog in the Inuit Cultures of the Canadian Arctic', *Anthropos* 97.1: 89–105.

Lawson, Edwin D. (1984). 'Personal Names. 100 Years of Social Science Contributions', *Names* 32: 45–73.

Lawson, Edwin D. (1987). *Personal Names and Naming. An Annotated Bibliography*. New York: Greenwood.

Lawson, Edwin D. (1995). *More Names and Naming. An Annotated Bibliography*. Westport, CT: Greenwood.

Lawson, Edwin D. (1996a). 'Personal Name Stereotypes', in Ernst Eichler, et al. (eds.), *Namenforschung/Name Studies/Les noms propres. Ein internationals Handbuch zur Onomastik/International Handbook of Onomastics/Manuel international d'onomastique*, vol. 2. Berlin/New York: de Gruyter, 1744–7.

Lawson, Edwin D. (1996b). 'The Onomastic Treasures of the CIA', *Names* 44: 154–64.

Lawson, Edwin D., and Dance, Philip (2008). *Fredonia Personal Name Bibliography*. Available online at: <http://www.fredonia.edu/faculty/emeritus/edwinlawson/bibliographies/Fredonia_Personal_Name_Bibliography_8-1-08_Lawson_edit.pdf>.

Lawson, Edwin D., and Sheil, Richard F. (2013). *The Onomastic Treasure of the CIA*. Fredonia, NY: State University of New York. Available online at: <http://ciaforeignpersonalnames. edwindlawson.com/>.

Layne, Linda (2006). ' "Your Child Deserves a Name": Possessive Individualism and the Politics of Memory in Pregnancy Loss', in Gabriele vom Bruck and Barbara Bodenhorn (eds.), *The Anthropology of Names and Naming*. Cambridge: Cambridge University Press, 31–50.

Layton, Robert (1997). *An Introduction to Theory in Anthropology*. Cambridge: Cambridge University Press.

LCAB = Ó Donnchadha, Tadhg (ed.) (1931). *Leabhar Cloinne Aodha Buidhe*. Dublin: Irish Manuscript Commission.

Lebel, Paul (1956). *Principes et méthodes d'hydronymie française*. Paris: Université de Paris. Faculté des lettres.

Leech, Geoffrey N. (1966). *English in Advertising*. London: Longmans.

Leech, Geoffrey N. (1981). *Semantics. The Study of Meaning*. 2nd edn. Suffolk: Richard Clay.

Lefebvre, Henri (1991). *The Production of Space*. trans by. Donald Nicholson-Smith. Oxford: Basil Blackwell.

Leibring, Katharina (2000). *Sommargås och Stjärnberg. Studier i svenska nötkreatursnamn*. Uppsala: Kungl. Gustav Adolfs Akademien för Svensk Folkkultur.

Leibring, Katharina (2001). 'Pärla, Sommargås och Burman. Svenska husdjursnamn från 1700-talet till våra dagar', *Ortnamnssällskapets i Uppsala årsskrift*: 10–23.

Leibring, Katharina (2009). 'Zwartje, Flight of Delight and Chikai. Borrowed Names for Animal Names in Sweden', in Wolfgang Ahrens, Sheila Embleton, and André Lapierre (eds.), *Names in Multi-Lingual, Multi-Cultural and Multi-Ethnic Contact. Proceedings of the 23rd International Congress of Onomastic Sciences, August 17–22, 2008, York University, Toronto, Canada*. Toronto: York University, 658–64. Available online at: <http://yorkspace.library. yorku.ca/xmlui/bitstream/handle/10315/4002/icos23_658.pdf?sequence=1>.

Leibring, Katharina (2012a). 'Is Your Name a Good Investment? Socio-Economic Reasons for Surname Changes in Sweden', in Holger Wochele, Julia Kuhn, and Martin Stegu (eds.), *Onomastics Goes Business. Role and Relevance of Brands, Company and Other Names in Economic Contexts*. Berlin: Logos, 273–80.

Leibring, Katharina (2012b). 'Staffan i den Svenska Kattnamnsskatten', in Katharina Leibring, Leif Nilsson, Annette C. Torensjö, and Mats Wahlberg (eds.), *Namn på stort och smått. Vänskrift till Staffan Nyström den 11 december 2012*. Uppsala: Institutet för språk och folkminnen, 141–8.

Leibring, Katharina (2013). 'Djurnamn', in Staffan Nyström, et al. (eds.), *Namn och namnforskning. Ett digitalt läromedel*. Uppsala: Uppsala universitetet, 159–64. Available online at: <http://uu.diva-portal.org/smash/get/diva2:606610/FULLTEXT01>.

Leibring, Katharina (2014). 'Från Trogen till Tyson. Hundnamn i Sverige i förändring', in Anne-Sofie Gräslund and Ingvar Svanberg (eds.), *Från renhållningshjon till modeaccessoar. Föredrag vid ett symposium 15 februari 2013*. Uppsala: Kungl. Gustav Adolfs Akademien för Svensk Folkkultur, 121–37.

Leino, Antti (2007). 'Construction Grammar in Onomastics. The Case of Finnish Hydronyms', in Donatella Bremer, Michele Bani, Franco Belli, and Matteo Paolini (eds.), *I Nomi Nel Tempo e Nello Spazio. Atti del XXII Congresso Internazionale di Scienze Onomastiche. Pisa, 28 agosto-4 settembre 2005*, vol. 1. Pisa: Edizioni ETS, 297–309.

Lele, Veerendra (2009). '"It's not Really a Nickname, it's a Method". Local Names, State Intimates, and Kinship Register in the Irish *Gaeltacht*', *Journal of Linguistic Anthropology* 19: 101–16.

Lemghari, El Mustapha (2014). 'Complexité sous-catégorielle des noms propres métonymiques et continuum massif vs comptable', in Joan Tort i Donada and Montserrat Montagut i Montagut (eds.), *Els noms en la vida quotidiana. Actes del XXIV Congrés Internacional d'ICOS sobre Ciències Onomàstiques. Names in Daily Life. Proceedings of the XXIV ICOS International Congress of Onomastic Sciences*. Generalitat de Catalunya, Departament de Cultura. Available online at: <http://www.gencat.cat/llengua/BTPL/ICOS2011/039.pdf>.

Léonard, Carol (2009). 'Toponymie et contrepoids aux effets du paysage linguistique en situation de contact des langues', in Wolfgang Ahrens, Sheila Embleton, and André Lapierre (eds.), *Names in Multi-Lingual, Multi-Cultural and Multi-Ethnic Contact. Proceedings of the 23rd International Congress of Onomastic Sciences, August 17–22, 2008, York University, Toronto, Canada*. Toronto: York University, 677–87. Available online at: <http://yorkspace.library.yorku.ca/xmlui/bitstream/handle/10315/4004/icos23_677.pdf?sequence=1>.

Lerner, Gene H., and Kitzinger, Celia (eds.) (2007). *Discourse Studies* 9.4.

Lester, G. A. (ed.) (2002). *Three Late Medieval Morality Plays*. London: A. and C. Black.

Lev, Eimi, and Lewinsky, Anat (2004). 'The Presentation of Self in Online Life. The Importance of Nicknames in Online Environments'. Available online at: <http://gsb.haifa.ac.il/~sheizaf/AOIR5/40.html> [accessed 30 May 2013].

Lévi-Strauss, Claude (1962). *La pensée sauvage*. Plon: Paris.

Lévi-Strauss, Claude (1966). *The Savage Mind*. English translation. London: Weidenfeld and Nicolson.

Levith, Murray J. (1978). *What's in Shakespeare's Names*. London: George Allen and Unwin.

Lewicka, Maria (2008). 'Place Attachment, Place Identity and Place Memory. Restoring the Forgotten City Past', *Journal of Environmental Psychology* 28: 209–31.

Lewis, Carenza (2007). 'New Avenues for the Investigation of Currently Occupied Medieval Rural Settlement. Preliminary Observations from the Higher Education Field Academy', *Medieval Archaeology* 51: 133–63.

Lexic.us (n.d.). 'Definition of Ethnos'. *Lexicus Online Web Dictionary and Thesaurus*. Available online at: <www.lexic.us/definition-of/ethnos>.

Li Chang, William, and Li, Perichyi (2008). 'Luck of the Draw. Creating Chinese Brand Names', *Journal of Advertising Research* 48.4: 523–30.

Li, Fengru (2012). 'A Sociolinguistic Inquiry into Chinese Brand Naming Behaviors. Moral Dilemmas, Constraining Hieroglyphs and Economic Aspirations', in Reina Boerrigter and Harm Nijboer (eds.), *Names as Language and Capital. Proceedings Names in the Economy III, Amsterdam, 11–13 June 2009*. Amsterdam: Meertens Instituut, 58–63. Available online at: <http://depot.knaw.nl/12899/>.

Liberman, A. M., Cooper, F. S., Shankweiler, D. P. and Studdert-Kennedy, M. (1967). 'Perception of the Speech Code', *Psychological Review* 74.6: 431–61.

Lieberson, Stanley (2000). *A Matter of Taste. How Names, Fashions, and Culture Change*. New Haven, CT: Yale University Press.

Light, Duncan (2004). 'Street Names in Bucharest, 1990–1997. Exploring the Modern Historical Geographies of Post-Socialist Change', *Journal of Historical Geography* 30: 154–72.

Lillis, Theresa, and McKinney, Carolyn (2013). 'The Sociolinguistics of Writing in a Global Context. Objects, Lenses, Consequences', *Journal of Sociolinguistics* 17.4: 415–39.

Lindbergh, Charles (1927). *We—Pilot and Plane*. London: G. P. Putnam's Sons.

Lindeström, Per (1692). *Resa till Nya Sverige*. ed. by Alf Åberg. Stockholm: Natur och Kultur.

Lindkvist, Harald (1912). *Middle-English Place-Names of Scandinavian Origin*. Uppsala: University Press.

Literary Devices (n.d.). Available online at: <http://slim707.tripod.com/>.

Litteraturbanken (n.d.). Litteraturbanken. Gratis Eböcker. Svenska Klassiker i Digitala Versioner. Available online at: <http://litteraturbanken.se>.

Löbner, Sebastian (1985). 'Definites', *Journal of Semantics* 4: 279–326.

Locher, Miriam A., and Watts, Richard J. (2005). 'Politeness Theory and Relational Work', *Journal of Politeness Research* 1: 9–33.

Lockerbie-Cameron, Margaret A. L. (1991). 'The Men Named in the Poem', in Donald Scragg (ed.), *The Battle of Maldon AD 991*. Oxford: Blackwell, 238–49.

Lockheed Martin (2006). 'Lockheed Martin Joint Strike Fighter Officially Named Lightning II', 7 July. Available online at: <http://www.lockheedmartin.com/us/news/press-releases/2006/july/LOCKHEEDMARTINJOINTSTRIKEFIGHTEROFF.html> [accessed 28 October 2013].

Löfvenberg, Mattias T. (1942). *Studies on Middle English Local Surnames*. Lund: Gleerup.

Lombard, Carol G. (2011). 'The Sociocultural Significance of *Niitsitapi* Personal Names. An Ethnographic Analysis', *Names* 59: 42–51.

Lombard, Carol G. (2012). 'Addressing and Interpreting the Issue of Authenticity in Place Renaming. A South African Perspective', *Nomina Africana* 26.1: 54–61.

Lombardi, Mike (2004). 'Why 7's Been a Lucky Number', *Boeing Frontiers Online* 2.10. Available online at: <http://www.boeing.com/news/frontiers/archive/2004/february/i_history.html>. [accessed 28 October 2013].

Longley, Paul A., Goodchild, Michael F., Maguire, David J., and Rhind, David W. (2005). *Geographic Information Systems and Science*. 2nd edn. Chichester: Wiley.

Longley, Paul, Singleton, Alex, Webber, Richard, and Lloyd, Daryl (date unavailable). *Public Profiler: GB Names*. [online] Available at: <http://gbnames.publicprofiler.org/> [Accessed 30 March 2014].

Longnon, Auguste (1920-9). *Les Noms de Lieux de la France*. Paris: Champion.

Longobardi, Claudio (2006). 'The Meaning of First Names in Children's Developmental Psychology', in Eva Brylla and Mats Wahlberg (eds.), *Proceedings of the 21st International Congress of Onomastic Sciences, Uppsala, 19–24 August 2002*, vol. 2. Uppsala: Institutet för spark- och folkminnen, 189–99.

Longrie, Michael (1997). 'Billy Joel's History Lesson', *College Teaching* 45.4: 147–9.

Lothian, J. M., and Craik, T. W. (eds.) (1975). *Twelfth Night*. The Arden Shakespeare Second Series. London: Methuen.

Lotman, Jurij M. (1972). *Vorlesungen zu einer strukturalen Poetik*. München: Wilhelm Fink.

Lötscher, Andreas (2010). 'Die historischen Voraussetzungen für den Eigennamenstatus von Produktnamen', *Onoma* 43: 25–56.

Lou, Jackie Jia (2010). 'Chinese on the Side. The Marginalization of Chinese in the Linguistic and Social Landscapes of Chinatown in Washington, DC', in Elana Shohamy, Eliezer Ben-Rafael, and Monica Barni (eds.), *Linguistic Landscape in the City*. Bristol: Multilingual Matters, 96–114.

Lou, Jackie Jia (2013). 'Representing and Reconstructing Chinatown. A Social Semiotic Analysis of Place Names in Urban Planning Policies of Washington, D.C.', in Celine-Marie Pascale (ed.), *Social Inequality and the Politics of Representation. A Global Landscape*. London: Sage, 110–25.

Lou, Jackie Jia (2014). 'Locating the Power of *Place* in *Space*. A Geosemiotic Approach to Context', in John Flowerdew (ed.), *Discourse in Context*. London: Bloomsbury, 205–23.

Lounsbury, Floyd (1960). 'Iroquois Place-Names in the Champlain Valley', *Report on the New York–Vermont Interstate Commission on Lake Champlain Basin*. New York Legislative Document 9: 21–66.

Louwrens, L. J. (1994). 'A Linguistic Analysis of Sotho Geographical Names', *Nomina Africana* 8.1: 1–42.

Lowenthal, David (1962). 'Not Every Prospect Pleases. What is our Criterion for Scenic Beauty?', *Landscape* 12.2: 19–23.

Lower, Mark Antony (1849). *English Surnames. An Essay on Family Nomenclature*. 2 vols. London: John Russell Smith.

Lower, Mark Antony (1996 [1860]). *Patronymica Britannica. A Dictionary of the Family Names of the United Kingdom*. Bowie, MD: Heritage Classic.

Lubbe, J. (2003). 'Van heilige tot ikon: Die geskiedenis van die naamgewing van een van Bloemfontein se strate', *Nomina Africana* 17.1: 5–20.

Lucchelli, Federica, and De Renzi, Ennio (1992). 'Proper Name Anomia', *Cortex* 28: 221–30.

Lundahl, Ivar (1950). 'Några gamla nordiska sjö- och vattendragsnamn', *Namn och Bygd* 38: 38–57.

Lurati, Ottavio (1983). *Natura e cultura nei nomi di luogo di Castel San Pietro e del Monte Generoso. Un contributo alla toponomastica lombarda*. Castel San Pietro: Commune.

Lyons, Christopher (1999). *Definiteness*. Cambridge: Cambridge University Press.

Lyons, John (1977). *Semantics*. 2 vols. Cambridge: Cambridge University Press.

Mac Airt, Seán (ed. and trans.) (1951). *The Annals of Innisfallen*. Dublin: Dublin Institute for Advanced Studies.

Mac Airt, Seán, and Mac Niocaill, Gearóid (ed. and trans.) (1983). *The Annals of Ulster*. vol. 1. Dublin: Dublin Institute for Advanced Studies.

Mac an Bhaird, Alan (1991–3). 'Ptolemy Revisited', *Ainm* 5: 1–20.

Mac Gabhann, Fiachra (1997). *Place-Names of Northern Ireland, vol. 7. County Antrim II: Ballycastle and North-East Antrim*. Belfast: The Institute of Irish Studies.

Mac Giolla Easpaig, Dónall (1981). 'Noun + Noun Compounds in Irish Placenames', *Études Celtiques* 18: 151–63.

Mac Giolla Easpaig, Dónall (1996). 'Placenames of County Galway', in Gerard Moran and Raymond Gillespie (eds.), *Galway. History and Society*. Dublin: Geography Publications, 795–815.

Mac Giolla Easpaig, Dónall (2005). 'The Significance and Etymology of the Place-Name *Temair*', in Edel Bhreathnach (ed.), *The Kingship and Landscape of Tara*, Dublin: Four Courts, 423–48.

Mac Mathúna, Liam (1997). 'Observations on Irish *lann* "(Piece of) Land, (Church) Building" and Compounds', *Ériu* 48: 153–60.

Mac Neill, Eoin (1930). 'The *Vita Tripartita* of St. Patrick', *Ériu* 11, 1–41.

Macalister, R. A. S. (ed. and trans.) (1938–56). *Lebor Gabála Érenn. The Book of the Taking of Ireland*. 5 vols. Dublin: Irish Texts Society.

McArthur, Tom (2002). *The Oxford Guide to World English*. Oxford: Oxford University Press.

Macaulay, Ronald K. S. (2005). *Extremely Common Eloquence*. Amsterdam: Rodopi.

McCawley, James (1968). 'The Role of Semantics in a Grammar', in Emmon Bach and Robert T. Harms (eds.), *Universals in Linguistic Theory*. New York: Holt, Rinehart and Winston, 124–69.

McClure, Peter (1979). 'Patterns of Migration in the Late Middle Ages. The Evidence of English Place-Name Surnames', *The Economic History Review* 32.2: 167–82.

McClure, Peter (1981a). 'Nicknames and Petnames. Linguistic Forms and Social Contexts', *Nomina* 5: 63–76.

McClure, Peter (1981b). 'The Interpretation of Middle English Nicknames. A Review of Jan Jönsjö, *Studies on Middle English Nicknames. 1, Compounds*', *Nomina* 5: 95–104.

McClure, Peter (2010a). 'Middle English Occupational Bynames as Lexical Evidence. A Study of Names in the Nottingham Borough Court Rolls 1303–1455. Part 1, Methodology', *Transactions of the Philological Society* 108.2: 164–77.

McClure, Peter (2010b). 'Middle English Occupation Bynames as Lexical Evidence. A Study of Names in the Nottingham Borough Court Rolls 1303–1455. Part 2, Etymologies', *Transactions of the Philological Society* 108.3: 213–31.

McClure, Peter (2011a). 'Surnames as Sources in the OED'. Available online at: <www.oed.com/public/surnamesassources>.

McClure, Peter (2011b). 'Personal Names and the Development of English'. Available online at: <www.oed.com/public/personalnamesinoed>.

McCone, Kim (ed. and trans.) (2000). *Echtrae Chonnlai and the Beginnings of Vernacular Narrative Writing in Ireland. A Critical Edition with Introduction, Notes, Bibliography and Vocabulary*. Maynooth: Department of Old and Middle Irish, National University of Ireland.

McConnel-Ginnet, Sally (2006). '"What's in a Name?" Social Labeling and Gender Practices', in Janet Holmes and Miriam Meyerhoff (eds.), *The Handbook of Language and Gender*. Malden, MA/Oxford: Blackwell, 69–97.

McConvell, Patrick (2006). 'Shibbolethnonyms, Ex-Exonyms and Eco-Ethnonyms in Aboriginal Australia. The Pragmatics of Onymization and Archaism', *Onoma* 41: 185–214.

McCrank, John (Reuters) (2012). 'Cohen terug op die rakke', *Die Burger*, 31 January.

MacDonald, Angus (1941). *The Place-Names of West Lothian*. Edinburgh: Oliver and Boyd.

McGee, R. Jon, and Warms, Richard L. (2013). 'Lévi-Strauss, Claude', in R. Jon McGeeand and Richard L. Warms, *Theory in Social and Cultural Anthropology. An Encyclopedia*. Thousand Oaks: Sage, 474–8.

Machaba, Mbali (2000). 'Homestead Names as a Reflection of Social Dynamics in Zulu Settings', *Nomina Africana* 14.2: 45–58.

Machado, José Pedro (1984). *Dicionário Onomástico Etmológico da Língua Portuguesa*. Lisboa: Editorial Confluência.

Machholz, Donald E. (1989). 'Comet Corner', *Association of Lunar and Planetary Observers* 33.1: 25–8.

Maciejauskienė, Vitalija (1991). *Lietuvių Pavardžių Susidarymas 13–18 a.* Vilnius: Mokslas.

McIntosh, Angus, Samuels, Michael L., and Benskin, Michael (1986). *A Linguistic Atlas of Late Middle English, 1350–1450*. Aberdeen: Aberdeen University Press.

McKay, Patrick, and Muhr, Kay (2007). *Lough Neagh Places. Their Names and Origins*. Belfast: Cló Ollscoil na Banríona.

McKinley, Richard A. (1975). *Norfolk and Suffolk Surnames in the Middle Ages*. London: Phillimore.

McKinley, Richard A. (1977). *The Surnames of Oxfordshire*. London: Leopard's Head.

McKinley, Richard A. (1981). *The Surnames of Lancashire*. London: Leopard's Head.

McKinley, Richard A. (1988). *The Surnames of Sussex*. Oxford: Leopard's Head.

McKinley, Richard A. (1990). *A History of British Surnames*. London/New York: Longman.

Maclean, Charles (1990). *The CLAN Almanac*. Kent: Eric Dobby Publishing.

Macleod, Iseabail (2011). 'Scottish National Dictionary', in Iseabail Macleod and J. Derrick McClure (eds.), *Scotland in Definition. A History of Scottish Dictionaries*. Edinburgh: John Donald, 144–71.

MacLysaght, Edward (1957). *The Surnames of Ireland*. Dublin: Irish Academic Press.

MacLysaght, Edward (1985). *The Surnames of Ireland*. 6th edn. Dublin: Irish Academic Press.

McMahon, Barbara (2008). 'Parents Lose Custody of Girl', *The Guardian*, 24 July. Available online at: <http://www.theguardian.com/lifeandstyle/2008/jul/24/familyandrelationships.newzealand>.

MacNeill, Máire (1962). *The Festival of Lughnasa*. 2 vols. Oxford: Oxford University Press.

McWeeny, Kathryn H., Young, Andrew W., Hay, Dennis C., and Ellis, Andrew W. (1987). 'Putting Names to Faces', *British Journal of Psychology* 78: 143–9.

Maguire, Laurie (2007). *Shakespeare's Names*. Oxford: Oxford University Press.

Majtán, Milan (2009). 'Pomenúvanie kráv na Slovensku začiatkom 18. storočia (motivácia imien podľa súpisov bytčianskeho panstva', *Acta Onomastica* 50: 151–7.

Malinowski, Bronislaw (1922). *Argonauts of the Western Pacific. An Account of Native Enterprise and Adventure in the Archipelagoes of Melanesian New Guinea*. London: Routledge and Kegan Paul.

Malinowski, Bronislaw (2002 [1926]). *Malinowski Collected Works. Volume 3: Crime and Custom in Savage Society*. Abingdon: Routledge.

Malinowski, David (2009). 'Authorship in the Linguistic Landscape. A Multimodal-Performative View', in Elana Shohamy and Durk Gorter (eds.), *Linguistic Landscape. Expanding the Scenery*. Abingdon: Routledge, 107–25.

Malone, Kemp (ed.) (1962). *Widsith*. Rev. edn. Copenhagen: Rosenkilde and Bagger.

Manzo, Lynne (2005). 'For Better or Worse. Exploring Multiple Dimensions of Place Meaning', *Journal of Environmental Psychology* 25: 67–86.

Markey, T. L. (1982). 'Crisis and Cognition in Onomastics', *Names* 30: 129–42.

Márkus, Gilbert (2012). *The Place-Names of Bute*. Donington: Shaun Tyas.

Marlett, Stephen A. (2008). 'The Form and Use of Names in Seri', *International Journal of American Linguistics* 74: 47–82.

Marsden, R. G. (1905). 'Ships in the Reign of James I', *Transactions of the Royal Historical Society (New Series)* 19: 309–42.

Marsh, Robert C. (ed.) (1964). *Logic and Knowledge. Essays 1901–1950*. London: Allen and Unwin.

Marshall, Alice Kahler (1985). *Pen Names of Women Writers from 1600 to the Present*. Camp Hill, PA: Alice Marshall Collection.

Marslen-Wilson, William D. (1987). 'Functional Parallelism in Spoken Word Recognition', *Cognition* 25: 71–102.

Marten, Heiko F., Van Mensel, Luk, and Gorter, Durk (2012). 'Studying Minority Languages in the Linguistic Landscape', in Durk Gorter, Heiko F. Marten, and Luk Van Mensel (eds.), *Minority Languages in the Linguistic Landscape*. Basingstoke: Palgrave Macmillan, 1–15.

Martin, Marcienne (2006). *Le pseudonym sur Internet. Une nomination située au Carrefour de l'anonymat et de la sphere privée*. Paris: L'Harmattan.

Martin, Priscilla (1997). 'Allegory and Symbolism', in Derek Brewer and Jonathan Gibson (eds.), *A Companion to the Gawain-Poet*. Cambridge: D.S. Brewer, 315–28.

Martins, Isabel Pavão, and Farrajota, Luisa (2007). 'Proper and Common Names. A Double Dissociation', *Neuropsychologia* 45: 1744–56.

Masanov, Iurii I. (1969). *V mire psevdonimov, anonimov i literaturnykh poddelok.* Moskva: Izdatelstvo Vsesoiuznoi Knizhnoi Palaty.

Mashiri, Pedzisai (2004). 'More Than Mere Linguistic Tricks. The Sociopragmatic Functions of Some Nicknames Used by Shona-Speaking People in Harare', *Zambezia* 31: 22–45.

Mastrelli Anzilotti, Giulia (2003). *Toponomastica Trentina. I Nomi delle Località abitate.* Trento: Provincia autonoma di Trento Servizio Beni librari e archivistici.

Matley, Ian M. (1990). 'Topographic Terms of Southern Scotland. Their Distribution and Significance', *Scottish Geographical Magazine* 106.2: 108–12.

Matthews, Constance M. (1972). *Place-Names of the English-Speaking World.* London: Weidenfeld and Nicolson.

Matthews, Philip W. (2011). 'Wanganui and Whanganui. A Clash of Identities', *Onoma* 46: 167–208.

Matthews, Rupert (1993). *The Illustrated History of the 20th Century.* Grenville Books.

Mattisson, Ann-Christin (1982). 'Elementet *hus* i medeltida nordiska borgnamn', *Studier i nordisk filologi* 63: 17–37.

Mattisson, Ann-Christin (1986). *Medeltida nordiska borg- och sätesgårdsnamn på –holm.* Nomina Germanica 17. Uppsala: Uppsala University.

Mawer, Allen (1930). 'Some Unworked Sources for English Lexicography', in Niels Bøgholm, Aage Brussendorff, and Carl A. Bodelsen (eds.), *A Grammatical Miscellany Offered to Otto Jespersen on his Seventieth Birthday.* London: Allen and Unwin, 11–16.

Mawer, Allen, and Stenton, Frank M. (1929). *Introduction to the Survey of English Place-Names.* English Place-Name Society 1. Cambridge: Cambridge University Press.

Mawer, Allen, and Stenton, Frank M., with Houghton, F. T. S. (1927). *The Place-Names of Worcestershire.* English Place-Name Society 4. Cambridge: Cambridge University Press.

Mawer, Allen, and Stenton, Frank M., with Gover, J. E. B. (1930). *The Place-Names of Sussex. Part 2.* English Place-Name Society 7. Cambridge: Cambridge University Press.

Maxwell, Allen R. (1984). 'Kadayan Personal Names and Naming', in Elisabeth Tooker (ed.), *1980 Proceedings of the American Ethnological Society. Naming Systems.* Washington, DC: American Ethnological Society, 25–39.

Maybury-Lewis, David (1984). 'Names, Person, and Ideology in Central Brazil', in Elisabeth Tooker (ed.), *1980 Proceedings of the American Ethnological Society. Naming Systems.* Washington, DC: American Ethnological Society, 1–10.

Mayerthaler, Willy (1988). *Morphological Naturalness.* Ann Arbor: Karoma.

Maylor, Elizabeth A. (1997). 'Proper Name Retrieval in Old Age. Converging Evidence Against Disproportionate Impairment', *Aging, Neuropsychology, and Cognition* 4: 211–26.

Mayor, Michel, and Queloz, Didier (1995). 'A Jupiter-Mass Companion to a Solar-Type Star', *Nature* 378.6555: 355–9.

Mazzon, Gabriella (2010). 'Terms of Address', in Andreas H. Jucker and Irma Taavitsainen (eds.), *Historical Pragmatics.* Handbooks of Pragmatics 8. Berlin/New York: de Gruyter Mouton, 351–76.

Meeussen, Achille (1959). *Essai de grammaire rundi.* Tervuren: Koninklijk Museum van Belgisch-Congo.

Meier, Emi (1989). *Familiennamenbuch der Schweiz.* 3 vols, 3rd edn. Zurich: Schulthess Polygraphischer Verlag.

Meinig, Donald W. (ed.) (1979). *The Interpretation of Ordinary Landscapes. Geographical Essays.* Oxford: Oxford University Press.

Meiring, Barbara Amoret (1993). 'The Syntax and Semantics of Geographical Names', in P. S. Hattingh, Naftali Kadmon, Peter E. Raper, and Ingrid Booysen (eds.), *Training Course in Toponomy for Southern Africa*. Pretoria: University of Pretoria.

Meldgaard, Eva Villarsen (1993). *Kattens navn. 2000 danske kattenavne*. Værløse: Billesø and Baltzer.

Menk, Lars (2005). *A Dictionary of German-Jewish Surnames*. Teaneck, NJ: Avotaynu.

Meredith, Martin (2011). *The State of Africa*. Jeppestown: Jonathan Bell.

Merku, Pavle (1982). *Slovenski Priimki na Zahodni Meji*. Trieste: Mladika.

Mertz, Elizabeth (1983). 'A Cape Breton System of Personal Names. Pragmatic and Semantic Change', *Semiotica* 44: 55–74.

Mewett, Peter (1982). 'Exiles, Nicknames, Social Identities and the Production of Local Consciousness in a Lewis Crofting Community', in Anthony P. Cohen (ed.), *Belonging. Identity and Social Organisation in British Rural Cultures*. Manchester: Manchester University Press, 222–46.

Meyer, Charles. F. (1992). *Apposition in Contemporary English*. Cambridge: Cambridge University Press.

Michelena, Luis (1973). *Apellidos Vascos*. 3rd edn. San Sebastián: Txertoa.

Michener, James (1974). *Centennial*. London: Secker and Warburg.

Mikkonen, Pirjo, and Sirkka, Paikkala (1992). *Sukunimet*. Keuruu: Otava.

Milani, Tommaso (2014). 'Sexed Signs—Queering the Scenery', *International Journal of the Sociology of Language* 228: 201–25.

Miles, Joyce C. (1973). *House Names Around the World*. Detroit: Gale Research Company.

Miles, Joyce C. (1982). *The House Names Book. Ackybotha to Zeelust*. London: Unwin Paperbacks.

Mill, John Stuart (1973 [1843]). *A System of Logic, Ratiocinative and Inductive*. London: John W. Parker [reprinted in Robson (1973)].

Mills, A. D. (2001). *A Dictionary of London Place Names*. Oxford: Oxford University Press.

Mills, A. D. (2003). *A Dictionary of British Place-Names*. Oxford: Oxford University Press.

Mills, Sara (2003), 'Caught Between Sexism, Anti-Sexism and "Political Correctness". Feminist Women's Negotiations with Naming Practices', *Discourse Society* 14: 87–110.

Mills, Sara (2011). 'Discursive Approaches to Politeness and Impoliteness', in Linguistic Politeness Research Group (eds.), *Discursive Approaches to Politeness*. Mouton Series in Pragmatics 8. Berlin: de Gruyter Mouton, 19–56.

Milroy, James, and Milroy, Lesley (2012). *Authority in Language. Investigating Standard English*. 4th edn. London: Routledge.

Miner, Ellis D. (1998). *Uranus. The Planet, Rings and Satellites*. 2nd edn. New York, NY: John Wiley.

Mithun, Marianne (1984). 'Principles of Naming in Mohawk', in Elisabeth Tooker (ed.), *1980 Proceedings of the American Ethnological Society. Naming Systems*. Washington, DC: American Ethnological Society, 40–54.

Moberg, Lennart (1987). '*Alma* och *Silma*. Ett ånamnspar av principiellt intresse', *Namn och bygd* 75: 96–99.

Modéer, Ivar (1989). *Svenska Personnamn. Handbok för Universitetsbruk of Självstudier*. Anthroponymica Suecana 5. Lund: Studentlitteratur.

Moldanová, Dobrava (1983). *Naše Prĳmení*. Prague: Mladá Fronta.

Mølgaard, Maria (2012). 'Danmark—et bjergrigt land?' Unpublished Master's dissertation, University of Copenhagen.

Molino, Jean (1982). 'Le nom propre dans la langue', *Langages* 16.66: 5–20.

Moll, Francesc de B. (1982). *Els Llinatges Catalans (Catalunya, País Vaelencià, Illes Balears)*. Mallorca: Editorial Moll.

Moll, Johan (2011). 'Die aard en funksie van straatname soos geïllustreer deur straatnaam-toekenning en -verandering', *LitNet Akademies Jaargang* 8.3: 326–44.

Moltmann, Friederike (2013). *Names, Sortals, and the Mass-Count Distinction*. Available online at: <http://semantics.univ-paris1.fr/index.php/visiteur/contenu/afficher/menu/24>.

Mondada, Lorenza (2000). *Décrire la ville. La construction des savoirs urbains dans l'interaction et dans le texte*. Paris: Economica.

Mondada, Lorenza (2004). 'L'annuncio del nome del paziente come dispositivo strutturante per l'attività', *Rivista di Psicolinguistica Applicata* 2.3: 65–78.

Moore, Viv, and Valentine, Tim (1998). 'Naming Faces. The Effect of Age of Acquisition on Speed and Accuracy of Naming Famous Faces', *The Quarterly Journal of Experimental Psychology* 51A: 485–513.

Moore, Wilfred George (1971). *The Penguin Encyclopaedia of Places*. Harmondsworth: Penguin.

Moran, Gerard, and Gillespie, Raymond (eds.) (1996). *Galway. History and Society*. Dublin: Geography Publications.

Morgan, Lewis Henry (1860). 'The Indian Method of Bestowing and Changing Names', *Proceedings of the American Association for the Advancement of Science* 13: 340–3.

Morgan, Nigel, Pritchard, Annette, and Pride, Roger (2002). 'Introduction', in Nigel Morgan, Annette Pritchard, and Roger Pride (eds.), *Destination Branding. Creating the Unique Destination Proposition*. Oxford: Elsevier Butterworth-Heinemann, 3–16.

Morgan, T. J., and Morgan, Prys (1985). *Welsh Surnames*. Cardiff: University of Wales Press.

Moriarty, Máiréad (2012). 'Language Ideological Debates in the Linguistic Landscape of an Irish Tourist Town', in Durk Gorter, Heiko F. Marten, and Luk Van Mensel (eds.), *Minority Languages in the Linguistic Landscape*. Basingstoke: Palgrave Macmillan, 74–88.

Morlet, Marie-Thérèse (1991). *Dictionnaire Étymologique de Noms de Famille*. Paris: Perrin.

Morris, William (ed.) (1979). *The American Heritage Dictionary of the English Language*. Boston: Houghton Mifflin.

Mowzer, Saleem (1998). 'Apartheid Came to Taunt us in the Naming of Streets', *Cape Argus*, 17 November.

Mühleisen, Susanne (2011). 'Forms of Address and Ambiguity in Caribbean English-Lexicon Creoles. Strategic Interactions in a Postcolonial Language Setting', *Journal of Pragmatics* 43.6: 1460–71.

Muhr, Kay (1996). *Place-Names of Northern Ireland, vol. 6. County Down IV: North-West County Down/Iveagh*. Belfast: Cló Ollscoil na Banríona.

Muhr, Kay (1999). 'Water Imagery in Early Irish', *Celtica* 23: 193–210.

Muhr, Kay (2001). 'Territories, People and Place-Names in Co. Armagh', in Art J. Hughes and William Nolan (eds.), *Armagh History and Society*. Dublin: Geography Publications, 295–331.

Muhr, Kay (2002). 'The Early Place-Names of Co. Armagh', *Seanchas Ard Mhacha* 19.1: 1–54.

Muhr, Kay (2006). 'Dindshenchas', in John T. Koch (ed.) *Celtic Culture. A Historical Encyclopedia*. 5 vols. Santa Barbara/Denver/Oxford: ABC-Clio, 599–600.

Muhr, Kay (2008). 'Some Aspects of Manx and (Northern) Irish Monument Names', in Oliver J. Padel and David N. Parsons (eds.), *A Commodity of Good Names. Essays in Honour of Margaret Gelling*. Stamford: Shaun Tyas, 217–32.

Muhr, Kay (2011). 'Place-Names and the Understanding of Monuments', in Roseanne Schot, Conor Newman, and Edel Bhreathnacheds (eds.), *Landscapes of Cult and Kingship*. Dublin: Four Courts, 232–55.

Muhr, Kay (2014). 'The Place-Names of County Fermanagh', in Claire Foley and Ronan McHugh (eds.), *An Archaeological Survey of County Fermanagh*. 2 vols. Belfast: NIEA, 17–54.

Muir, Bernard J. (ed.) (1994). *The Exeter Anthology of Old English Poetry. An Edition of Exeter Dean and Chapter MS 3501*. 2 vols. Exeter: University of Exeter Press.

Müller, Sophus (1904). 'Vej, By og Bygd i Sten- og Bronzealderen', *Aarbøger for nordisk Oldkyndighed og Historie 1904*. Copenhagen: H.H. Thieles, 1–64.

Müller-Lisowski, Kate (1948). 'Contributions to a Study in Irish Folklore. Traditions about Donn', *Béaloideas* 18: 142–99.

Murdock, G. P. (1945). 'The Common Denominator of Cultures', in Ralph Linton (ed.), *The Science of Man in the World Crisis*. New York: Columbia University Press, 123–42.

Murray, James, et al. (1888–1928). *A New English Dictionary on Historical Principles*. 12 vols. Oxford: Oxford University Press.

Murray, John (2014). *Reading the Gaelic Landscape. Leughadh Aghaidh na Tìre*. Dunbeath: Whittles.

Murray, Kevin (2010). *Historical Dictionary of Gaelic Placenames*. Available online at: <http://12.129.114.39/placenames/Login.aspx>.

Murray, Thomas E. (1995). 'From Trade Name to Generic. The Case of *Coke*', *Names* 43.3: 165–86.

Muth, Sebastian (2014). 'Informal Signs as Expressions of Multilingualism in Chisinau. How Individuals Shape the Public Space of a Post-Soviet Capital', *International Journal of the Sociology of Language* 228: 29–53.

Myres, J. N. L. (1935). 'Britain in the Dark Ages', *Antiquity* 9: 455–64.

Namescape (2012–13). *Namescape Project. Mapping the Onymic Landscape*. Available online at: <http://blog.namescape.nl/>.

Nash, Joshua (2011). 'Insular Toponymies. Pristine Place-Naming on Norfolk Island, South Pacific and Dudley Peninsula, Kangaroo Island, South Australia'. PhD dissertation, University of Adelaide.

Nash, Joshua (2013). 'Landscape Underwater, Underwater Landscapes. Kangaroo Island Diving Site Names as Elements of the Linguistic Landscape', *Landscape Research* 38.3: 394–400.

Naumann, Horst (1989 [1984]). 'Soziolinguistische Aspekte der Onomastik', in Friedhelm Debus and Wilfried Seibicke (eds.), *Reader zur Namenkunde*, vol. 1. Hildesheim: Georg Olms, 391–401.

Neethling, Bertie (2000). 'The Developer's Dilemma. Finding the Right Name', *Nomina Africana* 14.1: 57–72.

Neethling, Bertie (2007). 'The Xhosa Speaker's English Name. Burden or Blessing?', in Eva Brylla and Mats Wahlberg (eds.), *Proceedings of the 21st International Congress of Onomastic Sciences, Uppsala, August 19–24 2002*, vol. 3. Uppsala: Institutet för språk- och folkminnen, 245–66.

Neethling, Bertie (2009a). 'Lifestyle, Worldview and Identity. Names on Customized Vehicle Registration Plates', in Wolfgang Ahrens, Sheila Embleton, and André Lapierre (eds.), *Names in Multi-Lingual, Multi-Cultural and Multi-Ethnic Contact. Proceedings of the 23rd International Congress of Onomastic Sciences, August 17–22, 2008, York University, Toronto, Canada*. Toronto: York University, 760–5. Available online at: <http://yorkspace.library.yorku.ca/xmlui/bitstream/handle/10315/4015/icos23_760.pdf?sequence=1>.

Neethling, Bertie (2009b). 'Names as a Vehicle Towards Transformation in the South African Wine Industry', in Eva Lavric, Fiorenza Fischer, Carmen Konzett, Julia Kuhn, and Holger Wochele (eds.), *People, Products, and Professions. Choosing a Name, Choosing a Language*. Frankfurt am Main: Peter Lang, 279–87.

Neethling, Bertie (2010a). 'Naming as a Manifestation of Black Economic Empowerment (BEE) in Post-1994 South Africa', *Onoma* 43: 381–96.

Neethling, Bertie (2010b). 'Reintroducing the Name "Bantu" in South Africa within its Linguistic Context', *Nomina Africana* 24.1: 76–103.

Neethling, Bertie (2012). 'Bynames as an Expression of Identity. A Student Profile at the University of the Western Cape', in Staffan Nyström, Eva Brylla, Katharina Leibring, Lennart Ryman, and Per Vikstrand (eds.), *Binamn. Uppkomst, bildning, terminology och bruk. Handlingar från NORNA:s 40:e symposium i Älvkarleö, Uppland, 29/9–1/10 2010*. NORNA-rapporter 88. Uppsala: NORNA-förlaget, 23–38.

Neethling, Bertie (2013). 'Renaming Streets in the City of Cape Town. Policy and Practice', *Nomina Africana* 27.1: 21–37.

Neethling, S. J. (1995). 'Connotative Toponyms. Christopher Torr's "Hot Gates"', *Nomina Africana* 9: 56–67.

Neill, Kenneth (2009). *An Archaeological Survey of County Armagh*. Belfast: Stationery Office.

Neumüller, Kristina (2007). *Vattensjön och Vattenån. Samband mellan sjönamn och ånamn i Medelpad*. Acta Academiae Regiae Gustavi Adolphi 96. Uppsala: Kungl. Gustav Adolfs Akademien för Svensk Folkkultur.

Nevala, Minna (2004). *Address in Early English Correspondence. Its Forms and Socio-Pragmatic Functions*. Mémoires de la Société Néophilologique de Helsinki 64. Helsinki: Société Néophilologique.

Nevala, Minna (2009). 'Altering Distance and Defining Authority. Person Reference in Late Modern English', *Journal of Historical Pragmatics* 10.2: 238–59.

Nevalainen, Terttu, and Raumolin-Brunberg, Helena (1995). 'Constraints on Politeness. The Pragmatics of Address Formulae in Early English Correspondence', in Andreas H. Jucker (ed.), *Historical Pragmatics. Pragmatic Developments in the History of English*. Amsterdam: John Benjamins, 541–601.

New, Boris, Pallier, Christophe, Brysbaert, Marc, and Ferrand, Ludovic (2004). 'Lexique 2. A New French Lexical Database', *Behavior Research Methods, Instruments, and Computers* 36: 516–24.

Newell, Stephanie (2010). 'Something to Hide? Anonymity and Pseudonyms in the Colonial West African Press', *The Journal of Commonwealth Literature* 45: 9–22.

Newell, Stephanie (2013). *The Power to Name: A History of Anonymity in Colonial West Africa*. Athens: Ohio University Press.

New Zealand History (n.d.). '1000 Māori place-names', in *Maori Language Week*. Available online at: <http://www.nzhistory.net.nz/culture/maori-language-week/1000-maori-place-names> [accessed 25 November 2013].

Nicholls, Kenneth (ed.) (1994). *The Irish Fiants of the Tudor Sovereigns during the Reigns of Henry VIII, Edward VI, Philip and Mary, and Elizabeth I*. 3 vols. Dublin: Edmund Burke Publisher.

Nicholson, Zara (2012). 'Biko Honoured as Gugulethu Road is Renamed', *Cape Times*, 25 September.

NickNameRegistered.com (2015). Available online at: <http://nicknameregister.com/>.

NickName.ru (2010–15). Available online at: <http://nick-name.ru/>.

Nicolaisen, W. F. H. (1957). 'Die alteuropäischen Gewässernamen der britischen Hauptinsel', *Beiträge zur Namenforschung* 8: 209–68.

Nicolaisen, W. F. H. (1967). 'Scottish Place-Names. Scandinavian Personal Names in the Place-Names of South-East Scotland', *Scottish Studies* 11: 223–36.

Nicolaisen, W. F. H. (1969). 'The Distribution of Certain Gaelic Mountain-Names', *Transactions of Gaelic Society of Inverness* 45: 113–28.

Nicolaisen, W. F. H. (1971). 'Great Britain and Old Europe', *Namn och Bygd* 59: 85–102.

Nicolaisen, W. F. H. (1974). 'Names as Verbal Icons', *Names* 22.3: 104–10.

Nicolaisen, W. F. H. (1976a). 'The Place-Names of Barsetshire', *Literary Onomastics Studies* 3: 1–21.

Nicolaisen, W. F. H. (1976b). 'Words as Names', *Onoma* 20.1: 143–63.

Nicolaisen, W. F. H. (1978). 'Are there Connotative Names?', *Names* 26: 40–7.

Nicolaisen, W. F. H. (1980). 'Onomastic Dialects', *American Speech* 55: 36–45.

Nicolaisen, W. F. H. (1982a). 'The Viking Settlement of Scotland. Evidence of Place-Names', in R. T. Farrell (ed.), *The Vikings*. Chichester: Phillimore, 95–115.

Nicolaisen, W. F. H. (1982b). 'Lexical and Onomastic Fields', in Kazimierz Rymut (ed.), *Proceedings of the Thirteenth International Congress of Onomastic Sciences, Cracow, August 21–25, 1978*, vol. 2. Warszawa/Kraków: Ossolineum, 209–16.

Nicolaisen, W. F. H. (1982c). ' "Old European Names" in Britain', *Nomina* 6: 37–42.

Nicolaisen, W. F. H. (1985). 'Socio-Onomastics', in Ernst Eichler, et al. (eds.), *Namenforschung/Name Studies/Les noms propres. Ein internationals Handbuch zur Onomastik/International Handbook of Onomastics/Manuel international d'onomastique*. Leipzig: Karl-Marx-Universität, 118–32.

Nicolaisen, W. F. H. (1987). 'Names in Derivative Literature and Parodies', *Literary Onomastics Studies* 14: 49–67.

Nicolaisen, W. F. H. (1987 [1975]). 'The Place-Names of Wessex', *Literary Onomastics Studies* 2: 58–82 [reprinted in Alvarez-Altman and Burelbach (1987): 35–45].

Nicolaisen, W. F. H. (1991). 'Scottish Analogues of Scandinavian Place Names', in Gordon Albøge, et al. (eds.), *Analogi i navngivning. Tiende Nordiske Navneforskerkongres, Brandbjerg 20.-24. maj 1989*. Uppsala: NORNA-förlaget, 147–55.

Nicolaisen, W. F. H. (1994). 'Viking Place Names in Scotland', *NORNA-rapporter* 54: 31–49.

Nicolaisen, W. F. H. (1995a). 'Is There a Northwest Germanic Toponymy? Some Thoughts and a Proposal', in Edith Marold and Christiane Zimmermann (eds.), *Nordwestgermanisch*. Berlin/New York: de Gruyter, 103–14.

Nicolaisen, W. F. H. (1995b). 'Name and Appellative', in Ernst Eichler, et al. (eds.), *Namenforschung/Name Studies/Les noms propres. Ein internationals Handbuch zur Onomastik/International Handbook of Onomastics/Manuel international d'onomastique*, vol. 1. Berlin/New York: de Gruyter, 384–93.

Nicolaisen, W. F. H. (1995c). 'Names in English Literature', in Ernst Eichler, et al. (eds.) *Namenforschung/Name Studies/Les noms propres. Ein internationals Handbuch zur Onomastik/International Handbook of Onomastics/Manuel international d'onomastique*, vol. 1. Berlin/New York: de Gruyter, 564–8.

Nicolaisen, W. F. H. (1996). *The Picts and Their Place Names*. Rosemarkie: Groam House Museum.

Nicolaisen, W. F. H. (1999). 'An Onomastic Autobiography, or, In the Beginning was the Name', in Dieter Kremer and Friedhelm Debus (eds.), *Onomastik. Akten des 18. Internationalen Kongresses für Namenforschung. Trier, 12.-17. April 1993*, vol. 3. Tübingen: Niemeyer.

Nicolaisen, W. F. H. (2001). *Scottish Place-Names. Their Study and Significance*. New edn. Edinburgh: John Donald.

Nicolaisen, W. F. H. (2004). 'The Functions of Suffixes in Early Scottish Hydronymy', in Thorsten Andersson and Eva Nyman (eds.), *Suffixbildungen in alten Ortsnamen. Akten eines internationalen Symposiums in Uppsala 14.–16. Mai 2004*. Acta Academiae Regiae Gustavi Adolphi 88. Uppsala: Kungl. Gustav Adolfs Akademien för Svensk Folkkultur, 109–17.

Nicolaisen, W. F. H. (2005). 'Place Names as Evidence in the History of Scots', in Christian J. Kay and Margaret Mackay (eds.), *Perspectives on the Older Scottish Tongue. A Celebration of DOST*. Edinburgh: Edinburgh University Press, 112–18.

Nicolaisen, W. F. H. (2007). 'Gaelic *sliabh* Revisited', in Sharon Arbuthnot and Kaarina Hollo (eds.), *Fil súil nglais. A Grey Eye Looks Back. A Festschrift in Honour of Colm Ó Baoll*. Ceann Drochaid: Clann Tuirc, 175–86.

Nicolaisen, W. F. H. (2008). 'On Names in Literature', *Nomina* 31: 89–98.

Nicolaisen, W. F. H. (2011 [1980]). 'Surnames and Medieval Popular Culture. Tension and Extension. Thoughts on Scottish Surnames and Medieval Popular Culture', *Journal of Popular Culture* 14: 119–30 [reprinted in Nicolaisen (2011): 81–94].

Nicolaisen, W. F. H. (2011 [1987]). 'Semantic Causes of Structural Changes in Place-Names', *NORNA-rapporter* 34: 9–19 [reprinted in Nicolaisen (2011): 198–208].

Nicolaisen, W. F. H. (2011 [1990]). 'Placenames and Politics', *Names* 38: 193–207 [reprinted in Nicolaisen (2011): 218–27].

Nicolaisen, W. F. H. (2011). *In the Beginning was the Name. Selected Essays by Professor W.F.H. Nicolaisen*. n.p.: Scottish Place-Name Society.

Nicolaisen, W. F. H., Gelling, Margaret, and Richards, Melville (1970). *The Names of Towns and Cities in Britain*. London: Batsford.

Niedzielski, Nancy, and Preston, Dennis R. (2000). *Folk Linguistics*. New York: de Gruyter.

Nikonov, Vladimir Andreevich (1966). *Kratkij toponimičeskij slovar*. Moskva: Mysl'.

Nikonov, Vladimir Andreevich (1974). *Imia i obshchestvo*. Moskva: Nauka.

Nilsen, Don L. F. (2005). 'Onomastic Play in Yann Martel's *Life of Pi*', *Onoma* 40: 103–10.

Nilsson, Leif (1987). 'Utländska namn i Uppland', *Upsala Nya Tidning*, 10 March.

NISRA—Northern Ireland Statistics and Research Agency (2015). Available online at: <http://www.nisra.gov.uk/>.

Niwa, Motoji (1981). *Seishi No Gogen*. Tokyo: Kadokawa Shoten.

Niwa, Motoji (1985). *Nihon Seishi Daijiten*. 3 vols. Tokyo: Kadokawa Shoten.

Nordlander, Johan (1880). 'Norrländska husdjursnamn. Hundnamn', *Svenska landsmål och svenskt folkliv* 1: 419 26.

Norman, Teresa (2003 [1996]). *A World of Baby Names. A Rich and Diverse Collection of Names from Around the Globe*. New York: Perigee.

North, Marcy L. (2003). *Anonymous Renaissance. Cultures of Discretion in Tudor-Stuart England*. Chicago, IL: University of Chicago Press.

NSL = Sandnes, Jørn, and Stemshaug, Ola (eds.) (1997). *Norsk stadnamnleksikon*. 4th edn. Oslo: Det norske samlaget.

Ntuli, D. B. (1992a). 'The Significance of Zulu Homestead Names', *Nomina Africana* 6.1: 14–23.

Ntuli, D. B. (1992b). 'House-Naming Among Some South African Communities', *Nomina Africana* 6.2: 28–34.

Nübling, Damaris (2012), 'Tiernamen (Zoonyme)', in Damaris Nübling, Fabian Fahlbusch, and Rita Heuser (eds.), *Namen. Eine Einführung in die Onomastik*. Tübingen: Narr, 191–205.

Nübling, Damaris, Fahlbusch, Fabian, and Heuser, Rita (2012). *Namen. Eine Einführung in die Onomastik*. Tübingen: Narr.

Nuessel, Frank (2008). 'A Note on Ethnophaulisms and Hate Speech', *Names* 56.1: 29–31.

Nyman, Eva (2000). *Nordiska ortnamn på* -und. Acta Academiae Regiae Gustavi Adolphi 70. Studier till en svensk ortnamnsatlas 16. Uppsala: Kungl. Gustav Adolfs Akademien för Svensk Folkkultur.

Nyström, Staffan (1995). 'Lexikon och onomastikon—två samverkande system', *Namn og nemne* 12: 81–7.

Nyström, Staffan (1996). 'Namnmönster, namnsystem, onomastikon: något om namnförrådets art och struktur', in Kristoffer Kruken (ed.), *Den ellevte nordiske navneforskerkongressen*. NORNA-rapporter 60. Uppsala: NORNA-förlaget, 133–48.

Nyström, Staffan (1998). 'Names in the Mind. Aspects of the Mental Onomasticon', in W. F. H. Nicolaisen (ed.), *Proceedings of the XIXth International Congress of Onomastic Sciences, Aberdeen, August 4–11, 1996. Scope, Perspectives and Methods of Onomastics*, vol. 1. Aberdeen: Department of English, University of Aberdeen, 229–35.

Ó Cadhla, Stiofán (2014). 'Gods and Heroes. Approaching the *Acallam* as Ethnography', in Aidan Doyle and Kevin Murray (eds.), *In Dialogue with the Agallamh. Essays in Honour of Seán Ó Coileáin*. Dublin: Four Courts, 125–43.

Ó Doibhlin, Éamon (1971). 'The Deanery of Tulach Óg', *Seanchas Ard Mhacha* 6.1: 141–82.

Ó Donnchadha, Tadhg (ed.) (1931). 'Cín Lae Ó Mealláin', *Analecta Hibernica* 3: 1–61.

Ó Mainnín, Micheál B. (1993). *Place-Names of Northern Ireland, vol. 3. County Down III: The Mournes*. Belfast: Cló Ollscoil na Banríona.

Ó Muraíle, Nollaig (2005). '*Temair*/Tara and Other Places of the Name', in Edel Bhreathnach (ed.), *The Kingship and Landscape of Tara*. Dublin: Four Courts, 449–77.

Ó Murchadha, Diarmuid (1997). *The Annals of Tigernach. Index of Names*. London: Irish Texts Society.

Ó Riain, Padraig (1972). 'Boundary Association in Early Irish Society', *Studia Celtica* 7: 12–29.

Ó Riain, Padraig (2009). *Lebor Gabála Érenn. Index of Names*. London: Irish Texts Society.

Ó Riain, Padraig (2011). *A Dictionary of Irish Saints*. Dublin: Four Courts.

Ó Suilleabháin, Seán (1942). *A Handbook of Irish Folklore*. Dublin: Educational Company of Ireland.

O'Brien, Elizabeth (2009). 'Pagan or Christian? Burial in Ireland During the 5th to 8th Centuries AD', in Nancy Edwards (ed.), *The Archaeology of the Early Medieval Celtic Churches*. Society for Medieval Archaeology Monographs 29. Leeds: Maney, 135–54.

O'Brien, Michael A. (ed.) (1962). *Corpus Genealogiarum Hiberniae*. Dublin: Dublin Institute for Advanced Studies.

O'Connor, Loretta, and Kroefges, Peter C. (2008). 'The Land Remembers. Landscape Terms and Place-Names in Lowland Chontal of Oaxaca, Mexico', *Language Sciences* 30.2-3: 291–315.

O'Donovan, John (ed.) (1990 [1856]). *Annals of the Kingdom of Ireland by the Four Masters*. 7 vols. Dublin: DeBurca.

O'Rahilly, Cecile (ed.) (1976). *Táin Bó Cuailnge. Recension I*. Dublin: Dublin Institute for Advanced Studies.

O'Rahilly, Thomas F. (1933). 'Notes on Irish Place-Names', *Hermathena* 23: 196–220.

O'Rahilly, T. F. (1946). *Early Irish History and Mythology*. Dublin: Dublin Institute for Advanced Studies.

O'Regan, Hana (2001). *Ko Tahu, Ko Au*. Christchurch: Horomaka Press.

Ochs, Elinor, Schegloff, Emanuel A., and Thompson, Sandra, A. (1996) (eds.). *Interaction and Grammar*. Cambridge: Cambridge University Press.

Odebode, Idowu (2010). 'Naming Systems During Yoruba Wars. A Sociolinguistic Study', *Names* 58: 209–18.

ODL = Law, Jonathan, and Martin, Elizabeth A. (eds.) (2009). *Oxford Dictionary of Law*. 7th edn. Oxford: Oxford University Press.

OED = *Oxford English Dictionary* (2015–). 3rd edn, in progress. Available at: <http://www.oed.com>.

Oelke, Daniela, Kokkinakis, Dimitrios, and Malm, Mats (2012). 'Advanced Visual Analytics Methods for Literature Analysis', in *Language Technology for Cultural Heritage, Social Sciences, and Humanities (LaTeCH). An EACL 2012 workshop*. Avignon, France.

Oelke, Daniela, Kokkinakis, Dimitrios, and Keim, D. A. (2013). 'Fingerprint Matrices. Uncovering the Dynamics of Social Networks in Prose Literature', *Computer Graphics Forum* 32: 371–80.

Office for National Statistics (2004). *Focus on Religion*. London: Office for National Statistics.

Old, Susan R., and Naveh-Benjamin, Moshe (2012). 'Age Differences in Memory for Names. The Effect of Prelearned Semantic Associations', *Psychology and Aging* 27: 462–73.

Ollins, Wally (2002). 'Branding the Nation. The Historical Context', in Nigel Morgan, Annette Pritchard, and Roger Pride (eds.), *Destination Branding. Creating the Unique Destination Proposition*. Oxford: Elsevier Butterworth-Heinemann, 17–25.

Olsson, Ingemar (1959). *Gotländska terrängord*. Stockholm: Stockholms Universitet.

Omoniyi, Tope, and White, Goodith (eds.) (2006). *Sociolinguistics of Identity*. London: Continuum.

Oppenheimer, Stephen (2003). *Out of Africa's Eden. The Peopling of the World*. Cape Town: Jonathan Ball.

Orbell, Margaret (1991). *Hawaiki. A New Approach to Maori Tradition*. Christchurch: Canterbury University Press.

Ormeling, Ferdinand J. (1993). 'The Importance of Geographical Names for Cartographic and Non-Cartographic Purposes', in P. S. Hattingh, Naftali Kadmon, Peter E. Raper, and Ingrid Booysen (eds.), *Training Course in Toponomy for Southern Africa*. Pretoria: University of Pretoria, 11–29.

Ormis, Ján Vladimír (1944). *Slovník slovenských pseudonymov*. Turčiansky sv. Martin: Slovenská národná knižnica.

Ortiz Trifol, Carmen (1982). *Toponimia Riojana*. Logroño: Ochoa.

OSNB = Ordnance Survey Name Books (1827–35). Compiled during the progress of the Ordnance Survey and preserved in Phoenix Park, but now in the National Archives, Dublin.

Osthoff, Hermann, and Karl Brugmann (1878). *Morphologische Untersuchungen auf dem Gebiete der indogermanischen Sprachen*. Leipzig: S. Hirzel.

Otterbjörk, Roland (1983). 'faruki, kurR och ublubR. Namnproblem i sörmländska runinskrifter', *Studia anthroponymica Scandinavica* 1: 21–44.

Owen, Hywel Wyn (2013). 'English Place-Names in Wales', in Jayne Carroll and David Parsons (eds.), *Perceptions of Place. Twenty-First Century Interpretations of English Place-Name Studies*. Nottingham: English Place-Name Society, 321–53.

Owen, Hywel, and Morgan, Richard (2007). *Dictionary of the Place-Names of Wales*. Ceredigion: Gomer.

Pablé, Adrian (2009). 'The "Dialect Myth" and Socio-Onomastics. The Names of the Castles of Bellinzona in an Integrational Perspective', *Language and Communication* 29.2: 152–65.

Pafford, J. H. P. (ed.) (1963). *The Winter's Tale*. The Arden Shakespeare Second Series. London: Methuen.

Pamp, Bengt (1985). 'Ten Theses on Proper Names', *Names* 33.3: 111–18.

Pamp, Bengt (1991). 'Onomastisk analogi', in Gordon Albøge, et al. (eds.), *Analogi i navngivning. Tiende Nordiske Navneforskerkongres, Brandbjerg 20.–24. maj 1989.* Uppsala: NORNA-förlaget, 154–74.

Pang, Kam-yiu S. (2009). 'Eponymy and Life-narratives. The Effect of Foregrounding on Proper Names', *Journal of Pragmatics* 42: 1321–49.

Panic, Olga (2003). 'Brand Names. A Linguistic Phenomenon', *SKY Journal of Linguistics* 16: 247–51.

Partridge, Clive (1989). *Foxholes Farm. A Multi-Period Gravel Site.* Hertford: Hertfordshire Archaeological Trust.

Patterson, Michael, and Williams, Daniel (2005). 'Maintaining Research Traditions on Place. Diversity of Thought and Scientific Progress', *Journal of Environmental Psychology* 25: 361–80.

Paunonen, Heikki, Vuolteenaho, Jani, and Ainiala, Terhi (2009). 'Industrial Urbanization, Working-Class Lads and Slang Toponyms in Early Twentieth-Century Helsinki', *Urban History* 36: 449–72.

Pawley, Andrew (2002). 'The Austronesian Dispersal: Languages, Technologies and People', in Peter S. Bellwood and Colin Renfrew (eds.), *Examining the Farming/Language Dispersal Hypothesis.* Cambridge: McDonald Institute for Archaeological Research, University of Cambridge, 251–73.

Pearce, T. M. (1962). 'The Names of Objects in Aerospace', *Names* 10: 1–10.

Pedersen, Aud-Kirsti (2009). 'Haldningar til offentleg bruk av minoritetsspråklege stadnamn i Noreg', in Lars-Erik Edlund and Susanne Haugen (eds.), *Namn i flerspråkiga och mång-kulturella miljöer: Handlingar från NORNA:s 36:e symposium i Umeå, 16–18 november 2006.* Umeå: Institutionen för språkstudier, Umeå universitet, 37–56.

Peirce, Charles S. (1955). 'Logic as Semiotic. The Theory of Signs', in Justus Buchler (ed.), *The Philosophical Writings of Peirce.* New York: Dover Books, 98–119.

Pellijeff, Gunnar (1980). 'Ortnamn i språkkontakt', in Thorsten Andersson, et al. (eds.), *Ortnamn och språkkontakt.* NORNA-rapporter 17. Uppsala: NORNA-förlaget, 13–27.

Penhallurick, Rob (2010). *Studying the English Language.* 2nd edn. London: Palgrave Macmillan.

Penn, Simon (1983). 'The Origins of Bristol Migrants in the Early Fourteenth Century. The Surname Evidence', *Transactions of the Bristol and Gloucestershire Archaeological Society* 101: 123–30.

Pennycook, Alastair (2009). 'Linguistic Landscapes and the Transgressive Semiotics of Graffiti', in Elana Shohamy and Durk Gorter (eds.), *Linguistic Landscape. Expanding the Scenery.* Abingdon: Routledge, 302–12.

Pennycook, Alastair (2010). 'Spatial Narrations. Graffscapes and City Souls', in Adam Jaworski and Crispin Thurlow (eds.), *Semiotic Landscapes. Language, Image, Space.* London: Continuum, 137–50.

Penrose, Jan, and Jackson, Peter (eds.) (1994). *Constructions of Race, Place and Nation.* Minneapolis, MN: University of Minnesota Press.

Pereira, Paul (1995). 'The ANC's Chappaquiddick?', *Fast Facts (Newsletter of the South African Institute for Race Relations).*

Peréz Hernández, Lorena (2011). 'Cognitive Tools for Successful Branding', *Applied Linguistics* 32.4: 369–88.

Pérez Hernández, Lorena (2013). 'A Pragmatic-Cognitive Approach to Brand Names. A Case Study of Rioja Wine Brands', *Names* 61.1: 33–46.

Peterson, Lena (2007). *Nordiskt runnamnslexikon*. 5th rev. edn. Uppsala: Institutet för språk och folkminnen.

Pfukwa, Charles (2012). 'Taking to the Streets. An Onomastic Analysis of Selected Suburbs of the City of Harare, Zimbabawe', *Nomina Africana* 26.1: 113–30.

Pietarinen, Ahti-Veikko (2010). 'Peirce's Pragmatic Theory of Proper Names', *Transactions of the Charles S. Peirce Society* 46.3: 341–63.

Pike, Jim (2000). *Locomotive Names. The Illustrated Dictionary*. Stroud: Sutton Publishing.

Pink, Sarah (2007). 'Walking with Video', *Visual Studies* 22.3: 240–52.

Pintens, Walter (2009). 'Namensrecht', in Jürgen Basedow, Klaus J. Hopt, and Reinhard Zimmermann (eds.), *Handwörterbuch des Europäischen Privatrechts*, vol. 2. Tübingen: Mohr Siebeck, 1093–96.

Pires, Matthew (2007). 'Investigating Non-universal Popular Urban Toponyms. Birmingham's Pigeon Park', *Onoma* 42: 131–54.

Piroth, Walter (1979). *Ortsnamenstudien zur angelsächsischen Wanderung: Ein Vergleich von -ingas, -inga-Namen in England mit ihren Entsprechungen auf dem europäischen Festland*. Frankfurter historische Abhandlungen 18. Wiesbaden: Steiner.

Pisoni, Alberto, Vernice, Mirta, Iasevoli, Luigi, Cattaneo, Zaira, and Papagno, Costanza (2015). 'Guess Who? Investigating the Proper Name Processing Network by Means of tDCS', *Neuropsychologia* 66: 267–78.

Pitkänen, Ritva Liisa (1998). 'The Nomenclatures of a Farmer and a Fisherman. Occupation as the Decisive Factor', in W. F. H. Nicolaisen (ed.), *Proceedings of the XIXth International Congress of Onomastic Sciences, Aberdeen, August 4–11, 1996. Scope, Perspectives and Methods of Onomastics*, vol. 1. Aberdeen: Department of English, University of Aberdeen, 277–84.

Pitkänen, Ritva Liisa (2010). 'Place Names—Users and Usage', in Eva Brylla and Mats Wahlberg (eds.), *Proceedings of the 21st International Congress of Onomastic Sciences, Uppsala, 19–24 August 2002*. Uppsala: Institutet för språk- och folkminnen, 401–9.

Pitt-Rivers, Julian A. (1954). *The People of the Sierra*. London: Weidenfeld and Nicolson.

Pitz, Martina (2008). 'Die gewaltsame Germanisierung lothringischer Orts- und Flurnamen unter dem Hakenkreuz', in Nicole Eller, Stefan Hackl, and Marek Ľupták (eds.), *Namen und ihr Konfliktpotential im europäischen Kontext*. Regensburg: Edition Vulpes, 171–86.

Placcius, Vincent (1708). *Theatrum anonymorum et pseudonymorum ex symbolis et collatione virorum per europam doctissimorum ac celerrimorum*. Hamburg: Spieringk for G. Liebernickel.

Placenamesni.org (2013). Available online at: <http://www.placenamesni.org>.

Platen, Christoph (1997). *'Ökonymie'. Zur Produktnamen-Linguistik im Europäischen Binnenmarkt*. Tübingen: Niemeyer.

Plummer, Charles (ed.) (1929 [1892–9]). *Two of the Saxon Chronicles Parallel with supplementary extracts from the others*. 2 vols. Oxford: Clarendon Press.

PNF 1 = Taylor, Simon, with Márkus, Gilbert (2006). *The Place-Names of Fife. Volume 1. West Fife between Leven and Forth*. Donington: Shaun Tyas.

PNF 2 = Taylor, Simon, with Márkus, Gilbert (2008). *The Place-Names of Fife. Volume 2. Central Fife between Leven and Eden*. Donington: Shaun Tyas.

PNF 3 = Taylor, Simon, with Márkus, Gilbert (2009). *The Place-Names of Fife. Volume 3. St Andrews and the East Neuk*. Donington: Shaun Tyas.

PNF 4 = Taylor, Simon, with Márkus, Gilbert (2010). *The Place-Names of Fife. Volume 4. North Fife between Eden and Tay*. Donington: Shaun Tyas.

PNF 5 = Taylor, Simon, with Márkus, Gilbert (2012). *The Place-Names of Fife. Volume 5. Discussion, Glossaries, Texts.* Donington: Shaun Tyas.

PNRB = Rivet, A. L. F., and Smith, Colin (1979). *The Place-Names of Roman Britain.* London: Batsford.

Podol'skaia, Natal'ia V. (1978). *Slovar' russkoi onomasticheskoi terminologii.* Moskva: Nauka.

Podsevatkin, Sergei (1999). *Entsiklopedia psevdonimov.* Moskva: Terra.

Poets.org (n.d.). 'Poetry and Music'. New York: Academy of American Poets. Available online at: <http://www.poets.org/poetsorg/collection/poetry-music>.

Postles, David (1995). *The Surnames of Devon.* Oxford: Leopard's Head Press.

Postles, David (1998). *The Surnames of Leicestershire and Rutland.* Oxford: Leopard's Head Press.

Power, Rosemary (2012). *Kilfenora. A Guide for Pilgrims.* Hogan Computers, Clare.

Pöyhönen, Juhani (1998). *Suomalainen Sukunimikartasto. Atlas of Finnish Surnames.* Suomalaisen Kirjallisuuden Seura. Jyväskylä.

Praniskas, Jean (1968). *Trade Name Creation—Process and Patterns.* The Hague/Paris: Mouton.

Pratt, Stella (2005). 'Summer Landscapes. Investigating Scottish Topographical Place-Names', *Nomina* 28: 93–114.

Pred, Allan (1990). *Lost Words and Lost Worlds. Modernity and the Language of Everyday Life in Late Nineteenth-Century Stockholm.* Cambridge: Cambridge University Press.

Pretty, Grace, Chipuer, Heather, and Bramston, Paul (2003). 'Sense of Place Amongst Adolescents and Adults in Two Rural Australian Towns. The Discriminating Features of Place Attachment, Sense of Community and Place Dependence in Relation to Place Identity', *Journal of Environmental Psychology* 23.3: 273–87.

Profous, Antonín (1947–60). *Místní jména v Čechách. Jejich vznik, původní vý́znam a změny.* 4 vols. Praha: Nakl. Československé Akad. Věd.

Proshansky, Harold (1978). 'The City and Self-Identity', *Environment and Behaviour* 10: 147–69.

Proshansky, Harold, Fabian, A., and Kaminoff, R. (1983). 'Place Identity. Physical World Socialisation of the Self', *Journal of Environmental Psychology* 3: 57–83.

Proz.com (2012). 'Pseudonyms—Good, Bad or Ugly'. Available online at: <http://www.proz.com/forum/business_issues/225556-pseudonymsgood_bad_or_ugly.html> [accessed 4 June 2013].

Pugsley, Christopher (2006). *Te Hokowhitu A Tu. The Maori Pioneer Battalion in the First World War.* Auckland: Reed Books.

Pütz, Horst P. (1989). 'Rechnergestützte Bearbeitung großer Datenmengen am Beispiel des entstehenden Lexikons', in Friedhelm Debus und Horst Pütz (eds.), *Namen in deutschen literarischen Texten des Mittelalters. Vorträge, Symposion Kiel, 9.-12. 9. 1987,* Neumünster: Wachholtz, 287–99.

Puzey, Guy (2009). 'Opportunity or Threat? The Role of Minority Toponyms in the Linguistic Landscape', in Wolfgang Ahrens, Sheila Embleton, and André Lapierre (eds.), *Names in Multi-Lingual, Multi-Cultural and Multi-Ethnic Contact. Proceedings of the 23rd International Congress of Onomastic Sciences, August 17–22, 2008, York University, Toronto, Canada.* Toronto: York University, 821–7. Available online at: <http://yorkspace.library.yorku.ca/xmlui/bitstream/handle/10315/4022/icos23_821.pdf?sequence=1>.

Puzey, Guy (2010). 'Inbhir Nis No More? Linguistic Landscapes and Language Attitudes in Scotland and Nova Scotia', in Moray Watson and Lindsay Milligan (eds.), *From Vestiges to the Very Day. New Voices in Celtic Studies.* Aberdeen: AHRC Centre for Irish and Scottish Studies, 77–89.

Puzey, Guy (2011a). 'New Research Directions in Toponomastics and Linguistic Landscapes', *Onoma* 46: 211–26.

Puzey, Guy (2011b). 'Signscapes and Minority Languages. Language Conflict on the Street', in Elisha Foust and Sophie Fuggle (eds.), *Word on the Street*. London: Institute of Germanic and Romance Studies, 33–51.

Puzey, Guy (2011c). 'Wars of Position. Language Policy, Counter-Hegemonies and Cultural Cleavages in Italy and Norway'. PhD dissertation, University of Edinburgh.

Puzey, Guy (2012). 'Two-Way Traffic. How Linguistic Landscapes Reflect and Influence the Politics of Language', in Durk Gorter, Heiko F. Marten, and Luk Van Mensel (eds.), *Minority Languages in the Linguistic Landscape*. Basingstoke: Palgrave Macmillan, 127–47.

Puzey, Guy, McLeod, Wilson, and Dunbar, Robert (2013). 'Approaches to Bilingual Corporate Identity: Final Report', report for Bòrd na Gàidhlig. Available online at: <http://www.gaidhlig.org.uk/Downloads/Approaches%20to%20Bilingual%20Identity_Final%20Report_%20August_2013.pdf> [accessed 17 October 2014].

Quérard, Joseph-Marie (1845–60). *Supercheries littéraires dévoilées*. 5 vols. Paris: L'éditeur.

Quinton, Eleanor (ed.) (2009). *The Church in English Place-Names*. Nottingham: English Place-Name Society.

Quirk, Randolph, Greenbaum, S., Leech, Geoffrey, and Svartvik, Jan (1985). *A Grammar of Contemporary English*. New edn. London: Longman.

Radley, Alan (1990). 'Artefacts, Memory and a Sense of the Past', in David Middleton and Derek Edwards (eds.), *Collective Remembering*. London: Sage, 46–59.

Raento, Pauliina, and Douglass, William A. (2001). 'The Naming of Gaming', *Names. A Journal of Onomastics* 49.1: 1–35.

Rainbolt, Martha (2002). 'Women Naming Women. The Use of Sobriquets by Aphra Behn, Anne Finch, and Katherine Philips', *Names* 50: 133–52.

Raine, J. ed. (1967 [1835]). *Wills and Inventories from the Registry at Durham*, vol. 2. Durham: Surtees Society.

Rajić, Ljubisa (2007). 'Stedsnavn og etnisk og politisk identitet i Serbia', *Nytt om namn* 46: 23–9.

Ramge, Hans (ed.) (1987). *Hessischer Flurnamenatlas*. Darmstadt: Putschke.

Ramge, Hans (1998). 'Flurnamen. Am Beispiel der Hessischen Namenforschung', in Norbert Nail (ed.), *Die Welt der Namen: Sechs namenkundliche Beiträge*. Marburg: Universitätsbibliothek, 79–100.

Ramge, Hans (ed.) (2002). *Südhessisches Flurnamenbuch*. Darmstadt: Hessische Historische Komission.

Ramsay, Guy (2003). 'Cherbourg's Chinatown. Creating an Identity of Place on an Australian Aboriginal Settlement', *Journal of Historical Geography* 29.1: 109–22.

Raper, Peter E. (1987). 'Aspects of Onomastic Theory', *Nomina Africana* 1.2: 78–91.

Rapoport, Amos (1977). *Human Aspects of Urban Form. Towards a Man-Environment Approach to Urban Form and Design*. Oxford: Pergamon.

Rappenglück, Michael A. (1996). 'The Pleiades in the "Salle des Taureaux", Grotte de Lascaux. Does a Rock Picture in the Cave of Lascaux Show the Open Star Cluster of the Pleiades at the Magdalenien Era (ca. 15,300 BC)?', in Carlos Jaschek and F. Atrio Barandela (eds.), *Actas del IV Congreso de la SEAC «Astronomía en la Cultura»*. Salamanca: Universidad de Salamanca, 217–25.

Rasinger, Sebastian M. (2014). 'Linguistic Landscapes in Southern Carinthia (Austria)', *Journal of Multilingual and Multicultural Development* 35.6: 580–602.

Rastle, Kathleen G., and Burke, Deborah M. (1996). 'Priming the Tip of the Tongue. Effects of Prior Processing on Word Retrieval in Young and Older Adults', *Journal of Memory and Language* 35: 586–605.

Raumolin-Brunberg, Helena (1996). 'Forms of Address in Early English Correspondence', in Terttu Nevalainen and Helena Raumolin-Brunberg (eds.), *Sociolinguistics and Language History. Studies Based on the Corpus of Early English Correspondence.* Amsterdam: Rodopi, 167–81.

Rautio Helander, Kaisa (2009). 'Toponymic Silence and Sámi Place Names During the Growth of the Norwegian Nation State', in Lawrence D. Berg and Jani Vuolteenaho (eds.), *Critical Toponymies. The Contested Politics of Place Naming.* Farnham: Ashgate, 253–66.

Read, Allen Walker (1982). 'The Incantatory Use of Place Names in American Poetry', *Literary Onomastics Studies* 9: 21–47.

Reaney, Percy H. (1958). *A Dictionary of British Surnames.* London: Routledge and Kegan Paul.

Reaney, Percy H. (1967). *The Origin of English Surnames.* London: Routledge and Kegan Paul.

Reaney, Percy H. (1997). *A Dictionary of English Surnames.* Rev. 3rd edn with corrections and additions by R. M. Wilson. Oxford: Oxford University Press.

Red'ko, Iulian K. (1966). *Suchasni Ukraïns'ki Prizvishcha.* Kiev: Naukova Dumka.

Redmonds, George (1973). *Yorkshire West Riding.* London: Phillimore.

Redmonds, George (1992). *Yorkshire Surnames Series. Part 2: Huddersfield & District,* Huddersfield: GR Books.

Redmonds, George (1997). *Surnames and Genealogy. A New Approach.* Boston, MA: New England Historic and Genealogical Society. Republished 2002, The Federation of Family History Societies.

Redmonds, George (2004a). *Christian Names in Local and Family History.* Kew, London: The National Archives.

Redmonds, George (2004b). *Names and History. People, Places and Things.* London: Hambledon and London.

Redmonds, George (2015). *A Dictionary of Yorkshire Surnames.* Donington: Shaun Tyas.

Redmonds, George, King, Turi, and Hey, David (2011). *Surnames, DNA, and Family History.* Oxford: Oxford University Press.

Reed, Gay Garland (2010). 'Fastening and Unfastening Identities. Negotiating Identity in Hawai'i', *Discourse. Studies in the Cultural Politics of Education* 22.3: 327–39.

Rees, Nigel, and Noble, Vernon (1985). *A Who's Who of Nicknames.* London: Allen and Unwin.

Reeves, William (1847). *Ecclesiastical Antiquities of Down, Connor and Dromore.* Dublin: Hodges and Smith.

Reeves, William (1857). *The Life of Saint Columba, Founder of Hy, Written by Adamnan.* Dublin: Irish Archaeological and Celtic Society.

Reeves, William (1900 [1860]). 'The Ancient Churches of Armagh'. Reprinted in *Ulster Journal of Archaeology* 6: 24–33.

Reichmayr, Michael (2005). *Von Ajda bis Žuži. Slawisches in österreichen Rindernamen. Eine sprachliche und kulturhistorische Analyse.* Wien: Pavelhaus.

Reisæter, Guro (2012). 'Immigrants in Norway and Their Choice of Names. Continuation or Adaptation', in Botolv Helleland, Christian-Emil Ore, and Solveig Wikstrøm (eds.), *Names and Identities.* Oslo Studies in Language 4.2. Oslo: University of Oslo, 224–34. Available online at: <https://www.journals.uio.no/index.php/osla/article/view/320/445>.

Relph, Edward (1976). *Place and Placelessness.* London: Pion.

Rendell, Peter G., Castle, Alan D., and Craik, Fergus I. M. (2005). 'Memory for Proper Names in Old Age. A Disproportionate Impairment?', *The Quarterly Journal of Experimental Psychology* 58: 54–71.

Rentenaar, Robert (1984). *Vernoemingsnamen: een onderzoek naar de rol van de vernoeming in de nederlandse toponymie*. Publikaties van het P.J. Meertens-Instituut voor dialectologie, volkskunde en naamkunde van de Koninklijke Nederlandse akademie van wetenschappen 5. Amsterdam: University of Amsterdam.

Rentenaar, Robert (1991). 'Discussion', in Gordon Albøge, et al. (eds.), *Analogi i navngivning. Tiende Nordiske Navneforskerkongres, Brandbjerg 20.–24. maj 1989*. Uppsala: NORNA-förlaget, 173.

Richardson, Ruth E. (1996). 'Field-Names with Roman Connections', *Transactions of the Woolhope Naturalists Field Club* 48: 453–69.

Riley, Philip (2007). *Language, Culture and Identity*. London: Continuum.

Riley, Robert (1992). 'Attachment to the Ordinary Landscape', in Irwin Altman and Setha Low (eds.), *Place Attachment*. New York: Plenum Press, 13–36.

Ripley, Tim (1998). 'Birth of Typhoon's World Market Challenge', *Flight Daily News*, 7 September.

Rippon, Stephen (2012). *Making Sense of an History Landscape*. Oxford: Oxford University Press.

Risjord, Mark W. (2007). 'Ethnography and Culture', in Stephen P. Turner and Mark W. Risjord (eds.), *Philosophy of Anthropology and Sociology*. Oxford: Elsevier, 399–428.

Rissanen, Matti (2010). 'On the Happy Reunion of English Philology and Historical Linguistics', in Jacek Fisiak (ed.), *Historical Linguistics and Philology*. Berlin: Mouton de Gruyter, 353–70.

Roback, Abraham A. (1979 [1944]). *Dictionary of Ethnic Slurs (Ethnopaulisms)*. Waukesha, WI: Maledicta Press.

Roberts, J. Timmons (1993). 'Power and Placenames: A Case Study from the Contemporary Amazon Frontier', *Names* 41: 159–81.

Robinson, Christopher L. (2012). 'The Stuff of which Names are Made. A Look at the Colorful and Eclectic Namecraft of Lord Dunsany', *Names* 60: 26–35.

Robinson, Christopher L. (2013). 'What Makes the Names of Middle-Earth So Fitting? Elements of Style in the Namecraft of J. R. R. Tolkien', *Names* 61: 65–73.

Robinson, Fred C. (1993). *The Tomb of Beowulf and Other Essays on Old English*. Oxford: Blackwell.

Robson, J. M. (ed.) (1973). *Collected Works of John Stuart Mill*, vol. 7. Toronto: University of Toronto Press.

Rodríguez-Salgado, M. J. et al. (1988). *Armada 1588–1988. An International Exhibition to Commemorate the Spanish Armada*. London: Penguin.

Rofe, Matthew W., and Szili, Gertrude (2009). 'Name Games I. Place Names as Rhetorical Devices', *Landscape Research* 34.3: 361–70.

Rogan, Bjarne (1994). 'Navn eller nummer? Motiver for navngiving av ting', in Kristinn Jóhannesson, Hugo Karlsson, and Bo Ralph (ed.), *Övriga namn. Handlingar från NORNA:s nittonde symposium i Göteborg, 4–6 december 1991*. NORNA-rapporter 56. Uppsala: NORNA-förlaget, 81–97.

Rogers, Colin D. (1995). *The Surname Detective. Investigating Surname Distribution in England, 1086–Present Day*. Manchester: Manchester University Press.

Rogers, Edward S., and Rogers, Mary Black (1978). 'Method for Reconstructing Patterns of Change. Surname Adoption by the Weagamow Ojibwa, 1870–1950', *Ethnohistory* 25: 319–45.

Ronneberger-Sibold, Elke (2006). 'Lexical Blends. Functionally Tuning the Transparency of Complex Words', *Folia Linguistica Historica* 40.1–2: 155–81.

Ronneberger-Sibold, Elke (2007a). '(Distorting) Mirror or Picture Puzzle. The Relation Between Brand Names and Social Values in the First Half of the Twentieth Century', in Eva Brylla and Mats Wahlberg (eds.), *Proceedings of the 21st International Congress of Onomastic Sciences, Uppsala, 19–24 August 2002*, vol. 3. Uppsala: Institutet för språk- och folkminnen, 324–37.

Ronneberger-Sibold, Elke (2007b). 'Sprachlich hybride Markennamen im Deutschen: Ein geschichtlicher Überblick', in Ludger Kremer and Elke Ronneberger-Sibold (eds.), *Names in Commerce and Industry. Past and Present*. Berlin: Logos, 187–211.

Ronneberger-Sibold, Elke (2012). 'Brand Names as Offers of Identity. An Overview over the 20th Century', in Holger Wochele, Julia Kuhn and Martin Stegu (eds.), *Onomastics Goes Business. Role and Relevance of Brands, Company and Other Names in Economic Contexts*. Berlin: Logos, 1–18.

Ronneberger-Sibold, Elke, and Wahl, Sabine (2013). 'Preferred Sound Shapes of German Brand Names', in Paula Sjöblom, Terhi Ainiala, and Ulla Hakala (eds.), *Names in the Economy. Cultural Prospects*. Newcastle: Cambridge Scholars, 232–49.

Roochnik, Paul, and Ahmed, Salahuddin (2003). 'Arabic and Muslim Family Names', in Patrick Hanks (ed.), *Dictionary of American Family Names*, vol. 1. New York: Oxford University Press, xcix–cii.

Room, Adrian (1982). *Dictionary of Trade Name Origins*. London/Boston/Henley: Routledge and Kegan Paul.

Room, Adrian (1985). *A Concise Dictionary of Modern Place-Names in Great Britain and Ireland*. Oxford/New York: Oxford University Press.

Room, Adrian (1997). *Placenames of the World. Origins and Meanings of the Names for Over 5000 Natural Features, Countries, Capitals, Territories, Cities and Historic Sites*. Jefferson, NC: Macfarland.

Rosaldo, Renato (1984). 'Ilongot Naming. The Play of Associations', in Elisabeth Tooker (ed.), *Naming Systems. 1980 Proceedings of The American Ethnological Society*. Washington, DC: American Ethnological Society, 11–24.

Rosch, Eleanor (1977). 'Human Categorization', in Neil Warren (ed.), *Studies in Cross-Cultural Psychology*, vol 1. London: Academic Press, 1–72.

Rose-Redwood, Reuben, Alderman, Derek, and Azaryahu, Maoz (2010). 'Geographies of Toponymic Inscription. New Directions in Critical Place-Name Studies', *Progress in Human Geography* 34.4: 453–70.

Ross, Lars A., and Olson, Ingrid R. (2012). 'What's Unique about Unique Entities? An fMRI Investigation of the Semantics of Famous Faces and Landmarks', *Cerebral Cortex* 22: 2005–15.

Rosser, Gervase (1989). *Medieval Westminster 1200–1350*. Oxford: Clarendon Press.

Roth-Gordon, Jennifer (2012). 'Linguistic Techniques of the Self. The Intertextual Language of Racial Empowerment in Politically Conscious Brazilian Hip Hop', *Language and Communication* 32.1: 36–47.

Rowlands, John (1999). 'The Homes of Surnames in Wales', in John Rowlands and Sheila Rowlands (eds.), *Second Stages in Researching Welsh Ancestry*. UK: Federation of Family History Societies, in conjunction with the Department of Continuing Education, University of Wales, Aberystwyth, 161–76.

Rowlands, John, and Rowlands, Sheila (1996). *The Surnames of Wales*. Birmingham: Federation of Family History Societies.

Rowlands, John, and Rowlands, Sheila (2014). *The Surnames of Wales*. 2nd edn. Llandysul: Gomer Press.

RRS i = Barrow, G. W. S. (ed.) (1960). *Regesta Regum Scottorum, Volume 1: Acts of Malcolm IV.* Edinburgh: Edinburgh University Press.

RRS ii = Barrow, G. W. S. (ed.) (1971). *Regesta Regum Scottorum, Volume 2: Acts of William I.* Edinburgh: Edinburgh University Press.

RRS iv = Neville, Cynthia J. and Simpson, Grant G. (eds.) (c.2012). *Regesta Regum Scottorum, Volume 4: Acts of Alexander III, King of Scots, 1249–1286.* Edinburgh: Edinburgh University Press.

RRS v = Duncan, A. A. M. (ed.) (1988). *Regesta Regum Scottorum, Volume 5: Acts of Robert I.* Edinburgh: Edinburgh University Press.

RRS vi = Webster, Bruce (ed.) (1982). *Regesta Regum Scottorum, Volume 6: Acts of David II.* Edinburgh: Edinburgh University Press.

Rumble, Alexander (2011). 'The Landscape of Place-Name Studies', in Nicholas J. Higham and Martin J. Ryan (eds.), *Place-Names, Language and the Anglo-Saxon Landscape.* Woodbridge: Boydell, 23–50.

Russell, Bertrand (1919). *Introduction to Mathematical Philosophy.* London: George Allen and Unwin.

Russell, Bertrand (1964 [1918]). 'The Philosophy of Logical Atomism', *The Monist* 29: 190–222 [reprinted in Marsh (1964): 175–281].

Russell, Bertrand (1973 [1905]). 'On Denoting', *Mind* 14: 479–493 [reprinted in Lackey (1973): 103–19].

Rygh, Oluf (1904). *Norske Elvenavne.* With additions and clarifications by Karl Rygh. Kristiania: Cammermeyers Boghandel.

Rymes, Betsy (1996). 'Naming as Social Practice. The Case of Little Creeper from Diamond Street', *Language in Society* 25: 237–60.

Rymut, Kazimierz (1990–4). *Słownik Nazwisk Współcześnie w Polsce Używanych.* 10 vols. Kraków: Instytut Języka Polskiego PAN.

Rymut, Kazimierz (1999–2002). *Nazwiska Polaków. Słownik Historyczno-Etymologiczny.* 2 vols. Kraków: Instytut Języka Polskiego PAN.

Rzetelska-Feleszko, Ewa (2008). 'Proper Names of Shops and Firms (Retail and Services) in Post-Communist Countries', in Donatella Bremer, Michele Bani, Franco Belli, and Matteo Paolini (eds.), *I Nomi Nel Tempo e Nello Spazio. Atti del XXII Congresso Internazionale di Scienze Onomastiche. Pisa, 28 agosto–4 settembre 2005*, vol. 2. Pisa: Edizioni ETS, 595–600.

S = Sawyer, P. H. (1968). *Anglo-Saxon Charters. An Annotated List and Bibliography.* London: Royal Historical Society. Rev. cdn. available at: <http://www.esawyer.org.uk/about/index.html> [accessed 28 February 2013].

Saarelma, Minna (2012a). 'Animal Names', in Terhi Ainiala, Minna Saarelma, and Paula Sjöblom (eds.), *Names in Focus. An Introduction to Finnish Onomastics.* trans. by Leonard Pearl. Helsinki: Finnish Literature Society, 202–9.

Saarelma, Minna (2012b). 'Personal Names', in Terhi Ainiala, Minna Saaerlma, and Paula Sjöblom (eds.), *Names in Focus. An Introduction to Finnish Onomastics.* trans. by Leonard Pearl. Helsinki: Finnish Literature Society, 124–200.

Sacks, Harvey (1992). *Lectures on Conversation.* Oxford: Blackwell.

Sacks, Harvey, and Schegloff, Emanuel A. (1979). 'Two Preferences in the Organization of Reference to Persons in Conversation and Their Interaction', in George Psathas (ed.), *Studies in Ethnomethodology.* New York/London: Irvington, 15–21.

Sacks, Harvey, Schegloff, Emanuel A., and Jefferson, Gail (1974). 'A Simplest Systematics for the Organization of Turn-Taking for Conversation', *Language* 50.4: 696–735.

Særheim, Inge (2007). *Stadnamn i Rogaland.* Bergen: Fagbokforlaget.

Salih, Mahmud H., and Bader, Yousef T. (1999). 'Personal Names of Jordanian Arab Christians. A Sociocultural Study', *International Journal of the Sociology of Language* 140: 29–43.

Salingar, L. G. (1970). 'T.S. Eliot. Poet and Critic', in Boris Ford (ed.), *The Modern Age, James to Eliot*. The Pelican Guide to English Literature 7. Harmondsworth: Penguin, 330–49.

Salo, Hanni (2012). 'Using Linguistic Landscape to Examine the Visibility of Sámi Languages in the North Calotte', in Durk Gorter, Heiko F. Marten, and Luk Van Mensel (eds.), *Minority Languages in the Linguistic Landscape*. Basingstoke: Palgrave Macmillan, 243–59.

Sandnes, Berit (2010). *From Starafjall to Starling Hill. An Investigation of the Formation and Development of Old-Norse Place-Names in Orkney*. E-book published by the Scottish Place-name Society. Available online at: <http://www.spns.org.uk/Starafjall.pdf>.

Sandnes, Jørn (1998). 'Uppsala, Bjørkøy og Rosenborg: oppkalling og mønsterstyrt navngiving i Skandinavia', *Namn och bygd* 86: 81–90.

Sandnes, Jørn, and Stemshaug, Ola (eds.) (1997). *Norsk stadnamnleksikon*. Oslo: Det Norske Samlaget.

Sandred, Karl Inge (1997). 'The Value of Onomastic Boundaries in Dialect Studies. Focus on Some Medieval Norfolk Field-Names of Scandinavian Origin', in Heinrich Ramisch and Kenneth Wynne (eds.), *Language in Time and Space. Studies in Honour of Wolfgang Viereck on the Occasion of his 60th Birthday*. Stuttgart: Steiner, 205–11.

Sandred, Karl Inge, and Lindström, Bengt (1989). *The Place-Names of Norfolk. Part 1*. English Place-Name Society 61. Nottingham: English Place-Name Society.

Sapir, Edward (1912). 'Language and Environment', *American Anthropologist* 14: 226–42.

Schaab, Eva (2012). 'Von Bello zu Paul: Zum Wandel und Struktur von Hunderufnamen', *Beiträge zur Namenforschung* 47: 131–61.

Schaefer, B.E. (2006). 'The Origin of the Greek Constellations', *Scientific American* 295.5: 96–101.

Schegloff, Emanuel A. (1972). 'Notes on a Conversational Practice. Formulating Place', in David Sudnow (ed.), *Studies in Social Interaction*. New York: The Free Press, 75–119.

Schegloff, Emanuel A. (1996). 'Some Practices for Referring to Persons in Talk-In-Interaction', in Barbara A. Fox (ed.), *Studies in Anaphora*. Amsterdam/Philadelphia: John Benjamins, 438–85.

Schegloff, Emanuel A. (2007). 'Categories in Action. Person-Reference and Membership Categorization', *Discourse Studies* 9.4: 433–61.

Scheidt, Lois Ann (2001). 'Avatars and Nicknames in Adolescent Chat Spaces'. Available online at: <http://www.researchgate.net/profile/Lois_Scheidt/publication/253226272_Avatars_and_Nicknames_in_Adolescent_Chat_Spaces/links/546e4f330cf29806ec2ebod1.pdf> or <http://www.academia.edu/2958619/Avatars_and_nicknames_in_adolescent_chat_spaces>.

Schimmel, Annemarie (1989). *Islamic Names*. Edinburgh: Edinburgh University Press.

Schmid, Wolfgang P. (1981). 'Die alteuropäische Hydronymie. Stand und Aufgaben ihrer Erforschung', *Beiträge zur Namenforschung (Neue Folge)* 16: 1–12.

Schmid, Wolfgang P. (1995). 'Alteuropäische Gewässernamen', in Ernst Eichler, et al. (eds.), *Namenforschung/Name Studies/Les noms propres. Ein internationals Handbuch zur Onomastik/International Handbook of Onomastics/Manuel international d'onomastique*, vol. 1. Berlin/New York: de Gruyter, 756–62.

Schmitt, Christian (1998). 'Aufgaben und Perspektiven einer romanischen Firmenonomastik', in W. F. H. Nicolaisen (ed.), *Proceedings of the XIXth International Congress of Onomastic Sciences, Aberdeen, August 4–11, 1996. Scope, Perspectives and Methods of Onomastics*, vol. 1. Aberdeen: Department of English, University of Aberdeen, 288–300.

Schneider, Klaus P., and Barron, Anne (2008). *Variational Pragmatics. A Focus on Regional Varieties in Pluricentric Languages*. Amsterdam: John Benjamins.

Schneider, Thomas F., and Erich Blatter (eds.) (2011). *Ortsnamenbuch des Kantons Bern [alter Kantonsteil] I: Dokumentation und Deutung*, vol. 4: N-B/P. Basel/Tübingen: A. Francke.

Schnetz, Josef (1952). *Flurnamenkunde*. München: Verlag Bayerische Heimatforschung.

Schnetz, Josef (1997). *Flurnamenkunde*. 3rd edn. München: Verlag. für Orts- u. Flurnamenforschung in Bayern e.V.

Schönfeld, Moritz (1955). *Nederlandse waternamen*. Amsterdam: De Koninklijke Nederlandse Akademie van Wetenschappen te Amsterdam.

Schot, Roseanne, Newman, Conor, and Bhreathnach, Edel (eds.) (2011). *Landscapes of Cult and Kingship*. Dublin: Four Courts.

Schürer, Kevin (2002). 'Regional Identity and Populations in the Past', in David Postles (ed.), *Naming, Society and Regional Identity*. Oxford: Leopard's Head Press, 202–27.

Schürer, Kevin (2004). 'Surnames and the Search for Regions', *Local Population Studies* 72: 50–76.

Schwanke, Martina (1992). *Name und Namengebung bei Goethe. Computergestützte Studien zu epischen Werken*. Beiträge zur Namenforschung (Neue Folge) 38. Heidelberg: Carl Winter.

Schwarz, Ernst (1950). *Deutsche Namenforschung II: Orts- und Flurnamen*. Göttingen: Vandenhoeck and Ruprecht.

Schwarz, Jan-Christian (2005). *'derst alsô getoufet daz in niemen nennen sol'. Studien zu Vorkommen und Verwendung der Personennamen in den Neidhart-Liedern*. Documenta Onomastica Litteralia Medii Aevi DOLMA, Reihe B Studien 4. Hildesheim/Zürich/New York: Georg Olms.

Schwerdt, Judith (2007), 'Hipponymie. Zu Benennungsmotiven bei Pferdenamen in Geschichte und Gegenwart', *Beiträge zur Namenforschung* 42: 1–43.

Schwitalla, Johannes (1995). 'Namen in Gesprächen', in Ernst Eichler, et al. (eds.), *Namenforschung/Name Studies/Les noms propres. Ein internationals Handbuch zur Onomastik/International Handbook of Onomastics/Manuel international d'onomastique*, vol. 1. Berlin/New York: de Gruyter, 498–504.

Schwitalla, Johannes (2010). 'Kommunikative Funktionen von Sprecher- und Adressatennamen in Gesprächen', in Nicolas Pepin and Elwys De Stefani (eds.), *Eigennamen in der gesprochenen Sprache*. Tübingen: Francke, 179–99.

Scollon, Ron, and Scollon, Suzie Wong (2003). *Discourses in Place. Language in the Material World*. Abingdon: Routledge.

Scotlandsplaces (n.d.). Available online at: <http://www.scotlandsplaces.gov.uk/>.

Scots Education Resources (2007). 'Cuddy Brae. Language at Letham, The Scots Language in a Scottish Primary School'. Available online at: <http://www.scotseducation.co.uk/reports.html> [accessed 20 September 2013].

Scots Language Centre (2015). Available online at: <http://www.scotslanguage.com/>.

Scott, Maggie (2007). 'Place-Names and the Scots Language. The Marches of Lexical and Onomastic Research', *Scottish Language* 26: 1–15.

Scott, Margaret (2004). 'Uses of Scottish Place-Names as Evidence in Historical Dictionaries', in Christian Kay, Carole Hough, and Irené Wotherspoon (eds.), *New Perspectives on English Historical Linguistics. Selected Papers from 12 ICEHL, Glasgow, 21–26 August 2002. Volume 2: Lexis and Transmission*. Amsterdam: John Benjamins, 213–24.

Scott, Margaret (2008a). 'Unsung Etymologies. Lexical and Onomastic Evidence for the Influence of Scots on English', in Marijke Mooijaart and Marijke van der Wal (eds.), *Yesterday's Words. Contemporary, Current and Future Lexicography*. Newcastle: Cambridge Scholars, 187–98.

Scott, Margaret (2008b). 'Words, Names and Culture. Place-Names and the Scots Language', *Journal of Scottish Name Studies* 2: 85–98.

Scott, Margaret, and Clark, Andrew (2011). 'Directions in English Place-Name Studies: An Invitation to Debate, with a Case Study of Salford Quays', *Nomina* 34: 27–50.

Scragg, Donald (ed.) (1991). *The Battle of Maldon AD 991*. Oxford: Blackwell.

Seargeant, Philip (2012). 'Between Script and Language. The Ambiguous Ascription of "English" in the Linguistic Landscape', in Christine Hélot, et al. (eds.), *Linguistic Landscapes, Multilingualism and Social Change*. Frankfurt: Peter Lang, 187–200.

Searle, John R. (1958). 'Proper Names', *Mind* 67: 166–73.

Searle, John R. (1983). *Intentionality. An Essay in the Philosophy of Mind*. Cambridge: Cambridge University Press.

Searle, William G. (1897). *Onomasticon Anglo-Saxonicum. A List of Anglo-Saxon Proper Names from the Time of Beda to that of King John*. Cambridge: Cambridge University Press.

Searles, Edmund (2007). 'Prophecy, Sorcery, and Reincarnation. Inuit Spirituality in the Age of Skepticism', in Jean-Guy Gouletand and Bruce G. Miller (eds.), *Extraordinary Anthropology. Transformations in the Field*. Lincoln: University of Nebraska Press, 158–82.

Searles, Edmund (2008). 'Inuit Identity in the Canadian Arctic', *Ethnology* 47: 239–55.

Sebba, Mark (2010). 'Discourses in Transit', in Adam Jaworski and Crispin Thurlow (eds.), *Semiotic Landscapes. Language, Image, Space*. London: Continuum, 59–76.

Seddon, George (1997). 'Words and Weeds: Some Notes on Language and Landscape', in George Seddon (ed.), *Landprints. Reflections on Place and Landscape*. Melbourne: Cambridge University Press, 15–27.

Sedgefield, Walter J. (1924). 'Methods of Place-Name Study', in Allen Mawer and Frank M. Stenton (eds.), *Introduction to the Survey of English Place-Names, Part 1*. Cambridge: Cambridge University Press, 1–14.

Seelmann, Kurt (2007). *Rechtsphilosophie*. München: C.H. Beck.

Seibicke, Wilfried (1982). *Die Personennamen im Deutschen*. Berlin/New York: Walter de Gruyter.

Seibicke, Wilfried (1996–2007). *Historisches deutsches Vornamenbuch*. 5 vols. Berlin: de Gruyter.

Seiler, Hansjörg (2009). *Einführung in das Recht*. Zürich: Schulthess.

Sekine, Satoshi, and Ranchod, Elisabete (eds.) (2009). *Named Entities. Recognition, Classification and Use*. Amsterdam/Philadelphia: John Benjamins.

'Sekon', G. A. [pseudonym of George Augustus Nokes] (1899). *Evolution of the Steam Locomotive, 1803–1898*. London: Railway Publishing Co.

Seligman, Charles G. (1966). *Races of Africa*. 4th edn. Oxford: Oxford University Press.

Selting, Margret, and Couper-Kuhlen, Elizabeth (2001) (eds.). *Studies in Interactional Linguistics*. Amsterdam/Philadelphia: John Benjamins.

Semenza, Carlo (2009). 'The Neuropsychology of Proper Names', *Mind and Language* 24.4: 347–69.

Semenza, Carlo (2011). 'Naming with Proper Names. The Left Temporal Pole Theory', *Behavioural Neurology* 24: 277–84.

Semenza, Carlo, and Zettin, Marina (1988). 'Generating Proper Names. A Case of Selective Inability', *Cognitive Neuropsychology* 5: 711–21.

Semenza, Carlo, and Zettin, Marina (1989). 'Evidence for Aphasia for the Role of Proper Names as Pure Referring Expressions', *Nature* 342: 678–9.

Semple, Sarah (2007). 'Defining the OE *hearg*. A Preliminary Archaeological and Topographic Examination of *hearg* Place-Names and their Hinterlands', *Early Medieval Europe* 15.4: 364–85.

Senft, Gunter (2008). 'Landscape Terms and Place Names in the Trobriand Islands—The Kaile'una Subset', *Language Sciences* 30: 340–61.

Sepotokele, Themba (2004). 'Names of Legends Now Grace Streets of Joburg's CBD', *The Star*, 15 October.

SEPN = Survey of English Place-Names (1924–). 90 volumes so far published. Cambridge and Nottingham: Cambridge University Press and English Place-Name Society.

Seppänen, Aimo (1971). 'Proper Names in a Transformational Grammar of English', *Neuphilologische Mitteilungen* 72: 304–38.

Seppänen, Aimo (1982). *Restrictive Modification and Article Usage with English Proper Names*. Umeå Papers in Linguistics 1. Umeå: Umeå University.

Shabalala, M. A. (1999). 'Homestead Names as a Reflection of Social Dynamics in Mabengela, Nkandla'. Unpublished Master's Dissertation, University of Natal, Piertermaritzburg.

Shamai, Shmuel (1991). 'Sense of Place. An Empirical Measurement', *Geoforum* 22.3: 347–58.

Sharp, Harold S. (1972). *Handbook of Pseudonyms and Personal Nicknames*. Metuchen, NJ: Scarecrow.

Sharpe, Erin, and Ewert, Alan (2000). 'Interferences in Place Attachment. Implications for Wilderness', *USDA Forest Service Proceedings* 3: 218–22. Available online at: <www.wilderness.net/library/documents/Sharpe_3-29.pdf>.

Sharpe, Tony (1991). *T.S. Eliot. A Literary Life*. New York: St. Martin's.

Sharrock, Roger (ed.) (1966). *John Bunyan. The Pilgrim's Progress*. London: Oxford University Press.

Shennan, Hay (1892). *Boundaries of Counties and Parishes in Scotland*. Edinburgh: William Green and Sons. Available online at: <http://www.scotlandsplaces.gov.uk/digital-volumes/published-gazetteers-and-atlases/hay-shennan-county-and-parish-boundaries-1892>.

Shippey, T. A. (1979). 'Creation from Philology in *The Lord of the Rings*', in Mary Salk and Robert T. Farrell (ed.), *J. R. R. Tolkien, Scholar and Storyteller*. Ithaca: Cornell University Press, 286–316.

Shohamy, Elana (2006). *Language Policy. Hidden Agendas and New Approaches*. Abingdon: Routledge.

Shohamy, Elana, and Gorter, Durk (eds.) (2009). *Linguistic Landscape. Expanding the Scenery*. Abingdon: Routledge.

Shohamy, Elana, and Waksman, Shoshi (2009). 'Linguistic Landscape as an Ecological Arena. Modalities, Meanings, Negotiations, Education', in Elana Shohamy and Durk Gorter (eds.), *Linguistic Landscape. Expanding the Scenery*. Abingdon: Routledge, 313–31.

Shohamy, Elana, Ben-Rafael, Eliezer, and Barni, Monica (eds.) (2010). *Linguistic Landscape in the City*. Bristol: Multilingual Matters.

Shorrocks, Graham (2000). 'Purpose, Theory and Method in English Dialectology. Towards a More Objective History of the Discipline', in Robert Penhallurick (ed.), *Debating Dialect. Essays on the Philosophy of Dialect Study*. Cardiff: University of Wales Press, 84–107.

Shu, Austin C. W. (1969). *Modern Chinese Authors. A List of Pseudonyms*. East Lansing, MI: Michigan State University.

Sidorova, Marina Iur'evna (2006). *Internet-lingvistika. Russkii iazyk*. Moskva: «1989.ru». Available online at: <www.philol.msu.ru/~sidorova/files/blogs.pdf>.

Siegrist, Hansmartin (1995). 'Stilistische Funktion der Namen im Spielfilm', in Ernst Eichler, et al. (eds.), *Namenforschung/Name Studies/Les noms propres. Ein internationals Handbuch zur Onomastik/International Handbook of Onomastics/Manuel international d'onomastique*, vol. 1. Berlin/New York: de Gruyter, 576–82.

Siliņš, Klāvs (1990). *Latviešu Personvārdu Vārdnīca*. Riga: Zinātne.

Simons, D. Brenton (1997). *The Langhornes of Langhorne Park*. Boston, MA: Newbury Street Press.

Simpson, Louis (ed.) (1970). *An Introduction to Poetry*. London: Macmillan.

Sims-Williams, Patrick (2006). *Ancient Celtic Place-Names in Europe and Asia Minor*. Publications of the Philological Society 39. Oxford: Blackwell.

Sing365.com (2010). 'Billy Joel. "We Didn't Start The Fire" Lyrics'. Comment 'Story Behind This Song' by Tata, posted 26 April 2010. Available online at: <http://www.sing365.com/music/lyric.nsf/We-Didn't-Start-The-Fire-lyrics-Billy-Joel/C753C82435AC97D148256870001F1100>.

Sjöblom, Paula (2006). *Toiminimen toimenkuva. Suomalaisen yritysnimistön rakenne ja funktiot*. English summary. Helsinki: Finnish Literature Society, 298–304.

Sjöblom, Paula (2007). 'Finnish Company Names. Structure and Function', in Ludger Kremer and Elke Ronneberger-Sibold (eds.), *Names in Commerce and Industry. Past and Present*. Berlin: Logos, 297–306.

Sjöblom, Paula (2008a). 'Namnens tolkning som en kognitiv process', in Guðrún Kvaran, Hallgrímur J. Ámundason, Jónína Hafsteinsdóttir, and Svavar Sigmundsson (eds.), *Nordiska namn—Namn i Norden. Tradition och förnyelse. Handlingar från Den fjortonde nordiska namnforskarkongressen i Borgarnes 11–14 augusti 2007*. Uppsala: NORNA-förlaget, 419–24.

Sjöblom, Paula (2008b). 'Jobs Vacant. Seeking to Employ a Good Company Name. The Structure, Meaning and Function of Finnish Company Names', *Namn och Bygd* 96: 67–82.

Sjöblom, Paula (2008c). 'Multimodality of Company Names', *Onoma* 43: 351–80.

Sjöblom, Paula (2009). 'The Linguistic Origin of Company Names in Finland', in Eva Lavric, Fiorenza Fischer, Carmen Konzett, Julia Kuhn, and Holger Wochele (eds.), *People, Products, and Professions. Choosing a Name, Choosing a Language*. Frankfurt am Main: Peter Lang, 289–95.

Sjöblom, Paula (2010). 'Multimodality of Company Names', *Onoma* 43: 351–80.

Sjöblom, Paula (2012). 'The Use of Proper Names in Early Finnish Newspaper Advertisements', in Oliviu Felecan (ed.), *Name and Naming. Synchronic and Diachronic Perspectives*. Newcastle: Cambridge Scholars, 424–36.

Sjöblom, Paula (2014). 'Commercial Names and the Unestablished Terminology', in Joan Tort i Donada and Montserrat Montagut i Montagut (eds.), *Els noms en la vida quotidiana. Actes del XXIV Congrés Internacional d'ICOS sobre Ciències Onomàstiques. Names in Daily Life. Proceedings of the XXIV ICOS International Congress of Onomastic Sciences*. Generalitat de Catalunya, Departament de Cultura. Available online at: <http://www.gencat.cat/llengua/BTPL/ICOS2011/012.pdf>.

Sjöblom, Paula, Ainiala, Terhi, and Hakala, Ulla (2013). *Names in the Economy. Cultural Prospects*. Newcastle: Cambridge Scholars.

Skaife, Robert H. (ed.) (1872). *The Register of the Guild of Corpus Christi in the City of York*, vol. 57. Durham: Surtees Society.

Skeat, Walter W. (ed.) (1969 [1888]). *Piers Plowman*, 2 vols. Oxford: Clarendon Press.

Skipper, James K. (1986). 'Nicknames, Coal Miners and Group Solidarity', *Names* 34: 134–45.

Skok, Petar (1972). *Etimologijski rječnik hrvatskoga ili srpskoga jezika*, vol. 2. Zagreb: Jugoslavenska Akad. Znanosti i Umjetnosti.

Sloboda, Marián, et al. (2010). 'Carrying Out a Language Policy Change. Advocacy Coalitions and the Management of Linguistic Landscape', *Current Issues in Language Planning* 11: 95–113.

Slotte, Peter (1976). 'Ortnamns räckvidd; namnbruk och namnkunnande', in Vibeke Dalberg, Botolv Helleland, Allan Rostvik, and Kurt Zilliacus (eds.), *Ortnamn och samhälle. Aspekter, begrepp, metoder*. Helsingfors: The Society of Swedish Literature in Finland, 125–40.

Slotte, Peter, Zilliacus, Kurt, and Harling, Gunilla (1973). 'Sociologiska namnstudier', in Kurt Zilliacus (ed.), *Synvinklar på ortnamn*. Helsingfors: The Society of Swedish Literature in Finland, 97–181.

Šmilauer, Vladimír (1970). *Příručka slovanské toponomastiky*. Praha: Academia.

Smith, A. H. (1937). *The Place-Names of the East Riding of Yorkshire and York*. English Place-Name Society 14. Cambridge: Cambridge University Press.

Smith, A. H. (1956a). 'Place-Names and the Anglo-Saxon Settlement', *Proceedings of the British Academy* 42: 67–88.

Smith, A. H. (1956b). *English Place-Name Elements. Parts 1–2*. English Place-Name Society 25-26. Cambridge: Cambridge University Press.

Smith, A. H. (1961a). *The Place-Names of the West Riding of Yorkshire. Part 1*. English Place-Name Society 30. Cambridge: Cambridge University Press.

Smith, A. H. (1961b). *The Place-Names of the West Riding of Yorkshire. Part 4*. English Place-Name Society 33. Cambridge: Cambridge University Press.

Smith, A. H. (1961c). *The Place-Names of the West Riding of Yorkshire. Part 6*. English Place-Name Society 35. Cambridge: Cambridge University Press.

Smith, A. H. (1964–6). *The Place-Names of Westmorland. Parts 1–2*. English Place-Name Society 42–43. Cambridge: Cambridge University Press.

Smith, A. H. (1990). 'Place-Names and the Anglo-Saxon Settlement'. Sir Israel Gollancz Memorial Lecture, 29 February 1956, in Eric Gerald Stanley (ed.), *British Academy Papers on Anglo-Saxon England*. Oxford: Oxford University Press, 205–226.

Smith, Grant (2005). 'Names as Art. An Introduction to Essays in English', *Onoma* 40: 7–27.

Smith, Grant (2006). 'A Semiotic Theory of Names', *Onoma* 41: 14–26.

Smith, Grant (2007). 'The Influence of Name Sounds in the Congressional Elections of 2006', *Names* 55.4: 465–72.

Smith, Grant (2009). 'Ethnic, Class, and Occupational Identities in Shakespeare's Names', in Wolfgang Ahrens, Sheila Embleton, and André Lapierre (eds.), *Names in Multi-Lingual, Multi-Cultural and Multi-Ethnic Contact. Proceedings of the 23rd International Congress of Onomastic Sciences, August 17–22, 2008, York University, Toronto, Canada*. Toronto: York University, 909–14. Available online at: <http://yorkspace.library.yorku.ca/xmlui/bitstream/handle/10315/4033/icos23_909.pdf?sequence=1>.

Smith, J. C. (ed.) (1909). *Spenser's Faerie Queene*. 2 vols. Oxford: Clarendon Press.

Smith-Bannister, Scott (1997). *Names and Naming Patterns in England, 1538–1700*. Oxford: Clarendon Books.

Smitherman, Geneva (2006). *Word from the Mother. Language and African Americans*. London: Routledge.

SND = Grant, William, et al. (eds.) (1931–76), *The Scottish National Dictionary*. 10 vols. Edinburgh: Scottish National Dictionary Association. Available online at: <http://www.dsl.ac.uk>.

SO = *Sveriges ortnamn: Ortnamnen i Skaraborgs län, Ortnamnen i Värmlands län, Ortnamnen i Östergötlands län*, etc.

Sobanski, Ines (1998). 'The Onymic Landscape of G. K. Chesterton's Detective Stories', in W. F. H. Nicolaisen (ed.), *Proceedings of the XIXth International Congress of Onomastic Sciences, Aberdeen, August 4–11, 1996. Scope, Perspectives and Methods of Onomastics*, vol. 3. Aberdeen: Department of English, University of Aberdeen, 373–8.

Sobanski, Ines (2000). *Die Eigennamen in den Detektivgeschichten Gilbert Keith Chestertons. Ein Beitrag zur Theorie und Praxis der literarischen Onomastik*. Frankfurt am Main: Peter Lang.

SOL = Wahlberg, Mats (ed.) (2003). *Svenskt ortnamnslexikon*. Uppsala: Språk- och folkminnesinstitutet.

Solin, Heikki (1998). 'Romerskt namnskick', in Thorsten Andersson, et al. (ed.), *Personnamn och social identitet*. Stockholm: KVHAA, 179–93.

Sonderegger, Stefan (1960). 'Das Alter der Flurnamen und die germanische Überlieferung', *Jahrbuch für fränkische Landesforschung* 20: 181–201.

Sonderegger, Stefan (1966–7). 'Die Ausbildung der deutsch-romanischen Sprachgrenze in der Schweiz im Mittelalter', *Rheinische Vierteljahrsblätter* 31: 223–90.

Sonderegger, Stefan (1985a). 'Terminologie, Gegenstand und interdisziplinärer Bezug der Namengeschichte', in Werner Besch, Oskar Reichmann, and Stefan Sonderegger (eds.), *Sprachgeschichte. Ein Handbuch zur Geschichte der deutschen Sprache und ihrer Erforschung*, vol. 2. Berlin: de Gruyter, 2067–87.

Sonderegger, Stefan (1985b). 'Probleme schweizerischer Namenforschung', in Rudolf Schützeichel (ed.), *Gießener Flurnamen Kolloquium, 1.–4. Oktober 1984*. Heidelberg: Winter, 448–63.

Sonderegger, Stefan (1997–8). 'Flurnamen im Spannungsfeld von Gegenwart und Geschichte', *Blätter für oberdeutscheNamenforschung* 34/35: 5–23.

Søndergaard, Bent (1972). *Indledende studier over den nordiske stednavnetype lev (löv)*. Navnestudier 10. Copenhagen: Akademisk Forlag.

Sørensen, Hølger S. (1958). *Word-Classes in Modern English, with Special Reference to Proper Names. With an Introductory Theory of Grammar, Meaning and Reference*. Copenhagen: G.E.C. Gad.

Sorvali, Irma (2013). 'Bread Packages as Verbal and Visual Signs', in Paula Sjöblom, Terhi Ainiala and Ulla Hakala (eds.), *Names in the Economy. Cultural Prospects*. Newcastle: Cambridge Scholars, 136–51.

South African Press Association (2012). 'ANCWL Praises Maxeke for Helping to Empower Woman', *Mail and Guardian*, 4 August.

Sperling, Florian (2012). *Familiennamensrecht in Deutschland und Frankreich*. Tübingen: Mohr Siebeck.

SPNS = Scottish Place-Name Society website (1995–2009). Available online at: <http://www.spns.org.uk/>.

Spolsky, Bernard (2004). *Language Policy*. Cambridge: Cambridge University Press.

Spolsky, Bernard (2009). 'Prolegomena to a Sociolinguistic Theory of Public Signage', in Elana Shohamy and Durk Gorter (eds.), *Linguistic Landscape. Expanding the Scenery*. Abingdon: Routledge, 25–39.

Spolsky, Bernard, and Cooper, Robert L. (1991). *The Languages of Jerusalem*. Oxford: Clarendon Press.

Šrámek, Rudolf (1996). 'Geschichtliche Entwicklung der Flurnamen an exemplarischen Beispielen: slavisch', in Ernst Eichler, et al. (eds.), *Namenforschung/Name Studies/Les noms propres. Ein internationals Handbuch zur Onomastik/International Handbook of Onomastics/ Manuel international d'onomastique*, vol. 2. Berlin/New York: de Gruyter, 1462–8.

Šrámek, Rudolf (2002). 'Versuch einer Bestimmung der Namenkunde als Ganzes', in Ana Isabel Boullón Agrelo (ed.), *Actas do XX Congreso Internacional de Ciencias Onomásticas, Santiago de Compostela, 20–25 setembro 1999*. CD-ROM. A Coruña: Fundación Pedro Barrié de la Maza, 885–96.

Šrámek, Rudolf (2007). *Beiträge zur allgemeinen Namentheorie*. Wien: Präsens.

Šrámek, Rudolf (2008). 'Typologisierendes zu Namenkonflikten', in Nicole Eller, Stefan Hackl, and Marek Ľupták (eds.), *Namen und ihr Konfliktpotential im europäischen Kontext*. Regensburg: Edition Vulpes, 11–16.

Stafford, Laura, and Kline, Susan L. (1996). 'Married Women's Name Choices and Sense of Self', *Communication Reports* 9.1: 85–92.

Ståhl, Harry (1976). *Ortnamn och ortnamnsforskning*. 2nd edn. Stockholm: AWE/Geber.

Starks, Donna, et al. (2012). 'Nicknames in Australian secondary schools', *Names* 60.3: 135–49.

Stemshaug, Ola (1997a). 'Elvenamn', in Jørn Sandnes and Ola Stemshaug (eds.), *Norsk stadnamnleksikon*. 4th edn. Oslo: Det norske samlaget, 37–40.

Stemshaug, Ola (1997b). 'Innsjønamn', in Jørn Sandnes and Ola Stemshaug (eds.), *Norsk stadnamnleksikon*. 4th edn. Oslo: Det norske samlaget, 40–3.

Stenroos, Merja, Mäkinen, Martti, and Særheim, Inge (eds.) (2012). *Language Contact and Development around the North Sea*. Current Issues in Linguistic Theory 321. Amsterdam and Philadelphia: John Benjamins.

Stenton, Frank Merry (1970 [1924]). 'Personal Names in Place-Names', in Doris Mary Stenton (ed.), *Prepatory to Anglo-Saxon England. The Collected Papers of Frank Merry Stenton*. Oxford: Clarendon Press, 84–105.

Stevenage, Sarah V., and Lewis, Hugh G. (2005). 'By Which Name Should I Call Thee? The Consequences of Having Multiple Names', *The Quarterly Journal of Experimental Psychology* 58A: 1447–61.

Stevens, Ken (2008). 'Gowen Wilson of Hingham, Exeter, and Kittery', *The New England Historical and Genealogical Register*, vol. 162. Boston, MA: New England Historic Genealogical Society, 174–180.

Stewart, George R. (1945). *Names on the Land. A Historical Account of Place-Naming in the United States*. New York: Random House.

Stewart, George R. (1975). *Names on the Globe*. New York: Oxford University Press.

Stoichiţiou Ichim, Adriana (2013). 'Restaurant Names in the City of Bucharest', in Paula Sjöblom, Terhi Ainiala, and Ulla Hakala (eds.), *Names in the Economy. Cultural Prospects*. Newcastle: Cambridge Scholars, 89–105.

Stokes, Whitley (ed.) (1862). *Three Irish Glossaries. Cormac's Glossary, O'Davoren's Glossary and a Glossary to the Calendar of Oengus the Culdee*. London: Williams and Norgate. Available in electronic format at Early Irish Glossaries Database (2006–9), Department of Anglo-Saxon, Norse and Celtic, University of Cambridge: <http://www.asnc.cam.ac.uk/irishglossaries/>.

Stokes, Whitley (ed. and trans.) (1887). *The Tripartite Life of Patrick, with Other Documents Relating to that Saint*, London: Eyre and Spottiswoode.

Stokes, Whitley (1905). *The Martyrology of Oengus the Culdee*. London: Harrison and Sons.

Stokhof, W. A. L. (1983). 'Names and Naming in Ateita and Environment (Woisika, Alor)', *Lingua* 61: 179–207.

Stommel, Wyke (2007). '"Mein Nick bin ich!" Nicknames in a German Forum on Eating Disorders', *Journal of Computer-Mediated Communication* 13: 141–62.

Strandberg, Svante (1987a). 'Mönsternamngivning bland sjönamn. Struktur, namnseman-tik, kronologi', in Göran Hallberg, Stig Isaksson, Bengt Pamp, and Eero Kiviniemi (eds.), *Nionde nordiska namnforskarkongressen, Lund, 4–8 augusti 1985.* NORNA-rapporter 34. Uppsala: NORNA-förlaget, 247–61.

Strandberg, Svante (1987b). 'Rekonstruktion schwedischer Hydronyme', in *Egennamn i språk och samhälle. Nordiska föredrag på Femtonde internationella kongressen för namnforskning i Leipzig 13–17 augusti 1984.* Ortnamn och samhälle 9. Uppsala: Uppsala universitet, 61–6.

Strandberg, Svante (1988). 'Kontinentalgermanische Hydronymie aus nordischer Sicht', in Thorsten Andersson (ed.), *Probleme der Namenbildung. Rekonstruktion von Eigennamen und der ihnen zugrundeliegenden Appellative. Akten eines internationalen Symposiums in Uppsala 1.–4. September 1986.* Acta Universitatis Upsaliensis. Nomina Germanica 18. Uppsala: Uppsala universitet, 17–57.

Strandberg, Svante (1991). *Studier över sörmländska sjönamn. Etymologi, namnbildning och for-mutveckling.* Skrifter utg. genom Ortnamnsarkivet i Uppsala B 8. Uppsala: Ortnamnsarkivet i Uppsala.

Strandberg, Svante (1996). 'Hydronymisk forskning i de nordiska länderna. Likheter och olikheter', in Kristoffer Kruken (ed.), *Den ellevte nordiske navneforskerkongressen. Sundvollen 19.–23. juni 1994.* NORNA-rapporter 60. Uppsala: NORNA-förlaget, 59–73.

Strandberg, Svante (1998).'Schwedische Hydronymie: Aufgaben und Methoden', in W. F. H. Nicolaisen (ed.), *Proceedings of the XIXth International Congress of Onomastic Sciences, Aberdeen, August 4–11, 1996. Scope, Perspectives and Methods of Onomastics,* vol. 2. Aberdeen: Department of English, University of Aberdeen, 343–9.

Strandberg, Svante (1999). 'Med Nyköpingsån från källsjön till havet. En räcka sjö- och vattendragsnamn', *Saga och sed*: 53–72.

Strandberg, Svante (2002). 'Nordic Hydronymy', *Onoma* 37: 145–64.

Strandberg, Svante (2004a). 'Dehydronymische Ableitungstypen', in Thorsten Andersson and Eva Nyman (eds.), *Suffixbildungen in alten Ortsnamen. Akten eines internationalen Symposiums in Uppsala 14.–16. Mai 2004.* Acta Academiae Regiae Gustavi Adolphi 88. Uppsala: Kungl. Gustav Adolfs Akademien för Svensk Folkkultur, 27–44.

Strandberg, Svante (2004b). 'Dehydronymiska avledningstyper', in Svante Strandberg, Mats Wahlberg, and Björn Heinrici (eds.), *Namn. Hyllningsskrift till Eva Brylla den 1 mars 2004.* Namn och samhälle 15. Uppsala: Uppsala Universitet, 119–26.

Strandberg, Svante (2010). 'Probleme bei hydronymischer Rekonstruktion', in Lennart Elmevik and Svante Strandberg, *Probleme der Rekonstruktion untergegangener Wörter aus alten Eigennamen. Akten eines internationalen Symposiums in Uppsala 7.–9. April 2010.* Acta Academiae Regiae Gustavi Adolphi 112. Uppsala: Kungl. Gustav Adolfs Akademien för Svensk Folkkultur, 117–28.

Stricker, Hans (1981). *Die romanischen Orts- und Flurnamen von Wartau.* St Gallen: St. Galler Namenbuch.

Stricker, Hans, Banzer, Toni, and Hilbe, Herbert (1999). *Liechtensteiner Namenbuch. Vol. 3. Die Namen der Gemeinden Planken, Eschen, Mauren.* Vaduz: Historischer Verein für das Fürstentum Liechtenstein.

Stroud, Christopher, and Jegels, Dmitri (2014). 'Semiotic Landscapes and Mobile Narrations of Place. Performing the Local', *International Journal of the Sociology of Language* 228: 179–99.

Stroud, Christopher, and Mpendukana, Sibonile (2009). 'Towards a Material Ethnography of Linguistic Landscape. Multilingualism, Mobility and Space in a South African Township', *Journal of Sociolinguistics* 13.3: 363–86.

Stuart, David, and Houston, Stephen D. (1994). *Classic Maya Place Names*. Studies in Pre-Columbian Art and Archaeology 33. Washington, DC: Dumbarton Oaks Research Library and Collections.

Stueve, Ann, Gerson, Kathleen, and Fischer, Claude S. (1975). *The Structure and Determinants of Attachment to Place*. Berkeley, CF: Institute of Urban and Regional Development.

Sturges, Christopher M. and Haggett, Brian C. (1987). *Inheritance of English Surnames*. London: Hawgood.

Sue, Christina A., and Telles, Edward E. (2007). 'Assimilation and Gender in Naming', *American Journal of Sociology* 112.5: 1383–415.

Sunderland, Alan, Watts, Kathleen, Baddeley, Alan D., and Harris, John E. (1986). 'Subjective Memory Assessment and Test Performance in Elderly Adults', *Journal of Gerontology* 41: 376–84.

Surma, Genowefa (1988). 'Nazwy zwierząt w gminie Debrzno w woj. Słupskim', *Onomastica* 32: 169–75.

Suter, Elizabeth A. (2012). 'Negotiating Identity and Pragmatism. Parental Treatment of International Adoptees' Birth Culture Names', *Journal of Family Communication* 12: 209–26.

Sutherland, Elizabeth (1994). *In Search of the Picts*. London: Constable.

Suzman, Susan M. (1994). 'Names as Pointers. Zulu Naming Practices', *Language in Society* 23: 253–72.

Swennen, Geert (2001). 'Identiteit in Komputer-Mediated Communication. Een Analyse van Nicknames'. Unpublished Licentiate dissertation. Katholieke Universiteit Leuven.

Świerczyńska, Dobrosława (1983). *Polski pseudonim literacki*. Warszawa: PWN.

Swiss Civil Code (2014). English translation available online at: <http://www.admin.ch/ch/e/rs/2/210.en.pdf>.

Swissworld.org (n.d.) 'Swiss Mountains—Names'. Available online at: <http://www.swissworld.org/en/switzerland/swiss_specials/swiss_mountains/names/>.

Sykes, Bryan (2003). *Adam's Curse*. London: Transworld.

Sykes, Bryan, and Irven, Catherine (2000). 'Surnames and the Y Chromosome', *American Journal of Human Genetics* 66: 1417–19.

Szmrecsanyi, Benedikt (2013). *Grammatical Variation in British English Dialects: A Study in Corpus-Based Dialectometry*. Cambridge: Cambridge University Press.

Taavitsainen, Irma, and Jucker, Andreas H. (eds.) (2003). *Diachronic Perspectives on Address Term Systems*. Pragmatics and Beyond New Series 107. Amsterdam/Philadelphia: John Benjamins.

Takaki, Michiko (1984). 'Regional Names in Kalinga. Certain Social Dimensions of Place Names', in Elisabeth Tooker (ed.), *Naming Systems. 1980 Proceedings of The American Ethnological Society*. Washington, DC: American Ethnological Society, 55–77.

Talbot, Edward (c.1982). *The Locomotive Names of British Railways. Their Origins and Meanings*. Wildwood: Halcyon.

Tan, Peter K. W. (2004). 'Evolving Naming Patterns. Anthroponymics Within a Theory of the Dynamics of Non-Anglo Englishes', *World Englishes* 23.3: 367–84.

Tan, Peter K. W. (2011). 'Mixed Signals. Names in the Linguistic Landscape Provided by Different Agencies in Singapore', *Onoma* 46: 227–50.

Taylor, Archer, and Mosher, Fredric J. (1951). *The Bibliographical History of Anonyma and Pseudonyma*. Chicago: University of Chicago Press.

Taylor, Gary, and Spencer, Steve (2004). *Social Identities. Multidisciplinary Approaches*. London: Routledge.

Taylor, Richard (1974 [1855]). *Te Ika a Maui. Or New Zealand and Its Inhabitants*. Wellington: AH and AW Reed.

Taylor, Simon (ed.) (1998). *The Uses of Place-Names*. Edinburgh: Scottish Cultural Press.

Taylor, Simon (1999). 'Review of Gregory Toner, *Place-Names of Northern Ireland*, vol. 5; Kay Muhr, *Place-Names of Northern Ireland*, vol. 6; and Fiachra Mac Gabhann, *Place-Names of Northern Ireland*, vol. 7', *Nomina* 22: 159–67.

Taylor, Simon (2001). 'Place Names', in Michael Lynch (ed.), *Oxford Companion to Scottish History*. Oxford: Oxford University Press, 479–84.

Taylor, Simon (2004). 'Scandinavians in Central Scotland. *Bý*-Place-Names and Their Context', in Gareth Williams and Paul Bibire (eds.), *Sagas, Saints and Settlements*. Leiden/Boston: Brill, 125–45.

Taylor, Simon (2007a). '*Sliabh* in Scottish Place-names: Its Meaning and Chronology', *Journal of Scottish Name Studies* 1: 99–136.

Taylor, Simon (2007b). 'Gaelic in Glasgow. The Onomastic Evidence', in Sheila M. Kidd (ed.), *Glasgow: Baile Mòr Nan Gàidheal—City of the Gaels*. Glasgow: Roinn Na Ceiltis Oilthigh Ghlaschu, 1–19.

Taylor, Simon (2008). 'The Toponymic Landscape of the Gaelic Notes in the Book of Deer', in Katherine Forsyth (ed.), *Studies on the Book of Deer*. Dublin: Four Courts, 275–308.

Taylor, Simon (2009). 'Review of Victor Watts, *The Place-Names of County Durham*, Part 1, Stockton Ward, *Nomina* 32: 186–93.

Taylor, Simon (n.d.). 'Introduction and Notes to the Parish List'. Available online at: <http://www.spns.org.uk/ParishIntro.html>.

Taylor, Simon, and Cox, Richard A. V. (eds.) (2013). *The Journal of Scottish Name Studies 7*. Ceann Drochaid: Clann Tuirc. Available online at: <http://www.clanntuirc.co.uk/JSNS/V7/JSNS7.pdf>.

Taylor, Simon, with Márkus, Gilbert (2006–12). *The Place-Names of Fife*. 5 vols. Donington: Shaun Tyas.

Teacheroz (2009). '"We Didn't Start The Fire". The History Behind Billy Joel's Song'. Available online at <http://www.teacheroz.com/fire.htm> [accessed 4 June 2015].

Tempan, Paul (2004). 'Five Common Generic Elements in Irish Hill and Mountain Names. *Binn, Cnoc, Cruach, Mullach, Sliabh*'. Master's dissertation, Queen's University, Belfast.

Tempan, Paul (2009). 'Close Compounds in Irish Place-Names', in J. Derrick McClure, John M. Kirk, and Margaret Storrie (eds.), *A Land that Lies Westward. Language and Culture in Islay and Argyll*. Edinburgh: John Donald, 48–78.

Ten Have, Paul (1999). *Doing Conversation Analysis. A Practical Guide*. London: Sage.

Tent, Jan (2010). 'Two Unusual Names for the Australian Continent, Part 1', *Placenames Australia. Newsletter of the Australian National Placename Survey*, March, 6. Available online at: <http://www.anps.org.au/documents/March_2010.pdf>.

Tent, Jan (2013). 'The Ghost of Christmas Island Past', *Placenames Australia. Newsletter of the Australian National Placename Survey*, June, 8–9. Available online at: <http://www.anps.org.au/documents/June_2013.pdf>.

Tent, Jan, and Geraghty, Paul (2012). 'Where in the World is Ulimaroa? Or, How a Pacific Island Became the Australian Continent', *The Journal of Pacific History* 47.1: 1–20. Available online at: <http://www.tandfonline.com/doi/pdf/10.1080/00223344.2011.647396>.

Testenoire, Pierre-Yves (2008). 'Le nom propre en débat au tournant du siècle (Whitney–Bréal–Saussure)', in Jacques Durand, Benoit Habert, and Bernard Laks (eds.), *Congrès mondial de linguistique française*. Paris: Institut de Linguistique Française, 1001–14.

Teutsch, Andreas (2007). *Linguistische Aspekte der rechtlich basierten Markeneignung.* Studien zur Linguistik 14. Wien/Berlin: LIT.

Teutsch, Andreas (2012). 'Speakability of Trademarks', in Reina Boerrigter and Harm Nijboer (eds.), *Names as Language and Capital. Proceedings Names in the Economy III, Amsterdam, 11–13 June 2009.* Amsterdam: Meertens Instituut, 82–92. Available online at: <http://depot.knaw.nl/12899/>.

Teutsch, Andreas (2013). 'Names as Commercial Values—Names of Celebrities', in Oliviu Felecan and Alina Bugheşiu (eds.), *Onomastics in Contemporary Public Space.* Newcastle: Cambridge Scholars, 597–608.

Thies, Henning (1978). *Namen im Kontext von Dramen: Studien zur Funktion von Personennamen im englischen, amerikanischen und deutschen Drama.* Sprache und Literatur. Regensburger Arbeiten zur Anglistik und Amerikanistik 13. Frankfurt am Main/Bern/Las Vegas: Peter Lang.

Thipa, Henry M. (1985). 'Some Place Names. What Do They Tell?', *Logos* 5: 62–5.

Thomas, Keith (1983). *Man and the Natural World.* London: Allen Lane.

Thomason, Sarah Grey, and Kaufman, Terrence (1991). *Language Contact, Creolization, and Genetic Linguistics.* Berkeley/Los Angeles/Oxford: University of California Press.

Thompson, Riki (2009). 'Bilingual, Bicultural, and Binominal Identities. Personal Name Investment and the Imagination in the Lives of Korean Americans', *Journal of Language, Identity and Education* 5.3: 179–208.

Thomson, J. M. et al. (eds.) (1882–1914). *Registrum Magni Sigilli Regum Scottorum.* 11 vols. Edinburgh: The Scottish Record Society.

Thornton, Thomas F. (1997). 'Anthropological Studies of Native American Place Naming', *American Indian Quarterly* 21.2: 209–28.

Thuresson, Bertil (1950). *Middle English Occupational Terms.* Lund: C.W.K. Gleerup.

Thurlow, Crispin, and Jaworski, Adam (2010). 'Silence is Golden. The "Anti-Communicational" Linguascaping of Super-Elite Mobility', in Adam Jaworski and Crispin Thurlow (eds.), *Semiotic Landscapes. Language, Image, Space.* London: Continuum, 187–218.

Tia Mysoa (2008–). *This is Africa—My Simple Online Abode Blog.* Available online at: <http://tia-mysoa.blogspot.com>.

Tibón, Gutierre (1995 [1988]). *Diccionario Etimológico Comparada de los Apellidos Españoles, Hispanoamericanos y Filipinos.* Mexico: Fondo de Cultura Económica.

Tikka, Kaisa (2006). 'Paimion Vistan koululaisten leikkipaikannimiä. Katsaus leikkipaikannimien syntymiseen ja käyttöön'. Unpublished Master's dissertation, University of Turku.

Tinseth, Randy (2011). 'Behind the Scenes Story on Naming the Dreamliner', *Randy's Journal.* Available online at: <http://www.boeingblogs.com/randy/archives/2011/03/behind_the_scenes_story_on_nam.html> [accessed 28 October 2013].

Titford, John (2009). *The Penguin Dictionary of British Surnames.* London: Penguin.

Tomlin, Roger S. O. (1988). 'The Curse Tablets', in Barry Cunliffe (ed.), *The Temple of Sulis Minerva at Bath. Vol. 2: The Finds from the Sacred Spring.* Oxford: OUCA, 59–280.

Tomlin, Roger S. O. (1993). 'The Inscribed Lead Tablets', in Ann Woodward and Peter E. Leach (eds.), *The Uley Shrines. Excavation of a Ritual Complex on West Hill, Uley, Gloucestershire, 1977–79.* English Heritage Archaeological Reports 17. London: English Heritage, 113–26.

Toner, Gregory (1996). *Place-Names of Northern Ireland, vol. 5. County Derry I. The Moyola Valley.* Belfast: Cló Ollscoil na Banríona.

Toner, Gregory, and Ó Mainnín, Micheál B. (1992). *Place-Names of Northern Ireland, vol. 1. County Down I. Newry and South-West Down.* Belfast: Cló Ollscoil na Banríona.

Tönnies, Ferdinand (2002 [1887]). *Community and Society. Gemeinschaft und Gesellschaft.* trans. and ed. by C.P. Loomis. Mineola, NY: Dover.

Tooker, Elisabeth (ed.) (1984). *Naming Systems. 1980 Proceedings of the American Ethnological Society.* Washington, DC: American Ethnological Society.

Toussaint, Jacques (2007). 'Processing of Odonyms in Quebec, Canada. Progress Report'. *Ninth United Nations Conference on the Standardization of Geographical Names, New York, 21–30 August 2007*, 1–5. Available online at: <https://unstats.un.org/unsd/geoinfo/UNGEGN/docs/9th-uncsgn-docs/econf/9th_UNCSGN_e-conf-98-108-add1-en.pdf>.

Townland Index (1861): *Census of Ireland [1851]: General Alphabetical Index to the Townlands and Towns, Parishes and Baronies, Showing the Number of the Sheet of Ordnance Survey Maps in which they Appear*, Alexander Thom, Dublin. Electronic version available online at: <http://www.thecore.com/seanruad/index.html>.

Transport Scotland (2006). *Road Furniture in the Countryside. Guidance for Road and Planning Authorities and Statutory Undertakers.* Edinburgh: Transport Scotland.

Trask, Larry (1997). *The History of Basque.* London: Routledge.

Tuan, Yi-Fu (1974). *Topophilia. A Study of Environmental Perceptions, Attitudes and Values.* Englewood Cliffs, NJ: Prentice-Hall.

Tuan, Yi-Fu (1977). *Space and Place. The Perspective of Experience.* Minneapolis, MN: University of Minnesota Press.

Tuan, Yi-Fu (1991). 'Language and the Making of Place. A Narrative-Descriptive Approach', *Annals of the Association of American Geographers* 81.4: 684–96.

Tucker, Ken (2004). 'The Forenames and Surnames from the GB 1998 Electoral Roll Compared with those from the UK 1881 Census', *Nomina* 27: 5–40.

Tufi, Stefania, and Blackwood, Robert (2010). 'Trademarks in the Linguistic Landscape: Methodological and Theoretical Challenges in Qualifying Brand Names in the Public Space', *International Journal of Multilingualism* 7.3: 197–210.

Tungate, Mark (2007). *Adland. A Global History of Advertising.* London/Philadelphia: Kogan Page.

Turner, Noleen (2009). 'Odonymic Warfare. The Process of Renaming Streets in Durban, South Africa', *Nomina Africana* 23.1: 113–33.

Twigger-Ross, Clare, and Uzzell, David (1996). 'Place and Identity Processes', *Journal of Environmental Psychology* 16.3: 205–20.

Tyas, Shaun (2013). *The Dictionary of Football Club Nicknames in Britain and Ireland.* Donington: Paul Watkins.

Tylor, Edward Burnett (1871). *Primitive Culture.* London: John Murray.

Tyroller, Hans (1996a). 'Typologie der Flurnamen (Mikrotoponomastik): Germanisch', in Ernst Eichler, et al. (eds.). *Namenforschung/Name Studies/Les noms propres. Ein internationals Handbuch zur Onomastik/International Handbook of Onomastics/Manuel international d'onomastique*, vol. 2. Berlin/New York: de Gruyter, 1430–4.

Tyroller, Hans (1996b). 'Morhpologie und Wortbildung der Flurnamen: Germanisch', in Ernst Eichler, et al. (eds.). *Namenforschung/Name Studies/Les noms propres. Ein internationals Handbuch zur Onomastik/International Handbook of Onomastics/Manuel international d'onomastique*, vol. 2. Berlin/New York: de Gruyter, 1434–42.

Udolph, Jürgen (1994). *Namenkundliche Studien zum Germanenproblem.* Ergänzungsbände zum Reallexikon der Germanischen Altertumskunde 9. Berlin/New York: de Gruyter.

Udolph, Jürgen (1995a). 'Die Landnahme Englands durch germanische Stämme im Lichte der Ortsnamen', in Edith Marold and Christiane Zimmermann (eds.), *Nordwestgermanisch.*

Ergänzungsbände zum Reallexikon der Germanischen Altertumskunde 13. Berlin/New York: de Gruyter, 223–70.

Udolph, Jürgen (1995b). 'Flußnamen', *Reallexikon der Germanischen Altertumskunde* 9: 276–84.

Udolph, Jürgen (1996), 'Slavische Gewässernamengebung', in Ernst Eichler, et al. (eds.), *Namenforschung/Name Studies/Les noms propres. Ein internationals Handbuch zur Onomastik/International Handbook of Onomastics/Manuel international d'onomastique*, vol. 2. Berlin/New York: de Gruyter, 1539–47.

Udolph, Jürgen (2004). 'Suffixbildungen in alten Ortsnamen Nord- und Mitteldeutschlands', in Thorsten Andersson and Eva Nyman (eds.), *Suffixbildungen in alten Ortsnamen. Akten eines internationalen Symposiums in Uppsala 14.–16. Mai 2004*. Acta Academiae Regiae Gustavi Adolphi 88. Uppsala: Kungl. Gustav Adolfs Akademien för Svensk Folkkultur, 137–75.

Udolph, Jürgen (2006). 'England und der Kontinent: Ortsnamenparallelen (Ein Situationsbericht)', in Andrew J. Johnston, Ferdinand von Mengden, and Stefan Thim (eds.), *Language and Text. Current Perspectives on English and Germanic Historical Linguistics and Philology*. Heidelberg: Winter, 317–43.

Udolph, Jürgen (2012). 'The Colonisation of England by Germanic Tribes on the Basis of Place-Names', in Merja Stenroos, Martti Mäkinen, and Inge Særheim (eds.), *Language Contacts and Development around the North Sea*. Current Issues in Linguistic Theory 321. Amsterdam: John Benjamins, 23–52.

Ullmann, Stephen (1969). *Words and their Use*. London: F. Muller.

Unbegaun, Boris O. (1972). *Russian Surnames*. Oxford: Clarendon.

UNGEGN (2001). *Consistent Use of Place-Names*. New York: United Nations Group of Experts on Geographical Names. Available online at: <https://unstats.un.org/unsd/geoinfo/UNGEGN/docs/pubs/UNGEGNbrochure_en.pdf>.

UNGEGN (2014). United Nations Group of Experts on Geographical Names. New York: United Nations. Available online at: <http://unstats.un.org/unsd/geoinfo/ungegn/>.

Unger, Johann W. (2013). *The Discursive Construction of the Scots Language*. Discourse Approaches to Politics, Society and Culture 51. Amsterdam: John Benjamins.

Upton, Clive (2012). 'Modern Regional English in the British Isles', in Lynda Mugglestone (ed.), *The Oxford History of English*. 2nd edn. Oxford: Oxford University Press, 379–414.

Upton, Clive S. and Widdowson, John D. A. (1999). *Lexical Erosion in English Dialects*. Sheffield: National Centre for English Cultural Tradition.

US Air Force (2005). 'Designating and Naming Defense Military Aerospace Vehicles', *Air Force Instruction* 16-401(I), 14 April 2005. Available online at: <http://static.e-publishing.af.mil/production/1/af_a3_5/publication/afi16-401_ip/afi16-401_ip.pdf> [accessed 28 October 2013].

US Air Force (2006). '"Lightning II" Moniker Given to Joint Strike Fighter', 7 July. Available online at: <http://www.af.mil/News/ArticleDisplay/tabid/223/Article/130499/lightning-ii-moniker-given-to-joint-strike-fighter.aspx> [accessed 28 October 2013].

Utley, Francis Lee (1941). 'The One Hundred and Three Names of Noah's Wife', *Speculum* 16: 426–52.

Utterström, Gudrun (1998). 'Nova Suecia—ortnamn och språk', *Namn och Bygd* 86: 91–103.

Vaattovaara, Johanna (2009). *Meän tapa puhua. Tornionlaakso pellolaisnuorten subjektiivisena paikkana ja murrealueena*. Helsinki: Finnish Literature Society.

Valentine, Tim, and Darling, Stephen (2006). 'Competitor Effects in Naming Objects and Famous Faces', *European Journal of Cognitive Psychology* 18: 686–707.

Valentine, Tim, and Moore, Viv (1995). 'Naming Faces. The Effects of Facial Distinctiveness and Surname Frequency', *The Quarterly Journal of Experimental Psychology* 48A: 879–94.

Valentine, Tim, Brennen, Tim, and Brédart, Serge (1996). *The Cognitive Psychology of Proper Names. On the Importance of Being Ernest.* London: Routledge.

Valentine, Tim, Hollis, Jarold, and Moore, Viv (1999). 'The Nominal Competitor Effect. When One Name is Better Than Two', in Martin Hahn and S. C. Stoness (eds.), *Proceedings of the 21st Annual Meeting of the Cognitive Science Society.* Mahwah, NJ: Lawrence Erlbaum Associates, 749–54.

Van Dalen-Oskam, Karina (2005a). 'Dutch Literary Onomastics. Past, Present and Future', in Eva Brylla and Mats Wahlberg (eds.), *Proceedings of the 21st International Congress of Onomastic Sciences, Uppsala,19–24 August 2002*, vol. 1. Uppsala: Språk- och folkminnesin-stitutet, 398–406.

Van Dalen-Oskam, Karina (2005b). 'Vergleichende literarische Onomastik', in Andrea Brendler and Silvio Brendler (eds.), *Namenforschung morgen: Ideen, Perspektiven, Visionen,* Hamburg: Baar, 183–191. trans. as 'Comparative Literary Onomastics', at <http://www.huy-gens.knaw.nl/wp-content/bestanden/pdf_vandalenoskam_2005_Comparative_Literary_ Onomastics.pdf>.

Van Dalen-Oskam, Karina (2006). 'Mapping the Onymic Landscape', in Maria Giovanna Arcamone, Donatella Bremer, Davide de Camilli, and Bruno Porcelli (eds.), *I Nomi Nel Tempo e Nello Spazio. Atti del XXII Congresso Internatzionale di Scienze Onomastiche, Pisa, 28 Agosto–4 Settembre 2005*, vol. 3. Pisa: Edizioni ETS, 93–104.

Van Dalen-Oskam, Karina (2009). 'Professor Nummedal is niet alleen. Een analyse van de namen in Willem Frederik Hermans', *Nooit meer slapen'*, *Tijdschrift voor Nederlandse Taal-en Letterkunde* 125: 419–49. Available online at: <www.huygens.knaw.nl/vandalen>.

Van Dalen-Oskam, Karina (2012a). 'Immer nach Norden. Gebrauch und Funktion von Eigennamen im Roman *Oben ist es still* von Gerbrand Bakker. Ein Pilotprojekt zur vergleichenden literarischen Onomastik', trans. by Volker Kohlheim, *Beiträge zur Namenforschung (Neue Folge)* 47: 33–58. Available online at <http://xposre.nl/ep/noorden/>.

Van Dalen-Oskam, Karina (2012b). 'Who is Hvalbiff? Name and Identity in W. F. Hermans' *Beyond Sleep'*, in Botolv Helleland, Christian-Emil Ore, and Solveig Wikstrøm (eds.), *Names and Identities. Oslo Studies in Language* 4.2. Oslo: University of Oslo, 243–55, <https://www. journals.uio.no/index.php/osla/article/view/322/454>.

Van Dalen-Oskam, Karina (2012c). 'Personal Names in Literature. A Quantitative Approach', in Lars-Gunnar Larsson and Staffan Nyström (eds.), *Facts and Findings on Personal Names. Some European Examples. Proceedings of an International Symposium in Uppsala, October 20–21, 2011.* Uppsala: Kungliga Vetenskapssamhället, 153–68.

Van Dalen-Oskam, Karina (2013). 'Names in Novels. An Experiment in Computational Stylistics', *LLC. The Journal of Digital Scholarship in the Humanities* 28: 359–70. Also available online at: <http://llc.oxfordjournals.org/content/early/2012/03/09/llc.fqs007.full.pdf?keyty pe=ref&ijkey=xzKL6KhzbWesz1H>.

Van Dalen-Oskam, Karina, and Van Zundert, Joris (2004). 'Modelling Features of Characters. Some Digital Ways to Look at Names in Literary Texts', *Literary and Linguistic Computing* 19.3: 289–301.

Van de Velde, Mark L. O. (2003). 'Proper Names and the So-Called Class 1a in Eton', *Leuvense Bijdragen* 92: 43–59.

Van de Velde, Mark L .O. (2006). 'Multifunctional Agreement Patterns in Bantu and the Possibility of Genderless Nouns', *Linguistic Typology* 10.2: 183–221.

Van de Velde, Mark L. O. (2008). *A Grammar of Eton*. Berlin: Mouton de Gruyter.

Van de Velde, Mark L. O. (2009). 'Agreement as a Grammatical Criterion for Proper Name Status in Kirundi', *Onoma* 44: 219–41.

Van de Velde, Mark, and Ambouroue, Odette (2011). 'The Grammar of Orungu Proper Names', *Journal of African Languages and Linguistics* 32.1: 113–41.

Van Dijk, Teun A. (1992). 'Discourse and the Denial of Racism', *Discourse and Society* 3.1: 87–118.

Van Hamel, Anton G. (1933). *Compert Con Culainn and Other Stories*. Dublin: The Stationery Office.

Van Langendonck, Willy (1979). 'Definiteness as an Unmarked Category', *Linguistische Berichte* 63: 33–55.

Van Langendonck, Willy (1981). 'On the Theory of Proper Names', in Kazimierz Rymut (ed.), *Proceedings of the XIIIth International Congress of Onomastic Sciences (Kraków 1978)*, vol. 1. Kraków: Ossolineum, 63–78.

Van Langendonck, Willy (1994). 'Determiners as Heads?', *Cognitive Linguistics* 5: 243–259.

Van Langendonck, Willy (1996). 'Bynames', in Ernst Eichler, et al. (eds.), *Namenforschung/ Name Studies/Les noms propres. Ein internationals Handbuch zur Onomastik/International Handbook of Onomastics/Manuel international d'onomastique*, vol. 2. Berlin/New York: Walter de Gruyter, 1228–32.

Van Langendonck, Willy (1998). 'A Typological Approach to Place-Name Categories', in W. F. H. Nicolaisen (ed.), *Proceedings of the XIXth International Congress of Onomastic Sciences Aberdeen, August 4–11, 1996. Scope, Perspectives and Methods of Onomastics*, vol. 1. Aberdeen: Department of English, University of Aberdeen, 342–48.

Van Langendonck, Willy (1999). 'Neurolinguistic and Syntactic Evidence for Basic Level Meaning in Proper Names', *Functions of Language* 6.1: 95–138.

Van Langendonck, Willy (2007a). 'Trade and Brand Names. Proper or Common Nouns?', in Ludger Kremer and Elke Ronneberger-Sibold (eds.), *Names in Commerce and Industry. Past and Present*. Berlin: Logos, 23–33.

Van Langendonck, Willy (2007b). *Theory and Typology of Proper Names*. Trends in Linguistics. Studies and Monographs 168. Berlin/New York: Mouton de Gruyter.

Van Langendonck, Willy (2010). 'Names and Identity. On the Nomematic Approach. Review of Silvio Brendler, *Nomematik, Identitätstheoretische Grundlagen der Namenforschung (insbesondere der Namengeschichte, Namenlexikographie, Namengeographie, Namenstatistik und Namenstheorie)*', *Beiträge zur Namenforschung* 45.2: 193–220.

Van Langendonck, Willy, and Van de Velde, Mark (2007). 'Naar een universele theorie van eigennamen', *Handelingen van de Koninklijke Commissie voor Toponymie and Dialectologie* 74: 429–67.

Van Osta, Ward (1995). 'Von dem Irren im Kritisieren. Een repliek op Klaas Willems, *Naamkunde* 27: 179–88.

Vandebosch, Heidi (1998). 'The Influence of Media on Given Names', *Names* 46.4: 243–62.

Vandelanotte, Lieven, and Willemse, Peter (2002). 'Restrictive and Non-Restrictive Modification of Proprial Lemmas', *Word* 53.1: 9–36.

Vassallo, Edward, and Hiney, Jessica (2009). 'Private Lives and Publicity Rights', *World Trademark Review*, October/November: 42–5.

Vassere, Stefano (1996). 'Morphologie et formation des microtoponymes: domaine roman', in Ernst Eichler, et al. (eds.), *Namenforschung/Name Studies/Les noms propres. Ein internationals Handbuch zur Onomastik/International Handbook of Onomastics/Manuel international d'onomastique*, vol. 2. Berlin/New York: de Gruyter, 1442–7.

Veka, Olav (2000). *Norsk Etternamnleksikon.* Oslo: Det Norske Samlaget.

VEPN = Parsons, David N., and Styles, Tania, with Hough, Carole (1997–). *The Vocabulary of English Place-Names.* 3 vols so far published. Nottingham: Centre for English Name Studies/ English Place-Name Society.

Vieth, Werner H. (2006). 'Dialects. Early European Studies', in Kamal Brown (ed.), *Encyclopedia of Language and Linguistics.* 2nd edn, 14 vols. Oxford: Elsevier, 540–60.

Vikstrand, Per (2012). '*Solen skiner* och *Grisen skriker.* Namn på svenska rockgrupper 1960–2000', in Katharina Leibring, Leif Nilsson, Annette C. Torensjö, and Mats Wahlberg (eds.), *Namn på stort och smått. Vänskrift till Staffan Nyström den 11 december 2012.* Uppsala: Institutet för språk och folkminnen, 315–24.

Vikstrand, Per (2013). 'Namnet Uppsala', in Olof Sundqvist and Per Vikstrand (eds.), *Gamla Uppsala i ny belysning.* Gävle: Högskolan i Gävle, 135–60.

Viljamaa-Laakso, Marja (2008). 'No Logo—From the Thematic Year of Local Names to the Geography of the Market', in Eva Brylla and Mats Wahlberg (eds.), *Proceedings of the 21st International Congress of Onomastic Sciences, Uppsala, 19–24 August 2002,* vol. 4. Uppsala: Institutet för språk och folkminnen, 411–20.

Vincenz, Valentin (1983). *Die romanisten Orts- und Flurnamen von Buchs und Sevelen.* St. Gallen: St. Galler Namenbuch.

Vincenz, Valentin (1992). *Die romanischen Orts- und Flurnamen von Gams bis zum Hirschensprung.* St. Gallen: St. Galler Namenbuch.

Vincze, László (2010). 'Ungarische Markennamen', *Onoma* 43: 115–47.

Voigt, Gerhard (1982). *Bezeichnungen für Kunststoffe im heutigen Deutsch. Eine Untersuchung zur Morphologie des Markennamen.* Hamburg: Helmut Buske.

Vom Bruck, Gabriele, and Bodenhorn, Barbara (eds.) (2006a). *The Anthropology of Names and Naming.* Cambridge: Cambridge University Press.

Vom Bruck, Gabriele, and Bodenhorn, Barbara (2006b). ' "Entangled in Histories". An Introduction to the Anthropology of Names and Naming', in Gabriele vom Bruck and Barbara Bodenhorn (eds.), *The Anthropology of Names and Naming.* Cambridge: Cambridge University Press, 1–30.

Vrublevskaya, Oksana (2012). 'Die Pragmatik der Namen von ökonomischen Events', in Holger Wochele, Julia Kuhn, and Martin Stegu (eds.), *Onomastics Goes Business. Role and Relevance of Brand, Company and Other Names in Economic Contexts.* Berlin: Logos, 195–202.

Vuolteenaho, Jani, and Ainiala, Terhi (2009). 'Planning and Revamping Urban Toponymy: Ideological Alterations in the Linguistic Landscaping of Vuosaari Suburb, Eastern Helsinki', in Lawrence D. Berg and Jani Vuolteenaho (eds.), *Critical Toponymies. The Contested Politics of Place Naming.* Farnham: Ashgate, 227–51.

Vuolteenaho, Jani, and Berg, Lawrence D. (2009). 'Towards Critical Toponymies', in Lawrence D. Berg and Jani Vuolteenaho (eds.), *Critical Toponymies. The Contested Politics of Place Naming.* Farnham: Ashgate, 1–18.

Vuolteenaho, Jani, and Kolamo, Sami (2012). 'Textually Produced Landscape Spectacles? A Debordian Reading of Finnish Namescapes and English Soccerscapes', *COLLeGIUM. Studies Across Disciplines in the Humanities and Social Sciences* 13: 132–58.

Vuolteenaho, Jani, Ainiala, Terhi, and Wihuri, Elina (2007). 'The Change in Planned Nomenclature in Vuosaari, Helsinki', *Onoma* 42: 213–35.

Wagner, Heinrich (1971). *Studies in the Origin of the Celts and of Early Celtic Civilisation.* Belfast/Tubingen: (for the Institute of Irish Studies) Max Niemeyer.

Wagner, Heinrich (1981). 'The Origins of Pagan Irish Religion', *Zeitschrift fur Celtische Philologie* 38: 1–28.

Wahlberg, Mats (ed.) (2003). *Svenskt ortnamslexikon*. Uppsala: Språk- och Folkminnesinstitutet.

Wahlberg, Mats (2006). 'Systematized Name-Giving in the Area of "Other Names"—With Special Reference to Sweden', in Milan Harvalik (ed.), *Acta Onomastica. Věnováno k 70. narozeninám PhDr. Miloslavy Knappové, CSc.* Prague: Praha Ústav pro jazyk český AV ČR, 467–74.

Walker, Terry (2007). *Thou and You in Early Modern English Dialogues. Trials, Depositions, and Drama Comedy*. Amsterdam: John Benjamins.

Walker-Meikle, Kathleen (2012). *Medieval Pets*. Woodbridge: Boydell Press.

Walsh, Paul (1957). *The Place-Names of Westmeath*. Dublin: Dublin Institute for Advanced Studies.

Walther, Hans (1971a). *Namenforschung heute. Ihre Ergebnisse und Aufgaben in der Deutschen Demokratischen Republik*. Berlin: Akademie-Verlag.

Walther, Hans (1971b). *Namenkundliche Beiträge zur Siedlungsgeschichte des Saale- und Mittelelbegebietes bis zum Ende des 9. Jahrhunderts*. Deutsch-slawische Forschungen zur Namenkunde und Siedlungsgeschichte 26. Berlin: Akademie-Verlag.

Walther, Hans (1978). *Gesellschaftsentwicklung und Namenwandel*. Ortnamn och samhälle 3. Uppsala: Seminariet för nordisk ortnamnsforskning, Uppsala universitet.

Walther, Hans (1980). 'Zur Problematik, Typologi und Terminologie der sogenannten "Mischnamen" (onymischen Hybride)', in Thorsten Andersson, et al. (eds.), *Ortnamn och språkkontakt*. NORNA-rapporter 17. Uppsala: NORNA-förlaget, 143–62.

Walther, Hans, and Schultheis, Johannes (1989 [1974]). 'Soziolinguistische Aspekte der Eigennamen', in Rudolf Große and Albrecht Neubert (eds.), *Beiträge zur Soziolinguistik*. München: Hueber, 187–205 [reprinted in Friedhelm Debus and Wilfried Seibicke (eds.), *Reader zur Namenkunde I: Namentheorie*. Hildesheim: Georg Olms Verlag, 357–75].

Walton, John K. (2005). 'Power, Speed and Glamour. The Naming of Express Steam Locomotives in Inter-War Britain', *Journal of Transport History* 26.2: 1–19.

Wansbrough-White, Gordon (1995). *Names with Wings. The Names and Naming Systems of Aircraft and Engines Flown by the British Armed Forces 1878–1994*. Shrewsbury: Airlife.

Warchoł, Stefan (2004). 'Tiernamen', in Andrea Brendel and Silvio Brendler (eds.), *Namenarten und ihre Erforschung. Ein Lehrbuch für das Studium der Onomastik*. Hamburg: Baar, 773–94.

Ward-Jackson, C. H. (ed.) (1945). *Airman's Song Book*. London: Sylvan Press.

Warner, Richard (2006). 'St Patrick, the Kings of Clogher and the Standing Stones of Findermore', in Marion Meek (ed.), *The Modern Traveller to Our Past. Festschrift for Ann Hamlin*. No place: DPK, 169–76.

Waser, Erika (1998). 'Der wilde Hengst und der zahme Ochse: Tiernamen in Flurnamen', *Entlebucher Brattig* 16: 53–6.

Waser, Erika (2004). 'Flurnamen', in Andrea Brendler and Silvio Brendler (eds.), *Namenarten und ihre Erforschung. Ein Lehrbuch für das Studium der Onomastik*. Hamburg: Baar, 349–80.

Watson, J. Carmichael (ed.) (1941). *Mesca Ulad*. Medieval and Modern Irish Series 13. Dublin: Dublin Institute for Advanced Studies.

Watson, William J. (1926). *The History of the Celtic Place-Names of Scotland*. Edinburgh: William Blackwood.

Watts, Richard (2011). *Language Myths and the History of English*. Oxford: Oxford University Press.

Watts, Victor (2007). *The Place-Names of County Durham. Part 1*. ed. by Paul Cavill. English Place-Name Society 84. Nottingham: English Place-Name Society.

Watts, Victor (ed.), with Insley, John, and Gelling, Margaret (2004). *The Cambridge Dictionary of English Place-Names*. Cambridge: Cambridge University Press.

Webb, Colin de B., and Wright, John (eds. and trans.) (1976–2014). *The James Stuart Archive of Recorded Oral Evidence Relating to the History of the Zulu and Neighbouring People*. 6 vols. Pietermaritzburg: University of Natal Press.

Webster = Babcock, Philip (ed.) (1993). *Webster's Third New International Dictionary of the English Language. Unabridged*. Springfield, Massachusetts: Merriam-Webster.

Webster's Family Dictionary (1992). New York: Arrow Trading Company.

Weekley, Ernest (1916). *Surnames*. London: John Murray.

Weekley, Ernest (1917). *Surnames*. 2nd edn. London: John Murray.

Weinreich, Uriel (1953). *Languages in Contact. Findings and Problems*. New York: Linguistic Circle of New York.

Wells, John C. (1982). *Accents of English 2. The British Isles*. Cambridge: Cambridge University Press.

Werner, Otmar (1986). 'Eigennamen im Dialog', in Franz Hundsnurscher and Edda Weigand (eds.), *Dialoganalyse. Referate der 1. Arbeitstagung in Münster*. Tübingen: Niemeyer, 297–315.

Werner, Otmar (1995). 'Pragmatik der Eigennamen (Überblick)', in Ernst Eichler, et al. (eds.), *Namenforschung/Name Studies/Les noms propres. Ein internationals Handbuch zur Onomastik/International Handbook of Onomastics/Manuel international d'onomastique*, vol. 1. Berlin/New York: de Gruyter, 476–84.

Wessex Archaeology (2007). *Blacklands, Upper Row Farm, Laverton, Somerset. Archaeological Evaluation and Assessment of Results*. Report ref. 62504.01.

Whaley, Diana (2006). *A Dictionary of Lake District Place-Names*. Nottingham: English Place-Name Society.

Wheeler, Rebecca S. (2010). 'From Cold Shoulder to Funded Welcome. Lessons from the Trenches of Dialectally Diverse Classrooms', in Kristin Denham and Anne Loebeck (eds.), *Linguistics at School. Language Awareness in Primary and Secondary Education*. Cambridge: Cambridge University Press, 129–48.

Wheeler, Rebecca S., and Swords, Rachel (2004). 'Codeswitching. Tools of Language and Culture Transform the Dialectally Diverse Classroom', *Language Arts* 81.6: 470–80.

Wheeler, Rebecca S., and Swords, Rachel (2006). *Code-Switching. Teaching Standard English in Urban Classrooms*. Urbana, IL: National Council of Teachers of English.

Wheeler, Rebecca S., and Swords, Rachel (2010). *Code-Switching Lessons. Grammar Strategies for Linguistically Diverse Writers*. Portsmouth, NH: FirstHand Heinemann.

White, Dave, Virden, Randy, and van Riper, Carena (2008). 'Effects of Place Identity, Place Dependence, and Experience-Use History on Perceptions of Recreation Impacts in a Natural Setting', *Environmental Management* 42: 647–57.

Whitelock, Dorothy (1955). *English Historical Documents c. 500–1042*. London: Eyre and Spottiswoode.

Whitridge, Peter (2004). 'Landscapes, Houses, Bodies, Things. "Place" and the Archaeology of Inuit Imaginaries', *Journal of Archaeological Method and Theory* 11.2: 213–50.

Widdicombe, Sue (1998). 'Identity as an Analysts' and a Participants' Resource', in Charles Antaki and Sue Widdicombe (eds.), *Identities in Talk*. London: Sage Publications.

Wiesinger, Peter (2010). 'Älteres Wortgut in Orts- und Gewässernamen Oberösterreichs. Zur Rekonstruktion von Appellativen aus Propria im Bairisch-Althochdeutschen', in Lennart Elmevik and Svante Strandberg (eds.), *Probleme der Rekonstruktion untergegangener Wörter aus alten Eigennamen. Akten eines internationalen Symposiums in Uppsala 7.–9. April 2010.* Acta Academiae Regiae Gustavi Adolphi 112. Uppsala: Kungl. Gustav Adolfs Akademien för Svensk Folkkultur, 159–73.

Wikipedia (2013a). 'Race (human classification)'. Available online at: <http://en.wikipedia.org/wiki/Race_(human_classification)> [accessed 20 February 2013]

Wikipedia (2013b). 'Gringo'. Available online at: <http://en.wikipedia.org/wiki/Gringo> [accessed 30 February 2013]

Wikipedia (2013c). 'We Didn't Start The Fire (song)'. Available online at: <http://en.wikipedia.org/wiki/We_Didn%27t_Start_the_Fire>.

Wikipedia (2014a). 'Es'kia Mphahlele'. Available online at: <http://en.wikipedia.org/wiki/Es%27kia_Mphahlele>.

Wikipedia (2014b). 'List of Pseudonyms'. Available online at: <http://en.wikipedia.org/wiki/List_of_pseudonyms>.

Wikipedia (2014c). 'African Writers by Country'. Available online at: <http://en.wikipedia.org/wiki/List_of_African_writers_by_country>.

Wikipedia (2014d). 'North Korean People by Occupation'. Available online at: <http://en.wikipedia.org/wiki/Category:North_Korean_people_by_occupation>.

Wikipedia (2014e). 'List of Women Rhetoricians'. Available online at: <http://en.wikipedia.org/wiki/List_of_women_rhetoricians>.

Wikipedia (2014f). 'List of British Pornographic Actors'. Available online at: <http://en.wikipedia.org/wiki/List_of_British_pornographic_actors>.

Wikipedia (2014g). 'Naming law in Sweden'. Available online at: <http://en.wikipedia.org/wiki/Naming_law_in_Sweden>.

Wikipedia (2015a). 'Johan Heyns'. Available online at: <http://en.wikipedia.org/wiki/Johan_Heyns>.

Wikipedia (2015b). 'Street or Road Name'. Available online at: <http://en.wikipedia.org/wiki/Street_or_road_name>.

Wikipedia (2015c). 'Patter Song'. Available online at: <http://en.wikipedia.org/wiki/Patter_song>.

Wikipedia (n.d.). 'Geographical Indications and Traditional Specialities in the European Union'. Available online at: <http://en.wikipedia.org/wiki/Geographical_indications_and_traditional_specialities_in_the_European_Union>.

Wikstrøm, Solveig (2012). 'Surnames and Identities', in Botolv Helleland, Christian-Emil Ore, and Solveig Wikstrøm (eds.), *Names and Identities*. Oslo Studies in Language 4.2. Oslo: University of Oslo, 258–72. Available online at: <https://www.journals.uio.no/index.php/osla/article/view/323/448>.

Wilkerson, Douglas, and Takashi Wilkerson, Kyoko (2013). 'The Price of Home. Names and Prestige of Domicile in Japan', in Paula Sjöblom, Terhi Ainiala, and Ulla Hakala (eds.), *Names in the Economy. Cultural Prospects*. Newcastle: Cambridge Scholars, 55–72.

Williams, Daniel, and Vaske, Jerry (2003). 'The Measurement of Place Attachment. Validity and Generalizability of a Psychometric Approach', *Forest Science* 49.6: 830–40.

Williams, Robert J. (1993). *Pennyland and Hartigans. Two Iron Age and Saxon Sites in Milton Keynes*. Buckinghamshire Archaeological Society Monograph Series 4. Aylesbury: Buckinghamshire Archaeological Society.

Williams, William L. (1912). *He whakamahara ki ngā tangata o te hāhi*. Turanga: Ki te.

Williamson, Keith (2012). 'Historical Dialectology', in Alexander Bergs and Laurel Brinton (eds.), *English Historical Linguistics. An International Handbook*, vol. 2. Berlin: Mouton de Gruyter, 1421–37.

Williamson, May Gordon (1942). 'The Non-Celtic Place-Names of the Scottish Border Counties'. Unpublished PhD dissertation, University of Edinburgh.

Williamson, Tom, Liddiard Robert, and Partida, Tracey (2013). *Champion. The Making and Unmaking of the English Midland Landscape*. Liverpool: Liverpool University Press.

Wilson, Stephen (1998). *The Means of Naming. A Social and Cultural History of Personal Naming in Western Europe*. London: UCL Press.

Winchester, Angus (2011). 'Personal Names and Local Identities in Early Modern Cumbria', *Transactions of the Cumberland and Westmorland Antiquarian and Archaeological Society* 11: 29–49.

Windberger-Heidenkummer, Erika (2001). *Mikrotoponyme im sozialen und kommunikativen Kontext: Flurnamen im Gerichtsbezirk Neumarkt in der Steiermark*. Schriften zur deutschen Sprache in Österreich 30. Frankfurt am Main: Peter Lang.

Windberger-Heidenkummer, Erika (2011). 'Kontinuität und Diskontinuität von Flurnamen. Probleme und Beispiele', in Eckhard Meineke and Heinrich Tiefenbach (eds.), *Mikrotoponyme*. Heidelberg: de Gruyter.

Windt-Val, Benedicta (2009). '"Men han het Edvard …". Navn og navnebruk i Sigrid Undsets forfatterskap'. PhD dissertation, University of Oslo.

Winford, Donald (2003). 'Ideologies of Language and Socially Realistic Linguistics', in Sinfree Makoni, Geneva Smitherman, Arnetha F. Ball, and Arthur K. Spears (eds.), *Black Linguistics. Language, Society and Politics in Africa and the Americas*. London: Routledge, 21–39.

Withers, Charles (2000). 'Authorising Landscape. "Authority", Naming and the Ordnance Survey's Mapping of the Scottish Highlands in the Nineteenth Century', *Journal of Historical Geography* 26.4: 532–54.

Witkowski, Teodolius (1964). *Grundbegriffe der Namenkunde*. Deutsche Akademie der Wissenschaften zu Berlin. Vorträge und Schriften 91. Berlin: Akademie-Verlag.

Wochele, Holger (2007). 'Hotel Names in Italy and Romania—A Comparative Analysis', in Ludger Kremer and Elke Ronneberger-Sibold (eds.), *Names in Commerce and Industry. Past and Present*. Berlin: Logos, 317–29.

Wochele, Holger, Kuhn, Julia, and Stegu, Martin (eds.) (2012). *Onomastics Goes Business. Role and Relevance of Brand, Company and Other Names in Economic Contexts*. Berlin: Logos.

Wood, J. P. (1992). *Aircraft Nose Art. 80 Years of Aviation Artwork*. London: Salamander Books.

Wotjak, Gerd (1985). 'Zur Semantik der Eigennamen', *Namenkundliche Informationen* 48: 1–17.

Woulfe, Patrick (1923). *Irish Names and Surnames*. Dublin: M.H. Gill and Son.

Wright, John (2008). 'Reflections on the Politics of Being "Zulu"', in Benedict Carton, John Laband, and Jabulani Sithole (eds.), *Zulu Identities. Being Zulu, Past and Present*. Scottsville: University of KwaZulu-Natal Press: 35–43.

Wright, John, and Hamilton, Carolyn (1989). 'Traditions and Transformations. The Phongolo-Mzimkhulu Region in the Late Eighteenth and Early Nineteenth Centuries', in Andrew Duminy and Bill Guest (eds.), *Natal and Zululand from Earliest Times to 1910. A New History*. Pietermaritzburg: University of Natal Press and Shuter and Shooter.

Wright, Joseph (1898–1905). *The English Dialect Dictionary*. 6 vols. London: Henry Frowde. Available at: <http://www.uibk.ac.at/anglistik/projects/speed/>.

Wynn, Humphrey (1994). *The RAF Strategic Nuclear Deterrent Forces. Their Origins, Roles and Deployment 1946–1969—A Documentary History*. London: HMSO.

Yassin, Mahmoud Aziz F. (1978). 'Personal Names of Address in Kuwaiti Arabic', *Anthropological Linguistics* 20: 67–83.

Yeoh, Brenda (1992). 'Street Names in Colonial Singapore', *The Geographical Review* 82.3: 313–22.

Yida, Yuan and Jiaru, Qiu (2010). *Zhong Guo Xin Shi Da Ci Dian*—'The Comprehensive Dictionary of Surnames in China'. Nanchang: Jiangxi People's Publishing House.

Yli-Kojola, Maria (2005). 'Kurvinpussi vai Torikatu? Kouvolalaisten mielipiteitä kadunnimistä', in Terhi Ainiala (ed.), *Kaupungin nimet: kymmenen kirjoitusta kaupunkinimistöstä*. Helsinki: Finnish Literature Society, 178–201.

Young, Andrew W., Hay, Dennis C., and Ellis, Andrew W. (1985). 'The Faces That Launched a Thousand Slips. Everyday Difficulties and Errors in Recognizing People', *British Journal of Psychology* 76: 495–523.

Young, Andrew W., McWeeny, Kathryn H., Ellis, Andrew W., and Hay, Dennis C. (1986). 'Naming and Categorizing Faces and Written Names', *The Quarterly Journal of Experimental Psychology* 38A: 297–318.

Young, Andrew W., Ellis, Andrew W., and Flude, Brenda M. (1988). 'Accessing Stored Information About Familiar People', *Psychological Research* 50: 111–15.

Younge, Gavin (2006). 'Not Thought Of', *Artworks in Progress* 8. Michaelis School of Fine Art UCT, 74–7.

Yurdan, Marilyn (1990). *Irish Family History*. London: Batsford.

Zabeeh, Farhang (1968). *What is in a Name? An Inquiry into the Semantics and Pragmatics of Proper Names*. The Hague: M. Nijhoff.

Zabrodskaja, Anastassia (2014). 'Tallinn. Monolingual from Above and Multilingual from Below', *International Journal of the Sociology of Language* 228: 105–30.

Zadora-Rio, Elisabeth (2001). *Archéologie et Toponymie. Le Divorce*. Les Petits Cahiers d'Anatole 8. Tours: University of Tours. Available online at: <http://citeres.univ-tours.fr/doc/lat/pecada/F2_8.pdf>.

Zamora, Juan (1992). *Hugenottische Familiennamen im Deutschen*. Heidelberg: Winter.

Zerubavel, Eviatar (2003). *Time Maps. Collective Memory and the Social Shape of the Past*. Chicago, IL: University of Chicago Press.

Zilg, Antje (2009). '*WULEWU* würstel? Eine Darstellung produktgruppenspezifischer Aspekte italienischer Markennamen des Lebensmittelmarktes', in Wolfgang Ahrens, Sheila Embleton, and André Lapierre (eds.), *Names in Multi-Lingual, Multi-Cultural and Multi-Ethnic Contact. Proceedings of the 23rd International Congress of Onomastic Sciences, August 17–22, 2008, York University, Toronto, Canada*. Toronto: York University, 1088–96. Available online at: <http://yorkspace.library.yorku.ca/xmlui/bitstream/handle/10315/4054/icos23_1088.pdf?sequence=1>.

Zilg, Antje (2011). '*That's Amore*. Brand Names in the Italian Food Market', *International Journal of Applied Linguistics* 21.1: 1–25.

Zilg, Antje (2013). '*Tu y yo*. Aspects of Brand Names Related to Interaction and Identification', in Paula Sjöblom, Terhi Ainiala, and Ulla Hakala (eds.), *Names in the Economy. Cultural Prospects*. Newcastle: Cambridge Scholars, 269–81.

Zilliacus, Kurt (1966). *Ortnamnen i Houtskär. En översikt av namnförrådets sammansättning*. Studier i nordisk filologi 55. Helsingfors: Svenska litteratursällskapet.

Zinsli, Paul (1945). *Grund und Grat: die Bergwelt im Spiegel der schweizerdeutschen Alpenmundarten*. Bern: Francke.

Zinsli, Paul (1963). 'Die mittelalterliche Walserwanderung in Flurnamenspuren', in Paul Zinsli, and Oskar Bandle (eds.), *Sprachleben der Schweiz. Sprachwissenschaft, Namenforschung, Volkskunde.* Bern: Francke, 201–330.

Zinsli, Paul (1975). *Ortsnamen: Strukturen und Schichten in den Siedlungs- und Flurnamen der deutschen Schweiz.* 2nd edn. Frauenfeld: Huber.

Zinsli, Paul (1984). *Südwalser Namengut: Die deutschen Orts- und Flurnamen der ennetbirgischen Walsersiedlungen in Bosco-Gurin und im Piemont.* Bern: Stämpfli.

Zinsli, Paul (1991). *Walser Volkstum in der Schweiz, in Vorarlberg, Liechtenstein und Piemont: Erbe, Dasein, Wesen.* 6th edn. Chur: Bündner Monatsblatt.

Zipf, George K. (1949). *Human Behavior and the Principle of Least Effort.* New York: Addison-Wesley.

Zschieschang, Christian (2005). 'Flurnamen als Indikatoren hochmittelalterlicher Siedlumg—der Raum Wittenberg', in Armin Burkhardt, Ursula Föllner, and Saskia Luther (eds.), *Magdeburger Namenlandschaft. Onomastische Analyse zu Stadt und Region in Geschichte und Gegenwart.* Frankfurt am Main: Peter Lang, 187–210.

Subject Index

Index of Languages

OXFORD HANDBOOKS IN LINGUISTICS

Published titles

CPSIA information can be obtained
at www.ICGtesting.com
Printed in the USA
LVHW102102080721
692214LV00010B/487

9 780198 815532